C++ AND DATA STRUCTURES

C++ AND DATA STRUCTURES

An Algorithmic Approach and Program Design

FOR

(All Indian Universities, Engineering and Technical Colleges and Institutions, IIT's and IT Organizations)

R Singh • I Singh

Khanna Book Publishing Co. (P) Ltd.
Delhi

ISBN: 978-93-80016-79-5

First Edition 2010

Published by:
Khanna Book Publishing Co. (P) Ltd.
Regd. Off: 1694-95, 1st Floor, Nai Sarak, Delhi-110006 (India)
Phone: 011-23283211, 23256658
Fax: 011-23256658
E-mail: contact@khannabooks.com
Website: www.khannabooks.com

Cover Design & Layout by
Limited Colors, Delhi-92

Printed in India

Dedicated to God
and
Our Parents

PREFACE

The study of C++ programming and data structure is both exiting and challenging. It is exiting because it presents a wide range of programming techniques that make it possible to solve more complex problems. It is challenging because the complex nature of the data structures brings with it many concepts that change the way we approach to design of program. the book is divided into these two parts: C++ and Data Structures.

Part One provides a comprehensive discussion of the C++ programming language.

C++ is a general purpose programming language that is powerful, efficient & compact. Today, C++ becomes more popular can be both interesting & fun. This book presents a contemporary approach to programming, stressing the importance of clarity, legibility, modularity and efficiency in program design. Thus the reader is exposed to the principles of good programming practice as well as the specific rules of C++.

Complete C++ programs are presented throughout the text, beginning with the first chapter. The use of an interactive programming style is emphasized throughout the text. The chapters are mainly organized in increasing degree of complexity.

Chapter 1 describes the evolution of C++ language, Object oriented programming and some other related concepts and describes disadvantages of conventional programming languages and advantages and disadvantages of object oriented approach. It covers the important features of C++ such as object, class, inheritance, encapsulation, polymorphism etc. using graphical approach. The presentation of object oriented languages is given at the last of the chapter.

Chapter 2 it covers character set, keywords, identifiers, constants, variables and various data types are given in detail. It also deals with to operators and expressions. Library functions are also given in lucid manner.

Chapter 3 Covers Each and every control statement with the help of flowcharts and simple as well as complex programs.

Chapter 4 deals with arrays and strings. It covers one, two and multidimensional arrays and contains numerous examples. It also covers the concept of strings.

Chapter 5 describes another building block of C++ programming call functions. Types of functions, various categories of functions are described in detail with the help of diagrams and programs. Important concept of return statement and recursion is also given in lucid manner. It also presents detailed analysis of each and every storage class is covered with the help of programming examples.

Chapter 6 explains one of the complex concept, Pointers. It covers all concepts of pointers like array and pointer, function and pointer.

Chapter 7 covers structure and unions, various declaration types of structure, structure and pointers, structure and array, structure and function and complete description of unions.

Chapter 8 covers all the description of classes, object assignment, explanation of private, public and protected keyword. Overloading of member functions, nested classes, pointer to classes and objects are explained with the help of suitable examples.

Chapter 9 explains the special member function constructors and destructors. The characteristics of constructors and destructors are given in well manner. The constructors also support various properties of functions such as overloading, default arguments etc. The advanced concepts such as copy and dynamic constructor, constructor intializer constructor overloading, order of constructor and destructor invocation constructors and arrays etc. are dealt with in addition to how to make explicit call to constructors and destructors.

Chapter 10 presents you with extra ordinary feature of C++ language, i.e. operator overloading. It contains overloading of unary and binary operators, rules for operator overloading and various examples of operator overloading with friend functions. The type conversion from basic to class type, class type to basic, and class type to another class type is explained with suitable examples.

Chapter 11 one of the important concepts of OOP, i.e. inheritance is covered in detail. The effect of private, public and protected access specifiers in inheritance is explained in a lucid manner. Types of inheritance and execution sequence of constructors can destructors in inheritance are illustrated. In addition, virtual classes, abstract classes, advantages and disadvantages are discussed in detail. At the end detailed description of Aggregation and composition is given using suitable examples.

Chapter 12 covers the concept of binding, early and late binding, polymorphism, and virtual functions. In addition to rules for virtual functions, pure virtual functions, abstract classes and working of virtual function, virtual table and void pointers. Also object slicing and virtual destructors are discussed with suitable examples.

Chapter 13 covers different special functions like inline, friend, static, const, volatile etc with the help of examples and simple programs.

Part Two Discusses Detail Description of Data Structures.

Chapter 14 covers the introduction to data structures and it also includes various types of data structures array, linked list, stack, queues, trees, graphs, etc.

Chapter 15 deals with string processing. Various string operations are discussed. We also included various pattern matching algorithms brute-force, boyer-moore etc.

Chapter 16 describes the concept of algorithm design and complexity; it also covers the features of abstract data type, big O notation, and asymptotic notations, primitive and non-primitive data types with examples.

Chapter 17 deals with arrays. It covers one, two and multidimensional arrays and contains numerous examples. It also covers row major and column major arrays. Pointers and Records are also described at the end of the chapter.

Chapter 18 discusses linked list, another significant type of data structures. It covers various operations such as traversing a list, searching and retrieving an element from a list. Types of linked lists, single, double and circular linked list are also described in detail.

Chapter 19 describes another building block of data structures in stack. Terminologies of stack, pictorial representation of stack, push and pop operations and applications are discussed in the chapter. Evaluation of postfix expression and infix to postfix expression, Recursion, balancing symbols and parenthesis matching are also given at the end of the chapter. Direct and indirect recursive are explained through programs, and popular examples such as the Tower of Hanoi and factorial are also covered in the chapter.

Chapter 20 presents Queue data structure, Representation of queue, insertion and deletion of an element in a queue, its static and dynamic implementation, and its applications are covered in the chapter. In addition, circular queue, deque and priority queues are explained in detail.

Chapter 21 is devoted to sorting methods. Various sorting techniques such as selection insertion, bubble, tree, merge, heap sot methods have been elaborated with simple algorithms, and their explanation with the help of examples. Partition exchange and radix sort methods have been discussed and supported with programming examples. It also covers various searching techniques such as linear and binary search with the help of examples. Attention has also been paid on establishing the efficiency of some searching methods.

At the last appendix's are given to summarize the complete Description of C++ programming techniques.

This book can be used by a wide reader audience, ranging from beginning programmers to practicing professionals. It is well suited for advanced or beginning college level students as a complete book for an introductory programming cause, as a supplementary text, or as an effective independent study guide.

Many examples & programs are included as an integral part of the text.

Each and Every chapter contains clear statements of definitions and principles together with illustrative and other descriptive material.

Suggestions for improvement of the book will be gratefully accepted for future editions.

R SINGH
I SINGH

ACKNOWLEDGEMENT

First we would like to thanks almighty for giving us courage to bring up this book. I express my deep sense of gratitude to Mr. Mukul Seth who complimented me for writing books. We duly acknowledge the contribution of our colleagues Prof.Rachhpal Singh (Head), Prof. Harbhajan Singh, Prof. Sandeep Waraich, Prof. Sukhwinder Kaur, Prof. Kawaljit Kaur, Prof. Mani Arora, Mr. Baljinder Singh, Mr. Jagbir Singh, Mr. Sukhwant Singh, Mr. Avtar Singh Sandhu, Mr. Navjeet Singh, Mr. Manpreet Singh, Mrs. Mandeep Kaur, Mrs. Jyoti Maini, Ms. Navinderjit kaur and Mr. Kawaljeet Singh, Mr. Lovedeep Singh for their valuable co-operation and guidance. We are grateful to Mr. Puneet Khanna M/s Khanna Book Publishing for his encouragement and motivation during this project.

R SINGH

I SINGH

CONTENTS

Part II: Data Structures

Part - I
C++

1. Getting Started With C++
2. C++ Programming Basics
3. Control Statements
4. Arrays and Strings
5. Functions
6. Pointers
7. Structures and Unions
8. Classes
9. More About Classes
10. Operator Overloading
11. Inheritance
12. Polymorphism and Virtual Function
13. Exploring Special Functions

CHAPTER 1

Getting Started With C++

1.1 INTRODUCTION

A programming language is a set of instructions and a series of lexical conventions specifically designed to order computers what to do. When choosing a programming language to make a project, many different considerations can be taken. First, one must decide what is known as the *level* of the programming language. The level determines how near to the hardware the programming language is. In the lower level languages, instructions are written thinking directly on interfacing with hardware, while in "high level" ones a more abstract or conceptual code is written.

Generally, high level code is more portable, that means it can work in more different machines with a smaller number of modifications, whereas a low level language is limited by the peculiarides of the hardware which it was written for. Nevertheless, the advantage of low level code is that it is usually faster due to the fact that it is indeed written taking advantage of the possibilities of a specific machine.

A higher or lower level of programming is to be chosen for a specific project depending on the type of program that is being developed. For example, when a hardware driver is developed for an operating system obviously a very low level is used for programming. While when big applications are developed usually a higher level is chosen, or a combination of critic parts written in low level languages and others in higher ones.

Although there are languages that are clearly thought to be low level, like Assembly, whose instruction sets are adapted to each machine the code is made for, and other languages are inherently high level, like the Java, that is designed to be totally independent of the platform where is going to run. The C++ language is in a middle position, since it can interact directly with the hardware almost with no limitations, and can as well abstract lower layers and work like one of the most powerful high level languages.

Based on the C programming language, C++ was designed to be used in a C programming environment on a UNIX system. C++ retains most of C's efficiency and flexibility, incorporates all the features of C, and also supports features that are unavailable in the C language. Many of the added features were designed to support object-oriented programming.

1.2 THE BEGINNING OF THE MODERN AGE OF PROGRAMMING: C

The invention of C defines the beginning of the modern age of programming. Its impact should not be underestimated because it fundamentally changed the way programming was approached and thought about. Its design philosophy and syntax have influenced every major language since. C was one of the major, revolutionary forces in computing.

First of all, CPL (Combined Programming Language) was developed with the purpose of creating a language that was capable of both high level, machine independent programming and would still allow the programmer to control the behaviour of individual bits of information. The one major drawback of CPL was that it was too large for use in many applications. In 1967, Basic Combined Programming Language (BCPL), developed by Martin Richards at Cambridge University aimed to make the language easily understandable and scaled down version of CPL while still retaining its basic features.

Martin Richards

In 1969, Ken Thompson created the B language from Martin Richard's BCPL (Basic Combined Programming Language). He used assembly language and B to produce the initial versions of the UNIX operating system. BCPL and B were typeless languages in which variables were simply words in memory. Afterwards the BCPL was renamed called B-language from its first alphabet.

Ken Thompson

Finally in 1972, a co-worker of Ken Thompson, Dennis Ritchie, returned some of the generality found in BCPL to the B language in the process of developing the language we now know as C. Dennis Ritchie of Bell Laboratories later converted B into C by retaining most of B's syntax in 1972 and wrote the first compiler. C-language was renamed from the BCPL second alphabet.

Dennis Ritchie

Dennis Ritchie of USA designed C programming language in 1972 which was developed at "AT & T's Bell Laboratories". It's purpose was to operate on the UNIX operating system which was the most common operating system at that time.

Due to certain good characteristics of C i.e. it's powerful and dominant behavior make it's use quickly spread beyond Bell labs. In the late 70's C was so popular that it replaced many well known languages of that time. It was used in almost all sort of programs.

C grew out of the structured programming revolution of the 1970s. Prior to structured programming, large programs were difficult to write because the program logic tended to degenerate into what is known as "spaghetti code," a tangled mass of jumps, calls, and returns that is difficult to follow. Structured languages addressed this problem by adding well-defined control statements, subroutines with local variables, and other improvements. Using structured languages, it became possible to write moderately large programs.

Although there were other structured languages at the time, such as Pascal, C was the first to

successfully combine power, elegance, and expressiveness. Its terse, yet easy-to-use syntax coupled with its philosophy that the programmer (not the language) was in charge quickly won many converts. It can be a bit hard to understand from today's perspective, but C was a breath of fresh air that programmers had long awaited. As a result, C became the most widely used structured programming language of the 1980s.

Many different organizations began applying different versions of C. This caused a serious problem for system developers. A committee was formed in 1983 by the American National Standards Institute (ANSI) in order to solve this problem which resulted in the approval of another version of C in 1989 which is known as ANSI C. Almost every modern C compiler has tendency to withstand this standard. ANSI C was later also approved by the International Standards Organization (ISO) in 1990. We can say C is the basic beginner's language for the development of any system and application software. Latest version of the C language is C99.

1.3 THE NEED FOR C++

Given the preceding discussion, you might be wondering why C++ was invented. Since C was a successful computer programming language, why was there a need for something else?

The answer is complexity. Although C was one of the most liked and widely used professional programming languages in the world, the invention of C++ was necessitated by one major programming factor: **increasing complexity**. Over the years, computer programs have become larger and more complex. Even though C is an excellent programming language, it has its own limits. In C, once a program exceeds from 35,000 to 150,000 lines of code, it becomes so complex that it is difficult to grasp as a totality.

Throughout the history of programming, the increasing complexity of programs has driven the need for better ways to manage that complexity. C++ is a response to that need. The purpose of C++ is to allow this barrier to be broken. The essence of C++ is to allow the programmer to comprehend and manage larger, more complex programs.

To better understand the correlation between increasing program complexity and computer language development, consider the following.

Approaches to programming have changed dramatically since the invention of the computer. For example, when computers were first invented, programming was done by using the computer's front panel to toggle in the binary machine instructions. As long as programs were just a few hundred instructions long, this approach worked. As programs grew, assembly language was invented so that programmers could deal with larger, increasingly complex programs by using symbolic representations of the machine instructions. As programs continued to grow, high-level languages were developed to give programmers more tools with which to handle the complexity.

The first widely used computer language was, of course, FORTRAN. While FORTRAN was a very impressive first step, it is hardly a language that encourages clear, easy-to-understand programs. The 1960s gave birth to structured programming, which is the method of programming encouraged by languages such as C. With structured languages it was, for the first time, possible to write moderately complex programs fairly easily. However, even with structured programming methods, once a project reaches a certain size, its complexity exceeds what a programmer can manage. By the late 1970s, many projects were near or at this point. In response to this problem, a new way to program began to emerge: object-oriented programming (OOP). Using OOP, a programmer could handle larger, more complex programs. The trouble was that C did not support object-oriented programming. The desire for an object-oriented version of C ultimately led to the creation of C++.

1.4 C++ IS BORN

C++ was invented by Bjarne Stroustrup in 1979, at Bell Laboratories in Murray Hill, New Jersey. He initially called the new language "C with Classes." However, in 1983 the name was changed to C++. Stroustrup built C++ on the foundation of C, including all of C's features, attributes, and benefits. He also adhered to C's underlying philosophy that the programmer, not the language, is in charge. At this point, it is critical to understand that Stroustrup did not create an entirely new programming language.

Bjarne Stroustrup

Instead, he enhanced an already highly successful language. Most of the features that Stroustrup added to C were designed to support object-oriented programming. In essence, C++ is the object-oriented version of C. By building upon the foundation of C, Stroustrup provided a smooth migration path to OOP. Instead of having to learn an entirely new language, a C programmer needed to learn only a few new features before reaping the benefits of the object-oriented methodology.

When creating C++, Stroustrup knew that it was important to maintain the original spirit of C, including its efficiency, flexibility, and philosophy, while at the same time adding support for object-oriented programming. Happily, his goal was accomplished. C++ still provides the programmer with the freedom and control of C, coupled with the power of objects.

Although C++ was initially designed to aid in the management of very large programs, it is in no way limited to this use. In fact, the object-oriented attributes of C++ can be effectively applied to virtually any programming task. It is not uncommon to see C++ used for projects such as editors, databases, personal file systems, networking utilities, and communication programs. Because C++ shares C's efficiency, much high-performance systems software is constructed using C++. Also, C++ is frequently the language of choice for Windows programming.

1.5 THE EVOLUTION OF C++

The evolution of C++ begins with C. The reason for this is easy to understand: C++ is built upon the foundation of C. Thus, C++ is a superset of C. C++ expanded and enhanced the C language to support object-oriented programming (which is described later in this module). C++ also added several other improvements to the C language, including an extended set of library routines.

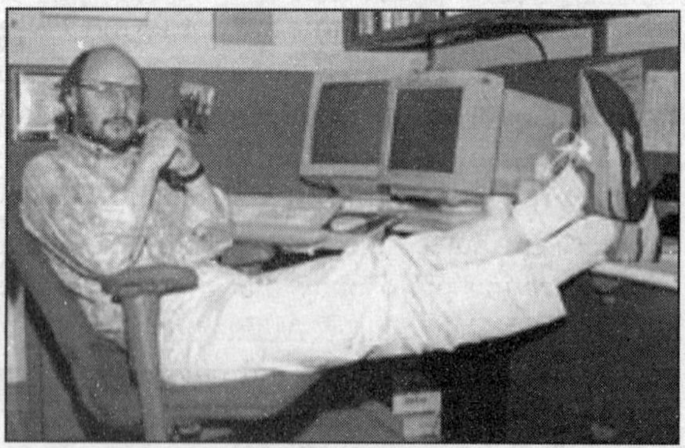

Bjarne Stroustrup

The C++ programming languages can be thought of as the C programming language with classes (and some other modern features are added). C++, an extension of C, was developed by Bjarne Stroustrup in the early 1980s at Bell Laboratories. C++ provides a number of features that "spruce up" the C language, but more importantly, it provides capabilities for object-oriented programming.

Most additions made by Stroustrup to C++ support object-oriented programming, sometimes referred to as OOP. (See the next sections for a brief explanation of object oriented programming.) Stroustrup states that some of C++'s object-oriented features were inspired by another object-oriented language called Simula67 and Algol68.

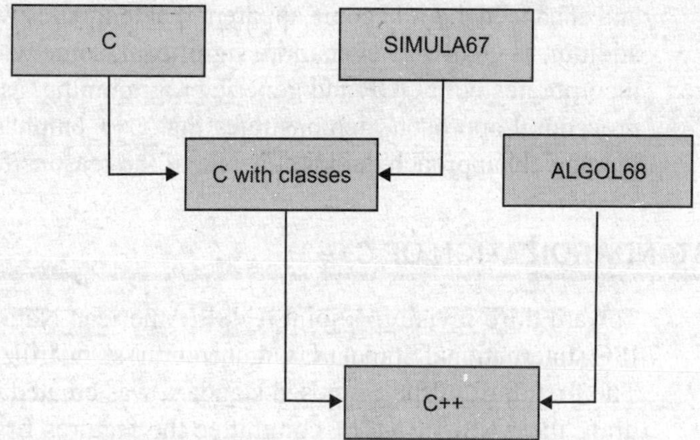

Figure 1.1: Evolution of C++

Therefore, C++ represents the blending of two powerful programming methods. Since C++ was first invented, it has undergone three major revisions, with each adding to and altering the language. The first revision was in 1985 and the second in 1990. The third occurred during the standardization of C++. Several years ago, work began on a standard for C++. Most of C is a subset of C++, and so most C programs are also C++ programs. (The reverse is not true; many C++ programs are definitely not C programs.) Unlike C, C++ has facilities for classes and so can be used for object-oriented programming.

Stroustrup added OOP features and generic programming support to C without significantly changing the C component. Thus C++ is a superset of C, meaning that any valid C program is a valid C++ program, too. There are some minor discrepancies, but nothing crucial. C++ programs can use existing C software libraries. Libraries are collections of programming modules that you can call up from a program. They provide proven solutions to many common programming problems, thus saving you much time and effort. This has helped the spread of C++.

The name C++ comes from the C increment operator ++, which adds one to the value of a variable. Therefore, the name C++ correctly suggests an augmented version of C. A computer program translates a real-life problem into a series of actions to be taken by a computer. While the OOP aspect of C++ gives the language the ability to relate to concepts involved in the problem, the C part of C++ gives the language the ability to get close to the hardware. This combination of abilities has enabled the spread of C++. It may also involve a mental shift of gears as you turn from one aspect of a program to another. Also, because C++ grafts OOP onto C, you can ignore C++'s object-oriented features. But you'll miss a lot if that's all you do. Only after C++ achieved some success did Stroustrup add templates, enabling generic programming. And only after the template feature had been used and enhanced did it become apparent that templates were perhaps as significant an addition as OOP—or even more significant, some would argue. The fact that C++ incorporates both OOP and generic programming, as well as the more traditional procedural approach, demonstrates that C++ emphasizes the utilitarian over the ideological approach, and that is one of the reasons for the language's success.

1.6 STANDARDIZATION OF C++

Toward third revision, a joint ANSI (American National Standards Institute) and ISO (International Standards Organization) standardization committee was formed. The first draft of the proposed standard was created on January 25, 1994. In that draft, the ANSI/ISO C++ committee the features first defined by Stroustrup and added some new ones as well. But in general, this initial draft reflected the state of C++ at the time.

Soon after the completion of the first draft of the C++ standard, an event occurred that caused the language to be greatly expanded: the creation of the Standard Template Library (STL) by Alexander Stepanov. The STL is a set of generic routines that you can use to manipulate data. It is both powerful and elegant, but also quite large. Subsequent to the first draft, the committee voted to include the STL in the specification for C++. The addition of the STL expanded the scope of C++ well beyond its original definition. While important, the inclusion of the STL, among other things, slowed the standardization of C++.

It is fair to say that the standardization of C++ took far longer than anyone had expected when it began. In the process, many new features were added to the language and many small changes were made. In fact, the version of C++ defined by the C++ committee is much larger and more complex than Stroustrup's original design. However, the standard is now complete. The final draft was passed out of committee on November 14, 1997. A standard for C++ is now a reality. The material in this book describes Standard C++, including all of its newest features. This is the version of C++ created by the ANSI/ISO standardization committee, and it is the one that is currently accepted by all major compilers.

1.7 C++ AND GENERIC PROGRAMMING

Generic programming is yet another programming paradigm supported by C++. It shares with OOP the aim of making it simpler to reuse code and the technique of abstracting general concepts. But whereas OOP emphasizes the data aspect of programming, generic programming emphasizes the algorithmic aspect. And its focus is different. OOP is a tool for managing large projects, whereas generic programming provides tools for performing common tasks, such as sorting data or merging lists. The term *generic* refers to create code that is type independent. C++ data representations come in many types—integers, numbers with fractional parts, characters, strings of characters, and user-defined compound structures of several types. If, for example, you wanted to sort data of these various types, you would normally have to create a separate sorting function for each type. Generic programming involves extending the language so that you can write a function for a generic (that is, not specified) type once and use it for a variety of actual types. C++ templates provide a mechanism for doing that.

1.8 C++ AND C

C++ is derived from the C language. We can say, it is a superset of C: Almost every correct statement in C is also a correct statement in C++, although the reverse is not true. The most important elements added to C to create C++ concern classes, objects, and object-oriented programming. However, C++ has many other new features as well, including an improved approach to input/output (I/O) and a new way to write comments. In fact, the practical differences between C and C++ are larger than you might think.

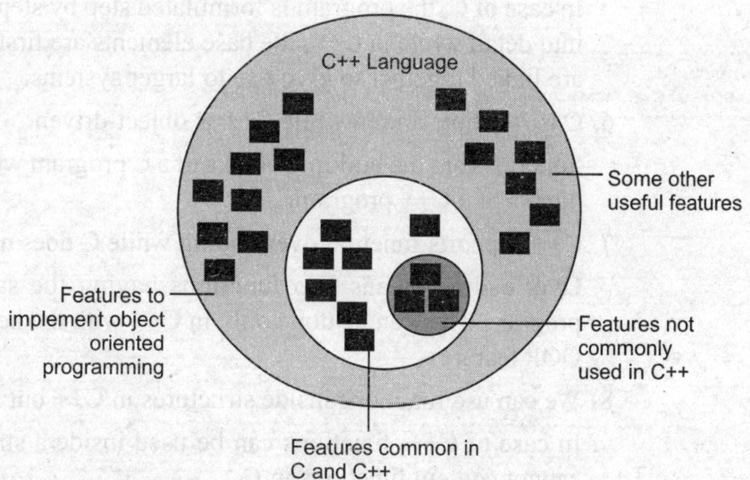

Figure 1.2: Shows the relationship of C and C++.

1.9 DIFFERENCE BETWEEN C AND C++

C++, as the name suggests is a superset of C. As a matter of fact, C++ can run most of C code while C cannot run C++ code. Here are the 20 major differences between C++ & C...

1. C came first, developed as a procedural block programming language back in 1972. While C++, created in 1979, was originally designed as an extension to C, and introduced the concept of object oriented programming techniques.
2. C follows the procedural programming paradigm while C++ is a multi-paradigm language(procedural as well as object oriented).

   In case of C, importance is given to the steps or procedure of the program while C++ focuses on the data rather than the process.

   Also, it is easier to implement/edit the code in case of C++ for the same reason.
3. In case of C, the data is not secured while the data is secured(hidden) in C++.

   This difference is due to specific OOP features like Data Hiding which are not present in C.
4. C is a low-level language while C++ is a middle-level language.

   C is regarded as a low-level language(difficult interpretation & less user friendly) while C++ has features of both low-level(concentration on whats going on in the machine hardware) & high-level languages(concentration on the program itself) & hence is regarded as a middle-level language.
5. C uses the top-down approach while C++ uses the bottom-up approach.

   In case of C, the program is formulated step by step, each step is processed into detail while in C++, the base elements are first formulated which then are linked together to give rise to larger systems.
6. C is function-driven while C++ is object-driven.

   Functions are the building blocks of a C program while objects are building blocks of a C++ program.
7. C++ supports function overloading while C does not.

   Overloading means two functions having the same name in the same program. This can be done only in C++ with the help of Polymorphism(an OOP feature)
8. We can use functions inside structures in C++ but not in C.

   In case of C++, functions can be used inside a structure while structures cannot contain functions in C.

9. The NAMESPACE feature in C++ is absent in case of C.

   C++ uses NAMESPACE which avoid name collisions. For instance, two students enrolled in the same university cannot have the same roll number while two students in different universities might have the same roll number. The universities are two different namespace & hence contain the same roll number(identifier) but the same university(one namespace) cannot have two students with the same roll number(identifier)

10. The standard input & output functions differ in the two languages.

    C uses scanf & printf while C++ uses cin>> & cout<< as their respective input & output functions

11. C++ allows the use of reference variables while C does not.

    Reference variables allow two variable names to point to the same memory location. We cannot use these variables in C programming.

12. C is a programming language for general purpose computers; C++ is an extension of the C programming language.

13. C is an imperative systems implementation language; C++ is used to design hardware.

14. C++ is used to design large and complex programs but C is used to design medium size programs.

15. A character constant in C is automatically converted into its equivalent ASCII, but it is not the case in C++.

16. In C main() function can be called within the program like the invocation of other functions. But in C++ it can be called with the help of classes.

17. In C register variables cannot be addressed, but in C++ it is possible.

18. The "stream.h" library in C++ provides a very useful alternative to "stdio.h" of C.

19. In C++, we use the feature of inheritance to make the code reusable but no such feature is available in C.

20. Abstraction is possible in case of C++ but not possible in C language.

1.10 CHARACTERISTICS OF C++

C++ has certain characteristics over other programming languages. The most remarkable are:

1. Object-oriented programming

The possibility to orientate programming to objects allows the programmer to design applications from a point of view more like a communication between objects rather than on a structured sequence of code. In addition it allows a greater reusability of code in a more logical and productive way.

2. *Portability*

You can practically compile the same C++ code in almost any type of computer and operating system without making any changes. C++ is the most used and ported programming language in the world.

3. *Brevity*

Code written in C++ is very short in comparison with other languages, since the use of special characters is preferred to key words, saving some effort to the programmer (and prolonging the life of our keyboards!).

4. *Modular programming*

An application's body in C++ can be made up of several source code files that are compiled separately and then linked together. Saving time since it is not necessary to recompile the complete application when making a single change but only the file that contains it. In addition, this characteristic allows to link C++ code with code produced in other languages, such as Assembler or C.

5. *C Compatibility*

C++ is backwards compatible with the C language. Any code written in C can easily be included in a C++ program without making any change.

6. *Speed*

The resulting code from a C++ compilation is very efficient, due indeed to its duality as high-level and low-level language and to the reduced size of the language itself.

1.11 OBJECT-ORIENTED PROGRAMMING

Central to C++ is object-oriented programming (OOP), it is necessary to understand its foundational principles. As just explained, OOP was the impetus for the creation of C++. Because of this, it is useful to understand OOP's basic principles before you write even a simple C++ program.

Object-oriented programming (OOP) is a currently popular and powerful programming technique. The three main characteristics of OOP are encapsulation, inheritance, and polymorphism. Encapsulation is a form of information hiding or abstraction. Inheritance has to do with writing reusable code. Polymorphism refers to a way that a single name can have multiple meanings in the context of inheritance.

Having made those statements, we must admit that they will hold little meaning for readers who have not heard of OOP before. However, we will describe all these terms in detail later in this chapter.

OOP is a powerful way to approach the job of programming. Programming methodologies have changed dramatically since the invention of the computer, primarily to accommodate the increasing complexity of programs. For example, when computers were first invented, programming was done by toggling in the binary machine instructions using the computer's front panel. As long as programs were just a few hundred instructions long, this approach worked. As programs grew, assembly language was invented so that a programmer could deal with larger, increasingly complex programs, using symbolic representations of the machine instructions. As programs continued to grow, high-level languages were introduced that gave the programmer more tools with which to handle complexity. The first widespread language was, of course, FORTRAN. Although FORTRAN was a very impressive first step, it is hardly a language that encourages clear, easy to understanding programs.

The 1960s gave birth to **structured programming**. This is the method encouraged by languages such as C and Pascal. The use of structured languages made it possible to write moderately complex programs fairly easily. Although the principles of structured programming improved the clarity, reliability, and ease of maintenance of programs, large-scale programming still remains a challenge. OOP brings a new approach to that challenge. Unlike procedural programming, which emphasizes algorithms, OOP emphasizes the data. Rather than try to fit a problem to the procedural approach of a language, OOP attempts to fit the language to the problem. The idea is to design data forms that correspond to the essential features of a problem. The topology of a structure program is inherently different than the topology of an OO program. Modules are nested into a calling tree, as shown below:

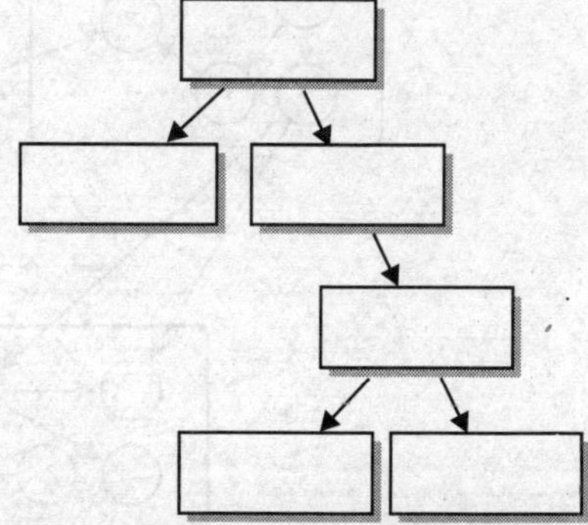

Figure 1.3: The topology of a structure program is a tree of modules

We all know that the structured languages are a powerful tool, even they reach their limit when a project becomes too large. Consider this: At each milestone in the development of programming, techniques and tools were created to allow the programmer to deal with increasingly greater complexity. Each step of the way, the new approach took the best elements of the previous methods and moved forward. Prior to the invention of OOP, many projects were nearing (or exceeding) the point where the structured approach no longer worked. Object-oriented methods were created to help programmers break through these barriers.

Object-oriented programming took the best ideas of structured programming and combined them with several new concepts. The result was a different way of organizing a program. In the most general sense, a program can be organized in one of two ways: around its code (what is happening) or around its data (who is being affected). Using only structured programming techniques, programs are typically organized around code. This approach can be thought of as **"code acting on data."** For example, a program written in a structured language such as C is defined by its functions, any of which may operate on any type of data used by the program. Object-oriented programs work the other way around. They are organized around data, with the key principle being "data controlling access to code." In an object-oriented language, you define the data and the routines that are permitted to act on that data. Thus, a data type defines precisely what sort of operations can be applied to that data.

An object-oriented program may thus be viewed as a collection of interacting *objects*, as opposed to the conventional model, in which a program is seen as a list of tasks (subroutines) to perform. In OOP, each object is capable of receiving messages, processing data, and sending messages to other objects and can be viewed as an independent 'machine' with a distinct role or responsibility. The actions (or "methods") on these objects are closely associated with the object.

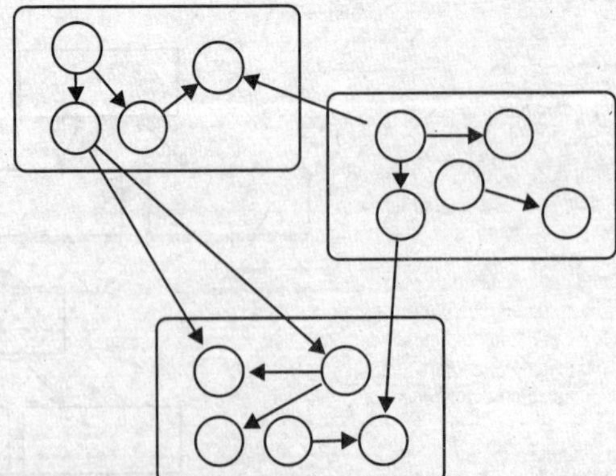

Figure 1.4: The topology of an OO program is communicating clusters of more tightly coupled objects

The topology of an OO program is inherently less ordered. Objects cluster together by those which communicate most frequently. Inter-cluster messages exist, but are less common than intra-cluster messages. Notice how much like a computer network this topology looks.

C++ accommodates OOP by providing classes, a kind of data type combining both data and algorithms.

C++ is not what some authorities would call a "**pure OOP language**." C++ tempers its OOP features with concerns for efficiency and what some might call "practicality." This combination has made C++ currently the most widely used OOP language, although not all of its usage strictly follows the OOP philosophy.

1.12 THE CHARACTER OF C++

C++ has classes that allow it to be used as an object-oriented language. It allows for overloading of functions and operators. C++'s connection to the C language gives it a more traditional look than newer object-oriented languages, yet it has more powerful abstraction mechanisms than many other currently popular languages. C++ has a template facility that allows for full and direct implementation of algorithm abstraction. C++ templates allow you to code using parameters for types. The newest C++ standard, and most C++ compilers, allow multiple namespaces to accommodate more reuse of class and function names. The exception handling facilities in C++ are similar to what you would find in other programming languages. Memory management in C++ is similar to that in C. The programmer must allocate his or her own memory and handle his or her own garbage collection. Most compilers will allow you to do C-style memory management in C++, since C is essentially a subset of C++. However, C++ also has its own syntax for a C++ style of memory management, and you are advised to use the C++ style of memory management when coding in C++. This book uses only the C++ style of memory management.

1.13 DISADVANTAGE OF CONVENTIONAL PROGRAMMING

The Conventional Programming which is a top down approach starts by first finding all the things that needs to be done and then decomposing each task into smaller tasks using functions. Each function can have its own data and logic and call other functions of the program. As programs grow ever larger and more complex, even the structured programming approach begins to show signs of strain. Analyzing the reasons for these failures reveals that there are weaknesses in the procedural paradigm itself. No matter how well the structured programming approach is implemented, large programs become excessively complex.

What are the reasons for these problems with procedural languages? There are two related problems. First, functions have unrestricted access to global data. Second, unrelated functions and data, the basis of the procedural paradigm, provide a poor model of the real world. The program written in these languages consists of a sequence of instructions that tells the compiler or interpreter to perform a given task. When program code is large then it becomes inconvenient to mange it. To overcome this problem, procedures or subroutines were adopted to make a program more understandable to the programmers. In many programs, important data variables are declared as global. In case of programs containing several functions, every function can access the global data as simulated in Figure 1.6.

1.13.1 Unrestricted Access

In a procedural program, one written in C for example, there are two kinds of data. Local data is hidden inside a function, and is used exclusively by the function. Local data is closely related to its function and is safe from modification by other functions.

However, when two or more functions must access the same data—and this is true of the most important data in a program—then the data must be made global. Global data can be accessed by any function in the program. The arrangement of local and global variables in a procedural program is shown in Figure 1.5.

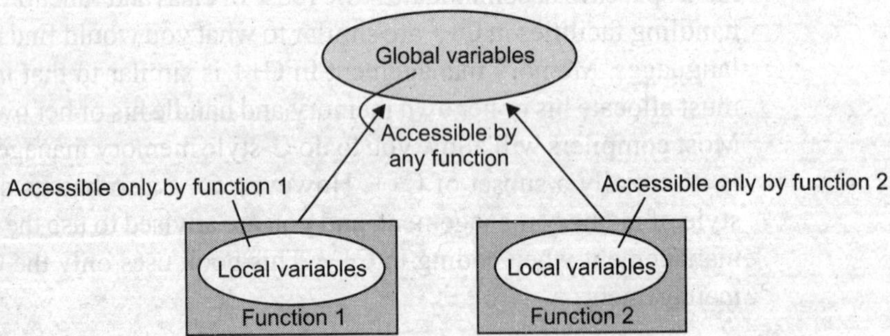

Figure 1.5: Local and global variables

In a large program, there are many functions and many global data items. The problem with the procedural paradigm is that this leads to an even larger number of potential connections between functions and data, as shown in Figure 1.6.

This large number of connections causes problems in several ways. First, it makes a program's structure difficult to conceptualize. Second, it makes the program difficult to modify. A change made in a global data item may necessitate rewriting all the functions that access that item.

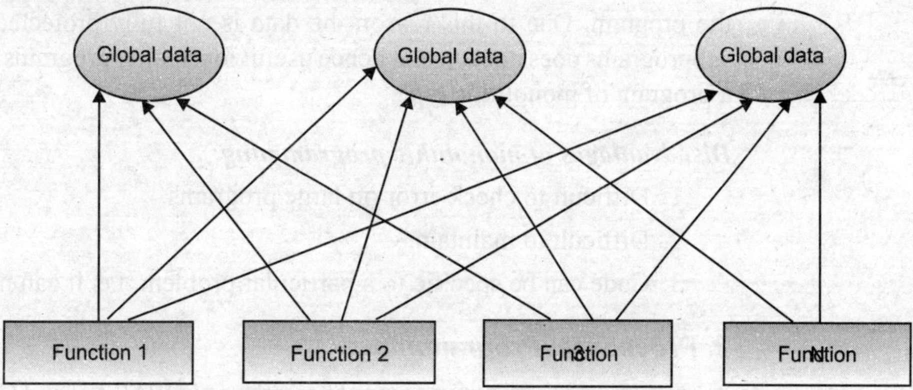

Figure 1.6: Functions accessing global data

1.13.2 Programming Paradigms

There are the different programming paradigms in the world of programming. Some of them are described here:

1. Monolithic Programming

Monolithic Programming indicates the program which contains a single function for the large program. It is always fight with modular programming to place the identity in programming world. In monolithic programming will not divide the program and it is a single thread of execution. When the program size increases it leads inconvenience and difficult to maintain.

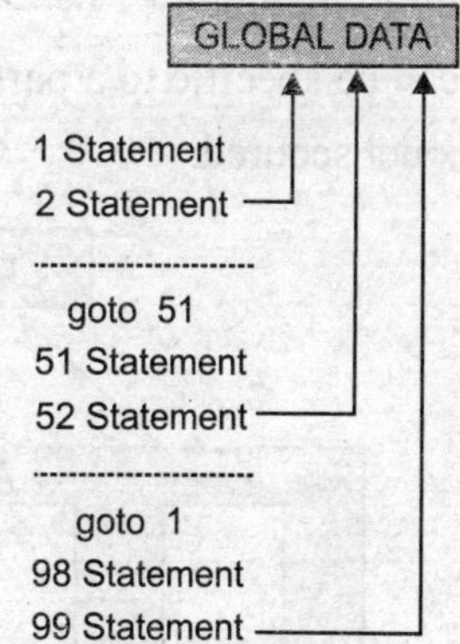

Figure 1.7: Monolithic programming

In monolithic programming languages such as BASIC and ASSEMBLY, the data variables declared are global and the statements are written in sequence. The program contains jumps statements such as goto, which transfer control to any statement as specified in it. The global data can be accessed from any portion of the program. Due to this reason the data is not fully protected. The concept of subprograms does not exit and hence useful for smaller programs. Figure 1.7 shows a program of monolithic type.

Disadvantages of monolithic programming:

1. Difficult to check error on large programs.
2. Difficult to maintain.
3. Code can be specific to a particular problem. i.e. it can not be reused.

2. Procedural Programming

In procedural programming languages such as FORTRAN and COBOL are the top down approaches in which programs are divided into a number of segments known as subprograms. In this approach, the data and functions are separated elements. Thus it focuses on functions apart from data. It shows different subprograms having access to the same global data. Here also, the data is not fully protected. Data is global and all the subprograms share the same data. Program flow control is achieved through the use of jumps (goto statements) and function calls. This approach avoids the repetition of code which is the main drawback of the monolithic programming. The basic drawback of procedural programming approach is that data is not secured as it can be accessible by all the functions. This approach is mainly used for medium sized applications.

Figure 1.8 describes a program of procedural type.

Disadvantages of procedural programming:

1. Difficult to maintain.
2. Code can be specific to a particular problem. i.e. it can not be reused.
3. Data is not secured.

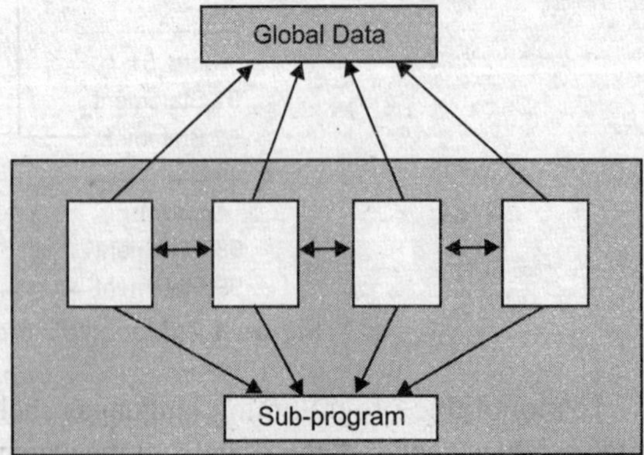

Figure 1.8: Procedural programming

3. Structured Programming

In structured programming languages such as PASCAL and C larger programs are developed. Structured programming help the programmer to divide the whole program into different modules and each module is separately developed and tested. Then the linker will link all these modules to form the complete program.

Each module has a set of related procedure. The use of modules and procedures makes the program more comprehensible. Each procedure has to perform different tasks. Each module has its own set of local variables and programs code as shown in Figure 1.9.

It also introduces the concept of user-defined datatypes and support modular programming. This approach emphasizes more on functions rather than data. It focuses on the development of large software applications in which different parts of the application are developed independently.

Advantage of structured programming:

1. Modular program are easier to code and debug.
2. Reduces the programming size.
3. Code can be reused in other programs.
4. Problem can be isolated to specific module so easier to find the error and correct it.

Disadvantages of structured programming:

1. Code can't be reused in same program.
2. Data is not secured.
3. It emphasis on functions rather than data.
4. Increase complexity when program becomes large.

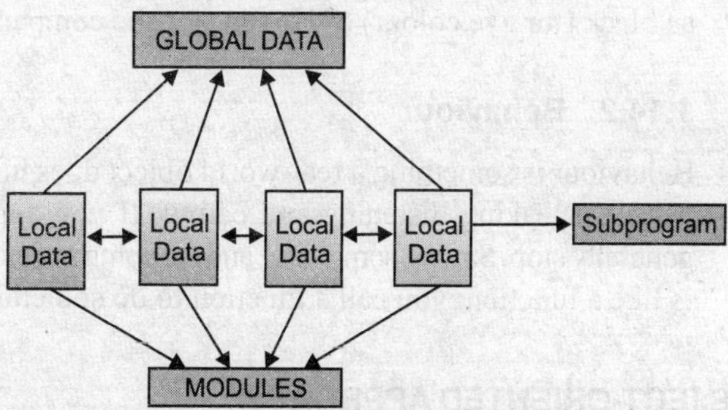

Figure 1.9: Structured programming

Following are drawbacks observed in monolithic, procedural, and structured programming languages:

1. **Data is not secured:** As the given data is global so unauthorized functions can access this data accidently and thus make it inconsistent. Data passes globally from one function to another. Most functions have access to global data. Hence, security to data is not provided.

   For example: Large size programs are divided into smaller programs known as functions. These functions can call one another. Hence, security is not provided.
2. **More emphasis on function rather than data:** In this approach more concentration is given to a function that performs some specific task and not to the data which given a second class status even though data is reason for program's existence.
3. **Non real world modeling:** The arrangement of separate data and functions doesn't model the real world modeling. In other words, the way the problem is solved using this approach is not close to reality.

1.14 REAL-WORLD MODELING

One of the most important problems with the procedural paradigm is that its arrangement of separate data and functions does a poor job of modeling things in the real world. In the physical world we deal with objects such as people, laptop and cars. Such objects aren't like data and they aren't like functions. Complex real-world objects have both attributes and behavior.

1.14 .1 Attributes

Examples of attributes (sometimes called its *features*) are, for people, eye colour and its job; and, for cars, colour and company. As it turns out, attributes in the real world are equivalent to data in a program: they have a certain specific values, such as black (for eye colour) or Honda (for the company of car).

1.14.2 Behaviour

Behaviour is something a real-world object does in response to some stimulus, for people, speaking, listening and eating. If you apply the brakes in a car, it will generally stop. Saying something and stopping are examples of behaviour. Behaviour is like a function: you call a function to do something and it does it.

1.15 OBJECT-ORIENTED APPROACH

Object-Oriented Approach is a better way of solving problems in computers compared to the procedural language programming such as in C. oops is designed around the data being operated upon as opposed to the operations, these operations are designed to fit data.

The fundamental idea behind object-oriented languages is to combine into a single unit both data and the functions that operate on that data. Such a unit is called an object. OOP uses objects as its fundamental building blocks. Each object is an instance of some class. Classes allow the mechanism of data abstraction for creating new data types. Inheritance allows building of new classes from existing classes. Hence if any of these elements are missing in a program we cannot consider that program as objected oriented program.

Object oriented programming attempts to solve the problems with only one approach; dividing the problems in sub-modules and using different objects. Objects of the program interact by sending messages to each other. The drawing below illustrates this clearly -

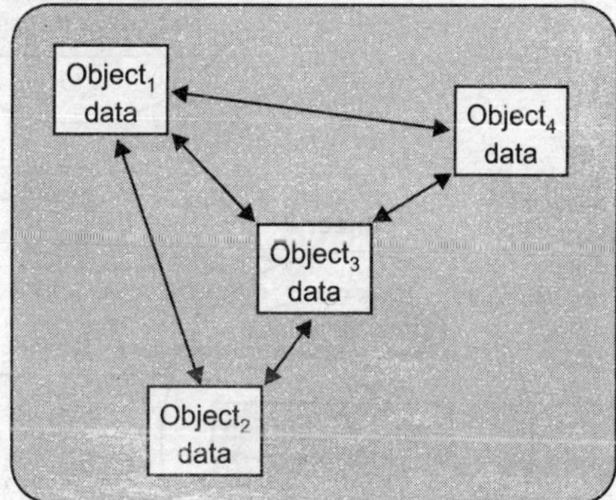

Figure 1.10: Object-Oriented approach

An object's functions, called member functions in C++, typically provide the only way to access its data. If you want to read a data item in an object, you call a member function in the object. It will access the data and return the value to you. You can't access the data directly. The data is hidden, so it is safe from accidental alteration. Data and its functions are said to be encapsulated into a single entity. Data encapsulation and data hiding are key terms in the description of object-oriented languages.

Abstraction is a term that is important for OOP. but it is not specific to this programming approach. There are a number of other programming approaches that use abstraction as well. While reusability is a concept that has often be associated with object oriented programming, it has existed since the 1950s, long before OOP was developed. If you want to modify the data in an object, you know exactly what functions interact with it: the member functions in the object. No other functions can access the data. This simplifies writing, debugging, and maintaining the program.

One characteristic which is found with many OOP languages is message passing programming abilities. It is not important how a computation is set up. However, an emphasis is placed on how text is split into modules. Object oriented programming languages place an importance on the code within a program. The computation model is insignificant. A C++ program typically consists of a number of objects, which communicate with each other by calling one another's member functions. The organization of a C++ program is shown in Figure 1.11.

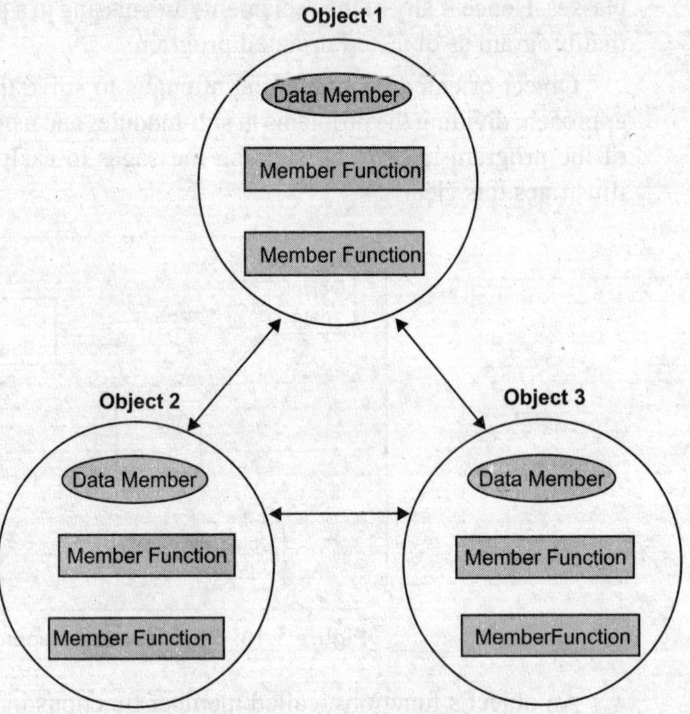

Figure 1.11: Object-Oriented paradigm

The member functions in C++ are also called methods in some other object-oriented languages (such as Smalltalk,). Also, data members are referred to as attributes or instance variables. Calling an object's member function is referred to as sending a message to the object.

One of the principal advantages of object-oriented programming is that they enable programmers to create modules that do not need to be changed when a new type of object is added. A programmer can simply create a new object that inherits many of its features from existing objects. This inherits technique is called inheritance. This makes object-oriented programs easier to modify.

Thus, C++ supports styles of programming that rely on fairly direct manipulation of hardware resources to deliver a high degree of efficiency plus higher-level styles of programming that rely on user-defined types to provide a model of data and computation that is closer to a human's view of the task being performed by a computer. These higher-level styles of programming are often called data abstraction, object-oriented programming, and generic programming.

For Example: You might want to think of objects as departments—such as sales, accounting, personnel, and so on—in a company. Departments provide an important approach to corporate organization. In most companies (except very small ones), people don't work on personnel problems one day, the payroll the next, and then go out in the field as salespeople the week after. Each department has its own personnel, with clearly assigned duties. It also has its own data: the accounting department has payroll figures, the sales department has sales figures, and the personnel department keeps records of each employee, and so on.

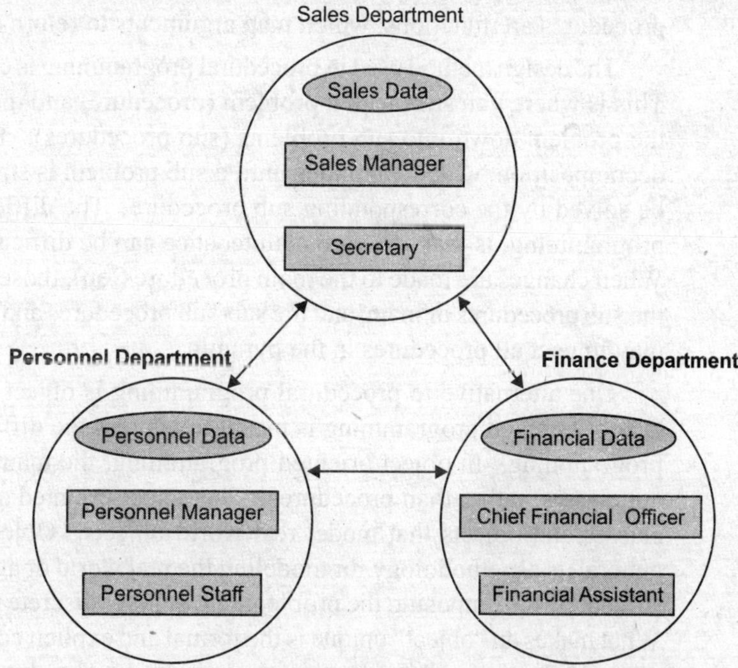

Figure 1.12: Corporate Organization using object oriented paradigm

The people in each department control and operate on that department's data. Dividing the company into departments makes it easier to comprehend and control the company's activities, and helps maintain the integrity of the information used by the company. The accounting department, for instance, is responsible for the payroll data. If you're a sales manager, and you need to know the total of all the salaries paid in the southern region in July, you don't just walk into the accounting department and start rummaging through file cabinets. You send a memo to the appropriate person in the department, then wait for that person to access the data and send you a reply with the information you want. This ensures that the data is accessed accurately and that it is not corrupted by inept outsiders. This view of corporate organization is shown in Figure 1.12. In the same way, objects provide an approach to program organization while helping to maintain the integrity of the program's data.

1.16 OBJECT-ORIENTED PROGRAMMING VS. PROCEDURAL PROGRAMMING

Programs are made up of modules, which are parts of a program that can be coded and tested separately, and then assembled to form a complete program. In procedural languages (i.e. C) these modules are procedures, where a procedure is a sequence of statements. In C for example, procedures are a sequence of imperative statements, such as assignments, tests, loops and invocations of sub procedures. These procedures are functions, which map arguments to return statements.

The design method used in procedural programming is called Top Down Design. This is where you start with a problem (procedure) and then systematically break the problem down into sub problems (sub procedures). This is called functional decomposition, which continues until a sub problem is straightforward enough to be solved by the corresponding sub procedure. The difficulties with this type of programming, is that software maintenance can be difficult and time consuming. When changes are made to the main procedure (top), those changes can cascade to the sub procedures of main, and the sub-sub procedures and so on, where the change may impact all procedures in the pyramid.

One alternative to procedural programming is object oriented programming. Object oriented programming is meant to address the difficulties with procedural programming. In object oriented programming, the main modules in a program are classes, rather than procedures. The object-oriented approach lets you create classes and objects that model real world objects. Object Orientation [OO], in general, is a methodology for modeling the real world or at least the problem being solved, by decomposing the problem into smaller discrete pieces called "Objects". What makes an "object" unique is the formal and explicit combination these smaller pieces' behavior with its' data into a single entity. The object's behaviors are called methods in OO terminology, while its data is called the Object's state. "Objects" will make up every part of the solution, that is, every part of the program will be made from objects. Formally, there are technical attributes of that must be present for a program (or a programming Language) to be considered Object Oriented, such as inheritance, polymorphism, encapsulation, and protection; aspects of these terms are still under debate in many programming circles, so no, 100% certain, absolutely clear definition is possible. The core concept, though, is that an "Object" is binding together of data and behavior, and Object Oriented programming, is the use of Objects while solving the problem.

The various differences between procedure oriented and Object oriented programming languages is written as in the below table:

Procedure Oriented Programming	Object-Oriented Programming
1. It emphasis on non-real world modeling i.e. have algorithmic approach.	It emphasis on real-world modeling by using objects.
2. Data is global so accessible to all the function of the program without any type of restrictions.	Data and functions are bind together into a single unit called object. So data and functions are only accessible to those objects which protect data from unauthorized access.
3. It uses procedural Programming and modular approach. Large Programs are divided into smaller programs (called functions)	It uses an object-oriented approach. Here large Programs are divided into smaller modules (called objects).
4. It does not emphasizes on what to do to solve a problem, as functions are action oriented	It emphasizes on what to do to solve a problem as functions are interface to the components or elements of the problem.
5. Data is in shareable mode and can be moved from one function to another function i.e. any external function can access the data.	Data is in non-sharable mode and is hidden. Data cannot be accessed by external functions.
6. Modification and maintenance of large and complex programs are time consuming and costly.	Modification and maintenance of large and complex programs are easy and less costly.
7. Functions communicate with each other by passing the arguments.	Messages communication between objects.
8. It uses procedure abstraction.	It uses data abstraction.
9. It is used for designing medium size problems.	It is used for designing large and complex problems.
10. It divides the problem into functions.	It divides the problems into number of entities called objects.
11. It uses top-down approach.	It uses bottom-up approach.
12. The examples are high level language like C, Fortran, Basic, Pascal etc.	The examples are Object Oriented language like C++, Java and C# (C-sharp) etc.

With OOP, every object can handle data, get messages, and transfer messages to other objects. The objects will all act as independent units in their own right, and they will be responsible for carrying out a certain process.

Because the objects are not dependent on each other, OOP is seen as being more flexible than older methods of programming. It has become quite popular, and it is now used in a number of advanced software engineering projects. Many programmers feel that object oriented programming is easier for beginners to learn than previous programming methods. Because it is easier to learn, it can also be analyzed and maintained without a large amount of difficulty. However, there are some people that feel that OOP is more complicated than older programming methods. To understand object oriented programming, there are a few concepts you will need to become familiar with.

The first concept that you will need to learn is called a “class.” A class creates the attributes of a thing, and it will also define the processes that the thing can carry out. For example, a class called “cats” will have the attributes which are commonly found with cats, such as the ability to purr. A class will bring about modularity within the objected oriented computer application. Someone who is not a programmer should be able to find a class. The reason for this is because the attributes of the class should be something that will make sense to them. It is also important for the code of a class to be self contained to a certain degree. When code is written with relevant names, it will be easier to understand. Making sure the code is self-contained will allow one part of the application to be updated without needing to change the other parts.

It is this modularity that makes OOP an effective programming method. It will also help the application solve the problems that it was designed for. The next concept that you will want to become familiar with is an “object.” An object can be defined as a specific instance of a class. As an example, while the class Cats will provide all the attributes that are found in all cats, the “object” named Betsy is a specific cat. While it shares the same attributes which are found in all cats, it has fur with a unique color. In object oriented programming, a programmer would say that the object Betsy is a run-time instance of the class Cats.

A class may also be divided into sub-groups. Certain variations of a class may not be a specific object. The class Cats may have a sub-group which consists of multiple cat breeds. For example, if Betsy were a Persian cat, it would be an instance of the Persian cat sub-group. Every object within an OOP language will share some attributes with the parent class, but it will also have unique attributes as well. The next concept that you will want to become familiar with is “method.” A method may also be called a “message” and can be defined as the abilities of an object. Because Betsy is a cat, Betsy can purr. Because of this, “purr” is a method that Betsy has.

Betsy may have a number of other methods. When a method is used within an object oriented programming language, it will only affect a single object. This is true even if the method is designed for the entire class. While all cats can purr, you will only need one cat to do it. Methods can further be broken down into commands, callbacks, or queries. A query will tell you about the state of the object, and a command will cause that object to carry out a task. A callback is a method that is composed of a part within an object. The part will notify its parent that an event has taken place, and the object may need to react to the event.

1.17 FEATURES OR CHARACTERISTICS OF OBJECT ORIENTED PROGRAMMING

One of the most important characteristics of OOP (Object Oriented Programming) is the data encapsulation concept, which means that there is a very close attachment between data items and procedures. The procedures (methods) are responsible for manipulating the data in order to reflect its behavior. The public interface, formed by the collections of messages understood by an object, completely defines how to use this object.

Programs that want to manipulate an object only have to be concerned about which messages this object understands, and do not have to worry about how these tasks are achieved or the internal structure of the object. The hiding of internal details makes an object abstract, and the technique is normally known as data abstraction. Normally, objects of a given type are instances of a class, whose definition specifies the private (internal) working of these objects as well as their public interface. Basically the creation of an object is referred to as instantiation, and it consists of a class definition with appropriate initial values.

Another powerful feature of OOP, is the concept of inheritance (derived classes in C++), meaning the derivation of a similar or related object (the derived object) from a more general based object. The derived class can inherit the properties of its base class and also adds its own data and routines. The concept above is known as single inheritance, but it is also possible to derive a class from several base classes, which is known as multiple inheritances. Overloading, in OOP, means the ability to assign multiple meanings to the names of operators and functions.

For example, the operator +, normally associated with arithmetic addition can be overloaded to add one list to another in a certain context. Polymorphism means the sending of a message to an object without concern about how the software is going to accomplish the task, and furthermore it means that the task can be executed in completely different ways depending on the object that receives the message (in C++, polymorphism is implemented through the use of virtual functions). When the decision as to which actions are going to be executed is made at run-time, the polymorphism is referred to as late binding (as in the case of virtual functions). If they are made at compile time then it is known as early binding.

1. Objects
2. Classes
3. Inheritance
4. Encapsulation
5. Abstraction
6. Polymorphism
7. Dynamic binding
8. Message passing
9. Reusability
10. Modularity
11. Dynamism
12. Delegation
13. Genericity
14. Extensibility
15. Persistence

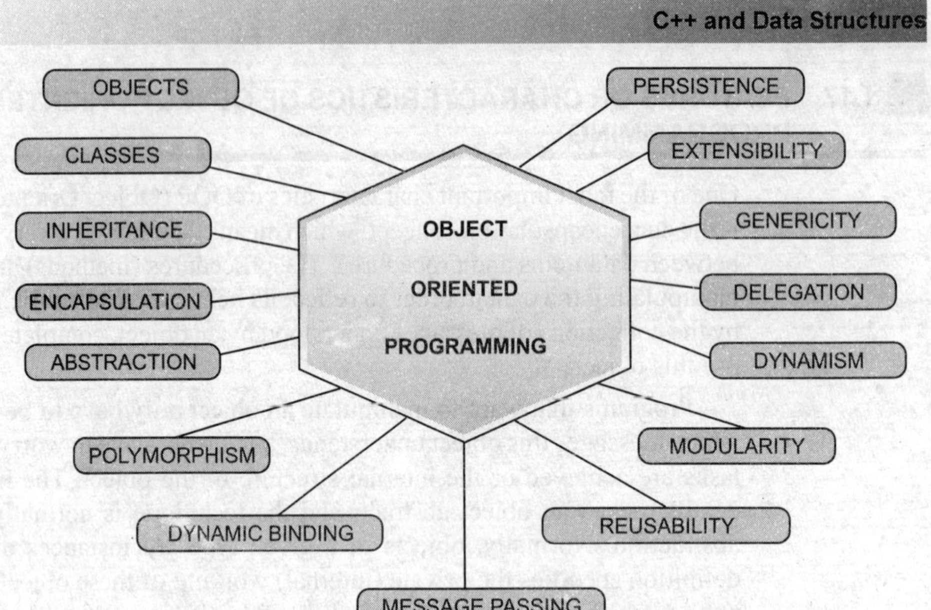

Figure 1.13: Features of Object Oriented Programming

1.18 OBJECTS

In object-oriented programming language C++, the data and functions (procedures to manipulate the data) are bundled together as a self-contained unit called an ***object.*** An object is a component of a program that knows how to perform certain actions and to interact with other pieces of the program. An object is a region of storage with associated semantics.

An object is a software bundle of related state and behaviour. Software objects are often used to model the real-world objects that you find in everyday life.

Definition: *"An object is a bundle of variables and related methods."*

The term "Object" that gives OOP it's name, refers to a *conceptual* object that represents an item in our program or system. This could be anything from an online form or a computer file, to a real world object such as a car.

This representation consists of ***attributes*** - the characteristics of our object; and ***methods*** - a set of functions and calculations that are either performed to modify the object itself, or are involved in some external effect.

Objects are further subdivided into physical objects and logical objects. For example a person, a place, a bank account, a table, a chair etc. are physical objects.

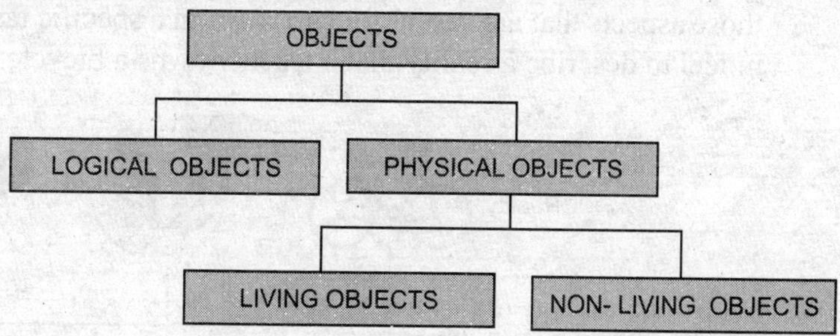

Figure 1.14: Different types of objects

An inventory, dictionary sale purchase files, library software are logical objects. An object has attributes like person has head, ear, eyes, arms and legs and has function of eating, walking, listing and speaking etc. A non-living object like a chair has four legs, back, made-up of wooden/steel/iron/plastic etc and is used to be seated.

In OOP perspective, an object is nothing but an instance of a class that contains real values instead of variables.

Given below are some objects that we use in our daily life:

Figure 1.15: Graphical representation of some objects

The real-world objects (any living or non- living thing) share two characteristics: they do have state and behaviour. For example, dogs have a state (like name, color, etc) and behaviour (like barking, fetching etc). Also consider for example a Bicycle have a state such as current gear, current wheels, number of gears etc and behaviour such as braking, accelerating etc.

After the real-world objects Software objects have been modelled in that, they too, have states and behaviours. A software object maintains states in the variables and implements behaviour by methods.

Object-orientation is so called because this method sees things that are part of the real world as objects. A phone is an object in the same way as a bicycle, a human being, or insurance policies are objects. In everyday life, we simplify objects in our thinking – we work with models. Software development does essentially the same: objects occurring in reality are reduced to a few features that are relevant in the current situation. Instead of real objects, we work with symbols. Properties and composition of objects correspond only roughly to reality; the model selects only those aspects that are useful for carrying out a specific task. In figure 1.16, we use model to describe a reality that a teacher owns a bicycle and he reads a book.

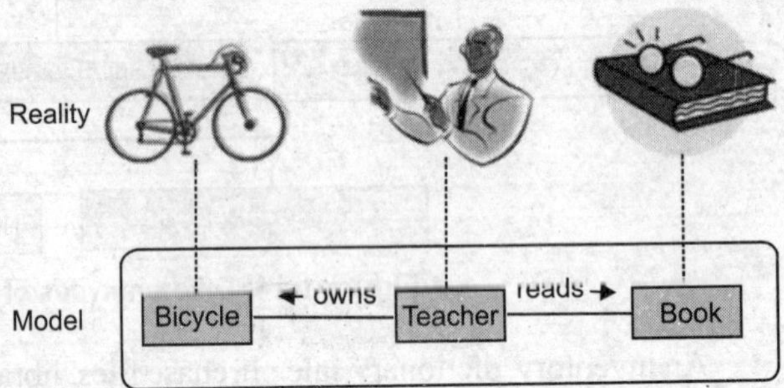

Figure 1.16: Complex realities are made more manageable by abstract models.

1.18.1 Interaction Between Object

An object can be considered a "thing" that can perform a set of activities. The set of activities that the object performs defines the object's behaviour. For example, a "Student Status" object can tell you its grade point average, year in school, or can add a list of courses taken. A "Student" object can tell you its name or its address.

Objects are the basic run-time entities in an object-oriented system. Programming problem is analyzed in terms of objects and nature of communication between them. When a program is executed, objects interact with each other by sending messages. Different objects can also interact with each other without knowing the details of their data or code.

The object's interface consists of a set of commands, each command performing a specific action. An object asks another object to perform an action by sending it a *message*. The requesting (sending) object is referred to as *sender* and the receiving object is referred to as *receiver*.

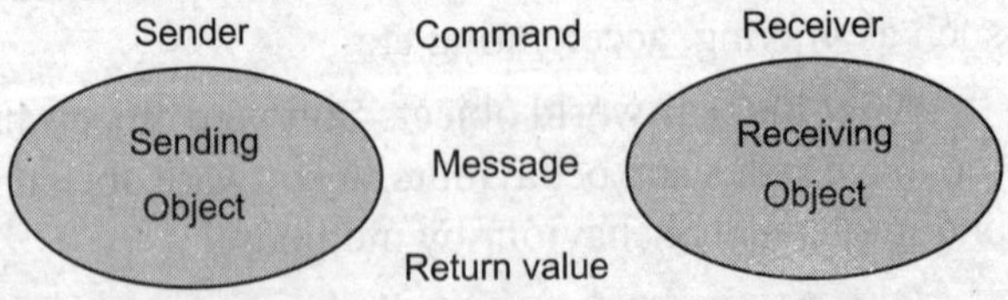

Figure 1.17: Sending and receiving object

Control is given to the receiving object until it completes the command; control then returns to the sending object.

For example, a **School** object asks the **Student** object for its *name* by sending it a *message* asking for its name. The receiving **Student** object returns the *name* back to the sending object.

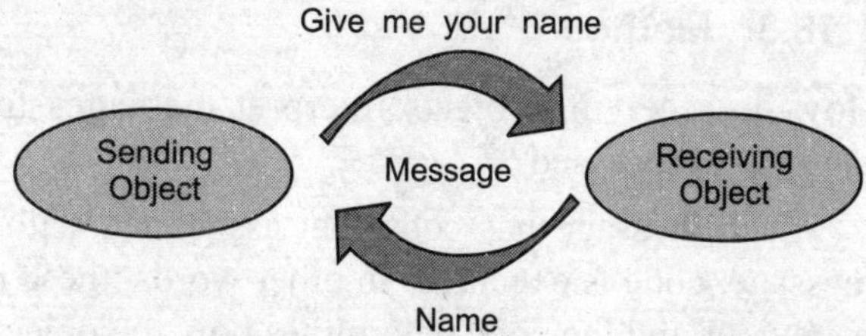

Figure 1.18: Sender sending message to receiver

A message can also contain information the sending objects needs to pass to the receiving object, called the *argument* in the message. A receiving object always returns a *value* back to the sending object. This returned value may or may not be useful to the sending object.

For example, the **School** object now wants to change the student's name. It does this by sending the **Student** object a message to set its name to a new name. The new address is passed as an argument in the message. In this case, the **School** object does not care about the return value from the message.

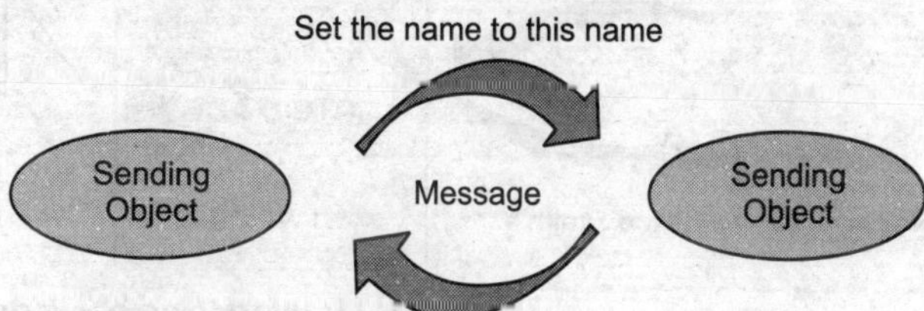

Figure 1.19: Interaction between objects

1.18.2 Sequential Operation

It is very common that a message will cause other messages to be sent, either to itself or to other objects, in order to complete its task. This is called ***sequential operation***. Control will not return to the original sending object until all other messages have been completed. For example, in the following diagram, Object A sends a message to Object B. For Object B to process that message it sends a message to Object C. Likewise, Object C sends a message to Object D. Object D returns to Object C who then returns to Object B who returns to Object A. Control does not return to Object A until all the other messages have completed.

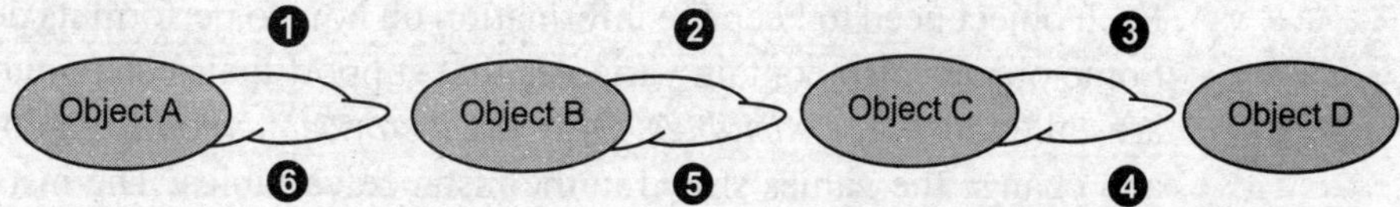

Figure 1.20: Sequential operation of objects

1.18.3 Method

How do receiving objects interpret messages from the senders? How are the messages processed?

Each message has code that associated with it. When an object receives a message, code is executed. In other words, these messages determine an object's behaviour and the code determines how the object carries out each message. The code that is associated with each message is called a *method*. The message name is also called the *method name* due to its close association with the method.

When an object receives a message, it determines what method is being requested and passes control to the *method*. An object has as many methods as it takes to perform its designed actions.

Refer to the following diagram, **name, name:**, and **name:address** are method names for the **Student** object. When the **Student** object receives the **name** message, the **name** message passes control to the *name* method defined in **Student**.

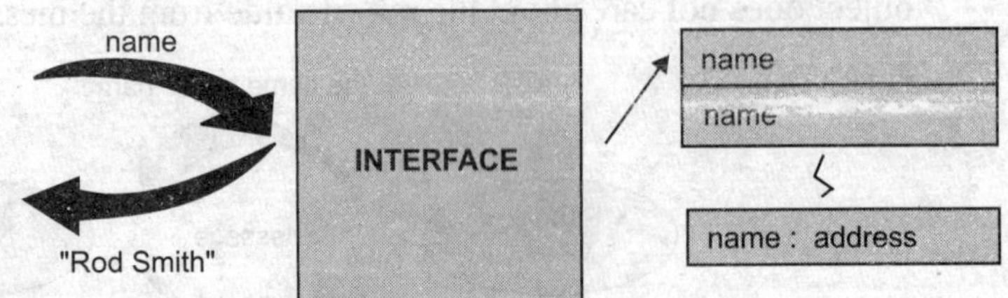

Figure 1.21: Interfacing between objects

Methods that operate on specific objects are instance methods and messages that invoke instance methods are called instance message. Methods that operate on specific classes are class methods. This will be discussed in more details in later chapter.

Methods are similar to subroutines, procedures, or functions found in procedural languages (C, Pascal). For example, a method name equates to a subroutine name, and the code for the method equates to the code found in a subroutine. Sending a message to an object is similar to calling a subroutine.

1.18.4 Object's Data

Each object need to keep the information on how to perform its defined behaviour. Some objects also contain variables that support their behaviour. These variables are called *instance variables*. Only the *instance method* for an object can refer to and change the values stored in the instance variables. The instance methods for other objects cannot refer to this object's data. An object may only access another object's data by sending it messages. This is called *encapsulation* and assures that there is a secure process for getting to an object's data.

Refer to the following diagram, the instance variables *variableOne* through *variableX* can only be accessed by the sender via instance methods *methodOne* through *methodN*. The sender can not refer to the variables directly by itself.

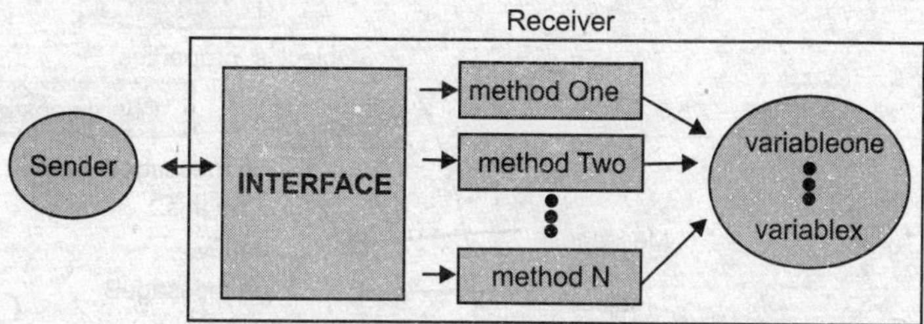

Figure 1.22: Representing different methods

Unlike procedural programming where common data areas are often used for sharing information, object-oriented programming discourages direct access to common data (other than the use of *global variables*) by other programs. Only the object that "owns" the data can change its content. Other objects can view or change this data by sending message to the "owner."

The instance variable names can be identical to the method names that associate with them. For example, the **Student** object has methods of **name, address,** and **major** as well as instance variables of *name*, *address*, and *major*. Smalltalk distinguishes variable identifier and a method identifier by the identifier's position in the expression.

The **figure** below illustrates diagrammatically what a programming shell in an object oriented programming environment "looks" like:

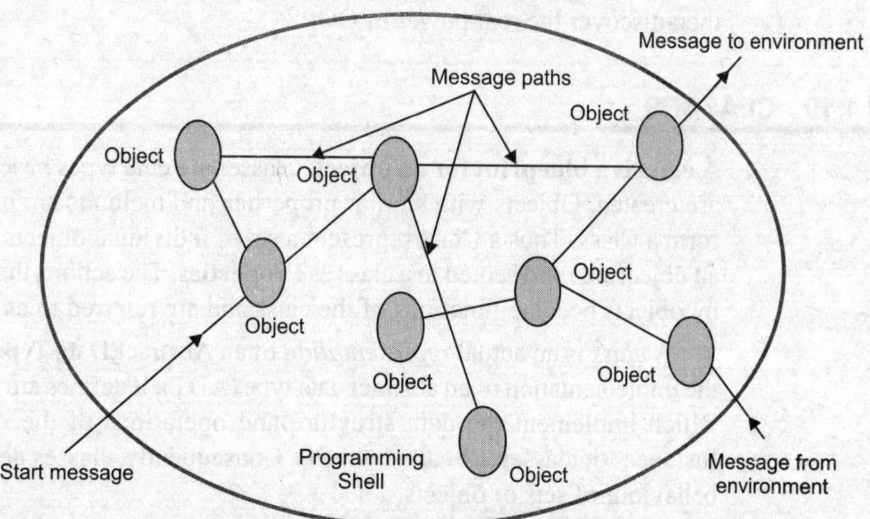

Figure 1.23: Diagram of objects created in an object oriented programming shell

Each object would have the following (diagrammatic) form:

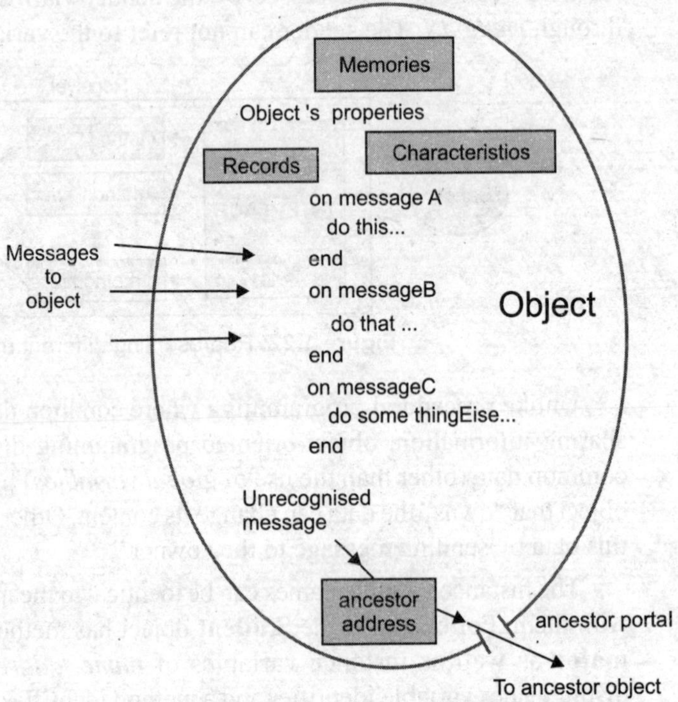

Figure 1.24: Diagram of an abstract object

Once you have understood that OOPS isn't about programming per se, you can then concentrate your thinking upon your ideas and your imagination. You will then discover the real power of OOPS.

1.19 CLASSES

A class is a blueprint for an object. Classes are data types based on which objects are created. Objects with similar properties and methods are grouped together to form a Class. Thus a Class represent a set of individual objects. Characteristics of an object are represented in a class as **Properties**. The actions that can be performed by objects become functions of the class and are referred to as **Methods**.

A *class* is an actual *representation* of an Abstract Data Type (ADT). A class is the implementation of an abstract data type (ADT). It defines attributes and methods which implement the data structure and operations of the ADT, respectively. Instances of classes are called objects. Consequently, classes define properties and behaviour of sets of objects.

Actually the concept of class should come first rather than the concept object.

Once a class has been defined, we can create any number of objects belonging to that class. For example, mango, apple and orange are members of the class **fruit**. If fruit has been defined as a class than the statement *fruit mango* will create an object mango belonging to the class fruit. All the objects in a class will share some common property. Some will less, some will more. This depends on inheritance.

Definition: *"A class is a collection of objects of similar type. Once a class is defined, any number of objects can be created which belong to that class."*

A *class* is a mechanism for creating user-defined data types. It is similar to the C language structure data type. In C, a structure is composed of a set of data members. In C++, a class type is like a C structure, except that a class is composed of a set of data members and a set of operations that can be performed on the class.

Classes are generally declared using the keyword class, with the following format:

```
class class_name
{
access_specifer_1:
member1;
access_specifier_2:
member2;
...
} object_name;
```

Where class_name is a valid identifier for the class, object_names is an optional list of names for objects of this class. The body of the declaration can contain members that can be both data or function declarations, and optionally access specifiers (private, public or protected).

In the object-oriented world, these categories are represented by classes, where a class is a description of the common properties of a category of objects.

For example consider we have a Class of *Cars* under which *Santro, Xing, Alto* and *WaganR* represents individual Objects. In this context each *Car* Object will have its own, Model, Year of Manufacture, Colour, Top Speed, Engine Power etc., which form **Properties** of the *Car* class and the associated actions i.e., object functions like Start, Move, and Stop form the **Methods** of *Car* Class.

No memory is allocated when a class is created. Memory is allocated only when an object is created, i.e., when an instance of a class is created. A class in C++ is an encapsulation of data members and functions that manipulate the data. The class can also have some other important members which are architecturally important.

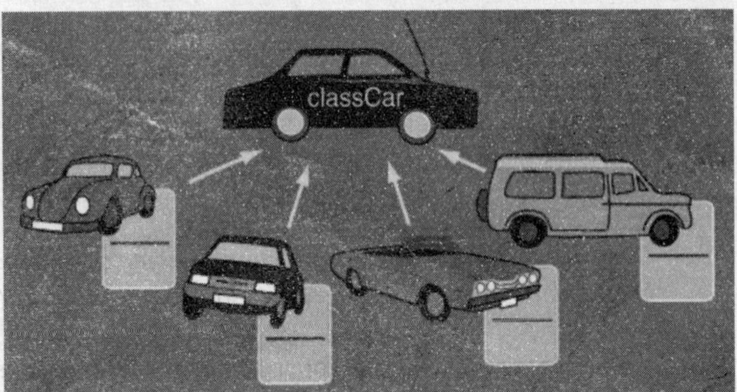

Figure 1.25: Class car having different types of cars having different

Given below are some examples of class data type:

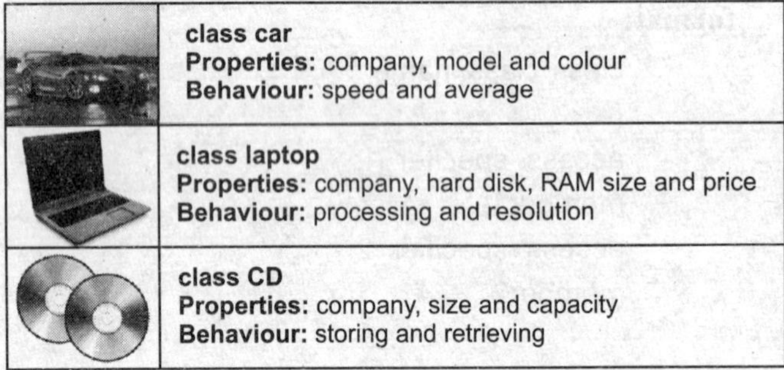

	class car **Properties:** company, model and colour **Behaviour:** speed and average
	class laptop **Properties:** company, hard disk, RAM size and price **Behaviour:** processing and resolution
	class CD **Properties:** company, size and capacity **Behaviour:** storing and retrieving

1.19.1 Understanding Classes Within Object Oriented Programming

To fully understand object oriented programming, you will want to be familiar with classes. When you look at the world around you, it will become obvious that many objects are the same type. For example, the car you drive is just one of the millions of cars that exist in the world.

In the OOP terminology, the car you drive is an instance of the class cars. Each car will have a state, and it will have behaviour as well. However, the state and behaviour of one car is not dependent on the state and behaviour of other cars. An example of a behaviour a car will have is braking, while the state of the car could be having four wheels.

In the object oriented programming, it is possible to have a large number of objects of the same type that have a number of identical attributes. An example of these objects could be video clips or rectangles. The advantage of processing objects which are the same type is that you can generate a diagram for them. This diagram is called a "class." So, the class is a diagram that contains the methods and variables which are related to a specific group of objects. For example, the class of a car would provide the variables that would allow all cars to have a state. In addition to this, the class would also provide information that is related to the methods that will allow changes to take place in the car.

Once the car class has been created, it will be possible for you to create a large number of car objects from this class. Once the instance of the car class has been created, it is the responsibility of the system to generate enough memory for the object and its variables. Every instance will be given a copy of the variables that have been created in the class. For example, MyCar and YourCar would be separate instances, but both would be part of the same class, which is a car. They will have values for the variables which will differ from each other. Not only can instance variables be created, but instances can be created for the class itself.

The class variable will hold information that will be held by every instance of a class. As an example, imagine if all cars have the same brake systems. In this situation, creating an instance variable to contain the brake systems is not effective. Every instance would need to have a separate copy of the variable, even though the value will be equal. In this situation, you will want to create a class variable that will hold the same brake system, and every instance will have this variable. When a single object alters the variable, this change will become evident in all the other objects. It is also possible for a class to define class methods.

Class method can be generated from a class, but you will need to generate an instance method on a specific instance. Objects have powerful advantages because they have modularity and the ability to hide information. Classes are powerful because they can be reused. Just a car company's use the same diagram to build cars multiple times, computer programmers will use an identical class multiple times to create a large number of objects. If you have read about objects, you may notice the similarities between them and classes. Many people who study object oriented programming become confused when dealing with classes and objects.

In the real world, the difference between classes and objects is obvious. For example, you can tell the difference between a car diagram and an actual car. However, when you are dealing with software, the differences aren't always easy to spot.

One reason for this is because objects which exist in software are the electronic versions of objects that exist in the real world. In addition to this, the word "object" is often used to talk about a class or an instance. An object can be categorized under a large number of classes. While some of these classes may be specific, others could be more generalized. For example, a Bloodhound would be a specific dog class. However, it could be processed in a larger class such as scenthound, or a larger superclass like Canidae.

1.19.2 Difference between Object and Class

Object	Class
1. Object is an instance of a class.	Class is a set of objects that share common properties and behaviour.
2. Data and functions that operate on that data are bind together to form an object.	A collection of similar type of objects is called a class.
3. Object is real world entities.	Class is a logical entity.
4. Objects occupy some space in memory.	Class doesn't consume space in memory.
5. Car, table and television are examples of objects.	Car is an example of class which has santro, indica, innova objects.

1.20 INHERITANCE

Inheritance is the process by which objects can acquire the properties of objects of other class. In OOP, *inheritance* provides reusability, like, adding additional features to an existing class without modifying it. This is achieved by deriving a new class from the existing one. The new class will have combined features of both the classes.

In object-oriented methodology, inheritance enables you to extend the functionality of an existing class. You create a class that inherits the attributes and behaviour of another class. In addition, the new class can consist of a few new attributes and behaviours that are specific to the class. In terms of classes and objects, attributes refer to the data and behaviour refers to the methods.

For example, you might have the Student class that consists of the basic characteristics of students, such as name, date of birth, and gender. You can extend the functions of the student class to a day scholar, who in addition to characteristics of the Student class contains its own features, such as locker number and residential address.

Definition: *"Inheritance is the process of forming a new class from an existing class or base class. The base class is also known as parent class or super class, the new class that is formed is called derived class. Derived class is also known as a child class or sub class."*

The derived classes have all the features of the base class and the programmer can choose to add new features specific to the newly created derived class.

For example, a programmer can create a *base* class named fruit and define *derived* classes as mango, orange, banana, etc. Each of these derived classes, (mango, orange, banana, etc.) has all the features of the *base* class (fruit) with additional attributes or features specific to these newly created derived classes.

Mango would have its own defined features, orange would have its own defined features, banana would have its own defined features, etc.

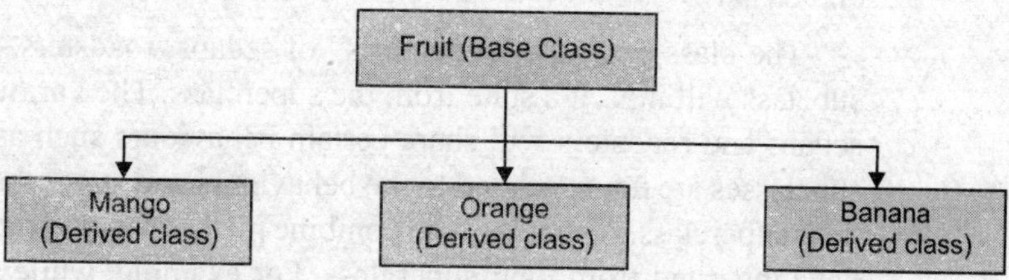

Figure 1.26: Base class defined three derived classes

This concept of *Inheritance* leads to the concept of *polymorphism.*

1.20.1 Features of Inheritance

Following are the various features of OOPs:

1. Inheritance helps in reducing the overall code size of the program, which is an important concept in object-oriented programming.
2. Inheritance enables you to add new features and functionality to an existing class without modifying the existing class.
3. Inheritance also enables you to share data and methods among multiple classes.

1.20.2 Hierarchical Classifications

Inheritance is the process by which one object can acquire the properties of another object. This is important because it supports the concept of hierarchical classification. If you think about it, most knowledge is made manageable by hierarchical (that is, top-down) classifications. **For example**, a Red Delicious apple is part of the classification apple, which in turn is part of the fruit class, which is under the larger class food. That is, the food class possesses certain qualities (edible, nutritious, and so on) which also, logically, apply to its subclass, fruit. In addition to these qualities, the fruit class has specific characteristics (juicy, sweet, and so on) that distinguish it from other food. The apple class defines those qualities specific to an apple (grows on trees, not tropical, and so on). A Red Delicious apple would, in turn, inherit all the qualities of all preceding classes and would define only those qualities that make it unique.

Without the use of hierarchies, each object would have to explicitly define all of its characteristics. Using inheritance, an object need only define those qualities that make it unique within its class. It can inherit its general attributes from its parent. Thus, it is the inheritance mechanism that makes it possible for one object to be a specific instance of a more general case.

For example, sedans, sports cars, and roadsters are all types of cars. In the object oriented language, sports cars, sedans, and roadsters are subclasses of the class cars.

The class cars is a "superclass" of sedans, roadsters, and sports cars. Every subclass will inherit a state from the superclass. The various types of cars such as sedans and roadsters will share certain behaviours such as braking. Despite this, subclasses are not restricted to the behaviours and states that they have taken from their superclass. A subclass can combine methods and variables with the traits they have inherited from their superclass. For example, while a sedan may have four doors, sports cars will generally have two. It is also possible for subclasses to override any methods that they have inherited, and they can create unique implementations for these methods.

As an example of this, you can "override" certain traits within a car to allow it to do different things. It is also possible to use more than just one level of inheritance. An inheritance structure can be generated which can be as deep as you want it to be. This inheritance structure is called a class hierarchy. The variables and methods can extend through the levels of the class hierarchy. In most cases, a hierarchy that is deep tends to have behaviours which are distinct. However, there are a number of important things you should know about a class hierarchy.

1.20.3 Types of Inheritance

There are five different inheritances supported in C++:

1. Single Inheritance
2. Multiple Inheritance
3. Multilevel Inheritance
4. Hierarchical Inheritance
5. Hybrid Inheritance

1. **Single inheritance:** If a class is derived from a single base class, it is called as single inheritance.

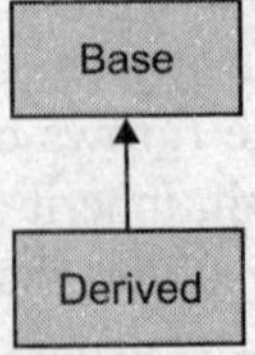

2. **Multiple inheritance:** If a class is derived from more than one base class, it is known as multiple inheritance.

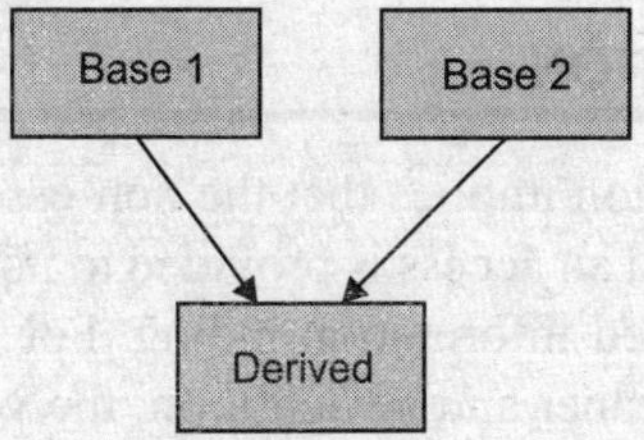

3. **Multilevel inheritance:** The classes can also be derived from the classes that are already derived. This type of inheritance is called multilevel inheritance.

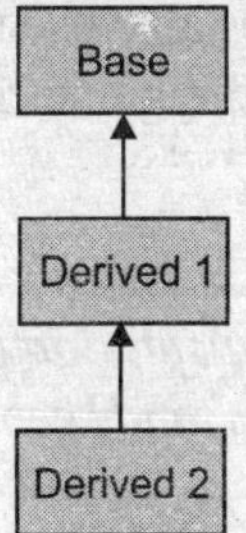

4. **Hierarchical inheritance:** If a number of classes are derived from a single base class, it is called as hierarchical inheritance.

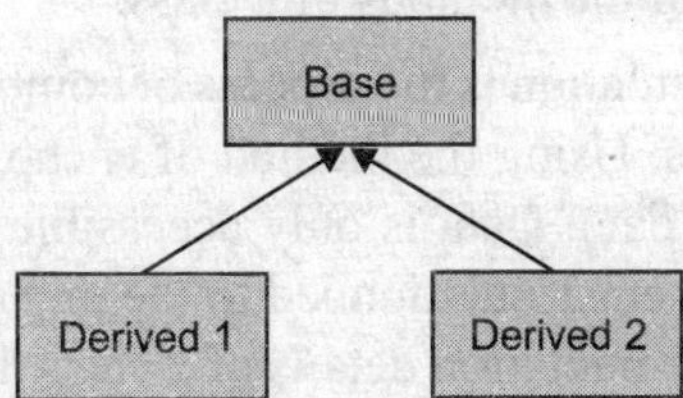

5. **Hybrid inheritance:** The combination of one or more types of inheritance is called hybrid inheritance.

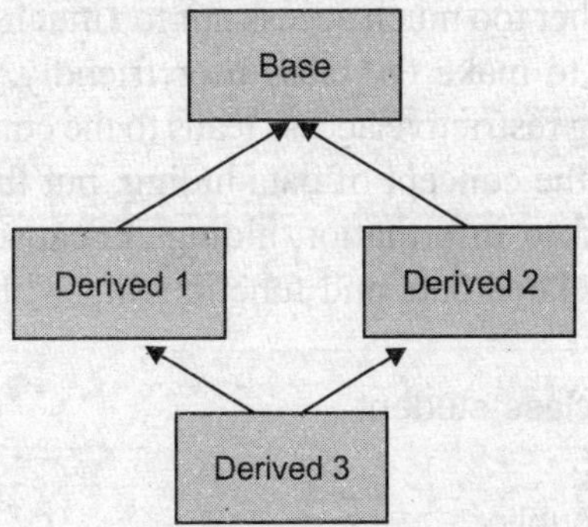

1.21 ENCAPSULATION

Encapsulation implies that the non-essential details of an object are hidden from the user and an access is provided to its essential details. Therefore, encapsulation is also called information hiding. For example, when you plug in the cord of a vacuum cleaner and switch it on, the vacuum cleaner starts functioning. An end-user need not know the working principle of a vacuum cleaner to convert electricity into suction power. The switch of the vacuum cleaner encapsulates the complex process of conversion of electricity into suction power. The complexity of an object is hidden as a result of encapsulation.

Computer games also use the feature of encapsulation. The user only needs to know how to play the game. However, the complex working of game is hidden from the user.

Definition: *"Encapsulation is the mechanism that binds together code and the data it manipulates, and keeps both safe from outside interference and misuse."*

In object-oriented methodology, need of encapsulation arises because the emphasis is on designing classes in such a manner that the classes share data and methods among themselves. Encapsulation is the feature that provides security to the data and the methods of a class.

Encapsulation is the process of combining data and functions into a single unit called class. Using the method of encapsulation, the programmer cannot directly access the data. Data is only accessible through the functions present inside the class. Data encapsulation led to the important concept of data hiding. Data hiding is the implementation details of a class that are hidden from the user. The concept of restricted access led programmers to write specialized functions or methods for performing the operations on hidden members of the class. Attention must be paid to ensure that the class is designed properly.

Neither too much access nor too much control must be placed on the operations in order to make the class user friendly. Hiding the implementation details and providing restrictive access leads to the concept of abstract data type. Encapsulation leads to the concept of data hiding, but the concept of encapsulation must not be restricted to information hiding. Encapsulation clearly represents the ability to bundle related data and functionality within a single, autonomous entity called a class.

```
class student
{
public:
int sample();
```

```
int example(char *s);
int endfunc();
.........
......... //Other member functions
private:
int x;
float sq;
.........
......... //Other data members
};
```

In the above example, the data members integer x, float sq and other data members and member functions sample(),example(char* s),endfunc() and other member functions are bundled and put inside a single autonomous entity called class student. This exemplifies the concept of Encapsulation. This special feature is available in object-oriented language C++ but not available in procedural language C. There are advantages of using this encapsulated approach in C++. One advantage is that it reduces human errors. The data and functions bundled inside the class take total control of maintenance and thus human errors are reduced. It is clear from the above example that the encapsulated objects act as a black box for other parts of the program through interaction. Although encapsulated objects provide functionality, the calling objects will not know the implementation details. This enhances the security of the application.

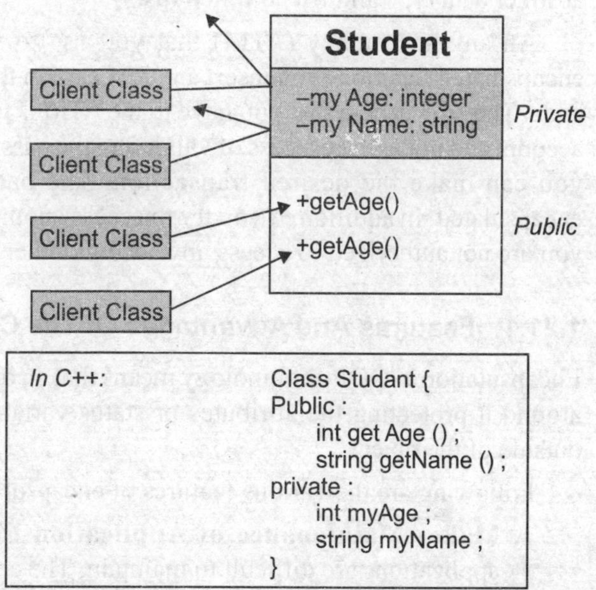

Figure 1.27: Diagram representing concept of Encapsulation

The key strength behind Data Encapsulation in C++ is that the keywords or the access specifiers can be placed in the class declaration as public, protected or private. A class placed after the keyword public is accessible to all the users of the class. The elements placed after the keyword private are accessible only to the methods of the class. In between the public and the private access specifiers, there exists the protected access specifier. Elements placed after the keyword protected are accessible only to the methods of the class or classes derived from that class.

In an object-oriented language, code and data may be combined in such a way that a self-contained "black box" is created. When code and data are linked together in this fashion, an *object* is created. In other words, an object is the device that supports encapsulation. Within an object, code, data, or both may be *private* to that object or *public*. Private code or data is known to and accessible only by another part of the object. That is, private code or data may not be accessed by a piece of the program that exists outside the object. When code or data is public, other parts of your program may access it even though it is defined within an object. Typically, the public parts of an object are used to provide a controlled interface to the private elements of the object.

The concept of encapsulation shows that a non-member function cannot access an object's private or protected data. This adds security, but in some cases the programmer might require an unrelated function to operate on an object of two different classes. The programmer is then able to utilize the concept of friend functions. Encapsulation alone is a powerful feature that leads to information hiding, abstract data type and friend functions.

An anytime money (ATM) that you use to withdraw money also has an encapsulated function. You insert an ATM card in the machine and provide the pin code. The only access that you have to the ATM is to provide the pin code for your account and not to the process of validating the password. If the pin code is correct, you can make the desired transaction. The backend transaction process is encapsulated. In addition, if you try to access another account, access is denied, as you are not authorized to access any account other than your account.

1.21.1 Features And Advantages Of The Concept Of Encapsulation

Encapsulation in OOP-terminology means that an object has something like a shell around it protecting the attributes or status variables from being accessed from outside of the object.

Following are the various features of encapsulation:

1. **Makes Maintenance of Application Easier:** Complex and critical applications are difficult to maintain. The cost associated with maintaining the application is higher than that of developing the application properly. To resolve this maintenance difficulty, the object-oriented programming

language C++ created the concept of encapsulation which bundles data and related functions together as a unit called class. Thus, making maintenance much easier on the class level.

2. **Improves the Understandability of the Application**
3. **Enhanced Security:** There are numerous reasons for the enhancement of security using the concept of Encapsulation in C++. The access specifier acts as the key strength behind the concept of security and provides access to members of class as needed by users. This prevents unauthorized access. If an application needs to be extended or customized in later stages of development, the task of adding new functions becomes easier without breaking existing code or applications, there by giving an additional security to existing application.

In order to benefit from the powerful feature of encapsulation in object-oriented programming language C++, the programmer must use encapsulation properly. To maximize the benefits of encapsulation, the user must minimize the implementation details in external interfaces as needed.

1.21.2 Encapsulation: Information Hiding

Encapsulation is a method for protecting data from unwanted access or alteration by packaging it in an object where it is only accessible through the object's interface.

Encapsulation is often referred to as ***information hiding***. But both are different. Infact *information hiding* is actually the result of Encapsulation. Encapsulation makes it possible to separate an object's implementation from its original behaviour - to restrict access of its internal data. This restriction facilitates certain details of an object's behaviour to be hidden. This allows protecting an object's internal state from corruption by its user.

It is the mechanism by which Abstraction is implemented. In other words you can say that it is the result of the Encapsulation. For example, the Laptop is an object that encapsulates many technologies/hardware that might not be understood clearly by most people who use it.

1.21.3 Encapsulation: Data Hiding

Data encapsulation, sometimes referred to as ***data hiding***, is the mechanism whereby the implementation details of a class are kept hidden from the user. The user can only perform a restricted set of operations on the hidden members of the class by executing special functions commonly called *methods*. The actions performed by the methods are determined by the designer of the class, who must be careful not to make the methods either overly flexible or too restrictive. This idea of hiding the details away from the user and providing a restricted, clearly defined interface is the underlying theme behind the concept of an *abstract data type*.

The advantage of using data hiding comes when the *implementation* of the class changes but the *interface* remains the same. For example, to create a stack class which can contain integers, the designer may choose to implement it with an array, which is hidden from the user of the class. The designer then writes the push() and pop() methods which puts integers into the array and removes them from the array respectively. These methods are made accessible to the user. Should an attempt be made by the user to access the array directly, a compile time error will result. Now, should the designer decide to change the stack's implementation to a linked list, the array can simply be replaced with a linked list and the push() and pop() methods rewritten so that they manipulate the linked list instead of the array. The code which the user has written to manipulate the stack is still valid because it was not given direct access to the array to begin with.

The concept of data hiding is supported in C++ through the use of the public, protected and private keywords which are placed in the declaration of the class. Anything in the class placed after the public keyword is accessible to all the users of the class; elements placed after the protected keyword are accessible only to the methods of the class or classes derived from that class; elements placed after the private keyword are accessible only to the methods of the class.

As a convention, calling a method of an object instantiated from a class is commonly referred to as sending a *message* to that object.

1.21.4 Coupling

The degree to which a module (class) depends on other classes. In a good design, you should try to minimize coupling. Classes should be self-contained units that have a low dependence on other classes, meaning understanding and using one class should not require an understanding of another. With low coupling a change in a module will not require changes in other modules.

Related to the concept of coupling is information hiding. Information hiding is the hiding of the implementation in a class or module that is most likely to change; this protects other parts of the program from change if the implementation is changed. Protecting an implementation involves providing a stable interface which other classes can use to access services provided by the class. Often encapsulation and information hiding are used interchangeably.

Example: Car and Driver

1.21.5 Cohesion

Cohesion is the measure within a module (class) of how well the members work together to provide a specific piece of functionality. Cohesion is measured by how strongly related and focused the responsibilities of a single class are. In good design, the cohesion should be maximized. Cohesion is decreased if the methods of a class have little in common, or methods carry out many activities.

If cohesion is low, modules may be difficult to understand, maintenance is difficult, because change may affect many modules, and modules cannot be reused, because it is unlikely that another application will have a use for the random grouping of functionality.

Example: Oven that has built-in radio and alarm clock.

1.22 ABSTRACTION

Abstraction is one of the most powerful and vital features provided by object-oriented C++ programming language. Modularity is very important in any programming language; it provides flexibility to users for using the programming language. This aspect is well achieved with high performance by the concept of abstraction in C++. In object-oriented programming language the programmer can abstract both data and code when needed.

The concept of abstraction relates to the idea of hiding data that are not needed for presentation. The main idea behind data abstraction is to give a clear separation between properties of data type and the associated implementation details. This separation is achieved in order that the properties of the abstract data type are visible to the user interface and the implementation details are hidden. Thus, abstraction forms the basic platform for the creation of user-defined data types called objects. Data abstraction is the process of refining data to its essential form. An Abstract Data Type is defined as a data type that is defined in terms of the operations that it supports and not in terms of its structure or implementation. Classes use the concept of abstraction and are defined as a list of abstract attributes.

In object-oriented programming language C++, it is possible to create and provide an interface that accesses only certain elements of data types. The programmer can decide which user to give or grant access to and hide the other details. This concept is called data hiding which is similar in concept to data abstraction.

Definition: *"Abstraction refers to the act of representing essential without including the background details or explanations."*

Abstraction is a process of identifying the relevant qualities and behaviors an object should possess. Let's take an example to understand abstraction. A Laptop consists of many things such as processor, motherboard, RAM, keyboard, LCD screen, wireless antenna, web camera, USB ports, battery, speakers etc. To use it, you don't need to know how internally LCD screens, keyboard, web camera, battery, wireless antenna, speaker's works.

Figure 1.28: Abstract machine

You just need to know how to operate the laptop by switching it on. The intrinsic details are invisible. Think about if you would have to call to the engineer who knows all internal details of the laptop before operating it. This would have highly expensive as well as not easy to use everywhere by everyone. So here the Laptop is an object that is designed to hide its complexity.

Think If you need to write a piece of software to track the students details of a school, you may probably need to create Students objects. People comes in all different backgrounds, educational qualifications, locations, hobbies, ages and have multiple religion, language but in terms of application, an student is just a name, age, class and roll number, while the other qualities are not relevant to the application. Determining what other qualities (background, qualifications, location, hobbies etc) are in terms of this application is abstraction.

This process of modeling is called abstraction and is illustrated in Figure 1.29 as below:

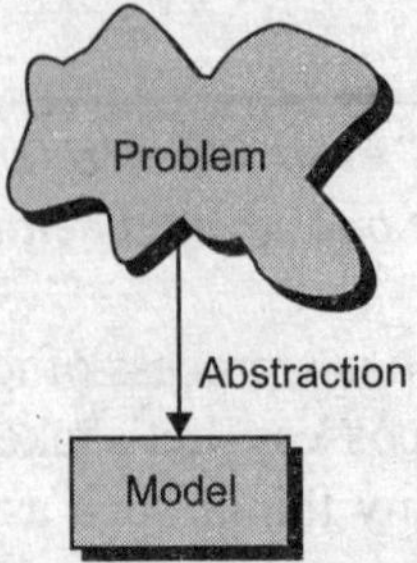

Figure 1.29: Create a model from a problem with abstraction

In object-oriented programming, abstraction means ignoring the non-essential details of an object and concentrating on its essential details. As discussed earlier, in an ATM, the user is not required to know the entire process of a transaction and how the data is stored. However, the program provides a restricted access to the user's account.

Similarly, when you want to send e-mail messages, you should know the processes of writing e-mail messages and sending it to the receiver. However, it is not necessary for you to know the entire process of sending the e-mail messages across the network.

To implement abstraction, you also use the encapsulation feature. Encapsulation hides the irrelevant details of an object and abstraction makes only the relevant details of an object visible. For example, the operation of a washing machine is hidden or encapsulated from the user. The details, like switching on and off the washing machine are the only details relevant for the user to know. This is implemented by abstraction. Rest of the working of the washing machine is encapsulated from the user.

In object-oriented software, complexity is managed by using abstraction. Abstraction is a process that involves identifying the critical behaviour of an object and eliminating irrelevant and complex details. A well thought out abstraction is usually simple, and easy to use in the perspective of the user, the person who is using your object.

1.22.1 How Types of Abstraction Differs

There are two broad types of abstraction; **functional abstraction** and **data abstraction**. The main difference between functional abstraction and data abstraction is that functional abstraction refers to a function that can be used without taking into account how the function is implemented. Data abstraction refers to the data that can be used without taking into account how the data are stored. There is also a difference in the way the access takes place in functional abstraction and data abstraction. In functional abstraction, access to the function is provided through a specific interface defined to invoke the function. In contrast, in data abstraction, access to the data is provided through a specific set of operations defined to examine and manipulate the data. For instance, when a programmer is using C++ standard data types, this means that users are using the concept of data abstraction. When using data types, the users are not concerned with how the data is stored but they are concerned with what operations are provided and what properties are supported.

1.22.2 Reasons for the Need Of Abstraction

1. **Flexibility in approach:** By hiding data or abstracting details that are not needed for presentation, the programmer achieves greater flexibility in approach.

2. **Enhanced Security:** Abstraction gives access to data or details that are needed by users and hide the implementation details, giving enhanced security to application.
3. **Easier Replacement:** With the concept of abstraction in object-oriented programming language, it is possible to replace code without recompilation. This makes the process easier and saves time for users.
4. **Modular Approach:** In object-oriented programming language C++, the abstraction concept helps users to divide the project application into modules and test each of them separately. Then all modules are integrated and ultimately tested together. This approach makes the application development easier.

There are various ways of achieving abstraction in object-oriented programming language C++. One approach is to take modular based code that is broken apart into smaller segments, known as functions. This functional or modular approach helps the code to be reused again and again when needed. For example, a programmer might write a function for computing an average and another programmer might write a function for computing salary. These functions can be reused when needed, by anyone. The modular based approach helps to centralize all data of a similar type, under the control of a type module. Defining module types allow the module to be an abstract data type. In many other programming languages, there is a small drawback associated with the approach to accessing module type.

In C++, this problem is resolved through the concept of **friend functions**. Friend functions resolve the problem by associating with one of the classes or some of its members as friends of the other class.

1.22.3 Data Abstraction

Data Abstraction increases the power of programming language by creating user defined data types. Data Abstraction also represents the needed information in the program without presenting the details.

The public interface, formed by the collections of messages understood by an object, completely defines how to use this object. Programs that want to manipulate an object only have to be concerned about which messages this object understands, and do not have to worry about how these tasks are achieved or the internal structure of the object. The hiding of internal details makes an object abstract, and the technique is normally known as data abstraction.

With abstraction you create a well-defined entity which can be properly handled. These entities define the *data structure* of a set of items. An entity with the properties just described is called an ***abstract data type*** **(ADT)**. However, data abstraction and data hiding are almost same.

For example: Car is a physical object which abstracts the details of engine, braking system, suspension, fuel injection etc. **Figure 1.30** represents abstract car without showing its parts explanations.

Figure 1.30: Abstract car

Figure given below is representing car with its explanations:

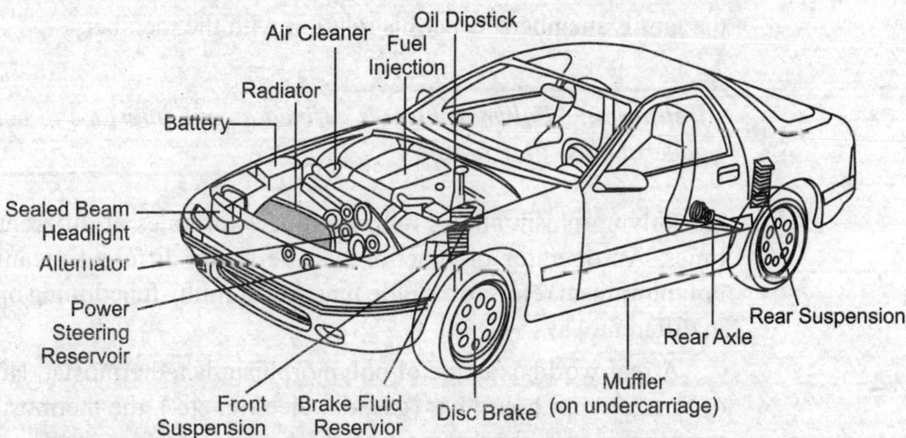

Figure 1.31: Car representing its background details or explanations

Abstraction refers to the act of representing essential without including the background details or explanations. Classes use the concept of abstraction and are defined as a list of abstract attribute such as size, weight and cost, and functions to operate on these attributes. Data abstraction ensures security of data from being unexpected viewing or changing or manipulating. Both the term data abstraction and data hiding are closely related and are often understood as one which is very much correct.

Abstract Data Type or Data Abstraction is a wide asked and thought question even in procedural or structured languages as data security or data hiding is essential for corporate users and to ensure the irrational manipulation or processing of data by other calls because of dynamic binding and multiple calls or value passing i.e. messages.

1.23 POLYMORPHISM

In object-oriented methodology, polymorphism is the feature that enables you to assign a different meaning or usage to an entity in different contexts. The entity can be a variable, method, or an object. In other words, Polymorphism allows a programmer to make use of an entity in several different forms without affecting the original identity of the entity.

Object-oriented programming languages support *polymorphism*, which is characterized by the phrase "one interface, multiple methods."

Polymorphism is derived from two Latin words-Poly, which means many, and morph, which means forms. Anything that exists in more than one form is known as a polymorph. You might have noticed that a person assumes different roles in different scenarios. For example, a person assumes various roles when he interacts with the members of his family. He is a father to his children, child to his parents, and husband to his wife. Although, the person is same, he behaves differently with the family members as per his relation with the member.

***Definition:** "Polymorphism is defined as one interface to control access to a general class of actions."*

Polymorphism allows routines to use variables of different types at different times. An operator or function can be given different meanings or functions. Polymorphism refers to a single function or multi-functioning operator performing in different ways.

A real-world example of polymorphism is a thermostat. No matter what type of furnace your house has (gas, oil, electric, etc.), the thermostat works the same way. In this case, the thermostat (which is the interface) is the same no matter what type of furnace (method) you have. For example, if you want a 70-degree temperature, you set the thermostat to 70 degrees. It doesn't matter what type of furnace actually provides the heat. This same principle can also apply to programming. For example, you might have a program that defines three different types of stacks. One stack is used for integer values, one for character values, and one for floating-point values. Because of polymorphism, you can define one set of names, **push()** and **pop()** , that can be used for all three stacks. In your program you will create three specific versions of these functions, one for each type of stack, but names of the functions will be the same. The compiler will automatically select the right function based upon the data being stored. Thus, the interface to a stack—the functions **push()** and **pop()** —are the same no matter which type of stack is being used. The individual versions of these functions define the specific implementations (methods) for each type of data.

For example: Example given below explains the concept of polymorphism. Function getarea() is used for different purposes but having same name.

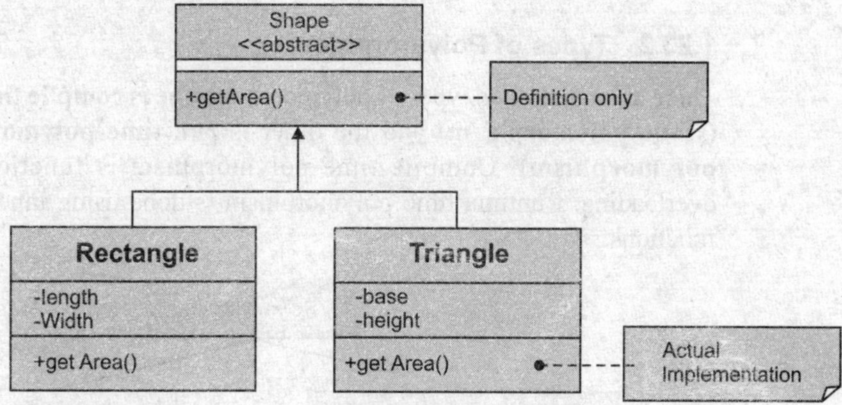

Figure 1.32: Explain the concept of polymorphism (+getArea())

For example: Example given below explains the concept of polymorphism.

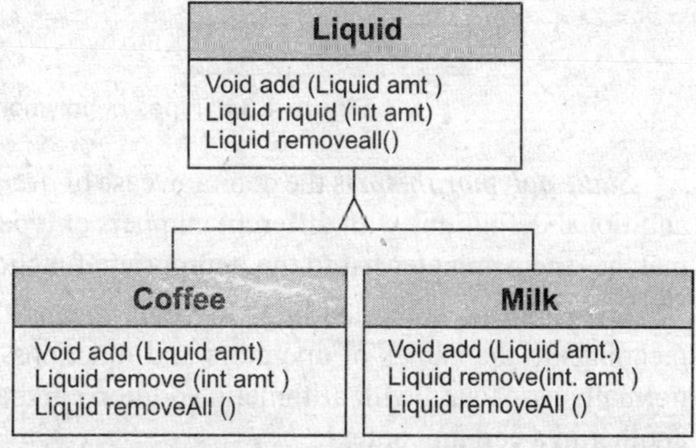

Figure 1.33: Concept of polymorphism (add(), remove())

Polymorphism plays an important role in allowing objects having different internal structures to share the same external interface. This means that a general class of operation may be accessed in the same manner even though specific actions associated with each operation may be accessed in the same manner even though specific actions associated with each operation may differ. Polymorphism is extensively used in implementing inheritance.

1.23.1 Features and Advantages of the Concept Of Polymorphism

Following are the features and advantages of polymorphism:

1. Using polymorphism, applications are Easily Extendable
2. It helps in reusability of code.

3. It provides easier maintenance of applications.
4. It helps in achieving robustness in applications.

1.23.2 Types of Polymorphism

There are mainly two types of polymorphism one is **compile time polymorphism (static polymorphism)** and the other is **run time polymorphism (dynamic polymorphism)**. Compile time polymorphism is functions and operators overloading. Runtime time polymorphism is done using inheritance and virtual functions.

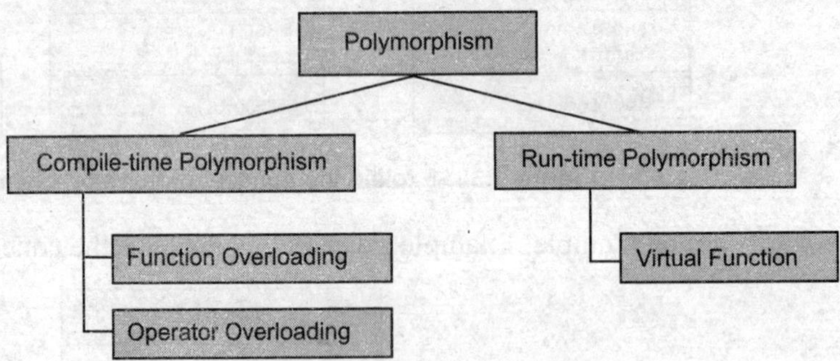

Figure 1.34: Types of polymorphism

Static polymorphism is the common case of *overriding* a function by providing additional definitions with different numbers or types of parameters. The compiler matches the parameter list to the appropriate function.

Overloading: Overloading, in OOP, means the ability to assign multiple meanings to the names of operators and functions. For example, the operator +, normally associated with arithmetic addition can be overloaded to add one list to another in a certain context.

Use of a single symbol to represent operators with different argument types, e.g. "-", used either, as a monadic operator to negate an expression, or as a dyadic operator to return the difference between two expressions. Another example is "+" used to add either integers or floating point numbers.

Dynamic polymorphism is much different and relies on parent classes to define *virtual functions* which child classes may redefine. When this virtual member function is called for an object of the parent class, the execution dynamically chooses the appropriate function to call - the parent function if the object really is the parent type, or the child function if the object really is the child type.

Virtual function: It can be also declared virtual, if the intention is late binding. This enables it to be bound at run time. Late binding is also referred to as dynamic binding. An advantage in declaring a function in an object as virtual is that, if the program that uses this object calls that function only conditionally, there is no need to bind the function early, during the compilation of the program. It will be bound only if the condition is met and the call of the function takes place. For example, you could have a polymorphic function called **draw()** that is associated with different graphical objects, like for rectangle, circle, and sphere. The details or methods of the functions are different, but the name **draw()** is common. If you now have a collection of these objects and pick up an arbitrary object without knowing exactly what it is (via a pointer, for example), you can still invoke the draw function for the object and be assured that the right draw function will be bound to the object and called.

In addition to the above types of polymorphism, there exist other kinds of polymorphism:

1. Run-time
2. Compile-time
3. Ad-hoc polymorphism
4. Parametric polymorphism

Other types of polymorphism defined:

1. ***Run-time:*** The *run-time* polymorphism is implemented with inheritance and virtual functions.
2. ***Compile-time:*** The *compile-time* polymorphism is implemented with templates.
3. ***Ad-hoc polymorphism:*** If the range of actual types that can be used is finite and the combinations must be individually specified prior to use, this is called *ad-hoc* polymorphism.
4. ***Parametric polymorphism:*** If all code is written without mention of any specific type and thus can be used transparently with any number of new types it is called *parametric* polymorphism.

1.24 DYNAMIC BINDING

Dynamic binding means that the code associated with a given procedure call is not known until the time of the call at run-time. Think as an object which has a certain function and that was inherited from its respective class. Thus every object of that class will inherit the function but won't have any effect unless or until it is called.

Definition: *"The concept of dynamic binding allows a variable to take different types dependent on the content at a particular time. This ability of a variable is called polymorphism."*

One important reason for having dynamic binding is that it provides a mechanism for selecting between alternatives which is arguably more robust than explicit selection by conditionals or pattern matching. When a new subclass is added, or an existing subclass changes, the necessary modifications are localized: you don't have incomplete conditionals and broken patterns scattered all over the program.

After this elaborate introduction, we now describe the major advantages of OOP.

Generally, the advantages are-

1. **Simplicity:** software objects model real world objects, so the complexity is reduced and the program structure is very clear;
2. **Modularity:** each object forms a separate entity whose internal workings are decoupled from other parts of the system;
3. **Modifiability:** it is easy to make minor changes in the data representation or the procedures in an OO program. Changes inside a class do not affect any other part of a program, since the only public interface that the external world has to a class is through the use of methods;
4. **Extensibility:** adding new features or responding to changing operating environments can be solved by introducing a few new objects and modifying some existing ones;
5. **Maintainability:** objects can be maintained separately, making locating and fixing problems easier;
6. **Re-usability:** objects can be reused in different programs.
7. It provides a clear ***modular*** structure for programs. This makes it good for defining abstract datatypes, where implementation details are hidden and the unit has a clearly defined interface.
8. It provides a good framework for code libraries, where supplied software components can be easily adapted and modified by the programmer. This is particularly useful for developing graphical user interfaces.
9. It makes it easy to maintain and modify existing code, as new objects can be created with small differences to existing ones.

1.25 MESSAGE PASSING

Object Oriented Programming (OOP) restructures the programming problem to allow for a higher level of abstraction. It groups operations and data into modular units called objects. These objects can be combined into structured networks to form a complete program, similar to how the pieces in a puzzle fit together to create a picture. In contrast to procedural programming, it focus on the interaction between data and functions, the design of objects and the interactions between those objects become the primary elements of object oriented program design.

By breaking down complex software projects into small, self-contained, and modular units, object orientation ensures that changes to one part of a software project will not adversely affect other portions of the software. Object orientation also aids software reuse. Once functionality is created in one program, it can easily be reused in other programs.

An object oriented program consists of a set of objects that communicate with each other. Object communicates with one another by sending data receiving information much same way as people passes messages to one another. A message for an object is a request for the execution of a procedure and therefore will invoke function in the receiving object that generates desire results.

Definition: *"It is the process of invoking an operation on an object. In response to a message the corresponding method is executed in the object."*

When a program is executed, the objects interact by **sending message** to one another. For example let us assume there is another object called 'Marks' which include the data Name (two objects can have same entity and function), Marks, Course etc. and associated functions are Total, Average, Display, Grade etc. Here the first object 'student' can communicate with the second object 'Marks' through the common data or functions. Any data can be called only and only by its respective functions. This is also known as data abstraction. **The figure** given below represents communication between different objects.

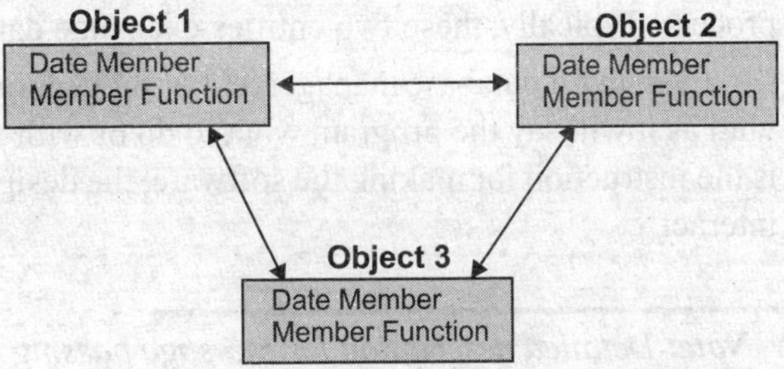

Figure 1.35: Message passing between objects

Objects are uniquely identifiable by a *name*. Therefore you could have two distinguishable objects with the same set of values.

Object oriented programming includes objects which communicate with each other.

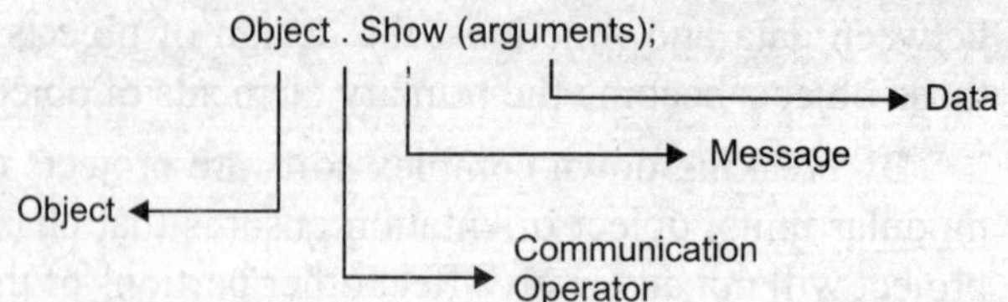

Figure 1.36: Description of object call using communication operator

In other words, an object is an instance of a class. It can be uniquely identified by its name and it defines a state which is represented by the values of its attributes at a particular time.

Objects are autonomous entities which only provide a well-defined interface. We'd like to talk of objects as if they are active entities. For example, objects are responsible for themselves; they might deny invocation of a method, etc. This distinguishes an object from a module, which is passive. Therefore, we don't speak of procedure calls. We speak of messages with which we ask an object to invoke one of its methods. Software objects interact and communicate with each other using messages. Example- the key word in a programming language 'employee salary (name)' will first refer first the object name which is here employee, then the message or variable which is here salary and then the information which is here name.

The Internet provides several objects. Two of the most well known ones are 'client' and 'server'. For example, you use an FTP client (object) to access data stored on an FTP server (object). Thus, you could view this as if the client **"sends a message"** to the server asking for providing data stored there. In the client/server environment we really have two remotely acting entities: the client and server process. Typically, these two entities exchange data in form of Internet messages.

Even in for database management or procedural languages, message passing is vital as it will say the program what to do or with what to work with. In a word, it is the instruction for making the software, the design and the hardware to work and interact.

Note: *Detailed description for message passing is given in objects.*

1.26 REUSABILITY

A main platform of object-oriented programming is code reusability. Rather than starting from scratch with each new application, a programmer will consult libraries of existing components to see if any are appropriate as starting points for the design of a new application.

This usage is achieved by the above explained terminology called as inheritance. Reusability is nothing but re-usage of structure without changing the existing one but adding new features or characteristics to it. It is very much needed for any programmers in different situations. Reusability gives the following advantages to users.

It helps in reducing the code size since classes can be just derived from existing one and one need to add only the new features and it helps users to save their time.

Definition: *"Reusability is the ability of software elements to serve for the construction of many different applications."*

This term refers to the ability for multiple programmers to use the same written and debugged existing class of data. This is a time saving device and adds code efficiency to the language. Additionally, the programmer can incorporate new features to the existing class, further developing the application and allowing users to achieve increased performance. This time saving feature optimizes code, helps in gaining secured applications and facilitates easier maintenance on the application.

For instance if there is a class defined to draw different graphical figures say there is a user who want to draw graphical figure and also add the features of adding colour to the graphical figure. In this scenario instead of defining a class to draw a graphical figure and colouring it what the user can do is make use of the existing class for drawing graphical figure by deriving the class and add new feature to the derived class namely add the feature of adding colours to the graphical figure. Class graphics is reused and class rectangle is created. Again class rectangle is reused and class square is created.

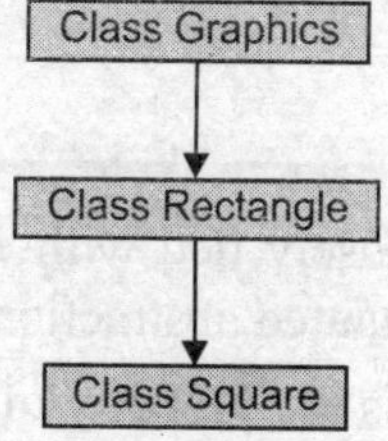

Figure 1.37: Reusing Code

Object oriented programming allows us to **reuse** our code. For example, the programmer has developed classes for any application, such as an inventory system. He can reuse these classes in similar type of applications programs without having any major changes. Reusability helps a programmer to concentrate and develop the software with more functionality otherwise he/she has to waste time to write the complete code from the scratch. The main advantages of reusability are time saving, easier software development, performance and efficiency during the software development.

1.26.1 Benefits of Reusability

Following are the various benefits of reusability:

1. **Reliability**. Components built by specialists in their field are more likely to be designed correctly and reliably. The reuse of these components across many applications will have given the developers of the components ample feedback to deal with any bugs and deficiencies.
2. **Efficiency**. The component developers are likely to be experts in their field and will have used the best possible algorithms and data structures.
3. **Time Savings.** By relying upon existing components there is less software to develop and hence applications can be built quicker.
4. **Decreased maintenance effort**. Using someone else's components decreases the amount of maintenance effort that the application developer needs to expend. The maintenance of the reused components is the responsibility of the component supplier.
5. **Consistency**. Reliance on a library of standard components will tend to spread a consistency of design message throughout a team of programmers working on an application. The library is the basis of a standard that will lend coherency and conformity to the design process.
6. **Investment**. Reusing software will save the cost of developing similar software from scratch. The investment in the original development is preserved if the developed software can be used in another project. The most reusable software tends to be that produced by the best developers. Reusing software is thus a way of preserving the knowledge and creations of the best developers.

1.27 MODULARITY

Modularity is closely tied with encapsulation; think of modularity as a way of mapping encapsulated abstractions into real, physical modules.

Modularity is the property of computer programs that measures the extent to which they have been composed out of separate parts called modules. In computing, a module is a software entity that groups a set of (typically cohesive) subprograms and data structures.

Programs that have many direct interrelationships between any two random parts of the program code are less modular than programs where those relationships occur mainly at well-defined interfaces between modules. In general usage, an interface is the point, area, or surface along which two substances or other qualitatively different things meet; it is also used metaphorically for the juncture between items.

Modular programming techniques are those which increase modularity. Structured programming can be seen as a subset or subdiscipline of procedural programming, one of the major programming paradigms. Procedural programming is a programming paradigm based upon the concept of the procedure call. In computer science, object-oriented programming, OOP for short, is a computer programming paradigm. In Software Engineering, the programming paradigm of aspect-oriented programming (AOP) (also called aspect-oriented software development (AOSD)) attempts to aid programmers in the Separation of concerns, or the breaking down of a program into distinct parts that overlap in functionality as little as possible. ...

One of the advantages of object oriented programming is that the process makes good use of modularity. That is, objects and tasks are grouped in a way that each module is capable of independent consideration. This can be a great help when making enhancements to a program, as modularity makes it possible to address the task of making alternations to the setup of one portion of the programming without impacting the structure and function of the other modules.

1.28 DYNAMISM

At one time in programming history, the question of how much memory a program would use was settled when the source code was compiled and linked. All the memory the program would ever need was set aside for it as it was launched. This memory was fixed; it could neither grow nor shrink.

In hindsight, it's evident what a serious constraint this was. It limited not only how programs were constructed, but what you could imagine a program doing. It constrained design, not just programming technique. Functions (like **malloc()**) that dynamically allocate memory as a program runs opened possibilities that didn't exist before.

Compile-time and link-time constraints are limiting because they force issues to be decided from information found in the programmer's source code, rather than from information obtained from the user as the program runs.

Although dynamic allocation removes one such constraint, many others, equally as limiting as static memory allocation, remain. For example, the elements that make up an application must be matched to data types at compile time. And the boundaries of an application are typically set at link time. Every part of the application must be united in a single executable file. New modules and new types can't be introduced as the program runs.

Object-oriented programming seeks to overcome these limitations and to make programs as dynamic and fluid as possible. It shifts much of the burden of decision making from compile time and link time to run time. The goal is to let program users decide what will happen, rather than constrain their actions artificially by the demands of the language and the needs of the compiler and linker.

Three kinds of dynamism are especially important for object-oriented design:

1. Dynamic typing, waiting until run time to determine the class of an object

2. Dynamic binding, determining at run time what method to invoke

3. Dynamic loading, adding new components to a program as it runs

1.29 DELEGATION

Delegation is a way of making object composition as powerful as inheritance. In delegation two objects are involved in handling a request receiving object delegates operations to its delegate. This is analogous to child class sending requests to the parent class.

Delegation allows the behaviour of an object to be defined in terms of the behaviour of another object.

ie, Delegation is alternative to class inheritance. Delegation refers to the delegating of responsibility and can be applied to inheritance. When a derived class does not have a desired attribute, it "delegates" responsibility to one of its base classes. In delegation systems, each object has a delegate list instead of a parent list. Thus, delegation's primary emphasis is

on message passing where an object could delegate responsibility of a message it couldn't handle to objects that potentially could (its delegates). Any object can be added to the delegate list, giving dynamic inheritance (of a sort). Typically, delegation and prototyping languages also have "part inheritance" in which fields and methods can be added and deleted from objects. This makes for easy "prototyping", which allows for objects to be constructed

piece by piece at run-time, although the term "prototyping" in the context of delegation languages usually refers to objects serving as prototypes for object instantiation, or exemplars.

1.30 GENERICITY

It is technique for defining software components that have more than one interpretation depending on the data type of parameters. Thus it allows the declaration of data items without specifying their exact data type. The compiler identifies the data type at run time. The programmer can create a function that can be used for any type of data. The template function in C++ allows generic programming.

1.31 EXTENSIBILITY

C++ allows the extension of the functionality of the existing software components. In C++ this is achieved through abstract classes and inheritance. It is a feature which allows the extension of the functionality of the existing software components.

1.32 PERSISTENCE

The phenomenon where the object (data) outlives the program execution time and exists between executions of a program is known as persistence. All data base systems support persistence. In C++ it is not supported. However the user can build it explicitly using file streams in a program.

1.33 ADVANTAGES OF OBJECT ORIENTED APPROACH

A major factor in the invention of Object-Oriented approach is to remove some of the flaws encountered with the procedural approach. In OOP, data is treated as a critical element and does not allow it to flow freely. It bounds data closely to the functions that operate on it and protects it from accidental modification from outside functions. OOP allows decomposition of a problem into a number of entities called objects and then builds data and functions around these objects. A major advantage of OOP is code reusability.

After this brief introduction, we now describe the major advantages of OOP.

1. **Real-World Modeling:** Object-oriented system tends to model the real world in a more complete fashion than do traditional methods. Objects are organized into classes of objects, and objects are associated with behaviors. The model is based on objects, rather than on data and processing.
2. **Improved Reliability and Flexibility:** Object-oriented system promise to be far more reliable than traditional systems, primarily because new behaviors can be "built" from existing objects. Because objects can be dynamically called and accessed, new objects may be created at any time. The new objects may inherit data attributes from one, or many other objects. Behaviors may be inherited from super-classes, and novel behaviors may be added without effecting existing systems functions.
3. **Scalable:** OO applications are more scalable then their structured programming roots. As an object's interface provides a roadmap for reusing the object in new software, it also provides you with all the information you need to replace the object without affecting other code. This makes it easy to replace old and aging code with faster algorithms and newer technology.

4. **Simplicity:** software objects model real world objects, so the complexity is reduced and the program structure is very clear;
5. **Modularity:** each object forms a separate entity whose internal workings are decoupled from other parts of the system;
6. **Modifiability:** it is easy to make minor changes in the data representation or the procedures in an OO program. Changes inside a class do not affect any other part of a program, since the only public interface that the external world has to a class is through the use of methods;
7. **Extensibility:** adding new features or responding to changing operating environments can be solved by introducing a few new objects and modifying some existing ones;
8. **Maintainability:** objects can be maintained separately, making locating and fixing problems easier;
9. **Re-usability:** objects can be reused in different programs.
10. **Information-hiding:** By interacting only with an object's methods, the details of its internal implementation remain hidden from the outside world.
11. **Code re-use:** If a class already exists, you can use objects from that class in your program. This allows programmers to implement/test/debug complex, task-specific objects, which you can then use in your own code.
12. **Easy Debugging:** If a particular object turns out to be a problem, you can simply remove it from your application and plug in a different object as its replacement. This is analogous to fixing mechanical problems in the real world. If a bolt breaks, you replace *it*, not the entire machine.

Some important features of Object oriented programming are as follows:

- Emphasis on data rather than procedure
- Programs are divided into Objects
- Data is hidden and cannot be accessed by external functions
- Objects can communicate with each other through functions
- New data and functions can be easily added whenever necessary
- Follows bottom-up approach
- Easy to maintain and modify existing code as new objects can be created with small differences to existing ones.
- An object oriented system uses encapsulation, data hiding, data abstraction and methods of communication between objects are properly defined, so the system can be understood very easily.
- Good framework for code libraries where supplied software components can be easily adapted and modified by the programmer. This is particularly useful for developing graphical user interfaces.

- Clear modular structure for programs which makes it good for defining abstract data types where implementation details are hidden and the unit has a clearly defined interface.

1.34 DISADVANTAGES OF OBJECT ORIENTED APPROACH

Although object oriented approach have many advantages but still it suffers from following disadvantages:

1. **Object-oriented Development is not a panacea:** Object-oriented Development is best suited for dynamic, interactive environments, as evidenced by its widespread acceptance in CAD/CAM and engineering design systems. Wide-scale object-oriented corporate systems are still unproved, and many bread-and-butter information systems applications (i.e. payroll, accounting), may not benefit from the object-oriented approach.
2. **Object-oriented Development is not a technology:** Although many advocates are religious in their fervor for object-oriented systems, remember that all the "HOOPLA" is directed at the object-oriented approach to problem solving, and not to any specific technology.
3. **Object-oriented Development is not yet completely accepted by major vendors:** Object-oriented Development has gained some market respectability, and vendors have gone from catering to a "lunatic fringe" to a respected market. Still, there are major reservations as to whether Object-oriented development will become a major force, or fade into history, as in the 1980's when Decision Support Systems made great promises, only to fade into obscurity.

Some other disadvantages are:

- Can run slower
- Can take more memory in case of dynamic binding
- Cannot use for making smaller software applications
- Not easy to learn and understand
- Difficult to understand flow control during complex objects
- Ignore some features of structured programming

1.35 APPLICATIONS OF OBJECT ORIENTED PROGRAMMING

Object Oriented Programming is a new way of approaching the job of programming. Object Oriented Programming (OOP) is a new way to solve complex system that has created lot of excitement and interest among software engineers.

The software developed using Object Oriented Programming is reliable, efficient, easily extended and modified. OOP is not only a way of programming but also a way of thinking abstractly about a problem using real world concepts rather than computer concepts. The applications of OOP are beginning to emerge in different areas.

The most common application area of OOP is GUI (Graphical User Interface) like Windows. In field of artificial intelligence, oops play a vital role for making expert systems. Many window systems have been developed using OOP technology. We can also develop different editors using Object Oriented Programming. OOP in combination with RDBMS can be used for developing Object Oriented Relational Database Management System (OORDBMS).

OOP Provides Many Applications

1. **Real time System:** A real time system is a system that give output at given instant and its parameters changes at every time. A real time system is nothing but a dynamic system. Dynamic means the system that changes every moment based on input to the system. OOP approach is very useful for Real time system because code changing is very easy in OOP system and it leads toward dynamic behavior of OOP codes thus more suitable to real time system.
2. **Simulation and Modeling:** System modeling is another area where criteria for OOP approach is countable. Representing a system is very easy in OOP approach because OOP codes are very easy to understand and thus is preferred to represent a system in simpler form.
3. **Hypertext and Hypermedia:** Hypertext and hypermedia is another area where OOP approach is spreading its legs. Its ease of using OOP codes that makes it suitable for various media approaches.
4. **Decision support system:** Decision support system is an example of Real time system that too very advance and complex system. More details is explained in real time system.
5. **CAM/CAE/CAD System:** Computer has wide use of OOP approach. This is due to time saving in writing OOP codes and dynamic behavior of OOP codes.
6. **Office Automation System:** Automation system is just a part or type of real time system. Embedded systems make it easy to use OOP for automated system.
7. **AI and expert System:** It is mixed system having both hypermedia and real time system.

Some other applications of OOPs:

1. Object Oriented Relational Database Management System (OORDBMS)
2. System Software
3. Office Automation System
4. Neural Networks
5. Fuzzy logics
6. Genetic programming
7. Parallel Programming
8. Digital Image Processing System
9. Graphical user Interface
10. Multimedia Applications
11. Network Management and Security System
12. Distributed System
13. Computer based Training Systems
14. Educational Systems

The concept of OOP is used to implement in different areas. The OOP technology improves the quality of software systems as well as enhances the reliability and productivity of the system.

1.36 OBJECT-ORIENTED LANGUAGES

There are almost two dozen major object-oriented programming languages in use today. But the leading *commercial* o-o languages are far fewer in number. These are:

1. C++
2. Smalltalk
3. Charm++
4. Java

Table 1.1 Properties of pure OOP and object based languages

	Pure Object-Oriented Languages			Object-Based Languages	
Properties	Java	Simula	Smalltalk	Eiffel	Ada
Encapsulation	Yes	Yes	Yes	Yes	Yes
Inheritance	Yes	Yes	Yes	Yes	No
Multiple Inheritance	No	No	Yes	Yes	No
Polymorphism	Yes	Yes	Yes	Yes	Yes
Binding					

	Pure Object-Oriented Languages			Object-Based Languages	
(Early and Late)	Both	Both	Late Binding	Early Binding	Early binding
Genericity	No	No	No	Yes	Yes
Class Libraries	Yes	Yes	Yes	Yes	Few
Garbage collection	Yes	Yes	Yes	Yes	No
Persistence	Yes	No	Promised	Less	Same as 3GL
Concurrency	Yes	Yes	Less	Promised	Hard

Table 1.2 Properties of extended traditional languages

	Pure Object-Oriented Languages			Object-Based Languages	
Properties	**Objective C**	**C++**	**Charm++**	**Objective Pascal**	**Turbo Pascal**
Encapsulation	Yes	Yes	Yes	Yes	Yes
Inheritance	Yes	Yes	Yes	Yes	Yes
Multiple Inheritance	Yes	Yes	Yes	---	----
Polymorphism	Yes	Yes	Yes	Yes	Yes
Binding					
(Early and Late)	Both	Both	Both	Late	Early
Genericity	No	Yes	Yes	No	No
Class Libraries	Yes	Yes	Yes	Yes	Yes
Garbage collection	Yes	No	No	Yes	Yes
Persistence	No	No	No	No	No
Concurrency	Poor	Poor	Yes	No	No

1.36.1 C++

C++ is an object-oriented version of C. It is compatible with C (it is actually a superset), so that existing C code can be incorporated into C++ programs. C++ programs are fast and efficient, qualities which helped make C an extremely popular programming language. It sacrifices some flexibility in order to remain efficient, however. C++ uses *compile-time binding,* which means that the programmer must specify the specific class of an object, or at the very least, the most general class that an object can belong to. This makes for high run-time efficiency and small code size, but it trades off some of the power to reuse classes.

C++ has become so popular that most new C compilers are actually C/C++ compilers. However, to take full advantage of object-oriented programming, one must program (and think!) in C++, not C. This can often be a major problem for experienced C programmers. Many programmers think they are coding in C++, but instead are only using a small part of the language's object-oriented power.

1.36.2 Smalltalk

Smalltalk is a pure object-oriented language. While C++ makes some practical compromises to ensure fast execution and small code size, Smalltalk makes none. It uses *run-time binding,* which means that nothing about the type of an object need be known before a Smalltalk program is run.

Smalltalk programs are considered by most to be significantly faster to develop than C++ programs. A rich class library that can be easily reused via inheritance is one reason for this. Another reason is Smalltalk's dynamic development environment. It is not explicitly compiled, like C++. This makes the development process more fluid, so that "what if" scenarios can be easily tried out, and classes definitions easily refined. But being purely object-oriented, programmers cannot simply put their toes in the o-o waters, as with C++. For this reason, Smalltalk generally takes longer to master than C++. But most of this time is actually spent learning object-oriented methodology and techniques, rather than details of a particular programming language. In fact, Smalltalk is syntactically very simple, much more so than either C or C++.

Unlike C++, which has become standardized, The Smalltalk language differs somewhat from one implementation to another. The most popular commercial "dialects" of Smalltalk are:

- VisualWorks from *ParcPlace-Digitalk, Inc.*
- Smalltalk/V and Visual Smalltalk from *ParcPlace-Digitalk Inc.*
- VisualAge from *IBM*

VisualWorks

VisualWorks is arguably the most powerful of Smalltalks. VisualWorks was developed by ParcPlace, which grew out of the original Xerox PARC project that invented the Smalltalk language. VisualWorks is *platform-independent,* so that an application written under one operating system, say, Microsoft Windows, can work without any modification on any of a wide range of platform supported by ParcPlace, from Sun Solaris to Macintosh. VisualWorks also features a *GUI* (Graphic User Interface) builder that is well-integrated into the product.

Smalltalk/V and Visual Smalltalk

Digitalk's versions of Smalltalk are somewhat smaller and simpler, and are specifically tailored to IBM compatible PCs. A Macintosh version was available, but support has since been abandoned. This does not bode well for Digitalk cross-platform efforts. Digitalk has a separate GUI builder, called PARTS Workbench (bundled with Visual Smalltalk), which allows quick construct of an application.

ParcPlace and Digitalk were merged into a single company, ParcPlace-Digitalk, Inc. The future of the Digitalk product line is uncertain, and it may just be spun off back into a separate company.

VisualAge

IBM's version of Smalltalk, VisualAge, is comparable to Smalltalk/V with PARTS. Both of these Smalltalks allow programmers to readily exploit machine-specific features, at the expense of some portability. IBM has adapted existing industry standards for such things as file management and screen graphics. When IBM talks, people listen, and IBM has made a substantial commitment to Smalltalk.

1.36.3 CHARM++

Charm ++ is also an object-oriented programming language. Charm++ is designed with the goal of enhancing programmer productivity by providing a high-level abstraction of a parallel program while at the same time delivering good performance on a wide variety of underlying hardware platforms. Programs written in Charm++ are decomposed into a number of cooperating message-driven objects called *chares*. When a programmer invokes a method on an object, the Charm++ runtime system sends a message to the invoked object, which may reside on the local processor or on a remote processor in a parallel computation. This message triggers the execution of code within the chare to handle the message asynchronously. The language provides features such as inheritance, strict type checking, overloading, and reusability. It is designed in order to work efficiently with different systems, together with shared memory systems and networking.

1.36.4 JAVA

Java is the latest, flashiest object-oriented language. It has taken the software world by storm due to its close ties with the Internet and Web browsers. It is designed as a portable language that can run on any web-enabled computer via that computer's Web browser. As such, it offers great promise as the standard Internet and Intranet programming language.

Java is a curious mixture of C++ and Smalltalk. It has the syntax of C++, making it easy (or difficult) to learn, depending on your experience. But it has improved on C++ in some important areas. For one thing, it has no pointers, low-level programming constructs that make for error-prone programs. Like Smalltalk, it has garbage collection, a feature that frees the programmer from explicitly allocating and de-allocating memory. And it runs on a Smalltalk-style virtual machine, software built into your web browser which executes the same standard compiled Java byte codes no matter what type of computer you have.

Java development tools are being rapidly deployed, and are available from such major software companies as IBM, Microsoft, and Symantec.

The following chart illustrates the popularity of different OOP languages in different year. Note that every time the overall popularity of using OOP is increasing.

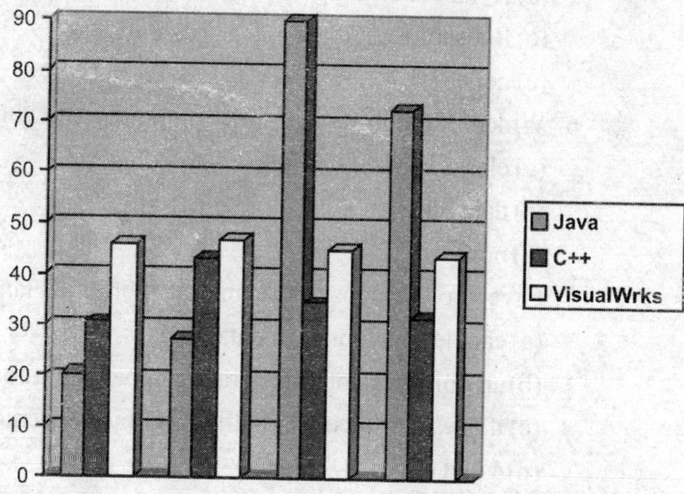

Figure 1.38: Graphical representation of OOPs popularity according to year 1990-2005.

Popularity of OOP languages in 1990, 1995, 2000, 2005.

OBJECTIVE TYPE QUESTIONS

1. CPP was developed in

   (a) 1972 (b) 1983

   (c) 1985 (d) 1999

2. CPP was developed by

   (a) Dennis Ritchie (b) Bjarne Stroustrup

   (c) both (d) none

3. CPP was developed at

   (a) USA (b) UK

   (c) Italy (d) none

4. Which is the characteristics of OOPS
   (a) Polymorphism (b) Abstraction
   (c) Encapsulation (d) Inheritance
   (e) all
5. Which of the following is not the characteristic of OOPS
   (a) Dynamic binding (b) Message passing
   (c) Reusability (d) all
   (e) none
6. Which of the following is a component of OOPS
   (a) class (b) object
   (c) data hiding (d) all
   (e) none
7. Give good reasons to use an object oriented language?
   (a) can define your own data types
   (b) an object oriented program can be taught to correct its own errors
   (c) it is easier to conceptualize an object oriented program
   (d) a and c
8. When a language has the capability to produce new data types, it is called
   (a) extensible (b) overloaded
   (c) encapsulated (d) reprehensible
9. Dividing a program into functions
   (a) is the key to object oriented programming
   (b) makes the program easier to conceptualize
   (c) makes the program run faster
   (d) both (b) and (c) above
10. In C++, a function contained within a class is called
    (a) a member function (b) an operator
    (c) a class function (d) a method
11. A normal C++ operator that acts in special ways on newly defined data type is called
    (a) classified (b) overloaded
    (c) encapsulated (d) glorified

EXERCISES

1. What do you mean by C++?
2. Why we need C++
3. Explain the evolution of C++
4. Explain the relationship between C and C++.
5. Difference between C and C++.
6. What are the characteristics of OOPs?
7. Explain the concept of object oriented programming.
8. Explain various disadvantages of conventional programming.
9. How C++ and OOPs related to each other.
10. Why we use object oriented approach?
11. What are the various paradigms of programming?
12. Difference between procedural and object oriented approach.
13. Explain the various features of Oops language.
14. What are objects/ Explain in detail.
15. Explain the role of class in OOPs.
16. What do you understand by abstraction and encapsulation?
17. What are the different types of inheritance?
18. How messages are passing between objects.
19. Explain the concept of polymorphism in detail.
20. What do you mean by dynamic binding?
21. What do you understand by reusability?
22. What are the advantages and disadvantages of OOPs?
23. What are the various application areas of OOPs?
24. What do you mean by modularity?
25. Explain other object oriented languages in detail.

CHAPTER 2

C++ Programming Basics

2.1 INTRODUCTION

This chapter examines the most fundamental element of the C (as well as the C++) language: tokens, character set, keywords, identifiers, constants, variables, and basic program construction. It also touches on a variety of other language features, including comments, type conversion, and const qualifier. These topics are not conceptually difficult, but you may find that the style in C++ is a little different compared with, say, BASIC or Pascal.

Like most other computer languages, C/C++ supports a number of different data types. This chapter also describes C++'s built in types and the basic facilities for constructing programs out of them. The C subset of C++ is presented together with C++'s additional support for traditional styles of programming. It also discusses the basic facilities for composing a C++ program out of logical and physical parts.

2.2 C++ TOKENS

As in the English language, in a paragraph all the words, punctuation mark and the blank spaces are called Tokens. Similarly in a C++ program all the C++ statements having Keywords, Identifiers, Constants , Strings, Operators and the Special Symbols are called C++ Tokens. C++ Tokens are the essential part of a C++ compiler and so are very useful in the C++ programming. A Token is an individual entity of a C++ program.

For example, some C++ Tokens used in a C++ program are :

Reserve words : long, do if, else etc.

Identifiers : Pay, salary etc.

Constant : 450.9,10,44 etc.

Strings	:	"Sukhwant", "2010-11" etc.
Operator	:	+, *, <, >=, &&,||, etc
Special symbols	:	(), {}, #, @, %, etc.

2.3 CHARACTER SET

Character set is the combination of English language(Alphabets and White spaces) and math's symbols(Digits and Special symbols). Character Set means that the characters and symbols that a C++ Program can understand and accept. These are grouped to form the commands, expressions, words, c-statements and other tokens for C++ Language. Character Set is the combination of alphabets or characters, digits, special symbols and white spaces same as learning English is to first learns the alphabets, then learn to combine these alphabets to form words, which in turn are combined to form sentences and sentences are combined to form paragraphs. More about a C++ program we can say that it is a sequence of characters. These character from the character set plays the different role in different way in the C++ compiler.

When we have to learn English language we start from beginning as given below:

When we have to learn C language we start from beginning as given below:

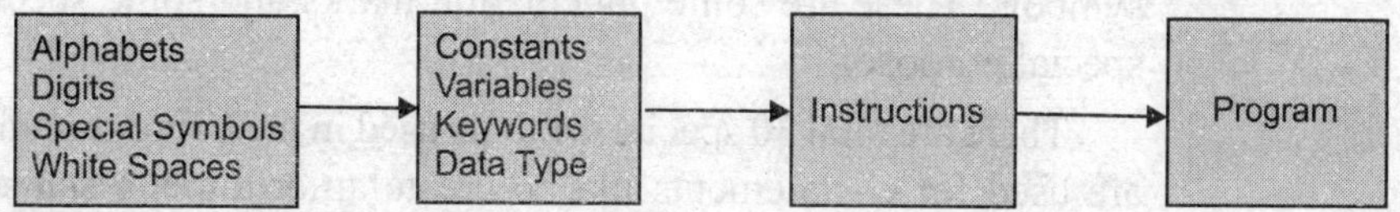

There are mainly four categories of the character set as shown in the Figure 2.1 below:

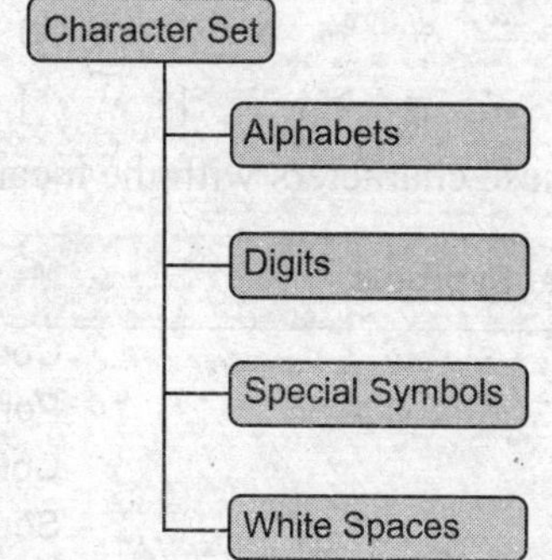

Figure 2.1: Categories of character set

1. Alphabets

Alphabets are represented by A-Z or a-z. C- Language is case sensitive so it takes different meaning for small and upper case letters. By using this character set C-statements and character constants can be written very easily. There are total 26 letters used in C-programming.

Upper Case Letters

A B C D E F G H I J K L M

N O P Q R S T U V W X Y Z

Lower Case Letters

a b c d e f g h i j k l m

n o p q r s t u v w x y z

2. Digits

Digits are represented by 0-9 or by combination of these digits. By using the digits numeric constant can be written easily. Also numeric data can be assigned to the C-tokens. There are total 10 digits used in the C-programming.

10 decimal digit

1 2 3 4 5 6 7 8 9 10

3. Special Symbols

All the keyboard keys except alphabet, digits and white spaces are the special symbols. These are some punctuation marks and some special symbols used for special purpose.

There are total 30 special symbols used in the C-programming. Special symbols are used for C-statements like to create an arithmetic statement +, -, * etc. , to create relational statement <, >, <=, >=, == etc. , to create assignment statement =, to create logical statement &&, || etc. are required.

30 Graphics symbols

! " # % & ' ( ) * + ' - . / :

; < = > ? [\ ] ^ _ { | } ~ @

All these characters with the meanings are discussed in the table below:

Special Symbols	Meaning
,	Comma
.	Period
:	Colon
;	Semicolon
?	Question Mark

Special Symbols	Meaning
‘	Single Quote
“	Double Quote
(	Left Parenthesis
)	Right Parenthesis
[	Left Bracket
]	Right Bracket
{	Left Brace
}	Right Brace
<	Left Angle Bracket or less than symbol
>	Right Angle Bracket or greater than symbol
=	Equal to Sign
!	Exclamation Mark
|	Vertical Bar or Pipe symbol
/	Slash or Forward Slash
\	Backslash or Backward Slash
~	Tilde symbol
+	Plus sign
-	Minus sign or Hyphen sign
*	Asterisk sign
#	Number sign or Hash symbol
%	Percentage sign
^	Caret symbol
&	Ampersand sign
@	“At the rate” symbol
_	Underscore sign

4. White Spaces

White spaces has blank space, new line return, Horizontal tab space, carriage ctrl, Form feed etc. are all used for special purpose. Also note that Turbo-C Compiler always ignore these white space characters in both high level and low level programming.

2.4 KEYWORDS AND IDENTIFIERS

Every word in C++ language is a keyword or an identifier. Keywords in C++ language cannot be used as a variable name. They are specifically used by the compiler for its own purpose and they serve as building blocks of a C++ program. C++ language has some reserve words which are called keywords of C++ language. These are the part of the C++ Tokens.

There are 63 keywords currently defined for Standard C++. These are shown in Table 2.1. Together with the formal C++ syntax, they form the C++ programming language. Also, early versions of C++ defined the **overload** keyword, but it is obsolete. Keep in mind that C++ is a case-sensitive language and it requires that all keywords be in lowercase.

Table 2.1: Keywords used in C++

asm	auto	bool	break
case	catch	char	class
const	const_cast	continue	default
delete	do	double	dynamic_cast
else	enum	explicit	export
extern	false	float	for
friend	goto	if	inline
int	long	mutable	namespace
new	operator	private	protected
public	register	reinterpret_cast	return
short	signed	sizeof	static
static_cast	struct	switch	template
this	throw	true	try
typedef	typeid	typename	union
unsigned	using	virtual	void
volatile	wchar_t	while	

Identifier

The name of a variable, function, class, or other entity in C++ is called an **identifier**. C++ gives you a lot of flexibility to name identifiers as you wish. However, there are a few rules that must be followed when naming identifiers:

- The identifier can not be a keyword. Keywords are reserved.
- The identifier can only be composed of letters, numbers, and the underscore character. That means the name can not contains symbols (except the underscore) nor whitespace.
- The identifier must begin with a letter or an underscore. It can not start with a number.
- C++ distinguishes between lower and upper case letters. nvalue is different than nValue is different than NVALUE.

2.5 CONSTANTS

Constants refer to fixed values that the program may not alter. Constants can be of any of the basic data types. The way each constant is represented depends upon its type. Constants are also called literals.

***Definition:** "A constant value is the one which does not change during the execution of a program."*

Constant uses the secondary storage area. Constants are those quantities whose value does not vary during the execution of the program i.e. constant has fixed value. Constants in every language are the same. For example, in the C++ language some valid constant are: 52.7 , -43.4, +83.65, "Sukhwant", 'M', "2010" , "\n" etc.

In C++ language constants are of two types:

1. Numeric Constant
2. Non-Numeric Constant (Character Constant)

These are further sub-divided into more categories as shown in the Figure 2.2 below:

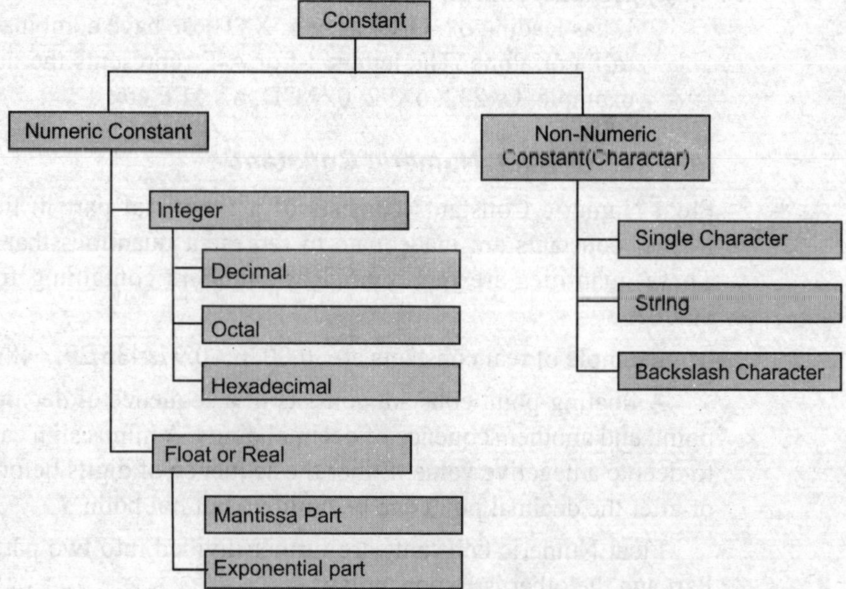

Figure 2.2: Different types of constants

2.5.1 Numeric Constant

These have numeric value having combination of sequence of digits i.e. from 0-9 as alone digit or combination of 0-9 with or without decimal point (precision value) having positive or negative sign. These are further sub-divided into two categories as:

(i) Integer Numeric Constant

(ii) Float or Real Numeric Constant

(i) Integer Numeric Constant

An Integer Numeric Constant is a sequence of digits(combination of 0-9 digits without any decimal point or without precision), optionally preceded by a plus or minus sign.

There are 3 types of integer numeric constant namely decimal integer, octal integers and hexadecimal integer.

(a) **Decimal Integer Numeric Constant:** These have no decimal point in it and is either be alone or be the combination of 0-9 digits. These have either +ve or –ve sign. For example: 1214, -1321, 10, 254, -78, +99 etc.

(b) **Octal Integer Numeric Constant:** These consist of combination of digits from 0-7 with positive or negative sign. It has leading with O or o (upper or lower case) means Octal or octal. For example: O317, O03, -O45 etc.

(c) **Hexadecimal Integer Numeric Constant:** These have hexadecimal data. It has leading ox, OX, Ox or x, X. These have combination of 0-9 and A-F (a-f) or alone. The letters a-f or A-F represents the numbers 10-15. For example: Ox232, oX92, 0xACD, oXAEF etc.

(ii) Float or Real Numeric Constant

Float Numeric Constants consists of a fractional part in their representation. Integer constants are inadequate to represent quantities that vary continuously. These quantities are represented by numbers containing fractional parts like 26.082.

Example of real constants are: 0.0026, -0.97, 435.29, +487.0, 3.4E-2, 4.5E5

A floating-point constant consists of a sequence of decimal digits, a decimal point, and another sequence of decimal digits. A minus sign can precede the value to denote a negative value. Either the sequence of digits before the decimal point or after the decimal point can be omitted, but not both.

Float Numeric constants are further divided into two parts. One is Mantissa Part and the other is Exponent Part.

(a) **Mantissa part :** The part without E and having a decimal point is called Mantissa Real part e.g. 45.5, -22.43, 0.5 etc. it is also called without exponent part.

(b) **Exponent part :** The exponent part has an E within it. It is also called a scientific notation. Here E has base value 10. It computes the power. For example: $4.2\text{x}10^{2}$ can be written as 4.2E2, $4.2\text{x}10^{-5}$ can be written as 4.2E-5. Similarly some more valid real numeric constant are as: 54.73 E –4, 51.9 E +11 etc.

2.5.2 Character Constant

Character constants have either a single character or group of characters or a character with backslash used for special purpose. These are further subdivided into three types:

(i) Single Character Constant

(ii) String Character Constant

(iii) Backslash Character Constant

(i) Single Character Constant

Single Character constants are enclosed between single quotes('). For example, 'a' and '%' are both character constants. So these are also called single quote character constant.

For example: 'a', 'M', '5', '+', '?' etc. are some valid single character constant.

(ii) String Character Constant

C++ supports another type of constant: the string. A string is a set of characters enclosed in double quotes ("). For example: "Mukul Seth" is a string.

You must not confuse strings with characters. A single character constant is enclosed in single quotes, as in 'a'. However, "a" is a string containing only one letter.

For example: "Avtar", "Hello", "2010", "2010-2020", "5+3", "?+!" etc. are some valid string character constant. These are used for printing purpose or display purpose in the C++ program's output statements. These can also be used for assigning the string data to the character (string) type variables.

(iii) Backslash Character Constants

Enclosing character constants in single quotes works for most printing characters. A few, however, such as the carriage return, can't be. For this reason, C++ includes the special backslash character constants, shown below, so that you may easily enter these special characters as constants.

These are also referred to as escape sequences. You should use the backslash codes instead of their ASCII equivalents to help ensure portability.

These are used for special purpose in the C++ language. These are used in output statements like cout etc.

Escape Sequences

A list of backslash character constant or escape sequence is as in the below table:

Constant	Meaning
'\a' or "\a"	Audible bell (Beep)
'b' or "\b"	Backspace (it moves one space back)
'\n' or "\n"	New line (Cursor moves to next line)
'\f' or "\f"	Form feed (move one page next). It is used in the printing the hard copy only.
'\t' or "\t"	Horizontal tab (it moves Eight spaces of tab).
'\v' or "\v"	Vertical tab (it moves Eight lines down). It does not work in the Turbo-C++ compiler.
'\r' or "\r"	Carriage return (it replaces a word or string from the beginning of the other string). For example, an output statement in a C++ program: cout<<"\n Flower is Beautiful \r Car"; will display the output: Car is Beautiful.
'\' ' or "\' "	It displays a single quote in output statement. For example, an output statement in a C++ program:cout<<"\n College \'s address"; will display the output: College 's address.
'\" ' or "\" "	It displays a double quote in output statement. For example, an output statement in a C++ program: cout<<"\n Programming is fun."; will display the output: Programming is fun.
'\?' or "\?"	It displays question mark.
'\0' or "\0"	Null character (it tells us the end of the string and used in string handling which we will study in more detail in later section)

2.6 VARIABLES

A variable is a value that can change any time. It is a memory location used to store a data value. A variable name should be carefully chosen by the programmer so that its use is reflected in a useful way in the entire program. Variable names are case sensitive.

Example of variable names are: Sun, number, Salary, Emp_name, average1 etc.

Any variable declared in a program should confirm to the following points:

1. They must always begin with a letter, although some systems permit underscore as the first character.
2. The length of a variable must not be more than 8 characters.
3. White space is not allowed and
4. A variable should not be a Keyword
5. It should not contain any special characters.

Examples of Invalid Variable names are: 123, (area), 6th, %abc etc.

A variable must be declared before it can be used. Variables can be declared at the start of any block of code, but most are found at the start of each function. Most local variables are created when the function is called, and are destroyed on return from that function. Variables uses the primary storage area.

Definition: *"Variables are those quantities whose value can vary during the execution of the program."*

Variables are basically memory locations which are given names and these locations are refereed in the program by variable names to read and write data in it. Variables are used for identification for entering the information or data. In variable you can enter integer value or real or character value (string value) according to the requirement. So we can say that variable are either of integer or float type or string type according to the data type used in C++ programming. Variables are used in C++ programs for reading data from the keyboard or from the file, process some formula and printing the information. In C++ language variables have no length for declaration, but some compilers allows either 31 character or 8 character long variables. It contains the name of a valid identifier.

For example:

area, simple, roll_no, name, student1 etc. are some valid variables.

A declaration begins with the type, followed by the name of one or more variables. For example,

```
int roll_no, marks;
```

Declarations can be spread out, allowing space for an explanatory comment. Variables can also be initialised when they are declared, this is done by adding an equals sign and the required value after the declaration.

```
int roll_no = 12;    // Variable roll_no stores value 12
int marks = 40;      // Variable marks stores value 40
```

Note that each variable in the C++ program has some features or properties associated with it called its **storage class** like auto, extern, static and register which are described in later section.

2.6.1 Declaration of Variables

Every variable used in the program should be declared to the compiler. The declaration does two things.

1. Tells the compiler the variables name.
2. Specifies what type of data the variable will hold.

The general syntax is:

```
datatype v1, v2, v3, .......... vn;
```

Where v1, v2, v3 are variable names. Variables are separated by commas. A declaration statement must end with a semicolon.

Example:

```
int sum;
int number, salary;
double average, mean;
```

2.6.2 Assigning Values To Variable

We can assign a value to a variable by using assignment operator (=). You can either assign a single value (constant) to a variable or by computing a formula and then the computed value can be assigned to that variable. Also you can assign a constant (fixed) value to a variable during the data type declaration statement.

The general syntax is:

```
variable1 = variable2;              a=b;
        or
variable = expression;              a = a + b;
        or
data type variable = constant;      int a =0;
```

For example, below are some valid assignment statements for assigning the values to the variable in different ways:

```
sum = 0;
int a = 22, c = 0;
float x = 22.25;
char x = 'R';
mul = a*b;
```

2.7 DATA TYPES

A programming language is proposed to help programmer to process certain kinds of data and to provide useful output. The task of data processing is accomplished by executing series of commands called program. A program usually contains different types of data types (integer, float, character etc.) and need to store the values being used in the program. C++ language is rich of data types. A C++ programmer has to employ proper data type as per his requirement.

C++ has different data types for different types of data and can be broadly classified as:

1. Primary data types
2. Secondary data types

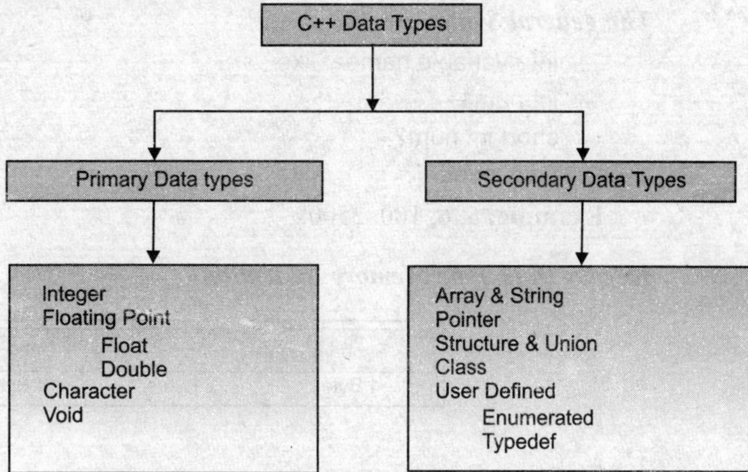

Figure 2.3: Different types of data types used in C++

2.7.1 Primary Data Types

A primary data type is used for representing a single value only. It is also called **Simple** or **Fundamental** data type. As these are used at primary level in the high level language, so these are called **Primary** data type. Simple data types has further some **Standard** data types.

These are sub-divided into four categories:

(i) Integer data type

(ii) Floating point data type (float and double)

(iii) Character data type

(iv) Void data type

(i) Integer Data Types

Integers are whole numbers with a range of values, range of values are machine dependent. Generally an integer occupies 2 bytes memory space and its value range limited to -32768 to +32768 (that is, -2^{15} to $+2^{15}-1$). A signed integer use one bit for storing sign and rest 15 bits for number.

To control the range of numbers and storage space, C++ has three classes of integer storage namely short int, int and long int. All three data types have signed and unsigned forms. A short int requires half the amount of storage than normal integer. Unlike signed integer, unsigned integers are always positive and use all the bits for the magnitude of the number. Therefore the range of an unsigned integer will be from 0 to 65535. The long integers are used to declare a longer range of values and it occupies 4 bytes of storage space.

The general Syntax is:

```
int <variable name>; like
int num1;
short int num2;
long int num3;
```

Example: 5, 6, 100, 2500.

Integer Data Type Memory Allocation

Short int	int	long int
1 Byte	2 Bytes	4 Bytes

(ii) Floating Point Types

These are further divided into two types:

(a) Float Data Type

The float data type is used to store fractional numbers (real numbers) with 6 digits of precision. Floating point numbers are denoted by the keyword float. These data type have at least one digit with a decimal point. These are also signed or unsigned. These data types require storage space (size) 32 bit and have range $3.4E^{-38}$ to $3.4E^{+38}$ for inputting the data.

The general Syntax is: float <variable name>; like

```
float num1;
```

Example: 9.1, 3.12.

(b) Double Data Type

When the accuracy of the floating point number is insufficient, we can use the double to define the number. The double is same as float but with longer precision and takes double space (8 bytes) than float. To extend the precision further we can use long double which occupies 10 bytes of memory space. These have double precision value having the 64 bits size and the range is $1.7E^{-308}$ to $1.7E^{+308}$.

Also there are long double or long float having 80 bits size and have a very high range $3.4E^{-4932}$ to $3.4E^{+4932}$.

The general Syntax is: double <variable name>; like

```
double num1;
long double num2;
```

Example: 9.125, 3.1254.

Floating Point Data Type Memory Allocation

float	double	long double
4 Byte	8 Bytes	10 Bytes

(iii) Character Data Type

Character type variable can hold a single character. As there are singed and unsigned int (either short or long), in the same way there are signed and unsigned chars; both occupy 1 byte each, but having different ranges. Unsigned characters have values between 0 and 255, signed characters have values from –128 to 127.

The general Syntax is: char <variable name>; like

```
char ch = 'a';
```

Example: a, b, g, S, j.

Character Data Type Memory Allocation

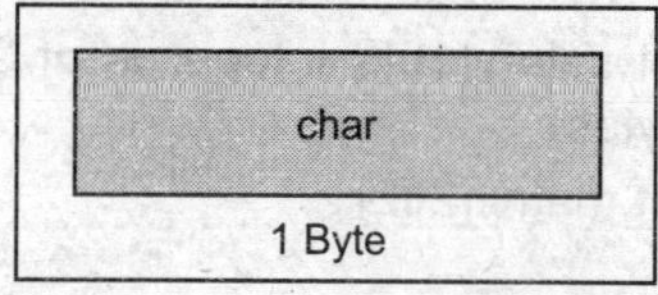

(iv) Void Data Type

The void type has no values therefore we cannot declare it as variable as we did in case of integer and float.

The void data type is usually used with function to specify its type. Like in our first C++ program we declared "main()" as void type because it does not return any value. The concept of returning values will be discussed in detail in the C++ function hub.

2.7.2 Secondary Data Types

Secondary data types are derived from the primary data type by adding some additional relationship with the various elements of the primary data types. Note that Secondary data type may be used for representing a single value or multiple values. As these data types have different structure depending on the C++ coding, these are also called Structured data type. These are also called Derived data type.

These are further sub divided into five categories:

(i) Array & String Data Type

(ii) Pointer Data Type

(iii) Structure & Union Data type

(iv) Class

(v) User Defined data types (enumerated and typedef)

(i) Array & String Data Type

Array and String data types are also called homogeneous data types. They are used to store same types of data elements together using common name.

(a) Array Data Type

Array is set of homogeneous(same type) data elements. Array is similar type of data collection name i.e. it is a collection of same types of elements. An array is a group of related data items, which share common name.

The General Syntax is:

```
data type array name [size];
        or
data type array-name [subscript1] [subscript2];
```

For Example:

int salary[10];(integer is of 2 bytes. Size 10 integers means 2*10=20 bytes)

int matrix[2][2];

(b) String Data Type

Combination of characters is called string. "I am a good baby" is a string. We can print or display the string by using the cout function as:

```
cout<<"\n I am a good baby \n";
```

String data type is used to store only character data. But if the string is stored in variable, then such type of variable should be of character type. Also character variable should be declared in the array form.

The General Syntax is:

```
data type string name [size];
        or
data type string-name [subscript1] [subscript2];
```

For Example:

```
char city [10];
char city [10][20];
```

(ii) Pointer Data Type

Pointer data types are used to handle the data at their memory addresses. We will study about the use and handling of the pointer data type in detail in the pointer chapter.

(iii) Structure & Union Data Type

Structure and union data types are also called heterogeneous data types. They are used to store different types of data elements together using common name.

(a) Structure Data Type

In C++, a structure data type is a collection of data elements that are referenced under one name, providing a convenient means of keeping related information together.

In the structure you can pack number of data elements having different data type with single structure, which is called structure name or tag name or structure tag.

The General Syntax is:

```
struct   structure-tag
{
data-type-1    structure element-1 or member-1;
data-type-2    structure element-1 or member-2;
data-type-3    structure element-1 or member-3;
..........................................................;
data-type-n    structure element-1 or member-n;
};
For Example:
struct student
{
char grade;
int rollno;
float fees;
double marks;
} st;
```

Structure Data Type Memory Allocation

Total size= char + int + float + double= 1+2+4+8=15 bytes

(b) Union Data Type

A union is a data type that declares a set of multiple data elements (called members or elements having different data-types) sharing the same name and memory area.

The compiler allocates sufficient memory to hold the largest variable of the union. All the members of union occupy the same memory locations called addresses. The old value of the already declared member will be destroyed and new value to the new member will be assigned in the memory by using the union concept.

Note that union declaration has more than one variable declaration, but only one can be used at a time. Also with the declaration of union, the Turbo-C++ compiler will automatically allocates the memory locations to the variable which has the long data type member element in the union (i.e. the priority list be: double, long float, float, long int, int, char). The general syntax used for the declaration of union be as follows:

The General Syntax is:

```
union union-tag
{
datatype-1 member-element-1;
......................................;
datatype-n   member-element-n;
}v1,v2,...vn;

For Example:
union student
{
char grade;
int rollno;
float fees;
double marks;
} st;
```

Union Data Type Memory Allocation

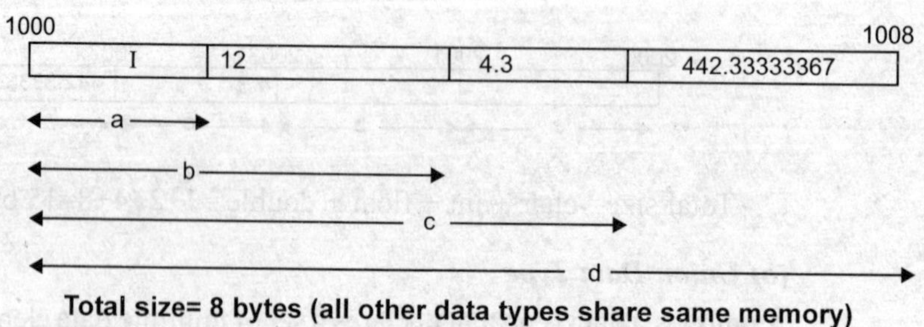

Total size= 8 bytes (all other data types share same memory)

(iv) Class

A class is an expanded concept of a data structure: instead of holding only data, it can hold both data and functions. An object is an instantiation of a class. In terms of variables, a class would be the type, and an object would be the variable. Classes are generally declared using the keyword class.

The General Syntax is:

```
class class_name
{
access_specifier_1:
member1;
access_specifier_2:
member2;
...
} object_names;
```

Where class_name is a valid identifier for the class, object_names is an optional list of names for objects of this class. The body of the declaration can contain members, that can be either data or function declarations, and optionally access specifiers. **For Example:**

```
class CRectangle
{
private:
int x, y;
public:
void set_values (int,int);
int area (void);
} rect;
```

(v) User Defined Type Declaration

C++ language supports a feature where user can define an identifier that characterizes an existing data type. This user defined data type identifier can later be used to declare variables. Two types of user defined data types are:

(a) Typedef Data Type

In C++ language a user can define an identifier that represents an existing data type. The user defined datatype identifier can later be used to declare variables.

In short its purpose is to redefine the name of an existing data type.

The General Syntax is:

```
typedef <type> <identifier>; like
typedef int number;
```

Now we can use number in lieu of int to declare integer variable.

For Example:

"int x1" or "number x1" both statements declaring an integer variable. We have just changed the default keyword "int" to declare integer variable to "number".

(b) Enumerated Data Type

This is also used for type definition, i.e. it allows the users to define a variable or an identifier, which is used for representation of existing data types. In other words, it provides us a way to define our own data type and also can define the value of a variable or an identifier stores into the main memory.

The General Syntax is:

```
enum  identifier {v1, v2, v3, ........,vn };
or
enum  identifier {v1, v2, v3, ......., vn} variable;
```

Here enum is the reserve word and v1,v2,v3,.....,vn all are the values which is also called enumeration constants. Also variable can be defined with the enumerated variable.

For Example:

```
enum month { Jan, Feb, Mar, ....., Dec};
        OR
enum  year {1999, 2000, 2001,.....,2005}y;
```

2.7.3 More on Data Types

C++ has two more data types: the types bool and wchar_t. The data types bool, and wchar_t are described below.

(i) The Boolean Data Type

The *Boolean* data type is also known as the logical data type and represents the concepts of true and false. The name "Boolean" comes from the mathematician George Boole; who in 1854 published: An Investigation of the Laws of Thought. Boolean algebra is the area of mathematics that deals with the logical representation of true and false using the numbers 0 and 1. The importance of the Boolean data type within programming is that it is used to control programming structures (if then else, while loops, etc.) that allow us to implement "choice" into our algorithms.

C++ defines a built-in Boolean type called bool. Objects of type bool can store only the values true or false, which are keywords defined by C++. Automatic conversions take place which allow bool values to be converted to integers, and vice versa. Specifically, any non-zero value is converted to true and zero is converted to false. The reverse also occurs; true is converted to 1 and false is converted to zero. The keyword bool is used to declare Boolean logic variables; that is, variables which can be either true or false.

In the following statement:

```
if (condexpr1) statement1;
```

If condexpr1 is **true**, statement1 is always executed; if condexpr1 is **false**, statement1 is never executed.

To declare a boolean variable, we use the keyword *bool*:

```
bool bValue;
```

When assigning values to boolean variables, we use the keywords *true* and *false*.

```
1.bool bValue1 = true;          // explicit assignment
2.bool bValue2(false);          // implicit assignment
```

In Conditional expressions have the type bool and so have values of type bool. For example, i!=0 now has **true** or **false** depending on the value of i.

The values true and false have the following relationship:

```
!false == true
!true == false
```

For example: The following code declares a boolean variable called *done*, initializes it to false, and then loops until that variable is set to true.

```
Bool done = false;
while( !done )
{
.............
}
```

The Boolean data type has the same attributes and acts or behaves similarly in all programming languages.

Most control structures use a *test expression* that executes either selection (as in the: if then else) or iteration (as in the while; do while; or for loops) based on the truthfulness or falseness of the expression. Thus, we often talk about the *Boolean expression* that is controlling the structure. Within many programming languages, this expression must be a Boolean expression and is governed by a tight set of rules. However, in C++ every data type can be used as a Boolean expression because the value of any data type within C++ can be demoted into a Boolean value.

Within most languages, expressions that yield Boolean data type values are divided into two groups. One group uses the relational operators within their expressions and the other group uses logical operators within their expressions.

Within the C++ programming language the Boolean data type is one of the standard or basic data types and is a member of the integer family.

(ii) The Wide Character Data Type

A wide character is a type of computer character datatype that generally has a size greater than the traditional 8-bit character. The increased datatype size allows for the use of larger coded character sets.

The keyword wchar_t is used to declare wide character variables. wchar_t size is implementation dependent, therefore development of portable applications cannot assume that popular character representation, such as Unicode, can fit into a wchar_t on every platform and using any compiler.

2.8 MODIFIERS IN C++ LANGUAGE

Except type **void**, the basic data types may have various modifiers preceding them. A type modifier alters the meaning of the base type to more precisely fit a specific need. The list of modifiers is shown here:

1. signed
2. unsigned
3. long
4. short

The **int** base type can be modified by **signed, short, long**, and **unsigned**. The **char** type can be modified by **unsigned** and **signed**. You may also apply **long** to **double**. Table 2.2 below shows all valid data type combinations supported by C++, along with their minimal ranges and typical bit widths. Remember, the table shows the range that these types will have.

Table 2.2: Data Types in C++, Size & Range of Data Types

Variable type	Keyword	Bytes required	Range
Character	char	1	–128 to 127
Unsigned character	unsigned char	1	0 to 255
Integer	int	2	–32768 to 32767
Short integer	short int	2	–32768 to 32767
Long integer	long int	4	–2,147,483,648 to 2,147,483,647
Unsigned integer	unsigned int	2	0 to 65535
Unsigned short integer	unsigned short int	2	0 to 65535
Unsigned long integer	unsigned long int	4	0 to 4,294,967,295
Float	float	4	1.2E-308 to
Double	double	8	2.2E-308 to
Long double	long double	10	3.4E-4932 to 1.1E+4932
Boolean value	bool	1	true or false
Wide character	wchar_t	2 or 4	1 wide character (65535)

2.9 BASIC STRUCTURE OF A COMPLETE C++ PROGRAM WITHOUT CLASSES

A C++ program can be developed from a general structure. The general structure of C++ program without classes is as shown below (which is also called overview of a C++ program):

1. Documentation Section
2. Preprocessor Directives or Compiler Directives Section
   (i) Link Section
   (ii) Definition Section
3. Global Declaration Section
4. Main C-program function called main ( )
5. Beginning of the program: Left brace {
   (i) Local declaration or local variable declaration;
   (ii) Executable Part or C-executable statements;
6. End of the main program: Right brace }
7. Sub-program Section or User-defined functions.
   Function 1( )
      { User Defined Program }
   Function 2( )
      { Sub Program }

Note that a function sub-program further has two section: local declaration part and the executable part of the function sub-program. We will study it in more detail in the later section.

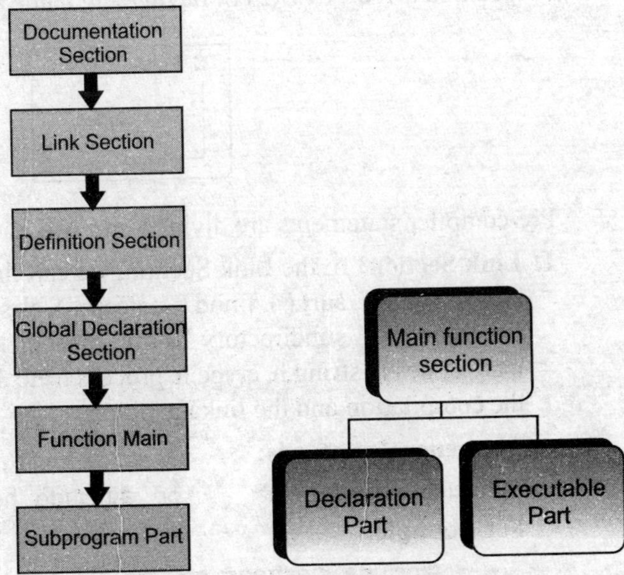

Figure 2.4: General structure of C++ program

2.9.1 Documentation Section

In Documentation section we give the Heading and Comments. Comment statement is the non-executable statement. Comment can be given in two ways:

1. **Single Line Comment:** Comment can be given in single line by using "//".

   The general syntax is: // Single Text line

   For Example: // Add Two Numbers (Heading of the program)

   C= a + b; // Store the value of a + b in C.(Comment to explain given statement)

2. **Multiple Line Comment:** Comment can be given in multiple lines starting by using "/*" and end with "*/".

   The general syntax is: /* Text Line1
   Text Line 2
   Text Line 3 */

   For Example: /* Write a C++ program to find the sum and
   average of five numbers. */

Note: Documentation section is an optional section.

2.9.2 Preprocessor Directives

These are compiler preprocessor statements. These are also optional statements, but becomes compulsory if your compiler has INCLUDE and LIB subdirectories in the specified drive TCPLUS or having any name as shown in the Figure below:

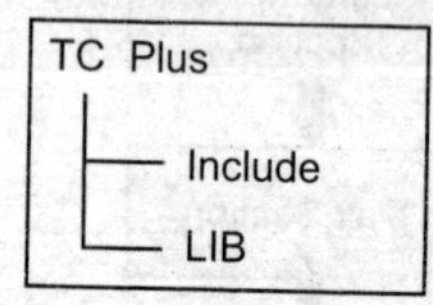

Pre-compiler statements are divided into two parts.

1. **Link Section:** In the Link Section, we can link the compiler function like cout<<, cin>>, sqrt ( ), fmod ( ), sleep ( ), clrscr ( ), exit(), strcat() etc. with the INCLUDE subdirectory having header files like iostream.h, conio.h, math.h, dos.h, string.h, ctype.h, process.h etc. It becomes very useful during the compilation and the linkage phase.

   The general syntax is:

   ```
   #include <header file>        or   #include "header file"
   ```

   For example:

   ```
   #include <iostream.h>
   ```

```
#include <conio.h>
#include "dos.h"
```

2. **Definition Section:** The second section is the Definition section by using which we can define a variable with its value. For this purpose define statement is used.

The general syntax is:

```
#define  variable name  value
```

For example:

```
#define  PI  3.142
#define  A  100
#define  NAME  "Jagminder"
```

2.9.3 Global Declaration Section

In this section, we declare some variables before starting of the main program or outside the main program. These variables are globally declared and used by the main function or sub function. These variables are called global variables. In some programs we use function sub-programs. So we declare some variables in the main program and function sub program having common name. This creates the duplicity or redundancy in defining the variables. So we can take the common variable declaration above the main program, which is also called global variable declaration. The global variables are automatically initialized with zero, hence there is no chance of garbage value. The global variable declaration can be done by the statement given below.

The general syntax is:

```
data type v1,v2,v3,........vn;
```

Here data types are int, float, char, double etc. v1,v2,v3,....vn is the list of global variables(v). For example: Following are the some valid global declaration statement as:

```
int a, b, c;
float x,y,z;
char ch, name[10], address[20];
```

2.9.4 main( )

main function is where a program starts execution. main( ) program is the C++ program's main structure in which we process some statements. The main function usually organizes at a high level the functionality of the rest of the program.

The general syntax is:

```
main ( )
```

2.9.5 Beginning of the Main Program: Left Brace {

(The beginning of the main program can be done by using left curly brace " { ").

(i) Local Variable Declaration

Variables which are declared and used in the main program are called local variables. These local variables are declared in local variable declaration section. Local variables are declared as:

The general syntax is: data type v1,v2,v3,..........vn;

Here data types are int, float, char, double etc. For example, some valid local variable declaration statements are as:

```
int a, b, c;
float x,y,z;
char ch, name[10], address[20];
```

(ii) Executable Statements

An executable statement is a procedural step in a middle level imperative programming language that calls for processing action by the computer, such as performing arithmetic, reading from and writing to an external medium, making a decision, etc. Each and Every C++ statements except control statements end with " ; " (semicolon).

For Example:

```
cout<<" Enter the name and rollno ";
cin>>name>>rn;
```

2.9.6 Ending Of The Main Program: Right Brace }

(The right curly brace "}" is used to end the main program).

2.9.7 User Defined Function Section

In this section, we define the function sub-program or called program, which are called by a calling statement from the main program. Further, in this section every function sub-program has local declaration variable section and executable statement section similar to the main program. Every function sub-program ends with the return statement with or without any argument and return the computed value to the main program according to the user's requirement.

The general syntax of function sub-program is as:

```
Function function-name(parameter)
{
local declaration;
```

```
executable statements;
return(argument);
}
```

The functions are made to simplify the main program, one discrete task is written in a function sub-program to make it simple. When user wants to do a particular task again and again in the program, then instead of writing the group of statements again and again in the main program , we can write it once in the function sub-program in a compact mode and call it again and again in the main program according to the user's requirement.

Program 1: Write a C++ program to find the area of circle using basic structure of C++ program without classes.

1. Documentation Section: Use single line comment

```
// Program to find the area of circle using basic structure of C++ program
```

2. Preprocessor Directives: Link and Definition Section

```
#include <iostream.h>      // Link Section
#include <conio.h>  // Link Section
#define  PI  3.142  // Definition Section
```

3. Global Declaration Section

```
float r;
```

4. Main program starts

```
main ( )
```

5. Beginning of the main program: Left brace

```
{
(i) Local Variable Declaration
float area (float), c;
(ii) Executable Statements
cout<<"Enter the radius of the circle:";
cin>>r;
c = area(r);
cout<<"Area of circle is "<< c;
getch( );
6. Ending of the main program: Right brace
}
```

7. User Defined Function Section

```
float area (float s)
{
float p;
p = PI * r*r;
```

```
return (p);
}
Output:
Enter the radius of the circle: 2.5
Area of circle is 19.6375
```

2.10 BASIC STRUCTURE OF A COMPLETE C++ PROGRAM WITH CLASSES

A C++ program can be developed from a basic structure. The general structure of C++ program **with classes** is as shown below (which is also called overview of a C++ program):

1. Documentation Section
2. Preprocessor Directives or Compiler Directives Section
   (i) Link Section
   (ii) Definition Section
3. Global Declaration Section
4. Class declaration or definition
5. Main C++ program function called main ( )
6. Beginning of the program: Left brace {
   (i) Object declaration part;
   (ii) Accessing member functions(using dot operator);
7. End of the main program: Right brace }

Note: *A class declaration or definition is further has its own relevant structure with its access specifiers.*

2.10.1 Documentation Section

In Documentation section we give the Heading and Comments. Comment statement is the non-executable statement. Comment can be given in two ways:

(i) Single Line Comment: Comment can be given in single line by using "//".

The general syntax is: // Single Text line

For Example: // Add Two Numbers (Heading of the program)

C= a + b;   // Store the value of a + b in C.(Comment to explain given statement)

(ii) Multiple Line Comment: Comment can be given in multiple lines starting by using "/*" and end with "*/".

The general syntax is: /* Text Line1
Text Line 2
Text Line 3 */

For Example: /* Write a C++ program to find the sum and average of five numbers. */

Note: Documentation section is an optional section.

2.10.2 Preprocessor Directives

These are compiler preprocessor statements. These are also optional statements, but becomes compulsory if your compiler has INCLUDE and LIB subdirectories in the specified drive TCPLUS or having any name as shown in the Figure below:

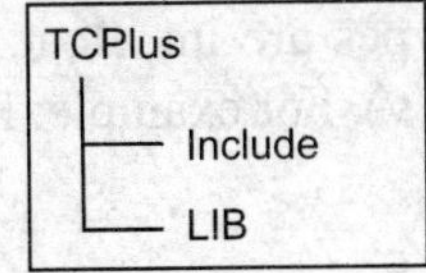

Pre-compiler statements are divided into two parts.

(i) **Link Section:** In the Link Section, we can link the compiler function like cout<<, cin>>, sqrt ( ), fmod ( ), sleep ( ), clrscr ( ), exit(), strcat() etc. with the INCLUDE subdirectory having header files like iostream.h, conio.h, math.h, dos.h, string.h, ctype.h, process.h etc. It becomes very useful during the compilation and the linkage phase.

The general syntax is: #include <header file> or #include "header file"

For example:

```
#include <iostream.h>
#include <conio.h>
#include "dos.h"
```

(ii) **Definition Section:** The second section is the Definition section by using which we can define a variable with its value. For this purpose define statement is used.

The general syntax is:#define variable name value

For example:

```
#define PI  3.142
#define A 100
#define NAME "Jagminder"
```

2.10.3 Global Declaration Section

In this section, we declare some variables before starting of the main program or outside the main program. These variables are globally declared and used by the main function or sub function. These variables are called global variables. In some programs we use function sub-programs. So we declare some variables in the main program and function sub program having common name. This creates the duplicity or redundancy in defining the variables. So we can take the common variable declaration above the main program, which is also called global variable declaration. The global variables are automatically initialized with zero, hence there is no chance of garbage value. The global variable declaration can be done by the statement given below.

The general syntax is:

data type v1,v2,v3,........vn;

Here data types are int, float, char, double etc. v1,v2,v3,.....vn is the list of global variables(v). For example: Following are the some valid global declaration statement as:

```
int a, b, c;
float x,y,z;
char ch, name[10], address[20];
```

2.10.4 Class Declaration or Definition

A class is an organization of data and functions which operate on them. Data types are called data members and the functions are called member functions. The combination of data members and member functions constitute a data object or simply an object.

The general syntax or general form of the class declaration is as follows:

```
class <name of class>
{
privat:
data members;
member functions();
public:
data members;
member functions();
protected:
data members;
member functions();
};
main()
{
<name of class> obj1;
obj1.member function();
```

```
obj1.member function();
getch();
}
```

(i) Class name or name of class

It is mainly the name given to a particular class. It serves as a name specifier for the class, using which we can create objects. The class is specified by keyword **"class"**.

For example: class Circle

Here Circle is the class name.

(ii) Data Members

These are the data-type properties that describe the characteristics of a class. We can declare any number of data members of any type in a class. We can say that the variables in C and data members in C++.

For example: float area;

(iii) Member Functions

These are the various operations that can be performed to data members of that class. We can declare any number of member functions of any type in a class. Member functions are access using object and dot operator.

For example: void read(); void display();

How member function access: c1.read();

Here c1 is object of class circle and operator dot (.) is used to access member functions.

(iv) Access Specifiers

Access specifiers are used to identify access rights for the data members and member functions of the class. Depending upon the access level of a class member, access to it is allowed or denied.

There are three main types of access specifiers in C++ programming language:

1. **private:** A *private* member within a class denotes that only members of the same class have accessibility. The *private* member is not accessible from outside the class.
2. **public:** *Public* members are accessible from outside the class.
3. **protected:** A protected access specifier is a stage between *private* and *public* access. If member functions defined in a class are *protected*, they cannot be accessed from outside the class but can be accessed from the derived class (inheritance).

Note: Every access specifier is discussed in detail in later chapters.

2.10.5 main( )

main function is where a program starts execution. main() program is the C++ program's main structure in which we process some statements. The main function usually organizes at a high level the functionality of the rest of the program.

The general syntax is: main ( )

2.10.6 Beginning of the Main Program: Left Brace {

(The beginning of the main program can be done by using left curly brace " { ").

(i) Object declaration part

We can declare objects of class inside the main program or outside the main program. A class declaration only uses to builds the structure of an object. The data members and member functions are combined in the class. The declaration of objects is same as declaration of variables of basic data types. Defining objects of class data type is known as class instantiation (instances of class). When we create objects during that moment, memory is allocated to them.

For example: c1 is the object of the class Circle. We can create any number of objects of a given class.

(ii) Accessing member functions(using dot operator)

The member function define in the class are access by using dot (.) operator. Suppose we have two member functions void read() and void display(). We have to access these member function in the main program.

The general syntax is:

```
Obj1. member function();
```

For example: c1.read();

Here c1 is object and read() is the member function of class Circle..

2.10.7 Ending of The Main Program: Right Brace }

(The right curly brace "}" is used to end the main program).

Program 2: Write a C++ program to find the area of circle using basic structure of C++ program with classes.

1. Documentation Section: Use single line comment

```
// Program to find the area of circle using basic structure of C++ program
```

2. Preprocessor Directives: Link and Definition Section

```
#include <iostream.h>        // Link Section
#include <conio.h>           // Link Section
#define  PI  3.142           // Definition Section
```
3. Global Declaration Section
```
float r;
```
4. Class declaration or definition
```
class Circle                 // Class definition (Circle class is created)
{
private:
float area;                  // Data member
public:
void read()                  // Member function
{
cout<<"Enter the radius of the circle:";
cin>>r;
}
void display()               // Member function
{
area = PI * r*r;
cout<<"Area of circle is "<< area;
}
};
```
5. Main program starts
```
main ( )
```
6. Beginning of the main program: Left brace
```
{
Circle c1;                   // Creates object c1 of class Circle
c1.read();                   // Call to member functions by object c1
c1.display();                // Call to member functions by object c1
getch( );
```
7. Ending of the main program: Right brace
```
}
```

2.11 CONSOLE INPUT AND OUTPUT

Like C, C++ does not have built-in input/output capability. All C++ compilers, however, come bundled with a systematic, object-oriented I/O package, known as the iostream classes. The stream is the central concept of the iostream classes. You can think of a stream object as a smart file that acts as a source and destination for bytes. A stream's characteristics are determined by its class and by customized insertion and extraction operators.

Through device drivers, the disk operating system deals with the keyboard, screen, printer, and communication ports as extended files. The iostream classes interact with these extended files. Built-in classes support reading from and writing to memory with syntax identical to that for disk I/O, which makes it easy to derive stream classes.

C++ programming language uses the concept of streams to perform input and output operations using the keyboard and to display information on the monitor of the computer.

2.11.1 Output Using Cout

The output stream manages output of the stream i.e., displays contents of variables on the screen. It uses << insertion operator before variable name. It uses the cout object perform consol write operation. the syntax and example of cout statements are as follows:

The general syntax is:

```
cout <<string;
```

Explanation of syntax:

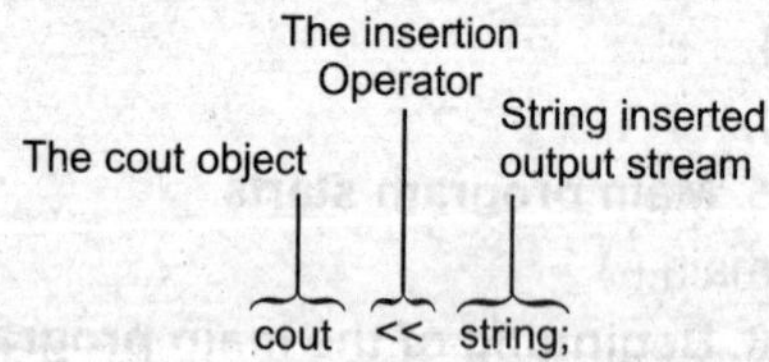

Example:

```
cout <<v1 <<v2 <<v3 .... <<vn;
```

where v1, v2, and v3 are variables. The above statement displays the contents of these variables on the screen. The cout statement allows us to use all 'C++' escape sequences like '\n', '\t', and so on.

Although the concepts behind the use of cout and << may be obscure at this point, using them is easy. They'll appear in almost every example program.

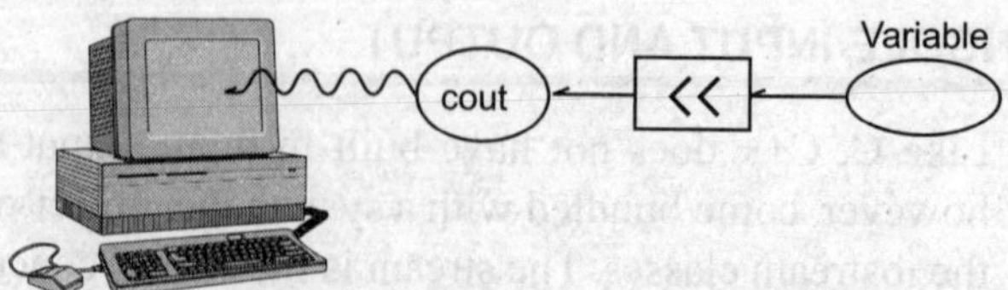

Figure 2.5: Using cout and the insertion operator <<.

By default, the device used for output is the screen of the computer. For outputting values the keyword *cout* is used, which is an object. The insertion operator << is used on the standard output *cout* stream. The syntax for using the standard output stream is *cout* followed by the operator << followed by the value to be inserted or output by the insertion operator.

For example:

```
int prog;
cin >> prog;
cout << prog;
```

In the above example, the variable *prog* is declared as an integer type variable. The next statement is the *cin* statement that waits for input from the user's keyboard. This information is then stored in the integer variable prog. The value of *prog* is displayed on the screen by the standard output stream *cout*. It is also possible to display a sentence as follows:

```
cout << " Training given by Lecturer";
```

The above gives output as:

Training given by Lecturer

If a programmer chooses to use constant strings of characters, they must be enclosed between double quotes " ".

In this situation, it is important to note the difference between the two statements below:

```
cout << "Lecturer";
cout << Lecturer;
```

In the above, the first statement displays on the screen as Lecturer. The second statement outputs the value of the variable Lecturer. As previously explained, the extraction operator >> can be used more than once in a single *cin* statement. Similarly, it is possible to use the insertion operator << more than once in a *cout* statement.

For example

```
cout << " Lecturer " << "gives" << "excellent training";
```

This produces output on the screen as:

Lecturer gives excellent training

The above concept is mainly used if the programmer chooses to print string constants followed by variables.

In this next example, the programmer chooses to display a combination of string *constants* and *variables*.

For example

```
int a=50;
cout << " Lecturer has given" << a << "numbers of trainings";
```

This produces the output as:

Lecturer has given 50 numbers of trainings

Below is one more example:

```
cout << "Lecturer";
cout << "Training";
```

The above produces output as:

Lecturer Training

An important point to note from the above example is *cout* does not give a line break unless specified. If the programmer chooses to display output in a new line, it must be explicitly specified in *cout* by using the \n which denotes *newline* character.

For example

```
cout << " Lecturer \n ";
cout << "Training";
```

gives output as

```
Lecturer
Training
```

There is also another way for specifying *newline* that is by using *endl* manipulator.

For example

```
cout << "Lecturer" << endl;
cout << "Training";
```

gives the same output as

Lecturer

Training

Program 1: Write a C++ program to demonstrate the use of *input* and *output* streams.

```
#include <iostream.h>
#include <conio.h>
void main()
{
int a,b,c;
cout << "Enter the value of a and b:";
cin >> a>>b;
c = a + b;
cout << "Value of c is:"<<c;
getch();
}
```

Output:

Enter the value of a and b: 2 4

Value of c is 6

More examples

```
int weight;
cout<<weight                    // Display integer value
float height;
cout<<height;                   // Displays float value
double volume;
cout<<volume;                   // Displays double value
char result [10];
cout<<result;                   // Reads char string
```

2.11.2 Input Using Cin

The input stream does read operation through keyboard. It uses cin as object. The cin statement uses >> (extraction operator) before variable name. The cin statement is used to read data through the input device. Its syntax and example are as follows.

The general syntax is:

```
cin >> variable;
```

Explanation of syntax:

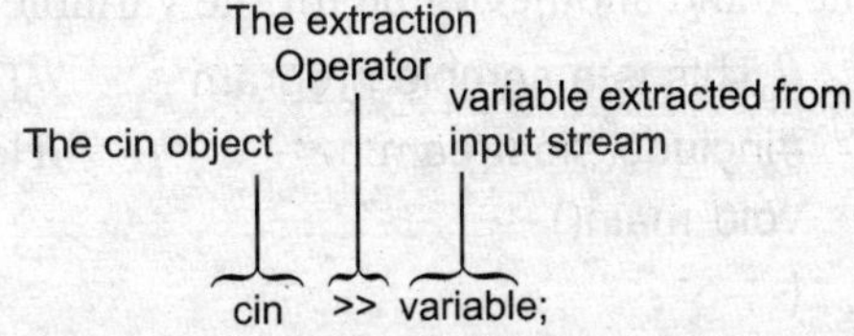

Example:

```
int v1;
float v2;
char v3;
cin >> v1 >> v2 >> v3....... >>vn;
```

Where v1, v2 and v3 are variable names. The above statement read the contents of these variables from one of the input device.

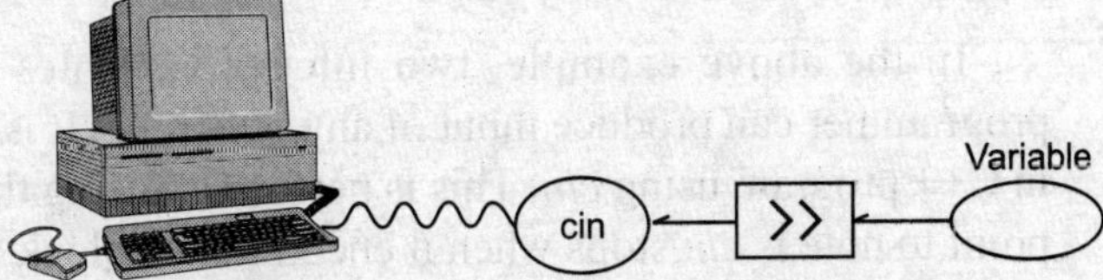

Figure 2.6: Using cin and the extraction operator >>.

Generally, the device used for input is the keyboard. For inputting, the keyword *cin* is used, which is an object. The overloaded operator of extraction, >>, is used on the standard input stream, in this case: *cin* stream. Syntax for using the standard input stream is cin *followed by the operator >> followed by the* variable *that stores the data extracted from the stream.*

For example:

```
int prog;
cin >> prog;
```

In the example above, the variable *prog* is declared as an integer type variable. The next statement is the *cin* statement. The *cin* statement waits for input from the user's keyboard that is then stored in the integer variable *prog*.

The input stream *cin* wait before proceeding for processing or storing the value. This duration is dependent on the user pressing the RETURN key on the keyboard. The input stream *cin* waits for the user to press the RETURN key then begins to process the command. It is also possible to request input for more than one variable in a single input stream statement. A single *cin* statement is as follows:

```
cin >> x >> y;
```

is the same as:

```
cin >> x;
cin >> y;
```

In both of the above cases, two values are input by the user, one value for the variable x and another value for the variable y.

```
// This is a sample program          //This is a comment Statement
#include <iostream.h>                //Header File Inclusion Statement
void main()
{
int sample, example;
cin >> sample;
cin >> example;
}
```

If a programmer wants to write comments in C++ program, the comments should follow after a pair of slashes denoted by //. All the characters after the // are ignored by C++ compiler and the programmer can choose to comment after the //
.

In the above example, two integer variables are input with values. The programmer can produce input of any data type. It is also possible to input strings in C++ program using *cin*. This is performed using the same procedures. The vital point to note is *cin* stops when it encounters a blank space. When using a cin, it is possible to produce only one word. If a user wants to input a sentence, then the above approach would be tiresome. For this purpose, there is a function in C++ called *getline*.

Program 2: Write a C++ program for cin to read.

```
#include <iostream.h>
#include<conio.h>
void main ()
{
int testScore1, testScore2, testScore3;
cout << "Enter test score #1: ";
cin >> testScore1;
cout << "Enter test score #2: ";
cin >> testScore2;
cout << "Enter test score #3: ";
cin >> testScore3;
cout << "Test score #1: " << testScore1 << endl;
cout << "Test score #2: " << testScore2 << endl;
cout << "Test score #3: " << testScore3 << endl;
getch();
}
```

Output:

```
Enter test score #1: 12
Enter test score #2: 12
Enter test score #3: 21
Test score #1: 12
Test score #2: 12
Test score #3: 21
```

```
More examples
int weight;
cin>>weight                 // Reads integer value
float height;
cin>>height;                // Reads float value
double volume;
cin>>volume;                // Reads double value
char result [10];
cin>>result;                // Reads char string
```

2.12 TYPICAL C++ DEVELOPMENT ENVIRONMENT

Let's consider the steps in creating and executing a C++ application using a C++ development environment (illustrated in **Figure 2.5**). C++ systems generally consist of three parts: a program development environment, the language and the C++ Standard Library. C++ programs typically go through six phases: edit, pre-process, compile, link, load and execute. The following discussion explains a typical C++ program development environment.

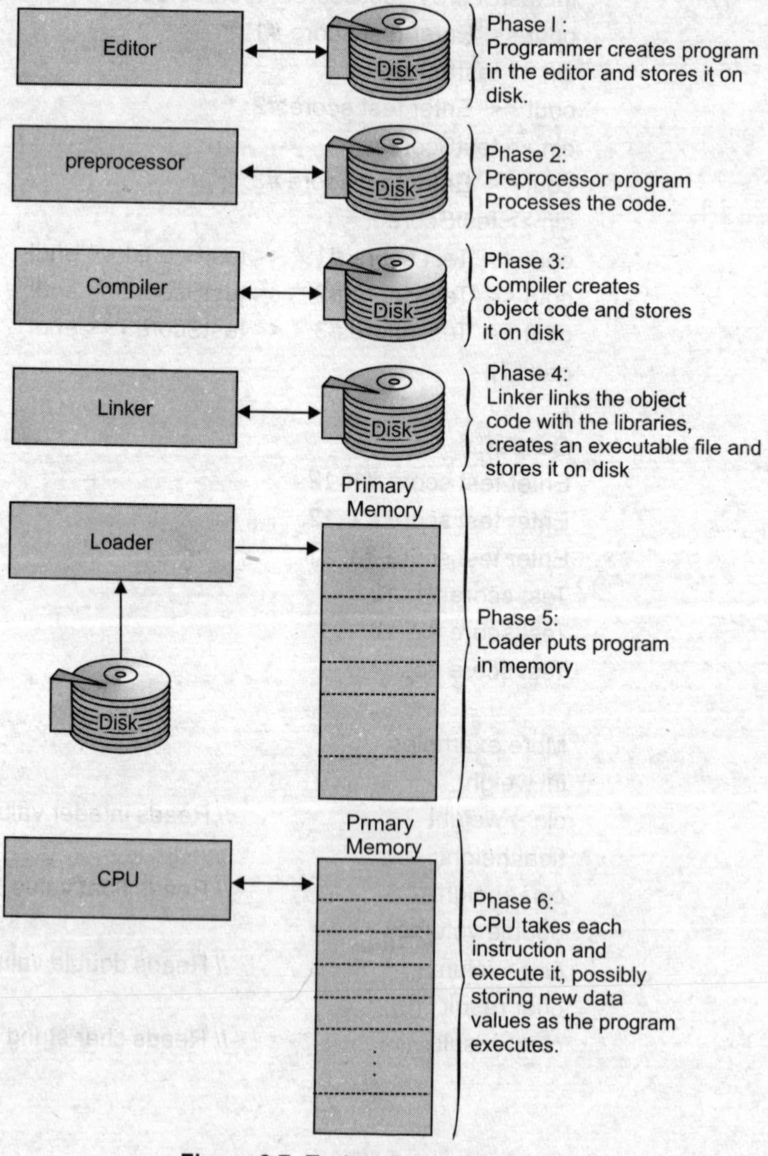

Figure 2.7: Typical C++ environment

2.12.1 Invoking Turbo C++

To start Turbo C++, move to directory in which you plan to develop C++ programs. Try to make directory of your own instead of developing programs in TCPLUS directory. (Suppose Turbo C++ compiler is at C drive of your computer)

For your own directory↵	for TCPLUS directory↵
C:\cd DirectoryName	C:\cd TCPLUS
(Change directory to name chosen	(Change directory to TCPLUD/Bin)
C:\DirectoryName>TC↵	C:\TCPLUS>cdBIN
	C:\TCPLUS>BIN>TC↵

***Note:** This ↵ sign tells to press Enter button.*

If you have the directory of your choice then after changing the directory, the path TC.EXE file should be set within the directory by the following command:

C:\DirectoryName>Path = C:\TCPLUS\BIN;%Path%↵

It is better for you to set path in AUTOEXEC.BAT File

After the path is set, we can run TC.EXE in cur own directory i.e.

C:\DirectoryName>TC↵

If you are using windows operating system, then first search for the drive in which TCPLUS is loaded or search for icon if any made on the desktop. Double clicking the Icon will open C++ environment.

You can also click the **Start button** and a Popup menu bar will appear. Then go for **Programs** option and click there, a cascading menu bar will appear, click TCPLUS from cascading menu once and then C++ IDE screen will be displayed. If either of the above two options fails, then select (C:\TC\BIN) directory from Window Explorer and execute TC.EXE by double clicking on it. A TC editor screen will be displayed on the screen as shown in Figure 2.6 below.

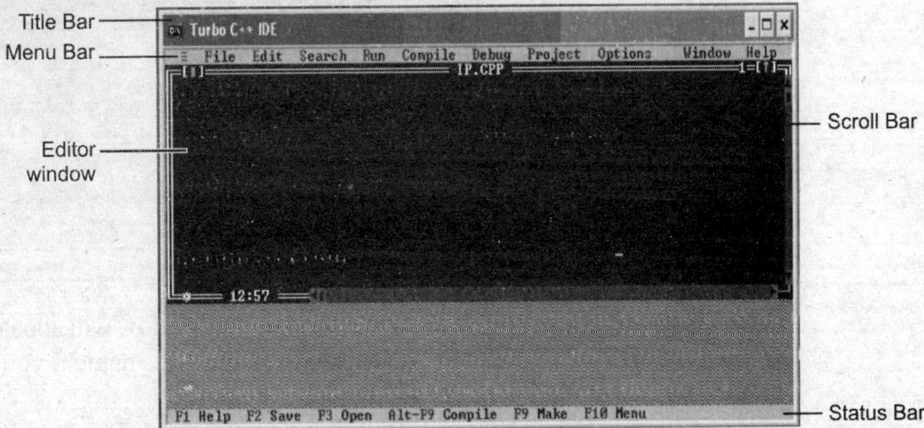

The IDE screen contains the following parts:

Title Bar: It indicates name of the running program or software.

Menu Bar: It contains number of menu items like File, Edit, Search, Run, Compile, Debug, Project, Options, Window and Help that are required for the development and execution of that Program.

Editor Window: The source code of the program is typed in the Editor Window.

Scroll Bar: It is used to move the page upward and downward vertically.

Status bar: It is displayed at the bottom of the screen and displays the status of the current activity on the screen.

2.12.2 Phase 1: Creating A Program

Phase 1 consists of editing a file with an editor. First of all you type a C++ program using the editor, make any necessary corrections and save the program on a secondary storage device, such as your hard drive. C++ source code filenames often end with the .CPP extension which indicates that a file contains C++ source code. See the documentation for your C++ compiler for more information on filename extensions.

First, select the new option from the file menu to open the new window to write your program.

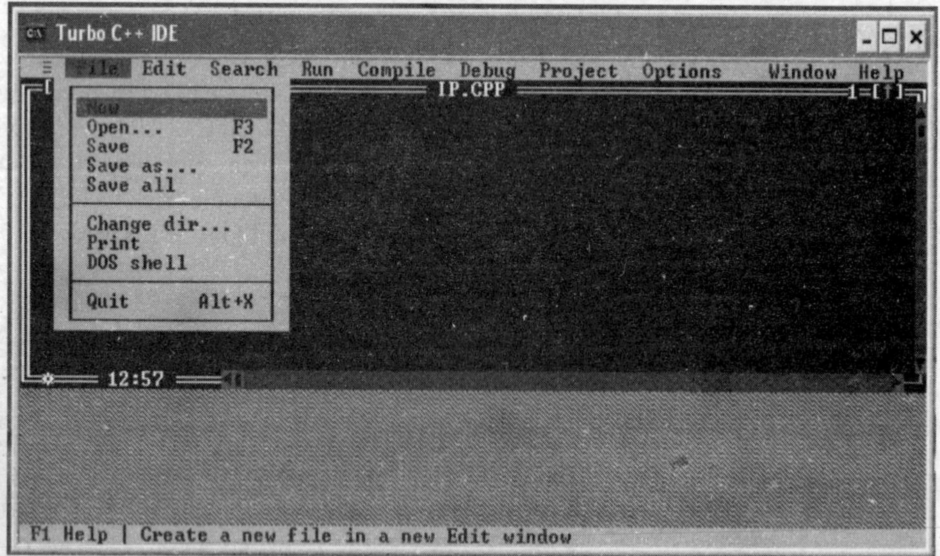

Selecting New from the File menu, an editor window will appear with a filename NONAME.CPP (by default). You need to change this name if you want to save the program.

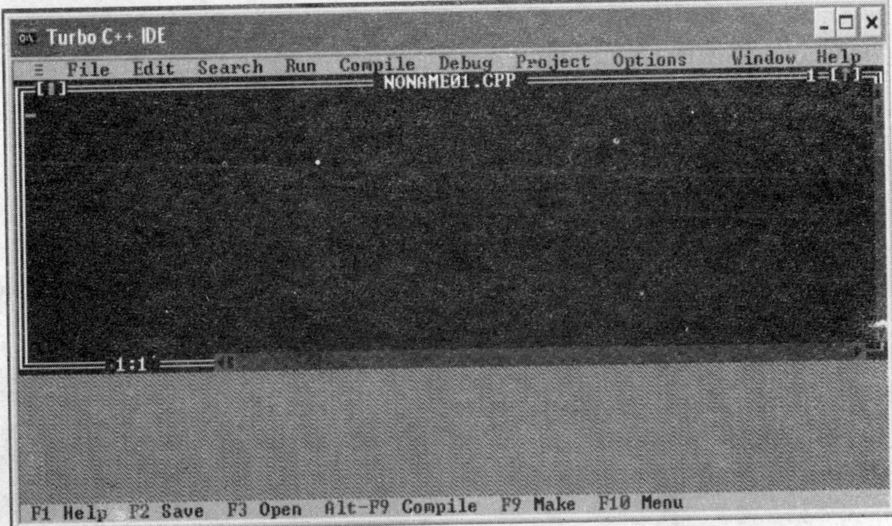

After new window will appear, the cursor will be positioned at the upper-left corner of the Editor Window. Now start typing the program.

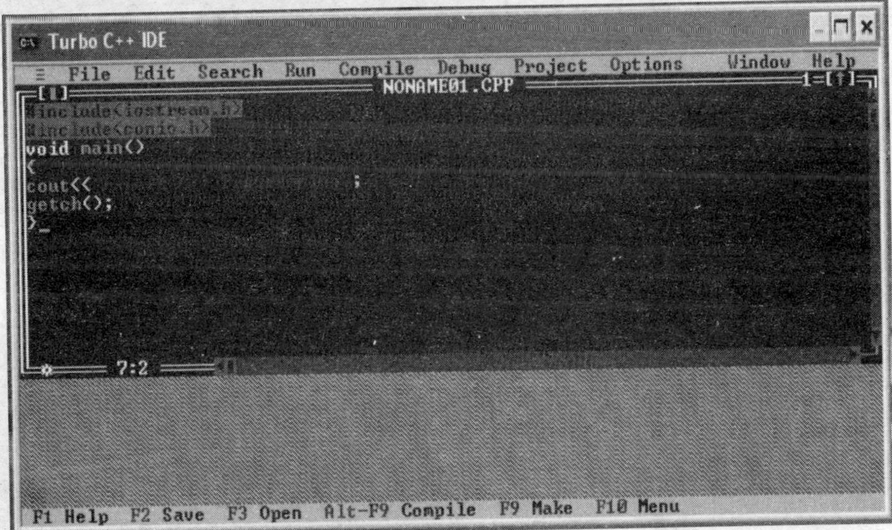

With the help of various keys we can type the programs by passing the ENTER key, the new line is inserted and drops the cursor to the start of the next line. The BACKSPACE key deletes the character to the left of the cursor. It is to be remembered that programs must be written using lowercase characters, as C++ is a case sensitive language.

Note: *For more information you can select contents from help menu.*

Saving the Program

After typing the C++ source code (Program) saves it to the disk by selecting SAVE from FILE menu or by pressing F2. Now the file will be saved with an extension (.CPP). Saving Programs before compiling is essential because if an error crashes the system, the changes made are lost.

If the program is saved for the first time, the backup file with extension (.BAK) is not formed but when we save it by making further changes in the same program, a copy of old file with the same name of program and extension (.BAK) is automatically formed.

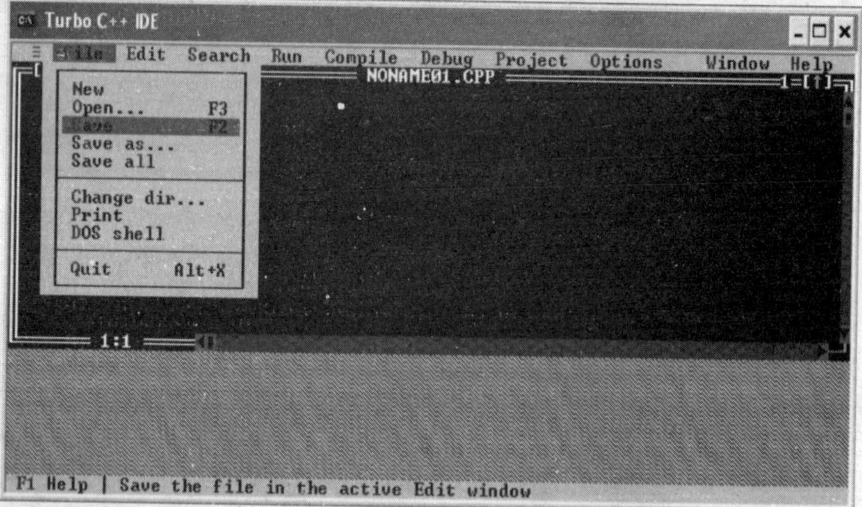

Suppose we can save program using another name then we use Save as option from file menu given below.

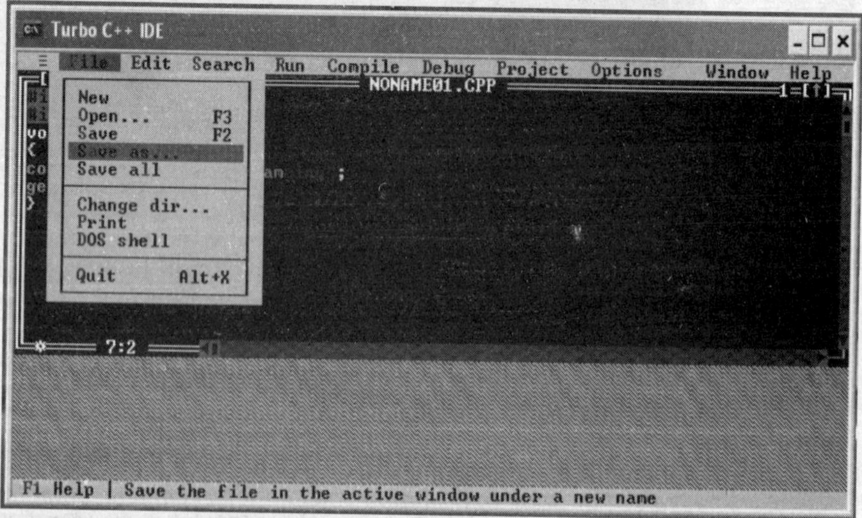

Now, the Save File as window is open as shown below. Write the name of the program in the first box with its extension .CPP and press ok.

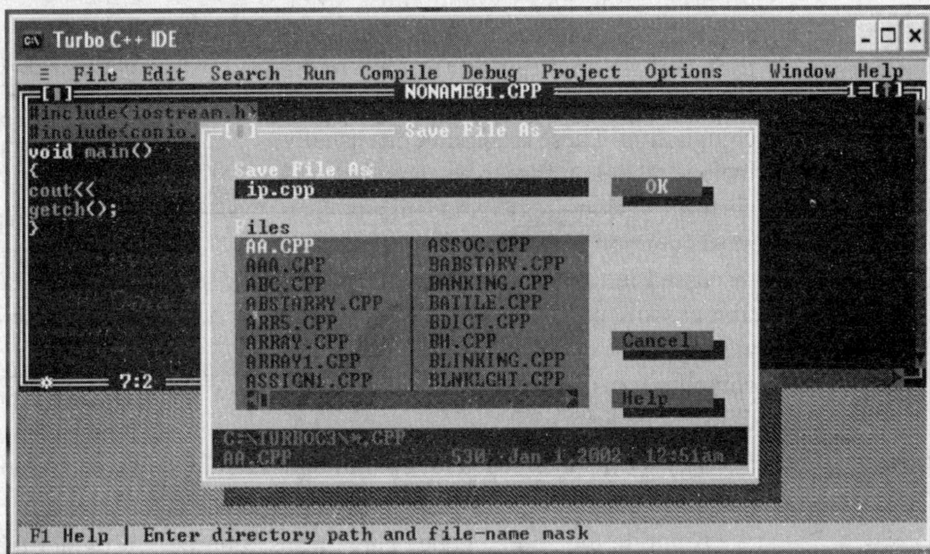

We will see that our program is Save as name (IP.CPP) as shown in Figure below.

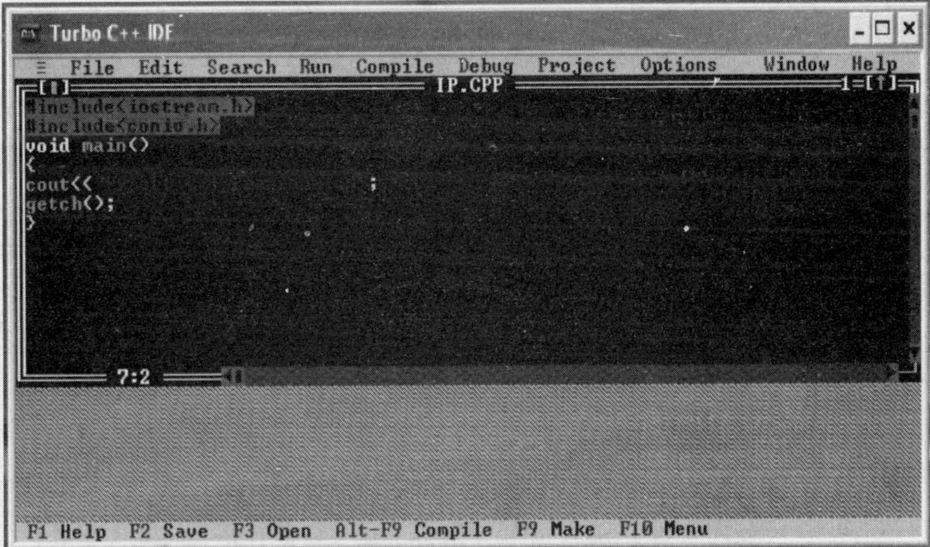

2.12.3 Phases 2 and 3: Pre-processing And Compiling A C++ Program

In phase 2, you give the command to compile the program. In a C++ system, a preprocessor program executes automatically before the compiler's translation phase begins (so we call preprocessing phase 2 and compiling phase 3). The C++ preprocessor obeys commands called preprocessor directives, which indicate that certain manipulations are to be performed on the program before compilation. These manipulations usually include other text files to be compiled, and perform various text replacements. The most common preprocessor directives are discussed in the early chapter; a detailed discussion of preprocessor features appears in next chapters. In phase 3, the compiler translates the C++ program into object code (.obj).

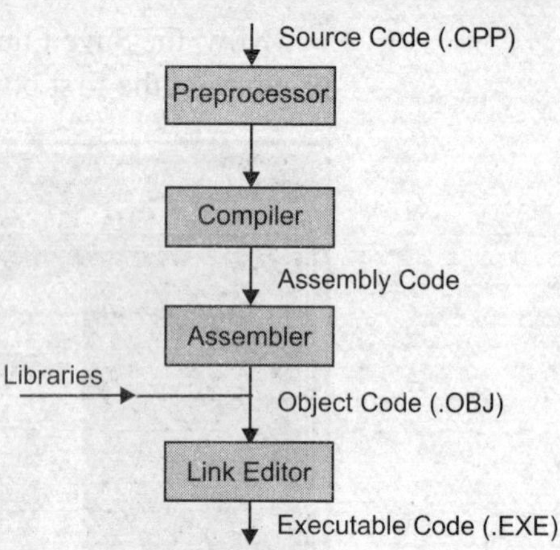

Figure 2.8: Compiling and Running a Complete C program

The shortcut key used for compiling is Alt+F9 key combination. This key will automatically make an object file.

Compile the source code. This means running a program that translates the source code to the internal language, called machine language, used by the host computer. The file containing the translated program is the object code for your program.

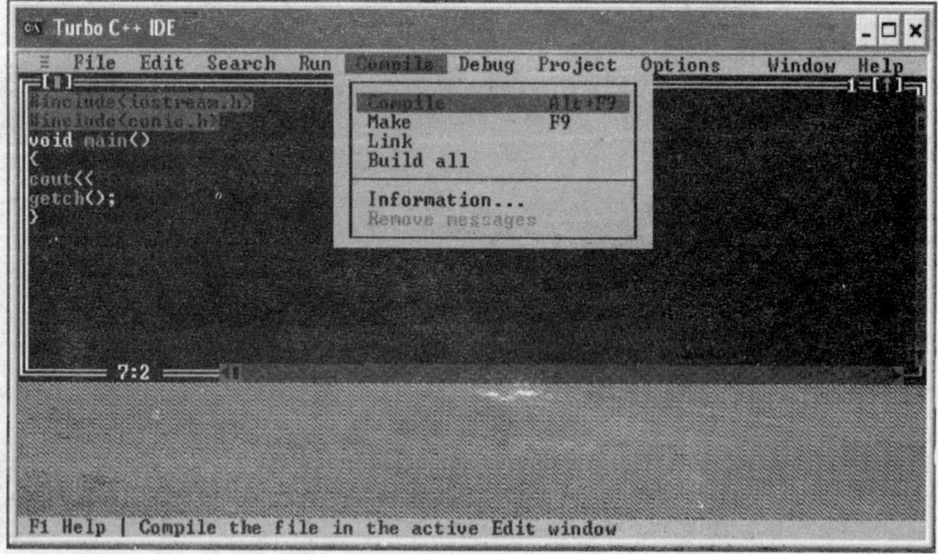

Compiling means checking the errors from our source code and convert source code to object code. The compiling box shown below indicates that there is no error in the source code and the object code file is created.

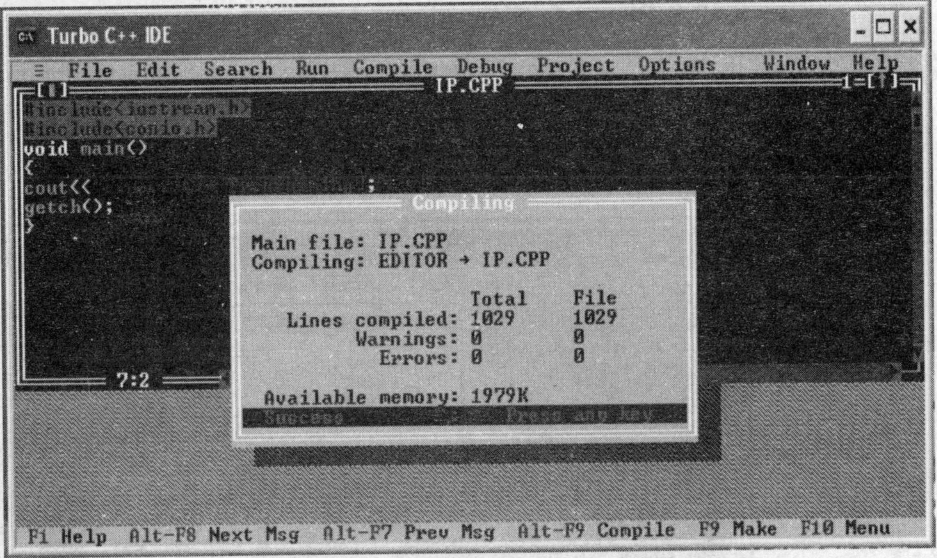

2.12.4 Phase 4: Linking

Phase 4 is called linking. C++ programs typically contain references to functions and data defined elsewhere, such as in the standard libraries or in the private libraries of groups of programmers working on a particular project. The object code produced by the C++ compiler typically contains "holes" due to these missing parts. A linker links the object code with the code for the missing functions to produce an executable image (with no missing pieces). If the program compiles and links correctly, an executable image is produced.

Link the object code with additional code. For example, C++ programs normally use libraries. A C++ library contains object code for a collection of computer routines, called functions, to perform tasks such as displaying information onscreen or calculating the square root of a number. Linking combines your object code with object code for the functions you use and with some standard startup code to produce a runtime version of your program. The file containing this final product is called the executable code.

2.12.5 Phase 5: Loading

Before a program can be executed, it must first be placed in memory. This is done by the loader, which takes the executable image from disk and transfers it to memory. Additional components from shared libraries that support the program are also loaded.

2.12.6 Phase 6: Execution

To run a C++ program after compilation, we use the Run option of Run menu or press Ctrl+F9 keys from the keyboard. It will result in creating a file with a same name as the source file but with (.EXE) extension like IP.EXE and it will also show the result of the program.

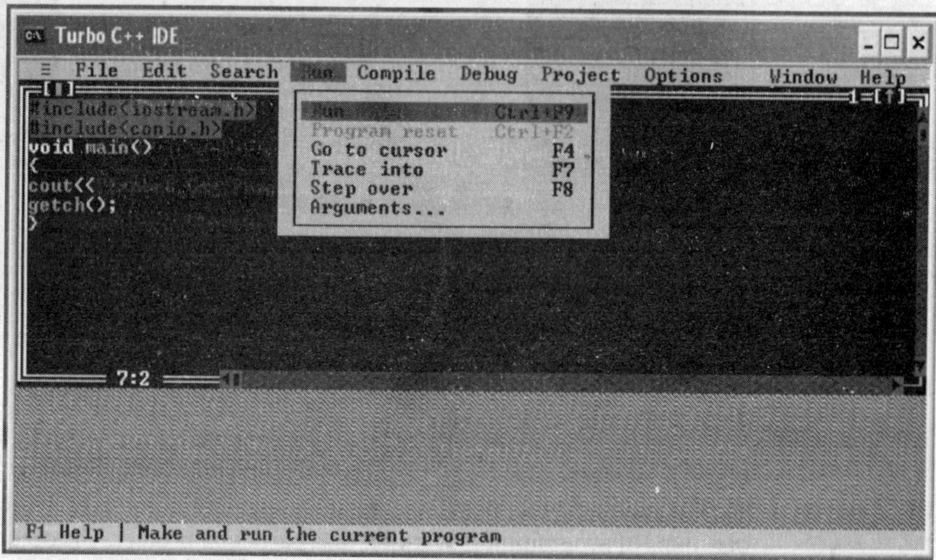

The output screen shown below:

2.12.7 Exiting From Turbo C++ IDE

When you have done your job (editing, compiling and running of the program), then you can quit from the Turbo C++ IDE by using the Quit option from the file menu or using shortcut key Alt + X combination.

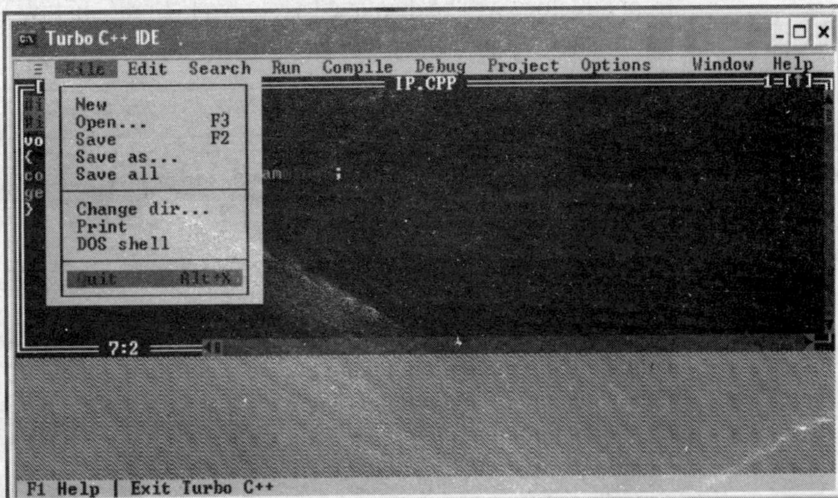

2.13 OPENING AN EXISTING FILE

If you are working in a DOS prompt and you want to open an existing file then simply write filename after the prompt (suppose your program IP.CPP is in the TCPLUS directory).

C:\TCPLUS>edit IP.CPP

It will open editor window containing this file.

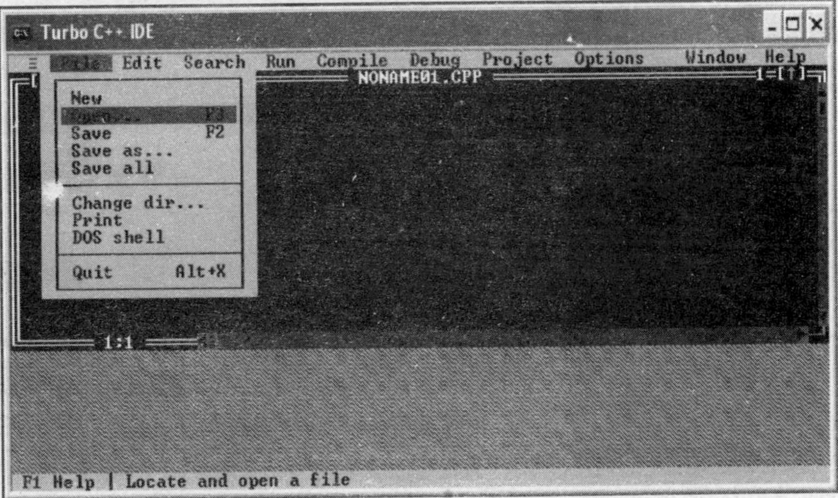

If you are already working in the IDE of Turbo C++ and you want to open an existing file, you simply select OPEN option from the FILE menu item and press ENTER or press F3.

As a result a OPEN dialog box containing list of existing all C++ files of current directory will be displayed as shown in Figure below. Select the appropriate file you want to open and press ENTER.

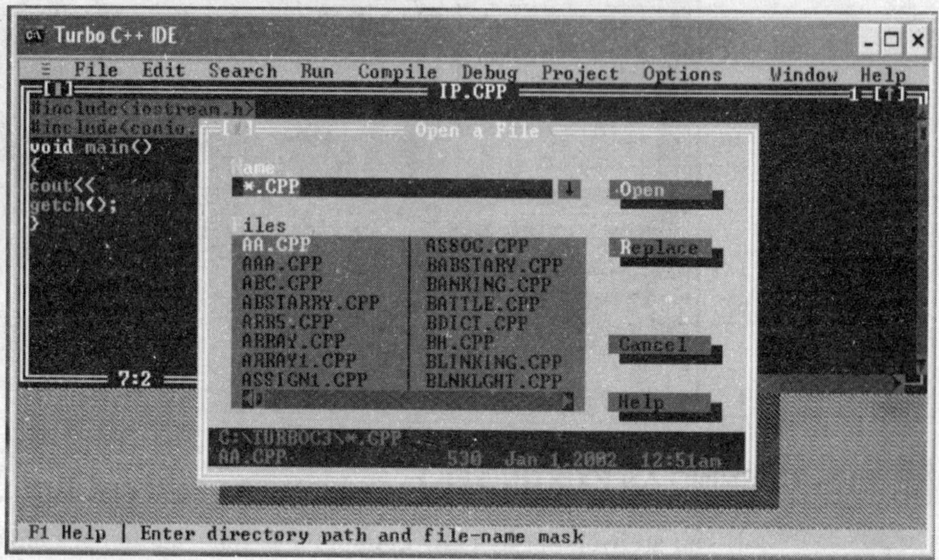

Now, the contents of the selected file will be displayed in the Editor Window.

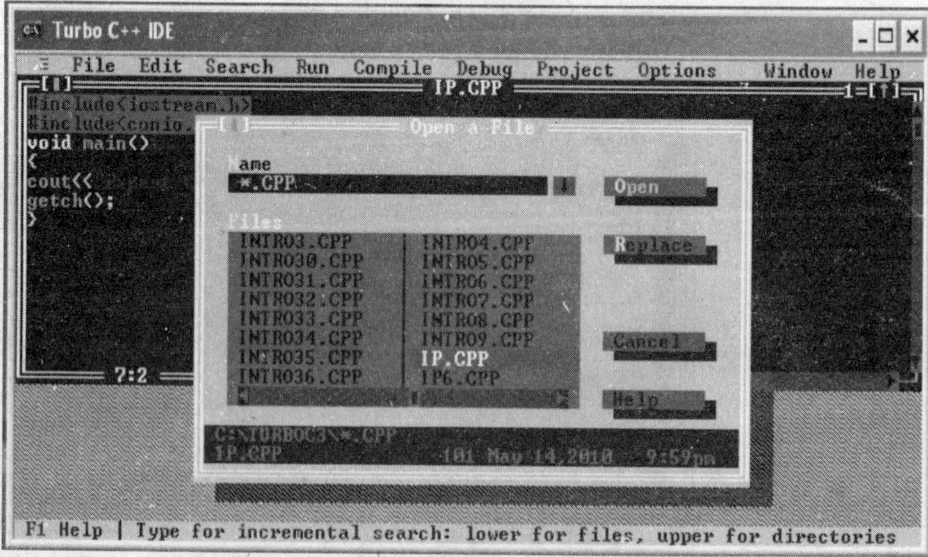

2.14 USING THE DOS SHELL

If you want to execute the executable C++ file having extension .EXE later on, then you can execute it on the DOS prompt without exiting from the C++ IDE. Some more DOS commands like renaming the file, copying the files, deleting the files, setting the date and time environment for the C++ program's using built-in date and time functions, displaying the version of the operating system being used and formatting the disk etc can be executed without exiting from the Turbo C++. When you select the DOS Shell option from the File menu, the DOS command prompt will be displayed.

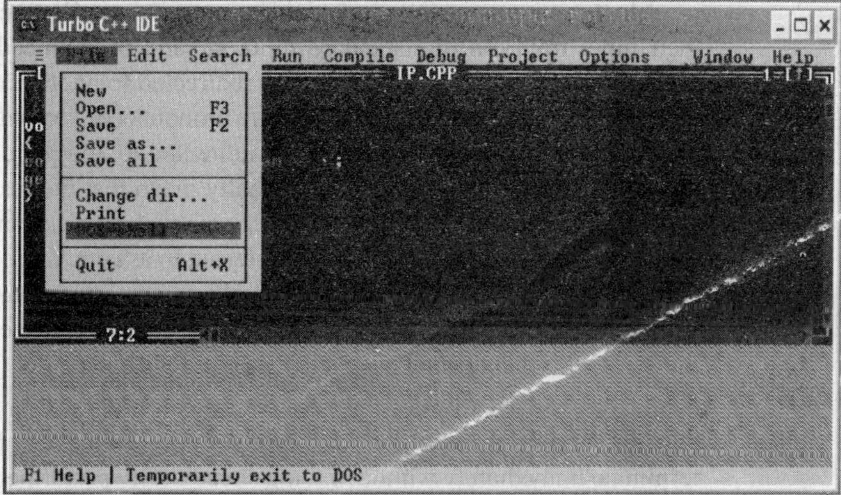

Now you can apply any Dos command operation on this prompt. You can execute any .EXE file created by the C++ IDE. When you have completed your job, then you can move to the Turbo C++ IDE by typing the **Exit** at the Dos prompt. This feature will save your time for the restarting of the Turbo C++ again.

Turbo C++ IDE
Type EXIT to return to Turbo C++. . .Microsoft(R) Windows DOS
(C)Copyright Microsoft Corp 1990-2001.
C:\TCPLUS>

If your executable file is in TCPLUS directory, then to execute the executable file we write C:\TCPLUS>IP.EXE

2.15 PROBLEMS THAT MAY OCCUR AT EXECUTION TIME

Each of the preceding phases can fail because of various errors that we discuss throughout the book. This would cause the C++ program to display an error message. If this occurs, you would have to return to the edit phase, make the necessary corrections and proceed through the remaining phases again to determine that the corrections fix the problem(s).

Most programs in C++ input and/or output data. Certain C++ functions take their input from cin (the standard input stream; pronounced "see-in"), which is normally the keyboard, but cin can be redirected to another device. Data is often output to cout (the standard output stream; pronounced "see-out"), which is normally the computer screen, but cout can be redirected to another device. When we say that a program prints a result, we normally mean that the result is displayed on a screen. Data may be output to other devices, such as disks and hardcopy printers. There is also a standard error stream referred to as cerr. The cerr stream (normally connected to the screen) is used for displaying error messages. It is common for users to assign cout to a device other than the screen while keeping cerr assigned to the screen, so that normal outputs are separated from errors.

Errors such as division by zero occur as a program runs, so they are called **runtime errors** or execution-time errors. Fatal runtime errors cause programs to terminate immediately without having successfully performed their jobs. Nonfatal runtime errors allow programs to run to completion, often producing incorrect results. [Note: On some systems, divide-by-zero is not a fatal error. Please see your system documentation.]

2.16 ERRORS IN C++

No one is perfect in this world; everyone commits some errors in one form or the other. Errors may occur due to the human mistakes. Error is an illegal operation performed by the user which results in abnormal working of the program.

Since errors prevent the program from being compiled or executed successfully, we have to remove them before compiling and executing.

There are mainly four types of errors:

1. Compile-time errors
2. Linker Errors
3. Run time Errors
4. Logical Errors (Semantic Errors)

2.16.1 Compile-time Errors

Compile-time errors are also called syntax errors. These errors occur either due to the typing mistake in the syntax or by writing wrong syntax. All these are detected by the compiler so it is also known as compiler errors. Some of the common compile time errors are missing semicolons at the end of statements, references to an undeclared variables, wrong number or type of arguments passed to a function etc. Also sometimes if you write the spelling of the else as eles, then it is also a syntax error. These all errors will be displayed in the message box along with the line number where message occurs. You can move from message window to the C++ edit window by pressing the function key F6. After correcting the error, you can again compile the program to run the program successfully.

2.16.2 Run Time Errors

Run time error occurs after the successfully execution of the program. Some common run time errors are division by zero (Divide Error), an attempt to compute the logarithm or the square root of a negative number (Domain Error), queue empty, null pointer assignments, stack overflow etc. Run Time Errors are difficult to find as thc compiler doesn't point to the line at which this error occurs. The error message is displayed only after the execution with a wrong output. Now, consider the previous program in which all the syntax errors are removed and program is successfully compiled. On execution of the program, if value of x is entered as 0 they it will generate a DIVIDE ERROR as division by zero is not possible. This will stop the program's execution without displaying the answer.

2.16.3 Linker Errors

Linker errors normally occur when after compilation we link the different object files with main's object file using Ctrl+F9 key (in Running phase). Some common linker errors are writing maik( ) instead of main( ), any user-defined function is called but not defined, any standard built-in function (abs, sqrt, floor, sin etc.) is called but its definition which is stored in library file which is not present. linker error will also stop the execution of the program. You will see a message "Linker Error" that will be displayed on the message window.

The Linker must find the definition of the function called otherwise it will create an executable file. To correct these errors return back to program using F6 key.

Sometimes program is correct with all the syntax and the logic is compiled successfully. But during linking if prototypes are not properly declared then an error will occur which is called linking error.

2.16.4 Logical Errors

Logical error occurs due to the non-expertise in the problem solving procedure. If you make the wrong logic to solve problems then the logical error occurs. Such errors which provide incorrect output but appear to be error free are called logical errors. Logical errors are often difficult to detect. The technique of finding and correcting this type of errors is called logical debugging. Errors like syntactic and execution errors are easier to find because they can just be located by generation of error messages on compilation or execution of a program.

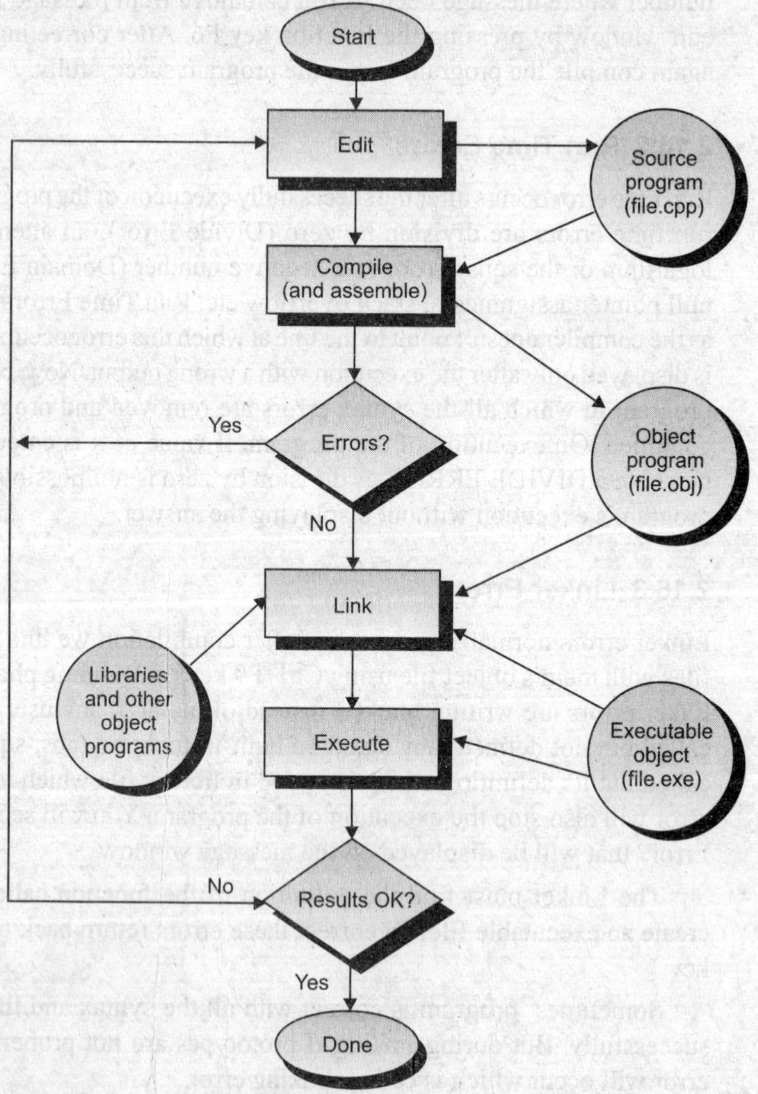

Figure 2.9: Flowchart showing Compiling, Running and Error checking a Complete C++ program

2.17 REVIEW OF TERMS

The terms that follow will be used frequently throughout the remainder of this reference. You should be completely familiar with them.

- **Source code** The text of a program that a user can read, commonly thought of as the program. The source code is input into the C++ compiler.
- **Object code** Translation of the source code of a program into machine code, which the computer can read and execute directly. Object code is the input to the linker.
- **Linker** A program that links separately compiled modules into one program. It also combines the functions in the Standard C++ library with the code that you wrote. The output of the linker is an executable program.
- **Library** The file containing the standard functions that your program can use. These functions include all I/O operations as well as other useful routines.
- **Compile time** The time during which your program is being compiled.
- **Run time** The time during which your program is executing.

2.18 FIRST C++ PROGRAM

You might be thinking that you have learnt lot about C++ language background and now eagerly want to try your first program in C++. To do so first of all you need a C++ compiler.

I assume that you have installed C++ compiler in your PC and now want to try your first program. Here is an example of your first C++ program which has been developed using Turbo C++ compiler.

Example - 1

```
#include <iostream.h>
#include<conio.h>
void main()
{
cout<<"Expert C++ Programming";
getch();
}
```

Just type the above line in the C++ editor and press Alt + F9 to compile that program. If there will be any mistakes, it will show "Error" message otherwise it will show "Success" message. Now press Ctrl + F9 to run compiled program and you will see similar output. If you cannot see anything then press Alt + F5 to see output window.

Turbo C++ Editor Window

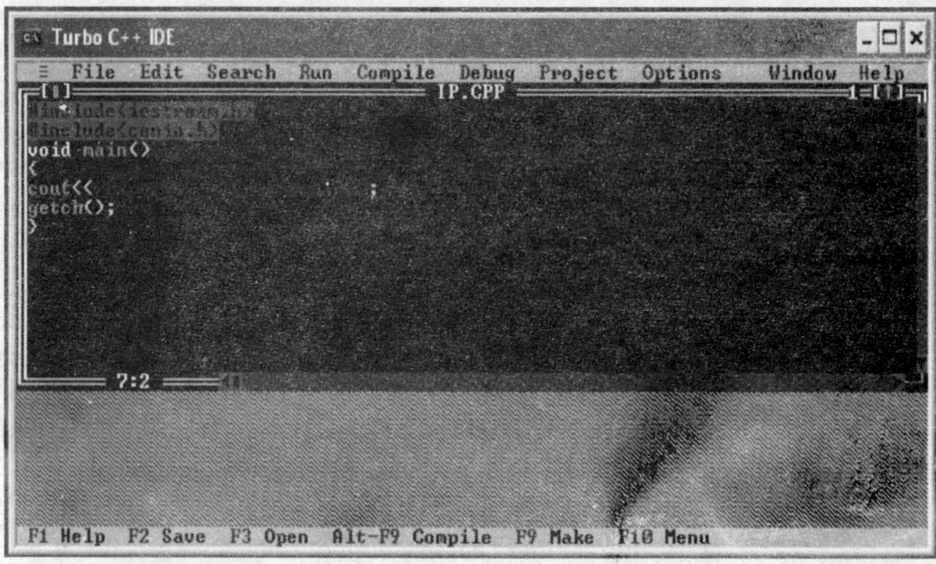

Program Output

Output after executing program.

Let's understand each and every line of this program. The very first line #include <iostream.h> tells the compiler to include a header file "iostream.h" in the program. Header file in C++ is nothing but collection of various functions. Here we are using cout<< from iostream.h header file. The second line #include <conio.h> tells the compiler to include a header file "conio.h" in the program. Header file in C++ is nothing but collection of various functions. Here we are using getch() from conio.h header file. The next line is void main() which is the beginning of the program. Every program must have a main() because program starts execution from this function. But what does the keyword void means before the main(). This means that main function will not return any value to the compiler. I know this is tough to understand now; these things will be discussed in detailed in function page.

The curly open and close braces { } defines the scope of the "main()" function means "main()" function's boundaries. The line between curly braces cout<<"Expert C++ Programming"; is the one of function defined in iostream.h whose job is to print message specified in double quotation. At the end of the line there is a semicolon (;) which is the end of that statement. C++ statements always end with a semicolon (;).

One thing you should keep in your mind that in C++ program, instructions declared in "main()", are executed from top to bottom. To understand it better let's extend the above program.

Example - 2

```
#include <iostream.h>
#include<conio.h>
void main()
{
clrscr();
cout<<"Expert C++ Programming";
cout<<"Welcome to Programming";
getch();
}
```

The top two lines include two header files "iostream.h" and "conio.h" respectively. The "iostream.h" header file contains "cout<<" and "conio.h" file contains "clrscr()" and "getch()". The "clrscr()" clears the output screen means any output shown by previously run program will be erased and that why we always put them at the beginning. Next is two "cout<<" statements which will print two different messages. The "getch()" waits for a keyboard input and if we press any key on keyboard the program exits. So we don't need to press Alt + F5 to see the output as we did in above program.

2.19 SYMBOLIC CONSTANTS

A symbolic constant is a constant that is represented by a name (symbol) in your program. Like a literal constant, a symbolic constant can't change. Whenever you need the constant's value in your program, you use its name as you would use a variable name. The actual value of the symbolic constant needs to be entered only once, when it is first defined.

Symbolic constants have two significant advantages over literal constants, as the following example shows. Suppose that you're writing a program that performs a variety of geometrical calculations. The program frequently needs the value ? (3.14) for its calculations. (You might recall from geometry class that ? is the ratio of a circle's circumference to its diameter.) For example, to calculate the circumference and area of a circle with a known radius, you could write

```
circumference = 3.14 * (2 * radius);
area = 3.14 * (radius)*(radius);
```

The asterisk (*) is C's multiplication operator. Thus, the first of these statements means "Multiply 2 times the value stored in the variable radius, and then multiply the result by 3.14. Finally, assign the result to the variable named circumference."

If, however, you define a symbolic constant with the name PI and the value 3.14, you could write

```
circumference = PI * (2 * radius);
area = PI * (radius)*(radius);
```

The resulting code is clearer. Rather than puzzling over what the value 3.14 is for, you can see immediately that the constant PI is being used.

The second advantage of symbolic constants becomes apparent when you need to change a constant. Continuing with the preceding example, you might decide that for greater accuracy your program needs to use a value of PI with more decimal places: 3.14159 rather than 3.14. If you had used literal constants for PI, you would have to go through your source code and change each occurrence of the value from 3.14 to 3.14159. With a symbolic constant, you need to make a change only in the place where the constant is defined. The rest of your code would not need to be changed.

2.19.1 Defining Symbolic Constants

C++ has two methods for defining a symbolic constant: the #define directive and the const keyword. **The #define directive is used as follows:**

```
#define CONSTNAME literal
```

This creates a constant named CONSTNAME with the value of literal. literal represents a literal constant, as described earlier. CONSTNAME follows the same rules described earlier for variable names. By convention, the names of symbolic constants are uppercase. This makes them easy to distinguish from variable names, which by convention are lowercase. For the previous example, the required #define directive for a constant called PI would be

```
#define PI 3.14159
```

Note that #define lines don't end with a semicolon (;). #defines can be placed anywhere in your source code, but the defined constant is in effect only for the portions of the source code that follow the #define directive. Most commonly, programmers group all #defines together, near the beginning of the file and before the start of the main() function.

2.19.2 How A #Define Works

The precise action of the #define directive is to instruct the compiler as follows: "In the source code, replace CONSTNAME with literal." The effect is exactly the same as if you had used your editor to go through the source code and make the changes manually. Note that #define doesn't replace instances of its target that occur as parts of longer names, within double quotes, or as part of a program comment. For example, in the following code, the instances of PI in the second and third lines would not get changed:

```
#define PI 3.14159 /* You have defined a constant for PI. */
#include<iostream.h>
#include<conio.h>
#define PI 3.14159
void main()
{
int r;
float area;
cout<<"Enter the radius:";
cin>>r;
area = PI * r * r;
cout<<"The Area of circle is "<<area;
getch();
}
```

2.19.3 Defining Constants with the Const Keyword

The second way to define a symbolic constant is with the const keyword. const is a modifier that can be applied to any variable declaration. A variable declared to be const can't be modified when the program is executed. A value is initialized at the time of declaration and is then prohibited from being changed. Here are some examples:

```
const int count = 100;
const float pi = 3.14159;
const long debt = 12000000, float tax_rate = 0.21;
```

const affects all variables on the declaration line. In the last line, debt and tax_rate are symbolic constants. As a side note, you should notice that in this example, debt was declared as a long and tax_rate was declared as a float.

If your program tries to modify a const variable, the compiler generates an error message. The following code would generate an error:

```
const int count = 100;
count = 200;   /* Does not compile! Cannot reassign or alter */
        /* the value of a constant. */
#include<iostream.h>
#include<conio.h>
void main()
{
int r;
float area;
const float pi = 3.14;
cout<<"Enter the radius:";
cin>>r;
area = PI * r * r;
cout<<"The Area of circle is "<<area;
getch();
}
```

***Note:** Most C++ programmers today use const instead of #define when declaring constants.*

2.20 DELIMETERS OF C++ LANGUAGE

C++ delimiters are the special characters used for special syntactic meaning. There are five powerful C++ delimiters used in a C++ program. These are described as:

Delimiter	Meaning
: (colon)	Used for label entry.
( ) (parenthesis)	Used for expression and enclosing the arguments in the function declaration.
[ ] (square bracket)	Used for describing the size for array.
{ }(curly braces)	Used for beginning and ending of function, blocks and main program.
; (semicolon)	Used at the end of every C++ statement except control statements.

2.21 OPERATORS AND EXPRESSIONS

C++ is very rich in built-in operators. Actually all the computation in the C++ language can be done through operators. In fact, it places more significance on operators than do most other computer languages. An operator can be defined as a thing which is used to represent the *operations* or *specific tasks* and the objects of the operations are referred to as *operands.*

An operator is a function which is can be given using expression 4 + 5 is equal to 9. Here 4 and 5 are called operands and + is called operator. Many of you are familiar with operators such as +, -, /, *, %. Arithmetic operators are the most common. Other operators are used for comparison of values, combination of logical states, and manipulation of individual binary digits. The binary operators are rather low level. Operators and values are combined to form expressions. The values produced by these expressions can be stored in variables, or used as a part of even larger expressions.

Now, we will teach about Operators, Arithmetic operators, Relational Operators, Logical Operators, Assignment Operators, Increments and Decrement Operators, Conditional Operators, Bitwise Operators and Special Operators.

2.22 OPERATORS

An operator is a symbol which helps the user to command the computer to do a certain mathematical or logical manipulations. Operators are used in C++ language program to operate on data and variables. C++ has a rich set of operators.

Definition: *"An operator is a symbol that operates on a certain data type and produces the output as the result of the operation."*

In C++, you can combine various operators of similar or different categories and perform an operation. In this case the C++ compiler tries to solve the expression as per the rules of precedence. Mainly operators are used to operate one, two or more than two operands depending upon their processing and given conditions.

2.23 CATEGORY OF OPERATORS

Operators are divided into three categories as given below:

2.23.1 Unary Operator

A unary operator is an operator, which operates on one operand, i.e. it operates on itself.

Operand1 **Operator**
Or
Operator Operand1

Here Operand1 may be a variable, a constant or an expression etc.

For Example: -b, ~a, x+1 etc.

2.23.2 Binary Operator

A binary operator is an operator, which operates on two operands.

Operand1 **Operator** Operand2

Here Operand1 and Operand2 may be a variable, a constant or an expression etc. and Operator must be either arithmetic type or relational type or logical type etc.

For Example: a + b, a>b, a && b etc.

2.23.3 Ternary Operator

A ternary operator is an operator, which operates on three operands.

Operand1 **Operator** Operand2 **Operator** Operand3

Here Operand1, Operand2, Operand3 may be a variable, a constant or an expression etc. and Operator must be either arithmetic type or relational type or logical type etc.

For Example: a +b +c, a>b>c, a && b || c etc.

2.24 TYPES OF OPERATOR

There are various operators used in C++ language. From every operator, C++ expression can be defined. By using some operators we can compute a formula, we can compare two expressions or variable values, or can create logical relationship between compound statements, can solve a conditional expression etc. There are mainly eight operators used in C++ language. **The relationship between these operators is shown in figure below:**

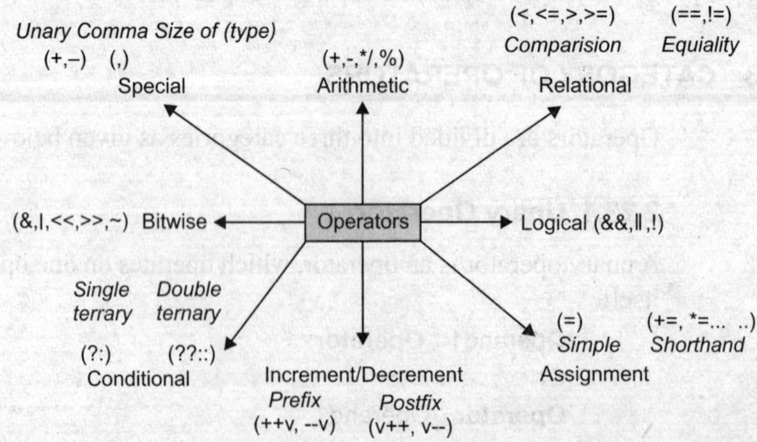

These are the various operators used in C++ language

1. Arithmetic operators
2. Relational operators
3. Logical operators
4. Assignment operators
5. Increment/Decrement operators
6. Conditional operators or Ternary operator
7. Bitwise operators
8. Special operators

2.25 EXPRESSIONS

An expression is a combination of variables constants and operators written according to the syntax of C++ language. In C++ every expression evaluates to a value i.e., every expression results in some value of a certain type that can be assigned to a variable.

2.25.1 Evaluation of Expressions

Expressions are evaluated using an assignment statement of the form

Variable = expression;

Variable is any valid C++ variable name. When the statement is encountered, the expression is evaluated first and then replaces the previous value of the variable on the left hand side. All variables used in the expression must be assigned values before evaluation is attempted.

There are various types of expressions occur in the C++ programming. These are as:

1. Arithmetic Expressions
2. Relational Expressions
3. Logical Expressions
4. Assignment Expressions
5. Increment/Decrement Expressions
6. Conditional or Ternary Expressions
7. Bitwise Expressions
8. Special Expressions

We will discuss every expression during the explanation of their related operators.

Example of evaluation statements are

x = a * b – c

y = b / c * a

z = a – b / c + d;

2.25.2 Rules for Evaluation of Expression

Following are the rules for evaluation of expression:

- First parenthesized sub expression left to right are evaluated.
- If parentheses are nested, the evaluation begins with the innermost sub expression.
- The precedence rule is applied in determining the order of application of operators in evaluating sub expressions.
- The associability rule is applied when two or more operators of the same precedence level appear in the sub expression.
- Arithmetic expressions are evaluated from left to right using the rules of precedence.
- When Parenthesis is used, the expressions within parenthesis assume highest priority.

2.26 ARITHMETIC OPERATORS

Arithmetic operators are used for arithmetic operations like Addition, Subtraction, Multiplication, Division etc. Mostly arithmetic operators are used in the all the computer languages. These arithmetic operators were designed at the time of Abacus computing machine.

They can be applied to almost any built-in data type allowed by C++. There are mainly five arithmetic operators used in C++ language. These all are given in the figure below:

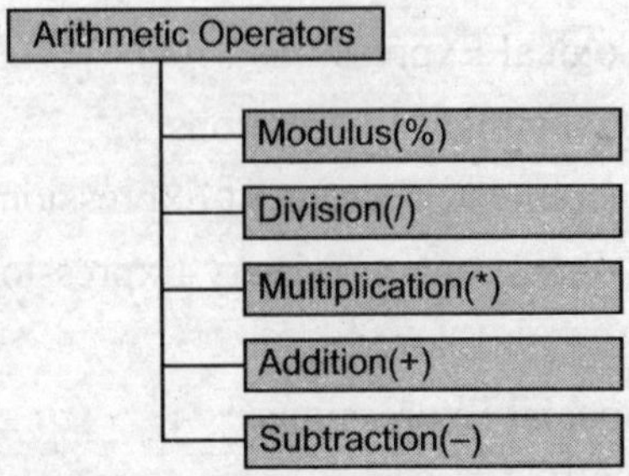

For example: Suppose A = 10 & B = 20 are two variables, then arithmetic operators used for different operations as:

Operator	Description	Example
+	Adds two operands	A + B will give 30
-	Subtracts second operand from the first	A - B will give -10
*	Multiply both operands	A * B will give 200
/	Divide numerator by denumerator	B / A will give 2
%	Modulus Operator and remainder of after an integer division	B % A will give 0

2.26.1 Arithmetic Expression

From the arithmetic operators, arithmetic expressions can be defined. There are mainly three types of arithmetic expressions linked with an arithmetic operator. These are explained as:

1. Integer Arithmetic Expression
2. Float Arithmetic Expression (or real arithmetic expression)
3. Mixed Mode Arithmetic Expression

1. Integer Arithmetic

When an arithmetic operation is performed on two whole numbers (a and b operands) or integers than such an operation is called as integer arithmetic. It always gives an integer as the result.

This is explained by the below examples as:

Suppose if a and b are two integer variables, then by using all the arithmetic operators different expressions with results be as:

```
int a ,b;
a = 5;          (both are of integer type)
b = 2;
Expression  Result
a + b = 7       (Integer)
a – b = 3       (Integer)
a * b = 10      (Integer)
a / b = 2       (Integer)
a % b = 1       (Integer)
```

In other words, we can say int with int, result be int. In integer division the fractional part is truncated.

2. Floating Point Arithmetic

When an arithmetic operation is preformed on two real numbers (a and b operands) or fraction numbers such an operation is called floating point arithmetic. The floating point results can be truncated according to the properties requirement. The remainder operator is not applicable for floating point arithmetic operands.

This can be explained by example as:

Suppose if a and b are the two float (real) variables, then by using all the arithmetic operators different expressions with the result be as:

```
float a, b;
a = 2.5;          (both a and b are of float type declared.)
b = 1.25;
```

Expression	**Result**
a + b = 3.75	(Real or float)
a – b = 1.25	(Real)
a * b = 3.124	(Real)
a / b = 2.0	(Real)

***Note:** Modulus operator can not be used as Real. In other word, we can say float with float result be float. Also if from two operands either be of double types, then result be of double type.*

3. Mixed Mode Arithmetic

When one of the operand is real(a) and other is an integer(b) and if the arithmetic operation is carried out on these 2 operands then it is called as mixed mode arithmetic. If any one operand is of real type then the result will always be real thus 15/10.0 = 1.5.

This can be explained by example as:

Suppose if a is of float type variable and b is of integer type variables (defined as: int b;), then by using all the arithmetic operators different expressions with the result be as:

```
float a;
int b;
a = 15.0;  ( one is of float type and other is of integer type defined.)
b = 10;
```

Expression	Result
a + b = 25.0	(real)
a – b = 5.0	(real)
a * b = 150.0	(real)
a / b = 1.5	(real)

Modulus can not be used in Mixed Mode Operations. From the above expressions note that if either of the operand be of real type, then the overall result be of real (float) type.

Note: In the arithmetic expression, if one operand be of character type (char), then the result be of character type. If one operand be of character type and the second operand be of integer type, then result be of integer type. Similarly if one operand be of character type and the second one be of either float or double type, then the result be of either float or double type respectively.

2.27 RELATIONAL OPERATORS

Often it is required to compare the relationship between operands and bring out a decision and program accordingly. This is when the relational operator comes into picture.

Relational operators compare between two operands and return in terms of true or false i.e. 1 or 0. In C++ and many other languages a true value is denoted by the integer 1 and a false value is denoted by the integer 0. Relational operators are used in conjunction with logical operators and conditional & looping statements.

It is required to compare the marks of 2 students, salary of 2 persons, we can compare them using relational operators.

Mainly relational operators are categorized into two sections. One is comparison section and second one is equality section. There are mainly six relational operators used in the C++ language. First four operators are in the comparison section and last two are in the equality section.

C++ supports the following relational operators.

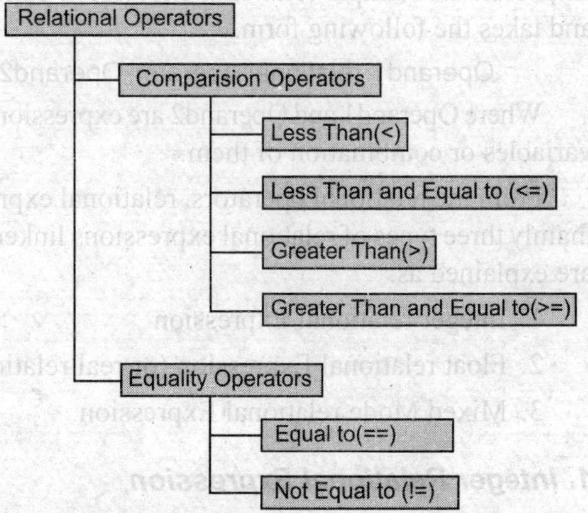

For example: Suppose A = 10 & B = 20 are two variables, then arithmetic operators used for different operations as:

Operator	Description	Example
==	Checks if the value of two operands is equal or not, if yes then condition becomes true.	(A == B) is not true.
!=	Checks if the value of two operands is equal or not, if values are not equal then condition becomes true.	(A != B) is true.
>	Checks if the value of left operand is greater than the value of right operand, if yes then condition becomes true.	(A > B) is not true.
<	Checks if the value of left operand is less than the value of right operand, if yes then condition becomes true.	(A < B) is true.
>=	Checks if the value of left operand is greater than or equal to the value of right operand, if yes then condition becomes true.	(A >= B) is not true.
<=	Checks if the value of left operand is less than or equal to the value of right operand, if yes then condition becomes true.	(A <= B) is true.

These operators are used in if statement, switch statement, conditional operator statement, while statement, do-while statement and for statement. These operators are mainly used for decision-making statement. These operators give the results in two branches, one is of True type and other is of false type (yes/no).

2.27.1 Relational Expression

The expression having two operands and one relational operator is called **Relational Expression**. A simple relational expression contains only one relational operator and takes the following form.

Operand1 relational operator Operand2

Where Operand1 and Operand2 are expressions, which may be simple constants, variables or combination of them.

From the relational operators, relational expressions can be defined. There are mainly three types of relational expressions linked with a relational operator. These are explained as:

1. Integer relational Expression
2. Float relational Expression (or real relational expression)
3. Mixed Mode relational Expression

1. Integer Relational Expression

When an relational operation is performed on two whole numbers (a and b operands) or integers than such an operation is called as integer relational. It always gives an integer as the result.

This is explained by the below examples as:

Suppose if a and b are two integer variables, then by using all the relational operators different expressions with results be as:

```
int a, b;
a = 3;          (both are of integer type)
b = 2;
Expression      Result
a > b           (True)
a >= b          (True)
a < b           ( False)
a < = b         ( False)
a == b          (False)
a ! = b         (True)
```

2. Float Relational Expression

When an relational operation is preformed on two real numbers(a and b operands) or fraction numbers such an operation is called floating point relational.

3. Mixed Mode Real Expression

When one of the operand is real(a) and other is an integer(b) and if the relational operation is carried out on these 2 operands then it is called as mixed mode relational.

2.28 LOGICAL OPERATORS

In the term logical operator the word logical refers to the ways in the relationship which can be connected together using the rules of formal logic.

A logical operator is used to compare or evaluate logical and relational expressions. These operations are used for compound relational expressions or logical expressions. When more than one relational expression occurs in a C++ expression using logical operators, then such type of expressions are called Compound Relational Expressions or logical expression. These are used in decision-making statement and some looping statements like if, switch, do while, while and for etc. These statements have either True (1) branch or false (0) branch. In other words, these are used to form complex expression to take the decision. There are mainly three logical operators used in C++ language as in the figure below:

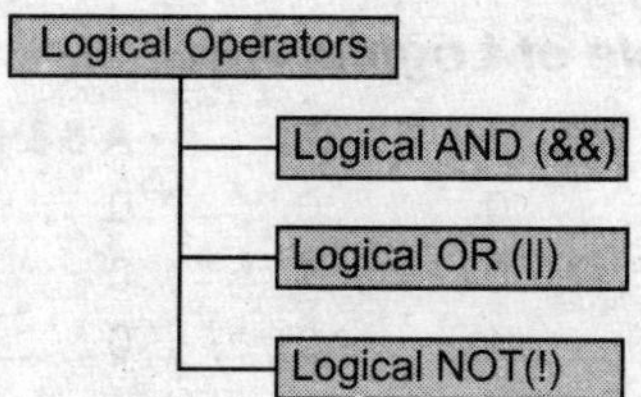

Logical AND (&&)

This operator is used to evaluate 2 conditions or expressions with relational operators simultaneously. If both the expressions to the left and to the right of the logical operator is true then the whole compound expression is true.

Example: a > b && x = = 10

The expression to the left is a > b and that on the right is x == 10 the whole expression is true only if both expressions are true i.e., if a is greater than b and x is equal to 10.

Logical OR (||)

The logical OR is used to combine 2 expressions or the condition evaluates to true if any one of the 2 expressions is true.

Example: a < m || a < n

The expression evaluates to true if any one of them is true or if both of them are true. It evaluates to true if a is less than either m or n and when a is less than both m and n.

Logical NOT (!)

The logical not operator takes single expression and evaluates to true if the expression is false and evaluates to false if the expression is true. In other words it just reverses the value of the expression.

Example:! (x >= y) the NOT expression evaluates to true only if the value of x is neither greater than or equal to y

For example: Suppose A = 10 & B = 20 are two variables, then arithmetic operators used for different operations as:

Operator	Description	Example
&&	Called Logical AND operator. If both the operands are non zero then condition becomes true.	(A && B) is true.
||	Called Logical OR Operator. If any of the two operands is non zero then condition becomes true.	(A || B) is true.
!	Called Logical NOT Operator. Use to reverses the logical state of its operand. If a condition is true then Logical NOT operator will make false.	!(A && B) is false

Truth table of Logical AND

A	B	A && B
0	0	0
0	1	0
1	0	0
1	1	1

Truth table of Logical OR

A	B	A || B
0	0	0
0	1	1
1	0	1
1	1	1

Truth table of Logical NOT

A	~ A
0	1
1	0

2.28.1 Logical Expression

From the logical operators, logical expressions can be defined. There are mainly three types of logical expressions linked with a logical operator. All the logical expression gives either true (non-zero) or false (zero) result.

These all are explained as:

1. Integer logical Expression
2. Float logical Expression (or real logical expression)
3. Mixed Mode logical Expression

1. Integer Logical Expression

When a logical operation is performed on two whole numbers (a and b operands) or integers than such an operation is called as integer logical.

2. Float Logical Expression

When an logical operation is preformed on two real numbers (a and b operands) or fraction numbers such an operation is called floating point logical.

3. Mixed Mode Real Expression

When one of the operand is real (a) and other is an integer (b) and if the logical operation is carried out on these 2 operands then it is called as mixed mode logical.

Note: *Note that in many expressions the relational and logical operators often works together. The key to the concept of relational and logical operator is the idea of **true** or **false**.*

2.29 ASSIGNMENT OPERATORS

The Assignment Operator (=) evaluates an expression on the right of the expression and substitutes it to the value or variable on the left of the expression. Assignment operators are further subdivided into two types:

1. Simple Assignment Operator
2. Short hand Assignment Operator

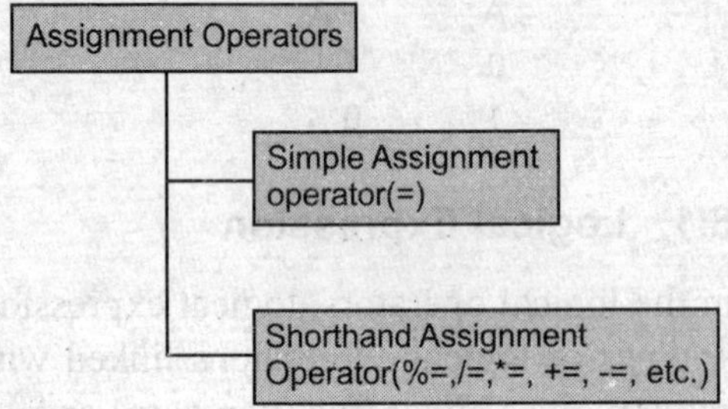

2.29.1 Simple Assignment Operator

Simple assignment operator is = (equal to). The general syntax of simple assignment operator is as:

```
var = constant value or variable or expression;
```

where var is the variable.

Example: x = a + b

Here the value of a + b is evaluated and substituted to the variable x.

2.29.2 Short Hand Assignment Operator

Arithmetic Assignment operators are a combination of arithmetic and the assignment operator. With this operator, the arithmetic operation happens first and then the result of the operation is assigned.

These operators have equal to (=) sign with all the arithmetic operators. The general syntax of short hand assignment or arithmetic assignment operator are as:

```
var operator = constant value or  expression;
```

where var is the variable.

Example: x + = 1 is same as x = x + 1

For example, some valid expressions having simple assignment and short hand assignment are as shown in table:

Statement with simple assignment operator	Statement with shorthand operator
a = a + 1	a += 1
a = a – 1	a -= 1
a = a * (n+1)	a *= (n+1)
a = a / (n+1)	a /= (n+1)
a = a % b	a %= b

For example: Suppose A = 10 & B = 20 are two variables, then arithmetic operators used for different operations as:

Operator	Description	Example
=	Simple assignment operator, Assigns values from right side operands to left side operand	C = A + B will assigne value of A + B into C
+=	Add AND assignment operator, It adds right operand to the left operand and assign the result to left operand	C += A is equivalent to C = C + A
-=	Subtract AND assignment operator, It subtracts right operand from the left operand and assign the result to left operand	C -= A is equivalent to C = C - A
*=	Multiply AND assignment operator, It multiplies right operand with the left operand and assign the result to left operand	C *= A is equivalent to C = C * A
/=	Divide AND assignment operator, It divides left operand with the right operand and assign the result to left operand	C /= A is equivalent to C = C / A
%=	Modulus AND assignment operator, It takes modulus using two operands and assign the result to left operand	C %= A is equivalent to C = C % A
<<=	Left shift AND assignment operator	C <<= 2 is same as C = C << 2
>>=	Right shift AND assignment operator	C >>= 2 is same as C = C >> 2
&=	Bitwise AND assignment operator	C &= 2 is same as C = C & 2
^=	bitwise exclusive OR and assignment operator	C ^= 2 is same as C = C ^ 2
|=	bitwise inclusive OR and assignment operator	C |= 2 is same as C = C | 2

2.29.3 Assignment Expression

Expression like a=10 or a=a+1 or a=a+b is called assignment expression because we use assignment operator (=) to assign the value to a variable. There are mainly two types of assignment expressions linked with an assignment operator.

These all are explained as:

1. Integer assignment Expression
2. Float assignment Expression (or real assignment expression)

1. Integer Assignment Expression

When all the operands are of integer type in an assignment expression (or an integer operand1 be assigned to another operand2, here operand2 should be a variable) having an assignment operator, then such type of expression is called an Integer assignment Expression.

2. Float Assignment Expression

When all the operands are of float type in an assignment expression (or a real operand1 be assigned to another operand2, here operand2 should be a variable) having an assignment operators, then such type of expression is called a float assignment Expression.

3. Short Notes on L-value And R-value

L-value and R-value can be easily computed from the assignment statement. L-value is called left value and R-value is called right value.

The general syntax is:

```
Operand1 = Operand2;
```

Here Operand1 is the L-values and the Operand2 is the R-values. For example, in the below statements:

```
c = a + b;
```

Here c is the L-value and the arithmetic expression (a+b) is the R-value.

Suppose x = 1; takes the value on the right (e.g. 1) and puts it in the memory referenced by x. Here x and 1 are known as L-VALUES and R-VALUES respectively L-values can be on either side of the assignment operator where as R-values only appear on the right.

So x is an L-value because it can appear on the left as we've just seen, or on the right like this: y = x; However, constants like 1 are R-values because 1 could appear on the right, but 1 = x; is invalid.

***Important Note:** Remember that there is a remarkable difference between the equality operator (= =) and the assignment operator (=). The equality operator is used to compare the two operands for equality (same value), whereas the assignment operator is used for the purposes of assignment.*

2.30 CONDITIONAL OR TERNARY OPERATOR

The conditional operator consists of 2 symbols the question mark (?) and the colon (:). The syntax for a ternary operator is as follows

```
Conditional Operator
(exp1? exp2 : exp3;)
```

The ternary operator works as follows: exp1 is evaluated first. If the expression is true then exp2 is evaluated & its value becomes the value of the expression. If exp1 is false, exp3 is evaluated and its value becomes the value of the expression. Note that only one of the expressions is evaluated.

Operator	Description	Example
? :	Conditional Expression	If Condition is true ? Then value X : Otherwise value Y

For Example

```
a = 10;
b = 15;
x = (a > b)? a: b
```

Here x will be assigned to the value of b. The condition follows that the expression is false therefore b is assigned to x.

For Example: Below is an if statement having a and b two variables as:

```
a = 10;
b = 5;
if (a > b)
{
c = a – b;
}
else
{
c = a + b;
}
```

The above if statement can be used by using the conditional operator in a single C++ statement as below:

```
c = (a > b)? a - b: a + b;
```

The above expression is also called conditional expression.

2.31 INCREMENT AND DECREMENT OPERATORS

These operators also fall under the broad category or unary operators but are quite distinct than unary minus. The increment (++) and decrement (– –) operators are very useful in C++ language. Increment operators are used to increment value one by one and decrement operators are used to decrement the value one by one. They are extensively used in for and while loops. These operators can be used in either the prefix or postfix notation as follows:

1. Prefix Increment / Decrement Operator
2. Postfix Increment / Decrement Operator

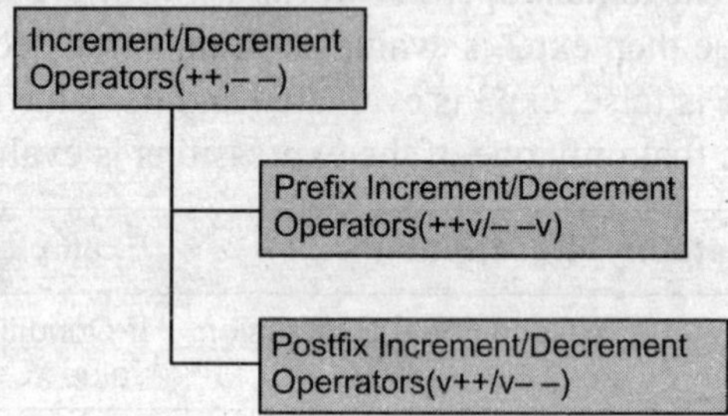

For example: Suppose A = 10 & B = 20 are two variables, then arithmetic operators used for different operations as:

Operator	Description	Example
++	Increment operator, increases integer value by one	A++ will give 11
– –	Decrement operator, decreases integer value by one	A– – will give 9

2.31.1 Prefix Operator

In the Prefix Increment operator, first of all value will be incremented and then incremented value will be assigned to a variable. Similarly in the prefix decrement operator first of all value will be decrement and then decremented value be assigned to the variable.

The general syntax is:

```
++ var;
-- var;
```

where var is the variable.

For Example: In case of prefix increment:

```
int a,b;
a = 10;
b = ++a;
cout<<a<<endl;
cout<<b<<endl;
```

Output:

```
11
11
```

In case of prefix decrement:

```
int a,b;
a = 10;
b = – –a;
cout<<a<<endl;
cout<<b<<endl;
```

Output:

```
9
9
```

2.31.2 Postfix Operator

In the postfix increment operator, first of all value will be assigned to the variable and then it will be incremented. Similarly in the postfix decrement operator, first of all value will be assigned and then it will be decremented.

The general syntax is:

```
var ++;
var - -;
```

where var is the variable.

For Example

In case of postfix increment:

```
int a,b;
a = 10;
b = a++;
cout<<a<<endl;
cout<<b<<endl;
```

Output:

```
10
11
```

In case of postfix decrement:

```
int a,b;
a = 10;
b = a– –;
cout<<a<<endl;
cout<<b<<endl;
```

Output:

```
10
9
```

2.32 BITWISE OPERATORS

We talked about the fact that computers work in binary numbers (0and 1). These are essentially streams of ones and zeros, each one referred to as a bit. Bits are formed into groups of 8 to form bytes. As such, it is not surprising that we, as programmers, will occasionally end up working at this level in our code. To facilitate this requirement, C++ provides a range of *bit operators*. Now, to understand how ones and zeros are formed into bytes to form numbers.

We will be working with the binary representation of two numbers. Firstly, the decimal number 171 is represented in binary as:

10101011

Secondly, the number 3 is represented by the following binary sequence:

00000011

Now that we have two binary numbers with which to work, we can begin to look at the C++ bitwise operators. There are six types of Bitwise operator. The table for Bitwise operators is as:

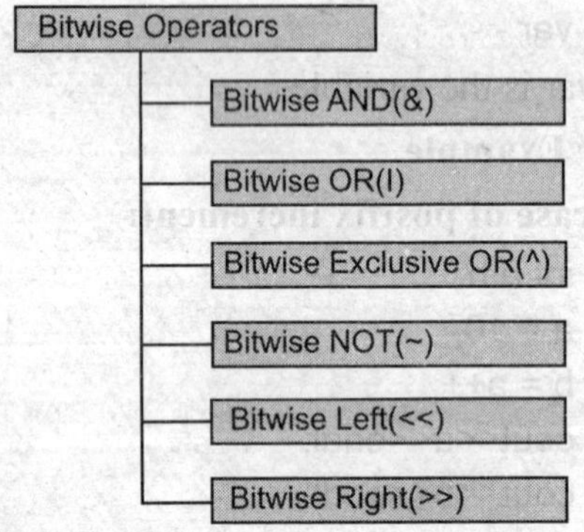

2.32.1 Bitwise Right Shift

A bitwise right shift is, as you might expect, the same as a left except that the shift takes place in the opposite direction. Note that since we are shifting to the right there is no opportunity to retain the lower most bits regardless of the data type used to contain the result. As a result the low order bits are discarded. Whether or not the vacated high order bit positions are replaced with zeros or ones depends on whether the *sign bit* used to indicate positive and negative numbers is set or not and, unfortunately, on the particular system and C++ implementation in use.

```
10101011 Right Shift one bit
========
01010101
```

The bitwise right shift is represented by the '>>' character sequence followed by the shift count:

```
int x = 171;
int z;
z = x >> 1;
cout<<z;
```

When executed, the above code will report the result of the shift as being 85, which equates to binary 01010101.

2.32.2 Bitwise Left Shift

The bitwise left shift moves each bit in a binary number a specified number of positions to the left. As the bits are shifted to the left, zeros are placed in the vacated right most (low order) positions. Note also that the once the left most (high order) bits are shifted beyond the size of the variable containing the value, those high orders are discarded:

```
10101011 Left Shift one bit
========
101010110
```

In C++ the bitwise left shift operator is represented by the '<<' sequence, followed by the number of bit positions to be shifted. For example, to shift left by 1 bit:

```
int x = 171;
int z;
z = x << 1;
cout<<z;
```

When compiled and executed, the above code will display a message stating that the result is 342 which, when converted to binary, equates to 101010110.

2.32.3 Bitwise Not

The Bitwise NOT is represented by a tilde sign(~). It makes complement of a given bit. Suppose bits are 1 results in a 0, If the bits are 0 results in 1. Its purpose is to convert 0 to 1 and 1 to 0 at individual bit of data. Taking our two example numbers, this would appear as follows:

```
10101011 NOT
========
01010100
```

As we can see, the only locations where both numbers have 1s are the last two positions. If we perform this in C++ code, therefore, we should find that the result is -84 (01010100):

```
int x = 171;
int z;
z = ~x; // Perform a bitwise NOT on the value held by variable x
cout<<z;
```

Output: -84

x_i	$\sim x_i$
0	1
1	0

We can do an example of bitwise ~. It's easiest to do this on 4 bit numbers (although only 2 bits are necessary to show the concept).

Variable	b_3	b_2	b_1	b_0
x	1	1	0	0
z = ~x	0	0	1	1

2.32.4 Bitwise AND

The Bitwise AND is represented by a single ampersand (&). It makes a bit by bit comparison of two numbers. Any corresponding position in the binary sequence of each number where both bits are 1 results in a 1 appearing in the same position of the resulting number. If either bit position contains a 0 then a zero appears in the result. Taking our two example numbers, this would appear as follows:

```
10101011 AND
00000011
========
00000011
```

As we can see, the only locations where both numbers have 1s are the last two positions. If we perform this in C++ code, therefore, we should find that the result is 3 (00000011):

```
int x = 171;
int y = 3;
int z;
z = x & y;        // Perform a bitwise AND on the values held by variables x
and y
cout<<z;
```

Output: 3

x_i	y_i	x_i & y_i
0	0	0
0	1	0
1	0	0
1	1	1

We can do an example of bitwise &. It's easiest to do this on 4 bit numbers, however.

Variable	b_3	b_2	b_1	b_0
x	1	1	0	0
y	1	0	1	0
z = x & y	1	0	0	0

2.32.5 Bitwise XOR

The bitwise XOR (commonly referred to as *exclusive OR* and represented by the caret '^' character) performs a similar task to the OR operation except that a 1 is placed in the result if one or other corresponding bit positions in the two numbers is 1. If both positions are a 1 or a 0 then the corresponding bit in the result is set to a 0.

For example:

```
10101011 XOR
00000011
========
10101000
```

The result in this case is 10101000 which convert to 168 in decimal. To verify this we can, once again, try some C++ code:

```
int x = 171;
int y = 3;
int z;
z = x ^ y;
cout<<z;
```

When executed, we get the following output:

```
168
```

x_i	y_i	x_i ^1 y_i
0	0	0
0	1	1
1	0	1
1	1	0

We can do an example of bitwise ^. It's easiest to do this on 4 bit numbers, however.

Variable	b_3	b_2	b_1	b_0
x	1	1	0	0
y	1	0	1	0
z = x ^ y	0	1	1	0

2.32.6 Bitwise OR

The bitwise OR also performs a bit by bit comparison of two binary sequences. Unlike the AND operation, the OR places a 1 in the result if there is a 1 in the first or second operand. The operator is represented by a single vertical bar character (|). Using our example numbers, the result will be as follows:

```
10101011 OR
00000011
========
10101011
```

If we perform this operation in a C++ example we see the following:

```
int x = 171;
int y = 3;
int z;
z = x | y;
cout<< z;
```

Output: 171

x_i	y_i	$x_i \mid y_i$
0	0	0
0	1	1
1	0	1
1	1	1

We can do an example of bitwise |. It's easiest to do this on 4 bit numbers, however.

Variable	b_3	b_2	b_1	b_0
x	1	1	0	0
y	1	0	1	0
z = x | y	1	1	1	0

Operator	Description	Example
&	Binary AND Operator copies a bit to the result if it exists in both operands	(A & B) will give 12 which is 0000 1100
|	Binary OR Operator copies a bit if it exists in eather operand	(A | B) will give 61 which is 0011 1101
^	Binary XOR Operator copies the bit if it is set in one operand but not both	(A ^ B) will give 49 which is 0011 0001
~	Binary Ones Complement Operator is unary and has the efect of 'flipping' bits	(~A) will give -60 which is 1100 0011

Operator	Description	Example
<<	Binary Left Shift Operator. The left operands value is moved left by the number of bits specified by the right operand	A << 2 will give 240 which is 1111 0000
>>	Binary Right Shift Operator. The left operands value is moved right by the number of bits specified by the right operand	A >> 2 will give 15 which is 0000 1111

2.32.7 Compound Bitwise Operators

As with the arithmetic operators, each bitwise operator has a corresponding compound operator that allows the operation and assignment to be performed using a single operator:

Operator	Description
x &= y	Perform a bitwise AND of x and y and assign result to x
x |= y	Perform a bitwise OR of x and y and assign result to x
x ^= y	Perform a bitwise XOR of x and y and assign result to x
x <<= n	Shift x left by n places and assign result to x
x >>= n	Shift x right by n places and assign result to x

2.33 SPECIAL OPERATORS

C++ supports some special operators of interest such as comma operator, size of operator, pointer operators (& and *) and member selection operators (. and ->) etc. Some types of special operators are as:

1. Unary Operator
2. Comma Operator
3. Sizeof Operator
4. Type Operator
5. Pointer Operator
6. Member Selection Operator

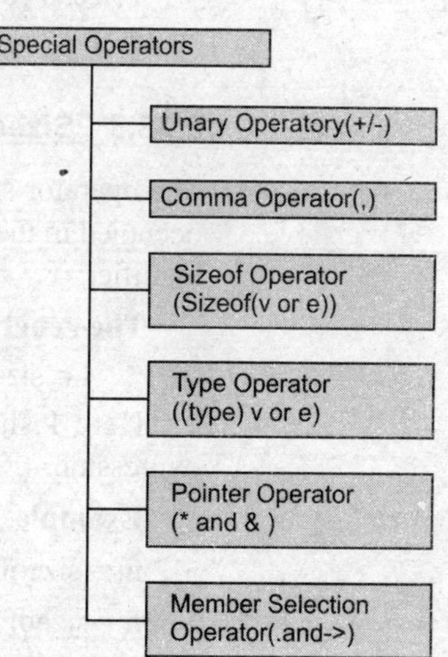

2.33.1 Unary Operator

These are used for identification of a number about whether it is signed or unsigned. These are + and -. Also increment / decrement operators ++, — are in the unary operator category as special operators. Suppose a = 3, then applying minus sign with the 3 digit, it will change the identification of 3 i.e. it is a –ve number. Similarly +7 identify the unary operator having plus sign. These two operators are used in below written expressions:

```
x = ++a – 7 * (-3) – (+2) * (-7);
y = 15 – (-12);
```

2.33.2 Comma Operator

The comma operator can be used to link related expressions together. A comma-linked list of expressions is evaluated left to right and value of right most expression is the value of the combined expression.

The general syntax is:

```
var =value, var2 =value, var3= value so on.
```

Where var is variable.

For example the statement

```
value = (x = 10, y = 5, x + y);
```

First assigns 10 to x and 5 to y and finally assigns 15 to value. Since comma has the lowest precedence in operators the parenthesis is necessary.

Some examples of comma operator are

In for loops: for (n=1, m=10, n <=m; n++,m++)

In while loops: While (c=getchar(), c != '10')

Exchanging values: t = x, x = y, y = t;

You can combine multiple expressions in a single expression using the comma operator.

2.33.3 Sizeof Operator

The operator size of gives the size of the data type or variable in terms of bytes occupied in the memory. The operand may be a variable, a constant or a data type qualifier.

The general syntax is:

```
I = sizeof (var or exp);
```

Here I should be of integer type. Here var is variable and exp is an expression.

Example

```
m = sizeof (sum);
n = sizeof (long int);
```

```
k = sizeof (235L);
a =  sizeof (b+c);
```

The size of operator is normally used to determine the lengths of arrays and structures when their sizes are not known to the programmer. It is also used to allocate memory space dynamically to variables during the execution of the program.

2.33.4 Type Operator (Type Conversion)

When an operator's operands are of different data types, C++ automatically converts them to the same data type. This can affect the results of mathematical expressions. This is called type conversion.

In C++ type conversion can be done by two ways, viz.

(i) Automatic Conversion (Implicit conversions)

When a value is converted to a higher type, it is said to be promoted. Let's look at the specific rules that govern the evaluation of mathematical expressions.

Rule1: chars, shorts, unsigned shorts are automatically promoted to int.

Rule2: When an operator works with two values of different data types, the lower data type is promoted to a higher data type.

Implicit conversions do not require any operator. They are automatically performed when a value is copied to a compatible type.

For example:

```
short a=2000;
int b;
b=a;
```

Here, the value of a has been promoted from short to int and we have not had to specify any type-casting operator. This is known as a standard conversion. Standard conversions affect fundamental data types, and allow conversions such as the conversions between numerical types (short to int, int to float, double to int...), to or from bool, and some pointer conversions.

Some of these conversions may imply a loss of precision, which the compiler can signal with a warning. This can be avoided with an explicit conversion.

Implicit conversions also include constructor or operator conversions, which affect classes that include specific constructors or operator functions to perform conversions.

For example:

```
class A {};
class B
{ public: B (A a) {} };
```

```
A a;
B b=a;
```

Here, a implicit conversion happened between objects of class A and class B, because B has a constructor that takes an object of class A as parameter. Therefore implicit conversions from A to B are allowed.

(ii) Explicit Type Casting

Type casting means to convert a higher data type to a lower data type. For the purpose of type casting we require to use the type case operator, which lets you manually promote or demote a value. It is a unary operator which appears as the data type name followed by the operand inside a set of parentheses.

The general syntax is: (datatype) v or e; where v is variable e is an expression.

For Example

```
int x, y;
float z;
x = 3;
y = 2;
z = x / y;
```

If we divide x by y, then result stored in the z variable be 1.0. But by using the type operator, we can get the float value as:

```
z = (float) x / y;
```

You can also convert one variable to the float type by using the type operator as:

```
c = (float) x;
```

2.33.5 Pointer Operator

There are two types of pointer operators used in C++ language. These are & (it is not Bitwise AND) and * (it is not multiplication sign or an arithmetic operator). We will discuss this operator in the Pointer chapter later on.

2.33.6 Member Selection Operator

These operators are used in structure and union. These operators are used to create a relationship between owner and member within a structure or union data. These are "." (dot operator) and → (relationship operator or member operator).

Operator	Description	Example
sizeof()	Returns the size of an variable.	sizeof(a), where a is interger, will return 4.
&	Returns the address of an variable.	&a; will give actaul address of the variable.
*	Pointer to a variable.	*a; will pointer to a variable.

2.34 ORDER OF PRECEDENCE OR HIERARCHY OF OPERATORS

C++ operators in order of precedence (highest to lowest). Their associatively indicates in what order operators of equal precedence in an expression are applied.

<table>
<tr><th>Operator</th><th>Description</th><th>Associatively</th></tr>
<tr><td>()</td><td>Parentheses (function call) (see Note 1)</td><td>left-to-right</td></tr>
<tr><td>[]</td><td>Brackets (array subscript)</td><td></td></tr>
<tr><td>.</td><td>Member selection via object name</td><td></td></tr>
<tr><td>-></td><td>Member selection via pointer</td><td></td></tr>
<tr><td>++ --</td><td>Postfix increment/decrement (see Note 2)</td><td></td></tr>
<tr><td>++ --</td><td>Prefix increment/decrement</td><td>right-to-left</td></tr>
<tr><td>+ -</td><td>Unary plus/minus</td><td></td></tr>
<tr><td>! ~</td><td>Logical negation/bitwise complement</td><td></td></tr>
<tr><td>(type)</td><td>Cast (change type)</td><td></td></tr>
<tr><td>*</td><td>Dereference</td><td></td></tr>
<tr><td>&</td><td>Address</td><td></td></tr>
<tr><td>sizeof</td><td>Determine size in bytes</td><td></td></tr>
<tr><td>* / %</td><td>Multiplication/division/modulus</td><td>left-to-right</td></tr>
<tr><td>+ -</td><td>Addition/subtraction</td><td>left-to-right</td></tr>
<tr><td><< >></td><td>Bitwise shift left, Bitwise shift right</td><td>left-to-right</td></tr>
<tr><td>< <=</td><td>Relational less than/less than or equal to</td><td>left-to-right</td></tr>
<tr><td>> >=</td><td>Relational greater than/greater than or equal to</td><td></td></tr>
<tr><td>== !=</td><td>Relational is equal to/is not equal to</td><td>left-to-right</td></tr>
<tr><td>&</td><td>Bitwise AND</td><td>left-to-right</td></tr>
<tr><td>^</td><td>Bitwise exclusive OR</td><td>left-to-right</td></tr>
<tr><td>|</td><td>Bitwise inclusive OR</td><td>left-to-right</td></tr>
<tr><td>&&</td><td>Logical AND</td><td>left-to-right</td></tr>
<tr><td>||</td><td>Logical OR</td><td>left-to-right</td></tr>
<tr><td>?:</td><td>Ternary conditional</td><td>right-to-left</td></tr>
<tr><td>=</td><td>Assignment</td><td>right-to-left</td></tr>
<tr><td>+= -=</td><td>Addition/subtraction assignment</td><td></td></tr>
<tr><td>*= /=</td><td>Multiplication/division assignment</td><td></td></tr>
<tr><td>%= &=</td><td>Modulus/bitwise AND assignment</td><td></td></tr>
<tr><td>^= |=</td><td>Bitwise exclusive/inclusive OR assignment</td><td></td></tr>
<tr><td><<= >>=</td><td>Bitwise shift left/right assignment</td><td></td></tr>
<tr><td>,</td><td>Comma (separate expressions)</td><td>left-to-right</td></tr>
</table>

Note 1: Parentheses are also used to group sub-expressions to force a different precedence; such parenthetical expressions can be nested and are evaluated from inner to outer.

Note 2: Postfix increment/decrement have high precedence, but the actual increment or decrement of the operand is delayed (to be accomplished sometime before the statement completes execution). So in the statement y = x * z++; the current value of z is used to evaluate the expression (i.e., z++ evaluates to z) and z only incremented after all else is done.

2.35 LIBRARY FUNCTIONS OR BUILT IN FUNCTION

One of the major features of C++ language is that C++ has many in built functions called library functions. C++ compiler is rich in Library functions as compared to other language's compilers. C++ compilers have mainly four types of functions. These functions are also called compiler function:

These are as:

1. Trigonometric functions
2. Hyperbolic functions
3. Mathematical functions
4. Miscellaneous functions

2.35.1 Trigonometric Functions

In C++ language trigonometric functions are built-in for solving trigonometric or polynomial equations. These are written as given below:

Trigonometric functions	Meanings
acos (x)	Arc cosine of x i.e., $\cos^{-1}x$
asine (x)	Arc sin of x i.e. $\sin^{-1}x$
atan (x)	Arc tangent of x i.e. $\tan^{-1}x$
atan2 (x, y)	Arc tangent of x/y i.e. $\tan^{-1}(x/y)$
cos (x)	cosine of x i.e. cos x
sin (x)	sin of x i.e. sin x
tan (x)	tangent of x i.e. tan x

2.35.2 Hyperbolic Functions

Hyperbolic functions are used to solve hyperbolic expressions. These are used in hyperbolic polynomials. There are mainly three hyperbolic standard functions used in C++ language. These are as given below:

Hyperbolic functions	Meanings
cosh (x)	hyperbolic cosine of x
sinh (x)	hyperbolic sin of x
tanh (x)	hyperbolic tangent of x

***Note:** In trigonometric and hyperbolic functions x & y are in Radians.*

2.35.3 Mathematical Functions

Mathematical functions are used to solve math functions they are include in math.h header file. These are used for solving some mathematical formulas. These are explained as given below:

Mathematical functions	Meanings
abs (x)	to find absolute value of x i.e. if x = –5 and y = abs (x) then y = 5 be the result and result will be integer
sqrt (s)	It finds the square root of x value and x > 0, i.e. if x = 16 and y = sqrt (x); then result be 4.
fabs (x)	to find the absolute value of x in float i.e. if x = –5.4 and y = fabs (x), then y = 5.4 and result will be float.
pow (x, y)	It computes the exponential formula x^y i.e. x can be written as y = pow (3, 2); For example: if x = 3, y = 2 and z = pow (x, y); be the expression, then result be 9.
log (x)	It returns the natural logarithm of x
log 10(x)	It returns the logarithm value having base 10 and x > 0.
exp (x)	It finds the e^x. Note that result will be in doubles.
fmod (x, y)	If finds the remainder of division x/y. Result will be always integer. For example: if x = 3, y = 2 and z = fmod (x, y); then result will be z = 2
rand (x)	It finds the random value of a +ve number. Result will be integer. For example, it

2.35.4 Miscellaneous Functions

All the miscellaneous functions are described given below:

Miscellaneous functions	Meanings
ceil (x)	x rounded upto the nearest integer value For example: if x = 2.2; and y = ceil (x); Then result of y = 3 Similarly if x = 2.9 and y = ceil (x); Then result of y = 3
floor (x)	x will be rounded down to the nearest integer value For example; if x = 2.2; and y = floor (x); Then result of y = 2. Similarly if x = 2.9; and y = floor (x); then result of y = 2.
toascii (x)	It will converts any character or numeric value to a ascii value. Result will always be intege.
tolower (c)	It converts any single character into lower case.
toupper (c)	It converts any single character into uppercase.

2.36 USE OF LIBRARY FUNCTIONS

To use a function, ensure that you have made the required #includes header file in your C++ program. Then the function can be called as though you had defined it yourself. It is important to ensure that your arguments have the expected types; otherwise the function will probably produce strange results.

Some libraries require extra options before the compiler can support their use. For example, to compile a program including functions from the math.h library the command might be

```
cc mathprog.cpp -o mathprog –lm
```

The final -lm is an instruction to link the maths library with the program. The manual page for each function will usually inform you if any special compiler flags are required. We have too include math.h file in our program if we are using math functions like sqrt(), abs() etc.

2.37 SHORTCUT KEYS OF TURBO C++

A hot key is one that works consistently. These are keys which are either used along like Function Keys (F1–F12) or with a key combination like Alt or Ctrl or shift or all of these with one single character only. Note that the bottom quick reference line of main Turbo-C++ screen normally shows the most appropriate hot function keys for your current situation. If you hold down the Alt key by itself for a few seconds, the quick reference line will switch to show you what Alt plus the function keys will perform. Below is the Table displaying the list of all the hot keys:

Function Key	Meaning
F1	Help menu
F2	Save the current program to disk.
F3	Provide a load window to enter file name for loading and saving.
F4	It is a toggle key. It zoom or Unzoom the active window.
F5	Traverse the program line by line.
F6	It is used to switch to the active window
F7	It moves the control to the Previous Error.
F8	It moves the control to the next error.
F9	It invoke the project-make.
F10	goto top line of the main menu and highlight the File Menu. In other words invoke the main menu.
Alt + F1	It is used to redisplay previous Help Screen.
Alt + F3	Pick file window
Alt + F9	Used for compilation Process. In the otherwords, it compile current file to .OBJ
Alt+F10	It is used to display version / Copy right notice.
Alt + C	Used to Pull Down Compile Menu.
Alt + D	Used to Pull Down Debug Menu
Alt + E	Used to Pull Down Edit Menu
Alt + F	Used to Pull Down File Menu
Alt + O	Used to Pull Down Option Menu
Alt + P	Used to Pull Down Project – Make Menu
Alt + R	Used to Run the current Menu
Alt + X	It is used to Exit from Turbo C++ and Move to the DOS Prompt or Window Desktop
Ctrl + F9	Used to run the program. convert compile file .obj to executed file .exe.
Ctrl + Del	To delete the selected text.
ESC	ESC is general menu – exit key. To exit from Turbo C++.

PROGRAMMING PROBLEMS

Program 1: Write a C++ program to display Hello: output String.

Program 2: Write a C++ program to display Hello and your name.

Program 3: Write a C++ program main function.

Program 4: Write a C++ program to assign value to a variable.

Program 5: Write a C++ program to finding the size of a type.

Program 6: Write a C++ program to convert feet to meters using doubles.

Program 7: Write a C++ program for float point constant number.

Program 8: Write a C++ program to read float number from console.

Program 9: Write a C++ program for pointer to long value.

Program 10: Write a C++ program to compute the gain and gain percentage of any computer device having cost price and selling price.

Program 11: Write a C++ program to compute the speed of a car if car covers 600meter long distance in 5 minutes.

Program 12: Write a C++ program to If a five-digit number is input through the keyboard, write a program to reverse the number.

Program 13: Write a C++ program to If a four digit number is input through the keyboard ,white a program to obtain the sum of the first and last digit of this number.

Program 14: Write a C++ program to In a town, the percentage of men is 52. The percentage of total literacy is 48. if total percentage of literate men is 35 of the total population, write a program to find the total number of illiterate men and women if the population of the town is 80,000.

Program 15: Write a C++ program a cashier has currency notes of denomination 10, 50 and 100. if the amount to be withdrawn is input through the keyboard, find the total number of currency notes of each denomination the cashier will have to give to the withdrawer.

Program 16: Write a C++ program if the total selling price of 15 items and the total profit earned on them is input through the keyboard, write a program to find the cost price of one item.

Program 17: Write a C++ program if a five-digit number is input through the keyboard, write a program to print a new number by adding one to each of its digits. For example, if the number that is input is 12391 then the output should be displayed as 23402.

Program 18: Write a C++ program to compute $(a+b)^3$.

Program 19: Write a C++ program to calculate gross salary of person.

Fill in the blanks

1. Every C++ program begins execution at the function ....
2. The .... begins the body of every function and the .... ends the body of every function.
3. Every C++ statement ends with a ....
4. The escape sequence \n represents the .... character, which causes the cursor to position to the beginning of the next line on the screen.
5. The escape sequence \t represents the .... character.
6. The .... statement is used to make decisions.

Answers:

1. main. 2. left brace ({), right brace (}). 3. semicolon. 4. newline. 5. horizontal tab. 6. if.

OBJECTIVE TYPE QUESTIONS

1. A C++ variable cannot start with
   (a) An alphabet
   (b) A number
   (c) A special symbol other than underscore
   (d) Both (2) & (3) above
2. Which is not a character of C++?
   (a) $ (b) ^
   (c) ~ (d) !
3. Which is not a keyword in C++?
   (a) const (b) main
   (c) sizeof (d) void
4. Identify the scalar data type in C++.
   (a) double (b) union
   (c) function (d) array
5. Identify the derived data type in C++.
   (a) int (b) float
   (c) union (d) char
6. Integral data type includes
   (a) enum (b) int
   (c) char (d) all the above

7. The qualifier that may proceed double is
   (a) signed (b) unsigned
   (c) short (d) long
8. A character constant is written within
   (a) double quotes (b) single quotes
   (c) options a and b (d) none of the above
9. String constants are represented within
   (a) single quotes (b) double quotes
   (c) options a and b (d) * and *\
10. An integer constant in C++ must have:
   (a) At least one digit (b) Atleast one decimal point
   (c) A comma along with digits (d) Digits separated by commas
11. A character variable can never store more than
   (a) 32 characters (b) 8 characters
   (c) 254 characters (d) 1 character
12. In C++ a variable cannot contain
   (a) Blank spaces (b) Hyphen
   (c) Decimal point (d) All the above
13. Which of the following is FALSE in C++
   (a) Keywords can be used as variable names
   (b) Variable names can contain a digit
   (c) Variable names do not contain a blank space
   (d) Capital letters can be used in variable names
14. A declaration float a,b; occupies .... of memory
   (a) 1byte (b) 4bytes
   (c) 8bytes (d) 16 bytes
15. What will be the maximum size of a double variable?
   (a) 1byte (b) 4bytes
   (c) 8bytes (d) 16 bytes
16. What will be the maximum size of a float variable?
   (a) 1byte (b) 4bytes
   (c) 8bytes (d) 16 bytes
17. String constants should be enclosed between ....
   (a) Single quotes (b) double quotes
   (c) both a and b (d) none of these

18. Character constants should be enclosed between ....
    (a) Single quotes (b) double quotes
    (c) both a and b (d) none of these
19. Identify the escape sequence(s)
    (a) \0 (b) \n
    (c) \f (d) all the above
20. Which is not a white space character(s)
    (a) \f (b) \v
    (c) \0 (d) blank
21. What is an object in C++?
    (a) constant (b) variable
    (c) identifier (d) keyword
22. Identify the C++ token(s)
    (a) keywords (b) constants
    (c) operators (d) all the above
23. Statement terminator is represented by
    (a) : (b) blank
    (c) ; (d) \n
24. Identify the number of tokens in the following:
    if (age == 21)
    (a) 4 (b) 5
    (c) 6 (d) 7
25. Identify the separators in C++.
    (a) white space character (b) comment
    (c) options a and b (d) semicolon
26. Among the following, which escape sequence does not have any specific meaning?
    (a) '\t' (b) '\a'
    (c) '\b' (d) '\c'
27. The escape sequence character '\x07' is equivalent to the character.
    (a) '\a' (b) '\b'
    (c) '\r' (d) '\f'
28. Which of the following is an example of compounded assignment statement?
    (a) a =5 (b) a+=5
    (c) a=b=c (d) a=b

29. The operator && is an example for .... operator.
    (a) Assignment (b) Increment
    (c) Logical (d) Rational
30. The operator & is used for
    (a) Bitwise AND (b) Bitwise OR
    (c) Logical AND (d) Logical OR
31. The operator / can be applied to
    (a) integer values (b) float values
    (c) double values (d) all of these
32. The equality operator is represented by
    (a) := (b) .EQ.
    (c) = (d) ==
33. Operators have hierarchy. It is used to know which operator
    (a) is most important (b) is used first
    (c) is faster (d) operates on large numbers
34. The bitwise AND operator is used for
    (a) Masking (b) Comparison
    (c) Division (d) Shifting bits
35. The bitwise OR operator is used to
    (a) set the desired bits to 1 (b) set the desired bits to 0
    (c) divide numbers (d) multiply numbers
36. Which of the following operator has the highest precedence?
    (a) * (b) ==
    (c) => (d) +
37. Which operator has the lowest priority?
    (a) ++ (b) %
    (c) + (d) ||
38. Which operator has the highest priority?
    (a) ++ (b) %
    (c) + (d) ||
39. Which is executed quickly?
    (a) p + + (b) + + p
    (c) options a and b (d) p + 1

40. p + + executes faster than p + 1 since
    (a) p uses register
    (b) single machine instruction is required for p + +
    (c) Options a and b (d) none of the above
41. Of the following, which are logical operators?
    (a) && (b) !
    (c) || (d) options a , b and c
42. In a C++ expression, how is a logical AND represented?
    (a) || (b) .AND
    (c) @@ (d) &&
43. Which of the following is a ternary operator?
    (a) ? : (b) *
    (c) sizeof (d) ^
44. Which of the following is not a bitwise operator?
    (a) & (b) ^
    (c) | (d) ||
45. The type cast operator is
    (a) & (b) cast ( )
    (c) // (d) " "
46. What would be the output of the expression 11 ^ 5?
    (a) 6 (b) 8
    (c) 14 (d) 15
47. The operator + in a+=4 means
    (a) a = a + 4 (b) a + 4 = a
    (c) a = 4 (d) a = 4 + 4
48. The number of binary arithmetic operators in C is
    (a) 5 (b) 4
    (c) 6 (d) 7
49. The number of unary arithmetic operators in C is
    (a) 1 (b) 4
    (c) 3 (d) 2
50. Identify the operator not used in C++.
    (a) ~ (b) %
    (c) ^ (d) * *

51. Which of the following statements will display the work “Hello” on the computer screen?

(a) cin << “Hello”; (b) cin >> “Hello”;

(c) cout << “Hello”; (d) cout >> “Hello”; (e) None

52. Which of the following is the extraction operator?

(a) >> (b) <<

(c) // (d) /*

(e) Both (a) and (b)

53. Which of the following statements allows the user to enter data at the keyboard?

(a) cin << currentPay; (b) cin >> currentPay;

(c) cout << currentPay; (d) cout >> currentPay;

(e) None

54. The standard output stream, which refers to the computer screen, is called ....

(a) cin (b) cout

(c) stin (d) stout

(e) None

55. The standard input stream, which refers to the keyboard, is called ....

(a) cin (b) cout

(c) stin (d) stout

(e) None

56. Which of the following is the insertion operator?

(a) >> (b) <<

(c) // (d) /*

(e) both (a) and (b)

EXERCISES

1. What are the C-tokens?
2. Explain the character set of C++ language.
3. What are keywords and identifiers?
4. What are constants? Explain different types of constants in detail.
5. What are variables? How we can declare and assign the value to a variable.
6. What are data types? Explain different data types in detail.

7. What are the various modifiers used in C++ language?
8. Explain the general or basic structure of a complete C++ program with or without classes.
9. Explain the concept of loading, editing, saving, compiling and executing a C++ program.
10. Explain local and global variables in detail.
11. What are the four C++ scopes?
12. What do you mean by symbolic constants? How we can define a symbolic constant.
13. How we can define constant with the const keyword.
14. Explain various delimiters of C++ language.
15. What do you mean by operator?
16. What are the different categories of operators?
17. What are the various types of operators used in the c programming?
18. Explain various arithmetic operators used in C++ language.
19. Explain various relational operators used in C++ language.
20. Differentiate between comparison and equality operator.
21. Explain various logical operators used in C++ language.
22. Differentiate between increment and decrement operator.
23. Explain various bitwise operators used in C++ language.
24. Explain the following expressions in detail.
    (a) Arithmetic Expression
    (b) Relational Expression
    (c) Logical Expression
25. Differentiate between simple assignment and shorthand assignment operator.
26. Write short notes on l-value and r-value.
27. Why conditional operator is called ternary operator?
28. What is the role of sizeof () operator?
29. How can you solve an arithmetic expression? Explain by taking an appropriate example.
30. Write down the hierarchy of operators or the order of precedence of all the operators used in the c programming?
31. What are the various types of library functions used in C++ language?
32. Explain various mathematical and trigonometric functions.
33. Differentiate between = and == operator.

34. How an expression with increment and decrement operators will be solved?
35. Explain the concept of compound bitwise operators.
36. Explain the concept of type operator (type conversion).
37. Explain the concept of output using cout.
38. Explain the concept of input using cin.

CHAPTER 3

Control Statements

3.1 INTRODUCTION

In programming, as in life, you have to make decisions and act on them. C++ provides control statements and loops to help your program take action. You may want to repeat a set of instructions based on some condition or state, for example, or even change the program execution sequence. The **control statements** are the statements whose execution results in a choice being made as to which of two or more paths should be followed.

This chapter discusses the three primary types of control structures: decision, looping and jumping. Actually all the function and statements used in the control statements can be used according to the given problem. These includes the conditional construct if and switch which control the flow in a particular directions according to the true or false facts. Similarly it includes the loop constructs while, do-while and for, which control the flow in a repetitive or iterative manners. Also jumping statements like break and continue, controls change the flow of programming according to the given conditions in the looping environment.

Most program control statements in any computer language including C++ rely on a conditional test that determines what action is to be taken. The conditional test produces either a true or false. Unlike many other computer languages that specify special value for true or false, a true value in C++ is any nonzero value including negative numbers. A false value is zero. This approach to true and false value is implemented in C++ primarily because it allows a wide range of routines to be coded very efficiently and easily with fast processing speed.

3.2 CONTROL STATEMENTS

A program consists of a number of statements which are usually executed in sequence. Programs can be much more powerful if we can control the order in which statements are run. To handle such types of statements, some flow controls required. These flow controls are called ***Control statements or Control structure***.

The C++ language program follows a sequential form of execution of statements. Many times it is required to alter the flow of sequence of instructions. C++ language provides statements that can alter the flow of a sequence of instructions. These statements are called as control statements.

Control statements are used to control the cursor in a program according to the condition or according to the requirement in a loop.

There are three types of control statements or flow controls:

1. Branching Statements
2. Looping Statements
3. Jumping Statements

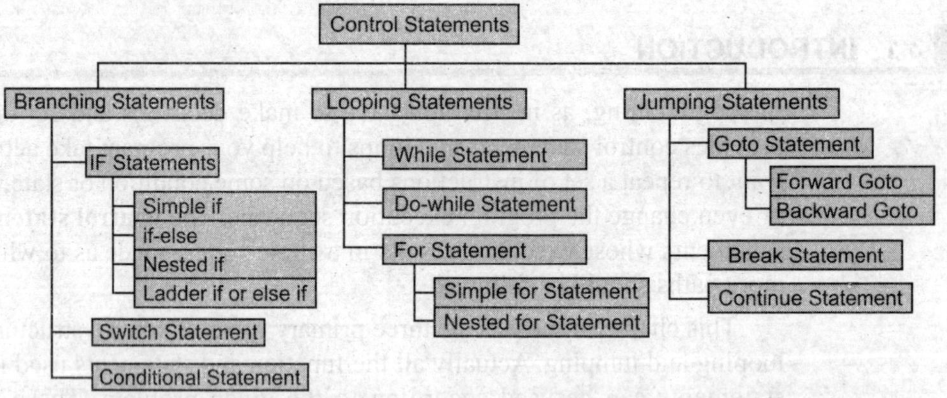

3.3 BRANCHING STATEMENTS OR DECISION MAKING STATEMENTS

We have seen that a C++ program is a set of statements, which are normally executed sequentially in the order in which they appear. This happens when no repetitions of certain calculations are necessary. However, in practice, we have a number of situations where we may have to change the order of execution of statements based on certain conditions are met.

C++ language possesses such decision making capabilities and supports the following statements known as Branching or decision-making statements.

C++ supports many branching statements depending upon their flow of control and according to their decision making policy. These are used when a condition arises in a statement. Branching Statement are of following categories:

1. If Statements
2. Switch Statement
3. Conditional Statement

3.3.1 If Statement

The if statement is the simplest form of the control statement. It is very frequently used in allowing the flow of program execution and decision making. *If* statement is a basic control flow structure of C++ programming language.

The if statement is a powerful decision making statement which can handle a single condition or group of statements. These have either true or false action.

There are mainly four types of if statements used in the C++ programming as:

(i) Simple if statement

(ii) if-else statement

(iii) nested if statement

(iv) else-if or ladder if or multi-condition if statement

(i) Simple if statement

The if statement is used when a unit of code need to be executed by a condition true or false. If the condition is true, the code in *if* block will execute otherwise it does nothing. In simple if statement, we have only one block called true-statement block.

The general syntax is:

```
if (condition)
{
/*True-statement block is executed.*/
}
Statement – x;
```

Flow-Chart of Simple if statement is:

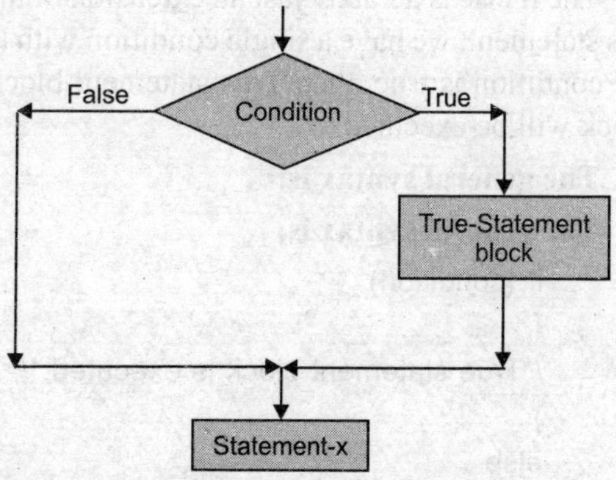

In the above flowchart, first of all condition will be checked. If the condition is true, then the True-statement block will be executed and after execution of this block, Statement– x will be executed. But if condition is false, then only statements-x will be executed.

Note: In both cases Statement-x will be executed.

Program 1: Write a C++ program to check whether the candidate's age is greater than 17 or not. Ifyes, display message "Eligble for voting".

```
#include<iostream.h>
#include<conio.h>
void main()
{
int age;
clrscr();
cout<<" Enter age:"<<endl;
cin>>age;
if(age>17)
cout<<"Eligible for voting";
getch();
}
```

Output:

```
Enter age:20
Eligible for voting
```

(ii) if-else statement

In this case you want to use both condition of *if* statement, you can use if-else statement. If the condition of *if* statement is false the code block in *else* will be executed.

The if else is actually just an extension of the general format of if statement. In this statement, we have a single condition with two different blocks. If the result of the condition is true, then True statement block is executed else False statement block will be executed.

The general syntax is:

The general syntax is:

```
if (condition)
{
/*True statement block is executed.*/;
}
else
{
/*False statement block is executed.*/;
}
Statement-x;
```

Flow-Chart of if-else statement is:

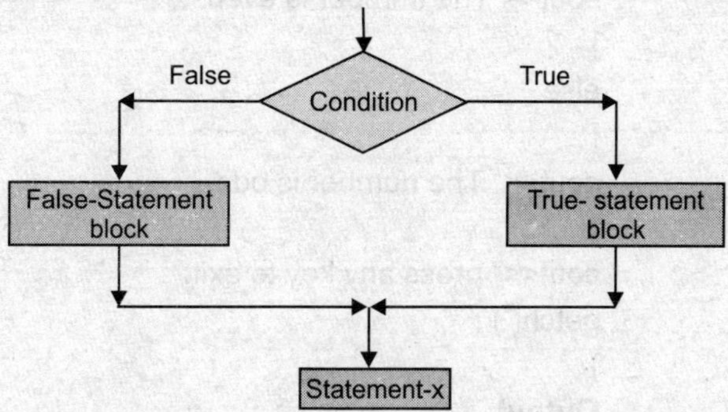

In the above flowchart, first of all condition will be checked. If condition is true then True statement block will be executed and after execution of true statement block, Statement-x will be executed, but if in case condition is false then first false block statements will be executed and then Statement-x will be executed.

Note: In both cases Statement-x will be executed.

Difference between if and If-else Statements

IF STATEMENT	IF ELSE STATEMENT
1. In if statement, if the condition is true then true block is executed & then statement x will be executed.	In if else statement, if the condition is true then true block is executed otherwise false block is executed. In both cases statement x will be executed.
2. Here we use two keywords called if and else.	Here we use only one keyword called if.
3. We have two blocks one is called true block other is false block.	We have only one block called true block.

Program 2: Write a C++ program to find out whether it is an odd number or even number. Any integer is input through the keyboard.

```
#include<iostream.h>
#include<conio.h>
void main()
{
int n ;
clrscr( ) ;
cout<<"Enter any number:" <<endl;
cin>>n) ;
if (n%2 = = 0)
```

```
{
cout<<"The number is even" ;
}
else
{
cout<<" The number is odd" ;
}
cout<<" press any key to exit.";
getch( ) ;
}
```

Output:

```
Enter any number:12
The number is even
Press any key to exit.
```

Compound Relational Tests

To perform compound relational tests, C++ language provides the necessary mechanisms. A compound relational test is simple one or more simple relational tests joined together by either the logical OR operators or logical AND. These operators are represented by character pairs && // respectively. To form complex expressions in C++, the compound operators can be used.

The general syntax is:

```
if (condition1 Logical operator condition2)
Or
if (condition1 Logical operator condition2 Logical operator condition3)
```

For Example:

```
if (condition1 && condition2)
if (condition1 // condition2 // condition3)
```

Program 3: Write a C++ program to verify is a number is divisible by 3 & 5 or not.

```
#include<iostream.h>
#include<conio.h>
void main()
{
int n;
cout<<"\n Enter the number:";
cin>>n;
if((n%3==0)&&(n%5==0))
{
```

```
cout<<"\n Its divisible by 3 and 5.";
}
else
{
cout<<"\n Its not divisible by 3 and 5.";
}
getch();
}
```

Output:

Enter the number:35

Its not divisible by 3 and 5.

(iii) Nested if Statement

The if statement may itself contain another if statement is called as nested if statement. This statement is some complex than the simple if or if-else statement, but is very useful to solve real world problems.

The general syntax is:

```
if (condition-1)
{
if (condition-2)
{
/*Truc statement blcok is executed (ST1).*/
}
else
{
/*False statement block is executed (SF1).*/
}
}
else
{
if (condition-3)
{
/*True statement block is executed (ST2)/*/
}
else
{
/*False statement block is executed (SF2).*/
}
}
Statement-x;
```

Flow-Chart of Nested-if statement is:

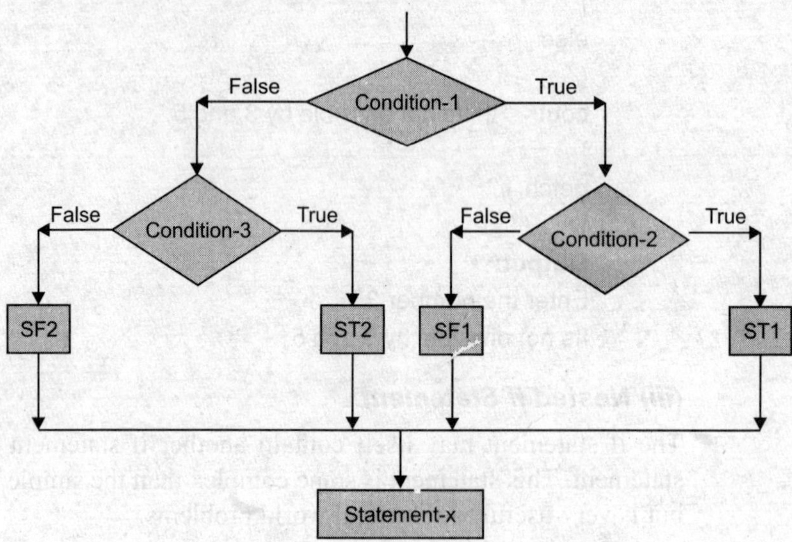

In the above flowchart, first of all condition-1 will be checked. If condition-1 is true, then further condition-2 will be checked. If condition-2 is true, then first true statement block (ST1) will be executed and after execution of ST1, statement-x will be executed. But if condition-2 is false, then first of all false statement block (SF1) will be executed and then statement-x will executed.

Similarly if condition-1 becomes false, then condition-3 will be checked. If condition-3 becomes true, then True statement block (ST2) will be executed and after execution of this block statement-x will be executed. But if condition-3 becomes false, then first false statement block (SF2) will be executed and then statement-x will executed.

***Note:** In all the cases statement-x will be executed.*

Difference between If-else and Nested-if Statements

IF ELSE STATEMENT	NESTED IF STATEMENT
1. It is easy to use & understand.	It is complex decision making statement.
2. Here we have only one condition & two blocks for execution (True & False).	Here we use number of conditions acc. to solve the problem.
3. We cannot use if within another if statement.	Here we use if statement within another if that,s why it is called nested if.

Program 4: Write a C++ program to find greatest number among three integer numbers.

```
#include<iostream.h>
#include<conio.h>
#include<dos.h>
void main()
{
int a,b,c,g;
cout<<endl;
cout<<"Enter the three numbers:";
cin>>a>>b>>c;
if(a>b)
{
if(a>c)
{
g=a;
}
else
{
g=c;
}
}
else
{
if(b>c)
{
g=b;
}
else
{
g=c;
}
}
cout<<endl;
cout<<"Greatest number is: "<<g;
getch();
}
```

Output:

Enter the three numbers: 20 30 10

Greatest number is: 30

(iv) Ladder if or else if statement

There is another way of putting ifs together when multipath decisions are involved. A multipath decision is a chain of ifs in which the statement associated with each else is an if.

When in a complex problem number of conditions arise in a sequence, then we can use Ladder-if or else if statement to solve the problem in a simple manner.

The general syntax is:

```
if (condition-1)
{
/*True statement block is executed (ST1).*/
}
else if (condition-2)
{
/*True statement block is executed (ST2).*/
}
else if (condition-3)
{
/*True statement block is executed (ST3).*/
}
...
...
else if (condition-n)
{
/*True statement block is executed (STn).*/
}
else
{
/*False statement block is executed (SFn).*/
}
statement-x;
```

Flow-Chart of Ladder-if statement is:

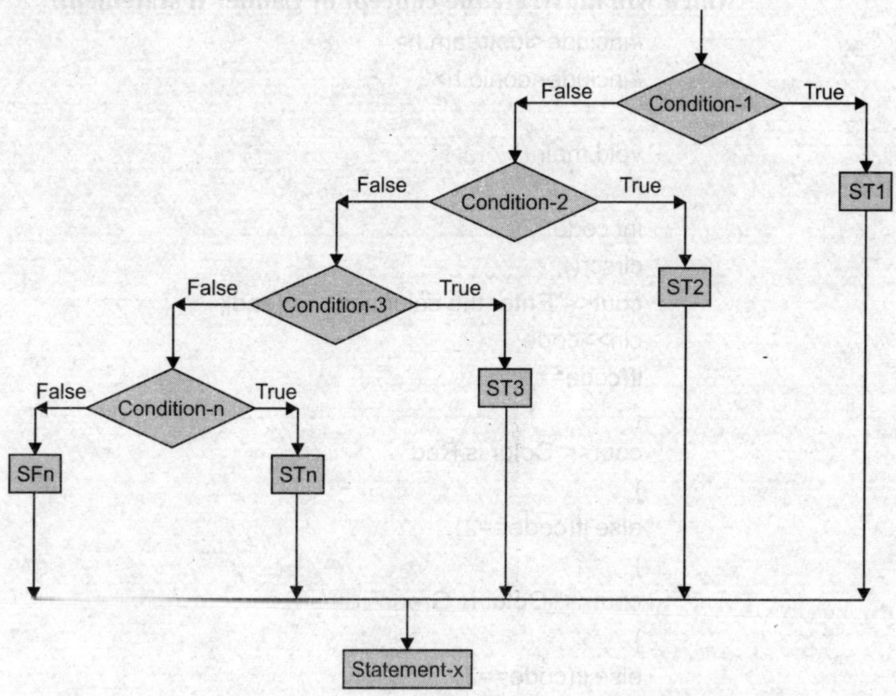

In the above flowchart, first condition-1 will be checked, if it is true then True statement block (ST1) will be executed, and then statement-x will executed, otherwise further next condition-2 will be checked. If the next condition-2 is true then True statement block (ST2) will be executed, and then statement-x will executed, otherwise further next condition will be checked and this process will continue till the end of the condition. If all the given condition becomes false then false statement block (SFn) is executed and then statement-x will executed.

Note: *In all the cases statement-x will be executed.*

Difference between Nested-if and Else-if Statements

Nested if statement	Lladder if or else-if statement
1. It is complex decision making statement.	It is more complex than nested if.
2. Here we apply any number of conditions but every condition can have two blocks (True & False).	Here we can apply any number of conditions but every condition can have one block called true block.

Program 5: Write a C++ program to display the color according to its code which will illustrate the concept of Ladder if statement.

```
#include<iostream.h>
#include<conio.h>

void main()
{
int code;
clrscr();
cout<<"Enter the color code:"<<endl;
cin>>code;
if(code==1)
{
cout<<"Color is Red";
}
else if(code==2)
}
cout<<" Color is Green";
}
else if(code==3)
{
cout<<" Color is White";
}
else if(code==4)
{
cout<<"Color is Yellow";
}
else
{
cout<<" No Color code defined";
}
cout<<endl;
cout<<" End of the Program ";
getche();
}
```

Output:

```
Enter the color code: 2
Color is Green
End of the Program
```

3.3.2 Switch Statement

When the multiple conditions occurs in a problem and it is difficult to solve such type of complex problem with the help of ladder if statement, then there is need of such type of statement which should have different alternatives or different cases to solve the problem in simple, easy and efficient way. For this purpose Switch statement is used. It is also called **Case Control statement** because it controls different cases and different blocks.

Unlike the If statement which allows a selection of two alternatives the switch statement allows a program to select one statement for execution out of a set of alternatives. During the execution of the switch statement only one of the possible statements will be executed the remaining statements will be skipped. The usage of multiple If else statement increases the complexity of the program since when the number of If else statements increase it affects the readability of the program and makes it difficult to follow the program. The switch statement removes these disadvantages by using a simple and straight forward approach.

The switch-case statement is a multi-way decision making statement. Unlike the multiple decision statement that can be created using ladder-if, the switch statement evaluates the conditional expression and tests it against the numerous constant values.

During execution, the branch corresponding to the value that the expression matches is taken. The value of the expressions in a switch-case statement must have to be an ordinal type i.e. integer, char, short, long, etc. Double and Float are not allowed.

The general syntax is:

```
switch (exp or var)
{
case value1:
/*True statemnt block is executed (ST1).*/
break;
case value2:
/*True statement block is executed (ST2).*/
break;
case value3:
/*True statement block is executed (ST3).*/
break;
...
...
case value n:
```

```
/*True statement block is executed (STn).*/
break;
default:
/*This block is executed when no condition met (Execute default action).*/
}
Statement-x;
```

Where exp is an arithmetic expression and var is the variable.

Flow-Chart of switch statement is:

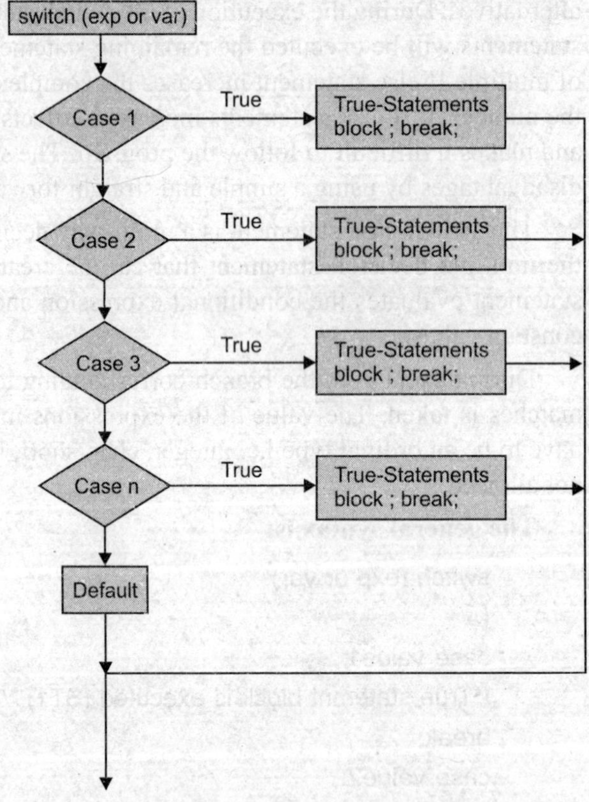

Working of Switch Statement

In the *switch* statement, the selection is determined by the value of an expression that you specify which is enclosed between the parentheses after the keyword *switch*. The data type of value which is returned by expression must be an integer value otherwise the statement will not compile.

The case constant expression must be an integer value and all values in case statement are equal. When a *break* statement is executed, it causes execution to continue with the statement following the closing brace for the switch. The *break* statement is not mandatory, but if you don't put a *break* statement at the end of the statements for a case, the statements for the next case in sequence will be executed as well, through to whenever another break is found or the end of the switch block is reached. This can lead some unexpected program logics happen.

The *default* statement is the default choice of the switch statement if all cases statement are not satisfy with the expression. The *break* after the default statements is not necessary unless you put another case statement below it.

Difference between Else-if and Switch Statements

Else if statement	Switch statement
1. It is complex statement.	It is easy to use & understand.
2. It cannot have different cases for different conditions.	It can have different cases for different conditions.
3. It is also called ladder if statement.	It is also called case control statement.
4. Here we use else if keyword.	Here we can use switch keyword.
5. In this we can use relational & logical operators.	In this we cannot use relational & logical operators.

Program 6: Write a C++ menu driven program which has following options:

1. Factorial of a number.
2. Prime or not
3. Odd or even
4. Exit

Once a menu item is selected the appropriate action should be teken and once this action is finished, the menu should reappear. Unless the user selects the 'Exit' option the program should continue to work.

```
#include<iostream.h>
#include<conio.h>
void main()
{
int choice, num, i ;
unsigned long int fact ;
clrscr();
while (1)
{
cout<<"1. Factorial\n";
cout<<"2. Prime\n";
```

```
cout<<"3. Odd / Even\n";
cout<<"4. Exit\n";
cout<<"\nYour choice ?";
cin>>choice ;
switch ( choice )
{
case 1 :
cout<<"\nEnter number:";
cin>>num ;
fact = 1 ;
for (i=1;i<=num ;i++)
fact = fact * i;
cout<<"\n Factorial value = \n"<< fact ;
break ;// Takes control out of switch
case 2 :
cout<<"\n Enter number:";
cin>>num ;
for(i=2;i<num;i++)
{
 if (num%i== 0 )
{
cout<<"\n Not a prime number.\n";
break ; // Takes control out of for loop
}
}
if (i==num)
cout<<"\n Prime number.\n";
break ; // Takes control out of switch
case 3 :
cout<<"\nEnter number:";
cin>>num ;
if ( num %2==0 )
cout<<"\n Even number.\n";
else
cout<<"\nOdd number.\n";
break ; // Takes control out of switch
case 4 :
exit( ) ; // Terminates program execution
}
}
```

```
getch();
}
```

Output:

```
1. Factorial
2. Prime
3. Odd / Even
4. Exit
Your choice ?1
Enter number:5
factorial value=120
1. Factorial
2. Prime
3. Odd / Even
4. Exit
Your choice ?2
Enter number:12
Not a prime number.
1. Factorial
2. Prime
3. Odd / Even
4. Exit
Your choice ?3
Enter number:12
Even number.
1. Factorial
2. Prime
3. Odd / Even
4. Exit
Your choice ?4
Exit
```

Nested Switch

The Switch statement may itself contain another switch statement is called as nested nested switch statement. This statement is some complex than the simple switch statement, but is very useful to solve real world problems.

Program 7: Write a C++ program to detect whether the entered number is even or odd. Use nested switch() case statement.

```
#include<iostream.h>
#include<conio.h>
```

```
void main()
{
int x,y;
clrscr();
cout<<"\n Enter a Number";
cin>>x;
switch(x)
{
case 0:
cout<<"\n Number is Even";
break;
case 1:
cout<<"\n Number is Odd";
break;
default:
y=x%2;
switch(y)
{
case 0:
cout<<"\n Number is Even";
break;
default:
cout<<"\n Number is Odd";
}
}
getch();
}
```

Output:

Enter a Number: 5
Number is Odd

3.3.3 Conditional Control Statement

This statement is based on conditional operator. This statement is used to solve the problem in a single line and is a fast executable operation. For this purpose, we can use conditional or ternary operator (? and :).

The general syntax is:

```
expression1 ? expression2: expression3;
```

It works like if-else statement that if expression1 is true then expression2 is executed but if expression1 is false then expression3 is executed. This is used for a single condition. Similarly for the nesting of condition, the conditional control statement has the general syntax as:

expression1? (expression2? expression3: expression4): expression5;

This is used for two conditions. Here first of all expression1 will be executed and if it is true, then further expression2 will be checked. If expression2 is true, then expression3 will be executed, otherwise expression4 will be executed. But if expression1 is false, then only the expression5 will be executed. This statement is work as nested if statement.

For example, Suppose if you want to compute the salary of a given function as described below on the basis of their basic pay (bp), then by using the nested conditional control statement in the C++ programming the procedure becomes very easier as compared to the nested if statement.

salary = { bp + 100 bp < 1000
2000 bp = 1000
4 bp + 2000 bp > 1000}

The program for the above said complex problem is as follows:

Program 8: Write a C++ program to solve the function by using the nested conditional statement.

```
#include<iostream.h>
#include<conio.h>
#include< dos.h>
void main()
{
int sal, bp;
clrscr();
cout<<"\n Enter the basic pay: ";
cin>>bp;
sal = (bp != 1000) ? ((bp < 1000) ? bp + 100 : 4 * bp + 2000) : 2000;
cout<<"\n Salary is Rs. "<< sal;
getche ( );
}
```

Output:

```
Enter the basic pay: 900
Salary is Rs. 1000.
```

3.4 LOOPING STATEMENTS

During looping a set of statements are executed until some conditions for termination of the loop is encountered. When a single statement or a group of statements will be executed again and again in a program (in an iterative way), then such type statement is called looping statements. A program loop therefore consists of two segments one known as body of the loop and other is the control statement. The control statement tests certain conditions and then directs the repeated execution of the statements contained in the body of the loop.

In looping process in general would include the following four steps:

1. Setting and initialization of a counter.
2. Execution of the statements in the loop.
3. Test for a specified conditions for the execution of the loop.
4. Incrementing the counter.

The test may be either to determine whether the loop has repeated the specified number of times or to determine whether the particular condition has been met.

A program loop consists of two segments:

(a) Body of the loop

(b) Control of loop

The control is tested always for execution of the body of the loop. Depending on the position of the control statement in the loop, a control may be classified into two parts:

(i) Entry Control loop

(ii) Exit Control loop

(i) Entry Control Loop

In this loop structure, first of all condition is checked, if it is true, then body of loop is executed, otherwise the control is moved out of the loop (we can exit from the loop, when the condition becomes false.)

For Example: The while loop and for loop is the example of the entry control loop.

(ii) Exit Control loop

In this loop structure, first of all body of loop is executed and then condition is checked. If condition is true, then again body of the loop is executed. If the condition is false, then control will move out from the loop.

For Example: The do-while statement is the example of the exit control loop.

C++ gives us a choice of three types of loop:

1. while Statement
2. do-while Statement
3. for Statement

3.4.1 While Statement

A loop statement allows you to execute a statement or block of statements repeatedly. The *while* loop is used when you want to execute a block of statements repeatedly with checked condition before making an iteration. While statement or while loop is an entry control loop.

The general syntax is:

```
while (test condition)
{
Body of Loop;
}
Statement-x;
```

Flow-Chart of while statement is:

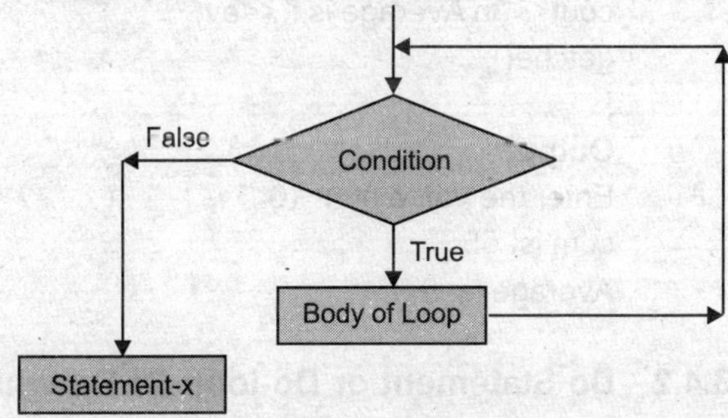

In the above flowchart, first of all condition is checked and if the condition is true then the body of the loop is executed. After the execution of the body, the test condition is once again checked and if it is true, the body is executed once again. This process of repeated execution of the body continues until the test condition finally becomes false and the control is transferred out of the loop. On exit, the program continues with the statements immediately after the body of the loop. The body of the loop may have one or more statements. The braces are needed only if the body contained two are more statements. But placing them is a good programming practice.

For example, Suppose if you want to find the average of first n positive integer numbers, then the program applied to compute the average by using the while loop is:

Program 9: Write a C++ program to find the average of N numbers using while() loop.

```
#include<iostream.h>
#include<conio.h>
void main()
{
int sum, n, i ;
float av;
cout<<"\n Enter the value of n:";
cin>>n;
sum=0;
i = 1;
while(i<=n)
{
sum= sum + i ;
i = i + 1;
}
cout<<"\n Sum is: "<<sum;
av=(float) sum/n;
cout<<"\n Average is :"<<av;
getche();
}
```

Output:

```
Enter the value of n: 10
sum is: 55
Average is: 5.5
```

3.4.2 Do Statement or Do-loop Or Do-while()

The do while loop is also a kind of loop, which is similar to the while loop in contrast to while loop, the do while loop tests at the bottom of the loop after executing the body of the loop. Since the body of the loop is executed first and then the loop condition is checked we can be assured that the body of the loop is executed at least once. do-while statement or do-loop is an exit control loop.

The general syntax is:

```
do
{
Body of Loop;
}
while (condition);
statement-x;
```

Flow-Chart of do-while statement is:

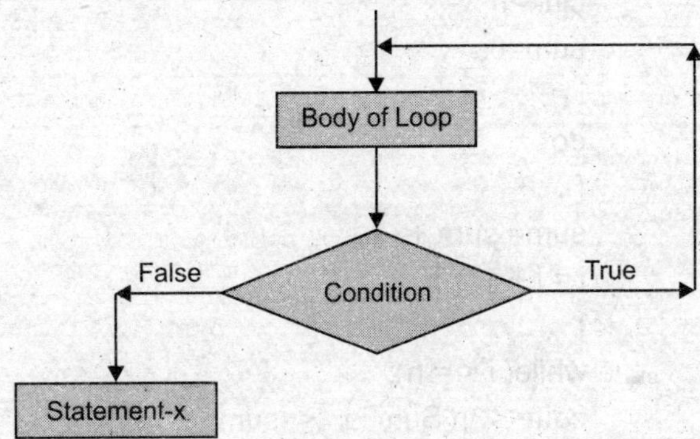

In the above flowchart, first of all the statement is executed, then condition is checked. If the condition is true then the body is executed again and this process continues till the condition becomes false. When the condition becomes false the loop terminates.

***Note:** Semicolon (;) must be at the end of the while condition.*

Difference between While and Do-while Statements

While statement	Do-while statement
1. It is also called entry control loop.	It is also called exit control loop.
2. In this statement, first of all condition is checked if condition is true then the body of loop is executed other-wise statement x will be executed.	In this statement, first of all body of loop is executed once then condition is checked if condition is true then again body of loop is executed otherwise statement x will be executed.
3. Here we use while keyword.	Here we can use do-while keyword.

For example as in the above said statement in the while loop, the average of n positive integer number by using the do-while loop can be computed as:

Program 10: Write a C++ program to find the average of N numbers using do-while() loop.

```
#include<iostream.h>
#include<conio.h>
void main()
{
int sum, n, i ;
float av;
```

```
cout<<"\n Enter the value of n:";
cin>>n;
sum=0;
i = 1;
do
{
sum= sum + i ;
i = i + 1;
}
while( i < = n);
cout<<"\n Sum is: "<<sum;
av=(float) sum/n;
cout<<"\n Average is :"<<av;
getch();
}
```

Output:

```
Enter the value of n: 10
sum is: 55
Average is: 5.5
```

***Note:** The do statement is similar to the while statement except that its termination condition is at the end of the body of the loop only. Thus, you want to use a do statement, if you want to perform the body of the loop at least once, regardless of the condition.*

3.4.3 For Statements or For Loop

The for statement allows for the controlled loop. The for loop works well where the number of iterations of the loop is known before the loop is entered. For statement is a powerful looping statement which can done initialization, test condition and increment/decrement in one step. It is fast and more efficient looping statements then while and do-while statement.

There are mainly two types of for statements used in the C++ programming as:

(i) Simple for statement

(ii) Nested for statement

(i) Simple for statement

The for loop is an entry-controlled loop that provides a more concise loop control structure. It is a looping statement, which repeat again and again till it satisfies the defined condition. It is one step loop, which initialize, check the condition and increment / decrement the step in the loop in a single statement.

The general syntax is:

```
for (initialization; test condition; increment/ decrement)
{
body of the loop;
}
statement-x;
```

Flow-Chart of for statement is:

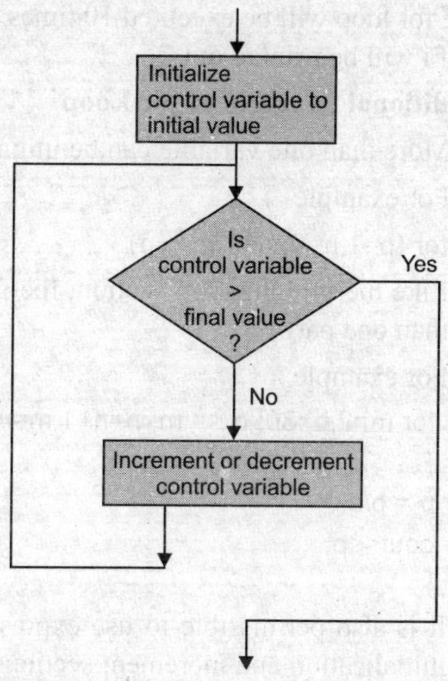

The execution of the for statement is as follows:

1. Initialization of the control variables is done first, using assignment statements
   such as **i = 1** and **count = 0**. The variables i and count are known as the loop control variables.
2. The value of the control variable is tested using the test-condition. The test-condition is a relational expression, such as **i<10** that determines when the loop will exit. If the condition is true, the body of the loop is executed; otherwise the loop is terminated and the execution continues with the statement that immediately follows the loop.
3. When the body of the loop is executed, the control is transferred back to the for statement after checking the last statement in the loop. Now, the control variable is incremented using an assignment statement such as **i = i+1** and the new value of the control variable is again tested to see whether it satisfies the loop condition. If the condition is satisfied, the body of the loop is again

executed. This process continues till the value of the control variable fails to satisfy the test-condition.

For Example

```
for( i = 0; i<10; i = i+1)
{
cout<<i;
}
```

The for loop will be executed 10 times. Each time a value equal to the current value of i will be printed out.

Additional Features of for Loop

1. More than one variable can be initialized at a time in the for statement.

   For example

   for (p=1,n=0; n<18; ++n)

2. Like the initialization section, the increment section may also have more than one part.

   For example

   ```
   for (a=2,b=30; n <= m; n=n+1,m=m-1)
   {
   p = b/a;
   cout<<p;
   }
   ```

3. It is also permissible to use expressions in the assignment statements of initialization and increment sections.

   For example

   for (w = (a+b); w>0; w=w/2) is valid.

4. One or more sections in the for statement can be omitted, if necessary. For example

   ```
   e = 2;
   for (; e != 10 ;)
   {
   cout<<e;
   e = e + 2;
   }
   ```

Both the initialization and increment sections are omitted in the for statement. In such cases, the sections are left blank. However, the semicolons separating the sections must remain. If the test-condition is not present, the for statement sets up an infinite loop.

Program 11: Write a C++ program to find the average of N numbers by using the for loop.

```
#include<iostream.h>
#include<conio.h>
void main()
{
int n, i, sum;
float av;
clrscr();
cout<<"\n Enter the value of N: ";
cin>>n;
for( i =1; i <=n; i++)
{
sum= sum+ i;
}
cout<<"\n Sum is: "<< sum;
av= (float) sum/n;
cout<<"\n Average is: "<< av;
getche(();
}
```

Output:

Enter the value of n: 10
Sum is: 55
Average is: 5.5

(ii) Nested for statement

When a for statement is executed within another for statement, then it is called nested for statement. We can apply number of nested for statements in C++ language.

The general syntax is:

```
for (initialization1; test condition1; increment1 / decrement)
{
    for (initialization2; test condition2; increment2 / decrement2)
    {
    inner-body of the loop.
    }
    outer-body of theloop;
}
statement-x;
```

For one value of outer loop, inner loop will repeat upto test condition2. So inner loop will be completed first and then outer loop will be completed. After completion of inner and outer loop, statement-x will be executed.

3.5 JUMPING STATEMENTS

There are three different controls used to jump from one C++ program statement to another and make the execution of the programming procedure fast. These three Jumping controls are:

1. goto statement
2. break statement
3. continue statement

3.5.1 Goto Statement

The goto statement is simple statement used to transfer the program control unconditionally from one statement to another statement. The go to moves the controls on a specified address called label or label name. The goto requires a label in order to identify the place where the branch is to be made. A label is a valid variable name followed by a colon.

The label is placed immediately before the statement where the control is to be transformed. A program may contain several goto statements that transferred to the same place when a program. The label must be unique. Control can be transferred out of or within a compound statement, and control can be transferred to the beginning of a compound statement. However the control cannot be transferred into a compound statement. The goto statement is discouraged in C++, because it alters the sequential flow of logic that is the characteristic of C ++ language.

Although it might not be essential to use the goto statement in a highly structured language like C++, there may be occasions when the use of goto is desirable. The goto is mainly of two types. One is conditional and the other is unconditional.

Also jump can be either in forward direction or in backward direction. The different types of goto statement are:

(i) Forward goto

(ii) Backward goto

(i) Forward goto

In this the control moves forward at a specified label either according to a condition or without condition.

The general syntax is:

Unconditional forward goto statement

```
ST1;
ST2;
goto label;
ST3;
ST4;
label:
      ST5;
      ST6;
```

Conditional forward goto statement

```
ST1;
ST2;
if(condition)
goto label;
ST3;
ST4;
label:
      ST5;
      ST6;
```

Note that here first statement ST1 and ST2 will be executed, then specified label (in C++ language it is label name) and execute the statements ST5 and ST6. It will skip a part of the program i.e. ST3 and ST4 statements.

This concept can be illustrated with the help of following C++ program as:

(ii) Backward goto

The backward go to or backward jump moves the control back to the specified addresses and so creates a loop.

In the case of conditional backward statement, it creates finite looping. But in the case of unconditional backward go to or jump, it creates infinite looping.

The general syntax is:

```
ST1;
label:
ST2;
ST3;
goto label;
ST4;
```

Unconditional backward goto statement

```
ST1;
label:
ST2;
ST3;
if(condition)
goto label;
ST4;
```

Conditional backward goto statement

Here first of all statements ST1, ST2 and ST3 will be executed. Then it will find a backward go to statement with a specified address and again ST2, ST3 statement will repeat either according to a condition or infinite times if there is no condition. Below written example is of conditional backward goto:

3.5.2 Break Statement

Sometimes while executing a loop it becomes desirable to skip a part of the loop or quit the loop as soon as certain condition occurs, for example consider searching a particular number in a set of 100 numbers as soon as the search number is found it is desirable to terminate the loop. C++ language permits a jump from one statement to another within a loop as well as to jump out of the loop. The break statement allows us to accomplish this task. A break statement provides an early exit from for, while, do and switch constructs. A break causes the innermost enclosing loop or switch to be exited immediately.

The general syntax is:

```
break;
```

The use of break statement within the while loop structure is:

```
while (condition)
 {
 ...
 if (condition2)
  {
  break;
  }
 }
statement-x;
```

By using the structure of the for loop, the break statement is used as:

```
for (initial value; condition, increment / decrement)
{
if (condition-1)
  {
  break;
  }
}
statement-x;
```

As in the above structure, when condition-1 becomes true, then it will break the loop and quit from the for loop and move to the statement-x, i.e. after exiting from the for loop, statement-x will be executed.

3.5.3 Continue Statement

During loop operations it may be necessary to skip a part of the body of the loop under certain conditions. Like the break statement C++ supports similar statement called continue statement. The continue statement causes the loop to be continued with the next iteration after skipping any statement in between.

Continue statement also comes with if statement. This statement is also used within any loop statement like do loop, while loop and for statement.

The general syntax is:

```
continue;
```

This statement will skip some part of iteration (loop) and comes to the next looping step i.e. it will increment / decrement the loop value, when continue occurs.

The use of the continue statement within the while loop is:

```
while (condition-1)
{
ST1;
ST2;
if (condition-2)
{
continue;
}
ST3;
ST4;
}
Statement-x;
```

Similarly, The use of the continue statement within the do-while loop is:

```
do
{
ST1;
ST2;
if (condition-2)
{
continue;
}
ST3;
ST4;
}while(condition1)
Statement-x;
```

Also by using the for loop the continue statement be described as:

```
for (initial value; condition-1; increment/decrement
{
ST1;
ST2;
if (condition-2)
{
continue;
}
ST3;
ST4;
}
Statement-x;
```

In all the above structure, First of all the statement ST1 and ST2 will be executed. When a condition met within the loop and if the condition becomes true, then the continue statement be executed and it will move to start the next looping iteration by skipping the statement ST3 and ST4. When condition becomes false, then the statement ST3 and ST4 will execute. After completion of the loop, the statement-x will be executed.

Difference between Break and Continue Statements

Break Statement	Continue Statement
1. Break statement is used to break any type of loop such as while, do while and for loop.	Continue statement is used to break current iteration.
2. Break statement terminates the loop body immedimately.	In continue statement the control returns to the top of the loop test conditions.
3. Here we use keyword break.	Here we can use keyword continue.

PROGRAMMING PROBLEMS

Program 1: Write a C++ program to calculate the square of those numbers only whose least significant digit is 5.

Program 2: Write a C++ program to calculateenergy bill. Read the starting and ending meter reading, The charges are as follows

No. Of Units Consumed	*Rates in (Rs.)*
200-500	3.50
100-200	2.50
Less than 100	1.50

Program 3: Write a C++ program if cost price and selling price of an item are input through the keyboard, write a program to determine whether the seller has made profit or incurred loss. Also determine how much profit he made or loss he incurred.

Program 4: Write a C++ program to a five-digit number is entered through the keyboard. Write a program to obtain the reversed number and to determine whether the original and reversed numbers are equal or not.Program 5: Write a C++ program to implement the company policy.

Program 5: Write a C++ program to implement the company policy.

The policy followed by a company to process customer orders is given by the following rules:

(a) If a customer order quantity less than or equal to that in stock and his credit OK, supply his requirement.

(b) If his credit is not OK do not supply. Send him intimation.

(c) If his credit is OK but the item in stock is less than his order quantity, supply what is in stock. Intimate to him that the balance will be shipped.

Program 6: Write a C++ program if the three sides of a triangle are entered through the keyboard, write a program to cheek whether the triangle is isosceles, equilateral, scalene or right –angled triangle.

Program 7: Write a C++ program to check whether a triangle is valid or not, when the three angles of the triangle are entered through the keyboard. A triangle is valid if the sum of all the three angles is equal to 180 degrees.

Program 8: Write a C++ program to given the length and breadth of a rectangle, write a program to find whether the area of the rectangle is greater than its perimeter. For example, the area of the rectangle with length = 5 and breadth = 4 is greater than its perimeter.

Program 9: Write a C++ program to given three points (x1, y1), (x2, y2) and (x3, y3), write a program to check if all the three points fall on one straight line.

Program 10: Write a C++ program in a company, worker efficiency is determined on the basis of the time required for a worker to complete a particular job. If the time taken by the worker is between 2 - 3 hours, then the worker is said to be highly efficient. If the time required by the worker is between 3 – 4 hours, then the worker is ordered to improve speed. If the time taken is between 4 – 5 hours, the worker is given training to improve his speed, and if the time taken by the worker is more than 5 hours, then the worker has to leave the company. If the time taken by the worker is input through the keyboard, find the efficiency of the worker.

Program 11: Write a C++ program to find grade of student according to marks obtained:

1.) % above or equal to 71-Grade A
2. % between 50 to 69-Grade B
3. % between 40 to 49-Grade C
4. % less than 40-Fail

Program 12: Write a C++ program to provide multiple functions such as

1. Addition
2. Subtraction
3. Multiplication
4. Division
5. Remainder Calculation
6. Larger out of two by using switch() statement.

Program 13: Write a C++ program to given the coordinates (x, y) of a centre of a circle and its radius, write a program which will determine whether a point lies inside the circle, on the circle or outside the circle.

(***Hint:*** Use sqrt ( ) and pow ( ) functions)

Program 14: Write a C++ program to generate the pyramid structure using numerical.

```
   0
  101
 21012
3210123
```

Program 15: Write a C++ program to display output:

```
*****
 ***
 **
  *
```

Program 16: Write a C++ program to display output:

```
****
***
**
*
```

Program 17: Write a C++ program to display output:

```
  1
 101
10101
```

Program 18: Write a C++ program to produce the following output:

```
   1
  2 3
 4 5 6
7 8 9 10
```

Program 19: Write a C++ program to display output:

```
1
25
368
47910
```

Program 20: Write a C++ program to display output:

```
4567645
 34543
  232
   1
```

Fill in the blanks

1. All programs can be written in terms of three types of control structures: ...., and ....
2. The .... branching statement is used to execute one action when a condition is true or a different action when that condition is false.
3. Repeating a set of instructions a specific number of times is called .... looping.
4. For statement is in the category of .... control structures.
5. Goto is of two types: .... and ....
6. The optional case of switch selection statement is ....

Answers

1. Branching, looping, and jumping. 2. if-else. 3. definite 4. Looping. 5. Forward, backward 6. default

OBJECTIVE TYPE QUESTIONS

1. C++ supports how many basic looping constructs
   (a) 2 (b) 3
   (c) 4 (d) 6
2. A statement differs from expression by terminating with a
   (a) ; (b) :
   (c) NULL (d) .
3. What should be the expression return value for a do-while to terminate
   (a) 1 (b) 0
   (c) -1 (d) NULL
4. Which among the following is a unconditional control structure
   (a) do-while (b) if-else
   (c) goto (d) for
5. Continue statement is used
   (a) to go to the next iteration in a loop
   (b) come out of a loop
   (c) exit and return to the main function
   (d) restarts iterations from beginning of loop
6. Structural programming approach makes use of
   (a) modules (b) control structures
   (c) user defined data types (d) all the above
7. A statement is differentiated from an expression
   (a) by terminating it with a semicolon
   (b) by terminating it with a newline character
   (c) by terminating it by a null
   (d) by terminating it by a blank space
8. A null statement can be represented by a
   (a) newline (b) blank space
   (c) semicolon (d) colon
9. A block is enclosed within a pair of
   (a) { } (b) ( )
   (c) [ ] (d) <>
10. Identify the unconditional control structure

(a) do-while (b) switch case

(c) goto (d) if

11. Identify the loop construct

(a) if-else (b) switch case

(c) goto (d) while

12. The number of loop constructs in C is

(a) 2 (b) 3

(c) 4 (d) 5

13. The minimum number of times the while loop is executed is

(a) 0 (b) 1

(c) 2 (d) cannot be predicted

14. The minimum number of times the for loop is executed is

(a) 0 (b) 1

(c) 2 (d) cannot be predicted

15. The minimum number of times the do-while loop is executed is

(a) 0 (b) 1

(c) 2 (d) cannot be predicted

16. The do-while loop is terminated when the conditional expression returns

(a) zero (b) 1

(c) non-zero (d) -1

17. The break statement is used to exit from:

(a) an if statement (b) a for loop

(c) a program (d) the main( ) function

18. A do-while loop is useful when we want that the statements within the loop must be executed:

(a) Only once (b) At least once

(c) More than once (d) None of the above

19. In what sequence the initialization, testing and execution of body is done in a do-while loop?

(a) Initialization, execution of body, testing

(b) Execution of body, initialization, testing

(c) Initialization, testing, execution of body

(d) None of the above

20. Which of the following statement is used to take the control to the beginning of the loop?

(a) exit (b) break
(c) continue (d) None of the above

21. Which conditional expression always returns false value ?
(a) if (a = = 0) (b) if(a = 0)
(c) if (a = 10) (d) if (10= = a)

22. Which conditional expression always return true value ?
(a) if(a= 1) (b) if(a = = 1)
(c) if(a = 0) (d) if(1= = a)

23. Infinite loop is
(a) useful for time delay (b) useless
(c) used to terminate execution (d) not possible

24. What is the value of x in the expression x = (a= 10, a*a) ?
(a) invalid expression (b) 0
(c) 10 (d) 100

25. Comma is used as
(a) a separate in C++ (b) an operator in C++
(c) a delimiter in C++ (d) terminator in C++

26. The continue statement is used in
(a) selective control structure only (b) loop control structure only
(c) options a and b (d) switch case control structure only

27. C++ is an example of
(a) object oriented language (b) structured programming language
(c) object based language (d) component based language

28. The syntax of if statement is
(a) if expression then program statement
(b) if (expression) program statement
(c) if(expression) then program statement
(d) if expression { program statement}

29. Which is the correct statement?
(a) while loop can be nested
(b) for loop can be nested
(c) option a and b
(d) one type of a loop cannot be nested in another type of loop.

30. The break statement is used to
    (a) continue the next iteration of the loop construct
    (b) exit the block where it exists and continue further sequentially
    (c) exit the outer most block even if it occurs inside the inner most block and continue further sequentially
    (d) terminate the program
31. Identify the wrong construct
    (a) for(expr 1; expr2;)
    (b) for(expr 1; expr3)
    (c) for(;expr;)
    (d) for(;;expr3)

EXERCISES

1. What do you understand by control statements?
2. What are the various types of control statements used in the C++ language?
3. Explain various branching statements in detail.
4. Differentiate between if and if-else statement.
5. Differentiate between if-else and else-if statement.
6. What do you mean by nested-if? How can you solve a problem with nested-if?
7. Differentiate between ladder if and switch statement.
8. What are the various advantages of switch statement?
9. Explain the working of switch statement.
10. What do you mean by conditional control statement?
11. Explain various looping statements in detail.
12. When is the for statement preferred over while statement and do-while? Give Example.
13. Explain various jumping statements in detail.
14. Differentiate between break and continue statements.
15. Differentiate between forward goto and backward goto statements. Explain with the help of example.

CHAPTER 4

Arrays and Strings

4.1 INTRODUCTION

An **Array** is a data structure that consists of a group of elements having a common name and these elements are accessed by using indexing. In most programming languages each element has the same data type and the elements of the array are stored in successive memory locations.

Array elements are usually numbered (as opposed to an associative array) and individual elements are accessed by their numeric position in the array. Some arrays are multi-dimensional, meaning that more than one index is needed to access an element. For instance, a two-dimensional array might be thought of as the elements in a plane that are indexed by x and y coordinates, while a three-dimensional array might be thought of as a volume that is indexed by x, y, and z coordinates and so on.

An array is simply a number of memory locations, each of which can store an item of data of the same data type and which are all referenced through the same variable name. An array data structure or simply array is a data structure consisting of a collection of elements (values or variables), each identified by one or more integer indices, stored so that the address of each element can be computed from its index tuple by a simple mathematical formula. For example, an array of 10 integer variables, with indices 0 through 9, may be stored as 10 words at memory addresses 2000, 2004, 2008, … 2036; so that the element with index i has address $2000 + 4 \times i$.

Array is same type of data collection i.e. it is a collection of same data type elements. An array is a group of related data items, which can share common name. It is the set of homogeneous data.

Arrays and lists order their items. An unordered set can be stored as an array or list in some random order, but there is an alternative. If data items can take on one of N data values—as for instance, data items for ages of employees in years, which must be positive integers less than 100—then we can represent sets as an N-element *bit array* (an array whose data items are bits) where a "true" in location K of the array means that the Kth possible is present in the set. Bit arrays can make set operations like intersection run very fast, and many computers have bit-handling instructions to speed things even more.

4.2 ARRAY

An array is used to process multiple elements with the same data type when a number of such elements are known. An array is a fixed-sized, homogeneous, and widely-used data type. By homogeneous, we mean that it consists of components which are all of the same type, called element type or base type. And by fixed sized, we mean that the number of components is constant, and so does not change during the lifetime of the structure. An array is also called a random-access data structure, because all components can be selected at random and are equally accessible.

An array can be used to structure several data objects in the programming languages. A component of an array is selected by giving its subscript, which is an integer indicating the position of the component in the sequence. Therefore, an array is made of the pairs (value, index); it means that with every index, a value is associated. If every index is one single value then it is called a one-dimensional array, whereas if every index is a n-tuple $\{i_1, i_2, i_3, \ldots, i_n\}$, the array is called a n-dimensional array.

An array is a particular method of storing elements of indexed data. Elements of data are stored sequentially in blocks within the array. Each element is referenced by an index, or subscript.

Think of a notebook with pages numbered 1 through 12. Each page may or may not contain information on it. The notebook is an array of pages. Each page is an element of the array 'notebook'. Programmatically, you would retrieve information from a page by referring to its number or subscript, i.e., notebook(4) would refer to the contents of page 4 of the array notebook.

Figure 4.1: The notebook (array) contains 12 pages (elements).

The index is usually a number used to address an element in the array.

An array is a systematic arrangement of objects, usually in rows and columns. Array is similar type of data collection name i.e. it is a collection of same data type elements. An array is a group of related data items, which share common name.

***Definition:** "It is the set of homogeneous data types (same data types)".*

Now question arises, why we need array. This can be explained by taking an example for preparing the grade of 100 students in an examination. So to solve this problem, we declare 100 different variables. But if in the next session, 50 more students sit in the examination, then there will be require number of changes in the program and also program becomes more complex. So to solve such type of problem, we need to define and declare array. Also processing speed becomes fast with the declaration and use of an array.

Also the concept of array can be explained by taking a problem with the C++ program. Let us suppose, there are five variables declared in a program having different type of data, but if we add more variable (50 variable), then it will create a problem for the declaration and use of variable. Also program becomes lengthy and complex. The program with problem (with array) and without problem (with array) be illustrated as:

Program without array having different variables

Program 1: Write a C++ program to display data without array.

```
#include<iostream.h>
#include<conio.h>
void main ( )
{
int a,b,c,d,e;
a=20;
cout<<a;
b=30;
cout<<b;
c=40;
cout<<c;
d=50;
cout<<d;
e=60;
cout<<e;
getch();
}
```

Output:

20 30 40 50

Program with array having same variable name:

Program 2: Write a C++ program to display data with array.

```
#include <iostream.h>
#include<conio.h>
void main ( )
{
int a[50], i, n;
cout<<"\n How many number you want to enter:";
cin>>n;
cout<<"\n Enter the"<<n<<"different elements in the array";
for(i=1; i<=n; i++)
{
cin>>a[i]);
}
cout<<"\n Different array elements are: \n ";
for(i=1; i<=n; i++)
{
cout<<a[i];
}
getch();
}
```

Output:

```
How many number you want to enter: 5
Enter the 5 different elements in the array:
20 30 40 50 60
Different array elements are:
20 30 40 50 60
```

So array will solve the problem with the use of lesser number of variable and variable having the same name.

Arrays are a data type which holds multiple variables of the same data type. Consider the case where a programmer needs to keep track of a number of people within an organisation. So far, our initial attempt will be to create a specific variable for each user. This might look like,

```
int name1 = 101;
int name2 = 232;
int name3 = 231;
```

It becomes increasingly more difficult to keep track of this as the number of variables increase. Arrays offer a solution to this problem.

An array is a multi-element box, a bit like a filing cabinet, and uses an indexing system to find each variable stored within it. In C++ indexing starts at **zero**.

Arrays, like other variables in C++ must be declared before they can be used. The replacement of the above example using arrays looks like,

```
int names[4];
names[0] = 101;
names[1] = 232;
names[2] = 231;
names[3] = 0;
```

We created an array called names, which has space for four integer variables. You may also see that we stored 0 in the last space of the array. This is a common technique used by C++ programmers to signify the end of an array.

Arrays have the following syntax, using square brackets to access each indexed value (called an element). **Syntax: x[i]**

So that x[5] refers to the sixth element in an array called x. In C++, array elements start with 0. Assigning values to array elements is done by,

x[10] = g; and assigning array elements to a variable is done by,

```
g = x[10];
```

In the following example, a character based array named word is declared, and each element is assigned a character. The last element is filled with a zero value, to signify the end of the character string (in C++, there is no string type, so character based arrays are used to hold strings). A cout statement is then used to print out all elements of the array.

Program 3: Write a C++ program to print Hello.

```
#include <iostream.h>
#include<conio.h>
void main()
{
char word[20];
word[0] = 'H';
word[1] = 'e';
word[2] = 'l';
word[3] = 'l';
word[4] = 'o';
word[5] = 0;
cout<<"The contents of word[] is "<< word;
getch();
}
```

Output:

The contents of word[] is Hello

Suppose salary of the 10 employees named by salary variables name and we write it sal1, sal2, sal3……sal10. We repeat the variable name of employees by using the subscript. Because of use of single subscript or more than one subscript, it is also called subscripted variable.

So Array's representation for the 10th employee is:

Salary [10];

Array has syntax:

Common name variable [size];
or
array-name [subscript1] [subscript2];

We can represent number of elements as a1, a2, … an . Where a is an array name and 1, 2, 3, … n are subscript. We can write the above array statement as:

a[i] , where i = 1, 2, 3, … n

Here i work as subscript and array-name a works as subscripted variable.

Array representation can be done as:

storage-type data-type array-name[size];
or
storage-type data-type array name[row size][column size];

4.3 ADVANTAGES OF ARRAY

Following are the advantages of array:

1. An array provides singe name .So it easy to remember the name of all element of an array.
2. You can use one name for similar objects and save them with the same name but different indexes.
3. Array name gives base address of an array .So with the help increment operator we can visit one by one all the element of an array.
4. Array has many application data structure.
5. Arrays are very useful when you are working with sequences of the same kind of data (similar to the second point but has a different meaning).
6. Arrays use as reference type.
7. Array is a static data structure thus the number of elements can be stored in it are somehow fixed.

4.4 DISADVANTAGES OF ARRAY

Following are the disadvantages of array:

1. Sometimes it's not easy to operate with many index arrays.
2. C environment doesn't have checking mechanism for array sizes.
3. An array uses reference mechanism to work with memory which can cause unstable behavior of operating system (unless special methods were created to prevent it) and often even "blues screen" and so on.
4. In an array the task of insertion and deletion is not easy because the elements are stored in contiguous memory location.
5. Each element of array is of same data type as well as same size. We can not work with elements of different data type.
6. An array is a static data structure. After declaring an array it is impossible to change its size.
7. A drawback of the simplicity of arrays is the possibility of referencing a non-existent element by using an index outside the range of valid indices. This is known as *exceeding the array bounds.* The result is, at best, a program working with incorrect data. At worst, the whole system can crash. This problem is particularly felt in the C++ programming language, the powerful syntax of which is unfortunately prone to this kind of error. Some other languages have built-in bounds checking, and will refuse to index an array outside of its permitted range.

4.5 TYPES OF ARRAY

The types of the array depend upon the given problem. Arrays are mainly of two types:

(i) Linear Array
(ii) Non-Linear Array

4.5.1 Linear Array

A data structure is said to be linear if its elements form a sequence or a linear list. This type of array is also called one Dimensional Array. This is also called list array. Another name of linear array is called **single-dimensional array**. In the linear array only one subscript is used. It is written either in row or in column form.

Syntax to define or declare linear array is:

```
data-type array-name [size];
```

where data types are integer (int), real(float), double and character(char) .

For example, some of the valid one dimensional array declaration statements are written as below:

```
int a[50];
float salary[30];
char name[20];
```

Suppose if you want to store the data "TEMPLE" in the array name city, then the representation for declaration be as:

```
char name[7];
```

We can declare that data type char for city variable and you can store maximum 8 character in the different cells of the city variable. So we see that when we declare character type array, size should be one cell more than the given data length, because last cell should be empty or null cell i.e. the end of the string has null character. It is denoted by "\0".

```
char name[7];
name
T     0
E     1
M     2
P     3
L     4
E     5
'\0'  6
```

Suppose if we want to assign values 5, 15, 30, 27, 53 is an array integer variable, then it can be written (in the computer memory) as:

```
number[0] = 55
number[1] = 35
number[2] = 40
number[3] = 47
number[4] = 33
```

We can declare these numbers in the array form as:

```
int number[5];
```

So when we assign different values to the declared array-name , then it can be written (in the computer memory) as :

```
number[0] = 55
number[1] = 35
number[2] = 40
number[3] = 47
number[4] = 33
```

Another name of declaration of array which have fixed or constant value is defined as:

static data-type array-name [size] = {list of values};

For example, the above said different values can be assigned to the array as :

```
static int numbers [5] = {55, 35, 40, 47, 33};
```

Now if we assign data as:

```
static int number[5] = {55, 35, 40};
```

then the different values assigned to different array variables as:

```
number[0]=55,
number[1]=35,
number[3]=40,
number[4]=0,
number[5]=0
```

Similarly we can declare and define values in float type of variables.

For example:

```
static float a[4] = {10.32, 5.06, 27.2};
Here a[0] = 10.32,
     a[1] = 5.06,
     a[2] = 27.2,
     a[3] = 0.0.
```

Also you can initialize static type of array as:

```
static int a[5] = {10, 11, 12, 22, 23};
```

It will take a[0] = 10, a[1] = 11, a[2] = 12, a[3] = 22, a[4] = 23

Also you can declare character type data in the array as:

```
static char name[ ] = {'B', 'A', 'B', 'Y'};
```

Here data to the character variable be assigned as:

```
name[0] = 'B',
name[1] = 'A',
name[2] = 'B',
name[3] = 'Y',
name[4] = '\0'
```

Similarly you can declare the name array variable as :

```
static char name[5] = {'B'., 'A', 'B', 'Y'};
```

For example, write a C++ program to find average of n numbers using array.

4.5.2 Non-linear Array

Non-linear array are further subdivided into n categories as:

Two Dimensional Array

Three Dimensional Array

N Dimensional Array

We will discuss here two and three-dimensional array only.

1. Two Dimensional Array

These arrays are also called double dimensional array or two subscripted array. Another name of two-dimensional array is Tabular or Rectangular Array. These arrays are in row and column form. So these are also called as Row-Column or square Array.

These arrays have two subscripts. We can write the double dimensional array in tabular form as:

$$\begin{matrix} a11 & a12 & a13 & \cdots & \cdots & \cdots & a1n \\ a21 & a22 & a23 & \cdots & \cdots & \cdots & a2n \\ \cdots & \cdots & \cdots & \cdots & \cdots & \cdots & \cdots \\ an1 & an2 & an3 & \cdots & \cdots & \cdots & ann \end{matrix}$$

The general syntax used for declaration of two dimensional array is as:

```
data type array-name [row size] [column size];
```

For example, some valid declarations are:

```
int a[10][10];
float b[50][50];
char name[10][20];
```

Also you can declare two dimensional array in static form i.e. these types of array declarations have fixed or constant values during declaration.

The syntax used for static two dimensional array is as follows:

static data-type array-name [row size][column size]= {list of value};

For example, suppose you want to assign some fixed value to a variable array named table by using the static two-dimensional array as.

```
static int table [2][3] = {2, 3, 4, 6, 8, 10};
```

Here the values assigned to the tabular array-name is as:

```
table[0][0] = 2
table[0][1] = 3
table[0][2] = 4
table[1][0] = 6
table[1][1] = 8
table[1][2] = 10
```

Also we can write the above statement as:

```
static int table[ ][ ] = {2, 3, 4, 6, 8, 10};
```

Above statement fails in some cases. Another way to write the above statement is as follows:

```
static int table[ ][ ] = {{2, 3, 4}, {6, 8, 10}};
or
static int table[ ][ ] = {{2,3}, {4, 6}, {8, 10}};
```

2. *Three Dimensional Array*

Three Dimensional Array is also called space array or xyz array. As it has three subscripts, so these are also called triple dimensional array.

The syntax used for three dimensional array is as:

```
data-type array-name [space size] [row size] [column size];
```

For example, it can be declared as:

```
int st[5] [2] [3];
float a[2][2][2];
char name[4][6][6];
```

Suppose there are five students in a class and get different marks in three subjects in two house tests, then their marks be displayed by using three dimensional-array as:

```
st[1][1][1] = 25 ,  st[1][1][2] = 23, st[1][1][3] = 40, st[1][2][1] = 50
st[1][2][2] = 5,  st[1][2][3] = 32, st[2][1][1] = 55, .........., st[5][2][3] = 15
```

3. *N-Dimensional or Multi-dimensional Array:*

This type of array has n size of rows, columns and spaces and so on.

The syntax used for declaration of this type of array is as follows:

```
Data-type array-name [s1][s2] ... ... ... [sn];
```

In this sn is the nth size of the array. This type of array is less used in C++ language.

4.6 STRINGS

A string is a collection of characters. In terms of programming, it can be defined as an array of characters. Any group of characters (except double quote sign) defined between double quote marks is a constant string. For example, if the following string

"Jagbir is a good programmer."

has to be displayed on the screen, then we will give

cout<<"\n Jagbir is a good programmer.\n";

in the program. The \" is to print the double quote itself onto the screen.

Combination of characters (group of character) is called string. "I am a good boy" is a string. We can print or display the string by using the cout function as:

cout<<"\n I am a good boy \n";

But if the string is stored in variable, then such type of variable should be of character type. Also character variable should be declared in the array form (single dimensional form if you read or write a single string, but if you want to read / write more than one string, then use two-dimensional array).

The use of string is as follows:

```
char city [20];
cout<< city;                    /* to print a single dimensional string */
    or
char city[5][20];
for (i=0; i <5; i++)            /* to print multi-dimensional strings */
{
cout<<city[i];
}
```

4.7 OPERATIONS ON STRING (HANDLING OF CHARACTER STRINGS)

String has number of operations in the C++ language, The common operations related to character strings are:

- Declaring and initializing string variables
- Reading and writing strings
- Combining strings together
- Comparing strings for equality
- Copying one string to another
- Find length of string
- Reverse a string
- Extracting a portion of a string

4.7.1 Declaration of String Variable

String variables are declared similar to any other array variables in C++. We can declare string variable by using the character data-type. For example if we want to declare a string variable city of a maximum size of 10 characters, then it can be done using one dimensional string declaration.

The general syntax is:

data-type array-name[size];

For Example:

char city[10]; (if it is a single string – one dimensional string array)

When the compiler assigns a character string to a character array, it automatically supplies a null character ('\0') at the end of the string. So the size of string should be such that it can hold the entire string plus one null character.

Also more than one string can be declared by using the double dimensional string array:

The general syntax is:

data-type array-name[row size][col. size];

For Example:

char city[10] [20]; (if it has multiple strings – two dimensional string array)

Similarly in this declaration you can read / write number of strings, but not more than 10 strings and every string has length not more than 19 characters. Last character always be a null character.

Null-terminated String

String is terminated by a special character which is called as null terminator or null parameter (/0). So when you define a string you should be sure to have sufficient space for the null terminator. In ASCII table, the null terminator has value 0.

4.7.2 Initialization of String Variable

Following the discussion on characters arrays, the initialization of a string must the following form which is simpler to one dimension array.

The general syntax is:

static data-type array-name[size] = {list of values};

For example, suppose you want to enter the string "january" to the city variable, then the procedure is as:

static char month1[ ]={'j','a','n','u','a','r','y'};

The data type always should be character type in the string handling.

Then the string month is initializing to January. This is perfectly valid but C++ offers a special way to initialize strings. The above string can be initialized char month1[]="January"; The characters of the string are enclosed within a part of double quotes. The compiler takes care of string enclosed within a pair of a double quotes. The compiler takes care of storing the ASCII codes of characters of the string in the memory and also stores the null terminator in the end.

The following example shows the use of string:

Program 4: Write a C++ program illustrate the use of string.

```
#include<iostream.h>
#include<conio.h>
void main()
{
char month[15];
cout<<"Enter the string:";
cin.get(month,15);
cout<<"The string entered is "<< month;
getch();
}
Output:
Enter the string: January
The string entered is January
```

***Note:** Character string always terminated by a null character ''. A string variable is always declared as an array & is any valid C++ variable name.*

In this example string is stored in the character variable month the string is displayed in the statement.

cout<<"The string entered is "<<month;

It is one dimension array. Each character occupies a byte. A null character (\0) that has the ASCII value 0 terminates the string. The figure shows the storage of string January in the memory recall that \0 specifies a single character whose ASCII value is zero.

0	1	2	3	4	5	6	7	8	9	10	11	12	13	14
J	**A**	**N**	**U**	**A**	**R**	**Y**	**\0**							

Character string terminated by a null character '\0'.

A string variable is any valid C++ variable name & is always declared as an array. The general form of declaration of a string variable is

```
Char string_name[size];
```

The size determines the number of characters in the string name.

Example:

```
char month[10];
char address[100];
```

The size of the array should be one byte more than the actual space occupied by the string since the complier appends a null character at the end of the string.

Also more than one string can be initialized by using the double dimensional string array:

The general syntax is:

```
static data-type array-name[row size][col. size] = {{list of row 1};
                                                    {list of row 2};
                                                    ……… …
                                                    {list of row n}};
```

For example, suppose if you want to assign three different cities data values to the city string variable, then this can be done as:

```
static char city[2][20] = { {'A', 'M', 'R', 'I', 'T', 'S', 'A', 'R', '\0'}
                            {'M', 'O', 'G', 'A', '\0'}}
```

0	1	2	3	4	5	6	7	8	9	10	11	12	13	14	15	16	17	18	19
A	M	R	I	T	S	A	R	\0											
M	O	G	A	\0															

Note that data-type always should be of character type.

***Note:** These are not valid initializations:*

String = "xyz";

String1 = String2;

To copy the chars in one string to another string we may do so on a character to character basis.

4.7.3 Reading and Writing A String

We can read the string by using the cin function. The function cin is used to read the character string from the terminal.

For example, if you want to read only single city data, then the procedure is as:

```
char city [10];
cin>>city;
```

Also if you want to read more than one strings (10 strings and every string have maximum 19 number of character, 20th is the null character), then the procedure is as follows:

```
char city [10][20];
for (i=0; i < 10; i++)
```

```
{
cin>>city[i];
}
```

Similarly the procedure to write or print the above said string(s) on monitor screen or to print on printer is as:

```
char city[10];
cout<<city;
```

The procedure for more than one string is as:

```
char city[10][20];
for (i=0; i < 10; i++)
{
cout<<city[i];
}
```

If you want to read two strings, then this can be done as:

```
char city1[10], city2[10];
cin>>city1>>city2;
```

The following points should be noted

1. When the field width is less than the length of the string, the entire string is printed.
2. The integer value on the right side of the decimal point specifies the number of characters to be printed.
3. When the number of characters to be printed is specified as zero, nothing is printed.
4. The minus sign in the specification causes the string to be printed left-justified.

We will see rest of the topics related to strings.

4.8 ARITHMETIC OPERATIONS ON CHARACTERS

We can also manipulate the characters as we manipulate numbers in C++ language. When ever the system encounters the character data it is automatically converted into a integer value by the system. We can represent a character as a interface by using the following method.

```
x='a';
cout<<x;
```

Will display 97 on the screen. Arithmetic operations can also be performed on characters for example x='z'-1; is a valid statement. The ASCII value of 'z' is 122 the statement the therefore will assign 121 to variable x.

It is also possible to use character constants in relational expressions for example

ch>'a' && ch <= 'z' will check whether the character stored in variable ch is a lower case letter. A character digit can also be converted into its equivalent integer value suppose un the expression a=character-'1'; where a is defined as an integer variable & character contains value 8 then a= ASCII value of 8 ASCII value '1'=56-49=7.

We can also get the support of the c library function to converts a string of digits into their equivalent integer values the general format of the function in x=atoi(string) here x is an integer variable & string is a character array containing string of digits.

4.8.1 ATOI ( ) Function (Character Converting Functions)

If you have character data enclosed within quotes i.e. in the string form, then you can convert it into integer form or numeric form by using the atoi ( ) function, the general syntax is as written below:

```
v1 = atoi (v2);
```

where v1 is an integer variable and v2 is of character type variable.

4.9 STANDARD LIBRARY STRING FUNCTIONS (#INCLUDE<STRING.H>)

This header file defines several functions to manipulate C++ strings.

Functions

Copying:

memcpy	Copy block of memory (function)
memmove	Move block of memory (function)
strcpy	Copy string (function)
strncpy	Copy characters from string (function)

Concatenation:

strcat	Concatenate strings (function)
strncat	Append characters from string (function)

Comparison:

memcmp	Compare two blocks of memory (function)
strcmp	Compare two strings (function)
strcoll	Compare two strings using locale (function)

strncmp	Compare characters of two strings (function)
strxfrm	Transform string using locale (function)

Searching:

memchr	Locate character in block of memory (function)
strchr	Locate first occurrence of character in string (function)
strcspn	Get span until character in string (function)
strpbrk	Locate character in string (function)
strrchr	Locate last occurrence of character in string (function)
strspn	Get span of character set in string (function)
strstr	Locate substring (function)
strtok	Split string into tokens (function)

Other:

memset	Fill block of memory (function)
strerror	Get pointer to error message string (function)
strlen	Get string length (function)
strlwr	Convert a string to lowercase(function)
strupr	Convert a string to uppercase(function)

Macros

NULL	Null pointer (macro)

Types

size_t	Unsigned integral type (type)

4.10 STRING HANDLING FUNCTIONS

C++ language is rich in library functions, but to handle or operate some operations with string, we use some powerful string-handling functions. All these function are linked with the "string.h" header file stored in the include sub-directory in the Turbo-C++ compiler. So note that all the string handling function requires to declare "string.h" header file in the link section before declaration and use.

Here we explain the five commonly used string handling function as:

(i) strcat ( )

(ii) strcmp ( )

(iii) strcpy ( )

(iv) strlen ( )

(v) strrev ( )

(vi) strlwr ( )

(vii) strupr ( )

(i) strcat ( )

The purpose of this string handling function strcat ( ) is to concatenate or combine two different strings together.

The general syntax is:

```
strcat(string1, string2);
```

Here string1 is combined with string2 and result will be stored {combined string} in string1.

Also we can concatenate more than one string by using nested concatenation:

```
strcat (strcat (string1, string2), string3);
```

(ii) strcmp( )

The purpose of this function is to compare two strings. It will check which string is alphabetically above the others. For comparison ASCII (American Standard Code for Information Interchange) values are used.

The general syntax is as:

```
strcmp (string1, string2);
```

If the ASCII difference of each character in the two different strings from the first alphabet (till null character of any string occurs first) is zero, then both the strings are equal. If difference is -ve, then string2 is larger than the string1, but if the difference is +ve, then string1 is larger than the string2.

```
char string1[20] , string2[20];
```

(iii) strcpy ( )

The purpose of this function is to copy one string into another string. Target or destination field should be larger than the source field. In other words size of the string1 should be larger to receive the contents of the string2.

The general syntax is:

```
strcpy (string1, string2);
```

It will copy the data from the string2 to the string1 variable. Also note that the length of the string1 should be larger than string2.

(iv) strlen ( )

The purpose of this function is to count the number of character in a string i.e. to find the length of the string.

The general syntax is:

```
n = strlen (string);
```

Where n should be of integer type and string variable should be of character type.

(v) strrev ( )

The purpose of this function is to reverse a string. This function takes string variable as its single (only one) argument. Here the first character becomes last and last character becomes first in a string.

The general syntax is:

```
strrev(st);
```

Here st is a string (character type) variable.

(vi) strlwr ( )

This function converts all characters in a string from uppercase to lowercase.

The general syntax is:

```
strlwr(string);
```

For example: strlwr("BABY") converts to baby.

(vii) strupr( )

This function converts all characters in a string from lower case to uppercase.

The general syntax is:

```
strupr(string);
```

For example: strupr("baby") will convert the string to BABY.

PROGRAMMING PROBLEMS

Program 1: Write a C++ Program to delete all the elements from array and fill leading blanks with zero.

Program 2: Write a C++ Program to merge two descending order sorted arrays and display it into ascending order.

Program 3: Write a C++ Program to sort numeric data using exchange sort.

Program 4: Write a C++ Program to remove duplicate numbers from an array.

Program 5: Write a C++ Program to convert a square matrix into a unit matrix.

Program 6: Write a C++ Program to convert two-dimensional arrays in one-dimensional array.

Program 7: Write a C++ Program to find maximum and minimum values from every of a matrix.

Program 8: Write a C++ Program to create a magic series by using the method of magic squares of odd digits.

Program 9: Write a C++ Program to interchange two matrices.

Program 10: Write a C++ Program to find whether a matrix is skew-symmetric or not.

Program 11: Given a matrix *A* of size *mxn*, write a program to print the sum of squares of the reciprocal of each row.

Program 12: Given a matrix *A* of size *mxn*, write a program to print the sum of squares of the reciprocal of each column.

Program 13: Write a C++ program to read a set of n integers between 1 and 10 and count the number of times each integer appears I the set. Print the integers in order of frequency, placing the number occurring the highest number of times first.

Program 14: Write a C++ Program to compute the frequency of letters in a sentence.

Program 15: Write a C++ Program to convert roman numerals into Arabic integers.

Program 16: Write a program to find inverse of matrix 3 x 3.

Program 17: Write a C++ Program to print the average percentage marks of any 50 students?

Program 18: Write a C++ program that returns the date after giving number of days and a date as input.

Program 19: Write a C++ program to Tic-Tac-Toe.

Program 20: Write a C++ program to a simple dictionary.

Program 21: Write a C++ program to find whether two strings are equal or not, if not equal then find the difference of these.

Program 22: Write a C++ program to get first and last name and print them together.

Program 23: Write a C++ program to extract m characters from a string starting with nth character.

Program 24: Write a C++ program to enter your name & outputs the ASCII codes of characters which represents your name.

Program 25: Write a C++ program to extract word from string.

Program 26: Write a C++ program to sort characters of string alphabetically.

Program 27: Write a C++ program to read a string and count the number of **characters** in it.

Program 28: Write a C++ program to finding occurrences of one string in another: strstr.

Program 29: Write a C++ program to a demonstration of seeking and finding.

Program 30: Write a C++ program to find substring.

Fill in the blanks

1. Lists and tables of values can be stored in ....
2. Array is the collection of .... data elements.
3. The elements of an array are related by the fact that they have the same .... and ....
4. The number like a[3] used to refer to a particular element of an array is called its ....
5. The process of placing the elements of an array in order is called .... the array.
6. The process of finding an array element from an array is called .... the array.
7. An array that uses two subscripts is referred to as a .... array.
8. Combination of characters (group of character) is called ....
9. String is terminated by a special character which is called as .... terminator
10. We can read the string by using the .... function.
11. String handling function strcat ( ) is to .... two different strings together.

Answers

1. arrays, 2. homogeneous 3. name, type. 4. subscript (or index). 5. sorting. 6. searching. 7. two-dimensional. 8. string. 9.null 10. cin 11. combine

OBJECTIVE TYPE QUESTIONS

1. An array of n elements will be declared in c as:

   (a) array[n] (b) array[n-1]

   (c) array[n+1] (d) array

2. The first element of a 0 based array can be accessed by:

   (a) array (b) array[0]

   (c) array[n-1] (d) array[n]

3. What will the piece of code reveal...

```
int a[] = {1,2,3,4,5,6,7,8,9,0};
printf("%d",a[2]);
printf("%d",2[a]);
```

** Regarding the fact that there are no syntax errors..

(a) 3 8 (b) Logical error

(c) 3 3 (d) 3

4. Memory is allocated in an array in:

   (a) Non Continues Way

   (b) Continues fashion

   (c) It may be any way, does not matter

   (d) Random but in some logical manner according to some algorithm.

5. A 'n' sized 1 based array indexed from:

   (a) [1] – [n] (b) [0] – [n]

   (c) [1] – [n-1] (d) [0] – [n-1]

6. How is this resolved.. Arr[2];

   (a) *(&Arr + 2) (b) Arr[0] + 2

   (c) The Second position from Arr[0] (d) *(Arr + 2)

7. Lower bound and Upper bound of an Array represent the following element..

   (a) Largest and Smallest Resp.

   (b) Smallest and Largest + 1

   (c) Smallest and Largest – 1

   (d) Smallest and Largest Resp.

8. In an Array the range specifies…

   (a) Scope of the Array (b) Nos. of Elements in the Array

   (c) The Group of the Array (d) Size – 1 of the Array

9. If Array's upper bound is specified by 'U' and lower bound is specified by 'L' then the range of the array will be.

   (a) U – L +1 (b) L + U – 1

   (c) U – L – 1 (d) L – U + 1

10. If Upper bound is represented by 99 and lower bound by 0 in a o based array, then the range of the array is..

    (a) 0 (b) 99

    (c) 100 (d) 101

11. A string is ended by…

    (a) The Last Character (b) The Null Character

    (c) The Dot Character (d) The First Character

12. Suppose that you want to declare an array of characters to hold a C++ string with exactly 9 letters. Which declaration is best?
(a) char s[8]; (b) char s[9];
(c) char s[10]; (d) char s[11];
(e) char s[12]

13. Which of the following can be used to describe arrays as well as hard disks?
(a) static (b) dynamic
(c) direct access (d) linked access
(e) linked

14. Of the following, which would access an element of an array of records?
(a) Data[i] (b) Data(i)
(c) Data(i,j) (d) Data.i
(e) Data[i].f

15. Arrays are also called as
(1) Dense lists (2) Predefined variables (3) Static data structures
(a) 1 and 2 (b) 2 and 3
(c) 1 and 3 (d) All

16. If a is an array (which actually is a pointer as such) and a pointer p;
The statement a = p, yields
(a) Address of p copied on a
(b) Address remains unchanged
(c) Leads to an error
(d) Address of a is copied on p instead.

17. Array is used to represent
(a) a list of data items of integer data type
(b) a list of data items of real data type
(c) a list of data items of different data type
(d) a list of data items of same data type

18. Array name is
(a) an array variable
(b) a keyword
(c) a common name shared by all elements
(d) not used in program

19. One-dimensional array is known as
(a) Vector (b) table
(c) Matrix (d) an array of arrays

20. The array elements are represented by
(a) index values (b) subscripted variables
(c) array name (d) size of an array

21. Array elements occupy
(a) subsequent memory locations
(b) random location for each element
(c) varying length of memory locations for each element
(d) no space in memory

22. The address of the starting element of an array is
(a) represented by subscripted variable of the starting element
(b) cannot be specified
(c) represented by the array name
(d) not used by the compiler

23. Identify the wrong statement
(a) Subscripts are also known as indices
(b) Array variables and subscripted variables are same
(c) Array variables and subscripted variables are different
(d) Array name and subscripted variables are same

24. Array subscripts in C++ always start at
(a) -1 (b) 0
(c) 1 (d) any value

25. Identify the correct declaration
(a) int a[10][10]; (b) int a[10,10];
(c) int a (10) (10); (d) int a (10,10);

26. Maximum number of elements in the array declaration int x[10]; is
(a) 9 (b) 10
(c) 11 (d) undefined

27. Maximum number of elements in the array declaration int y[5][8]; is
(a) 28 (b) 32
(c) 35 (d) 40

28. Two-dimensional array elements are sorted in

(a) column major order (b) row major order

(c) both options a and b (d) random order

29. Two-dimensional array elements are sorted

(a) row by row in the subsequent memory locations

(b) column by column in the subsequent memory location

(c) row by row in scattered memory locations

(d) column by column scattered memory locations

30. ANSI C recommends a compiler to support at least dimensions of an array

(a) 4 (b) 5

(c) 6 (d) 7

31. You can use the C++ .... function to assign a value to a String variable

(a) assign (b) copy

(c) string (d) strcopy

(e) strcpy.

32. To use the strcpy function, you must include the .... header file in your program

(a) assign.h (b) copy.h

(c) string.h (d) strcopy.h

(e) strcpy.h

33. The String data type is an extension of the .... data type

(a) character (b) double

(c) letter (d) long

(e) text

34. Which of the following creates a String named constant called partNo, whose value is AB45?

(a) const char [4] partNo = "AB45"; (b) const char [5] partNol = 'AB45';

(c) const char [5] partNo = "AB45"; (d) const char partNo [5] = 'AB45';

(e) None

35. Assume that a program contains the following three statements:

```
char itemName [10] = " ";
cout << "Enter the item: ";
cin >> itemName;
```

If, after executing the program, the user enters the two words Red Coat, C++ will store .... in the itemName variable

(a) coat (b) red

(c) red coat

36. If you want to store a maximum of 15 characters in a String variable, you need to tell C++ to put aside .... memory locations. (The 15 characters include the null character)

(a) 14 (b) 15

(c) 16 (d) either a or b will work

37. The syntax for declaring and initializing a String variable is char variablename[x] = initialvalue; In the syntax, x is a number that is .... the length of the string you want to store in the variable

(a) one less than (b) one more than

(c) the same as (d) two more than

38. You typically initialize a String variable to ....

(a) an asterisk (b) a space enclosed in single quotes

(c) the number 0 (d) a zero-length string

EXERCISES

1. What do you mean by array? How can you initialize it?
2. How you can declare one dimensional array.
3. How you can declare two dimensional arrays.
4. Why we use array?
5. Explain the memory representation of one dimensional array.
6. What are the various advantages of array?
7. What are the various disadvantages of array?
8. Explain the row-major representation of a 2D array in detail.
9. Explain the column-major representation of a 2D array in detail.
10. What are the various types of array? Explain each with an appropriate example?
11. Explain the concept of linear array in detail.
12. Explain the concept of Non-linear array in detail.
13. What are the various types of non-linear array in detail?
14. Differentiate between linear and non-linear array.
15. What do you mean by string? How can you initialize string?

16. How you can declare a string variable?
17. How you can initialize a string variable?
18. How you can read and write a string?
19. Explain the standard library of string functions.
20. Explain the various operations on string.
21. What are the various string handling functions? Explain all with the help of examples.
22. Differentiate between strcat() and strcpy().
23. How can you read and write string(s)?
24. How can you apply arithmetic operations on strings?
25. What is the role of atoi() function in the string?
26. How can you reverse a string?

CHAPTER 5

Functions

5.1 INTRODUCTION

We have mentioned earlier that one of the strengths of C++ language is that C++ functions are easy to define and use. C++ functions can be classified into two categories, namely, library functions and user-defined functions. Main is an example of user defined function. Sqrt() and abs() belong to the category of library functions. The main distinction between user-defined and library function is that the library functions are not required to be written by user while the user defined functions have to be developed by the user at the time of writing a program. However the user defined function can become a part of the C++ program library.

A function is a module or block of program code which deals with a particular task. Making functions is a way of isolating one block of code from other independent blocks of code.

Functions serve two purposes:

1. They allow a programmer to say: this piece of code does a specific job which stands by itself and should not be mixed up with anything else.
2. They make a block of code reusable since a function can be reused in many different contexts without repeating parts of the program text.

5.2 CATEGORIES OF FUNCTIONS

C++ functions can be classified into two categories, namely, library functions and user-defined functions.

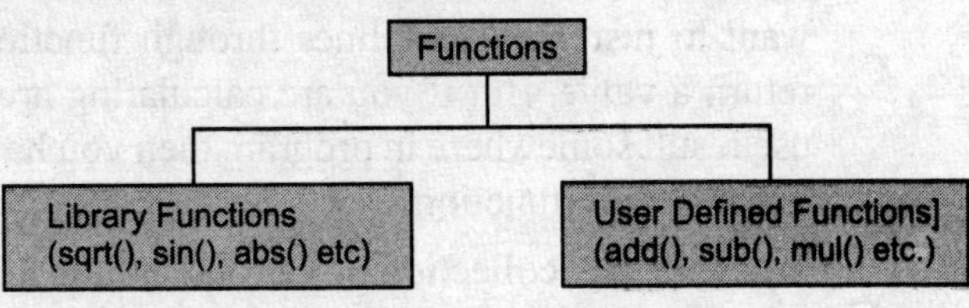

Note: *Library functions are described in Chapter 2.*

5.3 USER DEFINED FUNCTION OR SUBPROGRAM

A function is a block of statement that has a name and it has a property that it is reusable i.e. it can be executed from as many different points in a C++ Program as required.

A function is a self contained block of statements that perform a coherent task of the same kind Function helps to groups a number of program statements into a unit and gives it a name. This unit can be invoked from the other parts of a program. It is not possible by computer program to handle all the tasks by itself. Instead its requests other program like entities – called functions in C++ to get its tasks done.

Definition: "A function is a complete and independent program which is used (or invoked) by the main program or other subprograms. A subprogram receives values called arguments from a calling program, performs calculations and returns the results to the calling program".

In a C++ Program, the name of the function is unique and is Global. It means that a function can be accessed from any location with in a C++ Program. When the function is called, we pass information to the function called **arguments** specified. And the function either returns some values to the point it was called from or returns nothing.

So function in a C++ program has some properties discussed below.

1. Every function has a unique name. This name is used to call function from "main()" function. A function can be called from within another function.
2. A function is independent and it can perform its task without intervention from or interfering with other parts of the program.
3. A function performs a specific task. A task is a distinct job that your program must perform as a part of its overall operation, such as adding two or more integer, sorting an array into numerical order, or calculating a cube root etc.
4. A function returns a value to the calling program. This is optional and depends upon the task your function is going to accomplish. Suppose you

want to just show few lines through function then it is not necessary to return a value. But if you are calculating area of rectangle and wanted to use result somewhere in program then you have to send back (return) value to the calling function.

C++ language is collection of various inbuilt functions. If you have written a program in C++ then it is evident that you have used C++'s inbuilt functions. Cin, Cout, clrscr etc. all are C++'s inbuilt functions. You cannot imagine a C++ program without function.

5.4 FUNCTION DECLARATION AND DEFINATION

Function is block or part of program. When any program is very long or same code is repeating many times then we try to cut the program in different parts (or blocks) so that whole program became more understandable, easier to debug (error checking) and size of code will be lesser.

5.4.1 Declaration Of Function

We can declare the function by using function name.

The general syntax is:

```
data-type function-name (argument list);
```

Here data-type may be int, float, char and double.

Important Points Regarding the Declaration of Function

1. If function definition has written after the function call then it is necessary to declare the function before the function call because function call statement has no idea about prototype of calling function.
2. If function definition has written before the function call statement then it is not necessary to write function declaration.
3. If return type of function is signed int data type then it not necessary to write function declaration even though function definition has written after the function call.
4. Function's declaration doesn't reserve any memory space.
5. In declaration statement it is not necessary to write variable name in parameter of function.

5.4.2 How to Define a Function

There are two main parts of the functions. The function header and the function body.

The general syntax is:

```
<return type> FunctionName (Argument1, Argument2, Argument3......)
{
Statement1;
Statement2;
Statement3;
}
```

An example of function.

```
int sum (int a, int b)
{
int s;
s = a + b;
return s;
}
```

Function Header

```
int sum(int x, int y)
```

It has three main parts

1. The function name i.e. **sum**
2. The parameters (x and y) of the function enclosed in the parenthesis.
3. Return value type of the function i.e. **int**

Function Body

What ever is written with in { } is the body of the function.

The general syntax used for the definition and declaration of function is as:

```
#include<iostream.h>
#include<conio.h>
main()
{
Local declaration statement;
Executable statement;
Function name (actual parameters);
Executable statement;
}
Function name (formal or dummy parameters)
declaration of formal or dummy parameters;
{
Local declaration statement;
Executable statement;
return(variable or expression)
}
```

We can call a function from main program by using function name. Actually function is a division of a large program into small modules having some specific objective or task. Also multi-function can be called by using function name.

Note:

1. *Every function sub program should have last statement return statement.*
2. *Every function calling statement ends with the semicolon (;). Also note that the called statement or function comes from where function should not have semi-colon (;)*
3. *Every function is enclosed within {and} brackets similar to the main program.*

Program 1: Write a C++ program to illustrate the use of function structure.

```
#include<iostream.h>
#include<conio.h>
void main()
{
int p, sum(int, int);          //function declaration
p=sum(3,4);                    //function call
cout<<sum;
}
int sum( int a, int b)         //function definition
{
int s;                         //function body
s=a+b;
return s;                      //function returning a value
}
```

Output:

7

5.5 WHY WE USE FUNCTIONS

The most important reason to use functions is to aid in the conceptual organization of a program.

Another reason to use functions is to reduce program size. Any sequence of instructions that appears in program more than once is a candidate for being made into a function. The functions code is stored in only one place in memory, even though the function is executed many times in the course of the program.

Two main reasons for using functions:

1. Writing functions avoids rewriting the same code over and over. Suppose that there is a section of code in a program that calculates area of a triangle. If, later in the program we want to calculate the area of a different triangle we won't like to write the same instructions all over again. Instead we would prefer to jump to a "section of code" that calculates area and then jump back to the place from where you left off. This section of code is nothing but a function.

Function reduces the redundancy of code.

Program 2: Write a C++ program to find the sum of: 1! /5+ 2! /4+ 3! /3+ 4! /2+ 5! /1 without using function (Except main function). Where! Symbol indicates factorial of any number.

```
#include<iostream.h>
#include<conio.h>
void main()
{
int num, sum=0;
int fact1,fact2,fact3,fact4,fact5;
fact1=fact2=fact3=fact4=fact5=1;
num=0;
while(num<=0){
fact1 =fact1+fact1*num;
num++;
}
num=0;
while(num<=1){
fact2 =fact2+fact2*num;
num++;
}
num=0;
while(num<=2){
fact3 =fact3+fact3*num;
num++;
}
num=0;
while(num<=3){
fact4 =fact4+fact4*num;
num++;
}
```

```
num=0;
while(num<=4){
fact5 =fact5+fact5*num;
num++;
}
clrscr();
sum=fact1/1+fact2/2+fact3/3+fact4/4+fact5/5;
cout<<sum;
getch();
}
```

Program 3: Write a C++ program for the same code using function.

```
#include<iostream.h>
#include<conio.h>
void main()
{
int sum;
sum=fact(1)/1+fact(2)/2+fact(3)/3+fact(4)/4+fact(5)/5;
clrscr();
cout<<sum;
getch();
}
int fact(int x)
{
int num=0,fact=1;
while(num<=x-1)
{
fact =fact+fact*num;
num++;
}
return fact;
}
```

Compare the example one and two and find out the importance of function. You will find out function reduces the repetition of same code.

2. Using functions it becomes easier to write programs and keep track of what they are doing. If the operation of a program can be divided in to separate activities, and each activity placed in a different function, then each could be written and checked more or less independently. Separating the code in to modular functions also makes the program easier to design and understand.

Small modules are used to improve readability, portability as well as make the program easy to debug.

5.5.1 Use of Functions in C++ Serves Many Advantages

There are many advantages in using functions in a program they are:

1. It makes possible top down modular programming. In this style of programming, the high level logic of the overall problem is solved first while the details of each lower level functions is addressed later.
2. The length of the source program can be reduced by using functions at appropriate places.
3. It becomes uncomplicated to locate and separate a faulty function for further study.
4. A function may be used later by many other programs this means that a C++ programmer can use function written by others, instead of starting over from scratch.
5. Memory space can be properly utilized. Also less memory is required to run program if function is used.
6. A function can be used by many programs.
7. Function increases the execution speed of the program and makes the programming simple.
8. By using the function, program is portable as well as easy to understand.
9. A function can be used to keep away from rewriting the same block of codes which we are going use two or more locations in a program. This is especially useful if the code involved is long or complicated.
10. Programming teams does a large percentage of programming. If the program is divided into subprograms, each subprogram can be written by one or two team members of the team rather than having the whole team to work on the complex program
11. It removes the redundancy (occurrence of duplication of programs) i.e. avoids the repetition and saves the time and space.
12. Debugging and Testing becomes very easier and fast using the function sub-programming.
13. User can build its own customized library of different function used in daily routine having specific goal and link with the main program similar to the library functions.
14. Reliability is high in the function programming.

5.6 SCOPE OF FUNCTION VARIABLES

Following are the scope of function variables:

1. Only a limited amount of information is available within each function. Variables declared within the calling function can't be accessed unless they are passed to the called function as arguments. The only other contact a function might have with the outside world is through global variables.
2. Local variables are declared within a function. They are created a new each time the function is called, and destroyed on return from the function. Values passed to the function as arguments can also be treated like local variables.
3. Static variables are slightly different; they don't die on return from the function. Instead their last value is retained, and it becomes available when the function is called again.
4. Global variables don't die on return from a function. Their value is retained, and is available to any other function which accesses them.

5.7 RETURN STATEMENT

Return is keyword of C++. When the control reaches to the return keyword it immediately terminates the execution of that function and transfer the control to the calling function.

A function may or may not send back any value to the calling function. If it does, it is done through the return statement. While it is possible to pass to the called function any number of values, the called function can only return one value per call, at the most we can have

```
return;
or
return (variable);
or
return (expression);
```

The first, the 'plain' return does not return any value; it acts much as the closing brace of the function. When a **return** is encountered, the control is immediately passed back to the calling function. An example of the use of a simple **return** is as follows:

```
if(error)
return;                    //return nothing
```

The second form of **return** with an expression returns the value of the expression.

For example:

```
mul(x,y)
int x,y;
{
int p;
p = x*y;
return(p);          //return variable
}
```

We could have also combined the last two statements and makes third form as follows:

```
return(x*y);        //return expression
```

Now by default all functions return int type data. If a function wants to return some other type of value (can be float, character, string, structure, pointer, etc) whether it is user-defined or inbuilt data type, it can be achieved by giving a type specifier in the function header. **Example:**

```
double sum(w, r)
char rait(c)
```

When a value is returned it is automatically cast to the function's type. In functions that do computations using double, yet return int, the returned value will be truncated to an integer.

5.7.1 Features of Return Type of Function in C++ Programming

Following are the features of return type:

1. Default return type of function is signed int data type.
2. Function can return only one value at a time.
3. Storage classes allowed with return type are static, extern, typedef i.e. we cannot use auto and register storage class with the return type of any function.
4. Default return type of function is extern.
5. In return type we can use modifier like short, long, signed, unsigned, extern, static, const, volatile etc.

5.8 TYPES OF FUNCTION IN C++ PROGRAMMING LANGUAGES

In previous section, we are tried to explain what the function, its advantages is and how to declare a C++ function. And now we told you that there are five types of functions and they are:

1. Functions with no arguments and no return values.
2. Functions with arguments and no return values.
3. Functions with arguments and return values.

4. Functions with no arguments and return values.
5. Functions that return multiple values.

5.8.1 Functions With No Arguments and No Return Value

A C++ function without any arguments means you cannot pass data (values like int, char etc) to the called function. Similarly, function with no return type does not pass back data to the calling function. It is one of the simplest types of function in C++. This type of function which does not return any value cannot be used in an expression it can be used only as independent statement.

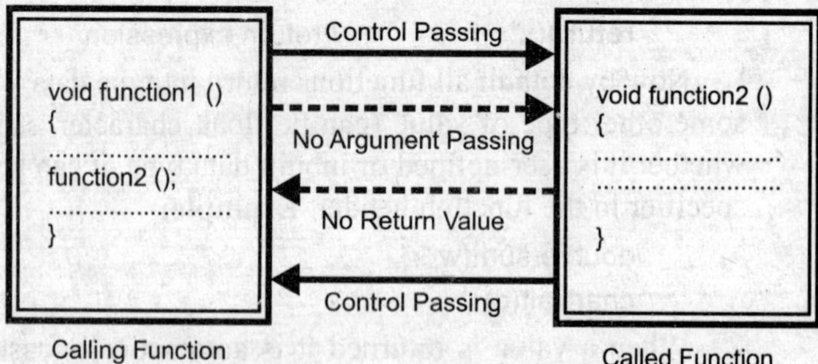

Logic of the functions with no arguments and no return value

5.8.2 Functions with Arguments and No Return Value

In our previous example what we have noticed that "main()" function has no control over the user defined function "printline()", it cannot control its output. Whenever "main()" calls "printline()", it simply prints line every time. So the result remains the same.

A C++ function with arguments can perform much better than previous function type. This type of function can accept data from calling function. In other words, you send data to the called function from calling function but you cannot send result data back to the calling function. Rather, it displays the result on the terminal. But we can control the output of function by providing various values as arguments.

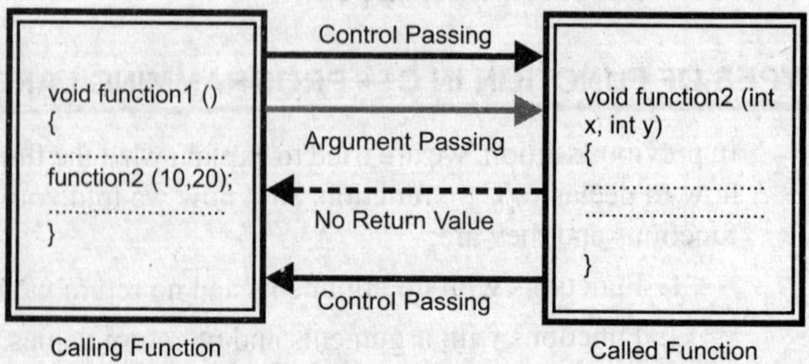

Logic of the function with arguments and no return value

5.8.3 Functions with Arguments and Return Value

This type of function can send arguments (data) from the calling function to the called function and wait for the result to be returned back from the called function back to the calling function. And this type of function is mostly used in programming world because it can do two way communications; it can accept data as arguments as well as can send back data as return value. The data returned by the function can be used later in our program for further calculations.

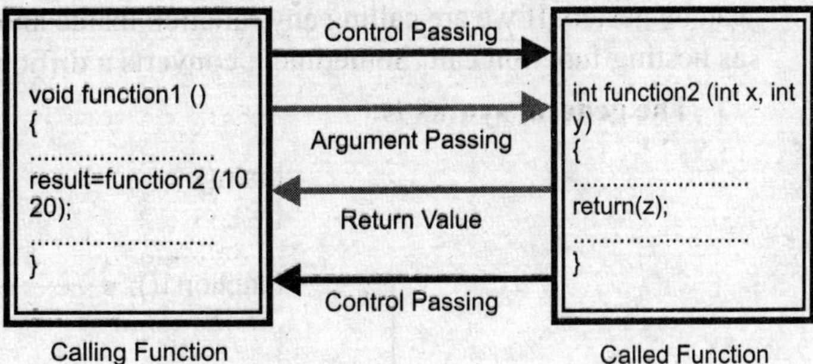

Logic of the function with arguments and return value

5.8.4 Functions with No Arguments but Returns Value

We may need a function which does not take any argument but only returns values to the calling function then this type of function is useful. The best example of this type of function is "cin.get()" library function which is declared in the header file "iostream.h". We can declare a similar library function of own. Take a look.

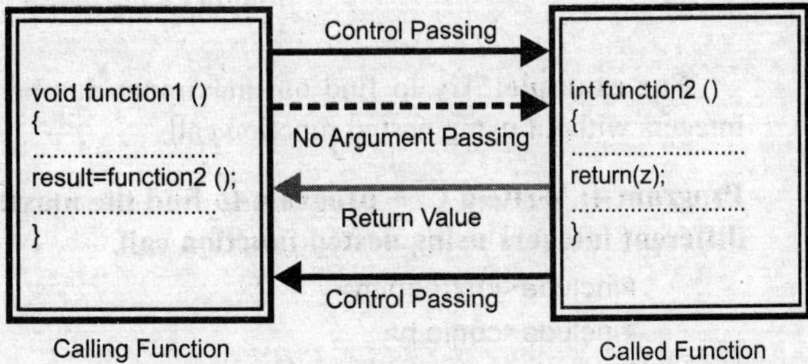

Functions with no arguments and return values

5.8.5 Functions that Return Multiple Values

So far, we have learned and seen that in a function, return statement was able to return only single value. That is because; a return statement can return only one value. But if we want to send back more than one value then how we could do this?

We have used arguments to send values to the called function, in the same way we can also use arguments to send back information to the calling function. The arguments that are used to send back data are called **Output Parameters**.

It is a bit difficult for novice because this type of **function uses pointer**.

5.9 NESTING OF FUNCTION CALL IN C++ PROGRAMMING

C++ permits nesting of two functions freely. There is no limit how deeply functions can be nested. If we are calling any function inside another function call is known as nesting function call. Sometime it converts a difficult program in easy one.

The general syntax is:

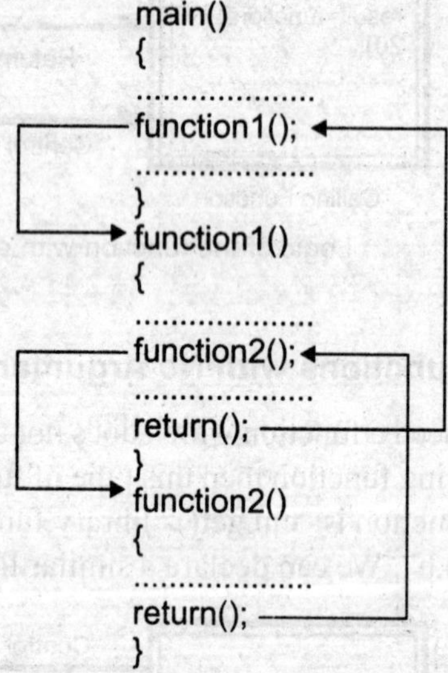

For example: Try to find out maximum number among the five different integers without using nested function call.

Program 4: Write a C++ program to find the maximum number among five different integers using nested function call.

```
#include<iostream.h>
#include<conio.h>
int max(int x, int y){return x>y ? x : y;}
void main()
{
int m;
m=max(max(4,max(11,6)),max(10,5));
cout<< m;
```

```
getch();
}
```

Output:

11

5.10 FUNCTION RECURSION IN C++

Recursion, in mathematics and computer science, is a method of defining functions in which the function being defined is applied within its own definition. The term is also used more generally to describe a process of repeating objects in a self-similar way. For instance, when the surfaces of two mirrors are almost parallel with each other the nested images that occur are a form of recursion.When a called function in turn calls another function, then a process of 'chaining' occurs. Recursion is a special case of this process or chain. So when a function calls itself, then it is called **recursion.** This chain continues till a specific condition met. If it has not any stop condition, then it will create an indefinite loop. Recursion is also called **self-reference loop**. It is alternative of loop. Any C++ program which is possible using loop it must be possible using function recursion.

Recursion is used to solve for the problems, which cannot be solved by the iterative procedure for, while and do loops. It is useful to solve repetitive problems, where input of one sub-program can be used as starting value having the previous output. A recursion procedure is also called well-defined function, if it satisfies the following conditions:

(i) A recursive function should have specific condition.

(ii) A recursive function should have smaller argument each time than the previous argument value in the every recursive loop.

For example, below written program is a recursive (unconditional recursion) procedure:

```
main ( )
{
cout<<"\n I LOVE MY BABY \n";
main ( );
}
```

It will display the result infinite times (indefinite loop) as:

```
I LOVE MY BABY
I LOVE MY BABY
I LOVE MY BABY
........................
```

Another example, which will illustrate the recursion based on condition, is to write a C++ program to find the factorial of a number is written below as:

Program 5: Write a C++ program to find the factorial of a number by using the Recursion.

```
#include <iostream.h>
#include <conio.h>
void main ( )
{
int n, factorial( );
clrscr();
cout<<"\n Enter the value of N: ";
cin>>n;
cout<<"\n Factorial of number "<<n<<" is  "<<factorial(n);
getch ( );
}
int factorial(n)
int n;
{
int m;
if (n = = 1)
{
return (n);
}
else
{
m = n * factorial(n-1);
return (m);
}
}
```

Output:

Enter the value of N: 5

Factorial of number 5 is 120

5.10.1 Important Points about Function Recursion in C++

Following are the important points about recursion:

1. **It is very slow process:** One problem with function recursion is it creates a function frame in each function call. This makes program very slow. This is main reason to introduce for, while and do-while loop in C++ event that it is also possible by using function recursion.
2. **Nature of function recursion is infinite loop or stack over flow:** Calling of same from its function body lead to infinite loop or stack over flow. But

with help of conditional statement if-else, switch-case we can able to stop the loop.

3. **It follows LIFO data structure:** In function recursion return value of each recursion is stored in stack. As we know stack is LIFO data structure.
4. **We cannot use break keyword in function recursion:** Keyword break can be use to stop any loop. Since function recursion is no a loop .So, we cannot use break and continue keyword.
5. We can not use goto keyword to switch the control from one function to another function.

5.10.2 Advantages of Recursion

Recursion is a process in which a function calls itself that is function calling itself is known as Recursion. The various advantages of recursion are:

(i) It is simple, easily understandable, concise, compact and transparent to view a c program.

(ii) Lesser number of programming statements (coding) required with the use of recursion.

(iii) It is very useful in solving mathematical (factorial, GCD, Fibonacci series etc.), trigonometric (compute hyperbolic trigonometric value), logical games (tower of Hanoi, generating random number in system simulation, puzzles) and algebraic problems (to solve Ackermann's function).

(iv) It is very useful where user-defined function or sub-program or procedure required.

(v) It is eminently useful if the solution to problem is in recursive terms.

(vi) It is more useful in the multiprocessing and multitasking environment.

(vii) It is very useful in solving the data structure problems like linked list, queues, stack, tree, Quick sort and merge sort etc.

(viii) Recursion saves the memory. In other words it utilizes the memory well.

5.10.3 Disadvantages of Recursion

The various disadvantages of recursion are:

(i) It requires more memory to store the automatic variable to solve the problems like stack and so waste the memory space. i.e. to consume more storage space.

(ii) If properly recursion procedure is not checked, then it will create a problem for the processing and procedure run out of memory.

(iii) In some problems, it is a time consuming process and is not efficient.

(iv) It will create indefinite looping process (non-terminating iteration), if condition not be applied at the proper place.

5.11 FUNCTION PROTOTYPES

The prototype of a function provides the basic information about a function which tells the compiler that the function is used correctly or not. It contains the same information as the function header contains. It is now considered good form to use **function prototypes** for all functions in your program. A prototype declares the function name, its parameters, and its return type to the rest of the program prior to the function's actual declaration. To understand why function prototypes are useful, enter the following code and run it:

```
#include <iostream.h>
void main()
{
cout<<add(3);
}
int add(int i, int j)
{
return i+j;
}
```

This code compiles on many compilers without giving you a warning, even though **add** expects two parameters but receives only one. It works because many C++ compilers do not check for parameter matching either in type or count. You can waste an enormous amount of time debugging code in which you are simply passing one too many or too few parameters by mistake. The above code compiles properly, but it produces the wrong answer.

To solve this problem, C++ lets you place function prototypes at the beginning of (actually, anywhere in) a program. If you do so, C++ checks the types and counts of all parameter lists. Try compiling the following:

```
#include <iostream.h>
int add (int,int);            /* function prototype for add */
void main()
{
cout<<add(3);
}
int add(int i, int j)
{
return i+j;
}
```

The prototype causes the compiler to flag an error on the cout function.

Place one prototype for each function at the beginning of your program. They can save you a great deal of debugging time, and they also solve the problem you get when you compile with functions that you use before they are declared. For example, the following code will not compile:

```
#include <iostream.h>
void main()
{
cout<<add(3);
}
float add(int i, int j)
{
return i+j;
}
```

Why, you might ask, will it compile when add returns an int but not when it returns a float? Because older C++ compilers default to an int return value. Using a prototype will solve this problem. "Old style" (non-ANSI) compilers allow prototypes, but the parameter list for the prototype must be empty. Old style compilers do no error checking on parameter lists.

Program 6: Write a C++ program to explain the concept of function prototyping.

```
#include <iostream.h>
#include<conio.h>
void main ( )
{
float a,b,
cout<<"\n Enter any number";
cin>>a;
b = square (a)
cout<<"\n square of "<<a<<" is "<<b;
getch();
}
square (float x)                /* Not using function prototype for
square() */
{
float y;
Y = x * x;
return (y);
}
```

the sample run of this program is Enter any number 2.5 square of 2.5 is 6.000000 Here 6 is not a square of 2.5 this happened because any C++ function, by default, always returns an integer value. The following program segment illustrates how to make square ( ) capable of returning a float value.

Program 7: Write a C++ program to explain the concept of function prototyping.

```
#include <iostream.h>
#include<conio.h>
void main ( )
{
float square ( );                    /* Using function prototype for square() */
float a, b;
cout<<"\n Enter any number ";
cin>>a;
b = square (a);
cout<<"\n square of "<<a<<" is "<<b;
getch();
}
float square (float x)
{
float y;
y= x *x;
return ( y);
}
```

Output:

Enter any number 2.5

square of 2.5 is 6.2500000

5.12 HANDLING OF NON-INTEGER FUNCTIONS

We have seen that C++ functions by default return **int** value. This is obvious to raise a question, whether there are other return types for functions. Yes there are, not only the basic data types like int, float, char but also user-defined types like structures and arrays.

For allowing other than the int return types we have the *type-specifier* for functions. This will help you to return other return types. We must do two things to enable a calling function to receive a non-integer value from a called function:

Note: The following explanations are in accordance to the older method of C++ functions, which doesn't declare function arguments on the same line as the function header. The modern or ANSI method declares the function on the same line as function header. There are also a few other subtle but important distinctions in the two methods.

1. The explicit type-specifier, corresponding to the data type required must be mentioned in the function header. The general form of the function definition is

```
type-specifier function-name (argument list)
argument declaration;
{
function statements;
}
```

The type-specifier tells the compiler, the type of data type the function is to return.

2. The called function must be declared at the start of the body in the calling function, like any other variable. This is to tell the calling function the type of data that the function is actually returning.

For example consider the following segment of program

```
main()
{
float x,a,b, mul();          //function declaration
double y, div();             //function declaration
//Program statements
x = mul(a,b);                //function call
y = div(a,b);                //function call
}
float mul(t,e)               //function definition
float t,e;
{
// Body
}
double div(i,o)              //function definition
float i,o;
{
//body
}
```

The declaration part of **main** function declares not only the variables but the functions **mul** and **div** as well. This only tells the compiler that mul return a float-type value and div a double-type value. Parentheses that follow mul and div specify that they are functions instead of variables.

If we have a mismatch between the type of data that the called function returns and the type of data that the calling function expects, we will have unpredictable results. We must, therefore be careful to make sure that both types are compatible.

In cases when the function doesn't return any values, in that situation we specify the return type as **void**. This has to be done in the declaration of the function in the main as well in the function header.

5.13 VOID FUNCTION

The functions that do not return any values can be explicitly defined as void. This prevents any accidental use of these functions in expressions.

When a void statement is used in function program, then it returns nothing. In other words, when we want to return no value to the calling program, then void function is used. Void function is used both in function definition and function declaration.

The general syntax is:

```
void function name( );
```

5.14 WHAT IS MAIN FUNCTION IN C++?

Main is user defined function because main is defined by user but it is different from other user defined function. Every c program starts from main function and end at the null statement. In any program there must be only one main function otherwise operating system will not able to decide from which main program should start.

Main function has three parameter:

1. Argument counter
2. Argument vector
3. Environment vector

5.15 FUNCTIONS AND ARRAYS

We can pass an entire array of values into a function just as we pass individual variables.

Arrays are declared with the function definition and so can be used in the function declaration statement. There are mainly two types of arrays defined in the previous chapter, so to passing the array to function is explained as:

5.15.1 Passing One-dimensional Array to Function

In this task it is essential to list the name of the array along with functions arguments without any subscripts and the size of the array as arguments.

The general syntax is:

function-name(array-name, array-size);

For example, passing of one-dimensional array values to the function subprogram can be illustrated in a valid statement as below:

big(a, n);

Will pass all the elements contained in the array a of size n.

For example, suppose if you want to find the biggest number among n numbers, then by using the function sub-program with the one dimension array, the C++ program shown below:

Program 8: Write a C++ program to illustrate the concept of passing of one-dimensional array to function.

```
#include<iostream.h>
#include<conio.h>
void main ( )
{
int a[50], x, i, b, big( ),n;
cout<<"Enter the size of array : ";
cin>>n;
cout<<"\n Enter the elements of Array : ";
for (i = 0; i < n; i++)
{
cin>>a[i];
}
b=big(a,n);
cout<<"Biggest number is "<<b;
getch( );
}
int big (x, m)
int x[ ], m;
{
int bi, i;
```

```
bi = x[0];
for (i=1; i < m; i++)
{
if(x [i ] > bi)
{
bi = x [i ];
}
}
return (bi);
}
```

Output:

```
Enter the size of array: 5
Enter the elements of Array:
10
40
45
20
15
Biggest number is 45
```

5.15.2 Passing Two-dimensional Array to Function

In the two-dimensional array, we have the array name, row size and column size.

The general syntax is:

function-name (array-name, row-size, column-size);

For example, passing of two-dimensional array values to the function subprogram can be illustrated in a valid statement as below:

trace(a,n,m);

Will pass all the elements contained in the array a of size n * m.

For example, write a C++ program to find sum of diagonal elements of a matrix using the two-dimensional array be as:

Program 9: Write a C++ program to illustrate the concept of passing two-dimensional array to the function.

```
#include <iostream.h>
#include<conio.h>
void main( )
{
int a[10][10], n, m, i, j, sum, trace( );
cout<<"\n Enter the number of row and columns in the matrix :";
```

```
cin>>n>>m;
cout<<"\n Enter the elements of matrix : ";
for(i=0; i<n; i++)
{
for(j=0; j< m; j++)
{
cin>>a[i][j];
}
}
sum=trace(a,n,m);
cout<<"\n Sum of diagonal elements is : "<<sum;
getch( );
}
int trace(x,p,q)
int p,q, x[p ][ ];
{
int i, j,s;
s=0;
for(i=0; i<p; i++)
{
for(j=0; j< q; j++)
{
if(i==j)
{
s=s+x[i][j];
}
}
}
return(s);
}
```

Output:

```
Enter the number of row and columns in the matrix: 3 3
Enter the elements of matrix:
4    5    8
2    6    9
9    4    2
Sum of diagonal elements is: 12
```

5.16 STORAGE CLASSES

To fully define a variable one needs to mention not only its type, but also its **'storage class'.** Every variable not only has a data type but also have a storage class. If don't specify any storage class of a variable in its declaration, the compiler will assume a storage class depending on the context in which the variable is used. Thus, variables have certain default storage classes. A variable name identifies some physical location within the computer where the string of bits representing the variable value is stored.

There are basically two kinds of locations in a computer where such a value may be kept memory and CPU registers. It is the variable's storage class, which determines in which of these two locations the value is stored.

Variable are stored in the memory in different ways by using the function. Every time the execution period (i.e. life time) and boundary (i.e. scope or visibility) of the variable vary in the function sub-programs. There are two mainly two types of variables.

1. **Local variable:** A local variable will be visible to the function in which it is declared, but not to other. It is declared inside the function. A local variable is also called automatic variable, because it is automatically created (when a function is called) and destroyed (when execution of function complete. i.e. when the function returns).
2. **Global variable:** A global variable is to visible to all the functions and it is declared outside the function. The proper place of declaration of global variable is at the beginning of the main program or before the function sub program. In other words before the declaration of all the function sub-programs.

The storage class determines the part of memory where storage is allocated for an object (particularly variables and functions) and how long the storage allocation continues to exist.

A scope specifies the part of the program which a variable name is visible, that is the accessibility of the variable by its name. In C++ program, there are four storage classes: automatic, register, static, and external.

Keep in mind that in the hardware terms we have primary storage such as registers, cache, memory (Random Access Memory) and secondary storage such as magnetic and optical disk.

5.17 STORAGE CLASS IN C++

A ***storage class*** is used to tell the compiler how to store the variables and functions within a program or code.

The general syntax is:

Storage-class type variable-name;

In c there are four types of storage class. They are:

1. Automatic storage class
2. Register storage class
3. Static storage class
4. External storage class

Storage class is modifier or qualifier of data types which decides:

1. In which area of memory a particular variable will be stored?
2. What will be the initial value of the variable, if the initial value is not specifically assigned (i.e, the default initial value).
3. What is the scope of the variable, i.e., in which functions the value of the variable would be available.
4. What is the life of the variables; i.e., how long would the variable exist.

5.18 AUTO KEYWORD IN C++

The auto keyword is used to place the specified variable into the stack area of memory. In most variable declaration, this is usually implicit one, e.g. int i;

1. Auto storage class
2. Properties of auto storage class

5.18.1 Auto Storage Class

Automatic variables or auto variables are default storage class of local variable. An auto variable cannot be declared globally. Automatic variables are declared inside a particular function and they are created when the function is called and destroyed when the function exits. Automatic variables are local or private to a function in which they are defined by default all variable declared without any storage specification is automatic. The value of variable remains unchanged to the changes that may happen in other functions in the same program and by doing this no error occurs.

The general syntax is:

Auto type variable-name;

That means the keyword auto just precedes the normal variable declaration.

Example:

```
#include <iostream.h>
#include<conio.h>
```

```
void main()
{
auto int i=10;
cout<<i;
getch();
}
```

Output:

10

Note: In C++ language all the variables which are defined within a function are automatic or in other words we can say that if we do not apply keyword auto before a variable which is defined within a function will be treated as an automatic variable.

5.18.2 Properties of Auto Storage Class

Following are the properties of auto storage class:

1. Default initial value of auto variable is garbage.
2. Visibility of auto variable is within the block where it has declared.
3. Scope of auto variable is within the block where it has declared.
4. From above example it is clear auto variable initialize each time.
5. An auto variable gets memory at run time.

5.19 REGISTER KEYWORD IN C++

The register keyword gives suggest to the compiler to place the particular variable in the fast register memory located directly on the CPU.

1. Register storage class
2. Properties of register storage class

5.19.1 Register Storage Class

A register storage class is very similar to auto storage class except one most important property. All register variable in C++ stores in CPU registers not in the memory. The lifetime and visibility of Register storage class is similar to that of auto default storage class. The default initial value is unpredictable; it may be some garbage value. These variables are accessed much quickly than other variables as they reside in the registers of the microprocessor.

As the registers of microprocessor are very small nearly 8 to 16 bits. So register variables are only of char or int data type.

The general syntax is:

```
register type variable-name;
```

Example:

```
#include <iostream.h>
#include<conio.h>
void main()
{
register int i=10;
cout<<i;
getch();
}
```

Output:

10

5.19.2 Properties of Register Storage Class

Following are the properties of register storage class:

1. In following declaration:

   register int a,

   We are only requesting not forcing to compiler to store variable a in CPU registers. Compiler will decide where to store in the variable a.
2. A register variable execute faster than other variables because it is stored in CPU registers so during the execution compiler has no extra burden to bring the variable from memory to CPU.
3. Since a CPU have limited number of register so it is programmer responsibility which variable should declared as register variable i.e. variable which are using many times should declared as a register variable.
4. We cannot dereference register variable since it has not any memory address.
5. Default initial value of register variable is garbage.
6. Scope and visibility of register variable is block.

5.20 STATIC KEYWORD IN C++

Keyword static is used for declaring static variables in C++. This modifier is used with all data types like int, float, double, array, pointer, structure, function etc.

1. Static storage class
2. Properties of static storage class

5.20.1 Static Storage Class

It is also used to declare the variables to be private to a certain file only when declared with global variables. Static can also be used with functions, making those functions visible only to file itself. The static keyword is used for extending the lifetime of a particular variable. The variable remains even after the function call is long gone (the variable is placed in the alterable area of memory),if you declare a static variable inside a function,. The static keyword can be overloaded.

The general syntax is:

```
static type variable-name;
```

Example:

```
#include <iostream.h>
#include<conio.h>
void main()
{
add();
add();
getch();
}
add()
{
static int i=10;
cout<<i<<endl;
i+=1;
}
```

Output:

```
10
11
```

5.20.2 Properties of Static Storage Class

Following are the properties of static storage class:

1. It is **not** default storage class of global variables. For example, analyze the following three programs and its output.
2. Default initial value of static integral type variables are zero otherwise null.
3. A same static variable can be declared many times but we can initialize at only one time.
4. We cannot write any assignment statement globally.
5. A static variable initializes only one time in whole program.

6. If we declared static variable locally then its visibility will within a block where it has declared.
7. If declared a static variable or function globally then its visibility will only the file in which it has declared not in the other files.
8. If we static variable has declared locally or globally its scope will always whole the program. (9) A static variables or functions have internal linkage. An internal linkage variables or functions are visible to the file where it has declared.

5.21 EXTERN KEYWORD IN C++

Keyword extern is used for declaring extern variables in C++. This modifier is used with all data types like int, float, double, array, pointer, structure, function etc.

1. Extern storage class
2. Properties of extern storage class

5.21.1 Extern Storage Class

The extern keyword is used to specify variable access the variable of the same name from some other file. In modular programs, this is very useful for sharing variables. **extern** is used to give a reference of a global variable that is visible to ALL the program files.

Variables which are common to all functions and accessible by all functions of a program are internal variables. External variables can be declared outside a function.

The general syntax is:

```
extern type variable-name;
```

Example:

```
#include <iostream.h>
#include<conio.h>
int i=10;
void main()
{
int i=2;
cout<<i;
display();
getch();
}
```

```
display()
{
cout<<endl<<i;
}
```

Output:

```
2
10
```

Note: The extern storage class is used only for **global variables**.

- *An extern variable is initialized by the program when the file is first loaded.*
- *Extern is a keyword which is used to represent external variable.*
- *The lifetime of the external variables remains as long as the program runs.*

5.21.2 Properties of Extern Storage Class

Following are the properties of extern storage class:

1. It is default storage class of all global variables as well all functions.
2. When we use extern modifier with any variables it is only declaration i.e. memory is not allocated for these variable. Hence in second case compiler is showing error unknown symbol i. To define a variable i.e. allocate the memory for extern variables it is necessary to initialize the variables.
3. If you will not use extern keyword with global variables then compiler will automatically initialize with default value to extern variable.
4. Default initial value of extern integral type variable is zero otherwise null.
5. We cannot initialize extern variable locally i.e. within any block either at the time of declaration or separately. We can only initialize extern variable globally.
6. If we declare any variable as extern variable then it searches that variable either it has been initialized or not. If it has been initialized which may be either extern or static* then it is ok otherwise compiler will show an error.
7. A particular extern variable can be declared many times but we can initialize at only one time.
8. We cannot write any assignment statement globally.

5.22 SCOPE AND VISIBILITY OF STORAGE CLASS IN C++

Following table shows the scope and visibility of storage classes:

Storage classes	How it has declared	Scope	Visibility
auto	Globally Locally	Block	Block
register	Globally Locally	Block	Block
Static	Globally Locally	Program Program	File Block
extern	Globally Locally	Program Program	Program Block

PROGRAMMING PROBLEMS

Program 1: Write a C++ program to find the Inverse of Matrix by using Function.

Program 2: Write a C++ program to a recursive function to obtain the running the running sum of first 25natural.

Program 3: Write a C++ program to a positive integer is entered through the keyboard, To obtain the prime factors of the number. Modify the function suitably to obtain the prime factors recursively.

Program 4: Write a C++ program to write a function which receives a float and an int from main( ), finds the product of these two and returns the product which is printed through main( ) .

Program 5: Write a C++ program to write a function power (a, b), to calculate the value of a raised to b.

Program 6: Write a C++ program to a 5-digit positive integer is entered through the keyboard, To calculate sum of digits of the 5-digit number:

(1) Without using recursion (2) Using recursion

Program 7: Write a C++ program to a positive integer is entered through the keyboard, write a function to find the binary equivalent of this number using recursion.

Program 8: Write a C++ program to a general- purpose function to convert any given year into its roman equivalent. The following table shows the roman equivalent of decimal numbers:

Decimal	Roman
1	i
5	v
10	x

50 l
100 c
500 d
1000 m

Program 9: Write a C++ program, which receives 5 integers and returns the sum, average and standard deviation of these numbers. Call this function from main( ) and print the results in

main( ).

Program 10: Write a C++ Program to print a palindrome number like 525 using function.

Program 11: Write a C++ Program to calculate of GCD of two numbers using function.

Program 12: Write a C++ Program to calculate number of days between two dates using function.

Program 13: Write a C++ Program to implement the tower of Hanoi using recursion.

Program 14: Write a C++ Program for adding, subtracting and multiplying matrices using separate functions for each operation and passing matrix as arguments to the functions.

Fill in the blanks

1. A function is invoked using a ....
2. The type of variable that is known only within the function in which it is defined is called a ....
3. The .... statement in a called function passes the value of an expression back to the calling function.
4. The keyword void means function have to returns....................
5. The three ways to return control from a called function to a caller are ...., ... and ....
6. A .... allows the compiler to check the number, data types and order of the arguments passed to a function.
7. Variables declared in a block or in the parameter list of a function are assumed to be of storage class .... unless specified otherwise.
8. Storage-class specifier .... is a recommendation to the compiler to store a variable in one of the computer's registers.
9. A variable declared outside any block or function is a .... variable.
10. For a local variable in a function to retain its value between calls to the function, it must be declared with the .... storage-class specifier.

11. A function that calls itself either directly or indirectly (i.e., through another function) is a .... function.

Answers

1. function call. 2. local variable. 3. return. 4. nothing. 5. return;, return expression; or return variable. 6. function prototype. 7. auto. 8. register. 9. extern. 10. static. 11. recursive.

OBJECTIVE TYPE QUESTIONS

1. The program execution starts from
   (a) the function which is first defined
   (b) main( ) function
   (c) the function which is last defined
   (d) the function other than main( )
2. How many main( ) functions can be defined in a C++ program ?
   (a) 1 (b) 2
   (c) 3 (d) any number of times
3. A function is identified by an open parenthesis following
   (a) a keyword
   (b) an identifier other than keywords
   (c) an identifier including keywords
   (d) an operator
4. A function with no action
   (a) is an invalid function
   (b) produces syntax error
   (c) is allowed and is known as dummy function
   (d) returns zero
5. Parameters are used
   (a) to return values from the called function
   (b) to send values from the calling function
   (c) options a and b
   (d) to specify the data type of the return value
6. Identify the correct statement
   (a) a function can be defined more than once in a program
   (b) function definition cannot appear in any order

(c) functions cannot be distributed in many files
(d) one function cannot be defined

7. The default return data type in function definition is
(a) void (b) int
(c) float (d) char

8. The parameters in a function call are
(a) actual parameters (b) formal parameters
(c) dummy parameters (d) optional

9. The parameters in a function definition are
(a) actual parameters (b) formal parameters
(c) dummy parameters (d) optional

10. The parameters passing mechanism used in C is
(a) call by reference (b) call by name
(c) call by value (d) options a and b

11. The storage class that can precede return data type in function declaration is
(a) extern (b) static
(c) options a and b (d) register

12. Recursive call results when
(a) a function calls itself
(b) a function calls another function, which in turn calls the function 1
(c) options a and b
(d) a function calls another function

13. The main( ) function calls in a C++ program
(a) allows recursive calls (b) does not allow recursive call
(c) is optional (d) is a built in function

14. The function main( ) is
(a) a built-in function (b) a user defined function
(c) optional (d) all the above

15. The function defined in math.h file for returning the arc tangent of x is
(a) tan_1(x) (b) atan(x)
(c) tanh(x) (d) arctan(x)

16. The function ceil(x) defined in math.h
(a) returns the value rounded down to the next lower integer
(b) returns the value rounded down to the next higher integer

(c) the next higher value

(d) the next lower value

17. The function floor(x) in math.h
    (a) returns the value rounded down to the next lower integer
    (b) returns the value rounded down to the next higher integer
    (c) the next higher value
    (d) the next lower value
18. The function strcpy(s1, s2) in string.h
    (a) copies s1 to s2 (b) copies s2 to s1
    (c) appends s1 to end of s2 (d) appends s2 to end of s1
19. The function strcat(s1, s2) in string.h
    (a) copies s1 to s2 (b) copies s2 to s1
    (c) appends s1 to end of s2 (d) appends s2 to end of s1
20. The function strcmp(s1, s2) returns zero
    (a) if s is lexicographically less than s2.
    (b) if s is lexicographically greater than s2
    (c) If both s1 and s2 are equal
    (d) If s1 is empty string
21. What function must all C++ programs have?
    (a) start( ) (b) main( )
    (c) return( ) (d) exit( )
22. Which of the following would compute the square of x in C++?
    (a) pow(2,x); (b) pow(x,2);
    (c) x* * 2; (d) power(x,2);
23. All standard C++ library < math.h > functions return what data type?
    (a) decimal (b) float
    (c) double (d) int
24. What does strcat append to the target string after the specified number of Characters have been copied?
    (a) nothing (b) null
    (c) \0 (d) -0
25. C++ allows
    (a) only call by value
    (b) only call by reference

(c) both

(d) only call by value and sometimes call by reference

26. Which of the following is a key word is used for a storage class

(a) printf (b) external

(c) auto (d) scanf

27. The storage class allowed for parameters is

(a) auto (b) static

(c) extern (d) register

28. Functions have

(a) file scope (b) local scope

(c) block scope (d) function scope

29. When a function is recursively called all automatic variables are

(a) stored in stack (b) stored in queue

(c) stored in array (d) stored in linked list

30. Global variables that are declared static are ....

Which one of the following correctly completes the sentence above?

(a) Deprecated by Standard C++

(b) Internal to the current translation unit

(c) Visible to all translation units

(d) Read-only subsequent to initialization

(e) Allocated on the heap

31. What does the "auto" specifier do?

(a) It automatically initializes a variable to 0;.

(b) It indicates that a variable's memory will automatically be preserved.

(c) It automatically increments the variable when used.

(d) It automatically initializes a variable to NULL.

(e) It indicates that a variable's memory space is allocated upon entry into the block.

EXERCISES

1. Explain different categories of functions.
2. What is user defined function or subprogram.
3. How can you declare and use user-defined function. Explain with an appropriate example?

4. Write detail explanation of syntax of function.
5. How to calculate size of a function in C++?
6. Why we use functions.
7. What are the various advantages of functions?
8. Explain the scope of function variables.
9. What is return statement?
10. Explain various features of return type of function in C++ programming.
11. What are the various types of function in C++ programming language?
12. Explain the concept of recursion in detail.
13. How to write function recursion program in easier way?
14. Write down important points about recursion in C++.
15. What are the various advantages of recursion?
16. What are the various disadvantages of recursion?
17. What do you mean by tail recursion?
18. Explain the concept of function prototypes in detail.
19. Explain the concept of handling of non-integer functions.
20. What do you mean by void function?
21. What is main function in C++?
22. Explain the relationship between functions and arrays.
23. How ca you design your own user-defined function library.
24. Write down important points about the functions.
25. What do you mean by scope of a variable?
26. Explain scope and visibility of storage classes.
27. What do you mean by auto keyword?
28. What is auto storage class?
29. Explain the properties of auto storage class.
30. What do you mean by register keyword?
31. What is register storage class?
32. Explain the properties of register storage class.
33. What do you mean by static keyword?
34. What is static storage class?
35. Explain the properties of static storage class.
36. What do you mean by extern keyword?
37. What is extern storage class?
38. Explain the properties of extern storage class.

CHAPTER 6

Pointers

6.1 INTRODUCTION

Many C++ programming learner thinks that pointer is one of the difficult topic in C++ language but it's not completely true. It is difficult to understand in comparison of other secondary (array, structure etc.) data types available in C++. Pointer in C++ seems to be difficult because it works directly with computer memory (RAM).

When we declare any variable in C++, for example integer variable, it occupies a memory according to its size (here 2 bytes). As it occupies a memory so it's natural to have an address for this location so that it can be referenced later by CPU for manipulation.

Pointers are an extremely powerful programming tool. They can make some things much easier, help improve your program's efficiency, and even allow you to handle unlimited amounts of data. For example, using pointers is one way to have a function modify a variable passed to it. It is also possible to use pointers to dynamically allocate memory, which means that you can write programs that can handle nearly unlimited amounts of data on the fly—you don't need to know, when you write the program, how much memory you need.

For most people it takes a little time and some practice to become fully comfortable with pointers, but once you master them you are a full-fledged C++ programmer.

C++ uses pointers in three different ways:

C++ uses pointers to create **dynamic data structures** — data structures built up from blocks of memory allocated from the heap at run-time.

C++ uses pointers to handle **variable parameters** passed to functions.

Pointers in C++ provide an alternative way to **access information stored in arrays**. Pointer techniques are especially valuable when you work with strings. There is an intimate link between arrays and pointers in C++.

In some cases, C++ programmers also use pointers because they make the code slightly more efficient. What you will find is that, once you are completely comfortable with pointers, you tend to use them all the time.

We will start this discussion with a basic introduction to pointers and the concepts surrounding pointers, and then move on to the three techniques described above. Especially on this chapter, you will want to read things twice. The first time through you can learn all the concepts. The second time through you can work on binding the concepts together into an integrated whole in your mind. After you make your way through the material the second time, it will make a lot of sense.

6.2 POINTER

In C++, a pointer is a variable that points to or references a memory location in which data is stored. In the computer, each memory cell has an address that can be used to access that location so a pointer variable points to a memory location we can access and change the contents of this memory location via the pointer.

Pointers are aptly named: they "point" to locations in memory.

Definition: *"A pointer is a memory variable that stores a memory address. Pointer can have any name that is legal for other variable and it is declared in the same fashion like other variables but it is always denoted by `*` operator."*

A pointer is a special kind of variable. Pointers are designed for storing memory address i.e. the address of another variable. Declaring a pointer is the same as declaring a normal variable except you stick an asterisk '*' in front of the variables identifier.

There are two new operators you will need to know to work with pointers. The **"address of"** operator '&' and the **"dereferencing"** operator '*'. Both are prefix unary operators.

When you place an ampersand in front of a variable you will get its address, this can be stored in a pointer variable. When you place an asterisk in front of a pointer you will get the value at the memory address pointed to.

For example: Suppose **a** is an integer variable and this variable have value 5 stored in the memory. It is represented as:

Variable name	Memory value	Memory address		Pointer variable
a	5	1025	←	ptr1(pointer)

Here the value 5 is stored at address 1025. We give name to memory address as ptr1. The ptr1 is a memory variable, which gives the address of the **a** variable having value 280. Then **ptr1 is called pointer**. Now variable ptr1, which is a memory variable and is stored further in the memory and again it has some memory address. Then the variable of that memory address is another pointer or pointer to pointer. Let it be **ptr2**. This series continues and there is no end. This is as shown:

Variable name	Memory value	Memory address		Pointer variable
a	5	1025	←	ptr1(pointer)
ptr1	1025	5000	←	ptr2(pointer to pointer)

6.2.1 Features of Pointers

Pointer is one of the most exciting features of C++ language and it has added power and flexibility to the language. Pointer is in C++ language because it offers following benefits to the programmers:

1. Pointer saves the memory space.
2. The memory is accessed efficiently with the pointers. The pointers assign memory space and it also releases. Dynamically memory is allocated.
3. Pointers can handle arrays and data table efficiently.
4. Pointers support dynamic memory management.
5. Pointer helps to return multiple values from a function through function argument.
6. Pointer increases program execution speed.
7. Pointer is an efficient tool for manipulating structures, linked lists, queues stacks etc.

6.2.2 Advantages of Pointers

Following are the advantages of pointers:

1. Function cannot return more than one value. But when the same function can modify many pointer variables and function as if it is returning more than one variable.
2. In the case of arrays, we can decide the size of the array at runtime by allocating the necessary space.
3. In the case of pointers to classes, we can use polymorphism and virtual classes to change the behavior of pointers to various types of classes at runtime.

6.2.3 Disadvantages of Pointers

Following are the disadvantages of pointers:

1. If sufficient memory is not available during runtime for the storage of pointers, the program may crash (least possible).
2. If the programmer is not careful and consistent with the use of pointers, the program may crash (very possible).

6.2.4 Rules of Using Pointers

Following are the rules of using pointers:

1. Always initialize a pointer by calling an allocator.
2. Always check to see if the allocation request failed.
3. Always deallocate memory controlled by a pointer when done with it.
4. Never access memory that has not been allocated - pay attention to the size of arrays.
5. Never access memory that has been deallocated.
6. Do not allocate and deallocate memory with wild abandon, because that can fragment the virtual memory address space, causing future allocation requests to fail—particularly in long running programs such as web servers.

6.3 DECLARING A POINTER VARIABLE

A pointer is a variable that contains the memory location of another variable in which data is stored. Using pointer, you start by specifying the type of data stored in the location. The asterisk helps to tell the compiler that you are creating a pointer variable. Finally you have to give the name of the variable.

The general syntax is:

```
datatype * pointer variable
```

We can declare pointers like this –

```
int *x;
float *f;
char *y;
```

In the first statement 'x' is an integer pointer and it tells to the compiler that it holds the address of any integer variable. In the same way 'f' is a float pointer which stores the address of any float variable and 'y' is a character pointer that stores the address of any character variable.

Program 1: Write a C++ program to illustrate the concept of accessing the address of pointer.

```
#include <iostream.h>
#include <conio.h>
void main()
{
int *ptr1 , a;
a = 5;
ptr1 = &a;
cout<<"\n Value"<<a<<" is stored at address "<<ptr1;
getch();
}
Output:
Value 5 is stored at address 1025
```

Note that the pointer variable or memory address always has integer data, which is also unsigned.

6.3.1 Pointer Operators ('*' AND '&')

Take a look on the following declaration,

```
int a=5;
```

When we make such declaration how C++ compiler treat this statement:

1. Reserve memory space for this integer value.
2. Name this memory location as a.
3. Store the value 5 at this location.

This can be illustrated by a simple diagram:

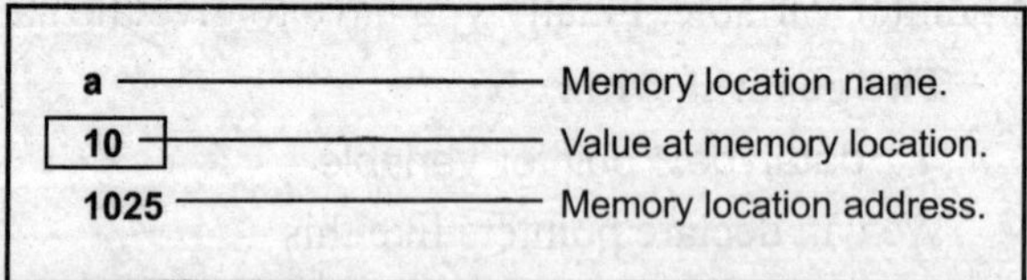

Figure 9.1: Integer variable location in memory

So when we declared an integer variable a and assigned value 5 then compiler occupied a 2 byte memory space at memory address 1025 and stored value 5 at that location. Compiler named this address a so that we can use a instead of 1025 in our program. But we can use address or variable in our program and both will point to the same value (example given below).

The memory address of a variable could differ from PC to PC and entirely depends on available free space in memory at time of program execution. As this differs from PC to PC thus we cannot rely on that address (numeric value representing variable address) and we cannot use this address in our program. But have you noticed one thing that address is an integer.

For Example: Simple pointer declaration and definition:

```
int a=5;
int * ptr;
ptr=&a;
```

Pictorial representation:

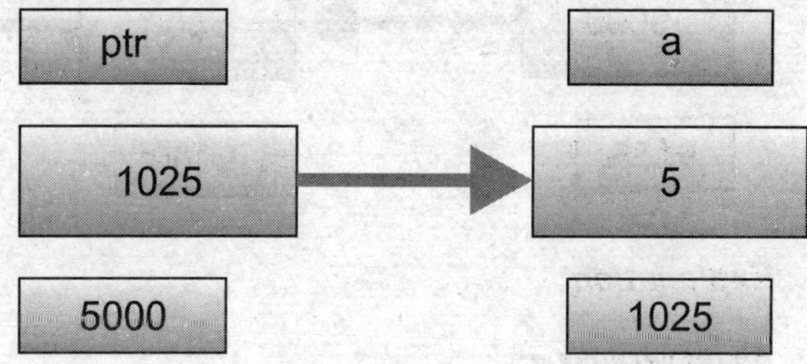

Explanation

About variable a:

1. Name of variable: a
2. Value of variable which it keeps: 5
3. Address where it has stored in memory: 1025 (assume)

About variable ptr:

4. Name of variable: ptr
5. Value of variable which it keeps: 1025
6. Address where it has stored in memory: 5000 (assume)

Note: *A variable where it will be stored in memory is decided by operating system. We cannot guess at which location a particular variable will be stored in memory.*

6.3.2 Pointers to Pointers

It is possible and often useful to create pointers to pointers.

For Example: Simple pointer to pointer declaration and definition:

```
int a=50;
int *ptr1;
int **ptr2;
ptr1=&a;
ptr2=&ptr1;
```

Pictorial representation of above pointer declaration and definition:

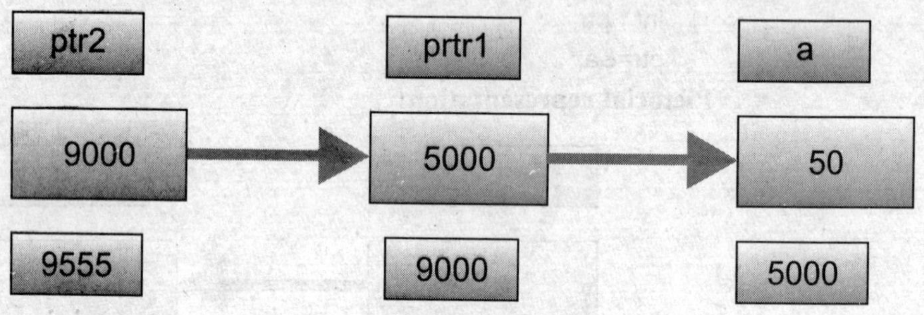

Explanation

About variable a:

1. Name of variable: a
2. Value of variable which it keeps: 50
3. Address where it has stored in memory: 5000 (assume)

About variable ptr1:

4. Name of variable: ptr1
5. Value of variable which it keeps: 5000
6. Address where it has stored in memory: 9000 (assume)

About variable ptr2:

7. Name of variable: ptr2
8. Value of variable which it keeps: 9000
9. Address where it has stored in memory: 9555 (assume)

Note:

** is know as indirection operator which gives content of any variable & is know as reference operator which gives address where variable has stored in memory.*

Cancellation rule of above two operators:

* and & operators always cancel to each other. i.e.

*&p=p

But it is not right to write:

&*p=p

Simple example:

Program 2: Write a C++ program to explain use of pointer to pointer.

```
#include<iostream.h>
#include<conio.h>
void main()
{
int x=25;
int *ptr=&x;            //statement one
int **temp=&ptr;        //statement two
cout<<x<<*ptr<<**temp;
}
```

Output: 25 25 25

Explanation:

As we know value of variable x is 25.

```
*ptr= *(&x) //from statement one
=*&x
=x //using cancellation rule
=25
**temp= **(&ptr)=*(*&ptr)=*ptr=*(&x)=*&x=x=25
```

6.4 ACCESSING THE ADDRESS OF THE MEMORY VARIABLE

The address of the memory variable can be accessed by using address operator (&). Now suppose a is a variable having value 5 and this variable is stored in the memory address at 1025. Then to represent address of the memory, we apply a variable ptr1, which is pointer or memory variable. We can store address of a variable in ptr1 pointer variable as by using & operator.

Program 3: Write a C++ program to illustrate the concept of displaying the address of a Pointer variable.

```
#include <iostream.h>
#include <conio.h>
#include<iostream.h>
#include<conio.h>
```

```
main ( )
{
int a, *ptr1;
a = 220;
ptr1 = &a;
cout<<"/n Value "<< a<<" is stored at address "<< &a;
cout<<"/n Value "<< a<<" is stored at address "<< ptr1;
cout<<"/n Value "<< *ptr1<<" is stored at address "<< ptr1;
cout<<"/n Value "<< *&a<<" is stored at address "<< &a;
getch( ) ;
}
Output:
Value 5 is stored at address 1025
Value 5 is stored at address 1025
Value 5 is stored at address 1025
Value 5 is stored at address 1025
```

6.5 POINTER EXPRESSIONS

In expressions, like other variables pointer variables can be used. For example if p1 and p2 are properly initialized and declared pointers, then the following statements are valid.

```
int x, y, *p1, *p2, z, a, b, c;
x = 1;
y = 2;
p1 = &x;
p2 = &y;
z = (* p1) / (* p2);
a = (* p1) + (* p2);
b = (* p1) x (* p2);
c = (* p1) - (* p2);
```

Note that *p1/*p2 is invalid, because / * becomes comment statement. So when we use pointer arithmetic expression we always use parenthesis.

C++ allows us to subtract integers to or add integers from pointers as well as to subtract one pointer from the other. We can also use short hand operators with pointers p1+=; sum+=*p2; etc., By using relational operators, we can also compare pointers like the expressions such as p1 >p2, p1== p2 and p1 != p2 are allowed.

```
int q, abc,*p1,*p2;
q =  280;
```

```
p1 =  &q;
abc =  200;
p2  =  &abc;
if (* p1 > *p2)
{
statement block;
}
```

Note that when value of a variable, which is linked to pointer variable p1, is greater than the value of another variable linked to the pointer variable p2. Then statement block will be executed.

6.6 SCALE FACTOR

Scale factor is a scale or measurement of the length of the cells of different data types in terms of bits or bytes. The scale factor for the different data types is as displayed in the below table as:

Data type	Memory space
char	1 byte
int	2 byte
float	4 byte
double	8 byte
long int	4 byte

You have noted that only pointers (addresses) can be incremented or decremented. These can not be applied on arithmetic operations, relational operations, logical operations and assignment operations.

6.7 POINTER AND FUNCTION

Pointer has deep relationship with function. We can pass pointer to the function and also pointer addresses can be passed to the function as pointer arguments. This can be represented by two ways as defined below:

1. Pointer for function parameters
2. Pointer to function

6.7.1 Pointer As Function Parameters

Most C++ programmers first use pointers to implement something called **variable parameters** in functions. You have actually been using variable parameters in the scanf function in C language — that's why you've had to use the **&** (the address operator) on variables used with scanf. Now that you understand pointers you can see what has really been going on.

The pointers are very much used in a function declaration. Sometimes only with a pointer a complex function can be easily represented and success. The usage of the pointers in a function definition may be classified into two groups. To understand how variable parameters work, lets see how we might go about implementing a **swap** function in C++. To implement a swap function, what you would like to do is pass in two variables and have the function swap their values(call by value).

(i) Call by value

We have seen that a function is invoked there will be a link established between the formal and actual parameters. A temporary storage is created where the value of actual parameters is stored. The formal parameters picks up its value from storage area the mechanism of data transfer between actual and formal parameters allows the actual parameters mechanism of data transfer is referred as call by value. The corresponding formal parameter represents a local variable in the called function. The current value of corresponding actual parameter becomes the initial value of formal parameter. The value of formal parameter may be changed in the body of the actual parameter. The value of formal parameter may be changed in the body of the subprogram by assignment or input statements. This will not change the value of actual parameters.

Program 4: Write a C++ program for call by value.

```
#include <iostream.h>
#include<conio.h>
void swap(int i, int j)
{
int t;
t=i;
i=j;
j=t;
}
void main()
{
int a,b;
a=5;
b=10;
cout<<"\n Value of a ="<<a<<" and Value of b = "<<b<<" before swap";
swap(a,b);
```

```
cout<<"\n Value of a ="<<a<<" and Value of b = "<<b<<" after swap";
getch();
}
```

Output:

Value of a = 5 and Value of b = 10 before swap

Value of a = 5 and Value of b = 10 after swap

Note: *When you execute above program, you will find that no swapping takes place. The values of* ***a*** *and* ***b*** *are passed to swap, and the swap function does swap them, but when the function returns nothing happens.*

To make this function work correctly you can use pointers(**call by reference**).

(ii) Call by reference

When we pass address to a function the parameters receiving the address should be pointers. The process of calling a function by using pointers to pass the address of the variable is known as call by reference. The function which is called by reference can change the values of the variable used in the call.

Program 5: Write a C++ program for call by reference.

```
#include <iostream.h>
#include<conio.h>
void swap(int *i, int *j)
{
int t;
t = *i;
*i = *j;
*j = t;
}
void main()
{
int a,b;
a=5;
b=10;
cout<<"\n Value of a ="<<a<<" and Value of b = "<<b<<" before swap";
swap(aa,bb);
cout<<"\n Value of a ="<<a<<" and Value of b = "<<b<<" after swap";
getch();
}
```

Output:

Value of a = 5 and Value of b = 10 before swap

Value of a = 10 and Value of b = 5 after swap

Explanation:

To get an idea of what this code does, print it out, draw the two integers **a** and **b**, and enter 5 and 10 in them. Now draw the two pointers **i** and **j**, along with the integer **t**. When **swap** is called, it is passed the *addresses* of **a** and **b**. Thus, **i** points to **a** (draw an arrow from **i** to **a**) and **j** points to **b** (draw another arrow from **b** to **j**). Once the pointers are initialized by the function call, ***i** is another name for **a**, and ***j** is another name for **b**. Now run the code in **swap**. When the code uses ***i** and ***j**, it really means **a** and **b**. When the function completes, a and b have been swapped.

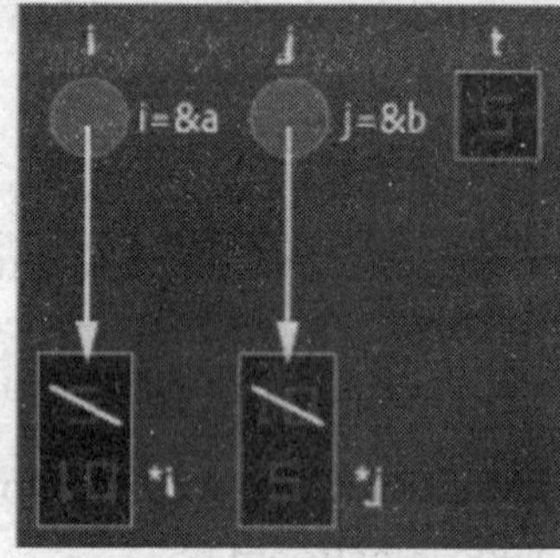

Suppose you accidentally forget the **&** when the **swap** function is called, and that the **swap** line accidentally looks like this: **swap(a, b);**. This causes a segmentation fault. When you leave out the **&**, the *value* of **a** is passed instead of its *address*. Therefore, **i** points to an invalid location in memory and the system crashes when ***i** is used.

Variable parameters are one of the most common uses of pointers in C++. Now you understand what's happening!

6.7.2 Pointer to Function

A function works like a variable. It has also similar data type declaration like the other variable. Pointer to a function variable occurs when you define a function as pointer by using '*'. As function has address location in memory the syntax used to declare pointer to function is as:

```
data-type (*function name)( ) ;
or
type  (*fptr)( );
```

Where type is the data type which may be integer, float or character, fptr () is function name and * (fptr) ( ) is pointer to function.

For example, the procedure to illustrate this concept is as follows:

```
int mul ( ), (*p1) ( );
p1 = & mul ;
```

By using the above example, we can say that mul( ) is a simple function. But p1 is pointer variable which work as pointer to function and in second statement the address of the mul( ) function is assigned to p1 variable which is the memory variable and you know memory variables or pointer. So p1( ) pointer function is linked to the function mul.

Program 6: Write a C++ program to multiply two numbers by using pointer to function concept.

```
#include <iostream.h>
#include<conio.h>
void main ( )
{
int mul( ), (*p1)( ), x, y, z;
cin>>x>>y;
p1 = &mul;
z = (*p1)(x, y);
cout<<z;
getch( );
}
int mul(int p, int q)
{
int m;
m = p * q;
return (m);
}
```

PROGRAMMING PROBLEMS

Program 1: Write a C++ program to print table w=3*x*x-2*x+1 and sin(x)-x varies in steps of 0.5.

Program 2: Write a C++ program using pointers to sort elements of array.

Program 3: Write a C++ program to represent the working of call by value and call by Reference.

Program 4: Write a C++ program to demonstrate that value x[i] and *(x+i) are equal.

Program 5: Write a C++ program to demonstrate array elements are stored in contiguous memory locations.

Program 6: Write a C++ program to function that receives a stored array of integer and an integer value, inserts the value in its correct place.

Program 7: Write a C++ program to reverse the string using pointer.

Program 8: Write a C++ program to find the area of triangle.

Program 9: Write a C++ program to find the area of sphere.

Program 10: Write a C++ program to print the ascii value of given character.

Program 11: Write a C++ program to print the upper case letters to lower case.

Program 12: Write a C++ program to print the lower case letters to upper case.

Program 13: Write a C++ program to read float value and print integer equivalent.

Program 14: Write a C++ program to read int value and print float equivalent.

Program 15: Write a C++ program to print a word form of given number is tens between 1 to 99.

Program 16: Write a C++ program to find a biggest of four given numbers.

Program 17: Write a C++ program to find a smallest of four given numbers.

Program 18: Write a C++ program to find a vowel or not of given character.

Program 19: Write a C++ program to switch statement using pointers.

Program 20: Write a C++ program to sum of first 100 numbers.

Fill in the blanks

1. Pointer is called .... variable.
2. A pointer is a variable that contains as its value the .... of another variable.
3. The three values that can be used to initialize a pointer are ...., ... and ....
4. Pointer and function are related using two techniques .... and ....

Answers

1. Memory addressable 2. address. 3. 0, NULL, an address. 4. call by value, call by reference.

OBJECTIVE TYPE QUESTIONS

1. Pointers are supported in

(a) FORTRAN (b) PASCAL

(c) C++ (d) Both options b and c

2. Pointer variable may be assigned
   (a) an address value represented in hexadecimal
   (b) an address value represented in octal
   (c) the address of another variable
   (d) an address value represented in binary
3. A pointer value refers to
   (a) an integer constant (b) a float value
   (c) any valid address in memory (d) any ordinary variable
4. Identify the correct declaration of pointer variables p1, p2.
   (a) int p1, p2; (b) int *p1, p2;
   (c) int p1, *p2; (d) int *p1, * p2;
5. The operators exclusively used in connection with pointers are
   (a) * and / (b) & and *
   (c) & and | (d) – and >
6. Identify the invalid expression for given register int r = 10;
   (a) r – 20 (b) &r
   (c) r + 15 (d) r / 10
7. Identify the invalid expression.
   (a) &274 (b) &(a + b)
   (c) &(a * b) (d) all the above
8. The operand of the address of operator is
   (a) a constant (b) an expression
   (c) a named region of storage (d) a register variable
9. The address of operator returns
   (a) the address of its operand (b) lvalue
   (c) both options a and b (d) rvalue
10. The indirection operator returns
    (a) the data object stored in the address represented by its operand
    (b) lvalue
    (c) both options a and b
    (d) rvalue
11. The operand of indirection operator is
    (a) pointer variable (b) pointer expression
    (c) both options a and b (d) ordinary variable

12. The operand of address of operator may be
    (a) an ordinary variable
    (b) an array variable
    (c) a pointer variable
    (d) any one of the above
13. After the execution of the statement int x; the value of x is
    (a) 0 (b) undefined
    (c) 1 (d) - 1
14. Pointer variable may be initialized using
    (a) static memory allocation (b) dynamic memory allocation
    (c) both options a and b (d) a positive integer
15. Identify the invalid pointer operator.
    (a) & (b) *
    (c) >> (d) none of the above
16. The number of arguments used in malloc( ) is
    (a) 0 (b) 1
    (c) 2 (d) 3
17. The number of arguments used in calloc( ) is
    (a) 0 (b) 1
    (c) 2 (d) 3
18. The number of arguments used in realloc( ) is
    (a) 0 (b) 1
    (c) 2 (d) 3
19. The function used for dynamic deallocation of memory is
    (a) destroy( ) (b) delete( )
    (c) free( ) (d) remove( )
20. The function call realloc(ptr, 0) is
    (a) same as free(ptr)
    (b) used to clear the values in the address represented by ptr
    (c) used to set the value of ptr to be 0
    (d) invalid
21. In the expression * cp + +
    (a) * cp is evaluated first and *cp is incremented by 1
    (b) * cp is evaluated first and cp is incremented by 1

(c) cp is incremented by 1 first and * is applied

(d) cp is incremented by 1 first and * is applied to the previous value of cp

22. The pointers can be used to achieve

(a) call by function (b) call by reference

(c) call by name (d) call by procedure

23. The first argument argc in main( ) counts

(a) the number of command line strings including the execution command

(b) the number of command line strings excluding the execution command

(c) the number of lines in a program

(d) the number of characters in a program

24. The arguments in main( ) function are known as

(a) program parameters

(b) command line arguments

(c) both options a and b

(d) memory in-line format conversion

25. The invalid address arithmetic is (are)

(a) adding two pointers (b) multiplying two pointers

(c) dividing two pointers (d) all the above

EXERCISES

1. What do you mean by pointers?
2. What are the various features of pointers?
3. What are the various advantages of pointers?
4. What are the various disadvantages of pointers?
5. Write down various rules of using pointers.
6. How can you declare a pointer?
7. How can you initialize a pointer?
8. How can you access values by using the pointers?
9. What are the various pointers arithmetic operations?
10. What do you mean by pointer addressing?
11. What is the function of atoi() function?
12. What is the role of scale factors in the array?
13. Explain the concept of pointers to pointers.
14. How can you access the address of the memory variable?

15. Explain the concept of pointer expressions.
15. Differentiate between call by value and call by reference.
16. How pointer arguments are passed?
17. How pointer arrays are passed as argument using function?
18. Differentiate between pointer to function and pointer as function argument.

CHAPTER 7

Structures and Unions

7.1 INTRODUCTION

In some programming contexts, you need to access multiple data types under a single name for easy manipulation; for example you want to refer to address with multiple data like house number, street, zip code, country C++ supports structure which allows you to wrap one or more variables with different data types. A structure can contain any valid data types like int, char, float even arrays and other structures.

Arrays are used to store large set of data and manipulate them but the disadvantage is that all the elements stored in an array are to be of the same data type. If we need to use a collection of different data type items it is not possible using an array. When we require using a collection of different data items of different data types we can use a structure. Structure is a method of packing data of different types. A structure is a convenient method of handling a group of related data items of different data types.

The C++ language gives you five ways to create a custom data type:

1. The structure, which is a grouping of variables under one name and is called an aggregate data type.
2. The union, which enables the same piece of memory to be defined as two or more different types of variables.
3. The bit-field, which is a special type of structure or union element that allows easy access to individual bits.
4. The enumeration, which is a list of named integer constants.
5. The typedef keyword, which defines a new name for an existing type.

First three features are described in this chapter. Last two features are already described (in Chapter 2).

7.2 STRUCTURE

A structure is a convenient tool for handling a group of logically related data items. Structure help to organize complex data is a more meaningful way. It is powerful concept that we may after need to use in our program Design. A structure is combination of different data types using the & operator, the beginning address of structure can be determined. This is variable is of type structure, then & variable represent the starting address of that variable.

A structure can be considered as a template used for defining a collection of variables under a single name. Structures help a programmer in grouping elements of different data types into a single logical unit. This is unlike arrays which permit a programmer to group only elements of same data type.

Definition: *"A structure is a collection of variables referenced under one name, providing a convenient means of keeping related information together."*

A structure declaration forms a template that can be used to create structure objects (that is, instances of a structure). The variables that make up the structure are called members. (Structure members are also commonly referred to as elements or fields.) Usually, the members of a structure are logically related. For example, suppose if you want to store a book in library using C++ program, then you give information about the title of the book, name of the author, number of pages in the book and the price of the book. Then before coding the problem you will examine it according to following table

Title of the book	Author	Pages	Price
Microprocessor	I Singh	500	285.50
Data Structure	I Singh	525	300.00
Soft Computing	R Singh	285	175.50

To elaborate this problem, we set some data-types and width (size) as shown below:

Field name	Data type	Width (in bytes)
Title	Character	20 bytes
Author	Character	15 bytes
Pages	Integer	2 bytes
Price	Float	4 bytes

Now to enter such type of data having different data types, only structure is the way to pack these all having a common name. To solve such type of problem, we have to use the structure data type. The keyword struct declares a structure to holds the details of four fields namely title, author, pages and price. These are members of the structures. Each member may belong to different or same data type as shown below:

```
struct lib_books
{
char title[20];
char author[15];
int pages;
float price;
};
```

Notice that the declaration is terminated by a semicolon. This is because a structure declaration is a statement. Also, the structure tag lib_books identifies this particular data structure and is its type specifier. We can declare a structure outside the main program and also can be declared within the main program.

The general syntax is:

```
struct tag_name
{
data type member-1;
data type member-2;
data type member-3;
......................;
data type member-n;
};
main ( )
{
struct tag_name  s1,s2,.......sn;
local declaration statements;
executable statements;
}
```

Where s1,s2,.....sn are the list of Structure variables.

The above structure can also be declared as:

```
struct tag_name
{
data type member-1;
data type member-2;
data type member-3;
......................;
data type member-n;
} s1,s2,.......sn;
main ( )
{
```

```
local declaration statements;
executable statements;
}
```

Another form to define the structure within the main program is as:

```
main ( )
{
struct tag_name
{
data type member-1;
data type member-2;
data type member-3;
.......................;
data type member-n;
};
struct tag_name  s1,s2,.......sn;
local declaration statements;
executable statements;
}
```

Note that structure-tag is an optional tag.

Now suppose if you take book1, book2, book3 as three different variables linked with the library structure, then these variables have the common structure of any book in the library can be represented as below:

```
struct lib_books
{
char title[20];
char author[15];
int pages;
float price;
};
main ( )
{
struct lib_books book1, book2, book3;
}
```

We can also declare the above written example in another way as follows:

```
struct lib_books
{
char title[20];
char author[15];
int pages;
```

```
float price;
} book1, book2, book3;
main ( )
{
local declaration statements;
executable statements;
}
```

Another way to write the same problem is as follows:

```
main ( )
{
struct lib_books
{
char title[20];
char author[15];
int pages;
float price;
};
struct lib_books book1, book2, book3;
local declaration statements;
executable statements;
}
```

Note that all the elements in the structure are related to each other logically.

Structure can also be used with the typedef declaration as:

```
typedef struct
{
data type member-1;
data type member-2;
data type member-3;
........................;
data type member-n;
}s1,s2,...sn;
```

For example:

```
typedef struct
{
char firstName[20];
char lastName[20];
char SSN[10];
float gpa;
}student;
```

Now you can use *student* directly to define variables of *student* type without using struct keyword. Following is the example: student st1;

7.3 ACCESSING STRUCTURE MEMBER OR ASSIGNING VALUES TO STRUCTURE MEMBER

Suppose we have a structure about library having information about the title of the book, name of the author, number of pages and the price of the book.

Now if we take book1 structure variable and assign value "I SINGH" to the author of the book, "MICROPROCESSOR" to the title of the book, "500" to the number of the pages and "Rs. 285.50" as the price of the book. To access structure members or assigning value to structure member we can use dot operator (.) between structure name and structure member name as follows:

The general syntax is:

```
structure_name.structure_member
```

For example:

```
book1.pages = 500;
book1.price = 285.50;
```

Program 1: Write a C++ program to read and write the library data by using structure.

```
#include<iostream.h>
#include<conio.h>
void main ( )
{
struct lib_books
{
char title[20];
char author[15];
int pages;
float price;
};
struct lib_books book1;
strcpy(book1. title, "MICROPROCESSOR");
strcpy(book1. author, "I SINGH");
book1.pages = 500;
book1.price = 285.50;
cout<<"\n Title of the book is "<<book1.title;
cout<<"\n Author of the book is "<<book1.author;
cout<<"\n Pages of the book are "<<book1.pages;
```

```
cout<<"\n Price of the book is "<<book1.price;
getch();
}
```

Output:

Title of the book is MICROPROCESSOR
Author of the book is I SINGH
Pages of the book are 500
Price of the book is 285.50

7.4 STRUCTURE AND ARRAY

Array and structure are two different concepts but array play very important role with structure. The two types of relationship of structure with array are discussed as:

1. Array of Structure
2. Array within Structure

7.4.1 Array of Structure

It is possible to define a array of structures of one-dimensional and multi-dimensional are declared by only changing the structure variables from fundamental type to an array type with no change in the structure declaration. We need to use an array than single variables.

The general syntax is:

For one dimensional:

```
struct tag_name
{
data type member-1;
data type member-2;
data type member[size];
......................;
data type member-n;
} struct tag_name variable-name[row-size];
```

For two dimensional:

```
struct tag_name
{
data type member-1;
data type member-2;
data type member[row-size][column-size];
......................;
data type member-n;
} struct tag_name variable-name[row-size] [column-size];
```

7.4.2 Array within Structure

There can also be structures containing arrays as its elements. Do not confuse this concept with array of structures. We can declare an array with in the structure.

The general syntax is:

For one dimensional:

```
struct tag_name
{
data type member-1;
data type member-2;
data type member[size];
......................;
data type member-n;
} structure variable list;
```

For two dimensional:

```
struct tag_name
{
data type member-1;
data type member-2;
data type member[row-size][column-size];
......................;
data type member-n;
} structure variable list;
```

7.5 DIFFERENCE BETWEEN ARRAY AND STRUCTURE

Array and structure are the different concepts so we have to explain the difference between both these concepts as given below:

ARRAY	STRUCTURE
An array is a collection of data items of same data types.	A structure is a collection of data items of different data types.
It has only declaration part.	It has declaration as well as definition part.
There is no keyword in array.	The keyword struct is used in structure.
An array name represents the address of the starting element.	A structure name is known as tag_name. It is a short hand notation of the declaration.
An array cannot have bit fields.	A structure may contain bit fields.
Array has Static memory allocation.	Structure has Dynamic memory allocation.
It uses the subscript to access the array elements.	It uses the dot(.)operator to access the structure members.

ARRAY	STRUCTURE

Example of array:
#include<iostream.h>
#include<conio.h>
void main()
{
int a[5];//only declare an array variable
....
....
}
	Example of structure:
	struct book_bank
	{
	char title[20];
	char author[15];
	int pages;
	float price;
	};struct book_bank book1, book2;
	// declaration of variable

7.6 STRUCTURE WITHIN STRUCTURE

A structure may be defined as a member of another structure. In such structures the declaration of the embedded structure must appear before the declarations of other structures. Structure with in a structure means nesting of structures.

The general syntax is:

```
struct tag_name1
{
data type member-1;
data type member-2;
data type member-3;
.......................;
data type member-n;
struct tag_name2
{
data type member-1;
data type member-2;
data type member-3;
......................;
data type member-m;
} s1;
member-element-m;
} s2;
```

The need of structure within structure is only in the case of number of structure member or member elements. In other words, we can say structure becomes too lengthy, so we sub-divide the structure into two or more than two substructures and embedded one structure within another according to their use and requirement.

Let us consider the following example of student's data. Suppose if we create a structure having the student's data with different data types (structure elements).

Some of the structure elements related with the personal information (like roll-no, name, address, mobile number and fees paid etc.) and others related with the examination information (like roll-no, physics-marks, computer-marks, math-.marks, total-marks, average-marks, grade, result etc). Then this problem can be represented as below:

```
/* Structure having number of elements packed in one structure */
struct student
{
int roll-no;
char name[20];
char addresess[50];
int mobile-no;
float fees;
char date-of-birth[08]
float phy-marks;
float comp-marks;
float math-marks;
float total-marks;
float average;
char grade;
char result[6];
}st[100];
```

These structures become lengthy and also waste the storage space, if a student take admission, but do not sit into the examination. So to remove such type of problems, we set the structure within structure procedure.

The above problem can be solved and processed easily by sub-dividing the structure and setting the structure within structure as:

```
struct  student
{
int  rollno;
char  name[20];
char   addresess[30];
int mobile-no;
float fees;
struct exam
{
float phy-marks;
float comp-marks;
float  math-marks;
```

```
float  total-marks;
float average;
char grade;
char result[5];
}e[50];
char date-of-birth[08];
}st[100];
```

The inner structure member element can be linked with the outer structure variable by using the structure dot operator (.). This can be represented as:

```
Outer-variable.Inner-variable.Inner-element;
```

7.7 STRUCTURE AND FUNCTION

Structure can be implemented with the function easily. For this process, passing of argument takes place similar to the array and variable. The relationship of structure with the function can be viewed from three angles as:

1. Passing Structure to a Function
2. Function Returning Structure
3. Passing array of Structure to Function

7.7.1 Passing Structure to A Function

A structure may be passed into a function as individual member or a separate variable. A program example to display the contents of a structure passing the individual elements to a function is shown below.

The general syntax is:

```
type-specifier function-name(structure-variable);    /*as actual argument
*/
type-specifier function-name(structure-variable)    /* as formal argument
*/
struct  tag_name  structure-variable;
{
.........
........
}
```

A complete structure of passing structure to the function as:

```
main()                    /* main program */
{
struct tag-name
{
```

```
data type member-1;
data type member-2;
data type member-3;
......................;
data type member-n;
}s1;
....................

....................
function-name(s1);
....................
getch();
}
datatype function-name(s2)   /* Function declaration */
struct tag-name  s2;
{
..........
..........
}
```

7.7.2 Function Returning Structure

All the values can be computed in the function body and then return a combined value of whole structure back to the calling statement.

7.7.3 Passing Array of Structure to Function

One of the difficult concept passing of an array of structures to the function is becomes very easy by using the passing of array as an individual element.

7.8 STRUCTURE AND POINTER

Sometimes it is useful to assign pointers to structures (this will be evident in the next section with self-referential structures). Declaring pointers to structures is basically the same as declaring a normal pointer.

The general syntax is:

```
struct  tag_name
{
datatype  member-1;
datatype  member-2;
.................;
datatype  member-n;
}s, *p;
```

Where s is the structure variable and p is the pointer variable. Note that structure variable is a pointer variable and there are no pointer variables work as structure member. Also the structure variable is an array of pointer variables pointing to a structure.

Structure can be directly handled by its address by using the pointer with structure. We use pointer with structure through structure variable. Array of structure variable directly stands for the address of zeroth element.

For example: Below is the declaration of a structure with the pointer displaying the information of a student as:

```
struct student
{
int rn;
char name[20];
char address[30];
float fees;
}s, *p;
```

Pointer variable p can be initialized as:

```
p=&s;
```

You can directly access the individual member element by using the following valid way:

```
(*p).rn;
(*p).name;
(*p).address;
(*p).fees;
```

Invalid way to access the members of structure:

```
*p.rn;
*p.name
```

Because user cannot access the member element directly with the pointer initialization, so always avoid to use pointer with structure without the use of parenthesis. Other way is that user can use the **arrow operator (- >)**. The general way to use arrow operator is as:

```
p - > structure member;
```

Here p is the pointer variable.

For example: Some of the valid declaration of pointer with structure using the arrow operator be as:

```
p - >rn;
p -> name;
p -> address;
p -> fees;
```

If the structure has variable as an array, then 0th element can be directly initialized and assigned to the pointer.

For example:

```
struct Account
{
int accnt-no;
float balance;
}a[10], *p;
```

then link can be created by using the assignment as:

```
p=a;
```

This can also be done as:

```
p=a[0];
```

Note: *The operator -> (arrow operator) has higher priority than "." (dot operator).*

7.9 SELF REFERENTIAL STRUCTURES

The self referential structures are structures that include an element that is a pointer to another structure of the same type.

The general syntax is:

```
struct tag_name
{
data type member-1;
data type member-2;
data type member-3;
.......................;
data type member-n;
struct tag_name *name;
};
```

where name refers to name of a pointer variable. Thus, the structure of type tag will contain a member that points to another structure of type tag. Such structures are known as self referential structure.

For example

```
struct list
{
char items[50];
struct list *next;
};
```

This is a structure of type list. The structure contains two members: a 40-element character array called items, and a pointer to structure of the same type called next. Therefore this is a self referential structure. Self-referential structures are very useful in applications that involve linked data structures, such as lists and trees. The basic idea of a linked data structure is that each component within the structure includes a pointer indicating where the next component can be found. Therefore, the relative order of the components can easily be changed simply by altering the pointers. In addition, individual components can easily be added or deleted, again by altering the pointers. As a result, a linked data structure is not confined to some maximum number of components. Rather, the data structure can expand or contract in size as required. Let us consider the example of the linked list.

For example: Linked List

A linked list is a *dynamic data structure*, which means that the memory to hold the INFO is created at run time (dynamic), and stored in a structured way (also called INFO structure). Also we can say Linked list is a linear INFO structure, i.e it is a linear collection of INFO elements called nodes, where the linear order is given by means of pointers. Each node consists of two fields, one containing the item and the other containing the address of the next item in the list. Each node contains two parts information part and link part. The last node of the linked list contains a special link part called Null Pointer (i.e. any invalid address).

Definition: *"A linked list is an ordered collection of data elements called nodes in which linear order is given by means of pointers. Each node has 2 parts: information (INFO) and link. The information part holds the useful information of the element. The link part or nextpointer part is used identifies the next node in the list."*

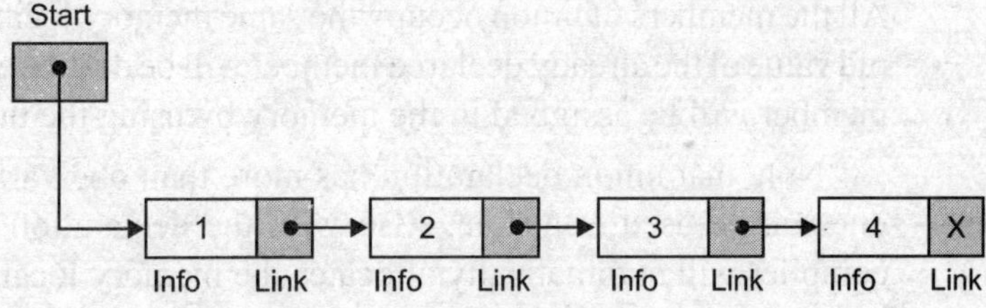

Figure 10.1: Linked list with four nodes.

A Linked List is generally an implementation structure. In other words, linked lists don't have an inherent ordering to them...making it difficult to insert/delete because no choice is made as to where things should be inserted or deleted. However, a linked list can be used to implement queues, stacks, and ordered linked lists (such as a sorted linked list). We may implement linked lists as an array, but it is much more common to implement them using a dynamic structure. The size of the list is only as big as the number of items in the list.

7.10 UNION

Unions like structure contain members whose individual data types may differ from one another. However the members that compose a union all share the same storage area within the computers memory where as each member within a structure is assigned its own unique storage area. Thus unions are used to observe memory. They are useful for application involving multiple members. Where values need not be assigned to all the members at any one time. Like structures union can be declared using the keyword union

If we are having the less memory to use in our program, for example 64K, we can use a single memory location for more than one variable this is called union.

You can use the unions in the following locations.

1. You can share a single memory location for a variable myVar1 and use the same location for myVar2 of different data type when myVar1 is not required any more.
2. You can use it if you want to user, for example, a long variable as two short type variables.
3. When you don't know what type of data is to be passed to a function, and you pass union this contains all the possible data types.

Definition: "A union is a variable which may hold members of different sizes and types."

The compiler allocates sufficient memory to hold the largest variable of the union. All the members of union occupy the same memory locations called addresses. The old value of the already declared member will be destroyed and new value to the new member will be assigned in the memory by using the union concept.

Note that union declaration has more than one variable declaration, but only one can be used at a time. Also with the declaration of union, the Turbo-C++ compiler will automatically allocates the memory locations to the variable which has the long data type member element in the union (i.e. the priority list be : double, long float, float, long int, int, char).

7.11 UNIONS DATATYPE

Unions are declared in the same fashion as structs, but have a fundamental difference. Only one item within the union can be used at any time, because the memory allocated for each item inside the union is in a shared memory location.

The general syntax is:

```
union union-tag
{
data type member-1;
data type member-2;
data type member-3;
......................;
data type member-n;
}u1, u2,...un;
```

One more way of declaration is as:

```
union union-tag
{
data type member-1;
data type member-2;
data type member-3;
......................;
data type member-n;
};
union tag-name  u1,u2,u3,.....un;
```

the declaration of variable can also be done as:

```
data-type union tag_name  u1,u2,u3,....,un;
```

Note that here data-type be optional. Also union tag is optional if you declare the variable with the union as:

```
union
{
data type member-1;
data type member-2;
data type member-3;
......................;
data type member-n;
}u1,u2,...un;
```

Union can also be used with the typedef declaration as:

```
typedef union
{
data type member-1;
data type member-2;
data type member-3;
```

```
.........................;
data type member-n;
}u1,u2,...un;
```

The size of union can be determined by using the size of operator either on the type of union or the union variable. if union is used within the structure , then the size of union be combination size of structure and union both. Also note that union can be declared outside the main program or within the main program (it is optional case).

To explain the concept of union, suppose there are four different type of member element declared with in the union having different data-type. Then by using the structure, these can be used as:

For Example:

```
struct student
{
char grade;
int rollno;
float fees;
double marks;
} st;
```

The storage of memory locations to these member are represented by using the structure be as below:

Structure Data Type Memory Allocation

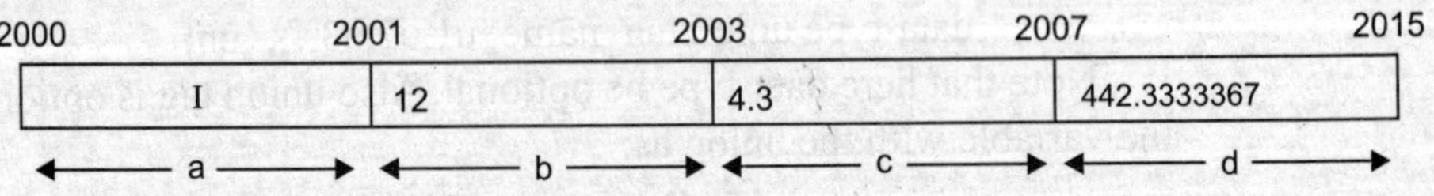

Total size= char + int + float + double= 1+2+4+8=15 bytes

The storage of memory locations to these member are represented by using the union be as below:

For Example:

```
union student
{
char grade;
int rollno;
float fees;
double marks;
} st;
```

Union Data Type Memory Allocation

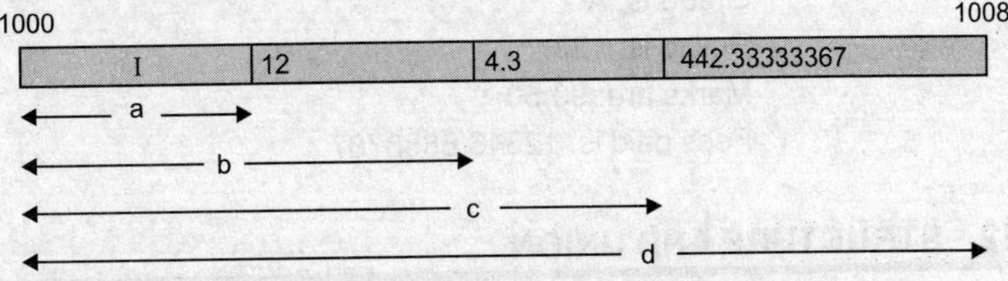

Total size= 8 bytes (all other data types share same memory)

For example, the concept of union can be explained by the C++ program as below to display the complete information of a student as:

Program 2: Write a C++ program to read and display student data using Union.

```
#include<conio.h>
#include<iostream.h>
void main()
{
union student
{
char grade;
int rollno;
float marks;
double fees;
}
union student s;
cout<<"\n Enter the garde, rollno, marks and fees of the student :";
cin>>s.grade>>s.rollno>>s.marks>>s.fees;
cout>>"\n Grade is:"<<s.garde;
cout<<"\n Rollno is:"<<s.rollno;
cout<<"\n Marks are :"<<s.marks;
cout<<"\n Fees paid  is: "<<s.fees;
getche();
}
Output:
Enter the garde, rollno, marks and fees of the student:
A
12
390.50
18766.8888787
```

```
Grade is: A
Rollno is: 122
Marks are: 90.50
Fees paid is: 12346.8888787
```

7.12 STRUCTURE AND UNION

The major difference between the structure and union be storage point of view. Structure and union are used as structures within union and union within structures.

A union can be used within the structure as

```
struct student
{
int rn;
char name[20];
union  subject
{
char grade;
int marks;
float percentage;
}v2;
}v1;
```

Also union of structure can be represented as below:

```
struct student
{
int rn;
char name[20];
}v1;
struct exam
{
char grade;
int marks;
float percentage;
}v2;
union  subject
{
struct student  info;
struct exam  result;
}v3;
```

So a structure can be used within the structure and it is also called **Union of Structure**.

7.13 DIFFERENCE BETWEEN STRUCTURE AND UNION

There are some similarities between structure and union that the both are heterogeneous data types. But some differences between both concepts given below:

STRUCTURE	UNION
Every member has its own memory Keyword struct is used	All members use the same memory Keyword union is used
All members may be initialized	Only its first member may be initialized
Different interpretations of the same memory location are not possible	Different interpretations of the same memory location are possible
Consumes more space compared to union All the members of the structure can be accessed at once.	Conservation of memory is possible In union only one member can be used at a time.
The size of the structure is equal to the sum of of all the variables of different data types defined in it.	The size of a union is equal to the size the largest element.
A structure can be passed as an argument to a function.	A union cannot be passed as an argument to a function.
Structure pointers can be created.	Union pointers cannot be created

For example:
struct example
{
int integer;
float floating_numbers;
}
the size allocated here is
sizeof(int)+sizeof(float);
	For example:
	union example
	{
	int integer;
	float floating_numbers;
	}
	size allocated is the size of the highest member.
	so size is=sizeof(float);

7.14 BIT-FIELDS

Unlike some other computer languages, C++ has a built-in feature, called a *bit-field*, which allows you to access a single bit.

C++ introduces a powerful tool bit level programming in which we can store data which size can be in bit. So there is not necessity to declare int or char data type for only one or two bit data. In this way we can save the memory space.

Bit-fields can be useful for a number of reasons, such as:

- If storage is limited, you can store several Boolean (true/false) variables in one byte.
- Certain devices transmit status information encoded into one or more bits within a byte.
- Certain encryption routines need to access the bits within a byte.

Although these tasks can be performed using the bitwise operators, a bit-field can add more structure (and possibly efficiency) to your code. A bit-field must be a member of a structure or union. It defines how long, in bits, the field is to be.

The general syntax is:

```
type name: length;
```

Here, *type* is the type of the bit-field, and *length* is the number of bits in the field. The type of a bitfield must be **int**, **signed**, or **unsigned**. Bit-fields are frequently used when analyzing input from a hardware device.

Structure using bit-fields:

```
struct
{
name1:bit_length;
name2:bit_length;
.........................................................................................
.........................................................................................
};
```

must be signed or unsigned int. If it signed int then minimum bit length must be two, one for sign and another for data.

Example:

```
void main()
{
struct employee
{
unsigned id: 8;
unsigned sex:1;
unsigned age:7;
};
struct employee emp1={203,1,23};
clrscr();
cout<<emp1.id<<emp1.sex<<emp1.age;
getch();
}
```

Output: 203 1 23

We can access the data member in same way.

How bit data is stored in the memory

Minimum size of structure which data member in bit is two byte i.e 16 bit. This is called word size of microprocessor. Word size depends on microprocessor. Turbo c is based on 8086 microprocessor which word size is two byte.

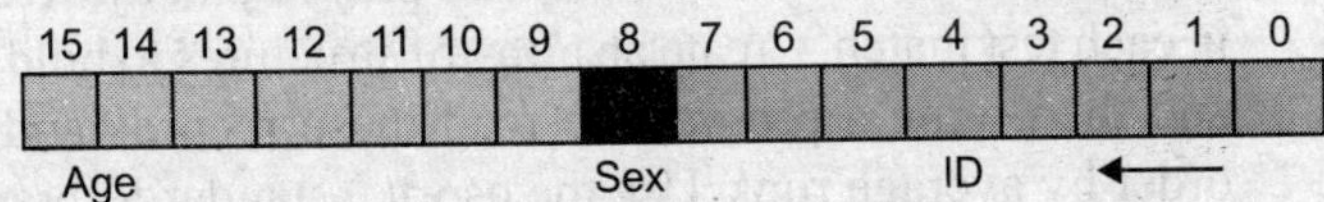

Bits are filed in from right to left direction 8 bit for id,1 bit for sex and 7 bit for age.

PROGRAMMING PROBLEMS

Program 1: Write a C++ program to sort student records according to grades.

Program 2: Write a C++ program to find total marks obtained by students in different subject.

Program 3: Write a C++ program to define a structure whose members are code having at maximum 4 characters name is a member having maximum25 characters and department is a member having maximum 20 characters and join date is a member of type date. Program to print the names of those employees who have completed at least one year of service.

Program 4: Write a C++ program to create a structure to specify data on student given below:

Roll number, Name, Department, Course, Year of joining Assume that there are not more than 450 students in the collage.

(a) Write a function to print name of all student who joined in a particular year.

(b) Write a function to print the data of a student whose roll number is given.

Program 5: Write a C++ program to create a structure to specify data of customers in a bank. The data to be stored is: Account number, Name, Balance in account. Assume of 200 customers in the bank.

(a) Write a function to print the account number and name of each customer with balance below Rs, 100.

(b) If a customer requests for withdrawal or deposit, it is given in the form:

Acct. no, amount, code (1 for deposit, 0 for withdrawal)

Write a program to give a massage, "The balance is insufficient for the specified withdrawal".

Program 6: Write a C++ program to an automobile company has serial number for engine parts starting from AA0 to FF9. The other characteristics of parts to be specified in a structure are: Year of manufacture, material and quantity manufactured.

(a) Specify a structure to store information corresponding to a part.

(b) Write a program to retrieve information on parts with serial numbers between BB1 and CC6.

Program 7: Write a C++ program to a record contains name of cricketer, his age, number of test matches that he has played and the average runs that he has scored in each test match. Create an array of structures to hold records of 20 such cricketers and then write a program to read these records and arrange them in ascending order by average runs. Use the qsort( ) standard library function.

Program 8: Write a C++ program that there is a structure called employee that holds information like employee code, name, data of joining. Write a program to create an array of structures and enter some data info if. Then ask the user to enter current date. Display the names of those employees whose tenure is 3 or more than 3 years according to the given current data.

Program 9: Write a C++ program for a book shop inventory management.

Program 10: Write a C++ Program to sort records of employees by using exchange sort method in structure.

OBJECTIVE TYPE QUESTIONS

1. Structure is a

(a) scalar data type (b) derived data type
(c) both options a and b (d) primitive data type

2. A Structure

(a) can be read as a single entity
(b) cannot be read as a single entity
(c) can be displayed as a single entity
(d) has member variables that cannot be read individually

3. Structure is a data type in which

(a) each element must have the same data type
(b) each element must have pointer type only
(c) each element may have different data type
(d) no element is defined

4. C++ provides a facility for user defined data type using

(a) pointer (b) function
(c) structure (d) array
(e) None of the above

5. The keyword used to represent a structure data type is
   (a) structure (b) struct
   (c) struc (d) structr
6. Structure declaration
   (a) describes the prototype (b) creates structure variable
   (c) defines the structure function (d) is not necessary
   (e) None of the above
7. Structure definition
   (a) describes the prototype (b) creates structure variable
   (c) defines the structure function (d) is not necessary
   (e) None of the above
8. The operator used to access the structure member is
   (a) * (b) .
   (c) [ ] (d) &
9. A structure
   (a) can be read as a single entity
   (b) cannot be read as a single entity
   (c) can be displayed as a single entity
   (d) has member variables that can not be individually read
10. A structure can have
    (a) pointers as its members (b) scalar data type as its members
    (c) structure as its members (d) all the above
11. A structure
    (a) allows array of structure
    (b) does not allow of structure
    (c) does not use array as its members
    (d) is a scalar data type
12. The operator exclusively used with pointer to structure is
    (a) . (b) ->
    (c) [ ] (d) *
13. If one or more members of a structure are pointers to the same structure, the structure is known as
    (a) nested structure (b) invalid structure
    (c) self referential structure (d) structured structure

14. If one or more members of a structure are other structures, the structure is known as
    (a) nested structure (b) invalid structure
    (c) self-referential structure (d) unstructured structure
15. Union is
    (a) a special type of structure (b) a pointer data type
    (c) a function data type (d) not a data type
16. The restriction with union is
    (a) the last member can only be initialized
    (b) the first member can only be initialized
    (c) any member can be initialized
    (d) union cannot be initialized
17. What is not possible with union?
    (a) array of union (b) pointer to union
    (c) self-referential union (d) none of the above
18. Structure is used to implement the data structures
    (a) stack (b) queue
    (c) tree (d) all the above
19. The nodes in a linked list are implemented using
    (a) self-referential structure (b) nested structure
    (c) array of structure (d) ordinary structure
20. A bit field can be of
    (a) int (b) float
    (c) double (d) all the above

EXERCISES

1. What do you understand by structure?
2. What is the structure tag and what is its purpose?
3. How can you declare it by using the different ways?
4. How can you access the elements of structure?
5. How can you assign value to the structure members or structure elements?
6. What do you mean by nesting of structure?
7. How can you link structure with array?
8. Differentiate between array of structure and array within the structure.

9. Differentiate between structure declaration and structure initialization.
10. How can you access the member elements by using the pointer with the structure?
11. What are the various ways to pass structure as arguments?
12. How can you relate the function with the structure?
13. What do you mean by union? How can you declare it?
14. Differentiate between structure and union.
15. Differentiate between union within the structure and union of structure.
16. Give an example of a structure declaration without the use of a tag. What are its advantages and disadvantages?
17. What are the restrictions on the use of nested structures?
18. How can structure members have storage class specifier or initializes?
19. How can you pass the entire structure as an argument to a function and return it?
20. Explain the method of passing a structure by value as an argument to a function with an example of prototype function declaration, function call and function decelerator.
21. Explain briefly the procedure of passing an array of structures to a function with prototype declaration, function call and function declaratory.
22. In what ways the initialization of the union is different from that of a structure?
23. What are the difficulties of processing a union?
24. How a structure is different from an array?
25. In what sense a structure can be recursive?
26. What a structure must include if it is a self-referential structure?
27. How can you use a union instead of structure?
28. Structure and union are the two sides of a coin or not. Explain it?
29. What are self referential structures? Write a program demonstrating use of self referential structure?
30. Explain the concept of bit-fields in detail.

CHAPTER 8

Classes

8.1 INTRODUCTION

C++ is a bunch of small additions to C, with a few major additions. One major addition is the object-oriented approach (the other addition is support for generic programming, which we'll cover later). As the name object-oriented programming suggests, this approach deals with objects. Of course, these are not real-life objects themselves. Instead, these objects are the essential definitions of real world objects. Classes are collections of data related to a single object type. Classes not only include information regarding the real world object, but also functions to access the data, and classes possess the ability to inherit from other classes. (Inheritance is covered in a later chapter.)

In object-oriented programming language C++, the data and functions (procedures to manipulate the data) are bundled together as a self-contained unit called an *object*. A *class* is an extended concept similar to that of *structure* in C programming language; this class describes the data properties alone. In C++ programming language, *class* describes both the properties (data) and behaviours (functions) of objects. *Classes* are not *objects*, but they are used to instantiate *objects*. Classes contain data known as data members and member functions. As a unit, the collection of data members and member functions is an object. Therefore, this unit of objects make up a class.

While C++ provides a number of basic data types (e.g. char, int, long, float, double, etc…) that are often sufficient for solving relatively simple problems, it can be difficult to solve complex problems using just these types. One of C++'s more useful features is the ability to define your own data types that better correspond to the problem being worked upon. You have already seen how enumerated types and structs can be used to create your own custom data types.

In C++, this is done via the **class** keyword. Using the class keyword defines a new user-defined type called a class. A class is similar syntactically to a structure. A class contains private as well as public parts. By default, all items defined in the class are private. To make parts of a class public (accessible to other parts of your program) you must declare them after the public keyword. All data members and member functions defined after public are accessible by all other functions in the program. Essentially, the rest of your program accesses an object through its public function. Although you can have public variables, you should try to limit or eliminate their use.

8.2 WHY WE NEED CLASSES

With the advancement in technology, the need was felt to create such type of data structure which holds the real world objects. Real-world objects have data type as person, chair, account number and balance. Also real world objects have some operations like ovens cook the food, accounts handles the interest and balance, cars move on the road etc and so on. So there is a way in C++ to combine all these properties of real-world objects. C++ helps by binding together the data-type properties.

So classes is a type which was developed that could just associate conventional function with the data structure and allow these functions to represent the active elements of the real-world object. At the end we can say, classes are needed to represent real-world entities that not only have data type properties (their characteristics or attributes) but also associated operations (their behavior or operations or functions). In other words classes are needed to allow structure to have data members as well as member functions.

8.3 OBJECT

Object is the basic unit of object-oriented programming. Objects are identified by its unique name. An object represents a particular instance of a class. There can be more than one instance of an object. Each instance of an object can hold its own relevant data.

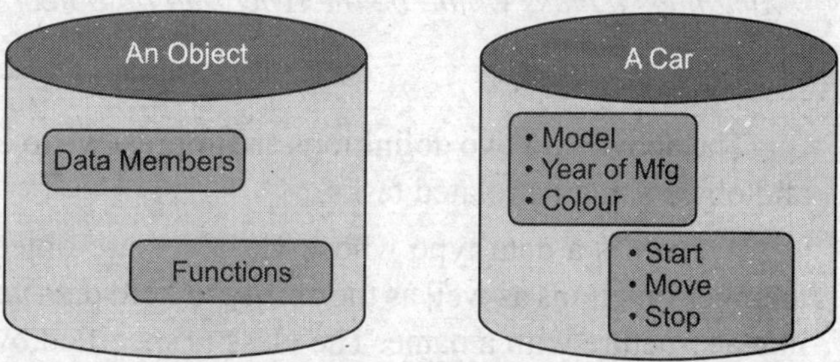

Figure 8.1: Object oriented approach

An Object is a collection of data members and associated member functions also known as methods.

Object-oriented programming solves many of the real world problems. In contrast to the other techniques, we now have a web of interacting *objects*, each house-keeping its own state (Figure 8.2).

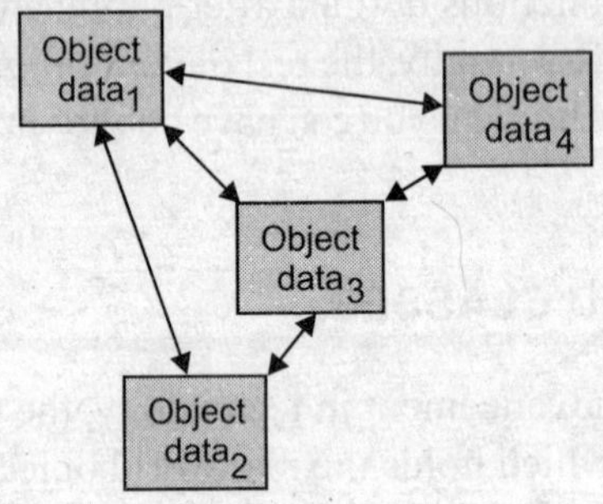

Figure 8.2: Object-oriented programming. Objects of the program interact by sending messages to each other.

8.4 CLASS

A class is the implementation of an abstract data type (ADT). It defines attributes and methods which implement the data structure and operations of the ADT, respectively.

A class is an expanded concept of a data structure: instead of holding only data, it can hold both data and functions.

Definition (Class): *"A class is an organization of data and functions which operate on them. Data structures are called data members and the functions are called member functions. The combination of data members and member functions constitute a data object or simply an object."*

Definition (object): *"An object is an instantiation of a class. In terms of variables, a class would be the type, and an object would be the variable."*

The above said two definitions are impressive to explain the concept of classes and objects and its related tasks.

A class is a data type whose variables are objects. Object as a variable has member functions as well as the ability to hold data values. A class is specified just like a structure with a name. The class is specified by keyword "class".

Classes are generally declared using the keyword class, with the following format:

```
class class_name
{
access_specifier_1:
member1;
access_specifier_2:
member2;
...
} object_names;
```

Where class_name is a valid identifier for the class, object_names is an optional list of names for objects of this class. The body of the declaration can contain members, which can be both data or function declarations, and optionally access specifiers.

All is very similar to the declaration on data structures, except that we can now include also functions and members, but also this new thing called access specifier. An access specifier is one of the following three keywords: private, public or protected. These specifiers modify the access rights that the members following them acquire:

- private members of a class are accessible only from within other members of the same class or from their friends.
- protected members are accessible from members of their same class and from their friends, but also from members of their derived classes.
- Finally, public members are accessible from anywhere where the object is visible.

8.4.1 General Structure of A Class

In general structure of a class, basically we have four main components:

1. Class name or name of class
2. Data Members
3. Member Functions
4. Access Specifiers
5. Declaring Objects

The general syntax or general form of the class declaration is as follows:

```
class <name of class>
{
private:
data members;
```

```
member functions();
public:
data members;
member functions();
protected:
data members;
member functions();
} obj1, obj2...objN;
```

1. Class name or name of class

It is mainly the name given to a particular class. It serves as a name specifier for the class, using which we can create objects. The class is specified by keyword **"class"**.

For example: In this example, Student is the class name or name specifier for the class. Class name has its own properties and behaviour. We can use class name to create objects like st1, st2. Each and every class which is created has unique name to create the difference between different classes.

```
class Student
{
privat:
int rn;
float fees:
public:
void read();
void show();
}st1, st2;
```

2. Data Members

These are the data-type properties that describe the characteristics of a class. We can declare any number of data members of any type in a class. We can say that the variables in C and data members in C++.

For example: int rn;

3. Member Functions

These are the various operations that can be performed to data members of that class. We can declare any number of member functions of any type in a class. They are referred to as a class interface. **For example:** void read(); void show();

4. Access Specifiers

Access specifiers are used to identify access rights for the data members and member functions of the class. Depending upon the access level of a class member, access to it is allowed or denied.

There are three main types of access specifiers in C++ programming language:

1. **private:** A *private* member within a class denotes that only members of the same class have accessibility. The *private* member is not accessible from outside the class.
2. **public:** *Public* members are accessible from outside the class.
3. **protected:** A protected access specifier is a stage between *private* and *public* access. If member functions defined in a class are *protected*, they cannot be accessed from outside the class but can be accessed from the derived class (inheritance).

Note: Every access specifier is discussed in detail in later sections.

---

5. Declaring Objects

A class declaration only uses to builds the structure of an object. The data members and member functions are combined in the class. The declaration of objects is same as declaration of variables of basic data types. Defining objects of class data type is known as class instantiation (instances of class).When we create objects during that moment, memory is allocated to them.

For example: st1, st2 are the objects of the class Student. We can create any number of objects of a given class.

An object is an abstract unit having following properties:

- It is individual.
- It points to a data members and member functions that are identifiable by the user.
- It holds data members as well as member functions method handles data.
- It's scope is limited to the block in which it is defined.

8.4.2 How To Write A Class

In Structure in C programming language, a structure is specified with a name. The C++ programming language extends this concept. A class is specified with a name after the keyword class.

The starting curly brace symbol, {is placed at the beginning of the code. Following the curly brace symbol, the body of the class is defined with the data members and member functions data. Then the class is closed with a curly brace symbol} and concluded with a semicolon (;).

```
class student
{
data members;
member functions;
.....................
};
```

There are different access specifiers for defining the data and functions present inside a class.

When defining access specifiers, the programmer must use the keywords: *private*, *public* or *protected* when needed, followed by a colon (:) and then define the data and member functions under it.

```
class student
{
private:
int rn;
public:
voidsum()
{
.....................
.....................
}
};
```

In the code above, the data member rn are defined as private access specifier. The member function sum() is defined as a public access specifier.

8.4.3 General Template of A Class

General structure for defining a class is:

```
class classname
{
acess specifier:
data member;
member functions;
access specifier:
data member;
member functions;
};
```

Generally, in class, all members (data) would be declared as private and the member functions would be declared as public. Private is the default access level for specifiers. If no access specifiers are identified for members of a class, the members are defaulted to private access.

```
class student
{
int rn,id;
public:
void sum()
{
...................
...................
}
};
```

In this example, data member's rn and id of the class student there are no access specifiers identified. student would have to give the default access specifier as private to these data members.

8.5 CREATION OF OBJECTS

Once the class is created, one or more objects can be created from the class as objects are instance of the class.

Juts as we declare a variable of data type *int* as: int x;

Objects are also declared as:

class name followed by object name;

student st1;

This declares st1 to be an object of class student.

For example a complete class and object declaration is given below:

```
class student
{
private:
int rn;
public:
void sum()
{
...................
...................
}
};
main()
```

```
{
student st1;
....................
....................
}
```

The object can also be declared immediately after the class definition. In other words the object name can also be placed immediately before the closing curly brace symbol} of the class declaration.

For example

```
class student
{
private:
int a,b;
pubic:
void sum()
{
....................
....................
}
}st1;
```

The above code also declares an object st1 of class student.

It is important to understand that in object-oriented programming language, when a class is created no memory is allocated. It is only when an object is created then the memory is allocated.

Program 1: Write a C++ program to declare class instance(create object).

```
#include <iostream.h>
#include<conio.h>
class myclass
{
int a;
public:
myclass(int x)
{
a = x;
}
int geta()
{
return a;
```

```
}
};
void main()
{
myclass ob(4);
cout << ob.geta();
getch();
}
```

Output:

4

8.6 HOW TO ACCESS C++ CLASS MEMBERS

By using dot operator or class member access operator, It is possible to access the class members after a class is defined and objects are created.

The general syntax to access class member:

```
Object_name.function_name (arguments);
```

The dot (.) used above is called the *dot operator* or *class member access operator*. The dot operator is used to connect the object and the member function. This concept is similar to that of accessing structure members in C programming language. The private data of a class can be accessed only through the member function of that class.

For example:

A class and object are defined below:

```
class student
{
int a, b;
public:
void sum(int,int);
} st1;
```

Then the member access is written as:

```
st1.sum(5,6);
```

Where st1 is the object of class student and sum() is the member function of the class.

The programmer now understands declaration of a *class*, creation of an object and accessibility of members of a *class*.

It is also possible to declare more than one object within a *class*:

```
class student
{
private:
int a;
public:
voidsum(int)
{
....................
....................
}
};
main()
{
student st1,st2;
....................
....................
}
```

In these two objects st1 and st2 are declared of class student.

8.7 RELATIONSHIP BETWEEN CLASS AND OBJECT

This relationship can be exist by associating one class having one object, one class having two objects and one class having multiple objects or N objects.

The relationship of class and object can be given as:

class classname obj 1, obj 2 ...... obj N;

For example: class student st1, st2 ……. stN;

Diagrammatic representation of classes and objects:

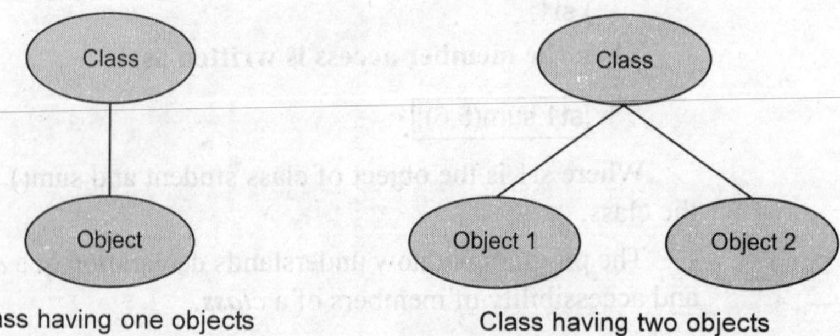

Class having one objects
Class having two objects

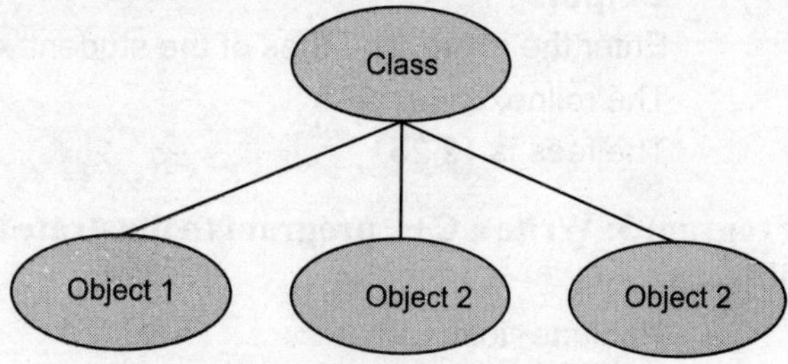

Class having multiple or N objects

For example: Programs given below represent relationship between classes and objects.

Program 2: Write a C++ program to illustrate the concept of class having one object.

```
#include<iostream.h>
#include<conio.h>
class student
{
private:
int rn;
float fees;
public:
void readdata()
{
cout<<"Enter the rollno. and fees of the student:";
cin>>rn>>fees;
}
void writedata()
{
cout<<"The rollno. is "<<rn<<endl;
cout<<" The fees is "<<fees<<endl;
}
};
void main()
{
student st;
st.readdata();
st.writedata();
getch();
}
```

Output:

Enter the rollno. and fees of the student: 4 12.25

The rollno. is 4

The fees is 12.25

Program 3: Write a C++ program to illustrate the concept of class having two objects.

```
#include<iostream.h>
#include<conio.h>
class student
{
private:
int rn;
float fees;
public:
void readdata()
{
cout<<"Enter the rollno. and fees of the student:";
cin>>rn>>fees;
}
void writedata()
{
cout<<"The rollno. is "<<rn<<endl;
cout<<" The fees is "<<fees<<endl;
}
};
void main()
{
student st1, st2;
st.readdata();
st.writedata();
st2.readdata();
st2.writedata();
getch();
}
```

Output:

Enter the rollno. and fees of the student: 4 12.25

The rollno. is 4

The fees is 12.25

Enter the rollno. and fees of the student: 5 12.55

```
The rollno. is 5
The fees is 12.55
```

Program 4: Write a C++ program to show the relationship of multiple data with multiple object.

```
#include<iostream.h>
#include<conio.h>
class currency
{
private:
int rupees ;
float paise ;
public:
void read ( )
{
cout<<"\n Rupees in integer is:" ;
cin >> rupees ;
cout<<"\n Paise in Real is:" ;
cin >> paise ;
}
void assign (int rs, float ps)
{
rupees = rs ;
paise = ps ;
}
void display ( )
{
cout<<"\n Rs."<<rupees<< "Ps." <<paise<<endl ;
}
};
void main ( )
{
currency c1, c2 ;
c1.assign (15, 3.75) ;
c2.read ( ) ;
cout<<"\n First Amount is:" ;
c1.display ( ) ;
cout<<"\n Second Amount is:" ;
c2.display ( ) ;
getch ( ) ;
```

```
}
```

Output:

Rupees is integer is : 420
Paise is real is : 36.2
First Amount is : Rs. 15 Ps. 3.75
Second Amt. is : Rs. 420 Ps. 36.2

Program 5: Write a C++ program to implement Class Rectangle.

```
#include <iostream.h>
#include<conio.h>
class Rectangle
{
int x, y;
public:
void set_values (int,int);
int area (void)
{
return (x*y);
}
};
void Rectangle::set_values (int a, int b)
{
x = a;
y = b;
}
void main ()
{
Rectangle rect;
rect.set_values (3,4);
cout << "area: " << rect.area();
getch();
}
```

Output:

area: 12

8.8 OBJECT ASSIGNMENT

In C++, we are using objects for all purposes one of the key concept is that how we can assign one object to another object. Answer is simple that by using assignment operator we can assign the one object to another object.

The general syntax is:

object1 = object2

Here, object2 is assign to object1.

Below is the programming example to illustrate this object assignment concept.

Program 6: Write a C++ program for Object assignment.

```
#include <iostream.h>
#include<conio.h>
class MyClass
{
int a, b;
public:
void setAB(int i, int j) { a = i, b = j; }
void display() {
cout << "\n a is " << a << '\n';
cout << "\n b is " << b << '\n';
}
};
void main()
{
MyClass ob1, ob2;
ob1.setAB(10, 20);
ob2.setAB(0, 0);
cout << "ob1 before assignment:";
ob1.display();
cout << "ob2 before assignment:";
ob2.display();
ob2 = ob1;                      // assign ob1 to ob2
cout << "ob1 after assignment:";
ob1.display();
cout << "ob2 after assignment:";
ob2.display();
ob1.setAB(-1, -1); // change ob1
cout << "ob1 after changing ob1:";
ob1.display();
cout << "ob2 after changing ob1:";
ob2.display();
getch();
}
```

Output:

```
ob1 before assignment:
a is 10
b is 20
ob2 before assignment:
a is 0
b is 0
ob1 after assignment:
a is 10
b is 20
ob2 after assignment:
a is 10
b is 20
ob1 after changing ob1:
a is -1
b is -1
ob2 after changing ob1:
a is 10
b is 20
```

Program 7: Write a C++ program to assign class object.

```
#include <iostream.h>
#include<conio.h>
class Box
{
public:
double length;
double width;
double height;
double volume()
{
return length * width * height;
}
};
void main()
{
Box firstBox = { 80.0, 50.0, 40.0 };
Box secondBox = firstBox;
secondBox.length *= 1.1;
secondBox.width *= 1.1;
```

```
secondBox.height *= 1.1;
cout << secondBox.length << secondBox.width << secondBox.height<<
endl;
cout << "Volume of second Box object is " << secondBox.volume()<<
endl;
getch();
}
```

Output:

```
885544
Volume of second Box object is 212960
```

8.9 ACCESS SPECIFIERS

There are mainly three types of access specifiers:

8.9.1 The Private Keyword

In the Private access specifier, a data member can be accessed and processed by the member function and the friend function of this class.

The private keyword is used to prevent direct access to data members or member functions by objects. Note that *private* member is not accessible from outside the class.

The general syntax of private keyword is:

```
private:
```

The private keyword is terminated by colon.

Consider the following example:

Program 8: Write a C++ program to illustrate the concept of private keyword.

```
#include<iostream.h>
#include<conio.h>
class student
{
private:
int rn;
float fees;
};
void main()
{
clrscr();
```

```
student st;
st.rn=32;                    //is not accessible
st.fees=44.50;               //is not accessible
cout<< "rollno:"<<st.rn;     //is not accessible
cout<<"fees:"<<st.fees;      //is not accessible
getch();
}
```

Output:

Error message:

```
st.rn=32;                    //is not accessible
st.fees=44.50;               //is not accessible
cout<< "rollno:"<<st.rn;     //is not accessible
cout<<"fees:"<<st.fees;      //is not accessible
```

Explanation: In the above program, data member's rn and fees are not accessible in the main program because rn and fees can be declared private in the class student. Due to the private keyword, the data members rn and fees are not accessible directly from outside the class.

To access the private members of a class, member functions of the same class are used. The member functions must be declared in the class using public access specifier. An object can access the private data members through the public member function.

8.9.2 The Public Keyword

In the Public access specifier, data members can be accessed and processed by all the member functions and the friend function by the other classes or outside this class.

The keyword public can be used to allow object to access the member variables of class directly like structure. The public keyword is written inside the class. Note that p*ublic* members are accessible from outside the class.

The general syntax of public keyword is:

```
public:
```

The public keyword is terminated by colon.

The member variables and functions declared followed by the keyword public can be accessed directly by the object. The declaration can be done as below:

```
class student                // class declaration
{
public:                      // public section begins
```

```
int rn;
float fees;
};
```

Consider the following example:

Program 9: Write a C++ program to illustrate the concept of public keyword.

```
#include<iostream.h>
#include<conio.h>
class student
{
public:                                 // public section begins
int rn;
float fees;
};                                      // end of class
void main ( )
{
clrscr ( );
student st1;                            //object declaration
st.rn=32;                               //is accessible
st.fees=44.50;                          //is accessible
cout<< "rollno:"<<st.rn;                     //is accessible
cout<<"fees:"<<st.fees;                      //is accessible
getch();
}
Output:
rollno: 32
fees: 44.50
```

Explanation: In the above program, data member's rn and fees are accessible in the main program because rn and fees can be declared public in the class student. Due to the public keyword, the data members rn and fees are accessible directly from outside the class.

Program 10: Write a C++ program to illustrate the use of a public variable.

```
#include <iostream.h>
#include<conio.h>
class myclass {
public:
int i, j, k; // accessible to entire program
};
void main()
```

```
{
myclass a, b;
a.i = 100;
a.j = 4;
a.k = a.i * a.j;
b.k = 12;
cout << a.k << " " << b.k;
getch();
}
```

Output:

400 12

8.9.3 The Protected Keyword

In the protected access specifier, the data members can be accessed and processed by the member function and the friend function of the class in which these are declared.

The access mechanism of protected keyword is same as private keyword. The main use of protected keyword is in inheritance of classes. Its detailed description is given in chapter ***inheritance.***

The general syntax of protected keyword is:

```
protected:
```

The protected keyword is terminated by colon.

Note that if member functions defined in a class are *protected*, they cannot be accessed from outside the class but can be accessed from the derived class (inheritance).

Consider the following example:

Program 11: Write a C++ program to illustrate the concept of protected keyword.

```
#include<iostream.h>
#include<conio.h>
class student
{
protected:
int rn;
float fees;
};
void main()
```

```
{
clrscr();
student st;
st.rn=32;                     //is not accessible
st.fees=44.50;                //is not accessible
cout<< "rollno:"<<st.rn;      //is not accessible
cout<<"fees:"<<st.fees;       //is not accessible
getch();
}
```

Output:

Error message:

```
st.rn=32;                     //is not accessible
st.fees=44.50;                //is not accessible
cout<< "rollno:"<<st.rn;      //is not accessible
cout<<"fees:"<<st.fees;       //is not accessible
```

Explanation: In the above program, data member's rn and fees are not accessible in the main program because rn and fees can be declared protected in the class student. Due to the protected keyword, the data member's rn and fees are not accessible directly from outside the class.

To access the protected members of a class, member functions of the same class are used. The member functions must be declared in the class using public access specifier. An object can access the protected data members through the public member function.

8.10 DEFINING MEMBER FUNCTIONS

Member function in the class can be defined with different access specifiers, either can be defined private or protected or public. There are two different ways to declare member functions.

These are described as below:

1. Member function inside the class
2. Member function outside the class

8.10.1 Member Function Inside the Class

Member function inside the class can be declared in public or private or protected section. When a member function is defined inside a class, then it processes all the operations just as in a simple function declaration. For example, below is the member function defined inside the class:

Program 12: Write a C++ program to illustrate the concept that the member function defined inside the class.

```
#include<iostream.h>
#include<conio.h>
class student
{
private:
int rn;
float fees;
public:
void readdata()
{
cout<<"Enter the rollno. and fees of the student:";
cin>>rn>>fees;
}
void writedata()
{
cout<<"The rollno. is "<<rn<<endl;
cout<<" The fees is "<<fees<<endl;
}
};
void main()
{
student st1;
st.readdata();
st.writedata();
getch();
}
```

Output:

```
Enter the rollno. and fees of the student: 4 12.25
The rollno. is 4
The fees is 12.25
```

Note that only small member functions are defined inside the class definition. Member functions defined inside the class are **inline functions**, by default with all its limitations. So if you define a member function inside a class then the function is automatically inline. e.g. void readdata ( ), void writedata ( ) member function of above class declaration are inline. inline function tells the compiler to replace the code for the body of the function at the place where it is called, so it saves the overheads of a function call i.e. time spent in loading and unloading of the function called. But the disadvantage of this inline member function is that when we call member function again and again it makes the size of program larger. So to avoid this problem we are decided to define member function outside the class.

8.10.2 Member Function Outside the Class

Due to drawbacks of inline function, we define member function outside the class definition. It is not always the case that the member function declaration and definition takes place within the class itself. Sometimes, declaration of member function alone can occur within the class. The programmer may choose to place the definition outside the class. In a situation such as this, it is important to understand the identifying member function of a particular class. This is performed by using the operator (::) this is called *scope resolution operator*.

The general syntax of defining member functions outside the class is:

```
return-type class-name :: function-name (arguments)
{
Body of member function;
}
```

Here return-type can be int, float, char, void or any standard data type.

For example:

```
class student
{
private:
in a;
public:
voidgetvalues() // Only Member Function declaration is done
};
voidstudent :: getvalues() // Here Member function is defined
{
........................
........................
}
main()
{
stidemt st1,st2;
........................
}
```

So the usage of scope resolution operator is as follows:

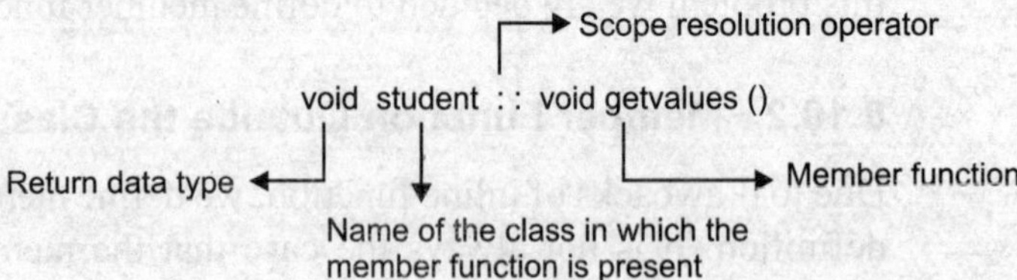

For example, below is the program defining member function outside the class:

Program 13: Write a C++ program to illustrate the concept that the member function defined outside the class.

```
#include<iostream.h>
#include<conio.h>
class student
{
private:
int rn;
float fees;
public:
void readdata();
void writedata();
};
void student :: readdata()          //definition outside the class
{
cout<<"Enter the rollno. and fees of the student:";
cin>>rn>>fees;
}
void student :: writedata()         //definition outside the class
{
cout<<"The rollno. is "<<rn<<endl;
cout<<" The fees is "<<fees<<endl;
}

void main()
{
student st1;
st.readdata();
st.writedata();
getch();
}
```

Output:

Enter the rollno. and fees of the student: 4 12.25

The rollno. is 4

The fees is 12.25

By using the scope resolution operator, same function can be used in any number of classes. The difference between a member function and a normal function is that a normal function can be invoked freely where the member function can be invoked by the object of the same class. The member function can invoke one another without using any object or dot operator.

Note: This operator (::) allows the programmer to use global and local variables of the same name in different ways.

Program 14: Write a C++ program by using member functions outside the body of class to find area of rectangle.

```
#include<iostream.h>
#include<conio.h>
class rectangle
{
private:
int m,n;
public:
void setdata(int,int);
void area();
};
void rectangle::setdata(int u,int v)
{
m=u;
n=v;
}
void rectangle::area()
{
int a=m*n;
cout<<"\nArea of rectangle= "<<a;
}
void main()
{
clrscr();
rectangle f,s;
```

```
f.setdata(10,20);
cout<<"Rectangle first:";
f.area();
s.setdata(20,30);
cout<<"\nRectangle second:";
s.area();
getch();
}
```

Output:

```
Rectangle first
Area of rectangle=200
Rectangle second
Area of rectangle=800
```

8.11 PRIVATE MEMBER FUNCTION

We know that to access private data of a class using public member function is possible. Now, we learn that how to declare member function in private section like data members. To execute private member function, it must be invoked by public member function of the same class.

A member function of a class can invoke by public member function of it own class. This method of invoking function is also called **nesting of member function.** When one member function invokes another member function, direct method of calling function is not used. The member function can be invoked by its name terminated by semicolon only like normal function. The following given program illustrates the concept of private member function.

Program 15: Write a C++ program to declare private member function and access it using public member function.

```
# include <iostream.h>
# include <conio.h>
class student
{
private:                // private section starts
int rn;
float fees;
void read( )            // private member function
{
rn = 12;
fees = 145.10;
```

```
}
public:                     // public section starts
void show ( )               // public member function
{
read( );                              // call to private member functions
cout <<"\n Rollno = "<<rn;
cout <<"\n Fees = "<<fees;
}
};
void main ( )
{
clrscr ( );
student st;                 // object declaration
// st.read ( );             // not accessible
st.show ( );                // call to public member function
getch();
}
```

Output:

```
Rollno = 12
Fees = 145.10
```

8.12 OVERLOADING MEMBER FUNCTIONS

Member functions are also overloaded in the same fashion as other ordinary functions. We learned that overloading is nothing but one function is defined with multiple definitions with same function name in the same scope. The program given below explains the concept of overloaded member function.

Program 16: Write a C++ program to overload member function of a class.

```
# include <iostream.h>
# include <stdlib.h>
# include <math.h>
# include <conio.h>
class student
{
public :
int rn (int);
double fees (double);
};
int student : : rn (int r)
```

```
{
int ans;
ans=abs (r);
return (ans);
}
double student : : fees (double f)
{
double ans;
ans=fabs (f);
return (ans);
}
void main ( )
{
clrscr ( );
student st;
cout <<\n Absolute value of -12 is "<<st.num (-12);
cout <<"\n Absolute value of -12.4142 is "<<st.num (-12.4142);
getch();
}
```

Output:

Absolute value of -12 is 12

Absolute value of -12.4142 is 12.4142

8.13 THE CONST MEMBER FUNCTION

The member functions of a class can also be declared as constant using const keyword. We cannot modify any data of constant functions in the class. The const keyword is suffixed to the function prototype as well as function definition. If const functions attempt to change the data, compiler will generate an error message.

The general syntax is:

```
return-type membe function-name() const
{
Body of const member function;
}
```

Program 17: Write a C++ program to declare const member function and attempt any operation within it.

```
# include <iostream.h>
# include <conio.h>
class A
```

```
{
int c;
public :
void add (int a, int b) const
{
// c=a+b;                // invalid statement. Can't modify any data in const
function
a+b;
cout <<"a+b = "<<_AX ;
}};
void main ( )
{
clrscr ( );
A a;
a .add (2, 4);
getch();
}
Output:
a+b = 6
```

Note: *Addition of a and b is performed in registers of CPU.*

8.14 OBJECTS AS FUNCTION ARGUMENTS

Similar to variables, objects can be passed on to functions. There are three methods to pass an argument to a function as given below:

1. **Passing of objects by its value** – In this type a copy of an object (actual object) is sent to function and assigned to object of calling function (Formal object). Both actual and formal copies of objects are stored at different memory locations. Hence, changes made in formal objects are not reflected to actual objects.
2. **Passing of objects by reference**– Address of object is implicitly sent to function.
3. **Passing of objects by address** – Address of the object is explicitly sent to function.

In pass by reference and address methods, an address of actual object is passed to the function. The formal argument is reference pointer to the actual object. Hence, changes made in the object are reflected to actual object. These two methods are useful because an address is passed to the function and duplicating of object is prevented.

The examples given below illustrate both methods of passing objects to the function as an argument.

Program 18: Write a C++ program to depict passing of objects by its value.

```
#include<iostream.h>
#include<conio.h>
class time
{
private:
int h,m;
public:
void readt();
void addt(time,time);
void showt();
};
void time::readt()
{
cout<<"\nEnter time in hours and minutes";
cin>>h>>m;
}
void time::addt(time u1,time u2)
{
int min=u1.m+u2.m;
int hrs=min/60;
m=min%60;
h=hrs+u1.h+u2.h;
}
void time::showt()
{
cout<<"\nTime obtained on adding= ";
cout<<h<<":"<<m;
}
void main()
{
clrscr();
time ob1,ob2,ob3;
ob1.readt();
ob2.readt();
ob3.addt(ob1,ob2);
ob3.showt();
getch();
```

```
}
```

Output:

Enter time in hours and minutes 12 20
Enter time in hours and minutes 9 00
Time obtained on adding=21:20

Program 19: Write a C++ program to depict passing of objects by reference.

```
#include<iostream.h>
#include<conio.h>
class ac
{
private:
int no; float bal;
public:
void read();
void show();
void tmoney(ac &,double);
};
void ac..read()
{
cout<<"Enter the account number= ";
cin>>no;
cout<<"Enter the balance= ";
cin>>bal;
}
void ac::show()
{
cout<<"\nAccount number is= "<<no;
cout<<"\nBalance is= "<<bal;
}
void main()
{
clrscr();
ac h1,h2;
cout<<"Enter account details of account first\n";
h1.read();
cout<<"Enter account details of account second\n";
h2.read();
cout<<"\nShowing account details before transfer\n";
h1.show();
```

```
h2.show();
double trans;
cout<<"\nEnter amount to transfer from account first to account second= ";
cin>>trans;
h1.tmoney(h2,trans);
cout<<"Showing account details after transfer of money ";
h1.show();
ht2.show();
getch();
}
```

Output:

```
Enter account details of account first
Enter the account number=501
Enter the balance=7000
Enter account details of account second
Enter the account number=502
Enter the balance=3000
Showing account details before transfer
Account number is=501
Balance is=7000
Account number is=502
Balance is=3000
Enter amount to transfer from account first to account second=500
Showing account details after transfer of money
Account number is=501
Balance is=6500
Account number is=502
Balance is=3500
```

Program 20: Write a C++ program to depict passing of objects by address.

```
# include <iostream.h>
# include <conio.h>
class life
{
int mfgyr;
int expyr;
int yr;
public :
void getyrs ( )
{
```

```
cout <<"\nManufacture Year: ";
cin >>mfgyr;
cout <<"\n Expiry Year : ";
cin >>expyr;
}
void period (life*);
};
void life : : period (life *y1)
{
yr=y1.expyr-y1->mfgyr;
cout <<"Life of the product : " <<yr;
}
void main ( )
{
clrscr ( );
life a1;
al .getyrs ( );
al .period (&a1);
}
```

Output:

Manufacture Year: 2008

Expiry Year: 2011

Life of the product: 3 Years

8.15 RETURNING AN OBJECT

We have learnt in previous chapters that how we can return variables and expression. Now, we can return objects. The program given below tells how we can return objects to function call.

Program 21: Write a C++ program to depict matrix addition by returning an object.

```
#include<iostream.h>
#include<conio.h>
#include<process.h>
class mat
{
private:
int x[10][10],u,v;
public:
```

```
void read();
mat add(mat);
void disp();
};
void mat::read()
{
cout<<"Enter order of u*v matrix";
cin>>u>>v;
cout<<"Enter elements:";
for(int i=0;i<u;i++)
for(int j=0;j<v;j++)
cin>>x[i][j];
}
void mat::disp()
{
for(int i=0;i<u;i++)
{
for(int j=0;j<v;j++)
cout<<x[i][j]<<'\t';
cout<<endl;
}}
mat mat::add(mat uu2)
{
if((u!=uu2.u)||(v!=uu2.v))
{
cout<<"Matrix addition not possible";
exit(0);
}
else
{
mat temp;
temp.u=uu2.u; temp.v=uu2.v;
for(int i=0;i<u;i++)
{
for(int j=0;j<v;j++)
temp.x[i][j]=x[i][j]+uu2.x[i][j];
}
return (temp);
}}
void main()
```

```
{
mat u1,u2,u3;
u1.read();
u2.read();
u3=u1.add(u2);
cout<<"On addition we get\n";
u3.disp();
getch();
}
Output:
Enter order of u*v matrix 2 2
Enter elements:1 3 5 7
Enter order of u*v matrix2 2
Enter elements:2 4 6 8
On addition we get
3   7
11  15
```

Program 22: Write a C++ program by returning objects for addition of distances.

```
#include<iostream.h>
#include<conio.h>
class dist
private:
int feet;
double inches;
public:
void get()
{
cout<<"Enter feet & inches";
cint>>feet>>inches;
}
void show()
{
cout<<"Addition"<<feet<<"\'-"<<inches<<"\"";
}
dist add(dist);
};
dist dist::add(dist h2)
{
```

```
dist tt;
tt.feet=feet+h2.feet;
tt.inches=inches+h2.inches;
if(tt.inches>=12.00)
{
tt.feet++;
tt.inches-=12.00;
}
return(tt);
}
void main()
{
clrscr();
dist obj1,obj2,obj3;
obj1.get();
obj2.get();
obj3=obj1.add(obj2);
obj3.show();
getch();
}
```

Output:

Enter feet & inches 6 3.0

Addition 9.0

8.16 SCOPES OF CLASSES AND OBJECTS

We have learnt in previous sections, the scope of data member and member function. Now we are introducing the concept that the scope or types of classes and objects. There are two types of classes and two types of objects are using in the OOPs.

8.16.1 Scope of Classes

First of all we are started from the various scopes of classes:

1. Global Class
2. Local Class

1. Global Class

A class is said to be global class if it is defined outside the main program. It means object of this class type can be declared anywhere in the program (global as well as local). For example, below is the declaration of global class:

Program 23: Write a C++ program to declare the Global class.

```
#include<iostream.h>
#include<conio.h>
class student                    //global class
{
private:
int rn;
float fees;
public:
void readdata()
{
cout<<"Enter the rollno. and fees of the student:";
cin>>rn>>fees;
}
void writedata()
{
cout<<"The rollno. is "<<rn<<endl;
cout<<" The fees is "<<fees<<endl;
}
}; student st1;                  //global object
void main()
{
clrscr();
st.readdata();
st.writedata();
getch();
}
```

Output:

```
Enter the rollno. and fees of the student: 4 12.25
The rollno. is 4
The fees is 12.25
```

2. Local Class

A class is said to be local class if it is defined inside the main program. It means the object of this class type can be declared only within the main program as local objects. For example, below is the declaration of local class as:

Program 24: Write a C++ program to declare the Local class.

```
Local class and local ojects
#include<iostream.h>
#include<conio.h>
```

```
void main()
{
class student                    //local class
{
private:
int rn;
float fees;
public:
void readdata()
{
cout<<"Enter the rollno. and fees of the student:";
cin>>rn>>fees;
}
void writedata()
{
cout<<"The rollno. is "<<rn<<endl;
cout<<" The fees is "<<fees<<endl;
}};
student st1;                     //local object
st.readdata();
st.writedata();
getch();
}
```

Output:

```
Enter the rollno. and fees of the student: 4 12.25
The rollno. is 4
The fees is 12.25
```

8.16.2 Scope of Objects

Now, we have to learn about scope of different objects:

1. Global Object
2. Local Object

1. Global Object

An object is said to be a global object if it is declared outside the main program and it is also available to all the other functions in the program. It means global object can be used anywhere in the program. Note that a global object can only be declared using a global class type. For example, below is the program, which explains the global object:

Program 25: Write a C++ program to declare the Global class.

```
#include<iostream.h>
#include<conio.h>
class student                    //global class
{
private:
int rn;
float fees;
public:
void readdata()
{
cout<<"Enter the rollno. and fees of the student:";
cin>>rn>>fees;
}
void writedata()
{
cout<<"The rollno. is "<<rn<<endl;
cout<<" The fees is "<<fees<<endl;
}
}; student st1;                  //global object
void main()
{
clrscr();
st.readdata();
st.writedata();
getch();
}
Output:
Enter the rollno. and fees of the student: 4 12.25
The rollno. is 4
The fees is 12.25
```

2. Local Object

An object is said to be a local object if it is declared inside the main program. It means local object is available only to the function in which it is declared and so it cannot be used outside the function declaring it. Note that a local object can be created from both global as well as local class. For example, below is the program which will explain the local object declaration:

Program 26: Write a C++ program to declare the Local Object.

```
#include<iostream.h>
#include<conio.h>
class student                    //global class
{
private:
int rn;
float fees;
public:
void readdata()
{
cout<<"Enter the rollno. and fees of the student:";
cin>>rn>>fees;
}
void writedata()
{
cout<<"The rollno. is "<<rn<<endl;
cout<<" The fees is "<<fees<<endl;
}
};
void main()
{
student st;                      //local object
st.readdata();
st.writedata();
getch();
}
```

Output:

```
Enter the rollno. and fees of the student: 4 12.25
The rollno. is 4
The fees is 12.25
```

8.17 DIFFERENCE BETWEEN CLASSES AND STRUCTURES

The major difference between class and structure is that the declaration of structure starts with the keyword struct whereas on the other hand, a class starts with the keyword class. For all other purposes both keywords are equivalent.

By default, the access specifier for members of a **class is private.** The default access specifier for a **structure is public.** This is an important difference to recognize and understand in object-oriented C++ programming language.

```
class student
{
int x;        //Here access specifier is private by default
};
```

whereas

```
struct student
{
int x;   //Here access specifier is public by default
};
```

The general syntax of structure and class are as follows:

Structure:

```
struct structure-name
{
data-type member1 ;
data-type member2 ;
..............................
datat-ype membern ;
} ;
struct structure-name v1, v2, ...... vn ;
```

Here member1, member2..... member n are data members and member functions of same or different types.

Class:

```
class class-name
{
private:
data members ;
public:
data members ;
member function ;
protected :
data members ;
member function ;
} ;
class function ;
} ;
class class-name obj1, ...... objn ;
```

In structure definition v1, v2, v3 ..... vn is the variable list, whereas in class definition obj1, obj2...... objn is the list of objects.

After the discussion, classes and structures can be differentiated as below:

STRUCTURE	CLASS
1. It contains heterogeneous variables and functions.	It contains heterogeneous data members and member functions.
2. The keyword is struct.	The Keyword is class.
3. All the members are public by default.	All the members are private by default.
4. The variable is used to access the members.	An object is used to access the members.
5. There is no data hiding features comes with structures.	Classes have data hiding concept. like private, protected and public.
6. Structures deals with variables only.	The classes deal with real-world objects.
7. The structure members can be directly accessed by the structure variables by any function anywhere in their scope (local or global).	The class members can not be accessed directly; these can be accessed through member functions.
8. 'this' pointer will not work in structure.	'this' pointer will work only in class.
9. Structures are value types and stored in stack memory.	Classes are reference types and stored in heap memory.
10. You can not do inheritance in structures. Struct cannot inherit from a structure.	You can do inheritance in structures. Class can inherit from a class.
11. Structures do not require constructors and destructors.	While classes requires constructors and destructors.
12. A structure can't be abstract data type.	A class is an abstract data type.
13. The structures are used in both c and c++.	A class is used only in c++ and other OOPs languages.

14. You cannot have instance Field initializers in structs.
struct MyStruct
{
int myVar = 10; // syntax error.
void MyFun( )
{
// statements
}
}
	Classes can have initializers.
	class MyClass
	{
	int myVar =10; // no syntax error.
	void MyFun( )
	{
	// statements
	}
	}

15. Structs are simple to use.	Classes are used for complex and large set data.

The concept of unions is different from that of classes declared with struct and class, since unions only store one data member at a time, but nevertheless they are also classes and can thus also hold function members. The default access in union classes is public.

Program 27: Write a C++ program How: Structures and Classes Are Related.

```
#include <iostream.h>
#include <string.h>
#include<conio.h>
struct str
{
void dstr(char *s);
void showstr();
private:
char str [255];
};
void str::dstr(char *s)
{
if(!*s)*str ='\0';
else strcat(str,s);
}
void str::showstr()
{
cout <<str <<"\n";
}
void main()
{
str s;
s.dstr("");
s.dstr("Hello");
s.dstr("there!");
s.showstr();
getch();
}
```

Output:

Hello there!.

Program 28: Write a C++ program How: Unions and Classes Are Related.

```
#include <iostream.h>
#include<conio.h>
```

```
union chng_byte
{
void chng();
void set_byte(unsigned short i);
void show_word();
unsigned short u;
unsigned char c [2];
};
void chng_byte::chng()
{
unsigned char t;
t=c[0];
c[0]==c[1 ];
c[1]==t;
}
void chng_byte::show_word()
{
cout <<u;
}
void chng_byte::set_byte(unsigned short i)
{
u =i;
}
void main()
{
chng_byte s;
s.set_byte(49034);
s.chng();
s.show_word();
getch();
}
```

Output:

49034

8.18 DATA HIDING OR ENCAPSULATION

In real life, it is common to use something without knowing how it actually works. For example, your TV remote provides buttons that allow you to do things like turn your TV on and off and adjust the volume. However, the detail of how the remote is actually implemented is hidden away. This is useful because it allows you to use the remote without having to worry about the details of why it works or how it was implemented. If gnomes broke into your house in the middle of the night and replaced the internals of your TV remote with a new (but compatible) technology, you'd probably never even notice.

Encapsulation is the idea of hiding the details of how something is implemented and instead exposing an interface to the user. This allows the user to use the item without having to worry about how it is implemented. Data hiding is also known as encapsulation.

In C++, access specifiers allow us to implement encapsulation within our classes. This is typically done by making ALL member variables of a class private, and providing public functions (often access functions) that allow the user to work with the class. Although this may seem more burdensome than providing public access directly, doing so actually provides several very useful benefits that help encourage class reusability and maintainability.

Perhaps most importantly, sometimes it turns out that the initial implementation of a class is too slow or uses too much memory, and a more complex solution is needed. Encapsulating the implementation means that the implementation of a class can be completely changed, and so long as the interface remains the same, the users of the class do not have to worry about the changes at all!

The keywords private and protected are used for hiding the data. **Table 6.3** shows the brief description of access specifiers. The following program explains data hiding:

Program 29: Write a C++ program to calculate simple interest. Hide the data elements of the class using private keyword.

```
# include <iostream.h>
# include <conio.h>
class bank
{
private :
float p;                              // principle amount
float r;                              // rate of interest
float t;                              // number of years
float si;
float amount;                         // total amount
public :
voin read ( )
{
cout <<" Principle Amount : "; cin>> p ;
cout <<" Rate of Interest    : "; cin>>r;
```

```
cout <<" Number of years  : "; cin>>t;
si= (p *r*t) /100;
amount = si + p;
}
void show( )
{
cout <<"\n Principle Amount : "<<p;
cout <<"\n Rate of Interest : "<<r;
cout <<"\n Number of years: "<<t;
cout <<"\n Interest        : "<<si;
cout <<"\n Total Amount    : "<<amount;
}
};
void main ( )
{
clrscr ( );
bank b ;
b.read ( );
b.show ( );
getch();
}
```

Output:

```
Principle Amount: 5000
Rate of Interest: 2
Number of years: 3
Principle Amount: 5000
Rate of Interest: 2
Number of years: 3
Interest: 300
Total Amount: 530
```

Table 8.1: Access specifiers and their scope

Access specifiers	Members of the class	Class objects
public	access possible	access possible
private	access possible	no access
protected	access possible	no access

Program 30: Write a C++ program to depict concept of abstraction , data hiding, encapsulation.

```
#include<math.h>
#include<iostream.h>
#include<conio.h>
#include<process.h>
class quadratic
{
private:
double a,b,c;
public:
void read();
void funcroots();
};
void quadratic::read()
{
cout<<"Enter coffiecients of Quadratic Eq. a,b,c= ";
cin>>a>>b>>c;
}
void quadratic::funcroots()
{
if(a==0)
{
cout<<"\nEquations is not quadratic";
exit(0);
}
else {
double disc;
disc=b*b-4*a*c;
if(disc<0)
cout<<"\nRoots are imaginary";
else if(disc==0)
{
double x=-b/(2*a);
cout<<"\nRoots are equal,x= "<<x;
}
else {
double m,n,t;
t=sqrt(disc);
```

```
m=(-b+t)/(2*a);
n=(-b-t)/(2*a);
cout<<"\nRoots are real and unequal"<<endl;
cout<<"m= "<<m<<endl;
cout<<"n= "<<n;
}}}
void main()
{
clrscr();
quadratic q1;
q1.read();
q1.funcroots();
getch();
}
```

Output:

Enter coffiecients of Quadratic Eq. a,b,c=2 4 3

Roots are imaginary

8.19 NESTED CLASS

A nested class is declared within the scope of another class. The name of a nested class is local to its enclosing class. Unless you use explicit pointers, references, or object names, declarations in a nested class can only use visible constructs, including type names, static members, and enumerators from the enclosing class and global variables.

***Definition:** "When a class is declared within another class, then such type of relation is called Nested class or nesting of class. The outer class is known as Enclosing class and the inner class, which is enclosed class, is known as Nested class."*

The general syntax of nested class is:

```
class outerclass_name
{
private:
data member ;
member function ;
public:
data member ;
```

```
member function ;
class innerclass_name
{
private
data member ;
member function ;
public :
data member ;
member function ;
} ;             //end of inner class
} ;             //end of outer class
class outerclass_name outer1;
class outerclass_name :: inner-class-nameinner1;
```

Note that simply declaring a class nested in another class does not mean that the enclosing class contains an object of the enclosed class.

For example:

```
// Example 1: Nested class
//
class OuterClass
{
class NestedClass
{
// ...
};
// ...
};
```

Nested classes are useful for organizing code and controlling access and dependencies. Nested classes obey access rules just like other parts of a class do; so, in Example 1, if NestedClass is public then any code can name it as OuterClass::NestedClass. Often nested classes contain private implementation details, and are therefore made private; in Example 1, if NestedClass is private, then only OuterClass's members and friends can use NestedClass.

Program 31: Write a C++ program to define inner class.

```
#include <iostream.h>
#include<conio.h>
#include <stdlib.h>
class OuterClass
{
public:
```

```
void outerFunction();
class InnerClass
{
public:
void innerFunction();
};
};
void OuterClass::outerFunction()
{
cout << "This is a function in the base class\n";
InnerClass myclass;
myclass.innerFunction();
}
void OuterClass::InnerClass::innerFunction()
{
cout << "This is a function in the InnerClass class \n";
}
void main()
{
OuterClass myclass;
myclass.outerFunction();
getch();
}
```

Output:

This is a function in the base class
This is a function in the InnerClass class

Note that private member of a class can be used within the member functions of the same class i.e. any private declared variable in outer class cannot be used in the public member function of inner class. Similarly private member of inner class cannot be used inside member function of any class other than the inner class itself.

Member functions of a nested class follow regular access rules and have no special access privileges to members of their enclosing classes. Member functions of the enclosing class have no special access to members of a nested class.

8.20 ARRAYS AND CLASSES

An array is a user-defined homogenous data type in which data is stored at contiguous memory locations. Mainly arrays are used to design a large size of data base. An array in a class can be private or public data member of the class. Note that private array member can be accessed by public member function only, but public array member are accessed directly using objects of this class. Arrays and classes have two types of relationship. One is the arrays within a class and second one is the array of class objects.

1. Array within classes
2. Array of class objects (Array of objects)

8.20.1 Array within Classes

The Array within classes can be declared as:

```
class class-name
{
private:
data-type array-name or data member [size];
public:
data member [size];
member function;
};
class class-name object list;
```

For example, below is the example describing the array within the class:

```
class student
{
private:
int rn[10] ;
float fees ;
public:
void read();
void write();
} ;
class student st ;
```

Here rn[10] is a private data member of class student. If you don't write private, then it is private by default.

Program 32: Write a C++ program to find electricity bill of a person.

```
unit     tarrif
>100     Rs.1.20 per unit
>200     Rs.2 per unit
>300     Rs.3 per unit
#include<iostream.h>
```

```
#include<conio.h>
class ebill
{
private:
int cno;
char cname[20];
int units;
double bill;
public:
void get()
{
cout<<"Enter custno,name and no. of units";
cin>>cno>>cname>>units;
}
void put()
{
cout<<"\nCustomer no is"<<cno;
cout<<"\nCustomer name  is"<<cname;
cout<<"\nNumber of units consumed"<<units;
cout<<"\nBill of Customer"<<bill;
}
void calc()
{
if(units<=100)
bill=units*1.20;
else if(units<=300)
bill=100*1.20+(units-100)*2;
else
bill=100*1.20+200*2+(units-300)*3;
}
};
void main()
{
ebill p1;
p1.get();
p1.calc();
p1.put();
getch();
}
```

Output:

```
Enter custno,name and no. of units 4 navtej 200
Customer no is 4
Customer name  is navtej
Number of units consumed 200
Bill of Customer 320
```

8.20.2 Array of Objects

The declaration of an array of class objects is very similar to the declaration of the array of structure in C++.

The general syntax is:

```
class class-name
{
private:
data member;
member function;
public:
data member;
member function;
};
class class-name object[size];
```

Below is the example to describe the array of class object:

```
class student
{
private:
int rn;
float fees;
public:
void read();
void write();
}
class student st[100] ;
```

Here student class can be accessed 100 times by using the st object.

Program 33: Write a C++ program to create an array of objects.

```
#include <iostream.h>
#include<conio.h>
class MyClass
```

```
{
int x;
public:
void setX(int i)
{ x = i; }
int getX()
{ return x; }
};
void main()
{
MyClass obs[4];
int i;
for(i=0; i < 4; i++)
obs[i].setX(i);
for(i=0; i < 4; i++)
cout << "obs[" << i << "].getX(): " << obs[i].getX() << "\n";
getch();
}
```

Output:

```
obs[0].getX(): 0
obs[1].getX(): 1
obs[2].getX(): 2
obs[3].getX(): 3
```

8.21 POINTERS TO CLASSES

It is perfectly valid to create pointers that point to classes. We simply have to consider that once declared, a class becomes a valid type, so we can use the class name as the type for the pointer.

The general syntax is:

class-name *pointer_object

For example:

```
CRectangle * prect;
```

* prect is a pointer to an object of class CRectangle.

As it happened with data structures, in order to refer directly to a member of an object pointed by a pointer we can use the arrow operator (->) of indirection.

Here is an example with some possible combinations:

Program 34: Write a C++ program for pointer to classes example.

```
#include <iostream.h>
#include<conio.h>
class CRectangle
{
int width, height;
public:
void set_values (int, int);
int area (void)
{
return (width * height);
}
};
void CRectangle::set_values (int a, int b)
{
width = a;
height = b;
}
void main ()
{
CRectangle a, *b, *c;
CRectangle * d = new CRectangle[2];
b= new CRectangle;
c= &a;
a.set_values (1,2);
b->set_values (3,4);
d->set_values (5,6);
d[1].set_values (7,8);
cout << "a area: " << a.area() << endl;
cout << "*b area: " << b->area() << endl;
cout << "*c area: " << c->area() << endl;
cout << "d[0] area: " << d[0].area() << endl;
cout << "d[1] area: " << d[1].area() << endl;
delete[] d;
delete b;
getch();
}
```

Output:

a area: 2

```
*b area: 12
*c area: 2
d[0] area: 30
d[1] area: 56
```

Next you have a summary on how can you read some pointer and class operators (*, &, ., ->, [ ]) that appear in the previous example:

expression	can be read as
*x	pointed by x
&x	address of x
x.y	member y of object x
x->y	member y of object pointed by x
(*x).y	member y of object pointed by x (equivalent to the previous one)
x[0]	first object pointed by x
x[1]	second object pointed by x
x[n]	(n+1)th object pointed by x

Be sure that you understand the logic under all of these expressions before proceeding with the next sections. If you have doubts, read again this section and/or consult the previous sections about pointers and data structures.

Program 35: Write a C++ program for using class pointer and class array together.

```
#include <iostream.h>
#include<conio.h>
class MyClass
{
private:
int Price;
int Count;
long Total;
public:
void Input(int P,int C)
{
Price=P;
Count=C;
}
void MyClass::Compute()
{
```

```
Total=(long) Price*Count;
}
void MyClass::Print(){
cout<<"Price="<<Price<<" Count="<<Count <<" Total="<<Total<<"\n";
}
};
void main()
{
MyClass *ob;
ob=new MyClass[6];
ob[0].Input(5,0);
ob[1].Input(3,5);
ob[2].Input(1,0);
ob[3].Input(5,20);
ob[4].Input(4,0);
ob[5].Input(8,5);
for(int i=0;i<6;i++)
ob[i].Compute();
for(int i=0;i<6;i++)
ob[i].Print();
delete ob;
getch();
}
```

Output:

```
Price=5 Count=0 Total=0
Price=3 Count=5 Total=15
Price=1 Count=0 Total=0
Price=5 Count=20 Total=100
Price=4 Count=0 Total=0
Price=8 Count=5 Total=40
```

8.22 POINTER TO OBJECTS

After the concept of pointer to classes now we are implemented the new concept of how pointers are related to objects. Following is the example of pointer to objects.

Program 36: Write a C++ program to explain the concept of pointer to object.

```
#include <iostream.h>
#include<conio.h>
class myclass
```

```
{
int i;
public:
void read(int j)
{
i = j;
}
int getInt()
{
return i;
}
};
void main()
{
myclass ob, *objectPointer;
objectPointer = &ob;                    // get address of ob
objectPointer->read(10);
cout << objectPointer->getInt();        // use -> to call getInt()
getch();
}
```

Output:

10

SOLVED PROGRAMMING

Program 1: Write a C++ program for class having Real Objects (car).

```
#include <iostream.h>
#include<conio.h>
class car                               //define class
{
private:
int model_no;
int engine_no;
float cost;
public:
void set(int mno,int eno,float c)       //set data
{
model_no =mno;
engine_no =eno;
```

```
cost =c;
}
void show()//display data
{
cout <<"Model " <<model_no;
cout <<",engine " <<engine_no;
cout <<",costs $" <<cost <<endl;
}
};
void main()
{
car car1;                                   //define object
car1.set(2009,184,20000.55); //call member function
car1.show();                             //call member function
getch();
}
```

Output:

Model 2009,engine_no 184,cost $20000.550781

Program 2: Write a C++ program for private fields.

```
#include <iostream.h>
#include<conio.h>
struct MyClass
{
int getI() { return i; } // these are public by default
void setI(int j) { i = j; }
private:
int i;
};
void main()
{
MyClass s;
s.setI(10);
cout << s.getI();
getch();
}
```

Output:

10

Program 3: Write a C++ program by returning objects for addition of distances.

```
#include<iostream.h>
#include<conio.h>
class dist
private:
int feet;
double inches;
public:
void get()
{
cout<<"Enter feet & inches";
cint>>feet>>inches;
}
void show()
{
cout<<"Addition"<<feet<<"\'-"<<inches<<"\"";
}
dist add(dist);
};
dist dist::add(dist h2)
{
dist tt;
tt.feet=feet+h2.feet;
tt.inches=inches+h2.inches;
if(tt.inches>=12.00)
{
tt.feet++;
tt.inches-=12.00;
}
return(tt);
}
void main()
{
clrscr();
dist obj1,obj2,obj3;
obj1.get();
obj2.get();
obj3=obj1.add(obj2);
```

```
obj3.show();
getch();
}
```

Output:

Enter feet & inches 6 3.0
Addition 9.0

Program 4: Write a C++ program for public fields and member functions.

```
#include <iostream.h>
#include<conio.h>
class MyClass
{
public:
int number;
void display();
};
void MyClass::display()
{
for(int i = 0; i<= number;i++)
{
cout<< "Hello World \n";
}
}
void main ()
{
MyClass myfirstobject;
myfirstobject.number =3;
myfirstobject.display();
getch();
}
```

Output:

Hello World
Hello World
Hello World
Hello World

Program 5: Write a C++ program to define class employee.

```
#include<iostream.h>
#include<conio.h>
#include<string.h>
```

```
class employee
{
char name [80 ];//private by default
public:
void putn(char *n);//these are public
void getn(char *n);
private:
double wage;
public:
void putw(double w);
double getw();
};
void employee::putn(char *n)
{
strcpy(name,n);
}
void employee::getn(char *n)
{
strcpy(n,name);
}
void employee::putw(double w)
{
wage =w;
}
double employee::getw()
{
return wage;
}
void main()
{
employee emp;
char name [80];
emp.putn("Rani");
emp.putw(25000);
emp.getn(name);
cout <<name <<" makes $";
cout <<emp.getw()<<" per year.";
getch();
}
```

Output:

Rahul makes $25000 per year.

Program 6: Write a C++ program to incrementing and decrementing an object pointer.

```
#include<iostream.h>
#include<conio.h>
class MyClass
{
int x;
public:
void setX(int val) { x = val; }
void display(){ cout << x << "\n"; }
};
void main()
{
MyClass ob[2], *p;
ob[0].setX(10);              // access objects directly
ob[1].setX(20);
p = &ob[0];                  // obtain pointer to first element
p->display();                // show value of ob[0] using pointer
p++;                         // advance to next object
p->display();                // show value of ob[1] using pointer
p—;                          // retreat to previous object
p->display();                // again show value of ob[0]
getch();
}
```

Output:

10
20
10

Program 7: Write a C++ program for adding rational numbers & display OUTPUT as numerator/denominator.

```
#include<iostream.h>
#include<conio.h>
class rational
{
private:
int n,d;
```

```
public:
void set(int a,int a1)
{
n=a;
d=a1;
}
void put() const
{
cout<<"Sum:";
cout<<n<<"/"<<d;
}
void add(rational u1, rational u2)
{
n=u1.n*u2.d+u2.n*u1.d;
d=u1.d*u2.d;
}
};
void main()
{
rational obj1,obj2,obj3;
obj1.set(15,5);
obj2.set(3,5);
obj3.add(obj1,obj2);
obj3.put();
getch();
}
```

Output:

Sum:90/25

Program 8: Write a C++ program for using class pointer and class array together.

```
#include <iostream.h>
#include<conio.h>
class MyClass
{
private:
int Price;
int Count;
long Total;
public:
```

```
void Input(int P,int C)
{
Price=P;
Count=C;
}
void MyClass::Compute()
{
Total=(long) Price*Count;
}
void MyClass::Print(){
cout<<"Price="<<Price<<"  Count="<<Count <<"  Total="<<Total<<"\n";
}
};
void main()
{
MyClass *ob;
ob=new MyClass[6];
ob[0].Input(5,0);
ob[1].Input(3,5);
ob[2].Input(1,0);
ob[3].Input(5,20);
ob[4].Input(4,0),
ob[5].Input(8,5);
for(int i=0;i<6;i++)
ob[i].Compute();
for(int i=0;i<6;i++)
ob[i].Print();
delete ob;
getch();
}
```

Output:

```
Price=5 Count=0  Total=0
Price=3 Count=5  Total=15
Price=1 Count=0  Total=0
Price=5 Count=20  Total=100
Price=4 Count=0  Total=0
Price=8 Count=5  Total=40
```

PROGRAMMING PROBLEMS

Program 1: Write a C++ program to initialize the public data members in a class.

Program 2: Write a C++ program to take objects as Data Types.

Program 3: Write a C++ program to declare class instance and use them.

Program 4: Write a C++ program for private and public variables and methods.

Program 5: Write a C++ program to find area of rectangle.

Program 6: Write a C++ program with help of objects and classes to find circumference & area of circle.

Program 7: Write a C++ program to using private member functions from class to find gross salary.

Program 8: Write a C++ program for example: one class, two objects.

Program 9: Write a C++ program to find average percentage of marks.

Program 10: Write a C++ program to using objects to perform all operations on complex numbers.

Program 11: Write a C++ program for use new to allocate memory for a class pointer.

Program 12: Write a C++ program to read and display student data to illustrate the concept of classes.

Fill in the blanks

1. A house is to a blueprint as a .... is to a class.
2. Every class definition contains keyword .... followed by the class's name.
3. A definition of a class is stored in a file with the .... filename extension.
4. Each and every parameter in a function header should specify both a .... and a ....
5. When each object of a class maintains its own copy of an attribute, the variable that represents the attribute is also known as a ....
6. Keyword public is a ....
7. Return type .... indicates that a function returns nothing.
8. When a member function is defined outside the class definition, the function header must include the class name and the .... , followed by the function name to access the member function to the class definition.

9. The source-code file and any other files that use a class can include the class's header file via an .... preprocessor directive.
10. Keyword private is a ....

Answers

1. object. 2. class. 3. .h 4. type, name. 5. data member. 6. access specifier. 7. void. 8. binary scope resolution operator (::). 9. #include. 10. access specifier

OBJECTIVE TYPE QUESTIONS

1. The scope resolution operator is
   (a) a comma (b) a semicolon
   (c) a colon (d) two colons
2. Two access specifers in C++ are
   (a) public and private (b) int and double
   (c) formal and informal (d) void and free.
3. In a class specifier, data or data or functions designated private are accessible
   (a) to any function in the program
   (b) only if you know the password
   (c) to member functions of that class
   (d) only to public members of the class.
4. The dot operator (or class member access operator) connects the following two entities (reading from left to right):
   (a) a class member and a class object
   (b) a class object and a class
   (c) a class and a member of that class
   (d) a class object and a member of that class
5. Classes are useful because they
   (a) are removed from memory when not in use
   (b) permit data to be hidden from other classes
   (c) bring together all aspects of an entity in one place
   (d) can closely model objects in the real word.
6. A program can directly access the .... members of a class
   (a) hidden (b) private
   (c) public (d) both b and c

7. The program can access the private members of a class ....
   (a) directly
   (b) only through other private members of the class
   (c) only through other public members of the class
   (d) None of the above – the program can not access the private members of a class in any way.
8. A pattern for creating an object is called a (n) ....
   (a) class (b) attributes
   (c) private (d) public
9. Which of the following is the scope resolution operator?
   (a) -> (b) ::
   (c) * (d) .
   (e) &
10. A blueprint for creating an object in C++ is called ....
    (a) a class (b) an instance
    (c) a map (d) a patterne
    (e) a sketch
11. To hide a data member from the program, you must declare the data member in the .... section of the class
    (a) concealed (b) confidential
    (c) hidden (d) private
    (e) restricted
12. To expose a data member to the program, you must declare the data member in the .... section of the class
    (a) common (b) exposed
    (c) public (d) unrestricted
    (e) user
13. Which of the following statements is false?
    (a) A class encapsulates all of an object's attributes and behaviors
    (b) An example of an attribute is the minutes variable in a time class
    (c) An example of a behavior is the setTime function in a time class
    (d) An object created from a class is referred to as an instance of the class.
14. Which of the following creates an animal object named dog?
    (a) animal "dog"; (b) animal dog;
    (c) dog "animal"; (d) dog animal;

15. Which of the following tells C++ that the displayBreed function is a member of the animal class?
    (a) displayBreed ( ) -> animal (b) displayBreed ( ) : : animal
    (c) displayBreed ( ) .animal (d) animal : : displayBreed ( )
    (e) animal ( ) -> displayBreed ( )
16. The best-written classes have ....
    (a) all functions private (b) all data public
    (c) no functions (d) None
17. Access specifiers are followed by ....
    (a) a comma (b) a semicolon
    (c) a colon (d) two colons
18. The scope resolution operator is ....
    (a) a comma (b) a semicolon
    (c) a colon (d) two colons
19. The default access specifier is ....
    (a) shielded (b) private
    (c) protected (d) public
20. Which of the following is an access specifier?
    (a) particular (b) shielded
    (c) protected (d) safe
21. The major advantage of data hiding is that ....
    (a) your programs can include more data
    (b) you no longer need functions
    (c) no one can ever use your data
    (d) your data will be used correctly.
22. Two access specifiers in C++ are
    (a) public and private (b) int and double
    (c) formal and informal (d) void and free.
23. Making class members inaccessible to non-member functions is an example of ....
    (a) polymorphism (b) data hiding
    (c) redundancy (d) recursion.
24. An object is a (n) .... of a class
    (a) owner (b) function
    (c) definition (d) instance.

25. The functions go in the .... section of a class definition
    (a) declaration (b) implementation
    (c) prototype (d) functioning
26. Which (if any) of the following is NOT a programmer-defined type?
    (a) An array (b) A structure
    (c) A class (d) All
27. Classes hold ....
    (a) data (b) methods
    (c) both data and methods (d) neither data nor methods.
28. You construct a class in two sections, known as the ....
    (a) header and body (b) type and parameters
    (c) declaration and implementation (d) pointer and variable
29. The declaration section holds ....
    (a) data members
    (b) data members and function prototypes
    (c) data members, function prototypes, and the functions themselves
    (d) None
30. A member function uses the correct object when you call it because ....
    (a) a copy of the object is passed to the function
    (b) the address of the object is passed to the function
    (c) the address of the function is passed to another function (d) the address of the object is returned from the function
31. To use this pointer with a member function, you ....
    (a) declare this as static
    (b) declare this as global
    (c) define this as equal to the address of the appropriate object
    (d) do nothing; it is automatically supplied for you

EXERCISES

1. Explain the basic concept of classes and objects.
2. What is the various access levels used in the declaration of classes?
3. Why classes are required?
4. How can you declare a class? Explain with an appropriate example.

5. Give the relationship of class and object?
6. Differentiate between structure and classes?
7. Differentiate between global and local classes?
8. Differentiate between global and local object?
9. What do you mean by classes within the classes? Explain with an example.
10. What are the various types of functions used in the classes?
15. Illustrate the concept of class with object using a C++ program?
16. What do you know about array of objects? Explain with an appropriate example.
17. What are the various class method definitions? Explain each with an example.
18. Differentiate among methods, objects and classes with an example for each?
19. Explain the concept of objects as function arguments.
20. Explain the overloading of member function.
21. What do you mean by const member function? Explain in detail.
22. Explain the concept of pointer to classes.
23. What do you mean by Nested classes? Explain with the help of example.
24. What do you mean by Private Keyword?
25. What do you mean by Public Keyword?
26. What do you mean by protected keyword?
27. Explain the concept of Pointer to objects.

CHAPTER 9

More About Classes

9.1 INTRODUCTION

Classes can have complicated internal structures, so object initialization and clean-up of a class is much more complicated then for any other data structures. Constructors and destructors are special member functions of classes that are used to construct and destroy class objects. The construction can be for example: **initialization for objects or memory allocation**. The destruction may involve **de-allocation of memory or other clean-up for objects.**

Constructors and destructors are declared within a class declaration (as like any other member function). A constructor or a destructor can be defined in-line or external to the class declaration. We may declare some default arguments when we make a constructor. There are some restrictions that apply to constructors and destructors:

- Constructors and destructors cannot have a return type (not even void).
- Pointers and references cannot be used on constructors and destructor's (It is not possible to get there address).
- Constructors and destructors cannot be declared static, const or volatile.
- Constructors cannot be declared with the keyword virtual.

***Note:** The same **access rules (private, public and protected)** apply to constructors and destructors as with any other member function.*

9.2 CONSTRUCTORS

Objects generally need to initialize variables or assign dynamic memory during their process of creation to become operative and to avoid returning unexpected values during their execution. A class can include a special function called constructor, which is automatically called whenever a new object of a class is created.

Constructors in C++ are special member functions of a class. They have the same name as the Class Name. There can be any number of overloaded constructors inside a class, provided they have a different set of parameters.

A **constructor** is a function that initializes the members of an object. A constructor only knows how to build an object of its own class.

There are some important qualities for a constructor to be noted:

- Constructors have the same name as the class.
- Constructors do not return any values
- Constructors are invoked first when a class is initialized. Any initializations for the class members, memory allocations are done at the constructor.

Definition: *"In C++ a constructor is a function with the same name as the class. Its purpose is to create a new instance of the class and initialize the member data of the instance."*

A constructor is a special method that is created when the object is created or defined. This particular method holds the same name as that of the object and it initializes the instance of the object whenever that object is created. The constructor also usually holds the initializations of the different declared member variables of its object. Unlike some of the other methods, the constructor does not return a value, not even void.

When your create an object, if you do not declare a constructor, the compiler would create one for your program; this is useful because it lets all other objects and functions of the program know that this object exists. This compiler created constructor is called the **default constructor**. If you want to declare your own constructor, simply add a method with the same name as the object in the public section of the object. When you declare an instance of an object, whether you use that object or not, a constructor for the object is created and signals itself.

9.2.1 Declaring and Defining Constructor

A member function with the same name as its class is a constructor function. Constructors cannot return values. Specifying a constructor with a return type is an error, as is taking the address of a constructor.

If a class has a constructor, each object of that type is initialized with the constructor prior to use in a program.

The general syntax used for defining Constructor is:

```
class class-name
{
private:
data-type data members;
public:
class name( ); {}          // constructor defined
or
class name(argument list);
{}
};
```

```
For example:
class X
{
private:
int i;
public:
X();                       // constructor for class X
{}
};
```

Constructors are called at the point an object is created. Objects are created as:

- Global (file-scoped or externally linked) objects.
- Local objects, within a function or smaller enclosing block.
- Dynamic objects, using the **new** operator. The **new** operator allocates an object on the program heap or "free store."
- Temporary objects created by explicitly calling a constructor.
- Temporary objects created implicitly by the compiler.
- Data members of another class. Creating objects of class type, where the class type is composed of other class-type variables, causes each object in the class to be created.
- Base class subobject of a class. Creating objects of derived class type causes the base class components to be created.

9.2.2 Use of Constructors

The main use of constructors is to initialize objects. The function of initialization is automatically carried out by the use of a special member function called a constructor.

A constructor performs various tasks that are not visible to you as the programmer, even if you write no code for the constructor. These tasks are all associated with building a complete and correct instance of class type.

Program 1: Write a C++ program for MyClass ob(4).

```
#include <iostream.h>
#include<conio.h>
class MyClass
{
int a;
public:
MyClass(int x)                    // constructor defined
{ a = x; }
int geta()
{ return a; }
};
void main()
{
MyClass ob(4);
cout << ob.geta();
getch();
}
Output:
4
```

9.3 PRIVATE CONSTRUCTORS

Occasionally, we do not want users outside of a class to use particular constructors. To enforce this behaviour, we can make constructors private. Just like regular private functions, private constructors can only be accessed from within the class. Let's take a look at an example of this:

```
#include <iostream.h>
#include<conio.h>
class Book
{
private:
int m_nPages;
// This constructor can only be used by Book's members
Book()                            // private default constructor
{
```

```
m_nPages = 0;
}
public:
// This constructor can be used by anybody
Book(int nPages)            // public non-default constructor
{
m_nPages = nPages;
}
};
void main()
{
Book cMyBook;               // fails because default constructor Book() is
private
Book cMyOtherBook(242);  // okay because Book(int) is public
getch();
}
```

One problem with public constructors is that they do not provide any way to control how many of a particular class may be created. If a public constructor exists, it can be used to instantiate as many class objects as the user desires. Often it is useful to restrict users to being able to create only one instance of a particular class. Classes that can only be instantiated once are called **singletons**. There are many ways to implement singletons, but most of them involve use of a private (or protected) constructor to prevent users from instantiating as many of the class as they want.

9.4 TYPES OF CONSTRUCTORS

Mainly constructors are classified in four categories. These are discussed as below:

1. Default constructor
2. Parameterized constructor
3. Copy constructor
4. Dynamic constructor

9.4.1 Default Constructor

If you do not declare any constructors in a class definition, the compiler assumes the class to have a default constructor with no arguments.

The general syntax is:

```
class-name ()               //default constructor
{}
```

This constructor has no arguments in it. Default Constructor is also called as *no argument constructor*.

For example:

```
class student
{
private:
int rn;
float fees;
public:
student();                    //constructor declared
...
};
student :: student()  // constructor defined outside the class using (::) operator.
{
rn=0;
fees=0.0;
}
```

Default constructors are further categorized in three ways as:

(i) Default constructor by compiler.

(ii) Default constructor by programmer without default argument.

(iii) Default constructor by programmer with default argument.

Program 2: Write a C++ program to illustrate the concept of class having default constructor.

```
#include<iostream.h>
#include<conio.h>
class student
{
private:
int rn;
float fees;
public:
void readdata()
{
cout<<"Enter the rollno. and fees of the student:";
cin>>rn>>fees;
}
void writedata()
```

```
{
cout<<"The rollno. is "<<rn<<endl;
cout<<" The fees is "<<fees<<endl;
}
};
void main()
{
student st;                //default constructor by compiler
st.readdata();
st.writedata();
getch();
}
```

Output:

```
Enter the rollno. and fees of the student: 4 12.25
The rollno. is 4
The fees is 12.25
```

Program 3: Write a C++ program to depict initialization of object using default constructor without default arguments.

```
#include<iostream.h>
#include<conio.h>
class rec
{
private:
int l,b;
public:
rec()                  //Default constructor defined without arguments
{
l=4;
b=3;
}
int area()
{
return(l*b);
}
};
void main()
{
rec obj;               //initialization of object without default arguments
cout<<"Area is"<<obj.area();
```

```
getch();
}
```

Output:

Area is 12

11.2

Program 4: Write a C++ program to depict initialization of object using default constructor with default arguments.

```
#include<iostream.h>
#include<conio.h>
class rec
{
private:
int l,b;
public:
rec(int u,int v)          //constructor defined with arguments
{
l=u;
b=v;
}
int area()
{
return(l*b);
}
};
void main()
{
rec obj(6,6);             //initialization of object with default arguments
rec obj1(2,8);
cout<<"Area is of rectangle first: "<<obj.area();
cout<<"Area is of rectangle second: "<<obj1.area();
getch();
}
```

Output:

Area is of rectangle first:36

Area is of rectangle second16

9.4.2 Parameterized Constructor

The constructor which may take arguments or parameters is called Parameterized constructor. The parameterized constructor allows us to initialize the various data elements of different objects with different value when they are created. This can be done by passing different values as arguments to the constructor function, when the objects are created.

This constructor works similar to the **Default constructor having default argument.** The basic difference is execution speed, which is more in the case of parameterized constructor.

The general syntax is:

```
class class name
{
private:
..........;
public:
class name (argument list)  //parameterized constructor
{ }
};
```

Program 5: Write a C++ program to implement CRectangle including a parameterized constructor:

```
#include <iostream.h>
#include<conio.h>
class CRectangle
{
int width, height;
public:
CRectangle (int,int);
int area () {return (width*height);}
};
CRectangle::CRectangle (int a, int b)
{
width = a;
height = b;
}
void main ()
{
CRectangle rect (3,4);
CRectangle rectb (5,6);
cout << "rect area: " << rect.area() << endl;
cout << "rectb area: " << rectb.area() << endl;
getch();
}
```

```
Output:
rect area: 12
rectb area: 30
```

a constructor that performs a action: it initializes the values of width and height with the parameters that are passed to it.

Notice how these arguments are passed to the constructor at the moment at which the objects of this class are created:

```
CRectangle rect (3,4);
CRectangle rectb (5,6);
```

Constructors cannot be called explicitly as if they were regular member functions. They are only executed when a new object of that class is created.

You can also see how neither the constructor prototype declaration (within the class) nor the latter constructor definition includes a return value; not even void.

9.4.2.1 Types of calls in parameterized constructor

We can use two types of call to invoke parameterized constructor:

(i) Implicit call

(ii) Explicit call

(i) Implicit call: Implicit call is by calling the constructor implicitly. There is no need to use assignment operator to assign the value to constructor. For example, below is the syntax of implicit call statement:

```
class-name object-name(values);
```

For example:

```
MyClass ob(4);                    //implicit call
```

It is very easy to use in shortcut initialization of values to parameter and is in the shorthand form.

Program 6: Write a C++ program for MyClass ob(4).

```
#include <iostream.h>
#include<conio.h>
class MyClass
{
int a;
public:
MyClass(int x) { a = x; }
int geta() { return a; }
};
void main()
{
```

```
MyClass ob(4);                          // implicit call
cout << ob.geta();
getch();
}
```

Output:

4

(ii) Explicit call: Explicit constructor is by calling the constructor explicitly. Here we use assignment operator to assign the value to constructor. For example, below is the syntax of implicit call statement:

```
class-name object-name = class-name(values);
```

For example:

```
MyClass ob = MyClass(4);        //Explicit call
```

Program 7: Write a C++ program for MyClass ob = MyClass(4).

```
#include <iostream.h>
#include<conio.h>
class MyClass
{
int a;
public:
MyClass(int x) { a = x; }
int geta() { return a; }
};
void main()
{
MyClass ob = MyClass(4);  //Explicit call
cout << ob.geta();
getch();
}
```

Output:

4

Program 8: Write a C++ program for constructors with One Parameter:A Special Case.

```
#include <iostream.h>
#include<conio.h>
class A
{
int a;
public:
```

```
A(int j)
{
a =j;
}
int get()
{
return a;
}
};
void main()
{
A aa =99;
cout <<aa.get();
getch();
}
```

Output:

99

Program 9: Write a C++ program for parameterized Constructors myclass.

```
#include <iostream.h>
#include<conio.h>
class myclass
{
int a, b;
public:
myclass(int i, int j)
{
a=i;
b=j;
}
void show()
{
cout << a << " " << b;
}
};
void  main()
{
myclass ob(3, 5);
ob.show();
getch();
```

```
}
```

Output:

3 5

Program 10: Write a C++ program to assign the public object member address to a pointer.

```
#include <iostream.h>
#include<conio.h>
class MyClass
{
public:
int i;
MyClass(int j)
{
i = j;
}
};
void  main()
{
MyClass myObject(1);
int *p;
p = &myObject.i;                    // get address of myObject.i
cout << *p;                        // access myObject.i via p
getch();
}
```

Output:

1

9.4.3 Copy Constructor

This constructor takes one argument. It is also called one argument constructor. The main use of copy constructor is to initialize the objects while in creation, also used to copy an object. The copy constructor allows the programmer to create a new object from an existing one by initialization.

Definition: *Copy constructor is*

- *a constructor function with the same name as the class*
- *used to make deep copy of objects.*

The general syntax to use a copy constructor is:

class-name (class-name or constructors-name & object-name);

or

constructor-name(class-name or constructors-name & object-name);

There are 3 important places where a copy constructor is called.

1. When an object is created from another object of the same type
2. When an object is passed by value as a parameter to a function
3. When an object is returned from a function

If a copy constructor is not defined in a class, the compiler itself defines one. This will ensure a shallow copy. If the class does not have pointer variables with dynamically allocated memory, then one need not worry about defining a copy constructor. It can be left to the compiler's discretion.

But if the class has pointer variables and has some dynamic memory allocations, then it is a must to have a copy constructor.

For example to invoke a copy constructor the programmer writes:

```
class-name obj2(obj1)
or
class-name obj2 = obj1;
```

Here obj1and obj2 are the objects of class.

Both the above formats can be used to invoke a copy constructor.

For Example:

```
#include <iostream.h>
#include <conio.h>
class student ()
{
private:
int rn;
public:
student ()
{ }
student (int r)
{
rn = r;
}
student (student & st)
{
rn = st.rn;
cout<<" Example of Copy Constructor";
```

```
}
void result()
{
cout<< rn;
}
};
void main()
{
student st1(50);
student st2(st1);
cout<< "\nst2 =";st2.result();
getch();
}
```

In the above the copy constructor takes one argument an object of type student which is passed by reference. The output of the above program is

Example of Copy Constructor

st2=50

Program 11: Write a C++ program for default Copy Constructor.

```
#include <iostream.h>
#include<conio.h>
class Height
{
private:
int feet;
float inches;
public:
Height():feet(0),inches(0.0)
{ }
Height(int ft,float in):feet(ft),inches(in)
{ }
void get()
{
cout <<"\n Feet:";
cin >>feet;
cout <<" inches:";
cin >>inches;
}
void show()
{
```

```
cout <<feet <<"-" <<inches ;
}
};
void main()
{
Height H1(6,4.0);
Height H2(H1);
Height H3 =H1;
cout <<"\nHeigh1 =";H1.show();
cout <<"\nHeigh2 =";H2.show();
cout <<"\nHeigh3 =";H3.show();
cout <<endl;
getch();
}
```

Output:

```
Heigh1 =6-4.0
Heigh2 =6-4.0
Heigh3 =6-4.0
```

9.4.3.1 The Copy Constructor and the Assignment Operator

Although using the assignment operator is fairly straightforward, correctly implementing an overloaded assignment operator can be a little trickier than you might anticipate. There are two primary reasons for this. First, there are some cases where the assignment operator isn't called when you might expect it to be. Second, there are some issues in dealing with dynamically allocated memory Some of the user has been confused during programming that they are using copy constructor or assignment operator in the program. We can illustrate this concept simply.

(i) The Assignment Operator

The **assignment operator** is used to copy the values from one object to another *already existing object*. The key words here are "already existing". Consider the following example:

1. student st(5); // calls student constructor
2. student st1; // calls student default constructor
3. st1 = st; // calls student assignment operator

In this case, st1 has already been created by the time the assignment is executed. Consequently, the student assignment operator is called. The assignment operator must be overloaded as a member function.

Assignment versus Initialization- Initialization means creating a new variable and then doing an assignment of a value to it so the only difference is the creation part of initialization. Assignment always works with a variable that exists. If we think in ints then the example below shows examples of assignment, copying and initialization.

```
int a= 9;          // initialization
a =10;             // assignment
int b=4;           // initialization
a = b;             // copying
```

With objects, the same is true, only assignment and copying can be more complicated if pointers or other non objects is involved.

What happens if the object being copied into does not already exist? To understand what happens in that case, we need to talk about the copy constructor.

(ii) The Copy Constructor

Consider the following example:

1. student st(5); // calls student constructor
2. student st1 = st; ; // calls student copy constructor!

Because the second statement uses an equals symbol in it, you might expect that it calls the assignment operator. However, it doesn't! It actually calls a special type of constructor called a copy constructor. A **copy constructor** is a special constructor that initializes a *new object* from an existing object.

The purpose of the copy constructor and the assignment operator are almost equivalent — both copy one object to another. However, the assignment operator copies to existing objects, and the copy constructor copies to newly created objects.

The difference between the copy constructor and the assignment operator causes a lot of confusion for new programmers, but it's really not all that difficult.

Summarizing:

1. If a new object has to be created before the copying can occur, the copy constructor is used.
2. If a new object does not have to be created before the copying can occur, the assignment operator is used.

There are three general cases where the copy constructor is called instead of the assignment operator:

1. When instantiating one object and initializing it with values from another object (as in the example above).
2. When passing an object by value.
3. When an object is returned from a function by value.

In each of these cases, a new variable needs to be created before the values can be copied — hence the use of the copy constructor.

Because the copy constructor and assignment operator essentially do the same job (they are just called in different cases), the code needed to implement them is almost identical.

9.4.4 Dynamic Constructor

Allocation of memory to objects at the time of their construction and at the execution time is a difficult task, but this problem is removed with the help of Dynamic Constructor. So the value provided at run time is called Dynamic constructor. The dynamic initialization is very handy to change the values without changing the program.

The memory allocation to objects in the Dynamic constructor can be allocated with the help of the **new** operator. Similarly the allocated memory can be released with the help of **delete** operator. You can read **new** and **delete** operator in the dynamic allocation later on. By using these dynamic operators, you can dynamically initialize the objects. This also helps in dynamic initialization of the copy constructor. The Dynamic initialization is explained by the below procedure as:

Program 12: Write a C++ program to depict use of new & delete operators.

```
#include<iostream.h>
#include<conio.h>
class rec
{
private:
int l;
int b;
public:
rec()
{
cout<<"Constructor with no parameter invoked";
}
void read()
{
cout<<"Enter length & breadth: ";
cin>>l>>b;
}
void area()
{
cout<<"Area is "<<l*b;
```

```
}
~rec()
{
cout<<"Destructor invoked";
}
};
void main()
{
rec *p;
p=new rec;
p->area();
cout<<"Destroying object\n ";
delete p;
cout<<"End of program";
getch();
}
```

Output:

```
Constructor with no parameter invoked
Enter length & breadth:4 3
Area is 12
Destroying object
Destructor invoked
End of program
```

Program 13: Write a C++ program to depict working of constructor & destructor in operations performed dynamically.

```
#include<iostream.h>
#include<conio.h>
#include<string.h>
class string
{
char *nm;
int len;
public:
string(char *s)
{
len=strlen(s);
nm=new char[len+1];
strcpy(name,s);
}
```

```
void com(string &ss2)
{
int k;
k=strcmp(nm,ss2.nm);
if(k==0)
cout<<"\nBoth objects have same name";
else
cout<<"\nBoth objects have different name";
}
void put()
{
cout<<"\nName of person"<<nm;
}
~string()
{
cout<<"\nRelease memory allocated to"<,nm;
delete[] nm;
}
};
void main()
{
string obj1("Mukul");
string obj2("Harleen");
obj1.put();
obj2.put();
obj1.com(obj2);
getch();
}
```

Output:

```
Name of person Mukul
Name of person Harleen
Both objects have different name
Release memory allocated to Harleen
Release memory allocated to Mukul
```

Program 14: Write a C++ program using reference variable to create dynamic objects.

```
#include<iostream.h>
#include<conio.h>
class rec
```

```
{
private:
int l;
int b;
public:
rec();
void get();
void area();
~rec();
};
rec::rec()
{
cout<<"Constructor with no parameter invoked";
}
void rec::get()
{
cout<<"Enter length & breadth: ";
cin>>l>>b;
}
void rec::area()
{
cout<<"Area is: "<<l*b;
}
rec::~rec()
{
cout<<"Destructor invoked";
}
void main()
{
rec &obj=*(new rec);
obj.get();
obj.area();
cout<<"End of program";
getch();
}
```

Output:

Constructor with no parameter invoked

Enter length & breadth:4 3

Area is:12

End of program

9.5 IMPORTANT POINTS ABOUT CONSTRUCTORS

Some important and special characteristics of constructor are as under:

1. Constructors are used to create, and can initialize, objects of their class type.
2. Constructors are just functions with the same name as the class.
3. Constructors are intended to initialize the members of the class when an instance of that class is created.
4. Constructors are not called directly (except through initializer lists)
5. Constructors are never virtual.
6. Constructor functions are called automatically when the objects are called.
7. A constructor initializes all the objects created under class.
8. The constructor must be defined in the public. The constructor must be a public member.
9. Overloading of constructors is possible.
10. If a class has a constructor, each object of that class will be initialized before any use is made of the objects.
11. If no constructor is defined, then compiler will provide default constructor automatically with Null initialization (It is not useful).
12. Member function can be accessed with in a constructor function.
13. A constructor can have default argument or default parameter.
14. Multiple constructors for the same class can be defined. They must have different parameters to distinguish them.
15. You cannot declare a constructor as virtual or static, nor can you declare a constructor as const, volatile, or const volatile.
16. You do not specify a return type for a constructor. A return statement in the body of a constructor cannot have a return value.
17. Constructor also obey the access rules i.e. private and protected constructors are available only for friend function and private member function whereas public constructor is used for all the member functions.
18. Mostly constructors are public.
19. Address of a constructor can not be copied i.e. it is not possible to take the address of a constructor.
20. An object of class with a constructor cannot be a member of a union.
21. Constructor can not be inherited i.e. the derived class constructor can call the base class constructor.

22. Memory allocation to objects can be provided to the constructor by using the **new** and **delete** operators.
23. Member functions may be called from within a constructor.
24. The name of constructor must be same as that of its class.

9.6 THE CONSTRUCTOR INITIALIZER

A constructor does not exist simply for cosmetic reasons. It can be used to initialize the member variables of an object. Therefore, a constructor provides a valuable alternative to a method initializer, the type of method we saw earlier.

To use a constructor to initialize the member variables of an object, provide as arguments the necessary variables that you intend to initialize. You do not have to initialize all member variables in the constructor, only those that need to be initialized. In fact, you should initialize only those members that you think the other objects or functions would need to provide when calling this object; this means that your object may have member variables that, either the external objects or functions do not need to modify (or access) or the member variable will be initialized later when called from the needed object or function.

Therefore, a constructor can also be used to call methods that hold the initial values of member variables.

Program 15: Write a C++ program using inline initialization in constructor.

```
#include <iostream.h>
#include<conio.h>
// Class to represent a box
class Box
{
public:
double length;
double breadth;
double height;
// Inline initialization
Box(double lv = 1.0, double bv = 1.0, double hv = 1.0):length(lv),
                    breadth(bv),height(hv)
{
cout << "Box constructor called" << endl;
}
// Function to calculate the volume of a box
double volume()
{
```

```
return length * breadth * height;
}
};
void main()
{
Box firstBox(80.0, 50.0, 40.0);
// Calculate the volume of the box
double firstBoxVolume = firstBox.volume();
cout << endl;
cout << "Size of first Box object is "
<< firstBox.length  << " by "
<< firstBox.breadth << " by "
<< firstBox.height
<< endl;
cout << "Volume of first Box object is " << firstBoxVolume
<< endl;
getch();
}
```

Output:

```
Box constructor called
Size of first Box object is 80 by 50 by 40
Volume of first Box object is 160000
```

Program 16: Write a C++ program to assign values using the member initialization syntax.

```
#include <iostream.h>
#include<conio.h>
class MyClass
{
const int numA; // const member
const int numB; // const member
public:
// Initialize numA and numB using initialization syntax.
MyClass(int x, int y) : numA(x), numB(y) { }
int getNumA()
{
return numA;
}
int getNumB()
{
```

```
return numB;
}
};
void main()
{
MyClass object1(7, 9), object2(5, 2);
cout << "Values in object1 are " << object1.getNumB() << " and " <<
object1.getNumA() << endl;
cout << "Values in object2 are " << object2.getNumB() << " and " <<
object2.getNumA() << endl;
getch();
}
```

Output:

```
Values in object1 are 9 7
Values in object2 are 2 5
```

9.7 CONSTRUCTORS AND ARRAYS

Arrays are constructed only using the default constructor. Default constructors are constructors that either accepts no arguments or for which all arguments have a default. Arrays are always constructed in ascending order. The initialization for each member of the array is done using the same constructor. Here we are representing the concept of array of objects as:

Program 17: Write a C++ program using array of objects to display area of multiple rectangles.

```
#include<iostream.h>
#include<conio.h>
class rec
{
private:
int l;
int b;
public:
rec(int a,int c)
{
l=a;
b=c;
}
void put()
```

```
{
cout<<"Area is: "<<l*b;
}};
void main()
{
rec obj[3]={rec(3,6),rec(2,5),rec(5,5)};
cout<<"Displaying areas of rectangles\n ";
for(int i=0;i<3;i++)
obj[i].put();
getch();
}
```

Output:

Displaying areas of rectangles

Area is:18

Area is:10

Area is:25

Program 18: Write a C++ program for an array of objects: call its method.

```
#include <iostream.h>
#include<conio.h>
class MyClass
{
public:
MyClass()
{
itsAge = 1;
itsWeight=5;
}
~MyClass() {}
int GetAge() const
{
return itsAge;
}
int GetWeight() const
{
return itsWeight;
}
void SetAge(int age)
{
itsAge = age;
```

```
}
private:
int itsAge;
int itsWeight;
};
void main()
{
MyClass myObject[5];
int i;
for (i = 0; i < 5; i++)
myObject[i].SetAge(2*i +1);
for (i = 0; i < 5; i++)
cout << " #" << i+1<< ": " << myObject[i].GetAge() << endl;
getch();
}
```

Output:

```
#1: 1
#2: 3
#3: 5
#4: 7
#5: 9
```

9.8 DESTRUCTOR

The destructor fulfills the opposite functionality. It is automatically called when an object is destroyed, either because its scope of existence has finished (for example, if it was defined as a local object within a function and the function ends) or because it is an object dynamically assigned and it is released using the operator delete. The destructor must have the same name as the class, but preceded with a tilde sign (~) and it must also return no value.

9.8.1 General Syntax of Destructor

A destructor is a function that has the same name as that of the class but is prefixed with a ~(tilde). Overloading a destructor is not possible. It can be explicitly invoked. In other words, a class can have only one destructor. A destructor cannot take arguments or specify a return value, or explicitly return a value.

The general syntax used for Destructor is:

```
~ constructor-name ();
or
~ class-name ();
```

The above is the general syntax of a destructor. In the above, the symbol tilde ~ represents a destructor which precedes the name of the class.

For example:

```
class student
{
private:
.........;
public:
student()
{ }
~ student()
{ }
};
```

Program 19: Write a C++ program to define and use the destructor.

```
#include <iostream.h>
#include<conio.h>
class myclass
{
int a;
public:
myclass();                    // constructor
~myclass();                   // destructor
void show();
};
myclass::myclass()            //constructor defined
{
cout << "In constructor\n";
a = 10;
}
myclass::~myclass()           // destructor defined
{
cout << "Destructing...\n";
}
void myclass::show()
{
cout << a << endl;
}
void main()
{
```

```
myclass ob;
ob.show();
getch();
}
Output:
In constructor
10
Destructing...
```

9.8.2 Use of Destructors

Destructors are also special member functions used in C++ programming language. Destructors have the opposite function of a constructor. The main use of destructors is to release dynamic allocated memory. Destructors are used to free memory, release resources and to perform other clean up. Destructors are automatically named when an object is destroyed. Like constructors, destructors also take the same name as that of the class name.

The use of destructors is especially suitable when an object assigns dynamic memory during its lifetime and at the moment of being destroyed we want to release the memory that the object was allocated.

Program 20: Write a C++ program for using destructor.

```
#include <iostream.h>
#include<conio.h>
class MyClass
{
public:
int x;
MyClass(int i);  // constructor
~MyClass();      // destructor
};
// a parameterized constructor.
MyClass::MyClass(int i)
{
x = i;
}
// Implement MyClass destructor.
MyClass::~MyClass()
{
cout << "Destructing object whose x value is " << x  <<" \n";
}
```

```
void main()
{
MyClass t1(5);
MyClass t2(19);
cout << t1.x << " " << t2.x << "\n";
getch();
}
```

Output:

```
5 19
Destructing object whose x value is 19
Destructing object whose x value is 5
```

9.8.3 Need for Destructor

As opposed to a constructor, a destructor is called when a program has finished using an instance of an object. A destructor does the cleaning behind the scenes. Like the default constructor, the compilers always create a default destructor if you don't create one. Like the default constructor, a destructor also has the same name as its object.

Destructors are usually used to de-allocate memory and do other cleanup for a class object and its class members when the object is destroyed. A destructor is called for a class object when that object passes out of scope or is explicitly deleted.

A destructor is a member function with the same name as its class prefixed by a ~ (tilde).

For example:

```
class X
{
public:
X();// Constructor for class X
{}
~X();// Destructor for class X
};
```

A destructor takes no arguments and has no return type. Its address cannot be taken. Destructors cannot be declared const, volatile, const volatile or static. A destructor can be declared virtual or pure virtual.

If no user-defined destructor exists for a class and one is needed, the compiler implicitly declares a destructor. This implicitly declared destructor is an inline public member of its class.

The compiler will implicitly define an implicitly declared destructor when the compiler uses the destructor to destroy an object of the destructor's class type.

9.9 IMPORTANT POINTS ABOUT DESTRUCTOR

Some important points about destructors:

1. Destructors take the same name as the class name.
2. Like the constructor, the destructor must also be defined in the public. The destructor must be a public member.
3. Destructor functions are invoked automatically when the objects are destroyed.
4. A Destructor may not be static.
5. These can not be inherited.
6. The Destructor does not take any argument which means that destructors cannot be overloaded.
7. No return type is specified for destructors.
8. An object of class with a Destructor cannot become member of a union.
9. Member function may be called from or accessed within a Destructor.
10. It is not possible to take the address of a Destructor.
11. No argument is provided to Destructor.
12. Destructor functions also access the three access levels private, protected and public similar to the constructor.
13. If a class has a Destructor, each object of that class will be reinitialized before the object goes out of scope.

9.10 ORDER OF CONSTRUCTOR AND DESTRUCTOR INVOCATION

The compiler automatically calls constructor and destructor. We can also call constructor and destructor in same fashion as we call normal user defined function. Every time an object is created and so automatically a constructor will be invoked. Now if there are number of objects declared simultaneously, then the question arises what will be the order of constructor and Destructor invocation. Note that the objects are constructed in the order they are defined and similarly these are destructed. Few examples are illustrated on this concept.

Program 21: Write a C++ program to depict execution of constructor and destructor.

```
#include<iostream.h>
#include<conio.h>
class ct
{
```

```
int id;
public:
ct(int i)
{
id=i;
cout<<"\n constructor ="<<id<<"runs";
}
~ct()
{
cout<<"\nobject ="<<id<<"destroyed";
}
};
void main()
{
ct c1(1);
ct c2(2);
ct c3(3);
coul<<"\nEnd of main";
getch();
}
```

Output:

```
constructor 1 runs
constructor 2 runs
constructor 3 runs
End of main
object 3 destroyed
object 2 destroyed
object 1 destroyed
```

Program 22: Write a C++ program to demonstrating the order in which constructors and destructors are called.

```
#include <string.h>
#include <iostream.h>
#include<conio.h>
class MyClass
{
public:
MyClass( int, string );          // constructor
~MyClass();                      // destructor
private:
```

```
int objectID;
string message;
};
MyClass::MyClass( int ID, string s )
{
objectID = ID;
message = s;
cout << "Object " << objectID << " constructor runs " << message << endl;
}
MyClass::~MyClass()
{
cout << "Object " << objectID << " destructor runs " << message << endl;
}
void create( void );
MyClass first( 1, "(global before main)" );
void main()
{
MyClass second( 2, "(local automatic in main)" );
static MyClass third( 3, "(local static in main)" );
create(); // call function to create objects
MyClass fourth( 4, "(local automatic in main)" );
getch();
}
void create( void )
{
cout << "\nCREATE FUNCTION: EXECUTION BEGINS" << endl;
MyClass fifth( 5, "(local automatic in create)" );
static MyClass sixth( 6, "(local static in create)" );
cout << "\nCREATE FUNCTION: EXECUTION ENDS" << endl;
}
```

Output:

```
Object 1 constructor runs (global before main)
Object 2 constructor runs (local automatic in main)
Object 3 constructor runs (local static in main)
CREATE FUNCTION: EXECUTION BEGINS
Object 5 constructor runs (local automatic in create)
Object 6 constructor runs (local static in create)
CREATE FUNCTION: EXECUTION ENDS
Object 5 destructor runs (local automatic in create)
```

Object 4 constructor runs (local automatic in main)
Object 4 destructor runs (local automatic in main)
Object 2 destructor runs (local automatic in main)
Object 6 destructor runs (local static in create)
Object 3 destructor runs (local static in main)
Object 1 destructor runs (global before main)

9.11 CONSTRUCTOR OVERLOADING

Like an ordinary method, a constructor can be overloaded. This means that you can have different constructors following the rules of overloading a function. Since we saw that a constructor can be used to initialize the member variables of its object, you can use multiple constructors to apply different initializations.

The general syntax is:

```
class class-name
{
private:
data-type member-elements;
public:
class-name ( ) { }                    // default constructor
class-name (one argument ) { }        // overloading of constructor
class-name (two argument ) { }        // overloading of constructor
~ class-name ( );                     // Destructor defined
};
```

A constructor can also be overloaded with more than one function that have the same name but different types or number of parameters. Remember that for overloaded functions the compiler will call the one whose parameters match the arguments used in the function call. In the case of constructors, which are automatically called when an object is created, the one executed is the one that matches the arguments passed on the object declaration:

Program 23: Write a C++ program again for class rectangle.

```
#include<iostream.h>
#include<conio.h>
class rec
{
private:
int l,b;
public:
rec()
```

```
{
l=b=0;
cout<<"Constructor with zero parameter\n";
}
rec(int a)
{
l=b=a;
cout<<"Constructor with one parameter\n";
}
rec(int a,int c)
{
l=a;
b=c;
cout<<"Constructor with two parameter\n";
}
int area()
{
return(l*b);
}
};
void main()
{
rec obj1;
rec obj2(3);
rec obj3(7,7);
cout<<"\nArea is of first rectangle : "<<obj1.area();
cout<<"\nArea is of square : "<<obj2.area();
cout<<"\nArea is of third rectangle : "<<obj3.area();
getch();
}
```

Output:

```
Area is of first rectangle :0
Area is of square :9
Area is of third rectangle :49
```

Program 24: Write a C++ program to illustrate the constructor and Destructor with the overloading of constructor.

```
// Program to define in different way about the overload constructors
#include<iostream.h>
#include<conio.h>
```

```
class integer
{
private:
int a;
public:
integer()
{
a=0;
cout<<endl<<"Constructor Called.";
}
integer(int i)
{
a=i;
cout<<endl<<"Constructor with argument called.";
}
~integer()
{
cout<<endl<<"Destructor Called.";
}
void get()
{
cout<<endl<<"Enter the value of integer:"<<endl;
cin>>a;
}
void show()
{
cout<<endl<<"The value of integer is:"<<'\t'<<a;
}
};
void main()
{
integer x, y(10);
x.get();
x.show();
y.show();
getch();
}
```

Output:

Constructor Called.

```
Constructor with argument called.
Enter the value of integer: 4
The value of integer is:    4
The value of integer is:    10
Destructor Called.
Destructor Called.
```

SOLVED PROGRAMMING

Program 1: Write a C++ program for constructor parameter with default value.

```
#include <iostream.h>
#include<conio.h>
#include <iomanip.h>
class MyClass
{
public:
MyClass(int a = 1, int b = 2, int c = 3)
{
MyClass::a = a;
MyClass::b = b;
MyClass::c = c;
};
void show_numbers(void)
{
cout << a << ' ' << b << ' '<< c << '\n';
};
private:
int a, b, c;
};
void main(void)
{
MyClass one(1, 1, 1);
MyClass defaults;
MyClass happy(101, 101, 101);
one.show_numbers();
defaults.show_numbers();
happy.show_numbers();
getch();
```

```
}
Output:
1 1 1
1 2 3
101 101 101
```

Program 2: Write a C++ program for constructor with 2 parameters.

```
#include <iostream.h>
#include<conio.h>
class MyClass
{
int h;
int i;
public:
MyClass(int j, int k)
{
h = j;
i = k;
}
int getInt()
{
return i;
}
int getHeight()
{
return h;
}
};
void main()
{
MyClass myObject[3] = {
MyClass(1, 2), // initialize
MyClass(3, 4),
MyClass(5, 6)
};
int i;
for(i=0; i<3; i++)
{
cout << myObject[i].getHeight();
cout << ", ";
```

```
cout << myObject[i].getInt() << "\n";
}
getch();
}
```

Output:

1, 2
3, 4
5, 6

Program 3: Write a C++ program to initialize variables and conduct calculation in constructor.

```
#include <iostream.h>
#include<conio.h>
class box
{
double line,width,heigth;
double volume;
public:
box(double a,double b,double c);
void vol();
};
box::box(double a,double b,double c)
{
line=a;
width=b;
heigth=c;
volume=line*heigth;
}
void box::vol()
{
cout<<"Volume is:"<<volume<<"\n";
}
void main()
{
box x(3.4,4.5,8.5),y(2.0,4.0,6.0);
x.vol();
y.vol();
getch();
}
```

Output:

```
Volume is: 28.9
Volume is: 12
```

Program 4: Write a C++ program to make a call class constructor or not during class array declaration.

```
#include <iostream.h>
#include<conio.h>
class powers
{
int x;
public:
powers()
{
x = 0;
cout << "\nno initializer\n\n";
}
powers(int n)
{
x = n;
cout << "\n\ninitializer:" << x;
}
int getx() { return x; }
void setx(int i) { x = i; }
};
void main()
{
powers ofTwo[] = {1, 2, 4, 8, 16}; // initialized
powers ofThree[5];               // uninitialized
getch();
}
```

Output:

```
initializer:1
initializer:2
initializer:4
initializer:8
initializer:16
no initializer
no initializer
no initializer
no initializer
no initializer
```

Program 5: Write a C++ program to overload the constructor.

```
#include <iostream.h>
#include<conio.h>
class MyClass
{
public:
int x;
int y;
// Overload the default constructor.
MyClass()
{
x = y = 0;
}
// Constructor with one parameter.
MyClass(int i)
{
x = y = i;
}
// Constructor with two parameters.
MyClass(int i, int j)
{
x = i; y = j;
}
};
void main()
{
MyClass t;        // invoke default constructor
MyClass t1(5);     // use MyClass(int)
MyClass t2(9, 10); // use MyClass(int, int)
cout << "t.x: " << t.x << ", t.y: " << t.y << "\n";
cout << "t1.x: " << t1.x << ", t1.y: " << t1.y << "\n";
cout << "t2.x: " << t2.x << ", t2.y: " << t2.y << "\n";
getch();
}
```

Output:

```
t.x: 0, t.y: 0
t1.x: 5, t1.y: 5
t2.x: 9, t2.y: 10
```

Program 6: Write a C++ program to depict working of copy constructor.

```
#include<iostream.h>
#include<conio.h>
class dist
{
private:
int feet;
float inch;
public:
dist(){}
dist(int f1,float in1)
{
feet=f1;
inch=in1;
}
dist(dist &d)
{
cout<<"Copy instructor invoked";
feet=d.feet;
inch=d.inch;
}
void show()
{
cout<<feet<<'\t'<<inch;
}
dist add(dist d)
{
dist t;
t.feet=feet+d.feet;
t.inch=inch+d.inch;
if(t.inch>=12.00)
{
t.inch-=12.00;
t.feet++;
}
return(t);
}
};
void main()
```

```
{
dist obj1(5,7);
dist obj2=obj1;
dist obj3;
obj3=obj1.add(obj2);
obj3.show();
getch();
}
```

Output:

```
Copy instructor invoked
Copy constructor invoked
Copy constructor invoked
obj3:-11 2
```

Program 7: Write a C++ program for Height class.

```
#include<iostream.h>
#include<conio.h>
class height
{
private:
int f;
double i;
public:
height(int f1)
{
f=f1;
i=0.0;
}
height(double f1)
{
f=int(f1);
i=(f1-int(f1))*12.0;
}
height()
{
f=i=0;
}
height(int f1,double in)
{
f=f1;
```

```
i=in;
}
void show()
{
cout<<"Feet="<<f<<"Inches="<<i<<"\n";
}
};
void main()
{
height obj1,obj2,obj3;
obj1=height(2);
obj2=height(3.5);
obj3=height(6,3);
obj1.show();
obj2.show();
obj3.show();
getch();
}
```

Output:

```
Feet=2  Inches=0
Feet=3 Inches=6
Feet=6 Inches=3
```

Program 8: Write a C++ program for a simple constructor and destructor.

```
#include <iostream.h>
#include<conio.h>
class MyClass
{
public:
int x;
MyClass();  // constructor
~MyClass(); // destructor
};
// Implement MyClass constructor.
MyClass::MyClass()
{
x = 10;
}
// Implement MyClass destructor.
MyClass::~MyClass()
```

```
{
cout << "Destructing...\n";
}
void main()
{
MyClass ob1;
MyClass ob2;
cout << ob1.x << " " << ob2.x << "\n";
getch();
}
```

Output:

```
10 10
Destructing...
Destructing...
```

PROGRAMMING PROBLEMS

Program 1: Write a C++ program to assign values to illustrate the parameterized constructor.

Program 2: Write a C++ program for the default constructor for class time is one that takes no arguments.

Program 3: Write a C++ program which use automatic conversions to assign new values.

Program 4: Write a C++ program to initialize variables and conduct calculation in constructor.

Program 5: Write a C++ program for calling default constructor when allocating an array dynamically.

Program 6: Write a C++ program for private and protected member variables.

Program 7: Write a C++ program for an array of objects: call its method.

Program 8: Write a C++ program to illustrate the constructor and Destructor with the overloading of constructor.

Program 9: Write a C++ program to generate Fibonacci series using the copy constructor.

Program 10: Write a C++ program for virtual copy constructor.

Program 11: Write a C++ program to demonstrating the order in which constructors and destructors are called.

Program 12: Write a C++ program using reference variable to create dynamic objects.

Fill in the blanks

1. Class members are accessed using the .... operator.
2. Class members specified as .... are accessible only to member functions of the class and friends of the class.
3. Class members specified as .... are accessible anywhere an object of the class is in scope.
4. The keyword .... specifies that an object or variable is not modifiable after it is initialized.

Answers

1. dot (.), 2. private. 3. public. 4. Const

OBJECTIVE TYPE QUESTIONS

1. A function that is called automatically each time an object is created is a
   (a) constructor (b) contractor
   (c) builder (d) architect
2. A class named student must have a constructor whose name is
   (a) student (b) ~student
   (c) constructor (d) any legal C++ name
3. A default constructor
   (a) takes no arguments
   (b) has default values for all its arguments
   (c) either a or b
   (d) neither a nor b
4. Providing two or more constructors for the same class ....
   (a) requires different argument lists
   (b) requires different constructor names
   (c) requires different constructor types
   (d) is illegal.
5. When the compiler cannot differentiate between two overloaded constructors, they are called ....
   (a) overloaded (b) destructed
   (c) ambiguous (d) dubious

6. A function that is called automatically each time an object is destroyed is a ....
   (a) constructor (b) destructor
   (c) destroyer (d) terminator.
7. You must preceed the destructor name with a (n)
   (a) exclamation point (b) octothorp
   (c) ampersand (d) tilde.
8. A function that is called automatically each time an object is destroyed is a
   (a) constructor (b) destructor
   (c) destroyer (d) terminator
9. When the compiler cannot differentiate between two overloaded constructors, they are called
   (a) overloaded (b) destructed
   (c) ambiguous (d) dubious
10. If you want to override constructor default values for an object you are instatiating, you must also override
    (a) all other parameters to that constructor
    (b) all parameters to the left of that value
    (c) all parameters to the right of that value
    (d) no other parameters to that constructor.
11. If you omit any constructor argument when you instantiate an object, you must use default values
    (a) for all parameters to the constructor
    (b) for all parameters to the right of the argument
    (c) for all parameters to the left of the argument
    (d) for no other parameters.
12. A constructor initialization list is preceded by
    (a) a semicolon (b) a colon
    (c) two colons (d) a space
13. The name of the constructor function for a class named animal is ....
    (a) animal (b) anbimalFunciton
    (c) conAnimal (d) pet (e) All
14. You place the constructor's prototype in the .... section of the class
    (a) confidential (b) hidden

(c) public (d) private

(e) restricted

15. Which of the following statements is false?

(a) You typically use a public member function to change the value in a private data member

(b) Because the constructor function does not return a value, you place the keyword void before the constructor's name

(c) the public member functions in a class can be accessed by any program that uses an object created from that class

(d) An instance of a class is considered an object

16. The features that allows you to use the same function name for separate functions that have different argument lists is called ....

(a) overriding (b) overloading

(c) constructing (d) destructing

17. If you want to override constructor default values for an object you are instantiating, you must also override ....

(a) all other parameters to that constructor

(b) all parameters to the left of that value

(c) all parameters to the right of that value

(d) no other parameters to that constructor.

18. A default constructor ....

(a) takes no arguments

(b) has default values for all its arguments

(c) either a or b

(d) neither a nor b

19. A function that is called automatically each time an object is created is a (n) ....

(a) constructor (b) contractor

(c) builder (d) architect

20. A variable w with a value 67 may be defined with ....

(a) int w = 67; (b) int w(67);

(c) int 67(w); (d) both a and b, but not c

21. A constructor may by ....

(a) provided automatically by C++ (b) written by you

(c) either a or b (d) neither a nor b

22. The return type you code for all constructors is ....
    (a) void
    (b) the class type
    (c) the same types as the first data member defined in the class
    (d) no type.
23. A class named Student must have a constructor whose name is ....
    (a) student
    (b) ~student
    (c) constructor
    (d) any legal C++ name

EXERCISES

1. What do you mean by Constructor? How can you declare it? Explain with an example?
2. Why are constructors used?
3. What are the various types of constructor used with the classes?
4. What are the various features of constructors?
5. What do you mean by **private constructors?**
6. Explain the relationship between the copy constructor and the assignment operator.
7. What do you mean by constructor initializer?
8. Explain the role of arrays in Constructor.
9. Explain the order of constructor and destructor invocation.
10. Differentiate between Constructor and Destructor.
11. What is the role of Copy Constructor in the Object Oriented programming?
12. How Dynamic Constructor helps in allocation of memory?
14. How is Default constructors used?
15. Why is the Parameterized Constructor used?
16. Differentiate between Default Constructor and Parameterized Constructor?
17. How do we invoke the constructor function?
18. What do you mean by the Destructor? How can you declare it? Explain with an example?
19. Why Destructors are used?
20. What are the various properties of Destructor?
21. How can you set the order of invocation of a constructor and Destructor?
22. What do you mean by constructor overloading? Explain with an appropriate example.

CHAPTER 10

Operator Overloading

10.1 INTRODUCTION

Operator overloading is a very important feature of Object Oriented Programming. Curious to know why!!? It is because by using this facility programmer would be able to create new definitions to existing operators.

In fact in other words a single operator can take up several functions as desired by programmers depending on the argument taken by the operator by using the operator overloading facility. Operators provide programmers with a concise notation for expressing manipulations of objects of fundamental types. Programmers can use operators with user-defined types as well. Although C++ does not allow new operators to be created, it does allow most existing operators to be overloaded so that, when these operators are used with objects, the operators have meaning appropriate to those objects. This is a powerful capability.

Operator overloading is an example of C++ polymorphism. Operator overloading extends the overloading concept to operators, letting you assign multiple meanings to C++ operators. The ability to overload operators is one of C++'s most powerful features. It allows the full integration of new class types into the programming environment.

After overloading the appropriate operators, you can use objects in expressions in just the same way that you use C++'s built-in data types. Operator overloading is not automatic you must write operator-overloading functions to perform the desired operations. Sometimes these functions are best made member functions; sometimes they are best as friend functions; occasionally they can be made global, non-friend functions.

10.2 OPERATOR OVERLOADING

Operator overloading provides the same concise and familiar expressions for user-defined types that C++ provides with its rich collection of operators for fundamental types.

Definition: *"Operator overloading extends the overloading concept to operators, letting you assign multiple meanings to C++ operators. Using this facility programmer would be able to create new definitions to existing operators."*

An operator is overloaded by writing a non-static member function definition or friend function definition as you normally would, except that the function name now it becomes the keyword operator followed by the symbol for the operator that can be overloaded. For example, the function name operator+ would be used to overload the addition operator (+). When operators are overloaded as member functions, they must be non-static, because they must be called on an object of the class and operate on that object. We can also use friend functions(non-member function) to overload different operators.

Note: *The operator overloaded functions must be either a member function i.e. non-static or friend function. But there is a big difference between the declarations of the operator overloaded using friend function and member function. In other words a friend function will have only one argument for the unary operators and two argument for the binary operators, whereas a member function have no arguments in the case of unary operator and one argument in the case of binary operators.*

10.2.1 Features of Operator Overloading

Following are the some major pros of different operator, using the operator overloading:

1. Operator overloading gives new meaning to existing operators.
2. Operator overloading works with objects.
3. Using the operator overloading, the major string operations can be done.
4. Coding becomes transparent with the help of operator overloading.
5. It makes the code more understandable.
6. Data conversion can also be done by using the operator overloading, i.e. it converts user defined data into basic data and vice versa.

7. By extending the meaning of operators, C++ operator overloading helps doing so.
8. Operator overloading can be applied to user defined data i.e. objects of user defined class.
9. It can change the complex statement into simple statement.
10. Also operator overloading decrease the size of complex program.
11. All the comparisons and string operations like concatenation etc. can be solved by using the operator overloading.
12. Operator overloading gives new direction to the OOP's.

After knowing about the feature of operator overloading now let us see how to define and use this concept of operator overloading in C++ programming language.

10.3 OPERATORS FOR FUNDAMENTAL TYPES

The meaning of how an operator works on objects of fundamental types cannot be changed by operator overloading. The programmer cannot, for example, change the meaning of how + adds two integers. Operator overloading works only with objects of user-defined types or with a mixture of an object of a user-defined type and an object of a fundamental type.

10.4 OPERATOR FUNCTION OR KEYWORD OPERATOR

You overload operators by creating operator functions. An *operator function* defines the operations that the overloaded operator will perform relative to the class upon which it will work. An operator function is created using the keyword **operator**. Operator functions can be either members or nonmembers of a class. Nonmember operator functions are almost always friend functions of the class, however. The way operator functions are written differs between member and nonmember functions. Therefore, each will be examined separately, beginning with member operator functions.

To overload an operator, a special function called operator function is used.

The general syntax of an operator function is:

```
return_type class_name :: operator operator_type( arguments )
{
Body of the function
}
```

Here, return_type is the datatype of the value returned by the specified operation like int, float, char, void etc.

The keyword operator is used to overload the specified operator

operator_type is the operator which has to be overloaded like +, -, —, ++, /, *, %, <, <=, >, etc.

The combination of the keyword operator and the operator_type i.e. operator operator_type represents the name of the function.

Another general syntax for defining an operator overloading is as follows:

```
return_type classname :: operator operator symbol (argument)
{
..................
statements;
}
```

Thus the above clearly specifies that operator overloading is defined as a member function by making use of the keyword operator.

In the above:

- return_type – is the data type returned by the function
- class name - is the name of the class
- operator – is the keyword
- operator symbol – is the symbol of the operator which is being overloaded or
- defined for new functionality
- :: - is the scope resolution operator which is used to use the function definition outside the class. The usage of this is clearly defined in our earlier section of How to define class members.

For example:

Suppose we have a class say Student and if the programmer wants to define a operator overloading for unary operator say ++, the function is defined as

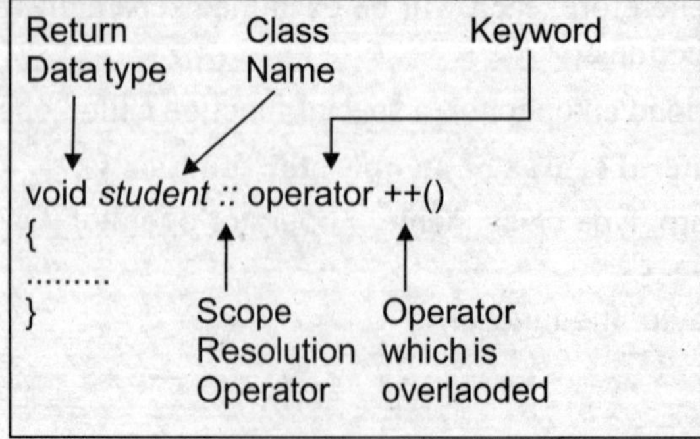

Inside the class Student the data type that is returned by the overloaded operator is defined as

```
class Student
{
private:
..........
public:
void operator ++( );
............
};
```

So the important steps involved in defining an operator overloading in case of unary operators are namely:

Inside the class the operator overloaded member function is defined with the return data type as member function or a friend function. The concept of friend function we will define in later sections. If in this case of unary operator overloading if the function is a member function then the number of arguments taken by the operator member function is none as seen in the below example. In case if the function defined for the operator overloading is a friend function which we will discuss in later section then it takes one argument.

The operator overloading is defined as member function outside the class using the scope resolution operator with the keyword operator as explained above.

10.5 OVERLOADING RULES

The following rules must be noted:

1. The order of operator evaluation remains unchanged. You cannot change the operator precedence rules.
2. You cannot change the operator associativity rules either. For example, the unary minus (-) operator associates from right to left.

   X = -Y; // Unary minus associates from right to left.

   X = Y-; // You CANNOT alter unary minus to go from left to right.
3. Note that an "operator" reserve word is used instead of the function name. Also the operator symbol is used after using the operator reserve word.
4. You cannot invent new operators that do not exist in the language. For instance, @ is not a valid C++ operator and cannot be overloaded.
5. Overloading some operators doesn't implictly define other operators for you. For example, overloading the + and = operators for a class doesn't mean that the += operator is overloaded automatically for you. You will need to write separate overload code for the += operator as well.
6. Overloaded operators must either be a nonstatic class member function or a global function. A global function that needs access to private or protected

class members must be declared as a friend of that class. A global function must take at least one argument that is of class or enumerated type or that is a reference to a class or enumerated type. For example:

```
class Point { public: Point operator<( Point & ); // Declare a member
operator // overload. ... // Declare addition operators.
friend Point operator+( Point&, int );
friend Point operator+( int, Point& ); };
```

The preceding code sample declares the less-than operator as a member function; however, the addition operators are declared as global functions that have friend access. Note that more than one implementation can be provided for a given operator. In the case of the preceding addition operator, the two implementations are provided to facilitate commutativity. It is just as likely that operators that add a Point to a Point, int to a Point, and so on, might be implemented.

7. Unary operators declared as member functions take no arguments; if declared as friend functions, they take one argument.
8. Binary operators declared as member functions take one argument; if declared as friend functions, they take two arguments.
9. If an operator can be used as either a unary or a binary operator (**&**, *, +, and -), you can overload each use separately.
10. Overloaded operators cannot have default arguments.
11. All overloaded operators except assignment (**operator=**) are inherited by derived classes.
12. The first argument for member-function overloaded operators is always of the class type of the object for which the operator is invoked (the class in which the operator is declared, or a class derived from that class). No conversions are supplied for the first argument.
13. You cannot change the way an operator works between native C++ types. For instance, you cannot change how + works between a double and an integer variable, as this operation is native to the compiler. You can however change how + works between a Complex class and a double variable, since Complex isn't a native C++ type.

10.6 TYPES OF OPERATOR OVERLOADING

The term operator overloading means giving the C++ operators such as (-, +, —, ++, *, /, >, <, >=, <= etc.), additional meanings while applying on user-defined data types.

For example, the statement:

```
z = x + y;
```

can be applied only to basic data-types such as float, int, double, long etc.

But consider a case where x, y and z are objects of a user-defined class. In this case, the above statement is not legal.

However, by making use of operator overloading, the above statement can be made legal. Operator overloading provides a flexibility to create new definitions for most of the C++ operators.

By using classes to create new variables and operator overloading to create definitions for operators, one can create a new language of one's own design.

The users can redefine or overload the following operators:

Operator	Name	Type
,	Comma	Binary
!	Logical NOT	Unary
!=	Inequality	Binary
%	Modulus	Binary
%=	Modulus assignment	Binary
&	Bitwise AND	Binary
&	Address-of	Unary
&&	Logical AND	Binary
&=	Bitwise AND assignment	Binary
( )	Function call	Binary
*	Multiplication	Binary
*	Pointer dereference	Unary
*=	Multiplication assignment	Binary
+	Addition	Binary
+	Unary Plus	Unary
++	Increment[1]	Unary
+=	Addition assignment	Binary
–	Subtraction	Binary
–	Unary negation	Unary
—	Decrement[1]	Unary
–=	Subtraction assignment	Binary
–>	Member selection	Binary
–>*	Pointer-to-member selection	Binary
/	Division	Binary
/=	Division assignment	Binary
<	Less than	Binary
<<	Left shift	Binary
<<=	Left shift assignment	Binary

Operator	Name	Type
<=	Less than or equal to	Binary
=	Assignment	Binary
==	Equality	Binary
>	Greater than	Binary
>=	Greater than or equal to	Binary
>>	Right shift	Binary
>>=	Right shift assignment	Binary
[ ]	Array subscript	Binary
^	Exclusive OR	Binary
^=	Exclusive OR assignment	Binary
|	Bitwise inclusive OR	Binary
|=	Bitwise inclusive OR assignment	Binary
||	Logical OR	Binary
~	One's complement	Unary
delete	**Delete**	Binary
new	**New**	Binary
conversion operators	conversion operators	Unary

Two versions of the unary increment and decrement operators exist: preincrement and postincrement.

The operators shown in the following table cannot be overloaded. The table includes the preprocessor symbols # and ##.

Nonredefinable Operators

Operator	Name
.	Member selection
.*	Pointer-to-member selection
::	Scope resolution
? :	Conditional
#	Preprocessor convert to string
##	Preprocessor concatenate

We have seen that different types of operators. Broadly classifying operators are of two types namely:

1. Unary Operators overloading
2. Binary Operators overloading

10.6.1 Unary Operators Overloading

As the name implies takes operate on only one operand. Some unary operators are namely ++ called as Increment operator, – – called as Decrement Operator, logical not (!) , ~, unary minus.

A unary operator for a class can be overloaded as a non-static member function with no arguments or as a friend function with one argument; that argument must be either an object of the class or a reference to an object of the class. Member functions that implement overloaded operators must be non-static so that they can access the non-static data in each object of the class. Remember that static member functions can access only static data members of the class.

As said before operator overloading helps the programmer to define a new functionality for the existing operator. This is done by using the keyword operator.

The general syntax is:

```
return_type class_name :: operator operator_type( arguments )
{
Body of the function
}
```

Some commonly used unary operators are unary minus (–), increment (++) and decrement (– –) operators.

The unary operators are shown in the following table:

Operator	Name
!	Logical NOT
&	Address-of
~	One's complement
*	Pointer dereference
+	Unary plus
++	Increment
–	Unary negation
– –	Decrement
conversion operators	conversion operators

Of the operators shown in preceding table, the postfix increment and decrement operators (++ and – –) are treated separately in Increment and Decrement.

Conversion operators are also discussed in a separate topic; see Conversion Functions.

Let us start by overloading the unary minus operator. The unary minus operator. changes the sign of an operand when applied to basic data-type (int, float, double etc.).

The following program, demonstrates how to overload this operator so that it can be applied to an object in much the same way as is applied to an int or float type variable.

Program 1: Write a C++ program illustrates the overloading of unary minus (-) operator

```
#include <iostream.h>
#include <conio.h>
class Minus
{
private:
int a, b, c;
public:
Minus( )                    // Default Constructor
{ }
Minus(int A, int B, int C)
{
a = A;
b = B;
c = C;
}
void display(void);
//********Declaration of the operator function**********
void operator - ( );
}; // End of the Class Definition

//***********Member Function Definitions*************
inline void Minus :: display(void)
{
cout << "\t a = " << a << endl;
cout << "\t b = " << b << endl;
cout << "\t c = " << c << endl;
}
//*********Definition of the operator function***********
inline void Minus :: operator - ( )
{
a = -a;
b = -b;
c = -c;
}
```

```
//*************Main Function Definition**************
void main(void)
{
Minus M(5, 10, -15);
cout << "\n Before activating the operator - ( )\n";
M.display( );
-M;
cout << "\n After activating the operator - ( )\n";
M.display( );
}
```

Output:

```
Before activating the operator - ( )
a= 5
b= 10
c= -15
After activating the operator - ( )
a= -5
b= -10
c= 15
```

For example, in the above program the declarative of the operator function is given as:

```
void operator – ( );
```

this declarative tells the compiler to call this member function, whenever the – operator is encountered, provided the operand is of type Minus.

In the main ( ) function of this program, the object M of type Minus is declared and initialized to

```
( 5, 10, -15 ) as:
Minus M( 5, 10, -15 );
```

Before activating the operator function, the values of a, b and c are displayed as:

```
a = 5
b = 10
c = -15
```

After the statement

```
-M;
```

the operator function gets activated and the values of a, b and c are displayed as:

```
a = -5
b = -10
c = 15
```

In the above program, the function operator – ( ) takes no argument.

This function is a member function, and the member functions can directly access the members of an object for which they have been called.

Therefore, the operator function for overloading the unary minus operator (-) does not require any argument.

Operator Function With Return Value

The operator – ( ) function defined in the above program has a problem. If one wants to use a statement such as:

```
M2 = -M1;
```

in the main ( ), the compiler will complain! The reason is that the operator function operator – ( ) has been defined to have a return type of void, while the assignment statement is being asked to return a variable of type Minus. Thus, the statements such as

```
M2 = -M1 ;
```

in the main( ) can be made available by following definition of the operator function:

```
Minus operator – ( )
{
Minus temp ;
temp.a = -a ;
temp.b = -b ;
temp.c = -c ;
return temp ;
}
```

Program 2: Write a C++ program illustrates the overloading of unary minus (-) operator and return value.

```
#include <iostream.h>
#include <conio.h>
//******Class Definition********
class Minus
{
private:
int a, b, c ;
public:
//*********Member Functions**************
Minus( ) // Default Constructor
{ }
Minus(int A, int B, int C)
{ a = A ; b = B ; c = C ; }
```

```
void display(void)
{
cout << "\t a = " << a << endl ;
cout << "\t b = " << b << endl ;
cout << "\t c = " << c << endl ;
}

//********Operator Function Definition *******
Minus operator - (void) // Declarative with the return type Minus
{
Minus temp ;
temp.a = -a ;
temp.b = -b ;
temp.c = -c ;
return temp ;
}
} ; // End of the class definition

//*******Main Functiion************
void main(void)
{
Minus M1(5, 10, -15); // Initialization of the object M1 of type Minus
cout << "\n Before activating the operator -( ):\n" ;
M1.display( ) ;
Minus M2 ; // Definining the object M2 of type Minus
M2 = -M1 ; // Activates the function operator -( ) and
// assigns the value of -M1 to M2
cout << "\n After activating the operator -( ):\n" ;
M2.display( ) ;
getch();
}
```

Output:

```
Before activating the operator - ( )
a= 5
b= 10
c= -15
After activating the operator - ( )
a= -5
b= -10
c= 15
```

In the above program, the operator – ( ) function creates a new object, named as temp of type Minus, for returning the values.

This type of object is known as **temporary object**. The values of the member data i.e. a, b and c are assigned to this temporary object temp as:

```
temp.a = -a ;
temp.b = -b ;
temp.c = -c ;
```

Finally, the function returns the object temp as:

```
return temp ;
```

Thus, the statement like

```
M2 = -M1 ;
```

can be used in the main( ) function.

Program 3: Write a C++ program illustrates the overloading the increment operator (++) with return value.

```
#include<iostream.h>
#include<conio.h>
class Increment
{
private:
int count ;
public:
//*****Member Function Definitions******
Increment( ) // Default Constructor
{ count = 0 ; }
Increment(int C) // Constructor with Argument
{ count = C ; }
Increment operator ++ ( ) // Operator Function Definition
{
count++ ;
return Increment(count);
}
void display(void) // Function for displaying the output
{
cout << count << endl ;
}
}; // End of the class definition
void main(void)
{
Increment I1, I2(5), I3, I4 ;
```

```
cout << "\n Before activating the operator ++( )\n" ;
cout << " I1 = " ;
I1.display( );
cout << " I2 = " ;
I2.display( );
++I1 ; // I1 and I2 are incremented
I2++ ;
cout << "\n After activating the operator ++( )\n" ;
cout << " I1 = " ;
I1.display( );
cout << " I2 = " ;
I2.display( ) ;
I3 = ++I1 ; /* Here, the objects I1 and I2 are incremented again and their
I4 = I2++ ; values are assigned to the objects I3 and I4 respectively */
cout << " I3 = " ;
I3.display( ) ;
cout << " I4 = " ;
I4.dicplay( ) ;
getch();
}
```

Output:

```
Before activating the operator ++ ( )
I1=0
I2=5
After activating the operator ++ ( )
I1=1
I2=6
I3=2
I4=7
```

In the above program, when the increment operator ++ is overloaded using the function operator ++ ( ) there is no distinction between prefix and postfix notation. That is why all the statements

```
I1++;
++I2;
and
I3 = I1++;
I4 = ++I2;
```

have the same effect i.e. they are incremented using the prefix notation only.

In order to make both notations of the increment operator (prefix & postfix) to work, the programmer must define two separate functions as:

```
operator ++ ( ) // For prefix
operator ++ ( int ) // For postfix
```

The operator function for overloading postfix increment operator uses a dummy argument int, which is automatically set to 0 by the postfix operator ++.

This dummy argument allows the compiler to distinguish the two forms (prefix, postfix) of the increment operator.

In reality it is not an argument and it does not mean an integer.

It is simply a signal to the compiler to create the postfix notation of the operator.

Program 4: Write a C++ program for Overloading ->.

```
#include <iostream.h>
#include<conio.h>
class A
{
public:
int i;
A *operator->()
{
return this;
}
};
void main()
{
A a;
a->i =100;
cout <<a.i <<" "<<a->i;
getch();
}
```

Output:

```
100 100
```

10.6.2 Binary Operators Overloading

Binary operators, when overloaded, are given new functionality. The function defined for binary operator overloading, as with unary operator overloading, can be member function or friend function. The difference is in the number of arguments used by the function. In the case of binary operator overloading, when the function is a member function then the number of arguments used by the operator member function is one. When the function defined for the binary operator overloading is a friend function, then it uses two arguments.

Binary operator overloading, as in unary operator overloading, is performed using a keyword operator.

To overload an operator, a special function called operator function is used.

The general syntax is:

```
return_type claa_name :: operator_type( arguments )
{
Body of the function
}
```

Binary operators can be overloaded in a similar manner as unary operators.

We should note the following features of an operator function for a binary operator:

1. It receives only one class type argument explicitly, in case of a member function. For a friend function, two class types are received as arguments.
2. It returns a class type.

   Consider the following expression:

   C = A + B;

The above expression contains three objects namely A, B and C of which A and B are the operands while C is the one to which the sum of A and B is assigned to. In the above expression, the operator function is supposed to add two user defined data types and return a user defined data type.

The following table shows a list of operators that can be overloaded.

Redefinable Binary Operators

Operator	Name
,	Comma
!=	Inequality
%	Modulus
%=	Modulus/assignment
&	Bitwise AND
&&	Logical AND
&=	Bitwise AND/assignment
*	Multiplication
*=	Multiplication/assignment
+	Addition
+=	Addition/assignment
–	Subtraction

–=	Subtraction/assignment
–>	Member selection
–>*	Pointer-to-member selection
/	Division
/=	Division/assignment
<	Less than
<<	Left shift
<<=	Left shift/assignment
<=	Less than or equal to
=	Assignment
==	Equality
>	Greater than
>=	Greater than or equal to
>>	Right shift
>>=	Right shift/assignment
^	Exclusive OR
^=	Exclusive OR/assignment
|	Bitwise inclusive OR
|=	Bitwise inclusive OR/assignment
||	Logical OR
delete	Delete
new	New

Binary operators which we can overloaded are arithmetic operators, comparison operators, arithmetic assignment operators, special operators etc.

Program 5: Write a C++ program for definition of operator+ ():

```
#include <iostream.h>
#include<conio.h>
class Values
{
int a,b;
public:
Values()
{}
Values(int aa,int bb)
{
a =aa;
b =bb;
}
void show()
{
cout <<a <<" ";
```

```
cout <<b <<"\n";
}
Values operator+(Values p);
};
Values Values::operator+(Values p)
{
Values temp;
temp.a =p.a +a;
temp.b =p.b +b;
return temp;
}
void main()
{
Values v1(20,30),v2(15,40);
v1.show();
v2.show();
v1 =v1 +v2;
v1.show();
getch();
}
Output:
20 30
15 40
35 70
```

Program 6: Write a C++ program for addition & multiplication of two matrices by overloading + and * operators.

```
#include<iostream.h>
#include<conio.h>
class mat
{
private:
int s[10][10];
int u,v;
public:
void show();
mat operator +(mat);
mat operator *(mat);
void read();
};
```

```
mat mat::operator+(mat uu2)
{
mat t;
t.u=u;
t.v=v;
cout<<t.u;
cout<<t.v;
for(int i=0;i<t.u;i++)
for(int j=0;j<t.v;j++)
t.s[i][j]=s[i][j]+uu2.s[i][j];
return t;
}
mat mat::operator*(mat uu2)
{
mat t;
t.u=u;
t.v=uu2.v;
for(int i=0;i<t.u;i++)
for(int j=0;j<t.v;j++)
{
t.s[i][j]=0;
for(int k=0;k<v;k++)
t.s[i][j]+=s[i][k]*uu2.s[k][j];
}
return t;
}
void mat::read()
{
cout<<"Enter order of matrix:\n";
cin>>u>>v;
cout<<"Enter  elements:\n";
for(int i=0;i<u;i++)
for(int j=0;j<v;j++)
cin>>s[i][j];
}
void mat::show()
{
for(int i=0;i<u;i++)
for(int j=0;j<v;j++)
```

```
cout<<s[i][j]<<"\t";
cout<<"\n";
}
void main()
{
mat obj1,obj2,obj3;
cout<<"Enter first matrix\n";
obj1.read();
cout<<"Enter second matrix\n";
obj2.read();
obj3=obj1+obj2;
cout<<"Result after addition\n";
obj3.show();
obj3=obj1*obj2;
cout<<"Result after multiplication\n";
obj3.show();
getch();
}
Output:
Enter first matrix
Enter order of matrix:2 2
Enter elements 3 4 1 2
Enter second matrix
Enter order of matrix:2 2
Enter elements 2 3 1 1
Rsult after addition
5 7
2 3
Result after multiplication
10 13
4 4
```

10.7 OPERATOR OVERLOADING USING A FRIEND FUNCTION

Friend functions are more useful in operator overloading. They offer better flexibility which is not provided by the member function of the class.

You can overload an operator for a class by using a nonmember function, which is usually a friend of the class. Since a **friend** function is not a member of the class, it does not have a **this** pointer. Therefore, an overloaded friend operator function is passed the operands explicitly. This means that a friend function that overloads a binary operator has two parameters, and a friend function that overloads a unary operator has one parameter. When overloading a binary operator using a friend function, the left operand is passed in the first parameter and the right operand is passed in the second parameter.

The general syntax of operator overloading with friend function is:

```
friend return_type operator operator_type( arguments )
{
Body of the function ;
}
```

10.8 USING A FRIEND TO OVERLOAD ++ OR – –

A friend function is used to overload the increment or decrement operators. Now, you must pass the operand as a reference parameter. This is because friend functions do not have **this** pointer. Here friend function takes one argument like

```
friend Values operator++(Values &p);
friend Values operator– –(Values &p);
```

Program 7: Write a C++ program Using a Friend to Overload ++ or - -.

```
#include <iostream.h>
#include<conio.h>
class Values
{
int a,b;
public:
Values()
{ }
Values(int aa,int bb)
{
a =aa;
b =bb;
}
void show()
{
cout <<a <<" ";
cout <<b <<"\n";
}
Values operator=(Values p2);
friend Values operator++(Values &p);
```

```
friend Values operator—(Values &p);
};
Values Values::operator=(Values p2)
{
a =p2.a;
b =p2.b;
return *this;
}
// friend;use a reference .
Values operator++(Values &p)
{
p.a++;
p.b++;
return p;
}
//p— a friend;use reference.
Values operator—(Values &p)
{
p.a—;
p.b—;
return p;
}
void main()
{
Values v1(20,30),v2;
v1.show();
++v1;
v1.show();
v2 =++v1;
v2.show();
—v2;
v2.show();
getch();
}
```

Output:

```
20 30
21 31
22 32
21 31
```

Program 8: Write a C++ program to Make op—, ++, = a friend; use reference.

```
#include <iostream.h>
#include<conio.h>
class Point
{
int x, y;
public:
Point() {}
Point(int px, int py)
{
x = px;
y = py;
}
void show()
{
cout << x << " ";
cout << y << "\n";
}
Point operator=(Point op2);
friend Point operator++(Point &op);
friend Point operator—(Point &op);
};
// Overload assignment for Point.
Point Point::operator=(Point op2)
{
x = op2.x;
y = op2.y;
return *this; // i.e., return object that generated call
}
// Now a friend; use a reference parameter.
Point operator++(Point &op)
{
op.x++;
op.y++;
return op;
}
// Make op— a friend; use reference.
Point operator—(Point &op)
{
```

```
op.x—;
op.y—;
return op;
}
void main()
{
Point ob1(10, 20), ob2;
ob1.show();
++ob1;
ob1.show(); // displays 11 21
ob2 =  ++ob1;
ob2.show(); // displays 12 22
—ob2;
ob2.show(); // displays 11 21
getch();
}
Output:
10 20
11 21
12 22
11 21
```

10.9 USING A FRIEND TO OVERLOAD +

A friend function is used to overload the binary operator (+). Now, it takes two arguments. Following is the example for overloading arithmetic operator (+).

Program 9: Write a C++ program for friend operator.

```
#include <iostream.h>
#include<conio.h>
class Num
{
friend Num operator+(Num ob, int i);
friend Num operator+(int i, Num ob),
int count;
public:
Num(int cc=0)
{
count=cc;
}
```

```
Num& operator=(int i);
void Show()
{
cout <<count<<endl;
}
};
Num& Num::operator=(int i)
{
count=i;
return *this;
}
Num operator+(Num ob, int i) // This handles ob+int.
{
Num temp;
temp.count=ob.count+i;
return temp;
}
Num operator+(int i, Num ob) // This handles int+ob.
{
Num temp;
temp.count=ob.count+i;
return temp;
}
void main()
{
Num obj;
obj=10;
obj.Show();
obj=10+obj;
obj.Show();
obj=obj+12;
obj.Show();
getch()
}
```

Output:

10

20

32

Both unary and binary operators are overloaded using friend function

Program 10: Write a C++ program to Operator Overloading Using a Friend Function.

```
//In this program,the operator+()function is made into friend:
#include <iostream.h>
#include<conio.h>
class Values
{
int a,b;
public:
Values()
{ }
Values(int aa,int bb)
{
a =aa;
b =bb;
}
void show()
{
cout <<a <<" ";
cout <<b <<"\n";
}
friend Values operator+(Values p1,Values p2);//friend
Values operator-(Values p2);
Values operator=(Values p2);
Values operator++();
};
//Now,+is overloaded using friend function.
Values operator+(Values p1,Values p2)
{
Values temp;
temp.a =p1.a +p2.a;
temp.b =p1.b +p2.b;
return temp;
}
Values Values::operator-(Values p2)
{
Values temp;
temp.a =a -p2.b;
```

```
temp.b =a -p2.b;
return temp;
}
Values Values::operator=(Values p2)
{
a =p2.a;
b =p2.a;
return *this;
}
Values Values::operator++()
{
a++;
b++;
return *this;
}
void main()
{
Values v1(20,30),v2(15,40);
v1.show();
v2.show();
++v1;
v1.show();
v2 =++v1;
v1.show();
v2.show();
v1=v2;
v1.show();
v2.show();
getch();
}
```

Output:

```
20 30
15 40
21 31
22 32
22 22
22 22
22 22
```

10.10 CREATING PREFIX AND POSTFIX FORMS OF THE INCREMENT AND DECREMENT OPERATORS

The increment and decrement operators fall into a special category because there are two variants of each:

- Preincrement and postincrement
- Predecrement and postdecrement

When you write overloaded operator functions, it can be useful to implement separate versions for the prefix and postfix versions of these operators. To distinguish between the two, the following rule is observed: The prefix form of the operator is declared exactly the same way as any other unary operator; the postfix form accepts an additional argument of type **int**.

Note: *When specifying an overloaded operator for the postfix form of the increment or decrement operator, the additional argument must be of type* ***int****; specifying any other type generates an error.*

10.10.1 Increment ++

You overload the prefix increment operator ++ with either a nonmember function operator that has one argument of class type or a reference to class type, or with a member function operator that has no arguments. The ++ (increment) operator adds 1 to the value of a scalar operand, or if the operand is a pointer, increments the operand by the size of the object to which it points. The operand receives the result of the increment operation. The operand must be a modifiable lvalue of arithmetic or pointer type. You can put the ++ before or after the operand. If it appears before the operand, the operand is incremented. The incremented value is then used in the expression. If you put the ++ after the operand, the value of the operand is used in the expression before the operand is incremented.

Program 11: Write a C++ program to increment time variable with ++operator.

```
#include <iostream.h>
#include<conio.h>
class Timer
{
private:
unsigned int time;
public:
Timer():time(0)
{ }
```

```
int get_time()
{
return time;
}
void operator ++()
{
++time;
}
};
void main()
{
Timer t1,t2;
cout <<"\nt1=" <<t1.get_time();
cout <<"\nt2=" <<t2.get_time();
++t1;
++t2;
++t2;
cout <<"\nt1=" <<t1.get_time();
cout <<"\nt2=" <<t2.get_time()<<endl;
getch();
}
```

Output:

```
t1=0
t2=0
t1=1
t2=2
```

Program 12: Write a C++ program to Overloaded ++operator in both prefix and postfix.

```
#include <iostream.h>
#include<conio.h>
class Timer
{
private:
int time;
public:
Timer():time(0)
{ }
Timer(int t):time(t)
{ }
```

```
int get_time()
{
return time;
}
Timer operator ++()
{
return Timer(++time);
}
Timer operator ++(int)
{
return Timer(time++);
}
};
void main()
{
Timer t1,t2;
cout <<"\nt1=" <<t1.get_time();
cout <<"\nt2=" <<t2.get_time();
++t1;
t2 =++t1;
cout <<"\nt1=" <<t1.get_time();
cout <<"\nt2=" <<t2.get_time();
t2 =t1++;
cout <<"\nt1=" <<t1.get_time();
cout <<"\nt2=" <<t2.get_time()<<endl;
getch();
}
Output:
t1=0
t2=0
t1=2
t2=2
t1=3
t2=2
```

10.10.2 Decrement - -

You overload the prefix decrement operator – – with either a nonmember function operator that has one argument of class type or a reference to class type, or with a member function operator that has no arguments. The – – (decrement) operator subtracts 1 from the value of a scalar operand, or if the operand is a pointer, decreases the operand by the size of the object to which it points. The operand receives the result of the decrement operation. The operand must be a modifiable lvalue. You can put the – – before or after the operand. If it appears before the operand, the operand is decremented, and the decremented value is used in the expression. If the – – appears after the operand, the current value of the operand is used in the expression and the operand is decremented.

Program 13: Write a C++ program to illustrate the overloading of post decrement operator.

```
#include<iostream.h>
#include<conio.h>
class A
{
int n;
public:
void input()
{
cin>>n;
}
void operator– –(int)
{
n– –;
cout<<"\nOperator overloaded function executed.\n";
}
void print()
{
cout<<n<<endl;
}
};
void main()
{
clrscr();
cout<<"Enter the number==>";
A a;
a.input();//INPUTTING
cout<<"The number is==>";
a.print();        //DISPLAYING
a– –; //DECRMENT BY OVERLOADED FUNCTION
cout<<"Now the number is==>";
```

```
a.print();        //AGAIN DISPLAYING
getch();
}
Output:
Enter the number==> 5
The number is==> 5
Now the number is==> 4
Operator overloaded function executed.
```

10.11 ASSIGNMENT AND ARITHMETIC ASSIGNMENT OPERATOR

The assignment operator (=) is, strictly speaking, a binary operator. Its declaration is identical to any other binary operator, with the following exceptions:

- It must be a nonstatic member function. No **operator=** can be declared as a nonmember function.
- It is not inherited by derived classes.
- A default **operator=** function can be generated by the compiler for class types if none exists.

The following example illustrates how to declare an assignment operator and arithmetic assignment operator:

Program 14: Write a C++ program to illustrate the concept of Overloading of Assignment and Arithmetic Assignment operator.

```
#include<iostream.h>
#include<conio.h>
class A
{
int p;
public:
void operator= (int n)
{
p=n;
}
void operator+= (A z)
{
p+=z.p;
}
void print()
{
```

```
cout<<"P is "<<p;
}
};
void main()
{
clrscr();
A a,a1;
a1=4;
a=3;
a.print();
a+=a1;
cout<<"\nNow ";
a.print();
getch();
}
```

10.12 COPY ASSIGNMENT OPERATORS

The copy assignment operator lets you create a new object from an existing one by initialization. A copy assignment operator of a struct A is a nonstatic non-template member function that has one of the following forms:

- A::operator=(A)
- A::operator=(A&)
- A::operator=(const A&)
- A::operator=(volatile A&)
- A::operator=(const volatile A&)

If you do not declare a copy assignment operator for a struct A, the compiler will implicitly declare one for you which will be inline public. The following example demonstrates implicitly defined and user-defined copy assignment operators:

Program 15: Write a C++ program to illustrate the copy assignment operator.

```
#include <iostream>
#include<conio.h>
struct A
{
A& operator=(const A&)
{
cout << "A::operator=(const A&)" << endl;
```

```
return *this;
}
A& operator=(A&)
{
cout << "A::operator=(A&)" << endl;
return *this;
} };
class B
{
A a;
};
struct C
{
C& operator=(C&)
{
cout << "C::operator=(C&)" << endl;
return *this;
}
C() { }
};
void main()
{
B x, y;
x = y;
A w, z;
w = z;
C i;
const C j();
// i = j;
}
Output:
A::operator=(const A&)
A::operator=(A&)
```

10.13 OVERLOADING OF RELATIONAL OPERATORS

All relational operators are binary, and should return either true or false. The six relational operators <, >, <=, >=, ==, and != can be overloaded the same way that the less than operator is overloaded in the program given below.

Program 16: Write a C++ program to overloaded 'less-than' operators with double value.

```
#include <iostream.h>
#include<conio.h>
#include <stdlib.h>                  // For random number generator
#include <time.h>                    // For time function
class Box
{
public:
Box(double aLength, double aWidth, double aHeight):length(aLength),
width(aWidth), height(aHeight) {}
double volume() const
{
return length*width*height;
}
double getLength()  const { return length; }
double getWidth() const { return width; }
double getHeight()  const { return height; }
int operator<(const Box& aBox) const
{
return volume() < aBox.volume();
}
int operator<(const double aValue) const
{
return volume() < aValue;
}
private:
double length;
double width;
double height;
};
void main()
{
Box firstBox(17.0, 11.0, 5.0);
if(firstBox < 100000)
{
cout << "less than";
}
else
```

```
{
cout << "not less than";
}
getch();
}
```

Output:

less than

10.14 OVERLOADING OF LOGICAL OPERATORS

The! Operator is unary, && and || are binary. It should be noted that in normal use, && and || have "short-circuit" behavior, where the right operand may not be evaluated, depending on the left operand. When overloaded, these operators get function call precedence, and this short circuit behavior is lost.

Program 17: Write a C++ program Write a program to overload logical not(!) to find factorial.

```
#include<iostream.h>
#include<conio.h>
class f
{
int num;
public:
f(int n)
{num=n;}
int operator!();
};
int f::operator!()
{
int fact1=1;
for(int i=2;i<=num;i++)
fact1=fact1*1;
return(fact1);
}
void main()
{
f fc(7);
int fact;;
fact=!fc;
cout<<"Factorial="<<fact;
```

```
getch();
}
```

Output:

Factorial=5040

Program 18: Write a C++ program for Another Demo: Overload the == and && relative to MyClass class.

```
#include <iostream.h>
#include<conio.h>
class MyClass
{
int x, y;
public:
MyClass()
{
x=0;
y=0;
}
MyClass(int i, int j)
{
x=i;
y=j;
}
void getXY(int &i, int &j)
{
i=x;
j=y;
}
int operator==(MyClass object2);
int operator&&(MyClass object2);
};
// Overload the == operator for MyClass.
int MyClass::operator==(MyClass object2)
{
return x==object2.x && y== object2.y;
}
// Overload the && operator for MyClass.
int MyClass::operator&&(MyClass object2)
{
return (x && object2.x) && (y && object2.y);
```

```
}
void  main()
{
MyClass object1(10, 10), object2(5, 3), object3(10, 10), object4(0, 0);
if(object1==object2)
cout << "object1 same as object2\n";
else
cout << "object1 and object2 differ\n";
if(object1==object3)
cout << "object1 same as object3\n";
else
cout << "object1 and object3 differ\n";
if(object1 && object2)
cout << "object1 && object2 is true\n";
else
cout << "object1 && object2 is false\n";
if(object1 && object4)
cout << "object1 && object4 is true\n";
else
cout << "object1 && object4 is false\n";
getch();
}
```

Output:

```
object1 and object2 differ
object1 same as object3
object1 && object2 is true
object1 && object4 is false
```

10.15 OVERLOADING STREAM INSERTION AND STREAM EXTRACTION OPERATORS

C++ is able to input and output the fundamental types using the stream extraction operator >> and the stream insertion operator <<. The class libraries provided with C++ compilers overload these operators to process each fundamental type, including pointers and C-like char * strings. The stream insertion and stream extraction operators also can be overloaded to perform input and output for user-defined types.

Program 19: Write a C++ program Class level ostream operator and istream operator.

```
#include <iostream.h>
#include<conio.h>
#include<fstream.h>
class ThreeD
{
int x,y,z;
public:
ThreeD(int i,int j,int k)
{
x=i;
y=j;
z=k;
}
friend ostream& operator<<(ostream& stream,ThreeD ob);
friend istream& operator>>(istream& stream,ThreeD ob);
};
ostream& operator<<(ostream& stream,ThreeD ob)
{
stream<<ob.x<<' '<<ob.y<<' '<<ob.z<<'\n';
return stream;
}
istream& operator>>(istream& stream,ThreeD  ob)
{
stream>>ob.x>>ob.y>>ob.z;
return stream;
}
void main()
{
ThreeD o1(1,2,3),o2(4,5,6);
ofstream out("test");
if(!out)
{
cout<<"Cannot open OUTPUT file\n";
return 1;
}
cout<<o1<<o2;
out.close();
```

```
ifstream in("test");
if(!in)
{
cout<<"Cannot open input file\n";
return 1;
}
ThreeD o3(0,0,0),o4(0,0,0);
in>>o3>>o4;
getch();
}
```

Output:

```
1 2 3
4 5 6
```

10.16 OVERLOADING NEW AND DELETE OPERATOR

It is possible to overload **new** and **delete**. You might choose to do this if you want to use some special allocation method. For example, you may want allocation routines that automatically begin using a disk file as virtual memory when the heap has been exhausted. Whatever the reason, it is a very simple matter to overload these operators.

Program 20: Write a C++ program to demonstrate overloaded new and delete.

```
#include <iostream.h>
#include<conio.h>
#include <new.h>
#include <stdlib.h>
class MyClass
{
int x, y, z;
public:
MyClass()
{
x = y = z = 0;
cout << "Constructing 0, 0, 0\n";
}
MyClass(int i, int j, int k)
{
x = i;
y = j;
```

```
z = k;
cout << "Constructing " << i << ", ";
cout << j << ", " << k;
cout << '\n';
}
~MyClass( )
{
cout << "Destructing\n";
}
void *operator new(size_t size);
void *operator new[](size_t size);
void operator delete(void *p);
void operator delete[](void *p);
void show() ;
};
void *MyClass::operator new(size_t size)
{
void *p;
cout << "Allocating MyClass object.\n";
p = malloc(size);
if(!p)
{
bad_alloc ba;
throw ba;
}
return p;
}
void *MyClass::operator new[](size_t size)
{
void *p;
cout << "Allocating array of MyClass objects.\n";
p = malloc(size);
if(!p)
{
bad_alloc ba;
throw ba;
}
return p;
}
```

```
void MyClass::operator delete(void *p)
{
cout << "Deleting MyClass object.\n";
free(p);
}
void MyClass::operator delete[](void *p)
{
cout << "Deleting array of MyClass objects.\n";
free(p);
}
void MyClass::show()
{
cout << x << ", ";
cout << y << ", ";
cout << z << endl;
}
void  main()
{
MyClass *objectPointer1, *objectPointer2;
try {
objectPointer1 = new MyClass[3];     // allocate array
objectPointer2 = new MyClass(5, 6, 7); // allocate object
}
catch (bad_alloc ba)
{
cout << "Allocation error.\n";
return 1;
}
objectPointer1[1].show();
objectPointer2->show();
delete [] objectPointer1; // delete array
delete objectPointer2;    // delete object
getch();
}
```

Output:

```
Allocating array of MyClass objects.
Constructing 0, 0, 0
Constructing 0, 0, 0
Constructing 0, 0, 0
```

```
Allocating MyClass object.
Constructing 5, 6, 7
0, 0, 0
5, 6, 7
Destructing
Destructing
Destructing
Deleting array of MyClass objects.
Destructing
Deleting MyClass object.
```

10.17 OVERLOADING SOME SPECIAL OPERATORS

C++ defines array subscripting, function calling, and class member access as operations. The operators that perform these functions are the **[ ], ( ),** and –>, respectively. These rather exotic operators may be overloaded in C++, opening up some very interesting uses.

One important restriction applies to overloading these three operators: They must be nonstatic member functions. They cannot be friends.

10.17.1 Overloading [ ]

The subscript operator, **[ ]**, is a binary operator which must be a nonstatic member function that takes a single argument. This argument can be of any type and designates the desired array subscript. The subscript operator, [], is used when accessing array elements, e.g. s[3]. This operator too may be overloaded.

Therefore, the general form of a member **operator[ ]()** function is as shown here:

Program 21: Write a C++ program to overload operator [].

```
#include <iostream.h>
#include<conio.h>
class MyClass
{
int a[3];
public:
MyClass(int i, int j, int k)
{
a[0] = i;
a[1] = j;
a[2] = k;
```

```
}
int operator[](int i)
{
return a[i];
}
};
void main()
{
MyClass object(1, 2, 3);
cout << object[1];
getch();
}
```

Output:

2

10.17.2 Function Call

The function-call operator, invoked using parentheses, is a binary operator. The function call operator must be a member function, but has no other restrictions - it may be overloaded with any number of parameters of any type, and may return any type.

primary-expression (expression-listopt)

In this, *primary-expression* is the first operand, and *expression-list*, a possibly empty list of arguments, is the second operand. The function-call operator is used for operations that require a number of parameters. This works because *expression-list* is a list instead of a single operand. The function-call operator must be a nonstatic member function. Let's begin with an example

Program 22: Write a C++ program Overloading ().

```
#include <iostream.h>
#include<conio.h>
class Values
{
int a,b;
public:
Values()
{ }
Values(int aa,int bb)
{
a =aa;
b =bb;
```

```
}
void show()
{
cout <<a <<" ";
cout <<b <<"\n";
}

Values operator+(Values p);
Values operator()(int i,int j);
};
Values Values::operator()(int i,int j)
{
a =i;
b =j;
return *this;
}
Values Values::operator+(Values p)
{
Values temp;
temp.a =p.a +a;
temp.b =p.b +b;
return temp;
}
void main()
{
Values v1(20,30),v2(15,40);
v1.show();
v1(25,35);
v1.show();
v1 =v2 +v1(50,50);
v1.show();
getch();
}
```

Output:

```
20 30
25 35
65 90
```

10.17.3 Overloading ->

The -> pointer operator, also called the *class member access* operator, is considered a unary operator when overloading.

The general syntax is:

class-type *operator->()

where *class-type* is the name of the class to which this operator belongs. The member access operator function must be a nonstatic member function.

This operator is used (often in conjunction with the pointer-dereference operator) to implement "smart pointers" that validate pointers prior to dereference or count usage.

The . member access operator cannot be overloaded.

Program 23: Write a C++ program to define operator: pointer reference.

```
#include <iostream.h>
#include<conio.h>
class myclass
{
public:
int i;
myclass *operator->()
{
return this;
}
};
void  main()
{
myclass ob;
ob->i = 10;
cout << ob.i << " " << ob->i;
getch();
}
```

Output:

10 10

10.17.4 Overloading the Comma Operator

The comma operator (,) can be overloaded. It is a binary operator, and like all overloaded operators, you can make an overloaded comma perform any operation you want.

Here is a program that illustrates the effect of overloading the comma operator.

Program 24: Write a C++ program overloading the Comma Operator.

```
#include <iostream.h>
#include<conio.h>
class Values
{
int a,b;
public:
Values()
{}
Values(int aa,int bb)
{
a=aa;
b=bb;
}
void show()
{
cout <<a <<" ";
cout <<b <<"\n";
}
Values operator+(Values p);
Values operator,(Values p);
};
Values Values::operator,(Values p)
{
Values temp;
temp.a =p.a;
temp.b =p.b;
cout <<p.a <<" "<<p.b <<"\n";
return temp;
}
Values Values::operator+(Values p)
{
Values temp;
temp.a =p.b +a;
temp.b =p.b +b;
return temp;
}
```

```
void main()
{
Values v1(20,30),v2(15,40),v3(25,35);
v1.show();
v2.show();
v3.show();
cout <<"\n";
v1 =(v1,v2+v2,v3);
v1.show();
getch();
}
Output:
20 30
15 40
25 35
55 80
25 35
25 35
```

10.18 TYPE CONVERSION

You already know that the = operator will assign a value from one variable to another, in statements like

var1 = var2;

where var1 and var2 are integer variables. You can also assign a value of one user-defined object to another object. Note that both the objects should be same types. When both the user-defined objects are of same type and you assign the value of one object to another object using assignment operator, then the values of all the member data items are simply copied into a new object.

Thus, assignments between types, whether they are basic types or user-defined types, are handled by the compiler with no effort on our part, provided that the same data type is used on both sides of the equal sign. Now question arises, what happen if the variable or objects are of different data types during data conversion assignment operation? Also how the compiler handles the conversion of basic data types. Answer to this question we will first review how the compiler handles the conversion of basic types, which it does automatically. After that we will explore several situations where the compiler doesn't handle things automatically and we need to tell it what to do. These include conversions between basic types and user-defined types, and conversions between different user-defined types.

The programmer should write the routines that convert basic data types to user-defined data types or vice versa.

There are three possibilities of data conversion as given below:

1. Conversion from basic data type to user-defined data type (class type)
2. Conversion from class type to basic data type
3. Conversion from one class type to another class type

10.18.1 Conversion From Basic Data Type To User-defined Data Type (Class Type)

The conversion from basic to class type easily carried out. It is automatically done by the compiler with the help of in-built routines or by applying typecasting. In this type the left-hand operand of = sign is always class type and right-hand operand is always basic type.

For example suppose a and b are two variables of int and float type respectively and an expression to assign a value of b variable to a variable is written as:

```
a = b;
```

Here compiler will require special routine to convert the value of b which is expressed in floating point format to a which is an integer format. So result be of integer type. Similarly we can convert from int to float, float to double, double to float, char to float and float to char etc. All the above conversions are implicit conversions.

We can also convert one type of data type to another type by using the casting operation. For this purpose we used "cast" operator.

The general syntax is:

```
v1 = (data type) v2;
```

Where v1 and v2 are the variables of different type. For example, casting can be done by using the below written statement as:

```
int x, y;
float z;
x = 3;
y = 2;
z = x / y;
```

If we divide x by y, then result stored in the z variable be 1.0. But by using the type operator, we can get the float value as:

```
z = (float) x / y;
```

You can also convert one variable to the float type by using the type operator as:

```
c = (float) x;
```

Program 25: Write a C++program to define constructor with no argument and with float argument. Explain how compiler take place conversion between types.

```
# include <iostream.h>
# include <conio.h>
class student
{
int rn;
float fees;
public:
student ( )
{
rn = 0;
fees = 0;
}
student (float m)
{
rn = 2;
fees = m;
}
void show ( )
{
cout <<"\n rn= "<<rn <<" fees = "<<fees;
cout <<"\n rn= "<<rn <<" fees = "<<fees;
}
};
void main ( )
{
clrscr ( );
student st;
st=1;
st.show ( );
st=2. 5;
st.show ( );
getch();
}
```

Output:

```
rn=2 fees = 1
rn=2 fees =1
```

```
rn=2 fees =2.5
rn=2 fees =2.5
```

10.18.2 Conversion From Class Type To Basic Data Type

Conversion from class type to basic data type (basic type like int, float, char, double etc.) and vice versa can be done if variable and class are of different type. The conversion from basic type to class type is easy to accomplish. In this type of conversion, the programmer explicitly needs to tell the compiler how to perform conversion from class of basic type. These instructions are written in a member function. Such type of conversion is also knows as overloading of type cast operators. The compiler first searches for the operator keyword followed by data type and if it is not defined, it applies the conversion functions. In this type, the left-hand operand is always of basic data type and right-hand operand is always of class type. While carrying this conversion, the conversion function should not have any argument and it cannot mention any return type. Program given below clear the concept of conversion between class type to basic type.

Program 26: Write a C++ program to convert class type data.

```
# include <iostream.h>
# include <conio.h>
class student
{
int rn;
float fees;
public:
student ( )
{
rn = 0;
fees = 0;
}
operator int ( )
{
return (rn);
}
operator float ( )
{
return fees;
}
student (float m)
{
```

```
rn = 3;
fees = m;
}
void show ( )
{
cout <<"\n rn= "<<rn <<" fees = "<<fees;
cout <<"\n rn= "<<rn <<" fees = "<<fees;
}
};
void main ( )
{
clrscr ( );
int j;
float fees;
student st;
st=7.5;
j = st;            // operator int ( ) is executed
fees = st;              // operator float ( ) is executed
cout <<"\n Value of j : "<<j;
cout <<"\n Value of fees : "<<fees;
getch();
}
```

Output:

Value of j: 3
Value of fees: 7.5

10.18.3 Conversion From One Class Type To Another Class Type

When an object of one class is assigned to object of another class, it is necessary to give the instructions to the compiler about this type of conversion. How to make conversion between these two user-defined data types? The method must be instructed to the compiler. There are two ways to convert object data type from one class to another. One is to define a conversion operator function in source class or a one-argument constructor in a destination class.

The general syntax is:

destination object = source object;

When we do conversion from one class to another class, then one class is called source class and other class is destination class. Suppose we have two classes one is hour other is minute. Since the conversion takes place from class minutes to class hour, minutes is known as the source class and hours is known as the destination class. You can do conversion either through a constructor or by using a conversion function.

```
hour = minute;
```

For example, below written is a program, which will convert minutes class to hours.

Program 27: Write a C++ program to convert class data type to another class data type.

```
# include <iostream.h>
# include <conio.h>
class minutes
{
int m;
public :
minutes ( )
{m ==240;}
get ( )
{return (m) ;}
void show ( )
{cout <<"\n Minutes = "<<m;}
class hours
{
int h;
public :
void operator = (minutes x);
void show ( )
{cout <<"\n Hours = "<<h;)
};
void hours : : operator = (minutes x)
{
h=x.get()/60;
}
void main ( )
{
clrscr ( );
minutes minute;
hours hour;
hour=minute;
minute.show ( );
hour.show();
```

```
getch();
}
```

Output:

Minutes = 240

Hours = 4

10.19 PITFALLS OF OPERATOR OVERLOADING AND CONVERSION

Operator overloading provides additional meaning to existing operators, this feature makes C++ more powerful. But this feature has some pitfalls.

Following are the pitfalls of operator overloading and type conversion:

1. **Having Same Semantics:** If you take a + operator, then it can be used for adding two numbers of two different objects of same class or different classes. Similarly you can concatenate two different strings to a third string by using + operator. The natural meaning of an operator does not change, while it is being overloaded.
2. **Having Same Syntax:** You can use any overloaded operator in the same way as these are used for some basic types. So an operator having a same symbol in a particular class creates a problem e.g. If a and b are two different basic types, then shorthand or arithmetic assignment operator having addition operation can be used as:

   ```
   a + = b;
   ```

   Also the above statement can be written as

   ```
   a = a + b;
   ```

   It means + operator is overloaded. So whether syntax is different but operation is same, which can not be changed at any cost and so made the syntax similar. Similarly you can not overload a binary operator to do unary operation and vice versa.
3. **Show Restriction:** Some times operator overloading create number of restrictions on using the same operator for different purposes e.g. the statement c = a + b ; will become meaningless if the number of overloaded operators grow too large and if they are used in non-intuitive ways, then the whole point of using them is lost and the listing becomes less readable instead of more.
4. **Do not create new operators:** As discussed earlier, only standard operators can be overloaded, do not create new operators for overloading. It helps the compiler not to be worried about the precedence of newly created operators.
5. **Having same hierarchy of operators:** Overloading the operators does not

change the precedence and associativity of the operators. The expressions are solved using the standard precedence and associativity rules.

6. The operators ( ), —>, [ ] and = must be overloaded as a member of the class and not using friend function.
7. **Avoid operator overloading to perform illogical operations:** Only an assignment operator among all overloaded operators can not be inherited by derived classes.
8. **Creates Ambiguity:** Some times operations done by overloading becomes ambiguous. e.g. If you create an overloading constructor and an overloading function having same operator, it arises the problem of ambiguity and it becomes difficult for the compiler to decide what to do .So to avoid ambiguity, operator should be used in a well-defined way.
9. **All the operators cannot be overloaded:** All the operators are not overloaded. Some of the operators like dot operator ,member operator or structure operator (.), the scope resolution operator (::), the pointer operator (®, ., *), address operators &, conditional operator (?:) and the logical operator (!) are not used for operator overloading and conversion of data type from one category to another.
10. Operators can be overloaded only explicitly.

SOLVED PROGRAMMING

Program 1: Write a C++ program to add two numbers using Binary operator overloading.

```
#include <iostream.h>
#include <conio.h>
class abc
{
private :
int a ;
abc ( )            // constructor defined
{
a = 0 ;
}
abc (int b)        // overloading constructor
{
a = b ;
}
abc operator + (abc obj1)
```

```
{
abc add ;                    // Binary operator overloading
add.a = a + abj1.a ;
return (add) ;
}
void display ( ) ;
~ abc ( ) {}
};
void abc : : display ( )
{
cout <<"\n Final values are"<< a ;
}
void main ( )
{
abc x (30) ;
abc y (20) ;
abc sum ;
sum = x + y;
x.display ( ) ;
y.display ( ) ;
sum.display ( ) ;
getch ( ) ;
}
```

Output:

Final values are 30
Final values are 20
Final values are 50

Program 2: Write a C++ program to overloaded 'less-than' operators with double value.

```
#include <iostream.h>
#include<conio.h>
#include <stdlib.h>              // For random number generator
#include <time.h>                // For time function
class Box
{
public:
Box(double aLength, double aWidth, double aHeight):length(aLength),
width(aWidth), height(aHeight) {}
double volume() const
{
```

```
return length*width*height;
}
double getLength()  const { return length; }
double getWidth() const { return width; }
double getHeight()  const { return height; }
int operator<(const Box& aBox) const
{
return volume() < aBox.volume();
}
int operator<(const double aValue) const
{
return volume() < aValue;
}
private:
double length;
double width;
double height;
};
void main()
{
Box firstBox(17.0, 11.0, 5.0);
if(firstBox < 100000)
{
cout << "less than";
}
else
{
cout << "not less than";
}
getch();
}
```

Output:

less than

Program 3: Write a C++ program Overloading De-reference operator.

```
#include <iostream.h>
#include<conio.h>
class MyType
{
public:
```

```
MyType (int arg = 0) : x(arg) {}
bool operator!=(const MyType& arg) const
{
return x != arg.x;
}
int operator*() const { return x; }
MyType& operator++()
{
++x;
return *this;
}
const MyType operator++(int)
{
MyType temp(*this);
++x;
return temp;
}
private:
int x;
};
template <class Iter>
double average(Iter a, Iter end)
{
double sum = 0.0;
for( ; a != end ;)
{
cout << *a++;
sum += *a++;
}
return sum;
}
void main()
{
MyType first(1);
MyType last(11);
cout << average(first, last) << endl;
getch();
}
```

Output:

1357930

Program 4: Write a C++ program to Overload assignment for Point.

```
#include <iostream.h>
#include<conio.h>
class Point
{
int x, y;
public:
Point() {} // needed to construct temporaries
Point(int px, int py)
{
x = px;
y = py;
}
void show()
{
cout << x << " ";
cout << y << "\n";
}
Point operator+(Point op2);
Point operator-(Point op2);
Point operator=(Point op2);
Point operator++();
};
// Overload + for Point.
Point Point::operator+(Point op2)
{
Point temp;
temp.x = op2.x + x;
temp.y = op2.y + y;
return temp;
}
// Overload - for Point.
Point Point::operator-(Point op2)
{
Point temp;
// notice order of operands
temp.x = x - op2.x;
temp.y = y - op2.y;
return temp;
```

```
}
// Overload asignment for Point.
Point Point::operator=(Point op2)
{
x = op2.x;
y = op2.y;
return *this; // i.e., return object that generated call
}
// Overload prefix ++ for Point.
Point Point::operator++()
{
x++;
y++;
return *this;
}
void main()
{
Point ob1(10, 20), ob2( 5, 30), ob3(90, 90);
ob1.show();
ob2.show();
++ob1;
ob1.show(); // displays 11 21
ob2 = ++ob1;
ob1.show(); // displays 12 22
ob2.show(); // displays 12 22
ob1 = ob2 = ob3; // multiple assignment
ob1.show(); // displays 90 90
ob2.show(); // displays 90 90
getch();
}
```

Output:

```
10 20
5 30
11 21
12 22
12 22
90 90
90 90
```

Program 5: Write a C++ program for double cast operator.

```
#include <iostream.h>
#include<conio.h>
class Power
{
double b;
int e;
double val;
public:
Power(double base, int exp)
{
b = base;
e = exp;
val = 1;
if(exp==0)
return;
for( ; exp>0; exp—)
val = val * b;
}
Power operator+(Power o)
{
double base;
int exp;
base = b + o.b;
exp = e + o.e;
Power temp(base, exp);
return temp;
}
operator double() { return val; } // convert to double
};
void main()
{
Power x(4.0, 2);
double a;
a = x;          // convert to double
cout << x + 1.2; // convert x to double and add 100.2
cout << "\n";
Power y(3.3, 3), z(0, 0);
z = x + y;  // no conversion
```

```
a = z;    // convert to double
cout << a;
getch();
}
Output:
17.2
20730.7
```

Program 6: Write a C++ program for conversions Between Objects and Basic Types.

```
#include <iostream.h>
#include<conio.h>
class Height
{
private:
const float MTF;
int feet;
float inches;
public:
Height():feet(0),inches(0.0),MTF(3.280833F)
{}
Height(float meters):MTF(3.280833F)
{
float fltfeet =MTF *meters;
feet =int(fltfeet);
inches =12*(fltfeet-feet);
}
Height(int ft,float in):feet(ft),
inches(in),MTF(3.280833F)
{}
void get()
{
cout <<"\nFeet:";cin >>feet;
cout <<"inches:";cin >>inches;
}
void show()
{cout <<feet <<"-" <<inches;}
operator float()
{
float fracfeet =inches/12;
```

```
fracfeet += feet;
return fracfeet/MTF;
}
};
void main()
{
float mtrs;
Height heigh1 =2.45F;
cout <<"\nheigh1 =";heigh1.show();
mtrs =heigh1;
cout <<"\nheigh1 =" <<mtrs <<" meters \n ";
Height heigh2(6,4.25);
mtrs =heigh2;
cout <<"\nheigh2 =" <<mtrs <<" meters \n ";
getch();
}
```

Output:

```
heigh1 =8-0.456493
heigh1 =2.45 meters
heigh2 =1.936754 meters
```

Program 7: Write a C++ program to convert money from dollars to rupees by using conversion function in destination class.

```
#define dolval 44.20
#include<iostream.h>
#include<conio.h>
class dollar
{
double dol;
public:
dollar(double doll)
{dol=doll;}
void show()
{cout<<"\nMoney in Dollars ="<<dol;}
double retdol()
{return(dol);}
};
class rupee
{
double rs;
```

```
public:
rupee(dollar d)
{rs=d.retdol()*dolval;}
void show()
{cout<<"\nMoney in Rs. ="<<rs;}
};
void main()
{
dollar obj1(3);
obj1.show();
rupee r=obj1;
r.show();
getch();
}
```

Output:

Money in Dollars=5

Money in Rs.=221

Program 8: Wrlte a C++ program to convert mts,cms dlstance to feet,lnches by using that function in source class.

```
#include<iostream.h>
#include<conio.h>
class dft
{
private:
int feet;
double inches;
public:
dft(){feet=inches=0;}
dft(int g,double h)
{
feet=g;
inches=h;
}
void put()
{
cout<<feet<<inch;
}
friend void add(dist,mtrcm);
};
```

```
class dmt
{
int mtr,cms;
public:
dmt(int u,int v)
{
mtr=u;cms=v;
}
void show()
{
cout<<mtr<<cms;
}
operator dft()
{
double mt;
mt=mtr+cms/100;
double dfeet;
dfeet=3.28*mt;
int feet1=int(dfeet);
double inches1=(dfeet-feet1)*12.00;
return dft(feet1,inches1);
}
};
void main()
{
dmt a=(2,22);
cout<<"distance in meters & centimeters";
a.put();
dft b;
b=a;
cout<<"\nDistance in feet & inches";
b.put();
getch();
}
```

PROGRAMMING PROBLEMS

Program 1: Write a C++ program to overload (++)operator.

Program 2: Write a C++ program to print the Fibbonacci series by using prefix increment unary operator.

Program 3: Write a C++ program to Overload the — relative to MyClass class using a friend.

Program 4: Write a C++ program to add the two different objects of the coordinate classes by using the concept of operator overloading.

Program 5: Write a C++ program + is overloaded using friend function.

Program 6: Write a C++ program Define -, + and = for the ThreeD class.

Program 7: Write a C++ program for Array class for 10 int value with overloaded functions: +, -, = =.

Program 8: Write a C++ program adds three additional overloaded operators to the loc class:the –,the =,and the unary ++.Pay special attention to how these functions are defined.

Program 9: Write a C++ program to overload all the Arithmetic Operators.

Program10: Write a C++ program Overloaded '+=' assignment operator.

Program 11: Write a C++ program Demo: Overload ().

Program 12: Write a C++ program The Subscript Operator ([]).

Program 13: Write a C++ program to return a reference from [].

Program 14: Write a C++ program Overload the < and >.

Program 15: Write a C++ program for Class ostream operator.

Program 16: Write a C++ program for ostream and istream operator for a class.

Program 17: Write a C++ program to Overload stream operator.

Program 18: Write a C++ program for a custom extractor (>>).

Program 19: Write a C++ program for a custom inserter (<<).

Program 20: Write a C++ program using a friend to overload <<.

Program 21: Write a C++ program to Overload New and Delete Operator.

Fill in the blanks

1. When we overload operator to do additional job that type of technique is called ....
2. Keyword .... introduces an overloaded-operator function definition.
3. To use operators on class objects, they must be overloaded, with the exception of operators .... , ... and ....
4. Unary and .... are the two types of operator overloading.

Answers

1. operator overloading. 2. operator. 3. assignment (=), address (&), comma (,).
4. binary.

OBJECTIVE TYPE QUESTIONS

1. Which of the following are types of overloading?
   (a) Function (b) operator
   (c) both a and b (d) none
2. In C++ programs, an assignment operator might be overloaded to
   (a) signal when assignment takes place
   (b) assign a separate ID number to each object
   (c) help keep track of the number of identical objects
   (d) all of the above
3. Following is not the operator overloading?
   (a) Unary (b) Binary
   (c) Assignment (d) ternery
   (e) none
4. Which of the following is advantage of operator overloading?
   (a) it works with objects (b) string operation can be done
   (c) coding becomes transparent (d) all
   (e) none
5. Which of the following is not prone of operator overloading?
   (a) change complex statement into simple
   (b) it decrease the size of program (c) cannot be applied to user defined data (d) data conversion can be done
6. Which of the following unary operator is used in operator overloading ?
   (a) ++ (b) ~
   (c) (d) all
   (e) none
7. Which of the following is binary operator in overloading ?
   (a) << (b) &&
   (c) := (d) all
   (e) none
8. Which of the following operator cannot be overloaded ?
   (a) :: (b) ?:
   (c) . (d) all
   (e) none

9. Which operator works on two operands ?
   (a) unary (b) binary
   (c) ternary (d) all
   (e) none
10. The major difference between unary and binary operator overloading is on the bases of
   (a) argument (b) objects
   (c) data member (d) member function
11. Data conversion can takes place between
   (a) basic types (b) objects and basic types
   (c) objects of different classes (d) all
12. Which of the following operator is not overloaded?
   (a) increment (b) comma
   (c) Assignment (d) scope resolution
   (e) none
13. Which of the following operator works on two operand?
   (a) unary (b) binary
   (c) ternary (d) all
   (e) none
14. Which of the following unary operator is used in operator overloading ?
   (a) ++ (b) ~
   (c) * (d) all
   (e) none
15. Which of the following operator works on one operand?
   (a) unary (b) binary
   (c) ternary (d) all
   (e) none
16. Which of the following is advantage of operator overloading?
   (a) it works with objects (b) string operation can be done
   (c) coding becomes transparent (d) all
   (e) none
17. Which of the following is binary operator in overloading ?
   (a) + (b) —
   (c) : (d) ::
   (e) none

18. Which of the following operator cannot be overloaded ?
    (a) :: (b) ?:
    (c) . (d) all
    (e) none
19. In C++, which of the following is most likely used to convert to a basic type to a user defined class ?
    (a) a one argument constructor
    (b) a built in conversion function
    (c) an overloaded = operator
    (d) a class conversion function that is a member of the class
    (e) None of the above
20. Data conversion can takes place between
    (a) basic types (b) objects and basic types
    (c) objects of different classes (d) all
    (e) None of the above

EXERCISES

1. What do you mean by operator overloading?
2. What are the various Features of operator overloading
3. What are the various types of operator overloading?
4. Differentiate between unary and binary operator overloading.
5. What do you mean by operator function or keyword operator?
6. Write the various overloading rules.
7. What you know about type conversion?
8. What are the various types of type conversion?
9. What are the various pitfalls of operator overloading?
10. What are the various advantages of Operator overloading?
11. What are the various operators used in Unary operator overloading?
12. What are the various operators used in Binary operator overloading?
13. What are the various problems occurs in the data conversions?
14. Discuss with the help of examples overloading binary operator with friend function.

CHAPTER 11

Inheritance

11.1 INTRODUCTION

Programmers seem to hate coding something from scratch; why code the same thing over and over again? Fortunately, it is possible to reuse code, thanks to one of the key concepts of object-oriented programming. That is inheritance, which is the subject of this concept. So if you're looking for a clear explanation of how inheritance works in C++, keep reading.

Reusability is a key feature within our everyday life. Computers are a prime example of this. If you've learned some electronics, you probably know this, and if not, let me tell you that a dividing circuit can be made simply with just a few transistors. It will work much faster than the digital circuit you will find inside a calculator. The only problem with the analog solution is that if you want to multiply with it tomorrow, you have to rebuild the circuit, while the digital circuit can just be reprogrammed.

Before we venture deeper into this subject, let me specify that to understand this concept fully you should know about classes (objects) and how you build them (private/public/protected members). First, we will present them.

The designers of object-oriented programming (in particular the creator of C++) thought in terms of reusability, and tried to implement a way to use code that is already written. If you have a family of objects that all have a few traits in common, why should you code separately for each of them?

It would be much more convenient to just write the common traits in a base class and later extend that with the specific objects. In the world of classes, inheritance solves this common problem. An object that holds the common traits and on which we will build the specific classes/objects is referred to as the base class, while the new class is known as the derived class.

In inheritance we can create new objects by directly acquiring the attributes and behaviours of other objects and then extending or specializing them. Like composition, inheritance is everywhere in real life. You inherited your parents genes, and acquired physical attributes from both of them. Technological products (computers, cell phones, etc…) often inherit features from their predecessors. C++ inherited many features from C, the language upon which it is based, and C itself inherited many of its features from the programming languages that came before it.

Consider an apple and a banana. Although an apple and a banana are different fruits, both have in common that they *are* fruits. Because apples and bananas *are* fruits, anything that is true of fruits is also true of apples and bananas. For example, all fruits have a name, a flavor, and are tangible objects.

Thus, apples and bananas also have a name, a flavor, and are tangible objects. Apples and bananas inherit these properties from the concept of fruit because they *are* fruit. Apples and bananas then define some of these properties in different ways (apples and bananas have different flavors), which is what makes them distinct from each other.

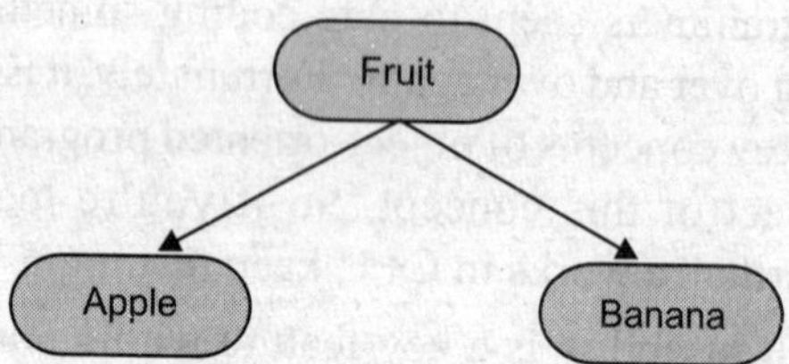

Figure 11.1: Inheritance

The object being inherited from is called the **parent** or **base**, and the object doing the inheriting is called the **child** or **derived** object. In the above picture, "fruit" is the parent, and both "apple" and "banana" are children. Unlike in composition, where each object has a *has-a* relationship with it's subobjects, in inheritance, each child has an *is-a* relationship with it's parent. An apple *is-a* fruit. A triangle *is-a* shape. Red *is-a* color.

By default, the children receive all of the properties of the parents. However, the children are then free to define or redefine inherited properties (bananas have that unique banana flavor), add new properties (eg. bananas add the property of being "starchy", which is not true of many other fruits), or even hide properties.

It is possible to define entire hierarchies of objects via inheritance. For example, a square is a rectangle, which is a quadrilateral, which is a shape. A right triangle is a triangle, which is also a shape.

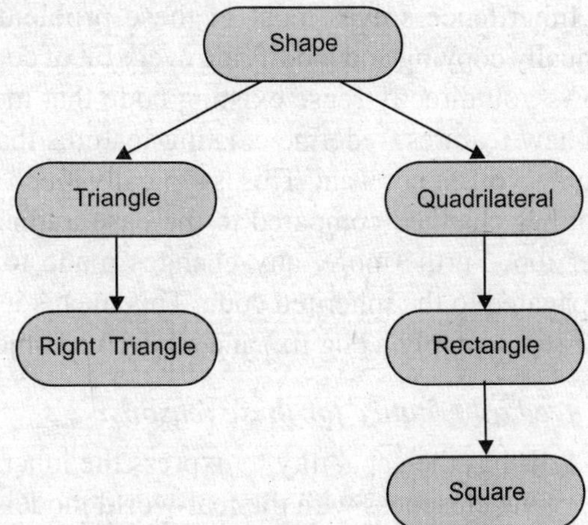

Figure 11.2: Hierarchical inheritance

11.2 WHY THE NEED FOR INHERITANCE IN C++?

One of the fundamental ideas behind object-oriented programming is that code should be reusable. However, existing code often does not do EXACTLY what you need it to. For example, what if you have a triangle and you need a square? In this case, we are presented with a number of choices on how to proceed, all of which have various benefits and downsides.

Perhaps the most obvious way to proceed is to change the existing code to do what you want. However, if we do this, we will no longer be able to use it for it's original purpose, so this is rarely a good idea.

A slightly better idea is to make a copy of some or all of the existing code and change it to do what we want. However, this has several major downsides. First, although copy-and-paste seems simple enough, it's actually quite dangerous. A single omitted or misplaced line can cause the program to work incorrectly and can take days to find in a complex program. Renaming a class via search-and-replace can also be dangerous if you inadvertently replace something you didn't mean to. Second, to rewrite the code to make it do what you want, you need to have an intimate understanding what it does. This can be difficult when the code is complex and not adequately documented. Third, and perhaps most relevant, this generally involves duplicating of existing functionality, which causes a maintenance problem. Improvements or bug fixes have to be added to multiples copies of functions that do essentially the same thing, which wastes programmer time. And that's assuming the programmer realizes multiple copies even exist! If not, some copies may not get the improvements or bug fixes.

Inheritance solves most of these problems in an efficient way. Instead of manually copying and modifying every bit of code your program needs, inheritance allows you directly reuse existing code that meets your needs. You only need to add new features, redefine existing features that do not meet your needs, or hide features you do not want. This is typically much less work (as you are only defining what has changed compared to the base, rather than redefining everything), and safer too. Furthermore, any changes made to the base code automatically get propagated to the inherited code. This means it is possible to change one piece of code (eg. to apply a bug fix) and all derived objects will automatically be updated.

We need inheritance for these reasons:

1. It has the capability to express the inheritance relationship, which ensures the closeness with the real-world models.
2. Reusability is another powerful reason for the need of inheritance. User can add some additional features in the sub-class and so can derive a new class from the existing class.
3. It has the transitive nature of inheritance. Here transitive nature means, if A is the friend of B and B is the friend of C, then C is the friend of A. In other words, if a class A inherits the properties of another class B, which further inherits the properties of sub-class C, then all the sub-classes of A will automatically inherits the properties of B and so on chain continue.
4. It has the capability to solve the complex problem into simple and in a hierarchical form.
5. By using Inheritance, the utilization of CPU becomes high and utilization of memory becomes low.

Note: *Inheritance solves the number of real world problem with its simplicity without any ambiguity and it also have the property of reusability.*

11.3 INHERITANCE

Inheritance is the process of creating new classes from the existing class or classes.

Using inheritance, one can create general class that defines **traits** common to a set of related items. This class can then be inherited (reused) by the other classes by using the properties of the existing ones with the addition of its own unique properties.

The old class is referred to as the base class and the new classes, which are inherited from the base class, are called derived classes.

C++ is rich in its data types. Inheritance is the concept to inherit the properties of one class to another class. This has also known as class structure again. For example, classes A contains two-member function ads and subtracts and class b contain two another functions multiply and divide.

Inheritance is the concept to inherit the properties of one class to another class. This has also known as class structure again. For example, classes A contains two-member function ads and subtracts and class b contain two another functions multiply and divide. We want to use all these function with one object then we need to use inheritance where class B inherits all the property of class, which is public, but class B cannot use the private properties of class A.

Definition: *"Inheritance is the process by which new classes called derived classes are created from existing classes called base classes. The derived classes have all the features of the base class and the programmer can choose to add new features specific to the newly created derived class."*

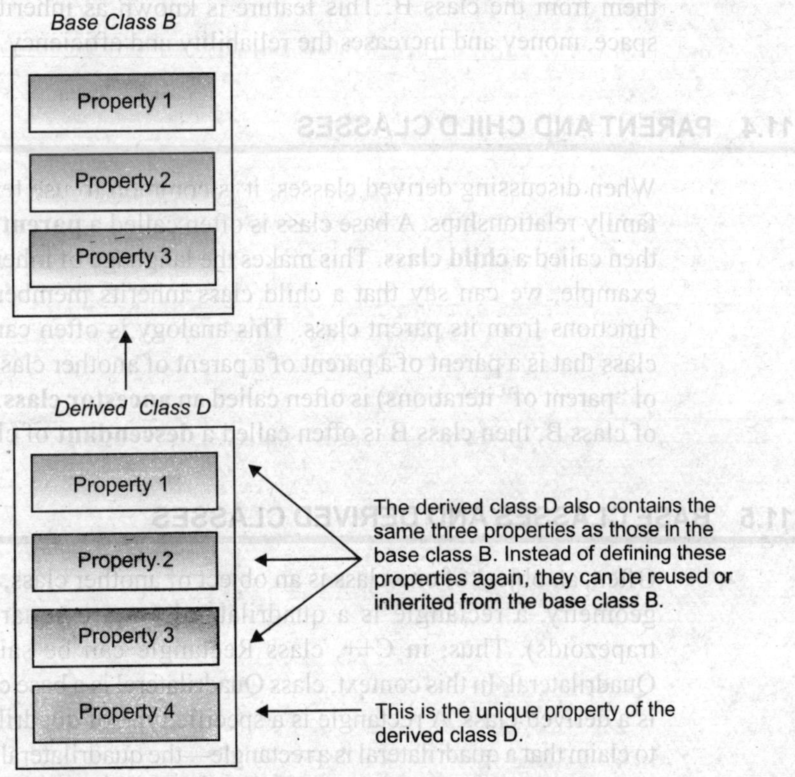

Figure 11.3: Base class and derived class

Inheritance is the process by which one object can acquire the properties of another object. This is important because it supports the concept of classification. If you think about it, most knowledge is made manageable by hierarchical classifications. For example, red delicious apple is the part of the apple class, which in turn is the part of the fruit class, which is under the food class. Without the use of classification, each object would have to define all of its characteristics explicitly. Using classifications, an object need to define only those qualities that make it unique within its class. It is the inheritance mechanism that makes it possible for one object to be specific instance of more general case.

In above figure, the class B contains the three member i.e. Property1, Property2 and Property3.

The second class named as D contains four members i.e. Property1, Property2, Property3 and Property4.

Out of these, three members (Property1, Property2, Property3) of the class D are same as that of class B, while the one member i.e. Property4 is unique.

In the class D, instead of defining all the three members again, one can reuse them from the class B. This feature is known as inheritance which saves time, space, money and increases the reliability and efficiency.

11.4 PARENT AND CHILD CLASSES

When discussing derived classes, it is common to use terminology derived from family relationships. A base class is often called a **parent class**. A derived class is then calied a **child class**. This makes the language of inheritance very smooth. For example, we can say that a child class inherits member variables and member functions from its parent class. This analogy is often carried one step further. A class that is a parent of a parent of a parent of another class (or some other number of "parent of" iterations) is often called an **ancestor class**. If class A is an ancestor of class B, then class B is often called a **descendant** of class A.

11.5 BASE CLASSES AND DERIVED CLASSES

Often, an object of one class is an object of another class, as well. For example, in geometry, a rectangle is a quadrilateral (as are squares, parallelograms and trapezoids). Thus, in C++, class Rectangle can be said to inherit from class Quadrilateral. In this context, class Quadrilateral is a base class, and class Rectangle is a derived class. A rectangle is a specific type of quadrilateral, but it is incorrect to claim that a quadrilateral is a rectangle—the quadrilateral could be a parallelogram or some other shape. Table 14.1 lists several simple examples of base classes and derived classes.

Table 14.1. Inheritance examples.

Base class	**Derived classes**
Student	GraduateStudent, UndergraduateStudent
Shape	Circle, Triangle, Rectangle, Sphere, Cube
Loan	CarLoan, HomeImprovementLoan, MortgageLoan
Employee	Faculty, Staff
Account	CheckingAccount, SavingsAccount

Because every derived-class object is an object of its base class, and one base class can have many derived classes, the set of objects represented by a base class typically is larger than the set of objects represented by any of its derived classes. For example, the base class Vehicle represents all vehicles, including cars, trucks, boats, airplanes, bicycles and so on. By contrast, derived class Car represents a smaller, more specific subset of all vehicles.

Inheritance relationships form treelike hierarchical structures. A base class exists in a hierarchical relationship with its derived classes. Although classes can exist independently, once they are employed in inheritance relationships, they become affiliated with other classes. A class becomes either a base class—supplying members to other classes, a derived class—inheriting its members from other classes, or both.

The mechanism of deriving a new class from an old one is called inheritance or derivation. It is the important and powerful facility of OOP's after classes and objects. The existing or old class is called **Base Class** or **Super Class** and the new created class is called **Derived Class or Sub class.**

The derived class inherits some or all of the properties from the base class. A class can also inherit properties from more than one class or from more than one level. With inheritance we are able to make use of the a-kind-of and is-a relationship. As described above, classes which are a-kind-of another class share properties of the latter.

Definition (Superclass/Subclass)

If class A inherits from class B, then B is called **superclass** of A. A is called **subclass** of B. Objects of a subclass can be used where objects of the corresponding superclass are expected. This is due to the fact that objects of the subclass share the same behaviour as objects of the super class.

Superclasses are also called parent classes. Subclasses may also be called child classes or just derived classes.

Of course, you can again inherit from a subclass, making this class the superclass of the new subclass. This leads to a hierarchy of superclass/subclass relationships. If you draw this hierarchy you get an inheritance graph.

A common drawing scheme is to use arrowed lines to indicate the inheritance relationship between two classes or objects. In our examples we have used "inherits-from". Consequently, the arrowed line starts from the subclass towards the super class as illustrated in below Figure 11.4:

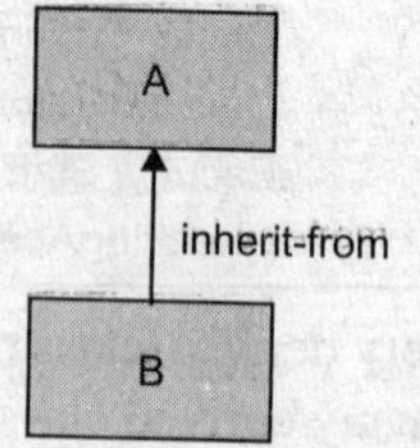

Figure 11.4: B Inherit-from A

In the literature you also find illustrations where the arrowed lines are used just the other way around. The direction, in which the arrowed line is used, depends on how the corresponding author has decided to understand it. Anyway, here the arrowed line is always directed towards the super class.

General Format for implementing the concept of Inheritance:

```
class derived_classname: access specifier base_classname
```

For example, if the *base* class is student and the derived class is marks it is specified as:

```
class marks: public student
```

The above makes marks have access to both *public* and *protected* variables of base class student.

Reminder about public, private and protected access specifiers:

1. If a member or variables defined in a class is private, then they are accessible by members of the same class only and cannot be accessed from outside the class.
2. Public members and variables are accessible from outside the class.
3. Protected access specifier is a stage between private and public. If a member functions or variables defined in a class are protected, then they cannot be accessed from outside the class but can be accessed from the derived class.

***Note:** Inheritance is the simplest form creating a relationship between Super class and Subclass.*

11.6 ADVANTAGES OF INHERITANCE

Following are the features or advantages of inheritance:

1. **Reusability:** Inheritance helps the code to be reused in many situations. The base class is defined and once it is compiled, it need not be reworked. Using the concept of inheritance, the programmer can create as many derived classes from the base class as needed while adding specific features to each derived class as needed.
2. **Saves Time and Effort:** The above concept of reusability achieved by inheritance saves the programmer time and effort. Since the main code written can be reused in various situations as needed.
3. **Increases Program Structure which results in greater reliability.**
4. **Polymorphism (to be discussed in detail in later sections)**

11.7 DISADVANTAGES OF INHERITANCE

Following are the disadvantages of inheritance:

1. Invoking member functions using objects create more compiler overheads.
2. In class hierarchy, various data elements remain unused, the memory allocated to them is not utilized.
3. Though object oriented programming is frequently propagandized as an answer for complicated projects. Inappropriate use of inheritance makes a program more complicated.

11.8 VARIOUS ISSUES ABOUT INHERITANCE

Inheritance is a concept of linking two or more classes with each other in a hierarchical manner so that their properties and functions can be shared. (One class will extend to another class.) This leads to the biggest advantage of re-usability of the members and avoids redundancy.

Inheritance leads to various issues such as:

1. What is Inherited
2. Types of inheritance
3. Accessibility modes (public, private and protected) in inheritance

11.8.1 What is Inherited?

When inheritance is done, various links and tables (index, virtual etc) are created which are used to provide the accessibility of the members of the base class in derived class and in other class hierarchy. This means saying **"public members are inherited"** is better to say as **"public members become accessible"**.

A derived class inherits every member of a base class except:

- its constructor and its destructor
- its friends
- its operator=() members

11.8.2 Types of Inheritance

There are five different inheritances supported in C++:

1. Simple / Single Inheritance
2. Multiple Inheritance
3. Multilevel Inheritance
4. Hierarchical Inheritance
5. Hybrid Inheritance

1. **Single inheritance:** If a class is derived from a single base class, it is called as single inheritance.

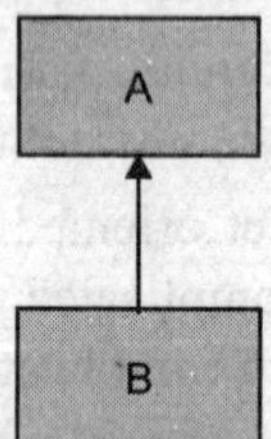

2. **Multiple Inheritance:** If a class is derived from more than one base class, it is known as multiple inheritance.

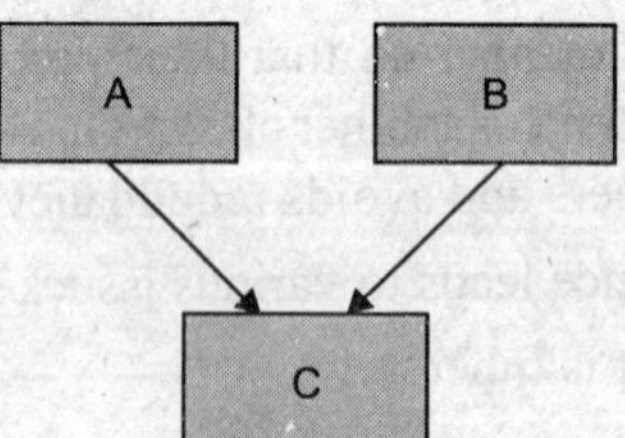

3. **Multilevel inheritance:** The classes can also be derived from the classes that are already derived. This type of inheritance is called multilevel inheritance.

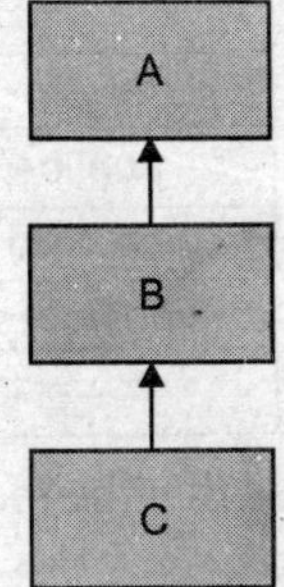

4. **Hierarchical inheritance:** If a number of classes are derived from a single base class, it is called as hierarchical inheritance.

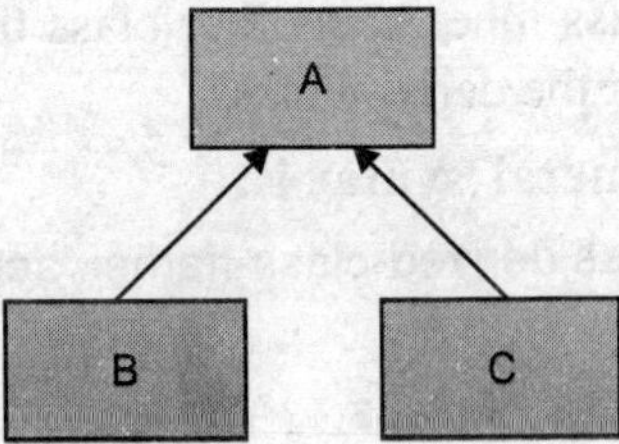

5. **Hybrid inheritance:** The combination of one or more types of inheritance is called hybrid inheritance.

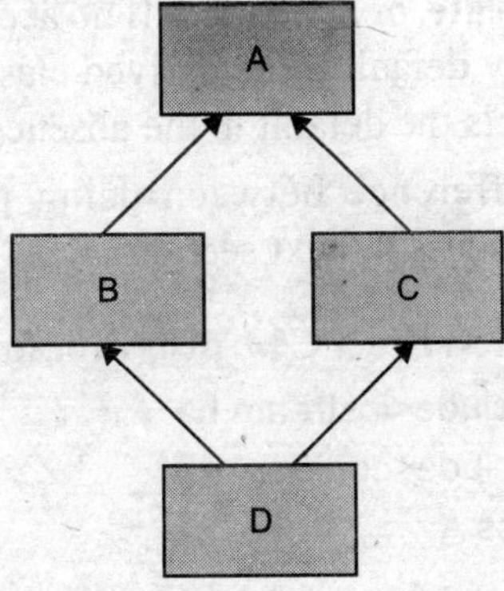

***Note :** we discuss all types in detail with programming examples in later section.*

11.8.3 Accessibility Modes and Inheritance

We can use the following chart for seeing the accessibility of the members in the Base class (first class) and derived class (second class).

		Inheritance Mode		
		public	protected	private
Members in base class	public	public	protected	private
	protected	protected	protected	private
	private	X	XX	
		Members in derived class		

Here X indicates that the members are not inherited, i.e. they are not accessible in the derived class.

11.9 BASE-CLASS ACCESS CONTROL

When a class inherits another class then the members of the base class become members of the derived class.

The general syntax is:

```
class derived-class-name : access specifier base-class-name
{
// body of class
};
```

The access status of the base-class members those are inside the derived class is determined by ***access specifier.*** The base-class access specifier must be either **public, private,** or **protected**. If no access specifier is present, the access specifier is private by default if the derived class is a class. If the derived class is a struct, then public is the default in the absence of an explicit access specifier.

The difference between using **public** or **private or protected** access specifier(discuss in next section).

Program 1: Write a C++ program for base-Class Access Control.

```
#include<iostream.h>
#include<conio.h>
class A
{
int i,j;
public:
void set(int a,int b)
{
i=a;
j=b;
}
void show()
```

```
{
cout <<i <<" "<<j <<"\n";
}
};
class B :public A
{
int k;
public:
B(int m)
{
k=m;
}
void show_k()
{
cout <<k <<"\n";
}
};
void main()
{
B b(4);
b.set(1,2);
b.show();
b.show_k();
getch();
}
Output:
1 2
4
```

11.10 PUBLIC INHERITANCE

Public inheritance is by far the most commonly used type of inheritance. In fact, very rarely will you use the other types of inheritance, so your primary focus should be on understanding this section. Fortunately, public inheritance is also the easiest to understand. When you inherit a base class publicly, all members keep their original access specifications. Private members stay private, protected members stay protected, and public members stay public.

The general syntax is:

```
class base
{
```

```
private:
data member;
..................;
public:
data member ;
..................;
protected:
data member;
..................;
};
class derived : public base
{
..................;
..................;
};
```

This is fairly straightforward. The things worth noting are:

1. Derived classes can not directly access private members of the base class.
2. The protected access specifier allows derived classes to directly access members of the base class while not exposing those members to the public.
3. The derived class uses access specifiers from the base class.
4. The outside uses access specifiers from the derived class.

To summarize in table form:

PUBLIC INHERITANCE			
Base access specifier	**Derived access specifier**	**Derived class access?**	**Public access?**
Public	Public	Yes	Yes
Private	Private	No	No
Protected	Protected	Yes	No

Program 2: Write a C++ program to demonstrate public inheritance.

```
#include<iostream.h>
#include<conio.h>
class BaseClass
{
int i, j;
public:
void set(int a, int b)
{
```

```
i = a; j = b;
}
void show()
{
cout << i << " " << j << "\n";
}
};
class DerivedClass : public BaseClass
{
int k;
public:
DerivedClass(int x)
{
k = x;
}
void showDerivedClass()
{
cout << k << "\n";
}
// i = 10; // Error! i is private to BaseClass and access is not allowed.
};
void main()
{
DerivedClass ob(3);
ob.set(1, 2); // access member of base class
ob.show();   // access member of base class
ob.showDerivedClass();   // uses member of derived class
getch();
}
Output:
1 2
3
```

Program 3: Write a C++ program to inherited as public.

```
#include<iostream.h>
#include<conio.h>
class base
{
protected:
int i, j;
```

```
public:
void set(int a, int b)
{
i=a;
j=b;
}
void show()
{
cout << i << " " << j << "\n";
}
};
class derived1 : public base
{
int k;
public:
void setk()
{
k = i*j;
}
void showk()
{
cout << k << "\n";
}
};
class derived2 : public derived1
{
int m;
public:
void setm()
{
m = i-j;
}
void showm()
{
cout << m << "\n";
}
};
void main()
{
```

```
derived1 ob1;
derived2 ob2;
ob1.set(2, 3);
ob1.show();
ob1.setk();
ob1.showk();
ob2.set(3, 4);
ob2.show();
ob2.setk();
ob2.setm();
ob2.showk();
ob2.showm();
getch();
}
```

Output:

```
2 3
6
3 4
12
-1
```

11.11 PRIVATE INHERITANCE

With private inheritance, all members from the base class are inherited as private. This means private members stay private, and protected and public members become private.

Note that this does not affect that way that the derived class accesses members inherited from its parent! It only affects the code trying to access those members through the derived class.

The general syntax is:

```
class base
{
private
data member;
....................;
public:
data member ;
................... ;
protected:
```

```
data member;
.................... ;
};
class derived : private base
{
.................... ;
.................... ;
};
```

To summarize in table form:

PRIVATE INHERITANCE			
Base access specifier	**Derived access specifier**	**Derived class access?**	**Public access?**
Public	Private	Yes	No
Private	Private	No	No
Protected	Private	Yes	No

Program 4: Write a C++ program to inherit base as private.

```
#include<iostream.h>
#include<conio.h>
class base
{
private:
int i;
public:
int j, k;
void seti(int x) { i = x; }
int geti() { return i; }
};
class derived: private base
{
public:
base::j;
base::seti;
base::geti;
int a;
};
void main()
{
```

```
derived ob;
ob.j = 20; // legal because j is made public in derived
//ob.k = 30; // illegal because k is private in derived
ob.a = 40; // legal because a is public in derived
ob.seti(10);
cout << ob.geti() << " " << ob.j << " " << ob.a;
getch();
}
Output:
10 20 40
```

Program 5: Write a C++ program for Public and Private Inheritance.

```
#include<iostream.h>
#include<conio.h>
class A //base class
{
private:
int privateA;
protected:
int protectA;
public:
int publicA;
};
class B :public A
{
public:
void fun()
{
int a;
a =privateA;//error:not accessible
a =protectA;//OK
a =publicA;//OK
}
};
class C :private A
{
public:
void funct()
{
int a;
```

```
a =privateA;//error:not accessible
a =protectA;//OK
a =publicA;//OK
}
};
void main()
{
int a;
B objB;
a =objB.privdateA;//error:not accessible
a =objB.protectA;//error:not accessible
a =objB.publicA;//OK (A public to B)
C objC;
a =objC.privateA;//error:not accessible
a =objC.protectA;//error:not accessible
a =objC.publicA;//error:not accessible (A private to C)
getch();
}
```

Output:

Run program (7 errors)

11.12 PROTECTED INHERITANCE

Protected inheritance is the last method of inheritance. It is almost never used, except in very particular cases. With protected inheritance, the public and protected members become protected, and private members stay private.

The general syntax is:

```
class base
{
private:
data member;
..................;
public:
data member ;
..................;
protected:
data member;
..................;
};
```

```
class derived : public base
{
.................;
.................;
};
```

Protected inheritance is similar to private inheritance. However, classes derived from the derived class still have access to the public and protected members directly. The public (stuff outside the class) does not.

To summarize in table form:

PROTECTED INHERITANCE			
Base access specifier	**Derived access specifier**	**Derived class access?**	**Public access?**
Public	Protected	Yes	No
Private	Private	No	No
Protected	Protected	Yes	No

11.12.1 More About Protected Members

The protected keyword is included in C++ to provide greater flexibility in the inheritance mechanism. If you use the qualifier protected, rather than private or public, before a member variable of a class, then for any class or function other than a derived class the effect is the same as if the member variable were labeled private. However, in the definition of a member function of a derived class the variable can be accessed by name. Similarly, if you use the qualifier protected before a member function of a class, then for any class or function other than a derived class the effect is the same as if the member variable were labeled private. However, in the definition of a member function of a derived class the protected function can be used.

Protected members are inherited in the derived class as if they were marked protected in the derived class. In other words, if a member is marked as protected in a base class, then it can be accessed by name in the definitions of all descendant classes, not just in those classes directly derived from the base class.

Program 6: Write a C++ program to inherit base as protected.

```
#include<iostream.h>
#include<conio.h>
class base
{
protected:
int i, j;
```

```
public:
void setij(int a, int b) { i=a; j=b; }
void showij() { cout << i << " " << j << "\n"; }
};
class derived : protected base
{
int k;
public:
void setk()
{
setij(10, 12);
k = i*j;
}
void showall()
{
cout << k << " ";
showij();
}
};
void main()
{
derived ob;
ob.setk();
ob.showall();
getch();
}
Output:
120 10 12
```

Program 7: Write a C++ program for inheritance for protected member .

```
#include<iostream.h>
#include<conio.h>
class BaseClass
{
protected:
int i, j;
public:
void set(int a, int b)
{
i = a;
```

```
j = b;
}
void show()
{
cout << i << " " << j << endl;
}};                        // i and j inherited as protected.
class DerivedClass1 : public BaseClass
{
int k;
public:
void setk()
{
k = i * j;
}
void showk()
{
cout << k << endl;
}};                        // i and j inherited indirectly through DerivedClass1.
class DerivedClass2 : public DerivedClass1
{
int m;
public:
void setm()
{
m = i - j;
}
void showm()
{
cout << m << endl;
}};
void main()
{
DerivedClass1 object1;
DerivedClass2 object2;
object1.set(2, 3);
object1.show();
object1.setk();
object1.showk();
object2.set(3, 4);
```

```
object2.show();
object2.setk();
object2.setm();
object2.showk();
object2.showm();
getch();
}
Output:
2 3
6
3 4
12
-1
```

11.13 RELATIONSHIP BETWEEN PRIVATE, PUBLIC AND PROTECTED INHERITANCE

When deriving a class from a base class, the base class may be inherited through public, protected or private inheritance. Use of protected and private inheritance is rare, and each should be used only with great care; we normally use public inheritance in this chapter. Figure 11.5 summarizes for each type of inheritance the accessibility of base-class members in a derived class. The first column contains the base-class access specifiers.

Base class member-access specifier	Type of inheritance		
	Public inheritance	**Protected inheritance**	**Private inheritance**
public	public in derived class Can be accessed directly by member functions friend functions and	protected in derived class Can be accessed directly by member functions and firend functions.	private in derived class Can be accessed directly by member functions and friend functions.
protected	protected in derived class Can be accessed directly by member functions friend functions and	protected in derived class Can be accessed directly by member functions and firend functions.	private in derived class Can be accessed directly by member functions and friend functions.
private	Hidden in derived class Can be accessed member functions and friend functions through public or protected member functions of the base class	Hidden in derived class Can be accessed member functions and friend functions through public or protected member functions of the base class	Hidden in derived class Can be accessed member functions and friend functions through public or protected member functions of the base class

Figure 11.5: Summary of base-class member accessibility in a derived class.

When deriving a class from a public base class, public members of the base class become public members of the derived class and protected members of the base class become protected members of the derived class. A base class's private members are never accessible directly from a derived class, but can be accessed through calls to the public and protected members of the base class.

When deriving from a protected base class, public and protected members of the base class become protected members of the derived class.

When deriving from a private base class, public and protected members of the base class become private members (e.g., the functions become utility functions) of the derived class. Private and protected inheritance are not is-a relationships.

11.14 SINGLE INHERITANCE

When only one class is derived from a single base class such derivation of a class is known as single inheritance. The derived class is not used as a base class. This type of inheritance uses one base and one derived class.

Definition: *"It is the process of creating a new class from an existing base class. The existing class is known as the base class and the newly created class is called derived class."*

Here only two classes have linked to each other.

The general syntax is:

```
class base
{
private:
data member;
.................;
public:
data member ;
.................;
protected:
data member;
.................;
};
class derived : public base
{
.................;
.................;
};
```

Here base is the Base class and derived is the Derived class.

Another more powerful general syntax used for defining a derived class in single inheritance is:

```
class derived : access specifier base
{
// data members and member function of the derived class;
};
```

Here access specifier controls the access and process of the inherited base class members in the derived class. The access specifier may be either private, public or protected and if no access specifier is defined, then by default the access specifier is considered as private. Base class name follows the colon(:).

Another general syntax is:

```
class A
{};
class B : publc A        //class B is derived from base class A
{};
```

For Example: class B is derived from base class A or class B inherits from base class A.

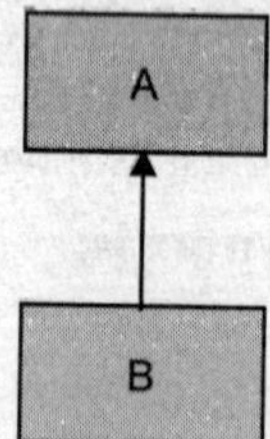

C++ Program to explain the relationship of base class and derived class.

Program 8: Write a C++ program to show single inheritance between two classes and one object.

```
#include<iostream.h>
#include<conio.h>
class student                          // Base class
{
private:
int rollno;                            //data member
};
class marks: public student            //class marks is derived from student
base class
{
```

```
private:
char name[20];
public:
void readdata()                              //member function
{
cout<<"\n Enter rollno:";
cin>>rollno;
cout<<"\n Enter name";
cin>>name;
}
void showdata()
{
cout<<"\n Rollno:"<<rollno;
cout<<"\n Name<<name;
}
};
void main()                                  //main program
{
clrscr();
marks m;
m.readdata();
m.showdata();
getch();
}
Output:
Enter rollno: 4
Enter name: Sukhwant
Rollno: 4
Name: Sukhwant
```

Program 9: Write a C++ program to show single inheritance between two classes and two objects.

```
#include<iostream.h>
#include<conio.h>
class student
{
private:
int rollno;
};
```

```
class marks: public student
{
private:
char name[20];
public:
void readdata()
{
cout<<"\n Enter rollno:";
cin>>rollno;
cout<<"\n Enter name";
cin>>name;
}
void showdata()
{
cout<<"\n Rollno:"<<rollno;
cout<<"\n Name<<name;
}
};
void main()
{
clrscr();
marks m1, m2;
m1.readdata();
m1.showdata();
m2.readdata();
m2.showdata();
getch();
}
```

Output:

```
Enter rollno: 4              // for object m1
Enter name: Sukhwant         // for object m1
Rollno: 4
Name: Sukhwant
Enter rollno: 12             // for object m2
Enter name: Avtar            // for object m2
Rollno: 12
Name: Avtar
```

11.15 CONSTRUCTOR, DESTRUCTOR, AND INHERITANCE

There are two major questions arises relative to constructors and destructors when inheritance is involved. First, how can parameters be passed to base-class constructor functions? Second, when are base-class and derived-class constructor and destructor functions called? These two important topics are discuss below.

11.15.1 Constructors in Inheritance (Base and Derived Classes)

A constructor in a base class does not inherited in the derived class, but you can invoke a constructor of the base class within the definition of a derived class constructor.

A constructor for a derived class uses a constructor from the base class in a special way. A constructor for the base class initializes all the data inherited from the base class. Thus, a constructor for a derived class begins with an invocation of a constructor for the base class.

Procedure to use base class constructor in derived class:

When defining a constructor for the derived class, you should include a call to a constructor of the base class. (within the initialization section of the constructor definition).

If you do not include a call to a constructor of the base class, then the default (zero-argument) constructor of the base class will automatically be called when the derived class constructor is called.

(1) No Argument Constructor

Program 10: Write a C++ program with no argument constructor in base & derived class.

```
#include<iostream.h>
#include<conio.h>
class b
{
public:
b()
{
cout<<"b's no parameter constructor";
}
};
class d:public b
{
```

```
public:
d()
{
cout<<"\nd's no parameter constructor";
}
};
void main()
{
d der;
getch();
}
Output:
b's no parameter constructor
d's no parameter constructor
```

11.15.2 Passing Parameters to Base and Derived Class Constructors

In some cases where only the derived class constructor requires one or more parameters, you simply use the standard parameterized constructor syntax **(see Chapter 12).** Now, we can also pass one or more parameters to base class contructors.

(1) One and Two Parameter Constructor

Program 11: Write a C++ program for contructor have one parameter,two parameters(inheritance).

```
#include<iostream.h>
#include<conio.h>
class b
{
int a;
public:
b(int a1)
{
a=a1;
cout<<"b's single parameter constructor";}
void show()
{
cout<<"\na= "<<a;}
};
class d:public b
```

```
{
int bs;
public:
d(int bb,int aa):b(aa)
{
bs=bb;
cout<<"\nd's constructor with two parameters ";}
void show()
{
b::show();
cout<<"\nbs= "<<bs;
}
};
void main()
{
d der(12,89);
der.show();
getch();
}
```

Output:

b's single parameter constructor
d's constructor with two parameters
a=12 bs=89

(2) Base and Derived Class Constructor

Program 12: Write a C++ program for one parameter,two parameter and three parameter base class, derived class constructors.

```
#include<iostream.h>
#include<conio.h>
class b
{
private:
int x;
public:
b11(int x1)
{
x=x1;
cout<<"b's with single parameter constructor\n";
x = x1;
```

```
}
};
class d1:public b
{
private:
int y;
public:
d1(int yy,int xx):b(xx)
{
cout<<"\nd1's constructor with two parameter ";
y=yy;
}
};
class d2:public d1
{
private:
int z;
public:
d2(int zz,int yy, int xx):d1(yy,xx)
{
cout<<"\nd3's constructor with three parameter ";
z=zz;
}
};
void main()
{
d2 der(10,20,30);
getch();
}
```

(3) Initialization of Base and Derived Class Constructor

Program 13: Write a C++ program to initialize member variables from base class.

```
#include<iostream.h>
#include<conio.h>
class BaseClass
{
int i, j;
public:
```

```
BaseClass(int x, int y)
{
i = x;
j = y;
}
void showij()
{
cout << i << ' ' << j << '\n';
}
};
class DerivedClass : public BaseClass
{
int k;
public:
DerivedClass(int a, int b, int c) : BaseClass(b, c)
{
k = a;
}
void show()
{
cout << k << ' '; showij();
}
};
void  main()
{
DerivedClass ob(1, 2, 3);
ob.show();
getch();
}
Output:
1 2 3
```

(4) Overloaded Constructor to Base Class

Program 14: Write a C++ program for adding a overloaded constructor to base class.

```
#include<iostream.h>
#include<conio.h>
#include <string.h>
class Shape
```

```
{
// private by default
double width;
double height;
public:
Shape()
{
width = height = 0.0;
}
Shape(double w, double h)
{
width = w;
height = h;
}
Shape(double x)
{
width = height = x;
}
void display()
{
cout << "Width and height are " << width << " and " << height << "\n";
}
double getWidth() { return width; }
double getHeight() { return height; }
void setWidth(double w) { width = w; }
void setHeight(double h) { height = h; }
};
class Triangle : public Shape
{
char style[20]; // now private
public:
Triangle()
{
strcpy(style, "unknown");
}
Triangle(char *str, double w, double h) : Shape(w, h)
{
strcpy(style, str);
}
Triangle(double x) : Shape(x)
```

```
{
strcpy(style, "isosceles");
}
double area()
{
return getWidth() * getHeight() / 2;
}
void showStyle()
{
cout << "Triangle is " << style << "\n";
}
};
void main()
{
Triangle t1;
Triangle t2("right", 8.0, 12.0);
Triangle t3(4.0);
t1 = t2;
cout << "Info for t1: \n";
t1.showStyle();
t1.display();
cout << "Area is " << t1.area() << "\n";
t2.showStyle();
t2.display();
cout << "Area is " << t2.area() << "\n";
t3.showStyle();
t3.display();
cout << "Area is " << t3.area() << "\n";
getch();
}
```

Output:

```
Info for t1:
Triangle is right
Width and height are 8 and 12
Area is 48
Triangle is right
Width and height are 8 and 12
Area is 48
Triangle is isosceles
```

```
Width and height are 4 and 4
Area is 8
```

(5) Shadow Function having Same Name in Base and Derived Class

Program 15: Write a C++ program for shadow function with the same name in base class.

```
#include<iostream.h>
#include<conio.h>
#include <stdlib.h>
class BaseClass
{
public:
void f();
};
void BaseClass::f()
{
cout << "Hey this is the base class!\n";
}
class DerivedClass:public BaseClass
{
public:
void f();
};
void DerivedClass::f()
{
cout << "Hey this is in the child class!!\n";
}
void main()
{
DerivedClass myclass;
myclass.f();
getch();
}
Output:
Hey this is in the child class!!
```

11.15.3 Destructors in Inheritance(base and Derived Classes)

If a base class has a correctly functioning destructor, it is relatively easy to define a correctly functioning destructor in a class derived from the base class. When the destructor for the derived class is invoked, it automatically invokes the destructor of the base class.

So there is no need for the explicit writing of a call to the base class destructor; it always happens automatically. In inheritance, destructors are executed in reverse order of constructor execution. Suppose if class B is derived from class A and class C is derived from class B, then

when an object of class C goes out of scope, first the destructor for the class C is called, then the destructor for class B is called, and finally the destructor for class A is called.

Note: *The order of destructor calls is the reverse of the order in which constructors are called.*

Here is an example to explain the concept of destructors in inheritance:

Program 16: Write a C++ program to call base's constructor and destructor from derived class.

```
#include<iostream.h>
#include<conio.h>
class BaseClass
{
public:
BaseClass() { cout << "Constructing base portion\n"; }
~BaseClass() { cout << "Destructing base portion\n"; }
};
class DerivedClass: public BaseClass
{
public:
DerivedClass() { cout << "Constructing derived portion\n"; }
~DerivedClass() { cout << "Destructing derived portion\n"; }
};
void main()
{
DerivedClass ob;
// do nothing but construct and destruct ob
getch();
}
```

Output:

```
Constructing base portion
Constructing derived portion
```

```
Destructing derived portion
Destructing base portion
```

Program 17: Write a C++ program to pass arguments to base class.

```
#include<iostream.h>
#include<conio.h>
class BaseClass
{
int i;
public:
BaseClass(int n)
{
cout << "Constructing base class\n";
i = n;
}
~BaseClass()
{
cout << "Destructing base class\n";
}
void showi()
{
cout << i << '\n';
}
};
class DerivedClass : public BaseClass
{
int j;
public:
DerivedClass(int n, int m) : BaseClass(m)
{
cout << "Constructing DerivedClass class\n";
j = n;
}
~DerivedClass()
{
cout << "Destructing DerivedClass class\n";
}
void showj()
{
cout << j << '\n';
```

```
}
};
void main()
{
DerivedClass o(10, 20);
o.showi();
o.showj();
getch();
}
Output:
Constructing base class
Constructing DerivedClass class
20
10
Destructing DerivedClass class
Destructing base class
```

11.15.4 When Constructor and Destructor Functions are Executed

It is possible to use constructor and/or destructor functions in base class and derived class, or both to contain. Now the time is to tell the order in which these functions are executed when an object of a derived class comes into existence and when it goes out of existence. Here are the examples to tell the order of constructor and destructor calls.

(1) Order of Constructor and Destructor Calls

Program 18: Write a C++ program for two parameter constructor(inheritance).

```
#include<iostream.h>
#include<conio.h>
class b
{
public:
b()
{
cout<<"b's no parameter constructor";
}
};
class d:public b
{
```

```
int a,b;
public:
d(int x,int y)
{
a=x;
b=y;
cout<<"\nd's constructor with two parameters ";}
};
void main()
{
d der(12,89);
getch();
}
```

Output:

b's no parameter constructor
d's constructor with two parameters

Program 19: Write a C++ program to call constructor from base class to initialize fields inherited from base class.

```
#include<iostream.h>
#include<conio.h>
class base
{
protected:
int i;
public:
base(int x)
{
i=x;
cout << "Constructing base\n";
}
~base()
{
cout << "Destructing base\n";
}
};
class derived: public base
{
int j;
public:
```

```
derived(int x, int y): base(y)
{
j=x;
cout << "Constructing derived\n";
}
~derived()
{
cout << "Destructing derived\n";
}
void show()
{
cout << i << " " << j << "\n";
}
};
void main()
{
derived ob(3, 4);
ob.show();
getch();
}
Output:
Constructing base
Constructing derived
4 3
Destructing derived
Destructing base
```

(2) Calling Base Class Constructor in Derived Class

Program 20: Write a C++ program to calling base class's constructor in derived class.

```
#include<iostream.h>
#include<conio.h>
class A
{
protected:
int i;
public:
A(int x)
{
```

```
i = x;
cout << "Constructing base class(A)\n";
}
~A()
{
cout << "Destructing base class(A)\n";
}
};
class B
{
protected:
int j;
public:
B(int x)
{
j = x;
cout << "Constructing base class(B)\n";
}
~B()
{
cout << "Destructing base class(B)\n";
}
};
class C: public A, public B
{
int k;
public:
C(int x, int y, int z): A(y), B(z)
{
k = x;
cout << "Constructing derived class (C)\n";
}
~C()
{
cout << "Destructing derived class(C)\n";
}
void show()
{
cout << i << " " << j << " " << k << "\n";
```

```
}
};
void main()
{
C c(1, 2, 3);
c.show();
getch();
}
Output:
Constructing base class(A)
Constructing base class(B)
Constructing derived class (C)
2 3 1
Destructing derived class(C)
Destructing base class(B)
Destructing base class(A)
```

11.16 OVERRIDING MEMBER FUNCTION

The member functions can also be used in a derived class, with the same name as those in the base class. One might want to do this so that calls in the program work the same way for objects of both base and derived classes.

The following program will illustrate this concept.

Program 21: Write a C++ program to Overriding a base class method in a derived class.

```
#include<iostream.h>
#include<conio.h>
class BaseClass
{
public:
// constructors
BaseClass()
{ cout << "BaseClass constructor...\n"; }
~BaseClass()
{ cout << "BaseClass destructor...\n"; }
//Other methods
void Talk()const
{ cout << "BaseClass sound!\n"; }
void Sleep()const
```

```
{cout << "I'm sleeping.\n"; }
protected:
int itsAge;
int itsWeight;
};
class DerivedClass : public BaseClass
{
public:
// Constructors
DerivedClass()
{ cout << "DerivedClass constructor...\n"; }
~DerivedClass()
{ cout << "DerivedClass destructor...\n"; }
// Other methods
void Walk()
{ cout << "walk...\n"; }
void Eat()
{ cout << "eat...\n"; }
void Talk()const
{ cout << "talk!\n"; }
};
void main()
{
BaseClass baseObject;
DerivedClass derivedObject;
baseObject.Talk();
derivedObject.Talk();
getch();
}
```

Output:

```
BaseClass constructor...
BaseClass constructor...
DerivedClass constructor...
BaseClass sound!
talk!
DerivedClass destructor...
BaseClass destructor...
BaseClass destructor...
```

Program 22: Write a C++ program to calling base method from overridden method.

```
#include<iostream.h>
#include<conio.h>
class BaseClass
{
public:
void Move() const
{
cout << "BaseClass move one step\n";
}
void Move(int distance) const
{
cout << "BaseClass move " << distance << " steps.\n";
}
protected:
int itsAge;
int itsWeight;
};
class DerivedClass : public BaseClass
{
public:
void Move()const;
};
void DerivedClass::Move() const
{
cout << "In dog move...\n";
BaseClass::Move(3);
}
void main()
{
BaseClass baseObject;
DerivedClass derivedObject;
baseObject.Move(2);
derivedObject.BaseClass::Move(6);
getch();
}
```

Output:

```
BaseClass move 2 steps.
BaseClass move 6 steps.
```

11.17 MULTIPLE INHERITANCE

It is the latest addition to the C++ language. When a class is derived from more than one class then that procedure is called multiple inheritance. A class can be derived by inheriting properties of more than one class.

Definition: *"In this type of inheritance, number of classes has inherited in a single class. Where two or more classes are, know as base class and one is derive class."*

The general syntax is:

```
class A                    //base class A
{};
class B                    //base class B
{};
class C : public A, public B
{
/*class C which is derived from base class A and base class B*/
};
```

For Example: if there are three classes A, B and C from which class A and class B are the base classes and class C is the derived from both base class A and base class B, then we can say that class C is multiple inherited from the base class A and B.

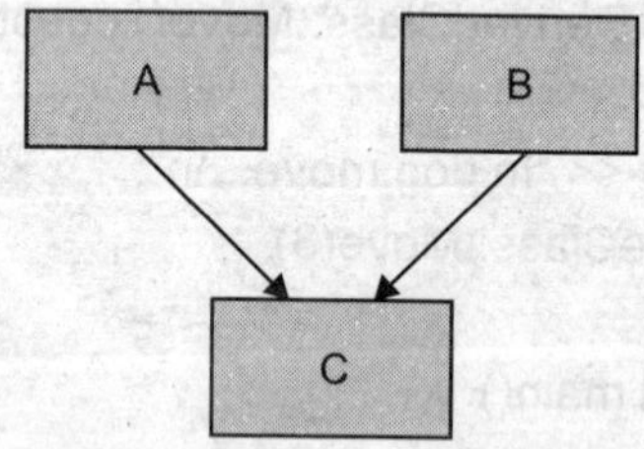

Program 23: Write a C++ program for multiple inheritance.

```
#include<iostream.h>
#include<conio.h>
class A
{
protected:
int x;
public:
```

```
void showx()
{
cout << x << "\n";
}
};
class B
{
protected:
int y;
public:
void showy()
{
cout << y << "\n";
}
};
class C: public A, public B
{
public:
void set(int i, int j)
{
x = i;
y = j;
}
};
void main()
{
C c;
c.set(10, 20);
c.showx();
c.showy();
getch();
}
Output:
10
20
```

Program 24: Write a C++ program for multiple base class constructing and destructing.

```
#include<iostream.h>
#include<conio.h>
```

```
class base1
{
public:
base1()
{
cout << "Constructing base1\n";
}
~base1()
{
cout << "Destructing base1\n";
}
};
class base2
{
public:
base2()
{
cout << "Constructing base2\n";
}
~base2()
{
cout << "Destructing base2\n";
}
};
class derived: public base1, public base2
{
public:
derived()
{
cout << "Constructing derived\n";
}
~derived()
{
cout << "Destructing derived\n";
}
};
void main()
{
derived ob;
```

```
getch();
}
```

Output:

```
Constructing base1
Constructing base2
Constructing derived
Destructing derived
Destructing base2
Destructing base1
```

11.17.1 Ambiguity Problem in Multiple Inheritance

The main problem that occurs with the inheritance is ambiguity. This problem can occur when data members and member functions are defined using the same name in both the base and the derived classes, then that same name creates an ambiguity in defining the single class. So to remove this problem, We are going to use scope resolution operator (**::**). It may be used to refer to any base member explicitly. This allows access to a name that has been redefined in the derived class.

For Example: How ambiguity occurs when the show() member function is accessed from the main ( ) program:

```
class base A
{
public :
int x;
show();
} ;
class base B
{
public :
int x,y;
show();
} ;
class derived C : public base A, public base B
{
public :
int z;
show();
} ;
void main ( )
{
```

```
derived C obj ;
obj. show();
}
```

Members are ambiguous without scope operator. When the member function **show()** is accessed by the class object, then the compiler cannot distinguish between the member function of the base class **base A** and the base class **base B.** So it is essential to declare the scope resolution operator explicitly to call a base class member as given below:

```
obj. base A : : getdata ( ) ;
obj. base B : : getdata ( ) ;
```

For Example: Program to demonstrate how ambiguity is avoided in multiple inheritance using scope resolution operator.

Program 25: Write a C++ program to avoid ambiguity in multiple inheritance.

```
#include<iostream.h>
#include<conio.h>
class A
{
private :
int i ;
public :
void readdata (int x) ;
void writedata ( ) ;
};
class B
{
private :
int j ;
public :
void readdata (int y) ;
void writedata ( ) ;
};
class C : : public A, public B
{ } ;
void A :: readdata (int x)
{
i = x ;
}
void A : : writedata ( )
{
```

```
cout <<"\n Value of i is ="<<i ;
}
void B :: readdata (int y)
{
j = y ;
}
void B : : writedata ( )
{
cout<<"\n value of j is ="<<j ;
}
void main ( )
{
class C obj ;
int x, y ;
cout<<"\n Enter the value of x" ;
cin>> x ;
obj. A :: readdata (x) ;
//Here member is ambiguous without scope
cout<<"\n Enter the value of y" ;
cin >> y ;
obj. B :: readdata (y) ;
obj. A :: writedata ( ) ;
obj. B :: writedata ( ) ;
getch();
}
```

11.18 HIERARCHICAL INHERITANCE

When two or more classes are derived from a single base class, then Inheritance is called the hierarchical inheritance. The representation of the hierarchical inheritance is shown in the following Figure 11.6.

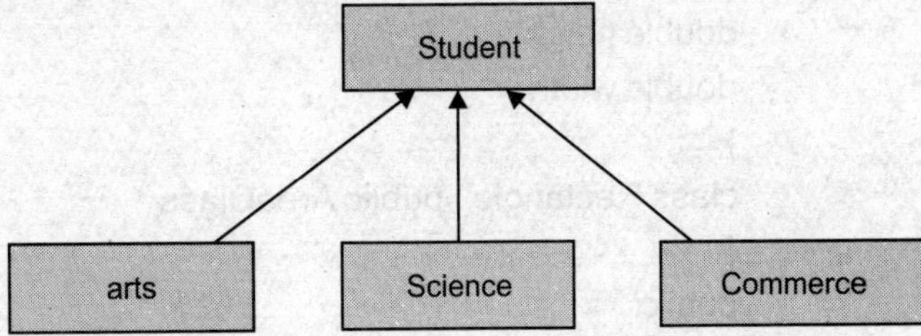

Figure 11.6: Hierarchical inheritance

In the above diagram, student is a base class, from which the three classes viz. arts, science and commerce have been derived.

Definition: *"This type of inheritance helps us to create a baseless for number of classes and those numbers of classes can have further their branches of number of class."*

The general syntax is:

```
class A                //base class
{};
class B : public A     // class B is derived from base class A
{};
class C : public A     // class C is derived from base class A
{};
```

For Example: Suppose class B and class C inherited from base class A or when two or more classes inherited from single base class that type of inheritance is called hierarchical inheritance.

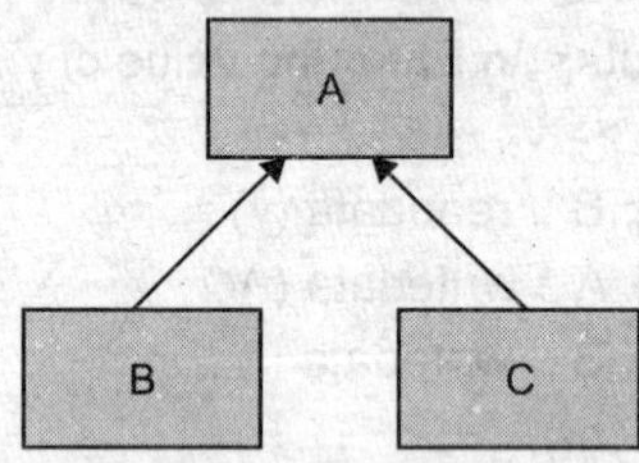

Program 26: Write a C++ program to share member variables between sub class

```
#include<iostream.h>
#include<conio.h>
class AreaClass
{
public:
double height;
double width;
};
class Rectangle : public AreaClass
{
public:
Rectangle(double h, double w)
{
```

```
height = h;
width = w;
}
double area()
{
return height * width;
}
};
class Isosceles : public AreaClass
{
public:
Isosceles(double h, double w)
{
height = h;
width = w;
}
double area()
{
return 0.5 * width * height;
}
};
class cyllnder : public AreaClass
{
public:
cylinder(double h, double w)
{
height = h;
width = w;
}
double area()
{
return (2 * 3.1416 * (width/2) * (width/2)) + (3.1416 * width * height);
}
};
void main()
{
Rectangle rectangleObject(10.0, 5.0);
Isosceles triangleObject(4.0, 6.0);
cylinder cylinderObject(3.0, 4.0);
```

```
cout << "Rectangle: " << rectangleObject.area() << endl;
cout << "Triangle: " << triangleObject.area() << endl;
cout << "Cylinder: " << cylinderObject.area() << endl;
getch();
}
```

Output:

```
Rectangle: 50
Triangle: 12
Cylinder: 62.832
```

11.19 MULTILEVEL INHERITANCE OR LEVEL OF INHERITANCE

It has been discussed so far that a class can be derived from a class. C++ also provides the facility of multilevel inheritance, according to which the derived class can also be derived by an another class, which in turn can further be inherited by another and so on.

The following figure will illustrate the meaning of the multilevel inheritance.

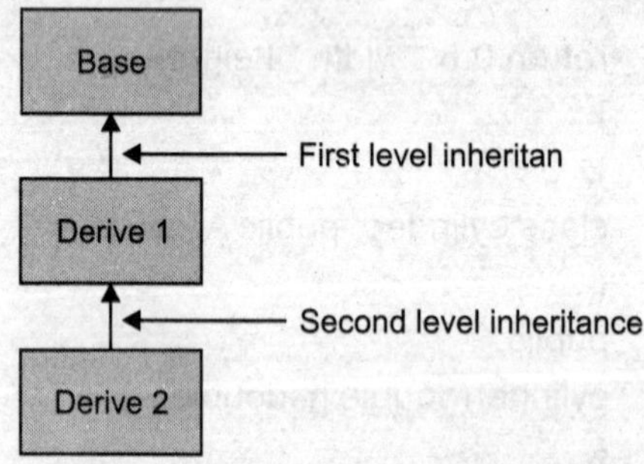

Figure 11.7: Multilevel inheritance

In the above figure, class Base represents the base class. The class Derive1 that is called first level of inheritance, inherits the class Base. The derived class Derive1 is further inherited by the class Derive2, which is called second level of inheritance.

Definition: *"In this type of inheritance, there are number of level and it has used in that cases where we want to use all properties in number of levels according to the requirement."*

The general syntax is:

```
class A
{};
```

```
class B : public A      //class B is derived from base class A
{};
class C : public B      //class C is derived from derived class B
{};
```

For Example: A inherited in class B and class B has inherited in class C for class B so on. Where class A is base class C. In another way we can say B is derived class A base class for C and A indirect base class for C and C indirect derived class for class A.

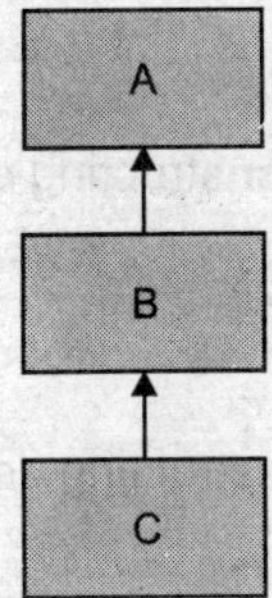

Program 27: Write a C++ program for three level inheritance.

```
#include<iostream.h>
#include<conio.h>
class base
{
public:
base()
{
cout << "Constructing base\n";
}
~base()
{
cout << "Destructing base\n";
}
};
class derived1 : public base
{
public:
derived1()
{
cout << "Constructing derived1\n";
}
```

```
~derived1()
{
cout << "Destructing derived1\n";
}
};
class derived2: public derived1
{
public:
derived2()
{
cout << "Constructing derived2\n";
}
~derived2()
{
cout << "Destructing derived2\n";
}
};
void main()
{
derived2 ob;
getch();
}
```

Output:

```
Constructing base
Constructing derived1
Constructing derived2
Destructing derived2
Destructing derived1
Destructing base
```

11.20 HYBRID INHERITANCE

In this type of inheritance, we can have mixture of number of inheritances but this can generate an error of using same name function from no of classes, which will bother the compiler to how to use the functions. Therefore, it will generate errors in the program. This has known as ambiguity or duplicity.

Definition: *"The combination of one or more types of inheritance is called hybrid inheritance."*

```
class A
{};
class B : public A      //class B is derived from base clase A
{};
class C : public A      //class C is derived from base class A
{};
class D : public B, D
{
//class D is derived from derived classes B and C
};
```

For Example: Suppose class B and class C inherited from base class A(using hierarchical inheritance) and class D is inherited from derived classes of A called class B and class C or we cam say class B and class C are the base classes of class D or class D is derived from both class B and class C(using multiple inheritance).

```
#include <iostream.h>
#include<conio.h>
class base
{
public:
int x;
};
class derived1 : public base
{
public:
int y;
};
class derived2 : public base
{
public:
int z;
};
class derived3 : public derived1, public derived2
{
public:
int mul;
};
void main()
{
derived3 ob;
```

```
ob.derived1::x = 10;
ob.y = 20;
ob.z = 30;
ob.mul = ob.derived1::x * ob.y * ob.z;
cout << ob.derived1::x << " ";
cout << ob.y << " " << ob.z << " ";
cout << ob.mul;
getch();
}
```

11.21 FRIEND FUNCTION AND INHERITANCE

In principle, private and protected members of a class cannot be accessed from outside the same class in which they are declared. However, this rule does not affect friends.

Friends are functions or classes declared as such.

If we want to declare an external function as friend of a class, thus allowing this function to have access to the private and protected members of this class, we do it by declaring a prototype of this external function within the class, and preceding it with the keyword friend:

Program 28: Write a C++ program to implement Hospital Management by 2 Classes with Common Friend Function.

```
#include<iostream.h>
#include<conio.h>
class A
{
char name[20],doctor[20],dis[20];
void input()
{
cout<<"Enter name of the patient==>";
cin>>name;
cout<<"Enter name of the doctor operating patient==>";
cin>>doctor;
cout<<"Enter name of the disease patient is suffering from==>";
cin>>dis;
}
void print()
{
cout<<"\nPatient's name is==>"<<name;
```

```
cout<<"\nDoctor operating "<<name<<" is ==>"<<doctor;
cout<<"\n"<<name<<" is suffering from==>"<<dis;
}
friend void input(int);
friend void output(int);
}a[50];
class B: public A
{
char ward;
int room,bed,days,bill,fees;
void input()
{
cout<<"Is patient living in private room?(y/n)==>";
cin>>ward;
if(ward=='y')
{
cout<<"Enter room number==>";
cin>>room;
}
else
{
cout<<"Enter bed number==>";
cin>>bed;
}
cout<<"Enter number of days patient living in hospital==>";
cin>>days;
cout<<"Enter the fees per day==>";
cin>>fees;
bill=fees* days;
}
void print()
{
if(ward=='y')
cout<<"\nPatient is in private room number==>"<<room;
else
cout<<"\nPatient is in public ward on bed number==>"<<bed;
cout<<"\nHe is living in hospital for "<<days<<" days";
cout<<"\nBill till date is==>"<<bill;
```

```
}
friend void input(int);
friend void output(int);
 }b[50];
void main()
{
clrscr();
int n;
cout<<"Enter number of patients==>";
cin>>n;
cout<<"Enter the information==>\n";
input(n);
clrscr();
cout<<"The database is==>\n";
output(n);
getch();
}
void input(int n)
{
for(int i=0;i<n;i++)
{
cout<<"\n Enter information of patient "<<i+1<<".==>\n";
a[i].input();
b[i].input();
}
}
void output(int n)
{
for(int i=0;i<n;i++)
{
cout<<"\n\n The information of patient "<<i+1<<" is==>\n";
a[i].print();
b[i].print();
}
}
```

Output:

```
Enter number of patients==>2
Enter the information==>
```

```
Enter information of patient 1==>
Enter name of the patient==> Heer
Enter name of the doctor operating patient==>Dr. Gagan
Enter name of the disease patient is suffering from==> Cold
Is patient living in private room?(y/n)==>"y
Enter room number==>22
Enter number of days patient living in hospital==>4
Enter the fees per day==>500
Enter information of patient 2==>
Enter name of the patient==> Himmat
Enter name of the doctor operating patient==>Dr. Homi
Enter name of the disease patient is suffering from==> BP
Is patient living in private room?(y/n)==>"y
Enter room number==>24
Enter number of days patient living in hospital==>6
Enter the fees per day==>500
The database is==>
The information of patient 1 is==>
Patient's name is==>Heer
Doctor operating Heer    is ==>Dr. Gagan
Heer is suffering from==> Cold
Patient is in private room number==>22
He is living in hospital for  4  days
Bill till date is==>2000
The information of patient 2 is==>
Patient's name is==>Himmat
Doctor operating Heer    is ==>Dr. Homi
Heer is suffering from==> Bp
Patient is in private room number==>24
He is living in hospital for  6  days
Bill till date is==>3000
```

11.22 POINTERS AND INHERITANCE

The private and public member variables of a class are stored in successive memory locations. A pointer to public member variable gives us access to private member variables.

The same is true for derived class. The member variables of base class and derived class are also stored in successive memory locations.

Program 29: Write a C++ program for a base pointer to access derived objects.

```
#include<iostream.h>
#include<conio.h>
class BaseClass
{
int i;
public:
void setInt(int num)
{
i = num;
}
int getInt()
{
return i;
}
};
class derived: public BaseClass
{
int j;
public:
void setJ(int num)
{
j = num;
}
int getJ()
{
return j;
}
};
void  main()
{
BaseClass *bp;
derived d;
bp = &d;            // BaseClass pointer points to derived object
bp->setInt(10);
cout << bp->getInt() << " ";
getch();
}
```

Output: 10

Program 30: Write a C++ program to demonstrate pointer to derived class.

```
#include<iostream.h>
#include<conio.h>
class BaseClass
{
int x;
public:
void setx(int i)
{
x = i;
}
int getx()
{
return x;
}
};
class DerivedClass : public BaseClass
{
int y;
public:
void sety(int i)
{
y = i;
}
int gety()
{
return y;
}
};
void  main()
{
BaseClass *p;                    // pointer to BaseClass type
BaseClass baseObject;            // object of BaseClass
DerivedClass derivedObject; // object of DerivedClass
p = &baseObject;                 // use p to access BaseClass object
p->setx(10);                     // access BaseClass object
cout << "Base object x: " << p->getx() << "\n";
p = &derivedObject;              // point to DerivedClass object
p->setx(99);                  // access DerivedClass object
```

```
derivedObject.sety(88);          // can't use p to set y, so do it directly
cout << "Derived object x: " << p->getx() << "\n";
cout << "Derived object y: " << derivedObject.gety() << "\n";
getch();
}
Output:
Base object x: 10
Derived object x: 99
Derived object y: 88
```

11.23 VIRTUAL BASE CLASSES OR VIRTUAL INHERITANCE

To overcome the ambiguity occured when multiple base classes are inherited, C++ uses the keyword virtual. The keyword virtual declares the specified class virtual.

For example, consider this incorrect program:

```
// This program contains an error so it will not compile.
#include <iostream.h>
#include<conio.h>
class base
{
public:
int x;
};
class derived1 : public base
{
public:
int y;
};
class derived2 : public base
{
public:
int z;
};
class derived3 : public derived1, public derived2
{
public:
int sum;
};
void main()
```

```
{
derived3 ob;
ob.x = 10;                        // this is ambiguous, which x???
ob.y = 20;
ob.z = 30;                        // x ambiguous here, too
ob.sum = ob.x + ob.y + ob.z; // also ambiguous, which x?
cout << ob.x << " ";
cout << ob.y << " " << ob.z << " ";
cout << ob.sum;
getch();
}
```

In the above program both **derived1** and **derived2** inherit **base**. However, **derived3** inherits both **derived1** and **derived2.** That means we have two copies of **base** present in an object of type **derived3**.

Now it means expression like ob.x = 10;

which **x** is being referred to, the one in **derived1** or the one in **derived2?** Because there are two copies of **base** present in object **ob**, there are two **ob.x**s! So that, the statement is inherently ambiguous.

There are two ways to remove the ambiguity from the preceding program. The first is to apply the scope resolution operator (As we discuss in previous section) to **x** and select the value of one **x. For example:**

```
// Use of explicit scope resolution to select one x.
#include <iostream.h>
#include<conio.h>
class base
{
public:
int x;
};
class derived1 : public base
{
public:
int y;
};
class derived2 : public base
{
public:
int z;
};
```

```
class derived3 : public derived1, public derived2
{
public:
int sum;
};
void main()
{
derived3 ob;
ob.derived1::x = 10;                    // scope resolved, use derived1's x
ob.y = 20;
ob.z = 30;                              // scope resolved
ob.sum = ob.derived1::x + ob.y + ob.z;  // also resolved here
cout << ob.derived1::x << " ";
cout << ob.y << " " << ob.z << " ";
cout << ob.sum;
getch();
}
```

When the **::** was applied, the program selected **derived1**'s version of **base**. However, this solution raises a deeper issue: What if only one copy of **base** is actually required? Is there some way to prevent two copies from being included in **derived3**?

Answer is that to use virtual keyword to make the **virtual** base classes.

When two or more objects are derived from a common base class, you can prevent multiple copies of the base class from being present in an object derived from those objects by declaring the base class as **virtual** when it is inherited. You can done this by preceding the base class' name with the keyword **virtual** when it is inherited.

For example, here we representing another version of the example program in which **derived3** contains only one copy of **base:**

```
// Use of virtual keyword to make the virtual base classes.
#include <iostream.h>
#include<conio.h>
class base
{
public:
int x;
};
class derived1 : virtual public base
{
```

```
public:
int y;
};
class derived2 : virtual public base
{
public:
int z;
};
class derived3 : public derived1, public derived2
{
public:
int sum;
};
void main()
{
derived3 ob;
ob.x = 10;                              // now unambiguous
ob.y = 20;
ob.z = 30;                              // unambiguous
ob.sum = ob.x + ob.y + ob.z; // unambiguous
cout << ob.x << " ";
cout << ob.y << " " << ob.z << " ";
cout << ob.sum;
getch();
}
```

Now, the keyword **virtual** precedes the rest of the inherited **class** specification. In both **derived1** and **derived2** have inherited **base** as **virtual**, any multiple inheritance involving them will cause only one copy of **base** to be present. Therefore, in **derived3**, there is only one copy of **base** and **ob.x = 10** is perfectly valid and unambiguous.

Note: *Even though both derived1 and derived2 specify base as virtual, base is still present in objects of either type.*

For example, the following sequence is perfectly valid:

```
// define a class of type derived1
derived1 ob;
ob.x = 12;
```

The only difference between a normal base class and a **virtual** one is what occurs when an object inherits the base more than once. If **virtual** base classes are used, then only one base class is present in the object. Otherwise, multiple copies will be found.

Program 31: Write a C++ program using virtual base classes.

```
#include<iostream.h>
#include<conio.h>
class Base
{
public:
virtual void print() const = 0; // pure virtual
};
class Derived1 : virtual public Base
{
public:
void print() const
{
cout << "Derived1\n";
}
};
class Derived2 : virtual public Base
{
public:
void print() const
{
cout << "Derived2\n";
}
};
class Multiple : public Derived1, public Derived2
{
public:
void print() const
{
Derived2::print();
}
};
void main()
{
Multiple both;
Derived1 one;
```

```
Derived2 two;
Base *array[ 3 ];
array[0] = &both;
array[1] = &one;
array[2] = &two;
for (int i = 0; i < 3; i++)
array[i]->print();
getch();
}
Output:
Derived2
Derived1
Derived2
```

11.24 AGGREGATION: CLASSES WITHIN CLASSES

Both aggregation and inheritance are class relationships that are more specialized than associations. It is necessary to compare and contrast them.

If a class B is derived by inheritance from a class A, we can say that "B is a *kind of* A." This is because B has all the characteristics of A, and in addition some of its own. It's like saying that a sparrow is a kind of bird: A sparrow has the characteristics shared by all birds (wings, feathers, and so on) but has some different features of its own.

For this reason inheritance is often called a "kind of" relationship.

Aggregation is called a "has a" relationship. Within aggregation, the lifetime of the part is not managed by the whole. To make this clearer, we need an example. For the past 12+ months I have been involved with the implementation of a CRM system, so I am going to use part of this as an example.

The CRM system has a database of customers and a separate database that holds all addresses within a geographic area. Aggregation would make sense in this situation, as a Customer 'has-a' Address. It wouldn't make sense to say that an Address is 'part-of' the Customer, because it isn't. Consider it this way, if the customer ceases to exist, does the address? I would argue that it does not cease to exist. Aggregation is shown on a UML diagram as an unfilled diamond (Figure 14.8).

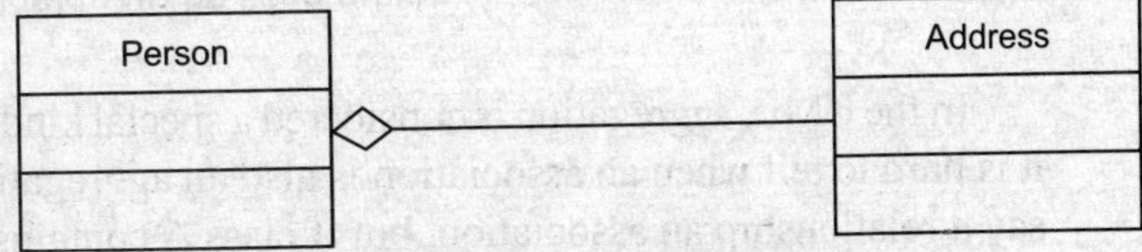

Figure 11.8: CRM system

Consider the following code:

```
class Address
{
. . .
}
class Person
{
Address address;
public :
Person(Address address)
{
this.address = address;
}
    . . .
}
```

Person would then be used as follows:

```
Address address = new Address();
Person person = new Person(address);
or
Person person = new Person( new Address() );
```

As you can see, Person does not manage the lifetime of Address. If Person is destroyed, the Address still exists. This scenario does map quite nicely to the real world.

For example: We say a library has a book or an invoice has an item line. Aggregation is also called a "part-whole" relationship: the book is part of the library. In object-oriented programming, aggregation may occur when one object is an attribute of another.

Here's a case where an object of class A is an attribute of class B:

```
class A
{
};
class B
{
A objA;                    // define objA as an object of class A
};
```

In the UML, aggregation is considered a special kind of association. Sometimes it is hard to tell when an association is also an aggregation. We can always safe to say a relationship an association, but if class A contains objects of class B, and is organizationally superior to class B, it is a good candidate for aggregation. An organization might have an aggregation of employees, or a stamp collection might have an aggregation of stamps.

Aggregation is shown in the same way as association in UML class diagrams, except that the

"whole" end of the association line has an open diamond-shaped arrowhead. Figure 11.9

shows how this looks.

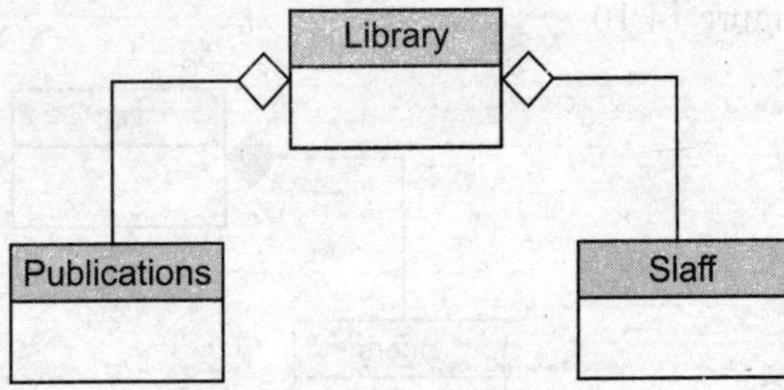

Figure 11.9: Aggregation

11.25 COMPOSITION

Composition is also called stronger form of aggregation. It has all the features of aggregation, plus two new features:

1. The part may belong to only one whole.
2. The lifetime of the part is the same as the lifetime of the whole.

In real-life, complex objects are often built from smaller, simpler objects. For example, a car is built using a metal frame, an engine, some tires, a transmission, a steering wheel, and a large number of other parts. A personal computer is built from a CPU, a motherboard, some memory, etc… Even you are built from smaller parts: you have a head, a body, some legs, arms, and so on. This process of building complex objects from simpler ones is called **composition** (also known as object composition).

More specifically, composition is used for objects that have a *has-a* relationship to each other. A car *has-a* metal frame, *has-an* engine, and *has-a* transmission. A personal computer *has-a* CPU, a motherboard, and other components. You *have-a* head, a body, some limbs.

So far, all of the classes we have used in our examples have had member variables that are built-in data types (eg. int, double). While this is generally sufficient for designing and implementing small, simple classes, it quickly becomes burdensome for more complex classes, especially those built from many sub-parts. In order to facilitate the building of complex classes from simpler ones, C++ allows us to do object composition in a very simple way — by using classes as member variables in other classes.

For example: A car is composed of doors (among other things). The doors can't belong to some other car, and they are bom and die along with the car. A room is composed of a floor, ceiling, and walls. While aggregation is a "has a" relationship, composition is a "consists of" relationship.

In UML diagrams, composition is shown in the same way as aggregation, except that the diamond-shaped arrowhead is solid instead of open. This is shown in Figure 14.10.

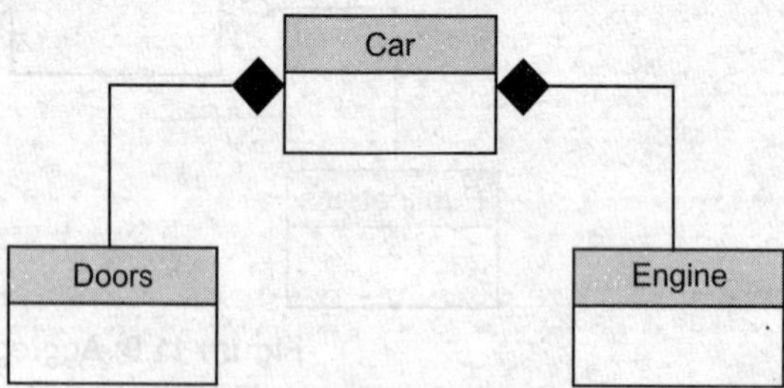

Figure 11.10: Composition

Even a single object can be related to a class by composition. In a car there is only one engine.

For example: To make the understanding of composition easier, we can say that composition gives us a 'part-of' relationship. Composition is shown on a UML diagram as a filled diamond (see Figure 11.11).

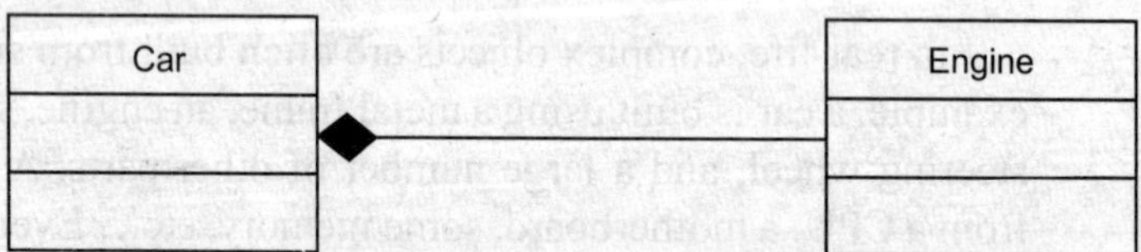

Figure 11.11: Engine is part-of car

If we were going to model a car, it would make sense to say that an engine is part-of a car. Within composition, the lifetime of the part (Engine) is managed by the whole (Car), in other words, when Car is destroyed, Engine is destroyed along with it.

As we know, inheritance gives us an 'is-a' relationship. So how do we express this in C++?

```
class Engine
{
...
```

```
}
class Car
{
Engine e = new Engine();
    .......
}
```

As you can see in the example code above, Car manages the lifetime of Engine.

11.26 COMPARING COMPOSITION AND INHERITANCE

So how exactly do composition and inheritance compare? Here are several points of comparison:

1. It is easier to change the interface of a back-end class (composition) than a superclass (inheritance). As the previous example illustrated, a change to the interface of a back-end class necessitates a change to the front-end class implementation, but not necessarily the front-end interface. Code that depends only on the front-end interface still works, so long as the front-end interface remains the same. By contrast, a change to a superclass's interface can not only ripple down the inheritance hierarchy to subclasses, but can also ripple out to code that uses just the subclass's interface.
2. It is easier to change the interface of a front-end class (composition) than a subclass (inheritance). Just as superclasses can be fragile, subclasses can be rigid. You can't just change a subclass's interface without making sure the subclass's new interface is compatible with that of its supertypes. For example, you can't add to a subclass a method with the same signature but a different return type as a method inherited from a superclass. Composition, on the other hand, allows you to change the interface of a front-end class without affecting back-end classes.
3. Composition allows you to delay the creation of back-end objects until (and unless) they are needed, as well as changing the back-end objects dynamically throughout the lifetime of the front-end object. With inheritance, you get the image of the superclass in your subclass object image as soon as the subclass is created, and it remains part of the subclass object throughout the lifetime of the subclass.
4. It is easier to add new subclasses (inheritance) than it is to add new front-end classes (composition), because inheritance comes with polymorphism. If you have a bit of code that relies only on a superclass interface, that code can work with a new subclass without change. This is not true of composition, unless you use composition with interfaces. Used together, composition and interfaces make a very powerful design tool.

5. The explicit method-invocation forwarding (or delegation) approach of composition will often have a performance cost as compared to inheritance's single invocation of an inherited superclass method implementation.
6. With both composition and inheritance, changing the implementation (not the interface) of any class is easy. The ripple effect of implementation changes remain inside the same class.

11.27 CHOOSING BETWEEN COMPOSITION AND INHERITANCE

So how do all these comparisons between composition and inheritance help you in your designs? Here are a few guidelines that reflect how I tend to select between composition and inheritance.

1. **Make sure inheritance models the *is-a* relationship:** My main guiding philosophy is that inheritance should be used only when a subclass *is-a* superclass. In the example above, an Apple likely is-a Fruit, so I would be inclined to use inheritance. An important question to ask yourself when you think you have an is-a relationship is whether that is-a relationship will be constant throughout the lifetime of the application and, with luck, the lifecycle of the code. For example, you might think that an Employee is-a Person, when really Employee represents a role that a Person plays part of the time. What if the person becomes unemployed? What if the person is both an Employee and a Supervisor? Such impermanent is-a relationships should usually be modelled with composition.
2. **Don't use inheritance just to get code reuse:** If all you really want is to reuse code and there is no is-a relationship in sight, use composition.
3. **Don't use inheritance just to get at polymorphism:** If all you really want is polymorphism, but there is no natural is-a relationship, use composition with interfaces.

11.28 DIFFERENCE BETWEEN COMPOSITION AND AGGREGATION

To summarize the differences between composition and aggregation:

Compositions

- Typically use normal member variables
- Can use pointer values if the composition class automatically handles allocation/deallocation
- Responsible for creation/destruction of subclasses

Aggregations

- Typically use pointer variables that point to an object that lives outside the scope of the aggregate class
- Can use reference values that point to an object that lives outside the scope of the aggregate class
- Not responsible for creating/destroying subclasses

SOLVED PROGRAMMING

Program 1: Write a C++ program to find Factorial of a number using inheritance.

```
#include<iostream.h>
#include<conio.h>
class A
{
int n;
public:
A(int p)
{
n=p;
}
long fact();
};
long A::fact()
{
long f=1;
for(int i=1;i<=n;i++)
f*=i;
return f;
}
class B:public A
{
public:
B(int p): A(p)
{
cout<<"Object created.\n";
}
void print()
```

```
{
cout<<"Factorial is==>"<<fact();
}
};
void main()
{
int n;
clrscr();
cout<<"Enter the number==>";
cin>>n;
B b(n);
b.print();
getch();
}
Output:
Enter the number==> 5
Object created.
Factorial is==> 120
```

Program 2: Write a C++ program for adding a constructor to Base class.

```
#include<iostream.h>
#include<conio.h>
#include <string.h>
class Shape
{
// private
double width;
double height;
public:
Shape(double w, double h)
{
width = w;
height = h;
}
void display()
{
cout << "Width and height are " << width << " and " << height << "\n";
}
double getWidth() { return width; }
double getHeight() { return height; }
```

```
void setWidth(double w) { width = w; }
void setHeight(double h) { height = h; }
};
class Triangle : public Shape
{
char style[20]; // now private
public:
Triangle(char *str, double w, double h) : Shape(w, h)
{
strcpy(style, str);
}
double area()
{
return getWidth() * getHeight() / 2;
}
void showStyle()
{
cout << "Triangle is " << style << "\n";
}
};
void main()
{
Triangle t1("isosceles", 4.0, 4.0);
Triangle t2("right", 8.0, 12.0);
cout << "Info for t1:\n";
t1.showStyle();
t1.display();
cout << "Area is " << t1.area() << "\n";
t2.showStyle();
t2.display();
cout << "Area is " << t2.area() << "\n";
getch();
}
```

Output:

```
Info for t1:
Triangle is isosceles
Width and height are 4 and 4
Area is 8
Triangle is right
```

Width and height are 8 and 12
Area is 48

Program 3: Write a C++ program for derived class constructors.

```
#include<iostream.h>
#include<conio.h>
class Timer
{
protected:
int time;
public:
Timer():time(0)
{ }
Timer(int t):time(t)
{ }
int get_time()
{
return time;
}
Timer operator ++()
{
return Timer(++time);
}
};
class Timert1 :public Timer
{
public:
Timert1():Timer()
{ }
Timert1(int t):Timer(t)
{ }
Timert1 operator —()
{
return Timert1(—time);}
};
void main()
{
Timert1 t1;
Timert1 t2(100);
cout <<"\nt1=" <<t1.get_time();
```

```
cout <<"\nt2=" <<t2.get_time();
++t1;
++t1;
++t1;
cout <<"\nt1=" <<t1.get_time();
—t2;
—t2;
cout <<"\nt2=" <<t2.get_time();
Timert1 t3 =—t2;
cout <<"\nt3=" <<t3.get_time();
cout <<endl;
getch();
}
Output:
t1=0
t2=100
t1=3
t2=98
t3=97
```

Program 4: Write a C++ program for inherit two base classes.

```
#include<iostream.h>
#include<conio.h>
class BaseClass1
{
public:
BaseClass1()
{
cout << "Constructing BaseClass1\n";
}
~BaseClass1()
{
cout << "Destructing BaseClass1\n";
}
};
class BaseClass2
{
int b;
public:
BaseClass2()
```

```
{
cout << "Constructing BaseClass2\n";
}
~BaseClass2()
{
cout << "Destructing BaseClass2\n";
}
};
// Inherit two base classes.
class DerivedClass : public BaseClass1, public BaseClass2
{
public:
DerivedClass()
{
cout << "Constructing DerivedClass\n";
}
~DerivedClass()
{
cout << "Destructing DerivedClass\n";
}
};
void main()
{
DerivedClass object;
getch();
}
Output:
Constructing BaseClass1
Constructing BaseClass2
Constructing DerivedClass
Destructing DerivedClass
Destructing BaseClass2
Destructing BaseClass1
```

Program 5: Write a C++ program for shadow base class function in its two children classes

```
#include<iostream.h>
#include<conio.h>
#include <stdlib.h>
class BaseClass
```

```
{
public:
void f(float);
};
void BaseClass::f(float price)
{
cout << "the base class!\n";
cout << price * .075f;
}
class DerivedClass1:public BaseClass
{
public:
void f(float);
};
void DerivedClass1::f(float price)
{
cout << "the child class 1\n";
cout << price * .010f << endl;
}
class DerivedClass2:public BaseClass
{
public:
void f(float);
};
void DerivedClass2::f(float price)
{
cout << "the child class 2\n";
cout << price * .005f << endl;
}
void main()
{
DerivedClass1 myclass;
DerivedClass2 anotherclass;
myclass.f(100);
anotherclass.f(100);
getch();
}
```

Output:

the child class 1

```
1
the child class 2
0.5
```

Program 6: Write a C++ program to directly inherit two base classes.

```
#include<iostream.h>
#include<conio.h>
class BaseClass1
{
int a;
public:
BaseClass1(int x)
{
a = x;
}
int geta()
{
return a;
}
};
class BaseClass2
{
int b;
public:
BaseClass2(int x)
{
b = x;
}
int getb()
{
return b;
}
};
class DerivedClass : public BaseClass1, public BaseClass2
{
int c;
public:
DerivedClass(int x, int y, int z) : BaseClass1(z), BaseClass2(y){
c = x;
}
```

```
void show()
{
cout << geta() << ' ' << getb() << ' ';
cout << c << '\n';
}
};
void  main()
{
DerivedClass object(1, 2, 3);
object.show();
getch();
}
Output:
3 2 1
```

Program 7: Write a C++ program for derived Class and base Class.

```
#include<iostream.h>
#include<conio.h>
class Timer  // base class
{
protected:
int time;
public:
Timer():time(0)    //zero arg const....
{ }
Timer(int t):time(t)          // one args  const...
{ }
int get_time()
{
return time;
}
Timer operator ++()
{
return Timer(++time);
}
};
class Timert1 :public Timer //derived class
{
public:
Timer operator —()
```

```
{
return Timer(—time);
}
};
void main()
{
Timert1 t1;
cout <<"\nt1=" <<t1.get_time();
++t1;
++t1;
++t1;
cout <<"\nt1=" <<t1.get_time();
—t1;
—t1;
cout <<"\nt1=" <<t1.get_time();
cout <<endl;
getch();
}
Output:
t1=0
t1=3
t1=1
```

Program 8: Write a C++ program for adding a overloaded constructor to base class.

```
#include<iostream.h>
#include<conio.h>
#include <string.h>
class Shape
{
// private by default
double width;
double height;
public:
Shape()
{
width = height = 0.0;
}
Shape(double w, double h)
{
```

```
width = w;
height = h;
}
Shape(double x)
{
width = height = x;
}
void display()
{
cout << "Width and height are " << width << " and " << height << "\n";
}
double getWidth() { return width; }
double getHeight() { return height; }
void setWidth(double w) { width = w; }
void setHeight(double h) { height = h; }
};
class Triangle : public Shape
{
char style[20]; // now private
public:
Triangle()
{
strcpy(style, "unknown");
}
Triangle(char *str, double w, double h) : Shape(w, h)
{
strcpy(style, str);
}
Triangle(double x) : Shape(x)
{
strcpy(style, "isosceles");
}
double area()
{
return getWidth() * getHeight() / 2;
}
void showStyle()
{
cout << "Triangle is " << style << "\n";
```

```
}
};

void main()
{
Triangle t1;
Triangle t2("right", 8.0, 12.0);
Triangle t3(4.0);
t1 = t2;
cout << "Info for t1: \n";
t1.showStyle();
t1.display();
cout << "Area is " << t1.area() << "\n";
t2.showStyle();
t2.display();
cout << "Area is " << t2.area() << "\n";
t3.showStyle();
t3.display();
cout << "Area is " << t3.area() << "\n";
getch();
}
```

Output:

```
Info for t1:
Triangle is right
Width and height are 8 and 12
Area is 48
Triangle is right
Width and height are 8 and 12
Area is 48
Triangle is isosceles
Width and height are 4 and 4
Area is 8
```

PROGRAMMING PROBLEMS

Program 1: Write a C++ program for public inheritance.

Program 2: Write a C++ program to show public inheritance.

Program 3: Write a C++ program to inherit base as private.

Program 4: Write a C++ program to implement inheritance using the private identifier.

Program 5: Write a C++ program to Inherit base as protected.

Program 6: Write a C++ program to inherit protected fields.

Program 7: Write a C++ program to demonstrate inheriting a protected base class.

Program 8: Write a C++ program for inheritance and protected Members.

Program 9: Write a C++ program for Protected Base-Class Inheritance.

Program 10: Write a C++ program for single parameter base class,derived class constructors.

Program 11: Write a C++ program for base class and derived class.

Program 12: Write a C++ program to access member of base and use member of derived class.

Program 13: Write a C++ program for multiple inheritance.

Program 14: Write a C++ program for pass parameter to two base classes.

Program 15: Write a C++ program to directly inherit two base classes.

Program 16: Write a C++ program to compute marks to explain the concept of Multiple Inheritance.

Program 17: Write a C++ program for an example of multiple base classes.

Program 18: Write a C++ program for multiple inheritance with employees and degrees

Program 19: Write a C++ program for multiple Inheritance to have the features from both parent.

Program 20: Write a C++ program to resolving Ambiguity in Case of Multiple Inheritance involving Common Base Classes.

Program 21: Write a C++ program to Implement Hospital Management by 2 Classes with Inheritance.

Program 22: Write a C++ program to display the processing of the grade using the concept of inheritance.

Fill in the blanks

1. .... is the process by which new classes called *derived* classes are created from existing classes called *base* classes.
2. A base class's .... members can be accessed only in the base-class definition or in derived-class definitions.
3. In a .... relationship, an object of a derived class also can be treated as an object of its base class.

4. In a .... relationship, a class object has one or more objects of other classes as members.
5. In single inheritance, a class represents .... relationship with its derived classes.
6. A base class's .... members are accessible within that base class and anywhere that the program has a handle to an object of that base class or to an object of one of its derived classes.
7. A base class's protected access members have a level of protection between those of public and .... access.
8. C++ provides for ...., which allows a derived class to inherit from many base classes, even if these base classes are unrelated.
9. When an object of a derived class is instantiated, the base class's .... is called implicitly or explicitly to do any necessary initialization of the base-class data members in the derived-class object.

Answers

1. Inheritance. 2. protected. 3. is-a or inheritance. 4. has-a or composition or aggregation. 5. hierarchical. 6. public. 7. private. 8. multiple inheritance. 9. constructor.

OBJECTIVE TYPE QUESTIONS

1. The process of extracting the relevant attributes of an object is known as ....

   (a) polymorphism (b) inheritance
   (c) abstraction (d) data hiding
2. If no constructors can specified for a derived class, objects of the derived class will use the constructors in the base class.

   (a) true (b) false
3. Adding a derived class to a base class requires fundamental changes to the base class

   (a) true (b) false
4. In heritance is a way to

   (a) make general class into more specific classes
   (b) add features to existing classes without rewriting them
   (c) pass arguments to objects of classes
   (d) improve data-hiding and encapsulation.

5. Advantages of inheritance include
   (a) facilitating class libraries
   (b) avoiding the rewriting of code
   (c) providing a useful conceptual framework
   (d) providing class growth through natural selection.
6. Inheritance is the principle that
   (a) classes with the same name must be derived from one another
   (b) knowledge of a general category can be applied to more specific objects
   (c) C++ functions may be used only if they have logical predecessors (d) one function name may invoke different methods.
7. A derived class may also be called a
   (a) subclass (b) super class
   (c) parent class (d) derived class
8. A derived class .... overside attributes of a parent class
   (a) may
   (b) may if the two classes have the same name
   (c) must
   (d) must not
9. A function in a derived class that has the same name as a function in the parent class
   (a) will override the base class function
   (b) will cause an error message to display
   (c) will be overridden by the base class function
   (d) will execude immediately often the base class function executes.
10. Reference variables and const class member
    (a) must be assigned values in any derived class
    (b) must never be initialized in a base class
    (c) must be initialized, rather than assigned values
    (d) must not exit if a class is to be a base class
11. When you create a derived class and instantiate on object
    (a) the parent class object must be constructed first
    (b) the child object must be constructed first
    (c) the parent class object must not be constructed
    (d) the child class object must not be constructed.

12. It is illegal to make objects of one class members of another class
    (a) true (b) false
    (c) depends upon the kind of object
13. A class hierarchy
    (a) describes "is a kind of" relationships
    (b) describes "has a" relationships
    (c) shows the same relationships as an organization chart
    (d) shows the same relationships as a family tree.
14. A class D can be derived from a class C, which is derived from a class B, which is derived from a class A
    (a) true (b) false
15. Assume a class derv that is privately derived from class Base. An object of class Derv located in main() can access
    (a) public members of Base (b) protected members of Base
    (c) private members of Base (d) public members of Derv
16. It is sometimes useful to specify a class from which no objects will ever be created
    (a) true (b) false
17. The scope-resolution operator usually
    (a) specifies a particular class (b) resolves ambiguities
    (c) limits the visibility of variables to a certain function
18. If a base class member is private, then ....
    (a) if a derived class uses the public access specifier, the data member becomes public
    (b) if a derived class uses the protected access specifier, the data member becomes protected
    (c) both a and b
    (c) neither a nor b
19. Private data can be accessed by ....
    (a) class member function (b) functions in derived classes
    (c) both a and b (d) neither a nor b
20. If a class will serve as a base class, most often the base class data members are ....
    (a) private (b) protected
    (c) public (d) polymorphic

21. Which of the following are never inherited?
    (a) Public data members (b) Constructor functions
    (c) Void functions (d) Overloaded + operators.
22. If a derived class uses the public access specifier, then ....
    (a) public base class members remain public in the derived class
    (b) protected base class members become public in the derived class
    (c) both a and b
    (d) neither a nor b
23. You separate a derived class name from its access specifier with ....
    (a) a colon (b) two colons
    (c) at least one space (d) a semicolon.
24. When a class serves as a base class to others, ...
    (a) all of its members are inherited
    (b) all of its members are inherited, except for any private members
    (c) all of its members are inherited except for any protected members
    (d) None
25. When a new class is derived from an existing class, the derived class member functions .... have names that differ from base class function names
    (a) may
    (b) may if the two classes have the same name
    (c) must
    (d) must not
26. When a class is derived from anther derived class, the newly derived class ....
    (a) may have more liberal access to a base class member than its immediate predecessor
    (b) may have the same type of access to a base class member as its immediate predecessor
    (c) may have more limited access to a base class member than its immediate predecessor
    (d) both b and c
27. A base class may also be called a ....
    (a) child class (b) subclass
    (c) derived class (d) parent class

28. A derived class may also be called a ....
    (a) subclass (b) super class
    (c) parent class (d) base class
29. A derived class .... override attributes of a parent class
    (a) may
    (b) may if the two classes have the same name
    (c) must
    (d) must not
30. Inheritance is the principle that ....
    (a) classes with the same name must be derived from one another
    (b) knowledge of a general category can be applied to more specific objects
    (c) C++ functions may be used only if they have logical predecessors
    (d) one function name may invoke different methods.
31. Compared with the classes from which key are derived, inherited classes may have ....
    (a) additional data members (b) additional member functions
    (c) both a and b (d) neither a nor b
32. To be called object-oriented, a programming language must allow ....
    (a) functions that return only a single value
    (b) #include files
    (c) inheritance
    (d) All
33. Code that has already been tested is said to be ....
    (a) inherited (b) reusable
    (c) reliable (d) polymorphic
34. A major advantage of inheritance is ....
    (a) reducing the time it takes to create new objects
    (b) not having to think about how objects will be used
    (c) reducing the amount of memory required to execute a program
    (d) enabling people who have not studied programming to create useful applications.
35. Object-oriented programmers primarily focus on ....
    (a) procedures to be performed
    (b) the step-by-step statements needed to solve a problem

(c) objects and the tasks that must be performed with those objects

(d) the physical orientation of objects within a program.

EXERCISES

1. What do you mean by Inheritance?
2. Why the need for inheritance in C++?
3. What are the various issues in inheritance.
4. What are the advantages and disadvantages of inheritance.
5. What are the various types of Inheritance?
6. Differentiate between base and derived class.?
7. What are the available accessibility modes in inheritance.
8. Explain the relationship between private , public and protected inheritance.
9. Explain the concept of private , public and protected access specifier.
10. Explain concept of constructor and destructor in inheritance.
11. Tell the order of constructor and destructor calls.
12. Explain the meaning of overriding member function.
13. How can you declare a derived base class constructor?
14. What do you mean by overriding member function? Explain with an appropriate example?
15. How inheritance occurs and works in different levels? Explain with an appropriate example?
16. What do you mean by multiple inheritances? How can you relate it with the single inheritance?
17. What is the ambiguity problem occurs with the multiple inheritance?
18. Explain the concept of level of inheritance.
19. Explain the relationship between friend function and inheritance.
20. What do you mean by hierarchical inheritance.
21. Explain the use of virtual base classes or virtual inheritance.
22. Explain the concept of aggregation and composition in detail.

CHAPTER 12

Polymorphism and Virtual Function

12.1 INTRODUCTION

Polymorphism is the ability to use an operator or function in different ways. Polymorphism gives different meanings or functions to the operators or functions. Poly, referring too many, morphism means forms or uses signifies the many uses of these operators and functions. A single function usage or an operator functioning in many ways can be called polymorphism. Polymorphism refers to codes, operations or objects that behave differently in different contexts.

Polymorphism, one of the three main attributes of an OOP language, denotes a process by which different implementations of a function can be accessed by the use of a single name. It is the capability to call different functions by just using one type of function call. It is useful since it can group classes and their functions together. Polymorphism is the most important part of Object-Oriented Programming. Some people feel that if they have an idea of what classes are they have stepped in the object-oriented world. But this is not true. Polymorphism is the core of object-oriented programming and if anybody stops here he's missing out the best part of Object Oriented Programming (OOP). And it is easy to grasp well.

Example: If you want to make a picture with circles, squares, lines and triangles we can make a class Shape and create an instance of it like this:

```
Shape *s[100];
```

Here all the addresses of the objects of the other classes are stored in the Shape Array. And then to draw the Picture all we have to do is:

```
for(int i=0;i<=100;i++)
s[i]->draw();
```

When the loop runs different draw functions of each class is called because the implementation of Functions from different classes are through the same function call.

The Array s[] has been defined to contain shape pointers and not square or triangle pointers.

12.2 POLYMORPHISM

Polymorphism is one of the most important principles of object oriented language. Polymorphism means many forms i.e. one interface multiple methods. The specific method to call depends on the nature of the situation. No matter what type of car it is the driving mechanism is the same. For example, you might have a program that defines three different types of stacks. One stack is used for integer values, one for character values, and one for floating-point values. Because of polymorphism, you can define one set of names, push() and pop() , that can be used for all three stacks. In your program you will create three specific versions of these functions, one for each type of stack, but names of the functions will be the same. The compiler will automatically select the right function based upon the data being stored. Thus, the interface to a stack—the functions push() and pop() —are the same no matter which type of stack is being used.

Definition: *"Polymorphism is defined as one interface to control access to a general class of actions."*

There are mainly two types of polymorphism one is **compile time polymorphism** and the other is **run time polymorphism**. Compile time polymorphism is functions and operators overloading. Runtime time polymorphism is done using inheritance and virtual functions.

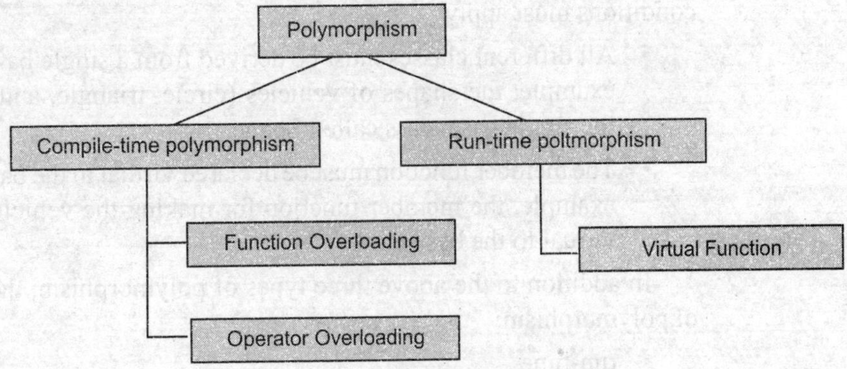

Figure 12.1: Types of polymorphism

Below is a simple example of the above concept of polymorphism:

6 + 10

The above refers to integer addition.

The same + operator can be used with different meanings with strings:

"student" + "Training"

The same + operator can also be used for floating point addition:

7.15 + 3.78

Polymorphism is a powerful feature of the object oriented programming language C++. A single operator + behaves differently in different contexts such as integer, float or strings referring the concept of *polymorphism*. The above concept leads to operator *overloading*. The concept of overloading is also a branch of *polymorphism*. When the exiting operator or function operates on new data type it is *overloaded*. This feature of polymorphism leads to the concept of *virtual methods*.

Polymorphism refers to the ability to call different functions by using only one type of function call. Suppose a programmer wants to code vehicles of different shapes such as circles, squares, rectangles, etc. One way to define each of these classes is to have a member function for each that makes vehicles of each shape. Another convenient approach the programmer can take is to define a base class named Shape and then create an instance of that class. The programmer can have array that hold pointers to all different objects of the vehicle followed by a simple loop structure to make the vehicle, as per the shape desired, by inserting pointers into the defined array. This approach leads to different functions executed by the same function call. Polymorphism is used to give different meanings to the same concept. This is the basis for *Virtual function* implementation.

In polymorphism, a single function or an operator functioning in many ways depends upon the usage to function properly. In order for this to occur, the following conditions must apply:

- All different classes must be derived from a single base class. In the above example, the shapes of vehicles (circle, triangle, and rectangle) are from the single base class called Shape.
- The member function must be declared virtual in the base class. In the above example, the member function for making the vehicle should be made as virtual to the base class.

In addition to the above three types of polymorphism, there exist other kinds of polymorphism:

- run-time
- compile-time
- ad-hoc polymorphism
- parametric polymorphism or pure polymorphism

Other types of polymorphism defined

run-time

The *run-time* polymorphism is implemented with inheritance and virtual functions.

compile-time

The *compile-time* polymorphism is implemented with templates.

ad-hoc polymorphism

If the range of actual types that can be used is finite and the combinations must be individually specified prior to use, this is called *ad-hoc* polymorphism.

parametric polymorphism

If all code is written without mention of any specific type and thus can be used transparently with any number of new types it is called *parametric* polymorphism.

12.3 BINDING

Binding refers to the act of associating an object or a class with its member. If we can call a method fn() on an object ob of a class c, we say that the object ob is binded with the method fn(). This happens at compile time and is known as static or compile - time binding. The calls to the virtual member functions are resolved during run-time. This mechanism is known as dynamic binding. The most prominent reason why a virtual function will be used is to have a different functionality in the derived class. The difference between a non-virtual member function and a virtual member function is the non-virtual member functions are resolved at compile time.

12.3.1 Compile Time Polymorphism or Static Binding

To understand the compile time polymorphism, come to the concept of the **function overloading**. Function overloading is the process of using the same function name for more than one operation.

The requirement in creating more than one function with the same name is that the compiler must be able to determine which function to use, on the basis of the number of arguments and the types of these arguments.

Since the compiler selects the appropriate function for a particular call at the compile time, hence this type of polymorphism is known as the **compile time polymorphism**, or **early binding**, or **static binding**.

Now, consider a case when both the base class and the derived class have the same function name, with the same number and type of arguments. In such situations, the compiler is unable to detect that what function should be invoked (member function of the base class or member function of the derived class). For example, consider the following program: having a base class B and a derived class D, inherited from the base class B. Each of these classes have the same member function Display( ).

Program 1: Write a C++ program for compile time polymorphism (without virtual function).

```
#include<iostream.h>
#include<conio.h>
class B                                    // Base Class
{
public:
void Display(void)
{
cout << "\n The member function of the base class B is invoked " ;
}
} ;
class D1 : public B                        // First derived class
{
public:
void Display(void)
{
cout << "\n The member function of the derived class D1 is invoked " ;
}
};
class D2 : public B                        // Second derived class
{
public:
void Display(void)
{
cout << "\n The member function of the derived class D2 is invoked " ;
}
};
void main(void)
{
B* base_ptr ;              // pointer to the object of the base class B
D1 der1_obj ;              // object of the first derived class D1
base_ptr = &der1_obj ;
base_ptr->Display( ) ;           // Accessing the member function
Display( )
```

```
D2 der2_obj ;                   // object of the second derived class D2
base_ptr = &der2_obj ;
base_ptr->Display( ) ;          // Accessing the member function
Display( )
getch();
}
```

Doesn't the compiler complain that we are assigning an address of one type D1 to a pointer of another B. The compiler is perfectly happy, because type checking has been relaxed in this situation. The rule is that pointers to objects of a derived class are type-compatible with pointers to object of the base class.

12.3.2 Run-time Polymorphism or Dynamic Binding

In place of static binding, one would like a binding method that is capable of determining which function should be invoked at run-time, on the basis of object type making call.

This type of binding is knows as **late or dynamic binding**, since the selection of the appropriate function is done dynamically at run-time. To achieve dynamic binding, C++ offers a special feature known as **virtual function**. A virtual function specification tells the compiler to create a pointer to a function but not to fill in the value of the pointer until the function is actually called.

Then at run-time and on the basis of the object making the call, the appropriate function address is used.

When a function with same name, same number of arguments and same type of arguments is used in both the base class and derived classes, the function in the base class can be made virtual by using a keyword virtual, preceding the function declaration.

For example, in the previous program, the function Display() in the base class B can be made virtual, by using the declaration as:

```
virtual void Display(void);
```

When a function is made virtual, C++ determines which function to use at run-time based on the type of the object pointed to by the base class pointer, rather than the type of the pointer. Now, consider the following program, which is same as that of the previous program, but the member function Display( ) in the base class B is made virtual.

Program 2: Write a C++ program for run time polymorphism.

```
// This program illustrates the use of the virtual function
#include<iostream.h>
#include<conio.h>
class B                                 // Base class
```

```
{
public:
virtual void Display(void)          // virtual function
{
cout << "\n The member function Display( ) " ;
cout << "of the \"Base Class B\" is invoked \n" ;
}
};
class D1 : public B                 // First derived class
{
public:
void Display(void)
{
cout << "\n The member function Display( ) " ;
cout << "of the \"Derived Class D1\" is invoked \n" ;
}
};
class D2 : public B                 // Second derived class
{
public:
void Display(void)
{
cout << "\n The member function Display() " ;
cout << "of the \"Derived Class D2\" is invoked " ;
}
};
void main(void)
{
B* base_ptr ;                 // pointer to the object of the base class B
D1 der1_obj ;                 // object of the first derived class D1
base_ptr = &der1_obj ;
base_ptr->Display( ) ;        // Accessing the member function Display( )
D2 der2_obj ;                 // object of the second derived class D2
base_ptr = &der2_obj ;
base->ptr->Display( ) ;       // Accessing the member function Display( )
getch();
}
```

12.4 STATIC VS DYNAMIC POLYMORPHISM

Static polymorphism is considered more efficient and dynamic polymorphism more flexible.

Statically bound methods are those methods that are bound to their calls at compile time. Dynamic function calls are bound to the functions during run-time. This involves the additional step of searching the functions during run-time. On the other hand, no run-time search is required for statically bound functions.

As applications are becoming larger and more complicated, the need for flexibility is increasing rapidly. Most users have to periodically upgrade their software, and this could become a very tedious task if static polymorphism is applied. This is because any change in requirements requires a major modification in the code. In the case of dynamic binding, the function calls are resolved at run-time, thereby giving the user the flexibility to alter the call without having to modify the code.

To the programmer, efficiency and performance would probably be a primary concern, but to the user, flexibility or maintainability may be much more important. The decision is thus a trade-off between efficiency and flexibility.

12.5 FEATURES AND ADVANTAGES OF THE CONCEPT OF POLYMORPHISM

Following are the various features and advantages of polymorphism:

1. ***Applications are easily extendable:*** Once an application is written using the concept of polymorphism, it can easily be extended, providing new objects that conform to the original interface. It is unnecessary to recompile original programs by adding new types. Only re-linking is necessary to exhibit the new changes along with the old application. This is the greatest achievement of C++ object-oriented programming. In programming language, there has always been a need for adding and customizing. By utilizing the concept of polymorphism, time and work effort is reduced in addition to making future maintenance easier.
2. Helps in reusability of code.
3. Provides easier maintenance of applications.
4. Helps in achieving robustness in applications.

12.6 FUNCTION OVERLOADING

One way that C++ achieves polymorphism is through the use of function overloading. In C++ enables several functions of the same name to be defined, as long as these functions have different sets of parameters (at least as far as the parameter types or the number of parameters or the orders of the parameter types are concerned). This capability is called **function overloading**. When an overloaded function is called, the C++ compiler selects the proper function by examining the number, types and order of the arguments in the call. Function overloading is commonly used to create several functions of the same name that perform similar tasks, but on different data types. For example, many functions in the math library are overloaded for different numeric data types.

Definition: *"In C++, two or more functions can share the same name as long as their parameter declarations are different. In this situation, the functions that share the same name are said to be overloaded, and the process is referred to as function overloading."*

Definition: *"Function overloading is the process of using the same name for two or more functions. The secret to overloading is that each redefinition of the function must use either different types of parameters or a different number of parameters. It is only through these differences that the compiler knows which function to call in any given situation."*

When you overload a function, you use the same name but you must use different parameters. If you don't the compiler won't know that they are different functions.

The general syntax to overload a function:

```
return type functionname(datatype arguments);
```

Here return type or data type is of int, float, double, char etc.

12.6.1 Why Function Overloading is Important

To see why function overloading is important, first consider three functions defined by the C subset: **abs(), labs(), and fabs().** The **abs()** function returns the absolute value of an integer, **labs()** returns the absolute value of a **long**, and **fabs()** returns the absolute value of a **double**. Although these functions perform almost identical actions, in C three slightly different names must be used to represent these essentially similar tasks. This makes the situation more complex, conceptually, than it actually is. Even though the underlying concept of each function is the same, the programmer has to remember three things, not just one. However, in C++, you can use just one name for all three functions, as this program illustrates:

Program 3: Write a C++ program to explain use of function overloading.

```
#include <iostream.h>
#include <conio.h>
```

```
// abs is overloaded three ways
int abs(int i);
double abs(double d);
long abs(long l);
void main()
{
cout << abs(-10) << "\n";
cout << abs(-11.0) << "\n";
cout << abs(-9L) << "\n";
getch();
}
int abs(int i)
{
cout << "Using integer abs()\n";
return i<0 ? -i : i;
}
double abs(double d)
{
cout << "Using double abs()\n";
return d<0.0 ? -d : d;
}
long abs(long l)
{
cout << "Using long abs()\n";
return l<0 ? -l : l;
}
```

Output:

```
Using integer abs()
10
Using double abs()
11
Using long abs()
9
```

This program creates three similar but different functions called abs(), each of which returns the absolute value of its argument. The compiler knows which function to call in each situation because of the type of the argument. The value of overloaded functions is that they allow related sets of functions to be accessed with a common name. Thus, the name abs() represents the general action that is being performed. It is left to the compiler to choose the right specific method for a particular circumstance. You need only remember the general action being performed. Due to polymorphism, three things to remember have been reduced to one. This example is fairly trivial, but if you expand the concept, you can see how polymorphism can help you manage very complex programs.

12.6.2 Advantage of Function Overloading

In overloaded functions, the function call determines which function definition will be executed. The biggest advantage of overloading is that it helps us to perform same operations on different datatypes without having the need to use separate names for each version.

Program 4: Write a C++ program for function overloading.

```
#include<iostream.h>
#include<conio.h>
int abslt(int);
long abslt(long);
float abslt(float);
double abslt(double);
void main()
{
int intgr=-5;
long lng=34225;
float flt=-5.56;
double dbl=-45.6768;
cout<<\" absoulte value of \"<<intgr<<\" = \"<<abslt(intgr)<<endl;
cout<<\" absoulte value of \"<<lng<<\" = \"<<abslt(lng)<<endl;
cout<<\" absoulte value of \"<<flt<<\" = \"<<abslt(flt)<<endl;
cout<<\" absoulte value of \"<<dbl<<\" = \"<<abslt(dbl)<<endl;
getch();
}
int abslt(int num)
{
if(num>=0)
return num;
else
 return (-num);
}
long abslt(long num)
{
```

```
if(num>=0)
return num;
else return (-num);
}
float abslt(float  num)
{
if(num>=0)
return num;
else return (-num);
}
double abslt(double  num)
{
if(num>=0)
return num;
else return (-num);
}
```

Output:

```
absoulte value of -5 = 5
absoulte value of 34225 = 34225
absoulte value of -5.56 = 5.56
absoulte value of -45.6768 = 45.6768
```

The above function finds the absolute value of any number int, long, float , double.

In C, the above is implemented as a set of different function abs()-for int, fabs()-for double ,labs()-for long. The use of overloading may not have reduced the code complexity /size but has definitely made it easier to understand and avoided the necessity of remembering different names for each version function which perform identically the same task.

***Note:** But overloading of functions with different return types are not allowed.*

12.7 TYPES OF FUNCTION OVERLOADING

Mainly the function can be overloaded using three ways:

1. Function having same name but different number of arguments
2. Function having same name but different datatypes
3. Function having same name but different datatypes and different number of arguments

12.7.1 Function having Same Name but Different Number of Arguments

A program given below having same function name func() but have different number of arguments like int func(int i), int func(int i,int j).

Program 5: Write a C++ program for function overloading (Different number of arguments).

```
#include <iostream.h>
#include<conio.h>
int func(int i);
int func(int i,int j);
void main()
{
cout <<func(20)<<" ";
cout <<func(6,8);
getch();
}
int func(int i)
{
return i;
}
int func(int i,int j)
{
return i*j;
}
```

Output:

20 48

12.7.2 Function Having Same Name but Different Datatypes

A program given below having same function name func() but have different datatypes like int func(int i), double func(double i).

Program 6: Write a C++ program for function overloading(Different data types).

```
#include <iostream.h>
#include<conio.h>
int func(int i);
double func(double i);
void main()
{
```

```
cout <<func(20)<<" ";
cout <<func(6.4);
getch();
}
double func(double i)
{
return i;
}
int func(int i)
{
return i;
}
```

Output:

20 6.4

As mentioned, the key point about function overloading is that the functions must differ in regard to the types and/or number of parameters. Two functions differing only in their return types cannot be overloaded. For example, this is an invalid attempt to overload **myfunc():**

```
int myfunc(int i); // Error: differing return types are
float myfunc(int i); // insufficient when overloading.
```

Sometimes, two function declarations will appear to differ, when in fact they do not.

For example, consider the following declarations.

```
void f(int *p);
void f(int p[]); // error, *p is same as p[]
```

Remember, to the compiler ***p** is the same as **p[ ]**. Therefore, although the two prototypes appear to differ in the types of their parameter, in actuality they do not.

12.7.3 Function having same Name but Different Datatypes and Different Number of Arguments

A program given below having same function name void show() but have different number of arguments like void show (char a), void show (char a, int n).

Program 7: Write a C++ program to illustrate the use of overloaded function show ( ) having different number of arguments in the different overloaded forms.

```
#include<iostream.h>
#include<conio.h>
void show (char a)
```

```
{
cout<<"\n Function taking single argument is: \n" ;
cout<<a;
}
void show (char  a, int n)
{
cout<<"\n Function taking double argument is: \n" ;
cout<< a ;
cout<<"\n" << n ;
}
void main ( )
{
void show(char);
void show(char, int);
char a[30] = "Khalsa College, Asr" ;
int n = 20 ;
show (a) ;
show (a, n) ;
getch( ) ;
}
```

Output:

```
Function taking single argument is:
Khalsa College, Asr
Function taking double argument is:
Khalsa College, Asr
20
```

Program 8: Write a C++ program to compute sum by using different types of function by using the concept of Function Overloading.

```
// Program to overload functions.
#include<iostream.h>
#include<conio.h>
int sum(int a,int b)
{
return a+b;
}
float sum(float a,float b)
{
return a+b;
}
```

```
void main()
{
int i,j;
float k,l;
int sum(int, int);
float sum(float, float);
cout<<"\nEnter two integer numbers:";
cin>>i>>j;
cout<<"\nSum of "<<i<<" & "<<j<<" is "<<sum(i,j);
cout<<"\nEnter two float numbers:";
cin>>k>>l;
cout<<"\nSum of "<<k<<" & "<<l<<" is "<<sum(k,l);
getch();
}
```

Output:

```
Enter two integer numbers: 5  7
Sum of 5 & 7 is 12
Enter two float numbers: 2.5  3.2
Sum of 2.5 & 3.2 is 5.7
```

12.8 POINTERS TO BASE CLASS

One of the key features of derived classes is that a pointer to a derived class is type-compatible with a pointer to its base class. Polymorphism is the art of taking advantage of this simple but powerful and versatile feature, which brings Object Oriented Methodologies to its full potential.

We are going to start by writing our program about the rectangle and the triangle taking into consideration this pointer compatibility property:

Program 9: Write a C++ program for pointer to base class.

```
// pointers to base class
#include <iostream.h>
#include <conio.h>
class CPolygon
{
protected:
int width, height;
public:
void set_values (int a, int b)
{
```

```
width=a; height=b;
}
};
class CRectangle: public CPolygon
{
public:
int area ()
{
return (width * height);
}
};
class CTriangle: public CPolygon
{
public:
int area ()
{
return (width * height / 2);
}
};
void main ()
{
CRectangle rect;
CTriangle trgl;
CPolygon * ppoly1 = &rect;
CPolygon * ppoly2 = &trgl;
ppoly1->set_values (4,5);
ppoly2->set_values (4,5);
cout << rect.area() << endl;
cout << trgl.area() << endl;
getch();
}
```

Output:

20

10

In function main, we create two pointers that point to objects of class CPolygon (ppoly1 and ppoly2). Then we assign references to rect and trgl to these pointers, and because both are objects of classes derived from CPolygon, both are valid assignations.

The only limitation in using *ppoly1 and *ppoly2 instead of rect and trgl is that both *ppoly1 and *ppoly2 are of type CPolygon* and therefore we can only use these pointers to refer to the members that CRectangle and CTriangle inherit from CPolygon. For that reason when we call the area() members at the end of the program we have had to use directly the objects rect and trgl instead of the pointers *ppoly1 and *ppoly2.

In order to use area() with the pointers to class CPolygon, this member should also have been declared in the class CPolygon, and not only in its derived classes, but the problem is that CRectangle and CTriangle implement different versions of area, therefore we cannot implement it in the base class. This is why we use virtual functions.

12.9 POINTERS TO DERIVED TYPES

We learned earlier in this chapter that a pointer of one type may not point to an object of another type. You'll now learn about the one exception to this general rule: a pointer to an object of a base class can also point to any object derived from that base class.

Similarly, a reference to a base class can also reference any object derived from the original base class. In other words, a base class reference parameter can receive an object of types derived from the base class, as well as objects within the base class itself.

Program 10: Write a C++ program for pointer to derived objects.

```
#include <iostream.h>
#include <string.h>
#include<conio.h>
class A
{
char author[80];
public:
void put_a(char *s)
{
strcpy(author, s);
}
void show_a()
{
cout << author << "\n";
}
};
```

```
class B : public A
{
char title[80];
public:
void put_t(char *num)
{
strcpy(title, num);
}
void show_t()
{
cout << "Title: ";
cout << title << "\n";
}
};
void main()
{
A *ptr;
A a;
B *bptr;
B b;
ptr = &a;
ptr->put_a("I Singh ");
ptr = &b;
ptr->put_a("R Singh ");
a.show_a();
b.show_a();
cout << "\n";
bptr = &b;
bptr->put_t("Exploring Vista");
ptr->show_a();
bptr->show_t( );
getch();
}
```

Output:

```
I Singh
R Singh

R Singh
Title: Exploring Vista
```

Program 11: Write a C++ program for pointer to derived objects.

```
#include <iostream.h>
#include <conio.h>
class BaseClass
{
int x;
public:
void setx(int i)
{
x = i;
}
int getx()
{
return x;
}
};
class DerivedClass : public BaseClass
{
int y;
public:
void sety(int i)
{
y = i;
}
int gety()
{
return y;
}
};
void main()
{
BaseClass *p;                  // pointer to BaseClass type
BaseClass baseObject;          // object of BaseClass
DerivedClass derivedObject; // object of DerivedClass
p = &baseObject;               // use p to access BaseClass object
p->setx(10);                   // access BaseClass object
cout << "Base object x: " << p->getx() << '\n';
p = &derivedObject;            // point to DerivedClass object
p->setx(99);                   // access DerivedClass object
```

```
derivedObject.sety(88);          // can't use p to set y, so do it directly
cout << "Derived object x: " << p->getx() << '\n';
cout << "Derived object y: " << derivedObject.gety() << '\n';
getch();
}
```

Output:

```
Base object x: 10
Derived object x: 99
Derived object y: 88
```

12.10 VIRTUAL FUNCTIONS

Polymorphism is also achieved in C++ using virtual functions. If a function with same name exists in base as well as parent class, then the pointer to the base class would call the functions associated only with the base class. However, if the function is made virtual and the base pointer is initialized with the address of the derived class, then the function in the child class would be called.

Virtual, as the name implies, is something that exists in effect but not in reality. The concept of virtual function is the same as a function, but it does not really exist although it appears in needed places in a program. The object-oriented programming language C++ implements the concept of virtual function as a simple member function, like all member functions of the class.

The functionality of virtual functions can be over-ridden in its derived classes. The programmer must pay attention not to confuse this concept with function overloading. Function overloading is a different concept and will be explained in previous sections of this chapter. Virtual function is a mechanism to implement the concept of polymorphism (the ability to give different meanings to one function).

Definition: *"A virtual function is a special type of function that resolves to the most-derived version of the function with the same signature. To make a function virtual, simply place the "virtual" keyword before the function declaration."*

Note that virtual functions and virtual base classes are two entirely different concepts, even though they share the same keyword.

12.10.1 Properties of Virtual Functions

Following are the various properties of virtual functions:

1. **Dynamic Binding Property:** Virtual Functions are resolved during run-time or dynamic binding. Virtual functions are also simple member functions. The main difference between a non-virtual C++ member function and a

virtual member function is in the way they are both resolved. A non-virtual C++ member function is resolved during compile time or static binding. Virtual Functions are resolved during run-time or dynamic binding

2. Virtual functions are member functions of a class.
3. Virtual functions are declared with the keyword virtual, detailed in an example below.
4. Virtual function takes a different functionality in the derived class.

12.11 HOW VIRTUAL FUNCTION SUPPORTS POLYMORPHISM

A virtual function is a member function that is declared within a base class and redefined by a derived class. To create virtual function, precede the function's declaration in the base class with the keyword virtual. When a class containing virtual function is inherited, the derived class redefines the virtual function to suit its own needs.

Base class pointer can point to derived class object. In this case, using base class pointer if we call some function which is in both classes, then base class function is invoked. But if we want to invoke derived class function using base class pointer, it can be achieved by defining the function as virtual in base class, this is how virtual functions support runtime polymorphism.

12.12 DESCRIBE THE VIRTUAL FUNCTION AND VIRTUAL TABLE

A virtual function in C++ is

- A simple member function of a class which is declared with "virtual" keyword
- It usually performs different functionality in its derived classes.
- The resolving of the function call is done at run-time.

A virtual table is a mechanism to perform dynamic polymorphism i.e., run time binding. Virtual table is used to resolve the function calls at runtime. Every class that uses virtual functions is provided with its own virtual functions.

Every entry in the virtual table is a pointer that points to the derived function that is accessible by that class. A hidden pointer is added by a compiler to the base class which in turn calls *_vptr which is automatically set when an instance of the class is created and it points to the virtual table for that class.

12.13 DECLARATION OF VIRTUAL FUNCTION

Virtual functions are member functions declared with the keyword virtual.

The general syntax to declare a Virtual Function uses:

```
class classname                //This denotes the base class of C++ virtual
function
{
public:
virtual void memberfunctionname() //This denotes the C++ virtual function
{
.............

............
}
};
```

Program 12: Write a C++ program for virtual member functions accessed with Pointers.

```
#include <iostream.h>
#include<conio.h>
class Base
{
public:
virtual void show()
{
cout <<"Base \n ";
}
};
class Derv1 :public Base
{
public:
void show()
{
cout <<"Derv1 \n ";
}
};
class Derv2 :public Base
{
public:
void show()
{
cout <<"Derv2 \n ";
}
};
```

```
void main()
{
Derv1 d1;
Derv2 d2;
Base *ptr;//pointer to base class
ptr =&d1;//put address of dv1 in pointer
ptr->show();//execute show()
ptr =&d2;//put address of dv2 in pointer
ptr->show();//execute show()
getch();
}
```

Output:

Derv1
Derv2

Program 13: Write a C++ program for Virtual Functions.

```
#include <iostream.h>
#include<conio.h>
class A
{
public:
virtual void func()
{
cout <<"Base class(A) virtual func().\n";
}
};
class B :public A
{
public:
void func()
{
cout <<"Derived class(B) func().\n";
}
};
class C :public A
{
public:
void func()
{
cout <<"Derived class(C) func().\n";
```

```
}
};
void main()
{
A *ptr,b;
B b1;
C c1;
//point to base
ptr =&b;
ptr->func();
ptr =&b1;
ptr->func();
ptr =&c1;
ptr->func();
getch();
}
```

Output:

Base class(A) virtual func().
Derived class(B) func().
Derived class(C) func().

12.14 RULES FOR VIRTUAL FUNCTIONS

Following are the rules for virtual functions:

1. The virtual function must be member of class
2. They cannot be static members
3. They are accessed by using object pointers
4. Prototype of base class function & derived class must be same
5. Virtual function in base class must be defined even though it is not used
6. A virtual function can be friend function of another class
7. We could not have virtual constructor
8. If a virtual function is derived in base class, it need not be necessarily redefined in the derived class
9. Pointer object of base class can point to any object of derived class but reverse is not true
10. When a base pointer points to derived class, incrementing & decrementing it will not make it point to the next object of derived class

12.15 NEED FOR VIRTUAL FUNCTION

The vital reason for having a virtual function is to implement a different functionality in the derived class.

For example: a Make function in a class Vehicle may have to make a Vehicle with red color. A class called FourWheeler, derived or inherited from Vehicle, may have to use a blue background and 4 tires as wheels. For this scenario, the Make function for FourWheeler should now have a different functionality from the one at the class called Vehicle. This concept is called Virtual Function.

Referring back to the Vehicle example, the declaration of Virtual function would take the shape below:

```
class Vehicle          //This denotes the base class of C++ virtual function
{
public:
virtual void Make()    //This denotes the C++ virtual function
{
cout <<"Member function of Base Class Vehicle Accessed"<<endl;
}
};
```

After the virtual function is declared, the derived class is defined. In this derived class, the new definition of the virtual function takes place.

When the class FourWheeler is derived or inherited from Vehicle and defined by the virtual function in the class FourWheeler, it is written as:

```
class Vehicle          //This denotes the base class of C++ virtual function
{
public:
virtual void Make()    //This denotes the C++ virtual function
{
cout <<"Member function of Base Class Vehicle Accessed"<<endl;
}
};
class FourWheeler : public Vehicle
{
public:
void Make()
{
cout<<"Virtual Member function of Derived class FourWheeler
Accessed"<<endl;
}
```

```
};
void main()
{
Vehicle *a, *b;
a = new Vehicle();
a->Make();
b = new FourWheeler();
b->Make();
}
```

In the above example, it is evidenced that after declaring the member functions Make() as virtual inside the base class Vehicle, class FourWheeler is derived from the base class Vehicle. In this derived class, the new implementation for virtual function Make() is placed.

The programmer might be surprised to see the function call differs and the output is then printed as above. If the member function has not been declared as virtual, the base class member function is always called because linking takes place during compile time and is therefore static.

In this example, the member function is declared virtual and the address is bounded only during run time, making it dynamic binding and thus the derived class member function is called.

To achieve the concept of dynamic binding in C++, the compiler creates a v-table each time a virtual function is declared. This v-table contains classes and pointers to the functions from each of the objects of the derived class. This is used by the compiler whenever a virtual function is needed.

12.16 USES OF VIRTUAL FUNCTIONS

In large, complex programs, virtual functions allow the programmer to simplify the programming process. If used correctly, the base class will successfully define the interface of its derived classes. However, the program will leave the implementation of this interface up to the derived classes. Therefore, the programmer can use one interface for multiple implementations. This capability also allows for the creation of class libraries, which establish standard interfaces, but allow the programmer to tailor these interfaces to any unique implementation situations that may arise. One of the most popular libraries around is the Microsoft Foundation Classes (MFC) library, which provides the interfaces necessary for programming in the Windows environment. This library frees the programmer from having to reinvent the Windows interfaces, instead allowing him or her to focus on the specific implementation of these interfaces.

Program 14: Write a C++ program for Virtual functions and polymorphism.

```
#include <iostream.h>
#include<conio.h>
class figure
{
protected:
double x, y;
public:
void set_dim(double i, double j=0)
{
x = i;
y = j;
}
virtual void show_area()
{
cout << "No area computation defined ";
cout << "for this class.\n";
}
} ;
class triangle : public figure
{
public:
void show_area()
{
cout << "Triangle with height ";
cout << x << " and base " << y;
cout << " has an area of ";
cout << x * 0.5 * y << ".\n";
}
};
class square : public figure
{
public:
void show_area()
{
cout << "Square with dimensions ";
cout << x << "x" << y;
cout << " has an area of ";
cout << x *  y << ".\n";
```

```
}
};
class circle : public figure
{
public:
void show_area()
{
cout << "Circle with radius ";
cout << x;
cout << " has an area of ";
cout << 3.14 * x * x << ".\n";
}
};
void main()
{
 figure *p; // create a pointer to base type
 triangle t; // create objects of derived types
 square s;
 circle c;
 p = &t;
 p->set_dim(10.0, 5.0);
 p->show_area();
 p = &s;
 p->set_dim(10.0, 5.0);
 p->show_area();
 p = &c;
 p->set_dim(9.0);
 p->show_area();
 getch();
}
```

Output:

Triangle with height 10 and base 5 has an area of 25.

Square with dimensions 10*5 has an area of 50.

Circle with radius 9 has an area of 254.34.

12.17 HOW DOES A VIRTUAL FUNCTION WORK?

Whenever a program has a virtual function declared, a v-table is constructed for the class. The v-table consists of addresses to the virtual functions for classes that contain one or more virtual functions. The object of the class containing the virtual function contains a virtual pointer that points to the base address of the virtual table in memory. Whenever there is a virtual function call, the v-table is used to resolve to the function address. An object of the class that contains one or more virtual functions contains a virtual pointer called the vptr at the very beginning of the object in the memory. Hence the size of the object in this case increases by the size of the pointer. This vptr contains the base address of the virtual table in memory. Note that virtual tables are class specific, i.e., there is only one virtual table for a class irrespective of the number of virtual functions it contains. This virtual table in turn contains the base addresses of one or more virtual functions of the class. At the time when a virtual function is called on an object, the vptr of that object provides the base address of the virtual table for that class in memory. This table is used to resolve the function call as it contains the addresses of all the virtual functions of that class. This is how dynamic binding is resolved during a virtual function call.

The following code shows how we can write a virtual function in C++ and then use the same to achieve dynamic or runtime polymorphism.

```
#include <iostream.h>
#include <conio.h>
class base
{
public:
virtual void display()
{
cout<<"\nBase";
}
};
class derived : public base
{
public:
void display()
{
cout<<"\nDerived";
}
};
void main()
{
base *ptr = new derived();
ptr->display();
getch();
}
```

In the above example, the pointer is of type base but it points to the derived class object. The method display() is virtual in nature. Hence in order to resolve the virtual method call, the context of the pointer is considered, i.e., the display method of the derived class is called and not that of the base. If the method was non virtual in nature, the display() method of the base class would have been called.

12.18 VIRTUAL FUNCTION ACCESS

The access for a virtual function is specified when it is declared. The access rules for a virtual function are not affected by the access rules for the function that later overrides the virtual function. In general, the access of the overriding member function is not known.

If a virtual function is called with a pointer or reference to a class object, the type of the class object is not used to determine the access of the virtual function. Instead, the type of the pointer or reference to the class object is used.

Virtual functions are accessed using a base class pointer. A pointer to the base class can be created. A base class pointer can contain the address of the derived object as the derived object contains the subset of base class object. Every derived class is also a base class. When a base class pointer contains the address of the derived class object, at runtime it is decided which version of virtual function is called depending on the type of object contained by the pointer.

In the following example, when the function f() is called using a pointer having type B*, bptr is used to determine the access to the function f(). Although the definition of f() defined in class D is executed, the access of the member function f() in class B is used. When the function f() is called using a pointer having type D*, dptr is used to determine the access to the function f(). This call produces an error because f() is declared private in class D.

```
class B
{
public:
virtual void f();
};
class D : public B
{
private:
void f();
};
void main()
{
D dobj;
```

```
B* bptr = &dobj;
D* dptr = &dobj;
// valid, virtual B::f() is public,
// D::f() is called
bptr->f();
// error, D::f() is private
dptr->f();
}
```

12.18.1 Characteristics of Virtual Function Access

Some most important characteristics used for virtual function declaration are as:

1. Virtual function should be declared in the base class. Note that when you define it in the base class, then there be no need to again define (redefine) in any derived class.
2. Virtual function should be member of some class. It is an error to declare a non-member function of a class Virtual e.g. virtual void add ( ) is valid.
3. Virtual function cannot be static member. E.g. virtual static int add ( ); is invalid.
4. Virtual function can be friend of another class.
5. Virtual function can be accessed by using object pointer.
6. In virtual function processing, Derived class pointer cannot be used to access an object of the base class.
7. Virtual function can be applied on Destructor. Note that constructor function cannot be virtual.
8. When virtual function is called through a pointer to a base class, the derived class function is activated.
9. Base class pointer can point to any object of derived class, but the pointer of derived class can not point to the object of Base class.
10. You cannot apply increment/decrement operation on the pointer to derived class object, when a base class pointer points to the object of derived class.
11. The keyword virtual should not be repeated in the definition outside the class declaration.
12. In the declaration of virtual destructor function, a destructor member function does not take any argument and no return type not even void.

12.18.2 Important Points

Following are the important points about virtual functions:

1. Virtual function is a polymorphism technique.
2. Refers to performing the same operation in a hierarchy of classes. Typically used in scenarios where the base class pointer is used to hold derived class objects and performs the same operation. Refer example below.
3. When a virtual function is called on a base class pointer the compiler decides to defer the decision on which function to call until the program is running thereby doing late binding.
4. The actual function called at run-time depends on the contents of the pointer and not the type.
5. Internally the compiler creates a VTABLE for each which has virtual functions.
6. Addresses of virtual functions are placed in the VTABLE. If a virtual function is not redefined in the derived class, the base class function address is used in VTABLE.
7. When objects are created compiler also places a VPTR pointing to starting address of VTABLE using which the correct function is invoked.

12.19 PURE VIRTUAL FUNCTION

A pure virtual function is a function which has no definition in the base class. Its definition lies only in the derived class ie it is compulsory for the derived class to provide definition of a pure virtual function. Since there is no definition in the base class, these functions can be equated to zero.

Definition: *"Pure Virtual Function is a Virtual function with no body."*

Pure virtual function is the function in the base class with no body. Since no body, you have to add the notation =0 for declaration of the pure virtual function in the base class.

The base class with pure virtual function can't be instantiated since there is no definition of the function in the base class. It is necessary for the derived class to override pure virtual function. This type of class with one or more pure virtual function is called abstract class which can't be instantiated, it can only be inherited.

12.19.1 Declaration of Pure Virtual Function

Since pure virtual function has no body, the programmer must add the notation =0 for declaration of the pure virtual function in the base class.

The general form of pure virtual function is:

```
virtual type func-name(parameter-list) = 0;
```

For example:

```
class classname
{
public:
virtual void virtualfunctioname() = 0 //This denotes the pure virtual function
in C++
};
```

The other concept of pure virtual function remains the same as described in the previous section of virtual function.

To understand the declaration and usage of Pure Virtual Function, refer to this example:

```
class A
{
public:
virtual void example()=0;      //Denotes pure virtual Function Definition
};

class B: public A
{
public:
void example()
{
cout<<"Welcome";
}
};
class C: public A
{
public:
void example()
{
cout<<"To Training";
}
};
void main()
{
A* arra[2];
B b;
C c;
arra[0]=&b;
```

```
arra[1]=&c;
arra[0]->example();
arra[1]->example();
getch();
}
```

Since the above example has no body, the pure virtual function example() is declared with notation =0 in the base class A. The two derived class named B and C are derived from the base class A. The pure virtual function example() takes up new definition. In the main function, a list of pointers is defined to the base class.

Two objects named b and c are defined for derived classes B and C. The address of the objects b and c are stored in the array pointers which are then used for accessing the pure virtual function example() belonging to both the derived class B and C and thus, the output is as in the above example.

The programmer must clearly understand the concept of pure virtual functions having no body in the base class and the notation =0 is independent of value assignment. The notation =0 simply indicates the Virtual function is a pure virtual function as it has no body.

Some programmers might want to remove this pure virtual function from the base class as it has no body but this would result in an error. Without the declaration of the pure virtual function in the base class, accessing statements of the pure virtual function such as, arra[0]->example() and arra[1]->example() would result in an error. The pointers should point to the base class A. Special care must be taken not to remove the statement of declaration of the pure virtual function in the base class.

Program 15: Write a C++ program to create pure virtual function.

```
#include <iostream.h>
#include<conio.h>
class area
{
double dim1, dim2;
public:
void setarea(double d1, double d2)
{
dim1 = d1;
dim2 = d2;
}
void getdim(double &d1, double &d2)
{
d1 = dim1;
```

```
d2 = dim2;
}
virtual double getarea() = 0; // pure virtual function
};
class rectangle : public area
{
public:
double getarea()
{
double d1, d2;
getdim(d1, d2);
return d1 * d2;
}
};
class triangle : public area
{
public:
double getarea()
{
double d1, d2;
getdim(d1, d2);
return 0.5 * d1 * d2;
}
};
void  main()
{
area *p;
rectangle r;
triangle t;
r.setarea(3.3, 4.5);
t.setarea(4.0, 5.0);
p = &r;
cout << "Rectangle has area: " << p->getarea() << '\n';
p = &t;
cout << "Triangle has area: " << p->getarea() << '\n';
getch();
}
```

Output:

Rectangle has area: 14.85

Triangle has area: 10

12.20 VIRTUAL BASE CLASS

When two or more objects are derived from a common base class, we can prevent multiple copies of the base class being present in an object derived from those objects by declaring the base class as virtual when it is being inherited. Such a base class is known as virtual base class. This can be achieved by preceding the base class' name with the word virtual.

Consider following example:

```
class A
{
public:
int i;
};
class B : virtual public A
{
public:
int j;
};
class C: virtual public A
{
public:
int k;
};
class D: public B, public C
{
public:
int sum;
};
void main()
{
D ob;
ob.i = 10;                    //unambiguous since only one copy of i is inherited.
ob.j = 20;
ob.k = 30;
ob.sum = ob.i + ob.j + ob.k;
cout << "Value of i is : "<< ob.i<<"\n";
cout << "Value of j is : "<< ob.j<<"\n"; cout << "Value of k is :"<< ob.k<<"\n";
cout << "Sum is : "<< ob.sum <<"\n";
getch();
}
```

Note: Detail description of virtual base class is described in Chapter inheritance.

12.21 VIRTUAL DESTRUCTOR

A virtual destructor is one that is declared as virtual in the base class and is used to ensure that destructors are called in the proper order. It is to be remembered that destructors are called in the reverse order of inheritance. If a base class pointer points to a derived class object and we some time later use the delete operator to delete the object, then the derived class destructor is not called.

If the destructor in the base class is not made virtual, then an object that might have been declared of type base class and instance of child class would simply call the base class destructor without calling the derived class destructor.

Hence, by making the destructor in the base class virtual, we ensure that the derived class destructor gets called before the base class destructor.

Program 16: Write a C++ program for Virtual Destructors.

```
#include <iostream.h>
#include<conio.h>
class Base
{
public:
~Base()
{
cout <<"Base destroyed \n ";
}
};
class Derv :public Base
{
public:
~Derv()
{
cout <<"Derv destroyed \n ";
}
};
void main()
{
Base *ptr =new Derv;
delete ptr;
```

```
getch();
}
```

Output:

Base destroyed

Program 17: Write a C++ program to demonstrate the object destruction sequence.

```
#include <iostream>
#include <conio.h>
class Base
{
public:
Base()
{
cout << "Base class constructor ..." << endl;
}
~Base()
{
cout << "Base class destructor ..." << endl;
}
};
class Derived : public Base
{
public:
Derived()
{
cout << "Derived class constructor ..." << endl;
}
~Derived()
{
cout << "Derived class destructor ..." << endl;
}
};
void main()
{
Base* base;
base = new Derived();
delete base;
getch();
}
```

Output:

Base class constructor ...
Derived class constructor ...
Base class destructor ...

Program 18: Write a C++ program to demonstrate the object destruction sequence using virtual destructor.

```
#include <iostream.h>
#include <conio.h>
class Base
{
public:
Base()
{
cout << "Base class constructor ..." << endl;
}
virtual ~Base()
{
cout << "Base class destructor ..." << endl;
}
};
class Derived : public Base
{
public:
Derived()
{
cout << "Derived class constructor ..." << endl;
}
~Derived()
{
cout << "Derived class destructor ..." << endl;
}
};
void main()
{
Base* base;
base = new Derived();
delete base;
getch();
}
```

Output:

Base class constructor ...
Derived class constructor ...
Derived class destructor ...
Base class destructor ...

Note: A constructor cannot be virtual because at the time when the constructor is invoked the virtual table would not be available in the memory. Hence we cannot have a virtual constructor.

12.21.1 Important Points

Following are the important points about virtual destructor:

1. Virtual destructor ensures that the object destruction happens from the most derived class towards the base class.
2. Significant in scenarios where derived classes object is assigned to a base class pointer.

12.22 PURE VIRTUAL DESTRUCTOR

Unlike ordinary member functions, a virtual destructor is not overridden when redefined in a derived class. Rather, it is extended: the lower-most destructor first invokes the destructor of its base class and only then, it is executed. Consequently, when you try to declare a pure virtual destructor, you may encounter compilation errors, or worse: a runtime crash. However, there's no need to despair—you can enjoy both worlds by declaring a pure virtual destructor without a risk. The abstract class should contain a declaration (without a definition) of a pure virtual destructor:

```
//Interface.h file
class Interface
{
public:
virtual ~Interface() = 0; //pure virtual destructor declaration
};
```

12.23 ABSTRACT CLASSES

Abstract classes act as expressions of general concepts from which more specific classes can be derived. You cannot create an object of an abstract class type; however, you can use pointers and references to abstract class types.

A class that contains at least one pure virtual function is considered an abstract class. Classes derived from the abstract class must implement the pure virtual function or they, too, are abstract classes.

An *abstract class* is a class that is designed to be specifically used as a base class. An abstract class contains at least one *pure virtual function.* You declare a pure virtual function by using a *pure specifier* (= 0) in the declaration of a virtual member function in the class declaration.

The following is an example of an abstract class:

```
class A
{
public:
virtual void f() = 0;
};
```

12.23.1 Uses of Abstract Class

1. Allows the base class to provide only an interface for its derived classes.
2. Prevents anyone from creating an instance of this class.
3. A class is made abstract if atleast one pure virtual function defined.

Program 19: Write a C++ program to demonstrate the definition of a abstract base class.

```
#include <iostream.h>
#include <conio.h>
class MyInterface
{
public:
virtual void Display() = 0;
};
class MyClass1 : public MyInterface
{
public:
void Display()
{
cout << "MyClass1" << endl;
}
};
class MyClass2 : public MyInterface
{
```

```
public:
void Display()
{
cout << "MyClass2" << endl;
}
};
void main()
{
// MyInterface obj;
// Cannot create instance of abstract class 'MyInterace' in function main()
// Error: Class 'MyInterface' is abstract because of 'MyInterface::Display()
= 0' in function main()
MyClass1 obj1;
obj1.Display();
MyClass2 obj2;
obj2.Display();
getch();
}
```

Output:

MyClass1
MyClass2

Program 20: Write a C++ program for abstract Classes and Pure Virtual Functions.

```
#include <iostream.h>
#include<conio.h>
class Base
{
public:
virtual void show()=0;  //This is pure virtual function
};
class Derv1 :public Base
{
public:
void show()
{
cout <<"Derv1 \n ";
}
};
```

```
class Derv2 :public Base
{
public:
void show()
{
cout <<"Derv2 \n ";
}
};
void main()
{
Base *ptr[2];  //array of pointers to base class
Derv1 d1;
Derv2 d2;
ptr[0]=&d1;  //put address of d1 in array
ptr[1]=&d2;  //put address of d2 in array
ptr[0]->show(); //execute show()in both objects
ptr[1]->show();
getch();
}
```

Output:

Derv1
Derv2

12.23.2 Restrictions on Using Abstract Classes

Abstract classes cannot be used for:

- Variables or member data
- Argument types
- Function return types
- Types of explicit conversions

Another restriction is that if the constructor for an abstract class calls a pure virtual function, either directly or indirectly, the result is undefined. However, constructors and destructors for abstract classes can call other member functions.

Pure virtual functions can be defined for abstract classes, but they can be called directly only by using the syntax:

abstract-class-name :: function-name**( )**

This helps when designing class hierarchies whose base classes include pure virtual destructors, because base class destructors are always called in the process of destroying an object.

Consider the following example:

```
// Declare an abstract base class with a pure virtual destructor.
class base
{
public:
base() {}
virtual ~base()=0;
};
// Provide a definition for destructor.
base::~base() {}
class derived:public base
{
public:
derived() {}
~derived(){}
};
void main()
{
derived *pDerived = new derived;
delete pDerived;
getch();
}
```

When the object pointed to by pDerived is deleted, the destructor for class derived is called and then the destructor for class base is called. The empty implementation for the pure virtual function ensures that at least some implementation exists for the function.

***Note:** In the preceding example, the pure virtual function base::~base is called implicitly from derived::~derived. It is also possible to call pure virtual functions explicitly using a fully qualified member-function name.*

12.24 THIS POINTER

The pointer 'this' is used as a pointer to the class object instance by the member function. The address of the class instance is passed as an implicit parameter to the member functions. It is a common knowledge that C++ keeps only one copy of each member function and the data members are allocated memory for all of their instances. These kinds of various instances of data are maintained use this pointer.

12.24.1 Important Notes on this Pointer

Following are the important points about this pointer:

1. **this** pointer stores the address of the class instance, to enable pointer access of the members to the member functions of the class.
2. **this** pointer is not counted for calculating the size of the object.
3. **this** pointers are not accessible for static member functions.
4. **this** pointers are not modifiable.

The **this** pointer is a pointer accessible only within the nonstatic member functions of a **class, struct**, or **union** type. It points to the object for which the member function is called. Static member functions do not have a **this** pointer.

The general syntax is:

```
this->member-identifier
```

Every class member function has a hidden parameter: the this pointer. this points to the individual object. Therefore, in each call to GetAge() or SetAge(), the this pointer for the object is included as a hidden parameter.

Program 21: Write a C++ program to use the this pointer explicitly.

```
// Using the this pointer
#include <iostream.h>
#include <conio.h>
class Rectangle
{
public:
Rectangle();
~Rectangle();
void SetLength(int length)
{ this->itsLength = length; }
int GetLength() const
{ return this->itsLength; }
void SetWidth(int width)
{ itsWidth = width; }
int GetWidth() const
{ return itsWidth; }
private:
int itsLength;
int itsWidth;
};
Rectangle::Rectangle()
```

```
{
itsWidth = 5;
itsLength = 10;
}
Rectangle::~Rectangle()
{}
void main()
{
Rectangle theRect;
cout << "theRect is " << theRect.GetLength() << " feet long.\n";
cout << "theRect is " << theRect.GetWidth() << " feet wide.\n";
theRect.SetLength(20);
theRect.SetWidth(10);
cout << "theRect is " << theRect.GetLength()<< " feet long.\n";
cout << "theRect is " << theRect.GetWidth()<< " feet wide.\n";
getch();
}
```

Output:

```
theRect is 10 feet long.
theRect is 5 feet wide.
theRect is 20 feet long.
theRect is 10 feet wide.
```

Explanation: The SetLength() and GetLength() accessor functions explicitly use the this pointer to access the member variables of the Rectangle object. The SetWidth and GetWidth accessors do not. There is no difference in their behavior, although the syntax is easier to understand.

If that were all there was to the this pointer, there would be little point in bothering you with it. The this pointer, however, is a pointer; it stores the memory address of an object. As such, it can be a powerful tool.

You don't have to worry about creating or deleting the this pointer. The compiler takes care of that.

Program 22: Write a C++ program using the 'this' pointer.

```
#include <iostream.h>
#include<conio.h>
class MyClass
{
int i;
public:
void setI(int val)
```

```
{
this->i = val;
}
int getI()
{
return this->i;
}
};
void main()
{
MyClass o;
o.setI(100);
cout << o.getI();
getch();
}
```

Output:

100

Program 23: Write a C++ program to access data members using 'this' pointer.

```
#include<iostream.h>
#include<conio.h>
class rec
{
private:
int l;
int b;
public:
void ds(int x,int y)
{
cout<<"Address of object that generates ds() call="<<this<<endl;
this->l=x;
this->b=y;
}
void ar()
{
cout<<"Address of object that generates ar() call="<<this<<endl;
cout<<"Area is: "<<this->l*this->b;
}
```

```
};
void main()
{
rec obj;
obj.ds(20,10);
obj.ar();
getch();
}
```

Output:

```
Address of object that generates ds() call=0x8fc0fff2
Address of object that generates ar() call=0x8fc0fff2
Area is:200
```

12.25 OBJECT SLICING

There is a distinct difference between passing the addresses of objects and passing objects by value when using polymorphism. All the examples you've seen here, and virtually all the examples you should see, pass addresses and not values. This is because addresses all have the same size, so passing the address of an object of a derived type (which is usually a bigger object) is the same as passing the address of an object of the base type (which is usually a smaller object). As explained before, this is the goal when using polymorphism – code that manipulates a base type can transparently manipulate derived-type objects as well.

If you upcast to an object instead of a pointer or reference, something will happen that may surprise you: the object is "sliced" until all that remains is the subobject that corresponds to the destination type of your cast.

12.25.1 Why we use Object Slicing

These are the various uses of object slicing:

1. Object slicing is a concept where additional attributes of a derived class object is sliced to form a base class object.
2. Object slicing doesn't occur when pointers or references to objects are passed as function arguments since both the pointers are of the same size.
3. Object slicing will be noticed when pass by value is done for a derived class object for a function accepting base class object.
4. Object slicing could be prevented by making the base class function pure virtual there by disallowing object creation.

Following is the example of object slicing:

```
#include <iostream.h>
```

```
#include <conio.h>
class Base
{
int i;
public:
Base(int ii = 0) : i(ii) {}
virtual int sum() const { return i; }
};
class Derived : public Base
{
int j;
public:
Derived(int ii = 0, int jj = 0) : Base(ii), j(jj) {}
int sum() const
{ return Base::sum() + j; }
};
void call(Base b)
{
cout << "sum = " << b.sum() << endl;
}
void main()
{
Base b(10);
Derived d(10, 47);
call(b);
call(d);
getch();
}
```

The function **call( )** is passed an object of type **Base** *by value* . It then calls the virtual function **sum( )** for the **Base** object. In **main( )**, you might expect the first call to produce 10, and the second to produce 57. In fact, both calls produce 10.

Two things are happening in this program. First, **call( )** accepts only a **Base** object, so all the code inside the function body will manipulate only members associated with **Base**. Any calls to **call( )** will cause an object the size of **Base** to be pushed on the stack and cleaned up after the call. This means that if an object of a class inherited from **Base** is passed to **call( )**, the compiler accepts it, but it copies only the **Base** portion of the object. It *slices* the derived portion off of the object, like this:

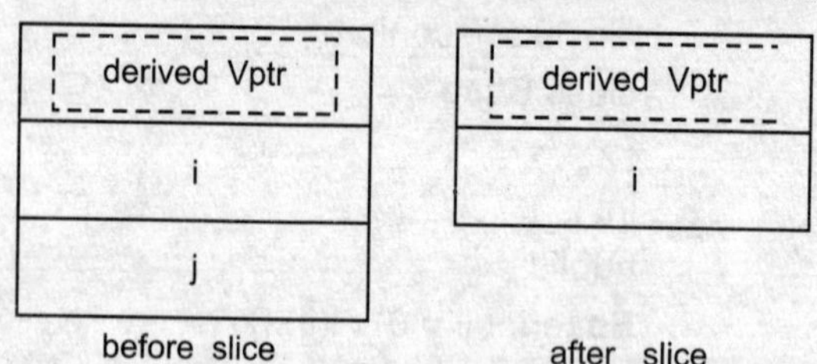

Now you may wonder about the virtual function call. Here, the virtual function makes use of portions of both **Base** (which still exists) and **Derived**, which no longer exists because it was sliced off! So what happens when the virtual function is called?

You're saved from disaster precisely because the object is being passed by value. Because of this, the compiler thinks it knows the precise type of the object (and it does, here, because any information that contributed extra features to the objects has been lost). In addition, when passing by value, it uses the copy-constructor for a **Base** object, which initializes the VPTR to the **Base** VTABLE and copies only the **Base** parts of the object. There's no explicit copy-constructor here, so the compiler synthesizes one. Under all interpretations, the object truly becomes a **Base** during slicing.

Object slicing actually removes part of the object rather than simply changing the meaning of an address as when using a pointer or reference. Because of this, upcasting into an object is not often done; in fact, it's usually something to watch out for and prevent. You can explicitly prevent object slicing by putting pure virtual functions in the base class; this will cause a compile-time error message for an object slice.

Program 24: Write a C++ program to demonstrate the concept of object slicing.

```
#include <iostream.h>
#include <conio.h>
class Base
{
int data1;
int data2;
public:
Base(int a, int b)
{
data1 = a;
data2 = b;
}
virtual void display()
{
```

```
cout << "I am Base class" << endl;
}
};
class Derived : public Base
{
int data3;
public:
Derived(int a, int b, int c) : Base(a, b)
{
data3 = c;
}
void display()
{
cout << "I am Derived class" << endl;
}
};
void somefunc ( Base obj )
{
obj.display();
}
void main()
{
Base b(10, 20);
Derived d(100, 200, 300);
somefunc(b);
somefunc(d);
}
```

Output:

I am Base class
I am Base class

SOLVED PROGRAMMING

Program 1: Write a C++ program to implement cube root with the help of function overloading.

```
#include<iostream.h>
#include<math.h>
int cuberoot (int x)
{
```

```
float q ;
q = sqrt (x) / 2.0;
x = x * 3.0;
q = q/10;
return (q) ;
}
double cuberoot (float x)
{
float q ;
q = sqrt (x) / 2.0;
x = x * 3.0;
q = q/10;
return (q) ;
}
float cuberoot (double (x))
{
double q ;
q = sqrt (x) / 2.0;
x = x / 3.0;
q = q / 1.0;
return (q)
}
void main ( )
{
int a, d ;
float b, e ;
double c, f ;
int cuberoot(int);
float cuberoot(float);
double cuberoot(double);
cout<<"\n Enter the integer number" ;
cin >> a ;
d = cuberoot (a);
cout<<"\n Cube root of "<< a <<" is" << d;
cout<<"\n Enter the float number" ;
cin >> b ;
e = cuberoot (b);
cout<<"\n Cuberoot of" << b <<" is" << e;
cout<<"\n Enter the double number" ;
cin >> c ;
```

```
f = cuberoot (c);
cout<<"\n Cuberoot of" << c <<" is" << f;
getch( ) ;
}
```

Program 2: Write a C++ program to compute the square root by using the concept of function overloading having different argument and also having the similar data types.

```
// function overloading with different argument, but similar data type
#include<iostream.h>
#include<conio.h>
#include<math.h>
class funct
{
public:
void funct(float a)
{
cout<<"A="<<sqrt(a)<<endl;
}
void funct(float x,float y)
{
cout<<"X="<<sqrt(x)<<"Y="<<sqrt(y)<<endl;
}
void funct(float b,float c,float d)
{
cout<<"B="<<sqrt(b)<<"C="<<sqrt(c)<<"D="<<sqrt(d)<<endl;
}
};
void main()
{
clrscr();
funct(16.0);
funct(16.0,9.0 );
funct(16.0,9.0,4.0);
getch();
}
```

Output:

```
A=4
X=4 Y=3
B=4 C=3 D=2
```

Program 3: Write a C++ program for a virtual function.

```
#include <iostream.h>
#include<conio.h>
class BaseClass
{
public:
virtual void who() { // specify a virtual function
cout << "Base\n";
}
};
class DerivedClass1 : public BaseClass
{
public:
void who() { // redefine who() for DerivedClass1
cout << "First derivation\n";
}
};
class DerivedClass2 : public BaseClass
{
public:
void who() { // redefine who() for DerivedClass2
cout << "Second derivation\n";
}
};
void main()
{
BaseClass base_obj;
BaseClass *p;
DerivedClass1 DerivedClass1_obj;
DerivedClass2 DerivedClass2_obj;
p = &base_obj;
p->who();  // access BaseClass's who
p = &DerivedClass1_obj;
p->who(); // access DerivedClass1's who
p = &DerivedClass2_obj;
p->who();  // access DerivedClass2's who
getch();
}
```

Output:

```
Base
First derivation
Second derivation
```

Program 4: Write a C++ program to call base virtual function explicitly.

```
#include <iostream.h>
#include<conio.h>
class Base
{
public:
virtual void foo( ) {cout << "Base::foo( )" << endl;}
};
class Derived : public Base
{
public:
virtual void foo( ) {cout << "Derived::foo( )" << endl;}
};
void main( )
{
Derived* p = new Derived( );
p->foo( );      // Calls the derived version
p->Base::foo( ); // Calls the base version
getch();
}
```

Output:

```
Derived::foo( )
Base::foo( )
```

Program 5: Write a C++ program for abstract base class.

```
#include <iostream.h>
#include<conio.h>
class CPolygon
{
protected:
int width, height;
public:
void set_values (int a, int b)
{
width=a;
height=b;
```

```
}
virtual int area (void) =0;
};
class CRectangle: public CPolygon
{
public:
int area (void)
{
return (width * height);
}
};
class CTriangle: public CPolygon
{
public:
int area (void)
{
return (width * height / 2);
}
};
void main ()
{
CRectangle rect;
CTriangle trgl;
CPolygon * ppoly1 = &rect;
CPolygon * ppoly2 = &trgl;
ppoly1->set_values (4,5);
ppoly2->set_values (4,5);
cout << ppoly1->area() << endl;
cout << ppoly2->area() << endl;
getch();
}
```

Output:

20

10

Program 6: Write a C++ program for pure virtual members can be called from the abstract base class.

```
#include <iostream.h>
#include<conio.h>
class CPolygon
```

```
{
protected:
int width, height;
public:
void set_values (int a, int b)
{
width=a;
height=b;
}
virtual int area (void) =0;
void printarea (void)
{
cout << this->area() << endl;
}
};
class CRectangle: public CPolygon
{
public:
int area (void)
{
return (width * height);
}
};
class CTriangle: public CPolygon
{
public:
int area (void)
{
return (width * height / 2);
}
};
void main ()
{
CRectangle rect;
CTriangle trgl;
CPolygon * ppoly1 = &rect;
CPolygon * ppoly2 = &trgl;
ppoly1->set_values (4,5);
ppoly2->set_values (4,5);
```

```
ppoly1->printarea();
ppoly2->printarea();
getch();
}
```

Output:

```
20
10
```

Program 7: Write a C++ program using virtual function to define inheritance.

```
#include <iostream.h>
#include<conio.h>
class area
{
double dim1, dim2;
public:
void setarea(double d1, double d2)
{
dim1 = d1;
dim2 = d2;
}
void getdim(double &d1, double &d2)
{
d1 = dim1;
d2 = dim2;
}
virtual double getarea()
{
cout << "You must override this function\n";
return 0.0;
}
};
class rectangle : public area
{
public:
double getarea()
{
double d1, d2;
getdim(d1, d2);
return d1 * d2;
}
```

```
};
class triangle : public area
{
public:
double getarea()
{
double d1, d2;
getdim(d1, d2);
return 0.5 * d1 * d2;
}
};
void main()
{
area *p;
rectangle r;
triangle t;
r.setarea(3.3, 4.5);
t.setarea(4.0, 5.0);
p = &r;
cout << "Rectangle has area: " << p->getarea() << '\n';
p = &t;
cout << "Triangle has area: " << p->getarea() << '\n';
getch();
}
```

Output:

```
Rectangle has area: 14.85
Triangle has area: 10
```

PROGRAMMING PROBLEMS

Program 1: Write a C++ program to find the average marks of three numbers to illustrate the concept of function overloading with the different data types.

Program 2: Write a C++ program to find rank of a student from the student database by using the concept of Function Overloading.

Program 3: Write a C++ program for Virtual functions: inheritance class.

Program 4: Write a C++ program using multiple virtual member functions called in turn.

Program 5: Write a C++ program for class with only virtual methods.

Program 5: Write a C++ program using virtual function to calculate area for different shapes.

Program 6: Write a C++ program why Virtual Functions: one interface, multiple methods.

Program 7: Write a C++ program using virtual methods.

Program 8: Write a C++ program to implementing pure virtual functions.

Program 9: Write a C++ program to deriving ADTs from other ADTs.

Program 10: Write a C++ program to show pure virtual functions using bank that wants to terminate emp on performance basis that if emp is manager then monthly target for keeping funds must not be less than Rs1000000. if emp is marketing executive then monthly target for opening accounts should must not be less than 20 accounts.

Fill in the blanks

1. .... is defined as one interface to control access to a general class of actions.
2. If a class contains at least one pure virtual function, it is a .... class.
3. Classes from which objects can be instantiated are called .... classes.
4. .... involves using a base-class pointer or reference to invoke virtual functions on base-class and derived-class objects.
5. Overridable functions are declared using keyword ....
6. .... is a concept where additional attributes of a derived class object is sliced to form a base class object.
7. In C++, it is possible to have various functions with the same name that operate on different types or numbers of arguments. This is called function ....
8. An object's non-static member functions have access to a "self pointer" to the object called the .... pointer.

Answers

1. Polymorphism 2. abstract. 3. concrete. 4. Polymorphism. 5. virtual. 6. Object slicing. 7.Overloading. 8.this

OBJECTIVE TYPE QUESTIONS

1. When a child class function is called, the compiler looks first for a matching function name in the ....

   (a) class of the object using the function name

(b) immediate ancestor class

(c) base class

(d) descendant class

2. A function in a derived class that has the same name as a function in the parent class ....
   (a) will cause an error message to display
   (b) will override the base class function
   (c) will be overridden by the base class function
   (d) will execute immediately after the base class function executes.
3. The keyword virtual indicates that ....
   (a) a derived class has public access to a base class
   (b) more than one base class exists
   (c) a base class should be used only once in inheritance
   (d) a derived class should have more than one base class constructed
4. Overloaded functions
   (a) are a group of functions with the same name
   (b) all have the same number and type of arguments
   (c) make life simpler for programmers
   (d) may fail unexpectedly due to stress.
5. Which of the following are the types of polymorphism?
   (a) overloading (b) overriding
   (c) overflow (d) all
   (e) none
6. Which of the following are the types of polymorphism?
   (a) overloading (b) virtual function
   (c) stack (d) both a and b
   (e) none
7. Virtual function are declared in
   (a) base class (b) derived class
   (c) both a and b (d) none
8. The function having no body is called ....
   (a) Virtual function (b) pure-virtual function
   (c) static function (d) all
   (e) none

9. Virtual function explain the concept of
   (a) polymorphism (b) encapsulation
   (c) inheritance (d) all
   (e) none
10. Virtual function uses the concept of
   (a) Run time binding (b) Compile time binding
   (c) Dynamic binding (d) Both a and c
   (e) None
11. Which type of binding is use in virtual function?
   (a) early binding (b) late binding
   (c) both (d) none
12. Polymorphism is also called
   (a) one interface multiple method (b) multi-interface multiple method
   (c) multiple interface one method (d) none
13. Which of the following is the way to overloaded, a function
   (a) By changing the data type of argument
   (b) By changing the number of argument
   (c) both
   (d) none
14. Ordinary function uses the concept of
   (a) Early binding (b) late binding
   (c) both a and b (d) none of the above
15. Virtual functions are redefined in
   (a) base class (b) derived class
   (c) both a and b (d) none
16. In pure virtual function, base class becomes
   (a) Abstract class (b) Actual class
   (c) Encapsulated class (d) inherited class
17. Pure virtual function is also called
   (a) Null (b) Empty virtual function
   (c) doing Nothing function (d) all
   (e) none

EXERCISES

1. Why do you mean by polymorphism? Explain its various types.
2. What do you mean by function overloading?
3. Why function overloading is used?
4. What do you know about binding?
5. Differentiate between compile time and run time Polymorphism.
6. Why virtual function is used?
7. Explain various types of function overloading.
8. Explain the concept of pointer to base class.
9. Explain the concept of pointer to derived class.
10. How can you declare a virtual function? Explain with an example?
11. Explain the Properties of virtual function.
12. What are the various rules of virtual function?
13. Why we need virtual function.
14. How virtual function works.
15. What are the uses of virtual function?
16. What are the various characteristics of virtual function?
17. Differentiate between virtual function and pure virtual function?
18. What are the various rules used in the virtual function?
19. Differentiate between late binding and the early binding.
20. What are the various properties of virtual function?
21. What are the various types of Polymorphism?
22. Write note on Abstract class.
23. What are the uses restrictions of abstract classes.
24. What is the role of virtual destructor in the polymorphism?
25. Explain the concept of this pointer.
26. What do you mean by object slicing?

CHAPTER 13

Exploring Special Functions

13.1 INTRODUCTION

In C++, we have different types of special functions like inline, friend, static, virtual etc. All these functions are used for different purposes. The powerful function used in OOPs is class function or member function. Class function binds the data member into a single entity, which is usable. Each and every function has its own keyword and unique identity. These functions make the object oriented programming more powerful. Now, we are describing these functions using concept of classes.

Following are the special functions used in C++:

1. Inline function
2. Friend function
3. Static function
4. Constant function
5. Virtual function
6. Volatile function

13.2 INLINE FUNCTION

The inline functions are a C++ enhancement designed to speed up programs. The coding of normal functions and inline functions is similar except that inline functions definitions start with the keyword inline. The distinction between normal functions and inline functions is the different compilation process.

Definition: *"Inline functions are functions where the call is made to inline functions. The actual code then gets placed in the calling program."*

13.2.1 Reason for the Need of Inline Function

Normally, a function call transfers the control from the calling program to the function and after the execution of the program returns the control back to the calling program after the function call. These concepts of function saved program space and memory space are used because the function is stored only in one place and is only executed when it is called. This concept of function execution may be time consuming since the registers and other processes must be saved before the function gets called.

The extra time needed and the process of saving is valid for larger functions. If the function is short, the programmer may wish to place the code of the function in the calling program in order for it to be executed. This type of function is best handled by the inline function. In this situation, the programmer may be wondering "why not write the short code repeatedly inside the program wherever needed instead of going for inline function?" Although this could accomplish the task, the problem lies in the loss of clarity of the program. If the programmer repeats the same code many times, there will be a loss of clarity in the program. The alternative approach is to allow inline functions to achieve the same purpose, with the concept of functions.

13.2.2 What Happens when an Inline Function is Written?

The inline function takes the format as a normal function but when it is compiled it is compiled as inline code. The function is placed separately as inline function, thus adding readability to the source program. When the program is compiled, the code present in function body is replaced in the place of function call.

13.2.3 General Format of Inline Function

Now, we are representing the general syntax for inline function.

The general syntax is:

```
inline datatype function_name(arguments)
```

The keyword inline specified in the above syntax, designates the function as inline function. For example, if a programmer wishes to have a function named mul with return value as integer and with no arguments as inline it is written as follows:

```
inline int mul( )
```

Program 1: Write a C program to explain the concept of inline functions.

```
#include <iostream.h>
#include <conio.h>
int mul(int);
void main( )
```

```
{
int x;
cout << "\n Enter the Input Value: ";
cin>>x;
cout<<"\n The Output is: " << mul(x);
getch();
}

inline int mul(int y)
{
return 5*y;
}
```

Output:

```
Enter the Input Value: 10
The Output is: 50
```

The output would be the same even when the inline function is written solely as a function. The concept, however, is different. When the program is compiled, the code present in the inline function mul( ) is replaced in the place of function call in the calling program. The concept of inline function is used in this example because the function is a small line of code.

The above example of **inline function**, when compiled, would have the structure as follows:

```
#include <iostream.h>
#include <conio.h>
int mul(int);
void main( )
{
int x;
cout << "\n Enter the Input Value: ";
cin>>x;
cout<<"\n The Output is: " << mul(x);      //The mul(x) gets replaced with
code return 5*y;
}
```

When the above program is written as **normal function** the compiled code would look like below:

```
#include <iostream.h>
#include <conio.h>
int mul(int);
void main( )
{
```

```
int x;
cout << "\n Enter the Input Value: ";
cin>>x;
cout<<"\n The Output is: " << mul(x);  //Call is made to the function mul
}
int mul(int y)
{
return 5*y;
}
```

A programmer must make wise choices when to use inline functions. Inline functions will save time and are useful if the function is very small. If the function is large, use of inline functions must be avoided.

13.2.4 Working of Inline Function

After writing any program, it is first compiled to get an executable code, which consists of a set of machine language instructions. When this executable code is executed, the operating system loads these instructions into the computer's memory, so that each instruction has a specific memory location. Thus, each instruction has a particular memory address.

After loading the executable program in the computer memory, these instructions are executed step by step. When the function call instruction is encountered, the program stores the memory address of the instructions immediately following the function call statement, loads the function being called into the memory, copies argument values, jumps to the memory location of the called function, executes the function codes, stores the return value of the function, and then jumps back to the address of the instruction that was saved just before executing the called function.

The **C++ inline function** provides an alternative. With inline code, the compiler replaces the function call statement with the function code itself (process called expansion) and then compiles the entire code. Thus, with inline functions, the compiler does not have to jump to another location to execute the function, and then jump back as the code of the called function is already available to the calling program.

Program 2: Write a C program to explain the concept of inline functions.

```
#include <iostream.h>
#include <conio.h>
inline void max(int a, int b)
{
cout << (a > b ? a : b);
```

```
}
void main()
{
int x, y;
cout<<" Enter the value of x and y:";
cin >> x >> y;
max(x, y);
getch();
}
```

Output:

```
Enter the value of x and y: 24 12
24
```

13.3 INLINE CLASS MEMBER FUNCTIONS

The inline specifier indicates the compiler that inline substitution is preferred to the usual function call mechanism for a specific function. This does not change the behavior of a function itself, but is used to suggest to the compiler that the code generated by the function body is inserted at each point the function is called, instead of being inserted only once and perform a regular call to it, which generally involves some additional overhead in running time.

The format for its declaration is:

```
inline type name ( arguments ... ) { instructions ... }
```

and the call is just like the call to any other function. You do not have to include the inline keyword when calling the function, only in its declaration.

Most compilers already optimize code to generate inline functions when it is more convenient. This specifier only indicates the compiler that inline is preferred for this function.

A function defined in the body of a class declaration is an inline function.

Program 3: Write a C++ program for inline method.

```
#include <iostream.h>
#include<conio.h>
class MyClass
{
int i; // private by default
public:
int getInt();
void setInt(int j);
};
```

```
inline int MyClass::getInt()
{
return i;
}
inline void MyClass::setInt(int j)
{
i = j;
}
void main()
{
MyClass s;
s.setInt(10);
cout << s.getInt();
getch();
}
```

Output:

```
10
```

> ***Note:*** *In the class declaration, the functions were declared without the* ***inline*** *keyword. The* ***inline*** *keyword can be specified in the class declaration; the result is the same.*

A given inline member function must be declared the same way in every compilation unit. This constraint causes inline functions to behave as if they were instantiated functions. Additionally, there must be exactly one definition of an inline function.

A class member function defaults to external linkage unless a definition for that function contains the **inline** specifier. The preceding example shows that these functions need not be explicitly declared with the **inline** specifier; using **inline** in the function definition causes it to be an inline function. However, it is illegal to redeclare a function as **inline** after a call to that function.

13.4 GUIDELINES FOR USING INLINE KEYWORD

Following are the guidelines for using inline keyword:

1. Always use inline function when you are sure it will give performance.
2. Always prefer inline function over macros.
3. Don't inline function with larger code size, one should always inline small code size function to get performance.

4. If you want to inline a function in class, then prefer to use inline keyword outside the class with the function definition.
5. In c++, by default member function declared and defined within class get inlined. So no use to specify for such cases.
6. If the function is virtual and its called virtually then it would not be inlined. So take care for such cases, same hold true for the use of function pointers.

13.5 ADVANTAGES OF INLINE FUNCTION

Following are the advantages of inline function:

1. It does not require function calling overhead.
2. It also save overhead of variables push/pop on the stack, while function calling.
3. It also save overhead of return call from a function.
4. It increases locality of reference by utilizing instruction cache.
5. After in-lining compiler can also apply intraprocedural optimization if specified. This is the most important one, in this way compiler can now focus on dead code elimination, can give more stress on branch prediction, induction variable elimination etc..

13.6 DISADVANTAGES OF INLINE FUNCTION

Following are the disadvantages of inline function:

1. May increase function sizes so that it may not fit on the cache, causing lots of cache miss.
2. After in-lining function if variables number which are going to use register increases than they may create overhead on register variable resource utilization.
3. It may cause compilation overhead as if some body changes code inside inline function than all calling location will also be compiled.
4. If used in header file, it will make your header file size large and may also make it unreadable.
5. If somebody used too many inline function resultant in a larger code size than it may cause thrashing in memory. More and more number of page fault bringing down your program performance.
6. Its not useful for embedded system where large binary size is not preferred at all due to memory size constraints.

13.7 FRIEND FUNCTION AND FRIEND CLASSES

The concept of encapsulation and data hiding indicate that non-member functions should not be able to access an object's private and protected data. The policy is if you are not a member, you can't get it. But there is a certain situation wherein you need to share your private or protected data with non-members. 'Friends' come here as a rescue.

In some circumstances, it is more convenient to grant member-level access to functions that are not members of a class or to all functions in a separate class. The **friend** keyword allows a function or class to gain access to the private and protected members of a class. You can declare friend functions or friend classes to access not only public members but also protected and private class members.

Any data which is declared **private** inside a class is not accessible from outside the class. A function which is not a member or an external class can never access such private data. But there may be some cases, where a programmer will need access to the private data from non-member functions and external classes. C++ offers some exceptions in such cases.

A class can allow non-member functions and other classes to access its own private data, by making them as **friends**. It gives two important points.

1. Once a non-member function is declared as a friend, it can access the private data of the class.
2. Similarly when a class is declared as a friend, the friend class can have access to the private data of the class which made this a friend.

13.8 FRIEND FUNCTION

A **friend** function is a function that is not a member of a class but has access to the class's private and protected members. Friend functions are not considered class members; they are normal external functions that are given special access privileges. Friends are not in the class's scope, and they are not called using the member-selection operators (. and –>) unless they are members of another class. A **friend** function is declared by the class that is granting access. The **friend** declaration can be placed anywhere in the class declaration. It is not affected by the access control keywords.

Definition: *"A friend function is a non-member function that grants access to class's private and protected members."*

A friend function is used for accessing the non-public members of a class. A class can allow non-member functions and other classes to access its own private data, by making them friends. Thus, a friend function is an ordinary function or a member of another class.

13.8.1 How to Define and Use Friend Function in C++

The friend function is written as any other normal function, except the function declaration of these functions is preceded with the keyword friend. The friend function must have the class to which it is declared as friend passed to it in argument.

13.8.2 Need for Friend Function

As discussed in the earlier chapters on access specifiers, when a data is declared as private inside a class, then it is not accessible from outside the class. A function that is not a member or an external class will not be able to access the private data. A programmer may have a situation where he or she would need to access private data from non-member functions and external classes. For handling such cases, the concept of Friend functions is a useful tool.

13.8.3 Advantages of Friend Functions

Following are the various advantages of friend functions:

1. A friend function may be declared friend of more than one class.
2. It does not have the class scope as it depends on function's original definition and declaration.
3. It does not require an object (of the class that declares it a friend) for invoking it. It can be invoked like a normal function.
4. Since it is not a member function, it cannot access the members of the class directly and has to use an object name and membership operator (.) with each member name.
5. It can be declared anywhere in the class without affecting its meaning.
6. A member function of the class operates upon the members of the object used to invoke it, while a friend function operates upon the object passed to it as argument.

13.8.4 Friend Functions have the Following Properties

Following are the various properties of friend functions:

1. Friend of the class can be member of some other class.
2. Friend of one class can be friend of another class or all the classes in one program, such a friend is known as GLOBAL FRIEND.

3. Friend can access the private or protected members of the class in which they are declared to be friend, but they can use the members for a specific object.
4. Friends are non-members hence do not get "this" pointer.
5. Friends, can be friend of more than one class, hence they can be used for message passing between the classes.
6. Friend can be declared anywhere (in public, protected or private section) in the class.

13.8.5 Important Points to Note While Using Friend Functions in C++

1. The keyword friend is placed only in the function declaration of the friend function and not in the function definition.
2. It is possible to declare a function as friend in any number of classes.
3. When a class is declared as a friend, the friend class has access to the private data of the class that made this a friend.
4. A friend function, even though it is not a member function, would have the rights to access the private members of the class.
5. It is possible to declare the friend function as either private or public.
6. The function can be invoked without the use of an object. The friend function has its argument as objects, seen in example below.

Program 3: Write a C++ program to understand the friend function.

```
#include<iostream.h>
#include<conio.h>
class minus
{
private:
int a,b;
public:
void test()
{
a=100;
b=200;
}
friend int compute(minus m1);
//Friend Function Declaration with keyword friend and with the object of class minus to which it is friend passed to it
};
int compute(minus m1)
```

```
{
//Friend Function Definition which has access to private data
return int(m.a+m.b)-5;
}
void main()
{
minus m;
m.test();
cout<<"The result is:"<<compute(m);
//Calling of Friend Function with object as argument.
getch();
}
```

Output:

The result is: 295

The function compute() is a non-member function of the class minus. In order to make this function have access to the private data a and b of class minus, it is created as a friend function for the class minus. As a first step, the function compute() is declared as friend in the class minus as:

friend int compute (minus m1)

The keyword friend is placed before the function. The function definition is written as a normal function and thus, the function has access to the private data a and b of the class minus. It is declared as friend inside the class, the private data values a and b are added, 5 is subtracted from the result, giving 295 as the result. This is returned by the function and thus the output is displayed as shown above.

Program 4: Write a C++ program to depict access of private data by a non member function.

```
#include<iostream.h>
#include<conio.h>
class d
{
int u;
public:
d(int uu)
{u=uu;}
friend void display(d);
};
void display(d t1)
{
cout<<t1.u;
```

```
}
void main()
{
clrscr();
d obj1(5);
display(obj1);
getch();
}
```

Output:

5

13.9 FRIEND CLASS

A **friend** class is a class all of whose member functions are friend functions of a class, that is, whose member functions have access to the other class's private and protected members.

A class can also be declared to be the friend of some other class. When we create a friend class then all the member functions of the friend class also become the friend of the other class. This requires the condition that the friend becoming class must be first declared or defined (forward declaration).

Definition: *"A friend class is a class whose member functions can access other class private and protected members."*

It is also possible to make an entire class a friend of another class. This gives all of the members of the friend class access to the private members of the other class.

We can also define a class CRectangle as friend of CSquare, granting that first class access to the protected and private members of the second one.

Program 5: Write a C++ program to understand the friend class CRectangle.

```
// friend class
#include<iostream.h>
#include<conio.h>
class CSquare;
class CRectangle
{
int width, height;
public:
int area ()
```

```
{return (width * height);}
void convert (CSquare a);
};
class CSquare
{
private:
int side;
public:
void set_side (int a)
{side=a;}
friend class CRectangle;
};
void CRectangle::convert (CSquare a)
{
width = a.side;
height = a.side;
}
void main ()
{
CSquare sqr;
CRectangle rect;
sqr.set_side(4);
rect.convert(sqr);
cout << rect.area();
getch();
}
```

Output:

16

In this example, we have declared CRectangle as a friend of CSquare so that CRectangle member functions could have access to the protected and private members of CSquare, more concretely to CSquare::side, which describes the side width of the square.

You may also see something new at the beginning of the program: an empty declaration of class CSquare. This is necessary because within the declaration of CRectangle we refer to CSquare (as a parameter in convert()). The definition of CSquare is included later, so if we did not include a previous empty declaration for CSquare this class would not be visible from within the definition of CRectangle.

Consider that friendships are not corresponded if we do not explicitly specify so. In our example, CRectangle is considered as a friend class by CSquare, but

CRectangle does not consider CSquare to be a friend, so CRectangle can access the protected and private members of CSquare but not the reverse way. Of course, we could have declared also CSquare as friend of CRectangle if we wanted to.

Another property of friendships is that they are *not transitive*: The friend of a friend is not considered to be a friend unless explicitly specified.

Program 6: Write a C++ program for friend Classes.

```
#include <iostream.h>
#include<conio.h>
class A
{
int a;
int b;
public:
A(int i,int j)
{
a =i;
b =j;
}
friend class B;
};
class B
{
public:
int val(A x);
};
int B::val(A x)
{
return x.a <x.b ?x.a :x.b;
}
void main()
{
A aa(10,20);
B bb;
cout <<bb.val(aa);
getch();
}
```

Output:

10

13.10 FRIEND AND ENCAPSULATION

Some people believe that the idea of having friend classes violates the principle of encapsulation because it means that one class can get at the internals of another. One way to think about this, however, is that friend is simply part of a class's overall interface that it shows the world. Just like an elevator repairman has access to a different interface than an elevator rider, some classes or functions require expanded access to the internals of another class.

Moreover, using friend allows a class to present a more restrictive interface to the outside world by hiding more details than may be needed by anything but the friends of the class. Finally, friends are particularly common in cases of operator overloading because it is often necessary for an overloaded operator to have access to the internals of the classes that are arguments to the operator.

Program 7: Write a C++ program for friend function Demo.

```
#include <iostream.h>
#include<conio.h>
class myclass
{
int num;
public:
myclass(int x)
{
num = x;
}
friend int isneg(myclass ob);
};
int isneg(myclass ob)
{
return (ob.num < 0) ? 1 : 0;
}
void  main()
{
myclass a(-1), b(2);
cout << isneg(a) << ' ' << isneg(b);
cout << endl;
getch();
}
```

Output:

1 0

13.11 STATIC FUNCTION

A class can contain **static** members, either data members or member functions. Static data members of a class are also known as "class variables", because there is only one unique value for all the objects of that same class. Their content is not different from one object of this class to another.

"The static keyword can be used to declare variables, functions, class data members and class functions."

By default, an object or variable that is defined outside all blocks has static duration and external linkage. Static duration means that the object or variable is allocated when the program starts and is deallocated when the program ends. External linkage means that the name of the variable is visible from outside the file in which the variable is declared. Conversely, internal linkage means that the name is not visible outside the file in which the variable is declared.

13.11.1 Uses of Static Keyword

Following are the various uses of static keyword:

1. When you declare a variable or function at file scope (global and/or namespace scope), the static keyword specifies that the variable or function has internal linkage. When you declare a variable, the variable has static duration and the compiler initializes it to 0 unless you specify another value.
2. When you declare a variable in a function, the static keyword specifies that the variable retains its state between calls to that function.
3. When you declare a data member in a class declaration, the static keyword specifies that one copy of the member is shared by all instances of the class. A static data member must be defined at file scope. An integral data member that you declare as const static can have an initializer.
4. When you declare a member function in a class declaration, the static keyword specifies that the function is shared by all instances of the class. A static member function cannot access an instance member because the function does not have an implicit this pointer. To access an instance member, declare the function with a parameter that is an instance pointer or reference.
5. You cannot declare the members of a union as static. However, a globally declared anonymous union must be explicitly declared static.

13.12 STATIC DATA MEMBERS

Classes can contain static data member and member functions. Class data members can be declared using the storage class specifier static in the class member list.

Only one copy of the static member is shared by all objects of a class in a program. When you declare an object of a class having a static member, the static member is not part of the class object.

Definition: *"When a data member is declared as static, only one copy of the data is maintained for all objects of the class."*

A typical use of static members is for recording data common to all objects of a class. You access a static data member by qualifying the class name using the:: (scope resolution) operator. In the following example, you can refer to the static member

Static data members are not part of objects of a given class type; they are separate objects. As a result, the declaration of a static data member is not considered a definition. The data member is declared in class scope, but definition is performed at file scope. These static members have external linkage. The following example illustrates this:

Program 8: Write a C++ program to share static variable among different class instances.

```
#include<iostream.h>
#include<conio.h>
class MyClass
{
static int a;
int b;
public:
void set(int i, int j)
{
a=i;
b=j;
}
void show();
};
int MyClass::a;
void MyClass::show()
{
cout<< "This is static a: " << a << endl;
cout<< "This is non-static b: " << b << endl;
}
void main(void)
```

```
{
MyClass x, y;
x.set(1,1);
x.show();
y.set(2,2);
y.show();
x.show();
getch();
}
```

Output:

```
This is static a: 1
This is non-static b: 1
This is static a: 2
This is non-static b: 2
This is static a: 2
This is non-static b: 1
```

13.13 STATIC MEMBER FUNCTIONS

Like data members, member functions, can also be declared as static. When a function is defined as static, it can access only static data members and member functions of the same class. The non-static members are not available to these functions. The static member function declared in public section can be invoked using its class name without using its objects. The static keyword makes the function free from the individual object of the class and its scope is global in the class without creating any side effect for other part of the program.

Definition: *"Static member functions are those functions that can be called without any object creation. Scope resolution operator is used to call a static member function."*

Static member functions have a class scope and they do not have access to the 'this' pointer of the class. When a member is declared as static, a static member of class, it has only one data for the entire class even though there are many objects created for the class. The main usage of static function is when the programmer wants to have a function which is accessible even when the class is not instantiated.

The programmer must note the following while using static member functions

Following are the important points to be noted when we are using static member function:

1. A static member function can only access static member data, static member functions and data and functions outside the class. The programmer must take note not to use static member function in the same manner as non-static member function, as non-static member function can access all of the above including the static data member.
2. A non-static member function can be declared as virtual but care must be taken not to declare a static member function as virtual.
3. The programmer must first understand the concept of static data while learning the context of static functions. It is possible to declare a data member of a class as static irrespective of it being a public or a private type in class definition. If a data is declared as static, then the static data is created and initialized only once. Non-static data members are created again and again. For each separate object of the class, the static data is created and initialized only once. As in the concept of static data, all objects of the class in static functions share the variables. This applies to all objects of the class.
4. A non-static member function can be called only after instantiating the class as an object. This is not the case with static member functions. A static member function can be called, even when a class is not instantiated.
5. A static member function cannot have access to the 'this' pointer of the class.

The general syntax is:

```
static return_data_type fucntionname()      //Static function defined with
keyword static
{
statement1;
//Statements for execution inside static function
statement2;
..........
..........
}
```

For example if a function show returning nothing is to be declared as static function it is done as follows:

```
static void show()
{
........;
.......;
}
```

13.13.1 Accessing Static Member Function

A normal member function is accessed using the object and an operator called the dot member access operator. The functions declared static or static functions are accessed using only the class name and the scope resolution operator, unlike in normal member functions where these are not used.

Program 9: Write a C++ program for declaration of static member function and how to access static member function.

```
#include <iostream.h>
#include <conio.h>
class Example
{
private:
static int sum;                    //Static data
int x;
public:
Example()                          //Constructor of the class
{
sum=sum+1;
x=sum;
}
~Example()                         //Destructor of the class
{
sum=sum-1;
}
static void show()                 //Static function show( ) defined with keyword
static
{
cout<<"\nResult is: "<<sum;
}
void number()                      //Normal member function number( )
{
cout<<"\nNumber is: "<<x;
}
};
void main()
{
Example e1;
Example::show();
```

```
//Static function show() accessed using class name example and the scope
resolution operator ::
Example e2,e3,e4;
Example::show();
e1.number();
//Normal member function accessed using object e1 and the dot member
access operator.
e2.number();
e3.number();
e4.number();
getch();
}
```

Output:

```
Result is: 1
Result is: 4
Number is: 1
Number is: 2
Number is: 3
Number is: 4
```

In the above example, the function show() is defined as static function and the integer data type sum is declared as static data type. Four objects e1, e2, e3 and e4 are created for the class Example. The constructor of the class Example increments the sum by 1 and the destructor of the class decrements sum by 1.

The static function is accessed using the class name Example and the scope resolution operator:: as

```
Example::show();
```

But the normal member function number() is accessed using the object name and the dot member access operator as

```
e1.number()
e2.number()
e3.number()
e4.number()
```

The first time the static function show() is called, there was one object created and thus, the sum is incremented by 1 in the constructor printing the result of sum as 1.When the static function show() is called the second time, there were three more objects e2,e3 and e4 created which results in the sum incremented thrice from 1 in the constructor of the corresponding class Example, resulting in the value of sum as 4, which is displayed in the second result. Applying the above explanation, it is clear that the static function operates on the class and not in object. To access static function the programmer can use the class name, followed by the scope resolution operator, as seen in example above.

Program 10: Write a C++ program for static Functions.

```
#include <iostream.h>
#include<conio.h>
class A
{
private:
static int a;
int b;
public:
A()
{
a++;
b =a;
}
~A()
{
a—;
cout <<"Destroy number b " <<b <<endl;
}
static void show_a()
{
cout <<"Value of a is " <<a <<endl;
}
void show_b()
{
cout <<"Value of b is " <<b <<endl;
}
};
int A :: a=0;
void main()
{
A a1;
A::show_a();
A a2,a3;
A::show_a();
a1.show_b();
a2.show_b();
```

```
a3.show_b();
getch();
}
```

Output:

```
Value of a is 1
Value of a is 3
Value of b is 1
Value of b is 2
Value of b is 3
Destroy number b 3
Destroy number b 2
Destroy number b 1
```

13.14 DIFFERENCES BETWEEN A STATIC MEMBER FUNCTION AND NON-STATIC MEMBER FUNCTION

Following are the difference between a static member function and non-static member function:

1. A static member function can access only static member data, static member functions and data and functions outside the class. A non-static member function can access all of the above including the static data member.
2. A static member function can be called, even when a class is not instantiated, a non-static member function can be called only after instantiating the class as an object.
3. A static member function cannot be declared virtual, whereas a non-static member functions can be declared as virtual
4. A static member function cannot have access to the 'this' pointer of the class.

The static member functions are not used very frequently in programs. But nevertheless, they become useful whenever we need to have functions which are accessible even when the class is not instantiated.

13.15 CONSTANT FUNCTION

By using the **const** keyword, we can declare constant data members, member functions and also constant objects. Constant means that the thing which we cannot modify when we once declare it.

The const keyword can be used to tell the compiler that a certain data member should not be modified once it has been initialized. It can also be used to declare functions of a class that do not alter any class data.

***Definition:** "A const member function is a member function that guarantees it will not change any class variables or call any non-const member functions."*

If a member function of a class does not alter any data in the class, then this member function may be declared as a constant function using the keyword const.

13.15.1 Constant Data Member

The keyword const (for constant) precedes the data type of a data member. It specifies that the value of a data member will not change throughout the program. Any attempt to alter the value of a data member defined with this qualifier will elicit an error message from the compiler.

The general syntax of constant data member is:

```
const data-type function-name(argument list)
```

For example:

```
const float PI = 3.14159F;
```

Program 11: Write a C++ program to assign values using the member initialization syntax.

```
#include <iostream.h>
#include<conio.h>
class MyClass
{
const int numA;                    // const member
const int numB;                    // const member
public:
// Initialize numA and numB using initialization syntax.
MyClass(int x, int y) : numA(x), numB(y) { }
int getNumA()
{
return numA;
}
int getNumB()
{
return numB;
}
};
void main()
{
```

```
MyClass object1(7, 9), object2(5, 2);
cout << "Values in object1 are " << object1.getNumB() << " and " <<
object1.getNumA() << endl;
cout << "Values in object2 are " << object2.getNumB() << " and " <<
object2.getNumA() << endl;
getch();
}
```

Output:

```
Values in object1 are 9 7
Values in object2 are 2 5
```

13.15.2 Constant Member Functions

Declaring a member function with the **const** keyword specifies that the function is a "read-only" function that does not modify the object for which it is called.

To declare a constant member function, place the **const** keyword after the closing parenthesis of the argument list. The **const** keyword is required in both the declaration and the definition. A constant member function cannot modify any data members or call any member functions that aren't constant.

The general syntax of constant member function is:

```
data-type function-name(argument list) const
```

Program 12: Write a C++ program for the implementation of constant member function.

```
//This program won't compile.
#include< iostream.h>
#include< conio.h>
class Demo
{
int i;
public:
int geti() const
{
return i;                // ok
}
void seti(int x) const
{
i = x;                   // error!
}
};
```

```
void main()
{
Demo ob;
ob.seti(1900);
cout << ob.geti();
getch();
}
```

This program will not compile because **seti()** is declared as **const**. This means that it is not allowed to modify the invoking object. Since it attempts to change **i,** the program is in error. In contrast, since **geti()** does not attempt to modify **i,** it is perfectly acceptable.

Program 13: Write a C++ program for adding rational numbers & display OUTPUT as numerator/denominator.

```
#include<iostream.h>
#include<conio.h>
class rational
{
private:
int n,d;
public:
void set(int a,int a1)
{
n=a;
d=a1;
}
void put() const
{
cout<<"Sum:";
cout<<n<<"/"<<d;
}
void add(rational u1, rational u2)
{
n=u1.n*u2.d+u2.n*u1.d;
d=u1.d*u2.d;
}
};
void main()
{
rational obj1,obj2,obj3;
```

```
obj1.set(15,5);
obj2.set(3,5);
obj3.add(obj1,obj2);
obj3.put();
getch();
}
```

Output:

Sum: 90/25

13.15.3 Constant Object

Some objects need to be modifiable and some do not. The programmer may use keyword const to specify that an object is not modifiable and that any attempt to modify the object should result in a compilation error.

A **const** object is defined the same for a user-defined type as a built-in type. When an object is declared as const, you can't modify it. It follows that you can use only const member functions with it, because they're the only ones that guarantee not to modify it.

The general syntax is:

```
const class-name object-name;
```

For example:

```
const Date BirthDate;
```

Program 24: Write a C++ program for the implementation of constant member function and constant object.

```
#include< iostream.h>
#include< conio.h>
class Date
{
private:
int month;
public:
Date( int mn, int dy, int yr );
int getMonth() const;           // A read-only function
void setMonth( int mn );                // A write function; can't be const
};
int Date::getMonth() const
{
```

```
return month;                  // Doesn't modify anything
}
void Date::setMonth( int mn )
{
month = mn;                    // Modifies data member
}
void main()
{
Date MyDate( 7, 4, 1998 );
const Date BirthDate( 1, 18, 1953 );   //constant object
MyDate.setMonth( 4 );                  // Okay
BirthDate.getMonth();                  // Okay
BirthDate.setMonth( 4 );               // Error
getch();
}
```

Once a function is declared as const, it cannot alter the data values of the class. The complier will generate an error message if such functions try to change the data value.

Some of the method members of an object, though using member variables of the same object, do not modify them. To make sure that such a method does not alter the value of a member variable, the method should be declared and implemented as constant.

Program 15: Write a C++ program for the implementation of constant member function and constant object.

```
#include< iostream.h>
#include< conio.h>
class student                  //student class
{
private:
int rn;
float fees;
public: //2-arg constructor
student (int r, float f) : rn(r), fees(f)
{ }
void get()                     //user input; non-const func
{
cout << "\nEnter rn: "; cin >> rn;
cout << "Enter fees: "; cin >> fees;
```

```
}
void show() const                    //display data; const func
{ cout << rn << "\'-" << fees << '\'"; }
};
void main()
{
const student st(4, 0.0);
// st.get();                         //ERROR: get() not const
cout << "st = ";
st.show(); //OK
cout << endl;
getch();
}
```

Now only const functions, such as show(), can be called for this object. Non-const functions, such as get(), which gives the object a new value obtained from the user, are illegal. In this way the compiler enforces the const value of st.

When you're designing classes it's a good idea to make const any function that does not modify any of the data in its object. This allows the user of the class to create const objects. These objects can use any const function, but cannot use any non-const function.

13.16 MUTABLE KEYWORD

The "mutable" is a C++ keyword. When we declare const, none of its data members can change. When we want one of its members to change, we declare it as mutable.

A "mutable" keyword is useful when we want to force a "logical const" data member to have its value modified. A logical const can happen when we declare a data member as non-const, but we have a const member function attempting to modify that data member.

The general syntax is:

```
mutable member-variable-declaration;
```

Sometimes there will be one or more members of a class that you want a const function to be able to modify even though you don't want the function to be able to modify any of its other members. You can accomplish this through the use of mutable keyword. It overrides const function.

Note: *A mutable member can be modified by a const member function.*

Program 16: Write a C++ program for the implementation of constant member function and constant object.

```
#include< iostream.h>
#include< conio.h>
class A
{
mutable int i;
int j;
public:
int geti() const
{
return i;
}
void seti(int x) const
{
i = x;              // modify the value of i(it is declare as mutable)
}
/* Error: not compile.
void setj(int x) const
{
j = x;              // do not modify value of j because it is not declare as mutable
}
*/
};
void main()
{
A a;
a.seti(10);
cout << a.geti();
getch();
}
```

Here, i is specified as mutable, so it may be changed by the seti() function. But, j is not mutable and setj() is unable to modify its value.

13.17 VIRTUAL FUNCTION

Virtual, as the name implies, is something that exists in effect but not in reality. The concept of virtual function is the same as a function, but it does not really exist although it appears in needed places in a program. The object-oriented programming language C++ implements the concept of virtual function as a simple member function, like all member functions of the class.

A virtual function is linked with the concept Polymorphism. We can already discuss this topic in previous chapter "**Polymorphism and Virtual Function**" in detail.

13.18 VOLATILE FUNCTION

Volatile variables are used for variables that can be modified by a process which is outside the control of the compiler, and a fresh copy of the variable need to be accessed on the chance that it might have been altered. Only volatile member functions can be called for volatile objects and volatile member functions can only call other volatile member functions. The compiler then ensures that no member function which acts on the object has any memory references optimized. In the absence of the volatile keyword, the compiler can optimize the member function code.

Use volatile for variables that you do not want the compiler to optimize, i.e, pointers to areas for interrupt handlers.

C++ also supports **volatile member functions**. You declare a member function with the volatile specifier to ensure that it can be called safely for a volatile object:

For example:

```
class A
{
int a;
public:
void fun() volatile;                // volatile member function
};
void main()
{
volatile A ob;                      // ob is a volatile object
ob.fun();                           // call a volatile member function safely
getch();
}
```

The object ob is declared volatile. When we Call a non-volatile member function from this object is unsafe, because ob's state might have been changed by a different thread in the meantime. We can call fun() safely by a volatile object, it's declared volatile too.

13.19 AUTOMATIC, STATIC AND GLOBAL OR EXTERNAL OBJECTS

In C++, objects can be declared with automatic storage class using the **auto** or **register** keyword. If no storage-class keyword is used for a local object (an object declared inside a function), **auto** is assumed. C++ initializes and declares these objects differently than objects declared with static storage classes.

You are also allowed to declare internal objects as **static**. Internal variables with this attribute have some interesting properties: they are initialized to zero when the program starts, they retain their value between entry to and exit from the statement containing their declaration and there is only one copy of each one, which is shared between all recursive calls of the function containing it. Internal statics can be used for a number of things. One is to count the number of times that a function has been called; unlike ordinary internal variables whose value is lost after leaving their function, statics are convenient for this.

The objects that are declared outside the main program are called **global objects or external objects.**

Extern keyword declares an object that is defined in another translation unit or in an enclosing scope as having external linkage.

Like the variables, we can also declare objects as automatic, static and external.

Program 17: Write a C++ program to show creation & destruction of automatic, static and global objects.

```
#include<iostream.h>
#include<conio.h>
#include<string.h>
class type
{
char msg[30];
public:
type(char s[])
{
strcpy(msg,s);
cout<<"Object created"<<msg<<"\n";
}
~type()
{
cout<<"Object destroyed"<<msg<<"\n";
}
};
```

```
type t1("global");                    //global or external objects
void main()
{
clrscr();
type t2("automatic");                 //automatic object
static type t3("static");             // static object
getch();
}
```

Output:

Object created automatic
Object created static
Object created automatic
Object created static
Object created global

SOLVED PROGRAMMING

Program 1: Write a C++ program for attractive inline functions.

```
#include <iostream.h>
#include<conio.h>
inline int f(int);
void main()
{
int target;
cout << "Enter a number to work with: ";
cin >> target;
cout << "\n";
target = f(target);
cout << "Target: " << target << endl;
target = f(target);
cout << "Target: " << target << endl;
target = f(target);
cout << "Target: " << target << endl;
getch();
}
int f(int target)
{
return 2*target;
}
```

Output:

Enter a number to work with: 12
Target: 24
Target: 48
Target: 96

Program 2: Write a C++ program to Print Fibonacci series by Static Variables.

```
#include<iostream.h>
#include<conio.h>
class fib
{
static int a,b;
int c;
public:
void print()
{
c=a+b;
cout<<c<<" ";
a=b;
b=c;
}
}f;
int fib::b=1;
int fib::a;
void main()
{
int n,i;
clrscr();
cout<<"Enter number of terms to be printed==>";
cin>>n;
if(n==0)
cout<<"No term to print.";
else
{
cout<<"The series is==>";
if(n==1)
cout<<"0";
else if(n>1)
{
cout<<"0 1 ";
```

```
for(i=1;i<=n-2;i++)
f.print();
}
}
getch();
}
```

Output:

Enter number of terms to be printed==> 20

The series is==> 0 1 1 2 3 5 8 13

Program 3: Write a C++ program for a static member functions.

```
#include <iostream.h>
#include<conio.h>
class MyClass
{
static int count;
public:
MyClass()
{
count++;
cout << "Constructing object " <<
count << endl;
}
~MyClass()
{
cout << "Destroying object " <<count << endl;
count—;
}
static int numObjects() { return count; }
};
int MyClass::count;
void main()
{
MyClass a, b, c;
cout << "There are now " << MyClass::numObjects() << " in existence.\n\n";
MyClass *p = new MyClass();
cout << "there are now " << MyClass::numObjects() << " in existence.\n\n";
delete p;
cout << " there are now " << a.numObjects() << " in existence.\n\n";
getch();
```

```
}
```

Output:

Constructing object 1
Constructing object 2
Constructing object 3
There are now 3 in existence.
Constructing object 4
there are now 4 in existence.
Destroying object 4
there are now 3 in existence.
Destroying object 3
Destroying object 2
Destroying object 1

Program 4: Write a C++ program for a friend function.

```
#include <iostream.h>
#include<conio.h>
class MyClass
{
int a, b;
public:
MyClass(int i, int j) { a=i; b=j; }
friend int friendFunction(MyClass x); // a friend function
};
// friendFunction() is a not a member function of any class.
int friendFunction(MyClass x)
{
int max = x.a < x.b ? x.a : x.b;
return max;
}
void main()
{
MyClass n(18, 111);
cout << "friendFunction(n) is " << friendFunction(n) << "\n";
getch();
}
```

Output:

friendFunction(n) is 18

Program 5: Write a C++ program for friend Classes.

```
#include <iostream.h>
#include<conio.h>
class A
{
private:
int data;
public:
A():data(90)
{}
friend class B;                          // B is a friend class
};
class B
{
public:
void func1(A a)
{
cout <<"\ndata=" <<a.data;
}
void func2(A a)
{
cout <<"\ndata=" <<a.data;
}
};
void main()
{
A a;
B b;
b.func1(a);
b.func2(a);
cout <<endl;
getch();
}
```

Output:

data=90
data=90

PROGRAMMING PROBLEMS

Program 1: Write a C++ program for Inline Functions.

Program 2: Write a C++ program for an Example of Static Data member.

Program 3: Write a C++ program for an Example of Static Member function.

Program 4: Write a C++ program for an Example of Static Class Data.

Program 5: Write a C++ program to depict working of friend function.

Program 6: Write a C++ program to depict member function can act as friend to function in other class.

Program 7: Write a C++ program to show entire class as friend of another.

Program 8: Write a C++ program to depict working of mutable keyword.

Program 9: Write a C++ program to depict working of volatile keyword.

Program 10: Write a C++ program to depict working of virtual function.

Program 11: Write a C++ program to depict working of auto, static and extern objects.

OBJECTIVE TYPE QUESTIONS

1. All the functions defined inside the class specified are inline by
   (a) auto (b) static
   (c) default (d) none
2. The inline function does not work under some circumstances is
   (a) if it contains static variable (b) if it is recursive
   (c) if it not return value (d) all
   (e) none
3. Which of the following is an advantage of inline function?
   (a) reduce the size of the object code
   (b) increase the execution speed of the program
   (c) compact the function calls
   (d) all
   (e) none
4. A friend function is a
   (a) static function (b) non-member function
   (c) member function (d) dynamic function
   (e) None

5. A friend function can access
   (a) private member (b) public member
   (c) protected member (d) all
   (e) none
6. Which of the following is the feature of the friend function
   (a) can be declared anywhere in the class
   (b) can be declared more than one class
   (c) works like normal function
   (d) all
   (e) none
7. The relationship using friend function is
   (a) unidirectional (b) bi-directional
   (c) both (d) none
8. Which of the following is not feature of friend function
   (a) it have not class scope (b) works like inline function
   (c) cannot access data members directly
   (d) all (e) none
9. Friend function can be declared
   (a) inside the class (b) outside the class
   (c) both a and b (d) none of the above
10. Constant function is used to
    (a) access the data (b) copy the data
    (c) modify the data (d) all
    (e) none
11. State function can access the data member of type
    (a) static (b) dynamic
    (c) global (d) all
    (e) none
12. If you want only one memory location to be reserted for a class variable, no matter how many objects are instantiated, you should declare the variable as
    (a) static (b) unary
    (c) dynamic (d) volatile

13. Static variables are sometimes called
    (a) class variables (b) functional variables
    (c) dynamic variables (d) auto variables
14. A static data member is given a value
    (a) within the class definition (b) outside the class definition
    (c) when the program is executed (d) never
15. A static data member is given a value ....
    (a) within the class definition (b) outside the class definition
    (c) when the program is executed (d) never
16. When you define an object that is a member of a class, such as Student Abby; ....
    (a) a block of memory is set aside and all data members are assigned valid values
    (b) a block of memory is set aside
    (c) no memory is set aside until values are defined
    (d) no memory is set aside, but valid values are assigned to data members.
17. If you want only memory location to be reserved for a class variable no matter how many objects are instantiated, you should declare the variable as ....
    (a) dynamic (b) unary
    (c) static (d) volatile
18. Static variables are sometimes called ....
    (a) class variables (b) functional variables
    (c) dynamic variables (d) auto variables
19. A friend function is a
    (a) static function (b) non-member function
    (c) member function (d) dynamic function
20. A friend function can access
    (a) private member (b) public member
    (c) protected member (d) all
    (e) none
21. Which of the following is the feature of the friend function
    (a) can be declared anywhere in the class
    (b) can be declared more than one class
    (c) works like normal function

(d) all
(e) none

22. The relationship using friend function is
(a) unidirectional (b) bi-directional
(c) both (d) none

23. Which of the following is not feature of friend function
(a) it have not class scope
(b) works like inline function
(c) cannot access data members directly
(d) all
(e) none

24. Friend function can be declared
(a) inside the class (b) outside the class
(c) both a and b (d) none of the above

25. Constant function is used to
(a) access the data (b) copy the data
(c) modify the data (d) all
(e) none

26. State function can access the data member of type
(a) static (b) dynamic
(c) global (d) all
(e) none

EXERCISES

1. What do you mean by inline function?
2. Why we need of inline function.
3. Explain the working of inline function.
4. Explain the concept of inline class member functions.
5. What are the advantages of inline function?
6. Explain the role of friend function.
7. Explain the concept of friend classes.
8. What are the advantages of friend function?
9. What are the properties of friend function?
10. Why we need friend function.

11. Explain the concept of friend function and encapsulation.
12. What do you mean by static function?
13. Explain the use of static keyword.
14. What do you mean by static data member?
15. What do you mean by static member function?
16. Differences between A Static Member Function and Non-Static Member Function
17. Explain the concept of constant member function.
18. Explain the concept of constant data member.
19. How we can declare constant objects.
20. What do you mean by mutable keyword?
21. Explain the concept of virtual function.
22. What do you understand by volatile function?
23. How we can declare automatic, static and global or external objects.

Part - II
Data Structures

14. Introduction to Data Structures
15. String Processing
16. Algorithm Design and Complexity
17. Arrays, Pointers and Records
18. Linked Lists
19. Stacks
20. Queues

CHAPTER 14

Introduction to Data Structures

14.1 INTRODUCTION

A data structure is considered as a way of storing data in a computer so that it can be used efficiently. A well-designed data structure uses few resources, both execution time and memory space to perform a variety of critical operations. Data structures are implemented using the data types, references and operations on them provided by a programming language.

This view has given rise to many formalized design methods and programming languages in which data structures, rather than algorithms, they are the key organizing factor. The Procedure-oriented programming languages like C++ allow data structures to be safely reused in different applications by hiding their verified implementation details. Different kinds of data structures are suited to different kinds of applications, and some are highly specialized to certain tasks. In the design of many types of programs, the choice of data structures is a primary design consideration, as experience in building large systems has shown that the difficulty of implementation and the quality and performance of the final result depends heavily on choosing the best data structure. After the data structures are chosen, the algorithms to be used often become relatively obvious. Sometimes things work in the opposite direction - data structures are chosen because certain key tasks have algorithms that work best with particular data structures. In either case, the choice of appropriate data structures is crucial.

14.2 ELEMENTARY DATA ORGANIZATION

14.2.1 Introduction to Computer

Computer is an information processing system, which is used to process raw data to produce information (meaningful data).

Computer data processing is any process that uses a computer program to enter data and summarize, analyze or otherwise convert data into usable information. The process may be automated and run on a computer. It involves recording, analyzing, sorting, summarizing, calculating, disseminating and storing data.

To be more precise, let us consider a simple example explaining raw data. Take the case of student roll no (5). When it is unprocessed i.e. it is only number when we process on it like Roll no. is 5.Then it is use to identify the student uniquely.

The processed data is called as information. So inputting of raw data and getting the information after processing is shown in the figure.

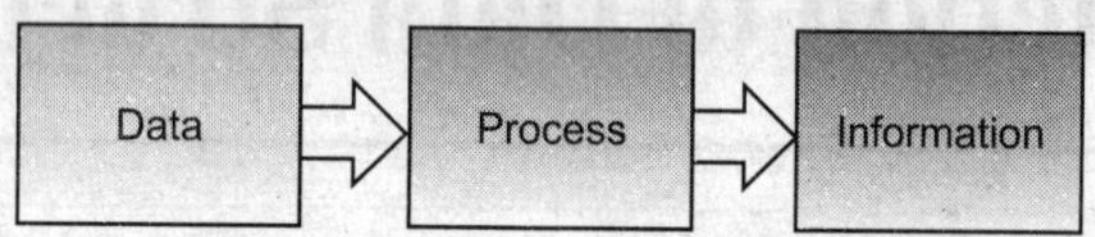

Figure 14.1: Processing of Data

14.2.2 Data and Data Item

Data are simply values or sets of values. Data is raw hand information collected by us. Data may be collected in the form of characters, words, and text and code numbers. Data are facts from which a conclusion can be drawn. Let us take an example of integers data is:

{23, 65, 87, 43}

Data of character type:

{A, B, ... , Z}

Data item is refers as single unit of values. Data items are divided into two sub items.

1. Group item
2. Elementary item

1. **Group item:** Data items, which are divided into sub items, are called as group items. For example, the name of student can be divided into subitems– first name, middle name and last name.
2. **Elementary item:** Data items, which are not divided into sub items, are called elementary items. For example, the Roll number of student cannot be divided into subitems.

14.2.3 Storage of Data

Now comes the idea of Data Storage. There are some guidelines for a data management system as:

1. Data must be represented and stored, for later accessing and processing.

2. Data must be organized for their selective and effective use.
3. Data must be processed for the effective support of user environment.
4. Data must be protected for retaining their value.

14.2.4 Data Organization

Data is organized in the form of fields, records and files.

Entity: An entity is called as set of certain attributes or properties with values. The values may be numeric or non numeric.

Example 14.1: In Student entity, Following are attributes and their corresponding values.

Attributes:	Roll no.	Name	Class	Address
Values:	1204	Avtar Singh	BCA	76 Aazad nagar, U.P

Field: A field refers to single elementary unit of information used to representing an attribute of an entity. The elements of a record are called as fields. A field is a specified area of record used for a particular kind of information.

Record: A record is defined as a finite, ordered collection of possibly heterogeneous elements of given entity. It is sometimes also called as simply a structure. In this structure, logically related data items of different types are grouped together under one name.

File: A file is the collection of records of the entities in a given entity set.

Key: Each record in a file may contain many of field items, but in each record there exists field that uniquely determines the record in the file. The uniquely field of a record is called as key field. The key of a record may be either an elementary item or a group item.

Primary key: The key, which is uniquely, self sufficient enough to determine the record in a file, is called as primary key. The example of primary key in above Student Entity is Roll no.

A file stores two types of records.

1. Fixed length records
2. Variable length records.

1. **Fixed length records-** All the records can have the same data items with the same amount of space assigned to each data item. There are fixed number of characters in each memory location.
2. **Variable length records-** All the records may contain different lengths. For example student records have variable length format.

14.2.5 Comparison of Fixed Length Storage and Variable Length Storage

Fixed Length Storage	Variable Length Storage
It gives more speed of processing records	Speed of processing is less as compared to fixed word-length storage
Memory space is not properly utilized	Memory space is properly utilized

14.3 DATA STRUCTURES

A data structure is a particular way of storing and organizing data in a computer so that it can be used efficiently. The term data structure refers to a scheme for organizing related pieces of information.

"The organized collection of data in mathematical or logical way is called data structure"

The study of different data structures includes:

1. Logical description of data.
2. Implementation detail of the data structure.
3. Quantitative analysis of the data structures, includes amount of memory required to store the data structure and the time required to process

The choice of particular data structure is depends mainly on two factors:

1. It must be rich in structure to represents real world relationship between data.
2. Structure should be simple and easy to use that the data can be access and process effectively when required.

Different kinds of data structures are suited to different kinds of applications, and some are highly specialized to certain tasks.

14.4 VARIOUS TYPES OF DATA STRUCTURES

Data structures are sometimes also called as data types. The complete hierarchical structure of data structure is represented as:

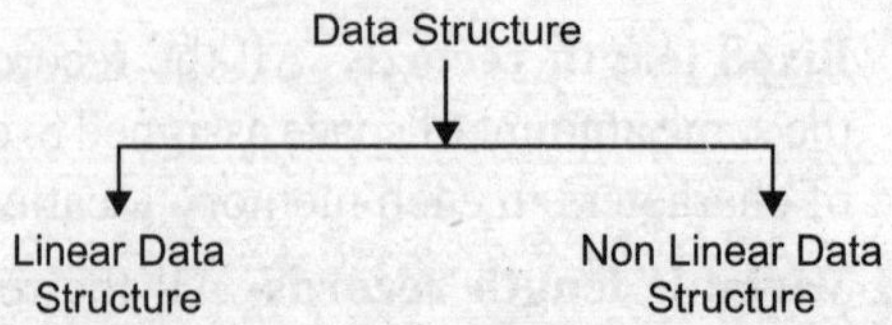

Figure 14.2: Types of Data structure

There are mainly two types of data structure:

1. **Linear Data Structures:** A data structure whose elements forms a proper sequence, or a having sequential structure, every element in the structure has a unique predecessor and unique successor. For examples: arrays, linked lists, stacks and queues.
2. **Non-linear Data Structure:** A data structure whose elements do not forms a sequence, or a having complex structure, there is no unique predecessor or unique successor. For examples: trees and graphs.

Other types are:

1. **Homogenous:** In this, data values of same types of data are stored as in an array.
2. **Non-homogenous:** In this, data values of different types are grouped as in structures and classes.
3. **Dynamic:** In dynamic data structures such as references and pointers, size and memory locations can be changed during program execution.
4. **Static:** Static keyword in C++ is used to initialize the variable to 0. The value of static variable remains in the memory throughout the program.

14.4.1 Linear Data Structure

Linear Data Structure is comprised of an ordered set of data elements. Let us consider linear list A having n data elements as

$$A = [A_0, A_1, A_2, A_3 \ldots A_{n-1}]$$

If n is zero, it is called as empty list.

1. *Array*

An array is a group of homogeneous collection of data of same data type and array data can be stored in contiguous memory locations.

Here, homogeneous data means, the data with same data type. Each data entry stored in an array is accessed with an array index or subscript. Either the subscript or index value keeps track of the serial location number or occurrence of each data entry that is stored.

Arrays are divided into two categories:

(i) Linear array

(ii) Non-linear array

For example, the array A[N] is a finite set of integer numbers as shown in Figure 14.3:

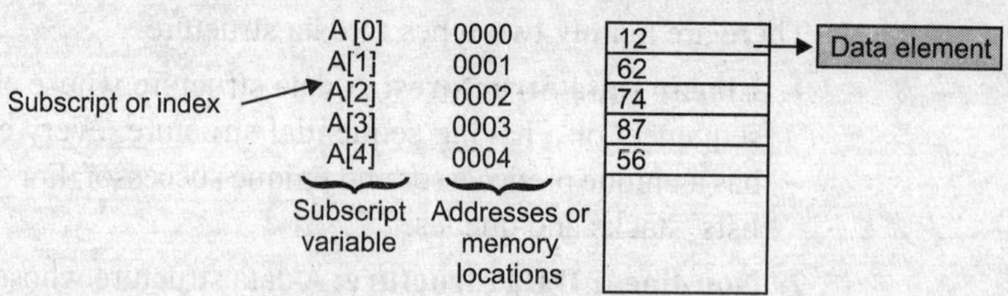

Figure 14.3: Array Addressing

Let us suppose array A[N] has finite no of data elements, say N, it means total number of elements in array A are N. Then A [N] will be called as subscript variable and N will be called as an index or subscript value. The index value of array starts from zero. The elements of array A will be accessed as A[0], A[1], A[2].... A[N-1], giving a total as N elements.

(i) Linear array or one-dimensional array

This is also called list array. Another name of linear array is single-dimensional array. These types are of ladder type. In the linear array only one subscript is used. It is written either in row or in column form.

Let us suppose array A[N] has finite no of data elements, say N, it means total number of elements in array A are N. Then its elements can be denoted as

$A_1, A_2, \ldots\ldots\ldots, A_N$	(Mathematical notation)
A(1), A(2),........, A(N)	(parenthesis notation)
A[0], A[1], A[2]......, A[N–1]	(bracket notation or in C language)

A[N] will be called as subscript variable and N will be called as an index or subscript value. The elements of array A will be accessed as A[0], A[1], A[2].... A[N–1], giving a total as N elements. So when we assign different values to the declared array, then it can be written (in the computer memory) as:

A[0] = 55 A[1] = 35

A[2] = 40 A[3] = 47

A[4] = 33

(ii) non-linear array or two dimensional array

These arrays are also called double dimensional arrays or two subscripted arrays. Another name of two-dimensional array is Tabular or Rectangular Array. These arrays are in both row and column form. These arrays have two subscripts. The example is two-dimensional array, which is set of finite no of homogeneous data elements and each element is accessed by two subscripts. For example, take the example of two dimensional integer Matrix A. A[i][j] will represent i^{th} row and j^{th} column in matrix A. Here i, j are called as indexes and A[i] [j] is called as subscripted variable. Every element of A can be accessed with the help of two subscripts i and j.

Let us suppose array A has finite number say N, M, of integer data elements. The elements of array can be accessed with subscripted variables. A two dimensional array is an array in which each element is itself an array.

Also an array having N number of rows and M number of columns as shown in the below Figure 14.4 can be called as N X M array.

In other words such types of array can store different values in those cells which is the intersection of rows and columns. We can say that values can be easily stored at particular space in the table.

As shown in the Figure 14.4, we can store the value either at A[0][0] or at a A[0][1] or A[0][2] or so on at the space A[i][j], where i is the number of rows varying from 0 to N and j is the number of columns varying from 0 to M.

	columns i=0	j=1 -----------------		j=M-1 upper limit of column
Rows i=0	A[0][0]	A[0][1]		
i=1	A[1][0]	A[1][1]		
- -				
- - i=N-1		A[i][j]		
Upper limit of row				

Example NxM array

Figure 14.4: Intersection of Rows And Columns (NXM array)

Now take simple example of matrix having 2 or more rows. In memory the array elements will be stored as shown in the Figure 14.5. Here we can see the A[0][0] is the array element number having value 5 stored at the address 0000, similarly the element A[0][1] has the vale 6 stored at the address 0001.

This procedure continues till we store the values according to either our requirement or according to the given set of values.

Here we can see that finally we have stored 9 value at the address 0003 in the address A[1][3] or a subscripted array.

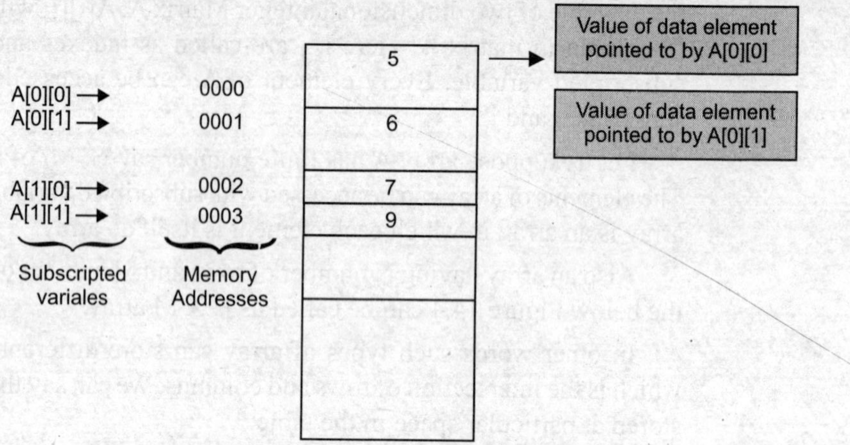

Figure 14.5: Storage of Array Elements

2. STRING

String is defined as an array of characters. Example of string is "AMRITSAR", where the double quotes (" ") are not part of string. The length of this string is 8. A string with length 0 is called as Null string or empty string, which is typically denoted as Null.

In memory Array representation of string named as str is shown in the Figure 14.6 as:

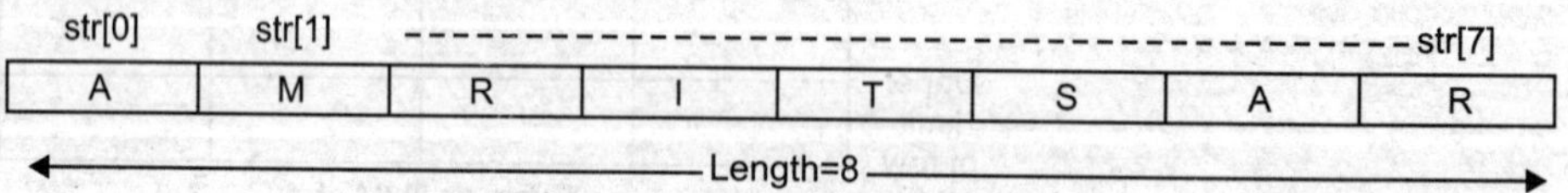

Figure 14.6: Array representation of String

An extra character is appended to the end of every string, called as NULL character '\0'. This null character denotes an end of string. Always remember that the total number of characters in the array is always 1 more than string length as shown in the Figure 14.7.

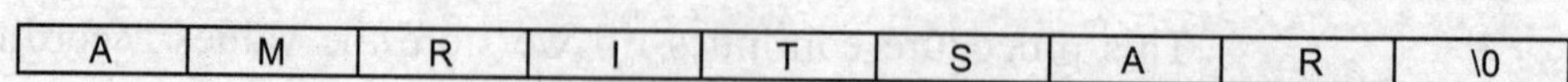

Figure 14.7: Array representation of string with NULL as last character

3. Linked List

A linked list is a data structure that consists of a sequence of data records such that in each record there is a field that contains a reference (i.e., a link) to the next record in the sequence.

Linked lists are among the simplest and most common data structures, and are used to implement many important abstract data structures, such as stacks, queues, hash tables, symbolic expressions, skip lists, and many more.

The principal benefit of a linked list over a conventional array is that the order of the linked items may be different from the order that the data items are stored in memory or on disk. For that reason, linked lists allow insertion and removal of nodes at any point in the list, with a constant number of operations.

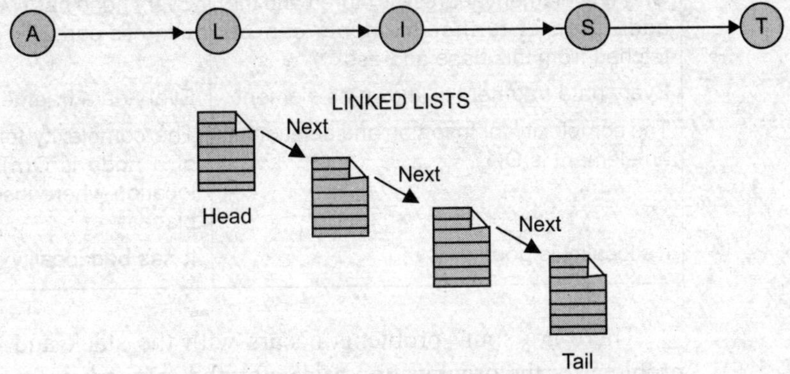

Figure 14.8: Different Views of Linked Lists

Definition: *"A linked list is an ordered collection of data in which each element contains the location of the next element, that is, each element has 2 parts: data and link. The data part holds the useful information, the data to be processed. The link is used to chain the data together. It contains a pointer that identifies the next node in the list".*

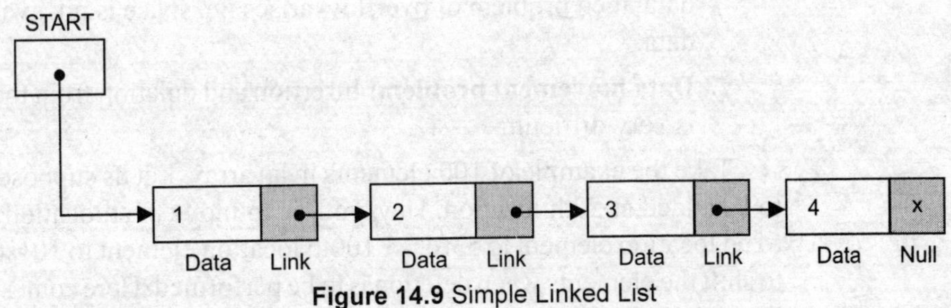

Figure 14.9 Simple Linked List

Linked lists are files or arrays with a pointer field included within each record or entry.

Disadvantages to Linked List

1. More primary memory is required to store size of the pointer field.
2. Processing time is more for accessing a unique data entry.

Difference between Array and Linked List

Array	Linked List
It uses contiguous memory space i.e. continuous memory.	Data in linked list can be stored at discontinues locations.
We can access data randomly.	Data access is sequential in this approach.
It is less flexible as compare to linked list.	It is more flexible as compare to an array.
Only first element address is stored and the addresses of further elements can be fetched from this base address.	Every node has two parts the data part and address part.
Every data fragment is known as element.	Every data fragment is known as node.
The complexity for insertion and deletion of an element is O(1).	The complexity for insertion and deletion of a node is O(n), where n denotes the location where insertion or deletion takes place.
It's locality is good.	It has bad locality.

There are some problems occurs with the stack and queue which create a problem for the organization of data by the data structures.

These problems are discussed as written below:

1. **Storage problem:** The storage space to stack, queue or in general to arrays, is allocated, when the program is written, and can not be changed while the program is running. The programmer has to decide on the maximum amount of memory that would be required for these arrays at the time of declarations. If the program is run with less amount of data, the reasonable space allocated, is wasted. On the other side, if the program is run with larger amount of data, then problem of overflow arises i.e. space is not available for the new data.
2. **Data movement problem:** Insertion and deletion from the middle of arrays is very difficult.

Take the example of 100 elements in an array. Let us suppose a new element is to be added at 50th location. Hey, you've to move 51st location element to 52nd, 52nd location element to 53rd, … 100th location element to 101st. Likewise we've to shift the elements when deletion is to be performed. Here comes the idea of linked lists. Linked lists are data structures that enable us to keep records in a file or entries in an array in logical order even though they may not be in physical order.

(i) Doubly linked list

In a doubly-linked list, each node contains, besides the next-node link, a second link field pointing to the previous node in the sequence. The two links may be called forward(s) and backwards.

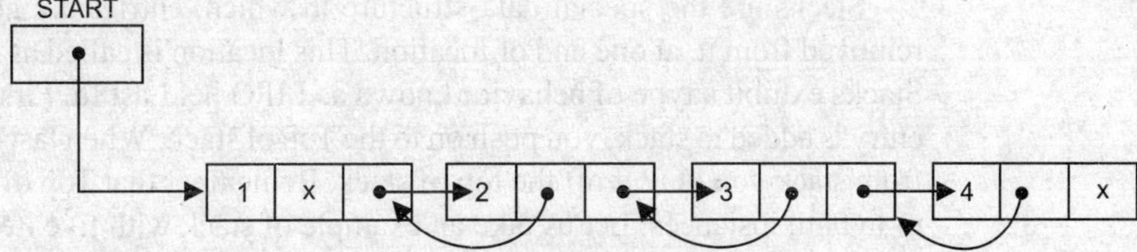

Figure 14.10: Doubly Linked List

(ii) Circular linked list

In a circularly linked list, all nodes are linked in a continuous circle, without using null. For lists with a front and a back (such as a queue), one stores a reference to the last node in the list. The next node after the last node is the first node. Elements can be added to the back of the list and removed from the front in constant time.

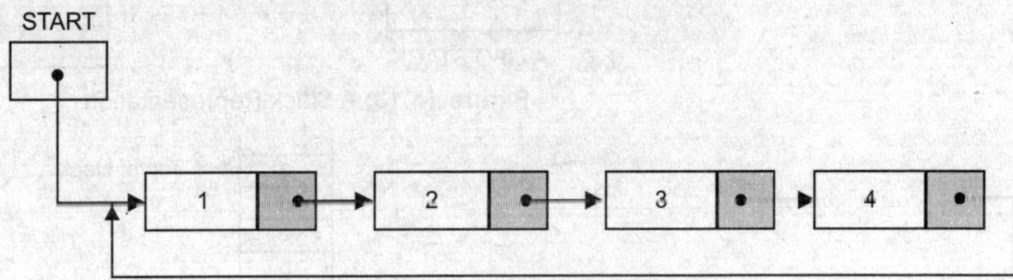

Figure 14.11: Circular Linked List

4. Stack

A stack is a last in, first out (LIFO) abstract data type and data structure. A stack can have any abstract data type as an element, but is characterized by only two fundamental operations, the push and the pop.

The two main operations applicable to a stack are:

1. **Push:** an item is put on top of the stack, increasing the stack size by one. As stack size is usually limited, this may provoke a stack overflow if the maximum size is exceeded.
2. **Pop:** the top item is taken from the stack, decreasing stack size by one. In the case where there was no top item (i.e. the stack was empty), a stack underflow occurs.

Figure 14.12: A Physical Stack of Plates

Stacks are the special data structure in which, entries are added to it or are removed from it, at one end or location. This location is called as Top of the stack. Stacks exhibit a type of behavior known as LIFO i.e. Last In, First Out. When any entry is added to stack, you push on to the Top of stack. When last entry is removed from stack you POP it off the top of stack. Remember that Top of stack is referred to in both instances. Let us take an example of stack with five items.

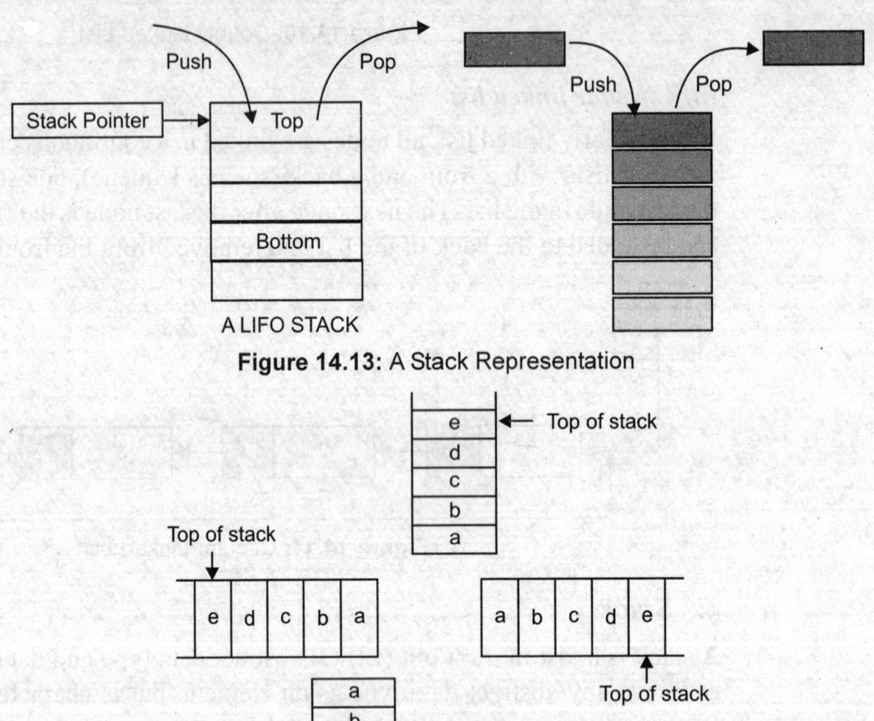

Figure 14.13: A Stack Representation

Figure 14.14: Different Views of Stacks

5. Queue

Queue is a linear data structure in which data can be added to one end and retrieved from the other. Just like the queue of the real world, the data that goes first into the queue is the first one to be retrieved. That is why queues are sometimes called as First-In-First-Out data structure.

In queues, as compared to stacks, entries are added to it at one end called as rear or tail of the queue, and are removed at other end called as front or head of the queue. The information in such list is processed in the same order as it was received i.e. on a First –In, First- Out (FIFO) or First-Come, First-Served (FCFS) basis. When a group forms a line it becomes a queue.

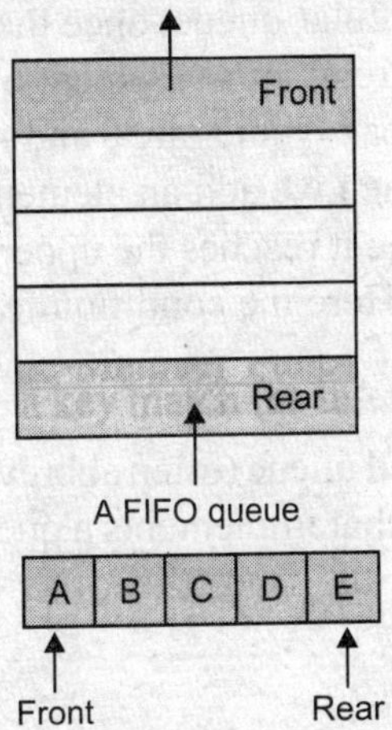

Figure 14.15: A Queue Representation

Student registration procedures in colleges and universities form the queue. As discussed, queues have front element and a rear element. The process of adding to queue is called as entering or inserting. The process of removing from queue is called as leaving or deleting. It does not matter when we draw queue growing from left to right or from right to left. Different views of Queue are as shown in the Figure 14.16:

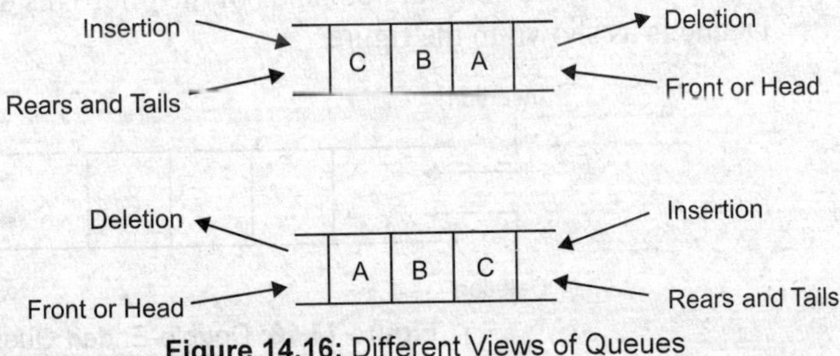

Figure 14.16: Different Views of Queues

(i) Circular queue

As the name suggests, this queue is not straight but circular, it looks like this

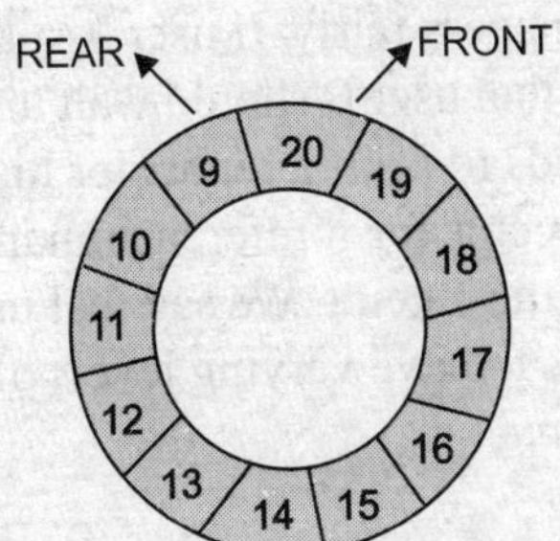

Figure 14.17: Circular Queue

In this Circular queue, once the queue is full, the "first" element of the queue becomes the "rear" most element of the queue. Initially when the queue is empty "front" and "rear" values are 0 and -1. Queue has got null values to all its elements. Every time when we add an element to the queue, the "rear" value increments by one till the time it reaches the upper limit of the queue after which it starts all over again from 0. Here the condition front>rear wont work

(ii) Double-ended queue

A double-ended queue (often abbreviated to deque, pronounced deck) is an abstract data structure that implements a queue for which elements can only be added to or removed from the front (head) or back (tail). It is also often called a head-tail linked list.

Definition: *A* deque *is a sequence where elements can be added and removed at both ends (front and rear) of the sequence, but not in the middle.*

In the preceding section we saw that a Queue comprises a pile of objects into which we insert items at one end and from which we remove items at the other end. In this section we examine an extension of the Queue, which provides a means to insert and remove items at both ends of the pile. This data structure is a *Deque*. A Deque is as shown in the figure:

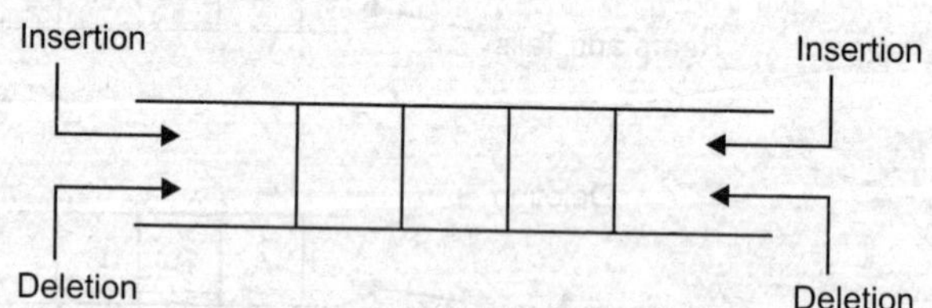

Figure 14.18: Double-Ended Queue

(iii) Priority queue

Previously, we've looked at the Queue data structure, which allowed accessing the data elements in first-come, first-serve fashion. Queues are useful for implementing resource managers fairly. If user A submits his print job to a printer before user B, it's only fair that user B should wait until user A is done to get his output. But what if user B needs to print a report for his meeting with the boss, while user A is just printing a receipt for a reference manual he just ordered. Obviously, user A can wait to print the receipt. We say that user B's job has higher *priority* than user A's. To allow jobs to have varying levels of priority, we replace our regular queue with a *priority queue*.

Definition: "A data structure that supports efficient insertions of new element and deletion of elements with the highest priority is known as Priority Queue".

In case the two or more elements have the same priority then these elements are processed in the order they were added to the Queue. The Queues are called "priority" Queues because they enable you to retrieve elements not by the insertion time (as in a stack or queue), nor by a key match (as in a dictionary), but by which element has the highest priority of retrieval.

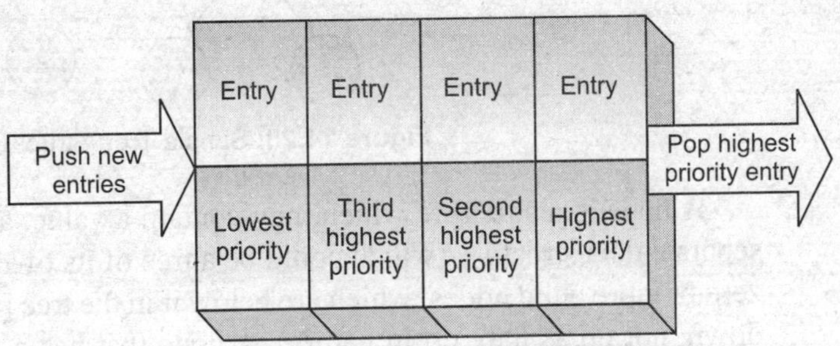

Figure 14.19: Priority Queue

Stack	Queue
It is based on the concept of LIFO stand for last in first out.	It is based on the concept of FIFO stand for first in first out.
It has only one end for insertion as well as deletion which is called TOP of stack.	It has two ends one Rear for insertion and another Front for deletion.
Stack has problem of dead entry.	Queue is free from dead entry problem.
it is mainly used for arithmetic calculation and sorting purpose.	It is mainly in operating system job processing and in simulation.
We can sort the data using stack.	Queue is not used in sorting purpose.
No concept of priority is available in Stack.	There are some queue which are based on priority concept

14.4.2 Non-Linear Data Structure

A data structure whose elements do not forms a sequence, or a having complex structure, there is no unique predecessor or unique successor. For example tree, graph, hash tables etc.

1. Tree

Tree is one of the most important nonlinear data structure. It is extremely useful whenever data naturally fit together in a hierarchical structure. It is an acyclic connected graph where each node has a set of zero or more children nodes, and at most one parent node.

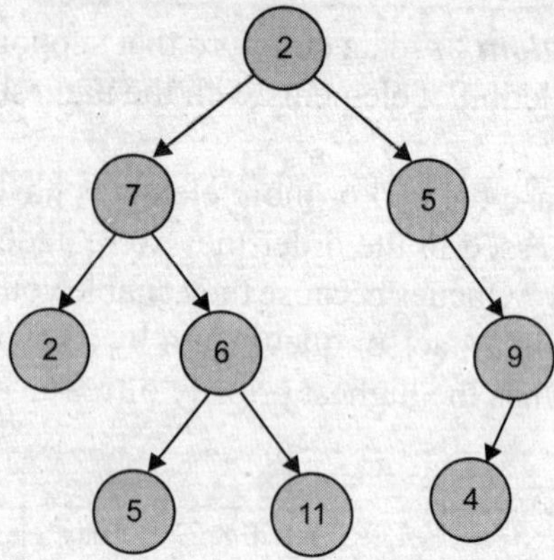

Figure 14.20: Simple Tree Structure

A node is a structure which may contain a value, a condition, or represent a separate data structure (which could be a tree of its own). Each node in a tree has zero or more child nodes, which are below it in the tree (by convention, trees grow down, not up as they do in nature). A node that has a child is called the child's parent node (or ancestor node, or superior). A node has at most one parent. Nodes that do not have any children are called leaf nodes. They are also referred to as terminal nodes.

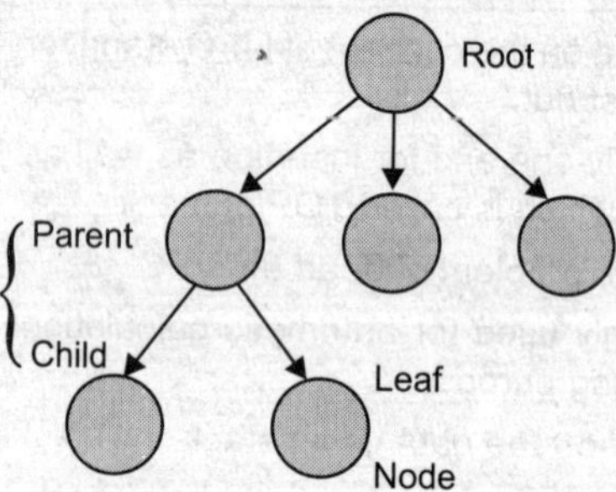

Figure 14.21: Representation of Tree Data Structure

Data contained in the tree exist in a logical relationship i.e. like that of parents to children. Each node, or child, in the tree may have one, many or no children.

A tree is defined as finite set 'T' having one or more nodes, such that there is specially designated node called the Root of the Tree, the remaining nodes are partitioned into disjoint sets T1, T2 … Tn and each of these sets is a tree, in turn.

The portioned trees are called as children or sub- trees of the Root.

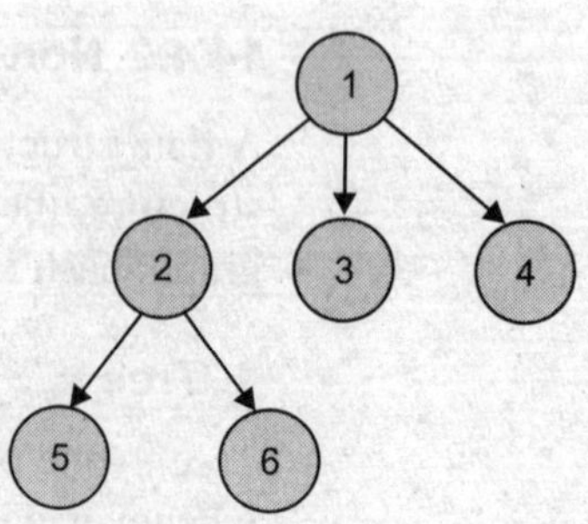

Figure 14.22: N-Tree Data Structure

2. Heaps

A heap is a specialized tree-based data structure that satisfies the heap property: if B is a child node of A, then key(A) ≥ key(B). A binary heap is a heap data structure created using a binary tree.

It can be seen as a binary tree with two additional constraints:

1. **The shape property:** the tree is an almost complete binary tree; that is, all levels of the tree, except possibly the last one (deepest) are fully filled, and, if the last level of the tree is not complete, the nodes of that level are filled from left to right.

2. **The heap property:** each node is greater than or equal to each of its children according to some comparison predicate which is fixed for the entire data structure.

   "Greater than" means according to whatever comparison function is chosen to sort the heap, not necessarily "greater than" in the mathematical sense (since the quantities are not always numerical). Heaps where the comparison function is mathematical "greater than" are called max-heaps; those where the comparison function is mathematical "less than" are called "min-heaps."

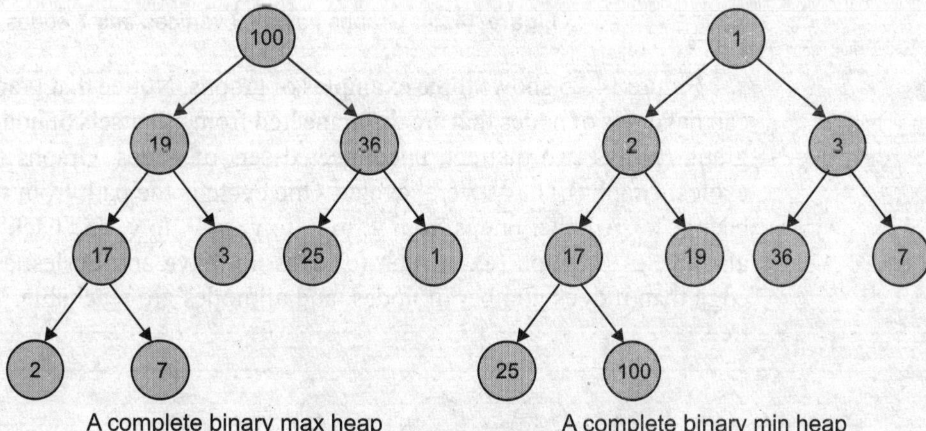

Figure 14.23: Binary Heaps

The several variants of heaps are the prototypical most efficient implementations of the abstract data type priority queues. Priority queues are useful in many applications. In particular, heaps are crucial in several efficient graph algorithms.

3. Graph

The tree structure is a special kind of graph in which the relationship between parent and child is hierarchical. A general graph is a structure that represents a less restrictive relationship between data elements.

Definition: *"A graph data structure consists mainly of a finite (and possibly mutable) set of ordered pairs, called edges or arcs, of certain entities called nodes or vertices. As in mathematics, an edge (x,y) is said to point or go from x to y."*

A graph is a set of points and a set of lines, with each line joining one point to another. The points are called the nodes of the graph and the lines are called the edges. A graph is a set of node and edges. Node is a data element of the graph; an edge is a path between two nodes.

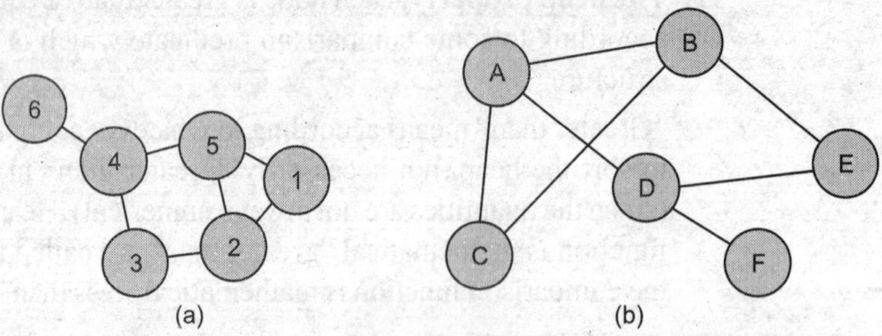

Figure 14.24: Graphs having 6 vertices and 7 edges

Figure 14.25 shows three examples of graphs. Notice that graphs, unlike trees, can have sets of nodes that are disconnected from other sets of nodes. For example, graph (a) has two distinct, unconnected sets of nodes. Graphs can also contain cycles. Graph (b) has several cycles. One cycle is the path from v_1 to v_2 to v_4 and back to v_1. Another one is from v_1 to v_2 to v_3 to v_5 to v_4 and back to v_1. (There are also cycles in graph (a).) Graph (c) does not have any cycles, as it has one less edge than it does number of nodes, and all nodes are reachable. Therefore, it is a tree.

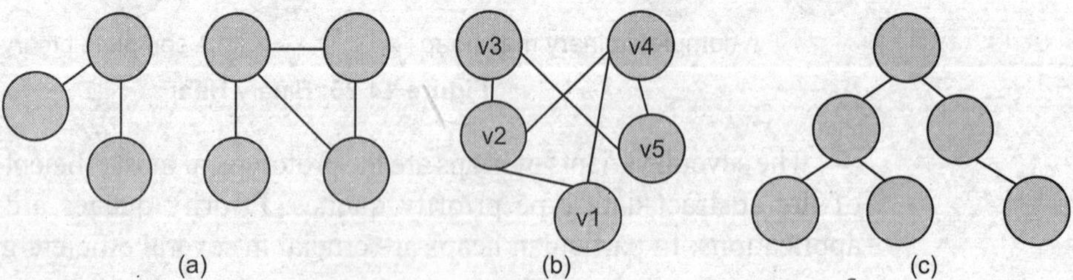

Figure 14.25: Three Examples of Graphs

Many real-world problems can be modeled using graphs. For example, search engines like Google model the Internet as a graph, where Web pages are the nodes in the graph and the links among Web pages are the edges. Programs like Microsoft

MapPoint that can generate driving directions from one city to another use graphs, modeling cities as nodes in a graph and the roads connecting the cities as edges.

4. Hash Tables

The simplest data structure is the **hash table**. The basis of a hash table is a **hash function**. A hash function is a function that takes an element of whatever data type you are storing (integer, string, etc) and outputs an integer in a certain range. This integer is used to determine the location in the table for that element.

The hash table itself consists of an array whose indices are the range of the hash function. A hash table or hash map is a data structure that uses a hash function to efficiently map certain identifiers or keys (e.g., person names) to associated values (e.g., their telephone numbers). The hash function is used to transform the key into the index (the hash) of an array element (the slot or bucket) where the corresponding value is to be sought.

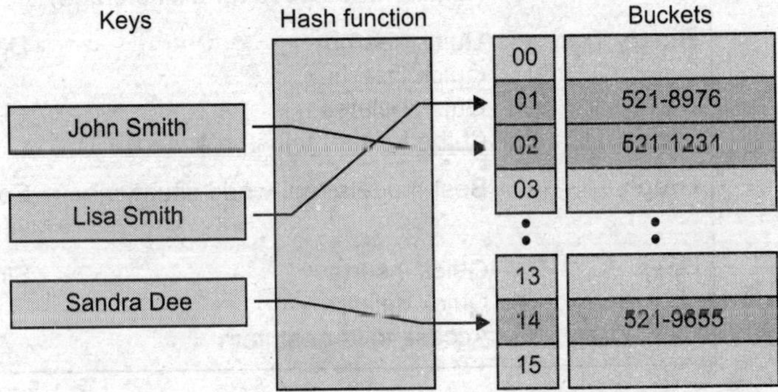

Figure 14.26: A small phone book as a hash table

Hash function

At the heart of the hash table algorithm is a simple array of items; this is often simply called the hash table. Hash table algorithms calculate an index from the data item's key and use this index to place the data into the array. The implementation of this calculation is the hash function, *f*:

$$\text{Index} = f(\text{key, Array Length})$$

The hash function calculates an index within the array from the data key. Array Length is the size of the array.

14.5 COMPARISON OF DATA STRUCTURES

Different characteristics having some advantages and disadvantages are as shown in a tabular form:

Data structure	Advantages	Disadvantages
Array	Quick inserts Fast access if index known	Slow search Slow deletes Fixed size
Ordered array	Faster search than unsorted array	Slow inserts Slow deletes Fixed size
Stack	Last-in, first-out access	Slow access to other items
Queue	First-in, first-out access	Slow access to other items
Linked List	Quick inserts Quick deletes	Slow search
Tree	Quick search Quick inserts Quick deletes (Tree always remains balanced) (Similar trees good for disk storage)	Complex to implement
Binary Tree	Quick search Quick inserts Quick deletes (If the tree remains balanced)	Deletion algorithm is complex
Graph	Best models real-world situations	Some algorithms are slow and very complex
Heap	Quick inserts Quick deletes Access to largest item	Slow access to other items

14.6 COMMON OPERATIONS ON DATA STRUCTURES

Data structure as we know that is a collection of data element arranged in either mathematical or logical form. Following are the operations, which are frequently used with data structures.

1. Creation: It is used to create data structure. **For example:**

(i) In C++ programming language, you often have used declaration statement.

int a;

That creates space for variable a, which store integer type of value or data.

(ii) In C++ programming language malloc (size) function also dynamically allocates a portion of memory of size, size and returns a pointer to an item of type char.

Syntax: pointer-variable = (data type *) malloc (size);

2. **Selection:** It accesses data within data structure. The form of the selection depends to a significant degree on the type of data structure being accessed.

3. **Updating:** It changes the data in structure. An assignment operator is an example of an update operation. The cost of performing an update operation is an important property, which must be considered in data structure.

4. **Deletion or Destroy:** It destroys the data structure, which was created with the help of creation operation. Destroy operation is not a necessary operation; it helps in the efficient use of memory. For example:

   (i) In C++ programming language, you have used free ( ) function to free the storage of a dynamically allocated variable using malloc ( ) Function.

   Syntax: free (pointer_variable)

   Calling free (p) makes the storage occupied by pointer p available for reuse, if necessary.

5. **Sorting:** This operation is used to arrange data in some logical order that is either in Ascending or Descending order. There are various type of sorting algorithm available with different space and time complexities. The commonly used algorithm for sorting are: Bubble sort, Quick Sort, Heap Sort, Insertion sort etc.

6. **Searching:** Computer systems are often used to store large amounts of data from which individually records must be retired according to some search criterion. Thus the efficient facilitate fast searching is an important issue this operation is used to search some particular item from list of items. There are two major method used for searching, known as Linear search and Binary Search.

7. **Traversing:** Traversing is one of the most common operations that mean to see each and every element at least once. The algorithm used to traverse an array is:

   For I=1 to 10

   Process A [I]

   I=I+1

   End for

8. **Copying:** This data structure operation is used to copy the contents of one object to another object.

9. **Concatenation:** This data structure is used to join two or more object into single object; this operation is normally used with string data structures.

10. **Merging:** It is similar to concatenation but the basic difference is that is can be applied on integers, floating pointer number as well.

11. **Splitting:** In this operation, records in a very large file are split into smaller files for processing.

14.7 APPLICATION OF DATA STRUCTURE

Thorough knowledge of a programming language is not a sufficient base upon which to make these decisions. The study of data structure will expose you to a vast collection of tried and proves methods used in designing efficient programs. Thus as you develop awareness of data structures you will begin to realize the considerations involved in large scale software projects. There are some applications of various data structure in such diverse area as:

1. It gives considerable help in Compiler design
2. It provides the methods of representing the data elements in the memory of computer efficiently.
3. It describe the physical and logical relationship between the data item
4. It provides considerable help in managing the Operating Systems
5. Data base management system
6. Statistical analysis packages
7. We can solve several numerical problems with the help of data structure.
8. It helps lot in Graphics applications.
9. Data structure find its major applications in Artificial intelligence
10. Data structure is also useful in Simulation
11. Data structures are used to find the shortest between two nodes in a network and to analyze the network completely.

The greatest difficulties of writing large computer program are not in deciding what the goals of the program should be, not even in finding methods that can be used to reach these goals. The president of a bassinet might say, " Let's get a computer to keep track of all our inventory information, accounting records and personnel file, and let it tell us when inventories need to be recorded and budget lines are overspent and let it handle the payroll," with enough time and effort, a staff of system analysts and programmers might be able to determine how various staff members are now doing these tasks and write program to do the work in the same way. The essence of programming and contemporary data processing requires efficient algorithms for accessing the data both in main memory and so secondary storage devices. The efficiency is fiercely linked to the structure of the data being preceded.

EXERCISES

1. What do you mean by computer?
2. Explain the concept of data and data item.
3. Explain the concept of data organization.
4. Comparison between fixed length storage and variable length storage?
5. What do you understand by data structures? Explain different types of data structure in detail.
6. Difference between Array and Linked List.
7. Difference between stack and queue.
8. Explain comparison of various data structures.
9. What are the various applications of data structure?
10. Differentiate between linear and non-linear data structure?
11. Explain common operations on data structures.

CHAPTER 15

String Processing

15.1 INTRODUCTION

In computer science, a string is a sequence of symbols that are chosen from a set or alphabet. In computer programming, a string is, essentially, a sequence of characters. A string is generally understood as a data structure storing a sequence of data values, usually bytes, in which elements usually stand for characters according to a character encoding, which differentiates it from the more general array data structure. In this context, the terms binary string and byte string are used to suggest strings in which the stored data does not (necessarily) represent text.

A variable declared to have a string data type usually causes storage to be allocated in memory that is capable of holding some predetermined number of symbols. When a string appears literally in source code, it is known as a string literal and has a representation that denotes it as such.

15.2 BASIC TERMINOLOGY

Computers are used for processing numerical data. Today, computers are used for processing non numerical data, called character data. Each programming language contains a character set that is used to communicate with the computer. Character set is the combination of English language(Alphabets and White spaces) and math's symbols(Digits and Special symbols). Character Set means that the characters and symbols that a computer can understand and accept. These are grouped to form the commands, expressions, words and statements.

Character Set is the combination of alphabets or characters, digits, special symbols and white spaces same as learning English is to first learns the alphabets, then learn to combine these alphabets to form words, which in turn are combined to form sentences and sentences are combined to form paragraphs.

When we have to learn English language we start from beginning as given below:

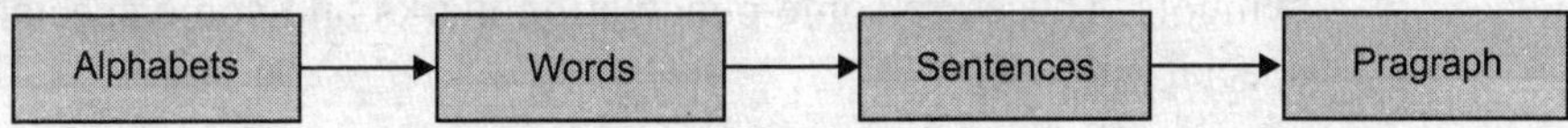

When we have to give instructions to computer we start from beginning as given below:

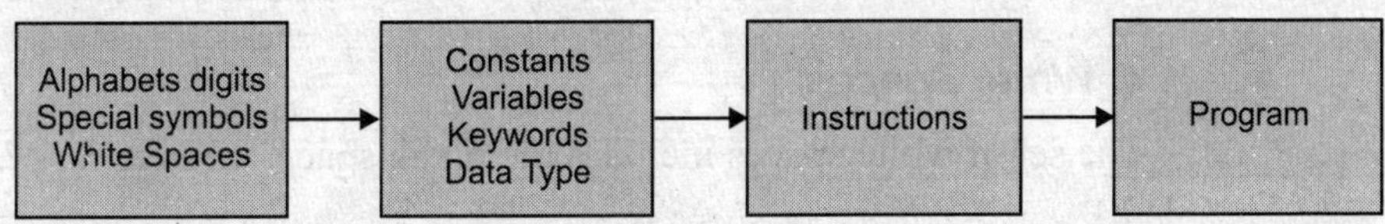

There are mainly four categories of the character set as shown in the figure 15.1 below:

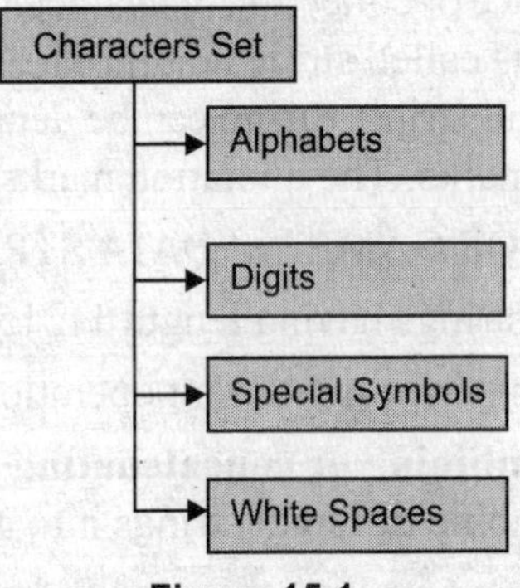

Figure 15.1

1. Alphabets

Alphabets are represented by A-Z or a-z. There are total 26 letters used in C++ programming.

Upper Case Letters

A B C D E F G H I J K L M N O P Q R S T U V W X Y Z

Lower Case Letters

a b c d e f g h i j k l m n o p q r s t u v w x y z

2. Digits

Digits are represented by 0-9 or by combination of these digits. By using the digits numeric constant can be written easily. There are total 10 digits used in the C++ programming.

10 Decimal Digits

0 1 2 3 4 5 6 7 8 9

3. Special Symbols

All the keyboard keys except alphabet, digits and white spaces are the special symbols. These are some punctuation marks and some special symbols used for special purpose.

30 Graphics symbols

! " # % & ' ( ) * + , - . / :

; < = > ? [\ ] ^ _ { | } ~ @

4. White Spaces

The set of white spaces includes the blank space, tabs etc.

15.3 STRINGS

The sequence or collection of characters is called a string. The number of characters in a string is called string length. The string having zero character is called empty string or null string. String can be denoted by enclosing their characters in double quotation marks. The quotation marks will work as string delimiters. Like

"END OF GAME" "DATA STRUCTURES" "KCA GATE1" " "

These strings having length 11, 15, 9 and 0 respectively.

We can perform different operations on strings as shown below:

(i) Combining or concatenating strings together: This operation is used to combine different strings into a single string.

For example: Let S_1 and S_2 be two strings.

S_1 = "Fat" and S_2 = "her". When we combine these two strings the result is Father.

(ii) Copy one string to another: This operation is used to copy one string into another string.

For example: Let S_1 and S_2 be two strings.

S_1 = "Fat" and S_2 = "her". When we copy string S_2 into S_1 then the result store in S_1 ="her". We have to confirm that the destination string where we stored data is larger than source string.

(iii) Comparing two strings: This operation is used to compare one string with another string to give the result that which string is larger. Here comparison can occur by using ASCII codes.

For example: Let S_1 and S_2 be two strings.

S_1 = "Fat" and S_2 = "her". Result is that the string S_2 is larger than S_1.

(iv) Extracting a portion of string (substring): This operation is used to extract a substring from a given string. It requires three type of information:

1. Name of given string.
2. The position of first character of the substring in the given string.
3. The length of the substring or the position of the last character of the substring.

Syntax: SUBSTRING (string, first character, length)

For example: Let be the given string S_1= Father.

SUBSTRING (Father, 2, 2) Result is at.

(v) To reverse a string: This operation is used to reverse the string.

Syntax: REVERSE (string)

For example: Let be the given string S_1= Father.

REVERSE (Father) Result is rehtaf.

(vi) To find length of the string: This operation is used to find the length of the string.

Syntax: LENGTH (string)

For example: Let be the given string S_1= Father.

LENGTH (Father) Result is 6.

We can also perform insertion and deletion on strings.

15.4 STORING STRINGS

Strings are stored in three types of structures:

1. Fixed-length structures
2. Variable-length structures
3. Linked structures

15.4.1 Fixed Length Structures

A file where all the records are of the same length is said to have **fixed length records**.

Some **fields** are always the same length (e.g. **Postcode** is always 7 characters). Some **fields** may need to be 'padded out' so they are the correct length

(e.g., Surname - If 15 characters are stored then Jenkins would be stored as 'JENKINS' – 7 characters followed by 8 spaces).

Advantage: Access is **fast** because the computer knows where each record starts. E.g., If each record is 120 bytes long then

- the 1st record starts at [Start of File] + 0 bytes

- the 2nd record starts at [Start of File] + 120 bytes
- the 3rd record starts at [Start of File] + 240 bytes etc.....

***Disadvantage**:* Using Fixed length records, the records are usually **larger** and therefore need **more storage space** and are **slower** to transfer (load or save).

In the Example

Table 15.1: Representation of fixed length structure

Number	Surname	Forename	Year	Form	Dob
92013	JONES	Sidney	12	B	23/04/78
92107	LAIDLAW	Lorraine	12	Y	12/11/79
92114	MERRITT	Mandy	12	G	08/03/79
92167	NASH	Natasha	12	B	19/08/78

...the field lengths may be...

Number :	5
Surname:	15
Forename:	15
Year:	2
Form:	1
DOB:	8

Each record would be **46 bytes** long.The first record of the example file would be stored as ...(each box represents one byte of storage).

<table>
<tr><td>9</td><td>2</td><td>0</td><td>1</td><td>3</td><td>J</td><td>O</td><td>N</td><td>E</td><td>S</td><td></td><td></td><td></td><td></td><td></td><td></td><td></td><td></td><td></td><td></td></tr>
<tr><td>S</td><td>i</td><td>d</td><td>n</td><td>e</td><td>y</td><td></td><td></td><td></td><td></td><td></td><td></td><td></td><td></td><td></td><td>1</td><td>2</td><td>B</td><td>2</td><td>3</td></tr>
<tr><td>/</td><td>0</td><td>4</td><td>/</td><td>7</td><td>8</td><td></td><td></td><td></td><td></td><td></td><td></td><td></td><td></td><td></td><td></td><td></td><td></td><td></td><td></td></tr>
</table>

15.4.2 Variable Length Structures

A record that has at least one variable-length field. The length of the entire record, therefore, varies according to what data is placed in the variable-length field.

One or more of the fields can be of **differing** lengths in each record.

Advantages

- the records will be **smaller** and will need less storage space
- the records will **load faster**

Disadvantages

- The computer will be unable to determine where each record starts so **processing** the records will be **slower**.

In the Example

Table 15.2: Representation of variable length structure

Number	Surname	Forename	Year	Form	Dob
92013	JONES	Sidney	12	B	23/04/78
92107	LAIDLAW	Lorraine	12	Y	12/11/79
92114	MERRITT	Mandy	12	G	08/03/79
92167	NASH	Natasha	12	B	19/08/78

Storage Method 1

When the record is stored, each field has a **field terminator** byte stored at the end of it, and there is often a **record terminator** at the end of the whole record.

The first record of the example would be stored as.....

9	2	0	1	3	*	J	O	N	E	S	*	S	i	d	n	e	y	*	1
2	*	B	*	2	3	/	0	4	/	7	8	%							

- ***** is a field terminator
- **%** is a record terminator

This record requires **33** bytes of storage.....but each record will be a different size.

Storage Method 2

Each field starts with a **byte** showing the **length** of the field. The whole record starts with a byte giving the size of the record. The first record of the example would be stored as....

34	5	9	2	0	1	3	5	J	O	N	E	S	6	S	i	d	n	e	y
2	1	2	1	B	8	2	3	/	0	4	/	7	8						

This record requires **34** bytes of storage....but again, each record would be a different size.

15.4.3 Linked Structures

In computer science, a linked structure is one of the fundamental INFO structures used in computer programming. It consists of a sequence of nodes, each containing arbitrary information fields and one or two references ("links") pointing to the next and/or previous nodes.

A linked structure is a *dynamic data structure*, which means that the memory to hold the INFO is created at run time (dynamic), and stored in a structured way (also called INFO structure). Also we can say Linked list is a linear INFO structure, i.e it is a linear collection of INFO elements called nodes, where the linear order is given by means of pointers. Each node consists of two fields, one containing the item and the other containing the address of the next item in the list. Each node contains two parts information part and link part. The last node of the linked list contains a special link part called Null Pointer (i.e. any invalid address).

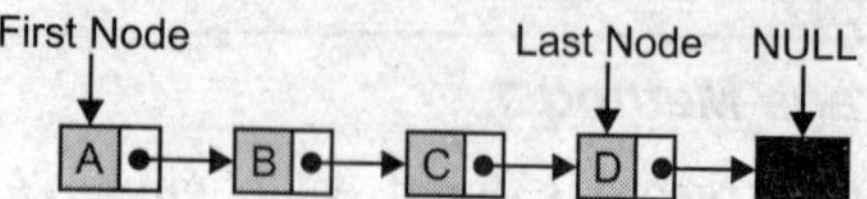

Figure 15.2: Linked structure represents first node, last node and null pointer.

Example 15.1: A Linked list made up of a number of "date" records/structures.

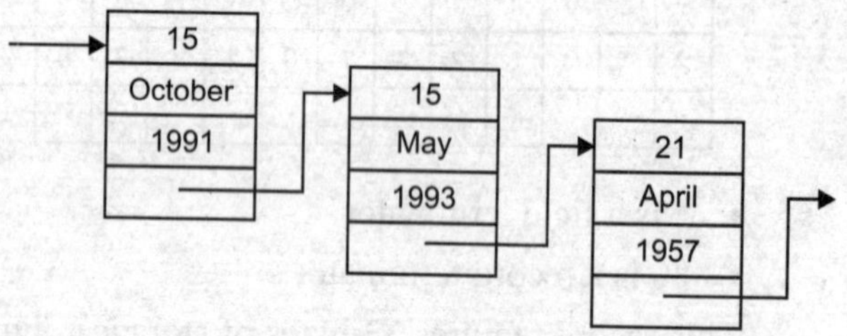

Figure 15.3: Linked structure having "date" records.

15.5 STRING SEARCHING ALGORITHM

String searching algorithms, sometimes called **string matching algorithms**, are an important class of string algorithms that try to find a place where one or several strings (also called patterns) are found within a larger string or text.

Let Σ be an alphabet (finite set). Formally, both the pattern and searched text are concatenations of elements of Σ. The Σ may be a usual human alphabet (for example, the letters A through Z in English). Other applications may use binary alphabet (S = {0,1}) or DNA alphabet (Σ = {A,C,G,T}) in bioinformatics.

In practice, how the string is encoded can affect the feasible string search algorithms. In particular if a variable width encoding is in use then it is slow (time proportional to N) to find the Nth character. This will significantly slow down many of the more advanced search algorithms. A possible solution is to search for the sequence of code units instead, but doing so may produce false matches unless the encoding is specifically designed to avoid it.

15.6 BASIC CLASSIFICATION

The various algorithms can be classified by the number of patterns each uses.

15.6.1 Single Pattern Algorithms

Let m be the length of the pattern and let n be the length of the searchable text.

Algorithm	Preprocessing time	Matching time
Naïve string search algorithm	0 (no preprocessing)	$\Theta((n-m+1)\ m)$
Rabin-Karp string search algorithm	$\Sigma(m)$	average $\Theta(n+m)$, worst $\Theta((n-m+1)\ m)$
Finite state automaton based search	$\Theta(m\ \|\Sigma\|)$	$\Theta(n)$
Knuth-Morris-Pratt algorithm	$\Theta(m)$	$\Theta(n)$
Boyer–Moore string search algorithm	$\Theta(m + \|\Sigma\|)$	$\Omega(n/m)$, $O(n)$
Bitap algorithm (shift-or, shift-and, Baeza-Yates-Gonnet)	$\Theta(m + \|\Sigma\|)$	$O(mn)$

Asymptotic times are expressed using O, Ω, and Σ notation

The **Boyer–Moore string search algorithm** has been the standard benchmark for the practical string search literature.

Algorithms using finite set of patterns

- Aho-Corasick algorithm
- Commentz-Walter algorithm
- Rabin-Karp string search algorithm

Algorithms using infinite number of patterns: Naturally, the patterns can not be enumerated in this case. They are represented usually by a regular grammar or regular expression.

15.6.2 Other Classification

Other classification approaches are possible. One of the most common uses preprocessing as main criteria.

Classes of string searching algorithms

	Text not preprocessed	Text preprocessed
Patterns not preprocessed	Elementary algorithms	Index methods
Patterns preprocessed	Constructed search engines	Signature methods

1. NAÏVE String Search

The simplest and least efficient way to see where one string occurs inside another is to check each place it could be, one by one, to see if it's there. So first we see if there's a copy of the needle in the first character of the haystack; if not, we look to see if there's a copy of the needle starting at the second character of the haystack; if not, we look starting at the third character, and so forth. In the normal case, we only have to look at one or two characters for each wrong position to see that it is a wrong position, so in the average case, this takes O(n + m) steps, where n is the length of the haystack and m is the length of the needle; but in the worst case, searching for a string like "aaaab" in a string like "aaaaaaaaab", it takes O(nm) steps.

2. *Finite State Automaton Based Search*

In this approach, we avoid backtracking by constructing a deterministic finite automaton (DFA) that recognizes strings containing the desired search string. These are expensive to construct—they are usually created using the powerset construction—but very quick to use. For example, the DFA shown to the right recognizes the word "MOMMY". This approach is frequently generalized in practice to search for arbitrary regular expressions.

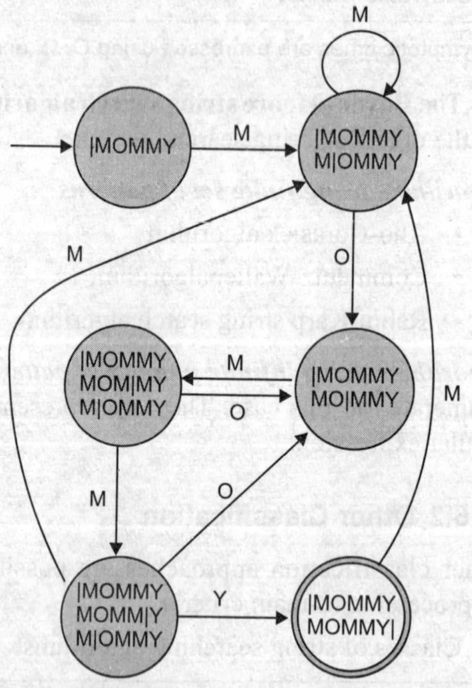

3. Stubs

Knuth–Morris–Pratt computes a DFA that recognizes inputs with the string to search for as a suffix, Boyer–Moore starts searching from the end of the needle, so it can usually jump ahead a whole needle-length at each step. Baeza–Yates keeps track of whether the previous j characters were a prefix of the search string, and is therefore adaptable to fuzzy string searching. The bitap algorithm is an application of Baeza-Yates' approach.

4. Index Methods

Faster search algorithms are based on preprocessing of the text. After building a substring index, for example a suffix tree or suffix array, the occurrences of a pattern can be found quickly. As an example, a suffix tree can be built in $\Theta(m)$ time, and all z occurrences of a pattern can be found in $O(m + z)$ time (if the alphabet size is viewed as a constant).

15.7 BRUTE FORCE ALGORITHM

In computer science, the brute force algorithm design pattern is a powerful technique for algorithm design when we have something we wish to search for or when we wish to optimize some function. In applying this technique in a general solution, we typically enumerate all possible configurations of the inputs involved and pick the best of all these enumerated configurations.

Brute-force search or **exhaustive search**, also known as **generate and test**, is a trivial but very general problem-solving technique that consists of systematically enumerating all possible candidates for the solution and checking whether each candidate satisfies the problem's statement.

Example 15.2: A brute-force algorithm to find the divisors of a natural number n is to enumerate all integers from 1 to n, and check whether each of them divides n without remainder. For another example, consider the popular eight queens puzzle, which asks to place eight queens on a standard chessboard so that no queen attacks any other. A brute-force approach would examine all the 64!/56!8! = 4,426,165,368 possible arrangements of 8 pieces in the 64 squares, and, for each arrangement, check whether any queen attacks any other.

Brute-force search is simple to implement, and will always find a solution if it exists. However, its cost is proportional to the number of candidate solutions, which, in many practical problems, tends to grow very quickly as the size of the problem increases. Therefore, brute-force search is typically used when the problem size is limited, or when there are problem-specific heuristics that can be used to reduce the set of candidate solutions to a manageable size.

15.7.1 Main Features of Brute Force Algorithm

- no preprocessing phase;
- constant extra space needed;
- always shifts the window by exactly 1 position to the right;

- comparisons can be done in any order;
- searching phase in **O**(mn) time complexity;
- 2n expected text characters comparisons.

15.7.2 Description

The brute force algorithm consists in checking, at all positions in the text between 0 and n-m, whether an occurrence of the pattern starts there or not. Then, after each attempt, it shifts the pattern by exactly one position to the right.

The brute force algorithm requires no preprocessing phase, and a constant extra space in addition to the pattern and the text. During the searching phase the text character comparisons can be done in any order. The time complexity of this searching phase is **O**(mn) (when searching for $a^{m-1}b$ in a^n for instance). The expected number of text character comparisons is 2n.

The C++ code

```
void BF(char *x, int m, char *y, int n) {
int i, j;
/* Searching */
for (j = 0; j <= n - m; ++j) {
for (i = 0; i < m && x[i] == y[i + j]; ++i);
if (i >= m)
OUTPUT(j);
}}
```

This algorithm can be rewriting to give a more efficient algorithm in practice as follows:

```
#define EOS '\0'
void BF(char *x, int m, char *y, int n) {
char *yb;
/* Searching */
for (yb = y; *y != EOS; ++y)
if (memcmp(x, y, m) == 0)
OUTPUT(y - yb);
}
```

The brute-force pattern matching algorithm compares the pattern **P** with the text **T** for each possible shift of **P** relative to **T**, until either

- a match is found, or
- all placements of the pattern have been tried

Brute-force pattern matching runs in time **O(nm)**

Example 15.3: Worst Case

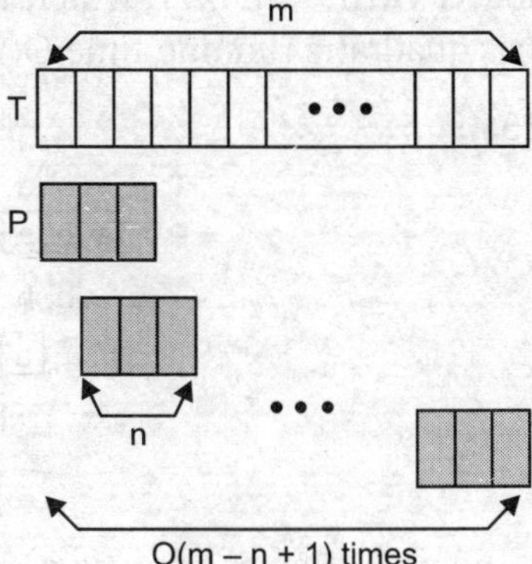

- **T = aaa … ah**
- **P = aaah**
- may occur in images and DNA sequences
- unlikely in English text

Algorithm 15.1: BruteForceMatch(T, P)

Step 1: Input text T of size n and pattern P of size m
Step 2: Output starting index of a substring of T equal to P or –1
if no such substring exists
Step 3: for i ← 0 to n – m
{ test shift i of the pattern }
Step 4: j ← 0
Step 5: while j < m – T[i + j] = P[j]
Step 6: j ← j + 1
Step 7: if j = m
return i {match at i}
else break while loop {mismatch}
return -1 {no match anywhere}
Step 8: End.

The brute-force pattern matching algorithm could not be simpler. It consists of two nested loops, with the outer loop indexing through all possible starting indices of the pattern in the text, and the inner loop indexing through each character of the pattern, comparing it to its potentially corresponding character in the text. Thus, the correctness of the brute-force pattern matching algorithm follows immediately.

The running time of brute-force pattern matching in the worst case is not good, however, because, for each candidate indeed in T, we can perform up to m character comparisons to discover that P does not match T at the current index. Referring to Algorithm, we see that the outer for-loop is executed at most n – m + 1 times, and the inner loop is executed at most m times. Thus, the running time of the brute-force method is O((n – m + 1), which is O(nm). Note that, when m = n/2, this algorithm has quadratic running time $O(n^2)$.

Example 15.4:

```
T  a b a c a b a b
P [a b a [b]]
     [a] b a b
       [a [b]] a b
          [a] b a b
            [a b a b]
```

Simple, but not efficient because it cannot avoid rescanning **T.**

15.8 BOYER-MOORE HEURISTICS

The **Boyer–Moore string search algorithm** is a particularly efficient string searching algorithm, and it has been the standard benchmark for the practical string search literature. It was developed by Bob Boyer and J Strother Moore in 1977. The algorithm preprocesses the target string (key) that is being searched for, but not the string being searched in (unlike some algorithms that preprocess the string to be searched and can then amortize the expense of the preprocessing by searching repeatedly). The execution time of the Boyer-Moore algorithm can be sub-linear: it doesn't need to check every character of the string to be searched, but rather skips over some of them. Generally the algorithm gets faster as the key being searched for becomes longer. Its efficiency derives from the fact that with each unsuccessful attempt to find a match between the search string and the text it's searching, it uses the information gained from that attempt to rule out as many positions of the text as possible where the string cannot match.

At first, we might feel that it is always necessary to examine every character in T in order to locate a pattern P as a substring. But this is not always the case, for the Boyer-Moore (BM) pattern matching algorithm, which we study in this section, can sometimes avoid comparisons between P and a sizeable fraction of the characters in T. The only caveat is that, whereas the brute-force algorithm can work even with a potentially unbounded alphabet, the BM algorithm assumes the alphabet is of fixed, finite size. It works the fastest when the alphabet is moderately sized and the pattern is relatively long. It works on following two heuristics:

Looking-Glass Heuristic: When testing a possible placement of P against T, begin the comparisons from the end of P and move backward to the front of P.

Character-Jump Heuristic: During the testing of a possible placement of P against T, mismatch of test character T[i] = c with the corresponding pattern character P[j] is handled as follows. If c is not contained anywhere in P, then shift

P completely past T[i] (for it cannot match nay character in P). Otherwise, shift P until an occurrence of character c in P gets aligned with T[i].

The looking-glass heuristic sets up the other heuristic to allow us to avoid comparisons between P and whole groups of characters in T. In this case at least, we can get to the destination faster by going backwards, for if we encounter a mismatch during the consideration of P at a certain location in T, then we are likely to avoid lots of needless comparisons by significantly shifting P relative to T using the character-jump heuristic. The character-jump heuristic pays off bit if it can be applied early in the testing of a potential placement of P against T.

Therefore, let us define how the character-jump heuristics can be integrated into a string pattern matching algorithm. To implement this heuristic, we define a function last (c) that takes a character c from the alphabet and specifies how far we shift the pattern P if a character equal to c is found in the text that does not match the pattern. In particular, we define last (c) as follows:

If c is in P, last (c) is the index of the last (right-most) occurrence of c in P. Otherwise, we conventionally define last (c) = –1.

If characters can be used as indices in arrays, then the last function can be easily implemented as a looking table. We leave the method for computing this table efficiently as a simple exercise. The last function will give us all the information we need to perform the character-jump heuristic. In Algorithm below, we show the BM pattern matching method. The ump step is illustrated in Figure 15.4.

Algorithm 15.2: BoyerMooreMatch(T, P, Σ)

```
Step 1: L ← lastOccurenceFunction(P, Σ )
Step 2: i ← m – 1
Step 3: j ← m – 1
Step 4: repeat if T[i] = P[j]
Step 5: if j = 0
return i { match at i }
else
i ← i – 1
j ← j – 1
else
{ character-jump }
l ← L[T[i]]
i ← i + m – min(j, 1 + l)
j ← m – 1
until i > n – 1
return –1 { no match }
Step 6: End.
```

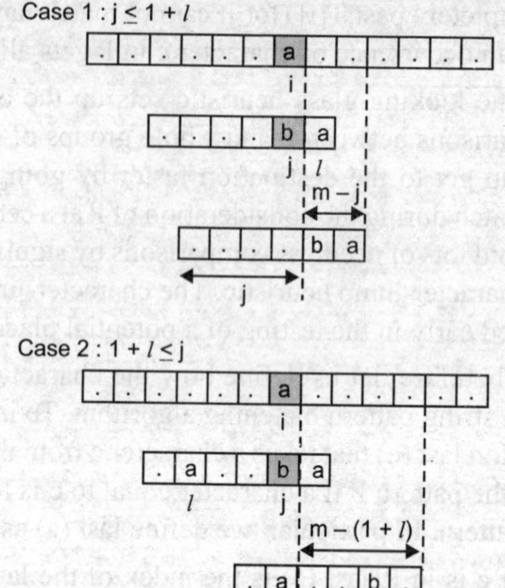

Figure 15.4: BM pattern matching method.

In Figure 15.5, we illustrate the execution of the Boyer-Moore matching algorithm.

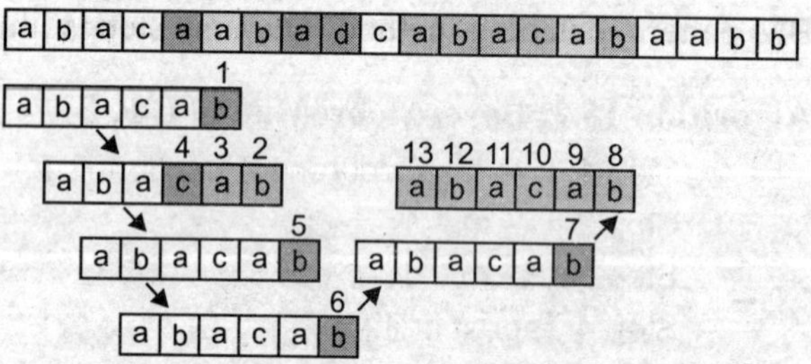

Figure 15.5: Execution of BM algorithm

15.8.1 Last-occurrence Function

Boyer-Moore's algorithm preprocesses the pattern **P** and the alphabet Σ to build the last-occurrence function **L** mapping Σ to integers, where **L(c)** is defined as

- the largest index **i** such that **P[i]** = **c** or
- –1 if no such index exists

Example 15.5 **Σ** = {a, b, c, d}

P = abacab

c	a	b	c	d
L(c)	4	5	3	–1

The last-occurrence function can be represented by an array indexed by the numeric codes of the characters The last-occurrence function can be computed in time **O(m + s)**, where **m** is the size of **P** and **s** is the size of Σ.

- If **P** contains **c**, shift **P** to align the last occurrence of **c** in **P** with **T[i]**
- Else, shift **P** to align **P[0]** with **T[i** + 1]

Example 15.6

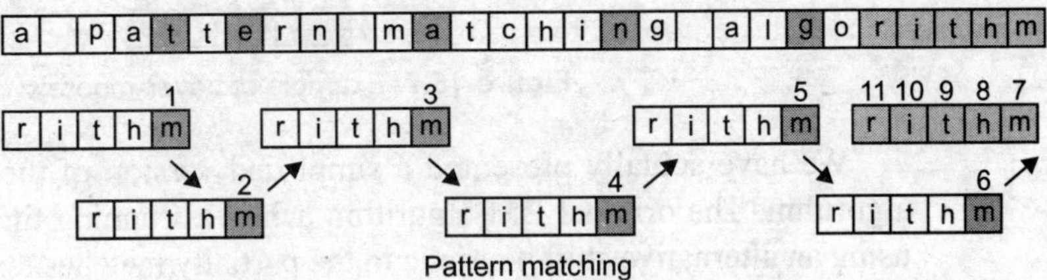

Figure 15.6: Example of pattern matching

The correctness of the BM pattern matching algorithm follows from the fact that each time the method makes a shift, it is guaranteed not to 'skip' over any possible matches. For last (c) is the location of the last occurrence of c in P.

The worst-case running time of the BM algorithm is O(nm + |Σ|. Namely, the computation of the last function takes time O(m + |Σ|). Namely, the computation of the last function takes time O(m + |Σ|) and the actual search for the pattern takes O(nm) times in the worst case, the same as the brute-force algorithm.

The worst-case performance, however, is unlikely to be achieved for English text.

Indeed, the BM algorithm is often able to skip over large portions of the text. (Figure 15.6) There is experimental evidence that on English text, the average number of comparisons done per text character is approximately 0.24 for a five-character pattern string. The payoff is not as great for binary strings or for very short patterns, however, in which case the KMP algorithm, discussed or, for very short patterns, the brute-force algorithm, may be better.

Example 15.7: Boyer-Moore's algorithm runs in time O(nm + s)

Example of worst case:

- **T** = **aaa … a**
- **P** = **baaa**

The worst case may occur in images and DNA sequences but is unlikely in English text.

Boyer-Moore's algorithm is significantly faster than the brute-force algorithm on English text

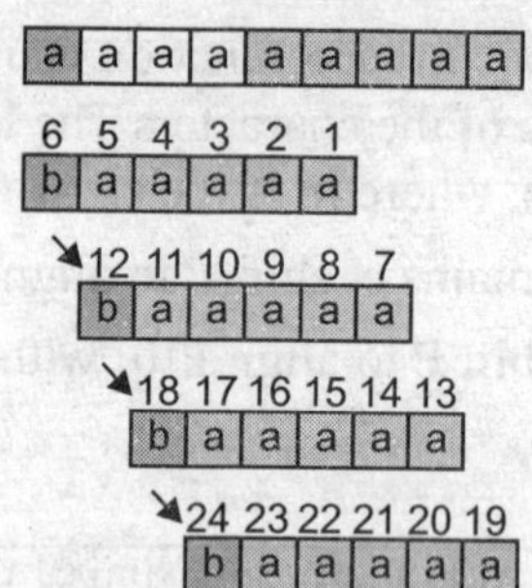

Figure 15.7: Example of boyer-moore's

We have actually presented a simplified version of the Boyer-Moore (BM) algorithm. The original BM algorithm achieves running time $O(n + m + |\Sigma|)$ by using an alternative shift neuristic to the partially matches text string, whenever it shifts the pattern more than the character-jump heuristic. This alternative shift heuristic is based on applying the main idea from the Knuth-Morris-Pratt pattern matching algorithm, which we discuss next.

15.9 KNUTH–MORRIS–PRATT ALGORITHM

The **Knuth–Morris–Pratt string searching algorithm** (or **KMP algorithm**) searches for occurrences of a "word" W within a main "text string" S by employing the observation that when a mismatch occurs, the word itself embodies sufficient information to determine where the next match could begin, thus bypassing re-examination of previously matched characters. The algorithm was conceived by Donald Knuth and Vaughan Pratt and independently by J. H. Morris in 1977, but the three published it jointly. In this article, we will be using zero-based arrays for our strings; thus the 'C' in W (shown below) will be denoted W. Knuth-Morris-Pratt's algorithm compares the pattern to the text in **left-to-right**, but shifts the pattern more intelligently than the brute-force algorithm. When a mismatch occurs, what is the **most** we can shift the pattern so as to avoid redundant comparisons?

Answer: the largest prefix of **P**[0..**j**] that is a suffix of **P**[1..**j**]

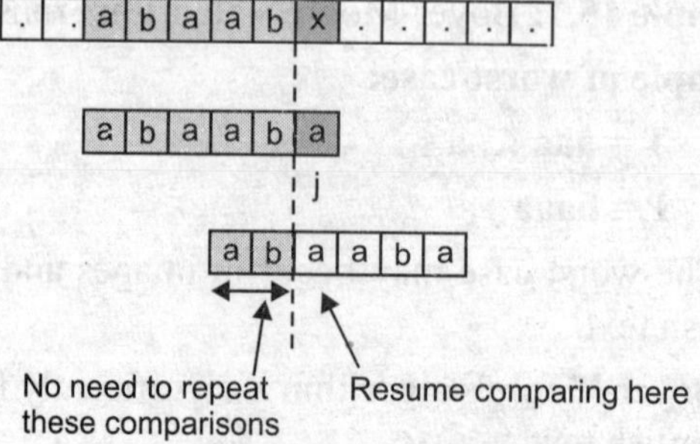

Figure 15.8: Knuth–Morris–Pratt

15.9.1 KMP Failure Function

Knuth-Morris-Pratt's algorithm preprocesses the pattern to find matches of prefixes of the pattern with the pattern itself.

The **failure function F(j)** is defined as the size of the largest prefix of **P[0..j]** that is also a suffix of **P[1..j]**.

Knuth-Morris-Pratt's algorithm modifies the bruteforce algorithm so that if a mismatch occurs at **P[j] ≠ T[i]** we set **j ← F(j – 1)**.

j	0	1	2	3	4	5
P[j]	a	b	a	a	b	a
F(j)	0	0	1	1	2	3

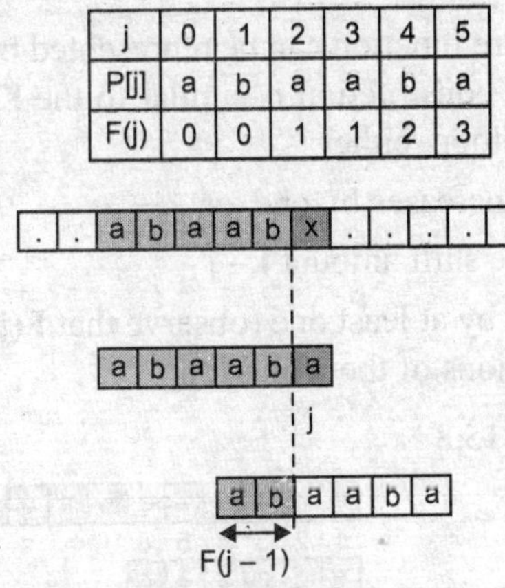

Figure 15.9: KMP failure function

15.9.2 The KMP Algorithm

The failure function can be represented by an array and can be computed in **O(m)** time At each iteration of the whileloop, either

- **i** increases by one, or
- the shift amount **i – j**

increases by at least one (observe that **F(j – 1) < j**). Hence, there are no more than 2**n** iterations of the while-loop. Thus, KMP's algorithm runs in optimal time **O(m + n)**.

Algorithm 15.3: KMPMatch(T, P)

```
Step 1: F ← failureFunction(P)
Step 2: i ← 0
Step 3: j ← 0
Step 4: while i < n
Step 5: if T[i] = P[j]
Step 6: if j = m – 1
return i – j { match }
else i ← i + 1
```

```
j ← j + 1
else if j > 0
j ← F[j – 1]
else i ← i + 1
return –1 { no match }
Step 7: End.
```

15.9.3 Computing The Failure Function

The failure function can be represented by an array and can be computed in **O(m)** time The construction is similar to the KMP algorithm itself At each iteration of the whileloop, either

- **i** increases by one, or
- the shift amount **i – j**

increases by at least one (observe that **F**(**j** – 1) < **j**). Hence, there are no more than 2**m** iterations of the while-loop.

Example 15.8

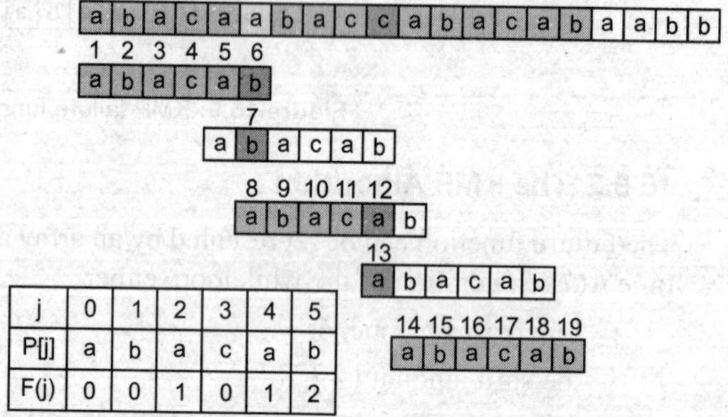

j	0	1	2	3	4	5
P[j]	a	b	a	c	a	b
F(j)	0	0	1	0	1	2

Figure 15.10: Compute failure function

Algorithm 15.4: Failure Function(P)

```
Step 1: F[0] ← 0
Step 2: i ← 1
Step 3: j ← 0
Step 4: while i < m
if P[i] = P[j]
{we have matched j + 1 chars}
F[i] ← j + 1
i ← i + 1
j ← j + 1
```

```
else if j > 0 then
{use failure function to shift P}
j ← F[j – 1]
else
F[i] ← 0 { no match }
i ← i + 1
Step 5: End.
```

15.9.4 Efficiency of the Search Algorithm

Assuming the prior existence of the table T, the search portion of the Knuth–Morris–Pratt algorithm has complexity O(k), where k is the length of S and the O is big-O notation. As except for the fixed overhead incurred in entering and exiting the function, all the computations are performed in the **while** loop, we will calculate a bound on the number of iterations of this loop; in order to do this we first make a key observation about the nature of T. By definition it is constructed so that if a match which had begun at S[m] fails while comparing S[m + i] to W[i], then the next possible match must begin at S[m + (i – T[i])]. In particular the next possible match must occur at a higher index than m, so that $T[i] < i$.

Using this fact, we will show that the loop can execute at most 2k times. For in each iteration, it executes one of the two branches in the loop. The first branch invariably increases i and does not change m, so that the index m + i of the currently scrutinized character of S is increased. The second branch adds i T[i] to m, and as we have seen, this is always a positive number. Thus the location m of the beginning of the current potential match is increased. Now, the loop ends if m + i = k; therefore each branch of the loop can be reached at most k times, since they respectively increase either m + i or m, and $m \le m + i$: if m = k, then certainly $m + i \ge k$, so that since it increases by unit increments at most, we must have had m + i = k at some point in the past, and therefore either way we would be done.

Thus the loop executes at most 2k times, showing that the time complexity of the search algorithm is O(k).

EXERCISES

1. Explain the basic terminology of strings.
2. What is Character Set?
3. What do you mean by strings? Explain various operations on string.
4. Explain the different operations on strings.
5. Explain various structures to storing strings.

6. Explain various string searching algorithms in detail.
7. Explain brute force algorithm in detail.
8. Explain boyer-moore heuristics in detail.
9. Explain knuth-morris-pratt algorithm with the help of example.
10. What do you mean by efficiency of the search algorithm?

CHAPTER 16

Algorithm Design and Complexity

16.1 INTRODUCTION

The word algorithm comes from the name of the famous Persian mathematician Mohammed al-Khowarizmi who is credited for inventing the rules for adding, subtracting, multiplying and dividing decimal numbers. An informal definition of an algorithm would state that it is 'a step by step procedure for solving a problem or accomplishing some end'. Harel defines it as 'an abstract recipe, prescribing a process which may be carried out by a human, a computer or by other means'. Although this can mean that algorithms may be applied in any context, our main interest is in how algorithms are implemented on a computer.

An algorithm is only useful if it can be translated into instructions that are executable. In other words, algorithms need to be implemented using a computer language. Several language paradigms, such as imperative, functional, and logic paradigms, are available to the algorithm implementor. The best-known one is the imperative (or procedural) paradigm which forms the basis for most common languages such as Pascal and C. Translating an algorithm into an imperative language involves building the solution using data structures such as variables and arrays and joining them with control structures such as conditional and loop statements. The main advantage of using imperative languages is that they have been designed with the computer architecture in mind, so the way the algorithm is executed by the computer is fairly straightforward. If another language paradigm is used, then the algorithm must be formulated using the constructs offered by this new paradigm. These constructs are then turned into machine code by the compiler for this language. For example, the functional language paradigm offers recursion as the main control structure, and non-updatable lists as one of the main data structures. The use of these higher level constructs eases the implementation of an algorithm but can make it harder to reason about the efficiency of the program.

The main motivation for using computers to implement algorithms is that of speed. As millions of instructions can be executed in only a few seconds, some problems that are too large to be solved by hand can be easily tackled. Then, an important question arises: given several algorithms for solving the same problem, which one should be selected for implementation? The answer is that the most efficient one should be used, that is, the one that takes less time to execute. Given that algorithms would have to work on large problems, the payoff for designing a 'good' algorithm can be significant at execution time.

At this stage, we must decide on the criteria that should be used to measure the efficiency of an algorithm. The exact execution time could constitute one possible measure but this approach suffers from several serious defects. First, this time varies according to the computer being used. Secondly, it depends on how various language constructs are translated into machine code by the compiler. In addition, it is often desirable to compare different algorithms before implementing them so as to avoid developing code unnecessarily. The usual technique used in analyzing an algorithm is to isolate an operation fundamental to the problem under study. This is called the complexity measure. Then, a walk through the algorithm reveals how many times the operation that corresponds to our measure is invoked. The result of the analysis is often expressed as a function of the size of the input. The size of the input is often related to the size of the data structure used in the algorithm.

This chapter describes concept of the algorithms, efficiency of an algorithm, Time and Space Complexity, it also describes various control structure that are building blocks for structured programming. Asymptotic notations: Big-Oh, Time-Space trade-off., Abstract Data Types (ADT).

16.2 PROBLEM ANALYSIS

A computer can be used to solve a problem by following set of stored instructions called a program. The problem solving process needs initial data, the operations that are to be performed and results in the form of output.

The following steps are required for problem solving:

(i) Define the Problem

The first step is to give a clear, concise problem statement. The problem definition should clearly specify the desired input and output. This step demands that user should have full knowledge of the background of the problem. A stated goal will help in the organization of the remaining steps.

For Example

- To compute the average of a set of data values.

- Given a quadratic equation, to compute its real and complex roots.
- To print a table of weight and height values for a normal human being.

(ii) Formulate a Mathematical Model

Most technical problems can be modelled mathematically. An existing model must be chosen or a new one if no standard mathematical model exists. This step also requires full knowledge of the problem and its underlying mathematical concepts.

For Example

- Average = (Value1+ Value2 +Value3) / 3
- Root = (-b + sqrt(b*b – 4*a*c))/ (2*a)

(iii) Develop an Algorithm

The next step is to devise and describe a precise plan of what you want the computer to do. This plan, expressed as a sequence of operations, is called an **algorithm**.

(iv) Coding the Program

The above algorithm cannot be as such understandable by the computer. It first must be written in a programming language as a program. A compiler or translator will then convert program into machine code that the computer can understand and act upon. Learning a computer language is required first to be a programmer so as to translate the algorithm derived in step 3 into a program.

(v) Testing the Program

If the program compiles correctly, use a simple set of test values to verify that the result is what you expected. If the results seem valid, test the program with a variety of "real" data sets. The mistakes if encountered in a program are called **bugs** and "debugging" code can take longer than writing the code.

To solve a problem some tools are used to simplify it and make it in the readable form. Following are the commonly used tools to solve the problem.

16.3 INTRODUCTION TO ALGORITHMS

16.3.1 Algorithm

An algorithm is a finite sequence of instructions, logic, an explicit, step-by-step procedure for solving a problem. An algorithm may be expressed as a pseudo code that is shorthand notation of English sentences.

Definition: "An algorithm is a finite set of instructions which, if followed, accomplish a particular task".

In addition every algorithm must satisfy the following criteria:

Step 1: Input: There are zero or more quantities which are externally supplied.

Step 2: Output: At least one quantity is produced.

Step 3: Definiteness: Each instruction must be clear and unambiguous.

Step 4: Finiteness: If we trace out the instructions of an algorithm, then for all cases the algorithm will terminate after a finite number of steps.

Step 5: Effectiveness: Every instruction must be sufficiently basic that it can in principle be carried out by a person using only pencil and paper. It is not enough that each operation be definite, but it must also be feasible.

A problem can be solved by using a computer only if an algorithm can be written for it. In addition, the use of algorithm provides many other benefits:-

1. While writing an algorithm, you identify the step-by-step procedure, the major decision points, and the variables necessary to solve the problem. This helps you in the development of the corresponding program.
2. Identification of the procedure and the decision points reduces the problem into a series of smaller problems of more manageable size. Therefore, problems that would be difficult or impossible to solve as a whole can be approached as a series of small solvable sub problems.
3. With the use of an algorithm, decision making becomes a more rational process. This is because algorithms comprise of sub tasks, where each sub task is atomic in nature and is supported by facts.
4. With the use of an algorithm, the same specified steps are used for performing the tasks. This makes the process more consistent and reliable.

Algorithm 16.1: Add Two Numbers

Step 1: Start

Step 2: Enter the value of A and B.

Step 3: A=10, B=5.

Step 4: Perform operation C = A + B.

Step 5: Store the result in C.

Step 6: End

Let us take one more example, to find biggest number between two given numbers. Think the logic, and you'll feel it's very easy to write the steps of an algorithm.

Algorithm 16.2: Find the Greater number among two numbers.

Step 1: Start

Step 2: Read two positive integer numbers 'A' and 'B'

Step 3: If A is greater than B, then go to step 4 else goto step 5.

Step 4: Print "A is greater than B" goto step 6.

Step 5: Print "B is greater than A"

Step 6: End.

Once these steps are performed on data specified in the problem, the desired result or output is obtained. Whenever an algorithm can be specified it makes sense to wonder about its behaviour.

This was realized by Charles Babbage, the father of Computers in 1830. An algorithm is a finite set of instructions, which when followed, perform a particular task.

16.3.2 Types of Algorithm

An algorithm is defined as "Step by step approach to solve any problem". There are mainly three types of algorithm exist, which are given as below:

1. Sequential Algorithm
2. Conditional Algorithm
3. Iterative Algorithm

1. **Sequential Algorithm:** an algorithm whose steps are executed sequentially i.e. execution of algorithm takes place in the same order in which an algorithm is developed. For example consider following algorithm to add two numbers

   Read A

   Read B

   C=A+B

   Print "Sum is"

   Print C

2. **Conditional Algorithm:** An algorithm whose execution depends upon certain conditions are called conditional algorithms. For example consider the following algorithm to check whether a given number is positive or negative.

   Read A

   If A>0 then

   Print "A is positive"

   Else

   Print "A is negative"

   End IF

3. **Iterative Algorithm:** an algorithm that repeat a statement of group of statement for number of times such an algorithm is called iterative algorithm. For example consider the following algorithm that will find the sum of first 100 Natural numbers:

```
Set S=0
For I=1 to 100
S=S+I
I=I+1
End For
Print "Sum of First 100 Natural numbers is"
Print S
```

Describing algorithms requires a notation for expressing a sequence of steps to be performed. The three most common options are (1) English, (2) pseudocode, or (3) a real programming language. Pseudocode is perhaps the most mysterious of the bunch, but it is best defined as a programming language that never complains about syntax errors. All three methods can be useful in certain circumstances, since there is a natural tradeoff between greater ease of expression and precision. English is the most natural but least precise language, while C and Pascal are precise but difficult to write and understand. Pseudocode is useful because it is a happy medium. The correct choice of which notation is best depends upon which of the three methods you are most comfortable with. I prefer to describe the *ideas* of an algorithm in English, moving onto a more formal, programming-language-like pseudocode to clarify sufficiently tricky details of the algorithm. A common mistake among my students is to use pseudocode to take an ill-defined idea and dress it up so that it looks more formal. In the real world, you only fool yourself when you pull this kind of stunt.

An algorithm can be described in several ways. One way is to give it a graphical form of notation which is known as Flow Chart. This form places each processing step in a "box" and uses arrows to indicate the next step. Different shaped boxes stand for different kinds of operations.

16.3.3 Flow-chart

A diagram that uses graphic symbols to depict the nature and flow of the steps in a process. To solve a problem in a sequence or stepwise diagrammatically or pictorially is called Flow Chart.

"A flowchart is a common type of chart, which represents an algorithm or process, showing the steps as boxes of various kinds, and their order by connecting these with arrows. Flowcharts are used in analyzing, designing, documenting or managing a process or program in various fields."

Flowcharts are tools used by programmers because they facilitate breaking down a problem into its simplest steps, each symbol in a flowchart can represent only one step in the algorithm. Flowcharts use easy-to-understand symbols to represent actions on data and the flow of data. The following are the basic flowchart symbols:

(i) Terminator or Start/Stop Box: The Terminator symbol is used to begin and end of each flowchart. It also has egg like shape called oval. It is used to indicates start/stop of a program.

(ii) Input/Output Box: Input boxes are used for input value to program and Output boxes are used for output value to outside world. This is also called read/write box and it has parallelogram shape.

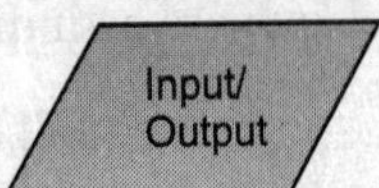

(iii) Process or Computation Or Assignment Box: It has square shape or rectangular shape. It indicates information processing e.g., addition, subtraction, or movement of data to computer memory.

(iv) Decision or Condition Box: Decision diamonds create two data flows from one. A Decision diamond always has True/False or Yes/No written on the left and right sides. It is also called decision making box.

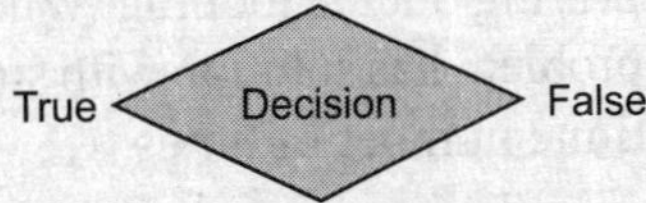

(v) Flow Line or Data Flow: Data Flows connect the different symbols, showing the order that is followed in the algorithm. Data Flows can only go in one direction, hence the arrow. When two or more data flows meet, they always meet at a connector. It has arrow shape.

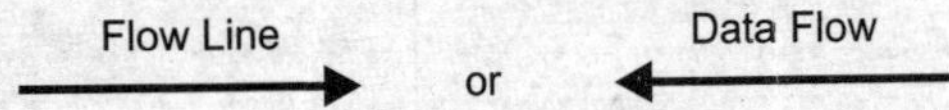

(vi) Loop or Iterative Box: This box has hexagon shape. It is used when a problem has repetitive steps or iterative steps i.e. a problem has solution with steps repeating again and again till a condition ends or definite number of times.

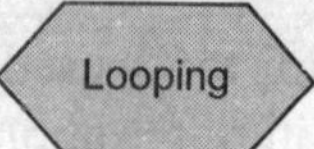

(vii) Connector or Flow Linker: This has circular shape. A small circle with any number or letter in it is used as a connector symbol. It connects various parts of a flow-chart which are far apart or spread over pages. This makes the flow chart simple and in short. It means it removes complexity of the flowchart.

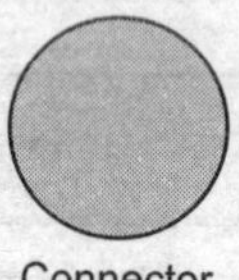

Connector

(viii) Function or Procedure or Sub-program Box: This symbol has a rectangle shape with two cuts or lines inside. It is used to denote a subprocess which is given elsewhere as indicated by connector symbol.

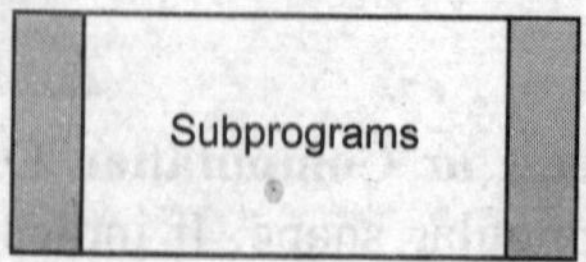

There are mainly three types of construct used in the programming which are useful in drawing the flow chart. The three programming constructs are known as:

Sequence construct that is used to carry out one step at a time, then next step and so on.

Selection construct performs an action based on the condition if it is true.

Iteration construct or looping construct performs an action as long as condition is true by carrying out the looping. When a problem has repetitive steps or iterative steps i.e. a problem has solution with steps repeating again and again till a condition ends or definite number of times.

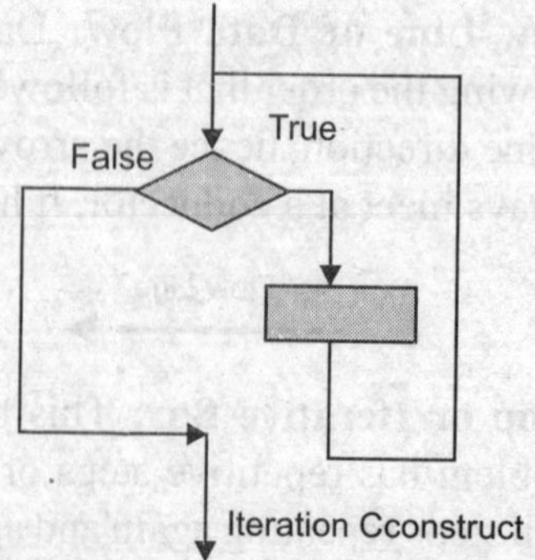

Iteration Cconstruct

The third construct known as Iteration is derived from the selection construct by transferring the control to the start position as along as the condition remains true. Once the condition becomes false, the control will be transferred to the next level after decision making.

Example 16.1: Flowchart to calculate the Average of set of values (Sequence Construct).

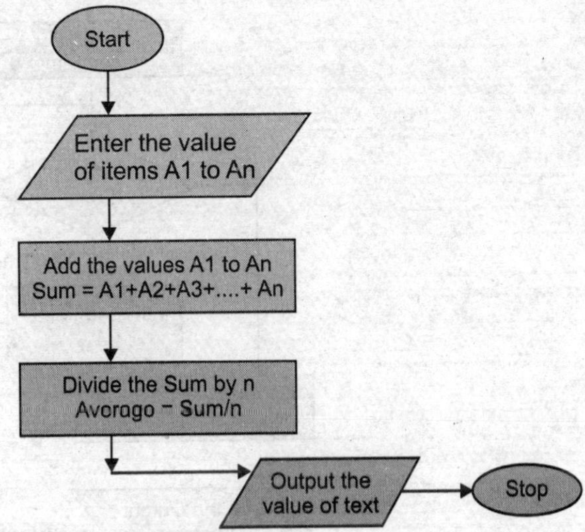

Example 16.2: Flowchart to find the largest number from two numbers (Selection Construct).

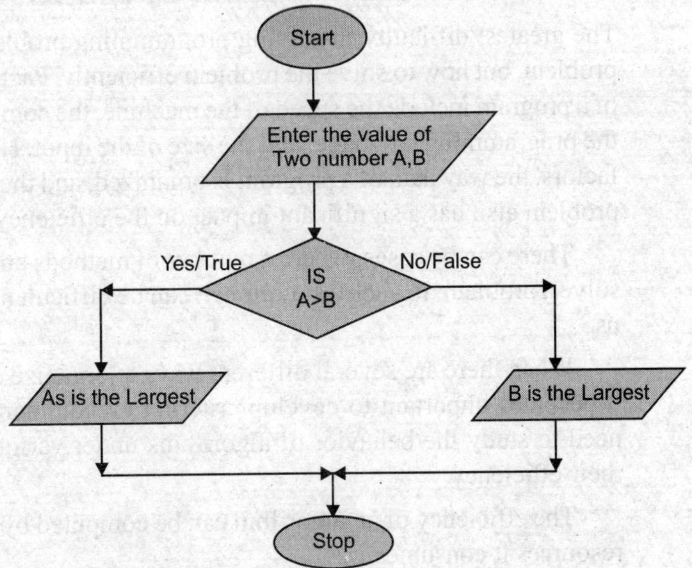

Example 16.3: Flowchart to Compute or Calculate the Average of N number i.e. From 1 to N (Iteration Construct or Looping Construct).

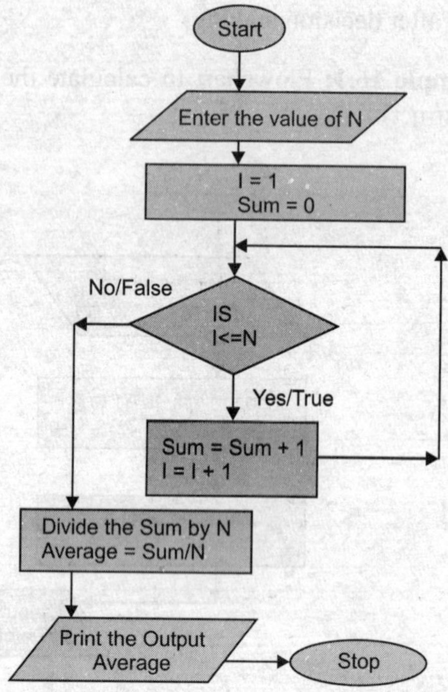

16.4 DETERMINING THE EFFICIENCY OF AN ALGORITHM

The greatest difficulty in solving programming problems is not how to solve the problem, but how to solve the problem efficiently. Factors that affect the efficiency of a program include the speed of the machine, the compiler. The operating system, the programming language, and the size of the input. However, in addition to these factors, the way data of a program is organized, and the algorithm used to solve the problem also has a significant impact on the efficiency of a program.

There can be cases, where a number of methods and algorithms can be used to solve a problem. In such a situation, it can be difficult to decide which algorithm to use.

When there are several different ways to organize data and devise algorithms, it becomes important to develop criteria to recommend a choice. Therefore, you need to study the behavior of algorithms under various conditions and compare their efficiency.

The efficiency of an algorithm can be computed by determining the amount of resources it consumes.

The primary resources that an algorithm consumes are:

1. **Time:** The CPU time required to execute the algorithm
2. **Space:** The amount of memory used by the algorithm for execution.

The lesser resources that an algorithm uses, the more efficient it is.

16.4.1 Efficiency of an Algorithm

Although, the efficiency of an algorithm depends on how efficiently it uses time and memory space, the scope of this course is limited to determining only the time efficiency of an algorithm.

To measure the time efficiency of an algorithm, you can write a program based on the algorithm, execute it, and measure the time it takes to run. The execution time that you measure in this case would depend on a number of factors such as:-

1. Speed of the machine
2. Compiler
3. Operating System
4. Programming language
5. Input data

However, to determine how efficiently an algorithm solves a given problem, you would like to determine how the execution time is affected by the nature of the algorithm. Therefore, you need to develop fundamental laws that determine the efficiency of a program in terms of the nature of the underlying algorithm.

To understand how the nature of an algorithm affects the execution, consider a simple example. Suppose assignment, comparison, write, and increment statements take a, b, c, and d time units to execute respectively. Now, consider the following code used to display the elements stored in an array:-

1. Set I = 0 // 1 assignment
2. While(I < n): // n comparisons
   (a) Display a[I] // n writes
   (b) Increment I by 1 // n increments

The execution time required for the preceding algorithm is given by:-

$$T = a + b X n + c X n + d X n$$

$$T = a + n(b + c + d)$$

Here, T is the total running time of the algorithm expressed as a linear function of the number of elements (n) in the array. From the preceding expression, it is clear that T is directly proportional to n.

In fact, the total running time T is directly proportional to the number of iterations involved in the algorithm. The number of iterations can be determined by counting the number of comparisons involved in the algorithm.

In the preceding code segment, a total of n comparisons are being made. Therefore, the total running time of the algorithm, T is directly proportional to n.

As T is directly proportional to n, an increase in the value of n will result in a proportional increase in the value of T, as shown in the following figure.

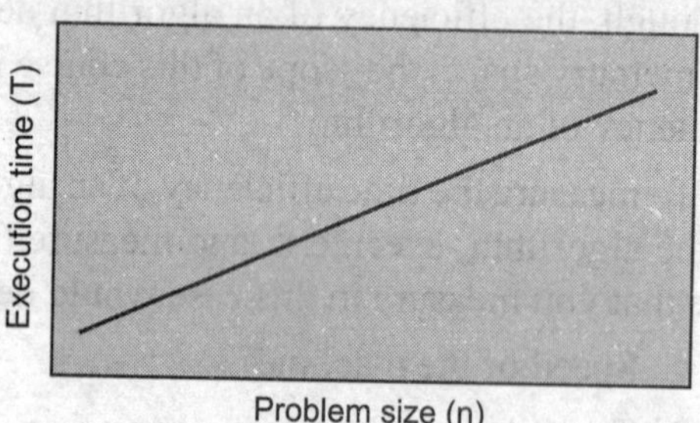

Now, consider the following algorithm:

Algorithm 16.3: Count number of comparisons.

Step 1: Set I = 0 // 1 assignment
Step 2: While (I < n): // n comparisons
  a. Set J = 0 // n assignments
  b. While (J < n): // n x n comparisons
    i. Display (a[I][J]) // n x n writes
    ii. Increment J by 1 // n x n increments
  c. Increment I by 1 // n increments

If you count the number of comparisons in the preceding code segment, they come out to be $(n^2 + n)$, which is a quadratic function of n. Therefore, the total running time is directly proportional to n^2.

Note: *Although the number of comparisons is $n^2 + n$, the value of n is very small as compared to the value of n^2 (especially when n is very large). Therefore, the value of n can be ignored for finding the approximate running time.*

As the running time is directly proportional to n^2, an increase in the value of n will result in a quadratic increase in the running time. This means that if the value of n is doubled, the running time will increase four times. The rate of change of T with an increase in the value of n is depicted in the following figure:

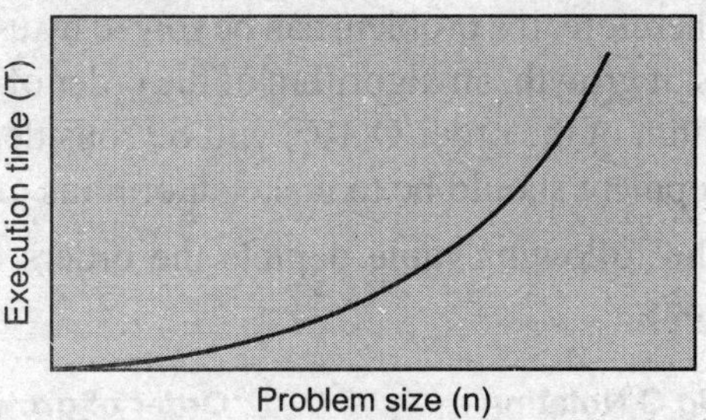

From the preceding discussion, you can conclude that the running time of a program is a function of n, where n is the size of the input data. The rate at which the running time of an algorithm increases as a result of an increase in the volume of input data is called the order of growth of the algorithm.

The order of growth of an algorithm is defined by using the big O notation. The big O notation has been accepted as a fundamental technique for describing the efficiency of an algorithm.

The following table lists some possible orders of growth, and their corresponding big O notations.

Order of Growth	Big O notation
Constant	O(1)
Logarithmic	O(log n)
Linear	O(n)
Log linear	O(n log n)
Quadratic	$O(n^2)$
Cubic	$O(n^3)$
Exponential	$O(2^n)$, O(10n)

16.4.2 Big O Notations

If an algorithm has a linear order of growth, the algorithm is said to be of the order O(n). Similarly, if an algorithm has a quadratic order of growth, the algorithm is said to be of the order $O(n^2)$.

16.4.3 Selecting an Efficient Algorithm

Now that you know how the efficiency of a particular algorithm is determined, let us see how this knowledge can be used to select an efficient algorithm.

According to their orders of growth, the big O notations can be arranged in an increasing order as:

$$O(1) < O(\log n) < O(n) < O(n \log n) < O(n^2) < O(n^3) < O(2^n) < O(10^n)$$

Therefore, if a problem can be solved by using algorithms each of the preceding orders of growth, an algorithm of the order of O(1) will be considered best, and an algorithm of the order $O(10^n)$ will be considered the worst. The goal of algorithm development should be to make algorithms of the smallest possible orders.

The following table depicts the orders of growth for the preceding big O notations.

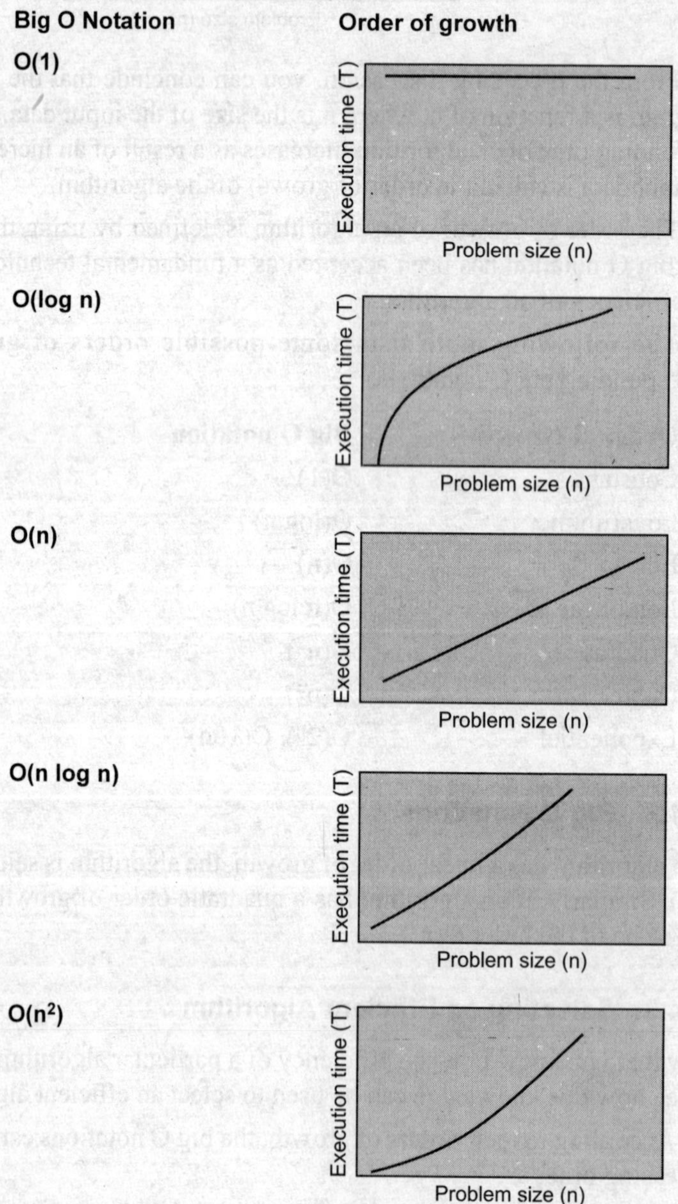

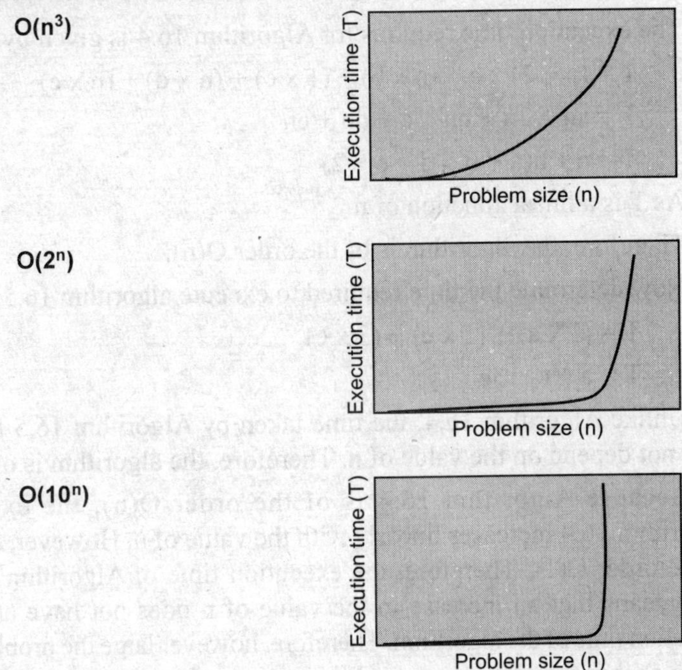

Now, consider that the assignment, comparisons, write and increment statements take a,b,c and d time units to execute, respectively. Also, suppose all arithmetic operations require e time units to execute. Now, consider the following two algorithms to find the sum of first n natural numbers:

Algorithm 16.4: Find sum of first n natural numbers.

Step 1: Set sum = 0 // 1 assignment
Step 2: Set i = 0 // 1 assignment
Step 3: While (i <= n) // n comparisons
a. Set sum = sum + i // n arithmetic operations, n assignments
b. Increment i by 1 // n increments
Step 4: Display (sum) // 1 write

Algorithm 16.5: Find sum of first n natural numbers.

Step 1: Set sum = (n x (n + 1))/2 // 3 arithmetic operations, 1 assignment
Step 2: Display (sum) // 1 write

Both Algorithm 16.4 and Algorithm 16.5 perform the same task, that is, both determine the sum of the first n natural numbers. Algorithm 16.4 adds each number iteratively to a variable sum. However, Algorithm 16.5 uses a formula to calculate the sum of the first n natural numbers.

The execution time requires for Algorithm 16.4 is given by:

T = (n + 2) x a + (n x b) + (1 x c) + (n x d) + (n x e)

T = an + 2n + bn + c + dn + en

T = c + n(a + b + d + e + 2)

As T is a linear function of n.

Therefore, the algorithm is of the order O(n).

Now determine the time required to execute algorithm 16.5:

T = (1 x a) + (1 x c) + (3 x e)

T = a + c + 3e

Unlike Algorithm 16.4, the time taken by Algorithm 16.5 is a constant, and does not depend on the value of n. Therefore, the algorithm is of the order O(1).

Because Algorithm 16.4 is of the order O(n), the execution time of Algorithm 16.4 increases linearly with the value of n. However, Algorithm 16.5 is of the order O(1). Therefore, the execution time of Algorithm 16.5 is constant. This means that an increase in the value of n does not have any impact on the execution time of the algorithm. Therefore, however large the problem be, Algorithm A solves it in the same amount of time.

Suppose for n = 10, both Algorithm 16.4 and 16.5 take 10 nanoseconds (ns) to execute. However when n is increased to 100, Algorithm 16.4 will take 100 ns to execute, but Algorithm 16.5 will take only 10 ns to execute, Similarly, when n is increased to 1000, Algorithm 16.4 will take 1000 ns to execute, but Algorithm 16.5 will take only 10 ns.

This means that when the problem is very large in size, Algorithm 16.5 would prove to be much more efficient than Algorithm 16.4.

16.4.4 Best, Worst, and Average Case Efficiency

Suppose you have a list of names in which you have to search for a particular name. You have designed an algorithm that searches the name in the list of n elements, by comparing the name to be searched with each element in the list sequentially.

The best case in this scenario would be if the first element in the list matches the name to be searched. The efficiency in that case would be expressed as O(1) because only one comparison was made.

Similarly, the worst case in this scenario would be if the complete list is traversed and the element is found at the end of the list or is not found in the list. The efficiency in that case would be expressed as O(n) because n comparisons were made.

Continuing with the same example, the average case efficiency can be obtained by finding the average number of comparisons. Here,

Minimum number of comparisons = 1

Maximum number of comparisons = n

Therefore, average number of comparisons = (n + 1)/2

(n + 1)/2 is a linear function of n. Therefore, the average case efficiency will be expressed as O(n).

The worst case efficiency of the preceding search program can be improved by using an alternate search algorithm that provides a better worst case efficiency.

16.5 ROLE OF DATA STRUCTURES

Multiple algorithms can be designed to solve a particular problem. However, the algorithm may differ in how efficiently they can solve the problem. In such a situation, an algorithm that provides the maximum efficiency should be used for solving the problem. Efficiency here means that the algorithm should work in minimal time and use minimal memory.

One of the basic techniques for improving the efficiency of algorithms is to structure the data that they operate on in such a way that the resulting operations can be efficiently performed. The way in which the various data elements are organized in memory with respect to each other is called a data structure.

Data can be organized in many different ways; therefore, you can create as many data structures as you want. However, there are some standard data structures that have proved useful over the years. These include arrays, linked lists, stacks, queues, trees and graphs. We will learn more about these data structures in the subsequent tutorials.

All these data structures are designed to hold a collection of data items. However, the difference lies in the way the data items are arranged with respect to each other and the operations that they allow. Because of the different ways in which the data items are arranged with respect to each other, some data structures prove to be more efficient that others to solve a given problem.

Suppose you have to write an algorithm that enables printer to service the requests of multiple users on a first-come-first-served (FCFS) basis. In this case, using a data structure that stores and retrieves the requests in the order of their arrival would be much more efficient than a data structure that stores and retrieves the requests in a random order.

In addition to improving the efficiency of an algorithm, the use of appropriate data structures also allows you to overcome some other programming challenges, such as:

- Simplifying complex problems
- Creating standard, reusable code components
- Creating programs that are easy to understand and maintain

Consider an example where you have to find the maximum value in a set of 50 numbers, In this scenario, you can either use 50 variables or a data structure, such as an array of size 50, to store the numbers. When 50 different variables are used to store the numbers, the algorithm to determine the maximum value among the numbers can be written as:

1. Accept 50 numbers and store them in num1, num2, num3, .. num50
2. Set max = num1
3. If num2 > max then: max = num2
4. If num3 > max then: max = num3:

   ....

   ....
5. If num50 > max then max = num50
6. Display max

On the other hand, when an array of size 50 is used, the algorithm can be written as:

1. Set max = num[0]
2. Repeat step3 varying i from 1 to 49
3. If num[i] > max then: max = num[i]
4. Display max

From the preceding two algorithms, it can be seen that the algorithm using an array manipulates memory much more efficiently than the algorithm using 50 variables. Also, the algorithm using an array involves few steps and is therefore, easier to understand and implement as compared to the algorithm that uses 50 variables.

Data structures also enable the creation of reusable code components. Suppose you have created a class to implement a data structure that stores and retrieves requests in the order of their arrival. Once the class is created, the same class can be used in several different applications that need to service the requests of multiple users on a FCFS basis.

This means that a data structure once implemented can be used as a standard component to provide a standard solution to a specific set of problems. The use of standard components helps simplify the maintenance process. This is because the standard components are time tested and therefore, do not need much maintenance.

16.6 COMPLEXITY OF ALGORITHMS

An algorithm is a sequence of statements, each of which has a clear meaning and can be performed with a finite amount of effort is a finite length of time. An algorithm is supposed to do two things.

1. Compute the correct answer given valid Input data.
2. Perform the computation in a reasonable time.

The second point is of course essential. A correct algorithm is useless if it is too slow. In such cases, we must find another algorithm or any be we will have to accept some approximation which allow us to use another algorithm, which runs in reasonable time but only generates an approximately correct results. Computer science is the science that deals with the issues of provide that an algorithm is correct and what its properties are such as how long time it can be expected to need in the average case or how much time it will use in the worst case.

These analyses are done without reference to any specific computer or programming language, the issue is how, many calculation steps (such as additions and multiplications or exchanges of items is an array) are needed to obtain the result and how this depends on the size of the problem. One of the most important properties of an algorithm is how its execution time increases as the problem is made large. By a larger problem, we mean sequences to align or longer sequences to align. This is so called algorithmic (or computational) complexity of the algorithm. As an algorithm is a sequence of steps to solve a problem, there may be more than one algorithm to solve a problem.

The choice of particular algorithm depends on following considerations:

1. **Performance requirements**

   Time Complexity (how much time algorithm required to run to completion?)

2. **Memory requirements**

   Space complexity (how much memory algorithm required to run to completion?)

3. **Programming requirements**

   Since programming requirement one difficult to analyze, precisely, complexity theory concentrate on performance and memory requirements. Specifically it is used to help in determining how the resource requirements of an algorithm grow in relation to the size of the data being manipulated.

Performance requirements one usually more critical than memory requirements, hence in general, it is not necessary to worry about memory unless they grow faster than performance requirements. Therefore in general the algorithms one analyzed only on the basic of performance requirements, i.e. running time.

16.6.1 Space Complexity

This is essentially the number of memory cells which an algorithm needs. A good algorithm keeps this number as small as possible, too. If the program is to run on multi user system it may be required to specify the amount of memory to be allocated to the program. A programme with sometime seek a trade off between space and time complexity. For example, a programme might choose a data structure that requires a lot of Storage in order to reduce the computation time. There is an element of art in making such tradeoffs but the programmer must make the choice from an informed point of view.

1. The programmer must have some verified basic on which to make the selection of a data structure or algorithm.
2. We may be interested to know in advance that whether deficient memory is available to run the program.
3. There may be several possible solutions with different space requirements.
4. Can be used to estimate the size of the largest problem that a program can solve.

In other words complexity refers to the rate at which the storage or time grows as a function of the problem size. The absolute growth depends on the machine used to execute program, the compiler used to construct the program and, many other factors we would like to have a way of describing the inherent complexity of a program, independent of machine/ compiler considerations. This means that we must not try to describe the absolute time or storage need. Space complexity is the measure of how much memory is used by a program relative to some measure of the size of the problems.

1. Most Primitives use constant space
2. Tail recursive calls also use constant space
3. General Recursive calls use linear space.

The amount of space needed by recursive functions is called the recursive stack space. For each recursive function, this space depends on the space needed by the local variables and the formal parameters. In addition, this space depends on the maximum depth of the recursion. In general the total space need by a program can be divided into parts.

1. A fixed part that is independent of particular problem and includes instruction space, space for constants, simple variables and fixed structured variables.
2. A variable part that includes structured variables whose size depends on the particular problem being solved, dynamically allocated space and the recursion stack space.

16.6.2 Time Complexity

The time complexity of an algorithm is the amount of time it needs to run to completion. To measure the time complexity accurately we can count the all sort of operations performed in an algorithm. If we know the time for each one of the primitive operations performed on given computer, we can easily computer the time taken by an algorithm to complete its execution. A key operation in our algorithm is an operation that takes maximum time among all possible operations in the algorithm. The time complexity can be expressed as a function of number of key operations performed.

16.6.3 Computational Complexity

Computational complexity is the study of how of a given resource a program uses. The resource in question is usually either space (how much memory) or time (how many basic operations). Complexity can be looked at from many angles:

1. **Worst-case** complexity is the most commonly discussed it give a guaranteed upper bound for how much of a resource a program will use.
2. **Average-case** complexity is often useful, but more difficult to compute.
3. **Best-case** complexity is rarely useful, except as a contrast with the average and worst cases. It given a guaranteed lower bound for how much of a resource a program will use.

16.7 ASYMPTOTIC NOTATION

A problem may have numerous algorithmic solutions. In order to choose the best algorithm for a particular task, you need to be able to judge how long a particular solution will take to run. Or, more accurately, you need to be able to judge how long two solutions will take to run, and choose the better of the two. You don't need to know how many minutes and seconds they will take, but you do need some way to compare algorithms against one another.

Asymptotic complexity is a way of expressing the main component of the cost of an algorithm, using idealized units of computational work. Consider, for example, the algorithm for sorting a deck of cards, which proceeds by repeatedly searching through the deck for the lowest card. The asymptotic complexity of this algorithm is the square of the number of cards in the deck. This quadratic behavior is the main term in the complexity formula, it says, e.g., if you double the size of the deck, then the work is roughly quadrupled.

The exact formula for the cost is more complex, and contains more details than are needed to understand the essential complexity of the algorithm. With our deck of cards, in the worst case, the deck would start out reverse-sorted, so our scans would have to go all the way to the end. The first scan would involve scanning 52 cards, the next would take 51, etc. So the cost formula is 52 + 51 + ... + 1. Generally, letting N be the number of cards, the formula is 1 + 2 + ... + N, which equals $(N + 1) * (N / 2) = (N^2 + N) / 2 = (1 / 2) N^2 + N / 2$. But the N^2 term dominates the expression, and this is what is key for comparing algorithm costs. (This is in fact an expensive algorithm; the best sorting algorithms run in sub-quadratic time.)

Asymptotically speaking, in the limit as N tends towards infinity, 1 + 2 + ... + N gets closer and closer to the pure quadratic function (1/2) N^2. And what difference does the constant factor of 1/2 make, at this level of abstraction. So the behavior is said to be $O(n^2)$.

Now let us consider how we would go about comparing the complexity of two algorithms. Let f(n) be the cost, in the worst case, of one algorithm, expressed as a function of the input size n, and g(n) be the cost function for the other algorithm. E.g., for sorting algorithms, f(10) and g(10) would be the maximum number of steps that the algorithms would take on a list of 10 items. If, for all values of n >= 0, f(n) is less than or equal to g(n), then the algorithm with complexity function f is strictly faster. But, generally speaking, our concern for computational cost is for the cases with large inputs; so the comparison of f(n) and g(n) for small values of n is less significant than the "long term" comparison of f(n) and g(n), for n larger than some threshold.

Note that we have been speaking about bounds on the performance of algorithms, rather than giving exact speeds. The actual number of steps required to sort our deck of cards (with our naive quadratic algorithm) will depend upon the order in which the cards begin. The actual time to perform each of our steps will depend upon our processor speed, the condition of our processor cache, etc., etc. It's all very complicated in the concrete details, and moreover not relevant to the essence of the algorithm.

16.8 BIG-O NOTATION

Big-O is the formal method of expressing the upper bound of an algorithm's running time. It's a measure of the longest amount of time it could possibly take for the algorithm to complete.

More formally, for non-negative functions, f(n) and g(n), if there exists an integer n0 and a constant c > 0 such that for all integers n > n0, f(n) d" cg(n), then f(n) is Big O of g(n). This is denoted as "f(n) = O(g(n))". If graphed, g(n) serves as an upper bound to the curve you are analyzing, f(n).

It is generally not possible to perform a simple analysis of an algorithm to determine the exact time required to execute it.

Following are the reasons for this:

(i) Exact time depends on the implementation of the algorithm and on the machine we are executing on.

(ii) Time requirement to be found in time analysis, depends on amount of input.

Since the data structure used by an algorithm can greatly affect the algorithm's performance, it is important that there exists a rigorous method by which to compare the efficiency of various data structures. What we, as developers utilizing a data structure, are primarily interested in is how the data structures performance changes as the amount of data stored increases. That is, for each new element stored by the data structure, how are the running times of the data structure's operations effected?

Methodical way of computing the running time of a block of code is to do follow these simple steps:

1. Determine the steps that constitute the algorithm's running time. Typically, you want to concern yourself with steps that involve the data structure itself, and not simple, atomic operations performed by the computer. In Figure 16.23, with the block of code we analyze its running time by only counting how many times the data structure needs to be accessed, and do not bother worrying about the time for creating and initializing variables.
2. Find the line(s) of code that perform the steps you are interested in counting. Put a 1 next to each of those lines.
3. For each line with a 1 next to it, see if it is in a loop. If so, change the 1 to 1 times the maximum number of repetitions the loop may perform. If you have two or more nested loops, continue the multiplication for each loop.
4. Find the largest single term you have written down. This is the running time.

Let's apply these steps to the blocks of code in Figure 16.23.

Referring to Figure 16.23, for example, Let us take simple example considering the statement x=x+1. We would determine two numbers for this statement. The first is the amount of time a single execution will take and the second is the number of times. i is executed. The multiplication of these numbers will give total time taken by this statement. The second statistics is the frequency count and it varies from data set to data set.

Now let us consider three different situations of the same statement in three different algorithms, considering these, we will calculate frequency count for all three types as shown in the Figure 16.23 as in the below Table:

Algorithm (a)	Algorithm (b)	Algorithm (c)
x = x+1	for (i=1; i<=n; i++)	for (I=1; i<=n; i++)
	x= x+1	for (j=1; j<=n; j++)
		x= x+1

Figure 16.23

In the case of (a), let us suppose that the statement x= x+1 is not contained within any loop. Then its frequency count is 1.

In the case of (b) the statement is executed n times (time taken to execute single statement i.e. 1) * (No. of times it is executed i.e. n). So frequency count is n.

In the case of (c), Time taken to execute single statement =1

No. of times it is executed = $n*n = n^2$

So frequency count is $1 * n^2 = n^2$

1, n , n^2 are said to be different and increasing order of magnitude.

An order notation has been developed to facilitate the handling of order of magnitude functions. It will be clear from definition.

Mathematical description of Big-oh notation

Assume f(n) and g(n) be two arbitrary functions, such that

f(n) = O (g (n)), read as f(n) is "big-oh" of g(n) or f(n) is of order g(n), if there exists positive constants n_0 and c , such that f(n) <= c * g(n) for all n> n_o.

Examples are:

(i) $100\ n^3 \Rightarrow 100 * n^3$ is $o(n^3)$

(ii) 1000 is 0(1)

(iii) n +log n is o (n) because log n < n

(iv) $2n^2 + 3\ n + 4$ is o (n^2)

Points to be kept in mind, while reading Big-oh definition are as:

- Complexity expressed in o-notation is only an upper bound and the actual complexity may be much lower.
- So this complexity can be treated as worst-case complexity.
- The constants c and n_o are unknown and are not necessarily small.

The different effects of constants on f(n) are as shown in the Figure 16.24:

N	log n	$\sqrt{n}$	n log n	n^2
10	3	3	30	100
100	6	10	600	10000
1000	9	31	9000	1000000
10000	13	100	130000	100000000

Figure 16.24: Effect of constants on f(n)

Some of common computing times of algorithms you'll study are:

n: When the time complexity of an algorithm is n, then the algorithm is said to be linear. This is the case, where processing has to be carried out on each individual element of the input. In this case time required by an algorithm is linearly proportional to 'n'.

n^2: When the time complexity of an algorithm is n^2 , then the algorithm is said to be Quadratic. As n^2 increases very rapidly with an increase in 'n', quadratic algorithms are practically useful only for relatively small problems

n^3: When the time complexity of an algorithm is n^3, then algorithm is said to be cubic. These types of algorithms are never practically useful.

logn: When the time complexity of an algorithm is log n, then the algorithm is said to be logarithmic. When a program is logarithmic, the program becomes slightly slower as 'n' increases. This time complexity usually occurs in algorithms, which solve big-problems by transforming it into smaller ones.

n log n: This type of time complexity occurs in those algorithms which solve a problem by breaking it up into smaller sub-problems and solve these sub-problems independently.

2^n : When the time complexity of an algorithm is 2^n, the algorithm is called as an exponential These are not suitable for practical use.

So in general, the most common computing times of algorithms, as discussed will be written as:

$$O(1) < 0(\log n) < 0(n) < 0(n \log n) < o(n^2) < 0(n^3) < 0(2^n)$$

16.8.1 How to Calculate Overall Time Complexity of an Algorithm?

The most common metric for calculating time complexity is Big Oh notation. This removes all constant factors so that the running time can be estimated in relation to N as N approaches infinity. In general you can think of it like this:

Code:

```
statement;
```

is constant. The running time of the statement will not change in relation to N.

Code:

```
for (i = 0; i < N; i++)
 statement;
```

is linear. The running time of the loop is directly proportional to N. When N doubles, so does the running time.

Code:

```
for (i = 0; i < N; i++)
{
 for (j = 0; j < N; j++)
 statement;
}
```

is quadratic. The running time of the two loops is proportional to the square of N. When N doubles, the running time increases by N * N.

Code:

```
while ( low <= high )
{
 mid = ( low + high ) / 2;
        if ( target < list[mid] )
 high = mid - 1;
        else if (target > list[mid])
 low = mid + 1;
        else break;
}
```

is logarithmic. The running time of the algorithm is proportional to the number of times N can be divided by 2. This is because the algorithm divides the working area in half with each iteration.

Code:

```
void quicksort (int list[], int left, int right)
{
 int pivot = partition (list, left, right);
 quicksort (list, left, pivot - 1);
 quicksort (list, pivot + 1, right);
}
```

is N * log (N). The running time consists of N loops (iterative or recursive) that are logarithmic, thus the algorithm is a combination of linear and logarithmic.

In general, doing something with every item in one dimension is linear, doing something with every item in two dimensions is quadratic, and dividing the working area in half is logarithmic.

There are other Big Oh measures such as cubic, exponential, and square root, but they're not nearly as common. Big Oh notation is described as O (<type>) where <type> is the measure.

The quicksort algorithm would be described as O (N * log (N)).

Note that none of this has taken into account best, average, and worst case measures. Each would have its own Big Oh notation. Also note that this is a VERY simplistic explanation. Big Oh is the most common. There are also other notations such as big omega, little o, and big theta.

16.8.2 Theory Examples

So, let's take an example of Big-O. Say that f(n) = 2n + 8, and g(n) = n2. Can we find a constant c, so that 2n + 8 <= n2? The number 4 works here, giving us 16 <= 16. For any number c greater than 4, this will still work. Since we're trying to generalize this for large values of n, and small values (1, 2, 3) aren't that important, we can say that f(n) is generally faster than g(n); that is, f(n) is bound by g(n), and will always be less than it.

It could then be said that f(n) runs in O(n2) time: "f-of-n runs in Big-O of n-squared time".

To find the upper bound - the Big-O time - assuming we know that f(n) is equal to (exactly) 2n + 8, we can take a few shortcuts. For example, we can remove all constants from the runtime; eventually, at some value of c, they become irrelevant. This makes f(n) = 2n. Also, for convenience of comparison, we remove constant multipliers; in this case, the 2. This makes f(n) = n. It could also be said that f(n) runs in O(n) time; that lets us put a tighter (closer) upper bound onto the estimate.

16.8.3 Practical Examples

O(n): printing a list of n items to the screen, looking at each item once.

O(log n): also "log n", taking a list of items, cutting it in half repeatedly until there's only one item left.

O(n^2): taking a list of n items, and comparing every item to every other item.

16.8.4 Big-omega Notation

For non-negative functions, f(n) and g(n), if there exists an integer n0 and a constant c > 0 such that for all integers n > n0, f(n) e" cg(n), then f(n) is omega of g(n). This is denoted as "f(n) = Ω(g(n))".

This is almost the same definition as Big Oh, except that "f(n) e" cg(n)", this makes g(n) a lower bound function, instead of an upper bound function. It describes the best that can happen for a given data size.

1. **Theta Notation:** For non-negative functions, f(n) and g(n), f(n) is theta of g(n) if and only if f(n) = O(g(n)) and f(n) = Ω(g(n)). This is denoted as "f(n) = Θ(g(n))".

   This is basically saying that the function, f(n) is bounded both from the top and bottom by the same function, g(n).

2. **Little-O Notation:** For non-negative functions, f(n) and g(n), f(n) is little o of g(n) if and only if f(n) = O(g(n)), but f(n) ≠ Θ(g(n)). This is denoted as "f(n) = o(g(n))".

   This represents a loose bounding version of Big O. g(n) bounds from the top, but it does not bound the bottom.

3. **Little Omega Notation:** For non-negative functions, f(n) and g(n), f(n) is little omega of g(n) if and only if f(n) = Ω(g(n)), but f(n) ≠ Θ(g(n)). This is denoted as "f(n) = ω(g(n))". Much like Little Oh, this is the equivalent for Big Omega. g(n) is a loose lower boundary of the function f(n); it bounds from the bottom, but not from the top.

16.8.5 How Asymptotic Notation Relates to Analyzing Complexity

Temporal comparison is not the only issue in algorithms. There are space issues as well. Generally, a trade off between time and space is noticed in algorithms. Asymptotic notation empowers you to make that trade off. If you think of the amount of time and space your algorithm uses as a function of your data over time or space (time and space are usually analyzed separately), you can analyze how the time and space is handled when you introduce more data to your program.

This is important in data structures because you want a structure that behaves efficiently as you increase the amount of data it handles. Keep in mind though those algorithms that are efficient with large amounts data are not always simple and efficient for small amounts of data. So if you know you are working with only a small amount of data and you have concerns for speed and code space, a trade off can be made for a function that does not behave well for large amounts of data.

16.8.6 A Few Examples of Asymptotic Notation

Generally, we use asymptotic notation as a convenient way to examine what can happen in a function in the worst case or in the best case. For example, if you want to write a function that searches through an array of numbers and returns the smallest one:

```
Function find-min(array a[1..n])
Let j = ∞
For i = 1 to n:
j = min(j, a[i])
Repeat
Return j
End
```

Regardless of how big or small the array is, every time we run find-min, we have to initialize the i and j integer variables and return j at the end. Therefore, we can just think of those parts of the function as constant and ignore them.

So, how can we use asymptotic notation to discuss the find-min function? If we search through an array with 87 elements, then the for loop iterates 87 times, even if the very first element we hit turns out to be the minimum. Likewise, for n elements, the for loop iterates n times. Therefore we say the function runs in time O(n).

What about this function:

```
Function find-min-plus-max(array a[1..n])
// First, find the smallest element in the array
Let j = ∞;
For i = 1 to n:
j = min(j, a[i])
Repeat
Let min = j
// Now, find the biggest element, add it to the smallest and
j = –∞;
For i = 1 to n:
j = max(j, a[i])
Repeat
Let max = j
// return the sum of the two
Return min + max;
End
```

What's the running time for find-min-plus-max? There are two for loops, that each iterate n times, so the running time is clearly O(2n). Because 2 is a constant, we throw it away and write the running time as O(n). Why can you do this? If you recall the definition of Big-O notation, the function whose bound you're testing can be multiplied by some constant. If f(x) = 2x, we can see that if g(x) = x, then the Big-O condition holds. Thus O(2n) = O(n). This rule is general for the various asymptotic notations.

16.9 SPACE VS TIME COMPLEXITY

In general, the amount of space used is less than the amount of time used because space cab be reused and time cannot. For most applications, we focus on time complexity, since memory tends to be cheap compared to time (three days). Some times, space is still and issue-particularly if the problem size is very large and the solution requires relatively low time complexity. (An example would be sorting very large (on the order of one billion element) data sets). A simple space example – adding two arrays of integers. Assume our array size is N and A.B are input arrays.

1. The following code requires N+N+N= 3N space:
2. int C [N}
3. for (int i=0; i < N; i++)
4. C (i) = A (i) + B (i);
5. Suppose we no larger need B- we can reuse it. The following code requires only N+N = 2N space:
6. For (int i = 0; i < N; i ++)
7. B (i) = A (i) + B (i);

Running –Time Analysis

How much time does each function require?

Actual time (i.e. seconds) hard to measure – varies from machine to machine and system to system

Consider time as number of basic operations:

1. One arithmetic op, e/g. + -*
2. One assignment
3. One read
4. One writes etc.

16.10 TIME SPACE TRADE OFF

To solve a given programming problem, many different algorithms may be used. Some of these algorithms may be extremely time-efficient and others extremely space-efficient. A space-time or time-memory tradeoff is a situation where the memory use can be reduced at the cost of slower program execution, or vice versa, the computation time can be reduced at the cost of increased memory use. As the relative costs of CPU cycles, RAM space, and hard drive space change — hard drive space has for some time been getting cheaper at a much faster rate than other components of computers— the appropriate choices for space-time tradeoffs have changed radically. Often, by exploiting a space-time tradeoff, a program can be made to run much faster.

The most common situation is an algorithm involving a lookup table: an implementation can include the entire table, which reduces computing time, but increases the amount of memory needed, or it can compute table entries as needed, increasing computing time, but reducing memory requirements.

A space-time tradeoff can be applied to the problem of data storage. If data is stored uncompressed, it takes more space but less time than if the data were stored compressed (since compressing the data reduces the amount of space it takes, but it takes time to run the compression algorithm). Depending on the particular instance of the problem, either way is practical.

In most of the cases, the space and time required by an algorithm are inversely related as:

i.e. $S \propto 1/T$ (Here $\propto$ is inversely proportional)

Where S is space required by an algorithm and T is time required by an algorithm. We can reduce the space requirements by increasing running time or vice-versa.

This situation is referred to as time-space tradeoff. Let us take a simple example of computing the exponential function x^n, where n is positive integer. The function x^n is defined as:

x * x * x * x ...... n times.

We will solve this problem with two different approaches as:

Approach 1

Algorithm 16.6: Let's discuss the algorithm of time-space tradeoff

Step 1: Start
Step 2: Read the variables n, x
Step 3: Assign the value of x to y
Step 4: Execute step 5 for n–1 times.
Step 5: Multiply the values of y & x and assign the calculated value to y
Step 6: Print the value of y
Step 7: End

This approach executes n-1 multiples, so **f1(n) = 0(n).**

Approach 2

This approach uses recursion. Let us consider the following function Exp(x,n), to find an exponent using recursion.

```
Exp (x, n)
{
if (n==1)
return x;
y = exp (x, n/2);
if (n%2==0)
return (y *y);
else
return (y * y* x);
}
```

This is a segment of a program to find exponent using recursion. Let us define it in an algorithm.

Algorithm 16.7: Let's discuss the algorithm of time-space tradeoff using recursion.

Step 1: Start

Step 2: Read the variables n, x

Step 3: if the value of n is 1 then print the value of x else goto step 4.

Step 4: Call the same function algorithm with value of x, value of n as n/2 and goto step 5

Step 5: If value of n is odd then assign the value of y *y *x to y and Print the same value else goto step 6.

Step 6: assign the value of y * y to y and print the same value

Step 7: End

Running times of two approaches discussed, are related to the number of multiplications they perform.

Thus for large exponents, the running time of approach 2 is much less than that of approach 1, however, memory space required by approach2 is much greater than approach 1, as it makes large number of recursive function calls.

16.11 INTRODUCTION TO PRIMITIVE DATA STRUCTURE AND NON PRIMITIVE DATA STRUCTURE

16.11.1 Primitive Data Structure

A new, primitive type is definable by enumerating the distinct values belonging to it. Such a type is called an *enumeration type*. Its definition has the form

TYPE T = $(c_1, c_2, \dots, c_n)$

T is the new type identifier, and the ci are the new constant identifiers.

Examples

TYPE shape = (rectangle, square, ellipse, circle)

TYPE color = (red, yellow, green)

TYPE sex = (male, female)

TYPE weekday = (Monday, Tuesday, Wednesday, Thursday, Friday, Saturday, Sunday)

TYPE currency = (franc, mark, pound, dollar, shilling, lira, guilder, krone, ruble, cruzeiro, yen)

TYPE destination = (hell, purgatory, heaven)

TYPE vehicle = (train, bus, automobile, boat, airplane)

TYPE rank = (private, corporal, sergeant, lieutenant, captain, major, colonel, general)

TYPE object = (constant, type, variable, procedure, module)

TYPE structure = (array, record, set, sequence)

TYPE condition = (manual, unloaded, parity, skew)

The definition of such types introduces not only a new type identifier, but at the same times the set of identifiers denoting the values of the new type. These identifiers may then be used as constants throughout the program, and they enhance its understandability considerably. If, as an example, we introduce variables

s, d, r, and b.

VAR s: sex

VAR d: weekday

VAR r: rank

then the following assignment statements are possible:

s := male

d := Sunday

r := major

b := TRUE

Evidently, they are considerably more informative than their counterparts

s := 1 d := 7 r := 6 b := 2

which are based on the assumption that c, d, r, and b are defined as integers and that the constants are mapped onto the natural numbers in the order of their enumeration. Furthermore, a compiler can check against the inconsistent use of operators. For example, given the declaration of s above, the statement

s :=s+1 would be meaningless.

If, however, we recall that enumerations are ordered, then it is sensible to introduce operators that generate the successor and predecessor of their argument. We therefore postulate the following standard operators, which assign to their argument its successor and predecessor respectively:

INC(x) DEC(x)

16.11.2 Standard Primitive Types

Standard primitive types are those types that are available on most computers as built-in features. They include the whole numbers, the logical truth values, and a set of printable characters. On many computers fractional numbers are also incorporated, together with the standard arithmetic operations. We denote these types by the identifiers

1. Integer
2. Real
3. Boolean
4. Char
5. Set

1. INTEGERS

The type INTEGER comprises a subset of the whole numbers whose size may vary among individual computer systems. If a computer uses *n* bits to represent an integer in two's complement notation, then the admissible values x must satisfy $-2^{n-1} \le x < 2^{n-1}$. It is assumed that all operations on data of this type are exact and correspond to the ordinary laws of arithmetic, and that the computation will be interrupted in the case of a result lying outside the representable subset. This event is called *overflow*. The standard operators are the four basic arithmetic operations of addition (+), subtraction (-), multiplication (*), and division (/).

Whereas the slash denotes ordinary division resulting in a value of type REAL, the operator DIV denotes integer division resulting in a value of type INTEGER. If we define the quotient q = m DIV n and the remainder r = m MOD n, the following relations hold, assuming n > 0:

q*n + r = m and 0 d" r < n

Examples:

31 DIV 10 = 3 31 MOD 10 = 1

-31 DIV 10 = -4 -31 MOD 10 = 9

We know that dividing by 10^n can be achieved by merely shifting the decimal digits n places to the right and thereby ignoring the lost digits. The same method applies, if numbers are represented in binary instead of decimal form. If two's complement representation is used (as in practically all modern computers), then the shifts implement a division as defined by the above DIV operaton. Moderately sophisticated compilers will therefore represent an operation of the form m DIV 2^n or m MOD 2^n by a fast shift (or mask) operation.

2. REAL

The type REAL denotes a subset of the real numbers. Whereas arithmetic with operands of the types INTEGER is assumed to yield exact results, arithmetic on values of type REAL is permitted to be inaccurate within the limits of round-off errors caused by computation on a finite number of digits. This is the principal reason for the explicit distinction between the types INTEGER and REAL, as it is made in most programming languages.

The standard operators are the four basic arithmetic operations of addition (+), subtraction (-), multiplication (*), and division (/). It is an essence of data typing that different types are incompatible under assignment. An exception to this rule is made for assignment of integer values to real variables, because here the semantics are unambiguous. After all, integers form a subset of real numbers. However, the inverse direction is not permissible: Assignment of a real value to an integer variable requires an operation such as truncation or rounding.

3. BOOLEANS

The two values of the standard type BOOLEAN are denoted by the identifiers TRUE and FALSE. The Boolean operators are the logical conjunction, disjunction, and negation. The logical conjunction is denoted by the symbol &, the logical disjunction by OR, and negation by "~". Note that comparisons are operations yielding a result of type BOOLEAN. Thus, the result of a comparison may be assigned to a variable, or it may be used as an operand of a logical operator in a Boolean expression.

```
p := x = y
q := (xd"y) & (y < z)
```

yield p = FALSE and q = TRUE.

Table 16.1 Boolean Operators.

p	q	p & q	p OR q	~p
True	True	True	True	False
True	False	True	False	False
False	True	True	False	True
False	False	False	False	True

The Boolean operators & (AND) and OR have an additional property in most programming languages, which distinguishes them from other dyadic operators.

Whereas, for example, the sum $x+y$ is not defined, if either x or y is undefined, the conjunction p&q is defined even if q is undefined, provided that p is FALSE.

This conditionality is an important and useful property. The exact definition of & and OR is therefore given by the following equations:

p & q = if p then q else FALSE

p OR q = if p then TRUE else q

4. CHARACTERS

The standard type CHAR comprises a set of printable characters. Unfortunately, there is no generally accepted standard character set used on all computer systems. Therefore, the use of the predicate "standard" may in this case be almost misleading; it is to be understood in the sense of "standard on the computer system on which a certain program is to be executed."

The character set defined by the International Standards Organization (ISO), and particularly its American version ASCII (American Standard Code for Information Interchange) is the most widely accepted set. The ASCII set is therefore tabulated in Appendix A. It consists of 95 printable (graphic) characters and 33 control characters, the latter mainly being used in data transmission and for the control of printing equipment.

In order to be able to design algorithms involving characters (i.e., values of type CHAR) that are system independent, we should like to be able to assume certain minimal properties of character sets, namely:

1. The type CHAR contains the 26 capital Latin letters, the 26 lower-case letters, the 10 decimal digits, and a number of other graphic characters, such as punctuation marks.
2. The subsets of letters and digits are ordered and contiguous
3. The type CHAR contains a non-printing, blank character and a line-end character that may be used as separators.

5. SET

The type SET denotes sets whose elements are integers in the range 0 to a small number, typically 31 or 63. Given, for example, variables

VAR r, s, t: SET

possible assignments are

r := {5}; s := {x, y .. z}; t := {}

Here, the value assigned to r is the singleton set consisting of the single element 5; to t is assigned the empty set, and to s the elements x, y, y+1, … , z-1, z.

The following elementary operators are defined on variables of type SET:

* set intersection

\+ set union

\- set difference

/ symmetric set difference

IN set membership

Constructing the intersection or the union of two sets is often called set multiplication or set addition, respectively; the priorities of the set operators are defined accordingly, with the intersection operator having priority over the union and difference operators, which in turn have priority over the membership operator, which is classified as a relational operator. Following are examples of set expressions and their fully parenthesized equivalents:

r * s + t = (r*s) + t

r - s * t = r - (s*t)

r - s + t = (r-s) + t

r + s / t = r + (s/t)

x IN s + t = x IN (s+t)

16.11.3 Non Primitive Data Structure

The data structures which are devcloped by programmer/User for his or her convenience are known as non primitive data structures. For example Array, Linked List, Stack etc.

1. FILE

A file is a collection of number of related records that may have the same or varying length. For example collection of all employee records for one company would be an employee file. Similarly collection of all inventory records for a company forms an inventory file. It is customary to set up a *master file* of permanent data and to use *transaction file* containing data of temporary nature. A file is a collection of related data stored in a particular area on the disk. There are two types of access on the files (two ways to access the files). These are sequential access files and random access file. In the sequential access files, the data or text can be store or read back sequentially. In the random access files, data can be accessed and processed randomly. Also files can be divided into two types. One is data file and second one is program file. There are two types of operations can be done on data i.e. data can be transferred between the console and the program and further can be transferred between program and a disk file.

16.11.4 Applications of Primitive Data Structures

1. Polynomial ADT

A polynomial can be represented with primitive data structures. For example, a polynomial represented as $a_k x^k \, a_{k-1} x^{k-1} + ... + a_0$ can be represented as a linked list. Each node is a structure with two values: a_i and i. Thus, the length of the list will be k. The first node will have (a_k, k), the second node will have (a_{k-1}, k–1) etc. The last node will be (a_0, 0).

The polynomial $3x^9 + 7x^3 + 5$ can be represented in a list as follows: $(3,9) \rightarrow (7,3) \rightarrow (5,0)$ where each pair of integers represent a node, and the arrow represents a link to its neighbouring node. Derivatives of polynomials can be easily computed by proceeding node by node. In our previous example the list after computing the derivative would represented as follows: $(27,8) \rightarrow (21,2)$. The specific polynomial ADT will define various operations, such as multiplication, addition, subtraction, derivative, integration etc. A polynomial ADT can be useful for symbolic computation as well.

2. Large Integer ADT

Large integers can also be implemented with primitive data structures. To conform to our previous example, consider a large integer represented as a linked list. If we represent the integer as successive powers of 10, where the power of 10 increments by 3 and the coefficient is a three digit number, we can make computations on such numbers easier. For example, we can represent a very large number as follows:

$$513(10^6) + 899(10^3) + 722(10^0).$$

Using this notation, the number can be represented as follows:

$$(513) \rightarrow (899) \rightarrow (722).$$

The first number represents the coefficient of the 10^6 term, the next number represents the coefficient of the 10^3 term and so on. The arrows represent links to adjacent nodes.

The specific ADT will define operations on this representation, such as addition, subtraction, multiplication, division, comparison, copy etc.

3. Window Manager ADT

A window interface can be represented by lists. Consider an environment with many windows. The first node in the list could represent the current active window. Subsequent windows are further along the list. In other words, the nth window corresponds to the nth node in the list.

The ADT can define several functions, such as Find_first_window which would bring a window clicked upon to the front of the list (make it active). Other functions could perform window deletion or creation.

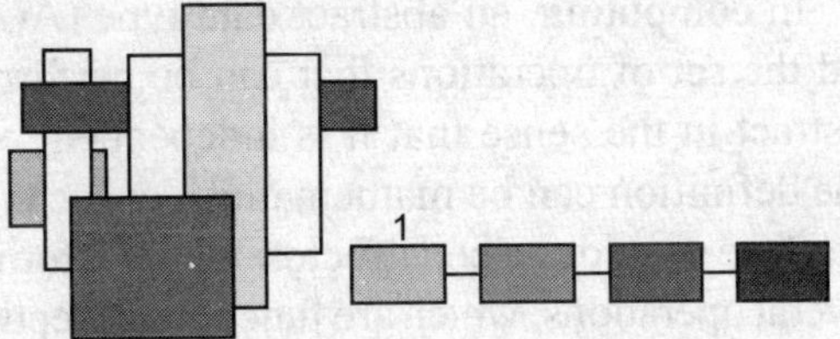

4. *Management of Free Space*

When memory is requested, a list of available blocks of memory might be useful. Again, a list could represent blocks in memory available to the user, with nodes containing pointers to these available blocks. The list can be used like a stack (LIFO). The last freed memory becomes the next available to the user. Such lists are called 'free space lists' or 'available space lists'. Since addition and deletion of nodes is at one end, these lists behave like stacks. All operations on free space lists can be done in O(1) time.

16.12 ABSTRACT DATA TYPE

An abstract data type or abstract data structure is a mathematical model for a certain class of data structures that have similar behavior; or for certain data types of one or more programming languages that have similar semantics. An abstract data type is defined indirectly, only by the operations that may be performed on it and by mathematical constraints on the effects (and possibly cost) of those operations.

For example, an abstract stack data structure could be defined by two operations: push, that inserts some data item into the structure, and pop, that extracts an item from it; with the constraint that each pop always returns the most recently pushed item that has not been popped yet. When analyzing the efficiency of algorithms that use stacks, one may also specify that both operations take the same time no matter how many items have been pushed into the stack, and that the stack uses a constant amount of storage for each element.

Abstract data types are purely theoretical entities, used (among other things) to simplify the description of abstract algorithms, to classify and evaluate data structures, and to formally describe the type systems of programming languages. However, an ADT may be implemented by specific data types or data structures, in many ways and in many programming languages; or described in a formal specification language. ADTs are often implemented as modules: the module's interface declares procedures that correspond to the ADT operations, sometimes with comments that describe the constraints. This information hiding strategy allows the implementation of the module to be changed without disturbing the client programs. Abstract data types are also an important conceptual tool in object-oriented programming and design by contract methodologies for software development.

In computing, an abstract data type (ADT) is a specification of a set of data and the set of operations that can be performed on the data. Such a data type is abstract in the sense that it is independent of various concrete implementations. The definition can be mathematical, or it can be programmed as an interface. The interface provides a constructor, which returns an abstract handle to new data, and several operations, which are functions accepting the abstract handle as an argument.

16.12.1 Examples

ADTs typically seen in textbooks and implemented in programming languages (or their libraries) include:

*String

*List

*Linked List

*Stack

*Queue

*Binary search tree

*Priority queue

*Complex number

*Associative array

*Multimap

The name "abstract data type" apparently was coined by researchers in software engineering and programming language design; while "abstract data structure" was coined by researchers in data structures and algorithms.

16.12.2 Defining an Abstract Data Type

Since ADTs are theoretical concepts, there are no standard conventions for defining them. A broad division may be drawn between "imperative" and "functional" definition styles.

16.12.3 Imperative Abstract Data Type

In the "imperative" view, which is closer to the philosophy of imperative programming languages, an abstract data structure is conceived as an entity that is mutable — meaning that it may be in different states at different times. Some operations may change the state of the ADT; therefore, the order in which operations are evaluated is important, and the same operation on the same entities may have different effects if executed at different times — just like the instructions of a computer, or the commands and procedures of an imperative language. To underscore this view, it is customary to say that the operations are executed or applied, rather than evaluated. The imperative style is often used when describing abstract algorithms.

16.12.4 Functional ADT

Another way to define an ADT, closer to the spirit of functional programming, is to consider each state of the structure as a separate entity. In this view, any operation that modifies the ADT is modeled as a mathematical function that takes the old state as an argument, and returns the new state as part of the result. Unlike the "imperative" operations, these functions have no side effects. Therefore, the order in which they are evaluated is immaterial, and the same operation applied to the same arguments (including the same input states) will always return the same results (and output states). In the functional view, in particular, there is no way (or need) to define an "abstract variable" with the semantics of imperative variables (namely, with fetch and store operations). Instead of storing values into variables, one passes them as arguments to functions.

16.12.5 Example: Abstract Stack (Functional)

For example, a complete functional-style definition of a stack ADT could use the three operations:

- push: takes a stack state and an arbitrary value, returns a stack state;
- top: takes a stack state, returns a valuc;
- pop: takes a stack state, returns a stack state;

with the following axioms:

- top(push(s,x)) = x (pushing an item onto a stack leaves it at the top)
- pop(push(s,x)) = s (pop undoes the effect of push)

In a functional-style definition there is no need for a create operation. Indeed, there is no notion of "stack instance". The stack states can be thought of as being potential states of a single stack structure, and two stack states that contain the same values in the same order are considered to be identical states. This view actually mirrors the behavior of some concrete implementations, such as linked lists with hash cons.

Instead of create(), a functional definition of a stack ADT may assume the existence of a special stack state, the empty stack, designted by a special symbol like Ë or "()"; or define a bottom() operation that takes no aguments and returns this special stack state. Note that the axioms imply that

- push(Λ,x) ≠ Λ

In a functional definition of a stack one does not need an empty predicate: instead, one can test whether a stack is empty by testing whether it is equal to Λ.

Note that these axioms do not define the effect of top(s) or pop(s), unless s is a stack state returned by a push. Since push leaves the stack non-empty, those two operations are undefined (hence invalid) when s = Λ. On the other hand, the axioms (and the lack of side effects) imply that push(s,x) = push(t,y) if and only if x = y and s = t.

As in some other branches of mathematics, it is customary to assume also that the stack states are only those whose existence can be proved from the axioms in a finite number of steps. In the stack ADT example above, this rule means that every stack is a finite sequence of values, that becomes the empty stack (Λ) after a finite number of pops. By themselves, the axioms above do not exclude the existence of infinite stacks (that can be poped forever, each time yielding a different state) or circular stacks (that return to the same state after a finite number of pops). In particular, they do not exclude states s such that pop(s) = s or push(s,x) = s for some x. However, since one cannot obtain such stack states with the given operations, they are assumed "not to exist".

16.12.6 Use of Abstract Data Type

Abstract Data Types can minimize depèndencies in your code, which is important when your code needs to be changed. Because you are abstracted away from lower-level details, some of the higher-level commonalities one data structure shares with a different data structure can be used to replace one with the other.

16.12.7 Why ADT?

Although most programming languages support some standard data types, they are not enough for most of applications. So programming languages usually support creating new data types in terms of "structured types". This can be done in "C" language by defining a "struct".

However just by defining a structured type, the operations applicable to objects of that type cannot be specified. This is why the concept of an Abstract Data Type is required.

16.12.8 Need and Importance of Structure

The most significant way that structured documents differ from unstructured ones is that structured documents include "rules." These rules proscribe the order in which text, graphics, and tables may be entered. For example, in an unstructured document, a paragraph has specific formatting— font, size, and spacing. In a structured document, this same paragraph adds to this formatting an exterior "wrapper" or "element" that governs the elements that appear before and after it. The elements rules come from a **document type definition** (DTD).

Basically, you move away from working with formatting and instead work with information rules for how things fit together and when things can occur. In most tools, the formatting is automated so that you can concentrate on your content while authoring rather than on formatting and layout.

16.12.9 Benefits of Structure

Structure brings to your documents a level of control that formatting alone cannot provide. Using structure has long-term and short-term benefits. These benefits include:

- re-use of information
- standardization of documents
- guided authoring
- improved information management

1. Information Control

Another consideration is information control. If data retrieval from documents is a goal, then structured documents are the obvious choice. Structured documents can interact with, or in some cases act as a database, with information sorted, extracted, and reused.

Another part of information control deserving of its own mention is translation. When sending documents for translation, regular word processing files would be sent for translation in full. With structure, however, additional data (part of a structured document's metadata) can include information on translation status. This means that each paragraph within a document can be marked as needing translation, translated already, modified since prior translation, and so forth. Companies doing the translation can then selectively translate new and modified content without retranslating content that has already been translated and has not changed.

2. Consistency

Documentation consistency issues also figure into the structured/unstructured debate. Structured data adds rules to prompt programmers, providing extra control. Consider simple example of workgroups in which many authors are working on same book. Each author holds biases and preferences, any of which can be good or bad. Multiple authors working the same document may each organize their chapter in a different way. Structure adds rules to prompt authors. So, structure is a very good direction to enforce consistency.

16.12.10 Separation of Interface and Implementation

When realized in a computer program, the ADT is represented by an interface, which shields a corresponding implementation. Users of an ADT are concerned with the interface, but not the implementation, as the implementation can change in the future. (This supports the principle of information hiding, or protecting the program from design decisions that are subject to change.)

The strength of an ADT is that the implementation is hidden from the user. Only the interface is published. This means that the ADT can be implemented in various ways, but as long as it adheres to the interface, user programs are unaffected.

There is a distinction, although sometimes subtle, between the abstract data type and the data structure used in its implementation. For example, a List ADT can be represented using an array-based implementation or a linked-list implementation. A List is an abstract data type with well-defined operations (add element, remove element, etc.) while a linked-list is a pointer-based data structure that can be used to create a representation of a List. The linked-list implementation is so commonly used to represent a List ADT that the terms are interchanged in common use.

Similarly, a Binary Search Tree ADT can be represented in several ways: binary tree, AVL tree, red-black tree, array, etc. Regardless of the implementation, the Binary Search Tree always has the same operations (insert, remove, find, etc.)

16.12.11 Abstract Data Structure

An abstract data structure is an abstract storage for data defined in terms of the set of operations to be performed on data and computational complexity for performing these operations, regardless of the implementation in a concrete data structure.

Selection of an abstract data structure is crucial in the design of efficient algorithms and in estimating their computational complexity, while selection of concrete data structures is important for efficient implementation of algorithms.

This notion is very close to that of an abstract data type, used in the theory of programming languages. The names of many abstract data structures (and abstract data types) match the names of concrete data structures.

16.12.12 Built-in Abstract Data Types

Because some ADTs are so common and useful in computer programs, some programming languages build implementations of ADTs into the language as native types or add them into their standard libraries. For instance, Perl arrays can be thought of as an implementation of the List or Deque ADTs and Perl hashes can be thought of in terms of Map or Table ADTs. The C++ Standard Library and Java libraries provide classes that implement the List, Stack, Queue, Map, Priority Queue, and String ADTs.

16.12.13 Rational Numbers as an Abstract Data Type

Rational numbers (numbers that can be written in the form a/b where a and b are integers) cannot be represented natively in a computer. A Rational ADT could be defined as shown below.

Construction: Create an instance of a rational number ADT using two integers, a and b, where a represents the numerator and b represents the denominator.

Operations: addition, subtraction, multiplication, division, exponentiation, comparison, simplify, conversion to a real (floating point) number.

To be a complete specification, each operation should be defined in terms of the data. For example, when multiplying two rational numbers a/b and c/d, the result is defined as ac/bd. Typically, inputs, outputs, preconditions, postconditions, and assumptions for the ADT are specified as well.

Stack Interface

The interface for a Stack ADT, written in C-style notation, might be:

```
long stack_create(); /* create new instance of a stack */
void stack_push(long stack, void *item); /* push an item on the stack */
void *stack_pop(long stack); /* get item from top of stack */
void stack_delete(long stack); /* delete the stack */
```

Usage

This ADT could be used in the following manner:

```
long stack;
struct foo *f;
stack = stack_create(); /* create a stack */
stack_push(stack, f); /* add foo structure to stack */
f = stack_pop(stack); /* get top structure from stack */
```

Implementation variants

The above stack ADT could be initially implemented using an array, and then later changed to a linked list, without affecting any user code.

The number of ways a given ADT can be implemented depends on the programming language. For example, the above example could be written in C using a struct and an accompanying set of data structures using arrays or linked lists to store the entries; however, since the constructor function returns an abstract handle, the actual implementation is hidden from the user. In object-oriented languages such as C++ and Java, ADTs are typically represented using the class construct where the data is represented by data members (attributes) and the operations are represented by member functions (methods). In addition, some languages such as C++ and Java provide a mechanism of enforcement (the private or protected keywords) to only allow the defined functions to operate on the data.

When using object-oriented ADTs, the user can often expand the ADT by creating a subclass of the ADT.

16.12.14 Implementation

Implementing an ADT means providing one procedure or function for each abstract operation. The ADT instances are represented by some concrete data structure that is manipulated by those procedures, according to the ADT's specifications.

Usually there are many ways to implement the same ADT, using several different concrete data structures. Thus, for example, an abstract stack can be implemented by a linked list or by an array.

An ADT implementation is often packaged as one or more modules, whose interface contains only the signature (number and types of the parameters and results) of the operations. The implementation of the module — namely, the bodies of the procedures and the concrete data structure used — can then be hidden from most clients of the module. This makes it possible to change the implementation without affecting the clients.

When implementing an ADT, each instance (in imperative-style definitions) or each state (in functional-style definitions) is usually represented by a handle of some sort.

In object-oriented programming languages, such as C++ and Java, an ADT is typically implemented as class, and each instance of the ADT is an object of that class. The module's interface typically declares the constructors as ordinary procedures, and most of the other ADT operations as methods of that class.

EXAMPLE: Implementation of the Stack ADT

As an example, here is an implementation of the stack ADT above in the C programming language.

Imperative-style interface

An imperative-style interface might be:

```
typedef struct stack_Rep stack_Rep;
/* Type: instance representation (an opaque record). */
typedef stack_Rep *stack_T;
/* Type: handle to a stack instance (an opaque pointer). */
typedef void *stack_Item;
/* Type: value that can be stored in stack (arbitrary address). */
stack_T stack_create(void);
/* Create new stack instance, initially empty. */
void stack_push(stack_T s, stack_Item e);
/* Add an item at the top of the stack. */
```

```
stack_Item stack_pop(stack_T s);
/* Remove the top item from the stack and return it . */
int stack_empty(stack_T ts);
/* Check whether stack is empty. */
```

This implementation could be used in the following manner:

```
#include <stack.h> /* Include the stack interface. */ stack_T t = stack_create(); /* Create a stack instance. */ int foo = 17; /* An arbitrary datum. */ t = stack_push(t, &f); /* Push the address of 'foo' onto the stack. */ ... void *e = stack_pop(t); /* Get the top item and delete it from the stack. */ if (stack_empty(t)) { ... } /* Do something if stack is empty. */ ...
```

This interface can be implemented in many ways. The implementation may be arbitrarily inefficient, since the formal definition of the ADT, above, does not specify how much space the stack may use, nor how long each operation should take. It also does not specify whether the stack state t continues to exist after a call s ← pop(t).

In practice the formal definition should specify that the space is proportional to the number of items pushed and not yet popped; and that every one of the operations above must finish in a constant amount of time, independently of that number. To comply with these additional specifications, the implementation could use a linked list, or an array (with dynamic resizing) together with two integers (an item count and the array size).

OBJECTIVE TYPE QUESTIONS

1. Data structure is
   (a) Physical and logical model of organization
   (b) Logical and mathematical model of organization
   (c) Physical and mathematical model of organization
   (d) All of the above
   (e) None
2. Which of the following data items lead to variable length record when included as item in the record?
   (a) Name of spouse (b) Name of children
   (c) Education (d) Pervious employee
   (e) All of the above
3. LIFO is related with
   (a) Stack (b) Queue
   (c) Both (d) None

4. The complexity of binary search is
   (a) Log n^2 (b) O log n^2
   (c) n/2 (d) None of the above
5. Before traversing data should be
   (a) Indexed (b) non-indexed
   (c) Either a or b (d) None
6. For ascending purpose, bubble sort has one major operation before interchanging as:
   (a) a[i]-a[i+1] (b) a[i]+a[i+1]
   (c) a[i]=a[i+1] (d) None
7. Complexity of Bubble sort is
   (a) O log n (b) O(n)
   (c) log n (d) None
8. Binary search comparison to linear search is
   (a) Fast (b) Slow
   (c) Both (d) None
9. Before applying binary search data should be:
   (a) Sorted (b) Unsorted
   (c) Both (d) None
10. The mid point in binary search should be of type:
    (a) integer (b) Real
    (c) Both (d) None
11. Information is represented by ....
    (a) data (b) characters
    (c) numeral (d) bits
12. In this method a positive integer is converted to negative by changing each bit to its opposite value.
    (a) one's complement (b) two's complement
    (c) both (a) and (b) (d) none of the above
13. The data type defined by the user is known as ....
    (a) abstract data type (b) built-in data type
    (c) classic data type (d) none of the above
14. The keyword class or struct can be used to create ....
    (a) abstract data type (b) built-in data type
    (c) logical data type (d) all of the above

15. An integer data type is ....

(a) primitive (b) non-linear

(c) (a) and (b) (d) non-primitive

EXERCISES

1 What do you understand by algorithms? Explain various types of algorithm in detail.
2. What is flow-chart?
3. How we can determine the efficiency of an algorithm?
4. Explain concept of Big O notations.
5. Explain in detail complexity of algorithms.
6. What do you mean by asymptotic notation?
7. What do you understand by time space trade off?
8. Difference between primitive data structure and non primitive data structure?
9. What are various applications of primitive data structures?
10. What is abstract data type? Explain various uses of ADT.
11. Explain the need and importance of structure.

CHAPTER 17

Arrays, Pointers and Records

17.1 INTRODUCTION

In computer science, Data structure is said to be linear if its element store in proper sequence or in form of simple linear list or linear relationship between the elements represented by means of sequential memory locations. An **Array** is a data structure that consists of a group of elements having a common name and these elements are accessed by using indexing. In most programming languages each element has the same data type and the elements of the array are stored in successive memory locations.

These are the various operations perform on array:

1. **Traversing-** Accessing and processing of each element exactly once.
2. **Searching-** Find the location of the element from the given array.
3. **Insertion-** Adding a new element in the array.
4. **Deletion-** Removing an element from the array.
5. **Sorting-** Arranging the elements in some type of order.
6. **Merging-** Combining two arrays into a single array.

Array elements are usually numbered (as opposed to an associative array) and individual elements are accessed by their numeric position in the array. Some arrays are multi-dimensional, meaning that more than one index is needed to access an element. For instance, a two-dimensional array might be thought of as the elements in a plane that are indexed by x and y coordinates, while a three-dimensional array might be thought of as a volume that is indexed by x, y, and z coordinates and so on.

An array is simply a number of memory locations, each of which can store an item of data of the same data type and which are all referenced through the same variable name. An array data structure or simply array is a data structure consisting of a collection of elements (values or variables), each identified by one or more integer indices, stored so that the address of each element can be computed from its index tuple by a simple mathematical formula. For example, an array of 10 integer variables, with indices 0 through 9, may be stored as 10 words at memory addresses 2000, 2004, 2008, … 2036; so that the element with index i has address 2000 + 4 × i.

Array is same type of data collection i.e. it is a collection of same data type elements. An array is a group of related data items, which can share common name. It is the set of homogeneous data.

Now question arises, why we need array. This can be explained by taking an example for preparing the grade of 100 students in an examination. So to solve this problem, we declare 100 different variables. But if in the next session, 50 more students sit in the examination, then it will require number of changes in the program and also program becomes more complex. So to solve such type of problem, we need to define and declare array. Also processing speed becomes fast with the declaration and use of an array.

The simplest of composite data structures is the *array*. It's just a group of data items stored in successive locations in computer memory. The data items can be any of the aforementioned basic types.

But arrays are a poor data structure when you must frequently change the data. The *linked lists*, often called just *lists*, are better. Linked lists store sequences of data items like arrays do, but the items do not have to be in successive locations in computer memory; each is paired with a pointer giving the memory location of the next data item in sequence, with the last data item in the list having a special pointer called *NULL*. So a list can be scattered around in computer memory, provided you keep item-pointer pairs together and store the location of the first data item. Linked lists need more space to store data items than an array would, but allow more flexibility in the use of computer memory. Lists are more common in artificial-intelligence programming than arrays, and in fact the programming language Lisp is built entirely around lists: lists even represent programs in Lisp.

Arrays and lists order their items. An unordered set can be stored as an array or list in some random order, but there is an alternative. If data items can take on one of N data values—as for instance, data items for ages of employees in years, which must be positive integers less than 100—then we can represent sets as an N-element *bit array* (an array whose data items are bits) where a "true" in location K of the array means that the Kth possible is present in the set. Bit arrays can make set operations like intersection run very fast, and many computers have bit-handling instructions to speed things even more.

17.2 ARRAY

An array is a data structure used to process multiple elements with the same data type when a number of such elements are known. An array is a fixed-sized, homogeneous, and widely-used data structure. By homogeneous, we mean that it consists of components which are all of the same type, called element type or base type. And by fixed sized, we mean that the number of components is constant, and so does not change during the lifetime of the structure. An array is also called a random-access data structure, because all components can be selected at random and are equally accessible.

An array can be used to structure several data objects in the programming languages. A component of an array is selected by giving its subscript, which is an integer indicating the position of the component in the sequence. Therefore, an array is made of the pairs (value, index); it means that with every index, a value is associated. If every index is one single value then it is called a one-dimensional array, whereas if every index is a n-tuple $\{i_1, i_2, i_3, \ldots, i_n\}$, the array is called a n-dimensional array.

An array is a particular method of storing elements of indexed data. Elements of data are stored sequentially in blocks within the array. Each element is referenced by an index, or subscript.

Think of a notebook with pages numbered 1 through 12. Each page may or may not contain information on it. The notebook is an array of pages. Each page is an element of the array 'notebook'. Programmatically, you would retrieve information from a page by referring to its number or subscript, i.e., notebook(4) would refer to the contents of page 4 of the array notebook.

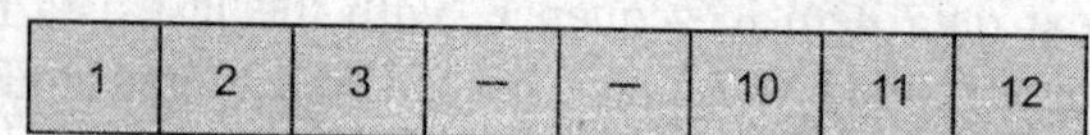

Figure 17.1: The notebook (array) contains 12 pages (elements).

The index is usually a number used to address an element in the array.

An array is a systematic arrangement of objects, usually in rows and columns. Array is similar type of data collection name i.e. it is a collection of same data type elements. An array is a group of related data items, which share common name.

"It is the set of homogeneous data (same type)".

Now question arises, why we need array. This can be explained by taking an example for preparing the grade of 50 students in an examination. So to solve this problem, we declare 50 different variables. But if in the next session, 10 more students sit in the examination, then there will be require number of changes in the program and also program becomes more complex. So to solve such type of problem, we need to define and declare array. Also processing speed becomes fast with the declaration and use of an array.

Also the concept of array can be explained by taking a problem with the C program. Let us suppose, there are four variables declared in a program having different type of data, but if we add more variable (50 variable), then it will create a problem for the declaration and use of variable. Also program becomes lengthy and complex.

Arrays are a data structure which hold multiple variables of the same data type. Consider the case where a programmer needs to keep track of a number of people within an organisation. So far, our initial attempt will be to create a specific variable for each user. This might look like,

```
int name1 = 101;
int name2 = 232;
int name3 = 231;
```

It becomes increasingly more difficult to keep track of this as the number of variables increase. Arrays offer a solution to this problem.

An array is a multi-element box, a bit like a filing cabinet, and uses an indexing system to find each variable stored within it. In C, indexing starts at **zero**.

Arrays, like other variables in C, must be declared before they can be used. The replacement of the above example using arrays looks like,

```
int names[4];
names[0] = 101;
names[1] = 232;
names[2] = 231;
names[3] = 0;
```

We created an array called names, which has space for four integer variables. You may also see that we stored 0 in the last space of the array. This is a common technique used by C programmers to signify the end of an array.

Arrays have the following syntax, using square brackets to access each indexed value (called an element). **Syntax: x[i]**

So that x[5] refers to the sixth element in an array called x. In C, array elements start with 0. Assigning values to array elements is done by,

x[10] = g;

and assigning array elements to a variable is done by,

g = x[10];

In the following example, a character based array named word is declared, and each element is assigned a character. The last element is filled with a zero value, to signify the end of the character string (in C, there is no string type, so character based arrays are used to hold strings). A printf statement is then used to print out all elements of the array.

Suppose salary of the 10 employees named by salary variables name and we write it sal1, sal2, sal3……sal10. We repeat the variable name of employees by using the subscript. Because of use of single subscript or more than one subscript, it is also called subscripted variable.

So Array's representation for the 10th employee is:

```
Salary [10];
```

Array has syntax:

```
Common name variable [size];
        or
array-name [subscript1] [subscript2];
```

We can represent number of elements as a1, a2, … an . Where a is an array name and 1, 2, 3, … n are subscript. We can write the above array statement as:

a[i] , where i = 1, 2, 3, … n

Here i work as subscript and array-name a works as subscripted variable.

Array representation can be done as:

```
storage-type data-type array-name[size];
        or
storage-type data-type array-name[row size][column size];
```

17.3 TYPES OF ARRAY

The types of the array depend upon the given problem. Arrays are mainly of two types:

(i) Linear Array
(ii) Non-Linear Array

17.4 LINEAR ARRAY

A data structure is said to be linear if its elements form a sequence or a linear list. This type of array is also called one Dimensional Array. This is also called list array. Another name of linear array is called **single-dimensional array**. In the linear array only one subscript is used. It is written either in row or in column form.

Syntax to define or declare linear array is:

```
data-type array-name [size];
```

where data types are integer (int), real(float), double and character(char).

For example, some of the valid one dimensional array declaration statements are written as below:

```
int a[50];
float salary[30];
char name[20];
```

Suppose if you want to store the data "TEMPLE" in the array name city, then the representation for declaration be as:

```
char name[7];
```

We can declare that data type char for city variable and you can store maximum 8 character in the different cells of the city variable. So we see that when we declare character type array, size should be one cell more than the given data length, because last cell should be empty or null cell i.e. the end of the string has null character. It is denoted by "\0".

char name[7];

name

T	0
E	1
M	2
P	3
L	4
E	5
'\0'	6

Suppose if we want to assign values 5, 15, 30, 27, 53 is an array integer variable, then it can be written (in the computer memory) as:

number[0] = 55

number[1] = 35

number[2] = 40

number[3] = 47

number[4] = 33

We can declare these numbers in the array form as:

int number[5];

17.4.1 Storage Structure of One Dimensional Array

The general form to use one dimensional array is given below:

```
int Age[10];
```

Here array_type declares base type of array which is the type of each element in array. In our example array_type is int and its name is Age. Size of the array is defined by array_size i.e. 10. We can access array elements by index, and first item in array is at index 0. First element of array is called lower bound and its always 0. Highest element in array is called upper bound.

1. Storage of an array in one statement

```
int Age [5] = {30, 22, 33, 44, 25};
```

2. Storage of an array separately

Look at the following C++ code which demonstrates the declaration and initialization of an array.

```
int Age [5];
Age [0]=30;
Age [1]=22;
Age [2]=33;
Age [3]=44;
Age [4]=25;
```

Array can also be initialized in a ways that array size is omitted, in such case compiler automatically allocates memory to array.

```
int Age [] = {30, 22, 33, 44, 25};
```

17.4.2 Representation of One-dimensional Array

An array is represented in memory by using a sequential mapping. The basic characteristic of the sequential mapping is that every element is at a fixed distance apart. Therefore, if the ith element is mapped into a location having an address a, then the $(i + 1)^{th}$ element is mapped into the memory location having an address (a + 1), as shown in Figure 17.2.

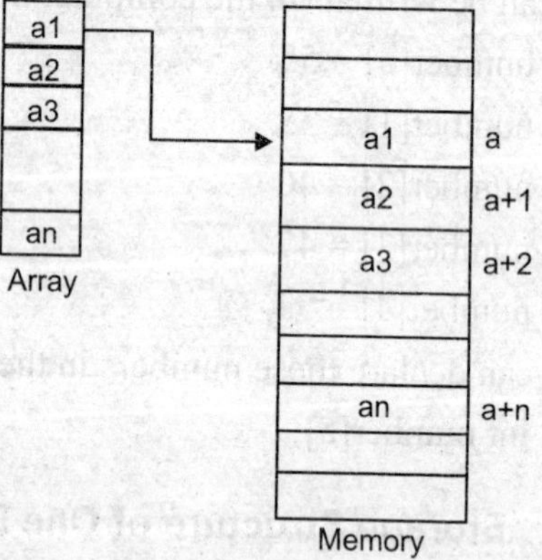

Figure 17.2: Representation of an array.

The address of the first element of an array is called the base address, so the address of the the ith element is

Base address + offset of the ith element from base address

Where the offset is computed as:

Offset of the ith element = number of elements before the ith * size of each element.

If LB is the lower bound, then the offset computation becomes:

$$\text{offset} = (i - LB) * \text{size}.$$

The fundamental concept of an array in any language is that of a sequential collection of values, all of the same type, all accessed by the same variable name. Individual values in an array are individually accessed by using the array name and an index (a number) to specify which value is being accessed.

For a starting example, consider this declaration:

int number;

This declares one variable of type integer capable of holding a single whole number. A diagram as shown in the Figure 17.3, this variable's memory allocation would look like this:

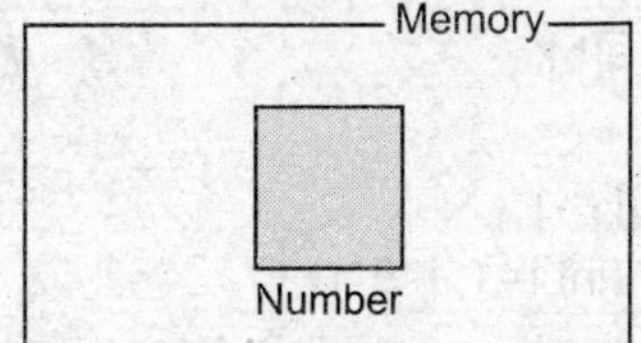

Figure 17.3: Representation of number in memory.

Compare this to the declaration of an array of integers:

int list[5];

In this case we have declared an array, which is capable of holding 5 integers. The 5 integers are located in the array, next to each other in memory, and indexed (numbered) from the first element (element 0) through to the last element (element 4). A diagram representing this array in memory would be as shown in the Figure 17.4 as:

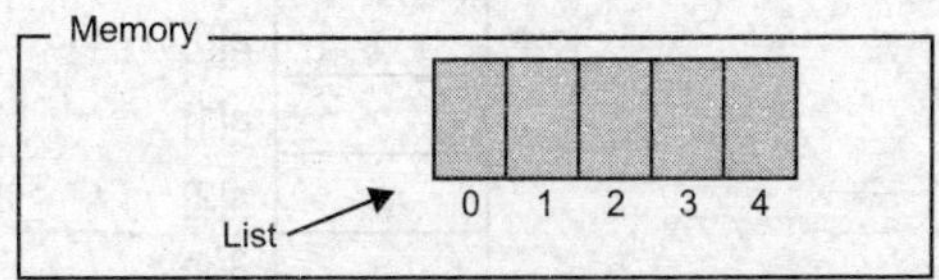

Figure 17.4: Representation of list in memory.

In C++ all arrays are indexed from 0 to n-1 where n is the size of the array. Arrays can be of any type, so for example, we can have:

```
int list[67];       // an array of 67 integers indexed from 0 to 66
char string[20];    // an array of 20 characters indexed from 0 to 19
float price[30];    // an array of floating point numbers indexed from 0 to 29
```

The elements in an array can be accessed and used by specifying the array name and, in square brackets, the index of the element you want to use. For example, to store 78.54 into the first element of the array price, we would write:

```
price[0] = 78.54;              // Note, first element is index 0
```

To store 100.25 into element 5 of the array price, we would write:

```
price[5] = 100.25;        // Note, this is the 6th element
```

To print the last element of the array price having value 220.32, we would write:

```
price[29]= 220.32;
```

When this index notation is used to access elements of an array, the individual elements can be treated as individual variables.

ARRAY MEMORY DIAGRAMS

Here is an array declaration and code to initialize it.

```
int a[5];                       // Allocates memory for 5 integers.
. . .
a[0] = 1;
for (int i=1; i<5; i++)
{
a[i] = a[i-1] * 2;
}
```

Arrays are often represented with diagrams that represent their memory use. The diagram below as shown in the figure 17.5 is one typical way to represent the memory used by an array. Each box represents the amount of memory needed to hold one array element. For integer this is usually 4 bytes.

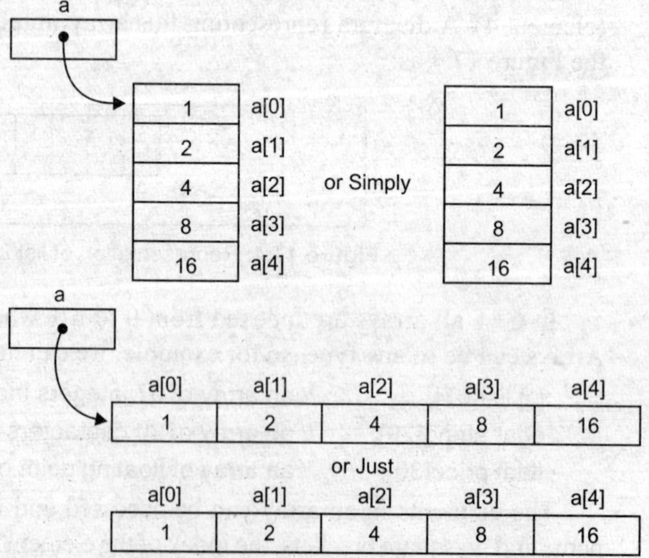

Figure 17.5: Various memory diagrams.

We can write the value of an element inside the box. Pointers hold the memory address of other data and are represented by a black disk with an arrow pointing to the data it references. The actual array variable, a in this example, is a pointer to the memory for all of its elements. A common shortcut is to omit writing the array variable, and write only the elements that hold the data because these are usually the focus of attention. Sometimes the cells are written horizontally, especially when showing arrays of characters.

17.4.3 Various Operations on Linear Array

Array can be used for handling same type of numbers or text data. Mainly there are various operations can be applied with the linear array.

These different operations are discussed as below:

1. Traversing or Visiting
2. Inserting
3. Deleting
4. Searching
5. Sorting
6. Merging
7. Reversing
8. Copying
9. Swapping

Here we will discuss Traversing, Inserting and deleting in this chapter in detail. The next three operations with their different methods will be discussed in the chapter 12 naming Sorting and Searching.

1. Traversing a linear array

Traversing means visiting and accessing each element of the array exactly once. Values are stored and retrieved from the array-type variable by indicating its position in an array. Because the array is an ordered collection, the position of an element is its index.

Figure 17.6 shows an array, seven elements long, containing numeric values. To traverse the array sequentially, we may use the algorithm in Figure 17.6 using the C++ syntax. The maximum number of comparisons is 7, and occurs when the key we are searching for as in A[6].

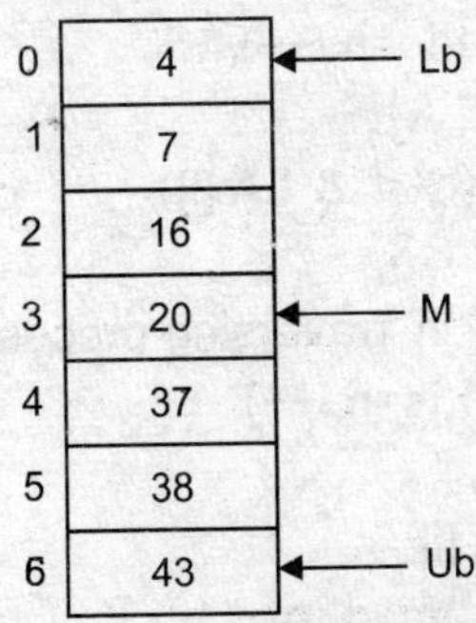

Figure 17.6: Traversing of linear array.

Algorithm 17.1: Traversing or Visiting a Linear Array

TRAVERSE (I, LB, UB)

Taking LA is a linear array having lower bound LB and upper bound UB. This algorithm is used to traverses linear array (LA) by applying an operation visiting to each element of LA.

Step 1: [Initialize Value of I.] Set I = LB.

Step 2: Repeat Steps 3 and 4 while I ≤ UB.

Step 3: [Visit each element exactly once.] Apply VISTING to LA [I].

Step 4: [Increment the value of I.] Set I= I + 1.

[End of while loop.]

Step 5: End.

Algorithm 17.2: Simple approach for traversing a Linear Array

TRAVERSE (I, LB, UB)

This algorithm traverses a linear array LA with lower bound LB and upper bound UB.

Step 1: Repeat Steps for I = LB to UB.

Apply PROCESS to LA [I].

[End of loop.]

Step 2: End.

Program 1: Write a C program to traversing or visiting a list (One dimensional array).

```
#include<stdio.h>
#include<conio.h>
void main()
{
int LA [50],i,n,p;
printf("\n How many numbers you want to insert: ");
scanf(" %d ", &n);
printf("\n Enter the Numbers:");
for(i=1;i<=n;i++)
{
scanf("%d",& LA [i]);
}
printf("\n Traversing process is: ");
for(i=1;i<=n;i++)
{
p= LA [i];
printf("\n%d",p);
```

```
}
getche();
}
Output:
How many numbers you want to insert: 5
Enter the Numbers:
44
22
33
11
55
Traversing process is:
44
22
33
11
55
```

Here the array LA is traversed starting from first element to last element. Each element is printed on the screen.

Note: To access the elements in the array the index is varied from lower bound to upper bound. Time to access every element is same. For array of size say, n, for loop executes n times. The traversal operation on linear arrays is of O(n).

2. Inserting in linear array

Inserting in array means, the operation of adding new element in the array is to be performed. Inserting an element at the end of the linear array can be easily done.

But, inserting an element at given position is little-bit complex.

Algorithm 17.3: Inserting into a Linear Array

INSERT (LA, N, J, ITEM).

Taking LA is a linear array with N elements and J is a positive in LA such that J ≤ N. This algorithm inserts an element ITEM into the Jth position in linear array (LA).

Step 1: [Initialize Value of I.] Set I = N.

Step 2: Repeat Steps 3 and 4 while I ≥ J.

Step 3: [Move Ith element downward position.] Set LA [I + 1] = LA [I].

Step 4: [Decrement the value of I.] Set I = I – 1.

[End of while loop.]

Step 5: [Insert new element in linear array.] Set LA [J] = ITEM.

Step 6: [Reset the value of N in LA.] Set N = N + 1.

Step 7: End.

Explanation:

Let us take an example of an array of size 8 as in Figure 17.7. Here N is 5 i.e. there are total 5 elements in the array.

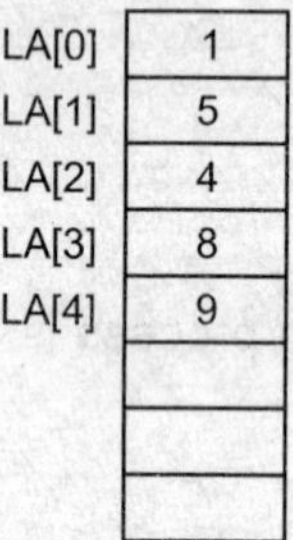

Figure 17.7: Linear array having 5 elements. (Before insertion)

Let us suppose an element 3 is to be inserted at position 2 i.e. at LA[1].

Step 1: I=N=5

Step 2: Repeat Steps 3 and 4 while I e" J.

Step 3: [Move Ith element downward position.]

Set LA [I + 1] = LA [I].

A[5+1]=A[5] i.e. the element stored at position 5 is moved downward by one position.

Step 4: [Decrement the value of I.]

Set I = I – 1.

So, after complete executions of step 3 and 4. Following statements have been executed:

LA[4+1]=LA[4]

LA[3+1]=LA[3]

LA[2+1]=LA[2]

LA[1+1]=LA[1]

Now position LA[1] is vacant so that new element can be inserted

Step 5: Insert new element in linear array.

Set LA [J] = ITEM=3

The element 3 has been inserted at required position

Step 6: [Reset the value of N in LA.] Set N = N + 1.

As now there are total 6 elements in array LA. So, now array LA will look like:

LA[0]	1
LA[1]	3
LA[2]	5
LA[3]	4
LA[4]	8
LA[5]	9

Figure 17.8: Linear array having 6 elements. (After insertion)

Step 7: End.

Note: *The worst case occurs when the element is to be inserted at the first position, as all elements (n) are to be moved down.*

The best case occurs when the element is inserted at the last position, as no element is moved down. Hence the complexity of insertion operation is O(n).

Program 2: Write a C++ program to insert an element in array at a specific position.

```
# include<iostream.h>
# include<conio.h>
# define size 21
class array
{
private:
int i, a[size];
public:
void read (int);
void insert (int, int, int); // for insertion of element
void display (int);
};
void array : : read (int n)
{
for(i=0;i<n;i++)
cin>>a[i];
}
void array : : display (int n)
```

```
{
for (i=0;i<n;i++)
cout<<a[i]<<" ";
}
void array : : insert (int n, int position, int info)
{
// back shifting
for (i=n-1;i>=(position-1);i--)
a[i+1]=a[i];
// insertion
a [position-1] = info;
}
void main ( )
{
array obj;
int n, pos, info;
clrscr ( );
cout <<"Read no of elements<=<<size-1<<"\n";
cin>>n;
cout<<"\n Read "<<n<<"elements\n";
obj.read (n);
cout<<"\nRead the element to be inserted: ";
cin>>info;
cout<<"\n\nRead the position of insertion<="<<n+1<<end1;
cin>>pos;
cout<<"\nGiven array is \n\n";
obj.display (n);
cout<<"\n\nElement to be inserted is "<<info;
cout<<"\n\nPosition of insertion is "<<pos<<"\n\n;
obj.insert (n, pos, info);
cout<<"\nArray after insertion is \n\n";
obj.display (n+1);
getch ( );
}
```

Output:

```
Read no of elements <=20
6
Read 6 elements
12      30      36      70      37      84
```

```
Read the element to be inserted: 50
Read the position of insertion <=7
4
Given array is
12    30    36    70    37    84
Element to be inserted is 50
Position of insertion is 4
Array after insertion is
12    30    36    50    70    37    84
```

Program 3: Write a C++ program for Insertion in a sorted array.

```
# include<iostream.h>
# include<conio.h>
# define size 21
class array
{
private:
int i, position,a[size];
public:
void read (int);
void insert (int, int, int); // for insertion of element
void display (int);
};
void array : : read (int n)
{
for(i=0;i<n;i++)
cin>>a[i];
}
void array : : display (int n)
{
for (i=0;i<n;i++)
cout<<a[i]<<" ";
}
void array : : insert (int n, int info)
{
if(info>=a[n-1])
a[n] = info;
else
{
```

```
position=0;
while(a[position]<=info)
position++;
for (i=n-1;i>=(position-1);i--)
a[i+1]=a[i];
a [position] = info;
}
}
void main ( )
{
array obj;
int n, info;
clrscr ( );
cout <<"Read no of elements<=<<size-1<<"\n";
cin>>n;
cout<<"\n Read "<<n<<"elements\n";
obj.read (n);
cout<<"\nRead the element to be inserted: ";
cin>>info;
cout<<"\nGiven array is \n\n";
obj.display (n);
cout<<"\n\nElement to be inserted is "<<info;
obj.insert (n, info);
cout<<"\nArray after insertion is \n\n";
obj.display (n+1);
getch ( );
}
```

Output:

```
Read no of elements <=20
6
Read 6 elements
12    30    36    39    50    84
Read the element to be inserted: 45
Given array is
12    30    36    39    50    84
Element to be inserted is 50
Array after insertion is
12    30    36    39    45    50    84
```

3. Deleting from linear array

Deleting from array means, the operation of deleting an element from array is to be performed. Deleting last element from array is simple. But deleting an element from given position is to be performed carefully.

Algorithm 17.4: Deleting from a Linear Array

DELETE (LA, N, J, ITEM)

Taking LA is a linear array with N elements and J is a positive in LA such that $J \leq N$. This algorithm deletes the Jth element from linear array (LA).

Step 1: Set ITEM = LA [J].

Step 2: Repeat for I = J to N – 1

[Move (I + 1)st element upward position.] Set LA [I] = LA [I + 1].

[End of loop.]

Step 3: [Reset the value of N in LA.] Set N = N – 1.

Step 4: End.

Explanation:

Let us take an example of an array of size 8 as in Figure 17.9. Here N is 5 i.e. there are total 5 elements in the array.

LA[0]	1
LA[1]	5
LA[2]	4
LA[3]	8
LA[4]	9

Figure 17.9: Linear array having 5 elements. (Before deletion)

Let us suppose an element 5 is to be deleted from the array and this element is stored at position J=1.

Step 1: Set ITEM = LA [J] = 5

Step 2: Repeat for I = J to N – 1

[Move (I + 1)st element upward position.]

Set LA [I] = LA [I + 1].

Step 3: [Reset the value of N in LA.] Set N = N – 1.

Step 4: End.

Now, there will be 4 total elements in the array as one element has been deleted. The array will look like:

LA[0]	1
LA[1]	4
LA[2]	8
LA[3]	9

Figure 17.10: Linear array having 4 elements. (After deletion)

***Note:** The worst case occurs when the element is deleted from the first position, as all the elements (n-1) are to be moved upward.*

The best case occurs when the element is deleted from the last position. In this case, no element is to be moved up.

Hence the complexity of deletion operation is O(n).

Program 4: Write a C++ program for deletion from a specific position.

```
# include<iostream.h>
# include<conio.h>
# define size 21
class array
{
private:
int i, a[size];
public:
void read (int);
void del (int, int);
void display (int);
};
void array : : read (int n)
{
for(i=0;i<n;i++)
cin>>a[i];
}
void array : : display (int n)
{
for (i=0;i<n;i++)
cout<<a[i]<<" ";
}
```

```
void array : : del (int pos, int n)
{
for (i=pos;i<=n-1;i++)
a[i-1]=a[i];
a [n-1] = 0.0; //for last element
}
void main ( )
{
array obj;
int n, pos;
clrscr ( );
cout <<"Read no of elements<=<<size-1<<"\n";
cin>>n;
cout<<"\n Read "<<n<<"elements\n";
obj.read (n);
cout<<"\nGiven array is \n\n";
obj.display (n);
cout<<"\n\nRead the position of deletion<="<<n<<end1;
cin>>pos;
cout<<"\n\nPosition of deletion is "<<pos<<"\n\n;
obj.del (pos,n);
cout<<"\nArray after deletion is \n\n",
obj.display (n-1);
getch ( );
}
```

Output:

```
Read no of elements <=20
6
Read 6 elements
32    30    36    10    37    84
Given array is
32    30    36    10    37    84
Read the position of deletion <=37
4
Position of deletion is 4
Array after deletion is
32    30    36    10    84
```

Program 5: Write a C++ program for deletion from an unsorted array.

```
# include<iostream.h>
# include<conio.h>
# define size 21
class array
{
private:
int i, position,a[size];
public:
void read (int);
void del (int, int, int);
void display (int);
};
void array : : read (int n)
{
for(i=0;i<n;i++)
cin>>a[i];
}
void array : : display (int n)
{
for (i=0;i<n;i++)
cout<<a[i]<<" ";
}
void array : : del (int info, int n)
{
for(i=0;i<n;i++)
{
if(a[i]= = info)
{
for (int pos =i+1;pos<n;pos++)
a[pos-1]=a[pos];
a [n-1] = 0.0;
retun(i);
}
}
return(-1);
}
void main ( )
{
```

```
array obj;
int n, info,flag;
clrscr ( );
cout <<"Read no of elements<=<<size<<"\n";
cin>>n;
cout<<"\n Read "<<n<<"elements\n";
obj.read (n);
cout<<"\nGiven array is \n\n";
obj.display (n);
cout<<"\nRead the element to be deleted: ";
cin>>info;
cout<<"\n\nElement to be deleted is "<<info;
flag=obj.del (info,n);
if(flag!= -1)
{
cout<<"\nArray after deletion is \n\n";
obj.display (n-1);
}
else
cout<<info<<"Not found in array\n";
getch ( );
}
Output:
Read no of elements <=20
6
Read 6 elements
32    30    36    39    10    84
Given array is
32    30    36    39    10    84

Read the element to be deleted: 36

Element to be deleted is 36
Array after deletion is
32    30    39    45    10    84
```

Program 6: Write a C++ program for deletion from a sorted array.

```
# include<iostream.h>
# include<conio.h>
# define size 21
```

```
class array
{
private:
int i, position,a[size];
public:
void read (int);
int del (int, int, int);
void display (int);
};
void array : : read (int n)
{
for(i=0;i<n;i++)
cin>>a[i];
}
void array : : display (int n)
{
for (i=0;i<n;i++)
cout<<a[i]<<" ";
}
int array : : del (int info, int n)
{
if((info<a[0]) || (info>a[n-1]))
return (-1);
else
{
int position =0;
while(a[position]<info)
position++;
if(a[position]= = info)
{
for(i=position+1;i<n;i++)
a[i-1]=a[i];
a [n-1] = 0.0;
retun(position);
}
else
return(-1);
}
void main ( )
```

```
{
array obj;
int n, info,flag;
clrscr ( );
cout <<"Read no of elements<=<<size<<"\n";
cin>>n;
cout<<"\n Read "<<n<<"elements in ascending order\n";
obj.read (n);
cout<<"\nGiven array is \n\n";
obj.display (n);
cout<<"\nRead the element to be deleted: ";
cin>>info;
cout<<"\n\nElement to be deleted is "<<info;
flag=obj.del (info,n);
if(flag!= -1)
{
cout<<"\nArray after deletion is \n\n";
obj.display (n-1),
}
else
cout<<info<<"Not found in array\n";
getch ( );
}
```

Output:

```
Read no of elements <=20
6
Read 6 elements in ascending order
12    30    36    39    50    84
Given array is
12    30    36    39    50    84

Read the element to be deleted: 50

Element to be deleted is 50
Array after deletion is
12    30    36    39    84
```

4. Searhing in linear array

The process of finding specified element in an array. Computer systems are often used to store large amounts of data from which individual records must be retrieved according to some search criterion. Thus the efficient storage of data to facilitate fast searching is an important issue. We are using two searching algorithm to find the element from a given array. Detailed description of searching and sorting is given in chapter 12.

Algorithm 17.5: Linear Search

LINEAR (LA, N, ITEM, LOC)

Taking LA is a linear array with N elements, and ITEM is a given item of information. This algorithm find the location LOC of ITEM in LA, or set LOC = 0 if the search is unsuccessful.

Step 1: [Insert ITEM at the end of LA.] Set LA [N + 1] = ITEM.

Step 2: [Initialize the value of LOC.] Set LOC = 1.

Step 3: [Search for ITEM.]

Repeat steps while LA [LOC] ≠ ITEM

Set LOC = LOC + 1

[End of while loop.]

Step 4: [Successful or Unsuccessful?] if LOC = N + 1, then Set LOC = 0.

Step 5: End.

Algorithm 17.6: Binary Search

BINARY (LA, LB, UB, ITEM, LOC)

Taking LA is a sorted array with lower bound LB and upper bound UB, and ITEM is a given item of information. The variables BEGIN, END and MIDLOC denote as beginning, ending and middle locations of elements of LA. This algorithm find the location LOC of ITEM in LA or if LOC not found set LOC = NULL.

Step 1: [Initialize starting variables.]

Set BEGIN = LB, END = UB and MIDLOC = INT ((BEGIN + END)/2).

Step 2: Repeat steps 3 and 4 while BEGIN ≤ END and LA [MIDLOC] ≠ ITEM.

Step 3: If ITEM < LA [MID], then

Set END = MIDLOC – 1.

Else

Set BEGIN = MIDLOC + 1.

[End of If statement.]

Step 4: Set MIDLOC = INT ((BEGIN + END)/2).

[End of Step 2 loop.]

Step 5: If LA [MIDLOC] = ITEM, then: Set LOC = MIDLOC else

Set LOC = NULL.

[End of If statement.]

Step 6: End.

Algorithm 17.7: Binary Search and Insertion

LA is a sorted array with N elements, and ITEM is a given item of information. This algorithm finds the location LOC of ITEM in LA or inserts ITEM in its proper place in LA.

SEARCH AND INSERTION (LA, LB, UB, ITEM, LOC, N, J)

Step 1: [Initialize starting variables.]

Set BEGIN = LB, END = UB and MIDLOC = INT ((BEGIN + END)/2).

Step 2: Repeat steps 3 and 4 while BEGIN ≤ END and LA [MIDLOC] ≠ ITEM.

Step 3: If ITEM < LA [MID], then

Set END = MIDLOC – 1.

Else

Set BEGIN = MIDLOC + 1.

[End of If statement.]

Step 4: Set MIDLOC = INT ((BEGIN + END)/2).

[End of Step 2 loop.]

Step 5: If ITEM < LA [MIDLOC], then:

Set LOC = MIDLOC.

Else:

Set LOC = MIDLOC + 1.

[End of If statment.]

Step 6: Insert ITEM into LA [LOC]

Step 7: [Initialize Value of I.] Set LOC = N.

Step 8: Repeat Steps 9and 10 while LOC ≥ J.

Step 9: [Move Ith element downward position.] Set LA [LOC + 1] = LA [LOC].

Step 10: [Decrement the value of I.] Set LOC = LOC – 1.

[End of while loop.]

Step 11: [Insert new element in linear array.] Set LA [J] = ITEM.

Step 12: [Reset the value of N in LA.] Set N = N + 1.

Step 13: End.

5. Sorting a linear array

Arranging elements in a specific order, either ascending or descending, is known as sorting. Many types of sorting techniques are available in data structures.

Algorithm 17.8: Bubble Sort

BUBBLE (LA, N, TEMP)

Taking LA is an array with N elements. TEMP is used as temporary variable

for interchanging values. This algorithm sorts the elements in LA.
Step 1: Repeat Steps 2 and 3 for J = 1 to N – 1.
Step 2: Set P = 1. [Initializes starting pointer P.]
Step 3: Repeat steps while P ≤ N – J [This loop executes for passes.]
(a) If LA [P] > LA [P + 1] then
Interchange LA [P] and LA [P + 1].
TEMP= LA [P].
LA [P] = LA [P + 1].
LA [P + 1] =TEMP.
[End of If statement.]
(b) Set P = P+1.
[End of Step 3 inner loop.]
[End of Step 1 outer loop.]
Step 4: End.

6. Merging Arrays

The merging means to concatenate or merge two arrays into a single one.

Suppose we have two sorted arrays A[] of m elements and B[] of n elements. Write a function merge which would merge this two arrays into new sorted array C[] in O(n) time as shown on the picture.

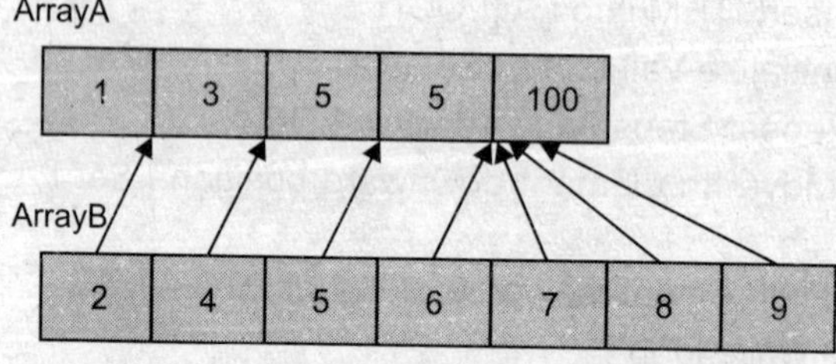

C++ code:

```
#include<iostream.h>
#include<conio.h>
void main()
{
int A[10],B[10],C[30],i,j,t,m,n,temp;
clrscr();
```

```
cout<<"\n Enter the number of elements of Array-A: ";
cin>>m;
cout<<"\n Enter the elements :\n";
for(i=1;i<=m;i++)
cin>>A[i];
cout<<"\n  Enter the number of elements of Array-B: ";
cin>>n;
cout<<"\n Enter the elements:  ";
for(i=1;i<=n;i++)
cin>>B[i];
t=m+n;
for(i=1;i<=m;i++)
C[i]=A[i];
for(i=1;i<=n;i++)
C[i+m]=B[i];
cout<<"\n  Merged array-C is:";
for(i=1;i<=t;i++)
cout<<C[i];
cout<<"\n  Sorted array -C is: ";
for(i=1;i<=m-1;i++)
{
for(j=1;j<=m-i;j++)
{
if(C[j]>C[j+1])
{
temp=C[j+1];
C[j+1]=C[j];
C[j]=temp;
}
else
continue;
}
}
for(i=1;i<=t;i++)
cout<<C[i];
getch();
}
```

7. *Reversing the Array*

Reverses the order of the elements of a given array. For example, if the given array contains five elements:

3 5 7 2 4

After reversing the order of elements, the result is

4 2 7 5 3

C++ code:

```
#include<iostream.h>
#include<conio.h>
void main()
{
int a[10],n,i,j,temp;
clrscr();
cout<<"Enter the size of array:";
cin>>n;
cout<<"\n Enter the elements of array:";
for(i=0;i<n;i++)
{
cin>>a[i];
}
for(i=0,j=n-1;i<n/2;i++,j—)
{
temp=a[i];
a[i]=a[j];
a[j]=temp;
}
cout<<"\n Elements of array after reversing are:";
for(i=0;i<n;i++)
{
cout<<a[i];
}
getch();
}
```

Output:

```
Enter the size of array: 2
Enter the elements of array: 40 50 60
Elements of array after reversing are: 60 50 40
```

8. Copying The Elements of One Array into Another in Reverse Order

C++ code:

```
#include <iostream.h>
#include <conio.h>
void main()
{
int arr1[5], arr2[5], i, j ;
clrscr( ) ;
cout<<"\nEnter 5 elements of array:";
for ( i = 0 ; i <= 4 ; i++ )
cin>>arr1[i] ;
for ( i = 0, j = 4 ; i <= 4 ; i++, j— )
arr2[j] = arr1[i];
cout<<"\nElements in reverse order:";
for ( i = 0 ; i <= 4 ; i++ )
cout<<arr2[i];
cout<<"\nPress any key to exit.";
getch( ) ;
}
```

Output:

```
Enter 5 elements of array: 7 4 8 1 3
Elements in reverse order:
3
1
8
4
7
Press any key to exit.
```

9. Swapping Two Arrays

The swapping means to interchange two arrays.

C++ code:

The C++ code for this is actually simpler than the description:

```
int nTemp;
nTemp = nArray[1];
nArray[1] = nArray[2];
nArray[2] = nTemp;
```

Of course, the above makes more sense when placed into a function:

```
void SwapElements( int * nArray, int nFirst, int nSecond)
{
int nTemp = nArray[nFirst];
nArray[nFirst] = nArray[nSecond];
nArray[nSecond] = nTemp;
}
```

Please feel free to clip the code sample, and use it in your own projects. Of course, if you need to swap different data types, then the code will need to be adjusted.

17.5 NON-LINEAR ARRAY

Non-linear array are further subdivided into *n* categories as:

1. Two Dimensional Array
2. Three Dimensional Array
3. N Dimensional Array

We will discuss here two and three-dimensional array only.

17.5.1 Two Dimensional Array

These arrays are also called double dimensional array or two subscripted array. Another name of two-dimensional array is Tabular or Rectangular Array. These arrays are in row and column form. So these are also called as Row-Column or square Array. These arrays have two subscripts. We can write the double dimensional array in tabular form as:

```
a11   a12   a13   ...   ...   ...   a1n
a21   a22   a23   ...   ...   ...   a2n
...   ...   ...   ...   ...   ...   ...
an1   an2   an3   ...   ...   ...   ann
```

The general syntax used for declaration of two dimensional array is as:

data type array-name [row size] [column size];

For example, some valid declaration are:

```
int a[10][10];
float b[50][50];
char name[10][20];
```

Also you can declare two dimensional array in static form i.e. these types of array declarations have fixed or constant values during declaration.

17.5.1.1 Storage Structure of Two Dimensional Array

The general form to use two dimensional array is given below:

```
int matrix [2][3];
```

Here array_type declares base type of array which is the type of each element in array. In our example array_type is int and its name is matrix. Size of the array is defined by array_name[row size][column size]; i.e. [2][3]. We can access array elements by index, and first item in array is at index [0][0]. First element of array is called lower bound and its always [0][0]. Highest element in array is called upper bound.

1. Storage of an array in one statement

```
int matrix [2][3] = {15, 70, 12, 22, 20, 18};
```

2. Storage of an array separately

Look at the following C++ code which demonstrates the declaration and initialization of an array.

```
int matrix [2][3];
```

Here the values assigned to the tabular array-name are as:

```
matrix [0][0] = 15
matrix [0][1] = 70
matrix [0][2] = 12
matrix [1][0] = 22
matrix [1][1] = 20
matrix [1][2] = 18
```

Also we can write the above statement as:

```
int matrix [ ][ ] = {15, 70, 12, 22, 20, 18};
```

Above statement fails in some cases. Another way to write the above statement is as follows:

```
int matrix [ ][ ] = {{15, 70, 12}, {22, 20, 18}};
or
int matrix [ ][ ] = {{15,70}, {12, 22}, {20, 18}};
```

Two-dimensioned arrays have two or more index values which specify the element in the array.

```
Two [i][j]
```

In the above example, the first index value i specifies a row index, while j specifies a column index.

17.5.1.2 Representation of Two-dimensional Array

1. Row-major representation

A two-dimensional array can be considered as a one-dimensional array whose elements are also one-dimensional arrays. So, we can view a two dimensional array as one single column of rows and map it sequentially as shown in Figure 17.11. Such a representation is called a row-major representation.

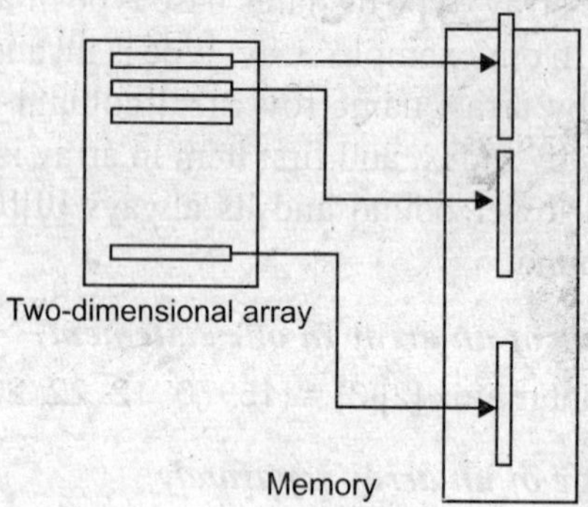

Figure 17.11: Row major representation of a two-dimensional array.

The address of the element of the ith row and the jth column therefore is:

addr(a[i, j]) = (number of rows placed before ith row * size of a row) + (number of elements placed before the jth element in the ith row * size of element)

where Number of rows placed before ith row = (i - LB1), and LB1 is the lower bound of the first dimension.

Size of a row = number of elements in a row * a size of element.

Number of elements in a row = (UB2 – LB2+1), where UB2 and LB2 are the upper and lower bounds of the second dimension, respectively.

Therefore:

addr(a[i, j]) = ((i – LB1) * (UB2 – LB2+1) * size) + ((j – LB2)*size)

Row-major Arrays

A Row-major array is a technique in which elements in an array are arranged row-wise. We can store elements row by row shown in figure below 17.12.

COLUMN-0	COLUMN-1	COLUMN-2	
X[0][0]	X[0][1]	X[0][2]	ROW-0
X[1][0]	X[1][1]	X[1][2]	ROW-1
X[2][0]	X[2][1]	X[2][2]	ROW-2

X[0][0]	X[0][1]	X[0][2]	X[1][0]	X[1][1]	X[1][2]	X[2][0]	X[2][1]	X[2][2]
	ROW-0			ROW-1			ROW-2	

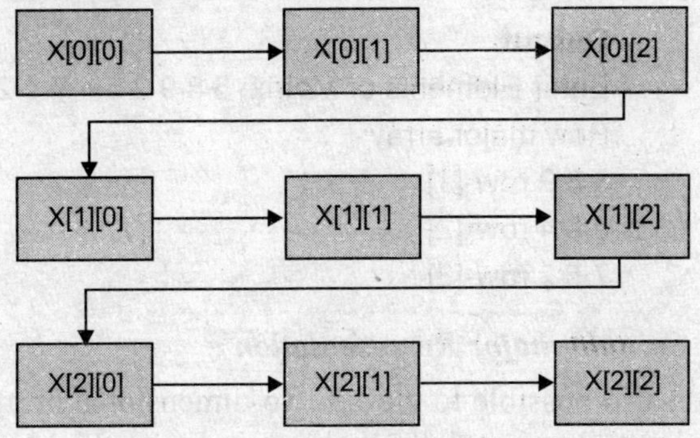

Figure 17.12: Row-major array

Program 7: Write a C++ program to implement an array by row-major method.

```
#include<iostream.h>
#include<conio.h>
void main()
{
int mat[3][3];
int i,j;
clrscr();
cout<<"Enter Elements of Matrix\n";
for(i=0;i<3;i++)
{
for(j=0;j<3;j++)
{
cin>>mat[i][j];
}
}
cout<<"\n Row major array: \n";
for(i=0;i<3;i++)
{
for(j=0;j<3;j++)
{
cout<<mat[i][j];
cout<<"row-["<<i+1<<"]\n";
}
}
getch();
}
```

Output:

Enter Elements of Matrix: 5 8 9 2 5 4 7 5 2
Row major array:
5 8 9 row-[1]
2 5 4 row-[2]
7 5 2 row-[3]

2. Column-major Representation

It is also possible to view a two-dimensional array as one single row of columns and map it sequentially as shown in Figure 17.13. Such a representation is called a **column-major representation.**

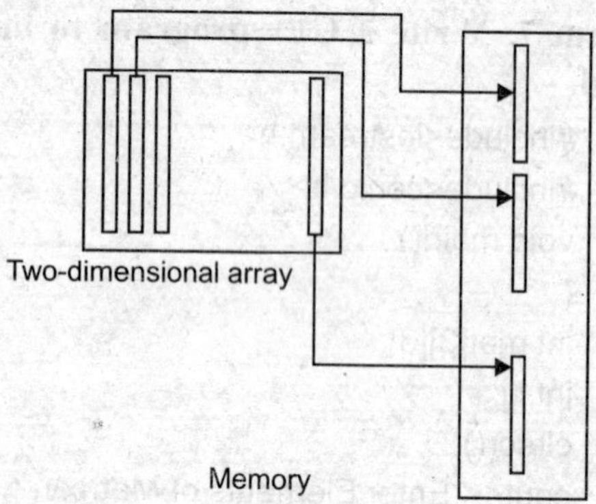

Figure 17.13: Column major representation of a two-dimensional array.

The address of the element of the ith row and the jth column therefore is:

addr(a[i, j]) = (number of columns placed before j^{th} column * size of a column) + (number of elements placed before the ith element in the jth column * size of each element)

Number of columns placed before j^{th} column = (j – LB2) where LB2 is the lower bound of the second dimension.

Size of a column = number of elements in a column * size of element Number of elements in a column = (UB1 – LB1 + 1), where UB1 and LB1 are the upper and lower bounds of the first dimension, respectively.

Therefore:

addr(a[i, j]) = ((j – LB2) * (UB1 – LB1+1) * size) + ((i – LB1)*size)

Column-major Arrays

In column major array elements are stored column-by-column as shown in Figure 17.13.

COLUMN-0	COLUMN-1	COLUMN-2	
X[0][0]	X[0][1]	X[0][2]	ROW-0
X[1][0]	X[1][1]	X[1][2]	ROW-1
X[2][0]	X[2][1]	X[2][2]	ROW-2

X[0][0]	X[1][0]	X[2][0]	X[0][1]	X[1][1]	X[2][1]	X[0][2]	X[1][2]	X[2][2]
COLUMN-0			COLUMN-1			COLUMN-2		

Program 8: Write a C++ program to implement an array by column-major method.

```
#include<iostream.h>
#include<conio.h>
void main()
{
int mat[3][3];
int i,j;
clrscr();
cout<<"Enter Elements of Matrix\n";
for(i=0;i<3;i++)
{
for(j=0;j<3;j++)
{
cin>>mat[i][j];
}
}
cout<<"\n Column major array: \n";
for(i=0;i<3;i++)
{
for(j=0;j<3;j++)
{
cout<<mat[i][j];
cout<<"\n";
}
}
getch();
}
```

Output:

Enter Elements of Matrix: 5 8 9 2 5 4 7 5 2

Column major array:

5 2 7

8 5 5

9 4 2

Program 9: Write a C++ program for addition of two matrices.

```
# include<iostream.h>
# include<conio.h>
# define s 5
class array
{
private:
int i, j, x[s] [s], y[s] [s], z[s] [s];
public;
void enter (int x[s] [s], int, int);
void display (int x[s] [s], int, int);
void mat_add (int x[s] [s], int y[s] [s], int z[s] [s], int, int);
};
void array : : enter (int x[s] [s], int row, int column)
{
for (i=0; i<row; i++)
cin>>x[i] [j];
}
}
void array : :display (int x[s] [s], int row, int column)
{
for (i=0; i<row; i++)
{
for (j=0; j<column;j++)
cout<<x[i] [j]<<'\t';
cout<<endl;
}
}
void array : : mat_add (int x[s] [s], int y[s] [s], int z[s] [s], int row, int column)
{
// Matrix addition
for (i=0; i<<row; i++)
{
for (j=0;j<column;j++)
z[i] [j] =x [i] [j] +y [i] [j];
}
}
void main ( )
{
```

```
array obj;
int a[s] [s], b[s] [s], c[s] [s], rowl, columnl, row2, column2;
clrscr ( );
cout<<\nEnter the order of first matrix <="<<s<<" * "<<s<<"\n";
cin>>row1>>column1;
cout<<\nEnter the order of second matrix <="<<s<<" * <<<s<<"\n};
cin>>row2<<column2;
if((row1= =row2) && (column1= =column2))
{
cout<<"\nEnter the first matrix of order "<<row1<<" * "<<column1<<end1;
obj.enter (a, row1, column1);
cout<<"\nEnter the second matrix of ordre "<<row2<<" *
"<<column1<<end1;
obj.enter(b, row2, column2);
clrscr ( );
cout<<"\nFirst matrix is \n\n";
obj.display (a, row1, column1);
cout<<"\nSecond matrix is \n\n";
obj.display(b, row2, column2);
obj.mat_add (a, b, c, row1, column1);
cout<<"\nAddition of two matrices is \n\n";
obj.display (c, row1, column1);
}
else
cout<<"\nMatrix addition is not possible";
getch ( );
}
```

Output:

```
Enter the order  of first matrix <=5 * 5
2    2
Enter the order of second matrix <=5 * 5
2    2
Enter the first matrix of order 2 * 2
1    4
3    6
Enter the second matrix of order 2 * 2
2    5
1    2
First matrix is
1    4
```

```
3	6
Second matrix is
2	5
1	2
Addition of two matrices is
3	9
4	8
```

Program 10: Write a C++ program for subtraction of two matrices.

```
# include<iostream.h>
# include<conio.h>
# define s 5
class array
{
private:
int i, j, x[s] [s], y[s] [s], z[s] [s];
public;
void enter (int x[s] [s], int, int);
void display (int x[s] [s], int, int);
void mat_add (int x[s] [s], int y[s] [s], int z[s] [s], int, int);
};
void array : : enter (int x[s] [s], int row, int column)
{
for (i=0; i<row; i++)
cin>>x[i] [j];
}
}
void array : :display (int x[s] [s], int row, int column)
{
for (i=0; i<row; i++)
{
for (j=0; j<column;j++)
cout<<x[i] [j]<<'\t';
cout<<endl;
}
}
void array: : mat_subtract (int x[s] [s], int y[s] [s], int z[s] [s], int row, int
column)
{
//Matrix subtraction
```

```
for (i=0;i<row;i++)
{
for (j=0;j<column;j++)
z[i] [j] =x [i] [j] -y [i] [j];
}
}
void main ( )
{
array obj;
int a[s] [s], b[s] [s], c[s] [s], rowl, columnl, row2, column2;
clrscr ( );
cout<<\nEnter the order of first matrix <="<<s<<" * "<<s<<"\n";
cin>>row1>>column1;
cout<<\nEnter the order of second matrix <="<<s<<" * <<<s<<"\n};
cin>>row2<<column2;
if((row1= =row2) && (column1= =column2))
{
cout<<"\nEnter the first matrix of order "<<row1<<" * "<<column1<<end1;
obj.enter (a, row1, column1);
cout<<"\nEnter the second matrix of ordre "<<row2<<" * "<<column1<<end1;
obj.enter(b, row2, column2);
clrscr ( );
cout<<"\nFirst matrix is \n\n";
obj.display (a, row1, column1);
cout<<"\nSecond matrix is \n\n";
obj.display(b, row2, column2);
obj.mat_add (a, b, c, row1, column1);
cout<<"\nAddition of two matrices is \n\n";
obj.display (c, row1, column1);
}
else
cout<<"\nMatrix addition is not possible";
getch ( );
}
```

Output:

```
Enter the order  of first matrix <=5 * 5
2      2
Enter the order of second matrix <=5 * 5
2      2
```

```
Enter the first matrix of order 2 * 2
5    4
8    2
Enter the second matrix of order 2 * 2
1    2
7    3
First matrix is
5    4
8    2
Second matrix is
1    2
7    3
Subtraction of two matrices is
4    2
1    -1
```

Program 11: Write a C++ program for multiplication of two matrices

```
# include<iostream.h>
# include<conio.h>
# define s 5
class array
{
private:
int i, j, x[s] [s], y[s] [s], z[s] [s];
public;
void enter (int x[s] [s], int, int);
void display (int x[s] [s], int, int);
void mat_add (int x[s] [s], int y[s] [s], int z[s] [s], int, int);
};
void array : : enter (int x[s] [s], int row, int column)
{
for (i=0; i<row; i++)
cin>>x[i] [j];
}
}
void array : :display (int x[s] [s], int row, int column)
{
for (i=0; i<row; i++)
{
for (j=0; j<column;j++)
```

```
cout<<x[i] [j]<<'\t';
cout<<endl;
}
}
void array : : mat_multiply (int x[s] [s], int y[s] [s], int z[s] [s], int row1, int
column1, int column2)
{
// Matrix multiplication
for (i=o; i<row1; i++)
{
for (j=0; jcolumn2;j++)
{
z[i] [j] =0;
for (k=0; k<column1; k++)
z[i] [j] +=x [i] [k] *y[k] [j];
}
}
}
void main ( )
{
array obj;
int a[s] [s], b[s] [s], c[s] [s], rowl, columnl, row2, column2;
clrscr ( );
cout<<\nEnter the order of first matrix <="<<s<<" * "<<s<<"\n";
cin>>row1>>column1;
cout<<\nEnter the order of second matrix <="<<s<<" * <<<s<<"\n};
cin>>row2<<column2;
if((row1= =row2) && (column1= =column2))
{
cout<<"\nEnter the first matrix of order "<<row1<<" * "<<column1<<end1;
obj.enter (a, row1, column1);
cout<<"\nEnter the second matrix of ordre "<<row2<<" *
"<<column1<<end1;
obj.enter(b, row2, column2);
clrscr ( );
cout<<"\nFirst matrix is \n\n";
obj.display (a, row1, column1);
cout<<"\nSecond matrix is \n\n";
obj.display(b, row2, column2);
obj.mat_add (a, b, c, row1, column1);
```

```
cout<<"\nAddition of two matrices is \n\n";
obj.display (c, row1, column1);
}
else
cout<<"\nMatrix addition is not possible";
getch( );
}
```

Output:

```
Enter the order of first matrix <=5 * 5
2    2
Enter the order of second matrix <=5 * 5
2    2
Enter the first matrix of order 2 * 2
1    3
4    5
Enter the second matrix of order 2 * 2
6    7
1    8
First matrix is
1    3
4    5
Second matrix is
6    7
1    8
Multiplication of two matrices is
9    31
29   68
```

17.5.2 Three Dimensional Array

Three Dimensional Array is also called space array or xyz array. As it has three subscripts, so these are also called triple dimensional array.

The syntax used for three dimensional array is as:

data-type array-name [space size] [row size] [column size];

For example, it can be declared as:

int st[5] [2] [3];

Suppose there are five students in a class and get different marks in three subjects in two house tests, then their marks be displayed by using three dimensional-array as:

st[1][1][1] = 55 , st[1][1][2] = 33, st[1][1][3] = 10, st[1][2][1] = 5

st[1][2][2] = 35, st[1][2][3] = 34, st[2][1][1] = 50, ..., st[5][2][3] = 75

17.5.3 N-dimensional or Multi-dimensional Array

This type of array has n size of rows, columns and spaces and so on.

The syntax used for declaration of this type of array is as follows:

Data-type array-name [s1][s2] ... ... [sn];

In this sn is the nth size of the array. This type of array is less used in C language.

17.6 MULTI DIMENSIONAL ARRAY

Up to now we have been talking about one-dimensional arrays (or alternatively, single-dimensional arrays. These arrays are by far the most common type of array, and so often we just say "array" when we mean this kind of array. However, it is possible to have arrays of multiple dimensions as well. For example, if you would find it useful to have an array with both rows and columns (i.e. with two dimensions) and more than that is called Multidimensional.

Ordinary arrays are indexed by a single integer. Also useful, particularly in numerical and graphics applications, is the concept of a multi-dimensional array, in which we index into the array using an ordered list of integers, such as in a[3,1,5]. The number of integers in the list used to index into the multi-dimensional array is always the same and is referred to as the array's dimensionality, and the bounds on each of these are called the array's dimensions. An array with dimensionality k is often called k-dimensional. One-dimensional arrays correspond to the simple arrays discussed thus far; two-dimensional arrays are a particularly common representation for matrices. In practice, the dimensionality of an array rarely exceeds three. Mapping a one-dimensional array into memory is obvious, since memory is logically itself a (very large) one-dimensional array. When we reach higher-dimensional arrays, however, the problem is no longer obvious.

Suppose we want to represent this simple two-dimensional array:

$$A \quad \begin{matrix} 1 & 2 & 3 \\ 4 & 5 & 6 \\ 7 & 8 & 9 \end{matrix}$$

It is most common to index this array using the RC-convention, where elements are referred in row, column fashion or $A_{row, col}$, such as:

$$A_{1,1} = 1, A_{1,2} = 2, ..., A_{3,2} = 8, A_{3,3} = 9$$

In computer science, a few common array indexing includes:

1. **Row-major order:** Used most notably by statically-declared arrays in C. The elements of each row are stored in order.

1	2	3	4	5	6	7	8	9

2. **Column-major order:** Used most notably in C. The elements of each column are stored in order.

1	4	7	2	5	8	3	6	9

Arrays of Arrays

A multidimensional array is an 'array of arrays'. A multidimensional array is the one in which each element of the array is an array itself. It is similar to tables in a database where each primary element (row) is a collection of secondary elements (columns). If the secondary elements do not contain a collection of other elements, it is called a 2-dimensional array (the most common type of multidimensional array), otherwise it is called an n-dimensional array where n is the depth of the chain of arrays. There are two types of multidimensional arrays in C++: 1. Rectangular array (one in which each row contains an equal number of columns) 2. Jagged array (one in which each row does not necessarily contain an equal number of columns)

The images below show what the different kinds of arrays look like. The figure also shows the indexes of different elements of the arrays. Remember, the first element of an array is always zero (0).

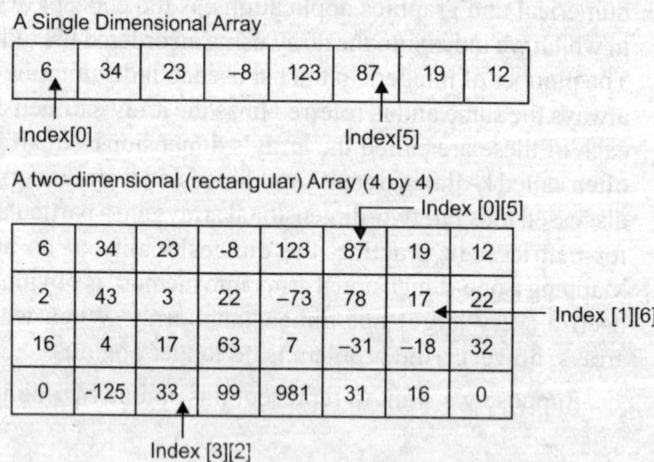

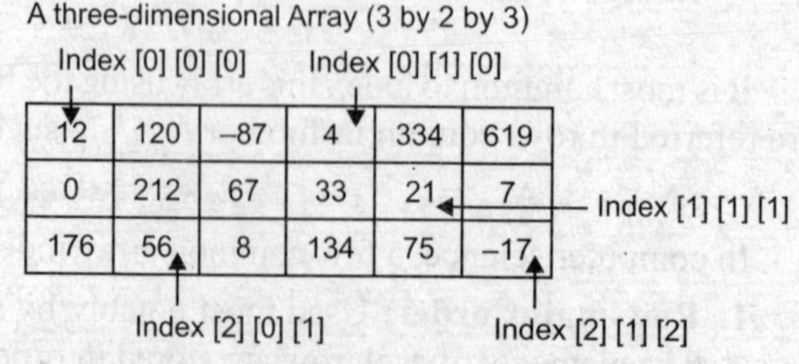

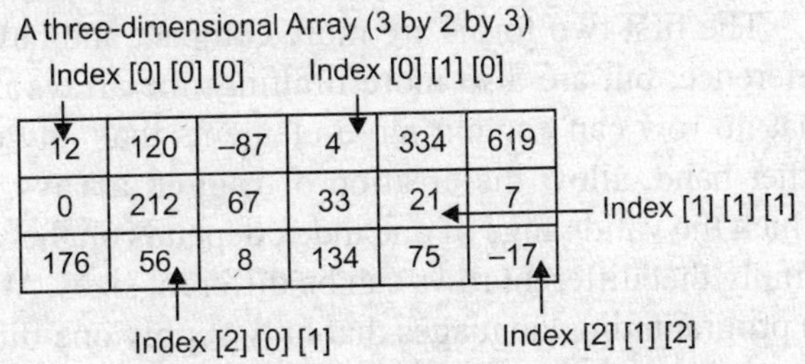

Figure 17.14: Various types of array

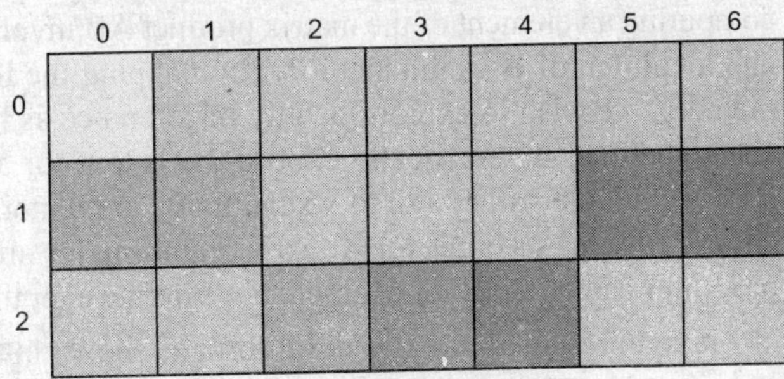

Figure 17.15: 2D jagged array

Multi-dimensional arrays are typically represented by one-dimensional arrays of references (Iliffe vectors) to other one-dimensional arrays. The subarrays can be either the rows or columns.

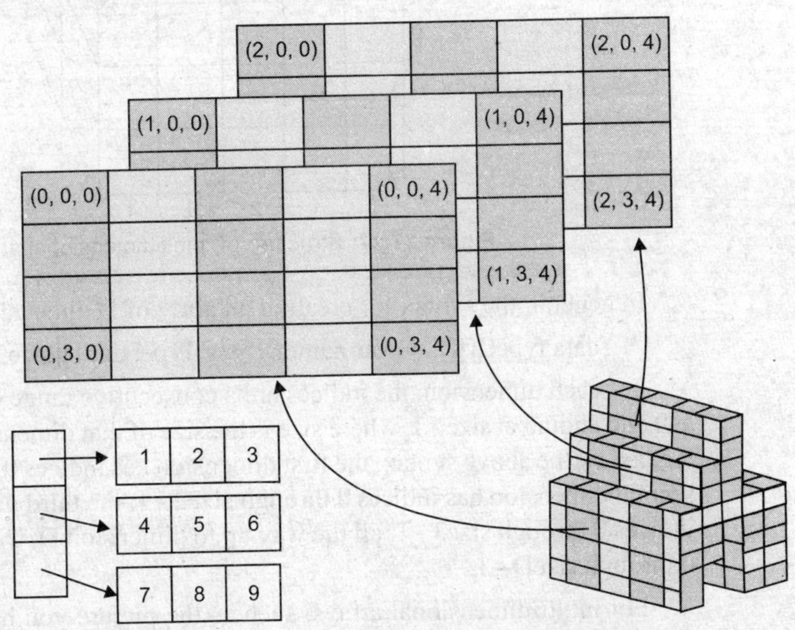

Figure 17.16: Representation of multidimensional arrays

The first two forms are more compact and have potentially better locality of reference, but are also more limiting; the arrays must be **rectangular**, meaning that no row can contain more elements than any other. Arrays of arrays, on the other hand, allow the creation of **ragged arrays**, also called **jagged arrays**, in which the valid range of one index depends on the value of another, or in this case, simply that different rows can be different sizes. Arrays of arrays are also of value in programming languages that only supply one-dimensional arrays as primitives.

In many applications, such as numerical applications working with matrices, we iterate over rectangular two-dimensional arrays in predictable ways. For example, computing an element of the matrix product **AB** involves iterating over a row of **A** and a column of **B** simultaneously. In mapping the individual array indexes into memory, we wish to exploit locality of reference as much as we can. **A** compiler can sometimes automatically choose the layout for an array so that sequentially accessed elements are stored sequentially in memory; in our example, it might choose row-major order for **A**, and column-major order for **B**. Even more exotic orderings can be used, for example if we iterate over the main diagonal of a matrix.

It is represented in a structural form as shown in the Figure 17.17 below:

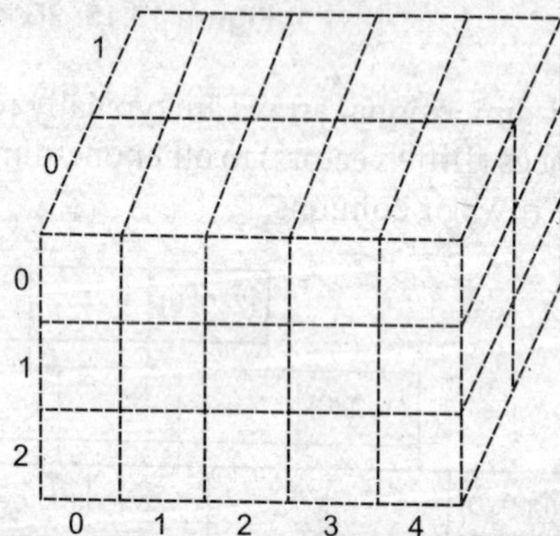

Figure 17.17: Structure of multidimensional arrays

In general, the syntax for creating an array of D dimensions is as follows:

data type[][][]...[] var name = new Type[size1][size2][size3]...[sizeD];

For each dimension, the indices are a consecutive range of integers beginning at 0 and ending at size - 1, where size is the size of that dimension. So, for the array created by the above syntax, the first dimension has indices 0 through size1 - 1, the second dimension has indices 0 through size2 - 1, the third dimension would have indices 0 through size3 - 1, all the way up to dimension D, which has indices from 0 through sizeD - 1.

For multi-dimensional arrays, such as the picture you have seen earlier, you decide which will be the first dimension, and which will the second dimension, and so on (if there are more than two dimensions), and then use the general syntax above. For example, for a two-dimensional array, we simplify the general syntax to two sets of brackets:

```
data type[][] varname = new
        Type[sizeOfFirstDimension][sizeOfSecondDimension];
```

In the two-dimensional array , if we wanted the number of rows in our picture to be the first dimension in our array (note there are four rows) and we wanted the number of columns in our picture to be the second dimension in our array (note there are five columns), and we wanted to hold values of type int, then we would write a statement such as the following one, in order to create that array:

```
int[][] theMatrix = new int[4][5];
```

and we have now created a two-dimensional array, with a variable name theMatrix, which has space for twenty integers. If we wanted to create an array to match the three-dimensional example from above, and we wanted the dimension with three cells (indexed with 0, 1, and 2) to be the first dimension, and we wanted the dimension with five cells (indexed with 0, 1, 2, 3, and 4) to be the second dimension, and we wanted the dimension with two cells (indexed with 0 and 1) to be the third dimension, and wanted the array to hold values of type char, then in order to create such an array, we would use the following statement:

```
char[][][] threeDarray = new char[3][5][2];
```

Note that the syntax for one-dimensional arrays – is just the above syntax, with D being equal to 1, since there is only one dimension. So, you would have exactly one pair of square brackets before the variable name, and one pair of square brackets with a size in it after the assignment operator – exactly as you saw in the previous notes packet:

```
Type[] varname = new Type[size1];
```

17.7 ACCESSING CELLS OF MULTI-DIMENSIONAL ARRAYS

Just as the syntax for creating a one-dimensional array was a special case of the more general syntax for creating a D-dimensional array, the syntax for accessing a one-dimensional array is a special case of the more general syntax for accessing a D-dimensional array.

Accessing a D-dimensional array is done with the following expression:

```
varname[index1][index2]...[indexD]
```

In the case of a two-dimensional array, you would have two sets of brackets:

```
varname[index1][index2]
```

In the case of a three-dimensional array, you would have three sets of brackets:

```
varname[index1][index2][index3]
```

and so on.

17.8 ADVANTAGES (PROS) AND DISADVANTAGES (CONS)

Arrays permit efficient (constant-time, O(1)) random access, but not efficient insertion and deletion of elements (which are O(n), where n is the size of the array). Linked lists have the opposite trade-off. Consequently, arrays are most appropriate for storing a fixed amount of data which will be accessed in an unpredictable fashion, and linked lists are best for a list of data which will be accessed sequentially and updated often with insertions or deletions.

Another advantage of arrays that has become very important on modern architectures is that iterating through an array has good locality of reference, and so is much faster than iterating through (say) a linked list of the same size, which tends to jump around in memory. However, an array can also be accessed in a random way, as is done with large hash tables, and in this case this is not a benefit.

Arrays also are among the most compact data structures; storing 100 integers in an array takes only 100 times the space required to store an integer, plus perhaps a few bytes of overhead for the pointer to the array (4 on a 32-bit system). Any pointer-based data structure, on the other hand, must keep its pointers somewhere, and these occupy additional space. This extra space becomes more significant as the data elements become smaller. For example, an array of ASCII characters takes up one byte per character, while on a 32-bit platform, which has 4-byte pointers, a linked list requires at least five bytes per character. Conversely, for very large elements, the space difference becomes a negligible fraction of the total space.

Because arrays have a fixed size, there are some indexes which refer to invalid elements - for example, the index 17 in an array of size 5. What happens when a program attempts to refer to these varies from language to language and platform to platform.

A drawback of the simplicity of arrays is the possibility of referencing a non-existent element by using an index outside the range of valid indices. This is known as exceeding the array bounds. The result is, at best, a program working with incorrect data. At worst, the whole system can crash (it is important to note that in cases where data integrity is critical, such as online banking, a crash may be preferable to working with incorrect data). This problem is particularly felt in the C++ programming language, the powerful syntax of which is unfortunately prone to this kind of error. Some other languages as Java have built-in bounds checking, and will refuse to index an array outside of its permitted range - although there may be alternative access functions which bypass the checks. Other languages, such as C++, offer facilities to create a data type that functions like a standard array with bounds checking, or offer such a data structure in their standard library. The advantage of providing both checked and unchecked versions, whichever way round the problem is approached, is that you can choose the unchecked version in the rare applications where bounds checking would impose an unreasonable performance penalty, without sacrificing safety in cases where performance is less critical.

17.9 APPLICATION OF ARRAYS

Whenever we require a collection of data objects of the same type and want to process them as a single unit, an array can be used, provided the number of data items is constant or fixed. Arrays have a wide range of applications ranging from business data processing to scientific calculations to industrial projects.

17.9.1 Implementation Of A Static Contiguous List

A list is a structure in which insertions, deletions, and retrieval may occur at any position in the list. Therefore, when the list is static, it can be implemented by using an array. When a list is implemented or realized by using an array, it is a contiguous list. By contiguous, we mean that the elements are placed consecutively one after another starting from some address, called the base address. The advantage of a list implemented using an array is that it is randomly accessible. The disadvantage of such a list is that insertions and deletions require moving of the entries, and so it is costlier. A static list can be implemented using an array by mapping the ith element of the list into the ith entry of the array, as shown in Figure 17.18.

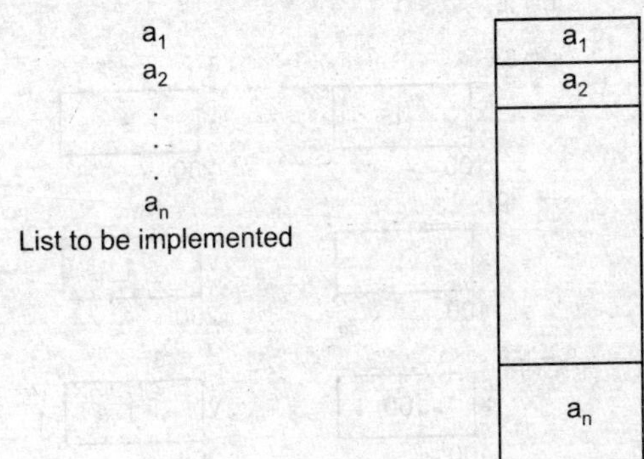

Figure 17.18: Implementation of a static contiguous list.

17.10 POINTER

A pointer is a variable which contains the address in memory of another variable. We can have a pointer to any variable type.

The *unary* or *monadic* operator **&** gives the "address of a variable".

The *indirection* or dereference operator * gives the "contents of an object *pointed to* by a pointer".

To declare a pointer to a variable do:

```
int *pointer;
```

Consider the effect of the following code:

```
int x = 1, y = 2;
int *ip;
ip = &x;
y = *ip;
x = ip;
*ip = 3;
```

It is worth considering what is going on at the *machine level* in memory to fully understand how pointer work. Consider Figure 17.19. Assume for the sake of this discussion that variable x resides at memory location 100, y at 200 and ip at 1000.

> ***Note:*** *A pointer is a variable and thus its values need to be stored somewhere. It is the nature of the pointers value that is* new.

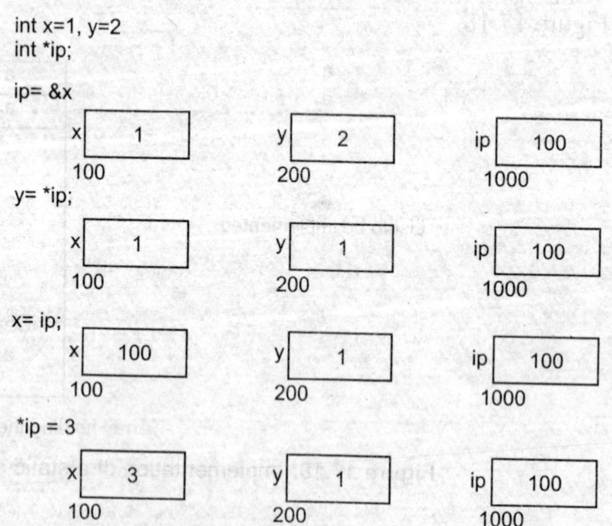

Figure 17.19: Pointer, Variables and Memory

Now the assignments x = 1 and y = 2 obviously load these values into the variables. ip is declared to be a *pointer to an integer* and is assigned to the address of x (&x). So ip gets loaded with the value 100.

Next y gets assigned to the contents of ip. In this example ip currently points to memory location 100 -- the location of x. So y gets assigned to the values of x -- which is 1.

We have already seen that C++ is not too fussy about assigning values of different type. Thus it is perfectly legal (although not all that common) to assign the current value of ip to x. The value of ip at this instant is 100.

Finally we can assign a value to the contents of a pointer (*ip).

***Important**: When a pointer is declared it does not point anywhere. You must set it to point somewhere before you use it.*

So ...

```
int *ip;
*ip = 100;
```

will generate an error (program crash!!).

The correct use is:

```
int *ip;
int x;
ip = &x;
*ip = 100;
```

We can do integer arithmetic on a pointer:

```
float *flp, *flq;
*flp = *flp + 10;
++*flp;
(*flp)++;
flq = flp;
```

***Note**: A pointer to any variable type is an address in memory — which is an integer address. A pointer is definitely NOT an integer.*

The reason we associate a pointer to a data type is so that it knows how many bytes the data is stored in. When we increment a pointer we increase the pointer by one "block" memory.

So for a character pointer ++ch_ptr adds 1 byte to the address.

For an integer or float ++ip or ++flp adds 4 bytes to the address.

Consider a float variable (fl) and a pointer to a float (flp) as shown in Figure 17.20.

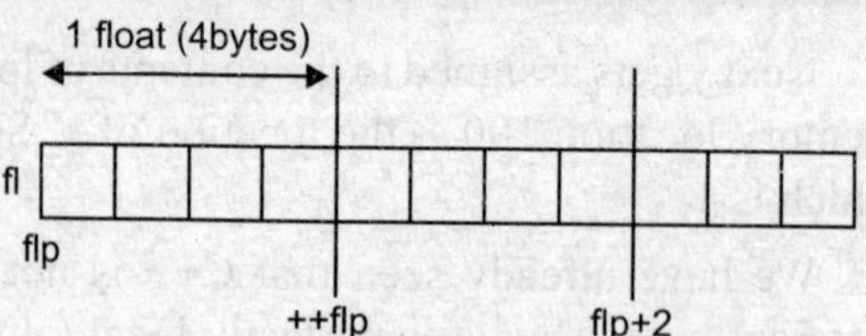

Figure 17.20: Pointer Arithmetic

Assume that flp points to fl then if we increment the pointer (++flp) it moves to the position shown 4 bytes on. If on the other hand we added 2 to the pointer then it moves 2 **float positions** *i.e* 8 bytes as shown in the Figure.

17.11 POINTERS AND ARRAYS

Pointers and arrays are very closely linked in C++.

Hint: *think of array elements arranged in consecutive memory locations.*

Consider the following:

```
int a[10], x;
int *pa;
pa = &a[0];            /* pa pointer to address of a[0] */
x = *pa;               /* x = contents of pa (a[0] in this case) */
```

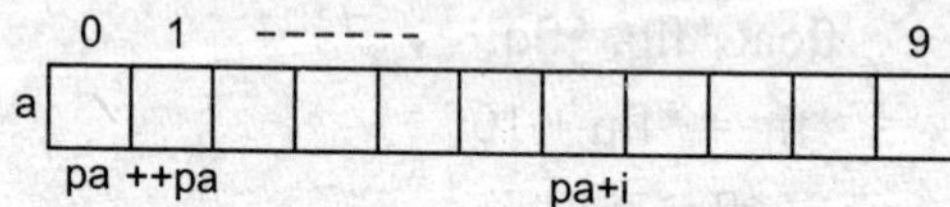

Figure 17.21: Arrays and Pointers

To get somewhere in the array (Figure 17.21) using a pointer we could do:

pa + i = a[i]

Warning: *There is no bound checking of arrays and pointers so you can easily go beyond array memory and overwrite other things.*

C++ however is much more subtle in its link between arrays and pointers.

For example we can just type

```
pa = a;
```

instead of

pa = &a[0]

and a[i] can be written as *(a + i).

i.e. &a[i] = a + i.

We also express pointer addressing like this:

pa[i] = *(pa + i).

However pointers and arrays are different:

1. A pointer is a variable. We can do pa = a and pa++.
2. An Array is not a variable. a = pa and a++ ARE ILLEGAL.

This stuff is very important. Make sure you understand it. We will see a lot more of this.

17.11.1 Arrays of Pointers

We can have arrays of pointers since pointers are variables.

Example use: *Sort lines of text of different length*

Note: *Text can't be moved or compared in a single operation.*

Arrays of Pointers are a data representation that will cope efficiently and conveniently with variable length text lines.

How can we do this?

1. Store lines end-to-end in one big char array (Figure 17.22). \n will delimit lines.
2. Store pointers in a different array where each pointer points to 1st char of each new line.
3. Compare two lines using strcmp() standard library function.
4. If 2 lines are out of order — swap pointer in pointer array (not text).

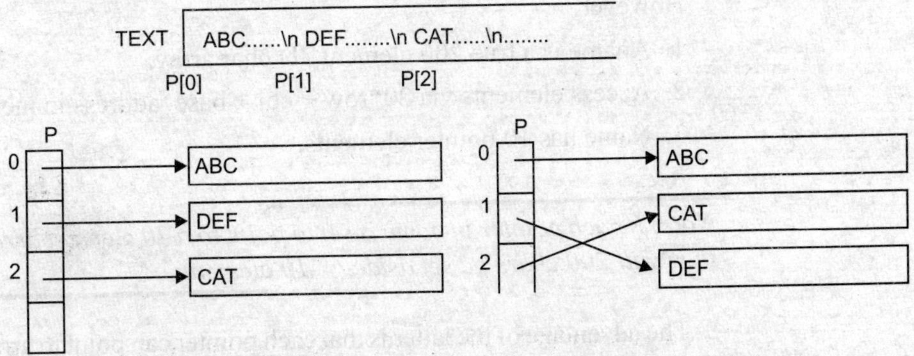

Figure 17.22: Arrays of Pointers (String Sorting Example)

This eliminates:

1. Complicated storage management.
2. High overheads of moving lines.

17.11.2 Multidimensional Arrays and Pointers

We should think of multidimensional arrays in a different way in C++:

A 2D array is really a 1D array, each of whose elements is itself an array Hence a[n][m] notation.

Array elements are stored row by row. When we pass a 2D array to a function we must specify the number of columns -- the number of rows is irrelevant. The reason for this is pointers again. C++ needs to know how many columns in order that it can jump from row to row in memory.

Consider int a[5][35] to be passed in a function:

We can do:

```
f(int a[][35]) {.....}
```

or even:

```
f(int (*a)[35]) {.....}
```

We need parenthesis (*a) since [] have a higher precedence than * So:

```
int (*a)[35]; declares a pointer to an array of 35 ints.
int *a[35]; declares an array of 35 pointers to ints.
```

Now lets look at the (subtle) difference between pointers and arrays. Strings are a common application of this.

Consider:

```
char *name[10];
char Aname[10][20];
```

We can legally do name[3][4] and Aname[3][4] in C++.

However

1. Aname is a true 200 element 2D char array.
2. Access elements via 20*row + col + base_address in memory.
3. Name has 10 pointer elements.

Note: *If each pointer in name is set to point to a 20 element array then and only then will 200 chars be set aside (+ 10 elements).*

The advantage of the latter is that each pointer can point to arrays be of different length.

Consider:

```
char *name[] = { "no month", "jan", "feb" ... };
char Aname[][15] = { "no month", "jan", "feb", ... };
```

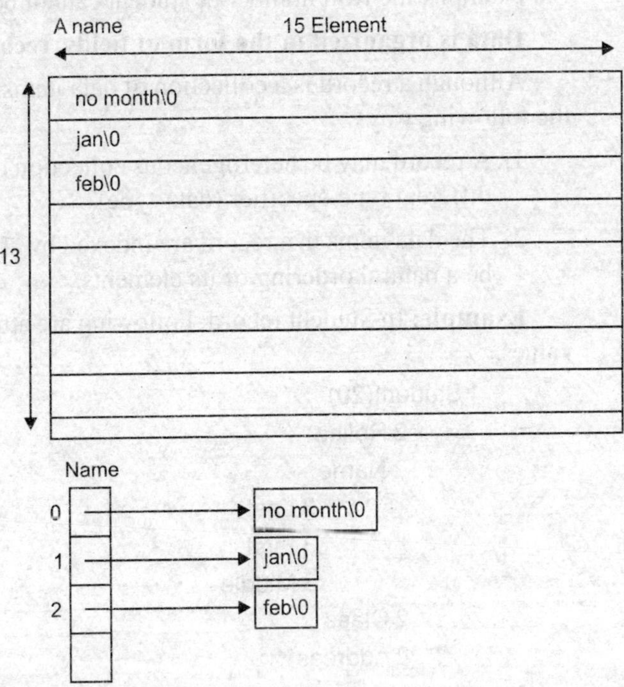

Figure 17.23: 2D Arrays and Arrays of Pointers

17.12 RECORDS

A record is a special type of data structure that, unlike arrays, collects different data types that define a particular structure such a book, product, person and many others. Collections of data are frequently organized into a hierarchy of field, records and files.

"A record is defined as a finite, ordered collection of possibly heterogeneous elements of given entity. It is sometimes also called as simply a structure. In this structure, logically related data items of different types are grouped together under one name."

A record is a collection of related data items, each of which is called a field or attribute, A field refers to single elementary unit of information used to representing an attribute of an entity. The elements of a record are called as fields. A field is a specified area of record used for a particular kind of information and a file is a collection of similar records. Data items, which are divided into sub items, are called as **group items**. For example, the name of student can be divided into subitems - first name, middle name and last name.

Data items, which are not divided into sub items, are called **elementary items**. For example, the Roll number of student cannot be divided into subitems.

Data is organized in the form of fields, records and files.

Although a record is a collection of data items, it differs from a linear array in the following ways:

1. A record may be heterogeneous collection of related fields. Every field has different type-specifier (data-type).
2. The data items in a record are indexed by attribute names, so there may not be a natural ordering of its elements.

Example: In Student record, Following are attributes and their corresponding values.

```
1 Student(20)
        2 Rollno
        2 Name
                3 Last
                3 First
                3 Middle
        2 Class
        2 Address
```

Table 17.1: Representation of Student record.

Attributes:	Student#	Rollno.	Name			Class	Address
			Last	First	Middle		
Values:	1	1201	Rair	Avtar	Singh	BCA	76A azad nagar, U.P
	2	1202	Sandhu	Avtar	Singh	BCA	34B galli nagar,U.P
	...	......	.....	...	......	.....	...
	...	......	.....	...	......	.....	...
	20	1220	Brar	Manbir	Singh	.....	67A Moga, Punjab

For example, suppose if you want to store a book in library using C++ program, then you give information about the title of the book, name of the author, number of pages in the book and the price of the book. Then before coding the problem you will examine it according to following table

Title of the Book	Name of Author	Pages of the Book	Price of the Book
C programming	Ikvinderpal Singh	450	300
Fundamental of C	Rachhpal Singh	500	200
Let Us C	Yashvant K.	700	300

To elaborate this problem, we set some data-types and width (size) as shown below:

Field name	Type	Width
Title	Character	20
Author	Character	20
Pages	Integer	8
Price	Real (Float)	7.2

In C++ language, to maintain such type of records we use structure data type, which is heterogeneous collection of related fields. Every field has different type-specifier (data-type).

```
struct      library
{
char        title [20] ;
char        author [20] ;
int         pages ;
float       price ;
};
```

17.13 RECORD STRUCTURES

A **record structure** is an aggregate entity containing one or more elements. (Record elements are also called fields or components.) You can use records when you need to declare and operate on multi-field data structures in your programs.

Creating a record is a two-step process:

1. You must define the form of the record with a multistatement **structure declaration.**
2. You must use a RECORD statement to declare the record as an entity with a name. (More than one RECORD statement can refer to a given structure.)

In computer science, a **record** (also called **tuple** or **struct**) is one of the simplest data structures, consisting of two or more values or variables stored in consecutive memory positions; so that each component (called a **field** or **member** of the record) can be accessed by applying different offsets to the starting address.

For example, a date may be stored as a record containing a 16-bit numeric field for the year, a three-letter field for the month, and an 8-bit numeric field for the day-of-month. As this example shows, the fields of a record need not all have the same size and encoding; therefore, in general one cannot easily obtain the field which has a run-time computed index in the field sequence, as one can do in an array.

A **record type** is a data type that describes such values and variables. Most modern computer languages allow the programmer to define new record types.

The definition includes specifying the data type of each field, its position in the record, and an identifier (name or label) by which it can be accessed. In type theory, product types are generally preferred due to their simplicity, but proper record types are studied in languages such as System F-sub. Since type-theoretical records may contain first-class function-typed fields in addition to data, they can express many features of object-oriented programming.

Records can exist in any storage medium, including main memory and mass storage devices such as magnetic tapes or hard disks. Records are a fundamental component of most data structures, especially linked data structures. Many computer files are organized as arrays of logical records, often grouped into larger physical records or blocks for efficiency.

The parameters of a function or procedure can often be viewed as the fields of a record variable; and the arguments passed to that function can be viewed as a record value that gets assigned to that variable at the time of the call. Also, in the call stack that is often used to implement procedure calls, each entry is an **activation record** or **call frame,** containing the procedure parameters and local variables, the return address, and other internal fields.

17.14 REPRESENTATION OF RECORDS IN MEMORY; PARALLEL ARRAYS

A **parallel array** is a data structure for representing arrays of records. It keeps a separate, homogeneous array for each field of the record, each having the same number of elements. Then, objects located at the same index in each array are implicitly the fields of a single record. Pointers from one object to another are replaced by array indices. This contrasts with the normal approach of storing all fields of each record together in memory. For example, one might declare an array of 100 names, each a string, and 100 ages, each an integer, associating each name with the age that has the same index.

An example in C++ using parallel arrays:

```
int ages[]  = {0,      17,      2,       52,      25};
char *names[] = {"None",   "Mike",   "Billy",   "Tom",      "Stan"};
int parent[] = {0 /*None*/, 3 /*Tom*/, 1 /*Mike*/, 0 /*None*/, 3 /*Tom*/};
for(i = 1; i <= 4; i++) {
printf("Name: %s, Age: %d, Parent: %s \n",
names[i], ages[i], names[parent[i]]);
}
```

Since records may contain homogeneous data, the elements of a record cannot be store in an array. Assuming the records contain non homogeneous data, the records may have to be stored in individual variables, one for each of its elementary data items. On the other hand, suppose one wants to store an entire file of records.

Note that all data elements belonging to the same identifier do have the same type. Such a file may be stored in memory as a collection of **parallel arrays**, where elements in different arrays with same subscript belong to the same record. This is illustrated in example below.

Example: Suppose a student list contains the name, roll no, class, mobile number of each student. We can store the file in four parallel arrays NAME, ROLLNO, CLASS, and MOBILE NO. as shown in figure for given subscript K, the elements NAME[K], ROLLNO[K], CLASS[K] and MOBILE NO.[K] belong to the same record.

Table 17.2: Representation of Student record.

Name	Roll no.	Class	Mobile no.
Sukhwant Singh	1	MCA	9889876519
Jagbir Singh	2	MCA	9871543298
Jagminder Singh	3	MCA	9845639856
Sukhminder Singh	4	MCA	9254378651
Prabhjeet Singh	5	MCA	9834276598

Parallel arrays have a number of practical advantages over the normal approach:

1. They can be used in languages which support only arrays of primitive types and not of records (or perhaps don't support records at all).
2. Parallel arrays are simple to understand and use, and are often used where declaring a record is more trouble than it's worth.
3. They can save a substantial amount of space in some cases by avoiding alignment issues. For example, one of the fields of the record can be a single bit, and its array would only need to reserve one bit for each record, whereas in the normal approach many more bits would "pad" the field so that it consumes an entire byte or a word.
4. If the number of items is small, array indices can occupy significantly less space than full pointers, particularly on architectures with large words.
5. Sequentially examining a single field of each record in the array is very fast on modern machines, since this amount to a linear traversal of a single array, exhibiting ideal locality of reference and cache behavior.

However, parallel arrays also have several strong disadvantages, which serves to explain why they are not generally preferred:

1. They have significantly worse locality of reference when visiting the records sequentially and examining multiple fields of each record, which is the norm.

2. They obscure the relationship between fields of a single record.
3. They have little direct language support (the language and its syntax typically express no relationship between the arrays in the parallel array.)
4. They are expensive to grow or shrink, since each of several arrays must be reallocated.

The bad locality of reference is the worst issue. However, a compromise can be made in some cases: if a structure can be divided into groups of fields that are generally accessed together, an array can be constructed for each group, and its elements are records containing only these subsets of the larger structure's fields. This is a valuable way of speeding up access to very large structures with many members, while keeping the portions of the structure tied together. An alternative to tying them together using array indexes is to use references to tie the portions together, but this can be less efficient in time and space. Some compiler optimizations, particularly for vector processors, are able to perform this transformation automatically when arrays of structures are created in the program.

17.15 FIXED LENGTH RECORDS

A file where all the records are of the same length is said to have **fixed length records**.

Some **fields** are always the same length (e.g. **Postcode** is always 7 characters). Some **fields** may need to be 'padded out' so they are the correct length

(e.g. Surname - If 15 characters are stored then Jenkins would be stored as 'JENKINS' - 7 characters followed by 8 spaces).

Advantage

Access is **fast** because the computer knows where each record starts.

E.g. If each record is 120 bytes long then

- The 1st record starts at [Start of File] + 0 bytes
- The 2nd record starts at [Start of File] + 120 bytes
- The 3rd record starts at [Start of File] + 240 bytes etc.....

Disadvantage

Using Fixed length records, the records are usually **larger** and therefore need **more storage space** and are **slower** to transfer (load or save).

In the Example

Table 17.3: Representation of fixed length record.

Number	Surname	Forename	Year	Form	DOB
92013	JONES	Sidney	12	B	23/04/78
92107	LAIDLAW	Lorraine	12	Y	12/11/79
92114	MERRITT	Mandy	12	G	08/03/79
92167	NASH	Natasha	12	B	19/08/78

...the field lengths may be..

Number : 5
Surname: 15
Forename: 15
Year: 2
Form: 1
DOB: 8

Each record would be **46 bytes** long.The first record of the example file would be stored as ...(each box represents one byte of storage)..

9	2	0	1	3	J	O	N	E	S										
S	i	d	n	e	y										1	2	B	2	3
/	0	4	/	7	8														

17.16 VARIABLE LENGTH RECORDS

A record that has at least one variable-length field. The length of the entire record, therefore, varies according to what data is placed in the variable-length field.

One or more of the fields can be of **differing** lengths in each record.

Advantages

- the records will be **smaller** and will need less storage space
- the records will **load faster**

Disadvantages

- The computer will be unable to determine where each record starts so **processing** the records will be **slower**.

In the Example

Table 17.4: Representation of variable length record.

Number	Surname	Forename	Year	Form	DOB
92013	JONES	Sidney	12	B	23/04/78
92107	LAIDLAW	Lorraine	12	Y	12/11/79
92114	MERRITT	Mandy	12	G	08/03/79
92167	NASH	Natasha	12	B	19/08/78

Storage Method 1

When the record is stored, each field has a **field terminator** byte stored at the end of it, and there is often a **record terminator** at the end of the whole record.

The first record of the example would be stored as.....

9	2	0	1	3	*	J	O	N	E	S	*	S	i	d	n	e	y	*	1
2	*	B	*	2	3	/	0	4	/	7	8	**%**							

* is a field terminator   **%** is a record terminator

This record requires **33** bytes of storage.....but each record will be a different size.

Storage Method 2

Each field starts with a **byte** showing the **length** of the field. The whole record starts with a byte giving the size of the record. The first record of the example would be stored as....

34	**5**	9	2	0	1	3	**5**	J	O	N	E	S	**6**	S	i	d	n	e	y
2	1	2	**1**	B	**8**	2	3	/	0	4	/	7	8						

This record requires **34** bytes of storage....but again, each record would be a different size.

17.17 MATRIX

A **matrix** is a rectangular array of numbers, such as

$$\begin{bmatrix} 1 & 9 & 13 \\ 20 & 55 & 4 \end{bmatrix}.$$

An item in a matrix is called an entry or an element. The example has entries 1, 9, 13, 20, 55, and 4. Entries are often denoted by a variable with two subscripts, as shown on the right.

A matrix is an ordered set of numbers listed rectangular form A matrix is a two dimensional array of numbers or expressions arranged in a set of rows and columns. An m × n matrix **A** has m rows and n columns and is written

m-by-n matrix

j changes

$a_{i,j}$ n columns

m rows

i changes

$$\begin{bmatrix} a_{1,1} & a_{1,2} & a_{1,3} & \cdots \\ a_{2,1} & a_{2,2} & a_{2,3} & \cdots \\ a_{3,1} & a_{3,2} & a_{3,3} & \cdots \\ \vdots & \vdots & \vdots & \ddots \end{bmatrix} \quad A = \begin{bmatrix} a_{11} & a_{12} & \cdots & a_{1n} \\ a_{2,1} & a_{2,2} & \cdots & a_{2n} \\ \vdots & \vdots & \ddots & \vdots \\ a_{m1} & a_{m2} & \cdots & a_{mn} \end{bmatrix}$$

Figure 17.24: Specific entries of a matrix are often referenced by using pairs of subscripts.

where the element aij, located in the ith row and the jth column, is a scalar quantity; a numerical constant, or a single valued expression. If m = n, that is there are the same number of rows as columns, the matrix is square, otherwise it is a rectangular matrix.

A matrix having either a single row (m = 1) or a single column (n = 1) is defined to be a vector because it is often used to define the coordinates of a point in a multi-dimensional space. (In this note the convention has been adopted of representing a vector by a lower case "bold-face" letter such as **x**, and a general matrix by a "bold-face" upper case letter such as **A**.) A vector having a single row, for example

$$x = [x_{11} \; x_{12} \; \cdots \; x_{1n}]$$

is defined to be a row vector, while a vector having a single column is defined to be a column vector

$$y = \begin{bmatrix} y_{11} \\ y_{21} \\ \vdots \\ y_{m1} \end{bmatrix}$$

Two special matrices are the square identity matrix, **I**, which is defined to have all of its elements equal to zero except those on the main diagonal (where i = j) which have a value of one:

$$I = \begin{bmatrix} 1 & 0 & \cdots & 0 \\ 0 & 1 & \cdots & 0 \\ \vdots & \vdots & \ddots & \vdots \\ 0 & 0 & \cdots & 1 \end{bmatrix}$$

and the null matrix **0**, which has the value of zero for all of its elements:

$$0 = \begin{bmatrix} 0 & 0 & \cdots & 0 \\ 0 & 0 & \cdots & 0 \\ \vdots & \vdots & \ddots & \vdots \\ 0 & 0 & \cdots & 0 \end{bmatrix}$$

A matrix is a rectangular arrangement of numbers. For example,

$$A = \begin{bmatrix} 9 & 8 & 6 \\ 1 & 2 & 7 \\ 4 & 9 & 2 \\ 6 & 0 & 5 \end{bmatrix}$$

An alternative notation uses large parentheses instead of box brackets:

$$A = \begin{pmatrix} 9 & 8 & 6 \\ 1 & 2 & 7 \\ 4 & 9 & 2 \\ 6 & 0 & 5 \end{pmatrix}$$

The horizontal and vertical lines in a matrix are called **rows** and **columns**, respectively. The numbers in the matrix are called its **entries** or its **elements**. To specify a matrix's size, a matrix with **m** rows and **n** columns is called an **m-by-n** matrix or **m × n** matrix, while **m** and **n** are called its **dimensions**. The above is a 4-by-3 matrix.

A matrix where one of the dimensions equals one is also called a **vector,** and may be interpreted as an element of real coordinate space. An m × 1 matrix (one column and m rows) is called a column vector and a 1 × n matrix (one row and n columns) is called a row vector. For example, the third row vector of the above matrix **A** is [4 9 2].

Most of this article focuses on **real and complex matrices,** i.e., matrices whose entries are real or complex numbers. More general types of entries are discussed below.

Square Matrix: If a matrix A has n rows and n columns then we say it's a square matrix.

In a square matrix the elements $a_{i,i}$, with i = 1,2,3,..., are called diagonal elements.

Remark. *There is no difference between a 1 x 1 matrix and an ordenary number.*

Diagonal Matrix: A diagonal matrix is a square matrix with all de non-diagonal elements 0.

The diagonal matrix is completely denoted by the diagonal elements.

Example [7 0 0]
[0 5 0]
[0 0 6]

The matrix is denoted by diagonal (7 , 5 , 6).

Row Matrix: A matrix with one row is called a row matrix

Column Matrix: A matrix with one column is called a column matrix

Matrices of the Same Kind: Matrix A and B are of the same kind if and only if A has as many rows as B and A has as many columns as B

The Tranpose of a Matrix: The n x m matrix A' is the transpose of the m x n matrix A if and only if

The ith row of A = the ith column of A' for (i = 1,2,3,..n)

So $a_{i,j} = a_{j,i}$' . The transpose of A is denoted T(A) or A^T

Zero-matrix: When all the elements of a matrix A are 0, we call A a 0-matrix. We write shortly 0 for a 0-matrix.

An identity matrix I: An identity matrix I is a diagonal matrix with all diagonal element = 1.

A scalar matrix S: A scalar matrix S is a diagonal matrix with all diagonal elements alike.

$a_{1,1} = a_{i,i}$ for (i = 1,2,3,..n)

The opposite matrix of a matrix: If we change the sign of all the elements of a matrix A, we have the opposite matrix -A. If A' is the opposite of A then $a_{i,j}' = -a_{i,j}$, for all i and j.

A symmetric matrix: A square matrix is called symmetric if it is equal to its transpose.

Then $a_{i,j} = a_{j,i}$, for all i and j.

A skew-symmetric matrix: A square matrix is called skew-symmetric if it is equal to the opposite of its transpose. Then $a_{i,j} = -a_{j,i}$, for all i and j.

Elementary matrix arithmetic—Matrix addition: The operation of addition of two matrices is only defined when both matrices have the same dimensions. If **A** and **B** are both (m × n), then the sum

$$\mathbf{C} = \mathbf{A} + \mathbf{B}$$

is also (m × n) and is defined to have each element the sum of the corresponding elements of **A** and **B**, thus

$$cij = aij + bij .$$

Matrix addition is both associative, that is

$$\mathbf{A} + (\mathbf{B} + \mathbf{C}) = (\mathbf{A} + \mathbf{B}) + \mathbf{C},$$

and commutative

$$\mathbf{A} + \mathbf{B} = \mathbf{B} + \mathbf{A}.$$

The subtraction of two matrices is similarly defined; if **A** and **B** have the same dimensions, then the difference

$$\mathbf{C} = \mathbf{A} - \mathbf{B}$$

implies that the elements of **C** are

$$cij = aij - bij.$$

Multiplication of a matrix by a scalar quantity: If **A** is a matrix and k is a scalar quantity, the product **B** = k**A** is defined to be the matrix of the same dimensions as **A** whose elements are simply all scaled by the constant k, bij = k × aij.

Matrix multiplication: Two matrices may be multiplied together only if they meet conditions on their dimensions that allow them to conform. Let **A** have dimensions m × n, and **B** be n × p, that is **A** has the same number as columns as the number of rows in **B**, then the product

$$\mathbf{C} = \mathbf{AB}$$

is defined to be an m × p matrix with elements

$$c_{ij} = \sum_{k=1}^{n} a_{ik} b_{kj}$$

The element in position ij is the sum of the products of elements in the ith row of the first matrix (**A**) and the corresponding elements in the jth column of the second matrix (**B**).

Notice that the product **AB** is not defined unless the above condition is satisfied, that is the number of columns of the first matrix must equal the number of rows in the second.

Matrix multiplication is associative, that is

$$\mathbf{A}(\mathbf{BC}) = (\mathbf{AB})\mathbf{C}$$

but is not commutative in general

$$\mathbf{AB} \neq \mathbf{BA}$$

In fact unless the two matrices are square, reversing the order in the product will cause the matrices to be nonconformal. The order of the terms in the product is therefore very important. In the product **C** = **AB**, **A** is said to pre-multiply **B**, while **B** is said to post-multiply **A**. It is interesting to note in passing that unlike the scalar case, the fact that **AB** = **0** does not imply that either **A** = **0** or that **B** = **0**.

Multiplication of a row matrix by a column matrix: This multiplication is only possible if the row matrix and the column matrix have the same number of elements. The result is a ordinary number (1 x 1 matrix).

To multiply the row by the column, one multiplies corresponding elements, and then adds the results. Example:

[1]
[2 1 3]. [2] = [19]
[5]

Multiplication of two matrices a.b: This product is defined only if A is a (l x m) matrix and B is a (m x n) matrix.

So the number of columns of A has to be equal to the number of rows of B.

The product C = A.B then is a (l x n) matrix.

The element of the ith row and the jth column of the product is found by multiplying the ith row of A by the jth column of B.

$$c_{i,j} = \text{sum}_k\ (a_{i,k}.b_{k,j})$$

Example

[1 2][1 3] = [5 7]
[2 1][2 2] [4 8]

[1 3][1 2] = [7 5]
[2 2][2 1] [6 6]

[1 1][2 2] = [0 0]
[1 1][-2 -2] [0 0]

From these examples we see that the product is not commutative and that there are zero divisors.

Algorithm 17.9: Matrix Multiplication

MATMUL(A, B, C, M, P, N)

Let A be an M X P matrix array, and let B be a P X N matrix array. This algorithm stores the product of A and B in an M x N matrix array C.

Step 1: Repeat Steps 2 to 4 for I = 1 to M:

Step 2: Repeat Steps 3 and 4 for I = 1 to N:

Step 3: Set C[I, J] := [Initializes C[I, J].]

Step 4: Repeat for J = 1 to P:

C[I, J] := C[I, J] + A[I, K] * B[K, J]

[End of Step 3 inner loop.]

[End of Step 2 middle loop.]

[End of Step 1 outer loop.]

Step 5: End.

Representing systems of equations in matrix form linear algebraic equations

The rules given above for matrix arithmetic allow a set of linear algebraic equations to be written compactly in matrix form. Consider a set of n independent linear equations in the variables xi for i = 1, 2. . . , n

$$\begin{array}{ccccccccc} a_{11}x_1 & + & a_{12}x_2 & + & \cdots & + & a_{1n}x_n & = & b_1 \\ a_{21}x_1 & + & a_{22}x_2 & + & \cdots & + & a_{2n}x_n & = & b_2 \\ \vdots & & \vdots & & \ddots & & \vdots & & \vdots \\ a_{n1}x_1 & + & a_{n2}x_2 & + & \cdots & + & a_{nn}x_n & = & b_n \end{array}$$

and write the coefficients aij in a square matrix **A** of dimension n

$$A = \begin{bmatrix} a_{11} & a_{12} & \cdots & a_{1n} \\ a_{21} & a_{22} & \cdots & a_{2n} \\ \vdots & \vdots & \ddots & \vdots \\ a_{n1} & a_{n2} & \cdots & a_{nn} \end{bmatrix}$$

the unknowns xij in a column vector **x** of length N

$$x = \begin{bmatrix} x_{11} \\ x_{21} \\ \vdots \\ x_{n1} \end{bmatrix}$$

and the constants on the right-hand side in a column vector

$$b = \begin{bmatrix} b_1 \\ b_2 \\ \vdots \\ b_n \end{bmatrix}$$

then equations may be written as the product

$$\begin{bmatrix} a_{11} & a_{12} & \cdots & a_{1n} \\ a_{21} & a_{22} & \cdots & a_{2n} \\ \vdots & \vdots & \ddots & \vdots \\ a_{n1} & a_{n2} & \cdots & a_{nn} \end{bmatrix} \begin{bmatrix} x_1 \\ x_2 \\ \vdots \\ x_n \end{bmatrix} = \begin{bmatrix} b_1 \\ b_2 \\ \vdots \\ b_n \end{bmatrix}$$

which may be written compactly as

$$\mathbf{Ax} = \mathbf{b}.$$

The transpose of a matrix

The transpose of an m×n matrix **A**, written $\mathbf{A}^{T}$, is the n×m matrix formed by interchanging the rows and columns of A. For example, if

$$A = \begin{bmatrix} a_{11} & a_{12} & a_{13} \\ a_{21} & a_{22} & a_{23} \end{bmatrix}$$

then in terms of the elements of the above matrix, the transpose is

$$A = \begin{bmatrix} a_{11} & a_{21} \\ a_{12} & a_{22} \\ a_{13} & a_{23} \end{bmatrix}$$

Notice that the transpose of a row vector produces a column vector, and similarly the transpose of a column vector produces a row vector. The transpose of the product of two matrices is the reversed product of the transpose of the two individual matrices,

$$(AB)^T = B^T A^T$$

The rules of matrix multiplication show that the product of a vector and its transpose is the sum of the squares of all of the elements

$$x(x^T) = \sum_{t=1}^{n} (x_i)^2$$

17.18 SPARSE MATRIX

A sparse matrix also known as sparse array in computing is an array where most of the elements have the same value (called the default value -- usually 0 or null) and only a few elements have a non-default value. Arrays are data structures used in programming languages, databases, and other computer systems. They use a value, called a subscript or an index, that indicates a position to locate a particular value.

"It is special type of matrix in which majority of elements are zero or Null. It requires different type of representation than simple array"

A naive implementation may allocate space for the entire array, but this is inefficient since there are only a few non-default values. If the sparsity is known in advance, more space-efficient implementations can be used which allocate space only for the non-default values. Example: An array with length of one million, where only the indices 1, 3, 120 and 999999 have non-default values, is sparse. It would be inefficient to allocate any space for the 999996 array elements with default values. Sparse array is also called Sparse Matrix.

In the mathematical subfield of numerical analysis a sparse matrix is a matrix populated primarily with zeros. Conceptually, sparsity corresponds to systems which are loosely coupled. Consider a line of balls connected by springs from one to the next; this is a sparse system. By contrast, if the same line of balls had springs connecting every ball to every other ball, the system would be represented by a dense matrix. The concept of sparsity is useful in combinatorics and application areas such as network theory, of a low density of significant data or connections.

Huge sparse matrices often appear in science or engineering when solving partial differential equations. When storing and manipulating sparse matrices on a computer, it is beneficial and often necessary to used specialized algorithms and data structures that take advantage of the sparse structure of the matrix. Operations using standard matrix structures and algorithms are slow and consume large amounts of memory when applied to large sparse matrices. Sparse data is by nature easily compressed, and this compression almost always results in significantly less memory usage. Indeed, some very large sparse matrices are impossible to manipulate with the standard algorithms.

17.18.1 Difference Between Sparse Matrix and Dense Matrix

A sparse matrix is a two-dimensional array in which most of the elements are null. Figure 1(a) and (b) indicate sparse and dense matrices. The matrix, which is not a sparse matrix, is called dense matrix. One cannot exactly determine the boundary between sparse and dense matrix. The sparse matrices are very useful in various applications. In sparse matrices, memory is wasted because the NULL values stored and hence to overcome wastage of memory a mechanism must be followed.

3	0	32	0	11
1	5	4	9	23
0	3	0	2	0
7	14	13	17	8
1	0	1	0	1

Figure 17.25: Dense matrix

3	0	32	0	11
1	0	0	0	0
0	0	0	2	0
0	0	0	0	0
1	0	1	0	1

Figure 17.26: Sparse matrix

Sparse matrices are classified as shown below in the figure 17.27

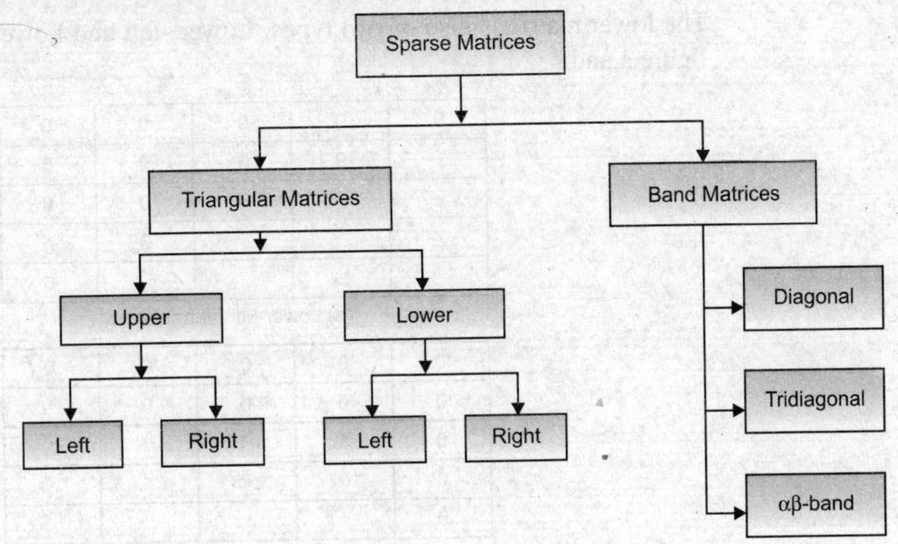

Figure 17.27: Different types of sparse matrices.

17.18.2 Upper Triangular Matrices

The upper matrix is a type of triangular matrix, which is also a type of sparse matrix. A sparse matrix is a matrix in which maximum of the elements are zero. The upper matrix is also of two types: Upper-left and Upper-right as shown in figure a and b.

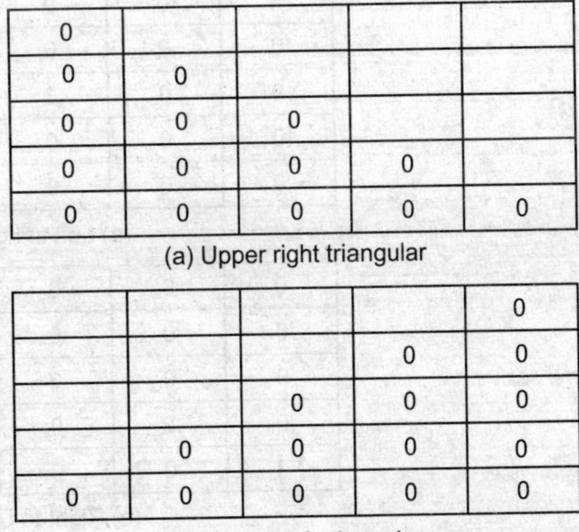

0				
0	0			
0	0	0		
0	0	0	0	
0	0	0	0	0

(a) Upper right triangular

				0
			0	0
		0	0	0
	0	0	0	0
0	0	0	0	0

(b) Upper left triangular

Figure 17.28: Representation of upper triangular matrices.

17.18.3 Lower Triangular Matrices

The lower matrix is a type of triangular matrix, which is also a type of sparse matrix. A sparse matrix is a matrix in which maximum of the elements are zero.

The lower matrix is also of two types: Lower -left and Lower -right as shown in figure a and b.

0	0	0	0	0
	0	0	0	0
		0	0	0
			0	0
				0

(a) Lower-left triangular

0	0	0	0	0
0	0	0	0	
0	0	0		
0	0			
0				

(b) Lower-right triangular

Figure 17.29: Representation of lower triangular matrices.

17.18.4 Diagonal Matrices

In diagonal matrices, only diagonal elements are non-zero and other values are NULL as shown in figures.

1	0	0	0	0
0	**2**	0	0	0
0	0	**3**	0	0
0	0	0	**4**	0
0	0	0	0	**5**

(a) Left to right

0	0	0	0	**5**
0	0	0	**4**	0
0	0	**3**	0	0
0	**2**	0	0	0
1	0	0	0	0

(b) Right to Left

Figure 17.30: Representation of diagonal matrices.

17.18.5 Tri-diagonal Matrices

These are two representations of the Tri-diagonal matrices.

1	1	0	0	0
1	2	8	0	0
0	4	3	3	0
0	0	5	4	5
0	0	0	8	5

(a) Left to Right

0	0	0	2	5
0	0	4	4	1
0	7	3	9	0
8	2	7	0	0
1	4	0	0	0

(b) Right to Left

Figure 17.31: Representation of Tri-diagonal matrices.

OBJECTIVE TYPE QUESTIONS

1. SPARSE Matrix is
   (a) Low proportion of zero (b) High proportion of zero
   (c) Both (d) None
2. Which of the following is the type of array?
   (a) Linear (b) Non-Linear
   (c) Both (d) None of the above
3. One Dimensional array is
   (a) Linear (b) Non-Linear
   (c) Both (d) None of the above
4. Linear search is
   (a) Fast Process (b) Slow Process
   (c) Both (d) None
5. Which of the following is the operation of array.
   (a) Sorting (b) Searching
   (c) Inserting (d) Deleting
   (e) All of the above (f) None of the above
6. Traversing is also called:
   (a) Sorting (b) Searching
   (c) Inserting (d) Deleting
   (e) Visiting (f) None of the above

7. An array is a .... type of data structure.
   (a) linear (b) non-linear
   (c) dynamic (d) (a) and (b)
8. Homogenous means ....
   (a) values of the same type (b) having all equal values
   (c) (a) and (b) (d) dissimilar values.
9. Array elements are stored in
   (a) successive memory locations (b) random memory locations
   (c) both (a) and (b) (d) none of the above
10. Accessing all elements of the array is known as
    (a) transverse (b) insertion
    (c) deletion (d) listing.
11. Merging of array elements means
    (a) combining two or more arrays (b) addition of elements of two arrays
    (c) interchanging elements of two arrays
    (d) none of the above.
12. Following one operation cannot be performed on arrays
    (a) merging (b) insertion
    (c) deletion (d) memory re-allocation.
13. Base address means
    (a) address of 0th element (b) address of array name
    (c) address of least element (d) none of the above.
14. Array elements are stored in
    (a) random memory locations (b) sequential memory locations
    (c) both of the above.
15. A character array always ends with
    (a) comma (,) (b) question mark (?)
    (c) null character (\0) (d) Full stop (.)
16. Arrays can not be initialized if they are
    (a) automatic (b) static
    (c) external (d) none of the above.
17. All the elements in the array must be
    (a) initialized (b) defined
    (c) none of the above.

EXERCISES

1. What do you mean by array? How we can declaration and initialization array.
2. How we can represent array in memory?
3. Explain different types of array in detail.
4. What are the various operations performed on linear array?
5. Write an algorithm for traversing a linear array.
6. Write an algorithm and C++ program for inserting element in linear array.
7. Write an algorithm and C++ program for deleting element from linear array
8. Write an algorithm for searching item from linear array.
9. Write an algorithm for sorting a linear array.
10. Write an algorithm and C++ program for merging two arrays.
11. Write an algorithm and C++ program for reversing the array.
12. Write an algorithm and C++ program for copying the elements of one array into another in reverse order.
13. What do you mean by multi dimensional array?
14. What is the various applications of arrays.
15. What is Pointer?
16. Explain concept of pointers and arrays.
17. What do you mean by Records?
18. What do you mean by Record structures?
19. Explain representation of records in memory using parallel arrays.
20. What do you mean by matrix? Write an algorithm for matrix multiplication.
21. What do you mean by sparse matrix?
22. Difference between sparse matrix and dense matrix.
23. What do you mean by diagonal matrices and tri-diagonal matrices?

CHAPTER 18

Linked Lists

18.1 INTRODUCTION

In computer science, a linked list is one of the fundamental INFO structures used in computer programming. It consists of a sequence of nodes, each containing arbitrary information fields and one or two references ("links") pointing to the next and/or previous nodes. The principle benefit of a linked list over a conventional list is that the order of the linked items may be different to the order that the INFO items are stored in memory or on disk, allowing the list of items to be traversed in a different order.

A linked list is a self-referential INFOtype because it contains a pointer or link to another INFO of the same type. Linked lists permit insertion and removal of nodes at any point in the list in constant time, but do not allow random access. Several different types of linked list exist: singly-linked lists, doubly-linked lists, and circularly-linked lists.

When dealing with many problems we need a dynamic list, dynamic in the sense that the size requirement need not be known at compile time. Thus, the list may grow or shrink during runtime. A linked list is a INFO structure that is used to model such a dynamic list of INFO items, so the study of the linked lists as one of the INFO structures is important.

Often in programming we are required to systematically store some type of information. A prime example of this is to use arrays but when you don't know the amount of information to be stored we need a dynamic INFO structure. One option for us is to use a linked list. A linked list works by creating a collection of objects (nodes) which both carry the INFO we want to store and a reference to the next node in the list.

So the first node in the list points to the next node and then the next points to the one after that until we reach the last node, which will point to null. This way all we really need to keep track of is the first node, as knowing it will enable us to access any node down the list (because they each point to each other, they are linked). And whenever you add a node it goes to the end of the list (as in the current last node begins to point to the new node and the new node, of course, to null [and it is the new last node now]). Linked lists allocate memory for an element when it's added. That's what makes them useful, because in practice though a lot of contexts may appear. Due to the allocation, you can't find every element one after another in memory.

That is why we must have a way to know where they are located: For the first allocated element that's easy, we put a pointer to it in the hash entry. For the second one we put a pointer in the first one to the second. For the third one we put a pointer in the second one and so on. In the last element the pointer to the next one equals 0. That's the way we know when we have reached the end of the linked list. In short words, an element in a linked list has the context information plus a pointer to the next element.

18.2 WHY WE USE LINKED LIST ?

Linked lists and arrays are similar since they both store collections of INFO. The terminology is that arrays and linked lists store "elements" on behalf of "client" code. The specific type of element is not important since essentially the same structure works to store elements of any type. One way to think about linked lists is to look at how arrays work and think about alternate approaches.

18.3 ARRAY REVIEW

Arrays are probably the most common INFO structure used to store collections of elements. An array is represented in memory using sequential mapping, which has the property that elements are fixed distance apart. But this has the following disadvantage: It makes insertion or deletion at any arbitrary position in an array a costly operation, because this involves the movement of some of the existing elements.

When we want to represent several lists by using arrays of varying size, either we have to represent each list using a separate array of maximum size or we have to represent each of the lists using one single array. The first one will lead to wastage of storage, and the second will involve a lot of INFO movement.

In most languages, arrays are convenient to declare and the provide the handy [ ] syntax to access any element by its index number. The following example shows some typical array code and a drawing of how the array might look in memory. The code allocates an array int scores[100], sets the first three elements set to contain the numbers 1, 2, 3 and leaves the rest of the array uninitialized...

```
void ArrayTest()
{
int scores[100];
// operate on the elements of the scores array...
  scores[0] = 1;
  scores[1] = 2;
  scores[2] = 3;
  }
```

Here is a drawing of how the scores array might look like in memory. The key point is that the entire array is allocated as one block of memory. Each element in the array gets its own space in the array. Any element can be accessed directly using the [ ] syntax.

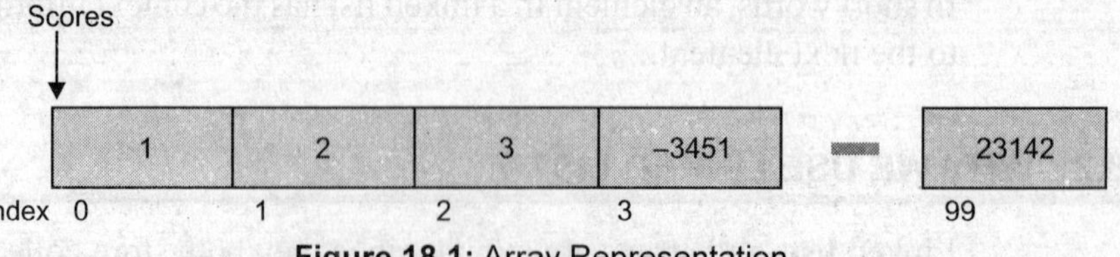

Figure 18.1: Array Representation

Once the array is set up, access to any element is convenient and fast with the [ ] operator. (Extra for experts) Array access with expressions such as scores[i] is almost always implemented using fast address arithmetic: the address of an element is computed as an offset from the start of the array which only requires one multiplication and one addition.

18.3.1 The Disadvantages of Arrays Are...

1. The size of the array is fixed — 100 elements in this case. Most often this size is specified at compile time with a simple declaration such as in the example above. With a little extra effort, the size of the array can be deferred until the array is created at runtime, but after that it remains fixed. (extra for experts) You can go to the trouble of dynamically allocating an array in the heap and then dynamically resizing it with realloc(), but that requires some real programmer effort.
2. Because of (1), the most convenient thing for programmers to do is to allocate arrays which seem "large enough" (e.g. the 100 in the scores example). Although convenient, this strategy has two disadvantages:
   (a) Most of the time there are just 20 or 30 elements in the array and 70% of the space in the array really is wasted.

(b) If the program ever needs to process more than 100 scores, the code breaks. A surprising amount of commercial code has this sort of naive array allocation which wastes space most of the time and crashes for special occasions (Extra for experts). For relatively large arrays (larger than 8k bytes), the virtual memory system may partially compensate for this problem, since the "wasted" elements are never touched.

3. (minor) Inserting new elements at the front is potentially expensive because existing elements need to be shifted over to make room. Linked lists have their own strengths and weaknesses, but they happen to be strong where arrays are weak. The array's features all follow from its strategy of allocating the memory for all its elements in one block of memory. Linked lists use an entirely different strategy.

As we will see, linked lists allocate memory for each element separately and only when necessary. So we have to use an alternative representation to overcome these disadvantages. One alternative is a linked representation. In a linked representation, it is not necessary that the elements be at a fixed distance apart. Instead, we can place elements anywhere in memory, but to make it a part of the same list, an element is required to be linked with a previous element of the list. This can be done by storing the address of the next element in the previous element itself. This requires that every element be capable of holding the INFO as well as the address of the next element. Thus every element must be a structure with a minimum of two fields, one for holding the INFO value, which we call a INFO field, and the other for holding the address of the next element, which we call link field.

Therefore, a linked list is a list of elements in which the elements of the list can be placed anywhere in memory, and these elements are linked with each other using an explicit link field, that is, by storing the address of the next element in the link field of the previous element.

18.4 LINKED LIST

A linked list is a *dynamic data structure*, which means that the memory to hold the INFO is created at run time (dynamic), and stored in a structured way (also called INFO structure). Also we can say Linked list is a linear INFO structure, i.e it is a linear collection of INFO elements called nodes, where the linear order is given by means of pointers. Each node consists of two fields, one containing the item and the other containing the address of the next item in the list. Each node contains two parts information part and link part. The last node of the linked list contains a special link part called Null Pointer (i.e. any invalid address).

Defination: "A linked list is an ordered collection of data elements called nodes in which linear order is given by means of pointers. Each node has 2 parts: information(INFO) and link. The information part holds the useful information of the element. The link part or nextpointer part is used identifies the next node in the list."

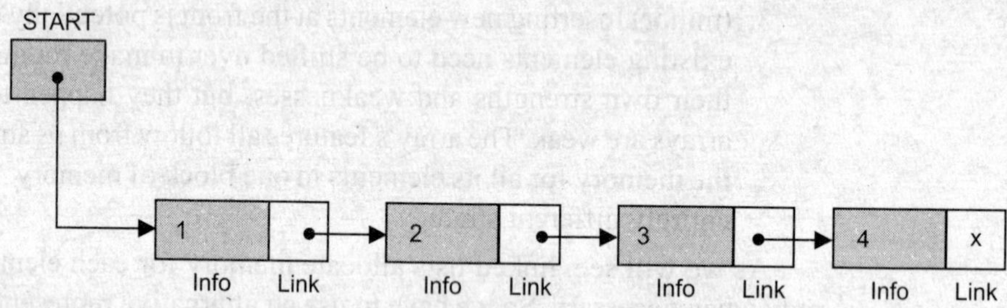

Figure 18.2: Linked list with four nodes.

A Linked List is generally an implementation structure. In other words, linked lists don't have an inherent ordering to them...making it difficult to insert/delete because no choice is made as to where things should be inserted or deleted. However, a linked list can be used to implement queues, stacks, and ordered linked lists (such as a sorted linked list). We may implement linked lists as an array, but it is much more common to implement them using a dynamic structure. The size of the list is only as big as the number of items in the list.

Example 18.1: A Linked list made up of a number of "date" records/structures.

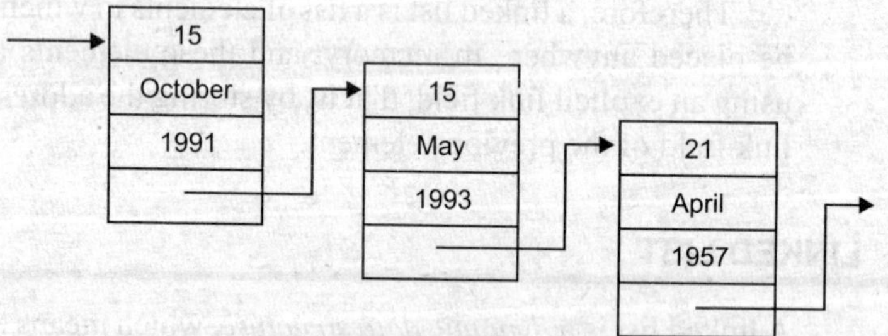

Figure 18.3: Linked list of "date" records.

18.4.1 Representation of Linked List

A linked list is a INFO structure which is built from structures and pointers. It forms a chain of "nodes" with pointers representing the links of the chain and holding the entire thing together. A linked list can be represented by a diagram like this one:

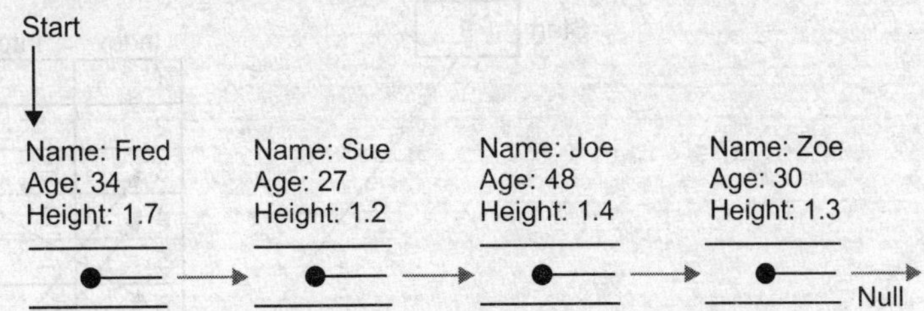

Figure 18.4: Linked list having student records.

This linked list has four nodes in it, each with a link to the next node in the series. The last node has a link to the special value NULL, which any pointer (whatever its type) can point to, to show that it is the last link in the chain. There is also another special pointer, called Start, which points to the first link in the chain so that we can keep track of it.

18.4.2 Array Implementation of Singly Linked List

The linked list requires two linear arrays. These are INFO and LINK.

INFO part contains the information

LINK Part contains the address of next node

Linked list also requires the pointer variable named START, which contains the address of the beginning of the list. We also need the NULL pointer, which is contained in the address part of the last node.

Let LIST be a linked list. Then LIST will be maintained in memory, unless otherwise specified or implied, as follows. First of all, LIST requires two linear arrays—we will call them here INFO and LINK—such that INFO[k] and LINK[k] contain, respectively, the information part and the next pointer field of a node of LIST. As noted above, LIST also requires a variable name—such as START — which contains the location of the beginning of the list, and a next pointer sentinel—denoted by NULL—which indicates the end of the list.

Since the subscripts of the arrays INFO and LINK will usually be positive, we will choose NULL = 0, unless otherwise stated.

The following example of linked lists indicates that the nodes of a list need not occupy adjacent elements in the arrays INFO and LINK, and that more than one list may be maintained in the same linear arrays INFO and LINK.

However, each list must have its own pointer variable giving the location of its first node.

Example 18.2: Figure 18.5 shows a linked list in memory where each node of the list contains a single character.

We can obtain the actual list of character, or, in other words, the string, as follow:

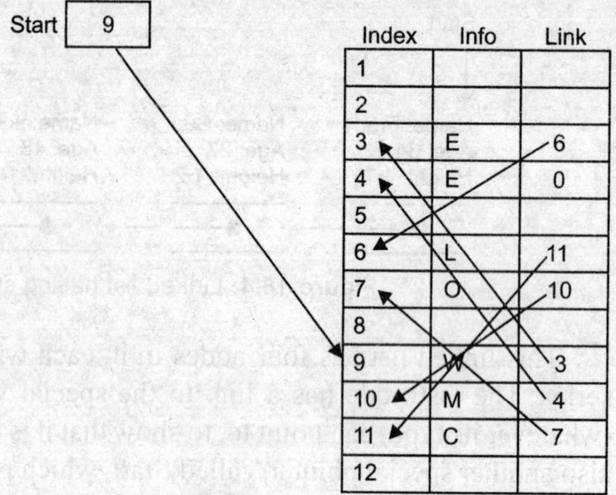

Figure 18.5: Memory representation of Linked List

START = 9, so INFO[9] = W is the first character.
LINK[9] = 3, so INFO[3] = E is the second character.
LINK[3] = 6, so INFO[6] = L is the third character.
LINK[6] = 11,so INFO[11] = C is the fourth character.
LINK[11] = 7,so INFO[7] = O is the fifth character.
LINK[7] = 10,so INFO[10] = M is the sixth character.
LINK[10] = 4,so INFO[4] = E is the seventh character.
LINK[4] = 0, the NULL value, so the list has ended.

In other words, WELCOME is the character string.

Example 18.3: Figure 18.6 pictures a linked list in memory where each node of the list contains a single character. We can obtain the actual list of characters, or, in other words, the string as follows:

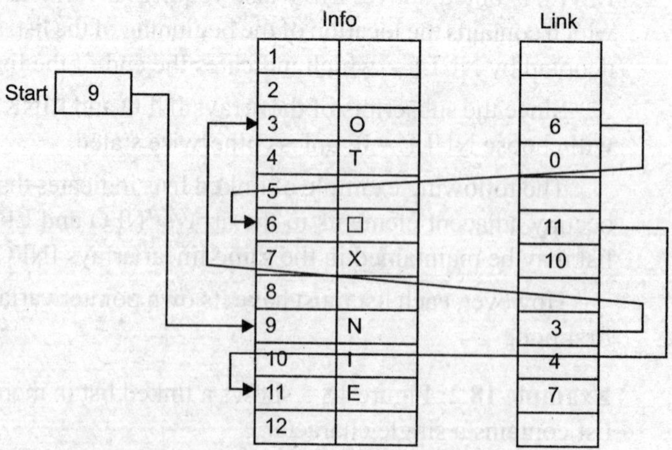

Figure 18.6: Memory representation of Linked List

START = 9, so INFO[9] = N is the first character.
LINK[9] = 3, so INFO[3] = O is the second character.
LINK[3] = 6, so INFO[6] = □ (blank) is the third character.
LINK[6] = 11, so INFO[11] = E is the fourth character.
LINK[11] = 7, so INFO[7] = X is the fifth character.
LINK[7] = 10, so INFO[10] = I is the sixth character.
LINK[10] = 4, so INFO[4] = T is the seventh character.
LINK[4] = 0, the NULL value, so the list has ended.

In other words, NO EXIT is the character string.

18.5 DYNAMIC DATA STRUCTURE: LINKED LISTS

The ADT known as a Linked List is the simplest example of a INFO structure providing the capability of 'dynamically adapting' to accommodate changes in the quantity of information stored. This structure also provides a basis for building more complex structures qualified by the precise regime in which applications wish to access individual records.

This is especially true when a very large collection (ca. 10^6+) of records is involved, and so in a typical modern INFObase setting, more sophisticated structures are needed. Linked lists and their basic variations do provide reasonable solutions in a number of systems' programming contexts, e.g. the management of processes in O/S environments; hardware modelling in simulation tools.

Definition: *A Linked List INFO structure,* ***L****, is recursively defined as:*

- **L** is the **empty** list, i.e. the list handle is the null reference.

  or

- **L** is of the form

  Head: L*

where ***Head*** *contains a datum item and* L^* *is a list. The notation ':' indicates that part of the 'Head' cell is a handle indicating (pointing at/referencing) the linked list* L^**. The Figure below gives an informal depiction of linked list structure.*

In Figure 18.7, the box labelled 'List Handle' indicates the name of the list. This contains a reference (or pointer) to the start of the list. Each list cell comprises two parts: the first (labelled 'Datum' in the diagram) contains the information held in the list element: this could be anything from a simple value over a primitive type to an arbitrary Object (which could itself be a linked list, but we will defer consideration of more complex structures such as this until later). The second element of a list cell (labelled 'Link' in Figure 18.7) is a pointer to the remainder of the list. In the (currently) final list cell, this pointer is set to the null reference.

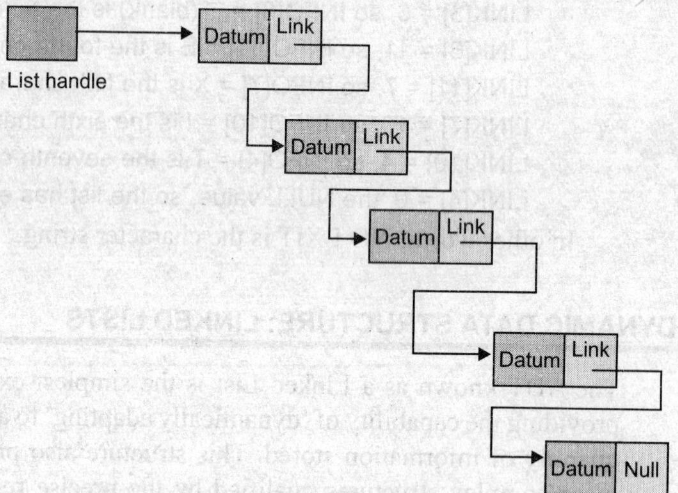

Figure 18.7: Linked List Structure

Most abstract INFO types are based on two "foundation INFO types". These are the array, and the linked list. Programming languages commonly provide the array as a part of the language, the linked list, though just as important is less likely to be provided in this way, it is however likely to be provided as a "library" item with a language.

Whereas an array provides a static collection of storage locations that may be accessed randomly using an index value, a linked list provides a dynamically allocated sequence of storage locations, each of which points to the next.

A good way to think of a linked list is as a chain, or string of beads. Each link not only contains the INFO, but also a pointer to the next link (Figure 18.8). As each INFO element is added, a link is created pointing from it to the next item in the list.

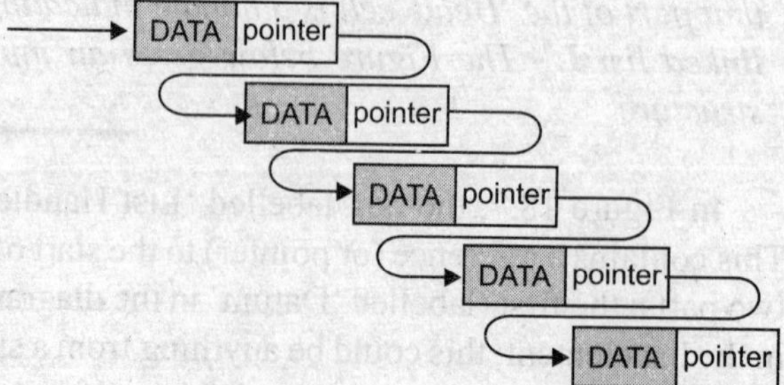

Figure 18.8: Structure of a linked list

Figure 18.8 shows a Singularly Linked List. This is the simplest of the linked INFO structures. At its most basic it is simply a sequence of dynamically allocated objects, each of which points to its successor in the list. There are however complications that lead to several implementations (Figure 18.9):

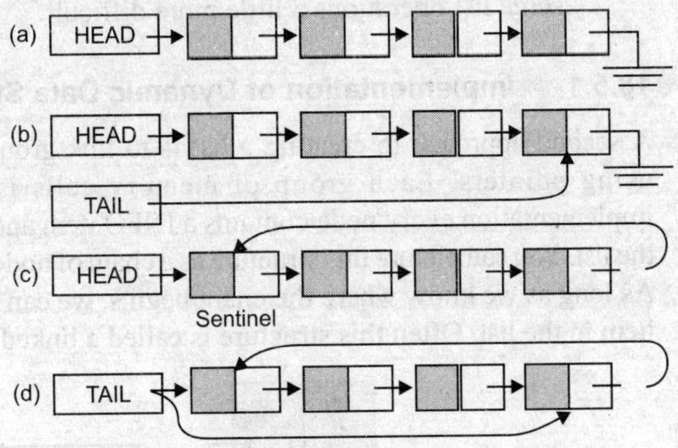

Figure 18.9: Singularly linked list varities

(a) Shows the simplest linked list. Each element refers to its successor; the last item in the list holds a null reference (doesn't point to anything). A single variable is used to point to the head of the list. The head pointer provides a mechanism for accessing the list from a programme. This pattern of list is easy to use for inserting and removing items from the head, but is inefficient when things are to be added to both ends of the list or in the middle. The tail of the list may only be found by traversing the whole list, making insertion and removal here quite a chore.

(b) Shows a list with two pointers, one each for the head and the tail. This alleviates the problem of finding the tail of a singularly linked list, but the increase in efficiency comes at the cost of the extra storage required for the tail pointer variable. Obviously this is a small overhead so is probably not a problem. It is still difficult however to remove items from the tail, or to access and add or remove items in the midst of the list.

(c) Shows two programming tricks that may be applied to singly linked lists. Firstly, c) is a circular list; the last element doesn't point to a null reference, but back to the head of the list. A circular list has identical operations for insertion at any point, be it the head, tail or at any arbitrary position within the list. The sentinel is used as it means that the head variable need never be changed. The sentinel is not used to hold any INFO, just point to (guard) the head of the list. The sentinel must be created when the list is initialised. The sentinel places extra storage requirements on the list. Insertion and removal of items of the list are still complex operations.

(d) The final implementation, shown is a circular list that does not use a sentinel [d)]. A single pointer variable is used to point at the tail of the list. As the head of the list follows the tail in a circular list, insertion at both the head and tail are easy. Unfortunately this type of implementation does makes some list operations a little more difficult.

18.5.1 Implementation of Dynamic Data Structure Using Pointer

A second approach to creating a list is to link groups of memory cells together using pointers. Each group of memory cells is called a node. With this implementation every node contains a INFO item and a pointer to the next item in the list. You can picture this structure as a chain of nodes linked together by pointers. As long as we know where the chain begins, we can follow the links to reach any item in the list. Often this structure is called a linked list.

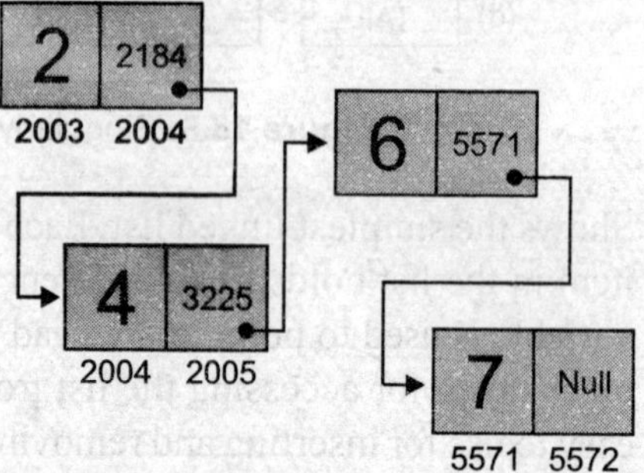

Figure 18.10: Dynamic Data Structure Using Pointer

Notice that the last memory cell in our chain contains a symbol called "Null". This symbol is a special value that tells us we have reached the end of our list. You can think of this symbol as a pointer that points to nothing.

18.5.2 Dynamic Implementation of Singly Linked List

A singly linked list is a sequence of INFO elements (of the same type) arranged one after another conceptually. Each element is stored in a node. Each node also contains a link that connects this node to the next node in the list. Here's a conceptual picture of a linked list containing N items, pointed to by a variable named L as shown in the figure 18.11:

Here's a conceptual picture of a linked list containing N items, pointed to by a variable named L:

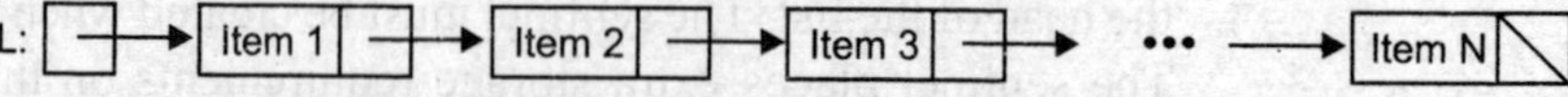

Figure 18.11: Dynamic implementation of single linked list.

Note that a linked list consists of one or more *nodes*. Each node contains some INFO (in this example, *item 1, item 2*, etc) and a pointer. For each node other than the last one, the pointer points to the next node in the list. For the last node, the pointer is null (indicated in the example using a diagonal line). The complete linked list structure as shown in the figure 18.12 below shows this a lot better than the above-described explanation:

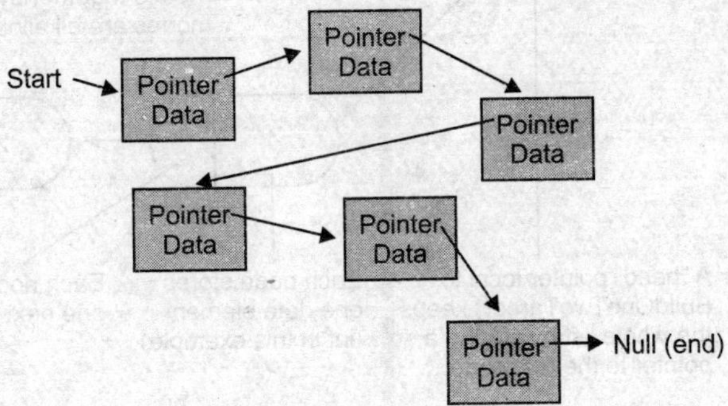

Figure 18.12: Structure of single linked list

In the diagram, each node is shown in the rectangles and contains a pointer to the next node in the list (shown by the arrows), and a INFO portion which holds the information for the node. The nodes are deliberately drawn in the diagram in a haphazard way to show that each node can exist in any portion of memory, not necessarily adjacent to or even close to the neighboring nodes in the list. The start of the list is also shown, which is just a pointer to the first node. From this start pointer any node can be referenced, for all but the first node though, other nodes will have to be "passed through" to get there. The end of the list is indicated by the final node pointing to NULL. Normally, when a linked list is initialized, the start pointer will hold NULL to indicate that the list is empty, but as soon as a node is added to the list, this changes.

18.5.3 Memory Allocation of Linked Lists Look Like

An array allocates memory for all its elements lumped together as one block of memory. In contrast, a linked list allocates space for each element separately in its own block of memory called a "linked list element" or "node". The list gets is overall structure by using pointers to connect all its nodes together like the links in a chain.

Each node contains two fields: a "INFO" field to store whatever element type the list holds for its client, and a "next" field which is a pointer used to link one node to the next node. Each node is allocated in the heap with a call to malloc(), so the node memory continues to exist until it is explicitly deallocated with a call to free(). The front of the list is a pointer to the first node. Here is what a list containing the numbers 1, 2, and 3 might look like...

The Drawing of List {1, 2, 3}

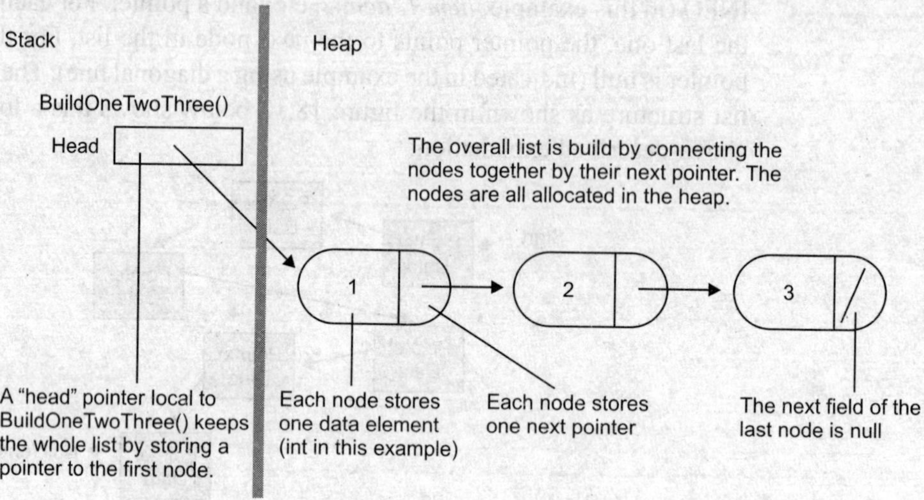

Figure 18.13: Memory Allocation of single Linked List.

The beginning of the linked list is stored in a "head" pointer which points to the first node. The first node contains a pointer to the second node. The second node contains a pointer to the third node, ... and so on. The last node in the list has its .next field set to NULL to mark the end of the list.

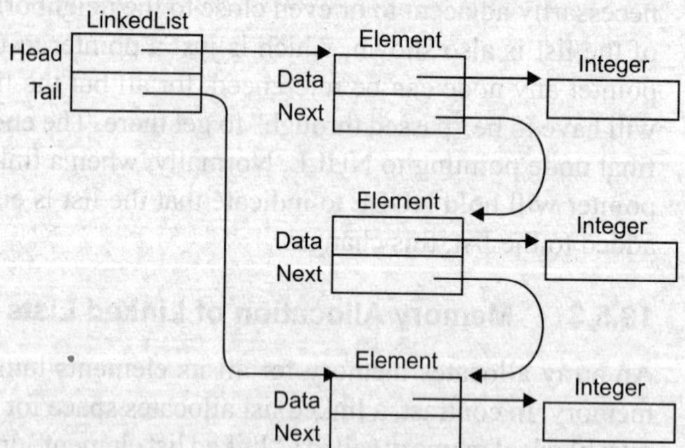

Figure 18.14: How a linked list resides in memory

Important Points:

- *Linked lists are used when the quantity of INFO is not known prior to execution.*
- *In linked lists, INFO is stored in the form of nodes and at runtime, memory is allocated for creating nodes.*

- *Due to overhead in memory allocation and deallocation, the speed of the program is lower.*
- *The INFO is accessed using the starting pointer of the list.*

18.5.4 Organization of Linked List

A linked list is a INFO structure used to maintain a dynamic series of INFO. Think of a linked list as a line of elephants in a circus where each elephant is holding on to the tail of the next elephant. If you know where the first elephant is, you can follow it's trunk to the next one. By following trunks, you can find any elephant in the chain. When you get to an elephant that isn't holding on to another elephant's tail, you know you are at the end.

Linked lists work in the same way, except programmers usually refer to nodes instead of elephants. A single node is defined the same way as any other user defined type or object, except that it also contains a pointer to a variable of the same type as itself.

C++ example node definition

```
typedef struct lnode
{
int INFO;
struct lnode *next;
}
listnode_t;
```

First node   Last node   Null

A → B → C → D →

Figure 18.15: Linked list represents first node, last node and null pointer.

Note that a linked list consists of one or more *nodes*. Each node contains some INFO (in this example, *item 1, item 2*, etc) and a pointer. For each node other than the last one, the pointer points to the next node in the list. For the last node, the pointer is null (indicated in the example using a diagonal line).

How INFO can be assigned and link by using pointers can be created is organized in the figure 18.16 as below:

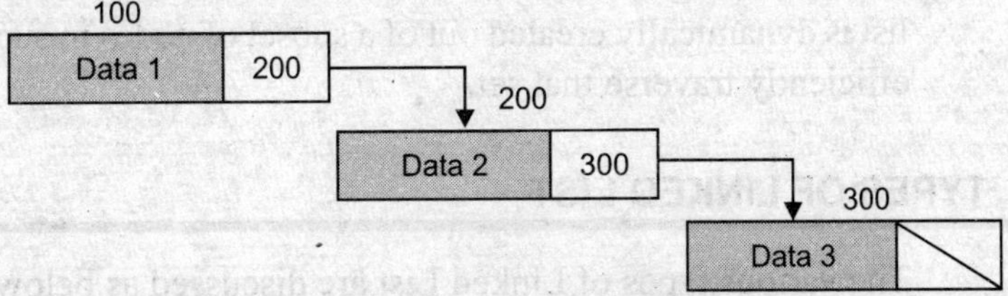

Figure 18.16: Linked list represents pointer addressess

Conceptual Picture: Representation of node conceptually having INFO and link part with a head value be as shown in the figure 18.17 below:

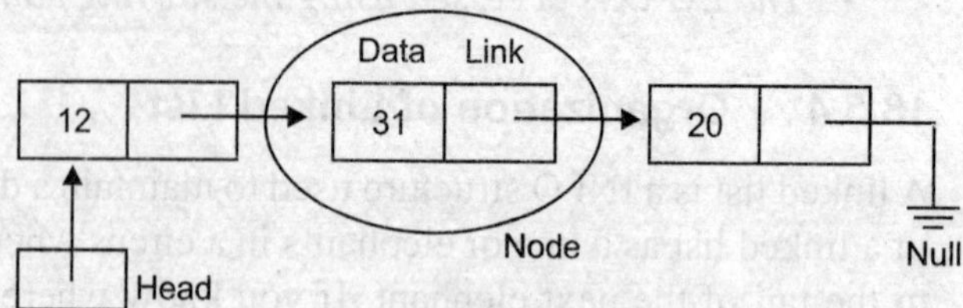

Figure 18.17: Head points to the first node.

Also the word addressing of every node shown in the Table 18.1 be shown in the table as:

Table 18.1: Defining a Node with word address and contents

Word Address	Contents
1000	31
1002	1008
1004	12
1006	1000
1008	20
1010	0
1012	1004

18.5.5 Applications of Linked Lists

Linked lists are used as a building block for many other INFO structures, such as **stacks, queues** and their variations.

The "INFO" field of a node can be another linked list. By this device, one can emulate arbitrary linked INFO structures with lists — a principle which is fundamental to **the Lisp programming language**, where linked lists are the primary (if not the only) INFO structuring mechanism.

Sometimes, linked lists are used to implement **associative arrays,** and are in this context called **association lists**. There is very little good to be said about this use of linked lists; they are easily outperformed by other INFO structures such as **self-balancing binary search trees** even on small INFO sets, sometimes a linked list is dynamically created out of a subset of nodes in such a tree, and used to more efficiently traverse that set.

18.6 TYPES OF LINKED LIST

The various types of Linked List are discussed as below:

1. Singular Linked List

2. Two Way Linked List or Doubly Linked List
3. Circular Linked List
4. Sorted Linked List
5. Endogenous/Exogenous Lists

18.7 SINGULAR LINKED LIST

Unless otherwise stated a particular type of linked list, the word "linked list" implies Singular linked list. A singly linked list is a sequence of INFO elements (of the same type) arranged one after another conceptually. Each element is stored in a node. Each node also contains a link that connects this node to the next node in the list.A singly linked list could be used to implement both stacks and queues, neither of which requires the ability to move backward through the list. A singly linked list could also be used for a sorted linked list.

18.7.1 Operations on A Linked List

Various Operations can be performed on this INFO structure, but we will be performing following list of operations stated below:

1. Traversing
2. Counting the items
3. Insertion
4. Deletion
5. Concatenating two lists
6. Searching
7. Reversing the direction of list
8. Copying linked list
9. Merging two lists
10. Erasing linked list
11. Spiliting linked list

18.7.1.1 Traversing A Linked List

Suppose we want to traverse a list in order to process each node exactly once. Suppose the list is sorted in memory as a linked list, our aim is to traverse the list starting from the first node to the end of the list.

In traversing algorithm we are using a pointer variable P which points to the node that is currently being processed. Therefore, LINK[P] points to the next node to be processed.

P = LINK[P]

This statement moves the pointer to the next node in the list, shown in figure 18.18:

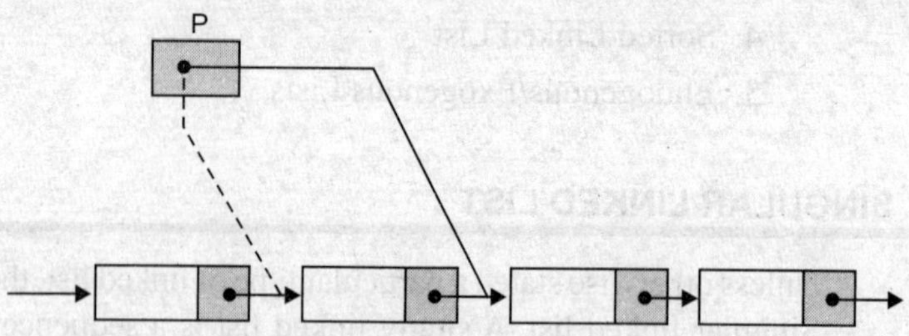

Figure 18.18: Pointer P performs traversing P = LINK[P].

First step, initialize P to START. Then process INFO [P], the information of the first node.Now, update PTR by assigning value to P = LINK [P], so that P points to next node. Then process INFO [P], the information of the next node.Again, update PTR by assigning value to P = LINK [P], and process INFO[P]. And so on. Continue until P ≠ NULL(tells the end of the list).

Algorithm 18.1: Traversing a Linked List

TRAVERSE (INFO, LINK, START, P)

Let LIST be a Linked list in memory. This algorithm traverses LIST, applying an operation PROCESS to each element of LIST. The variable P points to the node currently being processed.

Step 1: Set P = START. [Initializes pointer P.]

Step 2: Repeat Steps 3 and 4 while P ≠ NULL.

Step 3. Apply PROCESS to INFO [P].

Step 4: Set P = LINK [P]. [P now points to the next node.]

[End of Step 2 loop.]

Step 5: End.

This algorithm traverses the linked list applying an operation process to each element of the list.

This algorithm uses a pointer variable name P, which points to the node currently being processed. The step 4 P = Link [P], P now points to the next node.

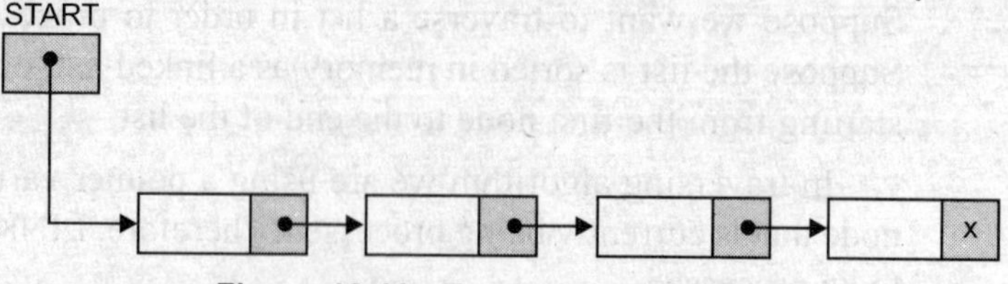

Figure 18.19 : Traversing a linked list

Program 1: Write a C++ program to create and display a linked list

```
#include <iostream.h>
# include <conio.h>
struct node
{
int info; // info field
node* link; //pointer to the link node
};
class link_list
{
private:
node* start;
public:
link_list ( ) //constructor
{
start=NULL; //initially the list has no node
}
void add_info (int i)
{
node* new_link= new node; //create a new node;
new_link->info=i;
new_link->=start; //make new node to point to the first node
start=new_link; // make new node as the first node in the list
}
void display ( ); //function prototype
}; //end of class
void link_list : : display ( )
{
node* move=start;
node* temp;
while (move)
{
cout<<move->info<<"->"; //display the info
temp= move;
move=move->link; //move to link node
delete temp; //delete the displayed node.
}
cout<<"NULL\n;
}
```

```
void main ( )
{
clrscr( );
link_list link;
for (int i=5; i<=10; i++)
link.add_info (i);
link.display( );
getch ( );
}
Output:
10->9->8->7->6->5->NULL
```

18.7.1.2 Counting the Number of Nodes of A Linked List

Counting is the next step after traversing the linked or during the traversing procedure. Counting means to find and display the number of node in a linked list till the Null part reaches.

Counting the number of nodes of a singly linked list requires maintaining a counter that is initialized to 0 and incremented by 1 each time a node is encountered in the process of traversing a list from the start.

Algorithm 18.2: Count the number num of nodes in a linked list.

COUNT (DATA, LINK, START, NUM)

Step 1: Set NUM = 0. [Initializes number NUM.]

Step 2: Set P = START. [Initializes pointer P.]

Step 3: Repeat Steps 4 and 5 while P ≠ NULL.

Step 4: Set NUM = NUM + 1. [Increment NUM by 1.]

Step 5: Set P = LINK [P]. [Updates pointer.]

[End of Step 3 loop.]

Step 6: End.

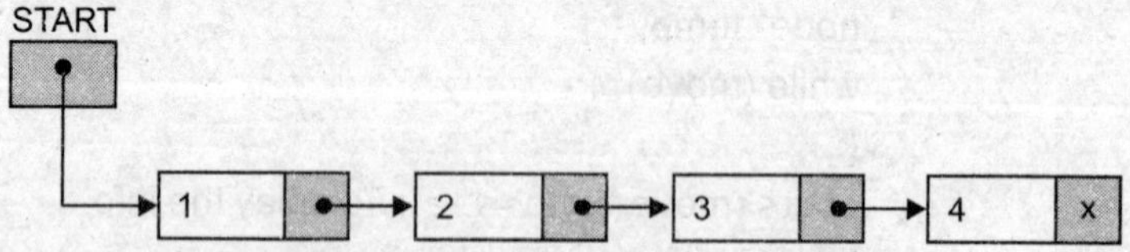

START → 1 → 2 → 3 → 4 x

Figure 18.20: Count total number of nodes of linked list

18.7.1.3 Inserting Into A Linked List

Before inserting or deleting element it is necessary to understand the concept of AVAIL list and Overflow and underflow as discussed below:

Avail List

In the preceeding sections, linked lists are implemented by using parallel arrays(shown in figure 18.21) and suppose insertions and deletions are performed on the linked list. Then the unused memory cells in the arrays will also be linked together to form a linked list using AVAIL as its pointer variable.

"A special list is maintained which consists of unused memory cells. This list, which has its own pointer, is called the list of free- storage or free-pool or Available free space list(AVAIL list)."

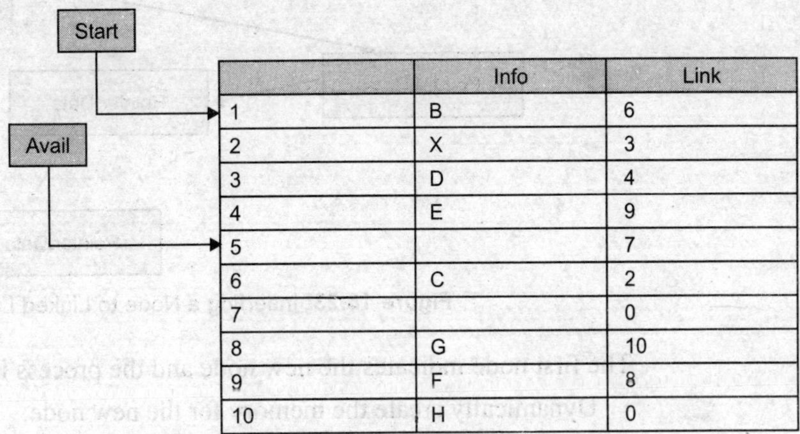

	Info	Link
1	B	6
2	X	3
3	D	4
4	E	9
5		7
6	C	2
7		0
8	G	10
9	F	8
10	H	0

Figure 18.21: Linked list using AVAIL as its pointer variable.

Here location LOC=5 is unused space called free space which is pointed by pointer variable AVAIL.Next free space is ponted by LINK[5] is 7.

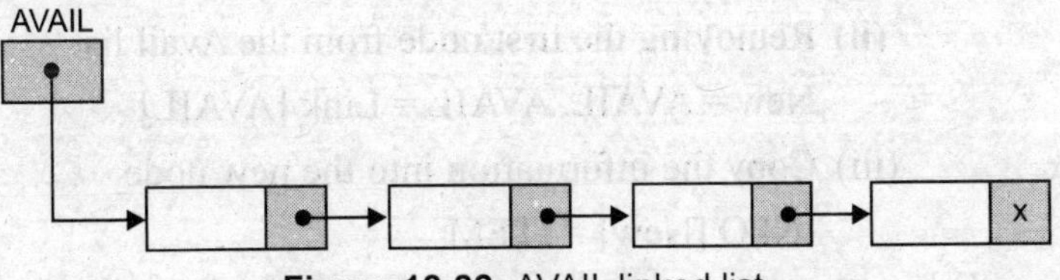

Figure 18.22: AVAIL linked list.

Overflow and Underflow

Overflow occurs when we want to insert a new INFO item, but there is no fre space i.e. AVAIL=NULL.

Underflow occurs when we want to delete some node from the linked list, b the list is already empty i.e. START = NULL.

Inserting A Node to A Linked List

Inserting a node isn't to difficult, but can be depending on how you implement list. With a simple single linked list, and not needing to worry about the positio the list the new node is added, it is a really easy task to add a node. This is done to the start of the list, as shown in the Figure 18.23 below:

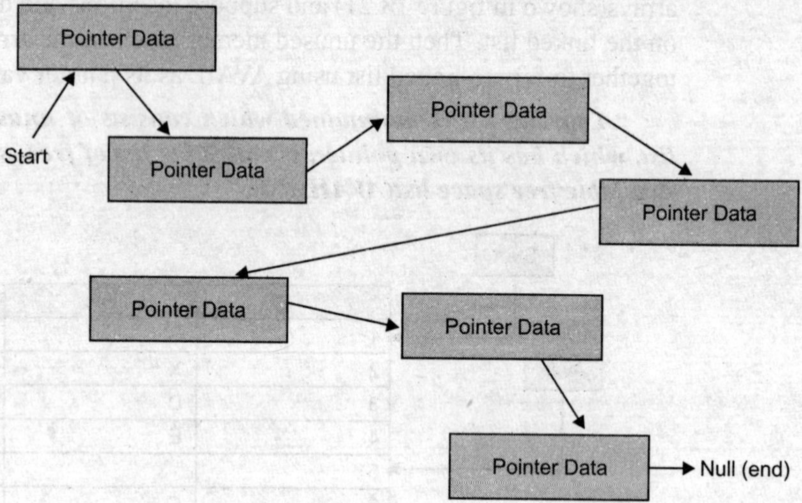

Figure 18.23: Inserting a Node to Linked List.

The first node indicates the new node and the process involves:

- Dynamically create the memory for the new node.
- Set the link pointer of the new node to equal the **start** pointer.

Set the start pointer to point to the new node. All the Insertion algorithms will include the following steps:

(i) Check for an overflow, if there is an overflow then exit

(ii) Removing the first node from the Avail list

New = AVAIL, AVAIL = Link [AVAIL]

(iii) Copy the information into the new node

INFO [New] = ITEM

The schematic diagram of first two steps is shown here:

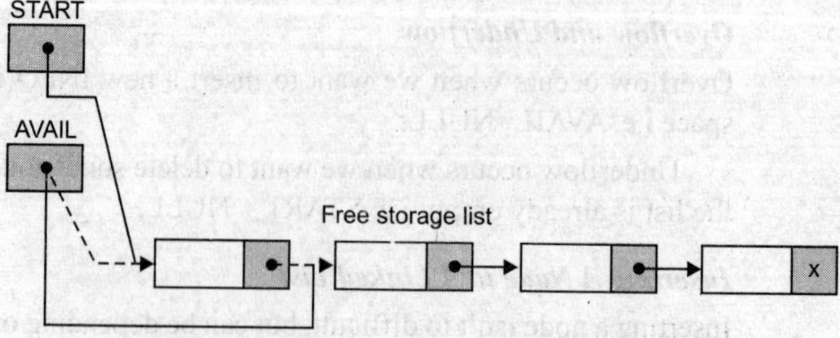

Figure 18.24: New = AVAIL and AVAIL = Link [AVAIL].

A. *Insertion at the Beginning of the Linked List*

Suppose our linked list is not sorted and then we have no reason that where we have to insert the new node.Then the easy way is to insert new node at the beginning of the list(shown in figure 18.25).

Algorithm 18.3: To insert new node at the beginning of a list.

INSBEGNOD (INFO, LINK, START, AVAIL, ITEM)

This algorithm inserts ITEM as the first node in the list.

Step 1: [OVERFLOW?] If AVAIL = NULL, then: Write: OVERFLOW, and End.

Step 2: [Remove first node from AVAIL list.]

Set NEW = AVAIL and AVAIL = LINK [AVAIL].

Step 3: Set INFO [NEW] = ITEM. [Copies new INFO into new node.]

Step 4: Set LINK [NEW] = START. [New node now points to original first node.]

Step 5: Set START = NEW. [Changes START so it points to the new node.]

Step 6: End.

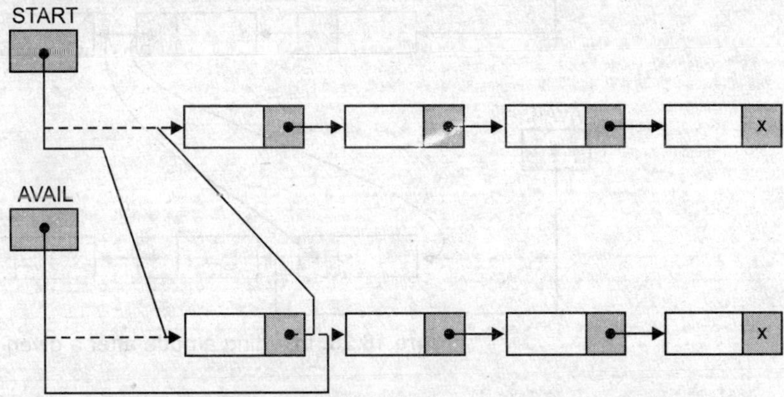

Figure 18.25: Insertion at the beginning of the Linked List.

B. *Inserting A Node After A Given Node*

The following algorithm which inserts ITEM into linked list so that ITEM follows Node N or, when LOC = NULL, so that ITEM is the first node.

Let the new node having location NEW. If LOC = NULL, then N is inserted as the first node described in previous algorithm. Otherwise, We insert the node after the given location by assigning

LINK [NEW] = LINK [LOC] and LINK [LOC] = NEW.

Algorithm 18.4: To insert new node after a given node into a linked list.

INSGVNNOD (INFO, LINK, START, AVAIL, LOC, ITEM)

This algorithm inserts ITEM so that ITEM follows the node with location LOC or insert ITEM at the first node when LOC = NULL.

Step 1: [OVERFLOW?] If AVAIL = NULL, then: Write: OVERFLOW, and End.

Step 2: [Remove first node from AVAIL list.]
  Set NEW = AVAIL and AVAIL = LINK [AVAIL].

Step 3: Set INFO [NEW] = ITEM. [Copies new INFO into new node.]

Step 4: If LOC = NULL, then [Insert as first node.]
    Set LINK [NEW] = START and START = NEW.
  Else: [Insert after node with location LOC.]
    Set LINK [NEW] = LINK [LOC] and LINK [LOC] = NEW.
  [End of if statement.]

Step 5: End.

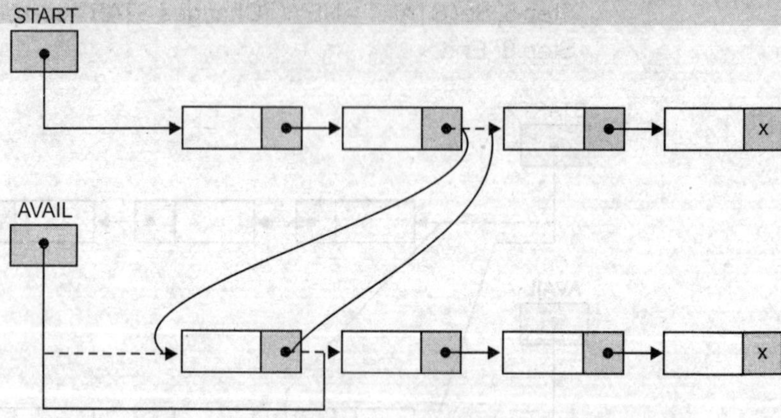

Figure 18.26: Inserting a node after a given node.

C. Insertion At The Last of the Linked List

Suppose the ITEM is to be inserted after the last node. First we have to reached at the last location and SAVE the last location then insert a new node at that point.

Algorithm 18.5: To find the location LOC of the last node in a sorted list.

FINDLOC (INFO, LINK, START, ITEM, LOC)

This algorithm finds the location LOC of the last node in a sorted list such that INFO [LOC] <ITEM, or sets LOC = NULL.

Step 1: [List empty?] If START = NULL, then: Set LOC = NULL, and Return.

Step 2: [Special case?] If ITEM < INFO [START], then: Set LOC = NULL, and Return.

Step 3: Set SAVE = START and P = LINK [START]. [Initializes pointers.]

Step 4: Repeat Steps 5 and 6 while P ≠ NULL.

Step 5: If ITEM < INFO [P], then

Set LOC = SAVE, and Return.

[End of If statement.]

Step 6: Set SAVE = P and P = LINK [P]. [Updates pointers.]

[End of Step 4 loop.]

Step 7: Set LOC = SAVE

Step 8: [Use Algorithm 18.4 to insert item after the last node with location LOC.]

Call INSGVNNOD (INFO, LINK, START, AVAIL, LOC, ITEM).

Step 9: End.

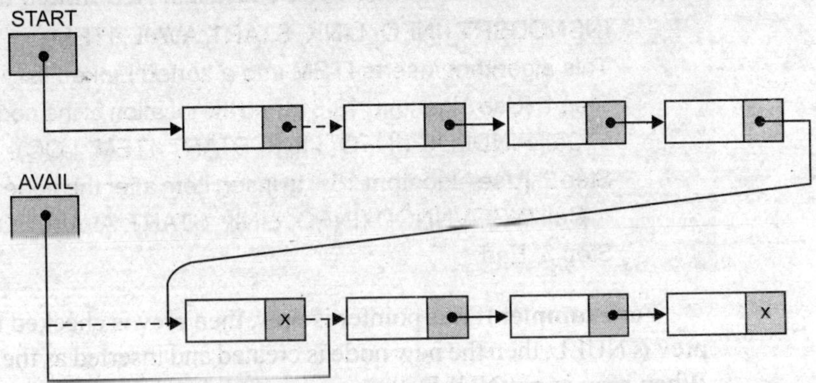

Figure 18.27: Insertion at the last Of The Linked List.

D. Inserting A New Node in A Sorted List

To insert a new node into an already sorted list, we compare the INFO value of the node to be inserted with the INFO values of the nodes in the list starting from the first node. This is continued until we get a pointer to the node that appears immediately before the node in the list whose INFO value is greater than the INFO value of the node to be inserted.

Suppose ITEM is to be inserted in a sorted linked list. Then ITEM must be inserted Between nodes X and Y.

$$INFO[X] < ITEM <= INFO[Y]$$

The given procedure first find the location LOC of node X , then insert the ITEM in between the node X and Y.

Traversing the list, using a pointer variable P and comparing ITEM with INFO [P] at each node. While traversing, keep track of the location of the proceeding node by using a pointer variable SAVE , as shown in figure 18.28. Thus SAVE and P are updated by assigning values:

SAVE = P and P = LINK [P].

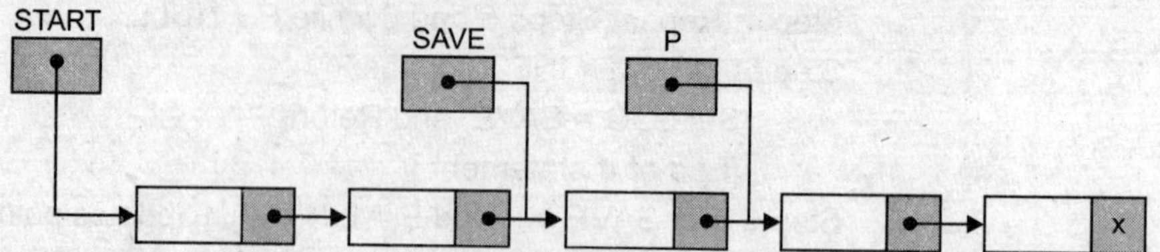

Figure 18.28: Save the proceeding node address and then P point towards next node.

The traversing continues as long as ITEM > INFO [P], or the traversing stopsITEM <= INFO [P]. Then P points to given node Y, so SAVE will contain the previous location X.

Algorithm 18.6: To insert new node into a sorted linked list.

INSNODSRT (INFO, LINK, START, AVAIL, ITEM)

This algorithm inserts ITEM into a sorted Linked list.

Step 1: [Use Algorithm 18.5 to find the location of the node preceding ITEM.]
  Call FINDLOC (INFO, LINK, START, ITEM, LOC).

Step 2: [Use Algorithm 18.4 to insert item after the node with location LOC.]
  Call INSGVNNOD (INFO, LINK, START, AVAIL, LOC, ITEM).

Step 3: End.

For example: If this pointer is prev, then prev is checked for a NULL value. If prev is NULL, then the new node is created and inserted as the first node in the list. When prev is not NULL, then a new node is created and inserted after the node pointed by prev, as shown in Figure 18.29.

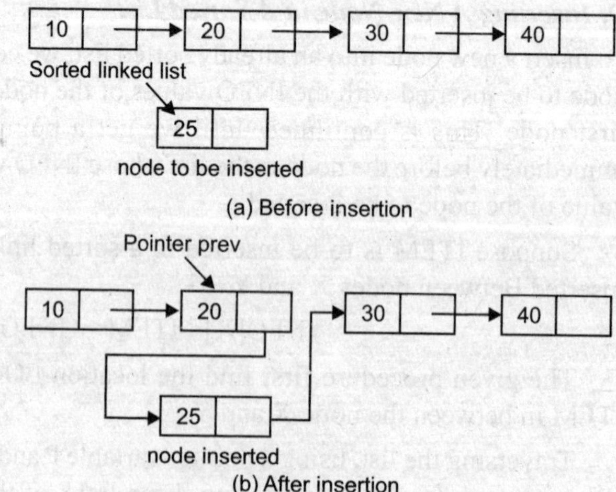

Figure 18.29: Insertion in a sorted list

Program 2: Write a C++ program to insert a node at the beginning or at the end of a linked list

```
#include <iostream.h>
# include <conio.h>
struct node
{
int info;                       // info field
node* link;                     //pointer to the link node
};
class link_list
{
private:
node* start;
public:
link_list ( )                   //constructor
{
start=NULL;                     //initially the list has no node
}
void create (int i)
{
node* new_node= new node; //create a new node;
new_node->info=i;
new_node->=start;    //make new node to point to the first node
start=new_node;      // make new node as the first node in the list
}
void display (int);        //function prototype
void beginning (int info)
{
node* new_node = new node;         //create a new node;
new_node->link=start;              //make new node to point to the first
node
start=new_node;
}
void end (int);               //function prototype
}; //end of class
//function definition display ( )
void link_list :: display (int delete_node)
{
node* move= start;
```

```
node* temp;
while (move)
{
cout<<move->info<<"->"; //display the info
temp=move;
move=move->link;             //move to link node
if (delete_node)
delete(temp);
}
cout<<"NULL";
}
//function definition end ( )
void link_list :: end (int info)
{
node* temp=start;
while (temp->link !=NULL)
temp=temp->link;
node* new_node= new node;                  // create a new node
new_node->info=info;
temp->link=new_node;
new_node->link=NULL;
}
void main ( )
{
int info, choice;
clrscr ( );
link_list link;
for (int i=5; i<=10; i++)
link.create (i);
cout<<"\n\nThe list before any operation is performed :\n\n";
link.display (0);
cout<<"\n\nRead the info field value of the node to be inserted: "'
cin>>info;
cout<<"\n\nRead the option (1, 2): ";
cout<<\n1. At the beginning";
cout<<"\n2. At the end\n";
cin>>choice;
switch (choice)
{
```

```
case 1: link.beginning (info);
break;
case 2: link.end (info);
break;
default: cout<<"Invalid choice readed\n";
}
cout<<"\n\nThe list after insertion is: \n\n;
link.display(1);
getch ( ); //freeze the screen
}
```

Output:

```
The list before any operation is performed:
10->9->8->7->6->5->NULL
Read the info field value of the node to be inserted: 12
Read the option (1, 2):
1. At the beginning
2. At the end
1
The list after insertion is:
12->10->9->8->7->6->5->NULL

The list before any operation is performed
10->9->8->7->6->5->NULL

Read the info field value of the node to be inserted: 4
Read the option (1,2):
1. At the beginning
2. At the end
2
The list after insertion is:
10->9->8->7->6->5->4->NULL
```

Program 3: Write a C++ program to insert a node at the desired position in a linked list

```
#include <iostream.h>
# include <conio.h>
# include<process.h>
struct node
{
int info;                    // info field
```

```
node* link;              //pointer to the link node
};
class link_list
{
private:
node* start;
public:
link_list ( )            //constructor
{
start=NULL;              //initially the list has no node
}
void create (int i)
{
node* new_node= new node; //create a new node;
new_node->info=i;
new_node->link=start;              //make new node to point to the first
node
start=new_node;                  // make net node as the first node in the list
}
void display (int);              //function prototype
void insert(int, int);           //function prototype
}; //end of class
//function definition display ( )
void link_list :: display (int delete_node)
{
node* move= start;
node* temp;
while (move)
{
cout<<move->info<<"->"; //display the info
temp=move;
move=move->link; //move to link node
if (delete_node)
delete(temp);
}
cout<<"NULL";
}
//function definition insert ( )
void link_list :: insert (int position, int info)
{
```

```
node* move=start;
int steps=1;
while (steps<position-1)
{
move=move->link;
steps++;
}
node* new_node= new node;        // create a new node;
new_node->info=info;
if (position= =1) //if node is to be inserted at the first place
{
new_node->link=start;
start=new_node;
}
else
{
new_node->link=move->link;
}
}
void main ( )
{
int value, info, choice, position, total=0;
clrscr( );
link_list link;
cout<<"Read the elements of the list terminated by negative number: \n";
cin>>value;
do
{
link.create(value);
total++; //increment with every node inserted
cin>>value;
}
while (value>=0);
cout<<"\n\nThe list before nay operation is performed (LIFO): \n\n;
link.display (0);
cout<<"\n\nTotal nodes: "<<total;
cout<<"\n\nRead the position where node is to be inserted: ";
cin>>position;
if(position<=0 || position >total+1) //check for valid position
```

```
{
cout<<\nWrong position inputted\n";
getch ( ); //freeze the screen
exit (1);
}
cout<<"\n\nRead the value of the node to be inserted: ";
cin>>info;
link.insert (position, info);
cout<<"\n\nThe list after insertion is: \n\n";
link.display(1);
getch ( );
}
```

Output:

```
Read the elements of the list terminated by negative number:
15    14    19    18    5    -99
The list before any operation is performed (LIFO):
5->18->19->14->15-> NULL
Total nodes: 5
Read the position where node is to be inserted: 3
Read the value of the node to be inserted: 17
The list after insertion is:
5->18->17->19->14->15-> NULL
```

Program 4: Write a C++ program to insert a node at the proper position in an arranged list

```
#include <iostream.h>
# include <conio.h>
struct node
{
int info;              // info field
node* link;            //pointer to the link node
};
class link_list
{
private:
node* start;
public:
link_list ( )          //constructor
{
start=NULL;            //initially the list has no node
```

```
}
void create (int i)
{
node* new_node= new node;        //create a new node;
new_node->info=i;
new_node->=start;        //make new node to point to the first node
start=new_node;          // make new node as the first node in the list
}
void reverse ( );        //function prototype
void display(int) ;      //function prototype
void insert (int);       //function prototype
};
void link_list :: reverse ( )
{
node* previous=start;
node* current=previous->link;
node* temp;
previous->link=NULL;
while(current !=NULL)
{
temp=current->link;
current->link=previous;
previous=current;
current=temp;
}
start=previous;
}
void link_list :: display (int delete_node)
{
node* move= start;
node* temp;
while (move)
{
cout<<move->info<<"->"; //display the info
temp=move;
move=move->link; //move to link node
if (delete_node)
delete (temp);
}
```

```
cout<<"NULL";
}
void link_list :: insert (int info)
{
node* move=start;
node* insert_after=move;
int is_first=0;
while (move->info<info && move != NULL)
{
is_first=1;
insert_after=move;
move=move->link;
}
node* new node= new node; //create a new node;
new_node->info=info;
if (is_first)
{
new_node->link=insert_after->link;
insert_after->link=new_node;
}
else
{
new_node->link=start;
start=new_node;
}
}
void main ( )
{
int value, info, choice;
clrscr ( );
link_list link;
cout<<"Read the elements of the list in ascending order terminated by"
<<"negative number: \n;
cin>>value;
do
{
link.create (value);
cin>>value;
}
```

```
while (value>=0);
cout<<"\n\nThe list before any operation is performed (LIFO) : \n\n;
link.display (0);
link.reverse ( );
cout<<"\n\nThe list after reversal is: \n\n";
link.display (0)l
cout<<"\n\nRead the value of the node to be inserted: ";
cin>>info;
link.insert (info);
cout<<"\n\nThe list after insertion is: \n\n";
link.display (1);
getch ( ); //freeze the screen
}
```

Output:

```
Read the elements of the list in ascending order terminated y negative number:
2    15    37    48    59    85    96    -99
The list before any operation is performed (LIFO):
86->75->49->38->27->15->2->NULL
The list after reversal is:
2->15->27->38->49->75->86->NULL
Read the value of the node to be inserted: 17

The list after insertion is:
2->15->17->27->38->49->75->86->NULL
```

18.7.1.4 Deletion from a Linked List

Deleting a node from a linked list is a lot harder than adding one; this is especially true in the case of a single linked list as is being used here. The problem is that the link from the *parent node* has to be set up to point to the *child node* of the node being deleted.

In other words, the link from the node before the node that is being deleted has to be changed to point to the same link as the one being deleted points to. The nodes don't hold information on their parent nodes, just child nodes, which is why it requires more work.

The diagram below shows the state of the list after the node in separate form in the Figure 18.30 is removed.

The process of deleting a node involves:

- Find the node to be deleted, remembering the previous node as the list is traversed through

- If the previous node is the start, set the start to be the child of the node being deleted
- otherwise set the link from the previous node to point to the same link as the node being deleted points to.
- Free up the memory for the deleted node.

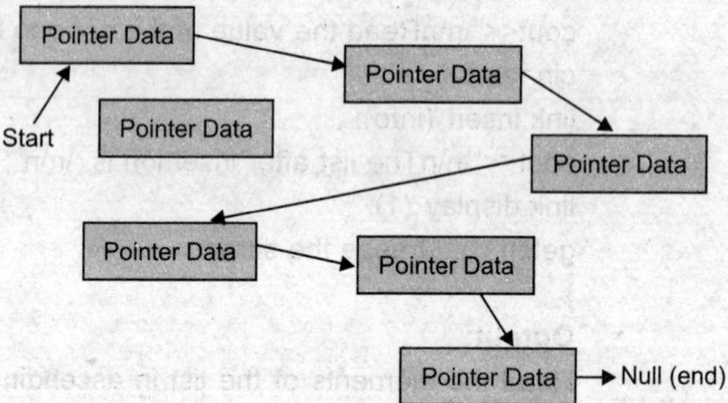

Figure 18.30: Deleting a Node from the Linked List.

All our deletions algorithms will return the memory space of the deleted node N to the beginning of the AVAIL list.Accordingly, all of our algorithms will include the following pair of assignments where LOC is the location of the deleted node N:

LINK [LOC] = AVAIL and AVAIL = LOC.

The operation is shown in Figure 18.31.

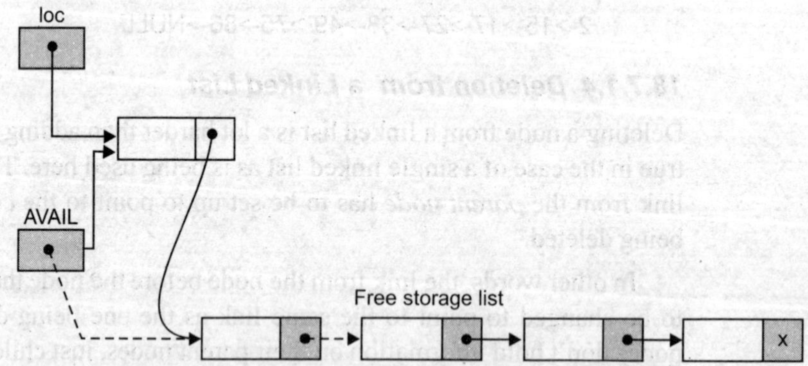

Figure 18.31: LINK [LOC] = AVAIL and AVAIL = LOC.

Garbage Collection

In many cases. we assumed that storage is allocated and freed one node at a time. There are two characteristics of nodes that make the above methods suitable. The first is that each node of a given type is of fixed size and the second is that the size clench node is fairly small. But in some cases a program might require a 'large amount of contiguous storage: which would be difficult to obtain uric block at a time, or a program may require storage blocks in a large variety of sizes. In such cases, memory management system must be able to process requests for variable length blocks. Thus processing certain types of data structures efficiently requires dynamic storage management capability.

Suppose some memory space becomes reusable because a node is deleted from a list or an entire list is deleted from a program then this space is available for future use. One way to bring this about is to immediately reinsert the space into free storage list, This is what we do when we implement linked lists through arrays. However, this method may be too time consuming for the operating system of a computer. Therefore, another method chosen by operating system of a computer is to periodically collect all the deleted space onto the free-storage list. The technique which does this collection is called garbage collection.

Under this method, nodes no longer in use remain allocated and undetected until all available storage has been allocated. A subsequent request for allocation cannot be satisfied until nodes that had been allocated but are no longer in use are recovered. When a request is made for additional nodes and there are none available a system routine called garbage collector is called. This routine searches through all the nodes in the system, identifies those that are no longer accessible from an external pointer and restores the inaccessible nodes to the available pool. The request for additional nodes is then fulfilled with some of the reclaimed nodes and the system continues processing the user request for more space. When available space is used up again, the garbage collector is called once again.

Garbage collection is usually done in two phases

The first phase called the marking phase involves marking of all nodes that are accessible from the external pointer.

The second phase called the collection phase which 'involves proceeding sequentially through memory and freeing all nodes that have not been marked.

Therefore, it can be said that first, the computer ruins through all lists, tagging those cells that are currently in use and then the computer runs through the mentor), collecting all untagged space on to the free-storage list. The garbage collection may take place when there is only some minimum amount of space left in the free storage list and when the CPU is idle and has time to do the collection.

Garbage collection is not an all-or-nothing proposition. It is possible to explicitly deallocate some common kinds of objects, and thus correspondingly decrease the frequency of garbage collections and garbage collection cost. It is possible to accommodate libraries that expect explicit deallocation calls. It is also possible to use the collector only as a debugging tool to locate leaks and remove it completely from the end product.

But for the sake of clarity, we'll look at the tradeoffs between exclusive use of explicit memory management (malloc/free or new/delete) and exclusive use of garbage collecting allocation.

A. Delete the Beginning Node from A Linked List

Suppose we are given location LOC of a node N in list. Furthermore, suppose we are given The location LOCP of the node Preceeding N or, when N is the first node, we are given LOCP = NULL.

Algorithm 18.7: To delete the node following a given node.

DELBEGNOD (INFO, LINK, START, AVAIL, LOC, LOCP)

This algorithm deletes the node N with location LOC. LOCP is the location of the node which precedes N or, when N is the first node, LOCP = NULL.

Step 1: If LOCP = NULL, then:

Set START = LINK [START]. [Deletes first node.]

Else:

Set LINK [LOCP] = LINK [LOC]. [Deletes node N.]

[End of If statement.]

Step 2: [Return deleted node to the AVAIL list.]

Set LINK [LOC] = AVAIL and AVAIL = LOC.

Step 3: End.

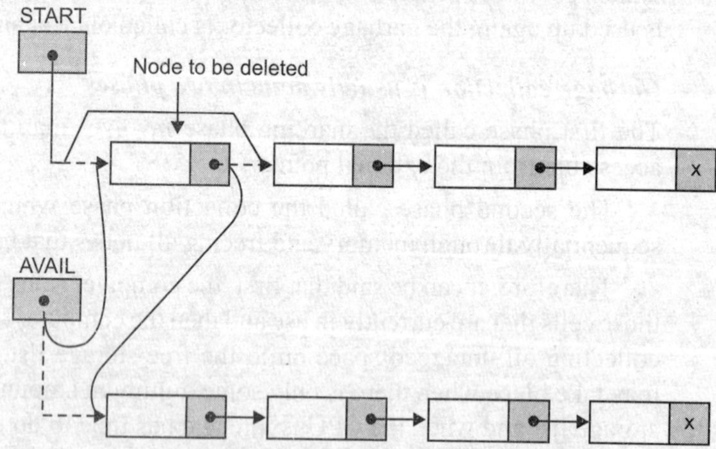

Figure 18.32: Delete the beginning node from a Linked List.

Set START = LINK [START].

This statement is used to delete the begining node from a list.

B. Deleting the Node with Given Item of Information

Algorithm 18.8: To find the location LOC of the node to be deleted.

FINDLOC (INFO, LINK, START, ITEM, LOC, LOCP)

This algorithm finds the location LOC of the first node N which contains ITEM and the location LOCP of the node preceding N. If ITEM does not appear in the list, then the procedure sets LOC = NULL; and if ITEM appears in the first node, then it sets LOCP = NULL.

Step 1: [List empty?] If START = NULL, then
        Set LOC = NULL and LOCP = NULL, and return.
    [End of If statement.]

Step 2: [ITEM in first node?] If INFO [START] = ITEM, then:
        Set LOC = START and LOCP = NULL, and Return.
    [End of If statement.]

Step 3: Set SAVE = START and P = LINK [START]. [Initializes pointers.]

Step 4: Repeat Steps 5 and 6 while P ≠ NULL.

Step 5: If INFO [P] = ITEM, then:
            Set LOC = P and LOCP = SAVE, and Return.
        [End of If statement.]

Step 6: Set SAVE = P and P = LINK [P]. [Updates pointers.]
    [End of Step 4 loop.]

Step 7: Set LOC = NULL. [Search unsuccessful.]

Step 8: Return.

Figure 18.33 is the schematic diagram of the assignment

Set LINK [LOCP] = LINK [LOC].

Which effectively deletes the node N when N is not the first node.

The simplicity of the algorithm comes from the fact that we are already given the location LOCP of the node which precedes node N.In many applications, we must first find LOCP.

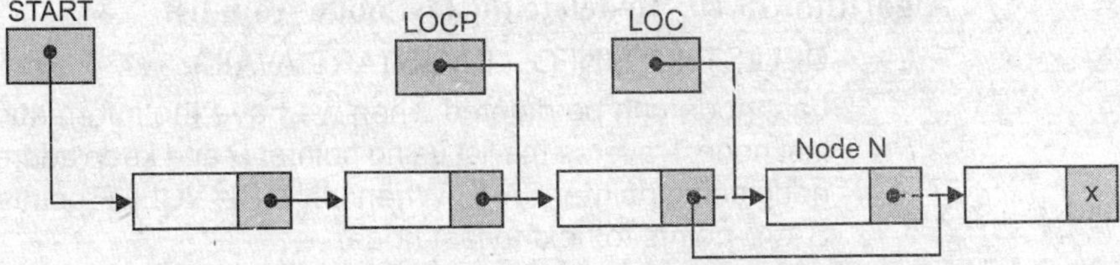

Figure 18.33: LINK [LOCP] = LINK [LOC]. [Deletes node N.]

This statement is used to delete the node N when N is not the first node.

Algorithm 18.9: To delete the node with a given item of information.

DELGVNNOD(INFO, LINK, START, AVAIL, ITEM)

This algorithm deletes from a Linked list the first node N which contains the given ITEM of information.

Step 1: [Use algorithm 10 to find the location of N and its preceding node.]
  Call FINDLOC(INFO, LINK, START, ITEM, LOC, LOCP)

Step 2: If LOC = NULL, then: Write: ITEM no in list, and End.

Step 3: [Delete node.]
  If LOCP = NULL, then
    Set LINK[LOCP] = LINK[LOC].
  [End of If statement.]

Step 4: [Return deleted node to the AVAIL list.]
  Set LINK[LOC] = AVAIL and AVAIL = LOC

Step 5: End.

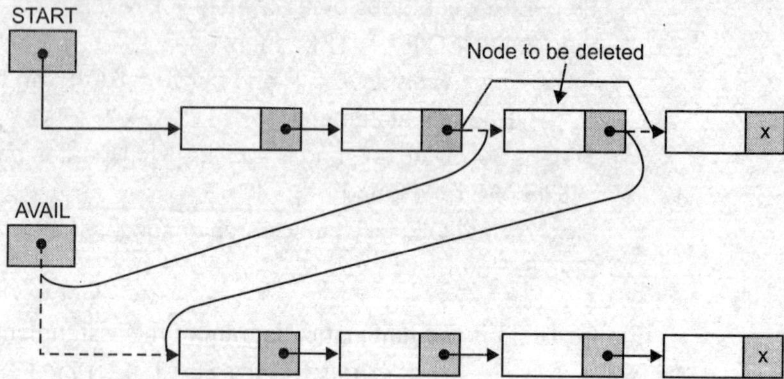

Figure 18.34: Deleting the node with given item of information.

C. Deleting the Last Node from List

In this operation, we have to delete the last node of the single linked list.

Algorithm 18.10: To delete the last node from list

DELLSTNOD(INFO, LINK, START, AVAIL)

Last node can be deleted when we have the information about next-to-last node.Traverse the list using pointer P and keep address of preceeding node using pointer SAVE.When LINK[P]=NULL P points to last node and SAVE points to next to last node.

Step 1: [List is empty?] If START = NULL, then Write: UNDERFLOW, and End.

Step 2: [List can contains only one element?]

If LINK[START] = NULL, then:

a. Set START = NULL. [Removes only node from list.]

b. Set LINK[START] = AVAIL and AVAIL = START. [Returns node to AVAIL list.]

c. End.

[End of If structure]

Step 3: Set P = LINK[START] and SAVE = START. [Initialize pointers P.]

Step 4: Repeat Steps while LINK[P] ≠ NULL. [Traverses list, go for last node.]

Set SAVE = P and P = LINK[P]. [Updates SAVE and P.]

[End of If statement.]

Step 5: Set LINK[SAVE] = LINK[P]. [Removes last node From LIST.]

Step 6: Set LINK[P] = AVAIL and AVAIL = P. [Returns node to AVAIL list.]

Step 7: End.

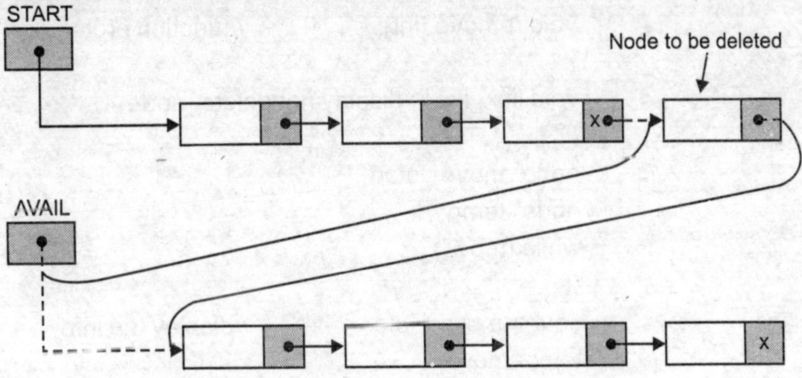

Figure 18.35: Deleting the last node from linked list.

Program 5: Write a C++ program to delete a node from a linked list

```
# include<iostream.h>
# include<conio.h>
# include<process.h> //for exit ( ) function
struct node
{
int info;                    //info field
node* link;                  //pointer to the link node
};
class link_list
{
private:
```

```
node* start;
public:
link_list ( )               //constructor
{
start=NULL;                 //initially the list has no node
}
void create (int i)
{
node* new_node= new node; //create a new node;
new_node->info=i;
new_node->link=start;             //make new node to point to the first
node
start=new_node;             // make new node as the first node in the list
}
void display ( );           //function prototype
void remove (int);          //function prototype
};
void link_list : : display (int delete_node)
{
node* move= start;
node* temp;
while (move)
{
cout<<move->info<<"->";     //display the info
temp=move;
move=move->link;            //move to link node
if (delete_node)
delete (temp);
}
cout<<"NULL";
}
void link_list : : remove (int position)
{
node* move=start;
int steps=1;
while (steps<position-1)
{
move=move->link;
steps++;
}
```

```
if (position= =1)                    // if to be inserted at the first place
{
node* temp= start;
start=start->link;
delete (temp);
}
else
{
node* temp= move->link;
move->link=move->link->link;
delete (temp);
}
}
void main ( )
{
int value, info, choice, number, total=0;
clrscr ( );
link_list link;
cout<<"Read the elements of the list terminated by negative number: \n;
cin>>value;
do
{
link.create(value);
total++; //increment with every node inserted
cin>>value;
} while (value>=0);
cout<<"\n\nThe list before any operation is performed (LIFO): \n\n";
link.display (0);
cout<<"\n\nTotal nodes: "<<total;
cout<<"\n\nRead the number of the node to be deleted: ";
cin>>number;
if(number<=0 | | number >total) //check for valid position
{
cout<<"\nWrong number inputted";
getch( ); //freeze the screen
exit (1);
}
total --;
link.remove (number);
cout<<"\n\nThe list after deletion is: \n\n";
```

```
link.display (1);
cout<<"\n\nTotal nodes: "<<total;
getch( );
}
```

Output:

Read the elements of the list terminated by negative number:
12 16 17 19 18 10 14 15 -99
The list before any operation is performed (LIFO):
15->14->10->18->19->17->16->12->NULL
Total nodes: 8
Read the number of the node to be deleted: 5
The list after deletion is:
15->14->10->18->17->16->12->NULL
Total nodes: 7

18.7.1.5 Concatenating Two Lists

Concatenating means to join or combine two different nodes into single node. Note that both the list should be ordered.

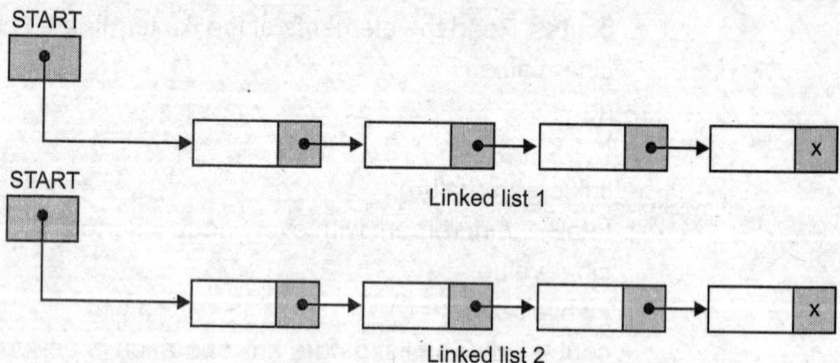

Figure 18.36: Two linked list

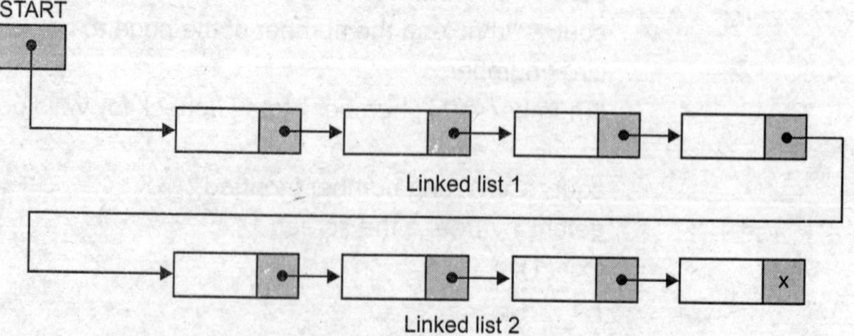

Figure 18.37: Concatenating two linked lists (linked list1 and linked list2)

Algorithm 18.11: To concatenate the two lists

This algorithm is used to concatenate two linked list into one.

CONCAT(START,LINK)

Step 1: Set P = START 1

Step 2: Repeat Step (3) while LINK [P] ≠ NULL

Step 3: P= LINK [P]

Step 4: Set LINK [P] = START 2

Step 5: End

Program 6: Write a C++ program to concatenate two linked lists

```
# include<iostream.h>
# include<conio.h>
# include<process.h>
struct node
{
int info;                    //info field
node* link;                  //pointer to the link node
};
class link_list
{
private:
node* start;
public:
link_list ( )                //constructor
{
start=NULL;                  //initially the list has no node
}
void create (int);                      //function prototype
void display (int);                     //function prototype
void concatenate (link_list);  //function prototype
};
void link_list : : create ( )
{
int value;
cin>>value;
do
{
node* new_node= new node;                        //create a new node;
new_node->info=value;
```

```
new_node->link=start;          //make new node to point to the first node
start=new_node;                //make new node as the first node in the list
cin>>value;
}
while (value>=0);
}
void link_list : : display (int delete_node)
{
node* move= start;
node* temp;
while (move)
{
cout<<move->info<<"->";                //display the info
temp=move;
move=move->link;                       //move to link node
if (delete_node)
delete (temp);
}
cout<<"NULL";
}
void link_list : : concatenate (link_list 11)
{
node* move=start;
while (move->link !=NULL)
move=move->link;
move->link=11.start;
}
void main ( )
{
clrscr ( );
link_list link1, link2;
cout<<"Read the elements of the first list terminated by"
<<"negative number: \n";
link1.create ( );
cout<<"Read the elements of the second list terminated by"
<<"negative number:\n;
link2.create ( );
cout<<"\n\nThe two lists before concatenation are: \n\n;
link1.display (0);
```

```
cout<<"\n\n";
link2.display (0);
link1.concatenate (1ink2);
cout<<"\n\nThe final list after concatenation is: \n\n;
link1.display (1);
getch ( );
}
```

Output:

Read the elements of the first terminated by negative number:

10 20 30 40 50 60 -99

Read the elements of the second list terminated by negative number:

15 25 35 45 55 65 -77

The two lists before concatenation are:

60->50->40->30->20->10->NULL

65->55->45->35->25->15->NULL

The final list after concatenation is:

60->50->40->30->20->10->65->55->45->35->25->15->NULL

18.7.1.6 Searching A Node in A Linked List

Searching a node in a Linked List is the same as finding the node before which or after another node is inserted. A pointer is defined and equated to pointer first. The pointer goes through the entire list. If the item is found, it displays the item found and name of the item on the screen otherwise it displays not found.

Algorithm 18.12: To search element from unsorted linked list

UNSORTSEARCH (INFO, LINK, START, ITEM, LOC)

LIST is a Linked list in memory. This algorithm find the location LOC of the node where ITEM first appears in LIST, or if item not exists in LIST set LOC = NULL.

Step 1: Set P = START. [Initializes pointer P.]

Step 2: Repeat Step 3 while P ≠ NULL.

Step 3:If ITEM = INFO [P], then;

Set LOC = P, and End.

Else:

Set P = LINK[P]. [P now points to the next node.]

[End of If statement.]

[End of Step 2 loop.]

Step 4: [If search is unsuccessful.] Set LOC = NULL

Step 5: End.

Algorithm 18.13: To search element from sorted linked list.

SORTSEARCH (INFO, LINK, START, ITEM, LOC)

LIST is a sorted list in memory. This algorithm find the location LOC of the node where ITEM first appears in LIST, or if item not exists in LIST set LOC = NULL.

Step 1: Set P = START. [Initializes pointer P.]

Step 2: Repeat Step 3 while P ≠ NULL.

Step 3: If ITEM > INFO[P], then

Set P = LINK[P]. [P now points to next node.]

Else if ITEM = INFO[P], then:

Set LOC = P, and End. [Search is successful.]

Else:

Set LOC = NULL, and End. [ITEM now exceeds INFO[P].]

[End of If statement.]

[End of Step 2 loop.]

Step 4: Set LOC = NULL.

Step 5: End.

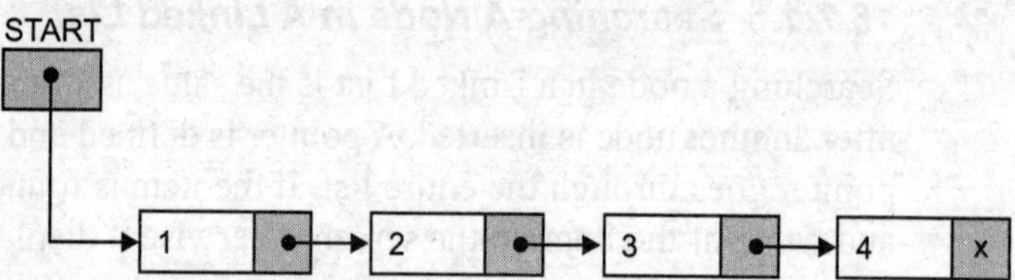

Figure 18.38: P = LINK[P] is used to search the given ITEM.

18.7.1.7 Reversing the Direction of Linked List

Reverse means to set the last node as first and first node as last and so on procedure continue.

Algorithm 18.14: To reverse the direction of linked list.

REVERSE(START, LINK, LOC)

This algorithm is used to reverse the given list.

Step 1: P = LINK [START]

Step 2: LINK [START] = NULL

Step 3: Repeat steps (4) & (5) while P ≠ NULL

Step 4: LOC= P, P = LINK [P]

Step 5: LINK [LOC] = START, START = LOC

Step 6: End

To reverse a list, we maintain a pointer each to the previous and the next node, then we make the link field of the current node point to the previous, make the previous equal to the current, and the current equal to the next, shown here.

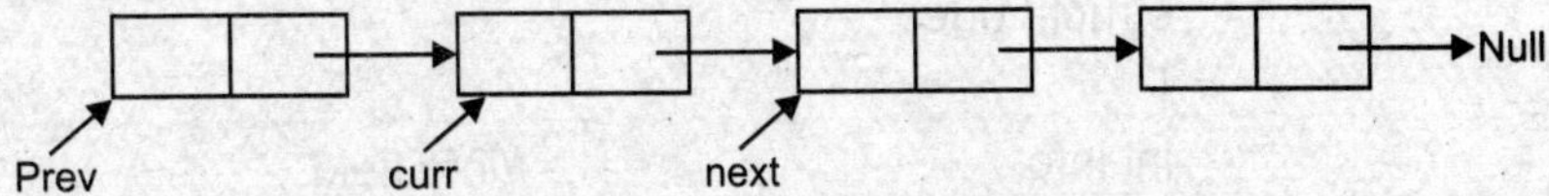

Figure 18.39: A linked list showing the previous, current, and next nodes at some point during reversal process.

Therefore, the code needed to reverse the list is

```
Prev = NULL;
while (curr !=NULL)
{
link =curr-> link;
curr-> link =prev;
prev=curr;
curr= link;
}
```

The working of a reverse function is shown here:

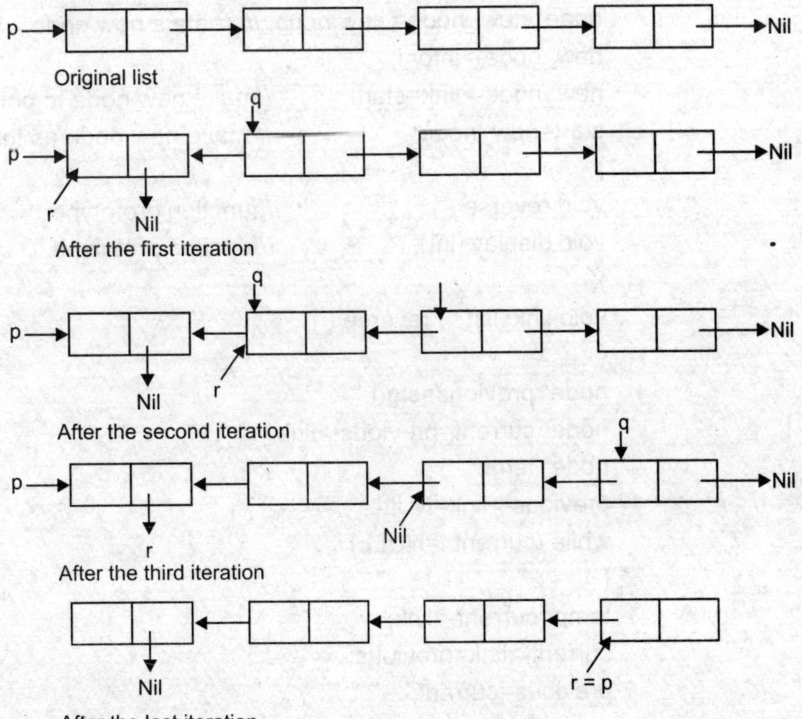

Figure 18.40: Reversal of a list.

Program 7: Write a C++ program to reverse a linked list

```
# include<iostream.h>
# include<conio.h>
struct node
{
int info;                          //info field
node* link;            //pointer to the link node
};
class link_list
{
private:
node* start;
public:
link_list ( )            //constructor
{
start=NULL;              //initially the list has no node
}
void create (int i)
{
node* new_node= new node; //create a new node;
new_node->info=i;
new_node->link=start;          //make new node to point to the first node
start=new_node;                // make new node as the first node in the list
}
void reverse ( );                //function prototype
void display (int);              //function prototype
};
void link_list : : reverse ( )
{
node* previous=start;
node* current=previous->link;
node* temp;
previous->link=NULL;
while (current !=NULL)
{
temp=current->link;
current->link=previous;
previous=current;
current=temp;
```

```
}
start=previous;
}
void link_list : : display (int delete_node)
{
node* move= start;
node* temp;
while (move)
{
cout<<move->info<<"->";     //display the info
temp=move;
move=move->link;            //move to link node
if (delete_node)
delete (temp);
}
cout<<"NULL";
}
void main ( )
{
int value, info, choice;
clrscr ( );
link_list link;
cout<<"Read the elements of the list terminated by negative number . \n";
cin>>value;
do
{
link.create (value);
cin>>value;
}
while (value>=0);
cout<<"\n\nThe list before any operation is performed (LIFO) : \n\n";
link.display (0);
link.reverse ( );
cout<<"\n\nThe list after reversal is: \n\n";
link.display (1);
getch ( ); //freeze the screen
}
```

Output:

Read the elements of the list terminated by negative number:

1 2 3 4 5 6 7 -99

The list before any operation is performed (LIFO):
7->6->5->4->3->2->1->NULL
The list after reversal is:
1->2->3->4->5->->6->7->NULL

18.7.1.8 Copying List1 into List2

Algorithm 18.15: To copy LIST1 list into LIST2 list

COPY(INFO, LINK, LIST1, LIST2, AVAIL)

This algorithm makes a copy of a list LIST1 using LIST2 as the list pointer variable of the new list.

Step 1: Set LIST2 = NULL.[Empty list.]

Step 2: [LIST1 is empty?] If LIST1 = NULL, then End.

Step 3: [Insert first node of LIST1 into LIST2.]
Call INSGVNLOC (INFO, LINK, LIST2, AVAIL, NULL, INFO [LIST1])
or:

(a) If AVAIL = NULL, then Write: OVERFLOW, and End.
(b) Set NEW = AVAIL and AVAIL = LINK[AVAIL]. [Removes first node from AVAIL list.]
(c) Set INFO [NEW] = INFO [LIST1]. [Copies INFO LIST1 into new node LIST2.]
[Insert new node as first node in LIST2.]
(d) Set LINK [NEW] = LIST2 and LIST2 = NEW.

Step 4: [Initializes pointers P and LOC.]
Set P = LINK [LIST1] and LOC = LIST2.

Step 5: Repeat Steps 6 and 7 while P ≠ NULL

Step 6: Call INSGVNLOC (INFO, LINK, LIST2, AVAIL, LOC, INFO [P]) or

(a) If AVAIL = NULL, then Write: OVERFLOW, and End.
(b) Set NEW = AVAIL and AVAIL = LINK [AVAIL].
(c) Set INFO [NEW] = INFO [P]. [Copies INFO into new node.]
(d) [Insert new node into LIST2 after the node with location LOC.]
Set LINK [NEW] = LINK [LOC], and LINK [LOC] = NEW.

Step 7:Set P = LINK [P] and LOC = LINK [LOC]. [Updates pointers P and LOC.]
[End of Step 5 loop.]

Step 8: End.

Check out this C++ program which creates an exact copy of a linked list:

```
copy_linked_lists(struct node *q, struct node **s)
{
if(q!=NULL)
```

```
{
*s=malloc(sizeof(struct node));
(*s)->data=q->data;
(*s)->link=NULL;
copy_linked_list(q->link, &((*s)->link));
}}
```

18.7.1.9 Merging of Two Sorted Lists

Merging of two sorted lists involves traversing the given lists and comparing the INFO values stored in the nodes in the process of traversing.

If p and q are the pointers to the sorted lists to be merged, then we compare the INFO value stored in the first node of the list pointed to by p with the INFO value stored in the first node of the list pointed to by q. And, if the INFO value in the first node of the list pointed to by p is less than the INFO value in the first node of the list pointed to by q, make the first node of the resultant/merged list to be the first node of the list pointed to by p, and advance the pointer p to make it point to the next node in the same list.

If the INFO value in the first node of the list pointed to by p is greater than the INFO value in the first node of the list pointed to by q, make the first node of the resultant/merged list to be the first node of the list pointed to by q, and advance the pointer q to make it point to the next node in the same list.

Repeat this procedure until either p or q becomes NULL. When one of the two lists becomes empty, append the remaining nodes in the non-empty list to the resultant list.

If the following lists are given as input, then what would be the output of the program after each pass? This is shown here:

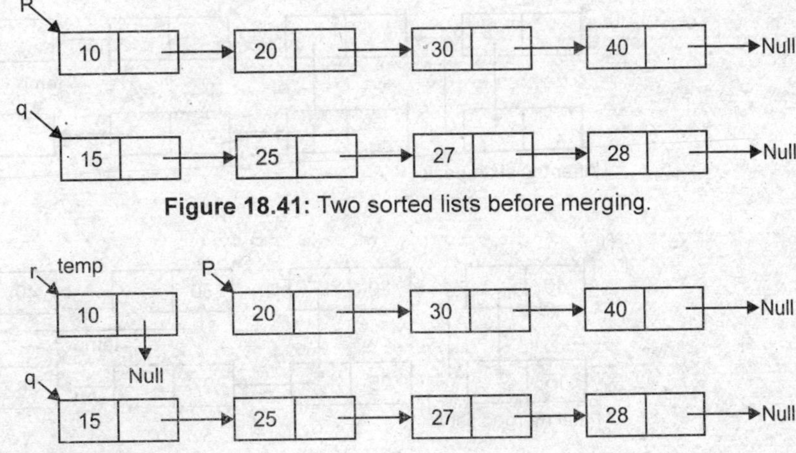

Figure 18.41: Two sorted lists before merging.

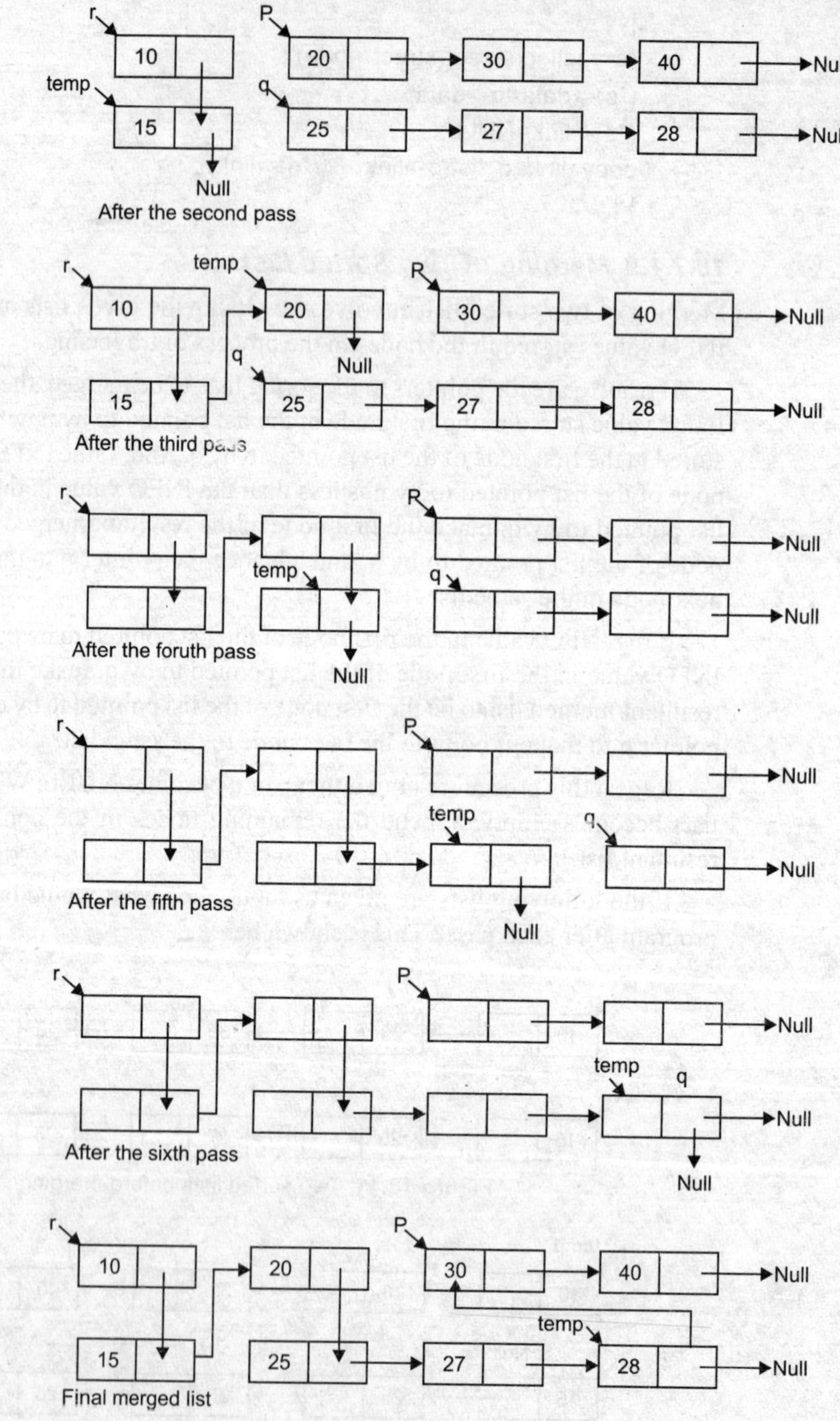

Figure 18.42: Final merged list.

Program 8: Write a C++ program to merge two linked lists by concatenating them first.

```
# include<iostream.h>
# include<conio.h>
struct node
{
int info;                     //info field
node* link;                   //pointer to the link node
};
class link_list
{
private:
node* start;
public:
link_list ( )                 //constructor
{
start=NULL;                   //initially the list has no node
}
void add_info ( );                   //function prototype
void display (int);                  //function prototype
void concatenate (link_list);  //function prototype
void sort ( );                       //function prototype
};
void link_list : : add_info ( )
{
int value;
cin>>value;
while (value>0)
{
node* new_link= new node;  //create a new node;
new_link->info=value;
new_link->link=start;            //make new node to point to the first node
start=new_node;                  //make new node as the first node in the list
cin>.value;
}
}
while (value>=0);
}
void link_list : : display (int delete_node)
```

```
{
node* move= start;
node* temp;
while (move)
{
cout<<move->info<<"->"; //display the info
temp=move;
move=move->link; //move to link node
if (delete_node)
delete (temp);
}
cout<<"NULL";
}
void link_list : : concatenate (link_list 11)
{
node* move=start;
while (move->link !=NULL)
move=move->link;
move->link=11.start;
}
void link_list : : sort ( )
{
node* top=start;
while (top->link != NULL)
{
int min=top->info;
node* move=top->link;
node* min_node;
while (move != NULL)
{
if (move->info <min)
{
min=move->info;
min_node=move;
}
move=move->link;
}
if (min != top->info)
{
```

```
int temp=top->info;
top->info =min;
min_node->info=temp;
}
top=top->link;
}
}
void main ( )
{
clrscr ( );
link_list link1, link2;
cout<<"Read the info of the first list terminated by negative number: \n";
link1.add_info ( );
cout<<"Read the info of the second list terminated by negative number:
\n";
link2.add_info ( );
cout<<"\nInputted linked lists before sorting are: \n\n";
link1.display (0);
cout<<end1<<end1;
link2.display (0);
link1.concatenate(link2);
link1.sort ( );
cout<<"\n\nMerged linked list is: \n\n";
link1.display (1);
getch ( );
}
```

Output:

```
Read the info of the first link list terminated by negative number.
12    42    32    22    72    -99
Read the info of the second link list terminated by negative number:
26    36    16    56    46    -66
Inputted link lists before sorting are:
72->22->32->42->12->NULL
46->56->16->36->26-> NULL
Merged linked list is:
12->16->22->26->32->36->42->46->56->72->NULL
```

18.7.1.10 Erasing A Linked List

Erasing a linked list involves traversing the list starting from the first node, freeing the storage allocated to the nodes, and then setting the pointer to the list to NULL.

If p is a pointer to the start of the list, the actions specified through the following code will erase the list:

```
while(p != NULL)
{
temp = p;
p = p->link;
free(t);
}
```

But a better strategy of erasing a list is to mark all the nodes of the list to be erased as free nodes without actually freeing the storage of these nodes. That means to maintain this list, a list of free nodes, so that if a new node is required it can be obtained from this list of free nodes.

The method of erasing a list requires adding all the nodes of the list to be erased to the list of free nodes, as shown here.

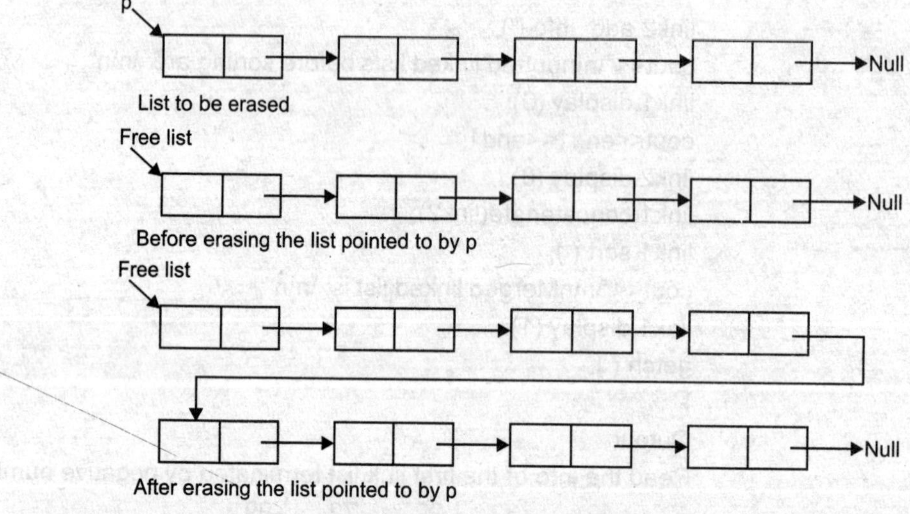

Figure 18.43: Final List After Erasing

18.7.1.11 Splitting A List

Once we build a linked list ,it can split int many sub-lists. The technique to splitting alist is very simple.

Consider a circular list containing 2n nodes, as shown in Figure 18.44.

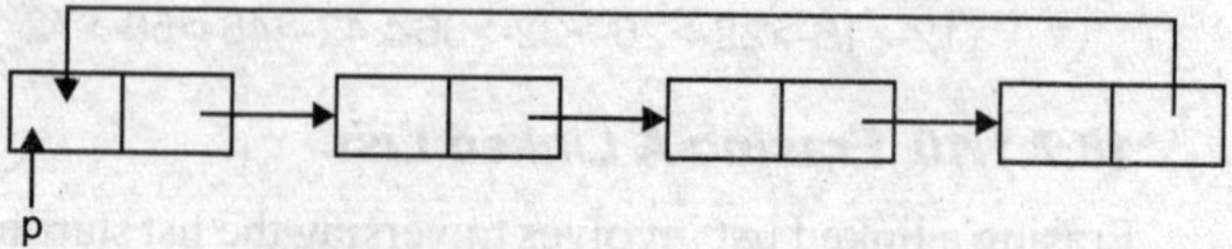

Figure 18.44: List containing 2n nodes

To split this list into two equal lists, it is required to traverse the list up to the nth node and store the link of the nth node, which is the address of $(n+1)^{th}$ node in the pointer, say q. After this, make the link field of the nth node point to the first node pointed to by p. Then traverse the list starting from the node pointed to by q up to the end. Then make the link field of the last node point to the node pointed to by q. The result of this is shown in Figure 18.45.

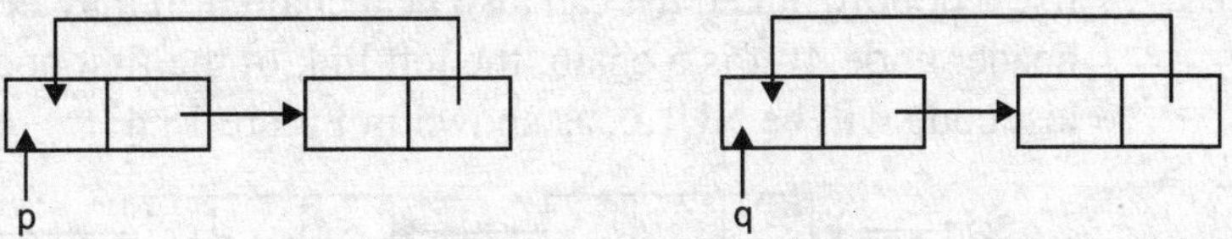

Figure 18.45: Splitting of a circular list

18.8 DOUBLY LINKED LIST

In a doubly linked list, also called a **two-way list**, each node is divided into three parts:

1. The first part, called the previous pointer field, contains the address of the preceding element in the list.
2. The second part contains the information of the list.
3. The third part, called the next pointer field, contains the address of the succeeding element in the list.

In addition, two pointer variables, named head and tail, are used that contain the address of first element and the address of last element of the list.

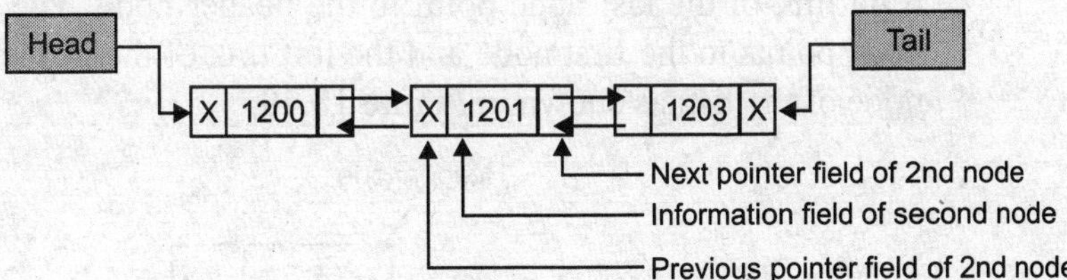

Figure 18.46: Two-way list.

The following are problems with singly linked lists:

1. A singly linked list allows traversal of the list in only one direction.
2. Deleting a node from a list requires keeping track of the previous node, that is, the node whose link points to the node to be deleted.
3. If the link in any node gets corrupted, the remaining nodes of the list become unusable.

These problems of singly linked lists can be overcome by adding one more link to each node, which points to the previous node. When such a link is added to every node of a list, the corresponding linked list is called a doubly linked list. Therefore, a doubly linked list is a linked list in which every node contains two links, called left link and right link, respectively. The left link of the node points to the previous node, whereas the right points to the next node. Like a singly linked list, a doubly linked list can also be a chain or it may be circular with or without a header node. If it is a chain, the left link of the first node and the right link of the last node will be NULL, as shown in Figure 18.47.

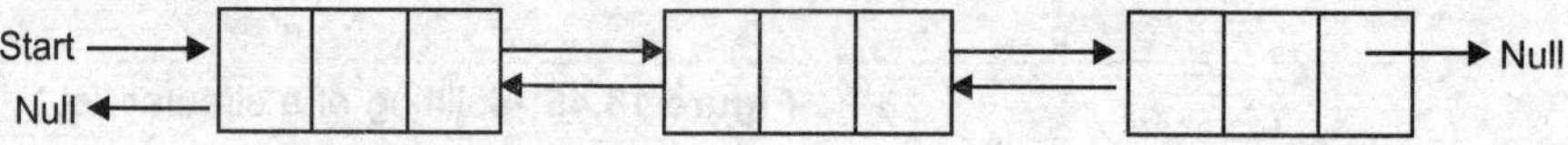

Figure 18.47: A doubly linked list maintained as chain

If it is a circular list without a header node, the right link of the last node points to the first node. The left link of the first node points to the last node, as shown in Figure 18.48.

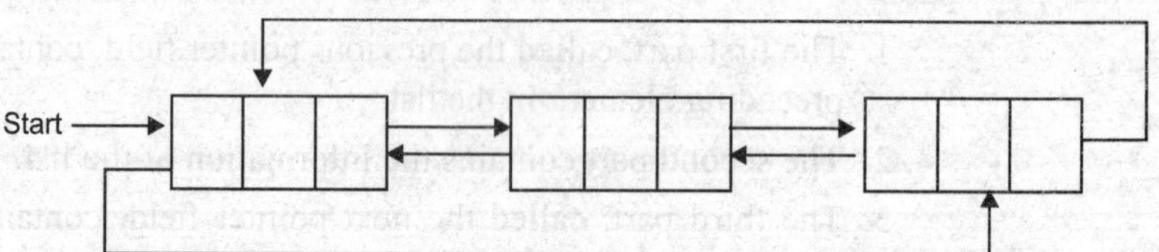

Figure 18.48: A doubly linked list maintained as a circular list

If it is a circular list with a header node, the left link of the first node and the right link of the last node point to the header node. The right link of the header node points to the first node and the left link of the header node points to the last node of the list, as shown in Figure 18.49.

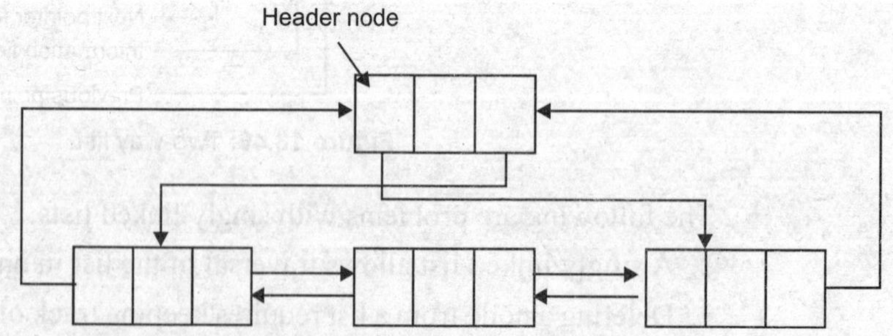

Figure 18.49: A doubly linked list maintained as a circular list with a header node

Therefore, the following representation is required to be used for the nodes of a doubly linked list.

```
struct dbnode
{
int INFO;
struct dnode *left,*right;
};
```

Recall that, given (only) a pointer to a node *n* in a linked list with N nodes, removing node *n* takes time O(N) in the worst case, because it is necessary to traverse the list looking for the node just before *n*. One way to fix this problem is to require **two** pointers: a pointer the node to be removed, and also a pointer to the node just before that one.

Another way to fix the problem is to use a **doubly linked** list. Here's the conceptual picture:

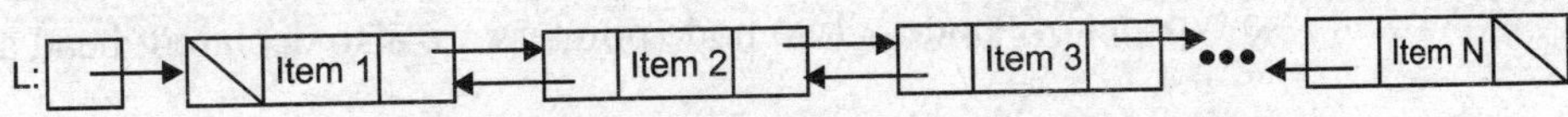

Figure 18.50: Representation of doubly linked list.

Each node in a doubly linked list contains **three** fields: the INFO, and two pointers. One pointer points to the previous node in the list, and the other pointer points to the next node in the list. The previous pointer of the first node, and the next pointer of the last node are both null.

To remove a given node *n* from a doubly linked list, we need to change the ***prev*** field of the node to its right, and we need to change the ***next*** field of the node to its left, as illustrated below.

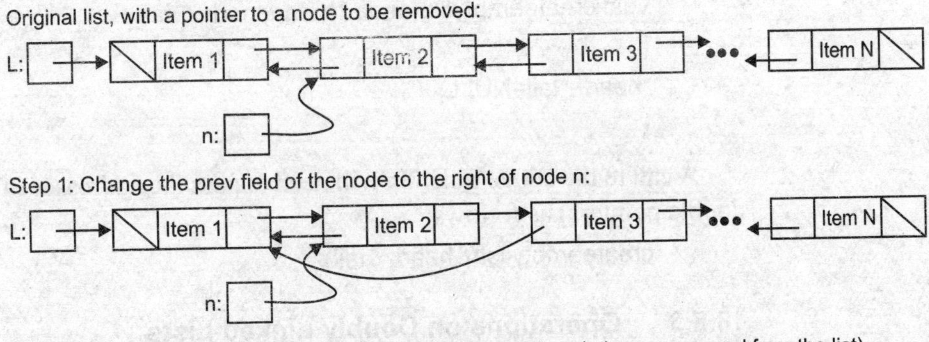

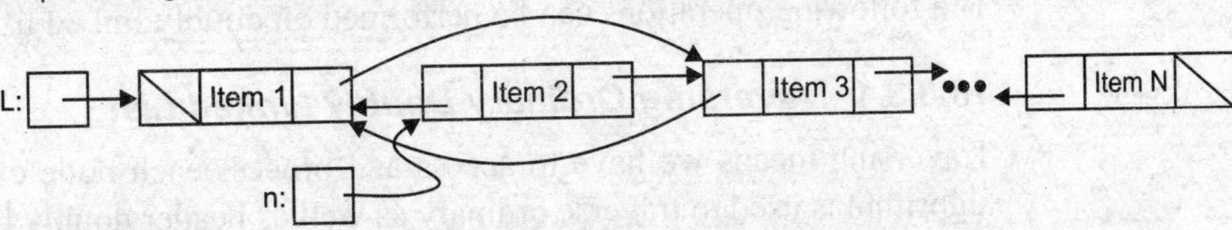

Figure 18.51: Conceptual diagram for removing node from doubly linked list.

18.8.1 Implementation of A Doubly Linked List

Suppose we want to store list of integers. Then, we define the following self-referential structure:

```
typedef struct nodetype
{
struct nodetype *prev;
int info;
struct nodetype *next;
}node;
node *head,*tail;
```

The above declaration defines a new INFO type called "struct nodetype" with a typedef of "node". Two node pointers are also declared: head and tail.

18.8.2 Creating an Empty List

- In the previous declaration, the variables head and tail are each declared as a pointer to a "node".
- These variables are not yet initialized.
- "head" is used to point to the first element of the list and "tail" is used to point to the last element of the list.
- Since the list will be empty in the beginning, the variables head and tail should be assigned a sentinel value to indicate the list is empty.

```
void createemptylist(node **head, node **tail)
{
*head=*tail=NULL;
}
```

A call to the above function will need to pass the addresses of head and tail (as double pointers) as follows:

```
createemptylist(&head, &tail);
```

18.8.3 Operations on Doubly Linked Lists

The following operations can be performed on doubly linked lists:

18.8.3.1 Traversing Ordinary Doubly Linked List

Traversing means we have to access and process each node exactly once. This algorithm is used to traverse ordinary as well as header doubly list.

Algorithm 18.16: To traverse the ordinary doubly linked list.

TRAVERSEDL(INFO, LINK, START, P)

Suppose we want to traverse LIST in order to process each element exactly once. If LIST is an ordinary doubly linked list Then use Algorithm 18.1:TRAVERSE(INFO, LINK, START, P).

Or

If LIST contains a header node. we can use algorithm 18.24 to traverse doubly header list.

Program 9: Write a C++ program to create and traverse a doubly linked list

```
# include<iostream.h>
# include<conio.h>
struct doubly
{
int info;
doubly* back;
doubly* front;
};
class doubly_class
{
private:
double* start;
public:
doubly_class ( )
{
start=new doubly;
start->front=NULL;
start->back=NULL;
start->info=-1;          // header node- can contain other information also
}
void create ( );         // function prototype
void display ( );        // function prototype
};
void doubly_class : : create ( )
{
int values;
doubly* new_node=new doubly;
new_node= start;
cout<<"\nRead the info terminated by negative number: \n;
cin>>value;
```

```
while (value>=0)
{
new_node->front=new doubly;
new_node->front->back=new_node;
new_node=new_node->front;
new_node->info=value;
new_node->front=NULL;
cin>>value;
}
}
void doubly_class : : display ( )
{
cout<<"\n\nTraversing in the forward direction: \n\n";
doubly* move=start;
do
{
move=move->info<<"<->";
}
while (move->front);
cout<<"NULL";
cout<<"\n\nTraversing in the back direction: \n\n;
do
{
cout<<move->info<<"<->";
move=move->back;
}
while (move->back);
cout<<'NULL";
}
void main( )
{
clrscr ( );
doubly_class d_list; // create an object
d_list.create ( );
d_list.display ( );
getch ( );
}
```

Output:

```
Read the info terminated by negative number:
12     13     11     14     16     15     -99
```

Traversing in the forward direction:

12<->13<->11<->14<->16<->15<->NULL

Traversing in the back direction:

15<->16<->14<->11<->13<->12<->NULL

18.8.3.2 Searching Ordinary Doubly Linked List

Searching means we have to find the given ITEM from the doubly linked list. This algorithm is used to find the ITEM from ordinary as well as header doubly list.

Algorithm 18.17: To search the ordinary doubly linked list.

SEARCHDL(INFO, LINK, START, ITEM, LOC)

Suppose we are given an ITEM of information. We have to find the location of ITEM in LIST. if LIST is an ordinary doubly linked list, Then we can use Algorithm 18.13

SORTSEARCH(INFO, LINK, START, ITEM, LOC).

Or

If LIST has a header node we can use algorithm 18 25 to search doubly header list. Advantage of two way list is that we can search the element from both directions(backward and forward).

18.8.3.3 Insertion into Doubly Linked List

Suppose we want to insert the node in the doubly linked list. We have three cases to insert the node.

One common operation for three cases is to insert the node in the doubly linked list. We remove the first node from the AVAIL list,then using the variable NEW to keep track of its location and then copy the new data ITEM into the NEW node that is;

NEW = AVAIL, AVAIL = FORW[AVAIL], INFO[NEW] = ITEM.

First case, is to insert the node at the beginning of the doubly linked list.

START = NEW, FORW[NEW] = LOCA.

BACK[NEW] = NULL, BACK[LOCA] = NEW.

Second case, is to insert the node after a given node in doubly linked list. Suppose we have the locations LOCA and LOCB in the doubly linked list.

We have to set the four pointers:

FORW[LOCA] = NEW, FORW[NEW] = LOCB,

BACK[LOCB] = NEW, BACK[NEW] = LOCA.

Third case, is to insert the node in the last of the doubly linked list. We have to set the three pointers:

FORW[LOCA] = NEW, FORW[NEW] = NULL,
BACK[NEW] = LOCA.

A. Insertion at the beginning of the doubly linked list

Algorithm 18.18: To insert new node at the beginning of the doubly linked list.

INSBEGNODDL(INFO, FORW, BACK, START, AVAIL, LOCA, LOCB, ITEM)

Step 1: [OVERFLOW?] If AVAIL = NULL, then: Write: OVERFLOW, and End.

Step 2: [Remove node from AVAIL list and copy new INFO into node.]
Set NEW = AVAIL, AVAIL = FORW[AVAIL], INFO[NEW] = ITEM.

Step 3: [Insert node into the beginning of two way list.]
Set START = NEW, FORW[NEW] = LOCA.
BACK[NEW] = NULL, BACK[LOCA] = NEW.

Step 4: End.

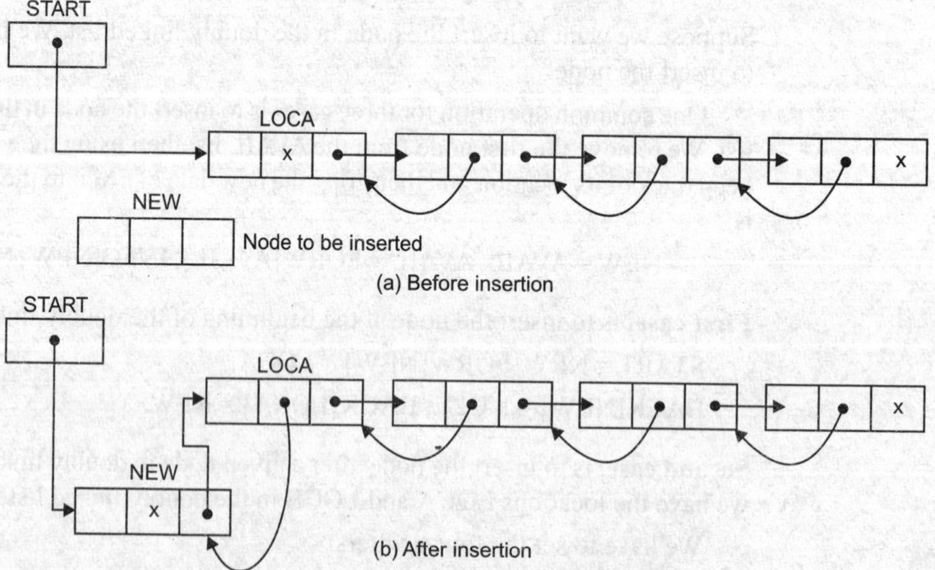

Figure 18.52: Insertion at the beginning of the doubly linked list.

B. Insertion of the node after a given node in the doubly linked list

Algorithm 18.19: To insert new node after a given node in the doubly linked list.

INSGVNNODDL(INFO, FORW, BACK, START, AVAIL, LOCA, LOCB, ITEM)

Step 1: [OVERFLOW?] If AVAIL = NULL, then: Write: OVERFLOW, and End.

Step 2: [Remove node from AVAIL list and copy new INFO into node.]
Set NEW = AVAIL, AVAIL = FORW[AVAIL], INFO[NEW] = ITEM.

Step 3: [Insert node into list.]
Set FORW[LOCA] = NEW, FORW[NEW] = LOCB,
BACK[LOCB] = NEW, BACK[NEW] = LOCA.

Step 4: End.

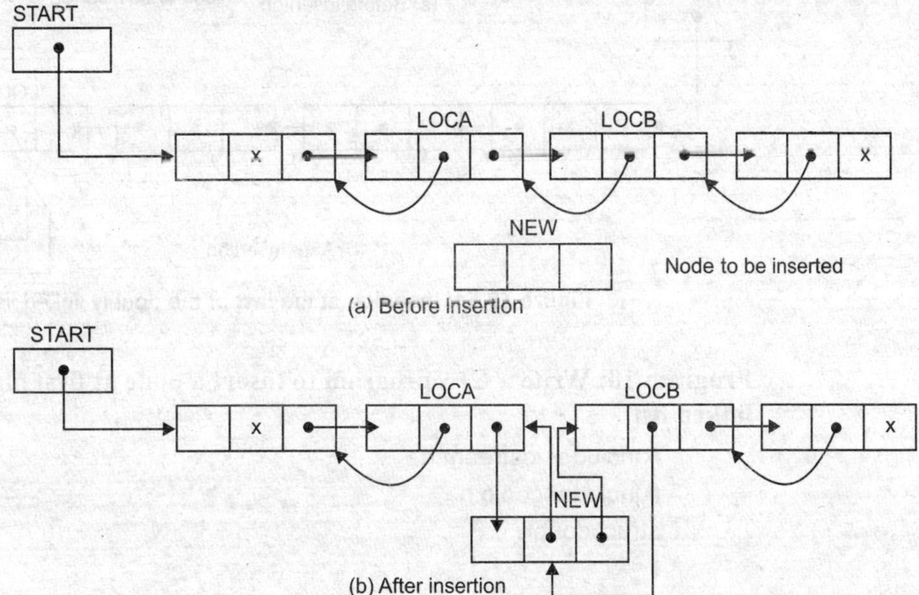

Figure 18.53: Insertion of the node after a given node in the doubly linked list.

C. Insertion at the Last of the Doubly Linked List

Algorithm 18.20: To insert new node in the last of the doubly linked list.

INSLSTNODDL(INFO, FORW, BACK, START, AVAIL, LOCA, LOCB, ITEM)

Step 1: [OVERFLOW?] If AVAIL = NULL, then: Write: OVERFLOW, and End.

Step 2: [Remove node from AVAIL list and copy new INFO into node.]
Set NEW = AVAIL, AVAIL = FORW[AVAIL], INFO[NEW] = ITEM.
Step 3: [Insert node into list.]
Set FORW[LOCA] = NEW, FORW[NEW] = NULL,
BACK[NEW] = LOCA.
Step 4: End.

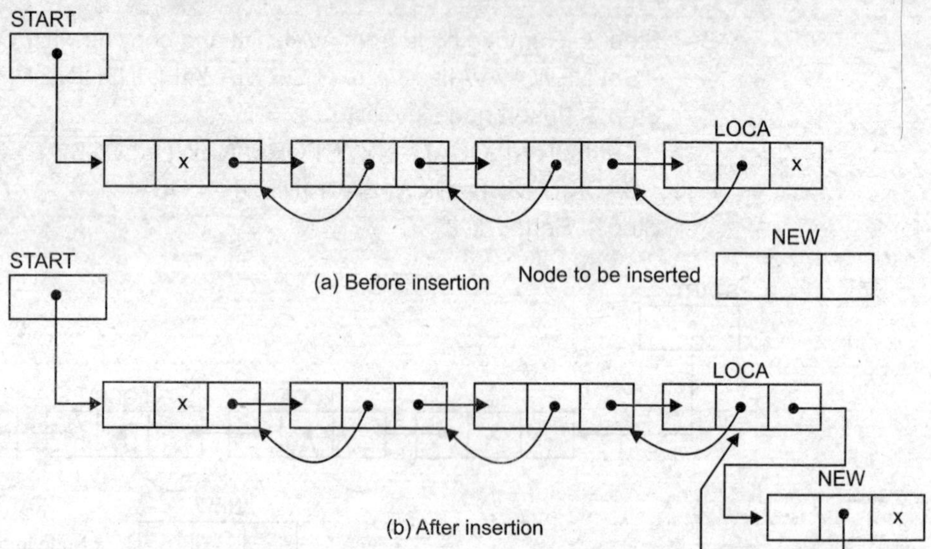

Figure 18.54: Insertion at the last of the doubly linked list.

Program 10: Write a C++ program to insert a node at first place in a doubly linked list

```
# include<iostream.h>
# include<conio.h>
struct doubly
{
int info;
doubly* back;
doubly* front;
};
class doubly_class
{
private:
double* start;
public:
```

```
doubly_class ( )
{
start=new doubly;
start->front=NULL;
start->back=NULL;
start->info=-1;          // header node- can contain other information also
}
void create ( );                    // function prototype
void insert_first (int info)
{
doubly* temp=new doubly;
temp-info=info;
temp->front=start->front;
start->front=back=temp;
temp->back=start;
start->front=temp;
}
void display ( );                   //function prototype
};
function definition create ( )
void doubly_class : : create ( )
{
int values;
doubly* new_node=new doubly;
new_node= start;
cout<<"\nRead the info terminated by negative number: \n;
cin>>value;
while (value>=0)
{
new_node->front=new doubly;
new_node->front->back=new_node;
new_node=new_node->front;
new_node->info=value;
new_node->front=NULL;
cin>>value;
}
}
void doubly_class : : display ( )
{
```

```
cout<<"\n\nTraversing in the forward direction: \n\n";
doubly* move=start;
do
{
move=move->front<<"<->";
cout<<move=start;
do
{
move=move->front;
cout<<move->info<<"<->";
}
while (move->front);
cout<<"NULL";
cout<<"\n\nTraversing in the back direction: \n\n";
do
{
cout<<move->info<<"<->;
move=move->back;
}
while (move->back);
cout<<"NULL";
}
void main ( )
{
clrscr ( );
int value;
doubly_class list;
list.create ( );
cout<<"\nBefore any operation:";
list.display ( );
cout<<"\n\nRead the info value of the first node:";
cin>>value;
list.insert_first (value);
cout<<"\nAfter insertion operation:";
list.display ( );
getch ( );
}
```

Output:

Read the info terminated by negative number:

20 10 40 50 70 60 -99

```
Before any operation:
Traversing in the forward direction:
20<->10<->40<->50<->70<->60<->NULL
Traversing in the back direction:
60<->70<->50<->40<->10<->20<->NULL
Read the info value of the first node: 17
After insertion operation:
Traversing in the forward direction:
17<->20<->10<->40<->50<->70<->60<->NULL
Traversing in the back direction:
60<->70<->50<->40<->10<->20<->17<->NULL
```

Program 11: Write a C++ program to insert a node at end in a doubly linked list

```
# include<iostream.h>
# include<conio.h>
struct doubly
{
int info;
doubly* back;
doubly* front;
};
class doubly_class
{
private:
double* start;
public:
doubly_class ( )
{
start=new doubly;
start->front=NULL;
start->back=NULL;
start->info=-1;            // header node- can contain other information also
}
void create ( );                    // function prototype
void insert_end(int);
void display ( );                   //function prototype
};
function definition create ( )
void doubly_class : : create ( )
```

```
{
int values;
doubly* new_node=new doubly;
new_node= start;
cout<<"\nRead the info terminated by negative number: \n;
cin>>value;
while (value>=0)
{
new_node->front=new doubly;
new_node->front->back=new_node;
new_node=new_node->front;
new_node->info=value;
new_node->front=NULL;
cin>>value;
}
}
void doubly_class :: insert_end (int info)
{
doubly* temp=new doubly;
temp->info=info;
doubly* move=start;
while (move->front)
move=move->front;
temp->front=NULL;
temp->back=move;
move->front=temp;
}
void doubly_class : : display ( )
{
cout<<"\n\nTraversing in the forward direction: \n\n";
doubly* move=start;
do
{
move=move->front<<"<->";
cout<<move=start;
do
{
move=move->front;
cout<<move->info<<"<->";
}
```

```
while (move->front);
cout<<"NULL";
cout<<"\n\nTraversing in the back direction: \n\n";
do
{
cout<<move->info<<"<->;
move=move->back;
}
while (move->back);
cout<<"NULL";
}
void main ( )
{
clrscr ( );
int value;
doubly_class list;
list.create ( );
cout<<"\nBefore any operation:";
list.display ( );
cout<<"\n\nRead the info value of the last node:";
cin>>value;
list.insert_end (value);
cout<<"\nAfter insertion operation:";
list.display ( );
getch ( );
}
```

Output:

```
Read the info terminated by negative number:
20    50    30    10    70    60    -99
Before any operation:
Traversing in the forward direction:
20<->50<->30<->10<->70<->60<->NULL
Traversing in the back direction:
60<->70<->10<->30<->50<->20<->NULL
Read the info value of the last node: 14
After insertion operation:
Traversing in the forward direction:
20<->50<->30<->10<->70<->60<->14<->NULL
Traversing in the back direction:
14<->60<->70<->10<->30<->50<->20<->NULL
```

Program 12: Write a C++ program to insert a node at the desired position in a doubly linked list

```
# include<iostream.h>
# include<conio.h>
struct doubly
{
int info;
doubly* back;
doubly* front;
};
class doubly_class
{
private:
double* start;
public:
doubly_class ( )
{
start=new doubly;
start->front=NULL;
start->back=NULL;
start->info=-1; // header node- can contain other information also
}
void create ( ); // function prototype
void insert ();
void display ( ); //function prototype
};
function definition create ( )
void doubly_class : : create ( )
{
int values;
doubly* new_node=new doubly;
new_node= start;
cout<<"\nRead the info terminated by negative number: \n;
cin>>value;
while (value>=0)
{
new_node->front=new doubly;
new_node->front->back=new_node;
new_node=new_node->front;
```

```
new_node->info=value;
new_node->front=NULL;
cin>>value;
}
}
void doubly_class : : insert ( )
{
int info, position;
cout<<"\n\nRead the info value of the node to be inserted: ";
cin>>info;
cout<<"Read the position where node is to be inserted: ";
cin>>position;
if (position<=0 | | position>total+1)
{
cout<<"\nInvalid position inputted";
getch ( );
exit (1);
}
doubly* temp=new doubly;
temp->info=info;
if (position= =1)
{
temp->front=start->front;
temp->back=start;
if (temp->front)
start->front->back=temp;
start->front=temp;
}
else
{
int steps=1;
doubly* move=start->front;
while (steps<position-1)
{
move=move->front;
steps++;
}
temp->front=move->front;
temp->back=move;
```

```
if (temp->front)
move->front->back=temp;
move->front=temp;
}total ++;
}
void doubly_class : : display ( )
{
cout<<"\n Total number of nodes:"<<total;
cout<<"\n\nTraversing in the forward direction: \n\n";
doubly* move=start;
do
{
move=move->front<<"<->";
cout<<move=start;
do
{
move=move->front;
cout<<move->info<<"<->";
}
while (move->front);
cout<<"NULL";
cout<<"\n\nTraversing in the back direction: \n\n";
do
{
cout<<move->info<<"<->;
move=move->back;
}
while (move->back);
cout<<"NULL";
}
void main ( )
{
clrscr ( );
int value;
doubly_class list;
list.create ( );
cout<<"\nBefore any operation:";
list.display ( );
list.insert ();
```

```
cout<<"\nAfter insertion operation:";
list.display ( );
getch ( );
}
```

```
Output:
Read the info terminated by negative number:
20    10    50    70    30    -99
Before any operation:
Total number of nodes: 5
Traversing in the forward direction:
20<->10<->50<->70<->30<->NULL
Traversing in the back direction:
30<->70<->50<->10<->20<->NULL
Read the info value of the node to be inserted: 16
Read the position where node is to be inserted: 4
After insertion operation:
Total number of nodes: 6
Traversing in the forward direction:
20<->10<->50<->16<->70<->30<->NULL
Traversing in the back direction:
30<->70<->16<->50<->10<->20<->NULL
```

18.8.3.4 Deletion From Doubly Linked List

Suppose we want to delete a node from two-way list. We have three choices to delete the node.

One common operation for three cases is to delete the node in the doubly linked list. We remove the first node and first node is assign to the AVAIL list that is;

FORW[LOCA] = AVAIL and AVAIL = LOCA

First case, is to delete the beginning node in the doubly linked list.

START = FORW[LOCA], BACK[LOCB]= NULL, START= LOCB.

Second case, is to delete the middle node from the doubly linked list. Suppose we have the locations LOCA,LOCN and LOCB in the doubly linked list.LOCN is the middle location to be delete. We have to set the two pointers:

FORW[LOCA] = LOCB, BACK[LOCB]=LOCA.

Third case, is to delete the last node of the doubly linked list.

FORW[LOCA] = NULL.

A. Deletion at the beginning of the doubly linked list

Algorithm 18.21: To delete the beginning node from doubly linked list.

DELBEGNODDL(INFO, FORW, BACK, START, AVAIL, LOC)
Step 1: [Delete node from two-way list.]
Set START = FORW[LOCA], BACK[LOCB]= NULL, START= LOCB.
Step 2: [Return node to AVAIL list.]
Set FORW[LOCA] = AVAIL and AVAIL = LOCA
Step 3: End.

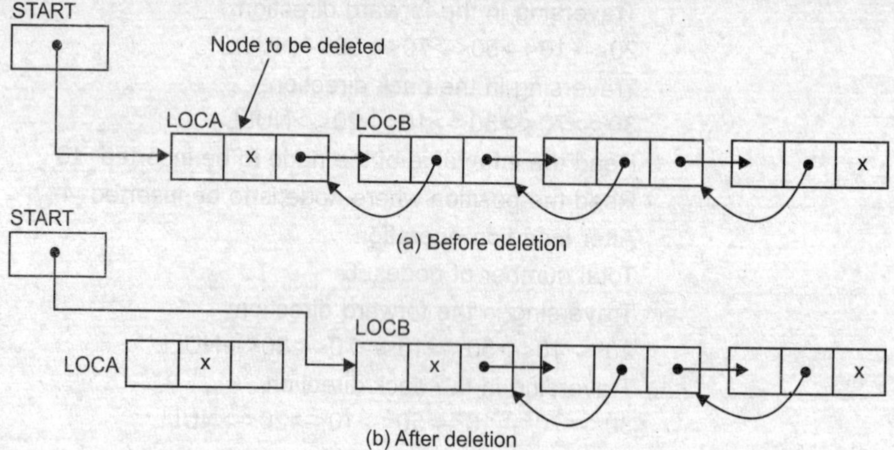

Figure 18.55: Deletion at the beginning of the doubly linked list.

B. Deletion the node after a given node of the doubly linked list

Algorithm 18.22: To delete the node with a given item of information from doubly linked list.

DELGVNNODDL(INFO, FORW, BACK, START, AVAIL, LOC)
Step 1: [Delete node from two-way list.]
Set FORW[LOCA] = LOCB, BACK[LOCB]=LOCA.
Step 2: [Return node to AVAIL list.]
Set FORW[LOCN] = AVAIL and AVAIL = LOCN
Step 3: End.

OR

Step 1: [Delete node from two-way list.]
Set FORW[BACK[LOC]] = BACK[LOC].
Step 2: [Return node to AVAIL list.]
Set FORW[LOC] = AVAIL and AVAIL = LOC
Step 3: End.

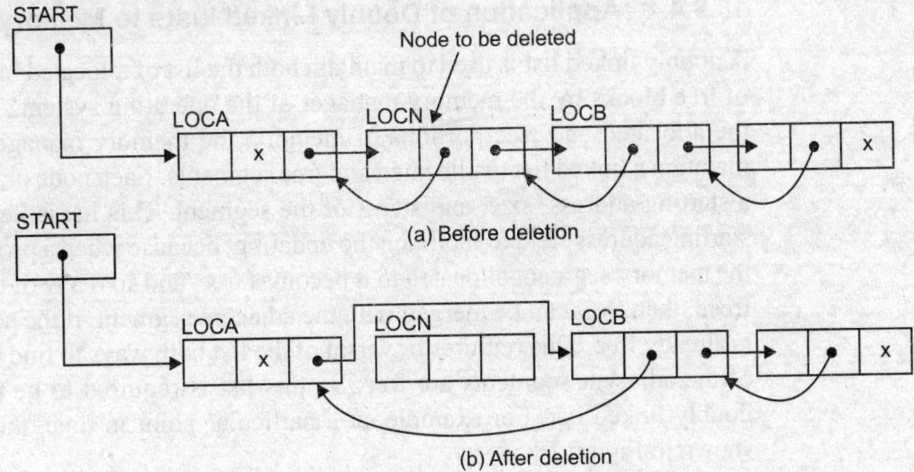

Figure 18.56: Deletion the node after a given node of the doubly linked list

C. Deletion at the last of the doubly linked list

Algorithm 18.23: To delete the last node from doubly linked list.

DELLSTNODDL(INFO, FORW, BACK, START, AVAIL, LOC)

Step 1: [Delete node from two-way list.]

Set FORW[LOCA] = NULL.

Step 2: [Return node to AVAIL list.]

Set FORW[LOCN] = AVAIL, and AVAIL = LOCN

Step 3: End.

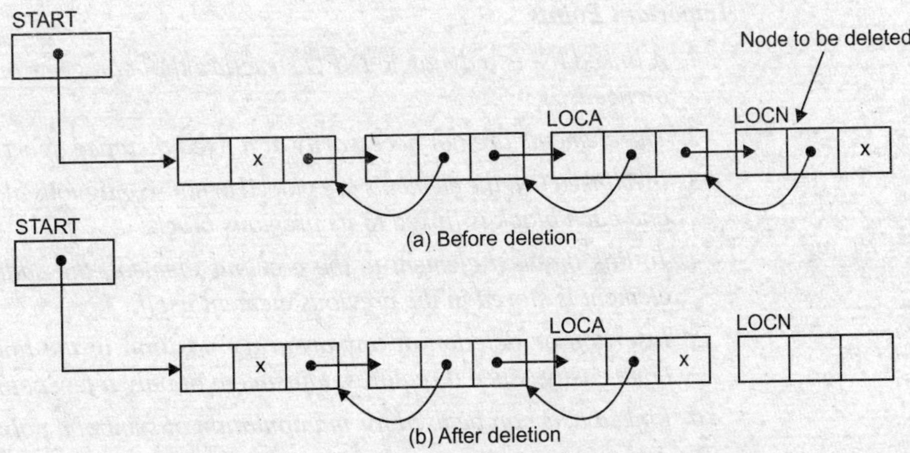

Figure 18.57: Deletion at the last of the doubly linked list

18.8.4 Application of Doubly Linked Lists to Memory Management

A doubly linked list is used to maintain both the list of allocated blocks and the list of free blocks by the memory manager of the operating system. To keep track of the allocated and free portions of memory, the memory manager is required to maintain a linked list of allocated and free segments. Each node of this list contains a starting address, size, and status of the segment. This list is kept sorted by the starting address field to facilitate the updating, because when a process terminates, the memory segment allocated to it becomes free, and so if any of the segments are freed, then they can be merged with the adjacent segment, if the adjacent segment is already free. This requires traversal of the list both ways to find out whether any of the adjacent segments are free. So this list is required to be maintained as a doubly linked list. For example, at a particular point in time, the list may be as shown in Figure 18.58.

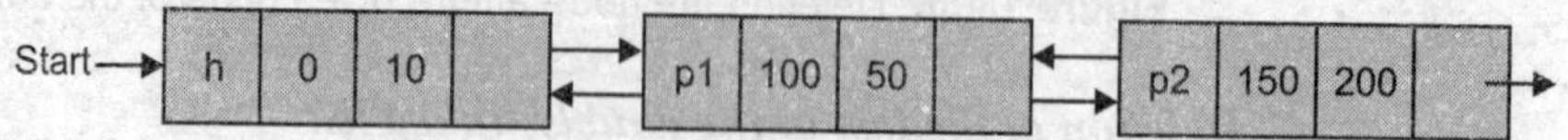

Figure 18.58: Before termination of process p1.

If the process p1 terminates, it is required to be modified as shown in Figure 18.59.

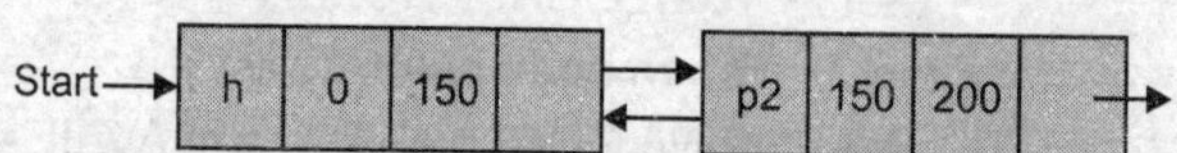

Figure 18.59: After termination of process p1.

Important Points

1. *A linked list is a dynamic INFO structure that can grow and shrink based on need.*
2. *The elements are not necessarily at a fixed distance apart.*
3. *In a linked list, the elements are placed in non-contiguous blocks of memory, and each block is linked to its previous block.*
4. *To link the next element to the previous element, the address of the next element is stored in the previous element itself.*
5. *Insertion or deletion at any arbitrary position in the linked list can be done easily, since it requires adjustment of only a few pointers.*
6. *Linked lists can be used for manipulation of symbolic polynomials.*
7. *A linked list is suitable for representation of sparse matrices.*
8. *A circular list is a list in which the link field of the last node is made to point to the start/first node of the list*

9. *A doubly linked list (DLL) is a linked list in which every node contains two links, called the left link and right link, respectively.*
10. *The left link of the node in a DLL is made to point to the previous node, whereas the right link is made to point to the next node.*
11. *A DLL can be traversed in both directions.*
12. *Having two pointers in a DLL provides safety, because even if one of the pointers get corrupted, the node still remains linked.*
13. *Deleting a particular node from a list, therefore, does not require keeping track of the previous node in a DLL.*

18.9 HEADER LINKED LISTS

A header linked list is a linked list which always contains a special node, called the header node, at the beginning of the list. The following are two kinds of widely used header lists:

1. A grounded header list is a header list where last node contains null pointer
2. Circular header list is a header list where the last node points back to the header node.

Figures 18.60 and 18.61 contains the diagram of these header lists.

The list pointer start always points to the header node. According to this, LINK[START]=NULL indicates that a grounded header list is empty, and LINK[START]= START indicates that a circular header list is empty.

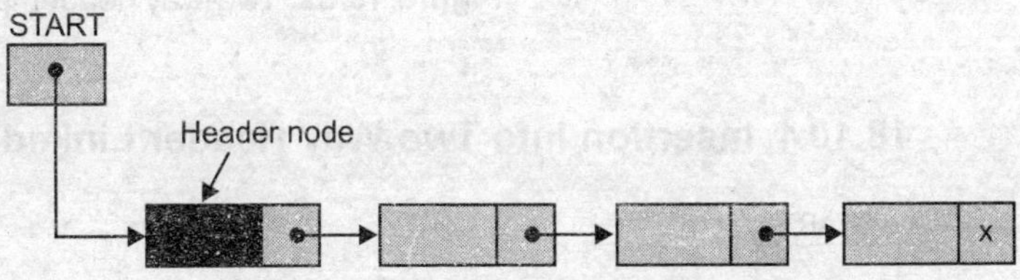

Figure 18.60: Grounded Header list

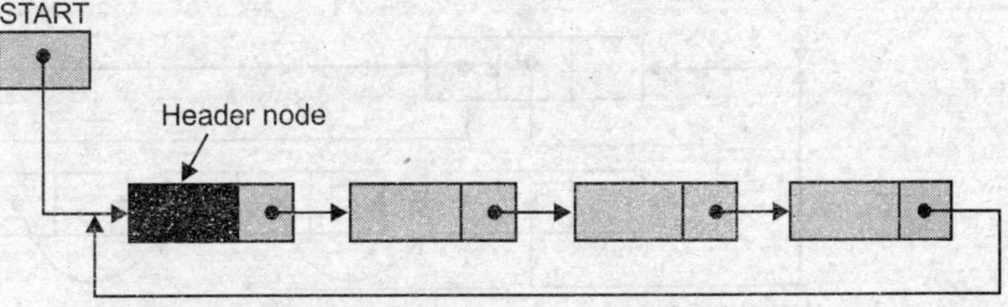

Figure 18.61: Circular Header list

Circular header list are frequently used instead of ordinary linked lists because many operations are much easier to state and implement using header list. This comes from two properties of circular header lists:

1. The null pointer is not used and hence all pointers contain valid addresses
2. Every ordinary node has predecessor, so the first node may not required a special case.

18.10 TWO-WAY HEADER LISTS

The advantages of a two-way list and a circular header list may be combined into a two-way circular header list as shown in figure below. The list is circular because the two end nodes point back to the header node. Observe that such a two-way list requires only one list pointer variable START, which points to the header node. This is because the two pointers in the header node point to the two ends of the list.

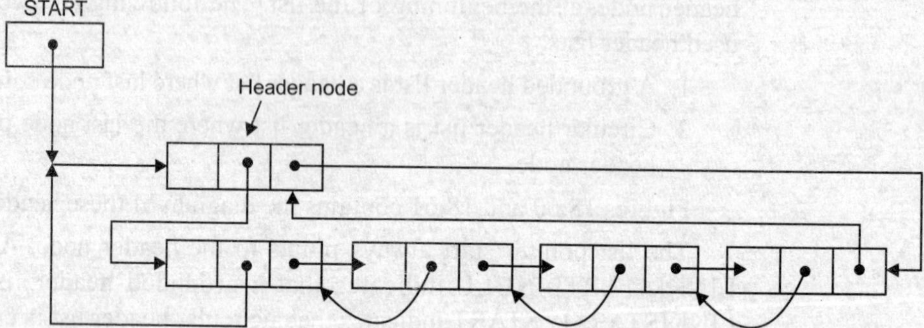

Figure 18.62: Two-way header list.

18.10.1 Insertion into Two Way Header Linked List

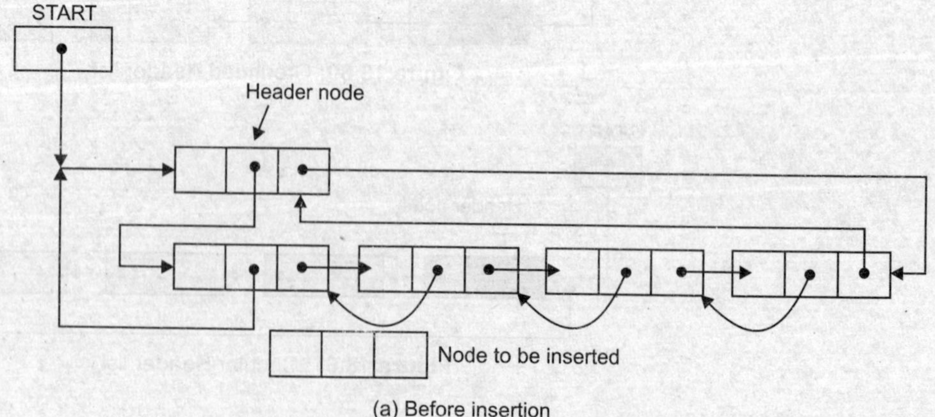

(a) Before insertion

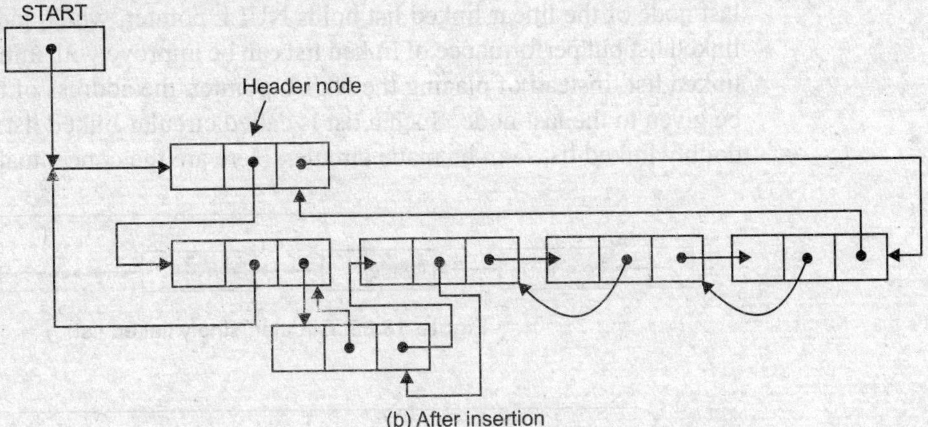

Figure 18.63: Insertion into two way header linked list

18.10.2 Deletion From Two Way Header Linked List

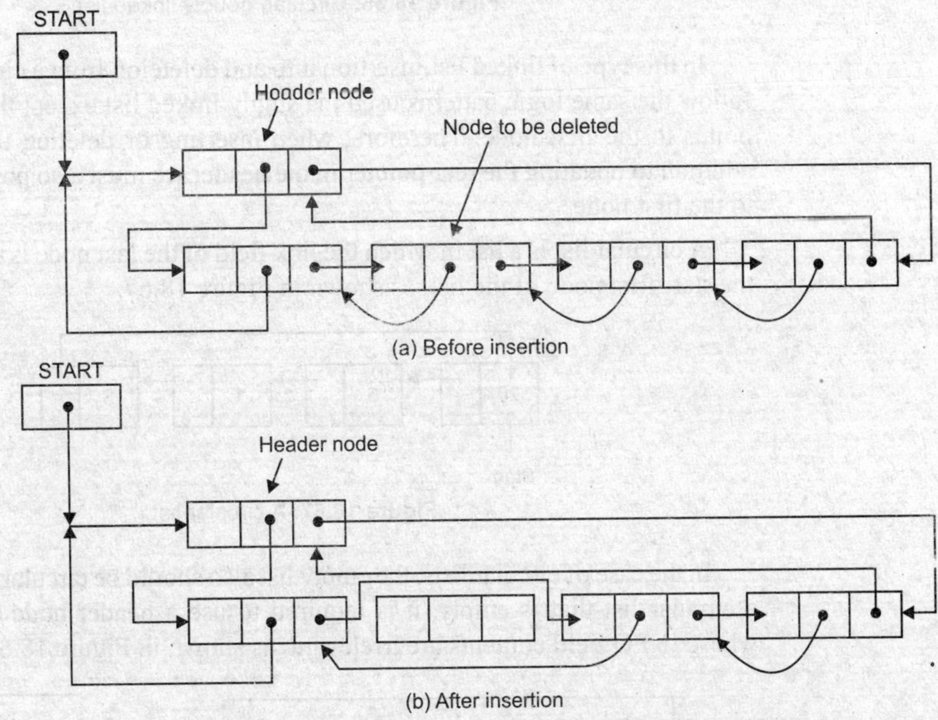

Figure 18.64: Deletion from two way header linked list

18.11 CIRCULAR LINKED LISTS

In circular linked list the last node points to header node. The linear linked list can be converted to circular linked list by linking the last node to the first node. The last node of the linear linked list holds NULL pointer, which indicates end of the linked list but performance of linked list can be improve with minor changes in the linked list. Instead of placing the NULL pointer, the address of the first node can be given to the last node, Such a list is called circular linked list. Both singly and doubly linked lists can be made circular. Here are the conceptual pictures:

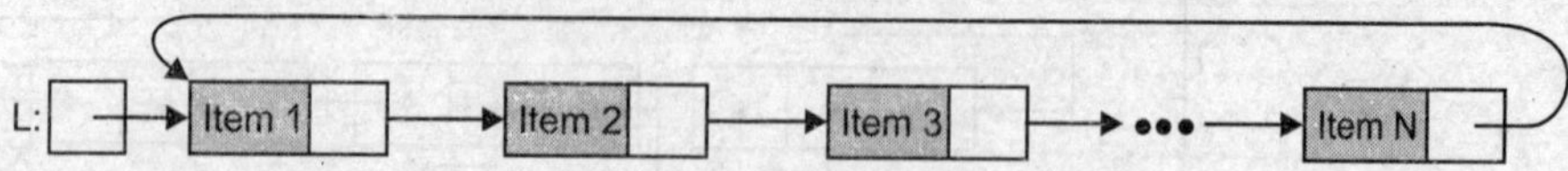

Figure 18.65: Circular, singly linked list.

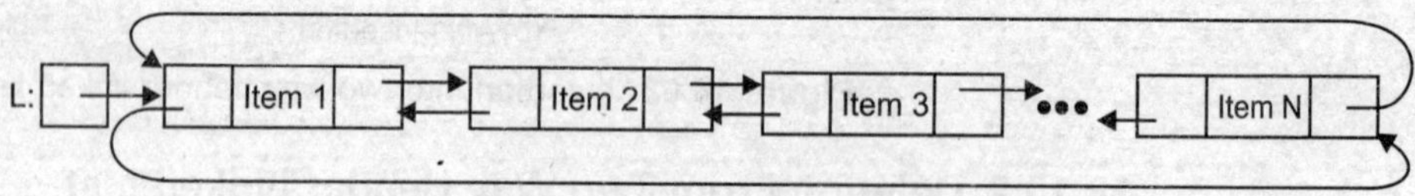

Figure 18.66: Circular, doubly linked list.

In this type of linked list,insertion into and deleteion from a circular linked list follow the same logic patterns used ina singly linked list except that the last node points to the first node. Therefore, when inserting or deleting the last node, in addition to updating the rear pointer in the header we must also point the link field to the first node.

A circular list is a list in which the link field of the last node is made to point to the start/first node of the list, as shown in Figure 18.67.

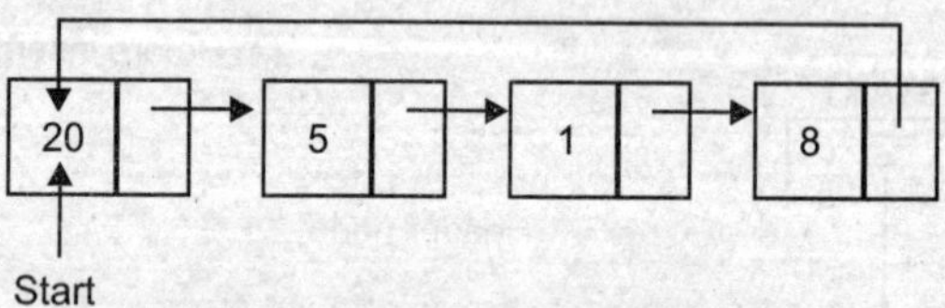

Figure 18.67: A circular list.

In the case of circular lists, the empty list also should be circular. So to represent a circular list that is empty, it is required to use a header node or a head-node whose INFO field contents are irrelevant, as shown in Figure 18.68.

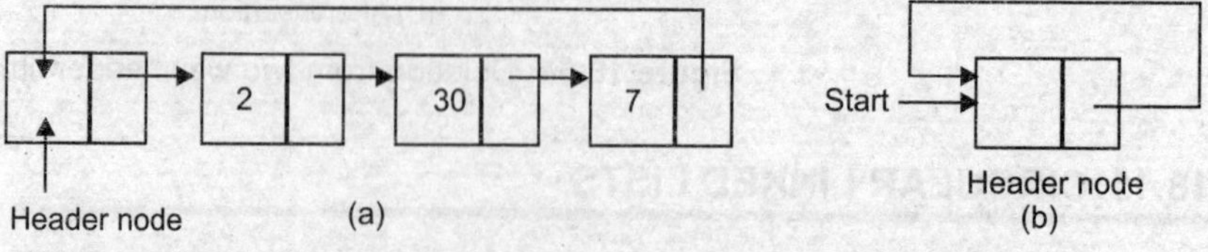

Figure 18.68: (a) A circular list with head node, (b) an empty circular list.

18.11.1 Operations on Circular Linked List

18.11.1.1 Traversing A Circular Linked List

This algorithm traverse the circular linked list.

Algorithm 18.24: Traversing a circular header list

TRAVERSECL (INFO, LINK, START, P)

Let LIST be a circular header list in memory. This algorithm traverses LIST, applying an operation PROCESS to each node of LIST.

Step 1: Set P = LINK[START]. [Initializes the pointer P.]

Step 2: Repeat Steps 3 and 4 while P ≠ START.

Step 3: Apply PROCESS to INFO[P].

Step 4: Set P = LINK[P]. [P now points to the next node.]

[End of Step 2 loop.]

Step 5: End.

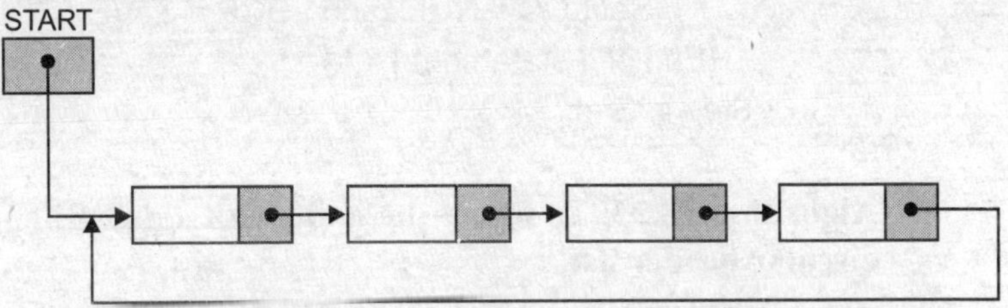

Figure 18.69: Traversing circular linked list.

18.11.1.2 Searching In Circular Linked List

Algorithm 18.25: To search element from circular header linked list

SRCHCL (INFO, LINK, START, ITEM, LOC)

LIST is a circular header list in memory. This algorithm finds the location LOC of the node where ITEM first appears in LIST or sets LOC = NULL.

Step 1: Set P = LINK[START].

Step 2: Repeat Steps while INFO[P] ≠ ITEM and P ≠ START

Set P = LINK[P]. [P now points to the next node.] [End of loop.]

Step 3: If INFO[P] = ITEM, then

Set LOC = P.

Else

Set LOC = NULL.

[End of If statement.]

Step 4: End.

18.11.1.3 Insertion in Circular Linked List

Algorithm 18.26: To find the location LOC of the specified node from a circular linked list.

FINDLOC (INFO, LINK, START, ITEM, LOC, LOCP)

This algorithm find the location LOC of the first node N which contains ITEM and also the location LOCP of the node preceding N when LIST is an ordinary linked list. The following is such an algorithm when LIST is a circular header list.

Step 1: Set SAVE = START and P = LINK [START]. [Initializes pointers.]

Step 2: Repeat Steps while INFO [P] ≠ ITEM and P ≠ START

Set SAVE = P and P = LINK [P]. [Updates pointers.]

[End of loop.]

Step 3: If INFO [P] = ITEM, then

Set LOC = P and LOCP = SAVE.

Else

Set LOC = NULL and LOCP = SAVE

[End of if statement.]

Step 4: End.

Algorithm 18.27: To insert the node with a given item of information from circular header list.

INSNODCHL(INFO, LINK, START, AVAIL, ITEM)

This algorithm insert the first node N which contains ITEM when LIST is an circular header list.

Step 1: [Use algorithm 18.26 to find the location of N and its preceding node.]

Call FINDLOC (INFO, LINK, START, ITEM, LOC, LOCP).

Step 2: [Use algorithm 18.4 to insert the node into a cicular linked list]

Call INSGVNNOD (INFO, LINK, START, AVAIL, LOC, ITEM)

Step 3: End.

A. Insertion of element at the beginning of the circular linked list

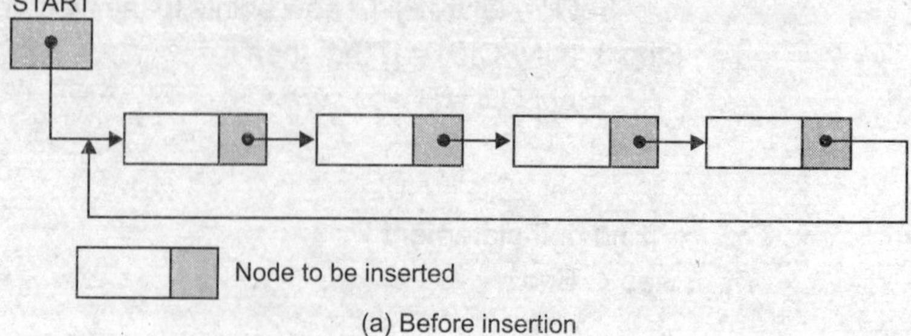

(a) Before insertion

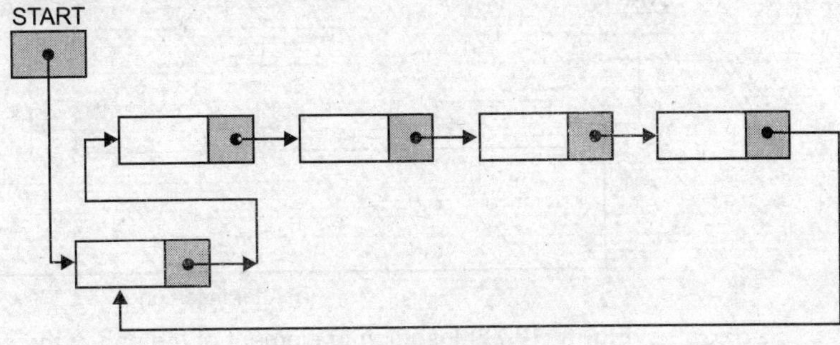

(b) After insertion

Figure 18.70: Insertion of element at the beginning of the circular linked list

B. Insertion of element at a given position in the circular linked list

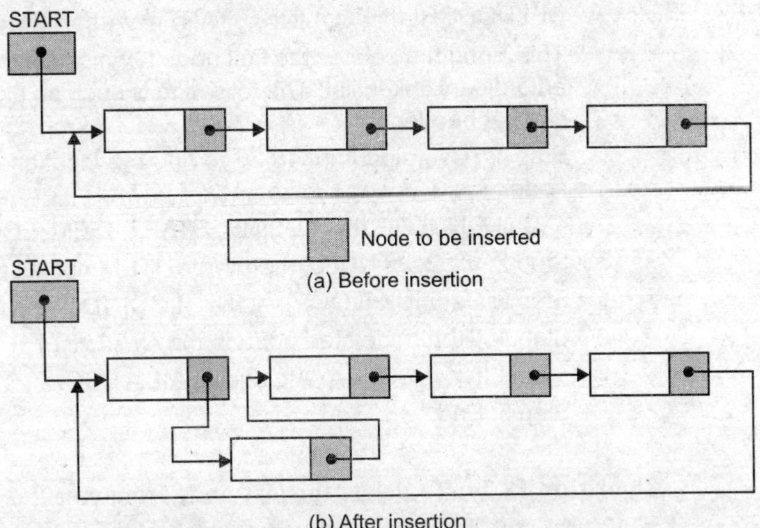

(a) Before insertion

(b) After insertion

Figure 18.71: Insertion of element at a given position in the circular linked list.

C. Insertion of element at the end of the circular linked list

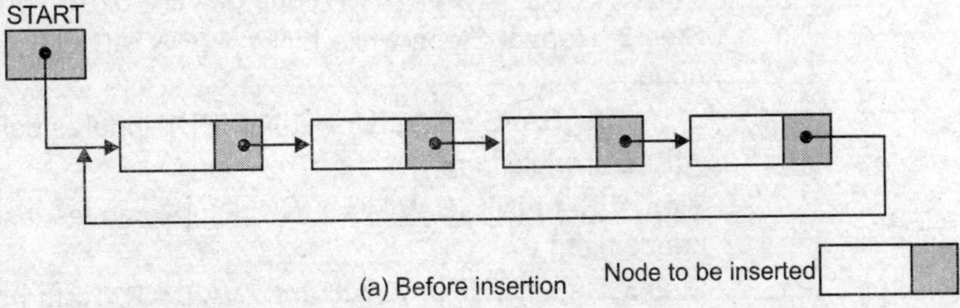

(a) Before insertion

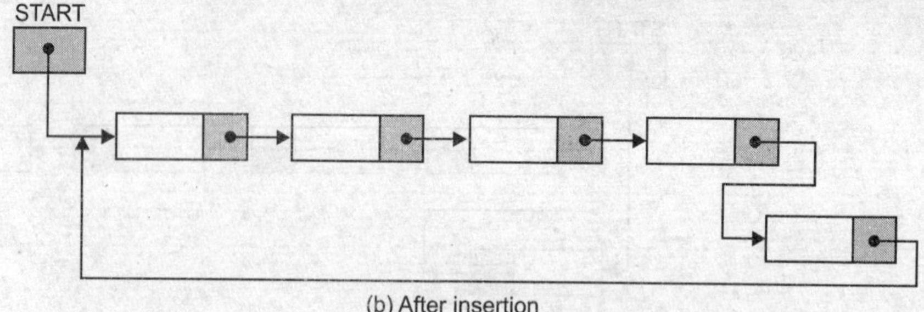

(b) After insertion

Figure 18.72: Insertion of element at the end of the circular linked list.

18.11.1.4 Deletion from Circular Linked List

Algorithm 18.28: To delete the node with a given item of information from circular header list.

DELNODCHL(INFO, LINK, START, AVAIL, ITEM)

This algorithm deletes the first node N which contains ITEM when LIST is an ordinary linked list. The following is such an algorithm when LIST is a circular header list.

Step 1: [Use algorithm 18.26 to find the location of N and its preceding node.]

Call FINDLOC (INFO, LINK, START, ITEM, LOC, LOCP).

Step 2: If LOC = NULL, then Write: ITEM not in list, and End.

Step 3: Set LINK [LOCP] = LINK [LOC]. [Deletes node.]

Step 4: [Return deleted node to the AVAIL list.]

Set LINK [LOC] = AVAIL and AVAIL = LOC.

Step 5: End.

Algorithm 18.29: To delete the last node from circular header list.

DELLSTNOD (INFO, LINK, START, AVAIL)

This algorithm deletes the last node from the header list.

Step 1: [List is empty?] If LINK [START] = NULL, then

Write: UNDERFLOW, and End.

Step 2: Set P = LINK [START] and SAVE = START. [Initializes pointers P.]

Step 3: Repeat Steps while LINK [P] ^{1} START [Traverses list go to last node.]

Set SAVE = P and P = LINK [P]. [Updates pcinters SAVE and P.]

[End of while loop.]

Step 4: Set LINK [SAVE] = LINK [P]. [Removes last node from circular header list.]

Step 5: Set LINK [P] = AVAIL and AVAIL = P. [Returns node to AVAIL list.]

Step 6: End.

A. Deletion of beginning node from the circular linked list

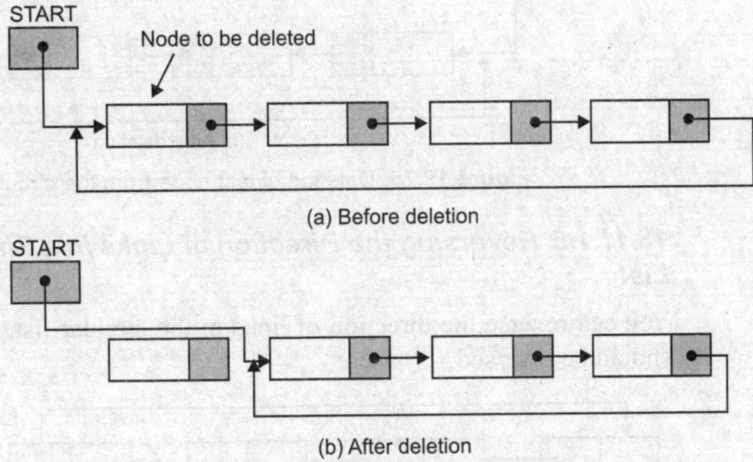

Figure 18.73: Deletion of beginning node from the circular linked list.

B. Deletion of node after a given node from the circular linked list

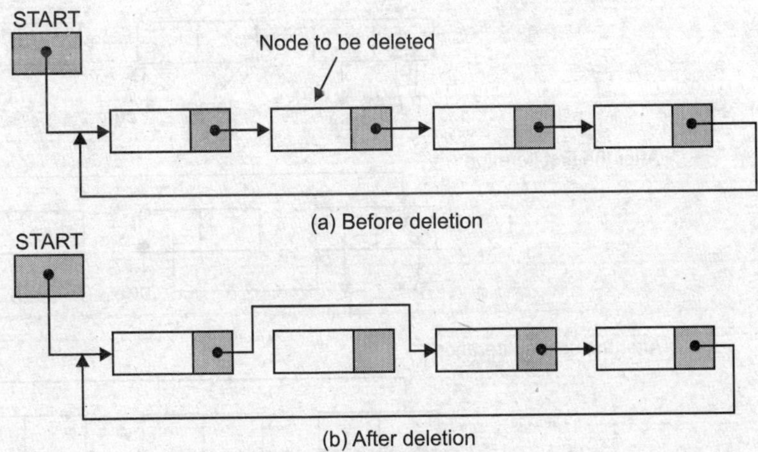

Figure 18.74: Deletion of node after a given node from the circular linked list.

C. Deletion of last node from the circular linked list

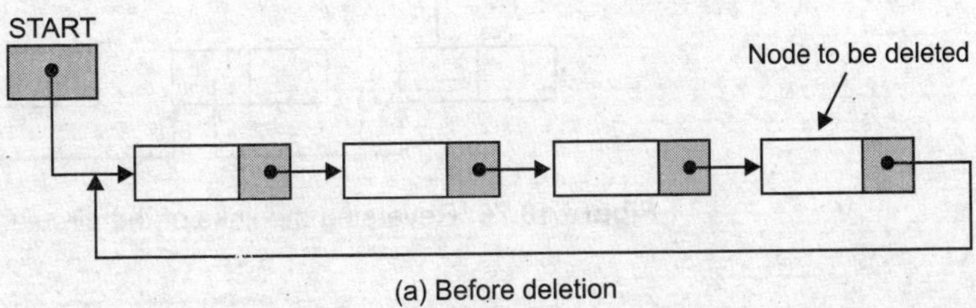

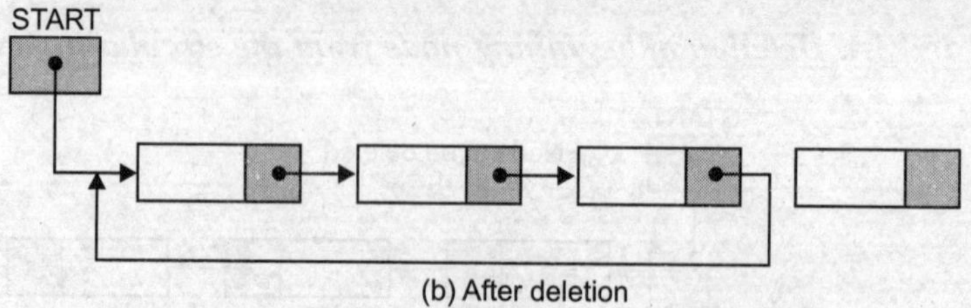

(b) After deletion

Figure 18.75: Deletion of last node from the circular linked list

18.11.1.5 Reversing the Direction of Links in a Singly Linked Circular List

You can reverse the direction of links in the circular list. If you do so, each link should be reversed.

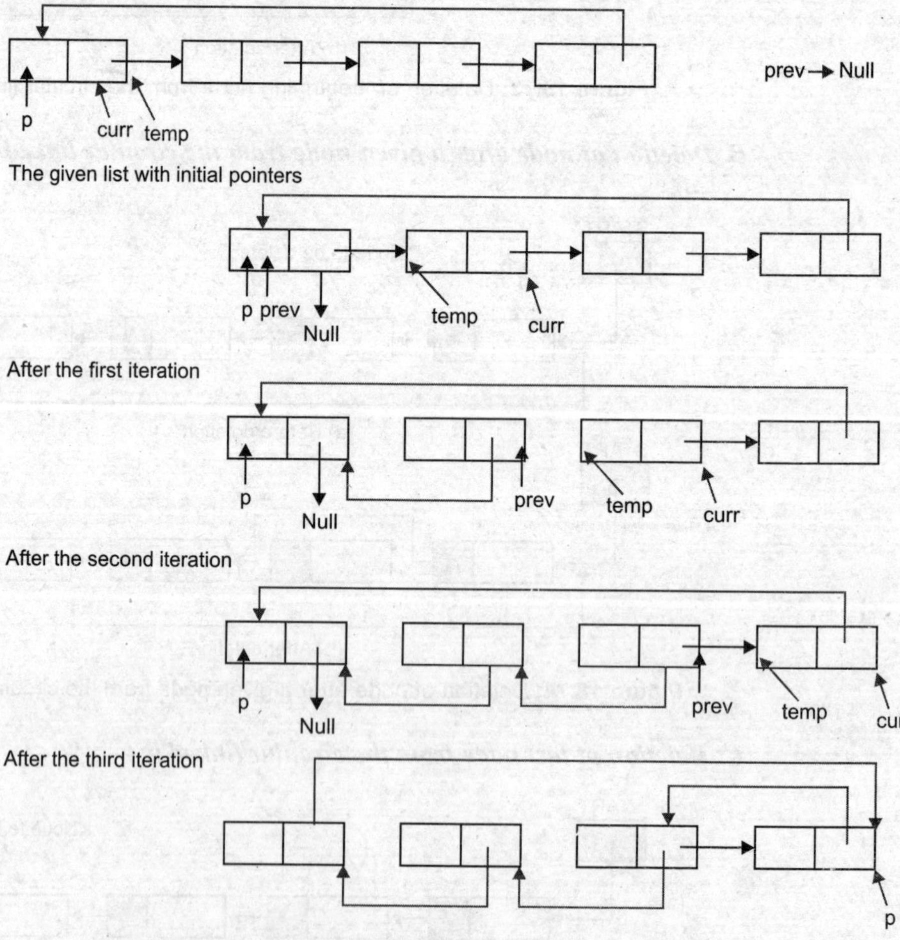

p curr temp prev → Null

The given list with initial pointers

p prev Null temp curr

After the first iteration

p Null prev temp curr

After the second iteration

p Null prev temp curr

After the third iteration

p

Figure 18.76: Reversing the links of the circular linked list

To reverse the links of a singly linked circular list, the list is required to be traversed from the start node until a node is encountered whose link points to the start node (that is, the last node in the list). For this, it is required to maintain the pointers to the current node and the previous node. An additional temporary pointer pointing to the current node is also required to be maintained. Initially, the current, temporary, and previous pointers are set as follows:

1. Set the current as well as the temporary pointer to the start pointer.
2. Set the previous pointer to NULL.
3. The pointers are manipulated in each iteration as follows:
   (i) Advance the current pointer to make it point to the next node.
   (ii) Set the link field of the node pointed to by the temporary pointer to the value of the previous pointer.
   (iii) Make the previous pointer point to the node pointed to by the temporary pointer.
   (iv) Make the temporary pointer point to the node pointed to by the current pointer.
   (v) When the last node is encountered, its link field is made to point to the previous node. After that, the link field of the node pointed to by the start pointer (first node) is made to point to this last node. And the start pointer is made to point to this last node. These manipulations are shown in Figure 18.76.

18.11.1.6 Merging of Two Circular Lists

You can merge two lists into one list. In order to merge or concatenate the two non-empty circular lists pointed to by p and q, it is required to make the start of the resultant list p. Then the list pointed to by p is required to be traversed until its end, and the link field of the last node must become the pointer q. After that, the list pointed to by q is required to be traversed until its end, and the link field of the last node is required to be made p.

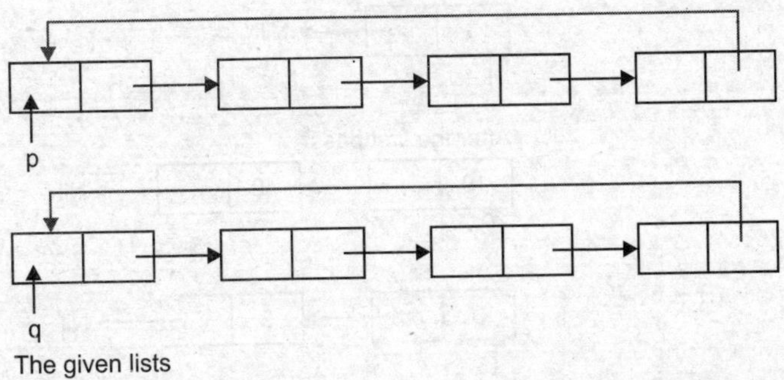

The given lists

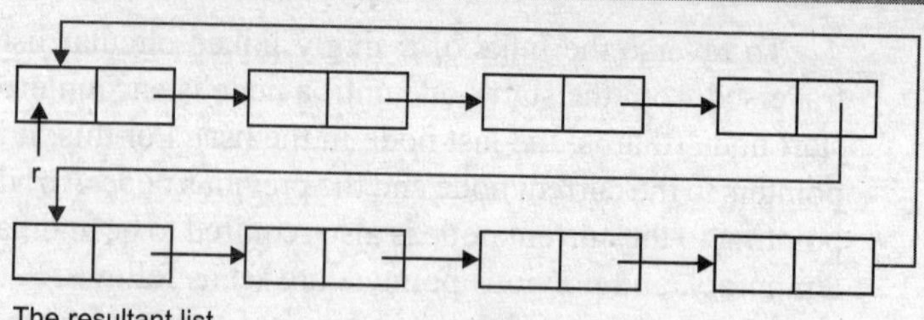

Figure 18.77: Merging of two circular lists

18.12 SORTED LINKED LISTS

To sort a linked list, first we traverse the list searching for the node with a minimum INFO value. Then we remove that node and append it to another list which is initially empty. We repeat this process with the remaining list until the list becomes empty, and at the end, we return a pointer to the beginning of the list to which all the nodes are moved.

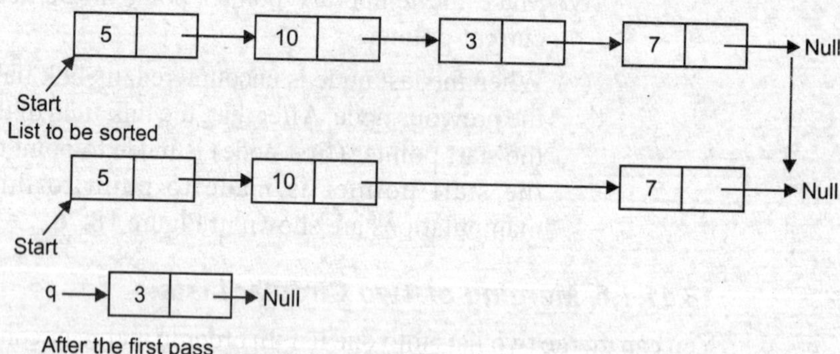

Figure 18.78: Sorting of a linked list.

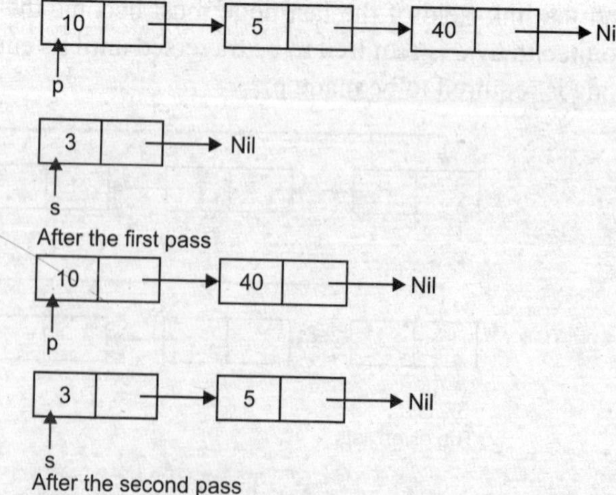

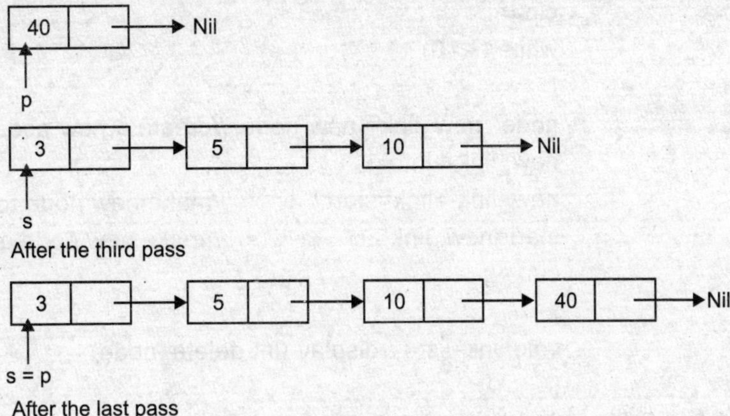

Figure 18.79: Sorting of a linked list.

Program 13: Write a C++ program to sort a linked list using selection sort method.

```
# include<iostream.h>
# include<conio.h>
struct node
{
int info;                    //info field
node* link;                  //pointer to the link node
};
class link_list
{
private:
node* start;
public:
link_list ( )                //constructor
{
start=NULL; //initially the list has no node
}
void add_info ( );                  //function prototype
void display (int);                 //function prototype
void sort( );                       //function prototype
}; //end of class
void link_list : : add_info ( )
{
int i;
cout<<"Read the info terminated by negative number\n;
```

```
cin>>i;
while (i>=0)
{
node* new_link= new node; //create a new node;
new_link->info=i;
new_link->link=start;          //make new node to point to the first node
start=new_link;                // make new node as the first node in the list
cin>>i;
}
void link_list : : display (int delete_node)
{
node* move= start;
node* temp;
while (move)
{
cout<<move->info<<"->";               //display the info
temp=move;
move=move->link;                      //move to link node
if(delete_node)
delete (temp);
}
cout <<"NULL";
}
void link_list : : sort ( )            // employs selection sort method
{
node* top=start;
while (top->link !=NULL)
{
int min=top->info;
node* move=top->link;
node* min_node;
while (move ! =NULL)
{
if (move->info <min)
{
min=move->info;
min_node=move;
}
move=move->link;
```

```
}
if (min != top->info)          // checks if node with minimum info found
{
int temp=top->info;
top->info =min;
min_node->info=temp;
}
top=top->link;
}
}
void main ( )
{
clrscr ( );
link_list link;
link.add_info ( );
cout<<"\nInputted link list before sorting is: \n\n";
link.display (0);
link.sort ( );
cout<<"\n\nInputted link list after sorting is: \n\n";
link.display (1);
getch ( );
}
```

Output:

```
Read the info terminated by negative number
24    15    37    29    47    30    80    25    -99
Inputted link list before sorting is:
25->80->30->47->29->37->15->24->NULL
Inputted link list after sorting is:
15->24->25->29->30->37->47->80->NULL
```

18.13 ENDOGENOUS / EXOGENOUS LISTS

Endogenous lists have the INFO stored in the structure's KEY. The KEY is INFO stored **within** the structure.

Exogenous lists have the INFO stored **outside** the structure. Instead of a KEY, the structure has a pointer to the INFO in memory. Exogenous lists do not require INFO to be moved when individual cells are moved in a list; only the pointers to INFO must be changed. This can save considerable cost when dealing with large INFO in each cell. Another benefit of exogenous lists is many cells can point to the same INFO. Again, this may be useful depending on the application.

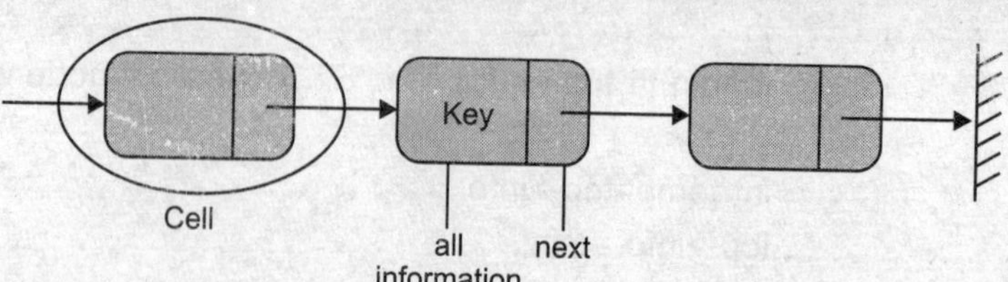

Figure 18.80: Exogenous lists

Here are example declarations of endogenous and exogenous structures:

```
struct endogenous
{
INFO_type key,
struct endogenous * next
};

struct exogenous
{
INFO_type * INFO,
struct exogenous * next
};
```

18.14 ADVANTAGES AND DISADVANTAGES OF USING LINKED LIST OVER ARRAY

Linked lists have several advantages over arrays. For one thing, a linked list allows a new element to be inserted or deleted in any position, with a constant number of operations (changing a couple of pointers). Linked lists can also save memory in applications that need one or more lists of unpredictable size, since the total space used will be proportional to the number of elements actually present in all lists (as opposed to the number of lists times the maximum size of each list).

Further memory savings can be achieved, in certain cases, by sharing the same tail elements among two or more lists. In this way, one can add new elements to the front of the list while keeping a reference to both the new and the old versions — which provides the simplest example of a persistent INFO structure.

On the other hand, compared to an array, the disadvantage of a linked list is that it only allows sequential access to elements, and only in one direction (from front to back). In particular, when removing or inserting an element in the middle of the list, one needs to know the address of the preceding element.

Another disadvantage of linked lists is the extra storage needed for the address fields, which often makes them impractical for lists of small INFO items such as characters or boolean values. Even more significant is the time cost of allocating memory separately for each new element (and, in some systems, of locating and recycling elements that cannot be reached; see garbage collection).

There are a number of techniques to reduce this overhead, such as using a free list or memory pool, storing the INFO itself inside the nodes, and CDR coding.The items in a linked list do not have to be stored in contiguous memory locations like an array.

18.14.1 Arrays vs Linked Lists

Arrays

1. Better for random access to any INFO value
2. Better if number of elements is known and doesn't vary much

Linked Lists

1. Better for additions and removals (other INFO elements do not need to be moved)
2. Better if number of elements varies greatly and is not known at runtime

18.14.2 Similarities between Linked List and Array

Both are used to store a sequence of similar INFO. Both are referred by the location of the first INFO/node.

18.14.3 Differences between Linked List and Array

Array INFO is ALWAYS continuous in memory, while link list nodes can be in anywhere and any order in the memory. Array's elements are accessed directly from the "distance" from the address to the first element. Linked list INFO is accessed indirectly. Each node will hold the location of the next node. To go to a particular element, we have to travel from node to node until we reach the node of interest.

When comparing the sequence implementations using linked lists and using arrays, we should consider:

- space requirements
- time requirements
- ease of implementation

In terms of space, each implementation has its advantages and disadvantages:

- In the linked-list implementation, one pointer must be stored for every item in the sequence, while the array stores only the items themselves.
- On the other hand, the space used for a linked list is always proportional to the number of items in the list. This is not necessarily true for the array

implementation as described: if a lot of items are added to a sequence and then removed, the size of the array can be arbitrarily greater than the number of items in the sequence. However, we could fix this problem by modifying the *remove Current* operation to shrink the array when it becomes too empty.

In terms of time:

- The array implementation requires O(N) worst-case time to add or remove an item with N items, because existing items need to be moved.
- In contrast, adding and removing items in a linked list can be implemented to require only O(1) time (if we maintain pointers to the last node in the list, and the node before the current one, as well as a pointer to the current node).

In terms of ease of implementation:

Straightforward implementations of both the array and linked-list versions seem reasonably easy. However, the methods for the linked-list version seem to require more special cases, and achieving O(1) times for adding and removing items in the linked-list version requires maintaining extra pointers (to the last node and to the node before the current one).

Good Points

Adding elements early in a linked list is cheaper than in a Vector since we do not need to move anything to make room for the new element. If we search for a value, on average we need to search half the list to find the value or to determine that it is not in a list so this is better than an unsorted vector.

Bad Points

There is no direct access to elements given an index as there is with vectors. To find an element by position, we need to start at the beginning of the list and count nodes as we walk the list. Adding nodes towards the end of a linked list is expensive because we need to walk the list to get to the spot where the addition will occur.

Linked lists often require more memory than Vectors. Each value in a linked list requires additional memory to hold a pointer. In a Vector, there may be wasted space due to unused capacity. The closer our vector is to full, the less wasted space there is.

18.14.4 Comparison of Linked List Variations

The major disadvantage of doubly linked lists (over singly linked lists) is that they require more space (every node has two pointer fields instead of one). Also, the code to manipulate doubly linked lists needs to maintain the *prev* fields as well as the *next* fields; the more fields that have to be maintained, the more chance there is for errors.

The major advantage of doubly linked lists is that they make some operations (like the removal of a given node, or a right-to-left traversal of the list) more efficient.

The major advantage of circular lists (over non-circular lists) is that they eliminate some special-case code for some operations. Also, some applications lead naturally to circular list representations. For example, a computer network might best be modeled using a circular list.

18.15 UTILITY OF LINKED LIST IMPLEMENTATIONS

1. Stacks can easily be implemented as a linked list. One needs a pointer to the top of the stack (which is the front of the list).

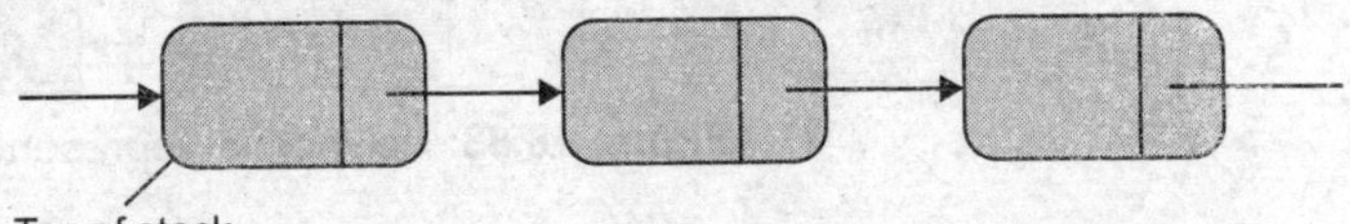

Figure 18.81: Stacks implemented using a linked list

2. Queues can easily be implemented as a linked list as well. One needs a pointer to the front of the queue (which is the front of the list); as well, one needs a pointer to the rear of the queue (which is the end of the list).

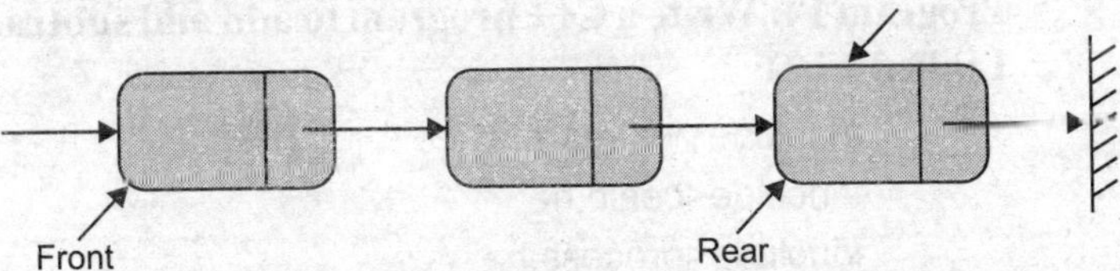

Figure 18.82: Queues implemented using a linked list

It is better, however, to implement a queue as a circular list. This circular list has a pointer to the list pointing at the **rear** rather than the front of the list.

3. Concatenating sublists can easily be done with a linked list. Conversely concatenating sublists with an array implementation is expensive.
4. Referencing sublists with a linked list implementation is expensive. Conversely, sublists can be referenced easily with an array implementation.

18.16 POLYNOMIAL REPRESENTATION

One of the problems that a linked list can deal with is manipulation of symbolic polynomials. By symbolic, we mean that a polynomial is viewed as a list of coefficients and exponents.

For example, the polynomial

$$3x^2 + 2x + 4$$

can be viewed as list of the following pairs

(3,2),(2,1),(4,0)

Therefore, we can use a linked list in which each node will have three fields, as shown in Figure 18.83.

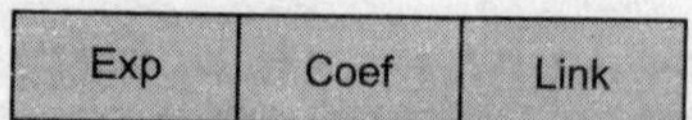

A polynomial $10x^4 + 5x^2 + 1$ can be represented as shown here:

Figure 18.83: Polynomial representation

If the polynomials to be added have n and m terms, respectively, then the linked list representation of these polynomials contains m and n terms, respectively.

Since polyadd traverses each of these lists, sequentially, the maximum number of iterations that polyadd will make will not be more than m + n. So the computation time of polyadd is O(m + n).

Program 14: Write a C++ program to add and subtract two polynomials (Using Linked List)

```
#include<iostream.h>
#include<conio.h>
#include<process.h>
// Creating a NODE Structure
struct node
{
int coe,exp;        // data
struct node *next; // link to next node and previous node
};
// Creating a class Polynomial
class polynomial
{
struct node *start,*ptrn,*ptrp;
public:
void get_poly(); // to get a polynomial
void show();      // show
void add(polynomial p1,polynomial p2); // Add two polynomials
void subtract(polynomial p1,polynomial p2); //Subtract2 polynomials
```

```
};
void polynomial::get_poly()     // Get Polynomial
{
char c='y';
ptrn=ptrp=start=NULL;
while(c=='y' || c=='Y')
{
ptrn=new node;
ptrp->next=ptrn;
if(start==NULL)
start=ptrn;
ptrp=ptrn;
cout<<"Enter the coefficient: ";
cin>>ptrn->coe;
cout<<"Enter the exponent: ";
cin>>ptrn->exp;
ptrn->next=NULL;
cout<<"Enter y to add more nodes: ";
cin>>c;
}
return;
}
void polynomial::show()  // Show Polynomial
{
struct node *ptr;
ptr=start;
while(ptr!=NULL)
{
cout<<ptr->coe<<"X^"<<ptr->exp<<" + ";
ptr=ptr->next;
}
cout<<" ";
}
void polynomial::add(polynomial p1,polynomial p2)  // Add Polynomials
{
struct node *p1ptr,*p2ptr;
int coe,exp;
ptrn=ptrp=start=NULL;
p1ptr=p1.start;
```

```
p2ptr=p2.start;
while(p1ptr!=NULL && p2ptr!=NULL)
{
if(p1ptr->exp==p2ptr->exp) // If coefficients are equal
{
coe=p1ptr->coe+p2ptr->coe;
exp=p1ptr->exp;
p1ptr=p1ptr->next;
p2ptr=p2ptr->next;
}
else if(p1ptr->exp>p2ptr->exp)
{
coe=p1ptr->coe;
exp=p1ptr->exp;
p1ptr=p1ptr->next;
}
else if(p1ptr->exp<p2ptr->exp)
{
coe=p2ptr->coe;
exp=p2ptr->exp;
p2ptr=p2ptr->next;
}
ptrn=new node;
if(start==NULL)
start=ptrn;
ptrn->coe=coe;
ptrn->exp=exp;
ptrn->next=NULL;
ptrp->next=ptrn;
ptrp=ptrn;
} // End of While
if(p1ptr==NULL)
{
while(p2ptr!=NULL)
{
coe=p2ptr->coe;
exp=p2ptr->exp;
p2ptr=p2ptr->next;
ptrn=new node;
if(start==NULL)
```

```
start=ptrn;
ptrn->coe=coe;
ptrn->exp=exp;
ptrn->next=NULL;
ptrp->next=ptrn;
ptrp=ptrn;
}
}
else if(p2ptr==NULL)
{
while(p1ptr!=NULL)
{
coe=p1ptr->coe;
exp=p1ptr->exp;
p1ptr=p1ptr->next;
ptrn=new node;
if(start==NULL)
start=ptrn;
ptrn->coe=coe;
ptrn->exp=exp;
ptrn->next=NULL;
ptrp->next=ptrn;
ptrp=ptrn;
}
}
} // End of addition
// Subtract two polynomials
void polynomial::subtract(polynomial p1,polynomial p2) // Subtract
{
struct node *p1ptr,*p2ptr;
int coe,exp;
ptrn=ptrp=start=NULL;
p1ptr=p1.start;
p2ptr=p2.start;
while(p1ptr!=NULL && p2ptr!=NULL)
{
if(p1ptr->exp==p2ptr->exp) // If coefficients are equal
{
coe=p1ptr->coe-p2ptr->coe;
exp=p1ptr->exp;
```

```
p1ptr=p1ptr->next;
p2ptr=p2ptr->next;
}
else if(p1ptr->exp>p2ptr->exp)
{
coe=p1ptr->coe;
exp=p1ptr->exp;
p1ptr=p1ptr->next;
}
else if(p1ptr->exp<p2ptr->exp)
{
coe=0-p2ptr->coe;
exp=p2ptr->exp;
p2ptr=p2ptr->next;
}
ptrn=new node;
if(start==NULL)
start=ptrn;
ptrn->coe=coe;
ptrn->exp=exp;
ptrn->next=NULL;
ptrp->next=ptrn;
ptrp=ptrn;
} // End of While
if(p1ptr==NULL)
{
while(p2ptr!=NULL)
{
coe=0-p2ptr->coe;
exp=p2ptr->exp;
p2ptr=p2ptr->next;
ptrn=new node;
if(start==NULL)
start=ptrn;
ptrn->coe=coe;
ptrn->exp=exp;
ptrn->next=NULL;
ptrp->next=ptrn;
ptrp=ptrn;
}
```

```
}
else if(p2ptr==NULL)
{
while(p1ptr!=NULL)
{
coe=p1ptr->coe;
exp=p1ptr->exp;
p1ptr=p1ptr->next;
ptrn=new node;
if(start==NULL)
start=ptrn;
ptrn->coe=coe;
ptrn->exp=exp;
ptrn->next=NULL;
ptrp->next=ptrn;
ptrp=ptrn;
}
}
} // End of subtraction
void main()
{
clrscr();
polynomial p1,p2,sum,diff;
cout<<"First Polynomial.";
p1.get_poly();
cout<<"Second polynomial.";
p2.get_poly();
clrscr();
cout<<"The First polynomial is: ";
p1.show();
cout<<"The second polynomial is: ";
p2.show();
cout<<"The sum of two polynomials is: ";
sum.add(p1,p2);
sum.show();
cout<<"The difference of two polynomials is: ";
diff.subtract(p1,p2);
diff.show();
getch();
}
```

18.17 REPRESENTATION OF SPARSE MATRICES

A matrix is a two-dimensional INFO object made of m rows and n columns, therefore having m × n values. When m=n, we call it a square matrix.

The most natural representation is to use two-dimensional array A[m][n] and access the element of ith row and j^{th} column as A[i][j]. If a large number of elements of the matrix are zero elements, then it is called a sparse matrix.

Representing a sparse matrix by using a two-dimensional array leads to the wastage of a substantial amount of space. Therefore, an alternative representation must be used for sparse matrices. One such representation is to store only non- zero elements along with their row positions and column positions. That means representing every non-zero element by using triples (i, j, value), where i is a row position and j is a column position, and store these triples in a linear list. It is possible to arrange these triples in the increasing order of row indices, and for the same row index in the increasing order of column indices. Each triple (i,j,value) can be represented by using a node having four fields as shown in the following:

```
Struct snode{
int row,col,val;
Struct snode *next;
};
```

row	col	value	Link

So a sparse matrix can be represented using a list of such nodes, one per non–zero element of the matrix. For example, consider the sparse matrix shown in Figure 18.84.

0	2	0	0	2	0
0	0	0	1	0	5
0	0	4	0	0	0
0	0	0	0	0	0
0	0	0	0	0	0

Figure 18.84: A sparse matrix.

This matrix can be represented using the linked list shown in Figure 18.85.

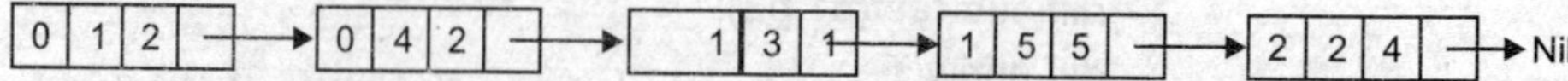

Figure 18.85: Linked list representation of sparse matrix of Figure 18.84.

In order to add two sparse matrices represented using the sorted linked lists as shown in the preceding program, the lists are traversed until the end of one of the lists is reached. In the process of traversal, the row indices stored in the nodes of these lists are compared.

If they don't match, a new node is created and inserted into the resultant list by copying the contents of a node with a lower value of row index. The pointer in the list containing a node with a lower value of row index is advanced to make it point to the next node. If the row indices match, column indices for the corresponding row positions are compared.

If they don't match, a new node is created and inserted into the resultant list by copying the contents of a node with a lower value of column index. The pointer in the list containing a node with a lower value of column index is advanced to make it point to the next node. If the column indices match, a new node is created and inserted into the resultant list by copying the row and column indices from any of the nodes and the value equal to the sum of the values in the two nodes. After this, the pointers in both the lists are advanced to make them point to the next nodes in the respective lists. This process is repeated in each iteration.

After reaching the end of any one of the lists, the iterations come to an end and the remaining nodes in the list whose end has not been reached are copied, as it is in the resultant list.

Consider the following sparse matrices:

Sparse matrix a

0	0	5	0
0	1	0	0
0	0	0	0
0	0	2	0

Sparse matrix b

0	0	0	0
0	3	0	1
0	0	0	0
0	0	5	0

Figure 18.86: Given two sparse matrices.

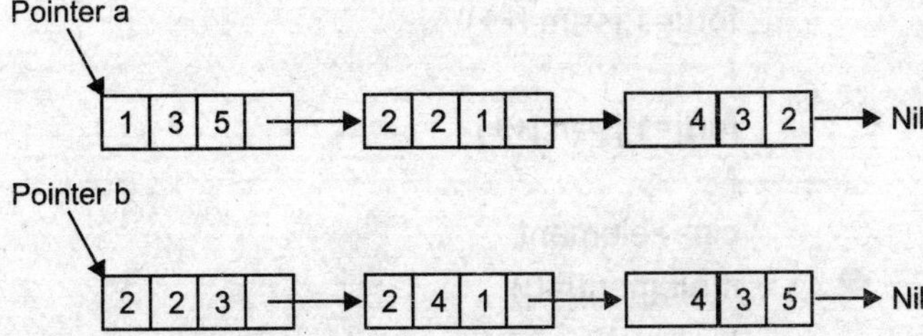

Figure 18.87: Linked representation of sparse matrices.

If the procedure sadd is applied to the above linked list representations then we get the resultant list, as shown in Figure 18.88.

Figure 18.88: Result of application of the procedure sadd.

This resultant list represents the matrix shown below:

0	0	5	0
0	4	0	1
0	0	0	0
0	0	7	0

Figure 18.89: Result of addition in matrix form.

This matrix is an addition of the matrices of a and b, respectively.

Program 15: Write a C++ program to add and subtract two sparse matrices.

```
#include<stdio.h>
#include<iostream.h>
#include<conio.h>
void main()
{
clrscr();
int sparse1[10][3],sparse2[10][3],sum[10][3],diff[10][3];
int m,n,p,q,t1,t2,s,d,element;
int i,j;
cout<<"Enter the number of rows and columns : ";
cin>>m>>n;
t1=t2=0;
cout<<"Enter the first matrix("<<m<<"*"<<n<<"):";
for(i=1;i<=m;i++)
{
for(j=1;j<=n;j++)
{
cin>>element;
if(element!=0)
{
t1=t1+1;
sparse1[t1][1]=i;
```

```
sparse1[t1][2]=j;
sparse1[t1][3]=element;
}
}
}
sparse1[0][1]=m;
sparse1[0][2]=n;
sparse1[0][3]=t1;
cout<<"Enter the second matrix("<<m<<"*"<<n<<"):";
for(i=1;i<=m;i++)
{
for(j=1;j<=n;j++)
{
cin>>element;
if(element!=0)
{
t2=t2+1;
sparse2[t2][1]=i;
sparse2[t2][2]=j;
sparse2[t2][3]=element;
}
}
}
sparse2[0][1]=m;
sparse2[0][2]=n;
sparse2[0][3]=t2;
// displaying the first sparse matrix
cout<<"The first sparse matrix is :Row       Column          Element";
cout<<"----------------------";
for(i=0;i<=t1;i++)
{
cout<<sparse1[i][1]<<"          "<<sparse1[i][2]<<"   "<<sparse1[i][3]<<"";
}
// displaying the second sparse matrix
cout<<"The second sparse matrix is :Row  Column          Element";
cout<<"----------------------";
for(i=0;i<=t2;i++)
{
cout<<sparse2[i][1]<<"          "<<sparse2[i][2]<<"   "<<sparse2[i][3]<<" ";
}
```

```
// Addition and subtraction
i=j=s=d=1;
while((i<=t1)&&(j<=t2))
{
if(sparse1[i][1]==sparse2[j][1])   // if rows are equal
{
if(sparse1[i][2]==sparse2[j][2]) // if columns are equal
{
sum[s][1]=diff[d][1]=sparse1[i][1];
sum[s][2]=diff[d][2]=sparse1[i][2];
sum[s][3]=sparse1[i][3]+sparse2[j][3];
diff[d][3]=sparse1[i][3]-sparse2[j][3];
i++;
j++;
if(sum[s][3]!=0)
s++;
if(diff[d][3]!=0)
d++;
}
else  // if columns are not equal
{
if(sparse1[i][2]<sparse2[j][2])
{
sum[s][1]=diff[d][1]=sparse1[i][1];
sum[s][2]=diff[d][2]=sparse1[i][2];
sum[s][3]=diff[d][3]=sparse1[i][3];
i++;
s++;
d++;
}
else
{
sum[s][1]=diff[d][1]=sparse2[j][1];
sum[s][2]=diff[d][2]=sparse2[j][2];
sum[s][3]=sparse2[j][3];
diff[d][3]=0-sparse2[j][3];
j++;
d++;
s++;
}
```

```
}
}
else   //   if rows are not equal
{
if(sparse1[i][1]<sparse2[j][1])
{
sum[s][1]=diff[d][1]=sparse1[i][1];
sum[s][2]=diff[d][2]=sparse1[i][2];
sum[s][3]=diff[d][3]=sparse1[i][3];
i++;
d++;
s++;
}
else
{
sum[s][1]=diff[d][1]=sparse2[j][1];
sum[s][2]=diff[d][2]=sparse2[j][2];
sum[s][3]=sparse2[j][3];
diff[d][3]=0-sparse2[j][3];
j++;
s++;
d++;
}
}
} // end of while
if(i<=t1)
{
for(p=i;p<=t1;p++)
{
sum[s][1]=diff[d][1]=sparse1[p][1];
sum[s][2]=diff[d][2]=sparse1[p][2];
sum[s][3]=diff[d][3]=sparse1[p][3];
s++;
d++;
}
}
else if(j<=t2)
{
for(p=j;p<=t2;p++)
{
```

```
sum[s][1]=diff[d][1]=sparse2[p][1];
sum[s][2]=diff[d][2]=sparse2[p][2];
sum[s][3]=sparse2[p][3];
diff[d][3]=0-sparse2[j][3];
s++;
d++;
}
}
// end of addition and subtraction
sum[0][1]=diff[0][1]=m;
sum[0][2]=diff[0][2]=n;
sum[0][3]=s-1;
diff[0][3]=d-1;
// displaying the sum matrix
cout<<"The sum is :Row     Column       Element";
cout<<"---------------------";
for(i=0;i<s;i++)
{
cout<<sum[i][1]<<"   "<<sum[i][2]<<"      "<<sum[i][3]<<"";
}
// displaying the difference matrix
cout<<"The difference is :Row     Column      Element";
cout<<"---------------------";
for(i=0;i<d;i++)
{
cout<<diff[i][1]<<"     "<<diff[i][2]<<"        "<<diff[i][3]<<"";
}
getch();
}
```

18.18 REVERSING LINKS IN THE CASE OF CIRCULAR LIST

Write a procedure for a singly linked circular list that reverses the direction of the links. First we have to maintains three pointers, prev, curr, and next, while traversing the list. They point to consecutive nodes in the list.

If the list is non-empty, then prev points to the head node while curr and next are accordingly assigned to the next elements in the list. The circular list is traversed until curr = = head of the list. At every step, curr->next points to prev. At the end of the loop, all the nodes in the list except the head node point to their original previous nodes.

Thus at the end of the loop, head->next is assigned prev which is the last node in the list.

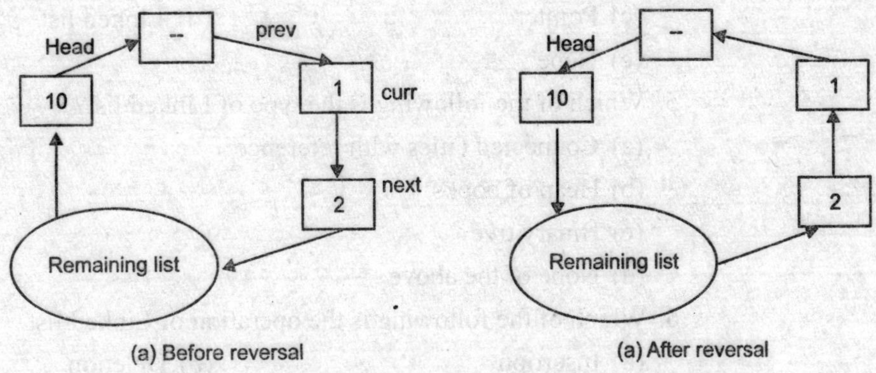

(a) Before reversal (a) After reversal

Figure 18.90: Reversing links in the case of circular list

Important Points :

1. *Note that the loop advances curr as curr=next rather than curr=curr->next, because curr->next gets changed in the loop.*
2. *The complexity of the reversal procedure is O(n).*
3. *If the head is maintained as a fixed node, that is, an empty list is denoted by a single node rather than NULL, then the functions operating on the list get simplified.*

OBJECTIVE TYPE QUESTIONS

1. Linked list is
   (a) Linear data structure (b) Non-linear data structure
   (c) Both (d) None
2. Which of the following operations can be performed on linked list?
   (a) Push (b) Pop
   (c) Insert a node (d) All of the above
   (e) None of the above
3. Linked list has how many nodes
   (a) One (b) Two
   (c) Three (d) Four
   (e) None of the above

4. Linked list can be implemented by using
   (a) Array (b) Queue
   (c) Pointer (d) Linked list
   (e) None
5. Which of the following is the type of Linked list?
   (a) Connected cities with reference
   (b) Heap of books
   (c) Binary tree
   (d) None of the above
6. Which of the following is the operation of Linked list
   (a) Insertion (b) Deletion
   (c) Create (d) Sorting
   (e) All of the above (f) None of the above
7. Which of the following is the linked list?
   (a) Singular Linked list (b) Two way linked list
   (c) Circular linked list (d) All of the above
   (e) None of the above
8. Which of the following is not the operation of Linked list:
   (a) Sorting (b) Merging
   (c) Inserting (d) All of the above
   (e) None of the above
9. Which of the following is the utility of linked list?
   (a) Stack (b) Queue
   (c) Concatenation (d) All of the above
   (e) None of the above
10. Traversing in Linked list means:
    (a) Sorting (b) Searching
    (c) Inserting (d) Deleting
    (e) Visiting (f) None of the above
11. The elements of static lists are stored in
    (a) successive memory locations
    (b) random memory locations
    (c) alternative memory locations
    (d) all of the above.

12. The elements of linked lists are stored in
    (a) successive memory locations (b) random memory locations
    (c) alternative memory locations (d) all of the above
13. Name the function that is used for memory allocation in implementation of linked list
    (a) malloc ( ) (b) realloc ( )
    (c) free ( ) (d) both (a) and (c).
14. If it is decided to create the linked list in C++, function that allocates memory is
    (a) malloc ( ) (b) new
    (c) delete (d) both (a) and (b)
15. The free () function is used to
    (a) release the memory (b) to unlink the node
    (c) to unlink the first and last node (d) None of the above
16. The pointer head points to the
    (a) first node (b) last node
    (c) either first or last node (d) None of the above
17. This type of linked list does not have null value in the last node
    (a) circular linked list (b) singly linked list
    (c) static list (d) None of the above
18. The first node of this type of linked list has NULL value
    (a) doubly linked list (b) doubly circular linked list
    (c) singly linked list (d) all of the above.
19. This type of linked list does not have first and last node
    (a) circular linked list (b) singly linked list
    (c) doubly linked list (d) static list.
20. When the malloc () function returns NULL value it means
    (a) memory is not allocated
    (b) memory is allocated but no data entered
    (c) memory is allocated
    (d) None of the above
21. If memory is not allocated, what further action will you suggest?
    (a) try again (b) exit from the program
    (c) both (a) & (b) (d) continue the program.

EXERCISES

1. Why we use linked list?
2. What is Linked list? Explain different types of linked list.
3. Explain various types of representation of linked list in memory.
4. What is Dynamic data structure.
5. Explain implementation of dynamic data structure using pointer.
6. Explain memory allocation of linked lists.
7. Write an algorithm and C ++program for different operations given below:

1. Traversing	2. Insertion
3. Deletion	4. Concatenating two lists
5. Searching	6. Reversing the direction of list
7. Copying linked list	8. Merging two lists
9. Erasing linked list	10. Spiliting linked list

8. What do you mean by Garbage collection?
9. What do you mean by Doubly linked list? Explain various operations performed on doubly linked list.
10. Explain various application of doubly linked lists to memory management.
11. What is Header linked list. Also explain two-way header lists.
12. What do you mean by Circular linked lists? Explain various operations performed on circular linked list.
13. What do you mean by Endogenous / exogenous lists?
14. What are different advantages and disadvantages of using linked list over array?
15. What are the differences between linked list and array?
16. Write comparison of linked list variations.
17. Explain representation of sparse matrices in detail.

CHAPTER 19

Stacks

19.1 INTRODUCTION

In computer science, a stack is a special type of data structure (a temporary abstract data type and data structure) which is based on the principle of Last In First Out (LIFO). Stacks are used extensively at every level of a modern computer system. For example, a modern PC uses stacks at the architecture level, which are used in the basic design of an operating system for interrupt handling and operating system function calls.

A stack is a last-in first-out data structure (LIFO). Conceptually, the stack data structure behaves like a stack of books or a stack of plates. New data is placed on the top of the stack, and when data is removed it is taken from the top. Your browser's back button likely stores a set of URLs in a stack. A stack-based computer system is one that stores temporary information primarily in stacks, rather than hardware CPU registers (a register-based computer system). The *stack* is a very common data structure used in programs. Stacks are the data structures in which, entries are added to it and removed from, at one end or location. This end is called as top of stack. The stack maintains an order of LIFO (Last in First Out).

19.2 DESCRIPTION OF STACK STRUCTURE

A stack is simply a list of elements with insertions and deletions permitted at one end called the stack top or top of stack. That means that it is possible to remove elements from a stack in reverse order from the insertion of elements into the stack. Thus, a stack data structure exhibits the LIFO (last in first out) property. Push and pop are the operations that are provided for insertion of an element into the stack and the removal of an element from the stack, respectively. Shown in Figure 19.1 are the effects of push and pop operations on the stack.

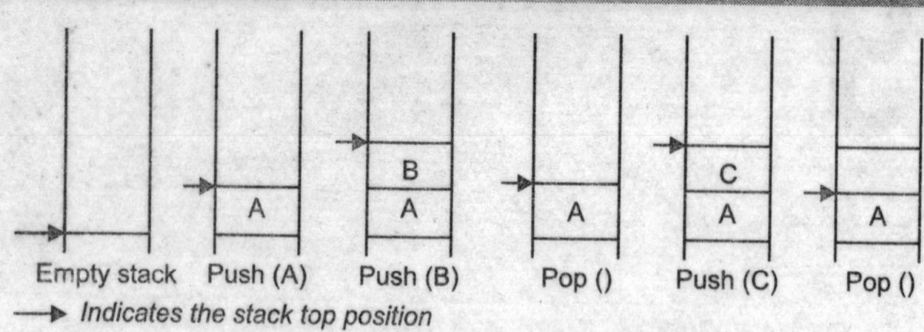

Figure 19.1: Stack operations.

The stack is a simple but important example of an abstract data type. It is used to store elements where the **L**ast element **in** is the **F**irst one **O**ut (LIFO). Anyone with a cluttered desk or an overfull sink of washing-up will be familiar with a stack. New elements are added or *pushed* onto the top of the stack. The first element to be removed or *popped* is taken from the top - the last one in. All recursive programming languages use an implicit system-stack to allocate space for local variables of routines as they are called. Some algorithms require the use of an explicit stack.

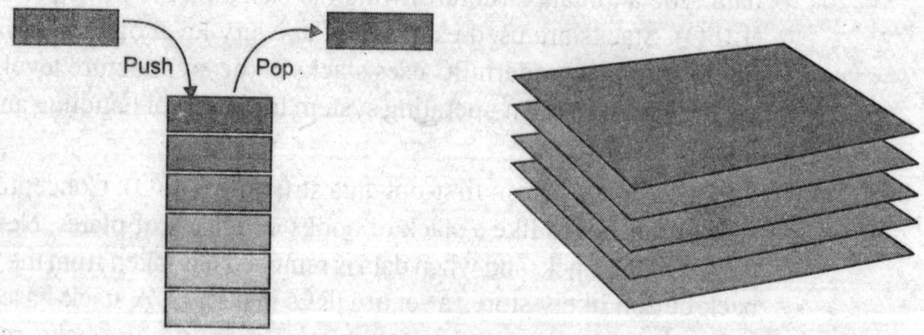

Figure 19.2: Diagrams of stacks.

Definition: *"Stack is a linear data structure that can be represented by using an array or linked list and is based on the methodology LIFO known as Last in First Out."*

Examples of Stack are:

- CD Rack
- Plates in cafeteria etc.

19.3 STACK

A stack is an ordered list in which all insertions and deletions are made at one end, called the top. Given a stack S= (a[1],a[2],.......a[n]) then we say that a1 is the bottommost element and element a[i]) is on top of element a[i-1], 1<i<=n.

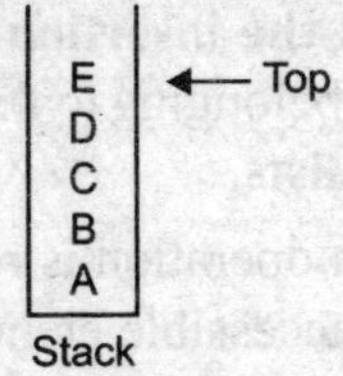

Figure 19.3: Stack Top.

The restrictions on a stack imply that if the elements A,B,C,D,E are added to the stack, n that order, then the first element to be removed/deleted must be E. Equivalently we say that the last element to be inserted into the stack will be the first to be removed. For this reason stacks are sometimes referred to as Last in First out (LIFO) lists.

19.3.1 Practical Approach: Stack

A **stack** is a temporary abstract data type and data structure based on the principle of Last in First out (LIFO). Stacks are used extensively at every level of a modern computer system. For example, a modern PC uses stacks at the architecture level, which are used in the basic design of an operating system for interrupt handling and operating system function calls. A common model of a stack is a plate or coin stacker. Plates are "pushed" onto to the top and "popped" off the top.

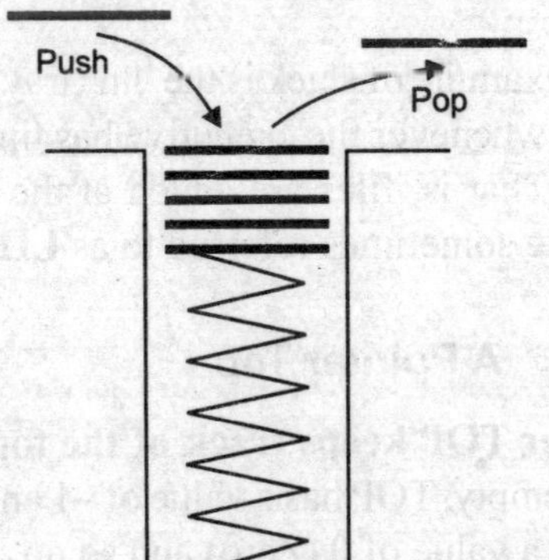

Figure 19.4: Stack operations push and pop.

There are two natural ways to implement a stack depending on the circumstances. A stack can be implemented by an array of elements. An integer "pointer" *top* indicates the element currently at the top of the stack. Initially top is zero for an empty stack. The array must be declared to have some fixed size. This is acceptable if an accurate estimate of the stack's maximum size can be made before the program runs. The other implementation uses a linked list. This is more suitable if an accurate estimate of the stack's maximum size cannot be made in advance.

Lists permit the insertion or deletion of an element to occur only at one end. A linear list belonging to this subclass is called a **stack**. They are also referred to as **pushdown lists**.

The insertion operation is referred to as **PUSH** and the deletion operation as **POP**. The most accessible element in a stack is known as the **TOP of the stack**. Since insertion and deletion operations are performed at one end of stack, the elements can only be removed in the opposite order from that in which they were added to the stack. Such a linear list is frequently referred to as a **LIFO** (Last-In First-Out) LIST.

Figure 19.5: Stack of files.

An example of stack is the "in" tray of a busy executive. The files pile up in the tray and whenever the executive has time to clear the files, he/she takes it off from the top. That is, files are added at the top and removed from the top. Therefore stacks are sometimes referred to as **LIFO structure**.

19.3.2 A Pointer Top

A pointer TOP keeps track of the top element in the stack. Initially when the stack is empty, TOP has a value of –1 and when the stack contains a single element, TOP has a value of 0 (Zero) and so on. Each time a new element is inserted in the stack, the pointer is incremented by 1. The pointer decrements by 1 each time a deletion is made from the stack.

Stack Structure

D = {d, F, A}

Where,

d : Array or a node (structure)

d = { a , TOP }

Here, **a :** Simple array or structure

TOP: Index or Pointer

F: PUSH, POP, DISPLAY, MODIFY

A: EMPTY, OVERFLOW, UNDERFLOW

19.4 STACK MODEL

A stack is a list with the restriction that inserts and deletes can be performed in only one position, namely the end of the list called the top. The fundamental operations on a stack are push, which is equivalent to an insert, and pop, which deletes the most recently inserted element. The most recently inserted element can be examined prior to performing a pop by use of the top routine. A pop or top on an empty stack is generally considered an error in the stack ADT. On the other hand, running out of space when performing a push is an implementation error but not an ADT error. Stacks are sometimes known as LIFO (last in, first out) lists. The model depicted in Figure 19.6 signifies only that pushes are input operations and pops and tops are output. The usual operations to make empty stacks and test for emptiness are part of the repertoire, but essentially all that you can do to a stack is push and pop.

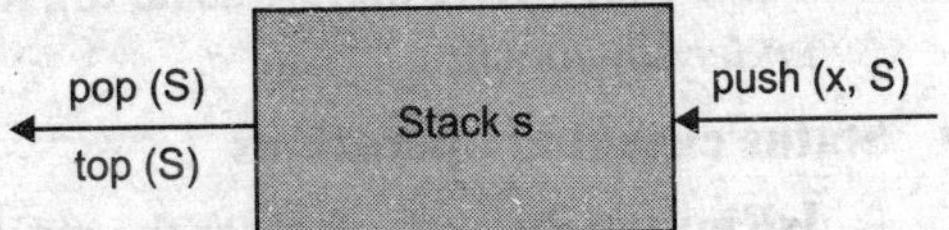

Figure 19.6: Stack model: input to a stack is by push, output is by pop.

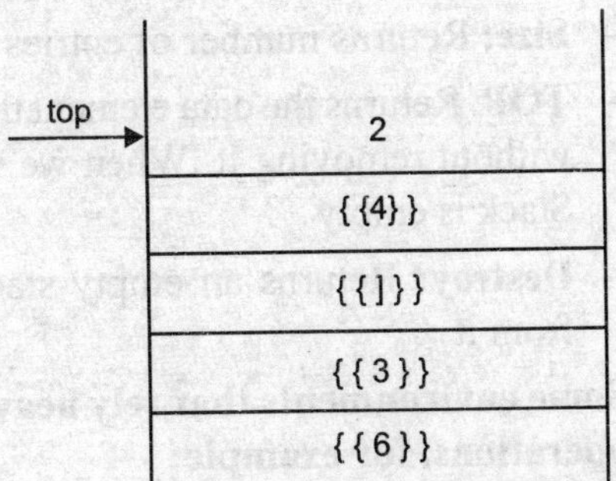

Figure 19.7: Stack model: only the top element is accessible.

Figure 19.7 shows an abstract stack after several operations. The general model is that there is some element that is at the top of the stack, and it is the only element that is visible.

19.5 COMMONLY USED STACK OPERATIONS

Now, let's think about a stack in an abstract way i.e., it doesn't hold any particular kind of thing (like books) and we aren't restricting ourselves to any particular programming language or any particular implementation of a stack.

Stacks hold objects, usually all of the same type. Most stacks support just the simple set of operations we introduced above; and thus, the main property of a stack is that objects go on and come off of the *top* of the stack (TOP).

Here are some operations, with their typical names, that are performed on stacks:

- **Initialization operation**
  - **Create:** Returns an empty stack.
- **Basic Operations**
  - **Push:** an item is put on top of the stack, increasing the stack size by one As stack size is usually limited, this may provoke a *stack overflow* if the maximum size is exceeded.
  - **Pop:** the top item is taken from the stack, decreasing stack size by one. In the case where there was no top item (i.e.the stack was empty), a *stack underflow* occurs.
- **Status checking operations**
  - **IsEmpty:** Reports whether the stack is empty or not?
  - **IsFull:** Reports whether the stack is full or not?
- **Other Operations**
  - **Size:** Returns number of entries in the stack.
  - **TOP:** Returns the data element that was most recently inserted into Stack without removing it. When we write TOP=0 or TOP=NULL, it means Stack is empty
  - **Destroy:** Returns an empty stack after deleting all the data elements from it
- **Some environments that rely heavily on stacks may provide additional operations, for example:**
  - **Dup**: the top item is popped and pushed again twice, so that an additional copy of the former top item is now on top, with the original below it.
  - **Swap** or **exchange**: the two topmost items are exchanged.
  - **Rotate**: the three topmost items exchange places in a rotary fashion. Two variants of this operation are possible; most often called **left** and **right rotate**.

19.5.1 Algorithm for Stack Operations

1. Push Operation

This operation is used to insert element onto the stack.

Algorithm 19.1: To insert element onto stack.

Push(S, TOP, X): This algorithm inserts an element X to the top of the stack which is represented by a vector S consisting MAX elements with a pointer TOP denoting the top element in the stack.

```
Step 1: [Check for stack underflow]
If (TOP>=max-1)
then write(stack overflow)
Return
Step 2: [Increment TOP]
TOP <— TOP+1
Step 3: [Insert element]
S[TOP] <— X
Step 4: [Finished]
Return
```

Explanation: Consider the stack S

Step 1: The first step of this algorithm checks for an overflow condition. If such a condition exists, then the insertion can't be performed and an appropriate error message results.

Here the value of n is 9 and, say 12 is the value which is to be pushed on to stack i.e. X is 12. As TOP is 7 which is less than the value of MAX i.e. 9, step 2 will be executed.

Position	Value
9	
8	
TOP → 7	2
6	8
5	9
4	7
3	6
2	5
1	1

Figure 19.8: Stack before push operation.

Step 2: Increment TOP by 1. Now TOP will be 8.

Step 3: Push the value of i i.e. 12 on to the stack at position pointed to by TOP use assignment

$$S[TOP] = S[8] = X = 12$$

Step 4: Return

The Stack after execution of push operation is:

Index	Stack
9	
TOP→ 8	12
7	2
6	8
5	9
4	7
3	6
2	5
1	1

Figure 19.9: Stack after push operation.

For example—Push (): This is the function which is used to insert and item in a Stack it should be noted that TOP will be incremented by 1 after every insertion. Suppose initially stack was empty now when we apply following operation we get:

push(1)
push(2)
push(3)

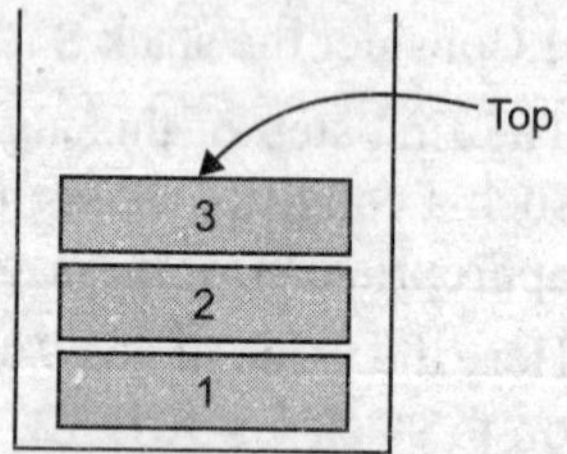

Figure 19.10: Stack perform push operations.

2. POP Operation

This operation is used to delete the element from the top of the stack.

Algorithm 19.2: To delete the element from top of stack.

Pop(S, TOP, X): This algorithm removes top element from the stack.
Step 1: [Check for the underflow on stack]
If (TOP<0)
then write(stack underflow)
Return
Step 2: [Hold the former top element of stack into X]
X <— S[TOP]
Step 3: [Decrement the TOP pointer or index by 1]
TOP <— TOP-1
Step 4: [finished-Return the popped item from the stack]
Return(X)

Explanation

Consider the stack S.

Step 1: As Underflow condition is checked for in the first step of the algorithm. If such a condition exists, then the deletion cannot be performed and an appropriate error message results. Here TOP is 7 which is greater than zero. So step 2 will be executed.

Step 2: Pop out the element stored on the top of the stack (data item stored on top of stack) X = S[7] = 2.

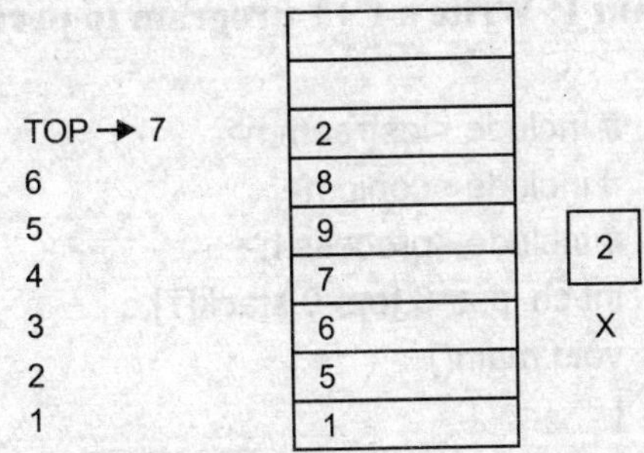

Figure 19.11: Stack before pop operation.

Step 3: The TOP is decremented by 1 and the value becomes TOP =6.

Step 4: Return

The stack after Pop Operation as:

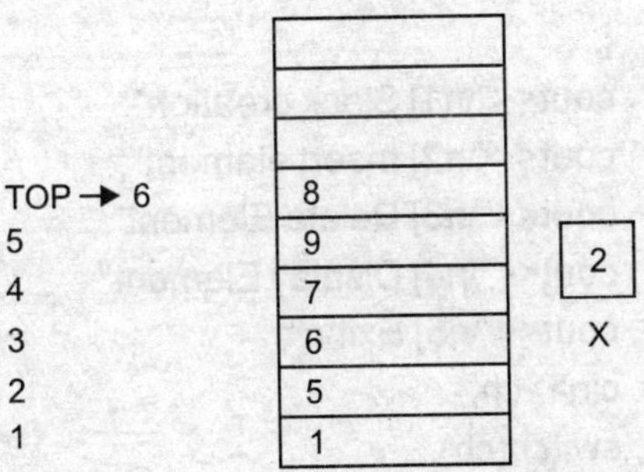

Figure 19.12: Stack after pop operation.

For example: Pop ()

This is the function which is for used for deletion (popping up) of an element from the stack It is similar to the deletion of an element at the end of a single linked list. This operation will decrement the value of TOP by 1. Now the following operation will do following changes in above stack.

Pop()

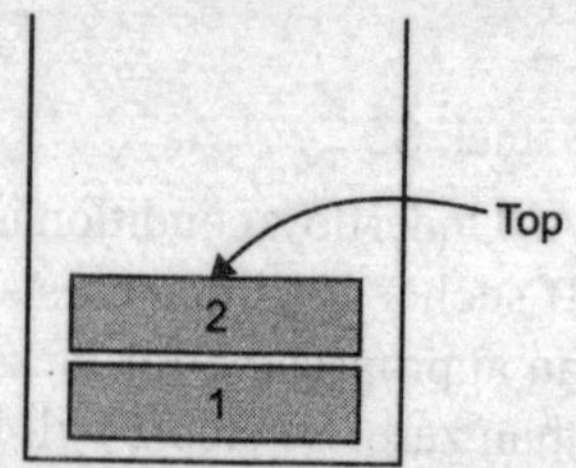

Figure 19.13: Stack perform pop operations.

Program 1: Write a C++ program to perform pop and push operation on the stack.

```
# include <iostream.h>
# include <conio.h>
# include <process.h>
int ch, p,z=6,top=0,stack[7],c;
void main()
{
void create ();
void push ();
void pop();
void show ();
clrscr ();
while(ch<5)
{
cout<<"\n1] Stack creation";
cout<<"\n2] Insert element";
cout<<"\n3] Delete Element";
cout<<"\n4] Display Element";
cout<<"\n5] Exit\n";
cin>>ch;
switch(ch)
{
case 1 : create();
continue;
case 2: push();
continue;
case 3: pop();
continue;
case 4: show ();
continue;
```

```
default: exit(0);
}
}
}
void create ()
{
cout<<"\n Enter number of elements in the stack (<7):";
cin>>c;
for (top=0;top<0;++top)
{
cout<<"Enter Element["<<top<<"]:-";
cin>>stack[top];
}
}
void push ()
{
if (top>=z)
{
cout<<"\n Stack is full";
getch();
}
else
{
cout<<"\n Enter number to be pushed:-";
cin>>stack[top];
top++;
}
}
void pop ()
{
if (top<=0)
{
cout<<"\nThe stack is empty";
getch();
}
else
top--;
}
void show()
```

```
{
for (p=top-1;p>=0;--p)
cout<<stack[p];
}
```

Output:

```
1] Stack creation
2] Insert element
3] Delete Element
4] Display Element
5] Exit
1

Enter number of elements in the stack (<7): 4
Enter Elements: 1 2 3 4
1] Stack Creation
2] Insert element
3] Delete Element
4] Display Element
5] Exit
4
0 4 3 2 1
1] Stack creation
2] Insert element
3] Delete Element
4] Display Element
5] Exit
```

3. Display Operation

This operation is used to display the element of the stack.

Algorithm 19.3: To display the element of the stack.

Display(S, TOP): This algorithm displays the contents of the stack i.e., vector S.

Step 1: [check for empty on stack]

if (TOP==-1)

then write('stack empty')

Return

Step 2: [Repeat through STEP 3 from i=TOP to 0]

Repeat through STEP 3 for i=TOP to 0 STEP-1]

Step 3: [Display the stack content]

write (S[i])

Step 4: [Finished]

Return

The first step of this algorithm checks for an empty condition. If such a condition exists, then the contents of the stack cannot be displayed and an appropriate error message results.

4. Peek Operation

This operation is used to print top most element of the stack.

Algorithm 19.4: To print top most element of the stack

Peek(S, TOP): This algorithm used to print top most element of the stack.

Step 1: [Check for the underflow on stack]

If (TOP<0)

then write(stack underflow)

Return

Step 2: [Print the value of Top most element]

write (S[TOP])

Step 3: [Finished]

Return

5. Dup Operation

This operation is used to first of all pop out the top item and then pushes the same item twice.

Algorithm 19.5: Dup operation first of all pops out the top item and then pushes the same item twice.

Dup(S, TOP, X): This algorithm will use both push and pop operations. Dup operation first of all pops out the top item and then pushes the same item twice.

An array stack, say stack S is declared with maximum size say, MAX, data item, say X and variable TOP points to the top of the stack.

Step 1: [Check for the underflow on stack]

If (TOP<0) then write (stack underflow)

Return Else go to step 9.

Step 2: [Pop out the data item into X using an assignment]. X = stack [TOP]

Step 3: [Decrement TOP by 1, as item has been popped out in step 2]. TOP <— TOP-1

Step 4: [Increment TOP]. TOP <— TOP+1

Step 5: [Push data item X onto stack using an assignment]. S [TOP] = X

Step 6: If (TOP>=max-1), then print that stack is full then Return else go to step 7.

Step 7: [Increment TOP]. TOP <— TOP+1

Step 8: [Push data item X onto stack using an assignment]

S[TOP] = X

Step 9: Return

Explanation

Consider the following stack with MAX =5, TOP=3 as shown in the Figure 19.14:

5	
4	
TOP→ 3	1
2	2
1	5

Figure 19.14: Stack with three elements

Step 1: Here TOP is 3 which is greater than 0, so step 2 will be executed.

Step 2: Pop the data item stored on top of the stack, and store it in variable X, using an assignment X = S[3] =1

Step 3: TOP = TOP-1 = 3-1=2

5	
4	
3	
TOP→ 2	2
1	5

Figure 19.15: Stack after step 3

Step 4: Increment TOP by 1. TOP = TOP +1 = 2+1 = 3.

Step 5: Push the value stored in X, i.e. 1 onto stack at position pointed to by TOP, using an assignment S [3] = X=1.

5	
4	
TOP→ 3	1
2	2
1	5

Figure 19.16: Stack after step 5

Step 6: As TOP now is 3 which is less than the value of MAX i.e. 5, so step 7 will be executed.

Step 7: Increment TOP by 1 and now TOP becomes TOP = TOP+1 = 3+1 =4

Step 8: Push the value stored in X, i.e. 1 onto stack at position pointed to by TOP using an assignment S[4] = X=1.

TOP→ 4	1
3	1
2	2
1	5

Figure 19.17: Stack after step 8

Step 9: Return

19. Swap Operation

This operation is used to interchange variables or values.

Algorithm 19.6: To swap two elements.

Swap(S, TOP, X): In the algorithm, an array stack S, say stack is declared with maximum size say, MAX, data items, say X and Y and variable TOP pointing to the top of the stack.

Step 1. [Check for the underflow on stack]

If (TOP<0) then write(stack underflow)

go to step 12 else Return

Step 2: if (MAX < 2) goto step 12 else return.

Step 3: [Pop out data item into X using an assignment]. X = S [TOP]

Step 4: [Decrement TOP by 1]

TOP= TOP-1.

Step 5: [Pop out data item, pointed to by TOP, into Y using the an assignment].

Y = S[TOP]

Step 6: [Decrement TOP by 1]. TOP= TOP-1.

Step 7: If (TOP<0) then write(stack underflow)

Step 8: [Increment TOP by 1]

TOP = TOP+1

Step 9: [Push the data item stored in X onto stack using an assignment]

S[TOP]=X

Step 10: [Increment TOP by 1]

TOP = TOP+1

Step 11: [Push the data item stored in Y onto stack using an assignment]

S[TOP]=Y

Step 12: Return

Explanation

Consider the same stack S referring to Figure 19.14, as discussed in dup operation.

Step 1: Here TOP is 3 which is greater than 0, so step 2 will be executed. As there are more than 2 data items in stack so step 3 is executed.

Step 2: if (MAX < 2) goto step 12 else return.

Step 3: Pop out the data item stored on top of the stack and store it in variable i, i.e. X = S[3] =1 (the value of data item located at location 3 pointed to by TOP).

5	
4	
3	
TOP→ 2	2
1	5

Figure 19.18: Stack after step 3

Step 4: TOP=TOP-1 =3-1=2. As TOP now is 2, which is greater than 0, so step 5 will be executed.

Step 5: Pop out the data item stored on Top of the stack and store it in variable Y, Y=S[TOP] = S[2] = 2 (the value of data item located at location 2 pointed to by TOP)

5	
4	
3	
2	
TOP→ 1	5

Figure 19.19: Stack after step 5

Step 6: Decrement TOP by 1, i.e. TOP = TOP-1 = 2-1=1.

Step 7: If (TOP<0) then write(stack underflow)

Step 8: Increment TOP by 1, i.e. TOP = TOP+1 = 1+1=2

Step 9: Push onto, data item stored in X, at location now pointed by TOP, i.e. stack [TOP] = S[2] =X = 1 (the value stored in X)

5	
4	
3	
TOP→ 2	1
1	5

Figure 19.20: Stack after step 9

Step 10: Increment TOP i.e. TOP = TOP+1 = 2+1=3

Step 11: Push onto, data item stored in Y, at location now pointed to by TOP, i.e. S[TOP] = S[3] = Y=2 (the value stored in Y). Final is Figure 19.21.

Index	Value
5	
4	
TOP→ 3	2
2	1
1	5

Figure 19.21: Stack after step 11

Step 12: Return

19.6 RIGHT ROTATE

Hint: *First of all check if n is greater than or equal to 3, because to perform rotation, we require at least three data items in the stack, then pop out the three uppermost data elements one by one adjusting pointer TOP accordingly. Store the popped out data elements in three different variables say X, Y, & Z.*

Then push the data item onto stack in the order X, Z, Y variables so that first element of stack, after right rotation, becomes the third, second becomes first and third becomes second.

All these operations, mentioned above, are performed in O (1) time. Stacks are either visualized growing from the bottom up, or growing from left to right, so that "topmost" becomes "rightmost". Let us take the same example of stack growing from left to right as shown in the Figure 19.22:

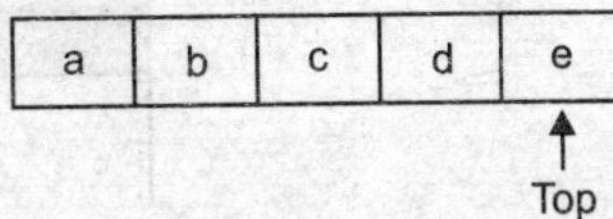

Figure 19.22: Stack growing from left to right

This means that a **right rotates** will move the first element to the third position, the second to the first and the third to the second. So the output for right rotate will be as shown in the Figure 19.23:

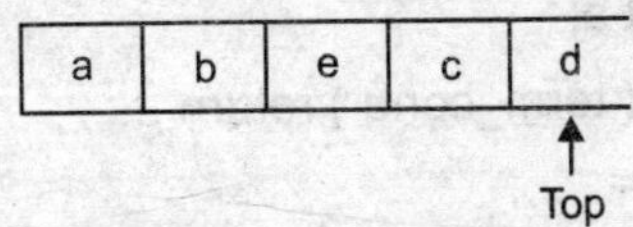

Figure 19.23: Stack after right rotate operation

19.7 STACK FRAMES

Almost invariably, programs compiled from modern high level languages (even C!) make use of a stack frame for the working memory of each procedure or function invocation. When any procedure or function is called, a number of words—the stack frame - is pushed onto a program stack. When the procedure or function returns, this frame of data is popped off the stack.

As a function calls another function, first its arguments, then the return address and finally space for local variables is pushed onto the stack. Since each function runs in its own "environment" or **context**, it becomes possible for a function to call itself — a technique known as recursion. This capability is extremely useful and extensively used - because many problems are elegantly specified or solved in a recursive way.

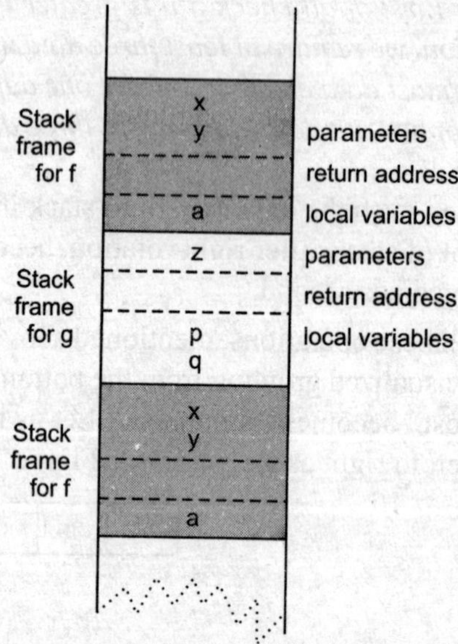

Figure 19.24: Stack frames.

Program stack after executing a pair of mutually recursive functions:

```
function f(int x, int y) {
int a;
if ( term_cond ) return ...;
a = .....;
return g(a);
}
function g(int z) {
```

```
int p,q;
p = ...; q = ...;
return f(p,q);
}
```

Note how all of function f and g's environment (their parameters and local variables) are found in the stack frame. When f is called a second time from g, a new frame for the second invocation of f is created.

19.8 MULTIPLE STACKS

Following pictures are two ways to do two stacks in array:

19.8.1 None Fixed Size of the Stacks

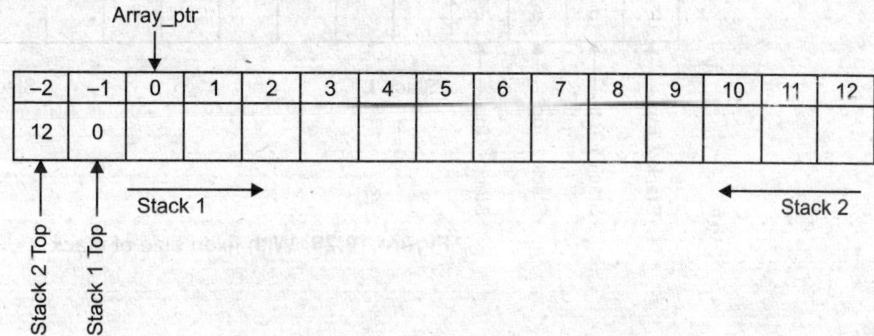

Figure 19.25: Without fixed size of stack.

- Stack 1 expands from the 0th element to the right
- Stack 2 expands from the 12th element to the left
- As long as the value of Top1 and Top2 are not next to each other, it has free elements for input the data in the array
- When both Stacks are full, Top1 and Top 2 will be next to each other
- There is no fixed boundary between Stack 1 and Stack 2
- Elements –1 and –2 are using to store the information needed to manipulate the stack (subscript for Top 1 and Top 2)

19.8.2 Fixed Size of the Stacks

- Stack 1 expands from the 0th element to the right
- Stack 2 expands from the 6th element to the left

- As long as the value of Top 1 is less than 6 and greater than 0, Stack 1 has free elements to input the data in the array
- As long as the value of Top 2 is less than 11 and greater than 5, Stack 2 has free elements to input the data in the array
- When the value of Top 1 is 5, Stack 1 is full
- When the value of Top 2 is 10, stack 2 is full
- Elements –1 and –2 are using to store the size of Stack 1 and the subscript of the array for Top 1 needed to manipulate Stack 1
- Elements –3 and –4 are using to store the size of Stack 2 and the subscript of the array for Top 2 needed to manipulate Stack 2

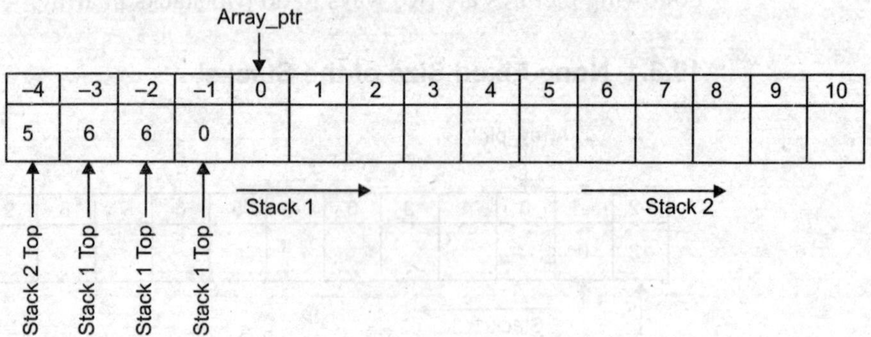

Figure 19.26: With fixed size of stack.

19.9 REPRESENTATION OF STACKS

A stack can be representation in memory using several data structures but usually it is representation using array or a linked list. The choice of representing stack has an array or a linked list depends upon whether the size of the stack is fixed or not. If the size of the stack is fixed then array representation of stack is more efficient as compared to linked list. We shall discuss both these representations in detail.

19.9.1 Array Representation of a Stack

For the sake of simplicity, we are using sequence array of Integer type items to explain the representation of stack. The top is represented by an integer denoting index of the location of top item of the stack. The stack items are placed from item[0] to item[top] continuously in that order with item[0] serving as bottom end. For instance to define a stack structure in C we can use the struct structure as shown below.

```
#define MAX 100
struct stack
{
int top ;
int item[MAX];
};
```

Once that have been done, an actual stack is s may be declared by

```
struct stack s;
```

A stack is represented as a normal array with the 0th element being the **top** of the stack. For example, the stack displayed to the left would become the following array:

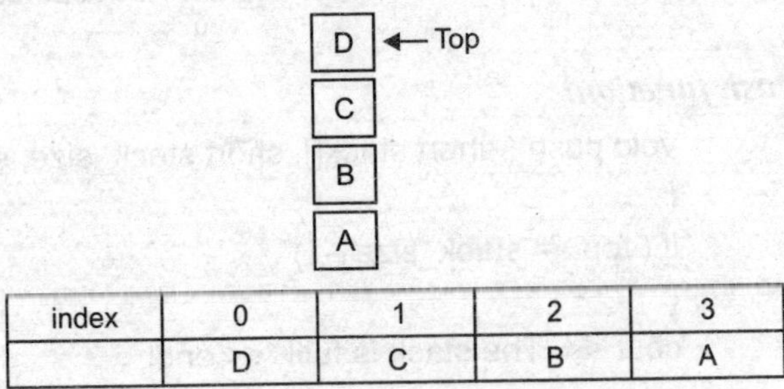

index	0	1	2	3
	D	C	B	A

Figure 19.27: Array representation of a stack.

Another way for Array Representation is as shown below:

0	1	2	3	4	5	6	7	...		
A	B	C	D							

top	4

Figure 19.28: Array representation of a stack with pointer top.

Algorithm 19.7: To insert or push an ITEM in the stack.

PUSH (STACK, TOP, MAXSTK, ITEM)

This algorithm pushes an ITEM onto a stack

Step 1: [When stack is already filled?]

If TOP = MAXSTK, then print: OVERFLOW, and Return.

Step 2: Set TOP = TOP+ 1. [Increment TOP by 1.]

Step 3: Set STACK [TOP] = ITEM. [Inserts ITEM in new TOP position of the stack.]

Step 4: End.

Explanation

Add: a push( ) operation adds an item to the topmost location on the stack.

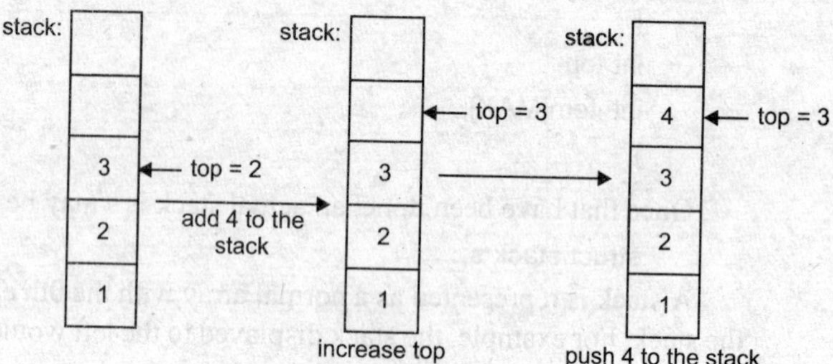

Figure 19.29: Push operation

Push function:

```
void push ( short stack[], short stack_size, short top, short item)
{
if ( top >= stack_size –1)
{
cout << "The stack is full!" << endl;
return;
}
stack[+ + top] = item;
}
```

POP operation

Algorithm 19.8: To delete or pop an ITEM from the stack.

POP (STACK, TOP, ITEM)

This algorithm deletes or pops the top element of STACK and assigns it to the variable name ITEM.

Step 1: [Stack has an item to be removed from it?]

If TOP = 0, then Print: UNDERFLOW, and Return.

Step 2: Set ITEM = STACK [TOP]. [Assign value of TOP element to ITEM.]

Step 3: Set TOP = TOP- 1. [Decrement TOP by 1.]

Step 4: End.

Explanation

Delete: a pop( ) operation removes an item from the topmost location on the stack

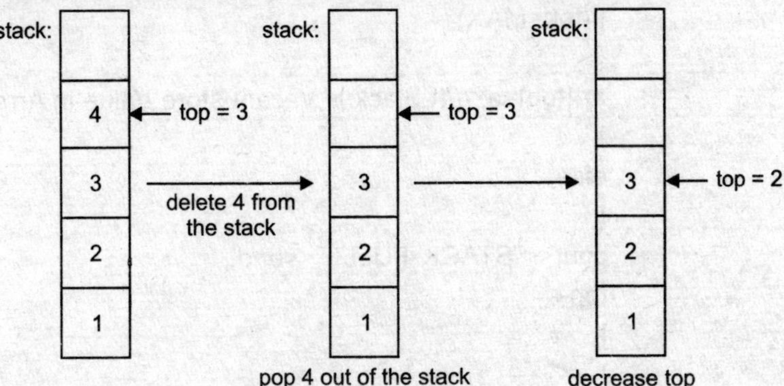

Figure 19.30: Pop operation

Pop function:

```
short pop (short stack[], short stack_size, short top)
{
if ( top = = –1)
{
cout << "The stack is empty!" << endl;
return 0;
}
return stack[top – – ] ;
}
```

Program 2: Write a C++ program to implement stack using arrays.

```
#include <iostream>
#include<conio.h>
#define MAX 10        // MAXIMUM STACK CONTENT
class stack
{
private:
int arr[MAX];   // Contains all the Data
int top;              //Contains location of Topmost Data pushed onto Stack
public:
stack()          //Constructor
{
top=-1;      //Sets the Top Location to -1 indicating an empty stack
}
void push(int a)  // Push ie. Add Value Function
{
top++;        // increment to by 1
```

```
if(top<MAX)
{
arr[top]=a;  //If Stack is Vacant store Value in Array
}
else
{
cout<<"STACK FULL!!"<<endl;
top--;
}
}
int pop()           // Delete Item. Returns the deleted item
{
if(top==-1)
{
cout<<"STACK IS EMPTY!!!"<<endl;
return NULL;
}
else
{
int data=arr[top];      //Set Topmost Value in data
arr[top]=NULL;          //Set Original Location to NULL
top--;                  // Decrement top by 1
return data;            // Return deleted item
}
}
};
void main()
{
stack a;
a.push(3);
cout<<"3 is Pushed\n";
a.push(10);
cout<<"10 is Pushed\n";
a.push(1);
cout<<"1 is Pushed\n\n";
cout<<a.pop()<<" is Popped\n";
cout<<a.pop()<<" is Popped\n";
cout<<a.pop()<<" is Popped\n";
getch();
}
```

Output:

3 is Pushed
10 is Pushed
1 is Pushed

1 is Popped
10 is Popped
3 is Popped

Program 3: Write a C++ program for Stack implementation as a class.

```
# include<iostream.h>
# include<process.h>
# include<conio.h>
# define SIZE 20
class stack
{
int a[SIZE];
int tos; // Top of Stack
public:
stack();
void push(int);
int pop();
int isempty();
int isfull();
};
stack::stack()
{
tos=0; //Initialize Top of Stack
}
int stack::isempty()
{
return (tos==0?1:0);
}
int stack::isfull()
{
return (tos==SIZE?1:0);
}
void stack::push(int i)
{
if(!isfull())
```

```
{
a[tos]=i;
tos++;
}
else
{
cerr<<"A ! Possible Data Loss !";
}
}
int stack::pop()
{
if(!isempty())
{
return(a[--tos]);
}
else
{
cerr<<"Stack is empty! What to pop...!";
}
return 0;
}
void main()
{
stack s;
int ch=1,num;
while(ch!=0)
{
cout<<"Stack Operations Mani Menu
1.Push
2.Pop
3.IsEmpty
4.IsFull
0.Exit
";
cin>>ch;
switch(ch)
{
case 0:
exit(1); //Normal Termination of Program
case 1:
```

```
cout<<"Enter the number to push";
cin>>num;
s.push(num);
break;
case 2:
cout<<"Number popped from the stack is: "<<s.pop()<<endl;
break;
case 3:
(s.isempty())?(cout<<"Stack is empty."):(cout<<"Stack is not empty.");
break;
case 4:
(s.isfull())?(cout<<"Stack is full."):(cout<<"Stack is not full.");
break;
default:
cout<<"Illegal Option. Please try again ";
}
}//end of while
getch();
}
```

Program 4: Write a C++ program for Stack implementation and reversed its contents.

```
# include<iostream.h>
# include<conio.h>
# define SIZE 20
class stack
{
int a[SIZE];
int tos; // Top of Stack
public:
stack();
void push(int);
int pop();
int isempty();
int isfull();
};
stack::stack()
{
tos=0; //Initialize Top of Stack
}
```

```
int stack::isempty()
{
return (tos==0?1:0);
}
int stack::isfull()
{
return (tos==SIZE?1:0);
}
void stack::push(int i)
{
if(!isfull())
{
cout<<"Pushing "<<i<<endl;
a[tos]=i;
tos++;
}
else
{
cerr<<"Stack overflow error !
Possible Data Loss !";
}
}
int stack::pop()
{
if(!isempty())
{
cout<<"Popping "<<a[tos-1]<<endl;
return(a[--tos]);
}
else
{
cerr<<"Stack is empty! What to pop...!";
}
return 0;
}
void reverse(stack s)
{
stack s2;
while(!s.isempty())
{
```

```
s2.push(s.pop());
}
cout<<"Reversed contents of the stack..."<<endl;
while(!s2.isempty())
{
cout<<s2.pop()<<endl;
}
}//end of fn.
void main()
{
clrscr();
stack s;
s.push(1);
s.push(2);
s.push(3);
reverse(s);
getch();
}
```

Representation of two stacks using an array

Two stacks are represented in an array twostacks[0…N–1], such that one stack starts from start of the array and grows towards its end while the other one starts from the end of the array and grows towards the start. Thus at any time, the maximum number of elements that the two stacks together can accommodate is N. Write functions Push(stacki, data) and Delete(stacki) to add element data and to delete an element from stack number stacki, 1 <= stacki <= 2. The functions should be able to add elements to the stacks as long as there are fewer than N elements in both stacks together.

1. The two stacks are characterized by their indices (stack pointers). Index 1 starts from –1 and goes up to N – 1 while index 2 starts from N and goes up to 0. When index 1 equals –1, it signifies that stack 1 is empty. When index 2 equals to N, that signifies that stack 2 is empty.
2. If the array is full, indices 1 and 2 point to consecutive elements. This situation is characterized as (index2 – index1 = = 1).

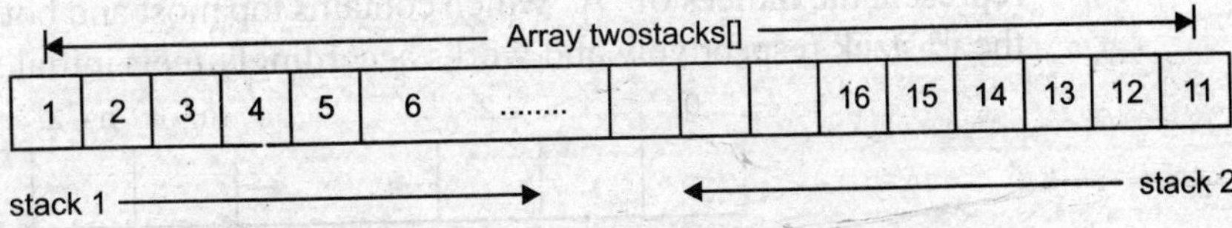

Figure 19.31: Representation of two stacks using an array

3. In Push(stacki,data), this condition is checked to signify overflow. If space is available, insertion of the element proceeds. If stacki == 1 then index 1 is incremented and the data is inserted at the index. If stacki == 2, index 2 is decremented and the data is inserted at the index.
4. In Delete(stacki), the condition for underflow is checked. If stacki == 1 then index 1 == –1 signifies underflow of stack 1. If stacki == 2 then index 2 == N signifies underflow of stack 2. If an element exists, then deletion of the element at the stack top proceeds. If stacki == 1 then index 1 is decremented, whereas if stacki == 2 then index 2 is incremented.

The problem of underflow and overflow

Overflow problem is faced in push operation in a stack. If we push an item to the stack, which is already full, this called as overflow. Underflow problem is faced in pop operation in a stack. if we pop a data item from the stack, which is empty; this state is called as underflow. The problem of underflow is easily manageable, but the problem of overflow takes the shape of time-space trade-off. In this case, it is advisable to have two combined stacks, so that if required one stack can use the space of other. Representing space of other multiple stacks in single array:

Anchored lists are more appropriate for stacks, where the non-anchored end of the list represents the top of the stack.

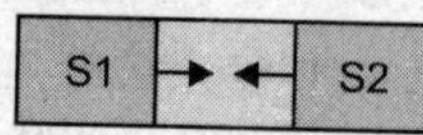

Figure 19.32: Concept of two stacks

Two stacks can be anchored at opposite ends of an array. As the stacks fill with data, they will "grow" towards each other. Figure 19.32 illustrates this concept. By filling the array with the two stacks anchored at opposite ends, the user can have the utility of two stacks while using the storage of one array.

In many applications, several stacks are required. Sometimes, we don't give memory space to different stacks; rather, we prefer to use single array to accommodate all stacks. Suppose "A" is an array of size "m" declared as, data type A [m].

Let us suppose n numbers of stacks are to be accommodated in single array "A" as shown in the Figure 19.33. We simply divide the array "A" in "n" approximately equal parts where the ith stack will be stored in "A" from index value of i * [m/n] to index value of (i * [m/n]-1). Let us suppose B [i] and C [i] represent the indices of "A" which contains top most and bottom most elements of the ith stack respectively and works accordingly their initial setting.

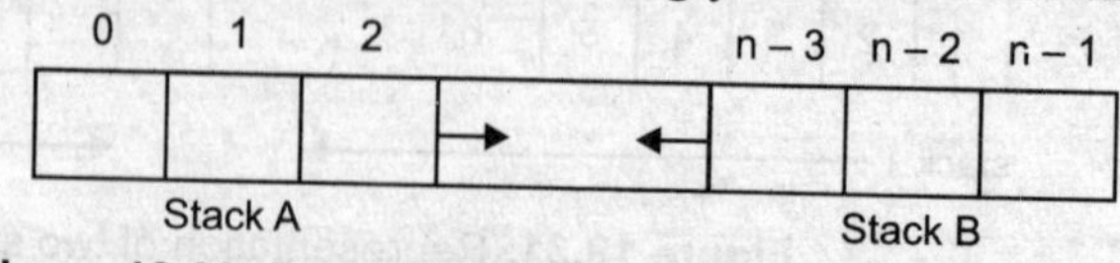

Figure 19.33: Representing two stacks in single array "A".

In this case, stack A, if required can use the space of stack B and vice-versa.

19.9.2 Representation of Stack using Linked-list

An alternative and efficient representation of stacks is possible by using linked lists for storing the data elements using dynamic memory. The advantages of linked list representation of stack over array representation are:

1. There is no need of knowing the stack size before implementing it, as dynamic memory allocation technique helps the programmer to declare the memory space at run time.
2. The stack is never full as long as the system has enough space for dynamic memory allocation.
3. Data movement, i.e. pushing or inserting and popping or deleting from stack is very easily handled with the concept of pointer in linked lists.

Remember that a stack implemented using linked list is called as linked stack.

Definition of linked list: *A linked list is a set of nodes (a node can be a structure or a class) defined arbitrarily in memory; a node has a special variable (pointer) of the same type as the structure/class, which points to the next memory location, thus making the list values continuous. The following picture shows how a linked list looks like when it is created. The first node of a list is referred to as head/start most of the time and the last node is referred to as tail/end, the tail/end of the list always points to NULL or 0 (zero), which is also referred to as grounding as shown in the Figure 19.34*

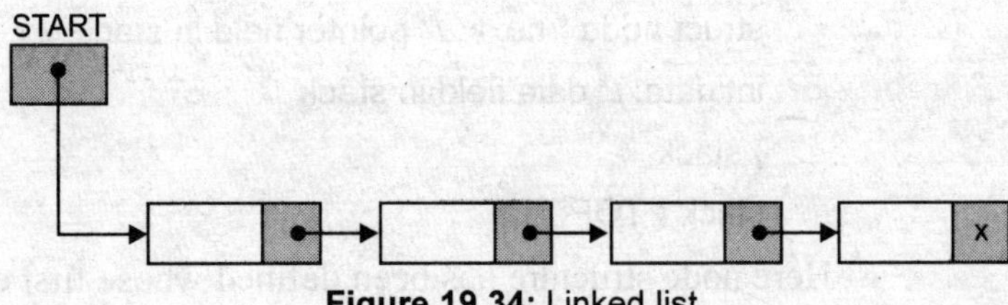

Figure 19.34: Linked list

Node organization

Basic element of a linked list is a "record" structure, of at least two fields (a class definition with these instance variables).

The object that holds the data and refers to the next element in the list, is called a **node**.

Data or Info next

data or Info component may actually be several fields or instance variables of any complexity. **next** is a pointer that points to the next element in the structure. There can be multiple reference fields but we won't consider that now.

Consider the stack of integers 10,20,30,40 (10 is the top, 40 the bottom). The logical order of the values in a stack is very clear; first comes the top element, next comes the element just below the top element, etc. In a linked implementation, the memory cell containing the top element will also contain a pointer to the second element, the memory cell containing the second element will contain a pointer to the third element, etc. What about the memory cell containing the bottom element?

There will be one memory cell for each element in the stack; in this memory cell we need to store *two* things: the value of the element, which is an integer in this example but could be anything, and a pointer to the memory cell of the next element. We can now draw the node-and-arc diagram representing Stack as shown in the Figure 19.35 as:

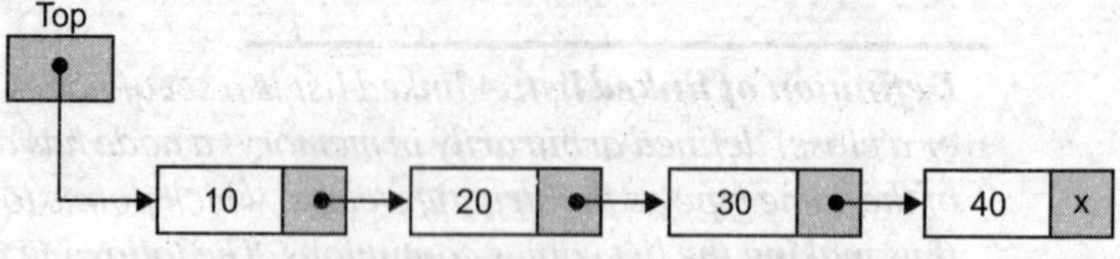

Figure 19.35: Node-and-arc representing stack

Formally a linked stack may be declared as:

```
typedef struct node
{
struct node * next ; /* pointer field in stack */
int data; /* data field in stack */
} stack;
stack * TOP;
```

Here node structure has been defined whose first element data holds the data element of the stack and the second element next holds the address of the element below it in the stack. Pointer variable TOP of type stack has also been declared.

Push operation

It's very similar to the addition in a dynamic linked list. The only difference is that here you'll add the new element only at the end of the list, which means addition can happen only from the TOP. Since a dynamic list is used for the stack, the Stack is also dynamic, means it has no prior size set. So, we don't have to check the Overflow condition in linked stack. This is as shown below:

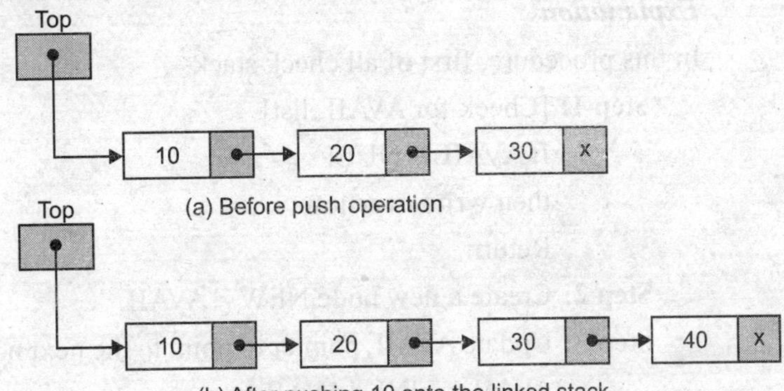

Figure 19.36: Push Operation

In Step [1] we create the new element to be pushed to the Stack.

In Step [2] the TOP most element is made to point to our newly created element.

In Step [3] the TOP is moved and made to point to the last element in the stack, which is our newly added element.

Algorithm 19.9: To insert node in the linked stack.

PUSH(AVAIL, TOP, LINK, NEW, INFO): Given a linked stack with pointer TOP pointing to the first node of the linked list. The AVAIL pointer points to the first node of the availability list. This algorithm pushes an ITEM onto the stack.

Step 1: [Check for AVAIL list]

If AVAIL = NULL

then write overflow

Return

Step 2: [Create a new node]

NEW = AVAIL

Step 3: [Update AVAIL, pointer]

AVAIL =LINK [AVAIL]

Step 4: [Copy ITEM into info part of new node]

INFO (NEW) = ITEM

Step 5: [Set link part of new node to top]

LINK (NEW) = TOP

Step 6: [TOP points to new node]

TOP =NEW

Step 7: Return

Explanation

In this procedure, first of all check stack.

Step 1: [Check for AVAIL list]
If AVAIL = NULL
then write overflow
Return

Step 2: Create a new node NEW = AVAIL

Step 3: Update AVAIL pointer to point to the next node of the availability list.
AVAIL =LINK [AVAIL]

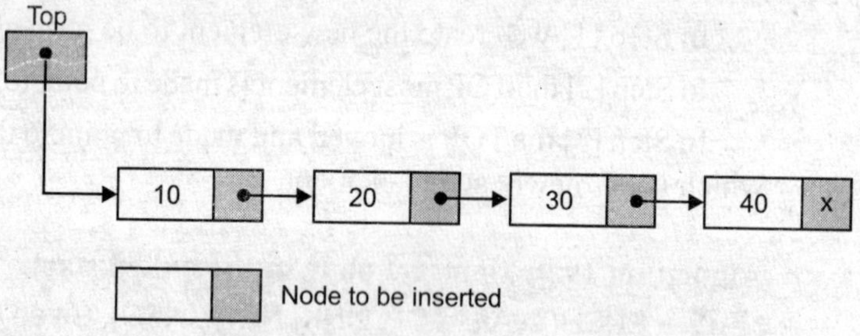

Figure 19.37: Before new node to be inserted.

Step 4: Now, Copy ITEM into INFO part of NEW node
INFO (NEW) = 5

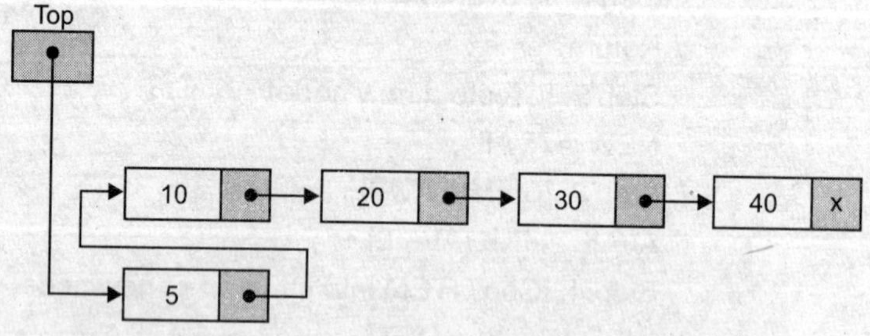

Figure 19.38: After insertion of new node having value 5.

Step 5: Set link part of NEW node to TOP
LINK (NEW) = TOP

Step 6: TOP points to new node
TOP =5

Step 7: Return

POP operation

This is again very similar to deletion in any Linked List, but you can only delete from the end of the list and that too, one at a time; and that makes it a stack. Here, we'll have a list pointer, "Next", which will be pointing to the last but one element in the List(stack). Every time we POP, the TOP most elements will be deleted and " Next " will be made as the TOP most element as shown below:

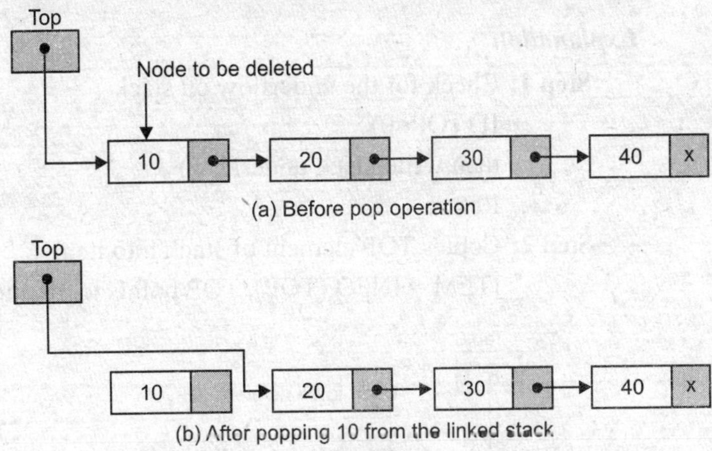

Figure 19.39: Pop operation.

In step [1] we delete topmost element 10 from linked stack

In step [2] we freed the TOP most element shown in Figure above

In step [3] we made the "Next" node as our TOP most element.

Algorithm 19.10: To delete node from linked stack.

POP(AVAIL, TOP, LINK, NEW, INFO, SAVE): Given a linked stack with pointer TOP pointing to the first node of the linked list. The AVAIL pointer points to the first node of the availability list. This algorithm pops the top element oh the linked stack and assign it to the local variable an ITEM. Here 'SAVE' is a local pointer variable ITEM and 'SAVE' is a local pointer variable which points to the deleted node.

Step 1: [Check for the underflow on stack]

If (TOP<0)

then write(stack underflow)

Return

Step 2: [Copies top element of stack into item]

ITEM = INFO (TOP)

Step 3: [Save TOP element]

SAVE =TOP

Step 4: [Reset TOP Element of stack into ITEM]

TOP = LINK [TOP]
Step 5: [Set link part to avail]
LINK (SAVE) = AVAIL
Step 6: [save pop node to avail list]
AVAIL = SAVE
Step 7: Return

Explanation

Step 1: Check for the underflow on stack
If (TOP<0)
then write(stack underflow)
Return

Step 2: Copies TOP element of stack into item
ITEM = INFO (TOP), TOP points to 10, then ITEM = 10

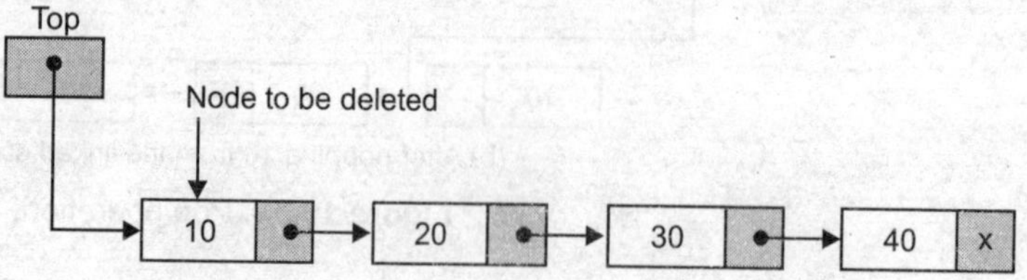

Figure 19.40: Before First node to be deleted.

Step 3: SAVE TOP element
SAVE =10

Step 4: Reset TOP Element of stack into ITEM, next ITEM is 20, now top points to 20.
TOP = 20

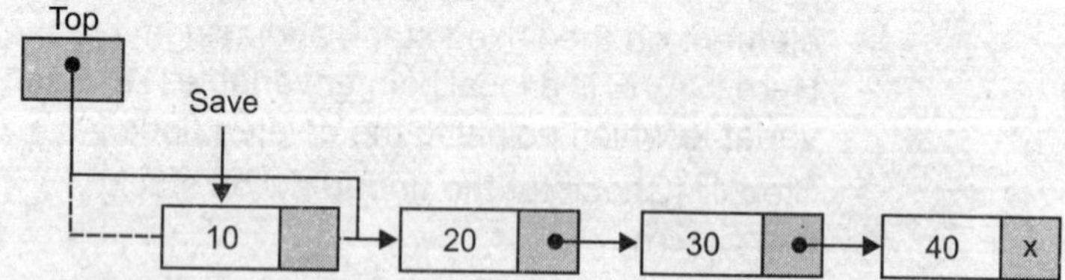

Figure 19.41: After deletion of first node having value 10.

Step 5: Set LINK part to AVAIL
LINK (SAVE) = AVAIL

Step 6: SAVE pop node to avail list
AVAIL = SAVE

Step 7: Return .

Implementation of a stack using linked representation

In earlier section we had used arrays to store the elements that get added to the stack. But when implemented as an array it suffers basic limitation of an array that is its size cannot increased or decreased once it is declared. As a result, one ends up reserving too much space or too less space for an array and in turn for a stack. This problem can be solved by stack using linked list. For this type of implementation, let us use singly linked list for storing stack elements. In this type of implementation the top of the stack is given by a pointer top pointing to the first item of the list, ie. in the beginning of the list. So the stack elements ordered from top to bottom in linked list from left to right name of the list pointing to the top of the stack. The advantage of the this strategy is the push, pop operation takes constant time.

In C++ the stack node can be defined as

```
struct node
{
int data ;
node * link;
};
```

The operations are done using pointer manipulations, below **pseudo-code** explain the stack operations

```
push (item x,stack s)
{
temp =new node;
temp → data=x; //putting value into the node
temp → link=top; //Assigning temp's link to the top of the stack
top=temp //updating the top
}
int pop (s)
{ if (s=NULL)
"Stack is empty";
int item;
temp=top;
item=temp →data;
top=top→link;
return item;
}
```

Initially the list is empty, so the top pointer is NULL. The push function takes a pointer to an existing list as the first parameter and a data value to be pushed as the second parameter, creates a new node by using the data value, and adds it to the top of the existing list. A pop function takes a pointer to an existing list as the first parameter, and a pointer to a data object in which the popped value is to be returned as a second parameter. Thus it retrieves the value of the node pointed to by the top pointer, takes the top point to the next node, and destroys the node that was pointed to by the top.

If this strategy is used for creating a stack with the previously used four data values: 10, 20, 30, and 40, then the stack is created as shown in Figure 19.42.

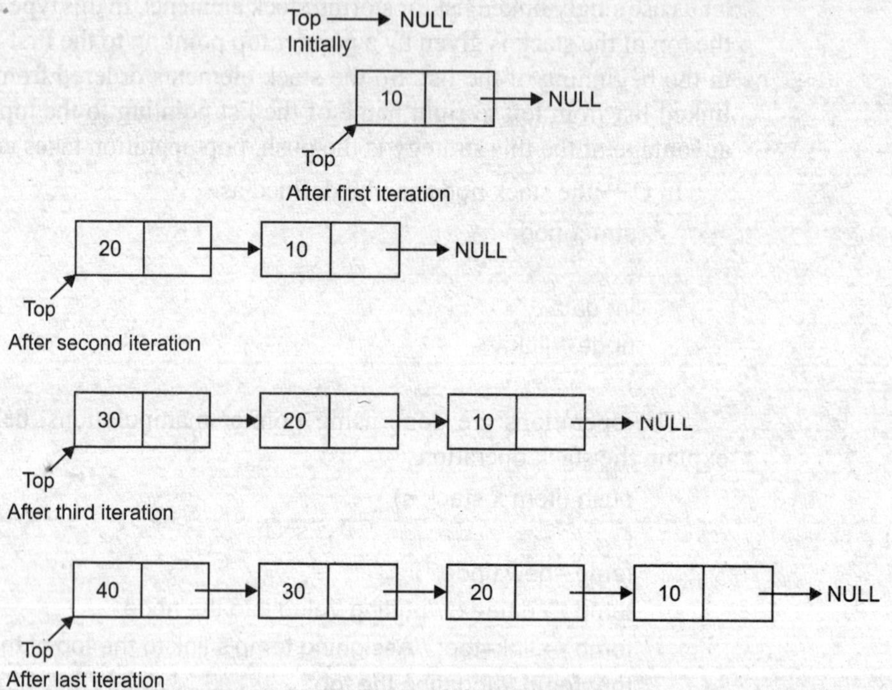

Figure 19.42: Linked stack.

Program 5: Write a C++ program to implement stack using linked list.

```
#include <iostream>
#include<conio.h>
struct node
{
int data;
node *link;
};
class lstack
{
private:
node* top;
```

```
public:
lstack()
{
top=NULL;
}
void push(int n)
{
node *tmp;
tmp=new node;
if(tmp==NULL)
cout<<"\nSTACK FULL";
tmp->data=n;
tmp->link=top;
top=tmp;
}
int pop()
{
if(top==NULL)
{
cout<<"\nSTACK EMPTY";
return NULL;
}
node *tmp;
int n;
tmp=top;
n=tmp->data;
top=top->link;
delete tmp;
return n;
}
~lstack()
{
if(top==NULL)
return;
node *tmp;
while(top!=NULL)
{
tmp=top;
top=top->link;
```

```
delete tmp;
}
}
};
void main()
{
lstack s;
s.push(11);
s.push(101);
s.push(99);
s.push(78);
cout<<"Item Popped = "<<s.pop()<<endl;
cout<<"Item Popped = "<<s.pop()<<endl;
cout<<"Item Popped = "<<s.pop()<<endl;
getch();
}
```

19.10 STACK APPLICATIONS

Five major applications of stacks are presented here. These examples are central to many activities that a computer must do and deserve time spent with them.

1. Expression evaluation
2. Backtracking (game playing, finding paths, exhaustive searching)
3. Memory management, run-time environment for nested language features.
4. Parenthesis matching
5. Balancing symbols

19.10.1 Expression Evaluation

In particular we will consider arithmetic expressions. Understand that there are boolean and logical expressions that can be evaluated in the same way. Control structures can also be treated similarly in a compiler.

This study of arithmetic expression evaluation is an example of problem solving where you solve a simpler problem and then **transform** the actual problem to the simpler one.

Aside: The NP-Complete problem. There are a set of apparently intractable problems: finding the shortest route in a graph (Travelling Salesman Problem), bin packing, linear programming, etc. that are similar enough that if a polynomial solution is ever found (exponential solutions abound) for one of these problems, then the solution can be applied to all problems.

Infix, Prefix and Postfix Notation

Infix Expression

In an expression if operator symbol is placed between two operands, it is called as infix expression and this way of writing an expression is called as Infix notation of an expression

Example is

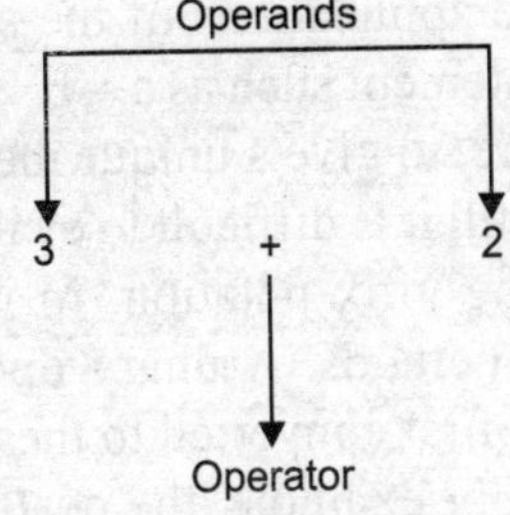

(How infix operation occurs)

Prefix Expression

In an expression if operator symbol is placed before its two operands, it is called as prefix expression or polish expression and this way of writing an expression is called as prefix or polish notation of an expression.

This notation was derived in 1920 by the polish mathematician Jan Lukasiewicz.

Example is:

The prefix or polish expression of infix expression 3+2 is +3 2 or +2 3.

Postfix expression

In an expression, if operator symbol is placed after its two operands, it is called as postfix expression or reverse polish expression and this way of writing an expression is called as postfix or reverse polish Notation (RPN) of an expression.

RPN was invented by Australian philosopher and computer scientist Charles Hamblin in the mid 1950s.

Example is:

The postfix or RPN of infix expression 3+2 is 3 2 + or 2 3 +

We are accustomed to write arithmetic expressions with the operation between the two operands: **a+b** or **c/d**. If we write **a+b*c**, however, we have to apply precedence rules to avoid the ambiguous evaluation (add first or multiply first?).

There's no real reason to put the operation between the variables or values. They can just as well precede or follow the operands. You should note the advantage of prefix and postfix: the need for precedence rules and parentheses are eliminated.

Infix	Prefix	Postfix
a + b	+ a b	a b +
a + b * c	+ a * b c	a b c * +
(a + b) * (c - d)	* + a b - c d	a b + c d - *

Postfix expressions are easily evaluated with the aid of a stack.

One of the applications of the stack is in expression evaluation. A complex assignment statement such as a = b + c*d/e–f may be interpreted in many different ways. Therefore, to give a unique meaning, the precedence and associativity rules are used. But still it is difficult to evaluate an expression by computer in its present form, called the infix notation. In infix notation, the binary operator comes in between the operands. A unary operator comes before the operand. To get it evaluated, it is first converted to the postfix form, where the operator comes after the operands. For example, the postfix form for the expression a*(b–c)/d is abc–*d/. A good thing about postfix expressions is that they do not require any precedence rules or parentheses for unique definition. So, evaluation of a postfix expression is possible using a stack-based algorithm.

Postfix expressions

Suppose we have a pocket calculator and would like to compute the cost of a shopping trip. To do so, we add a list of numbers and multiply the result by 1.06; this computes the purchase price of some items with local sales tax added. If the items are 4.99, 5.99, and 6.99, then a natural way to enter this would be the sequence

4.99 + 5.99 + 6.99 * 1.06 =

Depending on the calculator, this produces either the intended answer, 19.05, or the scientific answer, 18.39. Most simple four-function calculators will give the first answer, but better calculators know that multiplication has higher precedence than addition.

On the other hand, some items are taxable and some are not, so if only the first and last items were actually taxable, then the sequence

4.99 * 1.06 + 5.99 + 6.99 * 1.06 =

would give the correct answer (18.69) on a scientific calculator and the wrong answer (19.37) on a simple calculator. A scientific calculator generally comes with parentheses, so we can always get the right answer by parenthesizing, but with a simple calculator we need to remember intermediate results.

A typical evaluation sequence for this example might be to multiply 4.99 and 1.06, saving this answer as a_1. We then add 5.99 and a_1, saving the result in a_1. We multiply 6.99 and 1.06, saving the answer in a_2, and finish by adding a_1 and a_2, leaving the final answer in a_1. We can write this sequence of operations as follows:

4.99 1.06 * 5.99 + 6.99 1.06 * +

This notation is known as postfix or reverse Polish notation and is evaluated exactly as we have described above. The easiest way to do this is to use a stack. When a number is seen, it is pushed onto the stack; when an operator is seen, the operator is applied to the two numbers (symbols) that are popped from the stack and the result is pushed onto the stack. For instance, the postfix expression

6 5 2 3 + 8 * + 3 + *

is evaluated as follows: The first four symbols are placed on the stack. The resulting stack is

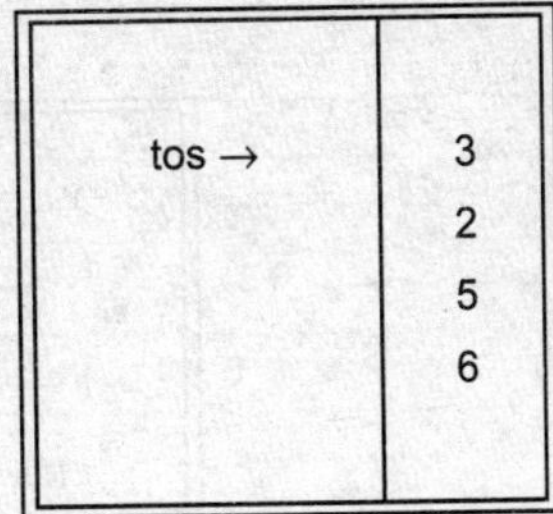

Next a '+' is read, so 3 and 2 are popped from the stack and their sum, 5, is pushed.

tos →
5
5
6

Next 8 is pushed.

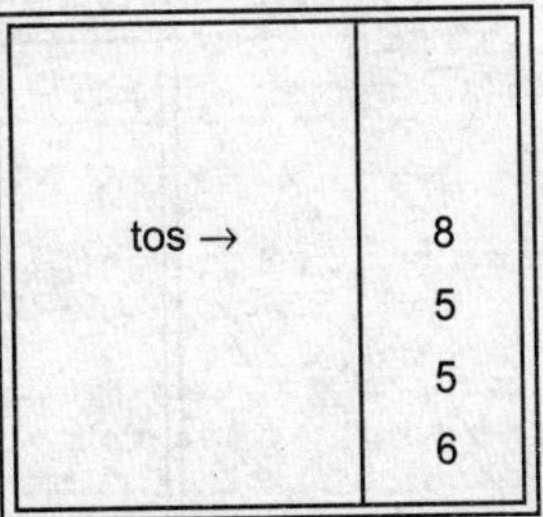

Now a '*' is seen, so 8 and 5 are popped as 8 * 5 = 40 is pushed.

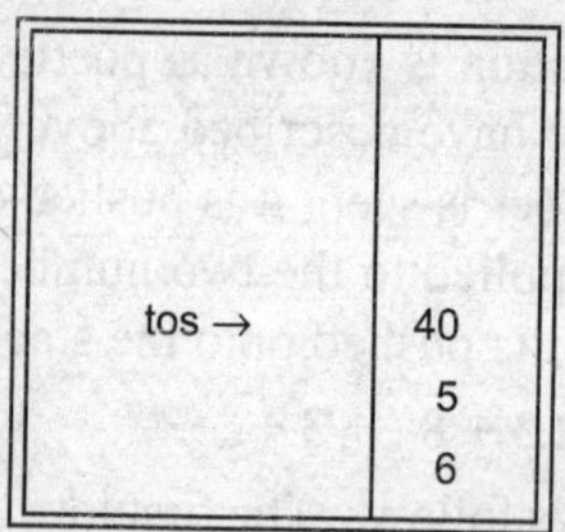

Next a '+' is seen, so 40 and 5 are popped and 40 + 5 = 45 is pushed.

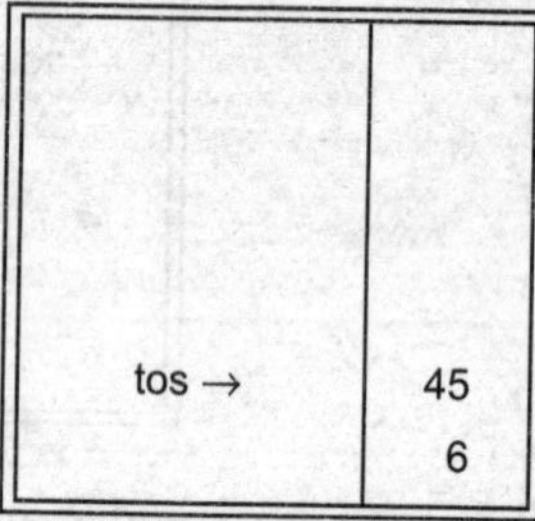

Now, 3 is pushed.

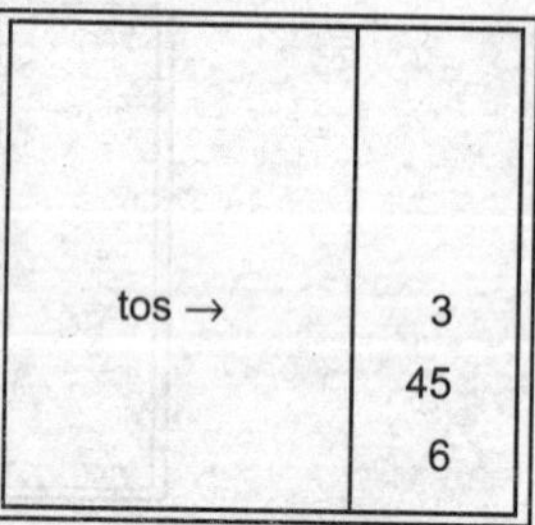

Next '+' pops 3 and 45 and pushes 45 + 3 = 48.

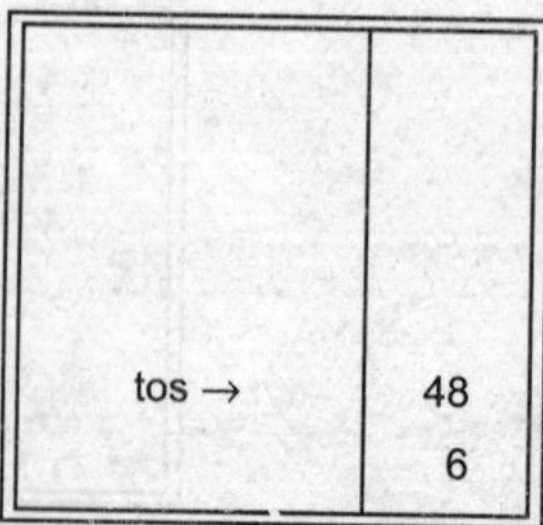

Finally, a '*' is seen and 48 and 6 are popped, the result 6 * 48 = 288 is pushed.

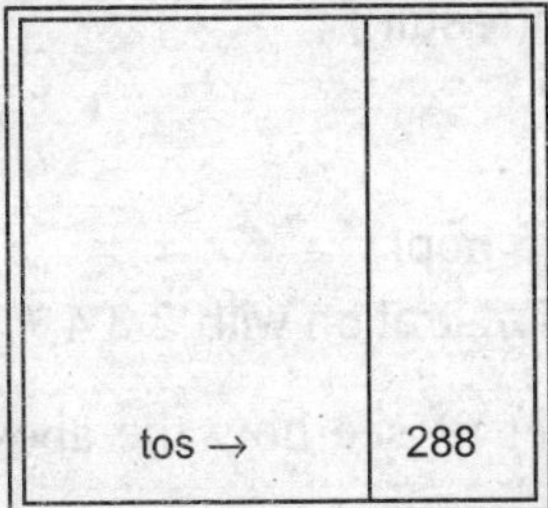

The time to evaluate a postfix expression is O(n), because processing each element in the input consists of stack operations and thus takes constant time. The algorithm to do so is very simple. Notice that when an expression is given in postfix notation, there is no need to know any precedence rules; this is an obvious advantage.

Algorithm 19.11: Postfix Evaluation

Assume we have a string of operands and operators, an informal, by hand process is

Scan the expression left to right

Skip values or variables (operands)

Step 1: When an operator is found, apply the operation to the preceding two operands

Step 2: Replace the two operands and operator with the calculated value (three symbols are replaced with one operand)

Step 3: Continue scanning until only a value remains—the result of the expression

The time complexity is O(n) because each operand is scanned once, and each operation is performed once.

Using stack it is very easy to evaluate postfix expression, the following pseudo code shows the procedure for evaluation.

A more formal algorithm:

```
create a new stack
while(input stream is not empty)
{
token = getNextToken();
if(token instanceof operand)
{
push(token);
} else if (token instance of operator)
op2 = pop();
op1 = pop();
result = calc(token, op1, op2);
```

```
push(result);
}
}
return pop();
Demonstration with 2 3 4 + * 5 -
```

Example: Let us see how the above algorithm will be implemented using an example.

Postfix String: 123*+4-

Initially the Stack is empty. Now, the first three characters scanned are 1,2 and 3, which are operands. Thus they will be pushed into the stack in that order.

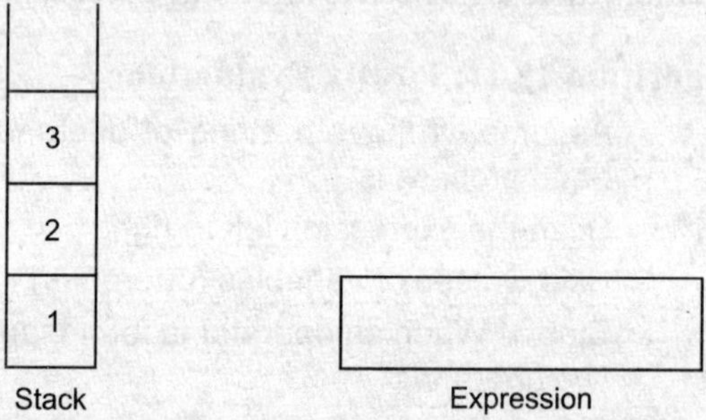

Next character scanned is "*", which is an operator. Thus, we pop the top two elements from the stack and perform the "*" operation with the two operands. The second operand will be the first element that is popped.

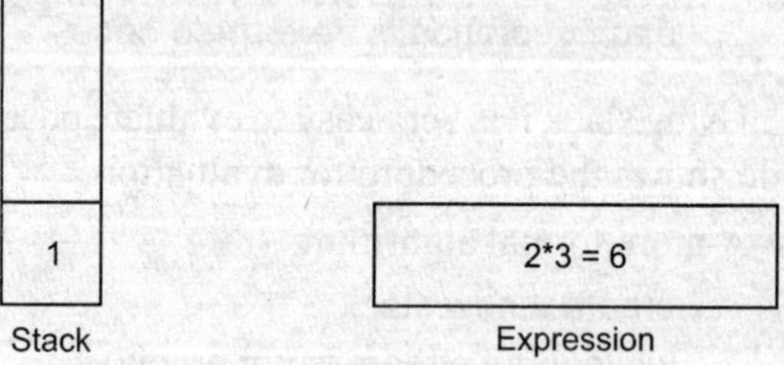

The value of the expression(2*3) that has been evaluated(6) is pushed into the stack.

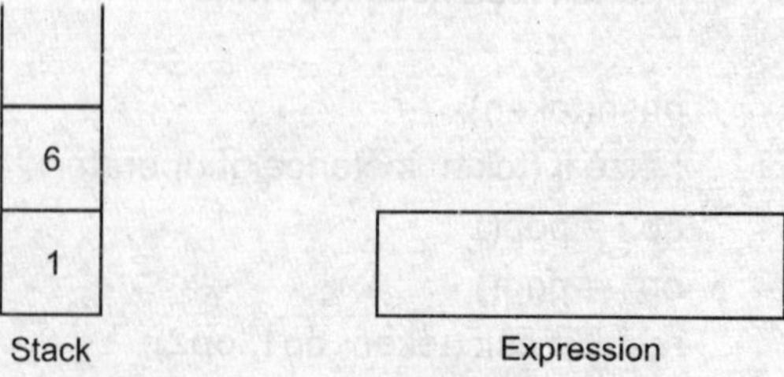

Next character scanned is "+", which is an operator. Thus, we pop the top two elements from the stack and perform the "+" operation with the two operands. The second operand will be the first element that is popped.

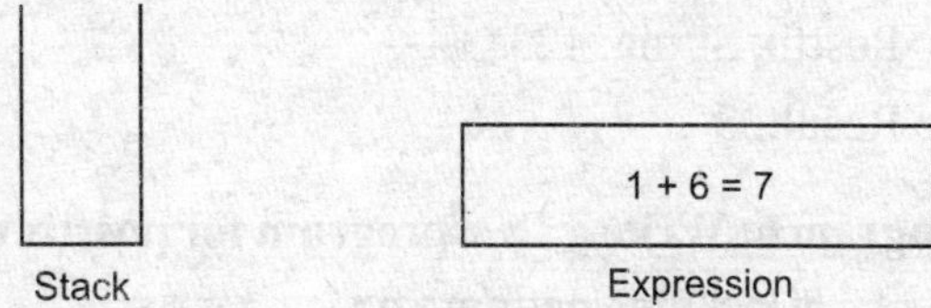

The value of the expression(1+6) that has been evaluated(7) is pushed into the stack.

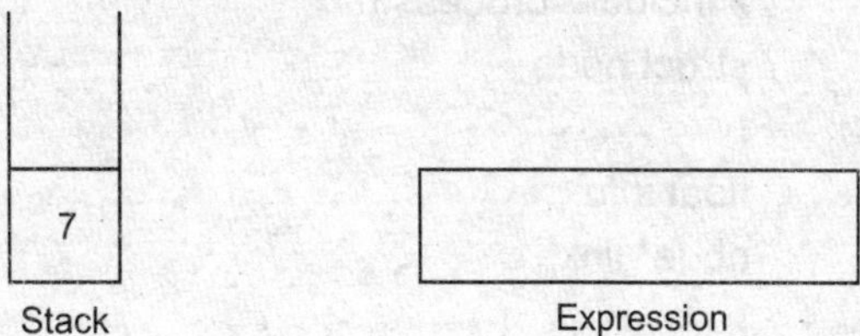

Next character scanned is "4", which is added to the stack.

Next character scanned is "-", which is an operator. Thus, we pop the top two elements from the stack and perform the "-" operation with the two operands. The second operand will be the first element that is popped.

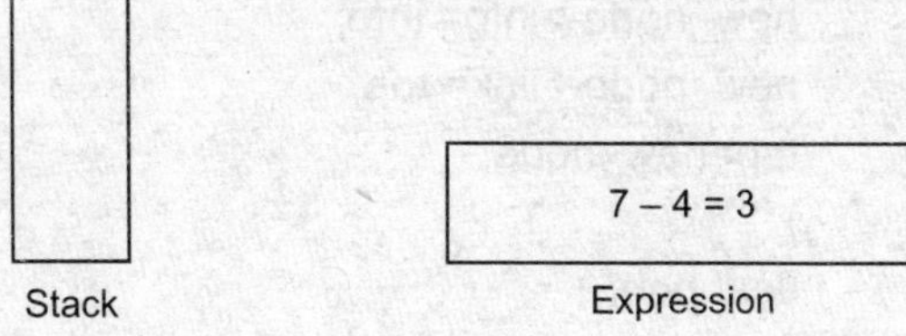

The value of the expression(7-4) that has been evaluated(3) is pushed into the stack.

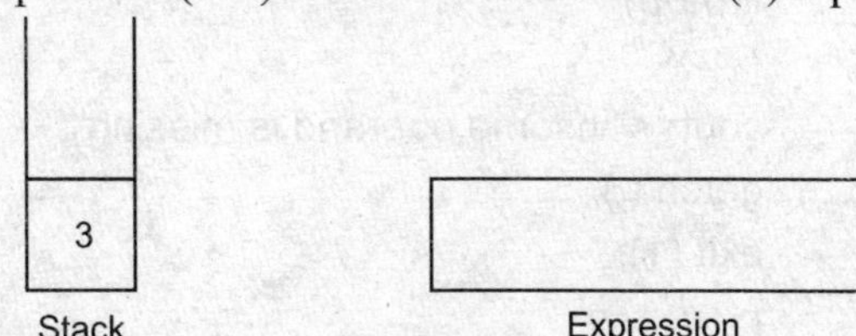

Now, since all the characters are scanned, the remaining element in the stack (there will be only one element in the stack) will be returned.

End result:

Postfix String: 123*+4-

Result: 3

Program 6: Write a C++ program for postfix expression evaluation using stack.

```
# include<iostream.h>
# include<conio.h>
# include<process.h>
struct node
{
float info;
node* link;
};
class stack
{
private:
node* top;
public:
stack ( )
{
top=NULL;
}
void push(float info)
{
node* new_node= new node;
new_node->info= info;
new_node->link= top;
top=new_node;
}
float pop( )
{
if (!top)
{
cout<<"\nsome operand is missing";
getch ( );
exit (1);
}
```

```
node* temp=top;
top=top->link;
return (temp->info);
}
int total ( ); // function prototype
};
{
int count=0;
node* temp=top;
while (temp)
{
count++;
temp=temp->link;
}
return (count);
}
void main ( )
{
clrscr ( );
stack s;
char ch;
int digit, temp;
float d1, d2;
float result;
cout<<"Enter the expression (with spaces) terminated by carriage return:
\n);
do
{
ch=getche ( );
switch (ch)
{
case '+': s.push (s.pop ( )+s.pop ( ));
break;
case '-': d1=s.pop ( );
d2=s.pop ( );
s.push (d2-d1);
break;
case '*': s.push (s.pop ( ) *s.pop ( ));
break;
case '/': d1=s.pop ( ) *s.pop ( ));
```

```
d2=s.push(d2/d1);
break;
case '\r': if (s.total ( ) >1)
cout<<endl<<s.total ( ) -1<<" operator(s) is (are) missing";
else
{
result= s.pop ( );
cout<<"\n\nResult of the evaluation is: "<<result;
}
getch ( );
exit (0);
default: digit=int (ch) -int ('0');
temp=0;
if(digit >=0 && digit <=9)
{
ch=getche( );
while (ch!=' ')
{
temp=int (ch) -int ('0');
digit=digit*10+temp;
ch=getche ( );
}
s.push (digit);
}
}
}
while (1);
}
```

Output:

Enter the expression (with spaces) terminated by carriage return:

5 6 2 + * 12 4 / +

Result of the evaluation is: 37

Infix to Prefix Notation

Algorithm 19.12: Infix to Prefix Notation

Step 1: Read the given infix expression into string called infix.

Step 2: Reverse the infix string and read one character at a time and perform the following operations:

If the read character is an operand, then add the operand to the prefix string.

If the read character is not an operand, then check

If the stack is not empty and precedence of the top of the stack operator is higher than the read operator, then pop the operator from stack and add this operator to the prefix string.

Else push the operator onto the stack.

Step 3: Repeat STEP 2 till all characters are processed from the input string.

Step 4: If stack is not empty, then pop the operator from stack and add this operator to the prefix string.

Step 5: Repeat STEP 4 till all the operators are popped from the stack.

Step 6: Reverse the prefix string and display the result of the given infix expression or the resultant prefix expression stored in a string called prefix from this algorithm.

Infix to postfix conversion

Consider the sum of A and B. We think applying the operator "+" to the operands A and B write the sum as A+B. This particular representation is called infix. There are two alternate notations for expressing the sum of A and B using the symbols A, B, and + These are

+ AB **prefix**

AB + **postfix**

The 'pre-', 'post-', and 'in-' refer to the relative position of the operator with respect to the two operands. In prefix notation the operator preceded the two operands, in postfix notation the operator follows the two operands, and in in-fix notation the operator in between the two operands. The precedence of the operator allows us to evaluate the expression unambiguously.

- Exponentiation Highest priority
- Multiplication, Division Next highest priority
- Addition, Subtraction lowest priority

If we wish to override these priorities we can do so by using a pair of parenthesis as shown below.

(A + B) * C

A * (B – C)

(A + B)/(C – D)

The expression with in a pair of parenthesis is always evaluated earlier than the other operations.

The prefix and postfix expressions have three features:

1. The Operands maintain the same order as in the equivalent infix expression.
2. Parenthesis are not need to designate the expressions unambiguously.
3. While evaluating the expression the priority of the operators is irrelevant.

```
// pseudo code for converting infix to postfix expression
operandStack=the empty Stack;
while(not end of the input)
{
element=next input character;
if(element is an operand);
add element to the postfix string
else
{
while (!empty(operandStack) and precedence (Stacktop( operand-
Stack,element ) ) )
{
topelement=pop(operandStack);
add topelement to postfix string;
}
push(operandStack,element);
}}
//output of the remaining operator
while(!empty(operandStack))
{
topelement=pop(operandStack);
add topelment to postfix string;
} // end if while loop
return the post string ;
```

Not only can a stack be used to evaluate a postfix expression, but we can also use a stack to convert an expression in standard form (otherwise known as infix) into postfix. We will concentrate on a small version of the general problem by allowing only the operators +, *, and (,), and insisting on the usual precedence rules. We will further assume that the expression is legal. Suppose we want to convert the infix expression

a + b * c + (d * e + f) * g

into postfix. A correct answer is a b c * + d e * f + g * +.

When an operand is read, it is immediately placed onto the output. Operators are not immediately output, so they must be saved somewhere. The correct thing to do is to place operators that have been seen, but not placed on the output, onto the stack. We will also stack left parentheses when they are encountered. We start with an initially empty stack.

If we see a right parenthesis, then we pop the stack, writing symbols until we encounter a (corresponding) left parenthesis, which is popped but not output.

If we see any other symbol ('+','*', '('), then we pop entries from the stack until we find an entry of lower priority. One exception is that we never remove a '(' from the stack except when processing a ')'. For the purposes of this operation, '+' has lowest priority and '(' highest. When the popping is done, we push the operand onto the stack.

Finally, if we read the end of input, we pop the stack until it is empty, writing symbols onto the output.

To see how this algorithm performs, we will convert the infix expression above into its postfix form. First, the symbol a is read, so it is passed through to the output. Then '+' is read and pushed onto the stack. Next b is read and passed through to the output. The state of affairs at this juncture is as follows:

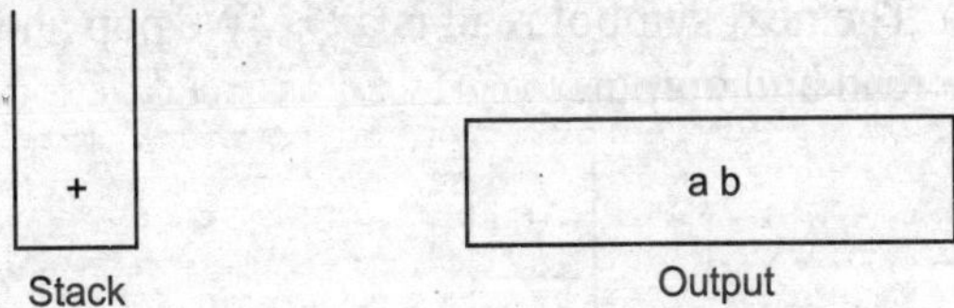

Next a '*' is read. The top entry on the operator stack has lower precedence than '*', so nothing is output and '*' is put on the stack. Next, c is read and output. Thus far, we have

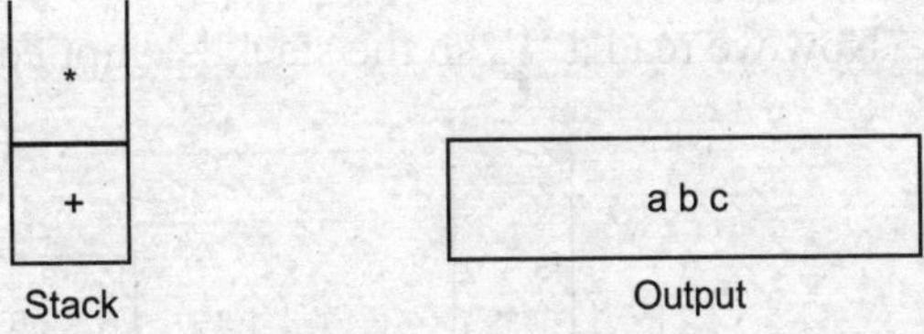

The next symbol is a '+'. Checking the stack, we find that we will pop a '*' and place it on the output, pop the other '+', which is not of lower but equal priority, on the stack, and then push the '+'.

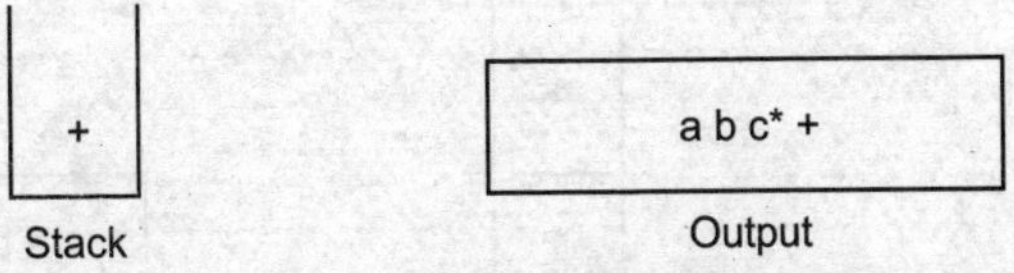

The next symbol read is an '(', which, being of highest precedence, is placed on the stack. Then d is read and output.

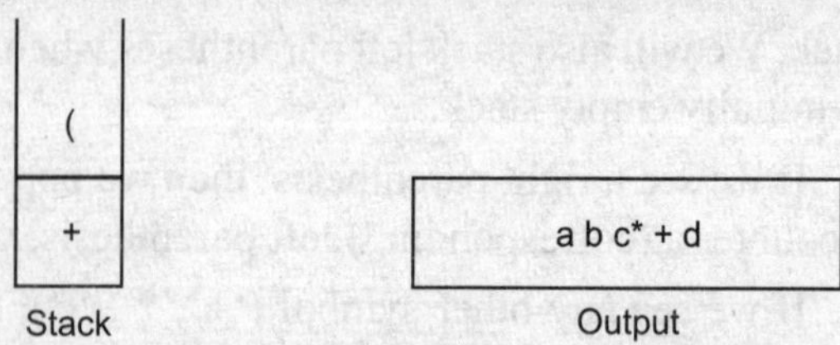

We continue by reading a '*'. Since open parentheses do not get removed except when a closed parenthesis is being processed, there is no output. Next, e is read and output.

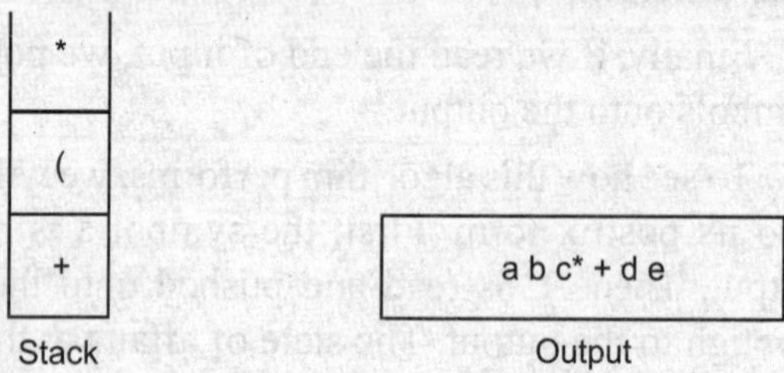

The next symbol read is a '+'. We pop and output '*' and then push '+'. Then we read and output.

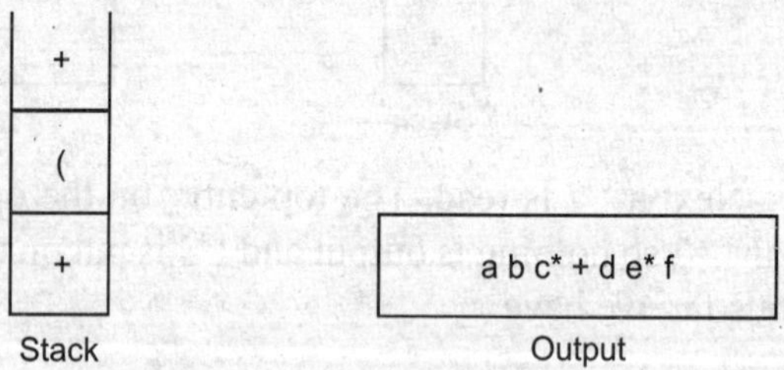

Now we read a ')', so the stack is emptied back to the '('. We output a '+'.

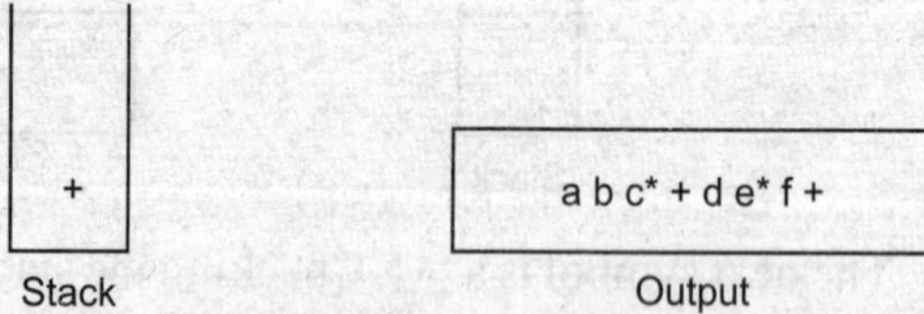

We read a '*' next; it is pushed onto the stack. Then g is read and output.

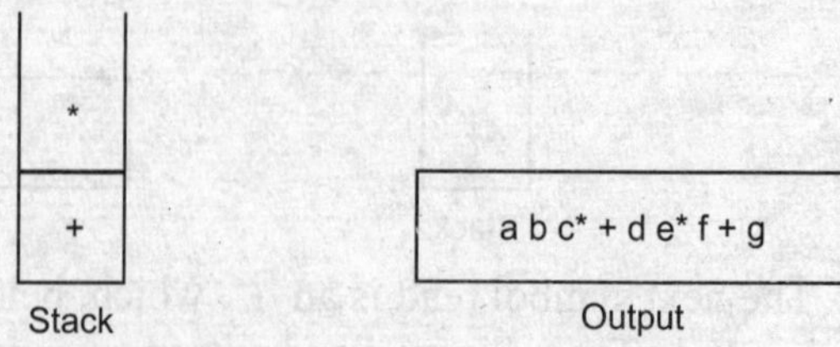

The input is now empty, so we pop and output symbols from the stack until it is empty.

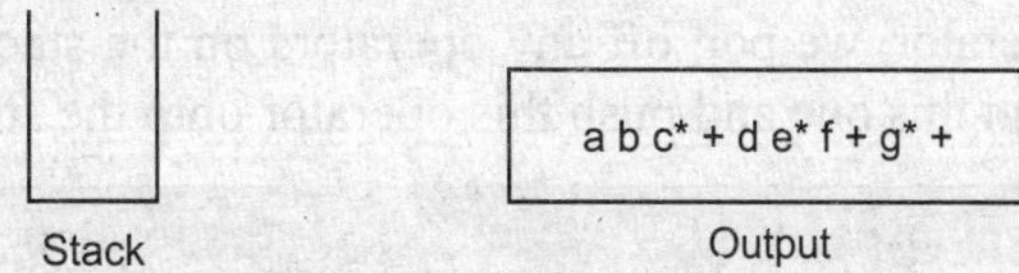

As before, this conversion requires only O(n) time and works in one pass through the input. We can add subtraction and division to this repertoire by assigning subtraction and addition equal priority and multiplication and division equal priority. A subtle point is that the expression a - b - c will be converted to ab - c- and not abc - -.

Our algorithm does the right thing, because these operators associate from left to right. This is not necessarily the case in general, since exponentiation associates right to left: 223 = 28 = 256 not 43 = 64. We leave as an exercise the problem of adding exponentiation to the repertoire of assignments.

Algorithm 19.13: Infix transformation to Postfix

This process uses a stack as well. We have to hold information that's expressed inside parentheses while scanning to find the closing ')'. We also have to hold information on operations that are of lower precedence on the stack. The algorithm is:

Step 1: Create an empty stack and an empty postfix output string/stream

Step 2: Scan the infix input string/stream left to right

Step 3: If the current input token is an operand, simply append it to the output string (note the examples above that the operands remain in the same order)

Step 4: If the current input token is an operator, pop off all operators that have equal or higher precedence and append them to the output string; push the operator onto the stack. The order of popping is the order in the output.

Step 5: If the current input token is '(', push it onto the stack

Step 6: If the current input token is ')', pop off all operators and append them to the output string until a '(' is popped; discard the '('.

Step 7: If the end of the input string is found, pop all operators and append them to the output string.

This algorithm doesn't handle errors in the input, although careful analysis of parenthesis or lack of parenthesis could point to such error determination.

For example consider the expression A+(B*C-(D/E)+F). To convert this infix to postfix expression we will perform the above mentioned steps i.e.We move from left to right in the infix expression. We keep on pushing elements onto the stack till we reach a operand.

Once we reach an operand, we add it to the output. If we reach a) symbol, we pop elements off the stack till we reach a corresponding (symbol. If we reach an operator, we pop off any operators on the stack which are of higher precedence than this one and push this operator onto the stack.

Symbol scanned	Stack	Expression	COMMENTS
A	(	A	
+	(+	A	
(	(+(	A	
B	(+(	AB	
*	(+(*	AB	
C	(+(*	ABC	
-	(+(-	ABC *	* has high priority
(	(+(-(	ABC*	
D	(+(-(	ABC*D	
/	(+(-(/	ABC*D	
E	(+(-(/	ABC*DE	
)	(+(-	ABC*DE/	) remove / and (from stack
+	(+(+	ABC*DE/-	
F	(+(+	ABC*DE/-F	
)	(+	ABC*DE/-F	
) SENTINEL		ABC*DE/-F+	

Program 7: Write a C++ program for infix to postfix conversion.

```
#include<iostream.h>
#include<string.h>
#include<stdlib.h>
#include<ctype.h>
#include<conio.h>
class expression
{
private:
char infix[100];
char stack[200];
int top;
int r;
char postfix[100];
public:
void convert();
int input_p(char);
int stack_p(char);
int rank(char);
```

```
};
int expression::input_p(char c)
{
if(c=='+' || c=='-')
return 1;
else if(c=='*' || c=='/')
return 3;
else if(c=='^')
return 6;
else if(isalpha(c)!=0)
return 7;
else if(c=='(')
return 9;
else if(c==')')
return 0;
else
{
cout<<"Invalid expression ::input error\n";
exit(0);
}
}
int expression::stack_p(char c)
{
if(c=='+' || c=='-')
return 2;
else if(c=='*' || c=='/')
return 4;
else if(c=='^')
return 5;
else if(isalpha(c)!=0)
return 8;
else if(c=='(')
return 0;
else
{
cout<<"Invalid expression  ::stack error\n";
exit(0);
}
}
int expression::rank(char c)
```

```
{
if(c=='+' || c=='-')
return -1;
else if(c=='*' || c=='/')
return -1;
else if(c=='^')
return -1;
else if(isalpha(c)!=0)
return 1;
else
{
cout<<"Invalid expression ::in rank\n";
exit(0);
}
}
void expression::convert()
{
cout<<"\n***************************************************\n"
<<"This program converts the given infix expression\n"
<<"in to postfix form"
<<"\n***************************************************\n";
cout<<"Enter an infix expression ::\n";
cin>>infix;
int l=strlen(infix);
infix[l]=')';
infix[l+1]='';
//Convertion starts
top=1;
stack[top]='(';
r=0;
int x=-1;
int i=0;
char next=infix[i];
while(next!='')
{
//Pop all the elements to outputin stack which have higher precedence
while( input_p(next) < stack_p(stack[top]) )
{
if(top<1)
{
```

```
cout<<"invalid expression ::stack error\n";
exit(0);
}
postfix[++x]=stack[top];
top-;
r=r+rank(postfix[x]);
if(r<1)
{
cout<<"Invalid expression ::r<1\n";
exit(0);
}
}
if(input_p( next ) != stack_p( stack[top]))
stack[++top]=next;
else
top-;
i++;
next=infix[i];
}
postfix[++x]=";
if(r!=1 || top!=0)
{
cout<<"Invalid expression ::error in rank or stack\n";
exit(0);
}
cout<<"\n\nThe corresponding postfix expression is ::\n";
cout<<postfix<<endl;
}
void main()
{
expression obj;
obj.convert();
getch();
}
```

Output:

```
************************************************
This program converts the given infix expression
in to postfix form
************************************************
Enter an infix expression ::
```

```
(a+b^c^d)*(c+d)
The corresponding postfix expression is ::
abcd^^+cd+*
Press any key to continue
```

Let us take another example of an expression (10-6) * (9/3)

Add closing brace to an end of expression.

Input expression is (10-6) * (9/3))

Following is the explanation of steps involved in algorithm:

Token read	Process	Stack contents (growing from left to right)	Result expression
(	Push	(	-
10	Print	(	10
-	Push	(-	6
6	Print	(-	10 6
)	Pop symbols until '(' appers ,Pop (	Empty	10 6 -
*	Push	*	10 6 -
(	Push	* (	10 6 -
9	Print	*(	10 6 - 9
/	Push	*(/	10 6 - 9
3	Print	*(/	10 6-9 3
)	Pop all symbols	*as '(' appears, we stop popping out	10 6 –9 3 /
End of expression		Empty	10 6 –9 3 / *

So the converted postfix expression is: 10 6 –9 3 / *

19.10.2 Backtracking

Backtracking is used in algorithms in which there are steps along some path (state) from some starting point to some goal.

- Find your way through a maze.
- Find a path from one point in a graph (roadmap) to another point.
- Play a game in which there are moves to be made (checkers, chess).

In all of these cases, there are choices to be made among a number of options. We need some way to remember these decision points in case we want/need to come back and try the alternative

Consider the maze. At a point where a choice is made, we may discover that the choice leads to a dead-end. We want to retrace back to that decision point and then try the other (next) alternative.

Again, stacks can be used as part of the solution. Recursion is another, typically more favored, solution, which is actually implemented by a stack.

Recursion

Recursion, in mathematics and computer science, is a method of defining functions in which the function being defined is applied within its own definition. The term is also used more generally to describe a process of repeating objects in a self-similar way. For instance, when the surfaces of two mirrors are almost parallel with each other the nested images that occur are a form of recursion. When a called function in turn calls another function, then a process of 'chaining' occurs. Recursion is a special case of this process or chain. So when a function calls itself, then it is called **recursion.** This chain continues till a specific condition met. If it has not any stop condition, then it will create an indefinite loop. Recursion is also called self-reference loop. Recursion is used to solve for the problems, which cannot be solved by the iterative procedure for, while and do loops. It is useful to solve repetitive problems, where input of one sub-program can be used as starting value having the previous output. A recursion procedure is also called well-defined function, if it satisfies the following conditions:

(i) A recursive function should have specific condition.

(ii) A recursive function should have smaller argument each time than the previous argument value in the every recursive loop.

For example, below written program is a recursive (unconditional recursion) procedure:

```
main ( )
{
printf ("\n I LOVE MY BABY \n");
main ( );
}
```

It will display the result infinite times (indefinite loop) as:

```
I LOVE MY BABY
I LOVE MY BABY
I LOVE MY BABY
........................
```

Another example, which will illustrate the recursion based on condition, is to write a C++ program to find the factorial of a number is written below as:

Program 8: Write a C++ program to find the factorial of a number by using the Recursion.

```
#include <iostream.h>
#include <conio.h>
void main ( )
```

```
{
int n, factorial( );
clrscr();
cout<<"\n Enter the value of N: ";
cin>>n;
cout<<"\n Factorial of number"<<n<<" is "<<factorial(n);
getch ( );
}
int factorial(n)
int n;
{
int m;
if (n = = 1)
{
return (n);
}
else
{
m = n * factorial(n-1);
return (m);
}
}
```

Output:

Enter the value of N: 5

Factorial of number 5 is 120

Working of Recursion

We hope you agree that it's difficult to visualize how the control flows from one function to another. Possibly given figure on next page would make the things a bit clearer.Assume that the number entered through scanf() is 5 as above program. Using the figure let's visualize what exactly happens when the recursive function factorial() gets called.

Go through the figure carefully. The first time when factorial() function is called from main() function, n collects value 5. From here, since n is not equal to 1, the if block is skipped and factorial() function is called again with the argument(n-1), i.e 4. This is a recursive call. Since n is still not equal to 1, factorial() function is called yet another time , with argument(4-1), i.e 3.This is again recursive call. Since again n is still not equal to 1, factorial() function is called yet another time, with the argument(3-1), i.e 2. This process will carry on until the value of argument n is 1. When the value of n is 1, control goes back to previous factorial()

function with the value 1, and m is evaluated as 2. And then control back to next previous factorial() function with the value 2 and m is again evaluated as 6.

Similarly, each factorial() function evaluates its m from the returned value, and finally 120 is return to main() function. The sequence would be grasped better by following the shown in the figure:

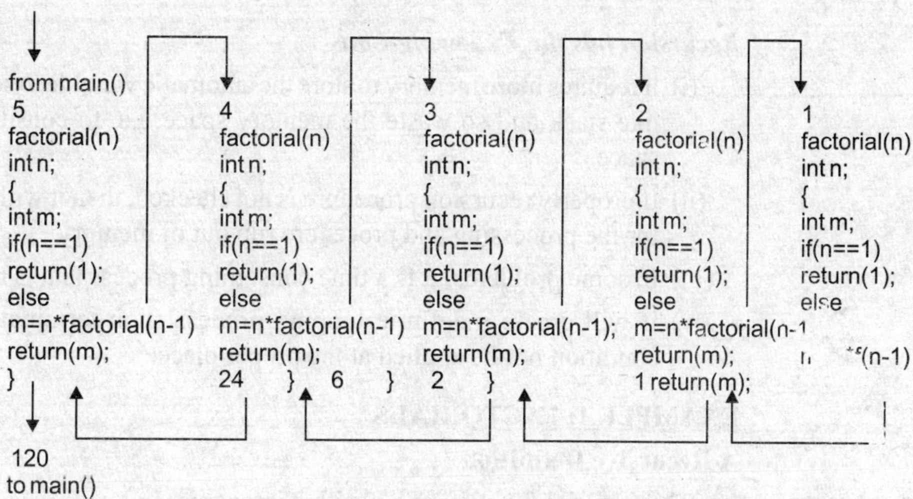

Note that while writing recursive function you have an if statement or a conditional statement somewhere in the recursive function to force the function to return without recursive calls being executed. If you don't do this and you call the function, you will fall in indefinite loop, and will never return from the called function.

Pros (Advantages) and Cons (Disadvantages) of Recursion

Recursion is a process in which a function calls itself that is function calling itself is known as Recursion. The various advantages of recursion are:

(i) It is simple, easily understandable, concise, compact and transparent to view a c program.

(ii) lesser number of programming statements (coding) required with the use of recursion.

(iii) It is very useful in solving mathematical (factorial, GCD, Fibonacci series etc.), trigonometric (compute hyperbolic trigonometric value), logical games (tower of Hanoi, generating random number in system simulation, puzzles) and algebraic problems (to solve Ackermann's function).

(iv) It is very useful where user-defined function or sub-program or procedure required.

(v) It is eminently useful if the solution to problem is in recursive terms.

(vi) It is more useful in the multiprocessing and multitasking environment.

(vii) It is very useful in solving the data structure problems like linked list, queues, stack, tree, Quick sort and merge sort etc.

(viii) Recursion saves the memory. In other words it utilizes the memory well.

Recursion has the Following Cons

(i) It requires more memory to store the automatic variable to solve the problems like stack and so waste the memory space. i.e. to consume more storage space.

(ii) If properly recursion procedure is not checked, then it will create a problem for the processing and procedure run out of memory.

(iii) In some problems, it is a time consuming process and is not efficient.

(iv) It will create indefinite looping process (non-terminating iteration), if condition not be applied at the proper place.

EXAMPLE 1: FACTORIALS

A Recursive Definition

The factorial function of a positive integer is

$$n! = n \times (n-1)\times \ldots\times 1$$

Formal Definition:

n! = 1 if n=0

= *n* (n-1)!* *If n>0*

Example:

3!= 3*2!

= 3*(2*1!)

= 3*(2*(1*0!))

= 3*(2*(1*1))

= 3*(2*1)

= 3*2 = 6

Factorials: A Recursive Definition:

Every recursive process or procedure consists of two parts:

- A smallest , base case that is processed without recursion
- A general method that reduces a particular case to one or more of the smaller

cases, thereby making progress toward eventually reducing the problem all the way to the base case

EXAMPLE 2: TOWERS OF HANOI

Here we will explain how recursion can be used as a tool in developing an algorithm to solve a particular problem like Tower of Hanoi. Let us suppose there are three needles named 1, 2 and 3. Let a finite number say, n of disks with decreasing size, are placed on needle 1.We are to place disks from needle 1 to needle3 using needle 2 as temporary storage.

Rules are:

- Move only one disk at a time.
- No larger disk can be on top of a smaller disk.
- Move all disks from the 1st needle to the 3rd needle.

Notation: To move disks from one tower to another we will use notation

move(64, 1, 3, 2) which means Move 64 disks from tower 1 to tower 3 using tower 2 as temporary storage.

The Solution (Divide and Conquer)

In Divide and Conquer method, the problem to be solved is divided into two or more sub problems which are solved separately. The solutions are then combined together to find the solution of the given problem.

The examples of this technique are Quick sort and binary search algorithms, which are discussed in searching and sorting chapter. A Divide and Conquer algorithm can be called as a recursive procedure as the algorithm calls itself when it is implemented to smaller sets. The problem of Towers of Hanoi can also be solved with the help of Divide and Conquer method. Here we will reduce the solution for n disks to a solution for n-1 disks and a solution for n=1 disk.

To move the bottom disk from tower 1: - There is no way to reach the bottom disk until the top 63 disks have been moved- and they (the 63 disks) must all be on tower 2 so that we can move the bottom disk from tower 1 to tower 3.

Therefore, if we want: move (64,1,3,2), We need:

1. move(63,1,2,3)

   // Move 63 disks from tower 1 to 2 (tower 3 temporary).
2. " Move disk 64 from tower 1 to tower 3."
3. move(63,2,3,1)

   // Move 63 disks from tower 2 to 3 (tower 1 temporary).

Now, move(63,2,3,1) is the same problem (and is a smaller problem) as move(64,1,3,2). Next: Repeat steps 1, 2 and 3 for move(63,2,3,1), and so on ...

The solution of the **Tower of Hanoi** problem for n=3, is explained in the Figure 3.18.

Now we want: move(3,1,3,2)

We need:

1. move(2,1,2,3) // move 2 disks from tower1 to tower 2(tower3 temporary)
2. move disk 3 from tower 1 to tower 3.
3. move(2,2,3,1) // move 2 disks from tower 2 to tower 3 (tower1 temporary).

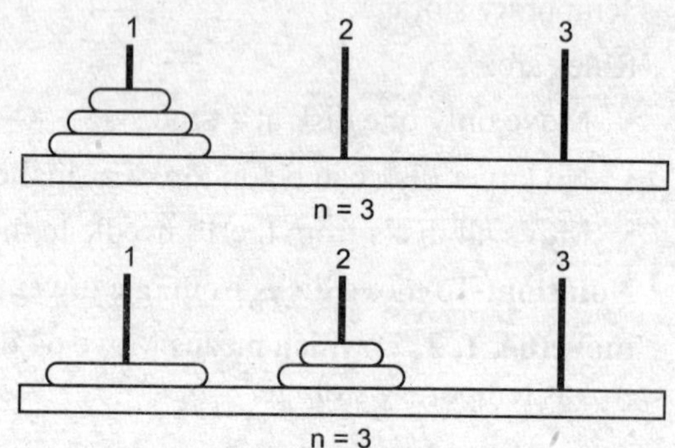

move (2, 1, 2, 3) i.e. Move top two disks from Tower 1 to Tower 2

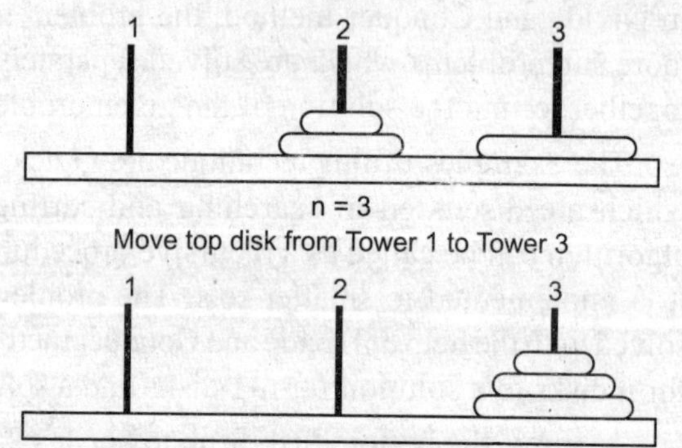

move (2, 2, 3, 1) i.e. Move top disks from Tower 2 to Tower 3

Figure 19.43: Towers of Hanoi problem solved with the help of Divide and Conquer algorithm in recursion

EXAMPLE 3: Ackermann Function

The Ackermann function is the simplest example of a well-defined total function, which is computable but not primitive recursive, providing a counterexample to the belief in the early 1900s that every computable function was also primitive recursive.

It grows faster than an exponential function, or even a multiple exponential function. The Ackermann function $A(x, y)$ is defined for integer x and y by:

$$A(x, y) = \begin{cases} y+1 & \text{if } x=0 \\ A(x-1,1) & \text{if } y=0 \\ A(x-1, A(x, y-1)) & \text{otherwise} \end{cases} \tag{1}$$

Special values for integer x include

$$A(0, y) = y + 1 \tag{2}$$

$$A(1, y) = y + 2 \tag{3}$$

$$A(2, y) = 2y + 3 \tag{4}$$

$$A(3, y) = 2^{y+3} - 3 \tag{5}$$

$$A(4, y) = \underbrace{2^{2^{\cdot^{\cdot^{2}}}}}_{y=3} - 3 \tag{6}$$

Expressions of the latter form are sometimes called power towers. $A(0, y)$follows trivially from the definition. $A(1, y)$can be derived as follows,

$$\begin{aligned} A(1, y) &= A(0, A(1, y-1)) = A(1, y-1) + 1 \\ &= A(0, A(1, y-2)) + 1 = A(1, y-2) + 2 \\ &= ¼ = A(1, 0) + y = A(0, 1) + y = y + 2 \end{aligned} \tag{7}$$

$A(2, y)$ has a similar derivation,

$$\begin{aligned} A(2, y) &= A(1, A(2, y-1)) = A(2, y-1) + 2 \\ &= A(1, A(2, y-2)) + 2 = A(2, y-2) + 4 \\ &= A(2, 0) + 2y = A(1, 1) + 2y = 2y + 3 \end{aligned} \tag{8}$$

Table of values

Values of A(x,y)

x\\y	**0**	**1**	**2**	**3**	**4**	**y**
0	1	2	3	4	5	y+1
1	2	3	4	5	6	y+2
2	3	5	7	9	11	2y+3
3	5	13	29	61	125	8*2^y-3
4	13	65533	2^{65536}-3	A(3,2^{65536}-3)	A(3,A(4,3))	$2^{2...2}$-3 (y+3 terms)
5	65533	A(4,65533)	A(4,A(5,1))	A(4,A(5,2))	A(4,A(5,3))	
6	A(5,1)	A(5,A(5,1))	A(5,A(6,1))	A(5,A(6,2))	A(5,A(6,3))	

It might be noted that for each item, we need to compute its predecessor in the row just to find the position (index in programming terms) at which to look up the item in the previous row. A(4,2) is greater than the number of particles in the universe raised to the power 200. A(5,2) is the item at index A(5,1) in the x=4 row, and cannot be written as a decimal expansion in the physical universe.

It is also amusing to note that beyond row 4,the values can only be written by resorting to the definition of the Ackermann function - writing them as decimal expansions, or as references to rows with lower x, would not be possible. A(5,0) is an exception, as is A(5,1) = A(6,0), which can at least have their index in row 4 expressed as a decimal expansion.

Tail Recursion

Tail recursion (or tail-end recursion) is a special case of recursion in which the last operation of the function, the tail call, is a recursive call. Such recursions can be easily transformed to iterations. Replacing recursion with iteration, manually or automatically, can drastically decrease the amount of stack space used and improve efficiency. This technique is commonly used with functional programming languages, where the declarative approach and explicit handling of state promote the use of recursive functions that would otherwise rapidly fill the call stack.

Definition: *A special form of* recursion *where the last operation of a function is a recursive call. The recursion may be optimized away by executing the call in the current stack frame and returning its result rather than creating a new stack frame.*

A recursive function is said to be *tail recursive* if there are no pending operations to be performed on return from a recursive call.

Tail recursive functions are often said to "return the value of the last recursive call as the value of the function." Tail recursion is very desirable because the amount of information which must be stored during the computation is independent of the number of recursive calls. Some modern computing systems will actually compute tail-recursive functions using an iterative process.

The "infamous" factorial function fact is usually written in a non-tail-recursive manner:

```
int fact (int n)
{
if (n == 0) return 1;
return n * fact(n - 1);
}
```

Notice that there is a "pending operation," namely multiplication, to be performed on return from each recursive call. Whenever there is a pending operation, the function is non-tail-recursive. Information about each pending operation must be stored, so the amount of information is not independent of the number of calls.

The factorial function can be written in a tail-recursive way:

```
int fact_aux(int n, int result)
{
if (n == 1) return result;
return fact_aux(n - 1, n * result)
}
int fact(n)
{
return fact_aux(n, 1);
}
```

The "auxiliary" function fact_aux is used to keep the syntax of fact(n) the same as before. The recursive function is really fact_aux, not fact. Note that fact_aux has no pending operations on return from recursive calls. The value computed by the recursive call is simply returned with no modification. The amount of information which must be stored is constant (the value of n and the value of result), independent of the number of recursive calls.

19.10.3 Memory Management

Any modern computer environment uses a stack as the primary memory management model for a running program. Whether it's native code (x86, Sun, VAX) or JVM, a stack is at the center of the run-time environment for Java, C++, Ada, FORTRAN, etc.

The discussion of JVM in the text is consistent with NT, Solaris, VMS, Unix runtime environments.

Each program that is running in a computer system has its own memory allocation containing the typical layout as shown below.

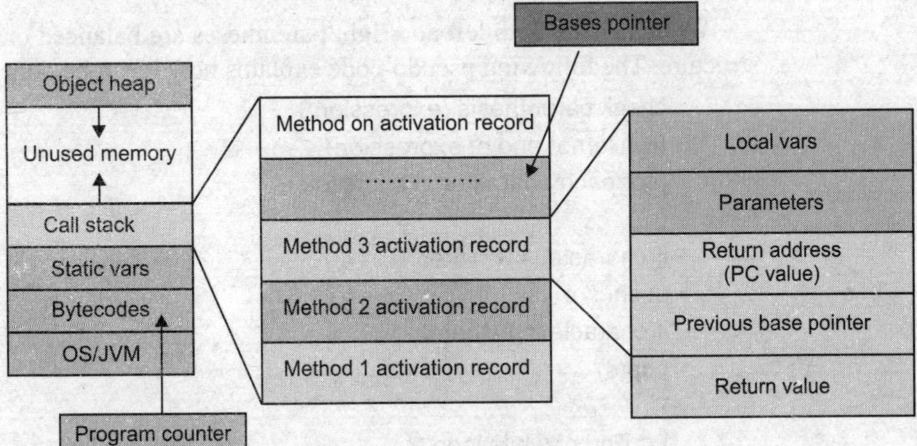

Figure 19.44: Memory management

Call and return process

When a method/function is called

1. An activation record is created; its size depends on the number and size of the local variables and parameters.
2. The Base Pointer value is saved in the special location reserved for it.
3. The Program Counter value is saved in the Return Address location.
4. The Base Pointer is now reset to the new base (top of the call stack prior to the creation of the AR).
5. The Program Counter is set to the location of the first bytecode of the method being called.
6. Copies the calling parameters into the Parameter region.
7. Initializes local variables in the local variable region.

While the method executes, the local variables and parameters are simply found by adding a constant associated with each variable/parameter to the Base Pointer.

When a method returns

1. Get the program counter from the activation record and replace what's in the PC.
2. Get the base pointer value from the AR and replace what's in the BP.
3. Pop the AR entirely from the stack.

19.10.4 Parenthesis Matching

The dynamic structure stack can be used checking for balanced parenthesis in an expression. For example expression given below

$$(1+(3\times5)-(2+((4-2)\times8)+100)-22\times(2+4))$$

We can check both left and right parentheses are balanced or not using stack structure. The following pseudo-code explains how it can be done.

```
check parenthesis (expression )
{ while(not end of expression)
{ for each character in expression
{
if(character = '(' ) then
push('(',s)
if(character=')') then
pop(s)
}
} /* End of while loop */
if(isEmpty(s)) then
```

```
"The expression is valid "
else
" Invalid expression"
} /* End of function check parenthesis */
```

Algorithm above works as for every open parenthesis push them into the stack and closing parenthesis pop from the stack. Finally the empty stack shows the parenthesis balanced expression.

19.10.5 Balancing Symbols

Compilers check your programs for syntax errors, but frequently a lack of one symbol (such as a missing brace or comment starter) will cause the compiler to spill out a hundred lines of diagnostics without identifying the real error.

A useful tool in this situation is a program that checks whether everything is balanced. Thus, every right brace, bracket, and parenthesis must correspond to their left counterparts. The sequence [()] is legal, but [(]) is wrong. Obviously, it is not worthwhile writing a huge program for this, but it turns out that it is easy to check these things. For simplicity, we will just check for balancing of parentheses, brackets, and braces and ignore any other character that appears.

The simple algorithm uses a stack and is as follows: Make an empty stack. Read characters until end of file. If the character is an open anything, push it onto the stack. If it is a close anything, then if the stack is empty report an error. Otherwise, pop the stack. If the symbol popped is not the corresponding opening symbol, then report an error. At end of file, if the stack is not empty report an error.

You should be able to convince yourself that this algorithm works. It is clearly linear and actually makes only one pass through the input. It is thus on-line and quite fast. Extra work can be done to attempt to decide what to do when an error is reported—such as identifying the likely cause.

Function Calls

The algorithm to check balanced symbols suggests a way to implement function calls. The problem here is that when a call is made to a new function, all the variables local to the calling routine need to be saved by the system, since otherwise the new function will overwrite the calling routine's variables. Furthermore, the current location in the routine must be saved so that the new function knows where to go after it is done. The variables have generally been assigned by the compiler to machine registers, and there are certain to be conflicts (usually all procedures get some variables assigned to register #1), especially if recursion is involved. The reason that this problem is similar to balancing symbols is that a function call and function return are essentially the same as an open parenthesis and closed parenthesis, so the same ideas should work.

When there is a function call, all the important information that needs to be saved, such as register values (corresponding to variable names) and the return address (which can be obtained from the program counter, which is typically in a register), is saved "on a piece of paper" in an abstract way and put at the top of a pile. Then the control is transferred to the new function, which is free to replace the registers with its values. If it makes other function calls, it follows the same procedure. When the function wants to return, it looks at the "paper" at the top of the pile and restores all the registers. It then makes the return jump.

Clearly, all of this work can be done using a stack, and that is exactly what happens in virtually every programming language that implements recursion. The information saved is called either an activation record or stack frame. The stack in a real computer frequently grows from the high end of your memory partition downwards, and on many systems there is no checking for overflow. There is always the possibility that you will run out of stack space by having too many simultaneously active functions. Needless to say, running out of stack space is always a fatal error.

In languages and systems that do not check for stack overflow, your program will crash without an explicit explanation. On these systems, strange things may happen when your stack gets too big, because your stack will run into part of your program. It could be the main program, or it could be part of your data, especially if you have a big array. If it runs into your program, your program will be corrupted; you will have nonsense instructions and will crash as soon as they are executed. If the stack runs into your data, what is likely to happen is that when you write something into your data, it will destroy stack information — probably the return address — and your program will attempt to return to some weird address and crash.

In normal events, you should not run out of stack space; doing so is usually an indication of runaway recursion (forgetting a base case). On the other hand, some perfectly legal and seemingly innocuous program can cause you to run out of stack space. The routine in Figure 19.45, which prints out a linked list, is perfectly legal and actually correct. It properly handles the base case of an empty list, and the recursion is fine. This program can be proven correct. Unfortunately, if the list contains 20,000 elements, there will be a stack of 20,000 activation records representing the nested calls of line 3. Activation records are typically large because of all the information they contain, so this program is likely to run out of stack space. (If 20,000 elements are not enough to make the program crash, replace the number with a larger one.)

This program is an example of an extremely bad use of recursion known as tail recursion. Tail recursion refers to a recursive call at the last line. Tail recursion can be mechanically eliminated by changing the recursive call to a goto preceded by one assignment per function argument. This simulates the recursive call because nothing needs to be saved — after the recursive call finishes, there is really no need to know the saved values. Because of this, we can just go to the top of the function with the values that would have been used in a recursive call. The program in Figure 19.46 shows the improved version. Keep in mind that you should use the more natural while loop construction. The goto is used here to show how a compiler might automatically remove the recursion.

Removal of tail recursion is so simple that some compilers do it automatically. Even so, it is best not to find out that yours does not.

```
void /* Not using a header */
print_list( LIST L )
{
/*1*/ if( L != NULL )
{
/*2*/ print_element( L->element );
/*3*/ print_list( L->next );
}
}
```

Figure 19.45: A bad use of recursion: printing a linked list

```
Void print_list( LIST L ) /* No header */
{
top:
if( L != NULL )
{
print_element( L->element );
L = L->next;
goto top;
}
}
```

Figure 19.46: Printing a list without recursion; a compiler might do this (you should not)

Recursion can always be completely removed (obviously, the compiler does so in converting to assembly language), but doing so can be quite tedious. The general strategy requires using a stack and is obviously worthwhile only if you can manage to put only the bare minimum on the stack. We will not dwell on this further, except to point out that although nonrecursive programs are certainly generally faster than recursive programs, the speed advantage rarely justifies the lack of clarity that results from removing the recursion.

Algorithm 19.14: Balance Symbol Checking

Step1: Read expression.

Step2: Create an empty stack.

Step3: Read symbols from left to right, repeat steps 4 and 5, until end of expression

Step4: If the symbol is an opening symbol then push it onto the stack else proceed.

Step5: If it is a closing symbol do the following:

Step5 a: if the stack is empty report an error and goto step8 else proceed

Step5 b: pop the stack If the symbol popped does not match the closing symbol report an error and goto step8 else proceed .

Step6: At the end of an expression if the stack is not empty report an error else proceed to next step

Step 7: Print Input expression is balanced

Step 8: Stop

Explanation

Step 1: Read an expression, say x = (( ))

Step 2: Write an empty stack.

Step 3: Start reading the symbols from left to right i.e. symbols will be read as in sequence as (( )). Scan the expression by repeating step 4 and 5 until

1 2 3 4

expression is completely read.

Step 4: The first symbol scanned is '('and it is opening symbol, so push it onto stack.

Next symbol scanned is again opening symbol '('. Push it on to stack

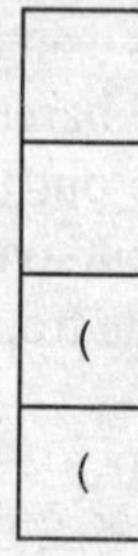

Step 5: Next symbol scanned is closing parenthesis ')',

(a) : so we will check whether stack is empty, which is not , so step 5b will be executed.

(b) Stack is to be popped, symbol popped is '('. It matches with the symbol scanned in step 5.

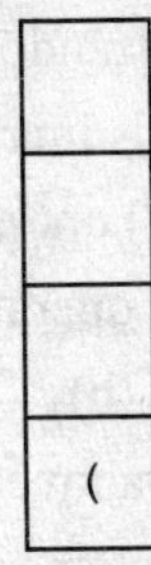

Read the last symbol ')', which is closing parenthesis, so step 5 will again be executed.

Step 5a: We will check if stack is empty, which is not, so step 5b will be executed.

Step 5b: Pop the stack i.e. pop '('. It matches with the symbol1 ')'

Step 6: Now expression is completely read, also stack is empty. So step 7 will be executed

Step 7: Print that input expression is balanced

OBJECTIVE TYPE QUESTIONS

1. The stack is based on the rule

(a) first-in-last-out (b) last-in-first-out

(c) both (a) and (b) (d) first-in-first-out

2. The push () operation is used

(a) to insert an element

(b) to remove an element

(c) to move an element

(d) all of the above.

3. The pop operation removes

(a) the element lastly inserted (b) first element of the stack

(c) any element randomly (d) None of the above

4. The top pointer is increased

(a) when push () operation is done

(b) when pop () operation is done

(c) both (a) and (b)

(d) None of the above

5. A stack holding elements equal to its capacity and if push is performed then such situation is called

(a) stack overflow (b) stack underflow

(c) illegal operation (d) None of the above

6. The prefix notation is also called as

(a) polish notation (b) postfix notation

(c) infix notation (d) None of the above

7. From the given options one is not a stack application

(a) template (b) recursion

(c) reverse string (d) conversion of number.

8. An expression containing more than one operation are solved according to

(a) priority of operators (b) priority of operands

(c) from left to right (d) right to left.

9. The following brackets changes the priority

(a) ( ) (b) [ ]

(c) { } (d) &

10. The postfix notation is also called as

(a) reverse polish notation (b) polish notation

(c) prefix notation (d) postfix notation.

11. Stack is

(a) Linear data structure (b) Non-linear data structure

(c) Both (d) None

12. Which of the following operations can be performed on stack?
    (a) Push (b) Pop
    (c) Insert (d) Both a and b
13. Overflow occurs if
    (a) Stack is full (b) Stack is empty
    (c) Stack is half (b) All of the above
14. Stack can be implemented by using
    (a) Array (b) Queue
    (c) Pointer (d) Linked list
    (e) None
15. Which of the following is the type of Stack?
    (a) Different cities (b) Heap of books
    (c) Binary tree (d) None of the above
16. Which of the following is the operation of stack
    (a) Tos (b) Peek
    (c) Create (d) Dup
    (e) All of the above (f) None of the above
17. Search is possible in stack
    (a) Yes (b) No
    (c) Fifty-fifty (b) None
18. Which of the following is the operation of Stack:
    (a) Sorting (b) Searching
    (c) Inserting (d) Deleting
    (e) All of the above
19. Which of the following is the application of stack
    (a) To set Infix expression
    (b) To set Prefix expression
    (c) To set postfix expression
    (d) All of the above
    (e) None of the above
20. Traversing in stack means:
    (a) Sorting (b) Searching
    (c) Inserting (d) Deleting
    (e) Visiting (f) None of the above

21. When a function calls itself is called
    (a) Recursion (b) Iteration
    (c) Function (d) none of the above.
22. In indirect recursion a function calls
    (a) Another function (b) itself
    (c) Only main () function (d) none of the above.
23. In tower of Hanoi the following one condition is not applicable:
    (a) At a time only one disk may be moved
    (b) the disc may be moved from any needle to another needle
    (c) No larger disk may be placed on the smaller one
    (d) The disks can be placed in any order.
24. The function declarator is used to
    (a) declare formal arguments (b) declare function prototype
    (c) function call (d) all of the above.

EXERCISES

1. Write description of stack structure.
2. What do you mean by Stack?
3. Explain the stack model?
4. What are the various commonly used stack operations?
5. Write an algorithm and C program **for stack operations:**
    1. Push 2. Pop
    3. Display operation 4. Peek **operation**
    5. Dup **operation** 6. Swap **operation**
    7. Right rotate
6. What do you mean by stack frames?
7. What do you mean by multiple stacks?
8. Explain various representations of stacks in detail.
9. Explain various applications of Stack.
10. Define prefix, Infix, and Postfix Expression.
11. What is the advantages of using postfix expressions as compared to Infix Expressions?
12. How an Arithmetic expression is evaluated?

13. Write an algorithm to convert an Infix to Postfix expression.
14. Convert the following Infix expressions to Postfix and Prefix expressions.
    (i) (a+(b/d)) *(c/e) + f
    (ii) ((a+b*c) / (e+f)) / g
    (iii) a ! b ! c
    (iv) (a-b) * (c/d) + e
    (v) (a *(b-c) / d) + (e / (f*g-h))
15. Write an algorithm to evaluate a Postfix expression.
16. Evaluate the following Postfix expressions:
    (i) 30 20 - 10 5 * 4 -
    (ii) 10 6 + 3 / 3 10 + 6 +
    (iii) 10 6 4 + *
17. Explain the procedure to convert an infix arithmetic expression to prefix or polish expression.
18. Explain concept of Backtracking.
19. What do you mean by Recursion? Explain the various applications of recursion.
20. Explain concept of Parenthesis matching.
21. Write an algorithm for balanced symbol checking.
22. Write the entire valid symbol from inputs set of following symbol.
    [(( )], { [( )], ({ }]), ({ [ ] }), ((({ { } }))) }

CHAPTER 20

Queues

20.1 INTRODUCTION

A queue is a particular kind of collection in which the entities in the collection are kept in order and the principal (or only) operations on the collection are the addition of entities to the rear terminal position and removal of entities from the front terminal position. This makes the queue a First-In-First-Out (FIFO) data structure.

Figure 20.1: Waiting line for service called queue.

In a FIFO data structure, the first element added to the queue will be the first one to be removed. This is equivalent to the requirement that whenever an element is added, all elements that were added before have to be removed before the new element can be invoked. A queue is an example of a linear data structure.

A queue is an abstract data type in which insertion occurs at one end (the rear) and deletion occurs at the other end (the front). A queue is defined to hold one type of data element. Only the elements indicated by front and rear can be accessed.

20.2 CONCEPT OF QUEUE

A queue is defined as a data structure, which holds a series of items to be processed on a **first in first out** basis (though some queues can be sorted in priority).

A queue differs from a stack in the way its removal operation behaves—a removal removes and returns the element that has resided in the queue for the longest period of time. For this reason, a queue is called a "first in, first out" data structure. A queue is represented in Figure 20.2 and 20.3 as shown below:

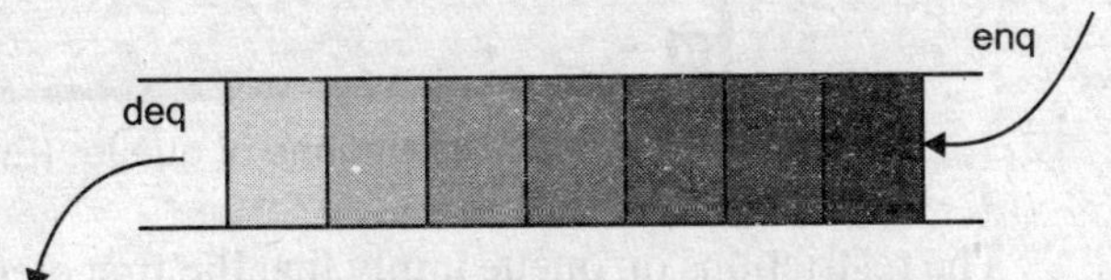

Figure 20.2: Representation of queue.

Figure 20.3: Explaining the concept of a Queue

A **queue** is an ordered list in which all insertions take place at one end, the **rear**, while all deletions take place at the other end, the **front**. When viewed as a queue with a[n] as the rear element one says that a[i+1] is behind a[i], 1<i<=n.

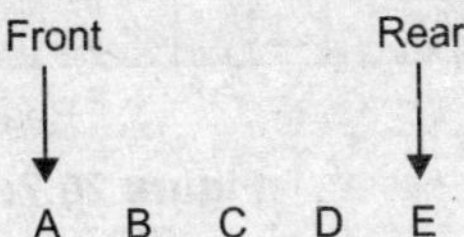

Figure 20.4: Queue having front and rear elements

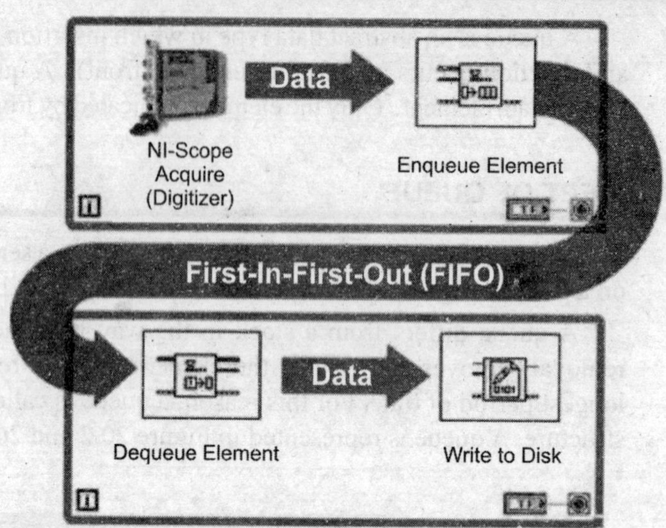

Figure 20.5: Various operations of queue. (Enqueue and Dequeue)

The restrictions on queue imply that the first element which is inserted into the queue will be the first one to be removed. Thus A is the first letter to be removed, and queues are known as First in First out (FIFO) lists. Note that the data object queue as defined here need not necessarily correspond to the mathematical concept of queue in which the insert/delete rules may be different.

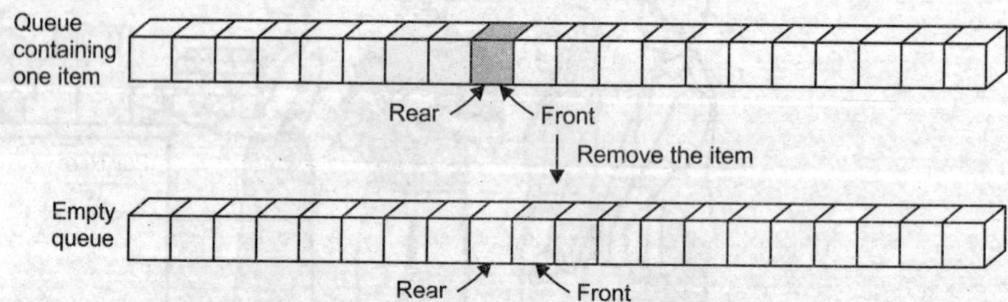

Figure 20.6: Remove the item from queue.

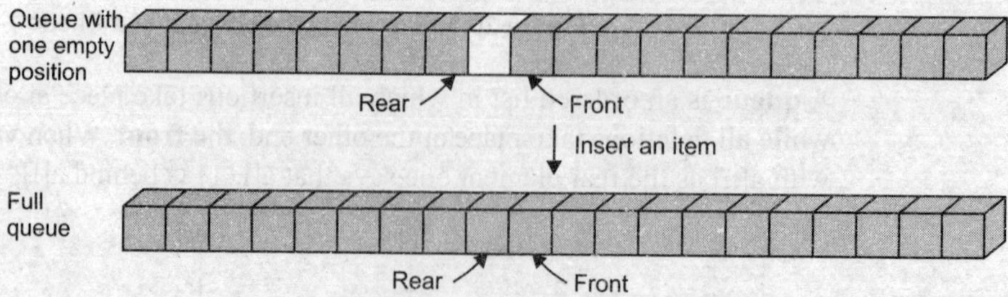

Figure 20.7: Insert an item in queue.

***Definition:** A data structure which is based on first come first serve having two different ends one for insertion(Rear) and another for deletion(Front) is called Queue.*

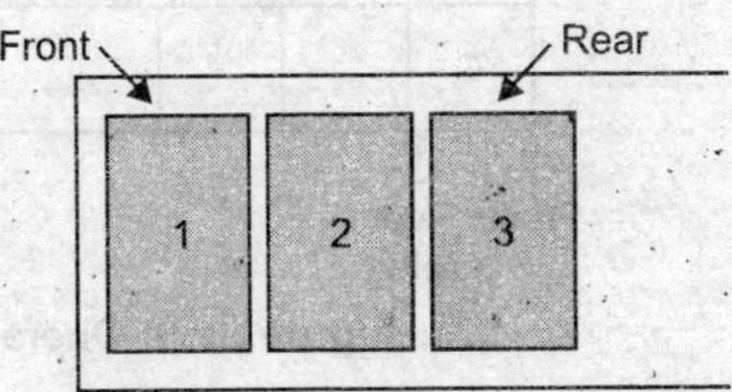

Figure 20.8: FIFO data structure

In a FIFO data structure, the first element added to the queue will be the first one to be removed. This is equivalent to the requirement that whenever an element is added, all elements that were added before have to be removed before the new element can be invoked. A queue is an example of a linear data structure. Queues provide services in computer science, transport and operations research where various entities such as data, objects, persons, or events are stored and held to be processed later. In these contexts, the queue performs the function of a buffer. Queues are common in computer programs, where they are implemented as data structures coupled with access routines, as an abstract data structure or in object-oriented languages as classes.

A **queue** is also a list of elements with insertions permitted at one end—called the rear, and deletions permitted from the other end—called the front. This means that the removal of elements from a queue is possible in the same order in which the insertion of elements is made into the queue. Thus, a queue data structure exhibits the **FIFO (first in first out)** property. Insert and delete are the operations that are provided for insertion of elements into the queue and the removal of elements from the queue, respectively. Shown in Figure 20.9 are the effects of insert and delete operations on the queue.

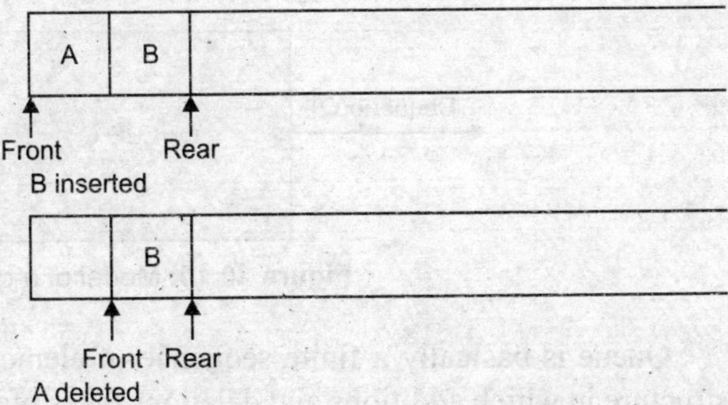

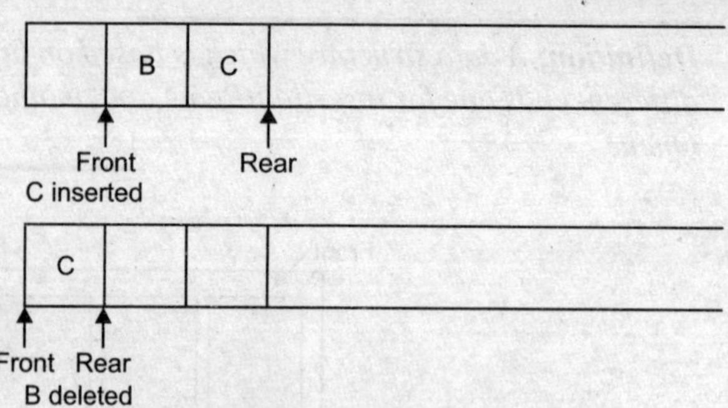

Figure 20.9: Operations on a queue.

The queue data structure is characterized by the fact that additions are made at the end, or tail, of the queue while removals are made from the front, or head, of the queue. For this reason, a stack is referred to as a FIFO structure (First-In First-Out). Queues occur naturally in situations where the rate at which clients' demand for services can exceed the rate at which these services can be supplied. For example, in a network where many computers share only a few printers, the print jobs may accumulate in a print queue. In an operating system with a GUI, applications and windows communicate using messages, which are placed in message queues until they can be handled.

20.3 QUEUE AS AN ABSTRACT DATA TYPE

Like stacks, queues are lists. With a queue, however, insertion is done at one end, whereas deletion is performed at the other end.

20.3.1 Queue Model

The basic operations on a queue are enqueue, which inserts an element at the end of the list (called the rear), and dequeue, which deletes (and returns) the element at the start of the list (known as the front). Figure 20.10 shows the abstract model of a queue.

Figure 20.10: Model of a queue

Queue is basically a finite sequence of elements of same type. It is a linear structure in which additions and deletions takes place at different ends. The end at which new elements are added is called the rear, and the end from which elements are deleted is called the front.

For Example:

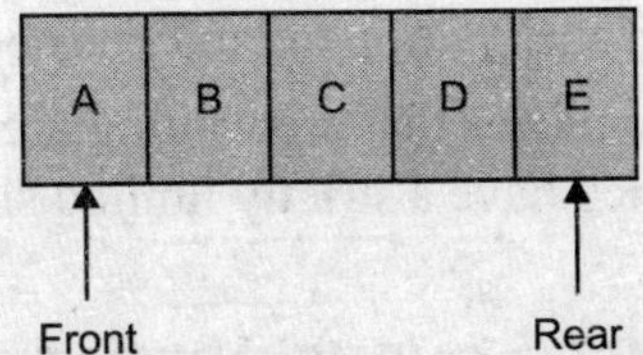

Figure 20.11: Queue having front and rear.

So a queue follows First-In-First-Out (FIFO) pattern of sequence. The FIFO property causes to operate like a line of people waiting to get their movie tickets for a show. We call the insert operation on a queue Enqueue, and we call the delete operation Dequeue. When an element is enqueued, it takes place at the rear end of the queue, the element dequeued is always the one at the front end of the queue.

20.4 APPLICATION OF QUEUES: SIMULATION OF AN AIRPORT

Simulation is the use of one system to imitate the behaviour of another system. A computer simulation is a program to imitate the behaviour of the system under study.

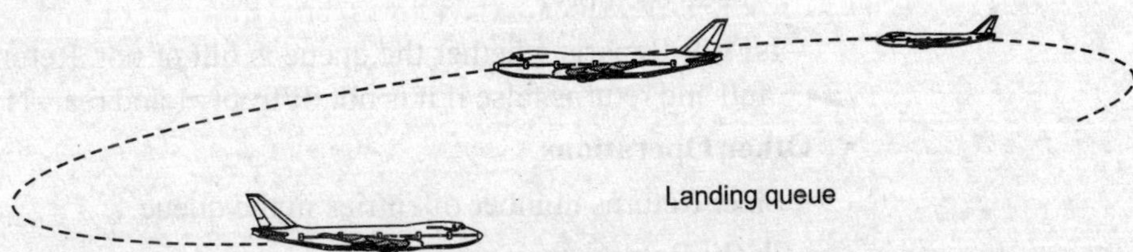

Figure 20.12: Landing queue.

Figure 20.13: Takeoff queue.

1. The same runway is used for both landings and takeoffs.
2. One plane can land or take off in a unit of time, but not both.
3. A random number of planes arrive in each time unit.
4. A plane waiting to land goes before one waiting to take off.
5. The planes that are waiting are kept in queues landing and takeoff, both of which have a strictly limited size.

20.5 COMMONLY USED QUEUE OPERATIONS

Here are some operations, with their typical names, that are performed on queues:

- **Initialization operation**
  - **Create:** Returns an empty queue.
- **Basic Operations**
  - **Enqueue:** Adds a new element at the rear of a queue.
  - **Dequeue:** Removes an element from the front of the queue and return it. (This operation cannot be performed if the queue is empty.)
- **Status checking operations**
  - **IsEmpty:** Reports whether the queue is empty or not. Returns true if queue is empty and returns false if it is not. If front=0 and rear=0 then queue is empty.
  - **IsFull:** Reports whether the queue is full or not. Returns true if queue is full and returns false if it is not. If front=1 and rear=N then queue is full.
- **Other Operations**
  - **Size:** Returns number of entries in the queue.
  - **Peek:** Returns the front of the queue without removing it.
  - **Rear:** Returns last element entered in queue.
  - **Equals:** checks if two queues are equal or not? Two queues are equal when their contents are equal (requires deep equality on each element of the queue).
  - **Destroy:** Returns an empty queue after deleting all the data elements from it.

All these operations, mentioned above, are performed in O(1) time.

20.6 ORDER PRODUCED BY A QUEUE

A static array can be used to implement the data structures. Consider, for example, a queue implemented as an array as shown in the Figure 20.14.

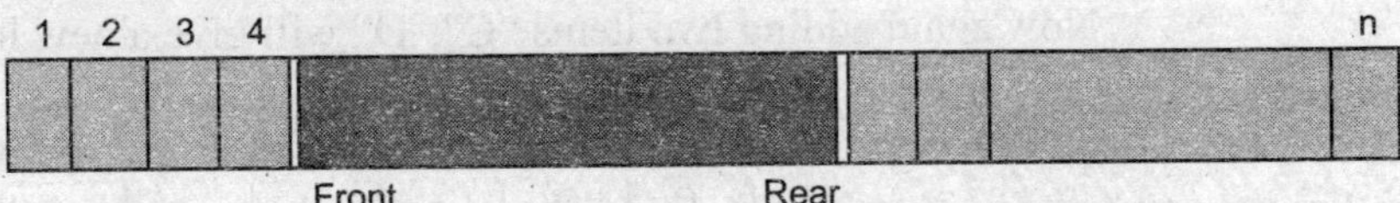

Figure 20.14: Queue with front and rear pointers.

As data is added to the rear of the queue, the cell labeled 'rear' (the cell containing the last enqueued data) is incremented to the right. If data is dequeued, the cell labeled 'front' (the cell containing the first enqueued data) is also incremented to the right. The following diagram shows an empty queue. It is identified as a series of ten locations, and two pointers named **front or head** and **rear or tail**. These two pointers keep track of where the front and rear of the queue is

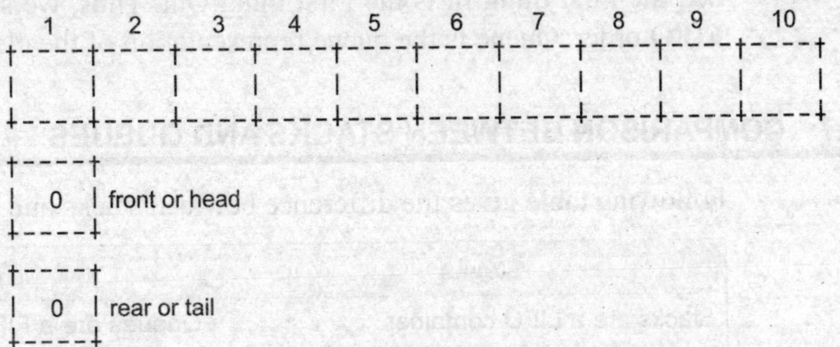

The front pointer is used to delete items, and the rear pointer insert items. Inserting two items called "A" and "B" will rearrange the queue to look like:

```
  1    2    3    4    5    6    7    8    9    10
+----+----+----+----+----+----+----+----+----+----+
| A  | B  |    |    |    |    |    |    |    |    |
+----+----+----+----+----+----+----+----+----+----+

+----+
| 1  | front or head
+----+

+----+
| 2  | rear or tail
+----+
```

Now deleting one item "A", will rearrange the Queue to look like:

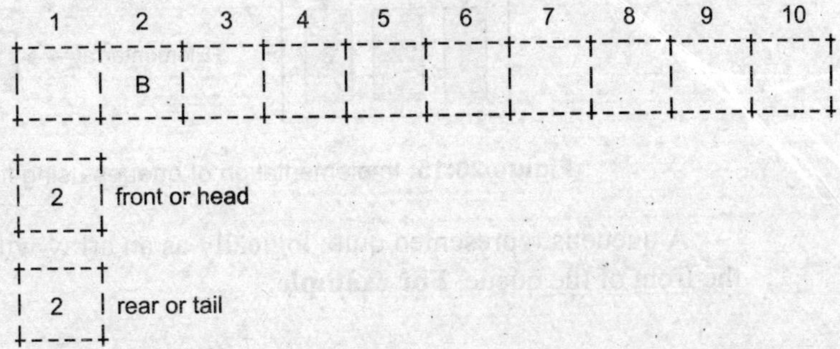

Now again adding two items "C","D" will give a new look to Queue:

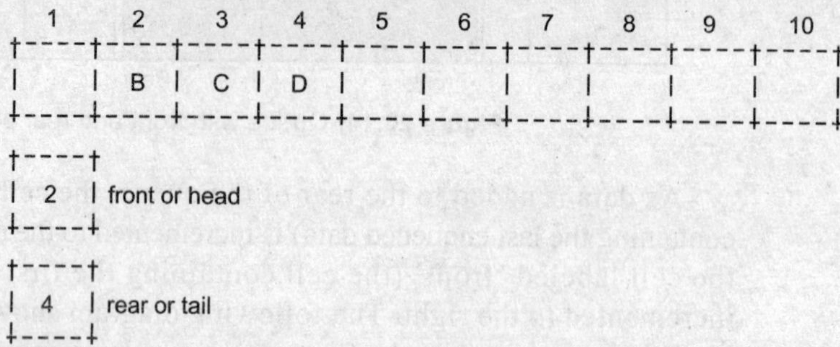

You'll notice that the queue enforces a certain order to the use of its contents, i.e., the First thing In is the First thing Out. Thus, we say that a queue enforces **FIFO** order. Queue is the queue representation of the elements in List.

20.7 COMPARISON BETWEEN STACKS AND QUEUES

Following table gives the difference between stacks and queues:

Stacks	Queues
Stacks are a LIFO container	Queues are a FIFO container
Store data in the reverse of order received	Store data in the order received
Stacks suggest applications where some sort of reversal or unwinding is desired.	Queues suggest applications where service is to be rendered relative to order received.
	From an ordering perspective, Queues are the "opposite" of stacks

20.8 IMPLEMENTATION OF QUEUES USING LINEAR ARRAYS

The Queue entries or data elements can be stored in an array. This is called as array representation of Queues. The queues represented using linear arrays are called as linear Queues. Operations mentioned on Queues can be implemented on an array.

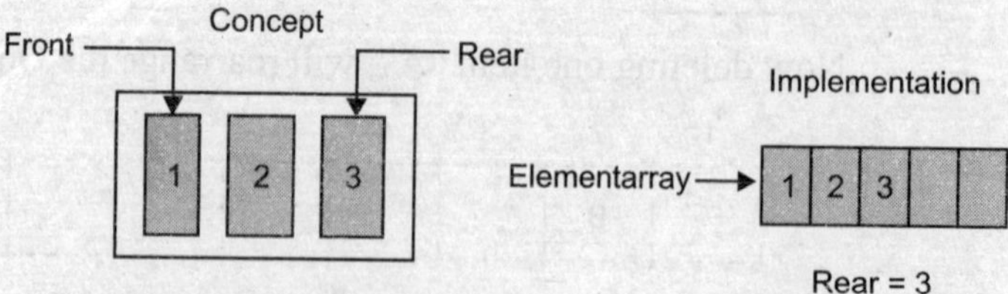

Figure 20.15: Implementation of queues using linear arrays.

A queue is represented quite logically as an array with the 0th element being the front of the queue. **For example:**

Figure 20.16: Front point to Todd.

The queue above would become the following array:

Index	0	1	2	3	4
	Todd	Bob	Phil	Kirt	Alice

Figure 20.17: Array index starting from zero.

Like a stack, a Queue usually holds things of the same type. We usually draw Queues horizontally. Here's a Queue of characters with 3 elements:

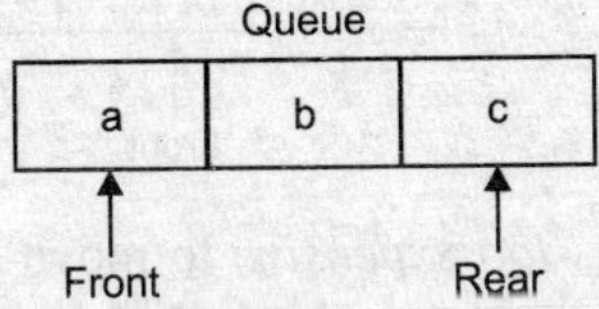

The main property of a queue is that objects go on the rear and come off of the front of the queue. One of the things we'll need to keep track of is the number of elements in the queue, i.e., not all the elements in the array may be holding elements of the queue at any given time. So far, the pieces of data we need for our array implementation of the queue are: an array and a count. So example mentioned above can be described as

Queue (made up of 'contents' and 'count')

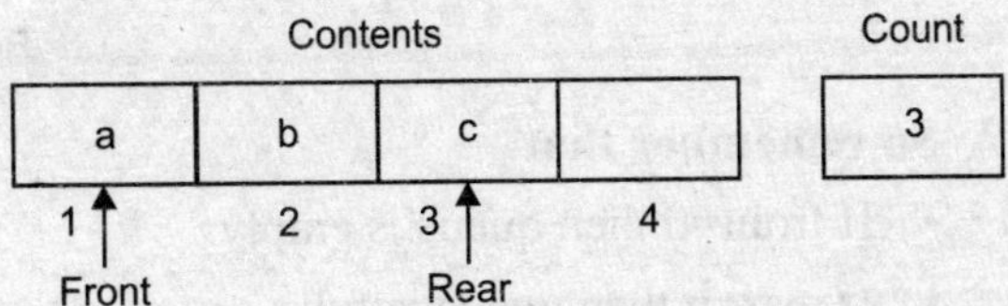

Where a is at the front and **c** is at the rear. Now, we enter a new element with Enqueue operation.

Queue (made up of 'contents' and 'count')

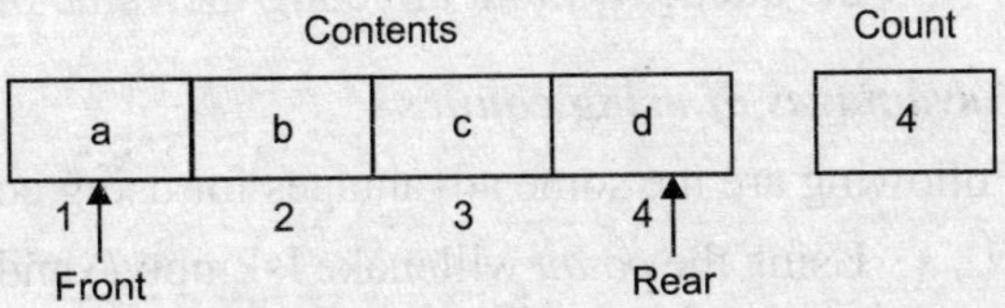

Now we remove an element with Dequeue operation and store it in variable ch

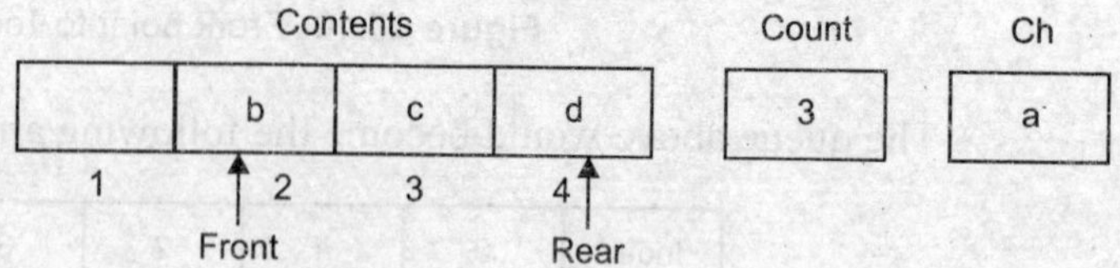

We have a problem because the *front* of the queue is no longer at array position 1. One solution would be to move all the elements down one, giving:

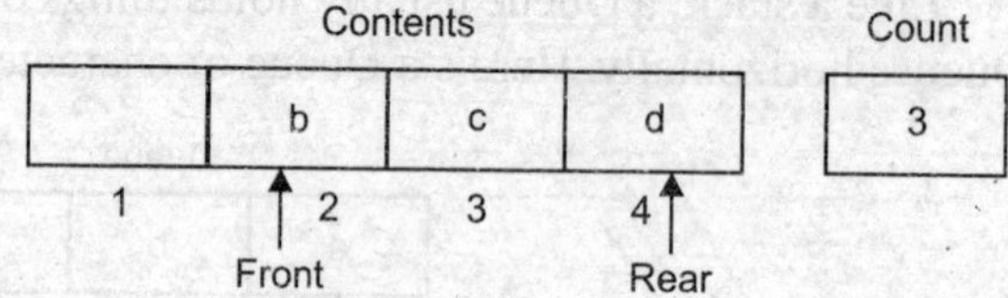

But it is *too expensive* to move everything down every time we remove an element.

Instead, we can use an additional piece of information to keep track of the front and rear, We can use the index of the elements at the front and rear, giving:

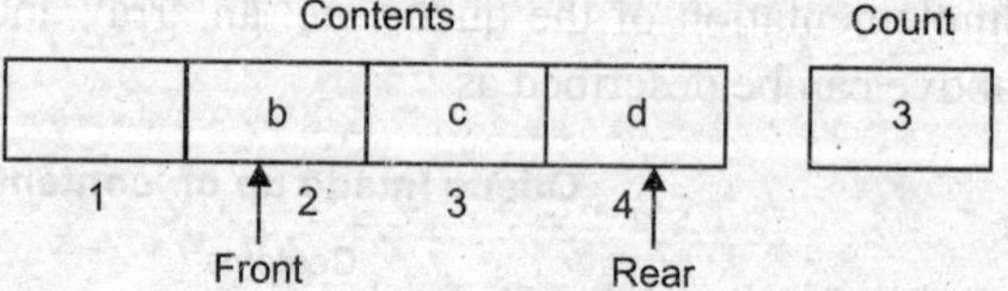

So remember that:

- If front=0 then queue is empty.
- If rear=n then queue is full.
- The value of rear is incremented by 1 when an element is entered in the queue, without affecting the value of front pointer.
- The value of the front is incremented by 1 when an element is deleted from the queue, without affecting the value of rear pointer.

Advantages of using count

Following are the some advantages for using count:

- Using the *count* will make IsEmpty() and IsFull() easy, although we'll have to make sure the count is updated properly in Enqueue and Dequeue operations. We haven't explored how to determine emptiness/fullness with rear or whether doing so presents any challenges.

- Using the count in Enqueue is similar to using rear. In both cases, the front won't move. With the count, we'll have to use count to calculate at which position to add new values.
- Using the count in Dequeue is not more difficult than using rear. In both cases, the front has to move.

20.8.1 Create Operation

Algorithm 20.1: To implement a queue using an array.

CREATEQ(N, FRONT, REAR, ITEM)

In the algorithm, an array Queue, say Queue is declared with maximum size as say, N and variables front and rear points to the first and last locations respectively of the Queue. The data item which is to be entered is stored in variable ITEM.

Step 1: Read the value of N i.e. total number of elements in Queue.

Step 2: Repeat steps 3 and 4 N times, starting from initial value of counter variable say] REAR = 1 to N.

Step 3: Read the value of element in ITEM.

Step 4: [Store the value entered of element in Queue current location using an assignment] QUEUE[REAR] = ITEM.

[Increment REAR by 1] REAR=REAR+1.

Step 5: [Decrement REAR by 1. So that it points to last element in Queue.]

REAR = REAR-1.

Step 6: End.

Explanation

Step 1: Let us create a QUEUE of size 4 i.e. the value of N is 4.

Step 2: Repeat steps 3 & step 4 for 4 times i.e. for REAR = 1 to 4

Step 3: Read the value of element, let us suppose user enters 10.

Step 4: Store this value into QUEUE in first location using an assignment

QUEUE [REAR] = QUEUE [1] = 10

Now if user enters the remaining elements as 20, 30, 40 using assignments

QUEUE [REAR+1] = QUEUE [1+1] = QUEUE [2] = 20

QUEUE [REAR+1] = QUEUE [2+1] = QUEUE [3] = 30

QUEUE [REAR+1] = QUEUE [3+1] = QUEUE [4] = 40

Queue will look like:

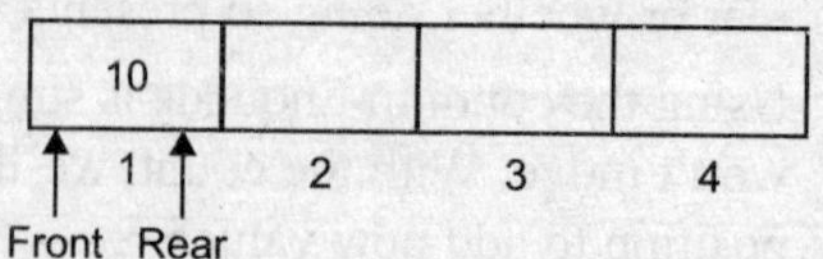

Figure 20.18: Queue Created for first element.

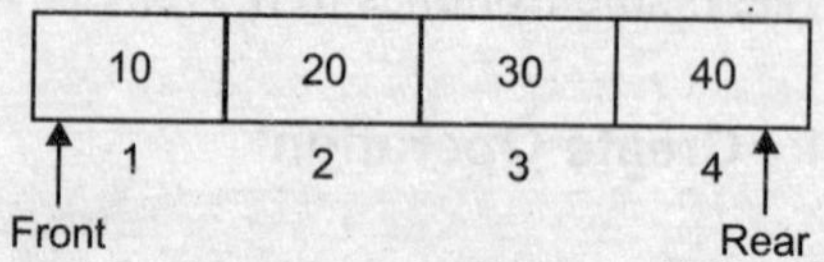

Figure 20.19: Final Queue Created.

After complete operation, FRONT pointer is 1 and REAR pointer is 4.

Step 5: After the step 3 & 4 have been executed for required no. of times i.e. 4 in this case, REAR will become 5 at step 5 so we should decrement it by 1 REAR=5-1= 4. So that it points to last element 4 in the QUEUE.

Step 6: End.

20.8.2 Enqueue Operation

Algorithm 20.2: To insert element in QUEUE structure.

INSRTQ(N, FRONT, REAR, ITEM)

This algorithm inserts an element ITEM into a queue. FRONT is used to delete the element from queue. REAR is used to insert element into queue.

Step1: [When the Queue is already filled?]

If FRONT = 1 and REAR = N, or if FRONT = REAR + 1, then

Write: OVERFLOW, and Return.

Step 2: [Find new value of REAR.]

If FRONT = NULL, then [Starting Queue initially empty.]

Set FRONT= 1 and REAR = 1.

Else if REAR = N, then

Set REAR = 1.

Else

Set REAR = REAR + 1.

[End of If statement.]

Step 3: Set QUEUE[REAR] = ITEM. [This inserts new element.]

Step 4: End.

Explanation

Consider the following Queue.

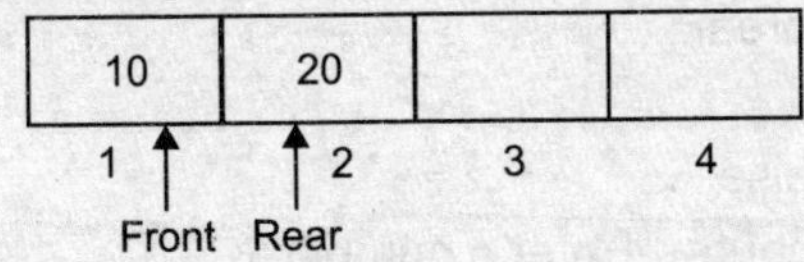

Figure 20.20: Before insertion. FRONT = 1 and REAR = 2.

Step 1: [When the Queue is already filled?]
If FRONT = 1 and REAR = 4, or if FRONT = 4 + 1, then
Write: OVERFLOW, and Return.

Step 2: [Find new value of REAR.]
If FRONT = NULL, then [Starting Queue initially empty.]
Set FRONT= 1 and REAR = 1.
Else if REAR = N, then
Set REAR = 1.
Else
Set REAR = REAR + 1. [SET REAR = 3]
[End of If statement.]

Step 3: Set QUEUE[3] = 30. [This inserts new element at position 3.]

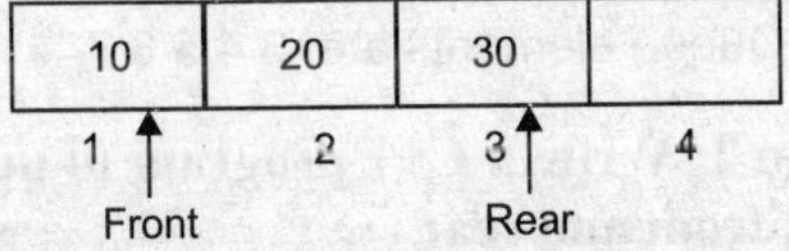

Figure 20.21: After insertion. FRONT = 1 and REAR = 3.

Step 4: End.

Program 1: Write a C++ program to insert elements in a queue.

```
# include <iostream.h>
# include <conio.h>
# include <process.h>
# define S 5
void main ()
{
int queue[S];
int r=0,n;
clrscr();
while (1) {
if (r>=S) {
cout<<"\n Queue overflow";
```

```
break;
}
else
cout<<"Enter a number:";
cin>>n;
queue[r]=n;
r++;
}
cout<<"\n Queue elements are:";
for (n=0;n<S;n++)
cout<<queue[n];
getch();
}
```

Output:

```
Enter a number: 3
Enter a number: 4
Enter a number: 5
Enter a number: 6
Enter a number: 7
Queue overflow
Queue elements are: 3 4 5 6 7
```

Program 2: Write a C++ program to perform insertion operation and show value of front and rear.

```
# include <iostream.h>
# include <conio.h>
void main ()
{
int queue[7];
int r=-1,f=-1,j;
clrscr();
while (r<6)
{
r++;
cout<<"rear="<<r<<"front="<<f<<" Enter element:";
cin>>queue[r];
if (r= =0) f=0;
}
cout<<"\n Queue elements are:";
for (j=0;<7;j++)
```

```
cout<<queue[j];
getch();
}
```

Output:

```
rear=-1 front=-1 Enter element:8
rear=0 front=0 Enter element:9
rear=1 front=0 Enter element:4
rear=2 front=0 Enter element:5
rear=3 front=0 Enter element:1
rear=4 front=0 Enter element:2
rear=5 front=0 Enter element:3
Queue elements are: 8 9 4 5 1 2 3
```

20.8.3 Dequeue Operation

Algorithm 20.3: To delete element from QUEUE structure.

DELQ(N, FRONT, REAR, ITEM)

This algorithm deletes an element from a queue and assigns it to the variable ITEM. FRONT is used to delete the element from queue. REAR is used to insert element into queue.

Step 1: [When the Queue is already empty?]

If FRONT = NULL, then Write: UNDERFLOW, and Return.

Step 2: Set ITEM =QUEUE[FRONT].

Step 3: [Find new value of front.]

If FRONT= REAR, then [Queue has only one element to start.]

Set FRONT = NULL and REAR = NULL

Else if FRONT = N, then

Set FRONT = 1

Else

Set FRONT = FRONT + 1.

[End of If statement.]

Step 4: End.

Explanation

Consider the following Queue:

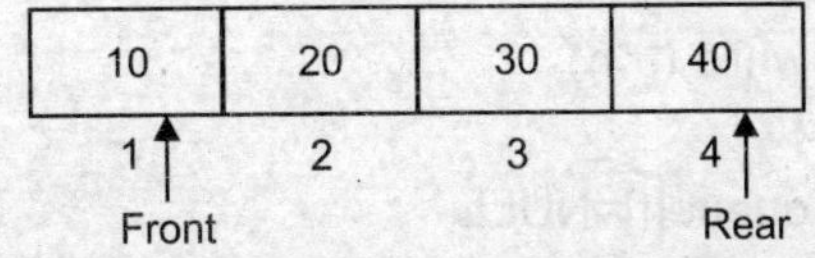

Figure 20.22: Before deletion. FRONT = 1 and REAR = 4.

Step 1: [When the Queue is already empty?]

If FRONT = NULL, then Write: UNDERFLOW, and Return.

Step 2: Set ITEM =QUEUE[1].[Element 10 is removed]

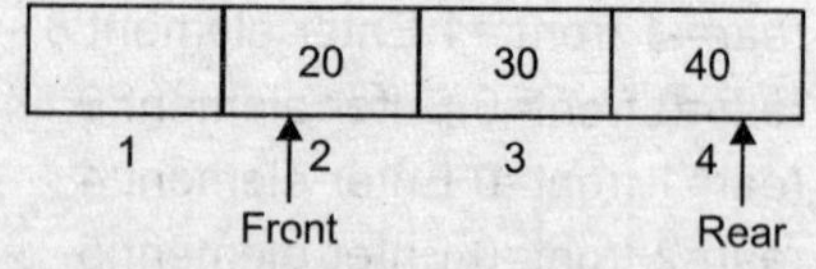

Figure 20.23: After deletion. FRONT = 2 and REAR = 4.

Step 3: [Find new value of front.]

If FRONT= REAR, then [Queue has only one element to start.]

Set FRONT = NULL and REAR = NULL

Else if FRONT = N, then

Set FRONT = 1

Else

Set FRONT = FRONT + 1. [SET FRONT =2]

[End of If statement.]

Step 4: End.

Program 3: Write a C++ program to perform deletion operation on queue and show value of front and rear.

```
# include <iostream.h>
# include <conio.h>
void main ()
{
int queue[7]={11,12,13,14,15,16,17};
int i,r=6,f=0,n;
clrscr();
cout<<"\nThe Elements of queue are as follows:-\n";
for(i=0;i<7;i++)
cout<<queue[i];
cout<<"\nInitial values rear="<<r<<"front="<<f;
cout<<"\nHow many elements u want to delete:";
cin>>n;
while (f<n)
{
queue[f]=NULL;
f++;
```

```
cout<<"\nrear="<<r<<" front="<<f;
}
cout<<"\n Queue elements are:";
for (n=0;n<7;n++)
cout<<queue[n];
getch();
}
```

Output:

```
The Elements of queue are as follows:-
11 12 13 14 15 16 17
Initial values rear=6 front=0
How many elements u want to delete: 3
rear=6 front=1
rear=6 front=2
rear=6 front=3
Queue elements are: 0 0 0 14 15 16 17
```

Program 4: Write a C++ program to perform different operations with queue such as insert, delete and display of elements.

```
# include <iostream.h>
# include <conio.h>
int queue[8];
int r;
void insert(void);
void del ();
void show (void);
void main ()
{
int c;
clrscr();
cout<<"\n1] Insert Element";
cout<<"\n2] Delete Element";
cout<< "\n3] Display element/s";
cout<<"\n4] Exit";
cout<<"\n Enter your choice:-";
cin>>c'
switch (c)
{
case 1: insert(); break;
case 2: del(); show();break;
```

```
case 3: show(); break;
default: exit(0);
}
main ();
getch();
}
void insert ()
{
Char ans='Y';
if (f>=7)
{
cout<<"\n Queue is full \n\n\n";
main ();
}
while (ans= ='Y'   ans= ='y')
{
cout<<"\n Enter element:-";
cin>>queue[r];
if (r= =7)
{
clrscr();
cout<<"\n Queue is Full";
getch();
break;
}
else
r++;
cout<<"\nContinue [Y/N]:-";
ans=getche();
}
}
void show()
{
int j;
for (j=0;j<r;j++)
cout<<queue[j];
getch();
}
void del ()
```

```
{
int j;
if (r= =0)
{
clrscr();
cout<<"\n Queue is empty \n\n\n";
main();
}
for (j=0;j<r;j++)
queue[j]= queue[j+1];
queue[r]=0;
r--;
}
```

Output:

```
1] Insert element
2] Delete element
3] Display element/s
4] Exit
Enter choice:- 1
Enter element:- 23
Continue [Y/N]:-y
Enter element:- 45
Continue [Y/N]:-
```

20.8.4 Peek Operation

Algorithm 20.4: To Print the front of the queue without removing it.

PEEKQ(N,FRONT, REAR)

In the algorithm, an array Queue, say Queue is declared with maximum size as say, n and variables front and rear points to the first and last locations respectively of the Queue.

Step 1: [When the Queue is already empty?]

If FRONT = NULL, then Write: UNDERFLOW, and Return.

Step 2: [Print the element stored at position]

If FRONT= REAR, then

FRONT=REAR=1 [Queue has only one element to print.]

Else Set FRONT = FRONT + 1. [Print elements one by one.]

[End of If statement.]

Step 3: End.

Explanation

Let us consider the following Queue

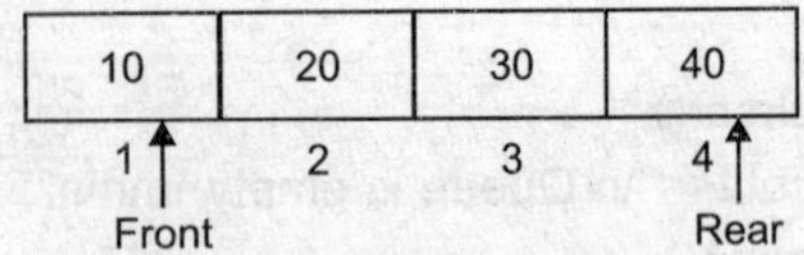

Figure 20.24: Print the FRONT = 10.

Step 1: [When the Queue is already empty?]
If FRONT = NULL, then Write: UNDERFLOW, and Return.

Step 2: [Print the element stored at position]
If FRONT= REAR, then [Queue has only one element to start.]
Set FRONT = NULL and REAR = NULL
Else if FRONT = N, then Set FRONT = 1
Else Set FRONT = FRONT + 1. [End of If statement.]

Step 3: End.

20.8.5 Rear Operation

Algorithm 20.5: To print last element entered in queue.

REARQ (N, FRONT, REAR,ITEM)

In the algorithm, an array Queue, say Queue is declared with maximum size as say, n and variables front and rear points to the first and last locations, respectively of the Queue.

Step 1: [When the Queue is already empty?]
If FRONT = NULL, then Write: UNDERFLOW, and Return.

Step 2: [Print the element stored at location pointed to by rear].
ITEM = QUEUE[REAR]

Step 3: End

Explanation

Let us consider the following Queue:

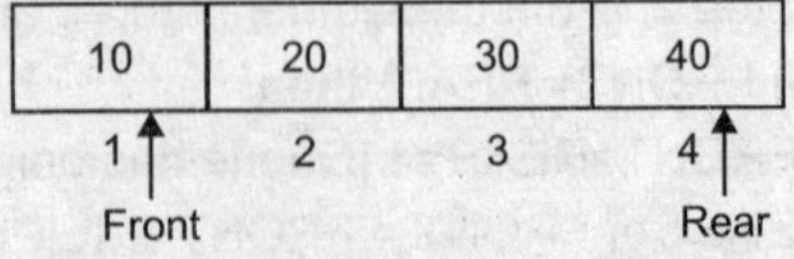

Figure 20.25: Print the REAR =40.

Step 1: [When the Queue is already empty?]
If FRONT = NULL, then Write: UNDERFLOW, and Return.

Step 2: [Print the element stored at location pointed to by rear].
Here it is 40. ITEM = QUEUE[4]. So 40 will printed.

Step 3: End

20.8.6 Equals Operation

Algorithm 20.6: To checks if two queues are equal or not? Two queues are equal when their contents are equal (requires deep equality on each element of the queue).

EQUALSQ (QUEUE1, QUEUE2, FRONT, N, M)

In the algorithm two array Queues say, Queue1 and Queue2 are declared with maximum size as say, n and m respectively and variables front and rear points to the first and last locations respectively of the Queues.

Step 1: IF QUEUE1[N] = QUEUE2[M] [if number of elements in QUEUE1 equal to number of elements in QUEUE2]
Then goto step 2. Else goto step 5.

Step 2: Repeat step 3 until FRONT > REAR.

Step 3: [Compare both queues]
IF QUEUE1[FRONT] = QUEUE2[FRONT] then
FRONT = FRONT +1
Else
goto step 5.

Step 4: Print the two Queues are equal.

Step 5: End.

Explanation

Consider the following two Queues:

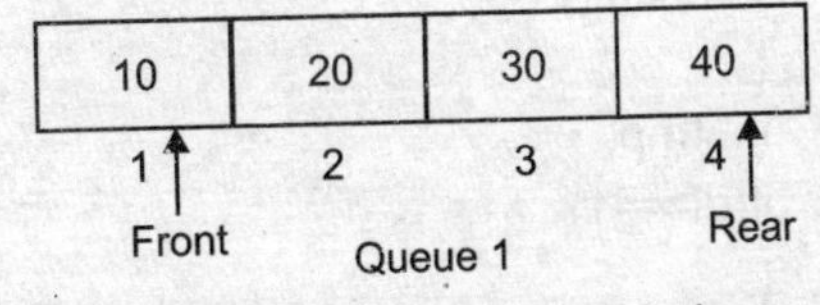

Figure 20.26: Queue1 having 4 elements.

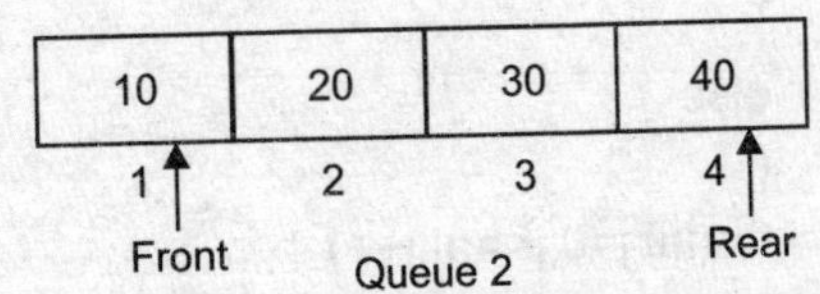

Figure 20.27: Queue2 having 4 elements.

Step 1: The total no of elements in QUEUE1 are 4 & total no of elements in QUEUE2 are 4, as these are equal so step 2 will be executed.

Step 2: Here front is 1 and rear is 4, as front is less than rear so steps 3 will be executed.

Step 3: Compare QUEUE1[FRONT] and QUEUE2[FRONT]. The value of these is 10, which is equal, so step 4 will be executed. FRONT = FRONT +1, So all the values of QUEUE1 will be compared with QUEUE2, till front is less than or equal to rear. As all these values are equal, so step 5 will be executed.

Step 4: Print that two Queues are equal

Step 5: End.

Program 5: Write a C++ program to implement queue using arrays.

```
#include <iostream>
#include<conio.h>
#define MAX 5          // MAXIMUM CONTENTS IN QUEUE
class queue
{
private:
int t[MAX];
int al;    // Addition End
int dl;    // Deletion End
public:
queue()
{
dl=-1;
al=-1;
}
void del()
{
int tmp;
if(dl==-1)
{
cout<<"Queue is Empty";
}
else
{
for(int j=0;j<=al;j++)
{
if((j+1)<=al)
{
tmp=t[j+1];
```

```
t[j]=tmp;
}
else
{
al--;
if(al==-1)
dl=-1;
else
dl=0;
} }
} }
void add(int item)
{
if(dl==-1 && al==-1)
{
dl++;
al++;
}
else
{
al++;
if(al==MAX)
{
cout<<"Queue is Full\n";
al--;
return;
}
}
t[al]=item;
}
void display()
{
if(dl!=-1)
{
for(int iter=0 ; iter<=al ; iter++)
cout<<t[iter]<<" ";
}
else
cout<<"EMPTY";
}
```

```
};
void main()
{
queue a;
int data[5]={32,23,45,99,24};

cout<<"Queue before adding Elements: ";
a.display();
cout<<endl<<endl;
for(int iter = 0 ; iter < 5 ; iter++)
{
a.add(data[iter]);
cout<<"Addition Number : "<<(iter+1)<<" : ";
a.display();
cout<<endl;
}
cout<<endl;
cout<<"Queue after adding Elements: ";
a.display();
cout<<endl<<endl;
for(iter=0 ; iter < 5 ; iter++)
{
a.del();
cout<<"Deletion Number : "<<(iter+1)<<" : ";
a.display();
cout<<endl;
}
getch();
}
```

Output:

```
Queue before adding Elements: EMPTY

Addition Number : 1 : 32
Addition Number : 2 : 32 23
Addition Number : 3 : 32 23 45
Addition Number : 4 : 32 23 45 99
Addition Number : 5 : 32 23 45 99 24

Queue after adding Elements: 32 23 45 99 24

Deletion Number : 1 : 23 45 99 24
```

Deletion Number : 2 : 45 99 24
Deletion Number : 3 : 99 24
Deletion Number : 4 : 24
Deletion Number : 5 : EMPTY

Program 6: Write a C++ program to implement Queue as a Class.

```
# include<iostream.h>
# include<conio.h>
# define SIZE 20
class queue
{
int a[SIZE];
int front;
int rear;
public:
queue();
~queue();
void insert(int i);
int remove();
int isempty();
int isfull();
};
queue::queue()
{
front=0;
rear=0;
}
queue::~queue()
{
delete []a;
}
void queue::insert(int i)
{
if(isfull())
{
cout<<" ******
Queue is FULL !!!
No insertion allowed further.
******";
return;
}
```

```
a[rear] = i;
rear++;
}
int queue::remove()
{
if(isempty())
{
cout<<" ******
Queue Empty !!!
Value returned will be garbage.
******";
return (-9999);
}
return(a[front++]);
}
int queue::isempty()
{
if(front == rear)
return 1;
else
return 0;
}
int queue::isfull()
{
if(rear == SIZE)
return 1;
else
return 0;
}
void main()
{
clrscr();
queue q;
q.insert(1);
q.insert(2);
cout<<" "<<q.remove();
cout<<" "<<q.remove();
cout<<" "<<q.remove();
getch();
}
```

20.9 MAJOR PROBLEM WITH SIMPLE QUEUE

Queue Migration is a problem commonly found in queues when implemented using arrays. As we remove the items from the queue, the queue migrates to one end and the other end remains empty. When we try to insert an element in the queue though there are empty spaces in the queue, it gives a message saying that the Queue is full.

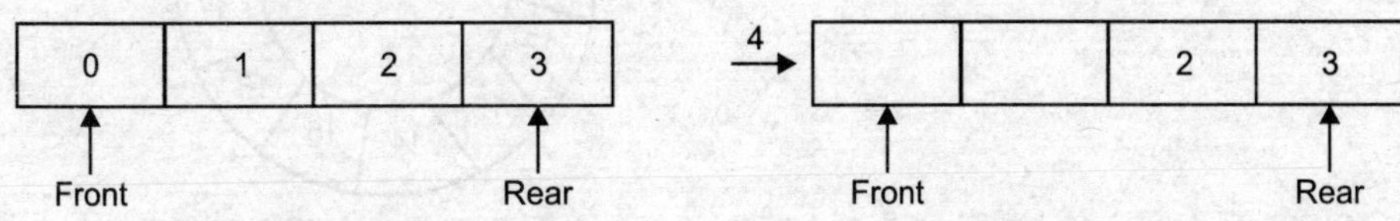

Figure 20.28: Queue Migration **Figure 20.29:** Queue Migration

Here in this Figure 20.28 The maximum size of the array is 4 and four elements 0,1,2,3 are inserted in the queue. When i delete two elements from it, the queue changes like Fig 20.29. Now i insert a number 4 in the queue, it returns a message 'Queue is Full'.

This problem could be solved by implementing a circular queue in next sections.

20.10 CIRCULAR QUEUE

The problem with the previous implementation is that the insert function gives a queue-full signal even if a considerable portion is free. This happens because the queue has a tendency to move to the right unless the 'front' catches up with the 'rear' and both are reset to 0 again (in the delete procedure). To overcome this problem, the elements of the array are required to shift one position left whenever a deletion is made. But this will make the deletion process inefficient. Therefore, an efficient way of overcoming this problem is to consider the array to be circular, as shown in Figure 20.30.

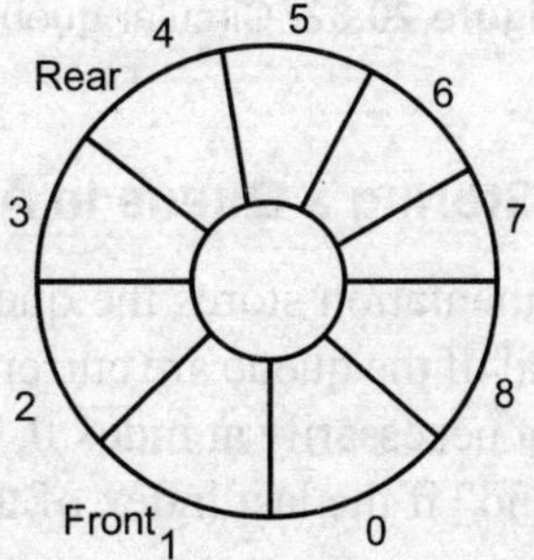

Figure 20.30: Circular queue.

Circular queue, as the name suggests, this queue is not straight but circular, it looks like this

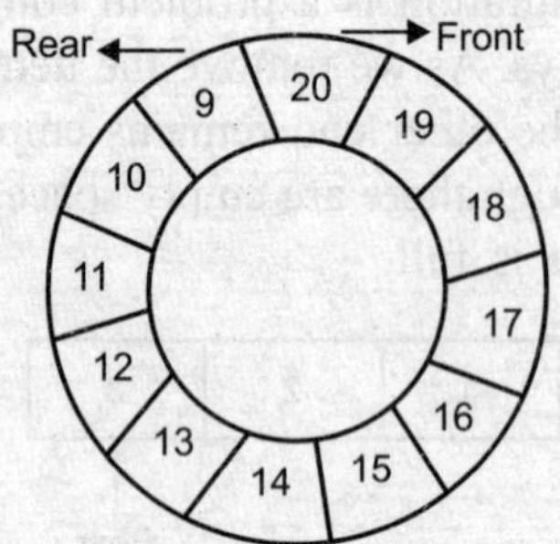

Figure 20.31: Circular Queue

In this Circular queue, once the queue is full, the "first" element of the queue becomes the "rear" most element of the queue. Initially when the queue is empty "front" and "rear" values are 0 and –1.

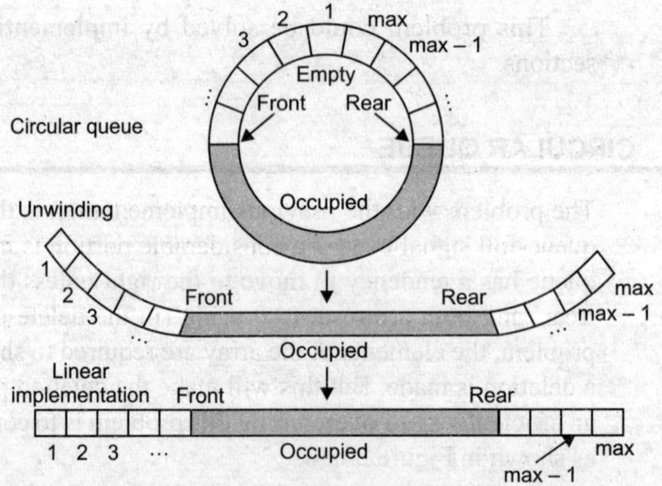

Figure 20.32: Circular queue, unwinding and linear implementation.

20.10.1 Storing a Queue In A Static Data Structure

This implementation stores the queue in an array. The array indices at which the head and tail of the queue are currently stored must be maintained. The head of the queue is not necessarily at index 0. The array can be a "circular array" – the queue "wraps round" if the last index of the array is reached.

EXAMPLE – storing a queue in an array of length 5

Add(A,Q)	A					Head: 0	Tail: 0
Add(D,Q)	A	D				Head: 0	Tail: 1
Add(Z,Q)	A	D	Z			Head: 0	Tail: 2
RemoveQ)		D	Z			Head: 1	Tail: 2
Add(X,Q)		D	Z	X		Head: 1	Tail: 3
Add(C,Q)		D	Z	X	C	Head: 1	Tail: 4
Remove(Q)			Z	X	C	Head: 2	Tail: 4
Add(F,Q)	F		Z	X	C	Head: 2	Tail: 0
Remove(Q)	F			X	C	Head: 3	Tail: 0

Figure 20.33: Storing a queue in a static data structure performing operation add and delete.

20.10.2 Enqueue Operation

Algorithm 20.7: To Insert an element in a circular queue.

INSRTCQ(N, FRONT, REAR, ITEM)

In the algorithm, a circular Queue, say Queue is declared with maximum size as say, n and variables front and rear points to the first and last locations, respectively of the circular Queue. The data item which is to be entered is stored in variable i.

Step 1: [When the Queue is already filled?]
If FRONT = 1 and REAR = N, or if FRONT = REAR + 1, then
Write: OVERFLOW, and Return.
Step 2: [Find new value of REAR.]
If FRONT = NULL, then [Starting Queue initially empty.]
Set FRONT= 1 and REAR = 1.
Else if REAR = N, then
Set REAR = 1.
Else
Set REAR = REAR + 1.
[End of If statement.]
Step 3: Set QUEUE[REAR] = ITEM. [This inserts new element.]
Step 4: End.

Explanation

Consider the following circular Queue with size as 4 i.e. N=4.

Step 1: As here FRONT =2 and REAR =4 so step 2 will be executed.

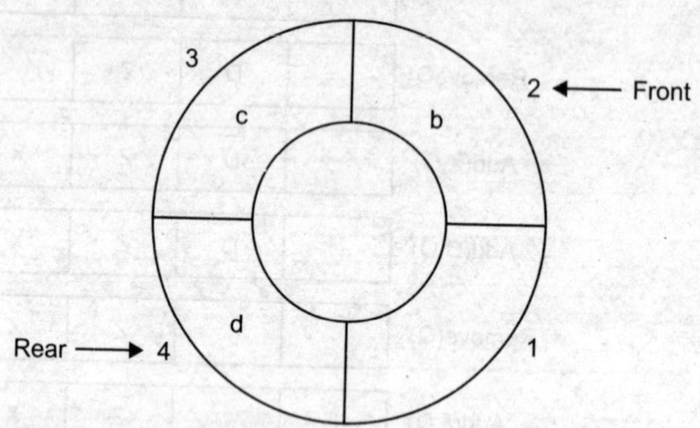

Figure 20.34: Before insertion of the element "e". FRONT = 2, REAR = 4.

Step 2: Here FRONT "'0, so step 3 will be executed.

Here REAR =N=4, so set REAR =1.

Now step 3 will be executed.

Step 3: Enter the element "e" stored in ITEM, in circular Queue, using an assignment QUEUE[REAR] = ITEM.

Queue will look like:

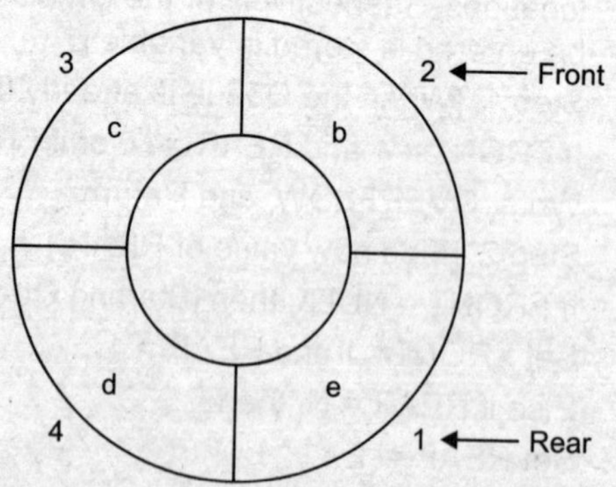

Figure 20.35: After insertion of the element 'e'. FRONT = 2, REAR = 1.

Step 4: End.

20.10.3 Dequeue Operation

Algorithm 20.8: To delete an element in a circular queue.

DELCQ(N, FRONT, REAR, ITEM)

In the algorithm, a circular Queue, say Queue is declared with maximum size as say, N and variables FRONT and REAR points to the first and last locations, respectively of the Queue.

Step 1: [When the Queue is already empty?]

If FRONT = NULL, then Write: UNDERFLOW, and Return.

Step 2: Set ITEM =QUEUE[FRONT].

Step 3: [Find new value of front.]

If FRONT= REAR, then [Queue has only one element to start.]

Set FRONT = NULL and REAR = NULL

Else if FRONT = N, then Set FRONT = 1

Else Set FRONT = FRONT + 1. [End of If statement.]

Step 4: End.

Explanation

Consider the following circular Queue with size as 4 i.e. n=4.

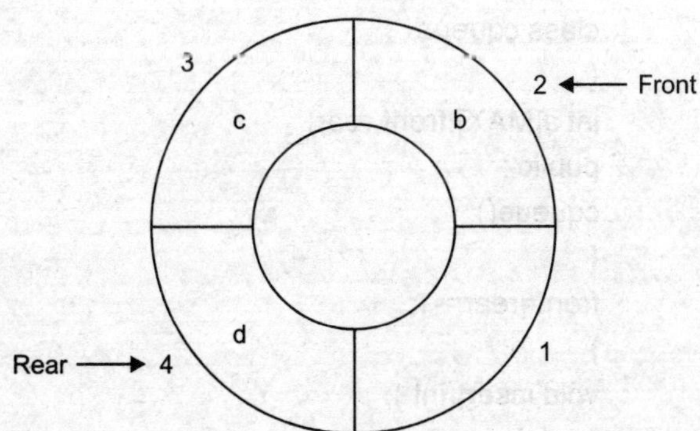

Figure 20.36: Before deletion of the element 'b'. FRONT = 2, REAR = 4.

Step 1: FRONT "" NULL. Goto step 2.

Step 2: Set ITEM =QUEUE[FRONT] , put value of FRONT=2

Set ITEM =QUEUE[2].

Step 3: [Increment front by 1 now front will become 3].

FRONT =FRONT + 1, last value of FRONT=2

After Increment, FRONT=2+1=3

Queue after deletion of an element will look like:

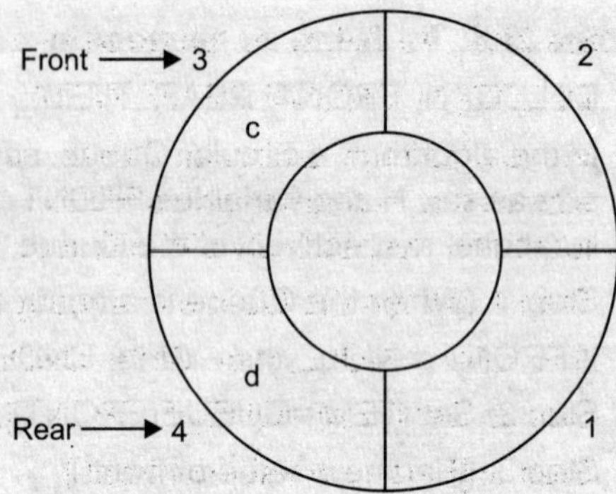

Figure 20.37: After deletion of the element 'b'. FRONT = 3, REAR = 4.

Step 4: End.

Program 7: Write a C++ program for Circular Queue Implementation using Arrays.

```
/* Circular Queues */
#include<iostream.h>
#include<conio.h>
const int MAX = 5;
class cqueue
{
int a[MAX],front,rear;
public :
cqueue()
{
front=rear=-1;
}
void insert(int );
int deletion();
void display();
};
void cqueue :: insert(int val)
{
if((front==0 && rear==MAX-1) || (rear+1==front))
cout<<" Circular Queue is Full";
else
{
if(rear==MAX-1)
```

```
rear=0;
else
rear++;
a[rear]=val;
}
if(front==-1)
front=0;
}
int cqueue :: deletion()
{
int k;
if(front==-1)
cout<<"Circular Queue is Empty";
else
{
k=a[front];
if(front==rear)
front=rear=-1;
else
{
if(front==MAX-1)
front=0;
else
front++;
}
}
return k;
}
void cqueue :: display()
{
int i;
if(front==-1)
cout<<"Circular Queue is Empty";
else
{
if(rear < front)
{
for(i=front;i<=MAX-1;i++)
cout<<a[i]<<"   ";
```

```
for(i=0;i<=rear;i++)
cout<<a[i]<<"   ";
}
else
{
for(i=front;i<=rear;i++)
cout<<a[i]<<"   ";
cout<<endl;
}
}
}
void main()
{
cqueue c1;
int ch,val;
char op;
do
{
clrscr();
cout<<"-----------Menu-------------";
cout<<"1.Insertion
2.Deletion
3.Display
4.Exit
";
cout<<"Enter Your Choice <1..4> ?";
cin>>ch;
switch(ch)
{
case 1 : cout<<"Enter Element to Insert ?";
cin>>val;
c1.insert(val);
break;
case 2 : val=c1.deletion();
cout<<"Deleted Element :"<<val<<endl;
break;
case 3 : c1.display();
break;
}
```

```
cout<<"Do you want to continue<Y/N> ?";
cin>>op;
}while(op=='Y' || op=='y');
getch();
}
```

Program 8: Write a C program to perform insert, delete operations with circular queue and display elements.

```
# include <iostream.h>
# include <conio.h>
# include <process.h>
int queue[8];int r,f=0,x=0;
void insert(void);
void del ();
void show (void);
void main ()
{
int c;
clrscr();
cout<<"\n1] Insert Element";
cout<<"\n2] Delete Element";
cout<<"\n3] Display element/s";
cout<<"\n4] Exit";
cout<<"\n Enter your choice:-";
cin>>c;
switch (c)
{
case 1: insert(); break;
case 2: del(); show();break;
case 3: show(); break;
default: exit(0);
}
main ();
getch();
}
void insert () {
int n;
char ch,ans='Y';
if (r>=7) {
while (queue[x]= =0) {
```

```
cout<<"\n Enter a Number:";
cin>>n;
queue[x]=n;
x++;
cout<<"\n Continue Y/N;
ch=getch();
if (ch!='Y')break;
}
cout<<"\n Queue is full \n\n\n";
main();
}
cout<<"\n Enter elements:";
while (ans= ='Y')
{
cin>>queue[r];
if (r= =7)
{
clrscr();
cout<<"\n Queue is Full";
getch();
break;
}
else
r++;
cout<<"\n Continue Y/N:";
ans=getche();
}
}
void show()
{
int j;
for (j=0;j<8++)
cout<<queue[j];
getch();
}
void del ()
{
int j;
if (r= =0)
```

```
{
clrscr();
cout<<"\n Queue is empty \n\n\n";
main();
}
if (f= =8) f=0;
queue[f]=0;
f++;
}
Output:
1] Insert Element
2] Delete Element
3] Display element
4] Exit
Enter your choice: 2
0 2 0 0 0 0 0 0
```

20.11 IMPLEMENTATION OF QUEUES USING LINKED LIST

An alternative and efficient representation of Queues is possible by using linked lists for storing the data elements using dynamic memory.

It is represented in the Figure 20.38 as shown below:

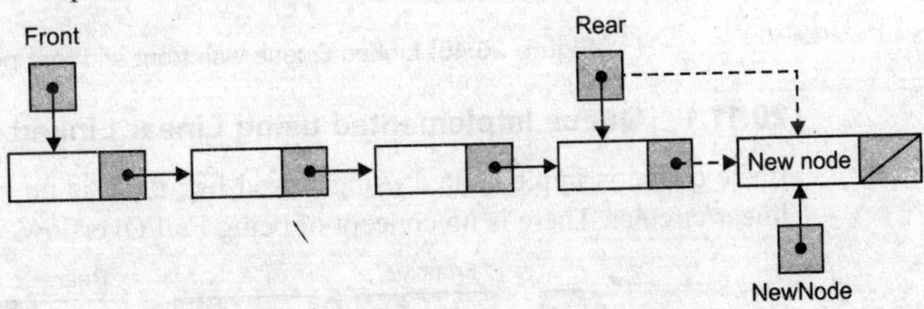

Figure 20.38: Queue using linked list

The advantages of linked list representation of Queues over array representation are:

1. There is no need of knowing the Queue size before implementing it, as dynamic memory allocation technique helps the programmer to declare the memory space at run time.
2. The Queue is never full as long as the system has enough space for dynamic memory allocation. So there is no need to check the IsFull or overflow condition of the Queue.

3. Data movement i.e. entering and deleting from Queue is very easily handled with the concept of pointer in linked lists

Remember that a Queue implemented using link list is called as linked Queue.

A linked list is a set of nodes (a node can be a struct or a class) defined arbitrarily in memory; a node has a special variable (pointer) of the same type as the structure/class, that points to the next memory location, thus making the list values continuous. The following picture shows how a linked list looks like when it is created. The first node of a list is referred to as head/start most of the time and the last node is referred to as tail/end, the tail/end of the list always points to NULL or 0 (zero), which is also referred to as grounding.

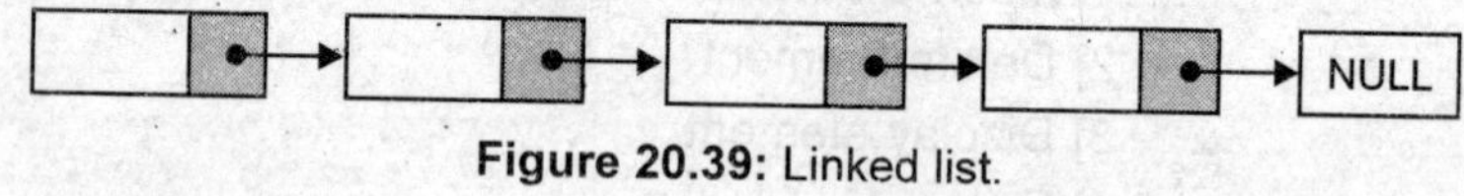

Figure 20.39: Linked list.

The following Figure 20.40 explains the same but with the concept of Queues:

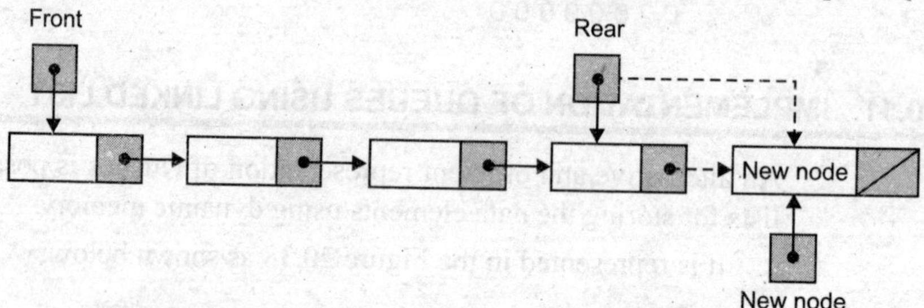

Figure 20.40: Linked Queue with front and rear pointers.

20.11.1 Queue Implemented using Linear Linked List

If the queue is implemented using linked list, there is no problem whether it is linear/circular. There is nò concept of being Full/Overflow.

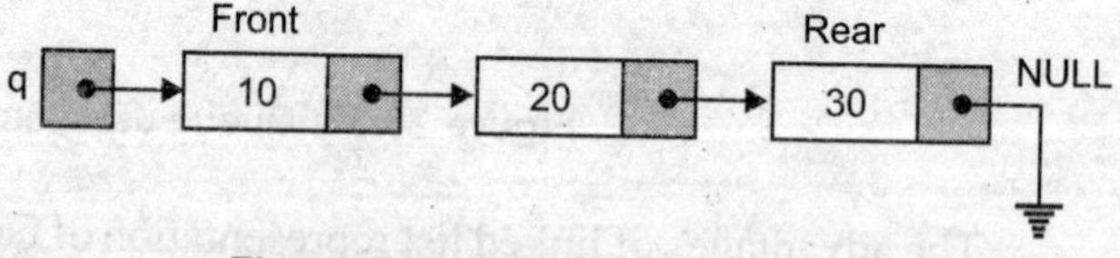

Figure 20.41: linear linked Queue

To check for Empty condition: Check whether q is NULL or not

For an element to be enqueued

//Create new(temp) or malloc(temp) temp.value = x

temp.next = NULL

rear.next = temp

For an element to be dequeued, it is just pointer jumping

front = front.next

q = q.next

Advantage

- No Queue Migration Problem
- Gives a natural way of handling queue

Disadvantage

- Pointer based Implementation is bit more complex and slower than array based implementation.

20.11.2 Queue Implemented using Circular Linked List

Instead of having a null pointer at the rear end, the pointer at the rear end points to the node at the front end of the list.

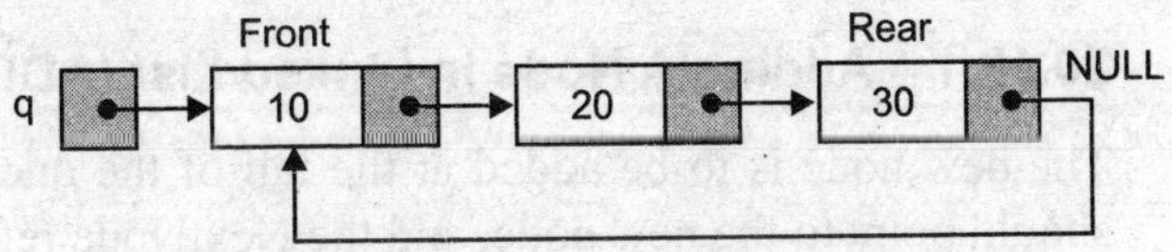

Figure 20.42: Circular linked queue

For an element to be enqueued

Pseudocode:

1. begin
2. Create newnode
3. if(front = null)
4. front = newnode
5. else
6. rear ! next = newnode
7. end //endif
8. rear = newnode
9. rear ! next = front
10. end

For an element to be dequeued

1. begin
2. if(front = rear)
3. delete front
4. else
5. q = front
6. front = q ! next
7. rear ! next = front
8. delete q
9. end //endif
10. end

20.12 STORING A QUEUE IN A DYNAMIC DATA STRUCTURE

As in the case of the stack, each node in a dynamic data structure contains data and a reference to the next node. A queue also needs a reference to the head node and a reference to the tail node. The following diagram describes the storage of a queue called Queue. Each node consists of data (DataItem) and a reference (NextNode).

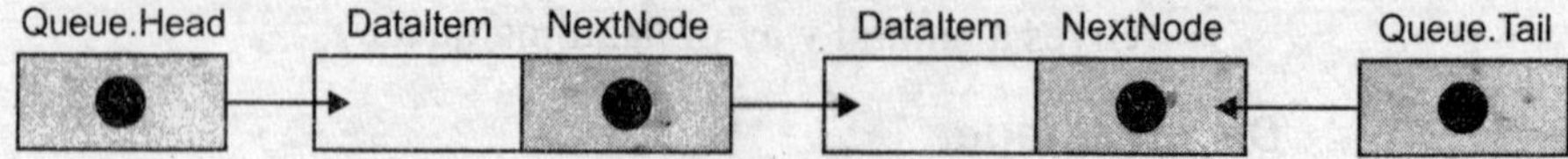

Figure 20.43: Representation of queue using linked list.

- The first node is accessed using the name **Queue.Head**.
- Its data is accessed using **Queue.Head.DataItem**
- The second node is accessed using **Queue.Head.NextNode**
- The last node is accessed using **Queue.Tail**

20.12.1 Adding A Node in Linked List (ADD)

The new node is to be added at the tail of the queue. The reference Queue.Tail should point to the new node, and the NextNode reference of the node previously at the tail of the queue should point to the DataItem of the new node.

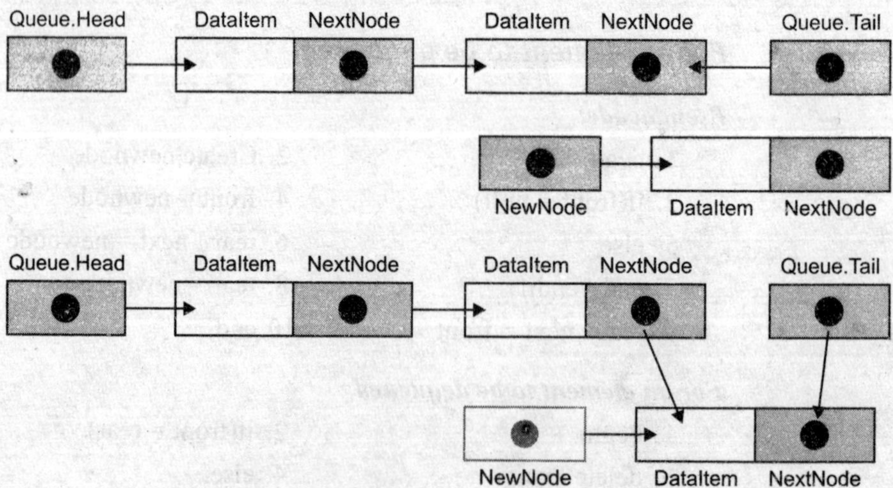

Figure 20.44: Adding a node in linked queue.

20.12.2 Removing A Node from the Linked List (REMOVE)

The value of Queue.Head.DataItem is returned. A temporary reference Temp is declared and set to point to head node in the queue (Temp = Queue.Head).

Queue.Head is then set to point to the second node instead of the top node.The only reference to the original head node is now Temp and the memory used by this node can then be freed.

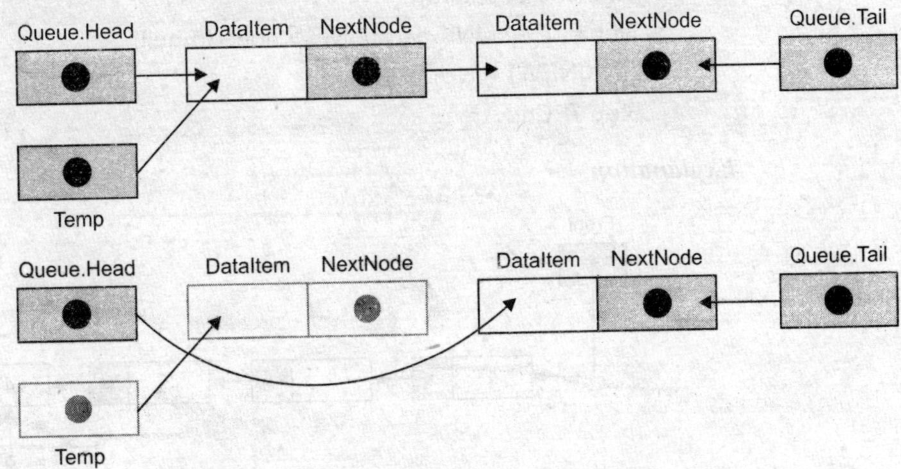

Figure 20.45: Removing a node from the linked queue.

20.12.3 Enqueue Operation

It's very similar to the addition in a dynamic linked list. The only difference is that here you'll add the new element only at the end of the list, since a dynamic list is used for the Queue, the queue is also dynamic, means it has no prior size set.

So, we don't have to check the Overflow condition in linked Queue.

Algorithm 20.9: To insert an element into linked queue.

(FRONT, REAR, AVAIL, ITEM)

The linked Queue say, Queue exists with two pointers front and rear pointing to first and last elements, respectively of the linked Queue.

Step 1: [Check for overflow, Avail list empty]

If AVAIL = NULL

Then write"overflow" return. [End of if structure]

Step 2: [Create a new node] NEW = AVAIL

Step 3: [Update AVAIL pointer] AVAIL = LINK[AVAIL]

Step 4: [save the ITEM into NEW node]INFO[NEW]=ITEM

Step 5: [Check queue is empty or not]

If FRONT = NULL then

a. FRONT =NEW

b. REAR = NEW

else[if queue is not empty]

a. [Update rear to point NEW node] LINK[REAR] = NEW
b. REAR = NEW
[End of if structure]
Step 6: [Set LINK part of NEW node to null]
LINK[NEW] = NULL
Step 7: End

Explanation

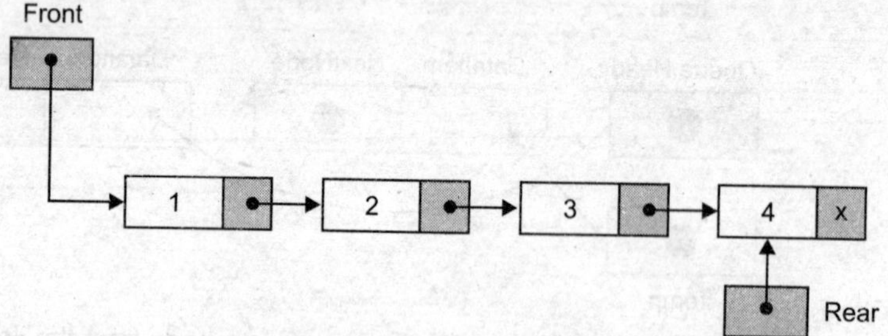

Figure 20.46: Before insertion FRONT = 1 and REAR = 4.

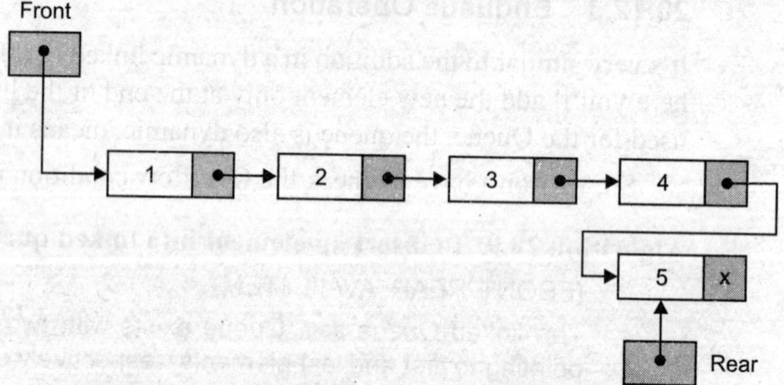

Figure 20.47: After insertion FRONT = 1 and REAR = 5.

20.12.4 Dequeue Operation

This is again very similar to deletion in any Linked List, but you can only delete from the head of the list, that makes it a Queue.

Algorithm 20.10: To delete an element from linked queue.

(FRONT, REAR, AVAIL, ITEM)

The linked Queue say, Queue exists with two pointers front and rear pointing to first and last elements, respectively of the linked Queue.

Step 1: [When the Queue is already empty?]

If FRONT = NULL, then Write: UNDERFLOW, and Return.

Step 2: Set ITEM =QUEUE[FRONT].
Step 3: [Assign Front to SAVE]
SAVE=FRONT
Step 4: [Reset FRONT to point to next node in LINK queue]
FRONT = LINK[SAVE]
Step 5: LINK[SAVE]= AVAIL
Step 6: [Save deleted node to AVAIL list] AVAIL = SAVE
Step 7: End.

Explanation

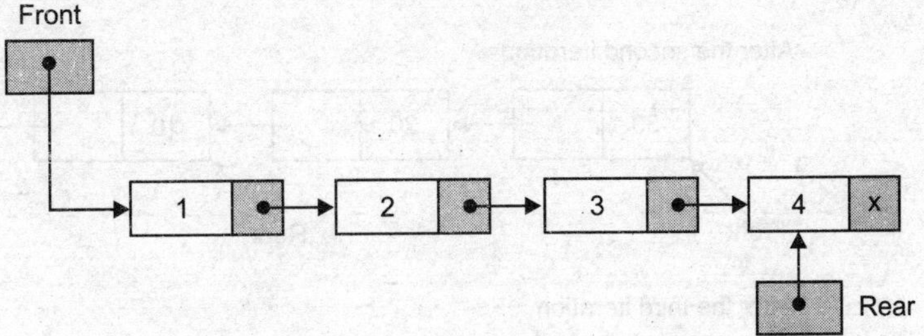

Figure 20.48: Before deletion FRONT = 1 and REAR = 4.

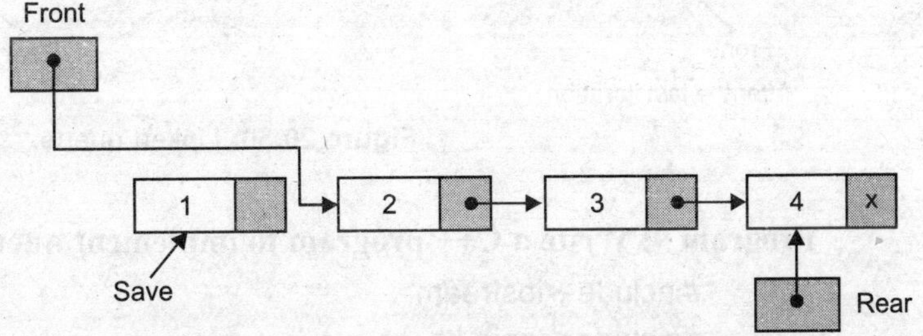

Figure 20.49: After deletion FRONT = 2 and REAR = 4.

For example: To create a linked queue. Initially, the list is empty, so both the front and rear pointers are NULL. The insert function creates a new node, puts the new data value in it, appends it to an existing list, and makes the rear pointer point to it. A delete function checks whether the queue is empty, and if not, retrieves the data value of the node pointed to by the front, advances the front, and frees the storage of the node whose data value has been retrieved.

If the above strategy is used for creating a queue with four data values —10, 20, 30, and 40, the queue gets created as shown in Figure 20.50.

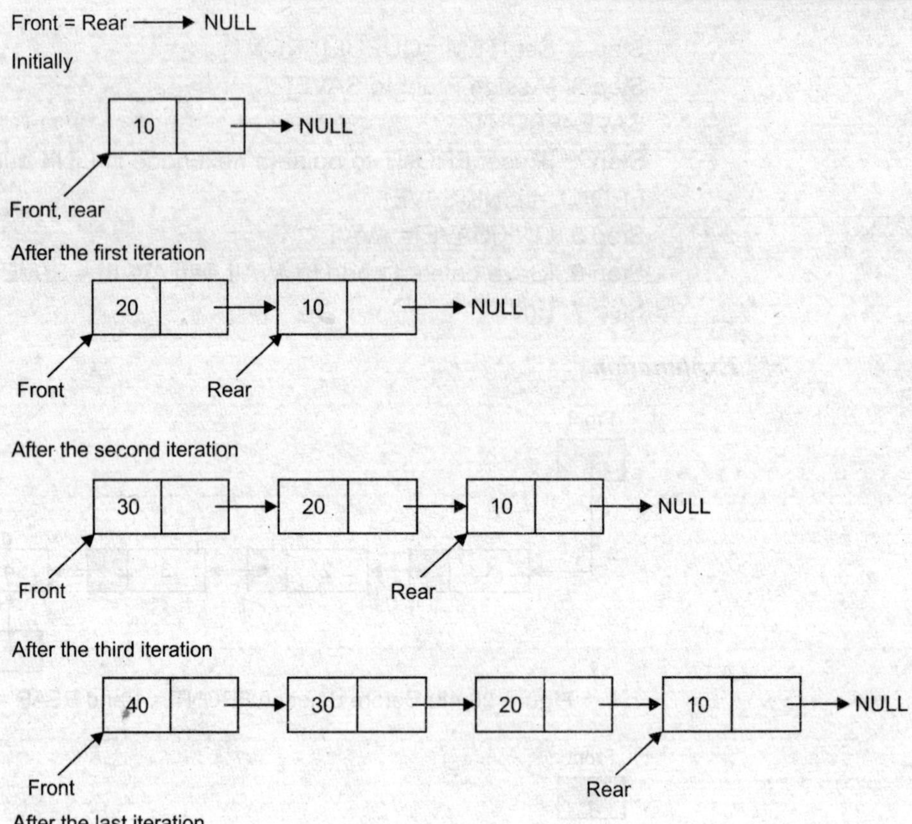

Figure 20.50: Linked queue.

Program 9: Write a C++ program to implement queue using liked list.

```
#include <iostream>
#include<conio.h>
struct node
{
int data;
node *link;
};
class lqueue
{
private:
node *front,*rear;
public:
lqueue()
{
```

```
front=NULL;
rear=NULL;
}
void add(int n)
{
node *tmp;
tmp=new node;
if(tmp==NULL)
cout<<"\nQUEUE FULL";
tmp->data=n;
tmp->link=NULL;
if(front==NULL)
{
rear=front=tmp;
return;
}
rear->link=tmp;
rear=rear->link;
}
int del()
{
if(front==NULL)
{
cout<<"\nQUEUE EMPTY";
return NULL;
}
node *tmp;
int n;
n=front->data;
tmp=front;
front=front->link;
delete tmp;
return n;
}
~lqueue()
{
if(front==NULL)
return;
node *tmp;
```

```
while(front!=NULL)
{
tmp=front;
front=front->link;
delete tmp;
}
}
};
void main()
{
lqueue q;
q.add(11);
q.add(22);
q.add(33);
q.add(44);
q.add(55);
cout<<"\nItem Deleted = "<<q.del();
cout<<"\nItem Deleted = "<<q.del();
cout<<"\nItem Deleted = "<<q.del();
getch();
}
```

20.13 DEQUE (DOUBLE ENDED QUEUES)

In computer science, a **deque** (short for double-ended queue) is an abstract data structure for which elements can be added to or removed from the front or back. This differs from a normal queue, where elements can only be added to one end and removed from the other. An input-restricted deque is one where deletion can be made from both ends, but input can only be made at one end. An output-restricted deque is one where input can be made at both ends, but output can be made from one end only. Both queues and stacks can be considered specializations of deques, and can be implemented using deques

Deque is usually pronounced deck, possibly due to the conceptual similarity to a deck of cards, where a card can be dealt from or returned to either the face or patterned side. In computer science, a **deque** (short for double-ended queue) is an abstract data structure for which elements can be added to or removed from the front or back. This differs from a normal queue, where elements can only be added to one end and removed from the other. Both queues and stacks can be considered specializations of deques, and can be implemented using deques.

***Definition:** A deque is a sequence where elements can be added and removed at both ends (front and rear) of the sequence, but not in the middle.*

In the preceding section we saw that a Queue comprises a pile of objects into which we insert items at one end and from which we remove items at the other end. In this section we examine an extension of the Queue, which provides a means to insert and remove items at both ends of the pile. This data structure is a Deque. A Deque is as shown in the Figure 20.51:

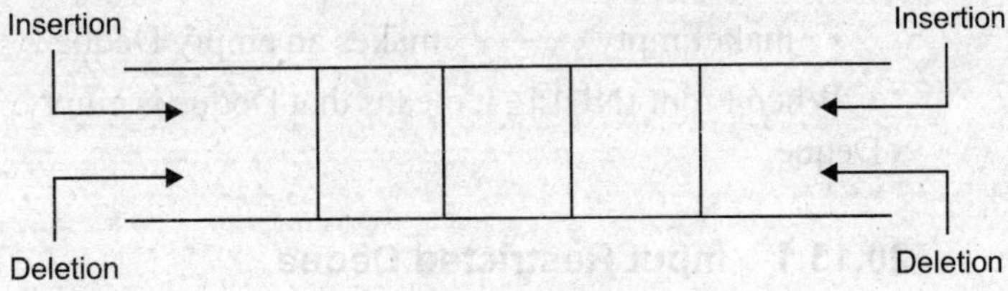

Figure 20.51: Deque

As an example let us suppose there is a deque with three elements as below:

Front = 4
Rear = 6

1	4	1

Now performing Enque front (3) operation will make Deque to look like:

3	1	4	1

Performing Enque rear operation will make Deque to look like:

3	1	4	1	5

Performing Deque front will delete 3, leaving Deque to look like

1	4	1	5

Performing Deque rear will delete 5, leaving Deque to look like

1	4	1

The word *Deque* is an acronym derived from *double-ended queue*

The operations that are defined on deques are:

- Enquefront inserts element at the front
- Enquerear inserts element at the rear
- getfront returns the item at the front
- getrear returns the item at the rear
- Dequefront returns and removes the item at the front
- Dequerear returns and removes the item at the rear
- IsEmpty returns true if the Deque is empty, false otherwise
- makeEmpty makes an empty Deque

When Front=NULL, it means that Deque is empty. There are two variations of a Deque.

20.13.1 Input Restricted Deque

It allows insertions at only one end of the list structure but allows performing deletions at both ends.

Program 10: Write a C++ program to demonstrate input restricted deque.

```
# include <iostream.h>
# include <conio.h>
int ird[5];
void main ()
{
int r=0,c=1,op,f=-1;
int insert(int);
void deleter(int,int);
void deletef(int,int);
void show(void);
while(1)
{
clrscr();
cout<<"\n (1) Insert";
cout<<"\n (2) Delete from rear";
cout<<"\n (3) Delete from front";
cout<<"\n (4) Display";
cout<<"\n (0) Exit";
cout<<"\n Enter Your choice:-";
cin>>op;
switch(op)
{
```

```
case 1:          while (c && r<5)
{
c=insert(r);
r++;
}
if (c= =0)
{
c=1;
r-;
}
else
if (f<0)
cout<<"\n Deque is full";
getch();
break;
case 2: deleter(-r,f);break;
case 3: deletef(r,++f); break;
case 4: show (); break;
default: exit(0);
}
}
getch();
}
void show ()
{
int j;
cout<<"\n Elements of deque are:";
for (j=0;j<5;j++);
getch();
}
int insert (int h)
{
int k;
cout<<"\n Enter an element (enter 0 to exit):";
cin>>k;
ird[h]=k;
return (k);
}
void deleter(int m,int n)
```

```
{
if (m<=n)
cout<<"Deque is empty";
else
{
cout<<"\n "<<m<<" The element deleted: "<<ird[m];
ird[m]=0;
}
getch();
}
void deletef(int f,int j)
{
if(f<j)
cout<<"Deque is empty";
else
{
cout<<"\n "<<j<<" The element deleted:- "<<ird[j];
ird[f]=NULL;
}
getch();
}
```

Output:

```
(1) Insert
(2) Delete from rear
(3) Delete from front
(4) Display
(0) Exit
Enter Your choice:- 1
Enter an element (enter 0 to exit): 2
Enter an element (enter 0 to exit): 3
Enter an element (enter 0 to exit): 5
Enter an element (enter 0 to exit): 8
Enter an element (enter 0 to exit): 6
Deque if full
(1) Insert
(2) Delete from rear
(3) Delete from front
(4) Display
(0) Exit
```

Enter Your choice:- 4
Elements of deque are: 2 3 5 8 6

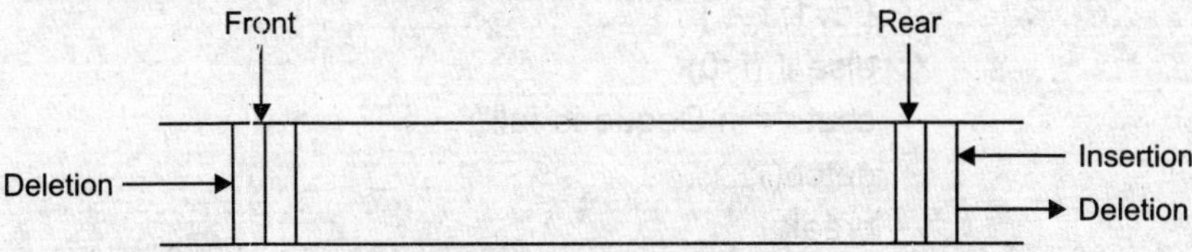

Figure 20.52: Input restricted deque.

20.13.2 Output-restricted Deque

It allows deletions at only one end of the list structure but allows performing insertions at both ends.

Program 11: Write a C++ program to demonstrate output restricted deque.

```
# include <iostream.h>
# include <conio.h>
# include <process.h>
int ird[5];
void main ()
{
int r=0,c=1,op,f=-1;
int insert(int);
int insertf(int);
void deletef(int);
void show(void);
clrscr();
while (1) {
cout<<"\n 1 Insert from rear:";
cout<<"\n 2 Insert from front";
cout<<"\n 3 Delete from front";
cout<<"\n 4 Display";
cout<<"\n 0 Exit";
cout<<"\n Enter Your choice:-";
cin>>op;
switch(op) {
case 1:
while (c && r<5)
{
c=insert(r);
r++;
```

```
}
if (c= =0)
{ c=1; r--; }
else if (f<0)
cout<<"\n Deque is full";
getch();
break;
case 2: f=insertf(f);break;
case 3: deletef(++f); break;
case 4: show (); break;
default: exit(0);
} }
getch();
}
void show () {
int j;
cout<<"\n Elements of deque are:";
for (j=0;j<5;j++);
getch();
}
int insertr (int h) {
int k;
cout<<"\n Enter an element (enter 0 to exit):";
cin>>k;
ird[h]=k;
return (k);
}
int insert(int m) {
int h;
if (ird[m]= =0 && m>=0) {
cout<<"\n Enter a element:";
cin>>h;
ird[m]=h;
} else
cout<<"\n no space available";
return -m;
}
void deletef(int f)
{ ird[f]=NULL;}
```

Output:

1 Insert from rear:
2 insert from rear
3 Delete from front
4 Display
0 Exit
Enter Your choice:- 1
Enter a element (enter 0 to exit): 1
Enter a element (enter 0 to exit): 2
Enter a element (enter 0 to exit): 3
Enter a element (enter 0 to exit): 0
1 Insert from rear:
2 insert from rear
3 Delete from front
4 Display
0 Exit
Enter Your choice: 4
Elements of deque are: 1 2 3 0 0

Figure 20.53: Ouput restricted deque.

20.13.3 Advantages of Deque

Deque provides random access in constant time

1. It provides Constant time i.e. of O (1), insert and delete operations at the front or the end.
2. A deque uses memory more effectively. if there isn't enough consecutive memory, the deque will use a series of smaller blocks.
3. The last or the first element can be obtained immediately

20.13.4 Disadvantages of Deque

1. Insert and delete operation in the middle take linear time.
2. There can be no splicing, no merges in comparison to lists.

20.14 PRIORITY QUEUE

Previously, we've looked at the Queue data structure, which allowed accessing the data elements in first-come, first-serve fashion. Queues are useful for implementing resource managers fairly. If user A submits his print job to a printer before user B, it's only fair that user B should wait until user A is done to get his output. But what if user B needs to print a report for his meeting with the boss, while user A is just printing a receipt for a reference manual he just ordered. Obviously, user A can wait to print the receipt. We say that user B's job has higher *priority* than user A's. To allow jobs to have varying levels of priority, we replace our regular queue with a *priority queue*.

Definition: *A priority queue is special type of queue that acts as an abstract data type in computer programming, supporting the following three operations:*

- *add an element to the queue with an associated priority*
- *remove the element from the queue that has the highest priority, and return it*
- *(optionally) peek at the element with highest priority without removing it*

The simplest way to implement a priority queue data type is to keep an associative array mapping each priority to a list of elements with that priority. If association lists are used to implement the associative array, adding an element takes constant time but removing or peeking at the element of highest priority takes linear (O(n)) time, because we must search all keys for the largest one.

A data structure that supports efficient insertions of new element and deletion of elements with the highest priority is known as Priority Queue.

In case the two or more elements have the same priority then these elements are processed in the order they were added to the Queue. The Queues are called "priority" Queues because they enable you to retrieve elements not by the insertion time (as in a stack or queue), nor by a key match (as in a dictionary), but by which element has the highest priority of retrieval.

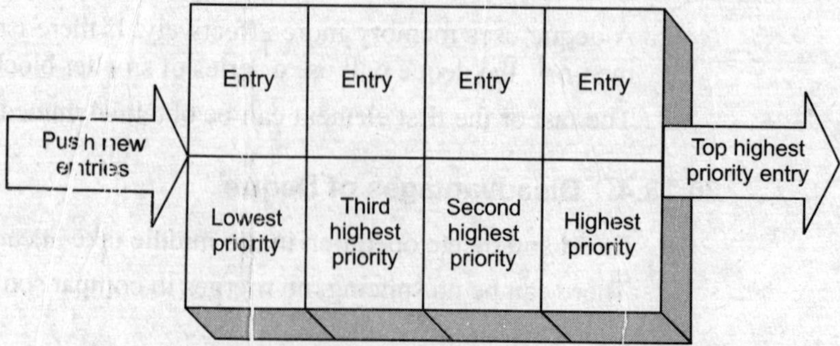

Figure 20.54: Shows a representation of a Priority Queue.

This type of Queue assigns a priority to every element that it stores. New elements are added to the Queue using the Insert operation, just as with a FIFO Queue. This Queue also has a delete operation, which differs from the FIFO Dequeue in one key area. When you call Delete for the priority queue, you don't get the oldest element in the queue. Instead, you get the element with the highest priority.

Applications of Priority Queues

Area	Examples
1. Operating systems.	task scheduling, interrupt handling
2. Event-driven simulation.	customers in a line
3. Numerical computation.	reducing round off error
4. Data compression.	Huffman codes
5. Graph searching.	shortest path
6. Computational number theory.	sum of powers
7. Artificial intelligence.	A* search

20.15 COMMONLY USED PRIORITY QUEUE OPERATIONS

Here are some operations, with their typical names, that are performed on Priority Queues:

- **Initialization operation**
  - **Create:** Returns an empty Priority Queue
- **Basic Operations**
  - **Insert:** Adds a new element in the Priority Queue.
  - **Delete:** returns and removes the element with the highest priority from the queue
- **Other Operations**
  - Replace the largest element with a new element in the Priority Queue.
  - Change the priority of an element in a Priority Queue
  - Join two Priority Queues into one
  - **FindMin:** Returns the element with highest Priority from the Queue, without removing it from the Queue.

Advantages

- operation FindMin is very efficient (of O (1))
- operations Insert and Delete are efficient (of O (logn))

- very useful in important application areas
- more efficient than Sorted Sequences
- more functionality than some related data types

Disadvantages

- Less functionality than Sorted Sequences.
- Less efficient than some related data types.

A priority queue is a collection of elements such that each element has been assigned a priority and such that the order in which elements are deleted and processed comes from the following rules:

1. An element of higher priority is processed before any element of lower priority.
2. Two element with same priority are processed according to the order in which they were added to the queue.

A simple example of a priority queue is a timesharing system: Programs of high priority are processed first, and programs with the same priority form a standard queue.

There are various ways of maintaining a priority queue in memory.

We discuss two of them here.

1. One way list and multiple queues
2. Array representation of a priority queue

20.16 ONE WAY LIST REPRESENTATION OF PRIORITY QUEUE

One way to maintain a priority queue in memory is by means of a one way list is, as follows:

1. Each node in the list will contain three items of information:
   - An information field calls INFO.
   - A priority number call PRT.
   - A next link number call LINK.
2. A node X precedes a node Y in the list.
   - When X has high priority than Y or
   - When both have same priority but X was added to the list before Y.

This means that the order in the one-way list corresponds to the order of the priority queue.

For example: A priority queue with seven elements show here:

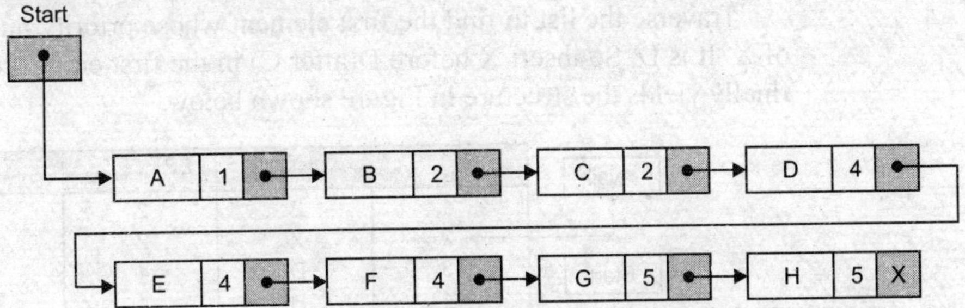

Figure 20.55: Schematic diagram of a priority queue using one way list.

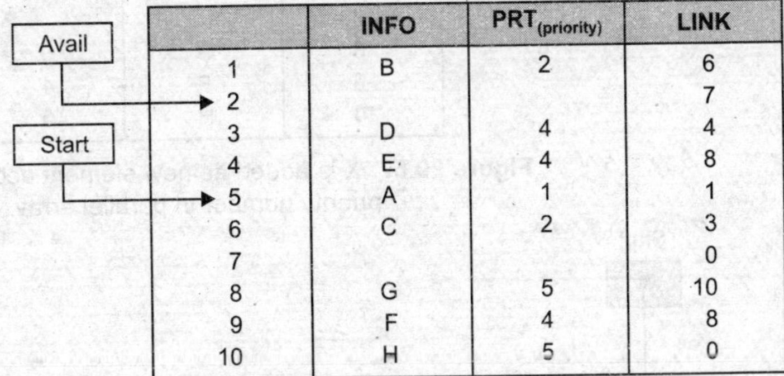

	INFO	PRT (priority)	LINK
1	B	2	6
2			7
3	D	4	4
4	E	4	8
5	A	1	1
6	C	2	3
7			0
8	G	5	10
9	F	4	8
10	H	5	0

Figure 20.56: Schematic diagram of a priority queue using linear arrays.

This Figure shows the way the priority queue may appear in memory using linear arrays INFO, PRT and LINK.

The main property of the one-way list representation of a priority queue is that the element in the queue that should be processed first always appears at the beginning of the one-way list. Accordingly, it is a very simple to delete and process an element from our priority queue.

20.16.1 Insert Operation in Linked List Representation of Priority Queue

The linked list of priority queue exists with the element to be processed at the beginning of the list. The element to be inserted say, item has priority number, say n.

Algorithm 20.11: This algorithm adds an ITEM with priority number N to a priority queue which is maintained in memory as a one-way list.

Step 1: Traverse the one-way list until finding a node X whose priority number exceeds N, Insert ITEM in front of node X.

Step 2: If no such node is found, insert ITEM as the last element of the list.

Step 3: End.

Traverse the list to find the first element whose priority number exceeds that of X. It is D, So insert X before D(after C) in the first empty cell, INFO[2]. This finally yields the structure in Figure shown below.

Avail

Start

	INFO	PRT(priority)	LINK
1	B	2	6
2	X	2	3
3	D	4	4
4	H	4	9
5	A	1	1
6	C	2	2
7			0
8	G	5	10
9	F	4	8
10	H	5	0

Figure 20.57: X is added as new element according to its priority number in parallel array.

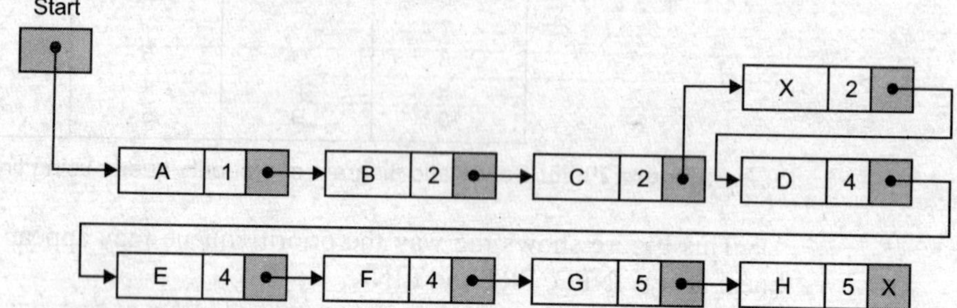

Figure 20.58: X is added as new element according to its priority number in linked list.

***Important point:** Observe that START and AVAIL are changed accordingly.*

20.16.2 Delete Operation in Linked List Representation of Priority Queue

The linked list of Priority Queue exists. The element to be deleted (with the highest priority number) is the first element in the list i.e. it is a sorted list.

Algorithm 20.12: This algorithm deletes and processes the first element in a priority queue which appears in memory as a one-way list.

Step 1: Set ITEM = INFO[START]. [This saves the data in the starting or first node.]

Step 2: Delete first node from the list.

Step 3: Process ITEM.

Step 4: End.

The first element in the one-way list is deleted. Specifically, First A is deleted and its memory cell INFO[5] is added to AVAIL list. This finally yields the structure in Figure shown below.

Avail → 1

Start → 5

	INFO	PRT(priority)	LINK
1	B	2	6
2	X	2	3
3	D	4	4
4	E	4	9
5			
6	C	2	2
7			0
8	G	5	10
9	F	4	8
10	H	5	0

Figure 20.59: A is deleted from parallel arrays.

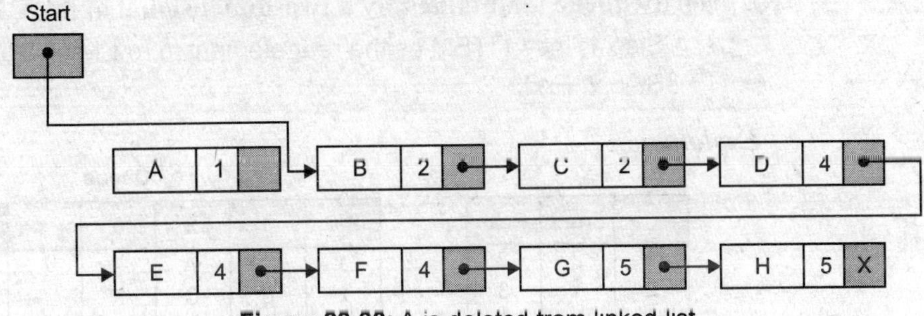

Figure 20.60: A is deleted from linked list.

***Important point:** Observe that START and AVAIL are changed accordingly.*

20.17 IMPLEMENTATION OF PRIORITY QUEUE USING ARRAY

As the elements of the Priority Queue are assumed to contain only their priority values, hence, the type of elements is assumed to be integer only. The most used way to implement a Priority Queue of say, n elements, is to store these elements in an array of integers in a completely unordered manner.

Remember that the lower the priority value, the higher the priority. One of the ways to maintain apriority queue in memory is to use a separate queue for each level of priority. Each such queue will appear in its own circular array and must have its own pair of pointers, FRONT and REAR. IN fact, if each queue is allocated the same amount of space, A Two-dimensional array queue can be used instead of the linear arrays. Figure shown below indicates this representation for the priority queue in fig above. Observe that FRONT[K] and REAR[K] contain, respectively, the front and rear elements of row K of queue, the row that maintains the queue of elements with priority number K.

	Front	Rear
1	2	2
2	1	3
3	0	0
4	5	1
5	4	5

(a)

Queue

R/C	1	2	3	4	5	6
1		A				
2	B	C	X			
3						
4	F				D	E
5				G	H	

(b)

Figure 20.61: Array representation of a priority queue.

20.17.1 Insert Operation

The priority queue, say PQ exists with n number of elements. The variable, value holds the value to be inserted in Queue.

Algorithm 20.13: This algorithm adds an ITEM with priority number M to a priority queue maintained by a two-dimensional array QUEUE.

Step 1: Insert ITEM as the rear element in row M of QUEUE.

Step 2: End.

Explanation

	Front	Rear
1	2	2
2	1	3
3	0	0
4	5	1
5	4	5

(a)

Queue

R/C	1	2	3	4	5	6
1		A				
2	B	C	X			
3						
4	F				D	E
5				G	H	

(b)

Figure 20.62: Before insertion priority queue look like.

Insert each element in its priority row. That is, add I as the rear element in row 3, add J as the rear element in row 4, add K as the rear element in row 1, add L as rear element in row 4, add M as rear element in row 2.This yields the structure in Figure given below. (Insertions with this array representation are usually simpler than insertions with the one-way list representation.)

	Front	Rear
1	2	3
2	1	4
3	1	1
4	5	3
5	4	5

(a)

Queue

R/C	1	2	3	4	5	6
1		A	K			
2	B	C	X	M		
3	I					
4	F	J	U		D	E
5				G	H	

(b)

Figure 20.63: After insertion priority queue look like.

Important point: *Observe that, In this case, FRONT and REAR are changed accordingly.*

20.17.2 Delete Operation

Algorithm 20.14: This algorithm deletes and processes the first element in a priority queue maintained by a two-dimensional array QUEUE.

Step 1: [Find first nonempty.]
Find the smallest K such that FRONT[K] “ NULL

Step 2: Delete and process the front element in row K of QUEUE.

Step 3: End.

Explanation

	Front	Rear
1	2	3
2	1	4
3	1	1
4	5	3
5	4	5

(a)

Queue

R/C	1	2	3	4	5	6
1		A	K			
2	B	C	X	M		
3	I					
4	F	J	U		D	E
5				G	H	

(b)

Figure 20.64: Before deletion priority queue look like.

First delete the elements with the highest priority in row 1. Since row 1 contains two elements, A and K, then the front element in row 2, B must also be deleted. This finally leaves the structure in Figure given below.

	Front	Rear
1	0	0
2	2	4
3	1	1
4	5	3
5	4	5

(a)

Queue

R/C	1	2	3	4	5	6
1						
2		C	X	M		
3	I					
4	F	J	U		D	E
5				G	H	

(b)

Figure 20.65: After deletion priority queue look like.

Important point: *Observe that, In this case, FRONT and REAR are changed accordingly.*

Program 12: Write a C++ program for Priority Queue.

```
#include<iostream.h>
#include<conio.h>
const int MAX=5;
class pqueue
{
int front,rear;
public:
struct data
{
int val,p,o;
}d[MAX];
pqueue()
{
front=rear=-1;
}
void insert(data d1);
data deletion();
void display();
};
void pqueue :: insert(data d1)
{
if(rear==MAX-1)
cout<<"Priority Queue is Full";
else
{
rear++;
d[rear]=d1;
if(front==-1)
front=0;
data temp;
for(int i=front;i<=rear;i++)
for(int j=i+1;j<=rear;j++)
{
if(d[i].p > d[j].p)
{
temp=d[i];
d[i]=d[j];
d[j]=temp;
```

```
}
else
{
if(d[i].p==d[j].p)
{
if(d[i].o > d[j].o)
{
temp=d[i];
d[i]=d[j];
d[j]=temp;
} }
} }
} }
data pqueue :: deletion()
{
data d1;
if(front==-1)
cout<<"Priority Queue is Empty";
else
{
d1=d[front];
if(front==rear)
front=rear=-1;
else
front++;
}
return d1;
}
void pqueue :: display()
{
if(front==-1)
cout<<"Priority Queue is Empty";
else
{
for(int i=front;i<=rear;i++)
{
cout<<"Object  :"<<i+1<<endl;
cout<<"Value ="<<d[i].val<<endl;
cout<<"Priority="<<d[i].p<<endl;
```

```
cout<<"Order =  "<<d[i].o<<endl;
}
}
}
void main()
{
pqueue p1;
data d1;
char op;
do
{
int ch;
clrscr();
cout<<"----------Menu-------------";
cout<<"1.Insertion
2.Deletion
3.Display
4.Exit
";
cout<<"Enter your Choice<1..4> ?";
cin>>ch;
switch(ch)
{
case 1 :  cout<<"Enter Value ?";
cin>>d1.val;
cout<<"Enter Priority?";
cin>>d1.p;
cout<<"Enter Order ?";
cin>>d1.o;
p1.insert(d1);
break;
case 2 :  d1=p1.deletion();
cout<<"Value = "<<d1.val<<endl;
cout<<"Priority = "<<d1.p<<endl;
cout<<"Order ="<<d1.o<<endl;
break;
case 3 :  p1.display();
break;
}
```

```
cout<<"Do You Want to Continue <Y/N> ?";
cin>>op;
}while(op=='Y' || op=='y');
getch();
}
```

20.18 IMPLEMENTATION OF PRIORITY QUEUE USING MULTIPLE QUEUES

Another way of representing a Priority Queue is to use a separate Queue for each priority number as shown in the Figure 20.66 below:

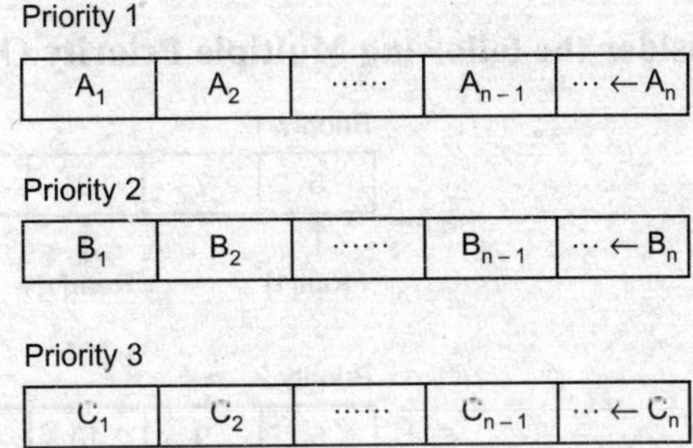

Figure 20.66: A Priority Queue as set of Queues

Each Queue has its own pair of front and rear pointers. Each Queue appears in circular array fashion. If each Queue is allocated the same amount of memory then these can be implemented using two-dimensional arrays. Remember that front[i] and rear[i] points to front and end of Queue with priority number i. See Figure 20.67.

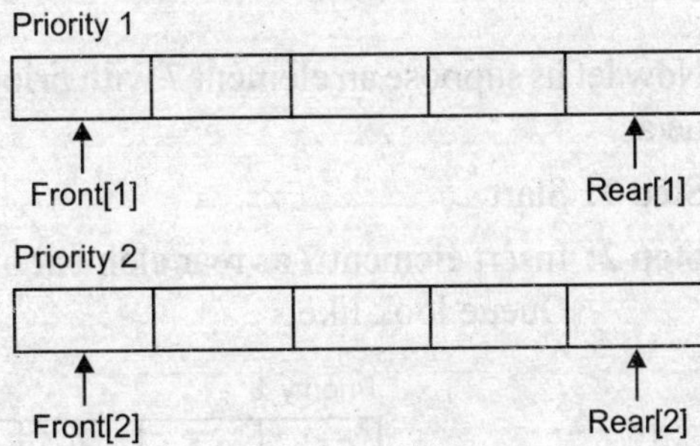

Figure 20.67: Priority Queue with pair of front and rear pointer

In order to process an element of the Priority Queue, element from the first non-empty highest priority number Queue is accessed. In case of Insert operation, a new element is inserted in the Priority Queue with given priority number.

20.18.1 Insert Operation in Priority Queue with Multiple Queue Representation

Algorithm 20.15: This algorithm inserts the element in priority queue using multiple queues. The Priority Queue with Multiple Queue representation exists. The element, say item with priority number, say n is to be inserted.

Step 1: Start

Step 2: Insert element, item as rear element in Queue with priority n

Step 3: End

Explanation

Consider the following Multiple Priority Queue:

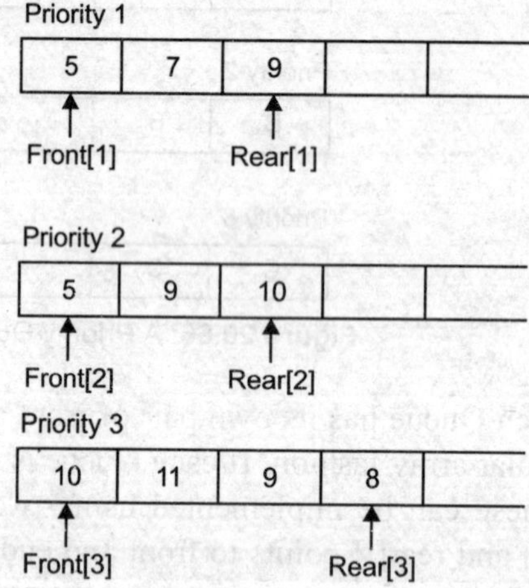

Figure 20.68: Before insertion priority queue look like

Now let us suppose an element 7 with priority 2, is to be added in above Priority Queue as:

Step 1: Start

Step 2: Insert element 7 as rear element of queue with priority 2. Now Priority Queue look like:

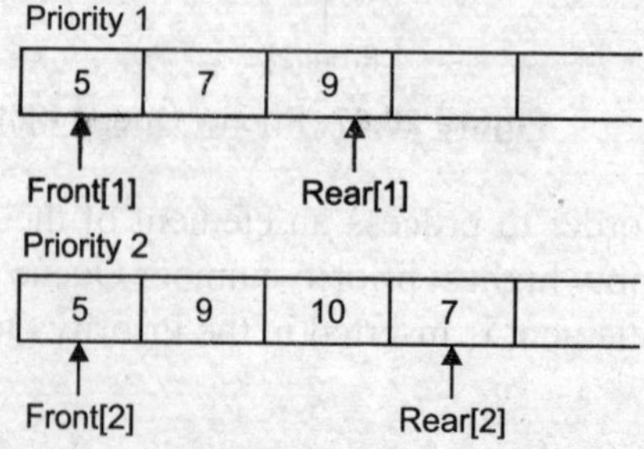

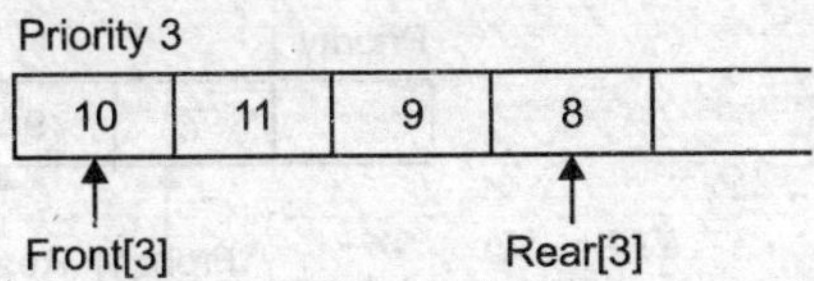

Figure 20.69: After insertion priority queue look like

Step 3: End.

20.18.2 Delete Operation in Priority Queue with Multiple Queue Representation

Algorithm 20.16: This algorithm inserts the element in priority queue using multiple queues. The Priority Queue with Multiple Queues representation exists. The first element in Priority Queue is to be deleted and processed.

Step 1: Start

Step 2: Find the smallest n so that front [n] '"NULL

Step 3: Delete first element in queue with priority number n

Step 4: End

Explanation

Let us consider the following Priority Queue:

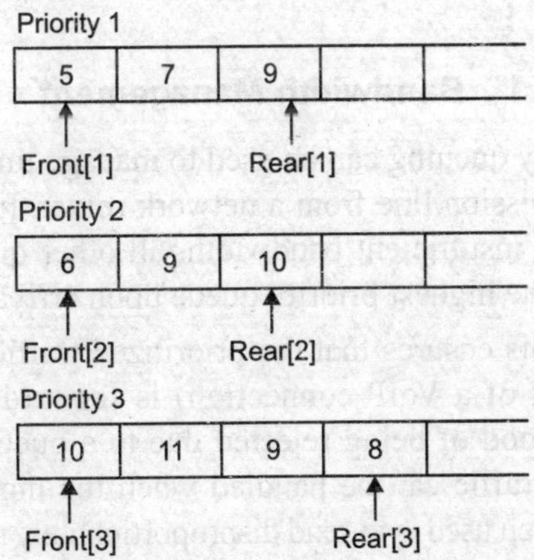

Figure 20.70: Before deletion priority queue look like

Step 1: Start

Step 2: Now find the smallest n so that front [n] '"NULL, In the above example Front [1] '"NULL

i.e. first element in Queue with priority 1 is not NULL and hence it is the element which will be deleted.

Step 3: Delete this first element. So Priority Queue will look like

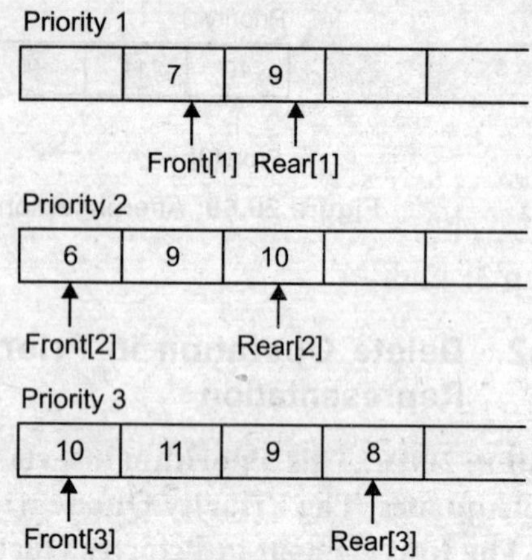

Figure 20.71: After deletion priority queue look like

Step 4: End.

20.19 APPLICATIONS OF PRIORITIY QUEUE

There are various applications areas where we apply priority queue some of them are:

20.19.1 Bandwidth Management

Priority queuing can be used to manage limited resources such as bandwidth on a transmission line from a network router. In the event of outgoing traffic queuing due to insufficient bandwidth, all other queues can be halted to send the traffic from the highest priority queue upon arrival.

This ensures that the prioritized traffic (such as real-time traffic, e.g. a RTP stream of a VoIP connection) is forwarded with the least delay and the least likelihood of being rejected due to a queue reaching its maximum capacity. All other traffic can be handled when the highest priority queue is empty. Another approach used is to send disproportionately more traffic from higher priority queues. Usually a limitation (policer) is set to limit the bandwidth that traffic from the highest priority queue can take, in order to prevent high priority packets from choking off all other traffic. This limit is usually never reached due to higher lever control instances such as the Cisco Callmanager, which can be programmed to inhibit calls which would exceed the programmed bandwidth limit.

20.19.2 Discrete Event Simulation

Another use of a priority queue is to manage the events in a discrete event simulation. The events are added to the queue with their simulation time used as the priority.

The execution of the simulation proceeds by repeatedly pulling the top of the queue and executing the event thereon.

20.19.3 Relationship to Sorting Algorithms

The semantics of priority queues naturally suggest a sorting method: insert all the elements to be sorted into a priority queue, and sequentially remove them; they will come out in sorted order. This is actually the procedure used by several sorting algorithms, once the layer of abstraction provided by the priority queue is removed. This sorting method is equivalent to the following sorting algorithms:

- Heapsort if the priority queue is implemented with a heap.
- Selection sort if the priority queue is implemented with an unordered array.
- Insertion sort if the priority queue is implemented with an ordered array.

20.20 APPLICATIONS OF QUEUES

There are various applications areas where we apply queue some of them are:

20.20.1 Scheduling and Buffering Queues

A queue is natural data structure for a system to serve the incoming requests. Most of the process scheduling or disk scheduling algorithms in operating systems use queues. Computer hardware like a processor or a network card also maintain buffers in the form of queues for incoming resource requests. A stack like data structure causes starvation of the first requests, and is not applicable in such cases. A mailbox or port to save messages to communicate between two users or processes in a system is essentially a queue like structure.

20.20.2 Search Space Exploration

Like stacks, queues can be used to remember the search space that needs to be explored at one point of time in traversing algorithms. Breadth first search of a graph uses a queue to remember the nodes yet to be visited.

20.20.3 Uses of Queues in Computer Systems

The purpose of a queue is to provide some form of buffering. Typical uses of queues in computer systems are:

- Process management
- Buffer between the fast computer and a slow printer

Everybody has experience with queues, as they are common place. Queues occur in cafeterias, petrol stations, shopping centers, any place where many people (customers) line up for few resources (cashier's, salespeople, petrol pumps etc).

20.20.4 Multiprogramming

One of the most important aspects of modern operating system is Multiprogramming. Multiprogramming is simply the ability for an operating system to execute many programs at once, and share different resources among them. These resources can vary from trying to writing to a disk, sharing memory, sharing CPU to managing ready and resource queues.

OBJECTIVE TYPE QUESTIONS

1. Queue is a
   (a) Linear data structure (b) Non-linear data structure
   (c) Both (d) None
2. Which of the following operations can be performed on Queue?
   (a) Push (b) Pop
   (c) Insertion (d) All of the above
   (e) None of the above
3. Queue has length
   (a) n (b) n-1
   (c) n+1 (d) All of the above
   (e) None of the above
4. Queue can be implemented by using
   (a) Array (b) Stack
   (c) Pointer (d) Linked list
   (e) None
5. Which of the following is the type of Queue?
   (a) Connected cities with reference (b) Heap of books
   (c) A Cinema Window (d) None of the above
6. Which of the following is the operation of Queue?
   (a) Insertion (b) Deletion
   (c) Create (d) Sorting
   (e) All of the above (f) None of the above
7. Which of the following is the Queue?
   (a) Singular queue (b) Deque
   (c) Priority queue (d) All of the above
   (e) None of the above

8. Which of the following is not the operation of Queue?
   (a) Sorting (b) Merging
   (c) Inserting (d) All of the above
   (e) None of the above
9. Which of the following is the utility of Queue?
   (a) Bus stop (b) Sorting
   (c) Concatenation (d) All of the above
   (e) None of the above
10. Traversing in Queue means:
   (a) Sorting (b) Searching
   (c) Inserting (d) Deleting
   (e) Visiting (f) None of the above
11. Queue follows the rule
   (a) FIFO (b) LIFO
   (c) LILO (d) FILO
12. The rear end of the queue is used
   (a) to insert an element (b) to remove an element
   (c) both (a) and (b) (d) None of the above
13. The front end of the queue is used
   (a) to insert an element (b) to remove an element
   (c) both (a) and (b) (d) None of the above
14. When an element is inserted in queue, the position of rear
   (a) increases (b) decreased
   (c) remains constant (d) None of the above
15. When an element is inserted in queue, the position of front
   (a) increments (b) decrements
   (c) unchanged (d) None of the above
16. Which one of the following is not a type of queue?
   (a) output restricted deque (b) circular queue
   (c) deque (d) priority queue.
17. In this queue elements can be inserted randomly
   (a) priority queue (b) simple queue
   (c) circular queue (d) None of the above
18. In the input restricted queue
   (a) deletion of element at both front and rear ends is done.

(b) insertion of element at both front and rear ends is done.

(c) deletion at only front end (d) all of the above

19. In this queue, smallest element of the queue is deleted first.

(a) ascending priority queue (b) descending priority queue

(c) circular queue (d) simple queue.

20. When the circular queue is full, and if one element is removed the next inserted element is stored at

(a) first location (b) last location

(c) intermediate location (d) None of the above

EXERCISES

1. Explain Concept of queue.
2. Why we call queue as an abstract data type.
3. Explain commonly used queue operations.
4. What is order produced by a queue.
5. Comparison between stacks and queues.
6. Explain implementation of queues using linear arrays.
7. Write an algorithm and C++ program for operations given below:

   1. Enqueue operation 2. Dequeue operation

   3. Peek operation 4. Rear operation

   5. Equals operation
8. Explain major problem with simple queue.
9. What do you understand by circular queue. Explain enqueue and dequeue operation with the help of an algorithm.
10. Explain implementation of queues using linked list.
11. What is Deque?
12. Explain input restricted deque and output-restricted deque with the help of program.
13. What do you mean by priority queue? Explain commonly used operations performed on priority queue.
14. Explain One way list representation of priority queue.
15. Explain implementation of priority queue using array.
16. Explain implementation of priority queue using multiple queues.
17. What are the various applications of priority queue.

CHAPTER 21

Sorting and Searching Techniques

21.1 INTRODUCTION

In the computer science, Sorting is technique to arranging elements in some order. Typically this is an operation that applied to arrays or other index able data structures. In Standard English, "to sort" means to arrange by kind or to classify. The term "sort" came to be used in Computer Science because the earliest automated ordering procedures used punched card machines, which classified cards by their holes, to implement *radix sort*.

To arrange items in a predetermined order. There are dozens of algorithms, the choice of which depends on factors such as the number of items relative to working memory, knowledge of the orderliness of the items or the range of the *keys*, the cost of comparing keys vs. the cost of moving items, etc. Most algorithms can be implemented as an *in-place sort*, and many can be implemented so they are *stable*, too.

21.2 SORTING

The sort operation may be defined in terms of an initial array, S, of N items and a final array, S′ , as follows:

1. $S_i' \leq S'_{i+1}$, $0 < i < N$
   (the items are in order) and
2. S′ is a *permutation* of S.

In terms of performance, sorting mostly comes in three flavors:

1. $O(n^2)$
2. O(n.log n) on average, but $O(n^2)$ at worst
3. O(n.log n)

The first class shouldn't be used for sorting really big arrays, say bigger than 2000 (there is no real limit; it depends on your time constraints). However they are usually very quick to code and debug, so always consider using them unless you are sure that they won't cut it. The algorithms in the second class are very seldom O(n^2), so it is fine to use them in most applications, particularly in computer Olympiads where you only have 5 or 10 test cases and are highly unlikely to get a really slow case, and even if you do you only lose some of your points.

Sorting time may depend on:

- Initial order of data
- Data structure used to represent data
- Memory available
- Size of record
- Sort algorithm
- Location of list: internal storage, external storage, etc.
- And many more

21.3 CLASSIFICATION OF SORTING ALGORITHMS

Sorting algorithms used in computer science are often classified by:

- **Computational complexity (worst, average and best behaviour):** In terms of the size of the list (n). Typically, good behaviour is O(n log n) and bad behaviour is O(n^2).

  Sort algorithms which only use an abstract key comparison operation always need at least O(n log n) comparisons on average; sort algorithms which exploit the structure of the key space cannot sort faster than O(n log k) where k is the size of the keyspace.
- **Memory usage (and use of other computer resources).**
- **Stability: Stable sorting algorithms** maintain the relative order of records with equal keys. That is, a sorting algorithm is *stable* if whenever there are two records R and S with the same key and with R appearing before S in the original list, R will appear before S in the sorted list.

  When equal elements are indistinguishable, such as with integers, stability is not an issue. However, say we were sorting these pairs of numbers by their first coordinate:

  (4, 3) (2, 1) (2, 7) (6, 6)

  In this case, two different results are possible, one which maintains the relative order records with equal keys, and one which doesn't:

  (2, 1) (2, 7) (4, 3) (6, 6) (order maintained)

  (2, 7) (2, 1) (4, 3) (6, 6) (order changed)

Unstable sorting algorithms may change the relative order of records with equal keys, stable sorting algorithms never so. Unstable sorting algorithms can be specially implemented to be stable. One way of doing this is to artificially extend the key comparison, so that comparisons between two objects with otherwise equal keys are decided using the order of the entries in the original data order as a tie-breaker. Remembering this order, however, often involves an additional space penalty.

There are different methods used for sorting the list or array. Some important methods are discusses in detail as below:

1. Bubble sort
2. Selection sort
3. Insertion sort
4. Quick sort
5. Heap sort
6. Merge sort
7. Radix sort
8. Bucket sort
9. Shell sort

21.4 BUBBLE SORT

Bubble sort is a simple sorting algorithm. It works by repeatedly stepping through the list to be sorted, comparing each pair of adjacent items and swapping them if they are in the wrong order. The pass through the list is repeated until no swaps are needed, which indicates that the list is sorted. Bubble sort belongs to $O(n^2)$ sorting algorithms, which makes it quite inefficient for sorting large data volumes. Bubble sort is **stable** and **adaptive**.The algorithm gets its name from the way smaller elements "bubble" to the top of the list. Because it only uses comparisons to operate on elements, it is a comparison sort.

21.4.1 Analysis

1. Performance

Bubble sort has worst-case and average complexity both Î(n^2), where n is the number of items being sorted. There exist many sorting algorithms with substantially better worst-case or average complexity of O(n log n). Even other Î(n^2) sorting algorithms, such as Insertion sort, tend to have better performance than bubble sort. Therefore bubble sort is not a practical sorting algorithm when n is large.

However, one significant advantage that bubble sort has over most other implementations, even QuickSort, is that the ability to detect that the list is sorted is efficiently built into the algorithm. Performance of bubble sort over an already-sorted list (best-case) is O(n). By contrast, most other algorithms, even those with better average-case complexity, perform their entire sorting process on the set and thus are more complex. However, Insertion sort also has this mechanism, and also performs better on a list that is substantially sorted (having a small number of inversions).

2. *Rabbits and Turtles*

The positions of the elements in bubble sort will play a large part in determining its performance. Large elements at the beginning of the list do not pose a problem, as they are quickly swapped. Small elements towards the end, however, move to the beginning extremely slowly. This has led to these types of elements being named rabbits and turtles, respectively.

Various efforts have been made to eliminate turtles to improve upon the speed of bubble sort. Cocktail sort achieves this goal fairly well, but it retains $O(n^2)$ worst-case complexity. Comb sort compares elements large gaps apart and can move turtles extremely quickly, before proceeding to smaller and smaller gaps to smooth out the list. Its average speed is comparable to faster algorithms like Quicksort.

3. *Step-by-step Example*

A bubble sort makes use of an array and some sort of "swapping" mechanism. Most programming languages have a built-in function to swap elements of an array. Even if a swapping function does not exist, only a couple of extra lines of code are required to store one array element in a temporary field in order to swap a second element into its place. Then the first element is moved out of the temporary field and back into the array at the second element's position.

Example 21.1: How a bubble sort works: Suppose you have a row of children's toy blocks with letters on them. They are in random order and you wish to arrange them in alphabetical order from left to right.

Step 1: Begin with the first block. In this case, the letter **G.** (a)

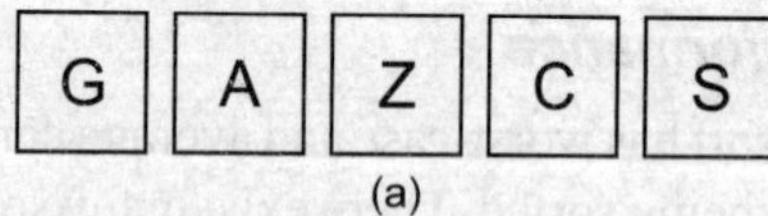

(a)

Step 2: Look at the block just to the right of it.

Step 3: If the block to the right should come before the block on the left, swap them so that they are in order (b)

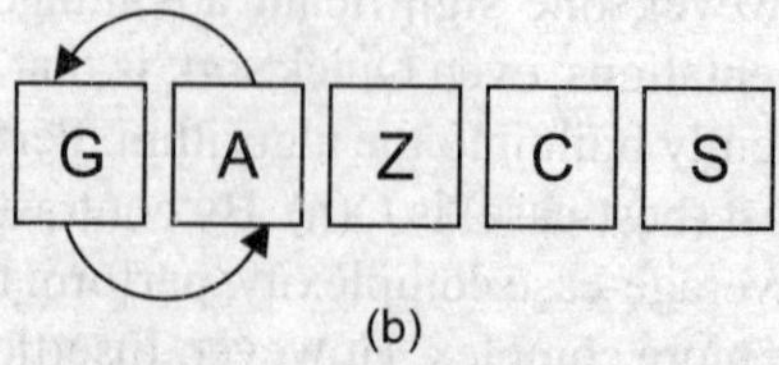

(b)

If you were doing this by hand, you might just pick the blocks to be moved with one in each hand and cross your arms to swap them. Or you might move the first one out of it's position temporarily, move the second one in its place, them move the first one to the now empty position (this is the difference between having a single function to do the swap, or writing some code to do it).

Step 4: Compare the next block in line with the first, and repeat step 3. Do this until you run out of blocks. Then begin step one again with the second block. (c,d,e)

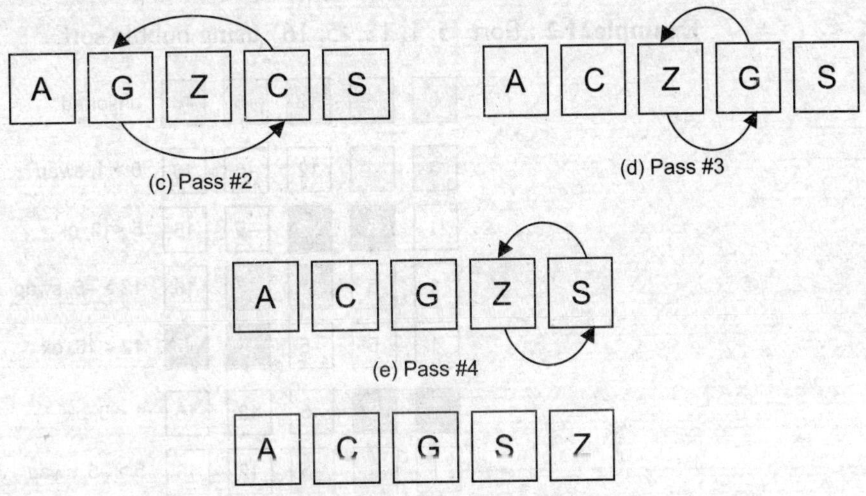

Figure 21.1: Bubble Sort.

21.4.2 Algorithm of Bubble Sort

1. Compare each pair of adjacent elements from the beginning of an array and, if they are in reversed order, swap them.
2. If at least one swap has been done, repeat step 1.
3. You can imagine that on every step big bubbles float to the surface and stay there. At the step, when no bubble moves, sorting stops.

Algorithm 21.1: BUBBLE(LA, N)

Here LA is an array with N elements. This algorithm sorts the elements in LA.

Step 1: START

Step 2: Repeat steps 3 and 4 For K=1 to N-1

Step 3: Set P =1 [Initializes pass pointer P]

Step 4: Repeat While P <=N-K [Execute Pass]

(a) if (LA[P] > LA [P+1]) then
Set TEMP=LA[P]
Set LA[P] = LA[P+1]
Set LA[P+1] = TEMP
[End of if Structure]
(b) Set P = P+1
[End of inner loop (While loop)]
[End of Step 1 Outer Loop.]
Step 5: End.

Example21.2 : Sort {5, 1, 12, -5, 16} using bubble sort.

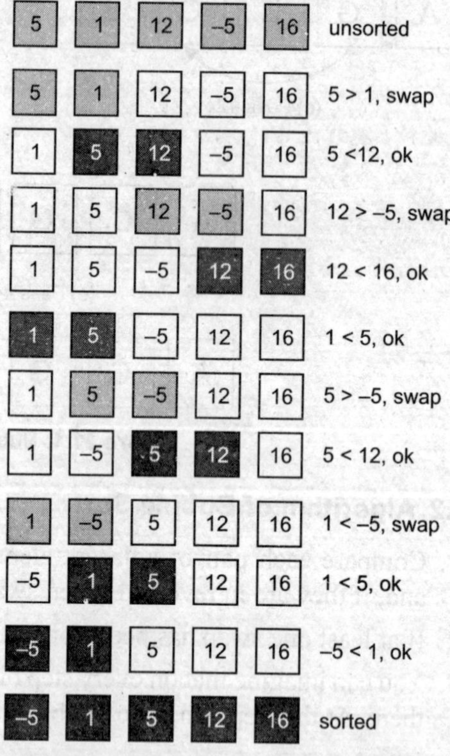

Figure 21.2: Example of bubble sort.

Program 1: Write a C++ program for Bubble sort(ascending order).

```
# include<iostream.h>
# include<conio.h>
# define size 20
class array
{
```

```
private:
int i;
float a[size];
public:
void read (int);
void display (int);
void bubble_sort (int);          // for sorting of elements
};
void array : : read (int n)
{
for (i=0;i<n;i++)
cin>>a[i];
}
void array : : display (int n)
{
for (i=0;i<n;i++)
cout<<a[i]<<" ";
}
void array : : bubble_sort (int n)
{
float temp; // temp is used here for swapping
int last;               // last denotes the position of last unsorted element
int pass;        // pass denotes the position of last unsorted element and
denotes pass counter
int exchngs;            // exchngs denotes the no of exchanges during a pass
pass=0;
last=n-1;
do
{
pass++;
exchngs=0;
for (i=0;i<last;i++)
{
if (a[i]>a[i+1])
{
exchngs++;
temp=a[i];
```

```
a[i] =a [i+1];
a[i+1] = temp;
} // for loop ends here
last --;
}
while ((exchngs !=0) && (pass !=n-1));
cout<<"\n\nNo of pass used for sorting = '<<pass;
}

void main ( )
{
array obj;
int n;
clrscr ( );
cout<<"read no of elements<="<<size<<"\n";
cin>>n;
cout<<"\nread "<<n>>" elements\n";
obj.read (n);
cout<<"\ngiven array is \n\n";
obj.display (n);
obj.bubble_sort (n); // function call selection_sort
cout<<"\n\nSorted array is\n\n";
obj.display(n);
getch ( );
}
```

Output:

```
read no of elements<=20
7
read 7 elements
14    25    12    28    15    -2    35
given array is
14    25    12    28    15    -2    35
No of pass used for sorting = 6
Sorted array is
-2    12    14    15    25    28    35
```

Complexity analysis

Average and worst case complexity of bubble sort is $O(n^2)$. Also, it makes $O(n^2)$ swaps in the worst case. Bubble sort is adaptive. It means that for almost sorted array it gives O(n) estimation. Avoid implementations, which don't check if the array is already sorted on every step (any swaps made). This check is necessary, in order to preserve adaptive property.

Turtles and rabbits

One more problem of bubble sort is that its running time badly depends on the initial order of the elements. Big elements (rabbits) go up fast, while small ones (turtles) go down very slow. This problem is solved in the Cocktail sort.

Turtle example 21.3: Thought, array {2, 3, 4, 5, 1} is almost sorted, it takes $O(n^2)$ iterations to sort an array. Element {1} is a turtle.

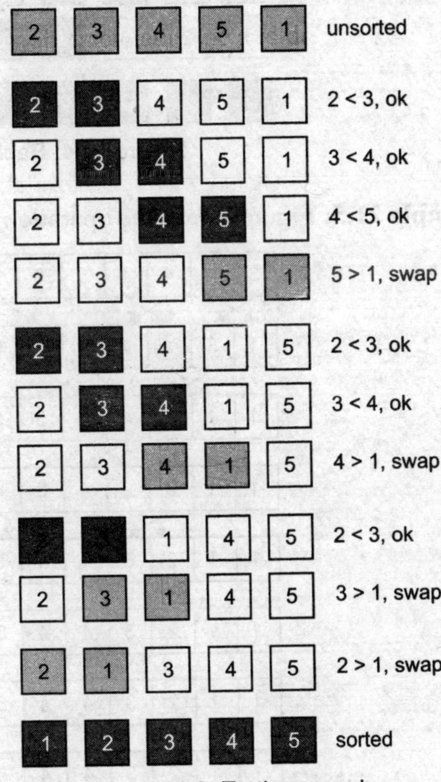

Figure 21.3: Turtle example.

Rabbit example21.4: Array {6, 1, 2, 3, 4, 5} is almost sorted too, but it takes O(n) iterations to sort it. Element {6} is a rabbit. This example demonstrates adaptive property of the bubble sort.

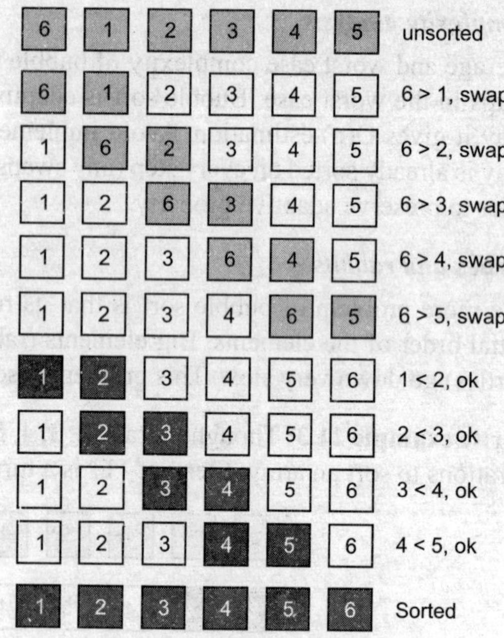

Figure 21.4: Rabbit example.

Example 21.5: Figure shows the operation of bubble sort.

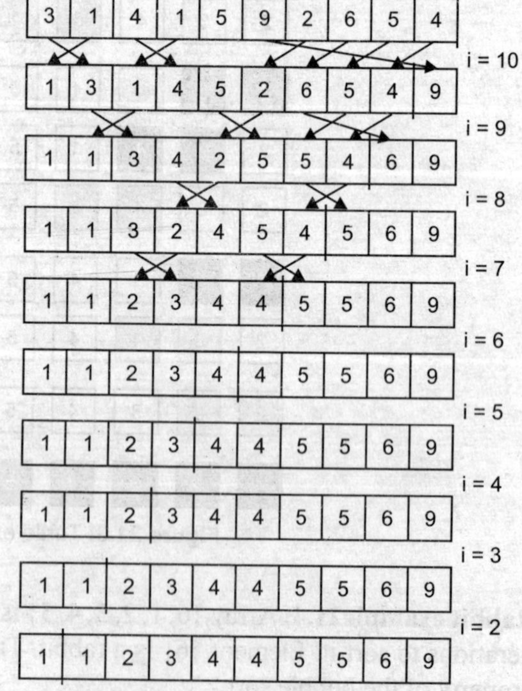

Figure 21.5: Bubble Sorting.

To sort the sequence $S = \{s_0, s_1, s_2, \ldots\ldots, s_{n-1}\}$, bubble sort makes n-1 passes through the data. In each pass, adjacent elements are compared and swapped if necessary. First, $s_0$and s_1 are compared; next, s_1 and s_2; and so on.

Notice that after the first pass through the data, the largest element in the sequence has *bubbled up* into the last array position. In general, after k passes through the data, the last k elements of the array are correct and need not be considered any longer. In this regard the bubble sort differs from the insertion sort algorithms—the sorted subsequence of k elements is never modified (by an insertion).

Figure also shows that while n-1 passes through the data are required to guarantee that the list is sorted in the end, it is possible for the list to become sorted much earlier! When no exchanges at all are made in a given pass, then the array is sorted and no additional passes are required. A minor algorithmic modification would be to count the exchanges made in a pass, and to terminate the sort when none are made.

The running time of bubble sort is $O(n^2)$.

21.4.3 Other Variations of Bubble Sort

1. Bubble Sort - Fixed Number of Passes

Bubble sort compares two values next to each other and exchanges them if necessary to put them in the correct order. There are many variations on bubble sort, but they all examine adjacent pairs.

This version of bubble sort makes a fixed number of passes (length of the array - 1). Each inner loop is one shorter than the previous one because the largest elements are being moved to the end of the array.

Algorithm 21.2: BubbleSort1 (x,n)

Where
x=Represents the list of elements
n=Represents the number of elements in the list
Step 1: [Initialize] i=0
Step 2: Repeat through step 7 while(i<n-1)
Step 3: j=0
Step 4: Repeat through step 6 while(j<n-i-1)
Step 5: if(x[j]>x[j+1]
TEMP=x[j]; x[j]=x[j+1]; x[j+1]=TEMP
Step 6: j++
Step 7: i++
Step 8: End.

Because this version of the bubble sort always makes n-1 passes over the array, it can't stop early if the array is already sorted.

2. Bubble Sort – stop when no exchanges

Algorithm 21.3: BubbleSort2(x,n)

Where
x=Represents the list of elements.
n=Represents the number of elements in the list.
Step 1: [Assume no exchanges] exchanges=false
Step 2: [Initialize] i=0
Step 3: Repeat through step 5 while(i<n-1)
Step 4: if(x[i]>x[i+1]]
TEMP=x[i]; x[i]=x[i+1]; x[i+1]=TEMP
exchanges=true [after exchange, must look again]
Step 5: i++
Step 6: go back step 1 while(exchanges)
Step 7: End.

This version of bubble sort continues making passes over the array as long as there were any exchanges. If the array is already sorted, this sort will stop after only one pass.

Disadvantage: This algorithm doesn't shorten the range each time by 1 as it could.

3. Bubble Sort — stop when no exchanges, shorter range each time

This version of bubble sort combines ideas from the previous versions. It stops when there are no more exchanges, and it also sorts a smaller range each time.

Algorithm 21.4: BubbleSort3(x, n)

Where
x=Represents the list of elements.
n=Represents the number of elements in the list.
Step 1: [Make loop smaller each time] n—
Step 2: [Assume this is last pass over array] exchanges=false
Step 3: [Initialize] i=0
Step 4: Repeat through step 6 while(i<n)
Step 5: if(x[i]>x[i+1])
TEMP=x[i]; x[i]=x[i+1] ;x[i+1]=TEMP
exchanges=true [after exchange, must look again]
Step 6: i++
Step 7: go back step 1 while(exchanges)
Step 8: End.

Disadvantage:

After the first pass it may not be necessary to examine the entire range of the array — only from where the lowest exchange occurred to where the highest exchange occurred. The parts above and below must already be sorted.

4. *Bubble Sort — Sort only necessary range*

Here's a version of bubble sort that, on each pass, looks only at the region of array where more exchanges might be necessary.

Algorithm 21.5: BubbleSortRange(x,n)

```
Where
x=Represents the list of elements.
n= Represents the number of elements in the list.
Step 1:  lowerbound=0      [First position to compare]
         upperbound=n      [First position NOT to compare]
         [Continue making passes while there is a potential exchange]
Step 2:  Repeat through step 11 while(lowerbound<=upperbound)
Step 3:  firstexchange=n   [Assume impossibly high index for low end]
         lastexchange=-1   [Assume impossibly low index for high end]
Step 4:  i=lowerbound              [Make a pass over the appropriate range]
Step 5:  Repeat through step 8 while(I<upperbound)
Step 6:  if x[i]>x[i+1])
TEMP=x[i]; x[i]=x[i+1] ; x[i+1]=TEMP
 [Remember first and last exchange indexes]
Step 7:  if(i<firstexchange)  [true only for first]then firstexchange=i
Step 8:  lastexchange=i             [Prepare limits for next pass]
Step 9:  lowerbound=firstexchange-1
Step 10: if(lowerbound<0) then lowerbound=0
Step 11: upperbound=lastexchange
Step 12: End.
```

Disadvantage

Notice that the largest unsorted element will always be moved all the way to its correct position in the array, but small elements are shifted down by only one place on each pass.

Note that in all these sorts the part that is sorted grows at only one end of the array. The ability to quit early is not symmetrical. The extreme values move all the way to the end in one direction, but only one place in the other direction. The algorithm can be improved by alternately "bubbling" in opposite directions.

Efficiency: O(n^2)

Pros

- Simple to implement and understand, but not much more so than several more efficient sorts
- Will be very quick on an already sorted list

Cons

- Probably the slowest sort ever invented

21.5 SELECTION SORT

Selection sort is one of the O(n^2) sorting algorithms, which makes it quite inefficient for sorting large data volumes. Selection sort is notable for its programming simplicity and it can over perform other sorts in certain situations (see complexity analysis for more details).

Selection sort is a sorting algorithm, specifically an in-place comparison sort. It has O(n^2) complexity, making it inefficient on large lists, and generally performs worse than the similar insertion sort. Selection sort is noted for its simplicity, and also has performance advantages over more complicated algorithms in certain situations.

Such algorithms construct the sorted sequence one element at a time by adding elements to the sorted sequence *in order*. At each step, the next element to be added to the sorted sequence is selected from the remaining elements.

Because the elements are added to the sorted sequence in order, they are always added at one end. This is what makes selection sorting different from insertion sorting. In insertion sorting elements are added to the sorted sequence in an arbitrary order. Therefore, the position in the sorted sequence at which each subsequent element is inserted is arbitrary.

Consequently, the sorts are implemented by exchanging array elements. Nevertheless, selection differs from exchange sorting because at each step we *select* the next element of the sorted sequence from the remaining elements and then we move it into its final position in the array by exchanging it with whatever happens to be occupying that position.

The simplest of the selection sorts is called *straight selection*. illustrates how straight selection works. In the version shown, the sorted list is constructed from the right (i.e., from the largest to the smallest element values).

At each step of the algorithm, a linear search of the unsorted elements is made in order to determine the position of the largest remaining element. That element is then moved into the correct position of the array by swapping it with the element which currently occupies that position.

Example 21.6: In the first step shown in Figure a linear search of the entire array reveals that 9 is the largest element. Since 9 is the largest element, it belongs in the last array position. To move it there, we swap it with the 4 that initially occupies that position. The second step of the algorithm identifies 6 as the largest remaining element an moves it next to the 9. Each subsequent step of the algorithm moves one element into its final position. Therefore, the algorithm is done after n-1 such steps.

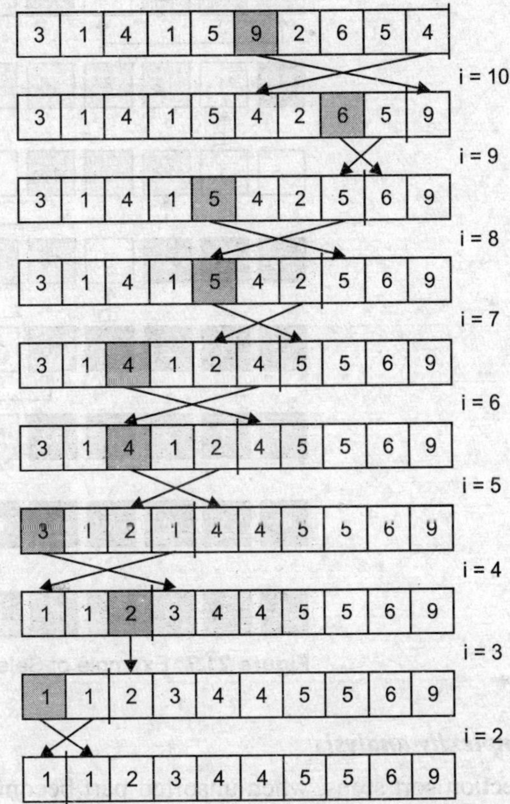

Figure 21.6: Straight Selection Sorting.

In all n-1 iterations of the outer loop are needed to sort the array. Notice that exactly one swap is done in each iteration of the outer loop. Therefore, n-1 data exchanges are needed to sort the list.

Furthermore, in the ith iteration of the outer loop, i-1 iterations of the inner loop are required and each iteration of the inner loop does one data comparison. Therefore, $O(n^2)$ data comparisons are needed to sort the list.

The total running time of the straight selection Do Sort routine is $O(n^2)$. Because the same number of comparisons and swaps are always done, this running time bound applies in all cases. I.e., the best-case, average-case and worst-case running times are all $O(n^2)$.

Let us see an example of sorting an array to make the idea of selection sort clearer.

Example 21.7: Sort {5, 1, 12, -5, 16, 2, 12, 14} using selection sort.

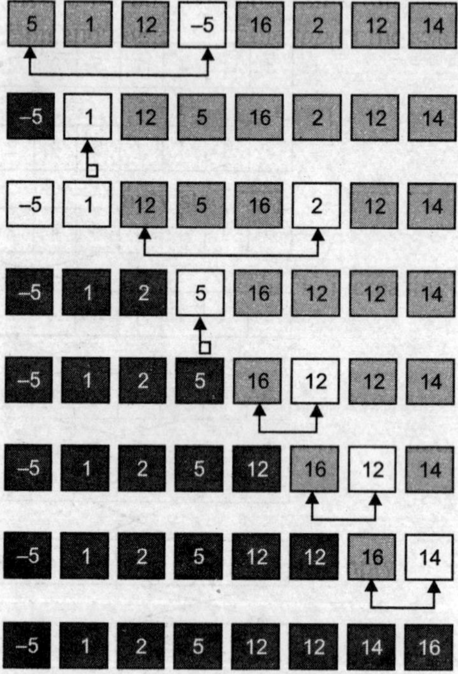

Figure 21.7: Example of Selection Sorting.

Complexity analysis

Selection sort stops, when unsorted part becomes empty. As we know, on every step number of unsorted elements decreased by one. Therefore, selection sort makes n steps (n is number of elements in array) of outer loop, before stop. Every step of outer loop requires finding minimum in unsorted part. Summing up, $n + (n - 1) + (n - 2) + ... + 1$, results in $O(n^2)$ number of comparisons. Number of swaps may vary from zero (in case of sorted array) to $n - 1$ (in case array was sorted in reversed order), which results in $O(n)$ number of swaps. Overall algorithm complexity is $O(n^2)$.

The idea behind selection sort is that to sort N items you make N passes through them.

1. On the first pass you find the largest value, and then swap it with the last item. Thus the largest item is now in position N.

2. On the second pass you scan through just the first N-1 entries. The largest of those items is swapped with the item in position N-1. Hence the largest item overall is now in the last position; the second largest item is now in the second last position.
3. This process is repeated, with one item being placed in its correct location each time.
4. After N passes, the entire collection of data is sorted.

A simple variation is to find the smallest item each time and put it at the front. To sort into descending order, the largest item is found each time and moved to the front (this is the algorithm that is used in the examples which follow).

21.5.1 Algorithm

The idea of algorithm is quite simple. Array is imaginary divided into two parts - sorted one and unsorted one. At the beginning, sorted part is **empty**, while unsorted one contains **whole array**. At every step, algorithm finds **minimal element** in the unsorted part and adds it to the end of the sorted one. When unsorted part becomes **empty**, algorithm stops.

When algorithm sorts an array, it swaps first element of unsorted part with minimal element and then it is included to the sorted part. This implementation of selection sort in **not stable**. In case of linked list is sorted, and, instead of swaps, minimal element is linked to the unsorted part, selection sort is **stable**.

The algorithm works as follows:

1. Find the minimum value in the list
2. Swap it with the value in the first position
3. Repeat the steps above for the remainder of the list (starting at the second position and advancing each time)

Effectively, the list is divided into two parts: the sublist of items already sorted, which is built up from left to right and is found at the beginning, and the sublist of items remaining to be sorted, occupying the remainder of the array.

Algorithm 21.6: SELECTIONSORT(A,N)

This algorithm sorts the array A with N elements.

Step 1: START

Step 2: Repeat Steps 3 and 4 For K=1,2,3,……,N-1

Step 3: Call MIN(A,K,LOC,N)

Step 4: [Interchange A[K] and A[LOC]]

Set TEMP=A[K]

Set A[K]=A[LOC]

Set A[LOC]=TEMP.
[End of Step 2 For loop]
Step 5: End.

Algorithm 21.7: MIN(A,K,N,LOC)

An array A is in memory. This algorithm finds the location LOC of the smallest elements among A[K], A[K+1], …………, A[N].

Step 1: Set MIN = A[K] and LOC = K [Initializes Pointers]

Step 2: Repeat For J = K+1, K+2,………, N.

If MIN>A[J] then

Set MIN = A[J] and LOC =A[J] and LOC =J.

[End of For loop of step 2]

Step 3: Return

Program 2: Write a C++ program for Selection sort.(ascending order)

```
# include<iostream.h>
# include<conio.h>
# define size 20
class array
{
private:
int i;
float a[size];
public:
void read (int);
void display (int);
void selection_sort (int); // for sorting of elements
};
void array : : read (int n)
{
for (i=0;i<n;i++)
cin>>a[i];
}
void array : : display (int n)
{
for (i=o;i<n;i++)
```

```
cout<<a[i]<<" ";
}
void array : : selection_sort (int n)
{
float  temp; // temp is used here for swapping
int min_index;
// min_index denotes the position of the least element during a pass
for (int pass=0; pass<n-1;pass++)
{
min_index=pass;
for (i=pass+1;i<n;i++)
{
if (a[i] <a[min_index])
min_index=i;
}
if (pass ! =min_index)
{
temp=a [pass];
a[pass]=a[min_index];
a[min_indcx]=temp;
}
}
}
void main ( )
{
array obj;
int n;
clrscr ( );
cout<<"read no of elements<="<<size<<"\n";
cin>>n;
cout<<"\nread "<<n>>" elements\n";
obj.read (n);
cout<<"\ngiven array is \n\n";
obj.display (n);
obj.selection_sort (n);
```

```
cout<<"\n\nSorted array is\n\n";
obj.display(n);
getch ( );
}
```

Output:

```
read no of elements<=20
7
read 7 elements
14    25    12    28    15    -2    35
given array is
14    25    12    28    15    -2    35
No of pass used for sorting = 6
Sorted array is
-2    12    14    15    25    28    35
```

21.6 INSERTION SORT

Insertion sort belongs to the $O(n^2)$ sorting algorithms. Unlike many sorting algorithms with quadratic complexity, it is actually applied in practice for sorting small arrays of data. **For instance, it is used to improve quicksort routine.** Some sources notice, that people use same algorithm ordering items, for example, hand of cards.

Insertion sort algorithm somewhat resembles selection sort. Array is imaginary divided into two parts - sorted one and unsorted one. At the beginning, sorted part contains **first element** of the array and unsorted one contains the rest. At every step, algorithm takes **first element** in the unsorted part and **inserts** it to the right place of the sorted one. When unsorted part becomes **empty**, algorithm *stops*. Sketchy, insertion sort algorithm step looks like this:

Sorted partitial result   Unsorted data

≤ x	> x	x	...

becomes

Sorted partitial result   Unsorted data

≤ x	x	> x	...

The idea of the sketch was originally posted here. Let us see an example of insertion sort routine to make the idea of algorithm clearer.

Example 21.8: Sort {7, -5, 2, 16, 4} using insertion sort.

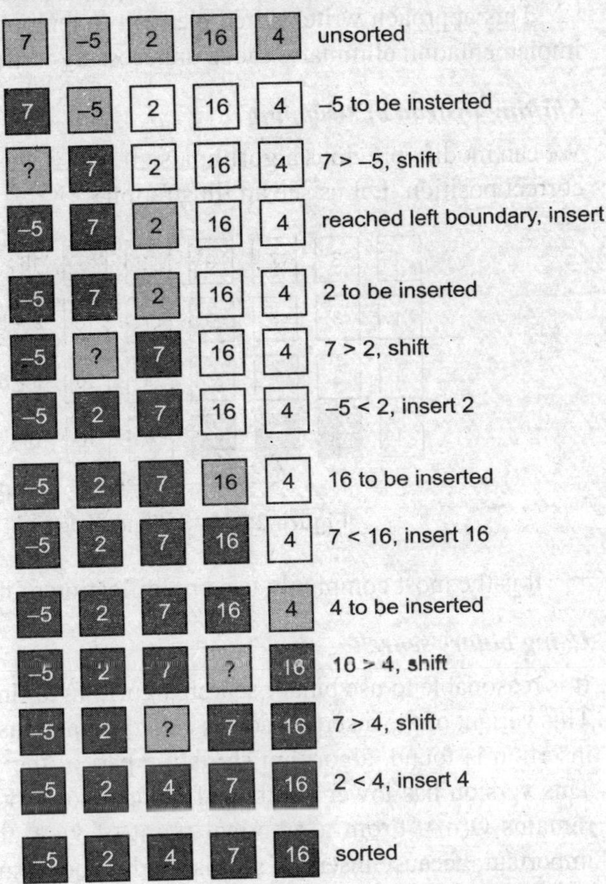

Figure 21.8: Example of Insertion Sort.

The ideas of insertion

The main operation of the algorithm is **insertion**. The task is to insert a value into the sorted part of the array. Let us see the variants of how we can do it.

"Shifting down" using swaps: The simplest way to insert next element into the sorted part is to sift it down, until it occupies correct position. Initially the element stays right after the sorted part. At each step algorithm compares the element with one before it and, if they stay in reversed order, swap them. Let us see an illustration.

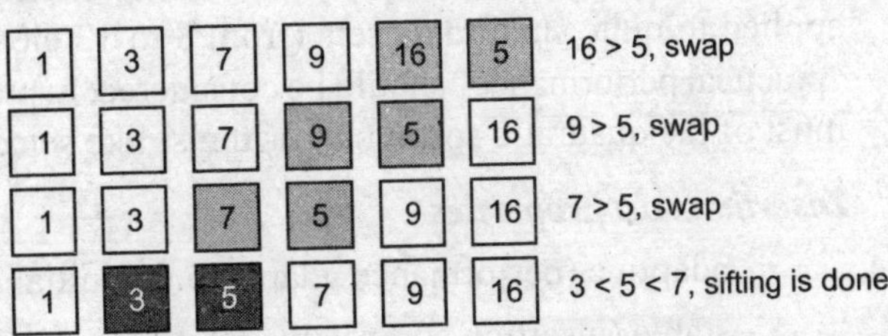

Figure 21.9: "Shifting down" using swaps.

This approach writes sifted element to temporary position many times. Next implementation eliminates those unnecessary writes.

Shifting instead of swapping

We can modify previous algorithm, so it will write sifted element only to the final correct position. Let us see an illustration.

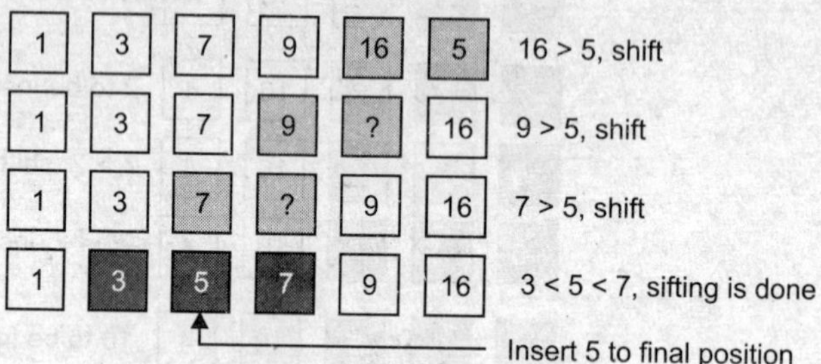

Figure 21.10: Shifting instead of swapping

It is the most commonly used modification of the insertion sort.

Using binary search

It is reasonable to use binary search algorithm to find a proper place for insertion. This variant of the insertion sort is called **binary insertion sort**. After position for insertion is found, algorithm shifts the part of the array and inserts the element. This version has lower number of comparisons, but overall average complexity remains $O(n^2)$. From a practical point of view this improvement is not very important, because insertion sort is used on quite small data sets.

Complexity analysis

Insertion sort's overall complexity is $O(n^2)$ on average, regardless of the method of insertion. On the almost sorted arrays insertion sort shows better performance, up to $O(n)$ in case of applying insertion sort to a sorted array. Number of writes is $O(n^2)$ on average, but number of comparisons may vary depending on the insertion algorithm. It is $O(n^2)$ when shifting or swapping methods are used and $O(n \log n)$ for binary insertion sort.

From the point of view of practical application, an average complexity of the insertion sort is not so important. As it was mentioned above, insertion sort is applied to quite small data sets (from 8 to 12 elements). Therefore, first of all, a "practical performance" should be considered. In practice insertion sort outperforms most of the quadratic sorting algorithms, like selection sort or bubble sort.

Insertion sort properties

- adaptive (performance adapts to the initial order of elements);
- stable (insertion sort retains relative order of the same elements);

- in-place (requires constant amount of additional space);
- online (new elements can be added during the sort).

Algorithm 21.8: INSERTION(A,N)

This algorithm sorts the array A with N elements. P is used as pointer.

Step 1: START

Step 2: Set A[0] = –∞ [Initializes sentinel element]

Step 3: Repeat steps 4 to 6 For K = 2, 3, 4,……, N.

Step 4: Set Temp = A[k] and P = K-1.

Step 5: Repeat While TEMP < A[P]

a. Set A[P+1] = A[P]. [Move Element Forward.]

b. Set P = P - 1.

[End of While Loop.]

Step 6: Set A[P+1] = TEMP. [Insert element in Proper Place.]

[End of for loop of Step 3]

Step 7: End.

Program 3: Write a C++ program for insertion sort.(ascending order)

```
# include<iostream.h>
# ınclude<conio.h>
# define size 20
class array
{
private:
int i;
float a[size];
public:
void read (int);
void display (int);
void insertion_sort (int); // for sorting of elements
};
void array : : read (int n)
{
for (i=0;i<n;i++)
cin>>a[i];
}
void array : : display (int n)
{
```

```
for (i=o;i<n;i++)
cout<<a[i]<<" ";
}
void array : : insertion_sort (int n)
{
int current, pos;
for (i=1;i<n;i++)
{
current=a[i]; // current denotes the element to be arranged
pos=0;
while ((pos<i) && (a[pos]<=current))
pos++;
//pos increased till values in array are <= current
if (pos !=i)
{
for (int j=i-1;j>=pos;j--)
a[j+1]=a[j];
// insertion
a[pos]=current;
}
}
}
void main ( )
{
array obj;
int n;
clrscr ( );
cout<<"read no of elements<="<<size<<"\n";
cin>>n;
cout<<"\nread "<<n>>" elements\n";
obj.read (n);
cout<<"\ngiven array is \n\n";
obj.display (n);
obj.insertion_sort (n);
cout<<"\n\nSorted array is\n\n";
obj.display(n);
```

```
getch ( );
}
```

Output:

```
read no of elements<=20
7
read 7 elements
14     25     12     28     15     -2     35
given array is
14     25     12     28     15     -2     35
No of pass used for sorting = 6
Sorted array is
-2     12     14     15     25     28     35
```

Efficiency: O(n^2)

Pros

- Fairly easy to implement with a linear search
- If a backwards linear search is used, it is much faster on an partially sorted array

Cons

- On an array, insertion is slow because all the elements after it have to be moved up.

Note: This sort isn't especially useful by itself (although it is a respectable O(n^2) sort), but forms the basis of Shell sort.

21.7 QUICKSORT

One of the most popular sorting algorithms is Quick Sort. Quick Sort executes in **O**(n lg n) on average, and **O**(n^2) in the worst-case. However, with proper precautions, worst-case behavior is very unlikely. Quick Sort is a non-stable sort. It is not an in-place sort as stack space is required.

Quicksort is a *divide-and-conquer* style algorithm. A divide-and-conquer algorithm solves a given problem by splitting it into two or more smaller subproblems, recursively solving each of the subproblems, and then combining the solutions to the smaller problems to obtain a solution to the original one.

To sort the sequence $S = \{s_0, s_1, s_2, \ldots\ldots, s_n\}$, quicksort performs the following steps:

1. Select one of the elements of S. The selected element, p, is called the *pivot* .
2. Remove p from S and then partition the remaining elements of S into two distinct sequences, L and G, such that every element in L is less than or equal to the pivot and every element in G is greater than or equal to the pivot. In general, both L and G are unsorted.
3. Rearrange the elements of the sequence as follows:

$$S \quad \underbrace{\{l_1, l_2, ..., l_{|L|}\}}_{L} : \underbrace{P}_{pivot} : \underbrace{\{g_1, g_2, ..., g_{|G|}\}}_{G}$$

   Notice that the pivot is now in the position in which it belongs in the sorted sequence, since all the elements to the left of the pivot are less than or equal to the pivot and all the elements to the right are greater than or equal to it

4. Recursively quicksort the unsorted sequences L and G.

The first step of the algorithm is a crucial one. We have not specified how to select the pivot. Fortunately, the sorting algorithm works no matter which element is chosen to be the pivot. However, the pivot selection affects directly the running time of the algorithm. If we choose poorly the running time will be poor.

Illustrates the detailed operation of quicksort as it sorts the sequence {3, 1, 4, 1, 5, 9, 2, 6, 5, 4}. To begin the sort, we select a pivot. In this example, the value 4 in the last array position is chosen. Next, the remaining elements are partitioned into two sequences, one which contains values less than or equal to 4 (L={3, 1, 2, 1}) and one which contains values greater than or equal to 4 (G = {5, 9, 4, 6, 5). Notice that the partitioning is accomplished by exchanging elements. This is why quicksort is considered to be an **exchange sort.**

After the partitioning, the pivot is inserted between the two sequences. This is called *restoring* the pivot. To restore the pivot, we simply exchange it with the first element of G. Notice that the 4 is in its correct position in the sorted sequence and it is not considered any further.

Now the quicksort algorithm calls itself recursively, first to sort the sequence L = {3, 1, 2, 1}; second to sort the sequence G = {9, 4, 6, 5, 5}. The quicksort of L selects 1 as the pivot, and creates the two subsequences L' = {1} and G' = {2, 3}. Similarly, the quicksort of G uses 5 as the pivot and creates the two subsequences L" = {5, 4} and G" = {9, 6}.

At this point in the example the recursion has been stopped. It turns out that to keep the code simple, quicksort algorithms usually stop the recursion when the length of a subsequence falls below a critical value called the cut-off. In this example, the cut-off is two (i.e., a subsequence of two or fewer elements is not sorted).

Example 21.9

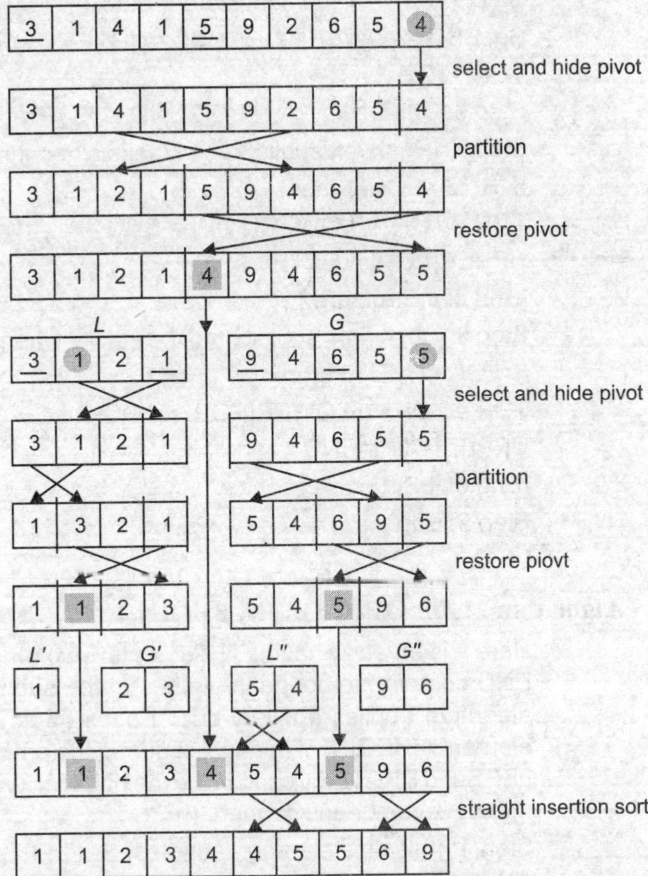

Figure 21.11: Quick Sorting

This means that when the algorithm terminates, the sequence is not yet sorted. However as Figure shows, the sequence is *almost* sorted. In fact, every element is guaranteed to be less than two positions away from its final resting place. In fact, if we know that every element of the sequence is at most d positions from its final resting place, the running time of straight insertion is O(dn) and since d=2 is a constant, the running time is O(n).

Algorithm 21.9: QUICKSORT

Step 1: START

Step 2: TOP=NULL [Initialize]

Step 3: [Push boundary values of a onto the stack when A has 2 or more elements]

If (N>1) then Set TOP = TOP+1, LOWER[1] = 1, UPPER[1]=N

Step 4: Repeat Steps 5 to 7 While TOP ≠ NULL
Step 5: [Pop sublist from Stacks]
Set BEG:=LOWER[TOP], END:=UPPER[TOP]
TOP:=TOP-1
Step 6: Call QUICK(A,N,BEG,END,LOC) Procedure
Step 7: [Push left sublist onto stacks when it has 2 or more elements]
If BEG <LOC-1 then:
TOP = TOP-1, LOWER[TOP] = BEG
UPPER[TOP]=LOC-1
[End of if Structure.]
Step 8: [push right sublist onto the stacks when it has 2 or more elements]
If LOC+1< END then:
TOP = TOP+1, LOWER[TOP] = LOC+1
UPPER[TOP]=END
[End of if Structure.]
Step 9: End.

Algorithm 21.10: QUICK(A, N, BEGIN, END, LOC)

Here A is an array having N elements. Two main parameters BEGIN and END contain the boundary values of the sublist of array A to which this algorithm applies applies. LOC Keeps track of the position of the first element A[BEGIN] of the sublist during the procedure. The local variables LEFT and RIGHT will contain the the boundary values of the list of elements that have not been scanned.

Step 1: [Initialize starting variables] Set LEFT = BEGIN, RIGHT = END AND LOC = BEGIN.
Step 2: [Scan elements from right to left.]
(a) Repeat Steps while A[LOC] ≤ A[RIGHT] and LOC ≠ RIGHT:
RIGHT = RIGHT – 1.
[End of while loop.]
(b) If LOC = RIGHT, then Return.
(c) If A[LOC]> A[RIGHT], then
(i) [Interchange elements A[LOC] and A[RIGHT].]
TEMP = A[LOC], A[LOC] = A[RIGHT].
A[RIGHT] = TEMP.
(ii) Set LOC = RIGHT.
(iii) GO to Step 3.
[End of If statement.]
Step 3: [Scan elements from left to right.]

(a) Repeat steps while A[LEFT] ≤ A[LOC] and LEFT ≠ LOC:
    LEFT = LEFT + 1
  [End of while loop.]
(b) If LOC = LEFT, then Return.
(c) if A[LEFT] > A[LOC], then
    (i) [Interchange elements A[LEFT] and A[LOC].]
        TEMP = A[LOC], A[LOC] = A[LEFT],
        A[LEFT] = TEMP.
    (ii) Set LOC = LEFT.
    (iii) Go to step 2.
[End of If statement.]

Table21.1 : Running Times for Exchange Sorting

Algorithm	Running time Best case	 Average case	 Worst case
bubble sort	$O(n^2)$	$O(n^2)$	$O(n^2)$
quicksort (random pivot selection)	$O(n \log n)$	$O(n \log n)$	$O(n^2)$

Program 4: Write a C++ program for Quick sort.(ascending order)

```
# include<iostream.h>
# include<conio.h>
# define size 20
class array
{
private:
float a[size];
int i, low, high, pivot_value, temp;
public:
void read (float *,int);
void display (float *,int);
void quick_sort (float *,int beq, int end);
};
void array : : read (float a[], int n)
{
for (i=0;i<n;i++)
cin>>a[i];
}
void array : : display (float a[], int n)
```

```
{
for (i=0;i<n;i++)
cout<<a[i]<<" ";
}
void array : : quick_sort (float arr[], int beg, int end)
{
lot=beg;
high=end;
pivot_value=arr [(beg+end)/2];
do
{
while (arr[low]>pivot_value)
high--;
if (low<=high)
{
temp = arr[low]
arr [low++] = arr[high];
arr [high--] = temp;
}
}while (low<=high);
if (beg<high)
quick_sort [arr, beg, high); // recursive call to the function
if (low<end)
quick_sort (arr, low, end); // recursive call to the function
}
void main ( )
{
array obj;
float a[size];
int n;
clrscr ( );
cout<<"read no of elements<="<<size<<"\n";
cin>>n;
cout<<"\nread "<<n<<" elements \n\n;
obj.read (a, n);
cout<<"\ngiven array is \n\n";
obj.display (a, n);
obj.quick_sort(a,0,n-1);
cout<<"\n\n Sorted array is\n\n";
```

```
obj.display(a,n))
getch ( );
}
```

Output:

```
read no elements<=20
7
read 7 elements
14    25    12    28    15    -2    35
given array is
14    25    12    28    15    -2    35
No of pass used for sorting = 6
Sorted array is
-2    12    14    15    25    28    35
```

21.8 HEAP SORT

The Quick Sort on the average improves performance over linear sort algorithms. In this section we consider another important nonlinear sort, the **heap sort**, which performs as well as the quick sort on the average and performs better than the quick sort in the worst cases. The heap sort has better all-around performance than any other internal sort that we present; however it is rather complex to program. J. W. J. Williams developed the heap sort in 1964. The heap sort is based upon use of a special type of binary tree (called a heap) to structure the sorting process.

Heap is a complete binary tree in which each node satisfies the heap condition. Heap has been defined as: descending heap (also called a **max heap**) and ascending heap (also called a **min heap**). In descending heap, the root of the tree (or the first element of the array) contains the largest element in the heap. Also note that any path from the root to a leaf (or indeed, any path in the tree that includes no more than one node at any level) is an ordered list in descending order. In ascending heap, the root contains the smallest element of the heap, and any path from the root to a leaf is an ascending ordered list.

To define a descending heap of size n as an almost complete binary tree of n nodes such that the content of each node is less than or equal to the content of its father. To define an ascending heap as a complete binary tree such that the content of each node is greater than or equal to the content of its father.

The structure satisfies the condition of descending heap as root of the tree and sub trees have higher value than the children. The roots of the sub trees are also higher the value of their children as shown in the Figure 21.12:

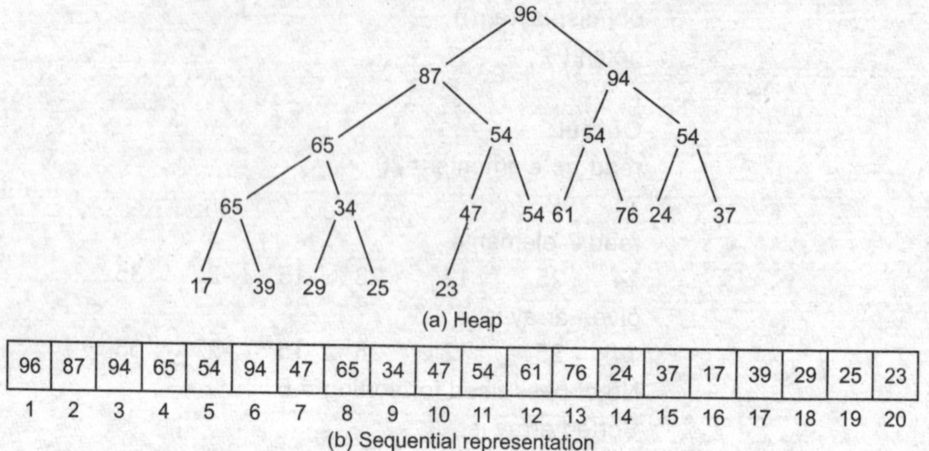

(a) Heap

96	87	94	65	54	94	47	65	34	47	54	61	76	24	37	17	39	29	25	23
1	2	3	4	5	6	7	8	9	10	11	12	13	14	15	16	17	18	19	20

(b) Sequential representation

Figure 21.12: Heap tree.

If the father is placed at say index 2, i.e., 87, its children will be placed at index 2*2 and (2*2)+1, i.e. 65 and 54.

21.8.1 Sorting Procedure

Heap sort involves three operations, insertion, deletion of nodes and building new heap tree in such a way so as to maintain the heap character of the tree. The sorting procedure of the Heap tree is very simple and the execution of this tree on computer is faster as compared to the other tree.

1. Inserting into a Heap

Suppose H is a heap with N elements, and suppose an ITEM of information is given. We insert ITEM into the heap H as follows:

1. First adjoin ITEM at the end of H so that H is still a complete tree, but not necessarily a heap.
2. Then let ITEM rise to its "appropriate place" in H so that H is finally a heap.

We illustrate the way this procedure works before stating the procedure formally.

Algorithm 21.11: INSHEAP(TREE, N, ITEM)

A heap H with N elements is stored in the array TREE, and an ITEM of information is given. This procedure inserts ITEM as a new element of H. Pointer P gives the location of ITEM as it rises in the tree, and PARENT denotes the location of the PARENT of ITEM.

Step 1: [Add new node to H and initialize P.]

Set N = N + 1 and P = N.

Step 2: [Find location to insert ITEM.]
Repeat Steps 3 to 6 while P > 1.
Step 3: Set PARENT = [P/2]. [Location of PARENTent node.]
Step 4: If ITEM ≤ TREE[PARENT], then:
Set TREE[P] = ITEM, and Return.
[End of If statement.]
Step 5: Set TREE[P] = TREE[PARENT]. [Moves node down.]
Step 6: Set P = PARENT. [Updates P.]
[End of Step 2 loop.]
Step 7: [Assign ITEM as the ROOTNOD of H.]
Set TREE[1] = ITEM.
Step 8: Return.

Example 21.10: Consider the heap H in Figure 21.12. Suppose we want to add ITEM = 71 to H. First we adjoin 71 as the next element in the complete tree; that is, we set TREE[21] = 71. Then 71 is the right child of TREE [10] = 47. The path from 71 to the root of H is pictured in Figure 21.13(a). We know find the appropriate place of 71 in the heap as follows:

(a) Compare 71 with its parent, 47. Since 71 is greater than 47, interchange 71 and 47; the path will now look Figure 21.13(b).

(b) Compare 71 with its new parent, 54. Since 71 is greater than 54, interchange 71 and 54; the path will now look like Figure 21.13(c).

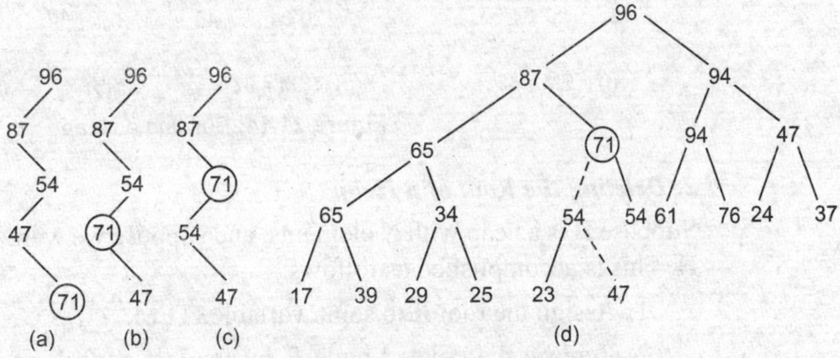

Figure 21.13: ITEM = 71 is Inserted

(c) Compare 71 with its new parent, 87. Since 71 does not exceed 87, ITEM = 71 has risen to its appropriate place in H.

Figure 21.13(d) shows the final tree. A dotted line indicate that an exchange has taken place.

Remark: *One must verify that the above procedure does always yield a heap as a final tree, that is that nothing else has been disturbed. This is easy to see, and we leave this verification to the reader.*

Example 21.11: Suppose we want to build a heap H from the following list of numbers:

34, 20, 40, 12, 50, 45, 67, 45

This can be accomplished by inserting the eight numbers one after the other into an empty heap H using the above procedure. Figure 21.14(a) through (h) shows the respective pictures of the heap after each of the eight elements has been inserted. Again, the dotted line indicated that an exchange has taken place during the insertion of the given ITEM of information.

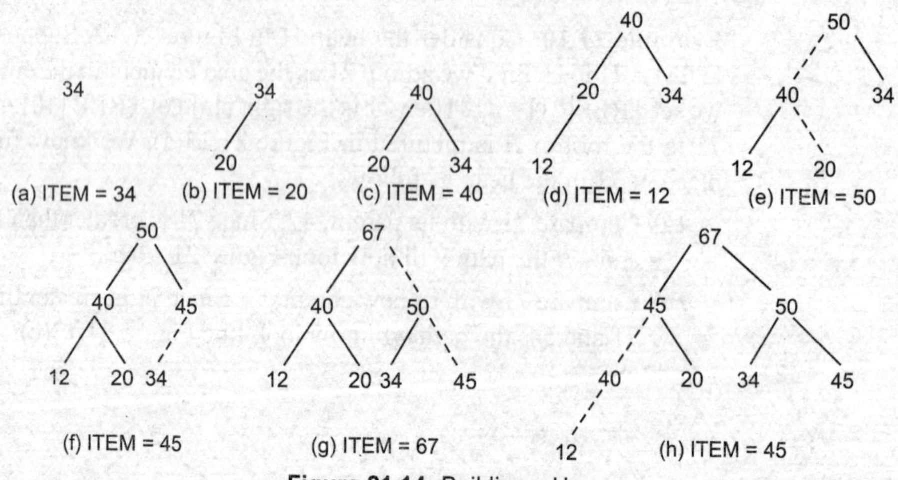

Figure 21.14: Building a Heap

2. Deleting the Root of a Heap

Suppose H is a heap with N elements, and suppose we want to delete the root R of H. This is accomplished as follows:

1. Assign the root R to some variable ITEM.
2. Replace the deleted node R by the last node L of H so that H is still a complete tree, but not necessarily a heap.
3. (Reheap) Let L sink to its appropriate place in H so that H is finally a heap.

Again we illustrate the way the procedure works before stating the procedure formally.

Algorithm 21.12: DELHEAP(TREE, N, ITEM)

A heap H with N elements is stored in the array TREE. This procedure assigns the ROOTNOD TREE[1] of H to the variable ITEM and then reheaps the remaining elements. The variable LAST saves the value of the original last node of H. The pointers P, LEFTNOD and RIGHTNOD give the locations of LAST and its LEFTNOD and RIGHTNOD children as LAST sinks in the tree.

Step 1: Set ITEM = TREE[1]. [Removes ROOTNOD of H.]

Step 2: Set LAST = TREE[N] and N = N – 1. [Removes last node of H.]

Step 3: Set P = 1, LEFTNOD = 2 and RIGHTNOD = 3. [Initializes pointers.]

Step 4: Repeat Steps 5 to 7 while RIGHTNOD ≤ N:

Step 5: If LAST ≥ TREE[LEFTNOD] and LAST ≥ TREE[RIGHTNOD], then:
Set TREE[P] = LAST and Return.
[End of If statement.]

Step 6: If TREE[RIGHTNOD] ≤ TREE[LEFTNOD], then:
Set TREE[P] = TREE[LEFTNOD] and P = LEFTNOD.
Else
Set TREE[P] = TREE[RIGHTNOD] and P = RIGHTNOD.
[End of If statement.]

Step 7: Set LEFTNOD = 2 * P and RIGHTNOD = LEFTNOD(2*P) + 1
[End of Step 4 loop.]

Step 8: If LEFTNOD = N and if LAST < TREE[LEFTNOD], then
Set TREE[P] = TREE[LEFTNOD] and P = LEFTNOD.

Step 9: Set TREE[P] = LAST.

Step 10: Return.

Example 21.12: Consider the heap H in Figure 21.15(a), where R = 93 is the root and L = 20 is the last node of the tree. Step 1 of the above procedure deletes R = 93, and Step 2 replaces R = 93 by L = 20. This gives the complete the tree in Figure 21.15(b), which is not a heap. Observe, however, that both the right and left subtrees of 20 are still heaps. Applying Step 3, we find the appropriate place of 20 in the heap as follows:

(a) Compare 20 with its two children, 83 and 68. Since 20 is less than the larger child, 83, interchange 20 and 83 so the tree now looks like Figure 21.15(c).

(b) Compare 20 with its two new children, 53 and 31. Since 20 is less than the larger child, 53, interchange 20 and 53 so the tree now looks like Figure 21.15(d).

(c) Compare 20 with its new children, 13 and 18. Since 20 is greater than both children, node 20 has dropped to its appropriate place in H.

Thus, Figure 21.15(d) is the required heap H without its original root R.

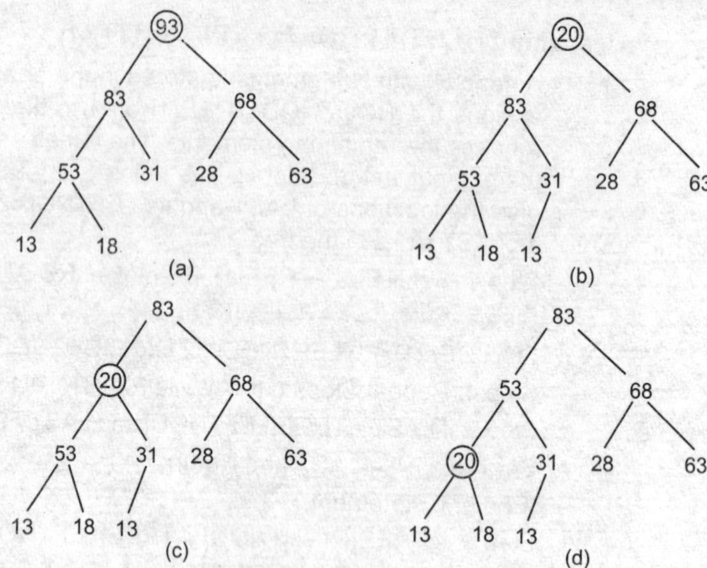

Figure 21.15: Reheaping.

Remark: *As with inserting an element into a heap, one must verify that the above procedure does always yield a heap as a final tree. Again we leave this verification to the reader. We also note that Step 3 of the procedure may not end until the node L reaches the bottom of the tree, i.e., until L has no children.*

21.8.2 Application to Sorting

Suppose an array A and N elements is given. The heapsort algorithm to sort A consists of the two following phases:

Phase A: Build a heap H out of the elements of A.

Phase B: Repeatedly delete the root element of H.

Since the root of H always contains the largest node in H, Phase B deletes the elements of A in decreasing order. A formal statement of the algorithm, which uses Procedures 21.11 and 21.12, follows.

Algorithm 21.13: HEAPSORT(A, N)

An array A with N element is given. This algorithm sorts the elements of A.

Step 1: [Build a heap H, using Algorithm 21.11.]

Repeat for I = 1 to N – 1

Call INSHEAP(A, I, A[I + 1])

[End of loop.]

Step 2: [Sort A by repeatedly deleting the ROOTNOD of H, using algorithm 21.12.]

Repeat while N> 1:

a. Call DELHEAP(A, N, ITEM).

b. Set A[N + 1] = ITEM.

[End of loop.]

Step 3: End.

The purpose of step 2(b) is to save space makes the sorting technique more efficient. That is we can use another array B to hold the sorted elements of A and replace step 2(b) as

Set B[N + 1] = ITEM.

***Note:** Step 2(b) not interfere with the algorithm, Since A[N+1] does not belong to the heap H.*

21.8.3 Complexity of Heapsort

Suppose the heapsort algorithm is applied to an array A with n elements. The algorithm has tow phases, and we analyze the complexity of each phase separately.

Phase A: Suppose H is a heap. Observe that the number of comparisons to find the appropriate place of a new element ITEM in H cannot exceed the depth of H. Since H is a complete tree, its depth is bounded by $\log_{2-}$ m where m is the number of elements in H. Accordingly, the total number g(n) of comparison to insert the n elements of A into H is bounded as follows:

$$g(n) \leq n \log_2 n$$

Consequently, the running time of Phase A of heapsort is proportional to $n \log_2 n$.

Phase B: Suppose H is a complete tree with m elements, and suppose the left and right subtrees of H are heaps and L is the root of H. Observe that reheaping uses 4 comparisons to move the node L one step down the tree H. Since the depth of H does not exceed $\log_2 m$, reheaping uses at most 4 $\log_{-}$ m comparison to find the appropriate place of L in the tree H. This means that the total number h(n) of comparison to delete the n elements of A from H, which requires reheaping n times, is bounded as follows:

$$h(n) \leq n \log_2 n$$

Accordingly, the running time of Phase B of heapsort is also proportional to $n \log_2 n$.

Since each phase requires time proportional to n $\log_2$ n, the running time to sort the n-element array A using heapsort is proportional to n $\log_2$ n, that is, f(n) = O(n $\log_2$ n). Observe that this gives a worst-case complexity of the heapsort algorithm. This contrasts with the following two sorting algorithms already studied:

1. **Bubble sort:** The running time of bubble sort is $O(n^2)$.
2. **Quicksort:** The average running time of quicksort is O(n $\log_2$n), the same as heapsort, but the worst-case running time of quicksort is $O(n^2)$, the same as bubble sort.

Efficiency: O(nlog n)

Pros

- Guaranteed to be O(n.log n)
- One of the few non-recursive **O(nlog n) sorts.**
- Fairly easy to debug, because it is non-recursive and because it consists of two smaller and unrelated parts.

Cons

- Not as fast on average as Quick sort.
- Quite a lot of code to implement the heap operations.

Note: *This isn't an especially useful sort, but the running time is guaranteed O(n.log n) and it is very light on memory consumption. Also, if you have already implemented a heap for some other reason, then this sort comes almost for free.*

It is possible to get some extra speed by constructing the heap in one pass: put everything into the heap ignoring the heap condition, then work through the heap from bottom to top, bubbling elements down the heap where necessary. This makes the heap creation take linear time.

21.9 MERGE SORTING

Merging is the combination of two or more sorted sequences into a single sorted sequence. In a two-way merge, two sorted sequences are merged into one. Clearly, two sorted sequences each of length n can be merged into a sorted sequence of length 2n in O(2n)=O(n) steps. However in order to do this, we need space in which to store the result. I.e., it is not possible to merge the two sequences *in place* in O(n) steps.

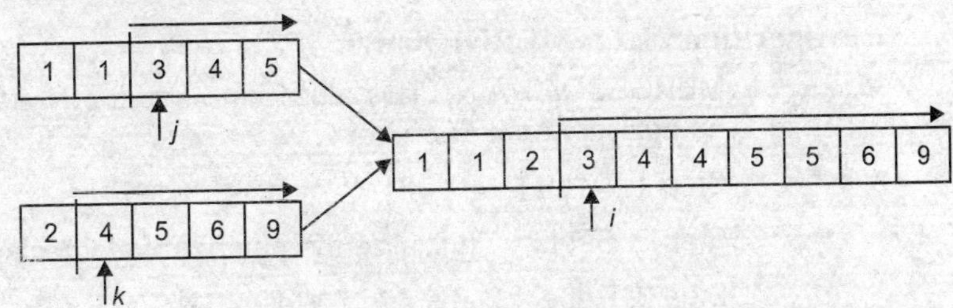

Figure 21.16: Two-Way Merging

Sorting by merging is a recursive, divide-and-conquer strategy. In the base case, we have a sequence with exactly one element in it. Since such a sequence is already sorted, there is nothing to be done. To sort a sequence of n>1 element:

1. Divide the sequence into two sequences of length[n/2] and[n/2];
2. Recursively sort each of the two subsequences; and then,
3. Merge the sorted subsequences to obtain the final result.

Example 21.13: Suppose the array a contain 14 elements as follows:

66,33,40,22,55,88,60,11,80,20,50,44,77,30

Each pass of the merge sort algorithm will start at the beginning of the array a and merge pairs of sorted subarray as follows:

Pass 1. Merge each pair of elements to obtain the following list of sorted pairs:

33, 66 22, 40 55, 88 11, 60 20, 80 44, 50 30, 70

Pass 2. Merge each pair of pairs to obtain the following list of sorted quadruplets:

22, 33, 40, 66 11, 55, 60, 88 20, 44, 50, 80 30, 70,

Pass 3. Merge each pair of sorted quardruplets to obtain the following two sorted subarrays:

11, 22, 33, 40, 55, 60, 66, 88 20, 30, 44, 50, 77, 80

Pass 4. Merge the two sorted subarrays to obtain the single sorted array

11 , 20 , 22 , 30 , 33 , 40 , 44 , 50 , 55 , 60 , 66 , 77 , 80 , 88

The original array A is now sorted.

Algorithm 21.14: MERGE SORT

MERGESORT(A,N): This algorithm sorts the N-element array A using an auxiliary array B.

Step 1: START

Step 2: Set L = 1 [Initialize the number of elements in the subarrays]

Step 3: Repeat Steps 4 to 7 While L<N

Step 4: Call MERGEPASS(A,N,L,B)

Step 5: Call MERGEPASS(B,N,2*L,A)

Step 6: Set L = 4*L

End of Step 3 of While loop

Step 7: End

Algorithm 21.15: MERGEPASS(A,N,L,B)

The N-element array A is composed of sorted subarrays where each subarray has L elements except possibly the last subarray, which may have fewer than L elements. The procedure merges the pairs of subarrays of A and assigns them to the array B.

Step 1: Set Q = INT(N/(2*L)), S = 2*L*Q and R = N-S

Step 2: [use procedure 2 to merge the Q pairs of subarrays]

Repeat For J=1, 2,.........,Q:

a. Set LB =1+(2*J-2)*L. [Find lower bound of first array]

b. Call MERGE(A,L,LB,A,B,LB+L,B,LB) [End of for loop]

Step 3: [only one subarrays left]

If R ≤ L then

Repeat For J=1,2,............., R

Set B(S+J) =A(S+J)

[End of the for loop]

Else

Call MERGE(A,L,S+1,A,R,L+S+1,B,S+1)

[End of if Structure]

Step 4: Return

Algorithm 21.16: MERGING(A,R,B,S,C)

Let A and B be sorted arrays with R and S elements, respectively. This algorithm merges A and B into an array C with N = R + S elements.

Step 1: Set NA = 1, NB = 1 and P = 1 [initialize]

Step 2: Repeat While NA ≤ R and NB ≤ S [Compare]

If (A[NA] < B[NB]) then

a. Set C[PTR] = A[NA] [Assign element from A to C]

b. Set P =P+1 and NA =NA+1 [Update Pointer P.]

Else

a. Set C[P] = B[NB] [Assign element from B to C]

b. Set P =P+1 and NB =NB+1 [Update Pointer]

End of if Structure

[End of While loop]

Step 3: [Assign remaining elements to C]

If (NA > R) then

Repeat For K=0,1,2,.............,S-NB

Set C[P+K] = B[NB+K]

[End of loop]

Else

Repeat For K=0, 1, 2,.............,R - NA:

Set C[P+K] = A[NA+K]

[End of loop]

[End of if Structure]

Step 4: End

Algorithm 21.17: MERGE(A, R, LBA, S, LBB, C, LBC)

This procedure merges the sorted arrays A and B into the arrays C.

Step 1: Set NA = LBA, NB = LBB, PTR = LBC, UBA = LBA + R – 1.

UBB = LBB + S – 1.

Step 2: Same as Algorithm 21.16 except R is replaced by UBA and S by UBB.

Step 3: Same as Algorithm 21.16 except R is replaced by UBA and S by UBB.

Step 4: Return.

Illustrates the operation of the two-way merge sort algorithm.

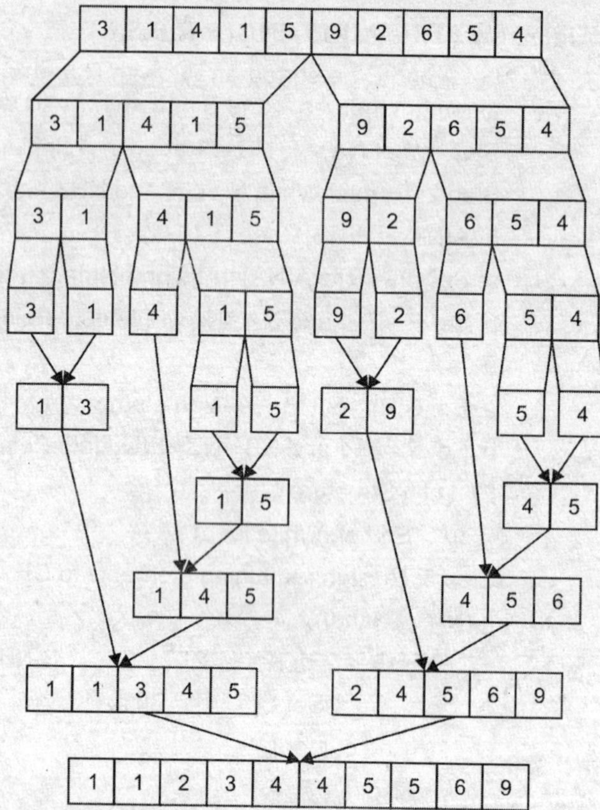

Figure 21.17: Two-Way Merge Sorting

Running Time Analysis

The running time of merge sort is determined by the running time of the recursive DoSort routine. (The main DoSort only adds a constant amount of overhead). The running time of the recursive DoSort routine is given by the following recurrence:

$$T(n)=\begin{cases} O(1) & n=1, \\ T(\lfloor n/2 \rfloor)+T(\lceil n/2 \rceil)+O(n) & n>1 \end{cases}$$

Where n = right – left + 1.

In order to simplify the solution of above Equation we shall assume that $n=2^k$ for some integer k>=0. Dropping the O()s from the equation we get

$$T(n)=\begin{cases} 1 & n=1, \\ 2T(n/2)+n & n>1 \end{cases}$$

which is easily solved by repeated substitution:

$$
\begin{aligned}
T(n) &= 2T(n/2) + n \\
&= 4T(n/4) + 2n \\
&= 8T(n/8) + 3n \\
&\vdots \\
&= 2^kT(n/2^k) + kn \\
&\vdots \\
&= nT(1) + n\log_2 n \\
&= n + n\log_2 n
\end{aligned}
$$

Therefore, the running time of merge sort is O(n log n).

A Lower Bound on Sorting

The preceding sections present three O(n log n) sorting algorithms—quicksort, heapsort, and the two-way merge sort. But is O(n log n) the best we can do? In this section we answer the question by showing that any sorting algorithm that sorts using only binary comparisons must make O(n log n) such comparisons. If each binary comparison takes a constant amount of time, then running time for any such sorting algorithm is also O(n log n).

Consider the problem of sorting the sequence S = {a, b, c} comprised of three distinct items. i.e., $a \neq b \wedge a \neq c \wedge b \neq c$. illustrates a possible sorting algorithm in the form of a *decision tree* . Each node of the decision tree represents one binary comparison. I.e., in each node of the tree, exactly two elements of the sequence are compared. Since there are exactly two possible outcomes for each comparison, each non-leaf node of the binary tree has degree two.

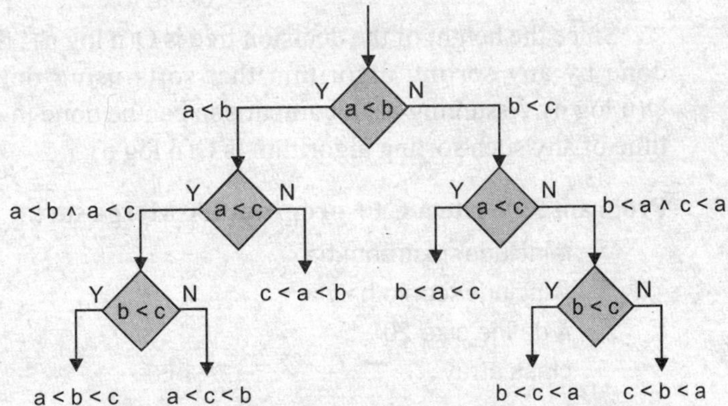

Figure 21.18: A Decision Tree for Comparison Sorting

For example, suppose that a<b<c. Consider how the algorithm shown in Figure ☐ discovers this. The first comparison compares a and b which reveals that a<b. The second comparison compares a and c to find that a<c. At this point it has

been determined that $a<b$ and $a<c$— the relative order of b and c is not yet known. Therefore, one more comparison is required to determine that $b<c$. Notice that the algorithm shown in Figure 21.18 works correctly in all cases because every possible permutation of the sequence S appears as a leaf node in the decision tree. Furthermore, the number of comparisons required in the worst case is equal to the height of the decision tree!

Any sorting algorithm that uses only binary comparisons can be represented by a binary decision tree. Furthermore, it is the height of the binary decision tree that determines the worst-case running time of the algorithm. In general, the size and shape of the decision tree is a function of the sorting algorithm and the number of items to be sorted.

Given an input sequence of n items to be sorted, every binary decision tree that correctly sorts the input sequence must have *at least* n! leaves—one for each permutation of the input. Therefore, it follows directly from Theorem that the height of the binary decision tree is *at least* $\log_2$ n!.

$$\lceil \log_2 n! \rceil \;^3\; \log_2 n!$$

$$^3 \sum_{i=1}^{n} \log_2 i$$

$$^3 \sum_{i=1}^{n/2} \log_2 n/2$$

$$^3\; n/2 \log_2 n/2$$

$$= W\ (n \log n)$$

Since the height of the decision tree is O(n log n) , the number of comparisons done by any sorting algorithm that sorts using only binary comparisons is O(n log n). Assuming each comparison can be done in constant time, the running time of any such sorting algorithm is O(n log n).

Program 5: Write a C++ program for Merge sort.

```
# include<iostream.h>
# include<conio.h>
# define size 20
class array
{
private:
float a[size];
int i, low, high, pivot_value, temp;
public:
```

```
void read (float *,int);
void display (float *,int);
void merge_sort (float *,int, int, int);
void merge_pass(float *,int ,int);
};
void array : : read (float a[], int n)
{
for (i=0;i<n;i++)
cin>>a[i];
}
void array : : display (float a[], int n)
{
for (i=0;i<n;i++)
cout<<a[i]<<" ";
}
void array : : merge_sort (float arr[], int top, int s, int bot)
{
float temparr [size];
int first, second, third;
first=top;
second=s+1;
third=top;
while ((first<=s) && (second<=bot))
{
if (arr [first]<=arr[second])
{
temparr [third]=arr [first];
first++;
}
else
{
temparr [third]=arr[second];
second++;
}
third++;
}
if (first<=s)
{
for (first=first;first<s;first++)
```

```
{
tempar [third]=arr[first];
third++;
}
}
else
{
for (second=second;second<=bot;second++)
{
temparr[third]=arr[second];
third++;
}
}
// copy the elements from temparr[] to arr[]
for (int i=top;i<=bot;i++)
arr[i]=temparr[i];
}
void array ::merge_pass (float app[], int m, int n)
{
if (n !=m)
{
int middle=(m+n) / 2;
merge_pass (app, m, middle);
merge_pass(app, middle+1, n);
merge_sort (app, m,middle,n); // invoke function merge_sort( )
}
}
void main ( )
{
array obj;
float a[size];
int n;
clrscr ( );
cout<<"read no of elements<="<<size<<"\n";
cin>>n;
cout<<"\nread "<<n<<" elements \n\n;
obj.read (a, n);
cout<<"\ngiven array is \n\n";
obj.display (a, n);
```

```
obj.merge_pass(a,0,n-1);
cout<<"\n\n Sorted array is\n\n";
obj.display(a,n))
getch ( );
}
Output:
read no elements<=20
6
read 6 elements
13    5    7    10    26    19
given array is
13    5    7    10    26    19
Sorted array is
5    7    10    13    19    26
```

21.10 BUCKET SORT

Bucket sort is possibly the simplest distribution sorting algorithm. The essential requirement is that the size of the universe from which the elements to be sorted are drawn is a small, fixed constant, say m.

Example 21.14: Suppose that we are sorting elements drawn from {0, 1,........, m-1}, i.e., the set of integers in the interval [0,m-1]. Bucket sort uses m counters. The ith counter keeps track of the number of occurrences of the ith element of the universe. Figure 21.19 illustrates how this is done.

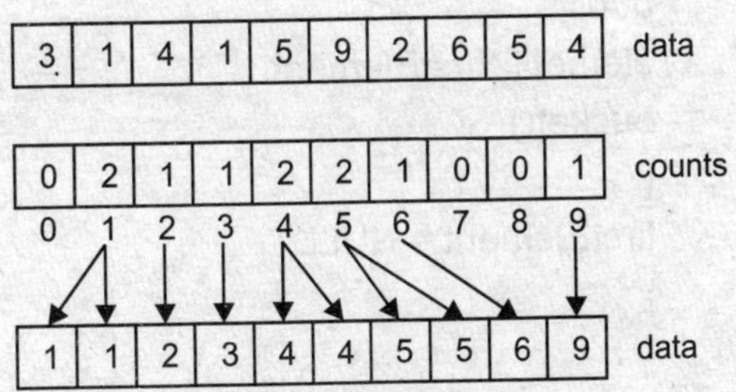

Figure 21.19: Bucket Sorting

In Figure 21.19, the universal set is assumed to be{0,1,......, 9}. Therefore, ten counters are required—one to keep track of the number of zeroes, one to keep track of the number of ones, and so on. A single pass through the data suffices to count all of the elements. Once the counts have been determined, the sorted sequence is easily obtained. E.g., the sorted sequence contains no zeroes, two ones, one two, and so on.

Thus, the running time of the bucket sort routine is O(m+n). Note that if m=O(n), the running time for bucket sort is O(n). I.e., the bucket sort algorithm is a *linear-time* sorting algorithm! Bucket sort breaks the O(n log n) bound associated with sorting algorithms that use binary comparisons because bucket sort does not do any binary comparisons. The cost associated with breaking the O(n log n) running time bound is the O(m) space required for the array of counters. Consequently, bucket sort is practical only for small m. E.g., to sort 16-bit integers using bucket sort requires the use of an array of $2^{16} = 65536$ counters.

Program 6: Write a C++ program for bucket sort.

```
#include <iostream.h>
#include<conio.h>
class element          //element
{
public:
int value;
element *next;
element()
{
value=NULL;
next=NULL;
}
};
class bucket        //bucket containing a perticular range of values
{
public:
element *firstElement;
bucket()
{
firstElement = NULL;
}
};
void main()
{
int lowend=0;     // minimum element
int highend=100;     //max element
int interval=10;     //number of intervals
const int noBuckets=(highend-lowend)/interval; //number of buckets required
bucket *buckets=new bucket[noBuckets];
bucket *temp;
```

```
for(int a=0;a<noBuckets;a++)  //creation of required buckets
{
temp=new bucket;
buckets[a]=*temp;
}
cout<<"--------The Elements to be Sorted using Bucket sort are -------------
-----\n";
int array[]={12,2,22,33,44,55,66,77,85,87,81,83,89,82,88,86,84,88,99};
for(int j=0;j<19;j++)  //sending elments into appropriate buckets
{
cout<<array[j]<<endl;
element *temp,*pre;
temp=buckets[array[j]/interval].firstElement;
if(temp==NULL)//if it is the first element of the bucket
{
temp=new element;
buckets[array[j]/interval].firstElement=temp;
temp->value=array[j];
}
else
{
pre=NULL;
while(temp!=NULL)     //move till the appropriate position in the bucket
{
if(temp->value>array[j])
break;
pre=temp;
temp=temp->next;
}
if(temp->value>array[j]) //if the new value is in betwen or at the begining
{
if(pre==NULL)  //insertion at first if the bucket has elements already
{
element *firstNode;
firstNode=new element();
firstNode->value=array[j];
firstNode->next=temp;
buckets[array[j]/interval].firstElement=firstNode;
}
else  //insertion at middle
```

```
{
element *firstNode;
firstNode=new element();
firstNode->value=array[j];
firstNode->next=temp;
pre->next=firstNode;
}
}
else// if the new value is to be created at last of bucket
{
temp=new element;
pre->next=temp;
temp->value=array[j];
}
}
}
cout<<"------------------------The Sorted Elements Are---------------\n";
for(int jk=0;jk<10;jk++)
{
element *temp;
temp= buckets[jk].firstElement;
while(temp!=NULL)
{
cout<<"*"<<temp->value<<endl;
temp=temp->next;
}
}
cout<<"--------------------------------END--------------------------------\n";
getch();
}
```

21.11 RADIX SORT

This section presents a sorting algorithm known as least-significant-digit-first radix sorting. Radix sorting is based on the bucket sorting algorithm discussed in the preceding section. However, radix sorting is practical for much larger universal sets than it is practical to handle with a bucket sort.

Radix sorting can be used when each element of the universal set can be viewed as a sequences of digits (or letters or any other symbols). For example, we can represent each integer between 0 and 99 as a sequence of two, decimal digits.

(E.g., the number five is represented as "05"). To sort an array of two-digit numbers, the algorithm makes two sorting passes through the array. In the first pass, the elements of the array are sorted by the least significant decimal digit. In the second pass, the elements of the array are sorted by the most significant decimal digit. The key characteristic of the radix sort is that the second pass is done in such a way that it does not destroy the effect of the first pass. Consequently, after two passes through the array, the data is contained therein is sorted. Each pass of the radix sort is implemented as a bucket sort. In the example we base the sort on decimal digits. Therefore, this is called a radix-10 sort and ten buckets are required to do each sorting pass.

Figure 21.20 illustrates the operation of the radix-10 sort. The first radix sorting pass considers the least significant digits. As in the bucket sort, a single pass is made through the unsorted data, counting the number of times each decimal digit appears as the least-significant digit. E.g., there are no elements that have a 0 as the least-significant digit; there are two elements that have a 1 as the least-significant digit; and so on.

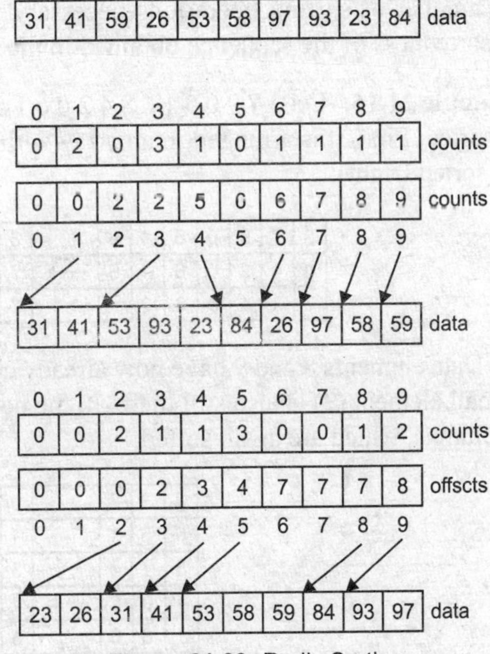

Figure 21.20: Radix Sorting

21.12 SHELL SORT

Shell sort developed by Donald L. Shell is a non-stable in-place sort. Shell sort improves on the efficiency of insertion sort by quickly shifting values to their destination. Average sort time is $O(n^{7/6})$ while worst-case time is $O(n^{4/3})$.

Shell sort is a sorting algorithm that is a generalization of insertion sort, with two observations:

- insertion sort is efficient if the input is "almost sorted", and
- insertion sort is typically inefficient because it moves values just one position at a time.

Shellsort is one of the oldest sorting algorithms, named after its inventor D.L. Shell (1959). It is fast, easy to understand and easy to implement. However, its complexity analysis is a little more sophisticated.

The idea of shellsort is the following:

(a) arrange the data sequence in a two-dimensional array

(b) sort the columns of the array

The effect is that the data sequence is partially sorted. The process above is repeated, but each time with a narrower array, i.e. with a smaller number of columns. In the last step, the array consists of only one column. In each step, the sortedness of the sequence is increased, until in the last step it is completely sorted. However, the number of sorting operations necessary in each step is limited, due to the presortedness of the sequence obtained in the preceding steps.

Example 21.15: Let 3 7 9 0 5 1 6 8 4 2 0 6 1 5 7 3 4 9 8 2 be the data sequence to be sorted. First, it is arranged in an array with 7 columns (left), then the columns are sorted (right):

3	7	9	0	5	1	6		3	3	4	0	5	1	5
8	4	2	0	6	1	6	⟶	7	4	4	0	5	1	5
7	3	4	9	8	2			7	7	9	9	8	2	

Data elements 8 and 9 have now already come to the end of the sequence, but a small element (2) is also still there. In the next step, the sequence is arranged in 3 columns, which are again sorted:

3	3	2		0	0	1
0	5	1		1	2	2
5	7	4		3	3	4
4	0	6	⟶	4	5	6
1	6	8		5	6	8
7	9	9		7	7	9
8	2			8	9	

Now the sequence is almost completely sorted. When arranging it in one column in the last step, it is only a 6, an 8 and a 9 that have to move a little bit to their correct position.

21.12.1 Implementation

Actually, the data sequence is not arranged in a two-dimensional array, but held in a one-dimensional array that is indexed appropriately. For instance, data elements at positions 0, 5, 10, 15 etc. would form the first column of an array with 5 columns. The "columns" obtained by indexing in this way are sorted with Insertion Sort, since this method has a good performance with presorted sequences.

The following program sorts an array *a* from index position 0 through *n*-1. The number of columns used for arranging data in each step is in array *cols*. Thus, data are arranged in 1391376 columns in the first step and in one column in the last step. (Note that essentially nothing is done if the number of columns *h* is larger than the number of data elements *n*.) Each column is sorted by Insertion Sort. First, data of the second row (beginning at $i = h$) are sorted to the correct position in their column, then data of the third row (when *i* reaches value $2h$) etc.

Example 21.16: In Figure 21.21(a) we have an example of sorting by insertion. First we extract 1 shift 3 and 5 down one slot and then insert the 1 for a count of 2 shifts. In the next frame two shifts are required before we can insert the 2. The process continues until the last frame where a total of 2 + 2 + 1 = 5 shifts have been made.

In Figure 21.21(b) an example of shell sort is illustrated. We begin by doing an insertion sort using a spacing of two. In the first frame we examine numbers 3-1. Extracting 1 we shift 3 down one slot for a shift count of 1. Next we examine numbers 5-2. We extract 2 shift 5 down and then insert 2. After sorting with a spacing of two a final pass is made with a spacing of one. This is simply the traditional insertion sort. The total shift count using shell sort is 1+1+1 = 3. By using an initial spacing larger than one we were able to quickly shift values to their proper destination.

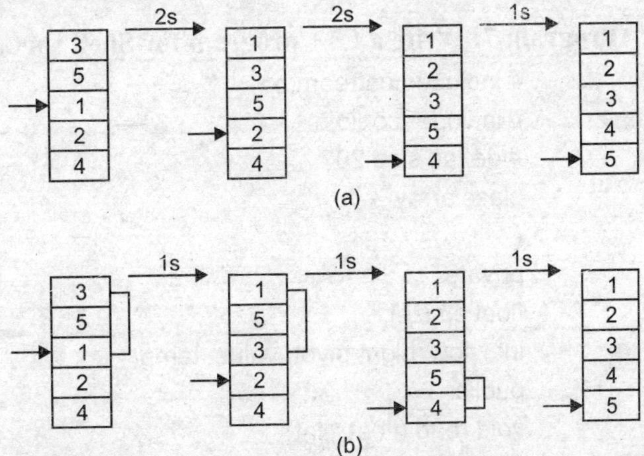

Figure 21.21: Shell Sort

Various spacings may be used to implement a shell sort. Typically the array is sorted with a large spacing the spacing reduced and the array sorted again. On the final sort spacing is one. Although the shell sort is easy to comprehend formal analysis is difficult. In particular optimal spacing values elude theoreticians. Knuth recommends a technique due to Sedgewick that determines spacing h based on the following formulas:

$h_s = 9 \cdot 2^s - 9 \cdot 2^{s/2} + 1$ if s is even

$h_s = 8 \cdot 2^s - 6 \cdot 2^{(s+1)/2} + 1$ if s is odd

These calculations result in values (h_0 h_1 h_2 ...) = (1 5 19 41 109 209 ...). Calculate h until $3h_t >= N$ the number of elements in the array. Then choose h_{t-1} for a starting value. For example to sort 150 items $h_t = 109$ ($3 \cdot 109 >= 150$) so the first spacing is h_{t-1} or 41. The second spacing is 19 then 5 and finally 1. The increment sequence used in this example code gives an $O(n^2)$ worst-case running time.

Algorithm 21.18: SHELL SORT

Step 1: input: an array a of length n with array elements numbered 0 to n – 1
Step 2: inc ← round(n/2)
Step 3: while inc > 0 do:
Step 4: for i = inc . n – 1 do:
TEMP ← a[i]
j ← i
Step 5: while j ≥ inc and a[j – inc] > TEMP do:
a[j] ← a[j – inc]
j ← j – inc
a[j] ← TEMP
Step 6: inc ← round(inc / 2.2)
Step 7: End.

Program 7: Write a C++ program for Shell sort.(ascending order)

```
# include<iostream.h>
# include<conio.h>
# define size 20
class array
{
private:
float a[size];
int i, low, high, pivot_value, temp;
public:
void read (float *,int);
void display (float *,int);
```

```
void shell_sort (float *,int beq, int end);
};
void array : : read (float a[], int n)
{
for (i=0;i<n;i++)
cin>>a[i];
}
void array : : display (float a[], int n)
{
for (i=0;i<n;i++)
cout<<a[i]<<" ";
}
void array : : shell_sort (float arr [], int n)
{
float temp;
int pass=0;
increment=1;
// choose sequence of increments
while (increment<=n)
increment = increment*3 + 1;
do
{
pass++;
increment /= 3;
cout<<"Iteration "<<pass<<" :\n;
do
{
exchngs=0;
for (i=0;i<n-increment;i++)
{
if(arr[i] >arr[i+increment] )
{
exchngs++; // increment no of exchanges
// swapping
temp = arr[i];
arr[i] = arr[i+increment);
arr[i+increment] = temp;
}
}
for (int j=0;j<n;j++)
```

```
cout<<arr[j]<<" ";
cout<<"exchngs= "<<exchngs<<"\n";
} while (exchngs);
} while (increment !=1);
}
void main ( )
{
array obj;
float a[size];
int n;
clrscr ( );
cout<<"read no of elements<="<<size<<"\n";
cin>>n;
cout<<"\nread "<<n<<" elements \n\n;
obj.read (a, n);
cout<<"\ngiven array is \n\n";
obj.display (a, n);
obj.shell_sort(a,n);
cout<<"\n\n Sorted array is\n\n";
obj.display(a,n))
getch ( );
}
```

Output:

```
read no elements<=20
6
read 6 elements
23    95    47    60    36    59
given array is
23    95    47    60    36    59
Trace of shell sort
Iteration 1:
23 59 47 60 36 95 exchngs=1
23 59 47 60 36 95 exchngs=0
Iteration 2:
23 47 59 36 60 95 exchngs=2
23 47 59 36 60 95 exchngs=1
23 36 47 59 60 95 exchngs=1
23 36 47 59 60 95 exchngs=0

Sorted array is
23    36    47    59    60    95
```

21.13 COMPARISON OF SORTING ALGORITHMS

The following chart compares sorting algorithms on the various criteria outlined above; the algorithms with higher constant terms appear first. Complexities below are in terms of n, the number of items to be sorted, k, the size of each key, and s, the chunk size used by the implementation. Many of them are based on the assumption that the key size is large enough that all entries have unique key values, and hence that $n << 2^k$, where << means "much less than."

Sort	Time			Space	Stability	Remarks
	Average	**Best**	**Worst**			
Bubble Sort	$O(n^2)$	$O(n^2)$	$O(n^2)$	Constant	Stable	Always use a modified bubble sort
Selection Sort	$O(n^2)$	$O(n^2)$	$O(n^2)$	Constant	Stable	Even a perfectly sorted input requires scanning the entire array
Insertion Sort	$O(n^2)$	O(n)	$O(n^2)$	Constant	Stable	In the best case (already sorted), every insert requires constant time
Heap Sort	O(n*log(n))	O(n*log(n))	O(n*log(n))	Constant	Instable	By using input array as storage for the heap, it is possible to achieve constant space
Merge Sort	O(n*log(n))	O(n*log(n))	O(n*log(n))	Depends	Stable	On arrays, merge sort requires O(n) space; on linked lists, merge sort requires constant space
Quick Sort	O(n*log(n))	O(n*log(n))	$O(n^2)$	Constant	Stable	Randomly picking a pivot value (or shuffling the array prior to sorting) can help avoid worst case scenarios such as a perfectly sorted array.
Radix sort	O(n. k/s)	—	O(n. k/s)	O(n)	Stable	Assumes uniform distribution of

Sort	Time			Space	Stability	Remarks
	Average	Best	Worst			
						elements from the domain in the array.
Bucket sort	O(n.k)	$O(n^2 .k)$	—	O(n.k)	Stable	Assumes uniform distribution of elements from the domain in the array.
Shell sort	—	$O(n \log^2 n)$	—	Constant	Instable	This sorting is generalization of insertion sort.

21.14 SEARCHING

Searching is a process of finding a given element in an array. Suppose LIST is collection of data maintained in memory by a table using some type of data structure. Searching is the operation which finds the location in memory of some given element of information or sends some message that element does not belong to LIST.

The search is said to be successful or unsuccessful according to whether the given element does or does not belong to LIST .The searching algorithm that is used depends mainly on the type of data structure that is used to maintain LIST in memory.

There are two frequently used methods of searching:

1. LINEAR SEARCH
2. BINARY SEARCH

21.14.1 Linear Search

If the elements in the array are unordered then linear search is performed comparing the given element against each element in the array in turn until match is found or the array comes to end and given element is not found.

Suppose LA is a linear array with n elements. In this searching method to search for a given ITEM in LA is to compare ITEM with each element of LA one by one. That is, first we test whether LA[1]= ITEM, and then we test whether LA[2]= ITEM, and so on. This method, which traverses LIST sequentially to locate ITEM, is called linear search.

In this searching algorithm, we first assign ITEM to LA[N+1], the position following the last element of LA. Then the outcome LOC = N+1

Where LOC denotes the position where ITEM first occurs in LA, signifies the search is unsuccessful. The purpose of this initial assignment is to avoid repeatedly testing whether or not we have reached the end of the array LA.

Algorithm 21.19: Linear Search

LINEAR (LA, N, ITEM, LOC)

Taking LA is a linear array with N elements, and ITEM is a given item of information. This algorithm find the location LOC of ITEM in LA, or set LOC = 0 if the search is unsuccessful.

Step 1: [Insert ITEM at the end of LA.] Set LA [N + 1] = ITEM.

Step 2: [Initialize the value of LOC.] Set LOC = 1.

Step 3: [Search for ITEM.]

Repeat steps while LA [LOC] ^{1} ITEM

Set LOC = LOC + 1

[End of while loop.]

Step 4: [Successful or Unsuccessful?] if LOC = N + 1, then Set LOC = 0.

Step 5: End.

Evaluation of Linear Search

The linear search is quite handy and efficient for short lists. It will be time consuming for a long lists.

If the given element is the first in the array, the number of comparisons will be 1. If the given element is last in the array, the number of comparisons will be n. This will cover best-case performance and worst-case performance.

Therefore, the average number of comparisons in linear search is:

$$\frac{1+2+3+...+n}{n}=\frac{n(n+1)}{2*n}=\frac{(n+1)}{2}$$

Thus the number of comparisons in the linear search will be O(n).

In case of sorted data, search will come to end as soon as value of the sorted data exceeds the value of element being searches.

In case of sorted data, assuming that values of data is uniformly distributed over the entire range of data, the number of comparisons will come down to n/2 on an average. In certain cases it may be preferable to sort the data before searching. The number of comparisons can also be reduced if most frequently accessed elements are placed in the beginning of the list.

Program 8: Write a C++ program for Linear Search.

```
# include<iostream.h>
# include<conio.h>
#define size 20
```

```
class array
{
private:
int i;
float a[size];
public:
void read (int);
void display (int);
int linear_search (int, float); // for searching of element
};
void array :: read (int n)
{
for (i=0,i<n;i++)
cin>>a[i];
}
void array : : display(int n)
{
for (i=0;i<n;i++)
cout<<a[i]<<" ";
}
int array : : linear_search (int n, float data)
{
// searching
i=0;
while (i<n)
{
if (a[i]= =data)
{
return (i);
}
else
i++;
}
return (-1);
}
void main ( )
{
array obj;
int n, position;
float data;
```

```
clrscr ( );
cout<<"read no of elements<="<<size<<"\n";
cin>>n;
cout<<"\nRead the element to be searched: ";
cin>>data;
cout<<"\ngiven array is \n\n";
obj.display (n);
cout<<"\n\nElement to be searched is "<<data;
// searching
position=obj.linear_search(n, data);
if (position= = -1)
cout<<"\n\nSearch is unsuccessful";
else
{
cout<<"\n\nSearch is successful \n\n";
cout<<data<<" found at position "<<position+1;
}
getch ( );
}
```

Output:

```
read no of elements<=20
8
read 8 elements
12    5     13    15    17    43    61    24
Read the element to be searched: 15
Given array is
12    5     13    15    17    43    61    24
Element to be searched is 15
Search is successful
15 found at position 4

read no of elements<=20
5
read 5 elements
14    17    14    13    38
Read the element to be searched: 15
Given array is
14    17    14    13    38
Element to be searched is 15
Search is unsuccessful
```

21.14.2 Binary Search

Binary search is a method by using which searching is fast in comparison to linear search but the main drawback of binary search is before binary search sorting is necessary.

In binary search the array list is divided into two equal parts (approximately). Suppose the elements of array list are in ascending order then if desired element is less than the middle element of array list, it will never be present in the second half of the array. Similarly if the desired element is greater than the middle element of array, it will never be present in the first half of the array list.

Thus we can focus our attention on one half of the array list. The process is repeated and in the next stage we have to search for the element only is one quarter of the array list. This process reduces the search length and search time.

There is an extremely efficient searching algorithm, called binary search, which can be used to find the location LOC of a given ITEM of information in LA.

The binary search algorithm applied to our array LA woks as follows. During each stage of algorithm, our search for ITEM is reduced to a segment of elements of LA:

LA[BEG], LA[BEG + 1], LA[BEG+2] , ...,LA[END].

Note that the variables BEG and END denote beginning and end locations of the segment. The algorithm compares ITEM with the middle element LA[MIDLOC] of the segment, where MIDLOC by

MIDLOC = INT ((BEGIN + END)/2)

If LA[MIDLOC] = ITEM, then the search is successful and set LOC = MIDLOC. Otherwise a new segment of LA is as follows:

(a) If ITEM < LA [MID], then ITEM is in left half of the segment:

LA[BEG], LA[BEG + 1], LA[BEG+2] , ...,LA[MID - 1].

Set END = MIDLOC – 1 and begin searching again.

(b) If ITEM > LA [MID], then ITEM is in right half of the segment:

LA[MID + 1], LA[MID +2], LA[BEG+3] , ...,LA[END].

Set BEGIN = MIDLOC + 1 and begin searching again.

We start with the entire array LA i.e. BEG =1 and END = n, or, more generally, with BEG = LB and END =UB.

If ITEM is not present in LA, then WE obtain

END < BEG

This condition signals that the search is unsuccessful and such a case we assign LOC = NULL. Here NULL means that item is not present in array LA.

Algorithm 21.20: Binary Search

BINARYSEARCH (LA, LB, UB, ITEM, LOC)

Taking LA is a sorted array with lower bound LB and upper bound UB, and ITEM is a given item of information. The variables BEGIN, END and MIDLOC denote as beginning, ending and middle locations of elements of LA. This algorithm find the location LOC of ITEM in LA or if LOC not found set LOC = NULL.

Step 1: [Initialize starting variables.]

Set BEGIN = LB, END = UB and MIDLOC = INT ((BEGIN + END)/2).

Step 2: Repeat steps 3 and 4 while BEGIN ≤ END and LA [MIDLOC] ≠ ITEM.

Step 3: If ITEM < LA [MID], then

    Set END = MIDLOC – 1.

    Else

    Set BEGIN = MIDLOC + 1.

    [End of If statement.]

Step 4: Set MIDLOC = INT ((BEGIN + END)/2).

  [End of Step 2 loop.]

Step 5: If LA [MIDLOC] = ITEM, then:

Set LOC = MIDLOC.

else

    Set LOC = NULL.

  [End of If statement.]

Step 6: End.

Explanation

Example 21.17

3	6	8	9	12
0	1	2	3	4

Suppose we want to search 9, then in first pass: MIDLOC = INT ((BEGIN + END)/2).

MIDLOC = (0+4)/2 = 2

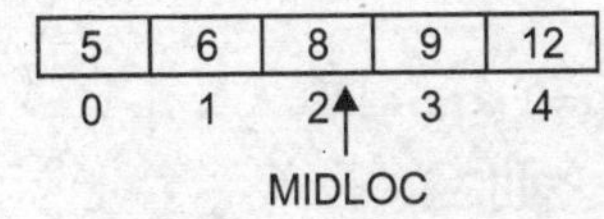

9 is greater than the middle element, then BEGIN = MIDLOC + 1. process is repeated in second half

MIDLOC = (3+4)/2 = 3

5	6	8	9	12
0	1	2	3	4

MIDLOC

If LA [MIDLOC] = ITEM means LA[3] = 9

LOC = MIDLOC LOC = 3

Now the position is found that is LOC = 3.

Evaluation of Binary Search

Binary search takes maximum $(\log_2 n)+1$ comparisons as compared to $(n+1)/2$ taken for a linear search. Even in the worst case binary search will take $\log_2 n$ running time. For a million items, it will take only 20 comparisons. Binary search is definitely an improvement over the linear search. It takes far less time as compared to the linear search. On the negative side data has to be sorted and access to middle of the time has to be maintained. Sorting becomes more costly in cases of large number of insertions and deletions.

Program 9: Write a C++ program for Binary Search.

```
# include<iostream.h>
# include<conio.h>
#define size 20
class array
{
private:
int i;
float a[size];
public:
void read (int);
void display (int);
int linear_search (int, float); // for searching of element
};
void array :: read (int n)
{
for (i=0;i<n;i++)
cin>>a[i];
}
void array : : display(int n)
```

```
{
for (i=o;i<n;i++)
cout<<a[i]<<"\t ";
}
int array : : binary_search (int n, float data)
{
int low, high, mid;
// searching
low=0;
high=n-1;
while(low<=high)
{
mid= (low+high) /2;
if (a[mid]= = data) // when element has been found
return (mid+1);
else
{
if (data>a [mid])
low= mid+1;
else high= mid-1;
}
}// while loop ends here
return (-1); // when element is not in array
}
void main ( )
{
array obj; //object created
int n, position;
float data;
clrscr ( );
cout<<"read no of elements<="<<size<<"\n";
cin>>n;
cout<<"\nRead the element to be searched: ";
cin>>data;
cout<<"\ngiven array is \n\n";
obj.display (n);
cout<<"\n\nElement to be searched is "<<data;
position=obj.binary_search(n, data);
```

```
if (position= = -1)
cout<<"\n\nSearch is unsuccessful";
else
{
cout<<"\n\nSearch is successful \n\n";
cout<<data<<" found at position "<<position;
}
getch ( );
}
```

```
Ouput:
read no of elements<=20
8
read 8 elements
12    5    13    15    17    43    61    24
Read the element to be searched: 15
Given array is
12    5    13    15    17    43    61    24
Element to be searched is 15
Search is successful
15 found at position 4

read no of elements<=20
5
read 5 elements
14    17    14    13    38
Read the element to be searched: 15
Given array is
14    17    14    13    38
Element to be searched is 15
Search is unsuccessful
```

21.15 IS BINARY SEARCH EFFICIENT THAN LINEAR SEARCH?

21.15.1 Efficiency of Linear Search

Having implemented the linear search algorithm, how would you measure its efficiency? A useful measure (or metric) would be general, applicable to any (search) algorithm. Since a more efficient algorithm would take less time to execute, one approach would be to write a program for each of the algorithms to be compared, and execute them, measuring the time each takes to finish. However, a better metric would allow algorithms to be evaluated before implementing them.

One such metric is the number of main steps the algorithm will require to finish. Of course, the exact number of steps depends on the input data. For the linear search algorithm, the number of steps depends on whether the target is in the list, and if so, where in the list, as well as on the length of the list. For search algorithms, the main steps are the comparisons of list values with the target value. Counting these for data models representing the **best case**, the **worst case**, and the **average case** produces the following table. For each case, the number of steps is expressed in terms of n, the number of items in the list.

Model	Number of Comparisons (for n = 100000)	Comparisons as a function of n
Best Case (fewest comparisons)	1 (target is first item)	1
Worst Case (most comparisons)	100000 (target is last item)	n
Average Case (average number of comparisons)	50000 (target is middle item)	n/2

The best case analysis doesn't tell us much. If the first element checked happens to be the target, any algorithm will take only one comparison. The worst and average case analyses give a better indication of algorithm efficiency.

Notice that if the list grows in size, the number of comparisons required to find a target item in both worst and average cases grows linearly. In general, for a list of length n, the worst case is n comparisons. The algorithm is called **linear search** because its complexity/efficiency can be expressed as a linear function: the number of comparisons to find a target increases linearly as the size of the list.

21.15.2 Efficiency of Binary Search

Is binary search more efficient than linear search? If so, how much more efficient is it? To evaluate binary search, count the number of comparisons in the best case and worst case. This analysis omits the average case, which is a bit more difficult, and ignores any differences between algorithms in the amount of computation corresponding to each comparison.

The best case occurs if the middle item happens to be the target. Then only one comparison is needed to find it. As before, the best case analysis does not reveal much.

When does the worst case occur? If the target is not in the array then the process of dividing the list in half continues until there is only one item left to check. Here is the pattern of the number of comparisons after each division, given the simplifying assumptions of an initial array length that's an even power of 2 (1024) and exact division in half on each iteration:

Items Left to Search	Comparisons So Far
1024	0
512	1
256	2
128	3
64	4
32	5
16	6
8	7
4	8
2	9
1	10

For a list size of 1024, there are 10 comparisons to reach a list of size one, given that there is one comparison for each division, and each division splits the list size in half. In general, if n is the size of the list to be searched and C is the number of comparisons to do so in the worst case. $\mathbf{C = \log_2 n}$. Thus, the efficiency of binary search can be expressed as a logarithmic function, in which the number of comparisons required to find a target increases only logarithmically with the size of the list. The following table summarizes the analysis for binary search.

Model	Number of Comparisons (for n = 100000)	Comparisons as a function of n
Best Case (fewest comparisons)	1(target is middle item)	1
Worst Case (most comparisons)	16(target not in array)	$\log_2 n$

21.15.3 Efficiency Comparison

Note that the worst-case number of comparisons is just 16 with 100,000 items, versus 100,000 for linear search! Furthermore, if the array were doubled in size to 200,000, the maximum number of comparisons for binary search would only increase by 1 to 17, whereas for linear search it would double from 100,000 to 200,000.

The following table shows how the maximum number of comparisons increases for binary search and linear search.

Array Size	Worst Case Comparisons	
	Linear Search	Binary Search
100,000	100,000	16
200,000	200,000	17
400,000	400,000	18
800,000	800,000	19
1,600,000	1,600,000	20

Remember following in case of Searching Algorithms

1. A common operation on arrays of records is to search the list to retrieve a particular record.
2. There are alternative algorithms for searching an array. The number of comparisons required is a useful metric for their efficiency.
3. Linear search examines each list item in turn until the target is located or the end of the list is reached.
4. Linear search efficiency for the worst case data model is a linear function of the number of items in the list.
5. If the list is sorted, a binary search strategy may be used.
6. Binary search uses the result of each comparison to eliminate half of the list from further searching.
7. Binary search efficiency for the worst case is a logarithmic function of list size.

OBJECTIVE TYPE QUESTIONS

1. Sorting is a
   (a) Linear data structure (b) Non-linear data structure
   (c) Data structure operation (d) None
2. Which of the following is the sorting method?
   (a) Bubble (b) Heap
   (c) Insertion (d) All of the above
3. Which of the following is not the sorting method?
   (a) Bubble (b) Heap
   (c) Deletion (d) All of the above
4. Sorting operation can be implemented by using
   (a) Array (b) Stack

(c) Pointer
(d) Linked list
(e) None

5. Which of the following is the type of Sorting?
(a) City names
(b) Heap of books
(c) Marks list
(d) All of the above

6. Which of the following is the operation of Fastest?
(a) Bubble
(b) Heap
(c) Insertion
(d) Selection

7. Which of the following is the operation of Slowest?
(a) Bubble
(b) Heap
(c) Insertion
(d) Selection

8. Which of the following is not the operation of has more phase of sorting?
(a) Bubble
(b) Heap
(c) Insertion
(d) Selection

9. Which of the following is the utility of Sorting?
(a) Arrangement of flower
(b) Arrangement of data
(c) Concatenation of data
(d) All of the above
(e) None of the above

10. Which sorting method starts with minimum value?
(a) Bubble
(b) Heap
(c) Insertion
(d) Selection

11. The process of arranging records in ordered manner is called
(a) sorting
(b) searching
(c) indexing
(d) None of the above

12. In insertion sort, the shifting of numbers are:
(a) shift greater number at end and smaller at beginning of the array
(b) shift greater number at the middle and smaller at right
(c) shift smaller at the center and greater at beginning
(d) None of the above

13. In this type of sort list is divided in two sub-lists:
(a) quick sort
(b) exchange sort
(c) merge sort
(d) None of the above

14. The exchange sort is also called:
    (a) bubble sort (b) merge sort
    (c) shell sort (d) None of the above
15. In the bubble sort the sorting is done with comparing
    (a) successive elements (b) first and last elements
    (c) last and middle elements (d) None of the above
16. In tree sort the elements are sorted with
    (a) inorder traversing (b) preorder traversing
    (c) post order traversing (d) None of the above
17. Radix sort method is based on
    (a) the positions of the digits (b) the squares of digits
    (c) the squares of digits (d) None of the above
18. For sorting the elements with partition exchange sort which method is used?
    (a) bubble sort (b) quick sort
    (c) heap sort (d) None of the above
19. In heap sort the numbers are initially arranged in
    (a) ascending order (b) descending order
    (c) binary tree (d) None of the above
20. With merge sort number of list that can be sorted are
    (a) one list (b) more than one lists
    (c) none of the above.
21. The process of finding a particular record is called
    (a) sorting (b) searching
    (c) indexing (d) None of the above
22. In this type of searching the records must be sorted
    (a) linear search (b) binary search
    (c) selection search (d) None of the above
23. Using bubble sort, the number of comparison for the letter PEOPLE is:
    (a) 20 (b) 10
    (c) 15 (d) 14
    (e) None

EXERCISES

1. What do you mean by sorting?
2. Explain the concept of bubble sort with the help of example.
3. Write an algorithm and C++ program for Bubble sort.
4. Explain the concept of selection sort with the help of example.
5. Write an algorithm and C++ program for Selection sort.
6. Explain the concept of insertion sort with the help of example.
7. Write an algorithm and C++ program for Insertion sort.
8. Explain the concept of quick sort with the help of example.
9. Write an algorithm and C++ program for Quick sort.
10. Explain the concept of heapsort with the help of example.
11. Write an algorithm and C++ program for Heap sort.
12. Explain the concept of merge sort with the help of example.
13. Write an algorithm and C++ program for Merge sort.
14. Explain the concept of radix sort with the help of example.
15. Write an algorithm and C++ program for Radix sort.
16. Explain the concept of bucket sort with the help of example.
17. Write an algorithm and C++ program for Bucket sort.
18. Explain the concept of shell sort with the help of example.
19. Write an algorithm and C++ program for Shell sort.
20. Write comparison of various sorting algorithms.
21. What do you mean by searching?
22. Write an algorithm and C++ program for linear search.
23. Write an algorithm and C++ program for binary search.
24. Difference between linear search and binary search.

APPENDIX 1

Operator Precedence and Associativity Chart

Operator	Type	Associativity
::	binary scope resolution	left to right
::	unary scope resolution	
()	parentheses	left to right
[]	array subscript	
.	member selection via object	
->	member selection via pointer	
++	unary postfix increment	
—	unary postfix decrement	
typeid	runtime type information	
dynamic_cast < type >	runtime type-checked cast	
static_cast< type >	compile-time type-checked cast	
reinterpret_cast< type >	cast for nonstandard conversions	
const_cast< type >	cast away const-ness	
++	unary prefix increment	right to left
—	unary prefix decrement	
+	unary plus	
-	unary minus	
!	unary logical negation	
~	unary bitwise complement	
sizeof	determine size in bytes	
&	address	
*	dereference	
new	dynamic memory allocation	
new[]	dynamic array allocation	

Operator	Type	Associativity
delete	dynamic memory deallocation	
delete[]	dynamic array deallocation	
(type)	C-style unary cast	right to left
.*	pointer to member via object	left to right
->*	pointer to member via pointer	
*	multiplication	left to right
/	division	
%	modulus	
+	addition	left to right
-	subtraction	
<<	bitwise left shift	left to right
>>	bitwise right shift	
<	relational less than	left to right
<=	relational less than or equal to	
>	relational greater than	
>=	relational greater than or equal to	
==	relational is equal to	left to right
!=	relational is not equal to	
&	bitwise AND	left to right
^	bitwise exclusive OR	left to right
|	bitwise inclusive OR	left to right
&&	logical AND	left to right
||	logical OR	left to right
?:	ternary conditional	right to left
=	assignment	right to left
+=	addition assignment	
-=	subtraction assignment	
*=	multiplication assignment	
/=	division assignment	
%=	modulus assignment	
&=	bitwise AND assignment	
^=	bitwise exclusive OR assignment	
|=	bitwise inclusive OR assignment	
<<=	bitwise left-shift assignment	
>>=	bitwise right-shift assignment	
,	comma	left to right

APPENDIX 2

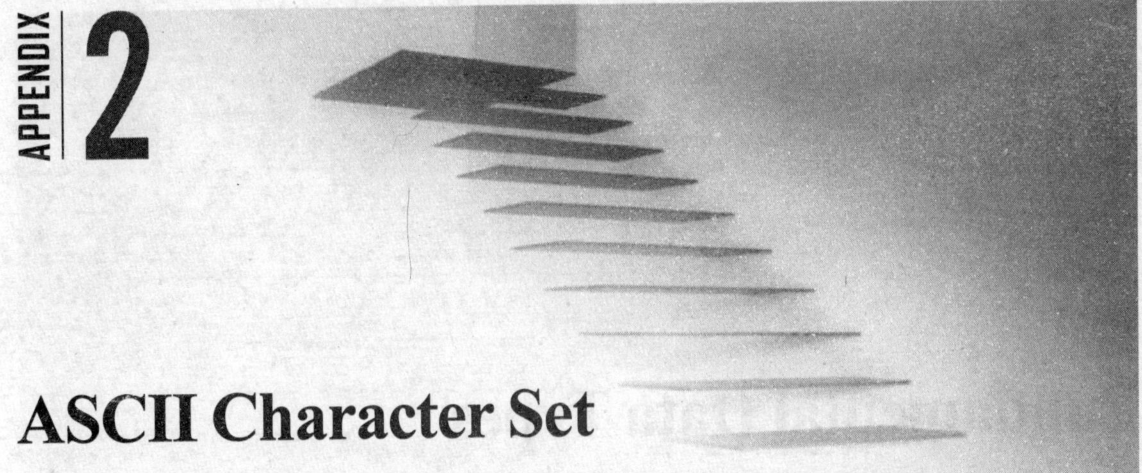

ASCII Character Set

ASCII CHARACTER SET

	0	1	2	3	4	5	6	7	8	9
0	nul	soh	stx	etx	eot	enq	ack	bel	bs	ht
1	nl	vt	ff	cr	so	si	dle	dc1	dc2	dc3
2	dc4	nak	syn	etb	can	em	sub	esc	fs	gs
3	rs	us	sp	!	"	#	$	%	&	'
4	(	)	*	+	,	-	.	/	0	1
5	2	3	4	5	6	7	8	9	:	;
6	<	=	>	?	@	A	B	C	D	E
7	F	G	H	I	J	K	L	M	N	O
8	P	Q	R	S	T	U	V	W	X	Y
9	Z	[	\	]	^	_	`	a	b	c
10	d	e	f	g	h	i	j	k	l	m
11	n	o	p	q	r	s	t	u	v	w
12	x	y	z	{	|	}	~	del		

The digits at the left of the table are the left digits of the decimal equivalent (0127) of the character code, and the digits at the top of the table are the right digits of the character code. For example, the character code for "R" is 82, and the character code for "0" is 48.

APPENDIX 3

Fundamental Data Types

Integral Types	Floating-Point Types
bool	float
char	double
signed char	long double
unsigned char	
short int	
unsigned short int	
int	
unsigned int	
long int	
unsigned long int	
wchar_t	

APPENDIX 4

C++ Keywords

This is a list of reserved keywords in C++. Since they are used by the language, these keywords are not available for re-definition (or overloading) by programmers.

Keyword	Description
and	alternative to && operator
and_eq	alternative to &= operator
asm	insert an assembly instruction
auto	declare a local variable
bitand	alternative to bitwise & operator
bitor	alternative to | operator
bool	declare a boolean variable
break	break out of a loop
case	a block of code in a switch statement
catch	handles exceptions from throw
char	declare a character variable
class	declare a class
compl	alternative to ~ operator
const	declare immutable data or functions that do not change data
const_cast	cast from const variables
continue	bypass iterations of a loop
default	default handler in a case statement
delete	make dynamic memory available
do	looping construct

Keyword	Description
double	declare a double precision floating-point variable
dynamic_cast	perform runtime casts
else	alternate case for an if statement
enum	create enumeration types
explicit	only use constructors when they exactly match
export	allows template definitions to be separated from their declarations
extern	tell the compiler about variables defined elsewhere
false	a constant representing the boolean false value
float	declare a floating-point variable
for	looping construct
friend	grant non-member function access to private data
goto	jump to a different part of the program
if	execute code based on the result of a test
inline	optimize calls to short functions
int	declare an integer variable
long	declare a long integer variable
mutable	override a const variable
namespace	partition the global namespace by defining a scope
new	allocate dynamic memory for a new variable
not	alternative to ! operator
not_eq	alternative to != operator
operator	create overloaded operator functions
or	alternative to || operator
or_eq	alternative to |= operator
private	declare private members of a class
protected	declare protected members of a class
public	declare public members of a class
register	request that a variable be optimized for speed
reinterpret_cast	change the type of a variable
return	return from a function
short	declare a short integer variable
signed	modify variable type declarations
sizeof	return the size of a variable or type
static	create permanent storage for a variable

Keyword	Description
static_cast	perform a nonpolymorphic cast
struct	define a new structure
switch	execute code based on different possible values for a variable
template	create generic functions
this	a pointer to the current object
throw	throws an exception
true	a constant representing the boolean true value
try	execute code that can throw an exception
typedef	create a new type name from an existing type
typeid	describes an object
typename	declare a class or undefined type
union	a structure that assigns multiple variables to the same memory location
unsigned	declare an unsigned integer variable
using	import complete or partial namespaces into the current scope
virtual	create a function that can be overridden by a derived class
void	declare functions or data with no associated data type
volatile	warn the compiler about variables that can be modified unexpectedly
wchar_t	declare a wide-character variable
while	looping construct
xor	alternative to ^ operator
xor_eq	alternative to ^= operator

APPENDIX 5

C++ Strings Library

The C++ strings library provides the definitions of the basic_string class, which is a class template specifically designed to manipulate strings of characters of any character type. It also include two specific instantiations: string and wstring, which respectively use char and wchar_t as character types.

string String class (class)

String class: String objects are a special type of container, specifically designed to operate with sequences of characters.

Unlike traditional c-strings, which are mere sequences of characters in a memory array, C++ string objects belong to a class with many built-in features to operate with strings in a more intuitive way and with some additional useful features common to C++ containers.

The string class is an instantiation of the basic_string class template, defined in <string> as:

```
typedef basic_string<char> string;
```

Member functions

(constructor)	Construct string object (constructor member)
operator=	String assignment (public member function)

Iterators:

begin	Return iterator to beginning (public member function)
end	Return iterator to end (public member function)
rbegin	Return reverse iterator to reverse beginning (public member function)
rend	Return reverse iterator to reverse end (public member function)

Capacity:

size	Return length of string (public member function)
length	Return length of string (public member function)
max_size	Return maximum size of string (public member function)
resize	Resize string (public member function)
capacity	Return size of allocated storage (public member function)
reserve	Request a change in capacity (public member function)
clear	Clear string (public member function)
empty	Test if string is empty (public member function)

Element access:

operator[]	Get character in string (public member function)
at	Get character in string (public member function)

Modifiers:

operator+=	Append to string (public member function)
append	Append to string (public member function)
push_back	Append character to string (public member function)
assign	Assign content to string (public member function)
insert	Insert into string (public member function)
erase	Erase characters from string (public member function)
replace	Replace part of string (public member function)
copy	Copy sequence of characters from string (public member function)
swap	Swap contents with another string (public member function)

String operations:

c_str	Get C string equivalent (public member function)
data	Get string data (public member function)
get_allocator	Get allocator (public member function)
find	Find content in string (public member function)
rfind	Find last occurrence of content in string (public member function)
find_first_of	Find character in string (public member function)
find_last_of	Find character in string from the end (public member function)
find_first_not_of	Find absence of character in string
find_last_not_of	Find absence of character in string from the end (public member function)
substr	Generate substring (public member function)
compare	Compare strings (public member function)

Index

B

C

Q

R